INTERACTIVE STUDENT CD

We are very proud to announce a significant expansion in learning resources permitted through the use of new technology. The textbook now contains a **CD-Rom** that provides complete **Baldrige case studies** and features new **multimedia cases** with **QuickTime™ videos**. Also included are **web links** to organizations that are tied to each chapter and a **Glossary of terms** from the textbook. These resources can be accessed using a web browser such as Internet Explorer or Netscape.

The CD-Rom also contains all of the major **spreadsheet templates** used in quantitative examples in Part 3. These files are saved in Microsoft® Excel 2000, 97 and 95 workbook formats and should be accessible to current systems.

THE MANAGEMENT AND CONTROL OF QUALITY
JAMES R. EVANS AND WILLIAM M. LINDSAY FIFTH EDITION

Introduction
Multimedia Cases
Cases
Spreadsheet Templates
Internet Resources
Baldrige Resources
Glossary
Web Site
Talk to Us
Home

Welcome to the Interactive Student CD for

The Management and Control of Quality, Fifth Edition

by Evans and Lindsay

For additional resources, click on the buttons to the left.

SOUTH-WESTERN THOMSON LEARNING

Site Search Site Map Decision Sciences Help

Web Sites of Many Businesses and Organizations Cited in this Book

3M Dental Products Division	http://www.mmm.com/dental/baldrige
ADAC Laboratories	http://www.adaclabs.com
American Express	http://www.americanexpress.com
American Productivity & Quality Center	http://www.apqc.org
American Society for Quality	http://www.asq.org
Analog Devices, Inc.	http://www.analog.com
Armstrong World Industries	http://www.armstrong.com
AT&T	http://www.att.com
Australian Quality Council	http://www.aqc.org.au
Avis	http://www.avis.com
BASF	http://www.basf.de
Black & Decker	http://www.blackanddecker.com
Boise Cascade Corporation	http://www.bc.com
Bureau of Labor Statistics	http://stats.bls.gov
CFI Group	http://www.cfigroup.com
Chrysler Corporation	http://www.chryslercorp.com
Cisco Systems, Inc.	http://www.cisco.com
Citigroup	http://www.citigroup.com
Coca-Cola	http://www.cocacola.com
Corning	http://www.corning.com
Custom Research, Inc.	http://www.cresearch.com
Dana Corporation	http://www.dana.com
Deer Valley Resort	http://www.deervalley.com
Deming Institute	http://deming.org
Digital Equipment Corporation	http://www.digital.com
Dunlavy Audio Labs, Inc.	http://www.dunlavyaudio.com
E.I. duPont de Nemours & Co.	http://www.dupont.com
Eastman Chemical	http://www.eastman.com
European Foundation for Quality Mangement	http://efqm.org/pressrel/custsat.htm
Federal Express (FedEx)	http://www.fedex.com
Fidelity Investments	http://www31.fidelity.comi80
Florida Power and Light	http://www.fplgroup.com
Ford Motor Company	http://www.ford.com
General Electric Corporation	http://www.ge.com
General Motors Corporation	http://www.gm.com
Granite Rock	http://www.graniterock.com
GTE Directories	http://directories.gte.net/INFO4.htm
Hershey Foods	http://www.hersheys.com
Hewlett-Packard	http://www.hp.com
The Home Depot	http://www.homedepot.com
Honda of America	http://www.honda.co.jp
IBM	http://www..ibm.com
Intel Corporation	http://www.intel.com
International Organization for Standardization	http://www.iso.ch

continued on inside back cover

The Management and Control of Quality

Fifth Edition

James R. Evans
University of Cincinnati

William M. Lindsay
Northern Kentucky University

Australia · Canada · Mexico · Singapore · Spain · United Kingdom · United States

The Management and Control of Quality, 5e by James R. Evans and William M. Lindsay

Vice President/Publisher: Dave Shaut
Senior Acquisitions Editor: Charles McCormick, Jr.
Senior Developmental Editor: Alice C. Denny
Senior Marketing Manager: Joseph A. Sabatino
Production Editors: Anne Chimenti, Elizabeth A. Shipp
Media Development Editor: Christine A. Wittmer
Media Production Editor: Robin K. Browning
Manufacturing Coordinator: Sandee Milewski
Internal Design: Jennifer Lambert
Cover Design: Rick Moore
Production House: Trejo Production
Printer: West Group

Printed in the United States of America
2 3 4 5 04 03 02

For more information contact South-Western, 5101 Madison Road, Cincinnati, Ohio, 45227 or find us on the Internet at http://www.swcollege.com

For permission to use material from this text or product contact us by
- **telephone: 1-800-730-2214**
- **fax: 1-800-730-2215**
- **web: http://www.thomsonrights.com**

Library of Congress Cataloging-in-Publication Data
Evans, James R. (James Robert)
The management and control of quality / James R. Evans, William M. Lindsay. — 5th ed.
p. cm.
Includes bibliographical references and index.
ISBN 0-324-06680-5
1. Quality control. 2. Total quality management. 3. Quality assurance. I. Lindsay, William M. II. Title.
TS156.E93 2001
658.5'62—dc21 2001020077

Chapter 5 Leadership and Strategic Planning 219

Contents

Brief Contents

PREFACE

Has quality lost its importance? The December 18, 2000 issue of *Business Week* includes an editorial entitled "The War for Better Quality Is Far From Won" written by Jeffrey E. Garten, Dean of the Yale School of Management. He observes: "Whatever happened to the hoopla surrounding quality control in Corporate America? Has the issue slipped from the front page because the war against big-time defects has been won? Or could Corporate America be deluding itself into thinking that quality no longer is the huge problem it once was?" Dean Garten points to the Firestone tire fiasco, recalls of circuit boards by Intel, automobile recalls, poor customer service quality, the lack of a quality framework for e-business, and the need for higher quality standards in biotechnology as reminders that quality problems still abound.

We agree completely—the war for better quality must continue. Today's business and non-profit organizations need to capitalize on the tremendous progress that has been made, particularly with respect to the Malcolm Baldrige National Quality Award. Recently, that award has been expanded to include nonprofit education and health care sectors, and there is increased use of the Baldrige Criteria for Performance Excellence for self-assessment among organizations in all economic sectors.

The Baldrige Criteria continues to evolve as it reflects the most effective management practices that lead to world-class performance. Solectron Corporation and The Ritz-Carlton Hotel Company have received second Baldrige Awards under significantly different criteria than when they initially won the Award, while at the same time expanding their operations globally. In short, the interest in and practice of high-performance quality management principles remains high. Comments from previous Baldrige recipients include: "The Baldrige Award truly embodies the American spirit . . . the Malcolm Baldrige National Quality Award has played a vital role in energizing U.S. companies, helping them gain a competitive edge in the emerging global marketplace. For each of us, the application process uncovered significant opportunities for improving efficiency and customer and employee satisfaction. The recognition of actually receiving the Award reinforced the need to continue improving performance in a marketplace that becomes more competitive every day." This book is intended to reflect and support these remarks.

CHANGES IN THE FIFTH EDITION

The fifth edition of *The Management and Control of Quality* continues to embrace the fundamental principles and historical foundations of total quality, and to promote high performance management practices that are reflected in the Baldrige Criteria. Several very positive changes have been made to allow for greater instructor flexibility and an improved focus on contemporary thinking.

Software Supplements

- We are very proud to announce a significant expansion in learning resources permitted through the use of new technology. The textbook now contains a CD-rom that provides complete Baldrige case studies and features new multimedia cases with QuickTime™ videos, web links to organizations that are tied to each chapter, and a Glossary of terms from the textbook. All this that can be accessed using a Web browser such as Internet Explorer or Netscape.
- In addition, the CD includes The Quality Gamebox, developed by PQ Systems in Dayton Ohio. It is a collection of simulations for teaching concepts of variability, some of which are used in Chapter 9. The CD-rom also contains all of the major spreadsheet templates used in quantitative examples in Part 3. These files are saved in Microsoft® Excel 2000, 97 and 95 workbook formats and should be accessible to current systems.

Continuing Our Contemporary Focus

- All chapters have been updated to reflect the most current thinking in the profession. Many new examples, Quality Profiles of all Baldrige winners to date, and new or revised Quality in Practice cases, questions, problems, and end-of-chapter cases are included. A new section, "Projects, Etc.," that provides ideas for student projects and practical field investigation has been added to most chapters.
- New cases and additional examples from organizations around the world emphasize the increasing importance of quality in the global economy. In addition, the increasingly important role of quality in e-commerce has been introduced in many chapters.

Chapter Reorganization to Increase Flexibility

- Several chapters from the fourth edition have been reorganized and streamlined resulting in a net reduction of one chapter. Our goal was to include an earlier treatment of TQ principles—particularly the notion of process thinking— in Chapter 1. This allows the instructor the flexibility to move directly to Part 3, Technical Issues in Quality, after covering just the first three chapters. Chapter 2 introduces systems thinking as a fundamental concept of total quality, and expands significantly the discussion of quality in health care and education. Chapter 3 now covers both traditional philosophies and contemporary award frameworks (including ISO 9000:2000) in an integrated fashion.
- Chapters 4 through 8 support the Baldrige Criteria and include updated examples of how organizations might respond on a Baldrige-based award application or self-assessment process. These examples use portions of a recent national examiner training case, which is provided on the CD-rom included in this

book. All of these chapters have been revised to conform closely to the spirit and content of the latest Criteria for Performance Excellence and recent research and practice. We have included new or updated descriptions of leadership theories, high-performance work design, motivation theories, cycle time reduction, the balanced scorecard, design of performance measurement systems, and measuring the return on quality.

- The technical chapters have been reorganized to focus on contemporary thinking and techniques. Chapter 9 is essentially new, and is devoted to statistical thinking and statistical tools. Included is a new and expanded section on experimental design and its application in quality. Chapter 10 focuses on tools for quality improvement, with particular emphasis on Six-Sigma methodology and applications. Chapter 11 includes a new section on the HACCP process and the role of quality control in food processing.
- We combined the two chapters on statistical process control from the fourth edition into one chapter plus an appendix. This provides a more integrated treatment of SPC concepts while still providing theoretical statistical topics in an optional appendix.
- The chapter on Building and Sustaining Total Quality Organizations is now the final chapter, and can be used as a capstone chapter whether the instructor chooses to emphasize the management issues in Part 2 or the technical issues in Part 3.

OVERVIEW OF THIS BOOK

Part 1 provides an introduction to quality management principles. Chapter 1 introduces the notion of quality, its history and importance, definitions, basic principles, and its impact on competitive advantage and financial return. Chapter 2 explores the role of total quality in all key economic sectors: manufacturing, service, health care, education, and the public sector. The philosophical perspectives supporting total quality, chiefly those of Deming, Juran, and Crosby, as well as award frameworks and ISO 9000 are presented in Chapter 3. This chapter also describes the Malcolm Baldrige National Quality Award and the Criteria for Performance Excellence as a framework for management planning and action to achieve TQ, and forms the basis for Part 2.

Part 2 focuses on the management system, which is concerned with planning to meet customers' needs; arranging to meet those needs through leadership and strategic planning; and accomplishing goals through the actions of people and work processes. All of this is done with an eye toward continuous improvement; and using data and information to guide the decision-making process. In Chapter 4, the focus is on understanding customers and their needs, and practices to achieve customer satisfaction. Leadership and strategic planning are the focus of Chapter 5. This chapter includes a discussion of quality and organizational structure and the Seven Management and Planning Tools, with an application to strategic planning. Chapter 6 deals with human resource practices, specifically, the design of high performance work systems and the management of human resources in a TQ environment. Chapter 7 outlines the scope of process management activities, including design, production and delivery, and supplier and partnering processes; and the philosophy of continuous improvement. In Chapter 8, the focus is on the use of data and information to measure and manage organizational performance. This chapter includes discussion of the linkage of measurement with strategy, the cost of quality, and measuring the return on quality.

Part 3 focuses on basic technical issues, tools, and techniques. Chapter 9 provides a general introduction to statistical thinking and the role of statistical tools and methodology in quality assurance, including experimental design and process capability. Chapter 10 focuses on quality improvement, including management models such as the Deming Cycle, Six-Sigma programs, and the Seven QC tools. Chapter 11 deals primarily with the design of the quality control system and metrology. Chapter 12 introduces statistical process control, focusing on the construction and use of control charts for both variable and attributes data. An optional appendix to Chapter 12 addresses some statistical issues associated with control charts. Chapter 13 addresses reliability in design and production.

Part 4 houses the final chapter of the book, which deals with building and sustaining quality organizations. Coverage includes building a quality infrastructure, understanding and sharing best practices, implementing a TQ strategy, and sustaining it in the midst of change.

Features and Pedagogy

Each chapter includes Review Questions, which are designed to help students check their understanding of the key concepts presented in the chapter. The management-oriented chapters also include Discussion Questions that are open-ended or experiential in nature, and designed to help students expand their thinking or tie practical experiences to abstract concepts. Most chapters have a section entitled Projects, Etc., which suggests projects that involve field investigation or other types of research. The technical chapters, as well as Chapter 7, Process Management, include Problems designed to help students develop and practice quantitative skills. Finally, each chapter includes several Cases, which are designed to help students apply the concepts to unstructured or more-comprehensive situations.

Throughout the book, "Quality Profiles" provide background, important practices, and results for organizations that embrace TQ principles, most of whom are Baldrige winners. At the end of each chapter, "Quality in Practice" case studies are presented that describe real applications of the chapter material. These cases reinforce the chapter concepts and provide opportunities for discussion and more practical understanding. Many of the cases are drawn from real, published, or personal experiences of the authors.

Possible Course Outlines

Because the textbook material is comprehensive, it normally cannot be covered fully in one course. The textbook is designed to be flexible in meeting instructor needs. We have used it in both undergraduate courses in operations management and in managerially oriented MBA electives.

We believe that undergraduate majors in industrial or operations management are best served by developing hands-on knowledge that they will be able to use in their entry-level jobs. Thus a typical course for these undergraduate students might be slanted toward the material in Parts 1, 3, and 4, with some overview of the topics in Part 2. For MBAs, coverage of most of the first 8 to 10 chapters along with Chapter 14 would be more appropriate.

Note on Company References and Citations

In today's ever-changing business environment, many companies and divisions are being sold or divested, resulting in name changes. For example, Texas Instruments Defense Systems & Electronics Group was sold to Raytheon and is now part of Raytheon Systems Company, and AT&T Universal Card Services was bought by CitiBank. Although we have made efforts to note these changes in the book, others will undoubtedly occur after publication. In citing applications of total quality in these companies, we have generally preserved their original names to clarify that the practices and results cited occurred under their original corporate identities.

INSTRUCTOR'S SUPPORT MATERIAL

The following support material is available from *http://www.swcollege.com* or the Thomson Learning Academic Resource Center at 800-354-9706. All of these instructor supplements are combined in the **Instructor's Resource CD** (ISBN: 0-324-06683-X).

- The **Instructors' Manual**—Prepared by author William Lindsay, contains teaching suggestions and answers to all end-of-chapter questions, exercises, problems, and cases.
- **Power Point™ presentation slides**—Prepared by author Jim Evans for use in lectures.
- **Test Bank** and **ExamView®** & **ExamView® Pro**—Prepared by Matthew Ford of Northern Kentucky University, the Test Bank includes true/false, multiple choice, and short answer questions for each chapter. ExamView computerized testing software allows instructors to create, edit, store, and print exams. ExamView Pro provides online (computer-based or Internet-based) testing.

ACKNOWLEDGMENTS

We are extremely grateful to all the quality professionals, professors, reviewers, and students who have provided valuable feedback and suggestions during the development of this and previous editions. Many people deserve special thanks, particularly our current editors at South-Western/Thomson Learning: Charles McCormick, Jr., Alice Denny, and Libby Shipp, and our previous editors at West Educational Publishing: Richard Fenton, Mary Schiller, and Esther Craig.

We will continue to do our best to improve this book in our quest for quality and to spread what we truly believe is a fundamentally important message to future generations of business leaders. We encourage you to contact us at our e-mail addresses shown below with any comments or improvement suggestions that you may have.

James R. Evans (james.evans@uc.edu)
William M. Lindsay (lindsay@nku.edu)

Part 1

The Quality System

Unless you live in Webster, New York, you probably have never heard of Trident Precision Manufacturing, Inc. The privately held company was formed in 1979 with three people. By 1996 it had grown to 167 people with revenues of $14.5 million. Rates of return on assets consistently exceed industry averages, customers rate the quality of Trident's products at 99.8 percent or better, and the company has never lost a customer to a competitor. In 1996 Trident received the Malcolm Baldrige National Quality Award, the United States' highest recognition for performance excellence.

How did Trident achieve such success? When CEO Nicholas Juskiw wrote his vision statement he said:

> *My Vision for Trident is one in which each of us shares in the responsibility, growth, and benefits of becoming a world-class organization. How will we, as a team, achieve this? Through quality! Not just the quality of each individual part but through Total Quality—in everything we say and do. . . . As a strong team, with each headed in the same direction, we can become the unquestionable leader that our Customers, Industry, and Community look up to.*

Trident's total quality quest began in 1988, when Juskiw attended a symposium offered by Xerox Corporation—one of the first U.S. companies to embrace the quality concept—about its Leadership Through Quality strategy. During the 1980s and 1990s, quality was a common buzzword from CEOs down to workers on the shop floor. Attention to quality revitalized many companies in the United States and many other nations, helped contribute to global trade, and increased the value of goods and services that all consumers purchase. During this time, quality became the feature article of every major business magazine and metropolitan newspaper.

Today, we hear much less about quality in business, except when things go wrong. As the *Los Angeles Times* reported, for example, "In the early 1990s government auditors found that McDonnell Douglas employees performed slipshod work, used out-of-date blueprints and improperly inspected parts—all as the financially troubled company was scrambling to keep planes rolling off the assembly line." Some have suggested that these flaws were tied to the January 31, 2000, crash of an Alaskan Airlines jet that killed 88 people, which had been delivered during that period of time.[1] And the Census Bureau mailed 120 million misaddressed letters for the 2000 census, described as a "regrettable mistake" that should have been caught by the government's quality control procedures.[2]

We believe that less attention is paid to quality today as the result of two forces—a "good-news, bad-news" type of story. The good news is that the principles of quality that were new to many organizations in the early 1980s have become a common part of routine management practice; in other words, quality is so ingrained in the cultures of many organizations that managers and employees need not consciously think about it. The bad news is that for many other organizations, quality was viewed as a short-term fix; when the hype and rhetoric passed, so did their quality efforts. Quality often still takes a backseat to economic pressures. Nevertheless, quality has not faded away, and will not fade away, simply because *it works*, with clear evidence that it improves the bottom line. Quality efforts are alive and well, perhaps under a different moniker in some organizations, and will remain an important part of a continual quest for improving performance across the globe.

Joseph Juran, one of the most respected leaders of quality in the twentieth century, suggested that the past century will be defined by historians as the century of productivity. He also stated that the next century has to be the century of quality. "We've made dependence on the quality of our technology a part of life."[3] As a member of the emerging generation of business leaders, you have an opportunity and a responsibility to improve the quality of your company and society, not just for products and services, but as Trident's vision states, in everything you say and do.

Part 1 introduces the basic concepts of quality. Chapter 1 discusses the history, definition, basic principles of quality, and the impact of quality on competitive advantage and business results. Chapter 2 describes the role of total quality in different types of organizations—manufacturing, service, health care, education, and government—and stresses the importance of taking a systems perspective of quality throughout an organization. Chapter 3 introduces the management philosophies on which modern concepts of quality are based, and managerial frameworks—particularly the Malcolm Baldrige Criteria for Performance Excellence—that guide today's organizational approaches to improvement and performance excellence. These topics provide the foundation for the key quality principles and practices that are the subject of the remainder of the book.

NOTES

1. Stanley Holmes and Jeff Leeds, "Quality Was Problem at Plant that Made Crashed Jet," *Cincinnati Enquirer*, February 20, 2000, A5.
2. D'Vera Cohn and Stephen Barr, "Census Mail Goes Out With Wrong Numbers," *Washington Post*, February 27, 2000, 1.
3. Thomas A. Stewart, "A Conversation with Joseph Juran," *Fortune*, January 11, 1999, 168–169.

Chapter 1

Introduction to Quality

Outline

Quality is not a new concept in modern business. In October 1887, William Cooper Procter, grandson of the founder of Procter & Gamble, told his employees, "The first job we have is to turn out quality merchandise that consumers will buy and keep on buying. If we produce it efficiently and economically, we will earn a profit, in which you will share."

Mr. Procter's statement addresses three issues that are critical to managers of manufacturing and service organizations: *productivity*, *cost*, and *quality*. Productivity (the measure of efficiency defined as the amount of output achieved per unit of input), the cost of operations, and the quality of the goods and services that create customer satisfaction all contribute to profitability. Of these three determinants of profitability, the most significant factor in determining the long-run success or failure of any organization is quality. Good quality of goods and services can provide an organization with a competitive edge. Good quality reduces costs due to returns, rework, and scrap. Good quality increases productivity, profits, and other measures of success. Most importantly, good quality generates satisfied customers, who reward the organization with continued patronage and favorable word-of-mouth advertising. Quality has even become a focal point for industry-union cooperation. In working with Chrysler Corporation (now Daimler-Chrysler) to improve quality, a vice president of the United Auto Workers (UAW) succinctly stated the importance of quality: "No quality, no sales. No sales, no profit. No profit, no jobs."

In this chapter we examine the notion of quality. We discuss its history, its importance in business, and its role in building and sustaining competitive advantage.

THE HISTORY AND IMPORTANCE OF QUALITY

In a broad sense, **quality assurance** refers to any action directed toward providing consumers with products (goods and services) of appropriate quality. Quality assurance, usually associated with some form of measurement and inspection activity, has been an important aspect of production operations throughout history.[1] Egyptian wall paintings circa 1450 B.C. show evidence of measurement and inspection. Stones for the pyramids were cut so precisely that even today it is impossible to put a knife blade between the blocks. The Egyptians' success was due to the consistent use of well-developed methods and procedures and precise measuring devices.

The Age of Craftsmanship

During the Middle Ages in Europe, the skilled craftsperson served both as manufacturer and inspector. "Manufacturers" who dealt directly with the customer took considerable pride in workmanship. Craft guilds, consisting of masters, journeymen, and apprentices, emerged to ensure that craftspeople were adequately trained. Quality assurance was informal; every effort was made to ensure that quality was built into the final product by the people who produced it. These themes, which were lost with the advent of the Industrial Revolution, are important foundations of modern quality assurance efforts.

During the middle of the eighteenth century, a French gunsmith, Honoré Le Blanc, developed a system for manufacturing muskets to a standard pattern using interchangeable parts. Thomas Jefferson brought the idea to America, and in 1798 the new U.S. government awarded Eli Whitney a contract to supply 10,000 muskets to the government in two years' time. The use of interchangeable parts necessitated careful control of quality. Whereas a customized product built by a craftsperson can be tweaked and hammered to fit and work correctly, random matching of mating parts provides no such assurance. The parts must be produced according to a carefully designed standard. Whitney designed special machine tools and trained unskilled workers to make parts following a fixed design, which were then measured and compared to a model. But he underestimated the effect of variation in production processes (an obstacle that continues to plague companies to this day). Because of the resulting problems, Whitney needed more than 10 years to complete the project. Nonetheless, the value of the concept of interchangeable parts was recognized, and it eventually led to the Industrial Revolution, making quality assurance a critical component of the production process.

The Early Twentieth Century

In the early 1900s the work of Frederick W. Taylor, often called the father of Scientific Management, led to a new philosophy of production. Taylor's philosophy was to separate the planning function from the execution function. Managers and engineers were given the task of planning; supervisors and workers, the task of execution. This approach worked well at the turn of the century, when workers lacked the education needed for doing planning. By segmenting a job into specific work tasks and focusing on increasing efficiency, quality assurance fell into the hands of inspectors. Manufacturers were able to ship good-quality products, but at great costs. Defects were present, but were removed by inspection. Plants employed hundreds, even thousands, of inspectors. Inspection was thus the primary means of quality control during the first half of the twentieth century.

Eventually, production organizations created separate quality departments. This artificial separation of production workers from responsibility for quality assurance led to indifference to quality among both workers and their managers. Concluding that quality was the responsibility of the quality department, many upper managers turned their attention to output quantity and efficiency. Because they had delegated so much responsibility for quality to others, upper managers gained little knowledge about quality, and when the quality crisis hit, they were ill-prepared to deal with it.

Ironically, one of the leaders of the industrial revolution, Henry Ford, Sr., developed many of the fundamentals of what we now call "total quality practices" in the early 1900s. This approach was discovered when Ford executives visited Japan in 1982 to study Japanese management practices. As the story goes, one Japanese executive referred repeatedly to "the book," which the Ford people learned was a Japanese translation of *My Life and Work*, written by Henry Ford and Samuel Crowther in 1926 (New York: Garden City Publishing Co.). "The book" had become Japan's industrial bible, and Ford Motor Company had strayed from its principles over the years. The Ford executives had to go to a used bookstore to find a copy when they returned to the United States.

The Bell System was the leader in the early modern history of industrial quality assurance.[2] It created an inspection department in its Western Electric Company in the early 1900s to support the Bell operating companies. Even though the Bell System achieved its noteworthy quality through massive inspection efforts, the importance of quality in providing telephone service across the nation led Bell to research and develop new approaches. In the 1920s employees of Western Electric's inspection department were transferred to Bell Telephone Laboratories. The duties of this group included the development of new theories and methods of inspection for improving and maintaining quality. The early pioneers of quality assurance—Walter Shewhart, Harold Dodge, George Edwards, and others including W. Edwards Deming—were members of this group. It was here that the term *quality assurance* was coined. These pioneers developed many useful techniques for improving quality and solving quality problems. Thus, quality became a technical discipline of its own.

The Western Electric group, led by Walter Shewhart, ushered in the era of statistical quality control (SQC). SQC is the application of statistical methods for controlling quality. SQC goes beyond inspection; it is focused on identifying and eliminating the problems that cause defects. Shewhart is credited with developing control charts, which became a popular means of identifying quality problems in production processes and ensuring consistency of output. Others in the group developed many other useful statistical techniques and approaches.

During World War II the U.S. military began using statistical sampling procedures and imposing stringent standards on suppliers. The War Production Board offered free training courses in statistical methods that had been developed within the Bell System. The impact on wartime production was minimal, but the effort developed quality specialists, who began to use and extend these tools within their organizations. Thus, statistical quality control became widely known and gradually adopted throughout manufacturing industries. Sampling tables labeled MIL-STD, for military standard, were developed and are still widely used today. The discipline's first professional journal, *Industrial Quality Control*, was first published in 1944, and professional societies—notably the American Society for Quality Control (now called the American Society for Quality, *http://www.asq.org*)—were founded soon after.

Post–World War II

After the war, during the late 1940s and early 1950s, the shortage of civilian goods in the United States made production a top priority. In most companies, quality remained the province of the specialist. Quality was not a priority of top managers, who delegated this responsibility to quality managers. Top management showed little interest in quality improvement or the prevention of defects and errors, relying instead on mass inspection.

During this time, two U.S. consultants, Dr. Joseph Juran and Dr. W. Edwards Deming, introduced statistical quality control techniques to the Japanese to aid them in their rebuilding efforts. A significant part of their educational activity was focused on upper management, rather than quality specialists alone. With the support of top managers, the Japanese integrated quality throughout their organizations and developed a culture of continuous improvement (sometimes referred to by the Japanese term *kaizen*, pronounced kī-zen). Back in 1951, the Union of Japanese Scientists and Engineers (JUSE) instituted the Deming Prize (see Chapter 3) to reward individuals and companies who meet stringent criteria for quality management practice.

Improvements in Japanese quality were slow and steady; some 20 years passed before the quality of Japanese products exceeded that of Western manufacturers. By the 1970s, primarily due to the higher quality levels of their products, Japanese companies had made significant penetration into Western markets. One of the more startling facts was reported in 1980 by Hewlett-Packard. In testing 300,000 16K RAM chips from three U.S. and three Japanese manufacturers, Hewlett-Packard found that the Japanese chips had an incoming failure rate of zero failures per 1,000 compared to rates of 11 and 19 for the U.S. chips. After 1,000 hours of use, the failure rate of the U.S. chips was up to 27 times higher. In a few short years, the Japanese had penetrated a major market that had been dominated by U.S. companies. The automobile industry is another, more publicized, example. The June 8, 1987, *Business Week* special report on quality noted that the number of problems reported per 100 domestic new car models in the first 60 to 90 days of ownership averaged between 162 and 180. Comparable figures for Japanese and German automobiles were 129 and 152, respectively. The U.S. steel, consumer electronics, and even banking industries also were victims of global competition. U.S. business recognized the crisis.

The U.S. Quality Revolution

The decade of the 1980s was a period of remarkable change and growing awareness of quality by consumers, industry, and government. During the 1950s and 1960s, when "made in Japan" was associated with inferior products, U.S. consumers purchased domestic goods and accepted their quality without question. During the 1970s, however, increased global competition and the appearance of higher-quality foreign products on the market led U.S. consumers to consider their purchasing decisions more carefully. They began to notice differences in quality between Japanese- and U.S.-made products, and they began to expect and demand high quality and reliability in goods and services at a fair price. Consumers expected products to function properly and not to break or fail under reasonable use, and courts of law supported them. Extensive product recalls mandated by the Consumer Product Safety Commission in the early 1980s and the intensive media coverage of the Challenger space shuttle disaster in 1986, in which the Challenger exploded shortly after takeoff killing all seven astronauts, increased awareness of the importance of quality. Consequently, consumers are more apt than ever before to compare, evaluate, and choose products critically for total value—quality, price, and serviceability. Magazines such as *Consumer Reports*, newspaper reviews, and the Internet make this task much easier.

Obviously, the more technologically complex a product, the more likely it is that something will go wrong. Government safety regulations, product recalls, and the rapid increase in product liability judgments have changed society's attitude from "let the buyer beware" to "let the producer beware." Businesses have seen that increased attentiveness to quality is vital to their survival. Xerox (see *Quality Profile*) discovered that its Japanese competitors were selling small copiers for what it cost

Quality Profile

Xerox Corporation Business Products and Systems

Xerox Business Products and Systems (BP&S), headquartered in Stamford, Connecticut, employs more than 50,000 people at 83 U.S. locations. It manufactures more than 250 types of document-processing equipment and generates more than half of the corporation's domestic revenues. Copiers and other duplicating equipment account for nearly 70 percent of BP&S revenues. The company attempts to define quality through the eyes of the customer. By analyzing a wide variety of data gathered by exhaustive collection efforts, including monthly surveys of about 40,000 equipment owners, the company identifies important customer requirements. This information is used to develop concrete business plans with measurable targets for achieving the quality improvements necessary for meeting customers' needs. Xerox measures its performance in approximately 240 key areas of product, service, and business performance relative to world leaders, regardless of industry.

In the five years of continuous improvement culminating in the firm's winning the Malcolm Baldrige National Quality Award in 1989, defects per 100 machines were decreased by 78 percent, unscheduled maintenance was decreased by 40 percent, and service response time was improved by 27 percent. These successes seem to affirm the Xerox Quality Policy statement that "Quality is the basic business principle at Xerox."

Source: Malcolm Baldrige National Quality Award Profiles of Winners, National Institute of Standards and Technology, Department of Commerce.

Xerox to make them. A Westinghouse (now CBS) vice president of corporate productivity and quality summed up the situation by quoting Dr. Samuel Johnson's remark: "Nothing concentrates a man's mind so wonderfully as the prospect of being hanged in the morning." Quality excellence became recognized as a key to worldwide competitiveness and was heavily promoted throughout industry.[3] Most major U.S. companies instituted extensive quality improvement campaigns, focused not only on improving internal operations, but also on satisfying external customers.

One of the most influential individuals in the quality revolution was W. Edwards Deming. In 1980 NBC televised a special program entitled "If Japan Can . . . Why Can't We?" The widely viewed program revealed Deming's key role in the development of Japanese quality, and his name was soon a household word among corporate executives. Although Deming had helped to transform Japanese industry three decades earlier, it was only then that U.S. companies asked for his help. From 1980 until his death in 1993, his leadership and expertise helped many U.S. companies—such as Ford Motor Company, General Motors, and Procter & Gamble—to revolutionize their approach to quality.

As business and industry began to focus on quality, the government recognized that quality is critical to the nation's economic health. In 1984 the U.S. government designated October as National Quality Month. In 1985 NASA announced an Excellence Award for Quality and Productivity. In 1987 the Malcolm Baldrige National Quality Award (see Chapter 3), a statement of national intent to provide quality leadership, was established by an Act of Congress. The Baldrige Award has become the most influential instrument for creating quality awareness among U.S. businesses. In 1988 President Reagan established the Federal Quality Prototype Award and the President's Award for governmental agencies.

From the late 1980s and through the 1990s, interest in quality grew at an unprecedented rate, fueled in part by publicity from the Malcolm Baldrige National Quality Award. Companies made significant strides in improving quality. In the automobile industry, for example, improvement efforts by Chrysler, General Motors, and Ford reduced the number of problems reported per 100 domestic cars in the first 60 to 90 days of ownership from about 170 in 1987 to 136 in 1991. The gaps between Japanese and U.S. quality began to narrow, and U.S. firms regained much of the ground they had lost.

By 1989 Florida Power and Light was the first non-Japanese company to be awarded Japan's coveted Deming Prize for quality; AT&T Power Systems (see *Quality Profile*) was the second in 1994. Quality practices expanded into the service sector and into such nonprofit organizations as schools and hospitals. By 1990, quality became the principal driver in nearly every organization's quest for success. By the mid-1990s thousands of professional books had been written, and quality-related consulting and training had blossomed into an industry. Companies began to share their knowledge and experience through formal and informal networking. New quality awards were established by the federal government under the Clinton administration. The majority of states in the United States developed award programs for recognizing quality achievements in business, education, nonprofits, and government. In 1999, Congress added nonprofit education and health care sectors to the Baldrige Award.

From Product Quality to Performance Excellence

Although quality initiatives focused initially on reducing defects and errors in products and services through the use of measurement, statistics, and other problem-solving tools, organizations began to recognize that lasting improvement could not

Quality Profile
AT&T Power Systems

AT&T Power Systems, based in Mesquite, Texas, employs 2,400 people and makes electrical power systems for telecommunications equipment. Although the company won Japan's Deming Prize in 1994, it set out on its quality journey in 1990 to improve its business, not to win an award. The objective was to improve quality without building extensive bureaucracy—a problem that had arisen at Florida Power and Light.

In early 1992 AT&T Power Systems worked with the Union of Japanese Scientists and Engineers (JUSE) consultants to implement total quality management processes. In mid-1993 they invited JUSE experts back to assess their quality systems. The consultants provided extensive feedback and indicated that the firm's performance could make it a contender for the Deming Prize.

In pursuing the award, the company submitted a 400-page application and subjected its managers to four days of questioning by Japanese examiners. All managers were called upon to describe their responsibilities in three minutes and to answer detailed questions, backed up by documentation, for the rest of an hour. (The Deming Prize is discussed in greater detail in Chapter 3.) Since beginning its push for quality, the company has increased its customer base sixfold and cut its inventories in half. It relies on more than 250 employee teams to identify and implement improvements.

Sources: "Bags Deming, Baldrige on Same Day," and "Deming Legacy Gives Firms Quality Challenge,"

be accomplished without significant attention to the quality of the management practices used on a daily basis. Managers began to realize that the approaches they use to listen to customers and develop long-term relationships, develop strategy, measure performance and analyze data, reward and train employees, design and deliver products and services, and act as leaders in their organizations are the true enablers of quality, customer satisfaction, and business results. In other words, they recognized that the "quality of management" is as important as the "management of quality." As organizations began to integrate quality principles into their management systems, the notion of **total quality management**, or **TQM**, became popular. Quality took on a new meaning of organization-wide performance excellence rather than an engineering-based technical discipline.

Unfortunately, with all the hype and rhetoric (and the unfortunate three-letter-acronym, "TQM"), companies scrambled to institute quality programs. In their haste, many failed. As a result, TQM met some harsh criticism. In reference to Douglas Aircraft, a troubled subsidiary of McDonnell Douglas Corporation, *Newsweek* stated, "The aircraft maker three years ago embraced 'Total Quality Management,' a Japanese import that had become the American business cult of the 1980s. . . . At Douglas, TQM appeared to be just one more hothouse Japanese flower never meant to grow on rocky ground."[4] Other articles in *The Wall Street Journal* ("Quality Programs Show Shoddy Results," May 14, 1992) and the *New York Times* ("The Lemmings Who Love Total Quality," May 3, 1992) suggested that total quality approaches were passing fads and inherently flawed. *Business Week* commentator John Byrne pronounced TQM "as dead as a pet rock" (June 23, 1997, p. 47). However, reasons for TQM failures usually are rooted in poor organizational approaches and management systems, and not in the foundation principles of quality management. In fact, *Business Week's*

Byrne went on to say that today's most popular management ideas focus on "good old-fashioned, strategic planning" and customer satisfaction, which are generic to the quality management philosophy. As the editor of *Quality Digest* put it: "No, TQM isn't dead. TQM failures just prove that bad management is still alive and kicking."

Today, the term *TQM* has virtually disappeared from business vernacular; however, the underlying principles of quality management are recognized as the foundation of high-performance management systems and an important factor for competitive success. Many organizations have integrated quality principles so tightly with daily work activities that they no longer view quality as something special. Unfortunately, many other organizations have barely begun.

Current and Future Challenges

The real challenge today is to ensure that managers do not lose sight of the basic principles on which quality management and performance excellence are based. The global marketplace and domestic and international competition have made organizations around the world realize that their survival depends on high quality.[5] Many countries, such as Korea and India, are mounting national efforts to increase quality awareness, including conferences, seminars, radio shows, school essay contests, and pamphlet distribution. Spain and Brazil are encouraging the publication of quality books in their native language to make them more accessible. These trends will only increase the level of competition in the future. Even the tools used to achieve quality a decade ago are no longer sufficient to achieve the performance levels necessary to compete in today's world. Many organizations are embracing highly sophisticated, statistically based tools as part of popular "Six-Sigma" initiatives (see Chapter 10). These require increased levels of training and education for managers and front-line employees alike, as well as the development of technical staff.

In 1999, the American Society for Quality identified eight key forces that will influence the future of quality in this new century:[6]

- *Partnering:* Superior products and services will be delivered through partnering in all forms, including partnerships with competitors.
- *Learning systems:* Education systems for improved transfer of knowledge and skills will better equip individuals and organizations to compete.
- *Adaptability and speed of change:* Adaptability and flexibility will be essential to compete and keep pace with the increasing velocity of change.
- *Environmental sustainability:* Environmental sustainability and accountability will be required to prevent the collapse of the global ecosystem.
- *Globalization:* Globalization will continue to shape the economic and social environment.
- *Knowledge focus:* Knowledge will be the prime factor in competition and the creation of wealth.
- *Customization and differentiation:* Customization (lot size of one) and differentiation (quality of experience) will determine superior products and services.
- *Shifting demographics:* Shifting demographics (age and ethnicity) will continue to change societal values.

Some of the implications of these forces are that organizations must reinterpret work to provide learning experiences for workers and use quality tools at all levels because they provide a common language and the means by which people work together; fewer professionals will be dedicated strictly to quality—the main function of quality professionals will be to train others in cutting-edge tools; and business leaders must take responsibility and be held accountable for the quality outcomes of their work processes.

As Tom Engibous, president and chief executive officer of Texas Instruments, commented on the present and future importance of quality in 1997: Quality will have to be everywhere, integrated into all aspects of a winning organization.

DEFINING QUALITY

Quality can be a confusing concept, partly because people view quality in relation to differing criteria based on their individual roles in the production-marketing chain. In addition, the meaning of quality has evolved as the quality profession has grown and matured. Neither consultants nor business professionals agree on a universal definition. A study that asked managers of 86 firms in the eastern United States to define quality produced several dozen different responses, including the following:

1. Perfection
2. Consistency
3. Eliminating waste
4. Speed of delivery
5. Compliance with policies and procedures
6. Providing a good, usable product
7. Doing it right the first time
8. Delighting or pleasing customers
9. Total customer service and satisfaction[7]

Thus, it is important to understand the various perspectives from which quality is viewed in order to fully appreciate the role it plays in the many parts of a business organization.[8]

Judgmental Criteria

One common notion of quality, often used by consumers, is that it is synonymous with superiority or excellence. In 1931 Walter Shewhart first defined quality as the goodness of a product. This view is referred to as the *transcendent* (*transcend*, "to rise above or extend notably beyond ordinary limits") definition of quality. In this sense, quality is "both absolute and universally recognizable, a mark of uncompromising standards and high achievement."[9] As such, it cannot be defined precisely—you just know it when you see it. It is often loosely related to a comparison of features and characteristics of products and promulgated by marketing efforts aimed at developing quality as an image in the minds of consumers. Common examples of products attributed with this image are Rolex watches and Mercedes-Benz and Cadillac automobiles.

Excellence is abstract and subjective, however, and standards of excellence may vary considerably among individuals. Hence, the transcendent definition is of little practical value to managers. It does not provide a means by which quality can be measured or assessed as a basis for decision making.

Product-Based Criteria

Another definition of quality is that it is a function of a specific, measurable variable and that differences in quality reflect differences in quantity of some product attribute, such as in the number of stitches per inch on a shirt or in the number of cylinders in an engine. This interpretation implies that higher levels or amounts of product characteristics are equivalent to higher quality. As a result, quality is often mistakenly assumed to be related to price: the higher the price, the higher the quality. Just consider the case of a Florida man who purchased a $262,000 Lamborghini only to find a leaky roof, a battery that quit without notice, a sunroof that detached when the car hit a bump, and doors that jammed![10] However, a product—a term used in this book to refer to either a manufactured good or a service—need not be expensive to be considered a quality product by consumers. Also, as with the notion of excellence, the assessment of product attributes may vary considerably among individuals.

User-Based Criteria

A third definition of quality is based on the presumption that quality is determined by what a customer wants. Individuals have different wants and needs and, hence, different quality standards. This interpretation leads to a user-based definition: quality is defined as *fitness for intended use*, or how well the product performs its intended function. Both a Cadillac and a Jeep Cherokee are fit for use, for example, but they serve different needs and different groups of customers. If you want a highway touring vehicle with luxury amenities, then a Cadillac may better satisfy your needs. If you want a vehicle for camping, fishing, or skiing trips, a Jeep might be viewed as better quality.

Nissan's experience provides an example of applying the fitness-for-use concept.[11] Nissan tested the U.S. market for Datsun in 1960. Although the car was economical to own, U.S. drivers found it to be slow, hard to drive, low-powered, and not very comfortable. In essence, it lacked most of the qualities that North American drivers expected. The U.S. representative, Mr. Katayama, kept asking questions and sending the answers back to Tokyo. For some time, his company refused to believe that U.S. tastes were different from its own. After many years of nagging, Mr. Katayama finally got a product that Americans liked, the 240Z. Eventually, the name Datsun was changed to Nissan in an attempt to remove the old quality image.

A second example is that of a U.S. appliance company whose ranges and refrigerators were admired by Japanese buyers. Unfortunately, the smaller living quarters of the typical Japanese home do not have enough space to accommodate the U.S. models. Some could not even pass through the narrow doors of Japanese kitchens. Although the products' performance characteristics were high, the products were simply not fit for use in Japan.

Value-Based Criteria

A fourth approach to defining quality is based on *value*; that is, the relationship of usefulness or satisfaction to price. From this perspective, a quality product is one that is as useful as competing products and is sold at a lower price, or one that offers greater usefulness or satisfaction at a comparable price. Thus, one might purchase a generic product, rather than a brand-name one, if it performs as well as the brand-name product at a lower price.

Competing on the basis of value became a key business strategy in the early 1990s. Procter & Gamble, for example, instituted a concept it calls value pricing—offering products at "everyday" low prices in an attempt to counter the common consumer practice of buying whatever brand happens to be on special. In this way, P&G hoped to attain consumer brand loyalty and more consistent sales, which would provide significant advantages for its manufacturing system. Competition demands that businesses seek to satisfy consumers' needs at lower prices. The value approach to quality incorporates a firm's goal of balancing product characteristics (the customer side of quality) with internal efficiencies (the operations side).

Manufacturing-Based Criteria

A fifth definition of quality is a manufacturing-based definition. That is, quality is defined as the desirable outcome of engineering and manufacturing practice, or *conformance to specifications*. **Specifications** are targets and tolerances determined by designers of products and services. Targets are the ideal values for which production is to strive; tolerances are specified because designers recognize that it is impossible to meet targets all of the time in manufacturing. For example, a part dimension might be specified as "0.236 ± 0.003 cm." This specification would mean that the target, or ideal value, is 0.236 centimeters, and that the allowable variation is 0.003 centimeters from the target (a tolerance of 0.006 cm.). Thus, any dimension in the range 0.233 to 0.239 centimeters is deemed acceptable and is said to conform to specifications. Likewise, in services, "on-time arrival" for an airplane might be specified as within 15 minutes of the scheduled arrival time. The target is the scheduled time, and the tolerance is specified to be 15 minutes.

For the Coca-Cola Company, for example, quality is "about manufacturing a product that people can depend on every time they reach for it," according to Donald R. Keough, former president and chief operations officer. Through rigorous quality and packaging standards, the company strives to ensure that its products will taste the same anywhere in the world a consumer might buy them. Even service organizations strive for consistency in performance; The Ritz-Carlton Hotel Company, which we discuss further in Chapter 2, seeks to ensure that its customers will have the same quality experience at any of their properties around the world. Conformance to specifications is a key definition of quality, because it provides a means of measuring quality. Specifications are meaningless, however, if they do not reflect attributes that are deemed important to the consumer.

Integrating Perspectives on Quality

Although product quality should be important to all individuals throughout a production-distribution system, how quality is viewed may depend on one's position in the system, that is, whether one is the designer, manufacturer, distributor, or customer. To understand this view more clearly, let us consider the production-distribution cycle that is illustrated in Figure 1.1. The customer is the driving force for the production of goods and services, and customers generally view quality from either the transcendent or the product-based perspective. The goods and services produced should meet customers' needs; indeed, business organizations' existences depend upon their ability to meet customer needs. It is the role of the marketing function to determine these needs. A product that meets customer needs can rightly be described as a quality product. Hence, the user-based definition of quality is meaningful to people who work in marketing.

The manufacturer must translate customer requirements into detailed product and process specifications. Making this translation is the role of research and development, product design, and engineering. Product specifications might address such attributes as size, form, finish, taste, dimensions, tolerances, materials, operational characteristics, and safety features. Process specifications indicate the types of equipment, tools, and facilities to be used in production. Product designers must balance performance and cost to meet marketing objectives; thus, the value-based definition of quality is most useful at this stage.

A great deal of variation can occur during manufacturing operations. Machine settings can fall out of adjustment; operators and assemblers can make mistakes; materials can be defective. Even in the most closely controlled process, specific

Figure 1.1 Quality Perspectives in the Production-Distribution Cycle

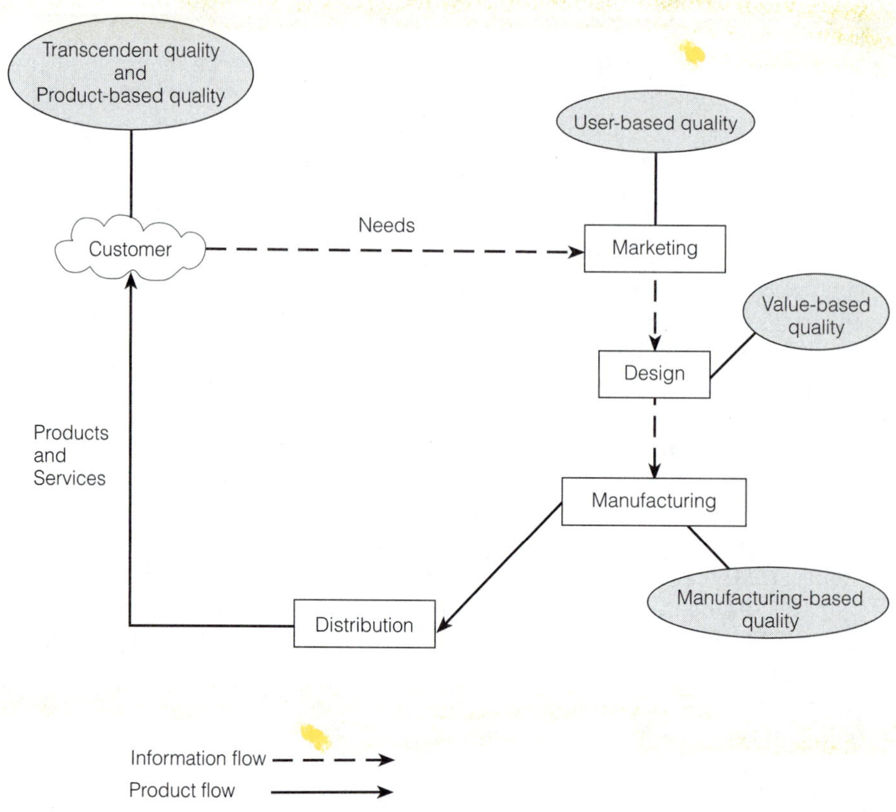

variations in product output are inevitable and unpredictable. The manufacturing function is responsible for guaranteeing that design specifications are adhered to during production and that the final product performs as intended. Thus, for production personnel, quality is described by the manufacturing-based definition. Conformance to product specifications is their goal.

The production-distribution cycle is completed when the product has been moved from the manufacturing plant, perhaps through wholesale and retail outlets, to the customer. Distribution does not end the customer's relationship with the manufacturer, however. The customer may need various services such as installation, user information, and special training. Such services are part of the product and cannot be ignored in quality management.

The need for different views of what constitutes quality at different points inside and outside an organization is now clear. All of these perspectives are necessary and must be embodied in an overall company philosophy in order to result in a product of true quality that will satisfy customers' needs. Hospital care offers a good illustration of how different views of quality can affect a single product. The transcendent definition of quality applies to the hospital's need to promote and maintain an image of excellence by ensuring the competency of its medical staff, the availability of treatments for rare or complicated disorders, or the presence of advanced medical technology. Subjective judgments of this kind of quality are made by patients and third-party organizations. Those who audit hospital efficiency and monitor treatment consistency and resource consumption define quality according to product-based dimensions. This view of quality is predominant among government and health care accrediting agencies.

Patients' perceptions of health care quality are focused on product-based and user-based criteria, and their expectations are high because of widely publicized improvements in medical care, advances in therapeutic drug treatments, and innovative surgery. Patient expectations have increased the pressure on hospitals to provide a variety of services to meet these expectations. As demand for flawless service increases, the medical staff and ancillary services must turn their attention to a manufacturing-based definition of quality. This view of quality is the one of accrediting agencies and the medical profession, which mandate conformance to various practices and determine licensing requirements for practice.

Customer-Driven Quality

Official definitions of quality terminology were standardized in 1978 by the American National Standards Institute (ANSI) and the American Society for Quality (ASQ).[12] These groups defined quality as "the totality of features and characteristics of a product or service that bears on its ability to satisfy given needs." This definition draws heavily on the product- and user-based approaches and is driven by the need to contribute value to customers and thus to influence satisfaction and preference. By the end of the 1980s, many companies had begun using a simpler, yet powerful, customer-driven definition of quality:

> *Quality is meeting or exceeding customer expectations.*

Partially true

To understand this definition, one must first understand the meanings of "customer." Most people think of a customer as the ultimate purchaser of a product or service; for instance, the person who buys an automobile for personal use or the guest who registers at a hotel. These customers are more precisely referred to as **consumers**. Clearly, meeting the expectations of consumers is the ultimate goal of any business. But before a product reaches consumers, it may flow through a chain of many firms or departments, each of which adds some value to the product. For example, an automobile engine plant may purchase steel from a steel company, produce engines, and then transport the engines to an assembly plant. The steel company is a supplier to the engine plant; the engine plant is a supplier to the assembly plant. The engine plant is thus a customer of the steel company, and the assembly plant is a customer of the engine plant. These customers are called **external customers**.

Every employee in a company also has **internal customers** who receive goods or services from suppliers within the company. An assembly department, for example, is an internal customer of the machining department, and managers are internal customers of the secretarial pool. Most businesses consist of many such "chains of customers." Thus, the job of an employee is not simply to please his or her supervisor; it is to satisfy the needs of particular internal and external customers. Failure to meet the needs and expectations of internal customers can result in a poor-quality product. For example, a poor design for a computerized hotel reservation system makes it difficult for reservation clerks to do their job, and consequently affects consumers' satisfaction. Understanding who are one's customers and what their expectations are is fundamental to achieving customer satisfaction, and it represents a radical departure from traditional ways of thinking in a functionally oriented organization. It allows workers to understand their place in the larger system and their contribution to the final product. (Who are the customers of a university, its instructors, and its students?)

Quality as customer satisfaction has been fundamental to Japanese business approaches. The president and CEO of Fujitsu Network Transmission Systems, a U.S. subsidiary of Fujitsu, Ltd., stated, "Our customers are intelligent; they expect us to continuously evolve to meet their ever-changing needs. They can't afford to have a thousand mediocre suppliers in today's competitive environment. They want a few exceptional ones."

QUALITY AS A MANAGEMENT FRAMEWORK

In the 1970s a General Electric task force studied consumer perceptions of the quality of various GE product lines.[13] Lines with relatively poor reputations for quality were found to deemphasize the customer's viewpoint, regard quality as synonymous with tight tolerance and conformance to specifications, tie quality objectives to manufacturing flow, express quality objectives as the number of defects per unit, and use formal quality control systems only in manufacturing. In contrast, product lines that received customer praise were found to emphasize satisfying customer expectations, determine customer needs through market research, use customer-based quality performance measures, and have formalized quality control systems in place for all business functions, not solely for manufacturing. The task force concluded that quality must not be viewed solely as a technical discipline, but rather as a management discipline. That is, quality issues permeate all aspects of business enterprise: design, marketing, manufacturing, human resource management, supplier relations, and financial management, to name just a few.

As companies came to recognize the broad scope of quality, the concept of **total quality (TQ)** emerged. A definition of total quality was endorsed in 1992 by the chairs and CEOs of nine major U.S. corporations in cooperation with deans of business and engineering departments of major universities, and recognized consultants:[14]

> *Total Quality (TQ) is a people-focused management system that aims at continual increase in customer satisfaction at continually lower real cost. TQ is a total system approach (not a separate area or program) and an integral part of high-level strategy; it works horizontally across functions and departments, involves all employees, top to bottom, and extends backward and forward to include the supply chain and the customer chain. TQ stresses learning and adaptation to continual change as keys to organizational success.*
>
> *The foundation of total quality is philosophical: the scientific method. TQ includes systems, methods, and tools. The systems permit change; the philosophy stays the same. TQ is anchored in values that stress the dignity of the individual and the power of community action.*

Procter & Gamble uses a concise definition: Total quality is the unyielding and continually improving effort by everyone in an organization to understand, meet, and exceed the expectations of customers.

Actually, the concept of TQ has been around for some time. A. V. Feigenbaum recognized the importance of a comprehensive approach to quality in the 1950s and coined the term **total quality control**.[15] Feigenbaum observed that the quality of products and services is directly influenced by what he terms the 9 Ms: markets, money, management, men and women, motivation, materials, machines and mechanization, modern information methods, and mounting product requirements. Although he developed his ideas from an engineering perspective, his concepts apply more broadly to general management.

The Japanese adopted Feigenbaum's concept and renamed it **companywide quality control**. Wayne S. Reiker listed five aspects of total quality control practiced in Japan.[16]

1. Quality emphasis extends through market analysis, design, and customer service rather than only the production stages of making a product.
2. Quality emphasis is directed toward operations in every department from executives to clerical personnel.
3. Quality is the responsibility of the individual and the work group, not some other group, such as inspection.
4. The two types of quality characteristics as viewed by customers are those that satisfy and those that motivate. Only the latter are strongly related to repeat sales and a "quality" image.
5. The first customer for a part or piece of information is usually the next department in the production process.

The term *total quality management* was actually developed within the Department of Defense and became popular with businesses in the United States during the 1980s. As we noted earlier, TQM has fallen out of favor, and many people simply use TQ, which we will do in this book.

Principles of Total Quality

Whatever the language, total quality is based on three fundamental principles.

1. A focus on customers and stakeholders
2. Participation and teamwork by everyone in the organization
3. A process focus supported by continuous improvement and learning

Despite their obvious simplicity, these principles are quite different from traditional management practices. Historically, companies did little to understand external customer requirements, much less those of internal customers. Managers and specialists controlled and directed production systems; workers were told what to do and how to do it, and rarely were asked for their input. Teamwork was virtually nonexistent. A certain amount of waste and error was tolerable and was controlled by post-production inspection. Improvements in quality generally resulted from technological breakthroughs instead of a relentless mindset of continuous improvement. With total quality, an organization actively seeks to identify customer needs and expectations, to build quality into work processes by tapping the knowledge and experience of its workforce, and to continually improve every facet of the organization.

Customer and Stakeholder Focus The customer is the principal judge of quality. Perceptions of value and satisfaction are influenced by many factors throughout the customer's overall purchase, ownership, and service experiences. To meet or exceed customer expectations, organizations must fully understand all product and service attributes that contribute to customer value and lead to satisfaction and loyalty. To accomplish this task, a company's efforts need to extend well beyond merely meeting specifications, reducing defects and errors, or resolving complaints. They must include both designing new products that truly delight the customer and responding rapidly to changing consumer and market demands. A company close to its customer knows what the customer wants, how the customer uses its products, and anticipates needs that the customer may not even be able to express. It also continually develops new ways of enhancing customer relationships.

A firm also must recognize that internal customers are as important in assuring quality as are external customers who purchase the product. Employees who view themselves as both customers of and suppliers to other employees understand how their work links to the final product. After all, the responsibility of any supplier is to understand and meet customer requirements in the most efficient and effective way possible.

Customer focus extends beyond the consumer and internal customer relationships, however. Employees and society represent important stakeholders. An organization's success depends on the knowledge, skills, creativity, and motivation of its employees and partners. Therefore, a TQ organization must demonstrate commitment to employees, provide opportunities for development and growth, provide recognition beyond normal compensation systems, share knowledge, and encourage risk-taking. Viewing society as a stakeholder is an attribute of a world-class organization. Business ethics, public health and safety, the environment, and community and professional support are necessary activities.

Participation and Teamwork Joseph Juran credited Japanese managers' full use of the knowledge and creativity of the entire workforce as one of the reasons for Japan's rapid quality achievements. When managers give employees the tools to make good decisions and the freedom and encouragement to make contributions, they virtually guarantee that better quality products and production processes will result. Employees who are allowed to participate—both individually and in teams—in decisions that affect their jobs and the customer can make substantial contributions to quality. In any organization, the person who best understands his or her job, along with how to improve both the product and the process, is the one performing it. This attitude represents a profound shift in the typical philosophy of senior management; the traditional view was that the workforce should be "managed," or to put it less formally, the workforce should leave their brains at the door. Good intentions alone are not enough to encourage employee involvement. Management's task includes formulating the systems and procedures and then putting them in place to ensure that participation becomes a part of the culture.

Empowering employees to make decisions that satisfy customers without constraining them with bureaucratic rules shows the highest level of trust. Marriott and Nordstrom are examples of two companies that empower and reward their employees for service quality. Marriott calls its customer service representatives "associates." Associates are permitted wide discretion to call on any part of the company to help customers and can earn lush bonuses for extraordinary work. Nordstrom's customer service stories are legendary, and include employees who have ironed a new shirt for a customer who needed it that afternoon, one who warmed customers' cars in winter while they shopped, and even one who refunded money for a set of tire chains, even though Nordstrom does not sell them![17]

Another important element of total quality is teamwork, which focuses attention on customer-supplier relationships and encourages the involvement of the total workforce in attacking systemic problems, particularly those that cross functional boundaries. Ironically, although problem-solving teams were introduced in the United States in the 1940s to help solve problems on the factory floor, they failed, primarily because of management resistance to workers' suggestions. The Japanese, however, began widespread implementation of similar teams, called quality circles, in 1962 with dramatic results. Eventually, the concept returned to the United States.

Today, the use of self-managed teams that combine teamwork and empowerment is a powerful method of employee involvement.

Traditionally, organizations were integrated vertically by linking all the levels of management in a hierarchical fashion (consider the traditional organization chart). TQ requires horizontal coordination between organizational units, such as between design and engineering, engineering and manufacturing, manufacturing and shipping, shipping and sales. Cross-functional teams provide this focus.

Partnerships with unions, customers, suppliers, and education organizations also promote teamwork and permit the blending of an organization's core competencies and capabilities with the complementary strengths of partners, creating mutual benefits. For example, many companies seek suppliers that share their own values. They often educate them in methods of improvement. If suppliers improve, then so will the company. For instance, Motorola requires suppliers to take courses in customer satisfaction and cycle time reduction at Motorola University. In addition, a 15-member council of suppliers rates Motorola's own practices and offers suggestions for improvement.[18]

Process Focus and Continuous Improvement The traditional way of viewing an organization is by surveying the vertical dimension—by keeping an eye on an organization chart. However, work gets done (or fails to get done) horizontally or cross-functionally, not hierarchically. A **process** is a sequence of activities that is intended to achieve some result. According to AT&T, a process is how work creates value for customers.[19] We typically think of processes in the context of production: the collection of activities and operations involved in transforming *inputs*, which are the physical facilities, materials, capital, equipment, people, and energy, into *outputs*, or the products and services. Common types of production processes include machining, mixing, assembly, filling orders, or approving loans. However, nearly every major activity within an organization involves a process that crosses traditional organizational boundaries as illustrated in Figure 1.2. For example, an order fulfillment process might involve a salesperson placing the order; a marketing representative entering it on the company's computer system; a credit check by finance; picking, packaging, and shipping by distribution and logistics personnel; invoicing by finance; and installation by field service engineers. A process perspective links all necessary activities together and increases one's understanding of the entire system, rather than focusing on only a small part. Many of the greatest opportunities for improving organizational performance lie in the organizational interfaces—those spaces between the boxes on an organization chart.

Continuous improvement refers to both incremental improvements that are small and gradual and breakthrough, or large and rapid, improvement. Improvements may take any one of several forms.

1. Enhancing value to the customer through new and improved products and services
2. Reducing errors, defects, waste, and their related costs
3. Increasing productivity and effectiveness in the use of all resources
4. Improving responsiveness and cycle time performance for such processes as resolving customer complaints or new product introduction

Major improvements in response time may require significant simplification of work processes and often drive simultaneous improvements in quality and productivity. Thus, response time, quality, and productivity objectives should be considered together. A process focus supports continuous improvement efforts by helping to understand these synergies and to recognize the true sources of problems.

Figure 1.2 Process Versus Function

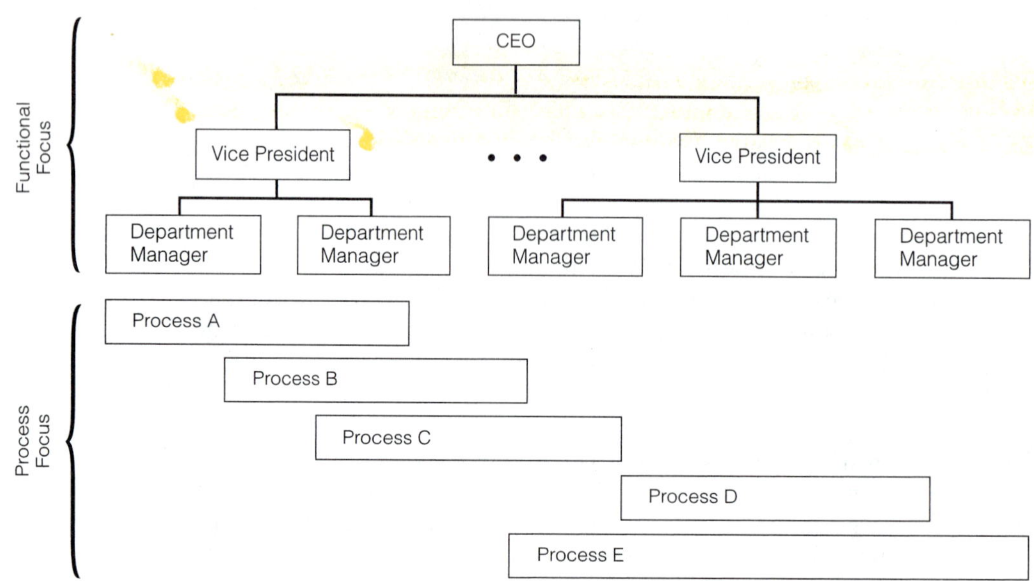

In 1950, when W. Edwards Deming was helping Japan with its postwar rebuilding effort, he emphasized the importance of continuous improvement. While presenting to a group of Japanese industrialists (collectively representing about 80 percent of the nation's capital), he drew the diagram shown in Figure 1.3. This diagram depicts not only the relationships among inputs, processes, and outputs, but also the roles of consumers and suppliers, the interdependency of organizational processes, the usefulness of consumer research, and the importance of continuous improvement of all elements of the production system. Deming told the Japanese that understanding customers and suppliers was crucial to planning for quality. He advised them that continuous improvement of both products and production processes through better understanding of customer requirements is the key to capturing world markets. Deming predicted that within five years Japanese manufacturers would be making products of the highest quality in the world and would have gained a large share of the world market. He was wrong. By applying these ideas, the Japanese penetrated several global markets in less than four years!

Real improvement depends on **learning,** that is, understanding why changes are successful through feedback between practices and results, which leads to new goals and approaches. A learning cycle has four stages:

1. Planning
2. Execution of plans
3. Assessment of progress
4. Revision of plans based upon assessment findings.

The concept of organizational learning is not new. It has its roots in general systems theory[20] and systems dynamics[21] developed in the 1950s and 1960s, as well as theories of learning from organizational psychology. Peter Senge, a professor at the Massachusetts Institute of Technology (MIT), has become the major advocate of the learning organization movement. He defines the **learning organization** as:

Figure 1.3 Deming's View of a Production System

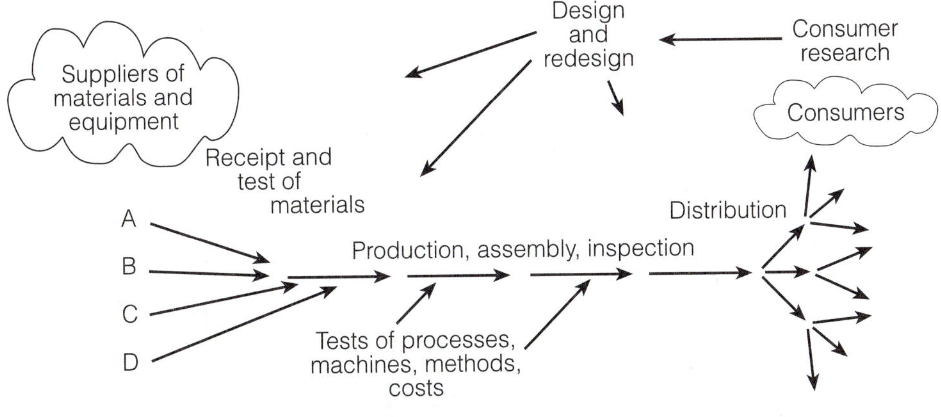

Source: Reprinted from *Out of the Crisis*, p. 5, by W. Edwards Deming, by permission of MIT and the W. Edwards Deming Institute. Published by MIT Center for Advanced Educational Services, Cambridge, MA 02139. © 1986 by The W. Edwards Deming Institute.

> *. . . an organization that is continually expanding its capacity to create its future. For such an organization, it is not enough merely to survive. "Survival learning" or what is more often termed "adaptive learning" is important—indeed it is necessary. But for a learning organization, "adaptive learning" must be joined by "generative learning," learning that enhances our capacity to create.*[22]

The conceptual framework behind this definition requires an understanding and integration of many of the concepts and principles that are part of the total quality philosophy. Senge repeatedly points out, "Over the long run, superior performance depends on superior learning."

Continuous improvement and learning should be a regular part of daily work; practiced at personal, work unit, and organizational levels; driven by opportunities to affect significant change; and focused on sharing throughout the organization. Organizational learning will be addressed further in Chapter 14.

Infrastructure, Practices, and Tools

The three principles of total quality need to be supported by an integrated organizational infrastructure, a set of management practices, and a set of tools and techniques, which all must work together as suggested in Figure 1.4. **Infrastructure** refers to the basic management systems necessary to function effectively and carry out the principles of TQ. It includes the following elements:

1. Customer relationship management
2. Leadership and strategic planning
3. Human resources management
4. Process management
5. Data and information management.

Practices are those activities that occur within each element of the infrastructure to achieve high performance objectives. For example, reviewing company performance

Figure 1.4 The Scope of Total Quality

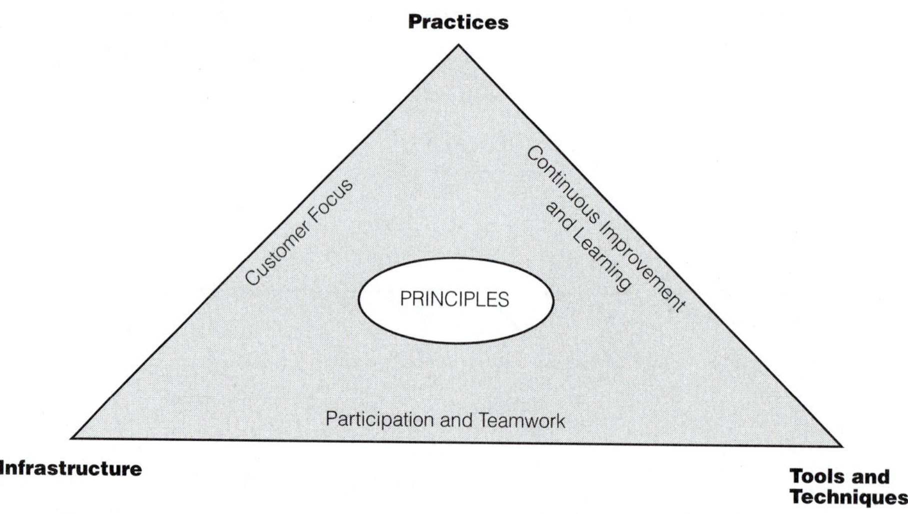

is a leadership practice; training and determining employee satisfaction are human resources management practices; and coordinating design and production/delivery processes to ensure troublefree introduction and delivery of products and services is a process management practice. **Tools** include a wide variety of graphical and statistical methods to plan work activities, collect data, analyze results, monitor progress, and solve problems. For instance, a chart showing trends in manufacturing defects as workers progress through a training program is a simple tool to monitor the effectiveness of the training; the statistical technique of experimental design is often used in product development activities. The relationships among infrastructure, practices, and tools are illustrated in Figure 1.5.

This section gives a brief overview of the major elements of a total quality infrastructure. We will expand on these topics and describe specific practices and tools in subsequent chapters. It is important to realize that total quality management practices and helpful tools continually evolve and improve. Therefore, discussion of each and every useful practice or tool is not possible within the scope of this book.

Figure 1.5 Relationships Among Infrastructure, Practices, and Tools

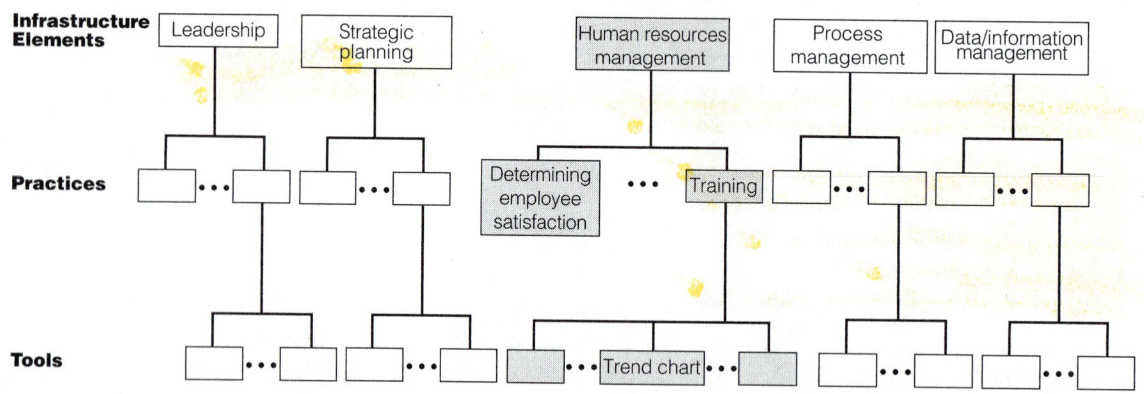

Customer Relationship Management Understanding customer needs, both current and future, and keeping pace with changing markets require effective strategies for listening to and learning from customers, measuring their satisfaction relative to competitors, and building relationships. Customer needs—particularly differences among key customer groups—must be linked closely to an organization's strategic planning, product design, process improvement, and workforce training activities. Satisfaction and dissatisfaction information are important because understanding them leads to the right improvements that can create satisfied customers who reward the company with loyalty, repeat business, and positive referrals. Satisfying customers requires prompt and effective response and solutions to their needs and desires as well as building and maintaining good relationships. These issues will be discussed in Chapter 4.

Leadership and Strategic Planning The success of any organization depends on the performance of the workers at the bottom of the pyramid. Ross Perot, the Texas billionaire founder of a large software consulting firm, once said that inventories can be managed, but people must be led. All managers, ideally starting with the CEO, must act as the organization's leaders for quality. Their task is to create clear values and high expectations for performance excellence, and then build these into the company's processes. Senior management should serve as role models to inspire and motivate the workforce and encourage involvement, learning, innovation, and creativity.

The pursuit of sustainable growth and market leadership through quality requires a strong future orientation and willingness to make long-term commitments to customers and stakeholders. Effective strategic business planning drives quality excellence throughout the organization and anticipates changes such as customers' expectations, new business and partnering opportunities, the global and electronic marketplace, technological developments, new customer segments, evolving regulatory requirements, community and societal expectations, and strategic changes by competitors. Plans, strategies, and resource allocations need to reflect these influences. Leadership and strategic planning are addressed further in Chapter 5.

Human Resource Management Meeting the company's quality and performance goals requires a fully committed, well-trained, and involved workforce. Front-line workers need the skills to listen to customers; manufacturing workers need specific skills in developing technologies; and all employees need to understand how to use data and information to drive continuous improvement. These goals can only be achieved through the design and management of appropriate work systems, reward and recognition approaches, education and training approaches, and a healthful, safe, and motivating work environment. Major challenges in this area include the integration of human resource practices and the alignment of human resource management with business directions and strategic change processes. Addressing these challenges requires effective use and understanding of employee-related data on knowledge, skills, satisfaction, motivation, safety, and well-being. These issues are discussed further in Chapter 6.

Process Management Process management involves the design of processes to develop and deliver products and services that meet the needs of customers, daily control of those processes so that they perform as required, and their continual improvement. Process management activities emphasize prevention and organizational learning; the costs of preventing problems at the design stage are much lower than costs of correcting problems that occur "downstream." Also, success in globally competitive markets requires a capacity for rapid change and flexibility, such as shorter product introduction cycles and faster and more flexible response to customers, which often means simplification of processes and the ability for rapid changeover from one process to another. Process management activities involve not only an organization's core capabilities, but also support processes, and supplier-partnering processes. Process management is the subject of Chapter 7.

Data and Information Management Modern businesses depend on data and information to support performance measurement, management, and improvement. Such measurements should derive from an organization's strategy and provide critical information about key processes, outputs, and results, which can then lead to improved customer service, operational, and financial performance. A comprehensive and balanced set of leading and lagging measures and indicators tied to customer and organization performance requirements provides a clear basis for aligning all activities with the organization's goals. These data must be supported by effective analysis capabilities to extract useful information and then to evaluate and compare that data with competitor and best practices benchmarks for purposes of decision making and operational improvement. We will discuss these issues further in Chapter 8.

QUALITY AND COMPETITIVE ADVANTAGE

Competitive advantage denotes a firm's ability to achieve market superiority. In the long run, a sustainable competitive advantage goes hand in hand with above-average performance. S. C. Wheelwright identified six characteristics of a strong competitive advantage:[23]

1. It is driven by customer wants and needs. A company provides value to its customers that competitors do not.
2. It makes a significant contribution to the success of the business.
3. It matches the organization's unique resources with opportunities in the environment. No two companies have the same resources; a good strategy uses the firm's particular resources effectively.
4. It is durable and lasting, and difficult for competitors to copy. A superior research and development department, for example, can consistently develop new products or processes that enable the firm to remain ahead of competitors.
5. It provides a basis for further improvement.
6. It provides direction and motivation to the entire organization.

Each of these characteristics relates to quality, suggesting that quality is an important source of competitive advantage.

The importance of quality in achieving competitive advantage was demonstrated by several research studies during the 1980s. PIMS Associates, Inc., a subsidiary of the Strategic Planning Institute, maintains a database of 1,200 companies and studies the impact of product quality on corporate performance.[24] PIMS researchers have found that:

1. Product quality is an important determinant of business profitability.
2. Businesses that offer premium-quality products and services usually have large market shares and were early entrants into their markets.
3. Quality is positively and significantly related to a higher return on investment for almost all kinds of products and market situations. (PIMS studies have shown that firms whose products are perceived as having superior quality have

more than three times the return on sales of firms whose products are perceived as having inferior quality.)

4. Instituting a strategy of quality improvement usually leads to increased market share, but at the cost of reduced short-run profitability.
5. High-quality producers can usually charge premium prices.

These findings can be summarized as in Figure 1.6. A product's value in the marketplace is influenced by the quality of its design. Improvements in design will differentiate the product from its competitors, improve a firm's quality reputation, and improve the perceived value of the product. This differentiation allows the company to command higher prices as well as to achieve a greater market share, which in turn leads to increased revenues, offsetting the costs of improving the design.

Improved conformance in production or service delivery leads to lower costs through savings in rework, scrap, resolution of errors, and warranty expenses. This viewpoint was popularized by Philip Crosby in his book *Quality Is Free*.[25] Crosby states:

> *Quality is not only free, it is an honest-to-everything profit maker. Every penny you don't spend on doing things wrong, over, or instead of, becomes half a penny right on the bottom line. In these days of "who knows what is going to happen to our business tomorrow," there aren't many ways left to make a profit improvement. If you concentrate on making quality certain, you can probably increase your profit by an amount equal to 5% to 10% of your sales. That is a lot of money for free.*

The net effect of improved quality of design and conformance is increased profits.

It is vital to focus quality improvement efforts on both design and conformance. Many organizations simply confine their quality efforts to defect elimination. In today's global marketplace, the absence of defects is a given, rather than a source of competitive advantage. Quality is simply the foundation for competitive advantage. Competitive success in today's market depends on such attributes as the speed of new product development, flexibility in production and delivery, and extraordinary customer service. For example, *Business Week* reported in 1998 that several wireless communications providers had replaced Motorola—a long-time quality leader—technology with others. A BellSouth spokesman said the products did not pass its "shake and bake test." After Qualcomm, Inc., released digital phones the size of cigarette packs, Motorola was nearly a year behind, and as a result, was quickly losing market share.[26] However, within a year, Motorola's wireless communications returned to profitability, including making a $1 billion, 10-year pact with Sun

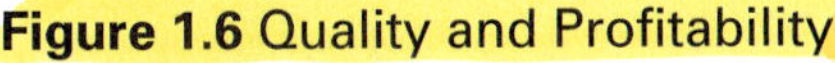

Figure 1.6 Quality and Profitability

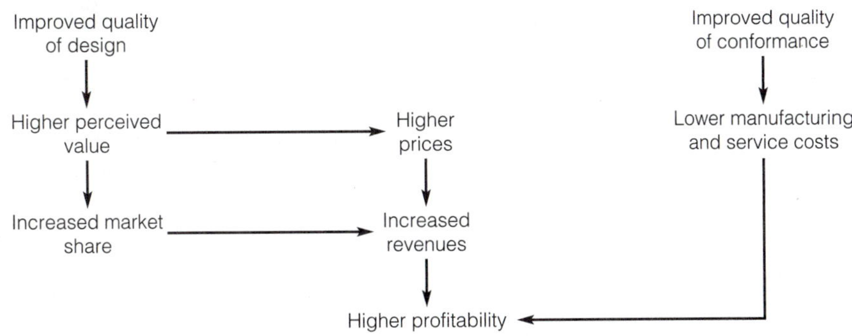

Microsystems to build wireless telecom equipment for the Internet with a 99.999 percent reliability. Only the most agile companies could make such a quick turnaround.

Quality and Business Results

As an old saying goes, "The proof is in the pudding." Companies that invest in quality management efforts experience outstanding returns and improvements in performance. The General Accounting Office (GAO) of the U.S. government studied 20 companies that were among the highest scoring applicants in the 1988 and 1989 Baldrige Award competition.[27] In nearly all cases, these companies achieved better employee relations, higher productivity, greater customer satisfaction, increased market share, and improved profitability, as summarized in the model shown in Figure 1.7. The solid lines show the causal effects; the dotted lines indicate the information feedback necessary for continuous improvement. The arrows in the boxes show the expected direction of the performance indicators. A more recent survey of almost 1,000 executives conducted by Zenger-Miller Achieve noted similar benefits from quality initiatives, including increased employee participation, improved product and service quality, improved customer satisfaction, improved productivity, and improved employee skills.[28]

Considerable evidence exists on the impact of quality initiatives on bottom-line results. The Commerce Department reported that an investment of $1,000 in common

Figure 1.7 The GAO Total Quality Model

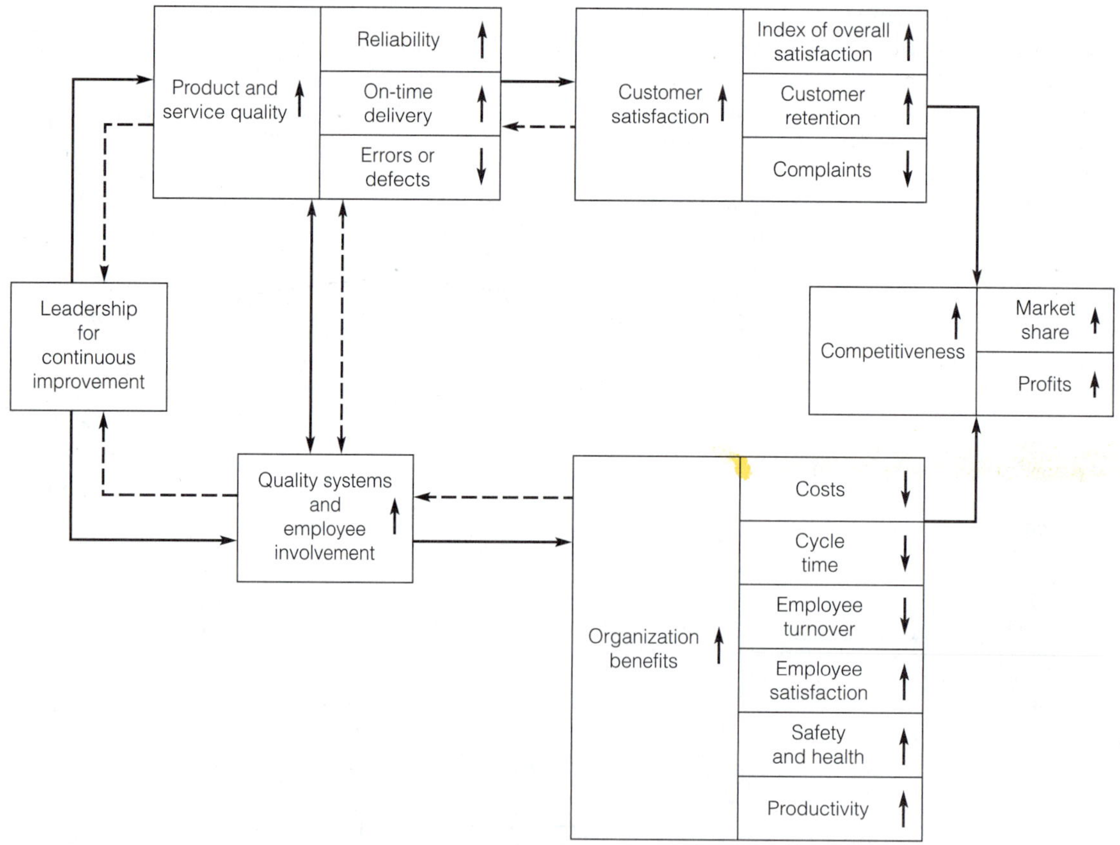

stock in each publicly traded company that won the Malcolm Baldrige National Quality Award through 1999 (or a proportional investment in winning subsidiaries of larger companies) would have outperformed the Standard & Poor's (S&P) 500 stock index by approximately 3.8 to 1, achieving an 841 percent return on investment, compared to a 222 percent return for the S&P 500. The group of five whole-company winners outperformed the S&P 500 by 4.8 to 1, achieving a 1,101 percent return on investment.

One of the most noted studies was published by Kevin Hendricks and Vinod Singhal in 1997.[29] Based on objective data and rigorous statistical analysis, the study showed that when implemented effectively, total quality management approaches improve financial performance dramatically. Using a sample of about 600 publicly traded companies that have won quality awards either from their customers (such as automotive manufacturers) or through Baldrige and state and local quality award programs, Hendricks and Singhal examined performance results from six years before to four years after winning their first quality award. The primary performance measure tracked was the percent change in operating income and a variety of measures that might affect operating income: percent change in sales, total assets, number of employees, return on sales, and return on assets. These results were compared to a set of control firms that were similar in size to the award winners and in the same industry. The analysis revealed significant differences between the sample and the control group. Specifically, the growth in operating income of winners averaged 91 percent versus 43 percent for the control group. Winners also experienced a 69 percent jump in sales (compared to 32 percent for the control group), a 79 percent increase in total assets (compared to 37 percent), a 23 percent increase in the number of employees (compared to 7 percent), an 8 percent improvement on return on sales (compared to 0 percent), and a 9 percent improvement on return on assets (compared to 6 percent). Small companies actually out performed large companies, and over a five-year period, the portfolio of winners beat the S&P 500 index by 34 percent.

A sample of specific operational and financial results that Baldrige winners have achieved include:

1. At Globe Metallurgical (see *Quality Profile*), from 1988 to 1992, exports grew from 2 percent to 20 percent of sales, while overall sales grew by 24 percent.
2. In 1992 Texas Instruments Defense Systems & Electronics Group had a 21 percent reduction in production cycle time with a 56 percent reduction in stock-to-production time.
3. Solectron, by focusing on customer satisfaction, experienced average yearly revenue growth of 46.8 percent, and by focusing on process quality saw average yearly net income growth of 57.3 percent over five years.
4 Armstrong World Industries Building Products Operations found that its cost-of-poor-quality index dropped by 37 percent, contributing $16 million in additional operating profit in 1994 alone. The company set industry safety records with more than 3 million hours without a lost-time injury, and made its highest-ever gainsharing and incentive payouts.
5. Boeing Airlift and Tanker Programs lowered rejection rates from 0.9 percent in 1994 to 0.08 percent in 1998 while improving net asset turnover by a factor of seven. Time spent on rework and repair was reduced by 54 percent from 1992 to 1998.
6. Texas Nameplate Company increased its national market share from less than 3 percent in 1994 to 5 percent in 1997, reduced its defects from 3.65 percent to about 1 percent of billings, and increased on-time delivery from 95 to 98 percent.

Quality Profile

Globe Metallurgical, Inc.

Globe Metallurgical, Inc., a small-business winner of the Malcolm Baldrige National Quality Award in 1988, has plants in Beverly, Ohio, and Selma, Alabama. The plants produce about 100,000 tons of alloys for more than 300 customers. In the early 1980s the company found itself faced with threats from foreign manufacturers. Globe's quality initiative was motivated by Ford Motor Company's Q-1 supplier program. To be considered as a long-term supplier for Ford, Globe launched a total quality approach. To begin, managers and supervisors viewed videotape lectures by W. Edwards Deming. The entire workforce was trained in statistical methods. Globe also developed a quality manual and offered quality-related education and training to its suppliers. It instituted practices to improve employee morale, such as improved benefit and pension plans, elimination of time clocks, and profit-sharing plans. A Quality-Efficiency-Cost steering committee led the total quality approach effort, supported by a variety of teams in which workers generated ideas for improvements.

Teamwork and statistical methods helped Globe achieve significant improvements in product quality. Greater consistency in final products—achieving specifications that fall within ranges more demanding than those imposed by customers—significantly lowered the chance of an out-of-specification shipment. This improvement also resulted in increased production rates and lower energy consumption. From 1985 to 1987, customer complaints decreased by 91 percent, and the accident rate, near the industry average in 1985, fell while the industry average rose.

Source: Malcolm Baldrige National Quality Award, Profiles of Winners, National Institute of Standards and Technology, Department of Commerce.

7. STMicroelectronics, Inc.–Region Americas reduced lost-day injuries from 1.01 per 100 workers in 1996 to 0.65 in 1999, which is 74 percent below the industry average, and employee satisfaction levels in 1999 exceeded the industry composite in 8 of 10 categories.

THREE LEVELS OF QUALITY[30]

An organization that is committed to total quality must apply it at three levels: the *organizational level*, the *process level*, and the *performer/job level*. At the organizational level, quality concerns center on meeting external customer requirements. An organization must seek customer input on a regular basis. Questions such as the following help to define quality at the organizational level:

1. Which products and services meet your expectations?
2. Which do not?
3. What products or services do you need that you are not receiving?
4. Are you receiving products or services that you do not need?

Customer-driven performance standards should be used as bases for goal setting, problem solving, performance appraisal, incentive compensation, nonfinancial rewards, and resource allocation.

At the process level, organizational units are classified as functions or departments, such as marketing, design, product development, operations, finance, purchasing, billing, and so on. Because most processes are cross-functional, the danger exists that managers of particular organizational units will try to optimize the activities under their control, which can suboptimize activities for the organization as a whole. At this level, managers must ask questions such as:

1. What products or services are most important to the (external) customer?
2. What processes produce those products and services?
3. What are the key inputs to the process?
4. Which processes have the most significant effect on the organization's customer-driven performance standards?
5. Who are my internal customers and what are their needs?

At the performer level (sometimes called the job level or the task-design level), standards for output must be based on quality and customer-service requirements that originate at the organizational and process levels. These standards include requirements for such things as accuracy, completeness, innovation, timeliness, and cost. For each output of an individual's job, one must ask:

1. What is required by the customer, both internal and external?
2. How can the requirements be measured?
3. What is the specific standard for each measure?

Viewing an organization from this perspective clarifies the roles and responsibilities of all employees in pursuing quality. Top managers must focus attention at the organizational level; middle managers and supervisors at the process level; and all employees must understand quality at the performer level. Getting everyone involved is the foundation of TQ.

QUALITY AND PERSONAL VALUES

Today, companies are asking employees to take more responsibility for acting as the point of contact between the organization and the customer, to be team players, and to provide more effective and efficient customer service. Rath & Strong, a Lexington, Massachusetts-based management consulting firm, polled almost 200 executives from *Fortune* 500 companies about activities that foster superior performance results for an organization.[31] The survey revealed that *personal initiative*, when combined with a customer orientation, has a positive impact on business success and sales growth rate. However, although 79 percent of all respondents indicated that employees are increasingly expected to take initiative to bring about change in the company, 40 percent of the respondents replied that most people in their company do not believe that they can make a personal contribution to the company's success. Alan Frohman, a senior associate with Rath & Strong, stated, "These results are significant because they suggest that although people are being expected to take personal initiative, most organizations have not figured out how to translate those expectations into positive behaviors."

Such behaviors reflect the personal values and attitudes of individuals. Unless quality is internalized at the personal level, it will never become rooted in the culture of an organization. Thus, quality must begin at a personal level. Employees who embrace quality as a personal value often go beyond what they are asked or normally expected to do in order to reach a difficult goal or provide extraordinary service to a customer. A good example involved a young girl who laid her dental retainer on a picnic table at Disney World while eating lunch.[32] She forgot about it until later in the day. The family returned to the spot, found the table cleaned up, and were at a loss to know what to do. They spotted a custodian, told him the problem, and the custodian sought permission from his supervisor to have the garbage bags searched by the night crew that evening! Two weeks later, the family received a letter from the supervisor explaining that, despite their best efforts, they had been unable to locate the retainer.

The concept of "personal quality" has been promoted by Harry V. Roberts, professor emeritus at the University of Chicago's Graduate School of Business, and Bernard F. Sergesketter, vice president of the Central Region of AT&T.[33] Personal quality may be thought of as personal empowerment; it is implemented by systematically keeping personal checklists for quality improvement. Roberts and Sergesketter developed the idea of a personal quality checklist to keep track of personal shortcomings, or defects, in personal work processes. The authors defended the use of a checklist to keep track of defects:

> *The word "defect" has a negative connotation for some people who would like to keep track of the times we do things right rather than times we do things wrong. Fortunately, most of us do things right much more than we do things wrong, so it is easier in practice to count the defects. Moreover, we can get positive satisfaction from avoiding defects—witness accident prevention programs that count days without accidents.*

An example of a personal quality checklist developed to improve professorial activities is provided in Figure 1.8. It can be used as a starting point for developing a

Figure 1.8 An Example of a Personal TQ Checklist

Week of: ______________________

Defect Category	M	T	W	TH	F	S	SU	Total
Search for something misplaced or lost, over 20 minutes								
Failure to discard incoming junk by end of day								
Putting a small task on the "hold" pile, over 2 hours								
Failure to respond to letter or phone call in 24 hours								
Lack of clarity in setting requirements/deadlines								
Excessive "general interest" reading; over 30 minutes/weekday								
Failure to provide weekly opportunity for feedback from a class								
Less than two hours of writing per day, 4 days/week								
Less than 8 hours of sleep on a weeknight								
Less than 3 exercise periods/week								
Take wife out for fewer than 1 meal/week								
Less than 0.5 hour meditation per weekday								

personal quality checklist (see the project later in the chapter). Note that each item on the checklist has a desired result, a way to measure each type of defect, and a time frame. Both work and personal defect categories are listed on the sheet. Sergesketter plotted defects that he observed during the first 18 months of his use of his own personal quality checklist on a run chart as shown in Figure 1.9. Many of the results were surprising.[34] For instance, he was surprised at the extent to which he was not returning phone calls the same day. He discovered that he had no way to count defects related to correspondence. As a result, he started to date stamp correspondence when it arrived and date stamp the file copy of the response. None of the items he measured was in the "four-minute mile" category, and yet he started out at a rate of 100 defects per month, but dropped drastically simply because he was aware of them. He also observed that when a person shares a defect list with others, they can help in reducing defects. Sergesketter noted, "I encourage and challenge you to start counting defects. It is impossible to reduce defects if we don't count them, and we can't reasonably ask our associates to count defects if we don't! I really believe that if several thousand of us here in the Central Region start counting defects, we will reduce them and differentiate ourselves from our competitors in a significant way."

Personal quality is an essential ingredient to make quality happen in the workplace, yet it has been neglected for a long time by most companies. Perhaps management, in particular, has operated under the idea that promoting quality is something that companies do to employees, rather than something they do with employees.

Maybe in the daily attempt to bring about change in the individual parts of the organizational universe, managers, employees, professors, and students will find that personal quality is the key to unlock the door to a wider understanding of what the concept really is all about.

Figure 1.9 Chart of Number of Defects/Month

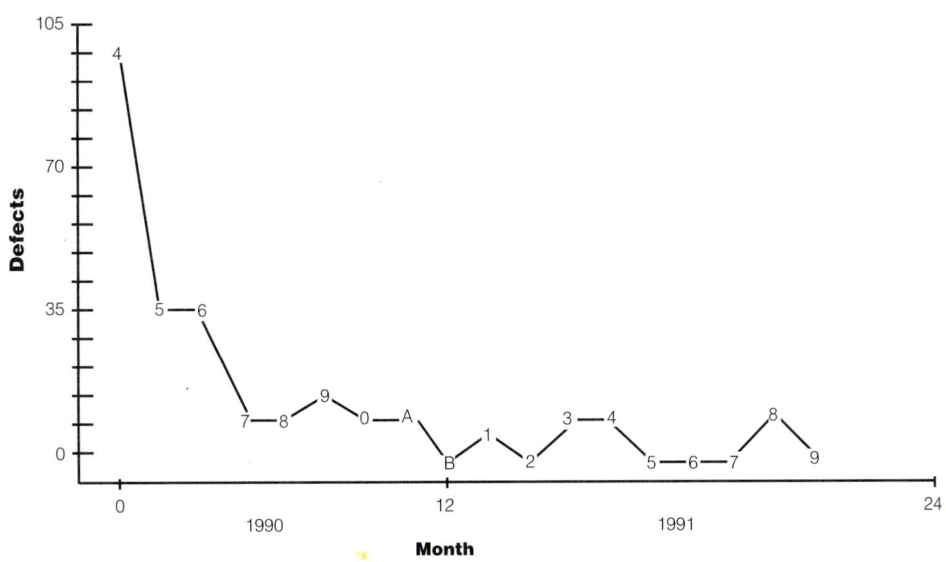

Source: Adapted with the permission of The Free Press, a Division of Simon & Schuster, Inc. from QUALITY IS PERSONAL: A Foundation for Total Quality Management by Harry V. Roberts and Bernard F. Sergesketter. © 1993 Harry V. Roberts and Bernard F. Sergesketter, p. 13.

Quality in Practice

The Xerox Transformation[35]

The Xerox 914, the first plain-paper copier, was introduced in 1959. Regarded by many people as the most successful business product ever introduced, it created a new industry. During the 1960s Xerox grew rapidly, selling all it could produce, and reached $1 billion in revenue in record-setting time. By the mid 1970s its return on assets was in the low 20-percent range. Its competitive advantage was due to strong patents, a growing market, and little competition. Such an environment would seem to prompt little need to focus on customers.

During the 1970s, however, IBM and Kodak entered the high-volume copier business—Xerox's principal market. Several Japanese companies introduced high-quality low-volume copiers, a market that Xerox had virtually ignored, and established a foundation for moving into the high-volume market. In addition, the Federal Trade Commission accused Xerox of illegally monopolizing the copier business. After negotiations, Xerox agreed to open approximately 1,700 patents to competitors. Xerox was soon losing market share to Japanese competitors, and by the early 1980s it faced a serious competitive threat from copy machine manufacturers in Japan; Xerox's market share had fallen to less than 50 percent. Some people even predicted that the company would not survive. Rework, scrap, excessive inspection, lost business, and other problems were estimated to be costing Xerox more than 20 percent of revenue, which in 1983 amounted to nearly $2 billion. Both the company and its primary union, the Amalgamated Clothing and Textile Workers, were concerned. In comparing itself with its competition, Xerox discovered that it had nine times as many suppliers, twice as many employees, cycle times that were twice as long, 10 times as many rejects, and seven times as many manufacturing defects in finished products. It was clear that radical changes were required.

In 1983 company president David T. Kearns became convinced that Xerox needed a long-range, comprehensive quality strategy as well as a change in its traditional management culture. Kearns was aware of Japanese subsidiary Fuji Xerox's success in implementing quality management practices and was approached by several Xerox employees about instituting total quality management. He commissioned a team to outline a quality strategy for Xerox. The team's report stated that instituting it would require changes in behaviors and attitudes throughout the company as well as operational changes in the company's business practices. Kearns determined that Xerox would initiate a total quality management approach, that they would take the time to "design it right the first time," and that the effort would involve all employees. Kearns and the company's top 25 managers wrote the Xerox Quality Policy, which states:

> *Xerox is a quality company.*
> *Quality is the basic business principle for Xerox.*
> *Quality means providing our external and internal customers with innovative products and services that fully satisfy their requirements.*
> *Quality improvement is the job of every Xerox employee.*

This policy led to a process called Leadership Through Quality, which has three objectives:

1. To instill quality as the basic business principle in Xerox, and to ensure that quality improvement becomes the job of every Xerox person.
2. To ensure that Xerox people, individually and collectively, provide our external and internal customers with innovative products and services that fully satisfy their existing and latent requirements.
3. To establish as a way of life management and work processes that enable all Xerox people to continuously pursue quality improvement in meeting customer requirements.

In addition, Leadership Through Quality is directed at achieving four goals in all Xerox activities:

- *Customer Goal*: To become an organization with whom customers are eager to do business.

- *Employee Goal:* To create an environment where everyone can take pride in the organization and feel responsible for its success.
- *Business Goal:* To increase profits and presence at a rate faster than the markets in which Xerox competes.
- *Process Goal:* To use Leadership Through Quality principles in all Xerox does.

Leadership Through Quality radically changed the way Xerox did business. All activities, such as product planning, distribution, and establishing unit objectives, now begin with a focus on customer requirements. "Benchmarking"—identifying and studying the companies and organizations that best perform critical business functions and then incorporating those organizations' ideas into the firm's operations—became an important component of Xerox's quality efforts. Xerox benchmarked more than 200 processes with those of noncompetitive companies. For instance, ideas for improving production scheduling came from Cummins Engine Company, ideas for improving the distribution system came from L.L. Bean, and ideas for improving billing processes came from American Express.

Measuring customer satisfaction and training are important components of the program. Every month, 40,000 surveys are mailed to customers, seeking feedback on equipment performance, sales, service, and administrative support. Any reported dissatisfaction is dealt with immediately and is usually resolved in a matter of days. When the program was instituted, every Xerox employee worldwide, and at all levels of the company, received the same training in quality principles. Training began with top management and filtered down through each level of the firm. Five years, four million labor-hours, and more than $125 million later, all employees had received quality-related training. In 1988 about 79 percent of Xerox employees were involved in quality improvement teams.

Several other steps were taken. Xerox worked with suppliers to improve their processes, implement statistical methods and a total quality process, and support a just-in-time inventory concept. Suppliers that joined in these efforts were involved in the earliest phases of new product designs and rewarded with long-term contracts.

Employee involvement and participation was also an important effort. Xerox had always had good relationships with its unions. In 1980 the company signed a contract with its principal union, the Amalgamated Clothing and Textile Workers, encouraging union members' participation in quality improvement processes. It was the first program in the company that linked managers with employees in a mutual problem-solving approach and served as a model for other corporations. A subsequent contract included the provision that "every employee shall support the concept of continuous quality improvement while reducing quality costs through teamwork."

Most important, management became the role model for the new way of doing business. Managers were required to practice quality in their daily activities and to promote Leadership Through Quality among their peers and subordinates. Reward and recognition systems were modified to focus on teamwork and quality results. Managers became coaches, involving their employees in the act of running the business on a routine basis.

From the initiation of Leadership Through Quality until Xerox's Business Products and Systems organization won the Malcolm Baldrige National Quality Award in 1989, some of the most obvious impacts of the Leadership Through Quality program included:

1. Reject rates on the assembly line fell from 10,000 parts per million to 300 parts per million.
2. Ninety-five percent of supplied parts no longer needed inspection; in 1989, 30 U.S. suppliers went the entire year defect-free.
3. The number of suppliers was cut from 5,000 to fewer than 500.
4. The cost of purchased parts was reduced by 45 percent.
5. Despite inflation, manufacturing costs dropped 20 percent.
6. Product development time decreased by 60 percent.
7. Overall product quality improved 93 percent.

Xerox has learned that customer satisfaction plus employee motivation and satisfaction result in increased market share and improved return on assets. In 1989 president David Kearns observed that quality is "a race without a finish line." The company continues to operate on the motto:

We are no longer the company we once were.
We are not yet the company we want to be.
We are a company dedicated to Continuous Quality Improvement.

Key Issues for Discussion

1. What aspects of Xerox's management practices would support the results they obtained? How do these practices lead to accomplishing the three Leadership Through Quality objectives?
2. Discuss the meaning of *Quality is a race without a finish line*. What is its significance to Xerox, or to any organization?

Quality in Practice
Building Trust Through Quality at Gerber[36]

The Gerber baby picture that accompanies everything from strained carrots and banana cookies to teething rings and diapers has developed into one of the most recognizable brand images in the world. According to Gerber, the company received the highest customer loyalty rating out of 3,500 U.S. corporate and product brands, topping companies such as Nike and Coca-Cola. To parents around the world, the Gerber baby means quality, and the Gerber company has long been a leader in using quality tools to uphold its reputation. While Gerber's quality programs have gone through various stages over the years, their goal has remained the same: to make sure consumers continue to see the Gerber baby, which has gone through periodic updatings of its own, as an emblem of excellence.

Gerber is the leader in the development, manufacturing, and marketing of foods and products for children from birth through age 3. The company dominates the U.S. retail baby food market with a 70% share against competitors Heinz and Beechnut, and rings up about $1 billion in annual sales. Gerber employs 6,200 people altogether at its headquarters and main processing plant in Fremont, Michigan, and its plants in Fort Smith, Arkansas; Costa Rica; Mexico; Poland; and Venezuela. Together these facilities produce 190 food products, which are labeled in 16 languages and distributed to more then 80 countries. Gerber's Baby Care product line (featuring items such as rattles, bottles, and eating utensils) was launched in 1960 and currently features some 300 products. This line is largely manufactured in Reedsburg, Wisconsin, and China. In 1994, Sandoz Ltd., a pharmaceutical manufacturer, purchased Gerber. The 1996 merger of Sandoz and Ciba Geigy, also known for producing pharmaceuticals, established the Novartis company. Located in Basel, Switzerland, Novartis positions Gerber as a primary member of its consumer health division.

The company began in the Gerber family kitchen in 1927. After watching her husband's messy attempt at straining peas for their daughter, Dorothy Gerber suggested that the task would be better accomplished at the family-owned canning plant. Daniel Gerber agreed and was so taken by the idea that within a year he had manufactured enough of five baby food flavors to begin national distribution. Understanding the concern parents have for what their babies consume, Gerber paid close attention to what went into the food and the processes involved in manufacturing it. This careful attention was one of the company's first steps toward committing to quality.

Although Gerber's quality systems have undergone several improvements over the years, teamwork was "one of the biggest things to hit quality at Gerber," says George Sheffier, a retired, 35-year Gerber veteran. He believes that fostering a team atmosphere taught Gerber how to help employees adjust to change, gave the company a head start on the diversity issues of the 1990s and was critical when Gerber began spreading quality techniques throughout its plants.

Gerber experimented with teams in the 1970s but by the end of the decade felt the company still lacked the benefits a solid team atmosphere provided. An attempt to implement the concept to a more intense degree in 1983 was met by employee skepticism. Realizing that management and supervisors were themselves having a difficult time adjusting to the team methodology, Gerber hired consultants to teach facilitation skills. Soon supervisors were holding meetings not only to familiarize workers with the team concept but to discuss change—how employees felt about it and what the company could do to help make it easier. As employees began feeling more comfortable working in teams, they voiced concerns about trouble spots in systems and processes. Gerber also learned that the team atmosphere was a necessity in linking quality to every process in the company.

Once employees recognized the value of teamwork, the company began taking quality functions out of the quality department and spreading them throughout the plant. The goal of integrating quality into manufacturing was to build quality into the product on a more consistent basis. By expanding quality responsibilities to front-line operations, Gerber hoped to increase process control and reduce line inspections. To accomplish this purpose, Gerber teamed QA staff with front-line operators in 1988 to establish procedures for each process. Although hesitant at first, front-line employees liked the fact that they were involved in the process from the start and were able to determine their own auditing criteria. Within 18 months, Gerber was able to cut its number of line inspectors and increase its quality auditing functions.

As quality became more widespread through the organization, Gerber needed to teach basic quality tools to its front-line operators. As with the team concept, however, employees accepted the new responsibilities once they realized the values of the tools. Employees came to prefer the use of these techniques, which enabled them to became more directly involved with the quality of the final product. The company also established management incentives for integrating quality into its manufacturing process. Many senior managers, for example, began to be compensated for maintaining a high level of consumer trust through the quality of the final product. Today, the company continues to improve the quality techniques it applies to each part of the manufacturing process. Its most recent project has been to install new software from SAS Institute Inc. The software gives employees instant access to data regarding the impact on the final product of each station in each process.

Even though Gerber has always tried to create systems that meet the expectations of parents, the company didn't always utilize feedback from its customers. Not until the company faced its largest crisis to date did Gerber realize the need to link the customer's voice with the quality system. This period, in the 1980s, was a defining point for Gerber, according to Gerber senior QA manager, Jim Fisher. The company lost some trust in the eye of the consumer, stemming from an instance of consumer tampering that brought Gerber unwanted national attention. Before the company had the opportunity to prove itself, the case snowballed into a media frenzy, leaving consumers questioning Gerber's quality. Gerber's history of continuous improvement and its well-documented manufacturing processes paid off, however. The investigation put the company under a microscope, with Fisher flying across the country to inspect bottles of food and the Food and Drug Administration (FDA) spending three weeks reviewing Gerber's systems and records. In the end, the FDA gave the company a clean bill of health, and any claims against Gerber dissipated once the FDA's report became available to the public.

What Gerber found was that it needed a system allowing consumers to contact it directly with suggestions, complaints, and questions pertaining to Gerber products or infant care in general. Gerber's consumer relations department, established and operated by Dorothy Gerber in 1938, continued to receive a steady flow of letters, but the system wasn't timely and the feedback wasn't closely tied to either the quality or the safety department. Consequently, Gerber opened its telephone information service (800-4-GERBER) in 1986. The system provided a notable change for the company's quality discipline as it allowed telephone operators to log customer information into a database. In turn, trend analysis could be conducted and consumer demands could be integrated into the product development process. Because parents are up with their infants throughout the night, the company extended the department's operating hours in 1991, capturing information 24 hours a day. Gerber takes a daily average of 2,400 calls, accommodating all languages, and employs a team of letter correspondents to answer the 45,000 letters it receives yearly.

The company has often demonstrated innovative and creative thinking, notably in its plan to eliminate pesticides from its foods. By thinking outside the box, Gerber was able to outshine its competition, exceed customer expectations, and prepare itself for future government requirements. In 1996, the U.S. Department of Agriculture (USDA) reconsidered the methods traditionally used to ensure food safety—spot checks of manufacturing conditions and random sampling of final products—and released its Hazard Analysis and Critical Control Point (HACCP) program (see Chapter 11). The program enforces principles such as analyzing all potential hazards associated with foods, identifying critical control points where hazards can be eliminated, and establishing procedures to monitor control points and verify properly working systems. The FDA and the USDA believed such guidelines would be proactive in stopping contaminated products from getting into the market.

Gerber came to the same conclusion—49 years earlier. In 1947 Gerber management came to believe that the best way to ensure the safety of its product was to control as much of the food-making process as possible. At that time the company began forming alliances with its growers, giving Gerber better control of produce cultivation and allowing it to keep track of the pesticides growers used. By the 1950s, Gerber had implemented a HACCP-like approach to its manufacturing process identifying critical control points and thus making its processes preventive rather than reactive. The Gerber product analysis laboratories were formed in 1963 to provide data on the composition of ingredients, monitor the quality of internal and external water sources and provide the analytical information needed to establish food formulations. The company also created procedures to monitor potential hazards and ensured correctly functioning processes by employing a thermal processing staff. The staff was to determine the amount of time a product needs to be cooked to become commercially sterile, conduct audits of production facilities to ensure that processing equipment was operating correctly, and review and improve thermal processing systems. The thermal processing staff grew so large that it became its own department in 1994, and it continues to work closely with Gerber's quality and safety departments today.

Gerber's dedication to performance excellence continues to serve the company well. Thinking beyond quality trends in pesticide control continues to put the company ahead of others as Gerber investigates what it calls environmental quality and examines environmental factors not traditionally considered, such as pollutants carried into the plant by a supplier. This innovative thinking enabled Gerber to introduce sugarless and starch-free formulations less than a year after a 1995 report criticized the baby food industry for its use of fillers. By linking quality practices throughout its processes and making statistical information available to all employees, Gerber continues to enhance its quality.

Key Issues for Discussion

1. How do the various definitions of quality discussed in this chapter relate to the quality practices at Gerber?
2. How does Gerber exhibit the fundamental principles of total quality—customer and stakeholder focus, participation and teamwork, and a process focus and continuous improvement?
3. How did quality help Gerber overcome the crisis it faced in the consumer-tampering situation? What lessons do their steps have for other companies?

Summary of Key Points

- Quality assurance refers to any action directed toward providing consumers with goods and services of appropriate quality. Although craftspeople were attentive to quality, the Industrial Revolution moved responsibility for quality away from the worker and into separate staff departments, which had the effect of making quality a technical, as opposed to managerial, function. This thinking carried through Western industry until about 1980.
- W. Edwards Deming and Joseph Juran taught techniques of quality control and management to the Japanese in the 1950s. Over the next 20 years, Japan made

massive improvements in quality, while the quality of U.S. products increased at a much slower rate.

- Four significant influences brought about the "quality revolution" in the United States in the 1980s: (1) consumer pressure, (2) changes in technology, (3) outdated managerial thinking, and (4) loss of national competitiveness. Quality assumed an unprecedented level of importance in the United States. The quality movement has influenced not only product and service improvements, but the way in which organizations are managed.
- Quality is defined from many viewpoints, including transcendent quality, product- and value-based quality, fitness for use, and conformance to specifications. The official definition of quality is "the totality of features and characteristics of a product or service that bears on its ability to satisfy given needs." Most businesses today define it as "meeting or exceeding customer expectations."
- Customers include consumers, who ultimately use a product; external customers, who may be intermediaries between the producer and the consumer; and internal customers, who are the recipients of goods and services from suppliers within the producing firm.
- Total quality is a total, companywide effort—through full involvement of the entire workforce and a focus on continuous improvement—that companies use to achieve customer satisfaction.
- Total quality is grounded in three core principles: (1) a focus on customers, (2) participation and teamwork, and (3) continuous improvement and learning. These principles are supported by an organizational infrastructure that includes customer relationship management, leadership and strategic planning, human resources management, process management, and data and information management, as well as a set of management practices and tools.
- Competitive advantage denotes a firm's ability to achieve market superiority over its competitors. Quality is a key source of competitive advantage, and studies have shown that quality is positively related to increased market share and profitability.
- Quality efforts have been criticized in the media as a passing fad and a flawed philosophy. However, a number of objective studies have shown that total quality principles are alive and well and that the benefits of TQ far outweigh its weaknesses.
- Quality begins at a personal level. The use of personal checklists is one way of reinforcing this idea and establishing positive values and ownership that pave the way for achieving a quality-oriented culture in an organization and in one's own life.
- Businesses should view quality at the organizational level, the process level, and the performer level. This perspective cuts across traditional functional boundaries and provides better information for achieving customer satisfaction.

Review Questions

1. Briefly summarize the history of quality before and since the Industrial Revolution. What caused the most significant changes?
2. What factors have contributed to the increased awareness of quality in modern business?
3. Explain the various definitions of quality. Can a single definition suffice? Why?

4. Distinguish among consumers, external customers, and internal customers. Illustrate how these concepts apply to a McDonald's restaurant, a Pizza Hut, or a similar franchise.
5. What is the concept of total quality? What does it mean for the way an organization is managed?
6. Describe the three fundamental principles of total quality.
7. What is a process? How does a process focus differ from traditional operations in an organization?
8. List some examples of the types of improvements an organization can make.
9. What is the difference between improvement and learning?
10. What are the important elements of a total quality infrastructure?
11. Explain the relationship among infrastructure, practices, and tools.
12. How does quality support the achievement of competitive advantage?
13. What did Philip Crosby mean by "Quality is free"?
14. Explain the role of quality in improving a firm's profitability.
15. What evidence exists to counter the claim that "Quality does not pay"?
16. Explain the three levels of quality and the key issues that must be addressed at each level.
17. Why is it important to personalize quality principles?

Discussion Questions

1. Discuss how either good or poor quality has affected you personally as a consumer. For instance, describe experiences in which your expectations were met, exceeded, or not met when you purchased goods or services. Did your experience change your regard for the company and/or its product? How?
2. Discuss the importance of quality to the national interest of any country in the world.
3. How might the definitions of quality apply to your college or university? Provide examples of its customers and ways in which their expectations can be met or exceeded.
4. Think of a product or a service that you are considering purchasing. Develop a list of fitness-for-use criteria that are meaningful to you.
5. Select a service activity with which you are familiar. If you were the manager of this activity, what "conformance to specifications" criteria would you use to monitor it?
6. Choose a product or service to illustrate how several definitions of quality can apply simultaneously.
7. How might quality management practices differ between a firm that might be characterized as "market-driven" and one that might be called "marketing-driven"?
8. Do you feel that your college or university is applying the principles of total quality? Why or why not?
9. What are some processes that you personally perform? What opportunities can you think of for improving them?
10. Choose some organization that you have read about or with which you have personal experience and describe their sources of competitive advantage. For each, state whether you believe that quality supports their strategy or does not support it.
11. Explain how the "three levels of quality" might apply to a college or university.

PROJECTS, ETC.

1. Develop a portfolio of advertisements from newspapers and magazines and illustrate how quality is used in promoting these products. Do the ads suggest any of the different definitions of quality?
2. Visit the Malcolm Baldrige National Quality Award Web site at *http://www.quality.nist.gov/* and summarize the key results of winners for the past two years. In addition, provide the latest report on stock performance of Baldrige-winning companies.
3. Prepare a "Quality in Practice" case similar to the Xerox and Gerber cases, using sources such as business periodicals, personal interviews, and so on. Focus your discussion on how their approach to total quality supports their competitive strategy.
4. Conduct some research on the HACCP program cited in the Gerber Quality in Practice case and report on the program's philosophy and implementation. How might similar approaches be used in other (nonfood) industries?
5. Develop your own personal quality checklist and analyze the results over an extended period of time. Use the following guidelines. After you have gathered data for a week or two, review the data for the purpose of analysis and improvement. Use charts to plot and analyze weekly results.
   - Each participant should initiate a personal quality improvement project and maintain and improve it during the rest of the term.
   - Consistent effort, rather than elegant precision in pursuing the project will be rewarded. That is, individual benefit, rather than "a grade," or perfection, is to be the major objective.
   - The personal quality checklist in Figure 1.8 provides a starting point for the project. Other tools and techniques (such as those listed in Chapter 10) may be incorporated at a later time.
   - Eight to ten items for personal tracking and improvement should be chosen. Table 1.1 provides possible checklist standards that may be useful; however, participants are not required to use only items from this list. Whatever is meaningful to you may be tracked.
   - After a week's data is gathered, a simple graph can be plotted to determine the level of "defects" encountered.
   - A suggested practice is that you share your personal checklist items and goals with your instructor, a colleague, spouse, or friend. Have that person ask you about your progress every week or so. If you are making regular progress, you should be happy to discuss it, and to show your charts and graphs.
   - Even if your progress is uneven, you should be able to show that you have improved on one or two items, which is progress. Don't be too self-critical!
   - An intermediate progress report should be built into the process around the middle of the pilot study period. The final report on the pilot project should be made at the end of the term. Consideration should be given to making personal quality a permanent part of your personal planning and improvement process.

   After completing the project, answer these questions:

   a. What did your analysis reveal?
   b. Did you experience the same thing that Sergesketter did when he found that certain items disappeared as problems in a short period of time, simply because he began to measure them?
   c. How did you feel about discussing your "defects" with others?
   d. How does the personal quality process tie into processes in a work environment?

Table 1.1 Suggested Standards for a Personal Quality Checklist

- Review class notes after each class
- Limit phone calls to 10 minutes, where possible
- No more than 10 hours of TV per week
- Get up promptly—no snooze alarm
- Complete all reading assignments as due
- Plan by using a brief outline of what is to be accomplished daily
- Refer to daily plan, each day
- Use stairs instead of elevator
- Follow up on job contacts within 24 hours
- Work in library (or other quiet place) to avoid interruptions
- Stick to one subject at a time while studying
- Don't doggedly persist in trying to clear up a confusing point (or "bug" in a computer program) when stuck; set it aside and return later; for example, no more than 10 minutes after searching for a problem
- Don't spend too much time on routine activities; for example, no more than 15 minutes for breakfast, decrease grooming time to no more than 20 minutes
- Remember names of people to whom you have been introduced
- In bed every night before midnight
- Good housekeeping standards around house, apartment, dorm room, by the end of the day
- Prompt payment of bills, before their due date
- Various dietary standards—eat vegetables, avoid fats (be specific!)
- Limit beer and/or cigarette consumption (be specific!)

Source: Adapted with permission of The Free Press, a Division of Simon & Schuster, Inc. from QUALITY IS PERSONAL: A Foundation for Total Quality Management by Harry V. Roberts and Bernard F. Sergesketter. Copyright © 1993 by Harry V. Roberts and Bernard F. Sergesketter, p. 35.

Cases

I. A Tale of Two Restaurants[37]

Kelley's Seafood Restaurant was founded about 15 years ago by Tim Kelley, who has run it from the start. The restaurant is profitable because of its excellent quality of food, but lately has been having problems with consistency because of numerous suppliers. The restaurant operations are divided into front-end (servers) and back-end (kitchen). Employees are cross-trained in all areas, and the kitchen staff continually seeks improvements in cooking. Servers, however, have few perks and are paid minimal wages, so turnover is a bit of a problem. Tim's primary criterion for selecting servers is their ability to show up on time. Little communication takes place between the front-end and back-end operations, other than fulfilling orders. Tim makes sure that any complaints are referred to him immediately by the servers.

The restaurant has no automation, as Tim believes that it would get in the way of customers' special requests. "This is the way we've done it for the past 15 years and how we will continue to do it," was his response to a suggestion of using a computerized system to speed up orders and eliminate delays. Tim used to hold staff meetings regularly, but recently they have dropped from once each week to one every five or six months. Most of his time is spent focusing on negative behavior, and he has often said "You can't find good people anymore."

Jim's SteakHouse is a family-owned restaurant in the same state. Jim uses only the freshest meats and ingredients from the best suppliers and serves extra large portions of food to help customers feel they are getting their money's worth. Jim pays his cooks high wages to attract quality employees. Servers get 70 percent of tips, bussers 20 percent, and the kitchen staff 10 percent to foster teamwork. Many new hires come from referrals from current employees. Jim interviews all potential employees and asks them many pointed questions relating to courtesy, responsibility, and creativity. The restaurant sponsors bowling nights, golf outings, picnics, and holiday parties for its employees. At Jim's, birthday customers receive a free dinner, children are welcomed with balloons, candy, and crayons, and big screen TVs cater to sports fans. Jim walks around and constantly solicits customer feedback. Jim visits many other restaurants to study their operations and learn new techniques. As a result of these visits, Jim installed computers to schedule reservations and enter orders to the kitchen.

Discussion Questions

1. Contrast these two restaurants from the perspective of TQ. How do they exhibit or not exhibit the fundamental principles of TQ?
2. What advice would you recommend to the owners?

II. A Total Quality Business Model[38]

Two young entrepreneurs, Rob and Diane, were contemplating an idea of developing a new type of takeout restaurant with limited dining facilities that would provide a wider variety of home-cooked cuisines than currently available. In developing their business model, they realized that a TQ-focused management infrastructure would be vital to success. Here are some of the ideas they are contemplating.

Customer Relationship Management

Rob and Diane realized that they must focus on the customers' perceived quality of both the product and service. They believe they must provide unexpected value to their customers and go beyond customer expectations to create lifetime customers. As part of training, employees will focus on "moment of truths"—the many instances when a customer forms an impression of the company, either through its products or interactions with its employees. These moments include a friendly greeting to each customer on arrival, recognizing repeat customers, offering samples of different items, answering questions, serving the products, and a genuine thank you on leaving. Another way to exceed expectations would be to accommodate any reasonable request. Employees would have the authority to do whatever it takes to satisfy the customer. When a complaint arises, the employee should act immediately to solve to the problem, listen attentively to the customer, and apologize. No matter what, the customer should always be thanked for bringing the complaint to the staff's attention.

To evaluate the customer's experience, the company would require shift managers to be the first customer on each shift, starting from the parking lot to check its cleanliness, In addition, they would use technology to track service times and complaints, and "mystery shoppers" each month throughout the system. Every quarter, all regional store and shift managers would meet to discuss their experiences and seek improvements.

Leadership and Strategic Planning

The leadership system would consist of regional vice presidents who would be responsible for all of the stores in a geographic area; regional managers, who would manage about a dozen stores within a region; and store managers, who would responsible for the day-to-day operations; and shift managers, who would manage the employees on each shift. This "cascading" structure would allow communications to be disseminated rapidly throughout the company, both top-down and bottom-up. A manager training and development program would ensure that managers at each level obtained the necessary skills for their job responsibilities. This program would not only address the needs of entry-level managers, but also those who move up the career ladder in the firm into higher leadership positions.

The company's vision would be simple: To be the consumer's choice for all varieties of fresh convenience meals. The strategy would be based on product quality (variety, freshness, value) and outstanding customer service. Rob and Diane realized that every employee needed to understand the company strategy, which would be emphasized during the employee orientation and management training and development programs. Managers would be responsible for ensuring that all hourly employees focus on these two goals through daily meetings, written quality check sheets completed on every shift, and an employee stock option program that would be tied to meeting these goals as well as profit targets.

Human Resource Management

All managers would be trained in several positions in order to gain a solid understanding of the duties and requirements of all employees, allowing them to cover certain positions if needed. Their expertise would enable them to train hourly employees and gain credibility with them. The training program for a new manager would be designed to be somewhat self-directed. The manager trainee would be given a skill checklist that included each skill that he or she should learn. Experienced trainers would be available to answer any questions and assist the manager trainee with any difficulties. Trainees would be given short evaluative tests and feedback from the trainer. Before their first day of work, all hourly employees would attend an orientation session, focused on making them feel welcome in their new work environment. The session would include a history of the company, mission, policies, and training procedures. To keep good people, the compensation program would have to be competitive in the industry. Managers would be required to visit local competitors to identify their compensation structure and make comparisons.

Job performance of all hourly employees would be reviewed periodically using performance appraisals by the store manager after the first 30, 90, and 180 days of employment, followed by annual appraisals. The appraisal would cover such topics as customer focus, quality of work, teamwork, and responsibility. It would also require the employee to identify future goals and objectives and plans for improving performance.

Process Management

All food production processes would be carefully documented so that all employees are aware of what specifications must be met, particularly those health and safety requirements that regulate temperature of food and proper storage. Managers would be responsible for taking periodic measurements and observations to ensure that all employees are following procedures. Managers would also be responsible for their relationships with food suppliers. Rob and Diane are thinking of identifying one large supplier for most of their food supplies.

Data and Information Management

All key data and information, such as inventories, financial reports and projections, customer feedback, employee and operational performance, would be collected and displayed in the kitchen area, so all employees can understand the results of their efforts. Information from all stores would be consolidated at corporate headquarters for evaluation and analysis.

Discussion Questions

1. What advice might you give Rob and Diane about the management practices they are proposing within each element of the TQ infrastructure? What additional practices might you suggest?
2. How might viewing the organization from the three levels of quality discussed in the chapter help improve their business plan?

III. Deere & Co.[39]

Deere & Company (*http://www.deere.com*), also known as John Deere after its founder, is a world-leading manufacturer, distributor, and financier of equipment for agriculture, construction, forestry, public works, and lawn and turf care. The company also provides credit and managed health care services. In August 1999, for the third straight year, Deere was named one of *Industry Week's* 100 Best-Managed Companies.

Deere's objective has consistently been to be the low-cost producer in the markets it serves; however, it seeks to do so while maintaining an image of quality and customer focus. Its slogan is "Achieving genuine value for customers worldwide." Because of the company's close ties to the agricultural industry, corporate performance in both sales and profits was highly variable during much of the 1980s and 1990s due to cycles of low prices and oversupplies of many agricultural products. During that period, the company made various adjustments in its product mix and manufacturing processes to enable it to better compete and survive in the global environment.

The following excerpts come from various Deere annual reports.

1984

In spite of the industry environment of low demand, the challenge is to do what we do better. Provide more value per dollar of purchase price. To accomplish this will require cost-effectiveness in all facets of our business, which includes being more flexible and more aggressive in adopting the most modern design and manufacturing technologies. . . . Product design is being systematically reviewed to provide improved performance and quality at a lower cost. . . . New manufacturing technologies such as robot welding have enabled Deere employees to become more efficient while producing parts of higher and more consistent quality. Underlying most changes in the forestry equipment line was a special emphasis on increased reliability.

1987

John Deere is determined to be the lowest-cost producer in our industries and to sustain a competitive advantage on a global basis. However, we all must perpetuate the company's reputation for providing the best quality and value to our customers. While we're making structural changes in our operations we must continue to adhere to these business principles. . . .

John Deere leadership in the agricultural equipment business is based on a line of products that has earned a reputation for excellent quality and reliability, on the skills and services we have to support the product line, and on our strong network of independent dealers. . . . In our continuing effort to improve the quality and performance of John Deere agricultural equipment, we have traditionally invested a higher percent of sales in product R&D than any of our major competitors. . . . The industrial equipment improvement reflects our strong product line and dedicated organization and our employees' determination to reduce costs, improve quality, and deliver the best value to the customer. . . . The total value of John Deere equipment is quality, reliability, dealer support, finance plans, resale value, and the company that stands behind it all.

1989

We must continue to ensure that John Deere products offer the customer the best value in all respects—in quality, reliability, features, resale price, and especially in value added by an independent network of well-placed, full-servicing dealers people can rely on.

1995

Deere's focus on continuous improvement takes a wide variety of forms, but is based on the simple concept that any product or process can be improved. We have placed great emphasis on enhancing the team-based culture of the company, in which salaried and hourly employees work cooperatively toward the common goal of creating ongoing, meaningful gains in productivity. . . . A key component of this operating philosophy is the company's growing utilization of team-based compensation systems that reward continuous improvements in productivity. . . . Our experience with initial pilot applications of these pay plans indicated that sustainable annual productivity improvements could be achieved in many operations. . . . These plans have already generated an average productivity gain that exceeds six percent. . . . The financial benefits of Deere's emphasis on continuous improvement are significant, and may be measured in a variety of ways. For example, looking at some important financial metrics for 1995, and comparing them with 1990, a year in which the production volume was similar, a clear trend of improvement emerges:

- *Return-on-assets performance improved to 8.5% from 6.1%.*
- *The debt-to-capitalization ratio declined to 26.3% from 35.5%.*
- *Tonnage produced per employee increased 25%.*
- *Net sales and revenues generated per employee were 50% higher.*
- *Dealer receivables as a percent of settlements, our proxy for retail sales, declined to 36% from 46%.*
- *Inventories measured at standard cost, as a percent of the cost of goods sold, dropped to 26% from 33%.*

1996

As we move ahead in the pursuit of genuine value, we continue to follow twin strategies of continuous improvement—embodying innovation, efficiency, effective business processes and a passion for *excellence—and profitable growth, which is being accomplished through the global pursuit of new markets and products. . . . Nothing stands as a better illustration of Deere's commitment to continuous improvement than our long record of investment in capital programs and research and development. In 1996, Deere invested a record amount of some $650 million in these areas, including $370 million for R&D alone. . . . Continuous improvement initiatives are setting the stage for our other strategy—that of profitable growth. . . . Our company's pursuit of genuine value as our primary strategic initiative provides a strong point of focus. In reaching to create value for our many constituencies, we have embarked on a series of exciting journeys that are fundamentally remaking our enterprise. For example, a strong company-wide total quality program continues to expand and intensify, yielding improved customer responsiveness, shortened cycle times, and reductions in costs and asset levels. Similarly, our effort to pursue profitable growth is taking us into dynamic new global markets of tremendous potential.*

1999

Genuine value captures the qualities we have been known for all along such as quality and integrity. But it also codifies the John Deere way of doing things and, thus, gives us a special identity. The basis of genuine value is that stakeholder value and stockholder value are interconnected. To this end, we believe that our strategies of continuous improvement, profitable growth and business innovation will lead to superior returns for our owners through the benefits provided to our customers, employees and neighbors. . . . We're continuing to invest heavily in new products and production facilities, have completed some very attractive acquisitions, and are progressing with an ambitious set of team-based initiatives that are improving quality and refining key business processes across the enterprise.

Continuous Improvement. *Highlighting our pursuit of genuine value through continuous improvement is an aggressive series of process-based initiatives targeting six-sigma levels of performance and customer satisfaction. During the year, some 900 projects involving the efforts of several thousand employees, were completed or in progress. Their goal: Streamlining business processes, large and small, and pursuing operational excellence throughout the company. . . . In support of the initiative stressing customer focus, our operating divisions are structuring their activities around the core processes of customer acquisition, order fulfillment, product development and customer support.*

Profitable Growth. *. . . our growth efforts are centered around international expansion in agricultural equipment, a focus on large customers in construction equipment, an unprecedented period of investment in commercial and consumer equipment, as well as a stepped-up emphasis on agribusiness and overseas markets in credit. Acquisitions and joint ventures are playing an increasingly important role in our growth plans as well. . . .*

Business Innovation. *. . . The company spent more than $700 million on new products and facilities designed to provide customers with greater productivity, value and convenience. . . . Innovation is also expected to spur the performance of the newly created John Deere Special Technologies Group. Its purpose includes developing advanced software, electronics, and communications solutions for John Deere customers, as well as creating new revenue streams by serving outside companies and customer groups. . . .*

While important, quality products and a venerable brand are only a start. We must remain passionate about enhancing quality, improving cycle times and embracing technology in order to keep our journey to preeminence on a steady course. . . . Nothing is likely to mean more to our future than how effectively we adapt information technology and, specifically, use the Internet as a springboard to promote our brand and sell our products. . . . For all their importance, products, processes and technology mean little without the right people behind them. . . . Our emphasis on building relationships has earned a loyal customer following, as well as a dedicated team of employees and dealers. Inasmuch as genuine value is truly a reciprocal process, their contributions and continued alle-

giance are crucial to the attainment of consistent world-class performance. In our view, those with an eye for enduring value will realize substantial benefit as Deere stakeholders and share in the excitement of raising genuine value to new heights.

Assignment

On the basis of this information, prepare a brief report discussing Deere & Company's evolution of quality. Relate your discussion to historical trends and issues discussed in this chapter. How has their perspective of quality changed? How has it helped them to stay competitive in a tough business environment over this time period? Do you think that their technology-focused efforts will help them to remain competitive in the future? You may also wish to study their recent annual reports to see how the company has progressed into the twenty-first century.

NOTES

1. Early history is reported in Delmer C. Dague, "Quality—Historical Perspective," in *Quality Control in Manufacturing* (Warrendale, PA: Society of Automotive Engineers, February 1981); and L. P. Provost and C. L. Norman, "Variation through the Ages," *Quality Progress* 23, no. 12 (December 1990), 39–44. Modern events are discussed in Nancy Karabatsos, "Quality in Transition, Part One: Account of the '80s," *Quality Progress* 22, no. 12 (December 1989), 22–26; and Joseph M. Juran, "The Upcoming Century of Quality," address to the ASQC Annual Quality Congress, Las Vegas, May 24, 1994. A comprehensive historical account may be found in J. M. Juran, *A History of Managing for Quality* (Milwaukee, WI: ASQC Quality Press, 1995).

2. M. D. Fagan, ed., *A History of Engineering and Science in the Bell System: The Early Years, 1875–1925* (New York: Bell Telephone Laboratories, 1974).

3. "Manufacturing Tops List of Concerns among Executives," *Industrial Engineering* 22, no. 6 (June 1990), 8.

4. "The Cost of Quality," *Newsweek*, September 7, 1992, 48–49.

5. Lori L. Silverman with Annabeth L. Propst, "Quality Today: Recognizing the Critical SHIFT," *Quality Progress*, February 1999, 53–60.

6. American Society for Quality: "Foresight 2020: The American Society for Quality Considers the Future," undated report.

7. Nabil Tamimi and Rose Sebastianelli, "How Firms Define and Measure Quality," *Production and Inventory Management Journal* 37, no. 3 (Third Quarter 1996), 34–39.

8. Four comprehensive reviews of the concept and definition of quality are David A. Garvin, "What Does Product Quality Really Mean?" *Sloan Management Review* 26, no. 1 (1984), 25–43; Gerald F. Smith, "The Meaning of Quality," *Total Quality Management* 4, no. 3 (1993), 235–244; Carol A. Reeves and David A. Bednar, "Defining Quality: Alternatives and Implications," *Academy of Management Review* 19, no. 3 (1994), 419–445; and Kristie W. Seawright and Scott T. Young, "A Quality Definition Continuum," *Interfaces* 26, no. 3 (May/June 1996), 107–113.

9. Garvin, see note 7, 25.

10. "Lamborghini Owner Says He Got $262,000 Lemon," *Cincinnati Enquirer*, June 23, 1998, B5.

11. Gregory M. Seal, "1990s—Years of Promise, Years of Peril for U.S. Manufacturers," *Industrial Engineering* 22, no. 1 (January 1990), 18–21.

12. ANSI/ASQC A3-1978, *Quality Systems Terminology* (Milwaukee, WI: American Society for Quality Control, 1978).

13. Lawrence Utzig, "Quality Reputation—Precious Asset," *ASQC Technical Conference Transactions*, Atlanta, 1980, 145–154.

14. Procter & Gamble, *Report to the Total Quality Leadership Steering Committee and Working Councils* (Cincinnati, OH: Procter & Gamble, 1992).

15. A. V. Feigenbaum, *Total Quality Control*, 3d ed., rev. (New York: McGraw-Hill, 1991), 77, 78.

16. Wayne S. Reiker, "Integrating the Pieces for Total Quality Control," *The Quality Circles Journal* (now *The Journal for Quality and Participation*) 6, no. 4 (December 1983), 14–20.

17. Ron Zemke and Dick Schaaf, *The Service Edge* (New York: New American Library, 1989), 352–355; William Davidow and Bro Utall, *Total Customer Service* (New York: Harper & Row, 1989), 86–87.

18. Myron Magnet, "The New Golden Rule of Business," *Fortune*, February 21, 1994, 60–64.

19. *AT&T's Total Quality Approach*, AT&T Corporate Quality Office (1992), 6.

20. L. von Bertalanffy, "The Theory of Open Systems in Physics and Biology," *Science* 111 (1950), 23–29.

21. J. W. Forrester, *Industrial Dynamics* (New York: John Wiley & Sons, 1961).

22. Peter M. Senge, *The Fifth Discipline: The Art and Practice of the Learning Organization* (New York: Doubleday Currency, 1990), 14.

23. S. C. Wheelwright, "Competing through Manufacturing," in *International Handbook of Production and Operations Management*, ed. Ray Wild (London: Cassell Educational, Ltd., 1989), 15–32.

24. *The PIMS Letter on Business Strategy*, no. 4 (Cambridge, MA: Strategic Planning Institute, 1986).

25. Philip Crosby, *Quality Is Free* (New York: McGraw-Hill, 1979).

26. Roger O. Crockett, Peter Elstrom, and Gary McWilliams, "Wireless Goes Haywire at Motorola," *Business Week*, March 9, 1998, 32.

27. U.S. General Accounting Office, "Management Practices: U.S. Companies Improve Performance Through Quality Efforts," GA/NSIAD-91-190 (May 1991).

28. "Progress on the Quality Road," *Incentive*, April 1995, 7.

29. Kevin B. Hendricks and Vinod R. Singhal, "Does Implementing an Effective TQM Program Actually Improve Operating Performance? Empirical Evidence from Firms That Have Won Quality Awards," *Management Science* 43, 9 (September 1997), 1258–1274. The results of this study have appeared in extensive business and trade publications such as *Business Week*, *Fortune*, and others.

30. Adapted from Alan P. Brache and Geary A. Rummler, "The Three Levels of Quality," *Quality Progress* 21, no. 10 (October 1988), 46–51.

31. Rath & Strong Executive Panel, Winter 1994 Survey on Personal Initiative, Summary of Findings.

32. David Armstrong, *Management by Storying Around* (New York: Doubleday Currency, 1992), 117–119.

33. Harry V. Roberts and Bernard F. Sergesketter, *Quality Is Personal: A Foundation for Total Quality Management* (New York: The Free Press, 1993).

34. Roberts and Sergesketter, see note 33, 13–14.

35. Information for this case was obtained from "Xerox Quest for Quality and the Malcolm Baldrige National Quality Award" presentation script; Norman E. Rickard, Jr., "The Quest for Quality: A Race Without a Finish Line," *Industrial Engineering*, January 1991, 25–27; Howard S. Gitlow and Elvira N. Loredo, "Total Quality Management at Xerox: A Case Study," *Quality Engineering* 5, no. 3 (1993), 403–432; and *Xerox Quality Solutions, A World of Quality* (Milwaukee, WI: ASQC Quality Press, 1993). Reprinted with permission of the Xerox Corporation.

36. Adapted from Mark R. Hagen, "Quality for the Long Haul at Gerber," *Quality Progress*, 33, 2 (February 2000), 29–34. © 2000. American Society for Quality (ASQ). Reprinted with permission.

37. Based on a student project prepared by Stacey Bizzell, Suzanne Lee, and Kenneth Shircliff. Their contribution is gratefully acknowledged.

38. Based on research conducted by Michael Judge, Melanie Landthaler, Pamela Stermer, and April Urso. We gratefully acknowledge their contribution.

39. Information courtesy of John Deere.

BIBLIOGRAPHY

Freund, Richard A. "Definitions and Basic Quality Concepts." *Journal of Quality Technology*, January 1985, 50–56.

Garvin, David A. *Managing Quality*. New York: The Free Press, 1988.

Hayes, Glenn E. "Quality: Quandary and Quest." *Quality* 22, no. 7 (July 1983), 18.

Hiam, Alexander. *Closing the Quality Gap: Lessons from America's Leading Companies*. Upper Saddle River, NJ: Prentice Hall, 1992.

Hunt, V. Daniel. *Managing for Quality: Integrating Quality and Business Strategy*. Homewood, IL: Business One Irwin, 1993.

Page, Harold S. "A Quality Strategy for the '80s." *Quality Progress* 16, no. 11 (November 1983), 16–21.

Schmidt, Warren H., and Jerome P. Finnigan. *The Race Without a Finish Line*. San Francisco: Jossey-Bass, 1992.

Van Gigch, John P. "Quality—Producer and Consumer Views." *Quality Progress* 10, no. 4 (April 1977), 30–33.

Wachniak, Ray. "World-Class Quality: An American Response to the Challenge." In *Quest for Quality: Managing the Total System*, ed. M. Sepehri. Norcross, GA: Institute of Industrial Engineers, 1987.

Chapter 2 Total Quality in Organizations

Outline

Jaguars (the automobiles, not the cats) have been traditionally known as beautiful but temperamental beasts.[1] In the 1970s people joked that to keep one on the road, a driver needed to own two. In 1989, a J. D. Power survey noted more defects per car than the hapless Yugo (ask your parents), which was voted the Worst Car of the Last Millennium in an automobile column reader poll.[2] However, after 10 years under the guidance of its new parent Ford Motor Company, Jaguar rose to the top of the 1999 J. D. Power Initial Quality Study, placing ahead of BMW, Mercedes-Benz, and Lexus. Ford accomplished feat this by investing billions of dollars in new quality and manufacturing programs, which included overhauling the 50-year-old manufacturing plant, teaching teamwork to top executives, providing a detailed written guide on how to select suppliers and organize production to ensure quality, and using its engineering expertise to help eliminate quality problems.

As noted in Chapter 1, modern quality management in the United States began in the manufacturing sector. However, the concept of quality has moved far beyond its manufacturing roots. By the 1990s businesses had increased their attention to service quality. They discovered that service quality is as critical to retaining customers as the tangible products they buy, and focused on such support processes as order entry, delivery, and complaint response. Pure service companies began to think in terms of "zero defections" and to explore new ways of developing customer loyalty. A hospital in Detroit, for example, promises to attend to its emergency room patients in 20 minutes or less. If unable to meet this promise, it provides the care free of charge.[3] Slogans such as Whatever It Takes and service guarantees are the norm in today's competitive environment. Nevertheless, many service industries have struggled with quality. In the airline industry, for example, the number of consumer complaints rose from 1.08 per 100,000 passengers in 1998 to 2.48 in 1999. The number of complaints about the top 10 airlines soared 89 percent in the first quarter 2000 from the previous year, and not because the airlines are ignoring the problems. Delta Airlines, for example, is spending millions of dollars in service enhancements: trying to respond to email within 48 hours and mail complaints within 2 weeks against a 2-month industry standard, and using technology to profile vulnerable passengers—unaccompanied children, wheelchair travelers, and connecting passengers—when flights must be cancelled for weather problems. But *USA Today* noted that most of the promises are aimed at better communication with customers, not problem-free flights.[4] As consumer expectations rise, a focus on quality permeates other sectors of the economy as well, including health care, education, and government.

For all types of organizations, quality is absolutely vital to keep customers, sustain profitability, and gain market share. This chapter explores the role of quality in manufacturing and service organizations, including education, health care, and government. We begin with the importance of viewing all organizations as systems, and focus on the role that each component of an organization plays in achieving high quality. We then present examples of quality efforts within these organizations.

QUALITY AND SYSTEMS THINKING

A **system** is the functions or activities within an organization that work together for the aim of the organization. A production system is composed of many smaller, interacting subsystems. For example, a McDonald's restaurant is a system that includes the order-taker/cashier subsystem, grill and food preparation subsystem, drive-through subsystem, purchasing subsystem, and training subsystem. These subsystems are linked together as internal customers and suppliers. Likewise, every organization is composed of many individual functions that are often seen as separate units on an organization chart. However, managers need to view the organization as a whole and concentrate on the important organizational links among these functions. For example, consider the infrastructure elements of a total quality system that we discussed in Chapter 1: customer relationship management, leadership and strategic planning, human resources management, process management, and data and information management. Senior leaders need to focus on strategic directions and on customers; strategies need to be linked to human resource plans and key processes in order to effectively align resources; human resources issues such as training and work system design must support the processes that manufacture products or deliver services; and data and information management provides the means for obtaining useful feedback to better understand the relationship between strategy and execution, and provide a means for improvement.

Russell Ackoff, a noted authority in systems thinking, explained the importance of systems thinking in the following way:

> *. . . a combination of the best practices by each part of a system taken separately does not yield the best system. We may not even get a good one. A company that has 12 facilities, each producing the same variations of the same type of beverage, had broken the production process down into 15 steps. It produced a table showing each factory (a column) and each of the 15 steps (rows). The company then carried out a study to determine the cost of each step at each factory (a costly study), which identified for each step the factory with the lowest cost. At each factory, the company tried to replace each of its steps that was not the lowest cost with the one used in the factory that had the lowest cost. Had this succeeded, each factory would be producing with steps that had each attained the lowest cost in any factory. It did not work! The lowest-cost steps did not fit together. The result was only a few insignificant cosmetic changes that did not justify the cost of the exercise.*[5]

Ackoff concluded that management should focus on the interactions of parts and of the system with other systems, rather than the actions of parts taken separately. Thus, successful management relies on a systems perspective. A systems perspective is one of the most important elements of total quality. As we discuss quality in manufacturing, service, and other sectors, think about how important a systems perspective is in achieving quality.

QUALITY IN MANUFACTURING

Well-developed quality assurance systems have existed in manufacturing for some time. However, these systems focused primarily on technical issues such as equipment reliability, inspection, defect measurement, and process control. The transition to a customer-driven organization has caused fundamental changes in manufacturing practices, changes that are particularly evident in areas such as product design, human resource management, and supplier relations. Product design activities, for example, now closely integrate marketing, engineering, and manufacturing operations (see Chapter 7). Human resource practices concentrate on empowering workers to collect and analyze data, make critical operations decisions, and take responsibility for continuous improvements, thereby moving the responsibility for quality from the quality control department onto the factory floor. Suppliers have become partners in product design and manufacturing efforts. Many of these efforts were stimulated by the automobile industry as Ford, GM, and Chrysler forced their network of suppliers to improve quality.

Exemplary quality leaders in the manufacturing sector include large companies such as Armstrong World Industries, AT&T (see *Quality Profile*), Boeing Airlift and Tanker Programs, Corning Telecommunications Products Division, Eastman Chemical Company, Motorola, and Solar Turbines Incorporated, and small companies such as Granite Rock Company, Inc., Sunny Fresh Foods, Texas Nameplate Company, Trident Precision Manufacturing, and Wainwright Industries. Leading practices of these and other outstanding manufacturing companies are featured throughout this book.

Quality Profile

AT&T Transmission Systems Business Unit

AT&T Transmission Systems Business Unit (TSBU) was one of six strategic business units within AT&T Network Systems Group when it won a Malcolm Baldrige National Quality Award in 1992. TSBU is now part of Lucent Technologies, Inc. Network Systems. TSBU was the largest of AT&T's manufacturing groups and a leading worldwide supplier of network telecommunications equipment for public and private telephone networks. Formally created in 1989, TSBU designs, manufactures, sells, and supports equipment and systems used to deliver telephone calls, data, and video, serving markets around the world. Challenged by AT&T Chairman Bob Allen, the unit introduced a more customer-focused TQM approach that calls for employees to align themselves along a set of goals and priorities identified by customers. This approach also required the organization to commit time, resources, and expertise to produce products and services that met and exceeded customers' expectations. As the foundation of its efforts, TSBU emphasized strategic planning, quality teams, and daily quality control.

Within six years, the unit achieved a 20-fold improvement in integrated circuit supplier quality and a 10-fold improvement in equipment product quality. Other improvements included 50 percent reduction in product development time, 40 percent reduction in inventory, $400 million in cost improvements, and 50 percent reduction in circuit pack returns. Measures of customer satisfaction showed consistent improvement. In 1991, as five major competitors reported financial losses, TSBU reported a profit and contributed substantially to AT&T's financial position.

Source: Malcolm Baldrige National Quality Award, Profiles of Winners, National Institute of Standards and Technology, Department of Commerce.

Manufacturing Systems

Figure 2.1 illustrates a typical manufacturing system and the key relationships among its functions. The quality concerns of each component of the system are described next.

Marketing and Sales Milton Hershey, the founder of Hershey Foods Corporation, understood the relationship between quality and sales. He used to say, "Give them quality. That's the best advertising in the world." For the first 68 years it was in business, Hershey Foods did not see a need to advertise its products in the mass media.[6] But marketing and sales involve much more than advertising and selling. Today, marketing and sales employees have important responsibilities for quality.

Marketing and sales personnel are responsible for determining the needs and expectations of consumers; specifically the products and product features that consumers want and the prices that consumers are willing to pay for them. This information enables a firm to define products that are fit for use and capable of being produced within the technological and budgetary constraints of the organization. Effective market research and active solicitation of customer feedback are necessary for developing quality products. Salespeople can help to obtain feedback on product performance from customers and convey this information to product designers and engineers. They should also help to ensure that customers receive adequate assistance and are completely satisfied.

Figure 2.1 Functional Relationships in a Typical Manufacturing System

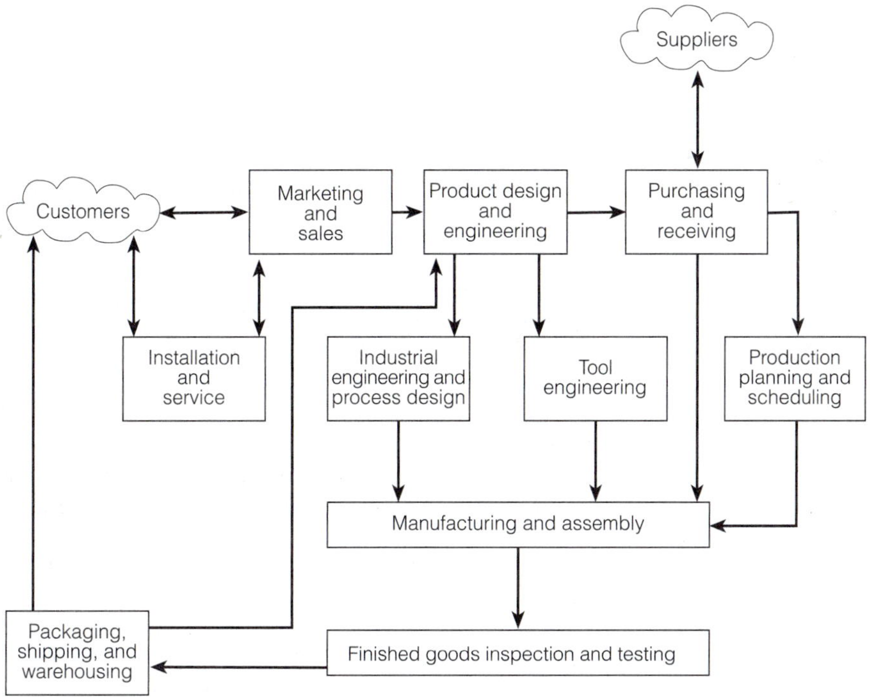

Sales representatives for Ames Rubber Corporation (see *Quality Profile*), a producer of rollers used in copiers, printers, and typewriters, take special note of such things as the volume of work a customer or prospective customer expects, the product features the customer seeks, and the customer's cost, service, and delivery requirements. Ames's sales department also conducts quarterly customer satisfaction surveys and monthly customer contact surveys. Customer satisfaction surveys collect data in the areas of products, service, information, and relationships. Customer contact surveys, which take the form of informal conversations, explore quality, cost, delivery, and service. All this information is used by the company to improve customer satisfaction. Chapter 4 explores customer focus and the marketing function further.

Product Design and Engineering The product design and engineering functions develop technical specifications for products and production processes to meet the requirements determined by the marketing function. Underengineered products will fail in the marketplace because they will not meet customer needs. Products that are overengineered, those that exceed the customer requirements, may not find a profitable market. Japanese automakers, for instance, discovered in the early 1990s that many consumers were unwilling to pay for some luxury features they had designed into their cars as standard features. Overengineering can also create a complacency that leads to poor quality. Poorly designed manufacturing processes result in poor quality or higher costs. Good design can help to prevent manufacturing defects and service errors and to reduce the need for the non-value-adding inspection practices that have dominated much of U.S. industry.

Quality Profile
Ames Rubber Corporation

Ames Rubber Corporation, based in Hamburg, New Jersey, produces rubber rollers used to feed paper, transfer toner, and fuse toner to paper in office machines such as copiers, printers, and typewriters. The company is the world's largest manufacturer of rollers for mid- to large-sized copiers. Ames also produces highly specialized parts for protecting the transaxles of front-wheel-drive vehicles. The company was founded in 1949; by 1993 it employed 445 "Teammates" at four sites, and had won the Malcolm Baldrige National Quality Award.

The company's organization chart clearly states its approach to business. External customers are on top, above the firm's unit managers and other managers, who are above the president. The entire business strategy is designed to ensure that the customer drives Ames Rubber's operations and goals. All products are made to order to customer design and specification. Its warranties are among the best in the industry and include a refund of the customer's portion of development costs for prototype parts if Ames fails to achieve the specifications.

Ames's total quality initiative began in 1987 when it invited Xerox personnel to train the executive committee. The process came to involve all Teammates (employees) in pursuing a common goal: full satisfaction of internal and external customers' needs through total quality in every endeavor. Between 1989 and 1993, the defect rate for Ames's largest customer, Xerox, was reduced from more than 30,000 parts per million to just 11. Over a five-year period, Teammate ideas saved the company more than $3 million. The company has demonstrated that total quality is not only good—it is profitable.

Source: Malcolm Baldrige National Quality Award, Profiles of Winners, National Institute of Standards and Technology, Department of Commerce.

Motorola (see *Quality Profile*) has been a role model for improving manufacturing quality through its product and process design activities. Motorola set an ambitious goal of *six-sigma quality*—a level of quality representing no more than 3.4 defects per million opportunities—for every process in the company. To reach this goal, Motorola determined that before it manufactures a product it must first determine the product characteristics that will satisfy customers (marketing's role); decide whether these characteristics can be achieved through the product's design, the manufacturing process, or the materials used; develop design tolerances that will assure successful product performance; conduct measurements to determine process variations from existing specifications; and then hone the product design, manufacturing process, or both, in order to achieve the desired results. Quality in product and process design is considered further in Chapter 7 and six sigma is discussed in Chapter 10.

Purchasing and Receiving The quality of purchased parts and services and the timeliness of their delivery are critical. A purchasing agent should be responsible for all aspects of procurement, including quality. The purchasing department can help a firm achieve quality in the following ways:

1. Selecting quality-conscious suppliers
2. Ensuring that purchase orders clearly define the quality requirements specified by product design and engineering

Quality Profile

Motorola, Inc.

Motorola has the distinction of being a recipient of the Malcolm Baldrige National Quality Award in the award's first year, 1988. Employing more than 130,000 workers at more than 50 facilities across the world, Motorola is among the 150 largest U.S. industrial corporations. Its principal product lines include communication systems and semiconductors, and it distributes its products through direct sales and service operations. An engineering-oriented company, it historically created new markets with innovative products—essentially telling customers what they wanted. As customers became more sophisticated and competition increased, Motorola shifted from a product focus to a customer focus, setting its fundamental objective as total customer satisfaction.

Two key beliefs guide the culture of the firm: respect for people and uncompromising integrity. Motorola's goals are to increase its global market share and to become the best in its class in all aspects—people, marketing, technology, product, manufacturing, and service. In terms of people, its objective is to be recognized worldwide as a company for which anyone would want to work.

Motorola was a pioneer in continual reduction of defects and cycle times in all the company's processes, from design, order entry, manufacturing, and marketing, to administrative functions. Employees in every function of the business note defects and use statistical techniques to analyze the results. Products that once took weeks to make are now completed in less than an hour. Even the time needed for closing the financial books has been reduced. It used to take a month and had been reduced to four days.

Sources: Ed Pena, "Motorola's Secret to Total Quality Control," *Quality Progress*, October 1990, pp. 43–45; A. William Wiggenhorn, "Stalking Quality at Motorola," presentation at the 1990 Council of Logistics Management Conference.

3. Bringing together technical staffs from both the buyers' and suppliers' companies to design products and solve technical problems
4. Establishing long-term supplier relationships based on trust
5. Providing quality improvement training to suppliers
6. Informing suppliers of any problems encountered with their goods
7. Maintaining good communication with suppliers as quality requirements and design changes occur.

An example of the quality consciousness of Japanese customers was related to a college class by the manager of a U.S. plant that was supplying stock to a Japanese manufacturer of semiconductor devices for electronics applications. The U.S. manager was justifiably proud of having the best quality material of this type available from any U.S. supplier, which was why his company had been chosen as a supplier. However, when the Japanese firm tested the first shipment of 9 million parts, it was quite upset with the lack of quality and informed the U.S. firm that it would have to do better or face being replaced by a Japanese supplier. The incoming inspection had detected five bad parts in the total shipment!

One facet of Motorola's Six-Sigma quality program is to reduce the number of suppliers and improve their capabilities and quality. Motorola provides extensive assistance and training to its suppliers and expects results in return. Suppliers are evaluated on the quality of delivered product and the timeliness of deliveries.

Only those suppliers that meet the company's expectations for superior quality are retained.

The receiving department is the link between purchasing and production. It must ensure through various inspection and testing policies that the delivered items are of the quality specified by the purchase contract. If the incoming material is of high quality, extensive inspection and testing is not necessary. Many companies now require that their suppliers provide proof that their processes can consistently turn out products of specified quality and give preferential treatment to those that can.

The quality of incoming materials and parts has become more critical as the use of flexible automation has increased. Many U.S. firms have implemented the Japanese management concept of just-in-time (JIT) scheduling. JIT requires that inventories be reduced to the barest minimum. To maintain production, the quality of materials must be high because no buffer inventories are kept to take up the slack.

Production Planning and Scheduling A production plan specifies long-term and short-term production requirements for filling customer orders and meeting anticipated demand. The correct materials, tools, and equipment must be available at the proper time and in the proper places in order to maintain a smooth flow of production. Poor quality often results from time pressures caused by insufficient planning and scheduling. Modern concepts of production planning and scheduling, such as JIT, have contributed to quality improvements and cost savings.

Manufacturing and Assembly The role of manufacturing and assembly in producing quality is to ensure that the product is made correctly. The linkage to design and process engineering, as noted earlier, is obvious; manufacturing cannot do its job without a good product design and good process technology. Once in production, however, no defects should be acceptable. If and when they do occur, every effort must be made to identify their causes and eliminate them. Inspecting-out already defective items is costly and wasteful.

Both technology and people are essential to high-quality manufacturing. Ames Rubber Corporation, for example, produces more than 17,000 custom parts by means of a wide range of manufacturing operations such as casting, extrusion, spraying, and molding. Each operation requires appropriate measuring methods and devices that can closely monitor the manufacturing process. Sophisticated measuring and testing equipment, such as laser measuring devices, ensure in-line process control. All Ames manufacturing staff understand the importance and use of statistics in controlling processes. At each production step, operators, inspectors, and supervisors collect and evaluate performance data. This process allows Ames to detect deviations from the processes immediately and to make the necessary adjustments.

Tool Engineering The tool engineering function is responsible for designing and maintaining the tools used in manufacturing and inspection. Worn manufacturing tools result in defective parts, and improperly calibrated inspection gauges give misleading information. These and other tool problems lead to poor quality and inefficiency. Engineers at Ames Rubber use statistical techniques to evaluate tooling and equipment and conduct periodic studies to ensure that Ames continues to meet or exceed product requirements.

Industrial Engineering and Process Design Manufacturing processes must be capable of producing items that meet specifications consistently. If they cannot, the result is excessive scrap, waste, and higher costs. The job of industrial engineers and process designers is to work with product design engineers to develop realistic specifications. In addition, they must select appropriate technologies, equipment, and work methods for producing quality products. For example, Nissan Motor Manufacturing has a fully automated paint system in which robots are programmed to move along with cars. Because the robots always know where the body is, the robot will stop if the line stops but continue the paint cycle until finished as a means of keeping paint quality consistent.[7] Industrial engineers also design facilities and arrange equipment to achieve a smooth production flow and to reduce the opportunities for product damage. Recently, industrial engineering as a profession has been incorporating activities more often taught in business schools.

Finished Goods Inspection and Testing The purposes of final product inspection are to judge the quality of manufacturing, to discover and help to resolve production problems that may arise, and to ensure that no defective items reach the customer. If quality is built into the product properly, such inspection should be unnecessary except for auditing purposes and functional testing. Electronic components, for example, are subjected to extensive "burn-in" tests that ensure proper operation and eliminate short-life items. In any case, inspection should be used as a means of gathering information that can be used to improve quality, not simply to remove defective items.

Packaging, Shipping, and Warehousing Even good-quality items that leave the plant floor can be incorrectly labeled or damaged in transit. Packaging, shipping, and warehousing—often termed *logistics activities*—are the functions that protect quality after goods are produced. Accurate coding and expiration dating of products is important for traceability (often for legal requirements), and for customers.

Installation and Service Products must be used correctly in order to benefit the customer. Users must understand a product and have adequate instructions for proper installation and operation. Should any problem occur, customer satisfaction depends on good after-sale service. In fact, service after the sale is one of the most important factors in establishing customer perception of quality and customer loyalty. At the Wallace Company (see *Quality Profile*), truck drivers saw the opportunity to do more than merely deliver materials to receiving docks. Where labor relations permit, they make deliveries to specific locations within plants and assist with unloading, stocking, and inventory counts. Many companies specify standards for customer service similar to the dimensions and tolerances prescribed for manufactured goods. At Wallace, for example, associates are expected to arrive for all appointments on time and to return customer phone calls within a prescribed time period. They are also responsible for knowing and observing their respective customers' rules and regulations, especially any that concern safety procedures.

In addition to the functions directly related to manufacturing the product, certain business support activities are necessary for achieving quality. Some of them are discussed here.

Finance and Accounting The finance function is responsible for obtaining funds, controlling their use, analyzing investment opportunities, and ensuring that the firm operates cost-effectively and—ideally—profitably. Financial decisions affect manufacturing equipment purchases, cost-control policies, price-volume decisions, and nearly all facets of the organization. In many organizations, however, financial managers do not understand how they can influence quality. Finance must authorize

Quality Profile
Wallace Company, Inc.

Wallace Company, Inc., was founded as a family-owned and operated industrial distributor of pipe, valves, fittings, and specialty products to the refining, chemical, and petrochemical industries. Corporate offices are in Houston, Texas, and nine branch offices are located in Texas, Alabama, and Louisiana. In 1990, the year Wallace won the Malcolm Baldrige National Quality Award, the company employed 280 people and had sales of $90 million. Their achievement demonstrated that quality is as applicable to small, family-owned businesses as it is to large manufacturing and service organizations.

Wallace's "associates"—its employees—are responsible for devising and carrying out plans for accomplishing the company's quality objectives. Participation on quality improvement teams, whose membership is voluntary and cuts across departmental and district-office boundaries, increased dramatically after 1985. As involvement increased, absenteeism, turnover, and work-related injuries dropped sharply. Between 1985 and 1987, the firm's market share almost doubled, its on-time deliveries jumped from 75 to 92 percent, and its operating profits increased by 740 percent.

Unfortunately, not long after winning the Baldrige, Wallace was forced to file for bankruptcy under Chapter 11, primarily because of recalled bank loans as the Texas oil industry fell on hard economic times. It was eventually purchased by another firm. Although quality may be necessary for competitiveness in today's business environment, it does not guarantee an organization's survival.

Source: Malcolm Baldrige National Quality Award, Profiles of Winners, National Institute of Standards and Technology, Department of Commerce.

sufficient budgeting for equipment, training, and other means of assuring quality. Financial studies can help to expose the costs of poor quality and opportunities to improve quality. Accounting data are useful in identifying areas for quality improvement and tracking the progress of quality improvement programs. Furthermore, inappropriate accounting approaches can hide poor quality.

Financial and accounting personnel who have contacts with customers can directly influence the service their company provides. At many companies, for example, employees chart invoice accuracy, the time needed to process invoices, and the time needed to pay bills. In addition, they can apply quality improvement techniques to improve their own operations. Financial personnel at Motorola, for example, were able to reduce the time needed to close the books from one month to four days.

Quality Assurance Every manager is responsible for studying and improving the quality of the process for which he or she is responsible; thus, every manager is a quality manager. Because some managers lack the technical expertise required for performing needed statistical tests or data analyses, technical specialists—usually in the "quality assurance department"—assist the managers in these tasks. Quality assurance specialists perform special statistical studies and analyses and may be assigned to work with any of the manufacturing or business support functions. It must be remembered that a firm's quality assurance department cannot assure quality in the organization. Its proper role is to provide guidance and support for the firm's total effort toward this goal.

Legal Services A firm's legal department attempts to guarantee that the firm complies with laws and regulations regarding such things as product labeling, packaging, safety, and transportation; designs and words its warranties properly; satisfies its contractual requirements; and has proper procedures and documentation in place in the event of liability claims against it. The rapid increase in liability suits has made legal services an important aspect of quality assurance.

We see that manufacturing is a rather complex system that can be viewed as a "chain of customers." This viewpoint suggests that a customer-driven quality focus must involve everyone in the organization. Quality is indeed everyone's responsibility.

QUALITY IN SERVICES

Service can be defined as "any primary or complementary activity that does not directly produce a physical product—that is, the nongoods part of the transaction between buyer (customer) and seller (provider)."[8] A service might be as simple as handling a complaint or as complex as approving a home mortgage. The North American Industry Classification System (NAICS) describes service organizations as those

> *primarily engaged in providing a wide variety of services for individuals, business and government establishments, and other organizations. Hotels and other lodging places; establishments providing personal, business, repair, and amusement services; health, legal, engineering, and other professional services; educational institutions, membership organizations, and other miscellaneous services are included.*

This classification of service organizations includes all nonmanufacturing organizations except such industries as agriculture, mining, and construction. Also usually included in this category are real estate, financial services, retailers, transportation, and public utilities.

Pure service businesses deliver intangible products. Examples would include a law firm, whose product is legal advice, and a health care facility, whose product is comfort and better health. However, service is a key element for many traditional manufacturing companies. For instance, manufacturers such as IBM and Xerox provide extensive maintenance and consulting services, which may be more important to the customer than tangible products.

The service sector has grown rapidly toward the end of the twentieth century. In 1945, 22.99 million people were employed by service-producing industries, and 18.5 million were employed by goods-producing industries. By the middle of 1997, 97.66 million people were employed by service-producing industries, while the number of people employed by goods-producing industries had grown only to 24.71 million. Thus, 79.8 percent of the nonfarm employees in the United States are working in services. More information about current labor statistics of this type can be found on the Bureau of Labor Statistics web pages at *http://stats.bls.gov/*.

The service sector began to recognize the importance of quality several years after manufacturing had done so. This delay can be attributed to the fact that service industries had not faced the same aggressive foreign competition as had manufacturing. Another factor is the high turnover rate in service industry jobs, which typically pay less than manufacturing jobs. Constantly changing personnel makes establishing a culture for continuous improvement more difficult. Also, the focus of quality changed from product defects to achieving customer satisfaction.

Companies that have become nationally prominent in the service industry for their quality efforts include large organizations such as AT&T Universal Card Services (see *Quality Profile*), BI, Dana Commercial Credit Corporation, Federal Express Corporation (FedEx), GTE Directories Corporation, and The Ritz-Carlton Hotel Company; and small companies such as Custom Research Inc. These companies will be featured throughout this book.

The importance of quality in services cannot be underestimated. The American Management Association estimates that the average company loses as many as 35 percent of its customers each year, about two-thirds of which are lost because of poor customer service. Studies have shown that companies can boost their profits almost 100 percent by retaining just 5 percent more of their customers than their competitors retain.[9] The reason is that the cost of acquiring new customers is much higher than the costs associated with retaining customers. Even with higher unit costs or a smaller market share, companies with loyal, long-time customers can financially outperform competitors with higher customer turnover.

The definitions of quality that apply to manufactured products apply equally to service products. The very nature of service implies that it must respond to the needs of the customer; that is, the service must "meet or exceed customer expectations." These expectations must be translated into performance standards and specifications similar to

Quality Profile
AT&T Universal Card Services

AT&T Universal Card Services (UCS) was launched on March 26, 1990. UCS markets and provides customer services for the AT&T Universal Card, a combined long-distance calling card and general purpose credit card. By September 1992 UCS had more than 10.2 million active accounts and nearly 16 million cardholders, making it the second largest bank card in the industry. The company, headquartered in Jacksonville, Florida, has 2,500 associates in four cities across the United States. The values that guide UCS include customer delight, commitment, teamwork, continuous improvement, trust and integrity, mutual respect, and a sense of urgency. UCS continually evaluates and improves the tools and technologies it uses to serve customers quickly and efficiently. The company is building a world-class integrated information analysis system to improve the quality of customer account inquiry, data access, and information analysis processes. These efforts translated into significant reductions in operating expenses, increases in productivity, and industry-leading customer satisfaction results.

Application processing cycle time improvements led UCS to a consistent three-day processing cycle time, when the industry average is 24 days, and the best in-class competitor takes 10 days. In their first two years of business, UCS received numerous recognitions and awards—including Best Product of 1990 by *Business Week*, Top Banking Innovation by *American Banker*, and Compass Award from the American Marketing Association for outstanding performance—all culminating in a 1992 Baldrige Award. UCS was sold to CitiBank in early 1998.

Source: Malcolm Baldrige National Quality Award, Profiles of Winners, National Institute of Standards and Technology, Department of Commerce.

standards of conformance that direct manufacturing activities. For example, a quick-service restaurant might be expected to serve a complete dinner within five minutes. In a fine restaurant, however, one might expect to have 10 to 15 minutes between courses, and might regard the service as poor if the time between courses is too short.

Contrasts With Manufacturing

The production of services differs from manufacturing in many ways, and these differences have important implications for quality management. The most critical differences are described here.

1. Customer needs and performance standards are often difficult to identify and measure, primarily because the customers define what they are, and each customer is different.
2. The production of services typically requires a higher degree of customization than does manufacturing. Doctors, lawyers, insurance salespeople, and food-service employees must tailor their services to individual customers. In manufacturing, the goal is uniformity.
3. The output of many service systems is intangible, whereas manufacturing produces tangible, visible products. Manufacturing quality can be assessed against firm design specifications (for example, the depth of cut should be 0.125 inch), but service quality can only be assessed against customers' subjective, nebulous expectations and past experiences. (What is a "good" sales experience?) Also, the customer can "have and hold" a manufactured product, but can generally only remember a service. Manufactured goods can be recalled or replaced by the manufacturer, but poor service can only be followed up by apologies and reparations.
4. Services are produced and consumed simultaneously, whereas manufactured goods are produced prior to consumption. In addition, many services must be performed at the convenience of the customer. Therefore, services cannot be stored, inventoried, or inspected prior to delivery as manufactured goods are. Much more attention must therefore be paid to training and building quality into the service as a means of quality assurance.
5. Customers often are involved in the service process and present while it is being performed, whereas manufacturing is performed away from the customer. For example, customers of a quick-service restaurant place their own orders, carry their food to the table, and are expected to clear the table when they have finished eating.
6. Services are generally labor intensive, whereas manufacturing is more capital intensive. The quality of human interaction is a vital factor for services that involve human contact. For example, the quality of hospital care depends heavily on interactions among the patients, nurses, doctors, and other medical staff. Banks have found that tellers' friendliness is a key factor in retaining depositors. Hence, the behavior and morale of service employees is critical in delivering a quality service experience.
7. Many service organizations must handle large numbers of customer transactions. For example, on a given business day, the Royal Bank of Canada might process more than 5.5 million transactions for 7.5 million customers through 1,600 branches and more than 3,500 banking machines, and FedEx might handle more than 1.5 million shipments across the globe. Such large volumes increase the opportunity for error.

These differences have made it difficult for many service organizations to apply total quality principles. The results of a survey conducted in the mid-1990s revealed that most smaller service firms had no TQ initiative, and many respondents believed that the unique characteristics of service described in the preceding list were contrary to their ability to define quality and measure clearly, and that understanding and fulfilling customer expectations are difficult because service customers usually do not complete a formal specification of the type, amount, and quality of service required.[10] These findings suggest that many service firms have not made the effort to fully understand the nature of TQ and its potential benefits, and the ways in which it can be implemented effectively.

Components of Service System Quality

Many service organizations such as airlines, banks, and hotels have well-developed quality systems. These systems begin with a commitment to the customers. For example, US Airways placed first in a 1999 survey of U.S. airline quality as measured by such attributes as on-time performance, denied boardings, mishandled luggage, and passenger complaints—one year after it finished dead last.[11] The airline launched a 12-point Customer Commitment program, that, as described by the president and CEO, ". . . is to ensure that we offer, and our customers receive, the service level that they are entitled to on a consistent basis—the highest level of service possible." The program included offering the lowest fares, providing timely information on flight delays or cancellations, providing on-time baggage delivery, giving customers 24 hours to cancel a purchased ticket without penalty, and responding promptly to complaints and requests for information. The airline devoted thousands of hours to developing procedures, refining programs, and implementing training plans.[12]

Service quality may be viewed from a manufacturing analogy, for instance, by putting it in terms of technical standards such as the components of a properly made-up guest room for a hotel, service transaction speed, or accuracy of information. However, managing intangible quality characteristics that usually depend on employee performance and behavior is more difficult. Thus, two key components of service system quality are *employees* and *information technology*. This statement does not imply that these factors are not important in manufacturing, of course, but they have special significance in services—just as engineering technology might have in manufacturing.

Employees Customers evaluate a service primarily by the quality of the human contact. A *Wall Street Journal* survey found that Americans' biggest complaints about service employees are of delivery people or salespeople who fail to show up when customers have stayed home at a scheduled time for them; salespeople who are poorly informed; and salesclerks who talk on the phone while waiting on you, say "It's not my department," talk down to you, or cannot describe how a product works.

Researchers have repeatedly demonstrated that when service employee job satisfaction is high, customer satisfaction is high, and that when job satisfaction is low, customer satisfaction is low.[13] Many service companies act on the motto, "If we take care of our employees, they will take care of our customers." At FedEx (see *Quality Profile*), for instance, the company credo is stated simply as People, Service, Profits. All potential decisions in the company are evaluated on their effects on the employees (people), on their customers (service), and the company's financial performance (profits), in that order. FedEx has a "no layoff" philosophy, and its "guaranteed fair treatment procedure" (discussed in Chapter 6) for handling employee grievances is

QUALITY PROFILE

FEDEX

Conceived by it chairman and chief executive officer Frederick W. Smith, FedEx launched operations in 1973 with a fleet of eight small aircraft. Five years later, the company employed 10,000 people and handled a daily volume of 35,000 shipments. By 1990, when FedEx was the first service company to win the Malcolm Baldrige National Quality Award, 90,000 employees at more than 1,650 sites were processing 1.5 million shipments daily, each one tracked by a central information system and delivered by a highly decentralized distribution network.

By constantly adhering to a management philosophy that emphasizes people, service, and profits, in that order, FedEx has achieved high levels of customer satisfaction and rapid sales growth. Extensive customer and internal data are used by cross-functional teams involved in the company's new product introduction process. Employees are encouraged to be innovative and to make decisions that advance quality and customer satisfaction goals. FedEx management continually sets higher goals for quality performance and customer satisfaction, investing heavily in state-of-the-art technology, and building on its reputation as an excellent employer. Company leaders are committed to management by fact, analysis, and improvement.

Sources: Malcolm Baldrige National Quality Award, Profiles of Winners, National Institute of Standards and Technology, Department of Commerce; FedEx Corporation Information Book.

used by firms in many industries as a model. Front-line workers can qualify for promotion to management positions, and the company has a well-developed recognition program for team and individual contributions to company performance.

In many companies, unfortunately, the front-line employees—salesclerks, receptionists, delivery personnel, and so on, who have the most contact with customers—receive the lowest pay, minimal training, little decision-making authority, and little responsibility (what is termed *empowerment*). High-quality service employees require reward systems that recognize customer satisfaction results and customer-focused behaviors, appropriate skills and abilities for performing the job, and supervisors who act more as coaches and mentors than as administrators. Training is particularly important; service employees need to be skilled in handling every customer interaction, from greeting customers to asking the right questions.

The Ritz-Carlton Hotel Company (see the *Quality in Practice* case at the end of this chapter) is one service company with an exemplary focus on its people.[14] The Ritz-Carlton motto is "Ladies and Gentlemen Serving Ladies and Gentlemen," and all employees are treated as guests would be treated. The company's focus is to develop a "skilled and empowered workforce operating with pride and joy" by ensuring that everyone knows what they are supposed to do, how well they are doing, and have the authority to make changes as necessary. For example, the role of the housekeeper is not simply to make beds, but to create a memorable experience for the customer. Each hotel has a director of human resources and a training manager, who are assisted by the hotel's quality leader. Each work area has a departmental trainer who is responsible for training and certifying new employees in his or her unit. The Ritz-Carlton uses a highly predictive "character-trait recruiting" instrument for determining candidates' fitness for each of 120 job positions. New employees receive two days' orientation in which senior executives personally demonstrate Ritz-Carlton methods and instill Ritz-Carlton values. Three weeks later, managers monitor the effectiveness of the instruction and then conduct a follow-up training session. Later, new employees must pass written and skill-demonstration tests in order to become certified in their work areas. Every day, in each work area, each shift supervisor conducts a quality line-up meeting and briefing session. Employees receive continuous teaching and coaching to refresh skills and improve their performance, reinforce their purpose on the job, and receive recognition for achievements. Through these and other mechanisms, employees receive more than 100 hours of quality education aimed at fostering a commitment to premium service, solving problems, setting goals, and generating new ideas. Employees are empowered to "move heaven and earth to satisfy a customer," to enlist the aid of other employees to resolve a problem swiftly, to spend up to $2,000 to satisfy a guest, to decide the business terms of a sale, to be involved in setting plans for their particular work area, and to speak with anyone in the company regarding any problem. The Ritz-Carlton has improved the turnover rate of employees steadily since 1989 to about 30% by 1999, well below industry averages.

Information Technology Information technology incorporates computing, communication, data processing, and various other means of converting data into useful information. Information technology is essential in modern service organizations because of the high volumes of information they must process and because customers demand service at ever-increasing speeds. Intelligent use of information technology not only leads to improved quality and productivity, but also to competitive advantage, particularly when technology is used to better serve the customer and to make it easier for customers to do business with the company.

Every service industry is exploiting information technology to improve customer service. Restaurants, for example, use handheld order-entry computer terminals to speed up the ordering process. An order is instantaneously transmitted to the kitchen or bar, where it is displayed and the guest check is printed. In addition to saving time, such systems improve accuracy by standardizing the order-taking, billing, and inventory procedures and reducing the need for handwriting. Credit authorizations, which once took several minutes by telephone, are now accomplished in seconds through computerized authorization systems. FedEx's handheld "SuperTracker" scans packages' bar codes every time packages change hands between pickup and delivery.

The Ritz-Carlton Hotel Company exploits information technology to remember each of its more than 800,000 customers. Knowledge of individual customer preferences, previous difficulties, family and personal interests, and preferred credit cards are stored in a database accessible to every hotel. This guest-profiling system allows each customer to be treated individually, by giving front-desk employees immediate access to such information as whether the guest smokes, whether he or she prefers scented or unscented soap, and what kind of pillow he or she prefers.

Another example is provided by Fidelity Investments.[15] Fidelity receives about 200,000 telephone calls each day, more than two-thirds of which are handled by a computer system without human intervention. A computer switching system monitors the call loads at Fidelity's four telephone centers and distributes calls among its more than 2,000 representatives. Fidelity is developing a "workstation of the future" that will allow its representatives to call up any customer's account on their terminal screen. Using this, Fidelity will be able to offer its customers up-to-the-second, personalized information and service while improving internal productivity.

Without a doubt, the largest impact of information technology for service has been in e-commerce. Customers can shop for almost any product; configure, price, and order computer systems; and take virtual test drives of automobiles and select options from thousands of possible combinations on the Internet in the convenience of their home. Information technology can be used to develop and enhance customer relationships. Amazon.com has been extremely successful at building relationships. They provide extensive information about products, such as reader reviews to help customers evaluate books, search used bookstores for out-of-print books, and even provide e-mail thank you letters a month or so after purchase. However, while information technology reduces labor intensity and increases the speed of service, it can have adverse effects on other dimensions of quality. Some people, including some customers, will argue that customer satisfaction is decreased as personal interaction is reduced. (Have you ever gotten irritated when wading through multiple menus on an automated telephone answering system?) Thus, service providers must balance conflicting quality concerns.

QUALITY IN HEALTH CARE

One service industry that has faced continuing pressure to improve quality—and one with the fastest growing interest in quality—is health care. Quality has been a focus for the industry for some time. In 1910, Ernest Codman, M.D., proposed the "end result system of hospital standardization." Under this system, a hospital would track every patient it treated long enough to determine whether the treatment was effective. If the treatment was not effective, the hospital would then attempt to determine why, so that similar cases could be treated successfully in the future. The American College of Surgeons (ACS) developed Minimum Standards for Hospitals in 1917 and began inspections the following year. The Joint Commission on Accreditation of Healthcare Organizations (JCAHO)—the principal accreditation agency for health care—was created in 1951 through a collaboration of ACS and several other agencies to provide voluntary accreditation. Its mission is "to continuously improve the safety and quality of care provided to the public through the provision of health care accreditation and related services that support performance improvement in health care organizations." By 1970, accreditation standards were recast to represent optimal achievable levels of quality, rather than minimum essential levels of quality. JCAHO issued new standards in 1992 requiring all hospital CEOs to educate themselves on continuous quality improvement (CQI) methods.[16] The new standards emphasize performance improvement concepts and incorporate quality improvement principles more fully in areas such as surgical case review, blood usage evaluation, and drug usage evaluation. Further information about the Joint Commission may be found at its Web site *http://www.jcaho.org*.

Similar to the Joint Commission, the National Committee for Quality Assurance (NCQA) is a private, not-for-profit organization dedicated to improving the quality of health care.[17] The organization's primary activities are assessing and reporting on the quality of the nation's managed care plans, work that has led to partnerships and collaborative efforts with many states, the federal government, employer and consumer groups, and many of the nation's leading corporations and business coalitions. NCQA's mission is to provide information that enables purchasers and consumers of managed health care to distinguish among plans based on quality, thereby allowing them to make more informed health care purchasing decisions. This goal encourages plans to compete based on quality and value, rather than on price and provider network. Efforts are organized around two activities, accreditation and performance measurement, which are complementary strategies for producing information to guide choice. These activities have been integrated under NCQA's accreditation program, which includes selected performance measures in such key areas as member satisfaction, quality of care, access, and service.

NCQA began accrediting managed care organizations (MCOs) in 1991 in response to the need for standardized, objective information about the quality of these organizations. Although the MCO accreditation program is voluntary and rigorous, it has been well received by the managed care industry, and almost half the health maintenance organizations (HMOs) in the nation, covering three quarters of all HMO enrollees, are currently involved in the NCQA accreditation process. For an organization to become accredited by NCQA, it must undergo a survey and meet certain standards designed to evaluate the health plan's clinical and administrative systems. In particular, NCQA's accreditation surveys look at a health plan's efforts to continuously improve the quality of care and service it delivers.

Other organizations, such as the Institute for Healthcare Improvement (IHI), have emerged to support quality improvement in health care. IHI's goals are improved health status, better clinical outcomes, reduced costs that do not compromise quality, greater access to care, an easier-to-use health care system, and improved satisfaction to patients and communities. IHI focuses on fostering collaboration, rather than competition, among health care organizations.

Despite accreditation and collaborative efforts aimed at quality, the industry faces considerable challenges. A 1998 study by the President's Advisory Commission on Consumer Protection and Quality in the Health Care Industry entitled *Quality First: Better Health Care for All Americans*, noted several types of quality problems in health care.[18] They include the following:

1. *Avoidable errors.* Too many Americans are injured during the course of their treatment, and some die prematurely as a result. For example, a study of injuries to patients treated in hospitals in New York State found that 3.7 percent experienced adverse events, of which 13.6 percent led to death and 2.6 percent to permanent disability, and that about one-fourth of these adverse events were due to negligence. A national study found that from 1983 to 1993, deaths due to medication errors rose more than twofold, with 7,391 deaths attributed to medication errors in 1993 alone.
2. *Underutilization of services.* Millions of people do not receive necessary care and suffer needless complications that add to health care costs and reduce productivity. For example, a study of Medicare patients with myocardial infarction found that only 21 percent of eligible patients received beta blockers, and that the mortality rate among recipients was 43 percent less than that for nonrecipients. An estimated 18,000 people die each year from heart attacks because they did not receive effective interventions.
3. *Overuse of services.* Millions of Americans receive health care services that are unnecessary, increase costs, and often endanger their health. For example, an analysis of hysterectomies performed by seven health plans estimated that one in six was inappropriate.
4. *Variation in services.* A pattern of wide variation continues throughout health care practice, including regional variations and small-area variations. These variations are a clear indicator that the practice of health care has not caught up with the science of health care to ensure evidence-based practice in the United States.

The Commission's report included more than 50 recommendations to address these issues, including the following:

1. *National aims for improvement of health care quality should be established, accompanied by appropriate, specific objectives for improvement.* These aims should be based on criteria that include focusing on common and/or costly conditions, areas where wide variability in practices exists, and improvements that have the greatest impact on reducing morbidity and mortality and improving functional capacity.
2. *Core sets of quality measures should be identified for standardized reporting by each sector of the health care industry.* These sets should reflect measurement priorities developed by taking into account both national aims for improvement and the information needs of consumers (especially vulnerable populations), purchasers, providers, health organizations, and public health and policy officials.
3. *All sectors of the health care industry should support the focused development of quality measures that enhance and improve the ability to evaluate and improve health care.* Types of measures that are needed include measures of aspects of health care that are not well addressed by existing measures; a wider range of health care outcome measures, including functional outcomes; measures that provide meaningful information about quality at the individual practitioner level; and summary measures that address quality across multiple dimensions.
4. *A widespread and ongoing consumer education strategy should be developed to deliver accurate and reliable information about health care quality to consumers and encourage them to consider information on quality when choosing health plans, providers, and treatments.* Education should address how health care experts define and identify good quality health care; how quality can vary across plans, facilities, health care organizations, and providers; why quality should be an important factor in making health care purchasing decisions; how to obtain comparative information on quality, their rights and responsibilities as health care purchasers and patients, and how they can play a role in improving health care quality.
5. *Information on health care quality should be developed to meet the needs of consumers.* Entities promulgating quality measures should obtain consumer input on issues consumers value and on the design of information reports that are intended, in part or in whole, for consumer use. Quality measures should be developed that are of interest to consumers in general, as well as consumers with particular health concerns (e.g., those with chronic or terminal illness, those receiving home care, those living with physical or mental disabilities, and those concerned with care of children).
6. *Interested parties should work together to develop a health care error reporting system to identify errors and prevent their recurrence.* The Federal Aviation Administration's Aviation Safety Reporting System (ASRS) may provide a useful model for a blame-free system of error reporting.
7. *Health care organizations should provide strong leadership to confront quality challenges.* Organizations should develop a culture that is supportive of leadership, innovation, and risk taking. They should strive to attract, reward, and retain strong leaders while providing mentoring opportunities for new generations of leaders.

8. *Organizations should become skilled at using and learning from quantitative information to measure progress toward quality improvement.* The key goal should be to improve the performance of systems of care as a whole rather than improving parts of the system at the expense of the whole. The commitment should be to evidence-based health care with processes put in place to systematically reevaluate established practices.
9. *Organizations should commit themselves to continuous improvement and the elimination of waste.* Health care organizations should recognize that most quality problems are due to faulty processes not individuals' failings. A clear link should be established between quality improvement and the elimination of wasteful processes.
10. *Organizations should make a commitment to reduce error and increase safety.* The health care industry should examine the possibility of establishing a national system for reporting and tracking errors.
11. *Organizations should build long-term relationships with all stakeholders.* Contracts with suppliers and other vendors should build quality improvement into long-term planning.
12. *Organizations should commit themselves to fundamental change in their work environment, involving and empowering all employees.* Employees should feel free to report errors and instances of improper care, as well as suggest innovations, regardless of their position within an organization.

These recommendations support the underlying philosophy of total quality that we described in Chapter 1.

While the national health care system as a whole may need a sweeping overhaul, many individual providers have turned toward quality as a means of achieving better performance and customer satisfaction. For example, Intermountain Health Care, a nonprofit system of 24 hospitals in Utah, has pursued quality as a strategic objective since 1985.[19] One hospital lowered the rate of postsurgical infections to less than one-fifth of the acceptable national norms through its use of statistical tools for quality improvement. At Boston's New England Deaconess Hospital, teams identify problems that add unnecessary days to hospital stays. In two years Deaconess achieved a 10 percent overall decrease in length of hospital stay. Nash General Hospital in Rocky Mount, North Carolina, examined processes within the Emergency Department and were able to reduce the length of stay by more than 50 percent.[20]

As another example, the Virginia Beach Ambulatory Surgery Center (VBASC) built a new outpatient surgical facility using the principles of total quality.[21] The center engaged employees in writing a policy and procedure manual. It continues to ask employee opinions on the quality of their work as individuals and the organization as a whole. Another part of the strategy encourages and supports professional development, and empowers employees to develop and manage innovative programs. In addition, it listens to customers and acts on their suggestions, views surgeons and their office staff as key customers, as part of its strong internal customer focus, and measures and objectively assesses everything it does. It evaluates its progress in these areas during monthly CQI meetings.

Although many health care organizations have seen measurable improvements from their quality initiatives, these improvements have been primarily in the areas of cost reduction and increased efficiency. A difficult challenge that most face is getting physicians involved in the quality process. Many are requiring their participation on teams and steering committees, creating a liaison role between management and physicians, using physicians as champions, and targeting training.[22]

QUALITY IN EDUCATION

Education represents one of the most interesting and challenging areas for quality improvement. Attacks on the quality of education in the United States, from kindergarten through the 12th grade (K–12) and at colleges and universities provided a rallying cry for education reform during the last decade.[23] Deming's view of a production system (see Figure 1.3 on page 21) can be applied to educational organizations as well as to traditional manufacturing and service organizations. Figure 2.2 applies Deming's model to the system of higher education. Suppliers include families, high schools, two-year colleges, and businesses. The inputs to the system are students, faculty, support staff, and so on. Outputs include people with new knowledge and abilities and research findings that are useful to organizations. The customers include the business community, graduate schools, society, students, and families. Processes include teaching, student counseling, and scientific research. Like manufacturing systems, educational systems can conduct customer research for evaluation and improvement. For example, by observing students, analyzing test results, and using other sources of student feedback, instructors assess their own effectiveness and develop strategies for improving it. Some colleges and universities survey their graduates and their graduates' employers to assess consumer satisfaction with their product. Such feedback helps colleges, departments, and faculty members to redesign curriculum and improve course content and facilitating services such as academic advising. A similar model could be developed for an individual classroom. (Who are the customers and suppliers? What are the key processes? What types of "consumer research" might be appropriate?) Viewing an educational institution in this fashion helps to better understand the role of quality management approaches in achieving educational objectives.

Aside from a few notable exceptions and pockets of excellence, educators, educational institutions, political groups and leaders, and even the public generally have been slow to attack the problem of educational decline on a systematic basis. One of the earliest and most widely publicized stories of the successful use of quality in education is that of Mt. Edgecumbe High School in Sitka, Alaska.[24] Mt. Edgecumbe is a public boarding school with some 200 students, often from problem homes in rural Alaska. Many are Native Americans, who are struggling to keep their culture alive while learning to live and work in American society. David Langford, a teacher, brought the quality concepts to Mt. Edgecumbe after hearing about them at a meeting at McDonnell-Douglas Helicopter Company. After reading many books by

Figure 2.2 Higher Education as a Production System

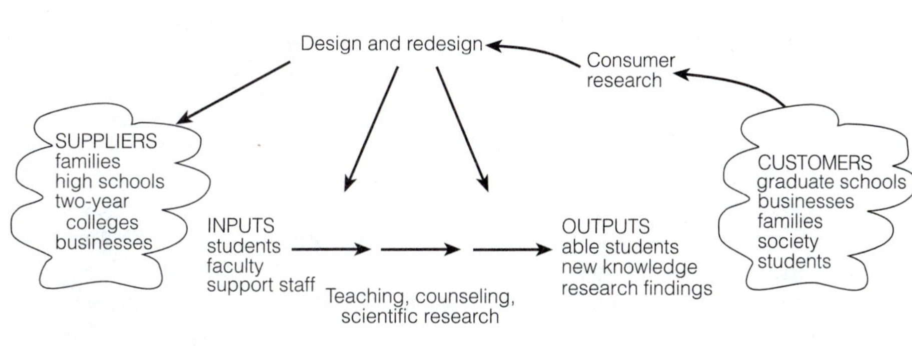

quality gurus such as Deming, Juran, and Crosby, Langford took some students in a computer club on a trip to Gilbert (Arizona) High School. There, they observed how Delores Christiansen taught continuous improvement in her business classes. They also visited companies in the Phoenix area that were using quality principles. The students, with the coaching of Langford, began to use quality concepts to improve school processes. For example, the students tackled the problem of too many tardy classmates. By investigating the reasons for tardiness, the students persuaded the administration to drop the punishment for tardy students, and were able to reduce the average number of late occurrences per week from 35 to 5.

As an even more radical change, the school dropped the traditional grading system. Instead, students use statistical techniques to keep track of their own progress. No assignment is considered finished until it is perfect. Eliminating grades has had a positive effect. One student, James Penemarl reported, "I found myself learning a lot more. It's not the teacher having to check my progress, it's me having to check my progress. See, however much I learn is up to me, and if I want to learn, I'm going to go out and learn." What they call CIP, or the Continuous Improvement Process, has been an obvious success (approximately 50 percent of students now go on to college), yet the messages that David Langford stresses in interviews about the school are (1) it takes time, effort, and persistence—it's not a "quick fix"; and (2) there's always room for improvement. Current information, experiences of teachers and students, and articles on applying TQ in secondary education can be obtained at Mt. Edgecumbe's Web site at *http://www.mehs.educ.state.ak.us/quality.html*.

Many other K–12 schools have implemented TQ initiatives. For example, the Conroe Independent School District just north of Houston, Texas, adopted a strategic plan in 1993 that included the following vision:

> *The school district in 2007 is a learning community united in its commitment to ensuring that all students graduate with confidence and competence. The schools and communities work together to provide performance standards that can be applied to the real world. This is achieved through the implementation of quality in instruction, operations, and leadership.*

The process developed to achieve this vision included a TQ implementation plan that relied heavily on training and teams. Initial projects included improving team teaching processes, accuracy in reporting data, purchasing processes, and communications and teamwork within the custodial department.[25]

Two other examples are Brazosport Independent School District (BISD) and Hunterdon Central Regional High School, which were the only two educational institutions to receive site visits for the Malcolm Baldrige National Quality Award in the first year of education sector eligibility (1999). BISD, 50 miles southwest of Houston, is the largest Exemplary school district in the state of Texas, a designation earned by only 121 districts based on tough accountability ratings. It is particularly noteworthy because of the socioeconomic diversity of its students. The success of BISD has been a never-ending journey of dedication and hard work, based on a philosophy of no excuses, and the belief that all children can learn regardless of family background, sex, or socioeconomic status. Figure 2.3 shows the results of standardized mathematics tests since 1991. BISD achieved such remarkable results by implementing a quality-based improvement strategy, using data to drive decision making, and empowering individuals most responsible for meeting customer requirements.

Hunterdon Central Regional High School is one of the largest, campus-style high school districts in New Jersey and a recipient of New Jersey Governor's Award for Performance Excellence. Hunterdon Central's vision statement, which commits the

Figure 2.3 Mathematics Standardized Test Results for Brazosport Independent School District

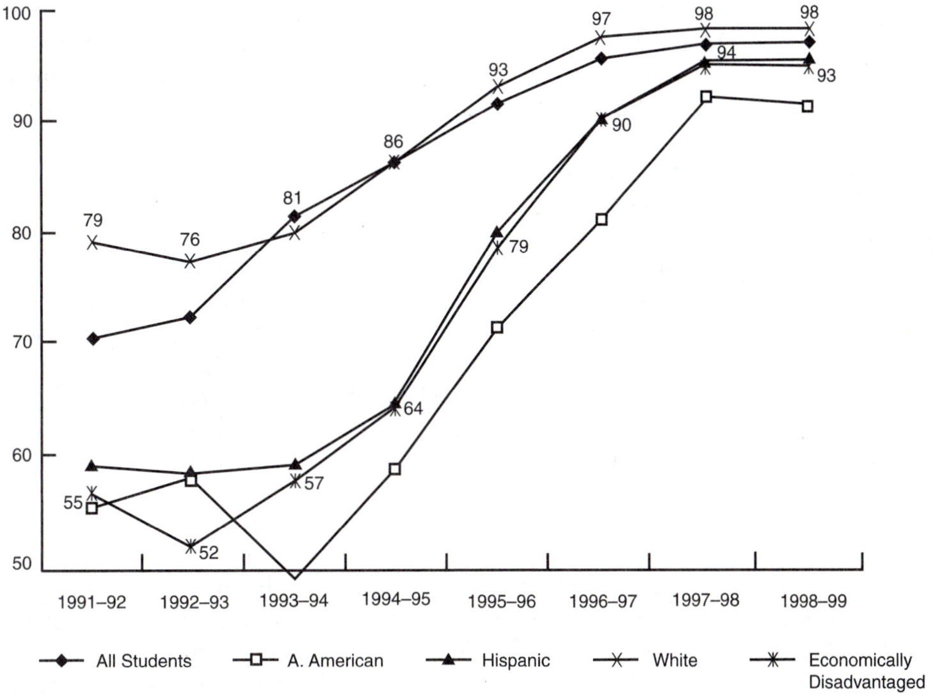
100
90
80
70
60
50
79
76
81
86
93
97
98
98
94
93
90
79
64
57
55
52
1991–92
1992–93
1993–94
1994–95
1995–96
1996–97
1997–98
1998–99
All Students
A. American
Hispanic
White
Economically Disadvantaged

Source: Brazosport Independent School District, Freeport, Texas.

school to a diverse curriculum that fosters lifelong learning in a changing society, is supported by five district aims.

1. Highest student achievement
2. Safe learning environment
3. Partnerships
4. High-performing workforce
5. Integrated management systems

The staff uses quality management as an assessment tool and employs quality principles to develop improvement strategies and effect change. Its quality policy is "Quality Systems and Services for Quality Learning"—the ultimate goal of all quality initiatives and processes of the district.

Koalaty Kid

The American Society for Quality (ASQ) has long promoted quality in elementary education through a program entitled *Koalaty Kid*.[26] This program was an outgrowth of activities at Frederick C. Carder Elementary School in Corning, New York, where Fred the Koala appears throughout the school on bulletin boards, at assemblies, in the cafeteria, and in the classrooms. In the 1980s, several teachers and the principal at Carder identified factors they deemed most important to student success in all areas where they felt their students needed improvement. First, they believed that reading was the key to all other learning, and observed that students did not read much beyond what was required in the classroom. Second, they found that all too often, students were handing in homework with numerous errors. When asked to correct them, students could do so easily when they knew how to do it, but simply didn't habitually do it right the first time. Third, they observed that the most successful students were those who felt confident of their abilities and comfortable with themselves.

Having identified these critical issues, they developed a plan to bring about change throughout the whole school. Reading became a primary focus. Students were invited to read books of their own choosing. Reading at home was encouraged with a system of contracts. Students demonstrated that they understood what they read through book reports, and each book was recorded. Students who met their contracts were recognized at assemblies, and incentives helped to encourage the habit. Second, the teachers communicated that the standard of work they expected in homework was best work the first time. When students handed in papers, they were asked to assess in their own minds, "Is this your best work?" Excellent papers were displayed on bulletin boards, and students were recognized for "Koalaty work." Third, teachers established schoolwide expectations for behavior, and made a point of "catching" students being good. This combination of efforts became known as "Koalaty Kid," and students eagerly strove to become "Koalaty Kids," to read more, do their best work the first time, and treat others with courtesy and respect.

In 1988, two ASQ members from Corning, Incorporated, visited the school and learned about Koalaty Kid. They immediately saw the parallels to total quality: critical issues had been identified, a plan for improvement was developed and implemented, clear expectations were communicated, a measurement system was put in place, and a consistent system of recognition and reward reinforced student success. Excited by what they saw in Carder School, the business people brought the Carder model to the attention of ASQ headquarters. The Society invested in a pilot program, providing incentives for reading and tracking increases in 26 pilot schools over two years. A Koalaty Kid steering committee, including educators, sponsors, and ASQ members, was formed to oversee the effort. In 1994 this grew into the Koalaty Kid Alliance, a membership organization with a board of directors. This has been the group to encourage a broader and more rigorous use of total quality tools in the schools. From 1995 to 1997 research was done by Penn State University on the effectiveness of the new Koalaty Kid training model. The researcher encouraged "the board and staff to move ahead aggressively with an expansion of the training initiative to additional elementary schools in the USA and abroad . . . implementing this approach at the middle school and high schools levels as well." (Executive Summary, Whitaker, 1997). Koalaty Keys, for middle school and high school ages, was created based on the same model as Koalaty Kid.

Because Koalaty Kid is an approach, not a prescribed program, schools can utilize it to achieve their own objectives. The four key factors are (1) active involvement of the whole school community, (2) committed leadership, (3) the employment of a system for continuous improvement, and (4) an environment that celebrates successes.

System for Continuous Improvement Koalaty Kid uses total quality principles—establishing consistent standards of excellence, setting and communicating clear expectations, focusing on continuous improvement (as opposed to finding fault and blaming), looking at a work task as a process, involving all who have a stake in the outcome in the improvement process, measuring results, and recognizing and rewarding success—for bringing about change. Using a set of quality "tools," teams define a system, assess a situation, analyze causes, try out improvement theories, study results, standardize improvement, and plan continuous improvement.

Active Involvement School administrators, teachers, sponsors, parents, and the students themselves work together on teams that are empowered to make decisions and implement change. Everyone who is ultimately affected by the school has an opportunity to influence its success. Together, they represent a larger resource than the school's paid staff. And because they represent all constituencies, they can often create change more swiftly and lastingly. Teams might manage some of the school's ongoing operations. They might identify and tackle tough issues. Or they might help the schools and students in any number of creative ways. It's up to the school leadership and the teams themselves to decide how they can best work toward achieving the school's goals.

Outside sponsoring organizations are vitally important to the success of Koalaty Kid schools. These businesses, institutions, community organizations, or ASQ sections participate on the school-based team. They may help the school in a variety of ways, depending on their own capabilities and the school's needs. Some provide funds for quality training, while others become a source of help for important school activities, expertise in troubleshooting quality processes, or enrichment for academic areas. Most important, their perspective as future employers or community representatives with a stake in the school's "output" helps to bring the school and its community closer together.

Parent involvement is critical to the success of Koalaty Kid schools. Parents work closely with their own children, monitoring homework assignments, reading aloud, identifying trouble spots, and communicating with students, teachers, and administrators about any factors that affect their children's success. In addition, they often serve as the core of the school's volunteer base. As volunteers, they may help the school in a variety of ways—supplementing the work of classroom teachers with one-on-one tutoring, raising funds for needed equipment, and participating actively in decision making on the school's teams.

The most important involvement comes from the students. Students as young as kindergartners, learn the tools of Total Quality and how to apply them within the process of continuous improvement. They learn how to solve their own problems and make date-driven decisions. These are competencies that prepare them for the future but also teach them how to be accountable for their own learning.

Committed Leadership Schools can change only if their designated leaders are committed to improvement. Change occurs quickly if these administrators are also capable of inspiring the faculty, students, parents, sponsors, and other administrators to work with them. Because of their positions, these individuals can allocate resources, call meetings, and generally "make things happen." However, leadership from others can also be effective, provided it is accepted and endorsed by those with ultimate decision-making authority. Leaders inspire others in the school community because of the depth and sincerity of their belief and commitment. Part of their ability to persuade others also comes from articulating their own clear understanding of where they are headed and the process they will use to get there. They constantly listen and learn, and they draw others with skill and ideas into the process. School leaders often find that undertaking the Koalaty Kid process inspires them to new levels in their own professional growth and a more profound understanding of their own roles as leaders.

Environment that Celebrates Successes Although many schools are now using team-based management and/or employing total quality, the fourth distinguishing feature of Koalaty Kid schools is the excitement that permeates the school environment. This excitement is focused on celebrating student successes, large and small. Displays of papers that meet or exceed requirements, photos of students recognized for exemplary behavior, and rosters of student achievements adorn classroom bulletin boards and school hallways. At assemblies and pep rallies, students cheer for one another's accomplishments as they are recognized. In hundreds of ways, the teachers, staff, volunteers, and parents communicate their delight when students reach goals.

Quality in Higher Education

Many colleges and universities have also made substantial commitments to quality efforts. One of the early success stories at the university level is Oregon State University (OSU).[27] After close study of the quality literature, a visit from Dr. W. Edwards Deming, company visits to Ford, Hewlett-Packard, and Dow, and attendance by the president and several top administrators at a seminar on problem-solving tools, administrators at OSU began the planning phase.

The pilot study at OSU was conducted in the physical plant area for a number of reasons: (1) quality was considered a high-priority issue; (2) it had a high probability of success; (3) management agreed that it was important; (4) no one else was working on it; and (5) it was also important to the customers of the organization. A multi-level team of 12 people chose to study the specific issues surrounding ways to "decrease turnaround time in the remodeling process." The team made and implemented a number of recommendations, including the following:

- Development of a project manager position
- Installation of a customer service center to enhance work scheduling, control, and follow-up
- Implementation of customer surveys to assess communications
- More consultation at the beginning of the process with customers
- Identification of equipment and materials that could be purchased during the design phase
- Shop participation to identify potential problems during the design phase.

The pilot project reduced the remodeling project time by 10 percent. Using customer surveys, the team studied many other processes, such as those in recruitment and admissions. However, note that such early efforts focused on administrative systems—the manufacturing analogy of quality—and not on the core processes of teaching or research.

Business has played an important role in fostering quality improvement efforts in higher education. In 1989 Xerox Corporation hosted the first Quality Forum, a gathering of academic and business leaders. Business leaders urged academia to teach quality principles and to use them in managing their organizations. Many companies established partnerships with colleges and universities. For example, Motorola's partnership with Purdue University led to the formation of the university's continuous quality improvement approach called *Excellence21*, a systemwide effort by the university to explore the principles of continuous improvement and total quality management. Projects continue to be developed in the following areas:

- Faculty and staff development and worklife enrichment
- Assessment of student learning outcomes
- Undergraduate education
- Graduate education

- Student related (student services)
- Administrative processes
- Technology[28]

Other universities established similar partnerships with industry leaders. However, these efforts revolved around project approaches. Two examples of schools that have addressed quality within their overall management systems are Northwest Missouri State University, a large public institution, and Babson College, a small private institution in Massachusetts focused on management education.

Northwest Missouri State University Northwest Missouri State University (Northwest) is a comprehensive, coeducational, publicly supported regional university.[29] An ever-changing institution focused on its customers and overall improvement, Northwest is future-oriented in its approach to the region's higher education needs and is distinguished by its longtime commitment to continuous quality improvement (CQI). Northwest serves 5,200 undergraduate students and 1,000 graduate students through 98 undergraduate degrees, 26 masters degrees, 4 educational specialist degrees, and a cooperative doctoral program in educational leadership. Twenty-one academic departments are housed in three colleges.

Northwest operates within a student-centered culture of quality (COQ) framework. Introduced in 1987 as a master plan to revitalize undergraduate education, the COQ plan was constructed by identifying 42 "best practices" and resulted in specific actions to improve their processes. The COQ has evolved from a set of activities into a shared set of university community values, namely, exceeding student and stakeholder expectations and striving for continuous learning and improvement at all institutional levels. Northwest has created a COQ based on educational researcher Alexander Astin's definition of quality: talent development. Success, therefore, is measured by the value the university adds to students, faculty, staff, and the region. The COQ, along with the deployment of other institutional programs, plans, processes and initiatives, supports and advances five institutional critical success factors (CSFs):

1. A focus on embedded continuous improvement efforts
2. An enriched living/learning environment
3. A safe and orderly, healthy, well-functioning and attractive campus
4. Financial flexibility
5. A symbiotic relationship with the northwest Missouri area.

These critical success factors have been a part of their early 1980s strategy to address student and stakeholder requirements.

In 1992, Northwest began to take a comprehensive systems approach through adoption of the Malcolm Baldrige National Quality Award (MBNQA) Criteria (which we discuss in the next chapter) as a framework for managing the organization. As part of this process, Northwest developed a set of nine university educational key quality indicators (KQIs), which drive planning, evaluation, and improvement of curricular and cocurricular programs and processes:

1. Communications competencies
2. Critical/creative thinking and problem-solving competencies
3. Computer competencies
4. Self-directed learning competencies
5. Competence in a discipline
6. Personal/social development

7. Teamwork/team-leading competencies
8. Multicultural competencies
9. Cultural enrichment

These educational KQIs are an outgrowth of their original COQ plan, which started with the identification of strategic trends and higher education best practices and continued through refinement stages of institution-wide instructional goals to the present educational KQIs. The KQI development is part of Northwest's Seven-Step Planning Process, which is used across all institutional levels. Academic departments develop their own KQIs for department-specific competencies and align with the educational KQIs to provide a total student educational experience. Northwest won a 1997 Missouri Quality Award. We encourage you to read their award application at the Web site cited in note 29.

Babson College Since 1990, Babson College has applied quality management in four areas:[30]

1. Teaching principles of quality management
2. Curriculum as a whole
3. Research in quality management
4. Using quality management as a way to run the institution.

As early as 1991, Babson taught full-semester courses on TQ at both the undergraduate and graduate levels, integrated quality principles across the curriculum, and engaged faculty in applied research on the subject. The influence of TQ in management of the college began with the development of the college's strategic plan for 1991–1995. Babson's top management (the "President's Cabinet") participated in TQ training in 1991, and the cabinet undertook a comprehensive review of the college's goal- and objective-setting processes utilizing TQ tools. The president established Babson's Office of Quality in 1992. The role of the Office of Quality was to address the following goals:

1. Design and facilitate the process of full engagement of continuous quality improvement at Babson College
2. Provide assistance to areas in the development of continuous quality improvement implementation plans
3. Review and monitor the progress of plans
4. Assist the Cabinet in defining annual strategic quality goals
5. Establish training needs, core course offerings, and curriculum
6. Deliver necessary training to the Cabinet and senior leadership
7. Participate with the Office of Human Resources and Affirmative Action in the development of recognition and reward systems that support continuous quality improvement
8. Formulate a communications strategy which supports continuous quality improvement, and coordinate events such as teamwork recognition days, quality fairs, quality camps, etc.
9. Maintain contacts with outside organizations and with state-of-the-art developments in the field of quality improvement
10. Train quality specialists and coordinate their deployment in response to specific requests for process coaching and facilitation support.

The many CQI activities that Babson conducted included a training needs analysis with development and testing of training materials, modification of organizational structures to include quality support, and identification of the major drivers of customer satisfaction. Cross-divisional/departmental teams are to pursue specific quality improvement objectives. It also undertook cost of quality analyses to identify priorities and provide broad direction for quality improvement efforts. The activities were followed by modification of recognition and reward systems to include continuous quality improvement as a criterion of performance for teams and individuals. By 1997, goals and actions for CQI were fully integrated in the college's planning, management, and review processes.

QUALITY IN THE PUBLIC SECTOR

Quality in the public sector—federal, state, and municipal governments—has not achieved growth and momentum as rapidly as in the private sector. Nevertheless, many public sector entities have made remarkable progress in incorporating the principles of quality into their operations.

Quality in the Federal Government

The federal government has a surprisingly long history of quality improvement activities. Quality circle programs, which are a form of team participation, were developed in the late 1970s at several Department of Defense installations, such as the Norfolk Naval Shipyard and the Cherry Point Naval Air Station. NASA began its quality improvement efforts in the early 1980s, both internally and with its suppliers.[31] Quality caught the attention of a number of agencies and managers when Executive Order 12637, "Productivity Improvement for the Federal Government," was signed by President Ronald Reagan in 1988.[32] The order required senior managers to monitor and improve both quality and productivity. It also encouraged them to use employee involvement, training, and participation in decision making, along with the more traditional methods of incentives, recognition, and rewards, to enhance the process.

One of the mechanisms set up to promote quality during the Reagan era was the Federal Quality Institute (FQI). The FQI was established within the U.S. Office of Personnel Management in Washington, D.C., as the primary source of leadership, information, and consulting services on quality management in the federal government. The institute, which no longer exists, provided such products and services as seminars, start-up assistance, national and regional conferences, support of quality awards, research, a listing of private sector consultants, an information network, and publications. In 1990 the FQI was given responsibility for administering the President's Quality Award and the Quality Improvement Prototype Award, which are the federal government's equivalent of the Malcolm Baldrige National Quality Award given to private sector organizations.

The focus on quality in the federal government continued during the Clinton administration. In fact, President Clinton had implemented a quality process in the state government of Arkansas while he was the governor. Just before his election to the presidency, he wrote an article upholding the values of quality as a way to enhance the operations of the federal government and to make it more customer-focused.[33]

Shortly after he assumed the presidency, Clinton approved an initiative to streamline government. Under the direction of Vice President Al Gore, a report entitled "Creating a Government That Works Better and Costs Less: Report of the National Performance Review" was written and published in the fall of 1993. In it, Vice President Gore made 384 recommendations and indicated 1,214 specific actions that the federal government should take to improve government operations and reduce costs. This National Performance Review (NPR) report triggered 11 executive orders and memoranda, signed by the president, which initiated the following actions:[34]

1. Eliminate one-half of executive branch internal regulations within three years.
2. Set customer service standards to ensure that service provided by agencies "equals the best in business."
3. Create a National Partnership Council to involve government employees and union representatives in championing changes called for by NPR.
4. Create the President's Community Advisory Board to help communities deliver integrated services instead of working from fragmented federal grants.
5. Streamline bureaucracy by requiring federal agencies to reduce staff by 252,000 people within five years and cut the supervisory ratio from 1:7 to 1:15; also cut office staff in half.
6. Improve agency rule-making procedures by streamlining the regulatory development process to save time and resources.
7. Implement management reform in the executive branch through newly designated chief operating officers, who work through the President's Management Council to lead the reinvention efforts.

One of the more recognizable results in improvements to federal services is the Internal Revenue Service. In the mid-1990s, the National Commission on Restructuring the Internal Revenue Service focused on ways of creating a more efficient system and structure that eases the burden of compliance and protects basic rights for the taxpayer, while ensuring that the Internal Revenue Service collects the proper amount of taxes. The Commission's objectives were that the taxpayer shall receive superior service from the IRS and that the IRS shall be accountable to the taxpayer for appropriated and collected revenues; that the IRS shall use contemporary, effective technology for ease of service and compliance; and that the administration of the laws governing federal revenue collection shall be done at the lowest cost possible to the government and in the least burdensome manner to the taxpayer while ensuring the protection of civil liberties and privacy. As a result of the Commission's 1997 report, *A New Vision for the IRS*, the IRS has made a concerted effort to improve the quality of its services and performance. Many improvements are evident, including faster telephone service, electronic filing, and a comprehensive Web site with downloadable forms, help files, and a host of other information.

State and Local Quality Efforts

State and local government agencies have gained momentum in developing their own quality programs and processes, albeit at a much slower rate than the private sector. Massachusetts, for example, has formed a Quality Improvement Council to oversee and facilitate a broad quality program. In North Carolina, pilot projects for improvement in the quality of services are under way in the Department of Administration and the Division of Motor Vehicles.

One of the earliest examples of a successful public-sector quality initiative involved the city of Madison, Wisconsin. Joseph Sensenbrenner, mayor of Madison from 1983 to 1989, was one of the leaders in bringing quality principles to city government.[35] After a 1983 audit disclosed problems at the city garage, such as long delays in repair and equipment unavailability, Sensenbrenner attempted to apply quality improvement approaches, where the manager and mechanics were surprised to see "top management" personally visible and committed to their problems. Sensenbrenner obtained the cooperation of the union president and formed a team to gather data from individual mechanics and the repair process itself. The team found that many delays resulted from insufficient stocking of repair parts, which, in turn, was caused by having more than 440 different types, makes, models, and years of equipment—all obtained by purchasing from the lowest bidder. Solving the problem required teamwork and breaking down barriers between departments. The concept of an internal customer was virtually unknown. When the 24-step purchasing policy was changed to three steps, employees were stunned and delighted that someone was listening to them. They studied the potential of a preventive maintenance program and discovered, for example, that city departments did not use truck-bed linings when hauling corrosive materials such as salt. Mechanics rode along on police patrols and learned that squad cars spent most time idling; this information was used to tune engines properly. Other departments helped gather data. As a result, the average vehicle turnaround time was reduced from nine days to three with a net annual savings of about $700,000.

The lessons learned in the city garage were expanded to other departments from painting to health. By the time Sensenbrenner left office in 1989, Madison's city departments each ran between 20 and 30 quality improvement projects at a time; five agencies focused on long-term commitment to new management practices, including continuous quality improvement skills and data-gathering techniques; the city provided training in quality to every employee; several state agencies eager to follow Madison's approach initiated joint efforts; and city workers continued to invent service improvements for internal and external customers.

A noteworthy effort over an extended period of time has resulted in the spread of TQ approaches throughout the government of Jefferson County, which contains the city of Louisville, Kentucky.[36] Key to this effort was Rebecca Jackson, county clerk, who introduced total quality and continuous improvement concepts to her office workforce of 320 employees soon after she was elected in 1989. She set about challenging her employees to develop a customer focus in offices as varied as the motor vehicle license tag department, local tax collections, voter registrations, county elections, public records office (deeds, mortgages, wills, etc.), and marriage and other professional licensing departments.

The voice of the customer was solicited and analyzed via customer comment cards that asked for feedback on staff work. More than 200 people responded every week. Each received a written reply, thanking them for their positive comments and outlining corrective action to be taken in problem areas. To build morale and serve as a catalyst for examining and improving procedures and processes, anyone who submitted a suggestion received a pen. Anyone whose suggestion was adopted was "mugged": he or she received a black mug imprinted with the office seal, which was presented with a certificate of appreciation at weekly meetings for top management.

Rebecca helped the staff to develop a set of common values, language, and tools. Formal training sessions were held for management and staff. Employees studied how the office worked, from the budgeting process to personnel policies. As a result, significant service time improvements were made. For example, the time needed to renew an auto tag was reduced from two hours to 30 minutes. Employees learned to treat people as customers, with smiles, greetings, and a "thank you" as they left. Employees acted as professionals by owning problems and finding solutions. A recent innovation under Rebecca's guidance has been to create a Web site where customers can find all of the popular forms and information, such as court docket files, budget information, application forms, studies, and reports available to download. This accessibility often saves people a trip to the courthouse just to pick up forms needed to obtain service.[37] Rebecca was so successful in turning around the operations of the County Clerk's Office, that in 1998 she was named Public Official of the Year, an award presented by the National Association of County Recorders, Election Officials, and Clerks.

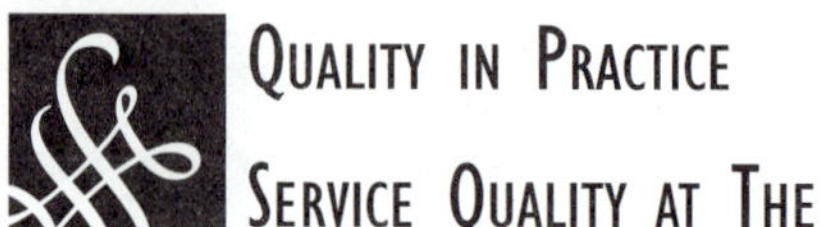

Quality in Practice

Service Quality at The Ritz-Carlton Hotel Company[38]

In 1992 The Ritz-Carlton Hotel Company became the first hospitality organization to receive the Malcolm Baldrige National Quality Award. In 1999 they became the second company to win the award a second time, a testament to their continuous journey of improvement. The hotel industry is intensely competitive, one in which consumers place high emphases on reliability, timely delivery, and value. The Ritz-Carlton focuses on the principal concerns of its main customers and strives to provide them with highly personalized, caring service. Attention to employee performance and information technology are two of the company's many strengths that helped it to achieve superior quality.

The Ritz-Carlton operates from an easy-to-understand definition of service quality that is aggressively communicated and internalized at all levels of the organization. Its Three Steps of Service, its motto, employee promise, credo, and its basics—collectively known as the Gold Standards—are shown in Figure 2.4, and instilled in all employees through extensive training approaches. They allow employees to think and act independently with innovation for both the benefit of the customer and the company. The company's approaches for selecting and training employees were discussed earlier in this chapter.

The Ritz-Carlton uses many sources of information to understand its customers, including alliances with travel partners, such as airlines and credit card companies; focus groups and customer satisfaction results; complaints, claims, and feedback from the salesforce; customer interviews; travel industry publications and studies; and even special psychological studies to understand what customers mean, not what they say, and how to appeal to the customer in the language they most understand.

A formal strategic planning process sets business directions to achieve the company's long-term vi-

Figure 2.4 The Ritz-Carlton Three Steps of Service, Motto, and Credo

Three Steps of Service

1
A warm and sincere greeting. Use the guest name, if and when possible.

2
Anticipation and compliance with guest needs.

3
Fond farewell. Give them a warm good-bye and use their names, if and when possible.

"We Are Ladies and Gentlemen Serving Ladies and Gentlemen"

The Ritz-Carlton®

Credo

The Ritz-Carlton Hotel is a place where the genuine care and comfort of our guests is our highest mission.

We pledge to provide the finest personal service and facilities for our guests who will always enjoy a warm, relaxed yet refined ambience.

The Ritz-Carlton experience enlivens the senses, instills well-being, and fulfills even the unexpressed wishes and needs of our guests.

Figure 2.5 Ritz-Carlton Service Quality Indicators

SQI Defects	Points
1. Missing Guest Preferences	10
2. Unresolved Difficulties	50
3. Inadequate Guestroom Housekeeping	1
4. Abandoned Reservation Calls	5
5. Guestroom Changes	5
6. Inoperable Guestroom Equipment	5
7. Unready Guestroom	10
8. Inappropriate Hotel Appearance	5
9. Meeting Event Difficulties	5
10. Inadequate Food/Beverage	1
11. Missing/Damaged Guest Property/Accidents	50
12. Invoice Adjustment	3

sion: "To Be the Premier Worldwide Provider of Luxury Travel and Hospitality Products and Services." Upper managers at the corporate and hotel level conduct monthly performance reviews of the strategic plan, focusing on key indicators that reflect employee pride and joy, customer loyalty, financial performance, and process performance. Quarterly reviews focus on opportunities for improvement and innovation. A variety of comparative data on competitors and other world-class organizations are used to evaluate and improve their practices. For example, data revealed that front desk turnover was higher than usual. The company found out that certain airlines were paying higher wages and attracting their employees. The Ritz-Carlton reevaluated its compensation policy to match the airlines and actually reduced its total costs by eliminating a supervisor who was required to monitor new employees.

The Ritz-Carlton gathers and uses customer-satisfaction and quality-related data on a daily basis. Information systems involve every employee and provide critical, responsive data on guest preferences, the introduction of error-free products and services, and opportunities for quality improvement. They track a set of Service Quality Indicators (SQI), shown in Figure 2.5, which represent the 12 most serious defects that can occur during regular operations. An index is computed and disseminated to the workforce daily and reviewed by hotel managers.

Each production and support process is assigned an "executive owner" at the corporate office and a "working owner" at the hotel level, who are responsible for the development and improvement of these processes. They have the authority to define the measurements and determine the resources needed to manage these processes. The "GreenBook," a handbook for employees, describes a nine-step quality improvement process to guide the design, control, and improvement of all processes, and is emphasized during new employee training and continual development. The Ritz-Carlton even has a process to overcome cultural resistance to change: (1) stress the importance of the change; (2) express confidence that the change can be made; (3) provide reasons why people should make the change as a group; and (4) allow time to accommodate the change.

These are only a few of The Ritz-Carlton's quality practices and the results have been impressive. At the time of winning its second Baldrige Award, overall "top box" customer satisfaction (using a scale of 1 to 5, with the "top box" being a 5) was 70 percent against 52 percent for its foremost competitor. Employee satisfaction on issues of decision-making authority, teamwork, communication, and empowerment exceeded service company norms by a significant margin. The time to process a new hire from walk-in to job offer dropped from 21 days to one day in three years. Total revenue per hours worked showed a steady upward trend, and pretax return on investment improved from 5.3 percent in 1995 to 12.9 percent in 1999. One lesson the hotel learned is not to underestimate the value of even one idea or quality improvement effort.

Key Issues for Discussion

1. What value does a focus on the Gold Standards have for The Ritz-Carlton Hotel Co.?
2. What must a company do to reduce job offer processing times so dramatically?
3. How does information play a central role in everything that The Ritz-Carlton Hotel Co. does?

Quality In Practice

Pinellas County Schools[39]

Pinellas County Schools is the seventh largest district in Florida and the 21st largest school district, out of more than 16,000, in the United States. It has more than 110,000 students in 82 elementary, 23 middle, and 16 high schools, along with five exceptional education schools, three alternative schools and three charter schools. The district employs more than 18,000 people in full- and part-time capacities. In 1991, Pinellas County Schools adopted a quality management philosophy in response to Florida's Blueprint 2000 education reform, and received a 1993 Florida Governor's Sterling Award in the Education Sector. Today, it is recognized as a leader in the support and promotion of education reform initiatives using quality principles.

Using the management philosophy of W. Edwards Deming (see Chapter 3) as a basis, district staff is training administrators, teachers, parents, and community leaders with the ultimate goal of producing students who are empowered and internally motivated learners. This ideal is clearly expressed in the district's vision statement: "The Pinellas County school district unites with the community to provide a quality education enabling each student to succeed." This broad-based approach to quality differentiates the school system's efforts from most companies employing quality management strategies. District officials realize that to reach their goal they must involve all stakeholders in the process, beginning with students and moving outward to teachers, administrators, parents, and the community at large. The following three strategic directions have been selected to sustain the school system's focus on critical elements that drive high-performing organizations.

1. Highest student achievement
2. Safe learning environment
3. Effective and efficient operation
   - Partnerships
   - High-performing workforce
   - Integrated management systems
   - Accountability systems

Central administration officials determined that three initiatives were essential for quality management strategies to be implemented in individual schools. First, Pinellas County Schools formed a District Quality Council to assure a common vision and constancy of purpose. The council integrated quality strategies with existing components of the comprehensive planning and budgeting system. In the second initiative, the Collaborative Quality Council piloted a collaborative collective bargaining process. The council's members—the superintendent, a deputy superintendent, quality coordinator, president of the teacher's association, executive director of the teachers' and support services' union and the president of the county council of PTAs—worked as a unit to develop collaborative decision-making and collective bargaining processes. Including the union in the beginning stages of the quality movement was a key step to success. Working together to establish short- and long-range goals allowed the two groups reach an early settlement in the bargaining process. The third initiative involved continuous training at all levels of the organization. The district in collaboration with the business community established a Quality Leadership Academy to support training. More than 100 businesses in the Tampa Bay area volunteered to be a part of this effort to provide quality training for employees, businesses, and community.

Pinellas County Schools also developed the "Superintendent's Quality Challenge," which is focused on recognizing and commending schools and departments whose teachers and administrators have demonstrated that they have internalized quality principles and values that drive them, and to guide quality-focused efforts for continual improvement. Schools receive feedback from external quality professionals and celebrate their progress annually.

From central administration to individual schools, the district is firmly committed to quality management. Departments throughout central administration, including architecture, data processing, finance, purchasing, transportation, maintenance, accounting, research, and warehousing, are in various stages of their journey. Departments begin with two full days of cross-functional training. Participants study quality management philosophy and learn to use the quality process tools. Working in groups of five or six, called quality teams, participants spend the last few hours of training applying what they have learned to their own situations. Team members select a real project within their department to which they apply quality processes. They spend the next four to six weeks developing flow charts, analyzing customer needs, discovering problems, and collecting data associated with the project. After completing that segment of the process, the departments meet with the quality trainer again. Each team within a department makes a presentation to the department to walk coworkers through the quality processes on their project.

The training has helped many departments increase efficiency and become more customer focused. For example, the central files staff processes requests for information from more than 70,000 current and former students' files. Since implementing quality processes, about 95 percent of requests are processed the day after they are received, compared to 80 percent before staff members began their quality journey.

Each school has a School Quality Advisory Council of parents, business leaders, administrators, and teachers. The councils develop the annual school improvement plan—concrete goals to move each school toward reform objectives. Council members are being trained to use quality process tools to continually assess their progress in relation to the plan's quality objectives.

All efforts in Pinellas are student-centered. Students are being taught processes to continually assess their learning progress based on clear objectives. Pinellas County Schools' officials are using student performance standards developed by the Florida Commission on Education Reform and Accountability, and the Secretary of Labor, and collecting survey data from the business community to develop world-class standards for student performance.

The district opened its first school developed within a total quality environment in the fall of 1992. The school, Marjorie Kinnan Rawlings Elementary, does not teach and administer in the "same old way." It is a model for reform in action for the district and the state. Before the building was completed, teachers began learning quality management strategies and their training continues. Teachers spend an afternoon each week in seminars. Rawlings' students are not just memorizing facts. They are learning how to learn. Students write everyday in every subject and are evaluated through outcome- and performance-based assessments. Rawlings received the Governor's Sterling Award in 1998.

Pinellas County Schools' second total quality-based school, Joseph L. Carwise Middle, opened in the fall of 1993. It has abandoned the traditional methods of school organization to embrace more innovative concepts. Carwise integrates all grade levels in all buildings. Students remain in the same building each year to build a sense of belonging. The school has no departments or department heads and no department budgets. Instead, each teacher is a member of a team and has a specific role to play on that team. Each teacher is given his or her own budget. Carwise teachers were some of the first to attend the district's quality boot camp, a three-day intensive quality training program.

Azalea Elementary School, one of Pinellas's schools currently trained in the Classroom Learning System (a set of classroom-based strategies for applying quality principles), received the Governor's Sterling Award in 2000 and has been benchmarked by many schools across the country.

These schools are examples of how the quality process is becoming meaningful to Pinellas County Schools' students. The process will bring the district closer to its goal of graduating more motivated learners who can become productive members of a global economy. The results confirm their efforts. In Comprehensive Tests of Basic Skills, the district's median scores exceeded the national median in all areas, and college-bound students' SAT scores exceed the national averages in both mathematics and verbal categories.

Key Issues for Discussion

1. Discuss how the practices at Pinellas County Schools reflect quality principles.
2. Thinking back on your own K–12 education, what things does Pinellas County do differently?

Summary of Key Points

- Quality management had its roots in manufacturing during the 1980s; soon after, service providers, health care, education, and government organizations began to study and implement quality management approaches.
- A system is the functions or activities within an organization that work together for the aim of the organization. Systems thinking is critical in applying quality principles because the organizational linkages among various functions of an organization must be in alignment to meet the needs of customers and other stakeholders.
- Quality plays an important role in each component of a manufacturing firm's production and business-support systems. All are linked together as a system of processes that supports the organization's objectives.
- Service represents the dominant sector of the U.S. economy. The differences between services and manufacturing require different approaches in designing and implementing quality assurance programs. Services can be viewed in the same context as manufacturing with Deming's model of a production system. The two key components of service quality are employees and information technology.
- The health care industry has faced considerable pressure from both the government and consumers to improve quality. Many organizations are involved in quality-related oversight and promotion of quality principles. While many efforts are underway, considerable work remains for the industry as a whole.
- Educational institutions are increasingly adopting quality management approaches. Significant results have been achieved by many K–12 school districts and institutions of higher education. Efforts by professional organizations, such as the American Society for Quality and its Koalaty Kid program, can help foster interest, but success rests on active involvement of the entire community, committed leadership, a system for continuous improvement, and an environment that celebrates success.
- The federal government, as well as state and local agencies, have also been active in promoting and improving quality in their operations. The 1993 National Performance Review report set the stage for the Clinton administration's "reinventing government" initiatives that use many quality concepts.
- Health care and educational organizations are beginning to adapt quality philosophies to their operations and administrative systems. Business-education partnerships have been formed to provide funding, research, and a forum for discussion of the application of quality to education.

Review Questions

1. What is a system? Why is systems thinking important to quality management?
2. Explain the quality concerns of each major function of a manufacturing system.
3. How can business support systems help to sustain quality in an organization? List the key business support activities and their role in quality.
4. What types of organizations fall under the definition of services? Why is service quality especially important in today's business environment?

5. How do service standards differ from manufacturing specifications? How are they similar?
6. Discuss the differences between manufacturing and service organizations. What are the implications of these differences for quality assurance?
7. Explain the roles of employees and information technology in providing quality service. How does The Ritz-Carlton Hotel Company use employees and information technology for quality service?
8. Summarize the status of quality in the health care industry. How do the recommendations of the President's Advisory Commission on Consumer Protection and Quality in the Health Care Industry address the basic principles of TQ described in Chapter 1?
9. Summarize the major quality initiatives used in education. How are the approaches at K–12 institutions similar and different from those used in the colleges and universities discussed in the chapter?
10. Describe some of the key quality initiatives that have been taken in the government sector.

Discussion Questions

1. Provide some examples of service organizations or activities that illustrate the critical differences of services in contrast with manufacturing.
2. Explain the analogy of Deming's model of a production system as used in manufacturing to the example provided for education. Can this model be applied universally with only changes in language and terminology?
3. Cite some examples from your own experience in which you felt service employees were truly empowered to serve you better.
4. How is information technology used to improve service at your college or university?
5. What role has the Internet played in improving service quality? What barriers to service quality might it have?
6. Discuss the implications of the following statements with respect to introducing TQ principles in a college classroom.[40] Do you agree with them? How do they reflect TQ principles? What changes in traditional learning approaches would they require for both students and instructors?
   a. Embracing a customer focus doesn't mean giving students all As and abandoning standards.
   b. If students fail, the system has failed.
   c. Faculty members are customers of those who teach prerequisites.
   d. Treating students as customers means allowing students to choose not to come to class.
   e. Completing the syllabus is not a measure of success.
   f. New and tenured instructors should visit each other's classrooms
   g. Eliminate performance appraisals based on classroom evaluations.
   h. No matter how good the test, luck will be involved.
7. Contrast the role of service quality at Amazon.com and Barnes & Noble (which operates traditional bookstores as well as an e-commerce site). What are the differences in their approaches? How might a company like Barnes & Noble exploit its dual marketing focus (stores and e-commerce) in a complementary fashion to provide services that Amazon.com would not be able to offer?

8. Cite one or more examples of times when you received either high or poor quality service from a physician's office, dentist's office, or hospital. What do you think contributed most to your experience—well-designed procedures, technology, or the behavior of the professionals or staff?
9. Thinking of your experiences at a post office, driver's license bureau, or other government agency, describe your perception of the quality of the service, and suggest some TQ approaches that might help the agency improve.

Projects, Etc.

1. Interview some key managers at a nearby manufacturing company and construct a diagram similar to Figure 2.1 showing the company's key functions and their relationships. Summarize the major quality concerns of each function and develop a relationship chart similar to that of Figure 2.2.
2. Interview some managers at a local service organization and summarize the role of employees and information technology in providing quality service. How are employees and information technology integrated into long-range improvement plans and strategies?
3. Develop a Deming-type diagram of a hospital as a production system. You might wish to talk with some health care professionals to better understand the terminology and key issues.
4. Arrange a tour of a local hospital or clinic. How is quality managed in the organization? What individuals or groups spearhead quality improvement efforts? Is the entire workforce involved to any degree? What quality-related improvements have they made in the past two years?
5. Interview administrative officials at your college or university to determine what quality efforts have been made to improve both administrative functions and educational effectiveness.
6. Arrange an interview with a local high school principal or school district superintendent. Determine whether any quality initiatives have been adopted during the past two years. Have teachers been trained in quality improvement approaches? How does the school or district gather information from its stakeholders? Are the interviewees aware of the Koalaty Kid program?
7. School boards provide a critical link between schools, parents, and the community. According to the National School Board Association, school boards must help to create a vision and structure for the school system while focusing on accountability to ensure results and advocacy for improved performance. Interview members of a local school board or parents of children in a public school district that you know to determine how well the school board addresses the following points:[41]
   a. Focuses on issues related to student achievement.
   b. Sets a common vision for student achievement and a clear definition of student success.
   c. Uses reliable data to make informed decisions about how to support student achievement goals and how to measure progress.
   d. Brings diverse opinions to bear and create community consensus on student achievement goals.
   e. Sets benchmarks and discusses progress toward student achievement goals
   f. Plays a leadership role in defining standards of achievement for all students.
   g. Develops and follows a process for maintaining accountability within the schools and the school board itself.

h. Models teamwork and partnership.
i. Has mechanisms for feedback from parents, administrators, teachers, and the greater community.
j. Creates policies that clearly support student achievement goals.

8. Have quality initiatives been adopted by your local government? Interview some local politicians and managers to answer this question. Can you, as a customer, obtain easy access to these people?

Cases

I. Shiny Hill Farms[42]

Shiny Hill Farms is a major pork processor, specializing in smoked meats, hams, sausages, and luncheon meats. The firm's largest facility slaughters more than 5,000 hogs each day. Throughout the food industry, quality is a high priority, and Shiny Hill Farms is no exception.

The quality assurance department (QA) seeks to prevent any defective products from reaching the consumer. QA's primary concern is controlling product weight, appearance, and shelf life throughout the manufacturing operations. Production operators are held accountable for their cuts on specific meat products. The cuts must be performed according to quality assurance specifications in order to obtain high yields. (Yield is the percentage of the live weight of the hog that can be sold.)

Quality assurance monitors all operations, from the killing of hogs through packaging. QA personnel inspect incoming animals, work with USDA inspectors, and monitor cooking temperatures. They check scales daily to ensure they are providing correct weights. If products fall outside specifications, it is the responsibility of QA personnel to notify operators that changes need to be made to bring quality up to standard. Many QA personnel monitor weights of packaged boxes continuously to ensure that they conform to weight specifications. They open boxes and weigh the packages as well as checking them for defects such as rips, leaks, and pinholes. Weights of packages near the bottom, middle, and top of each skid (pallet) are inspected. If these packages conform to weight specifications, then the entire skid is accepted and sent to the warehouse. If not, the skid is tagged for 100 percent inspection, and the process is studied to determine why the variations occurred. QA personnel analyze graphs of yields and packaging waste weekly.

Other functions throughout the company focus on quality. The sanitation department, for example, sanitizes all manufacturing machines and work surfaces before initial production runs each day. The research and development department plays an important role in improving quality. For example, it is continually seeking out and testing new methods of curing meat and of killing bacteria more effectively and efficiently. R&D also helps to develop new packaging that may improve consumers' perception of quality. In addition, it develops new products, such as "lite" luncheon meats that contain less fat and cholesterol, enlisting the aid of focus groups and taste panels.

A food processing plant is an intense, high-speed manufacturing setting. Shiny Hill Farms operators may have to make as many as 10 cuts each minute on a conveyor line. Engineering personnel replaced all old manufacturing lines with ergonomically correct lines. The production line was redesigned to a standard height with adjustable-height work stations to better meet operators' needs. Turnover of meat cutters averages between 30 and 40 percent. New cutters are shown a video on how to use machines and knives correctly in order to make quality cuts. On the line, they are expected to learn from experience—watching others and learning from their mistakes.

Discussion Questions

1. Describe the scope of quality efforts in this organization.
2. What is the role of the quality assurance department at Shiny Hill Farms? Does it promote the concept of total quality?
3. What suggestions do you have for improving Shiny Hill Farms' quality effort?

II. The Nightmare on Phone Street[43]

H. James Harrington, a noted quality consultant, related the following story in *Quality Digest* magazine:

> *I called to make a flight reservation just an hour ago. The telephone rang five times before a recorded voice answered. "Thank you for calling ABC Travel Services," it said. "To ensure the highest level of customer service, this call may be recorded for future analysis." Next, I was asked to select from one of the following three choices: "If the trip is related to company business, press 1. Personal business, press 2. Group travel, press 3." I pressed 1.*
>
> *I was then asked to select from the following four choices: "If this is a trip within the United States, press 1. International, press 2. Scheduled training, press 3. Related to a conference, press 4." Because I was going to Canada, I pressed 2.*
>
> *Now two minutes into my telephone call, I was instructed to be sure that I had my customer identification card available. A few seconds passed and a very sweet voice came on, saying, "All international operators are busy, but please hold because you are a very important customer." The voice was then replaced by music. About two minutes later, another recorded message said, "Our operators are still busy, but please hold and the first available operator will take care of you." More music. Then yet another message: "Our operators are still busy, but please hold. Your business is important to us." More bad music. Finally the sweet voice returned, stating, "To speed up your service, enter your 19-digit customer service number." I frantically searched for their card, hoping that I could find it before I was cut off. I was lucky; I found it and entered the number in time. The same sweet voice came back to me, saying, "To confirm your customer service number, enter the last four digits of your social security number." I pushed the four numbers on the keypad. The voice said: "Thank you. An operator will be with you shortly. If your call is an emergency, you can call 1-800-CAL-HELP, or push all of the buttons on the telephone at the same time. Otherwise, please hold, as you are a very important customer." This time, in place of music, I heard a commercial about the service that the company provides.*
>
> *At last, a real person answered the telephone and asked, "Can I help you?" I replied, "Yes, oh yes." He answered, "Please give me your 19-digit customer service number, followed by the last four digits of your social security number so I can verify who you are." (I thought I gave these numbers in the first place to speed up service. Why do I have to rattle them off again?)*
>
> *I was now convinced that he would call me Mr. 5523-3675-0714-1313-040. But, to my surprise, he said: "Yes, Mr. Harrington. Where do you want to go and when?" I explained that I wanted to go to Montreal the following Monday morning. He replied: "I only handle domestic reservations. Our international desk has a new telephone number: 1-800-1WE-GOTU. I'll transfer you." A few clicks later a message came on, saying: "All of our international operators are busy. Please hold and your call will be answered in the order it was received. Do not hang up or redial, as it will only delay our response to your call. Please continue to hold, as your business is important to us."*

Discussion Questions

1. Summarize the service failures associated with this experience.
2. What might the travel agency have done to guarantee a better service experience for Mr. Harrington?

NOTES

1. Heide Dawley and Keith Naughton, "How Jaguar Stopped Being a Punch Line," *Business Week*, June 7, 1999, 34–35.

2. Click and Clack, *Cincinnati Enquirer*, April 1, 2000, F2.

3. "Michigan Hospital Promises to Deliver," *Cincinnati Enquirer*, 17 July, 1991, A2.

4. Marilyn Adams, "Air Service Faces Continued Heat From Fliers," USAToday.com, Money, June 1, 2000.

5. Russell L. Ackoff, *Recreating the Corporation: A Design of Organizations for the 21st Century*, New York: Oxford University Press, 1999.

6. "A Profile of Hershey Foods Corporation" (Hershey Foods Corporation, Hershey, PA 17033), 7.

7. Jeff Sabatini, "Flawless (Nearly)," *Automotive Manufacturing & Production*, November 1999, 60–62.

8. D. A Collier, "The Customer Service and Quality challenge," *The Service Industries Journal*, 7, no. 1, January 1987, p. 79.

9. Frederick F. Reichheld and W. Earl Sasser, Jr., "Zero Defections: Quality Comes to Services," *Harvard Business Review* 68, no. 5 (September/October 1990), 105–112.

10. Dean S. Elmuti and Yunus Kathawala, "Small Service Firms Face Implementation Challenges," *Quality Progress*, April 1999, 67–75.

11. The Associated Press, "US Airways Makes Quality Turnaround," *Cincinnati Enquirer*, April 20, 1999, B7.

12. *http://www.usair.com/company/news/nw_99_1214b.htm.*

13. Ron Zemke, "Auditing Customer Service: Look Inside as Well as Out," *Employee Relations Today* 16 (Autumn 1989), 197–203.

14. Adapted from the 1992 and 1999 Ritz-Carlton's Malcolm Baldrige National Quality Award application summaries, Cheri Henderson, "Putting on the Ritz," *TQM Magazine* 2, no. 5 (November/December 1992), 292–296, and remarks by various Ritz-Carlton managers at the 2000 Quest for Excellence Conference, Washington D.C.

15. Quality '93: Empowering People with Technology, Advertisement in *Fortune*, September 20, 1993.

16. "New JCAHO Standards Emphasize Continuous Quality Improvement," *Hospitals*, August 5, 1991, 41–44.

17. This information is adapted from NCQA's Web site, *http://www.ncqa.org.*

18. *http://www.hcqualitycommission.gov.*

19. "Reinventing Health Care," *Fortune*, July 12, 1993, Advertisement section.

20. Maureen Bisognano, "New Skills Needed in Medical Leadership," *Quality Progress* (June 2000), 32–41.

21. Robert Burney, "TQM in a Surgery Center," *Quality Progress*, 27, no. 1 (January 1994), 97–100.

22. Nada R. Sanders, "Health Care Organizations Can Learn from the Experiences of Others," *Quality Progress* (February 1997), 47–49.

23. See, for example, Christina Del Valle, "Readin', Writin', and Reform," *Business Week/Quality Special Issue*, October 25, 1991, 140–142; Myron Tribus, "Quality Management in Education," *Journal for Quality and Participation*, January/February 1993, 12–21. See also Christopher W. L. and Paula E. Morrison, "Students Aren't Learning Quality Principles in Business Schools," *Quality Progress* 25, no. 1 (January 1992), 25–27; John A. Byrne, "Is Research in the Ivory Tower 'Fuzzy, Irrelevant, and Pretentious'?" *Business Week*, October 29, 1990, 62–66.

24. This section is adapted from an extensive account in Lloyd Dobyns and Clare Crawford-Mason, *Quality or Else* (Boston: Houghton-Mifflin, 1991), 221–230.

25. Kathleen A. Sharples, Michael Slusher, and Mike Swaim, "How TQM Can Work in Education," *Quality Progress*, 29, no. 5 (May 1996), 75–78.

26. Adapted from the *http://www.koalatykid.org* Web site. Permission to reprint is granted by the ASQ Koalaty Kid Alliance.

27. L. Edwin Coate, "TQM at Oregon State University," reprinted with permission from *Journal for Quality and Participation*, December 1990, 56–65. See also L. Edward Coate, *Implementing Total Quality Management in a University Setting* (Corvallis, OR: Oregon State University, July 1990); Ralph G. Lewis and Douglas H. Smith, *Total Quality in Higher Education* (Delray Beach, FL: St. Lucie Press, 1994).

28. Purdue *Excellence21*, *http://ex21.tech.purdue.edu.*

29. Adapted from Northwest's Missouri Quality Award application, available at *http://www.nwmissouri.edu.*

30. Susan West Engelkemeyer, "TQM in Higher Education: The Babson College Journey," *The Center for Quality Management Journal* 2, no. 1 (Winter 1993), pp. 28–33, and other documents available at *http://www.babson.edu/quality.*

31. Ned Hamson, "The FQI Story: Today and Tomorrow," *Journal for Quality and Participation* (July/August 1990), 46–49.

32. Executive Order No. 12637, vol. 7. *United States Code Congressional and Administrative News*, 100th Congress—Second Session (St. Paul, MN: West Publishing Co.), B21–B23.

33. Bill Clinton, "Putting People First," *Journal for Quality and Participation* (October/November 1992), 10–12.

34. Adapted from "What's Happening With the National Performance Review Recommenda-

tions?" *Federal Quality News* 2, no. 5 (December/January 1994), 8–9.

35. Joseph Sensenbrenner, "Quality Comes to City Hall," *Harvard Business Review* (March/April 1991), 64–75.

36. Adapted from *CQM Voice* 9, no. 1 (Spring 1998), published at: *http://cqmextra.cqm.org/voice.nsf/*.

37. See *http://www.co.jefferson.ky.us/*.

38. See note 12.

39. Most of this material was adapted from the Pinellas school Web site, *http://www.pinellas.k12.fl.us*, with permission of Pinellas County Schools. Contact Kenneth L. Rigsby, Ed.D., for more information.

40. Adapted from Ronald E. Turner, "TQM in the College Classroom," *Quality Progress*, 28, no. 10 (October 1995), 105–108.

41. "The Key Work of School Boards," National School Board Association brochure. NSBA, 1680 Duke Street, Alexandria, VA 22314.

42. Based on a student project prepared by Burton Phillips and Stefanie Steward. Their contribution is gratefully acknowledged.

43. H. James Harrington, "Looking for a Little Service," *Quality Digest*, May 2000; *http://www.qualitydigest.com*.

BIBLIOGRAPHY

Berry, Leonard L., Valarie A. Zeithaml, and A. Parasuraman. "Five Imperatives for Improving Service Quality." *Sloan Management Review*, Summer 1990, 29–38.

Freund, Richard A. "The Role of Quality Technology." In *Quality Assurance: Methods, Management, and Motivation*, ed. H. J. Bajaria, 10–13, Dearborn, MI: Society of Manufacturing Engineers, 1981.

Garvin, David A. *Managing Quality*. New York: The Free Press, 1988.

Harris, Adrienne. "The Customer's Always Right." *Black Enterprise* 21 (June 1991), 233–242.

Haywood-Farmer, John. "A Conceptual Model of Service Quality." *International Journal of Operations and Production Management* 8, no. 6 (1988), 19–29.

King, Carol A. "Service Quality Assurance Is Different." *Quality Progress* 18, no. 6 (June 1985), 14–18.

Lewis, Barbara R. "Quality in the Service Sector: A Review." *International Journal of Bank Marketing* 7, no. 5 (1989), 4–12.

Murray, David J. "Quality Assurance and Other Departments." In *Quality Assurance: Methods, Management, and Motivation*, ed. H. J. Bajaria, 41–46, Dearborn, MI: Society of Manufacturing Engineers, 1981.

Rosander, A. C. "Service Industry QC—Is the Challenge Being Met?" *Quality Progress* 13, no. 9 (September 1980), 33–34.

Scanlon, Frank, and John T. Hagan. "Quality Management for the Service Industries—Part 1." *Quality Progress* 16, no. 5 (May 1983), 18–23.

Shetty, Y. K., and Joel E. Ross. "Quality and Its Management in Service Businesses." *Industrial Management*, November/December 1985.

Thompson, Phillip, Glenn DeSouza, and Bradley T. Gale. "The Strategic Management of Service Quality." *Quality Progress* 18, no. 6 (June 1985), 20–25.

Williams, Roy H., and Ronald M. Zigli. "Ambiguity Impedes Quality in the Service Industries." *Quality Progress* 20, no. 7 (July 1987), 14–17.

Zemke, Ron. "The Emerging Art of Service Management." *Training* 29 (January 1992), 36–42.

Philosophies and Frameworks

Outline

In the 1890s, Caesar Ritz defined the standards for a luxury hotel. These standards evolved into the quality responsibilities of the employees—the Ladies and Gentlemen Serving Ladies and Gentlemen—of today's Ritz-Carlton Hotel Company (see *Quality in Practice* in Chapter 2): anticipating the wishes and needs of the guests, resolving their problems, and exhibiting genuinely caring conduct toward guests and each other. The Ritz-Carlton management recognized that the key to ensuring that these responsibilities are realized was to create a "Skilled and Empowered Work Force Operating with Pride and Joy."

The concept of "pride and joy" in work—and its impact on quality—is one of the foundations of the philosophy of W. Edwards Deming. Deming, along with Joseph M. Juran and Philip B. Crosby, are regarded as true "management gurus" in the quality revolution. Their insights on measuring, managing, and improving quality have had profound impacts on countless managers and entire corporations around the world. Because of their personalities, Deming, Juran, and Crosby have been likened, respectively, to a fire-and-brimstone preacher, a theologian, and an evangelist. Deming's gruff demeanor reportedly struck fear into many of the corporate executives who attended his seminars; Juran's *Quality Control Handbook* is often called the "bible" of quality; and Crosby is noted for his inspiring, motivational speaking. This chapter presents the philosophies of these three leaders and examines their individual contributions as well as their philosophical similarities and differences. In addition, it discusses the contributions of other key individuals who have helped to shape current thinking in quality management. These philosophies became the cornerstone for quality management practice, and the foundation for award frameworks, most notably the Deming Prize and Malcolm Baldrige National Quality Award, which we also discuss in this chapter.

THE DEMING PHILOSOPHY

No individual has had more influence on quality management than Dr. W. Edwards Deming. Deming received a Ph.D. in physics and was trained as a statistician, so much of his philosophy can be traced to these roots. He worked for Western Electric during its pioneering era of statistical quality control in the 1920s and 1930s. Deming recognized the importance of viewing management processes statistically. During World War II he taught quality control courses as part of the U.S. national defense effort, but he realized that teaching statistics only to engineers and factory workers would never solve the fundamental quality problems that manufacturing needed to address. Despite numerous efforts, his attempts to convey the message of quality to upper-level managers in the United States were ignored.

Shortly after World War II Deming was invited to Japan to help the country take a census. The Japanese had heard about his theories and their usefulness to U.S. companies during the war. Consequently, he soon began to teach them statistical quality control. His thinking went beyond mere statistics, however. Deming preached the importance of top-management leadership, customer/supplier partnerships, and continuous improvement in product development and manufacturing processes. Japanese managers embraced these ideas, and the rest, as they say, is history. Deming's influence on Japanese industry was so great that the Union of Japanese Scientists and Engineers established the Deming Application Prize in 1951 to recognize companies that show a high level of achievement in quality practices. Deming also received Japan's highest honor, the Royal Order of the Sacred Treasure, from the Emperor. The former chairman of NEC Electronics once said, "There is not a day I don't think about what Dr. Deming meant to us."

Although Deming lived in Washington, D.C., he remained virtually unknown in the United States until 1980, when NBC telecast a program entitled "If Japan Can . . . Why Can't We?" The documentary highlighted Deming's contributions in Japan and his later work with Nashua Corporation. Shortly afterward, his name was frequently on the lips of U.S. corporate executives. Companies such as Ford, GM, and Procter & Gamble invited him to work with them to improve their quality. To their initial surprise, Deming did not lay out "a quality improvement program" for them. His goal was to change entire perspectives in management, and often radically. Deming worked with passion until his death in December 1993 at the age of 93, knowing he had little time left to make a difference in his home country. When asked how he would like to be remembered, Deming replied, "I probably won't even be remembered." Then after a long pause, he added, "Well, maybe . . . as someone who spent his life trying to keep America from committing suicide."[1]

Foundations of the Deming Philosophy

Unlike other management gurus and consultants, Deming never defined or described quality precisely. In his last book, he stated, "A product or a service possesses quality if it helps somebody and enjoys a good and sustainable market."[2] The Deming philosophy focuses on bringing about improvements in product and service quality by reducing uncertainty and variability in the design and manufacturing process. In Deming's view, variation is the chief culprit of poor quality. In mechanical assemblies, for example, variations from specifications for part dimensions lead to inconsistent performance and premature wear and failure. Likewise, inconsistencies in service frustrate customers and hurt companies' reputations. To accomplish reductions in variation, Deming advocated a never-ending cycle of product design, manufacture, test, and sales, followed by market surveys and then redesign and so forth. He claimed that higher quality leads to higher productivity, which in turn leads to long-term competitive strength. The Deming "chain reaction" theory (see Figure 3.1) summarizes this view. The theory is that improvements in quality lead to lower costs because they result in less rework, fewer mistakes, fewer delays and snags, and better use of time and materials. Lower costs, in turn, lead to productivity improvements. With better quality and lower prices, a firm can achieve a higher market share

Figure 3.1 The Deming Chain Reaction

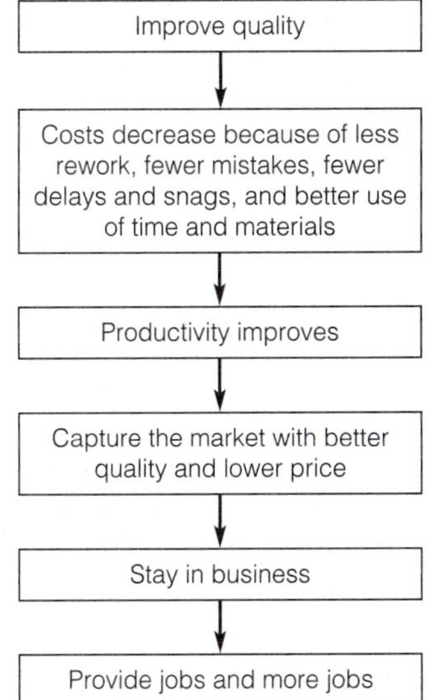

and thus stay in business, providing more and more jobs. Deming stressed that top management has the overriding responsibility for quality improvement.

Deming's philosophy underwent many changes as he continued to learn. In his early work in the United States, he preached his "14 Points" (see Table 3.1), which are discussed in detail later in the chapter. The 14 Points caused some confusion and misunderstanding among businesspeople, because Deming did not provide a clear rationale for them. Near the end of his life, however, he synthesized the underlying foundations of the 14 Points in what he called "A System of Profound Knowledge." Understanding the elements of this "system" provides critical insights needed for understanding and appreciating the 14 Points.

Deming's Profound Knowledge system consists of four interrelated parts:

1. Appreciation for a system
2. Understanding of variation
3. Theory of knowledge
4. Psychology.

Each of these parts is explained here.

Systems We noted the importance of systems in Chapter 2. The components of any system must work together if the system is to be effective. Traditional organizations typically manage according to the functions in vertical organization charts. However, when interactions occur among the parts of a system, managers cannot manage the system well by simply managing the parts; they must understand the horizontal, cross-functional processes and optimize the system. Suboptimization results in losses

Table 3.1 Deming's 14 Points

1. Create and publish to all employees a statement of the aims and purposes of the company or other organization. The management must demonstrate constantly their commitment to this statement.
2. Learn the new philosophy, top management and everybody.
3. Understand the purpose of inspection, for improvement of processes and reduction of cost.
4. End the practice of awarding business on the basis of price tag alone.
5. Improve constantly and forever the system of production and service.
6. Institute training.
7. Teach and institute leadership.
8. Drive out fear. Create trust. Create a climate for innovation.
9. Optimize toward the aims and purposes of the company the efforts of teams, groups, staff areas.
10. Eliminate exhortations for the workforce.
11. (a) Eliminate numerical quotas for production. Instead, learn and institute methods for improvement.
    (b) Eliminate MBO [management by objective]. Instead, learn the capabilities of processes and how to improve them.
12. Remove barriers that rob people of pride of workmanship.
13. Encourage education and self-improvement for everyone.
14. Take action to accomplish the transformation.

Source: Originally published in *Out of the Crisis* by W. Edwards Deming. Published by MIT Center for Advanced Educational Services, Cambridge, MA 02139. © 1986 by The W. Edwards Deming Institute. Revised by W. Edwards Deming in January 1990. Reprinted by permission of MIT and the W. Edwards Deming Institute.

to everybody in the system. According to Deming, it is poor management, for example, to purchase materials or service at the lowest price or to minimize the cost of manufacture if it is at the expense of the system. For instance, inexpensive materials may be of such inferior quality that they will cause excessive costs in adjustment and repair during manufacture and assembly. Minimizing the cost of manufacturing alone might result in products that do not meet designers' specifications and customer needs. Such situations result in a win-lose effect. Purchasing wins, manufacturing loses; manufacturing wins, customers lose, and so on. To manage any system, managers must understand the interrelationships among the systems' components and among the people that work in it.

Management must have an aim, a purpose toward which the system continually strives. Deming believes that the aim of any system should be for everybody—stockholders, employees, customers, community—and the environment to gain over the long term. Stockholders can realize financial benefits, employees can receive opportunities for training and education, customers can receive products and services that meet their needs and create satisfaction, the community can benefit from business leadership, and the environment can benefit from responsible management.

This theory applies to managing people also. All the people who work within a system can contribute to improvement, which will enhance their joy in work. Many factors within the system affect an individual employee's performance:

- The training received
- The information and resources provided
- The leadership of supervisors and managers
- Disruptions on the job
- Management policies and practices.

Few performance appraisals recognize such factors and often place blame on individuals who have little ability to control their environment. Pitting individuals or departments against each other for resources is self-destructive to an organization. The individuals or departments will perform to maximize their own expected gain, not that of the entire firm. Therefore, optimizing the system requires internal cooperation. Similarly, using sales quotas or arbitrary cost-reduction goals will not motivate people to improve the system and customer satisfaction; the people will perform only to meet the quotas or goals.

Variation The second part of Profound Knowledge is a basic understanding of statistical theory and variation. We see variation everywhere, from hitting golf balls to the meals and service in a restaurant. A device called a **quincunx** illustrates a natural process of variation. A computer-simulated quincunx is shown in Figure 3.2.[3] In a quincunx, small balls are dropped from a hole in the top and hit a series of pins as they fall toward collection boxes. The pins cause each ball to move randomly to the left or the right as it strikes each pin on its way down. Note that most balls end up toward the middle of the box. Figure 3.3 shows the frequency distribution of where the balls landed in one simulation. Note the roughly symmetrical, bell shape of the distribution. A normal distribution is bell-shaped. Even though all balls are dropped from the same position, the end result shows variation.

The same kind of variation exists in any production and service process, generally due to factors inherent in the design of the system, which cannot easily be controlled. Excessive variation results in products that fail or perform erratically and inconsistent service that does not meet customers' expectations. Deming suggests that management first understand, and then work to reduce variation through improvements in

Figure 3.2 A Quincunx in Action

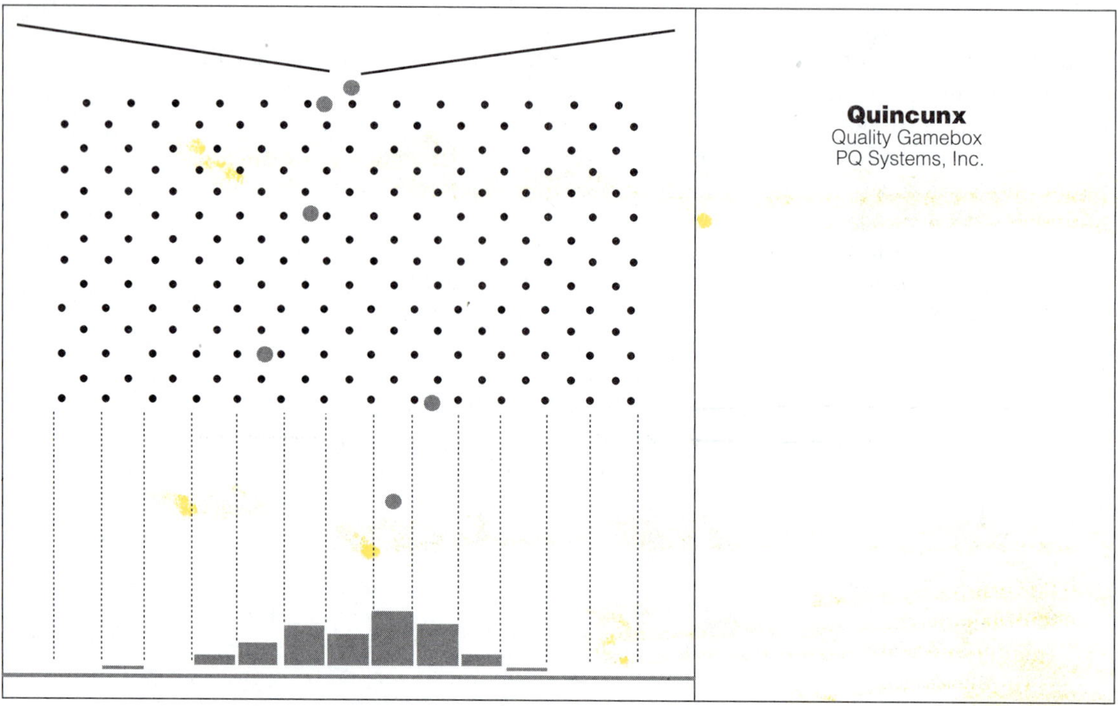

technology, process design, and training. With less variation, both the producer and consumer benefit. The producer benefits by needing less inspection, experiencing less scrap and rework, and having higher productivity and customer satisfaction. The consumer has the advantage of knowing that all products have similar quality characteristics and will perform consistently. This advantage can be especially critical when the consumer is another firm using large quantities of the product in its own manufacturing or service operations.

Statistical methods are the primary tool used to identify and quantify variation. Deming proposes that every employee in the firm be familiar with statistical techniques and other problem-solving tools. Statistics can then become the common language that every employee—from top executives to line workers—uses to communicate with one another. Its value lies in its objectivity; statistics leaves little room for ambiguity or misunderstanding. We will explore issues of variation and statistics further in Chapter 9.

Theory of Knowledge The third part of Profound Knowledge is the theory of knowledge, the branch of philosophy concerned with the nature and scope of knowledge, its presuppositions and basis, and the general reliability of claims to knowledge. Deming's system was influenced greatly by Clarence Irving Lewis, author of *Mind and the World* (Mineola, NY: Dover, 1929). Lewis stated "There is no knowledge without interpretation. If interpretation, which represents an activity of the mind, is always subject to the check of further experience, how is knowledge possible at all? . . . An argument from past to future at best is probable only, and even this probability must rest upon principles which are themselves more than probable."

Figure 3.3 Results from a Quincunx Experiment

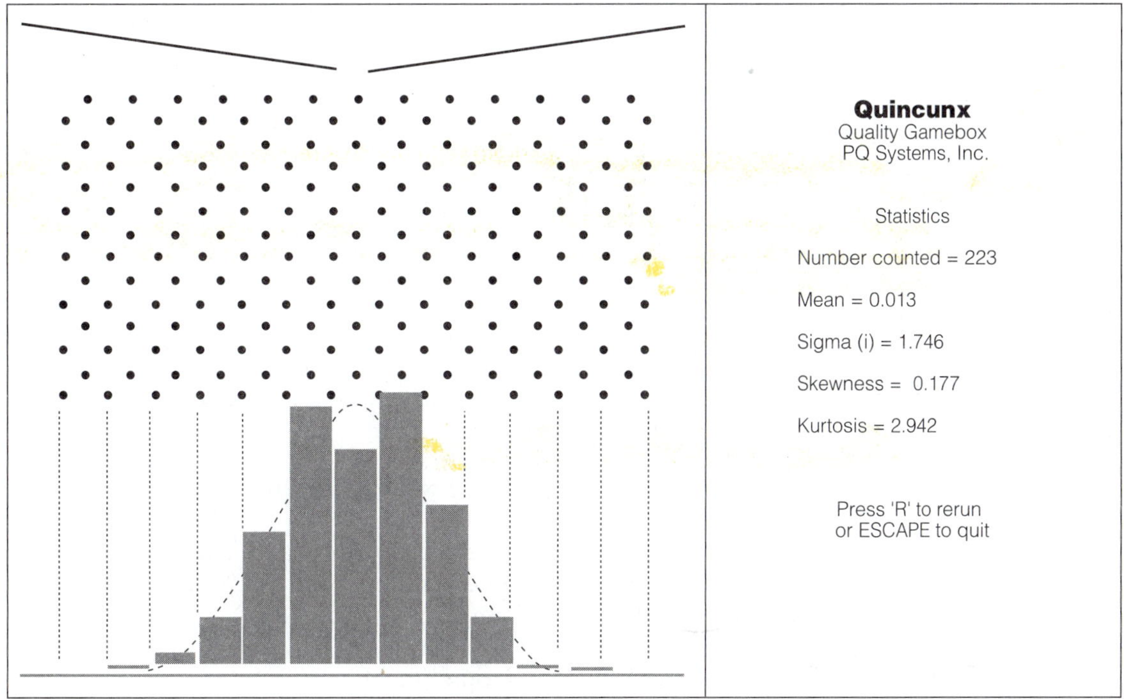

Deming emphasized that knowledge is not possible without theory, and experience alone does not establish a theory. Any rational plan, however simple, requires prediction concerning conditions, behavior, and comparison of performance. A statement devoid of prediction or explanation of past events conveys no knowledge. Experience only describes—it cannot be tested or validated—and alone is no help in management. Theory, on the other hand, shows a cause-and-effect relationship that can be used for prediction. Copying an example of success, without understanding it with theory, may lead to disaster. Many companies have jumped on the latest popular approach advocated by business consultants, only to see the approach fail. Methods that have sustained success are grounded in theory. This notion implies that management decisions must be based on facts, not instincts. Objective data and a systematic problem-solving process provide a rational basis for making decisions. They allow us to distinguish between improvement and change, and plan for learning and improvement.

Psychology Psychology helps us understand people, interactions between people and circumstances, interactions between leaders and employees, and any system of management. Much of Deming's philosophy is based on understanding human behavior and treating people fairly. People differ from one another. A leader must be aware of these differences and work toward optimizing everybody's abilities and preferences. Most managers operate under the assumption that all people are alike. However, a true leader understands that people learn in different ways and at different speeds, and manages the system accordingly.

People are motivated intrinsically and extrinsically. Fear does not motivate people; instead, it prevents the system from reaching its full potential. People are born with a need for love and esteem in their relationships with other people. Some circumstances provide people with dignity and self-esteem. Conversely, circumstances that deny people these advantages will smother intrinsic motivation. If people cannot enjoy their work, they will not be productive and focused on quality principles. Psychology helps us to nurture and preserve these positive innate attributes of people; otherwise, we resort to carrots and sticks that have no long-term values.

One of Deming's more controversial beliefs is that pay is not a motivator, which industrial psychologists have been saying for decades. The chairman of General Motors once stated if GM doubled the salary of every employee, nothing would change. Monetary rewards are a way out for managers who do not understand how to manage intrinsic motivation. When joy in work becomes secondary to getting good ratings, employees are ruled by external forces and must act to protect what they have and avoid punishment.

Peter Scholtes, a noted consultant, makes some salient observations about the failure to understand the components of Profound Knowledge:[4]

When people don't understand systems:

- They see events as individual incidents rather than the net result of many interactions and interdependent forces.
- They see the symptoms but not the deep causes of problems.
- They don't understand how an intervention in one part of [an organization] can cause havoc in another place or at another time.
- They blame individuals for problems even when those individuals have little or no ability to control the events around them.
- They don't understand the ancient African saying, "It takes a whole village to raise a child."

When people don't understand variation:

- They don't see trends that are occurring.
- They see trends where there are none.
- They don't know when expectations are realistic.
- They don't understand past performance so they can't predict future performance.
- They don't know the difference between prediction, forecasting, and guesswork.
- They give others credit or blame when those people are simply either lucky or unlucky, because people tend to attribute everything to human effort, heroics, frailty, error, or deliberate sabotage, no matter what the systemic cause.
- They are less likely to distinguish between fact and opinion.

When people don't understand psychology:

- They don't understand motivation or why people do what they do.
- They resort to carrots and sticks and other forms of induced motivation that have no positive effect and impair the relationship between the motivator and the one being motivated.
- They don't understand the process of change and the resistance to it.
- They revert to coercive and paternalistic approaches when dealing with people.
- They create cynicism, demoralization, demotivation, guilt, resentment, burnout, craziness, and turnover.

When people don't understand the theory of knowledge:

- They don't know how to plan and accomplish learning and improvement.
- They don't understand the difference between improvement and change.
- Problems will remain unsolved, despite their best efforts.

Very little in Deming's system of Profound Knowledge is original. Walter Shewhart developed the distinction between common and special causes of variation in the 1920s; business schools began to teach many of the behavioral theories to which Deming subscribed in the 1960s; management scientists refined systems theory in the 1950s through the 1970s; and scientists in all fields have long understood the relationships among prediction, observation, and theory. Deming's major contribution was to tie these concepts together. He recognized their synergy and developed them into a unified universal theory of management.

Deming's 14 Points

Deming was emphatic in his belief that managerial practices needed a radical overhaul. His 14 Points listed in Table 3.1 constitute the core of his program for achieving quality excellence. According to Deming, the 14 Points cannot be implemented selectively; they are an all-or-nothing commitment. We will consider each in turn.

Point 1: *Create a Vision and Demonstrate Commitment* An organization must define its values, mission, and vision of the future to provide long-term direction for its management and employees. Deming believed that businesses should not exist simply for profit; they are social entities whose basic purpose is to serve their customers and employees. To effectively serve customers, they must take a long-term view and invest in innovation, training, and research. In Japan, for instance, companies spend considerably more on research and development than in the United States. They willingly give up short-term profits knowing they will achieve a greater market share in the future.

The emphasis on short-term profits has eroded American industry. Short-term thinking is driven by quarterly dividends, annual performance appraisals, monthly sales quotas, and the fear of hostile takeovers. Job-hopping, where personal career advancement is placed ahead of the welfare of the firm, is one of Deming's "Deadly Diseases." The costs due to lost knowledge and experience, as well as the investments in hiring and training, are staggering. Take American sports, for example. How many teams can build a dynasty with free agency? Many players go to the highest bidder with little team loyalty. Consequently, employees work only for their boss or individual rewards, and not for the company's future.

Throughout the 1990s corporations frequently "downsized" in a desperate attempt to overcome the problems brought about by long-term ineffective management. Often, the problems result from a competitive crisis or financial losses. Edmund Faltermayer suggests a number of creative approaches that companies may take to reduce or eliminate layoffs.[5]

- Hiring freezes
- Restricting overtime
- Retraining or redeploying excess workers
- Switching positions to temporary or part-time
- Job sharing
- Employ consultants, instead of permanent staff
- Use voluntary leave and unpaid vacations
- Shorten the workweek
- Reduce pay
- Encourage early retirement
- Start lean and stay lean

Successful use of such strategies takes careful planning and disciplined management, but generally such alternatives are superior to wholesale layoffs.

Deming understood that business must adopt a long-term perspective and take responsibility for providing jobs and improving a firm's competitive position. This responsibility lies with top management, who must develop a vision and set the policies and mission of the organization. They must then act on the policies and show commitment.

Point 2: *Learn the New Philosophy* The world has changed in the last few decades. Old methods of management built on Frederick Taylor's principles, such as quota-driven production, work measurement, and adversarial work relationships will not work in today's global business environment. They create mistrust, fear, and anxiety and a focus on "satisficing," rather than "optimizing."

Production and service processes often contain considerable waste and inefficiencies. For example, several years ago one of the authors purchased a new dining room set, delivered directly from the factory. A brass knob was missing from one of the doors. The company was prompt in sending a replacement knob. In fact, a package containing six knobs arrived the following week. Later, another package of six arrived. A few weeks later a third package came. Imagine the cost to the company of administrative time as well as the items themselves! Eliminating defects is not enough. Companies must develop a quality consciousness and a new attitude that "good enough" just isn't.

Companies cannot survive if products of poor quality of conformance or poor fitness for use leave their customers dissatisfied. Instead, companies must take a customer-driven approach based on mutual cooperation between labor and management and a never-ending cycle of improvement. Everyone, from the boardroom to the stockroom, must learn the new philosophy.

Point 3: *Understand Inspection* Routine inspection acknowledges that defects are present, but does not add value to the product. Rather, it is rarely accurate, and encourages the production of defective products by letting someone else catch and fix the problem. The rework and disposition of defective material decreases productivity and increases costs. In service industries, rework cannot be performed; external failures are the most damaging to business.

Workers must take responsibility for their work, rather than leave the problems for someone else down the production line. Managers need to understand the concept of variation and how it affects their processes and seek to reduce the common causes of variation. Simple statistical tools can be used to help control processes and eliminate mass inspection as the principal activity in quality control. Inspection should be used as an information-gathering tool for improvement, not as a means of "assuring" quality or blaming workers.

Point 4: *Stop Making Decisions Purely on the Basis of Cost* Purchasing departments have long been driven by cost minimization without regard for quality. In 1931 Walter Shewhart noted that price has no meaning without quality.[6] Yet, by tradition, the purchasing manager's performance is evaluated by cost. What is the true cost of purchasing substandard materials? The direct costs of poor quality materials that arise during production or during warranty periods, as well as the loss of customer goodwill, can far exceed the cost "savings" perceived by purchasing. Purchasing must understand its role as a supplier to production. This relationship causes individuals to rethink the meaning of an "organizational boundary." It is not simply the four walls around the production floor. The supplier and manufacturer must be considered as a "macro organization."

Deming urged businesses to establish long-term relationships with a few suppliers, leading to loyalty and opportunities for mutual improvement. Management has long justified multiple suppliers for reasons such as providing protection against strikes or natural disasters but has ignored "hidden" costs such as increased travel to visit suppliers, loss of volume discounts, increased setup charges resulting in higher unit costs, and increased inventory and administrative expense. Most importantly, because each supplier's process is different, constantly changing suppliers solely on the basis of price increases the variation in the material supplied to production.

In contrast, a reduced supply base decreases the variation coming into the process, thus reducing scrap, rework, and the need for adjustment to accommodate this variation. A long-term relationship strengthens the supplier-customer bond, allows the supplier to produce in greater quantity, improves communication with the customer, and therefore enhances opportunities for process improvement. Suppliers know that only quality goods are acceptable if they want to maintain a long-term relationship. Statistical methods provide a common language for communication within that relationship.

Point 5: *Improve Constantly and Forever* Quality improvement will be discussed extensively in Chapter 10. Traditionally, Western management has viewed improvement in the context of large, expensive innovations such as robotics and computer-integrated manufacturing. Yet the success of Japanese manufacturers is due primarily to continuous incremental improvements. In Japan, improvement is a way of life.

Improvements are necessary in both design and production. Improved design comes from understanding customer needs and continual market surveys and other sources of feedback, and from understanding the manufacturing process and developing manufacturable designs. Improved production is achieved by reducing the causes of variation and establishing stable, predictable processes. Statistical methods provide a tool for improvement, which goes beyond production and includes transportation, engineering, maintenance, sales, service, and administration. When quality improves, productivity improves and costs decrease.

Point 6: *Institute Training* For continuous improvement, employees—both management and workers—require the proper tools and knowledge. People are an organization's most valuable resource; they want to do a good job, but they often do not know how. Management must take responsibility for helping them. Deming noted that in Japan, entry-level managers spend 4 to 12 years on the factory floor and in other activities to learn the aspects of production. All employees should be trained in statistical tools for quality problem solving. Not only does training result in improvements in quality and productivity, but it adds to worker morale, and demonstrates to workers that the company is dedicated to helping them and investing in their future. In addition, training reduces barriers between workers and supervisors, giving both incentive to improve further. For example, at Honda of America in Marysville, Ohio, all employees start out on the production floor, regardless of their job classification.

Point 7: *Institute Leadership* The job of management is leadership, not supervision. Supervision is simply overseeing and directing work; leadership means providing guidance to help employees do their jobs better with less effort. In many companies, supervisors know little about the job itself because the position is often used as an entry-level job for college graduates. The supervisors have never worked in the department and cannot train the workers, so their principal responsibility is to get the product out the door.

Supervision should provide the link between management and the workforce. Good supervisors are not police or paperpushers, but rather coaches, helping workers to do a better job and develop their skills. Leadership can help to eliminate fear from the job and encourage teamwork.

Point 8: *Drive Out Fear* Driving out fear underlies many of Deming's 14 Points. Fear is manifested in many ways: fear of reprisal, fear of failure, fear of the unknown, fear of relinquishing control, and fear of change. No system can work without the mutual respect of managers and workers. Workers are often afraid to report quality problems because they might not meet their quotas, their incentive pay might be reduced, or they might be blamed for problems in the system. One of Deming's classic stories involved a foreman who would not stop production to repair a worn-out piece of machinery. Stopping production would mean missing his daily quota. He said nothing, and the machine failed, causing the line to shut down for four days. Managers are also afraid to cooperate with other departments, because the other managers might receive higher performance ratings and bonuses, or because they fear takeovers or reorganizations. Fear encourages short-term thinking.

Managers fear losing power. One example is presented by Bushe.[7] After a statistical quality control program was implemented in an automotive plant, worker groups were sometimes able to offer better advice about system improvements than the corporate engineering staff, which ran counter to the plant's well-established culture. Middle managers were no longer the "experts." Their fear diminished their support for the program, which was eventually eliminated.

Point 9: *Optimize the Efforts of Teams* Teamwork helps to break down barriers between departments and individuals. Barriers between functional areas occur when managers fear they might lose power. Internal competition for raises and performance ratings contributes to building barriers. The lack of cooperation leads to poor quality because other departments cannot understand what their "customers" want and do not get what they need from their "suppliers." In Japan, companies emphasize that the next department or individual in the production process is actually the customer, and train their workers to manage such customer relationships.

Perhaps the biggest barrier to team efforts in the United States results from issues between union and management. With some notable exceptions, the history of management–labor relations in U.S. firms has been largely adversarial. Lack of sensitivity to worker needs, exploitation of workers, and poor management practices and policies have frequently resulted in strained relations between managers and their subordinates. Labor leaders also must bear their share of the blame. They have resisted many management efforts to reduce rigid, rule-based tasks, preferring to adhere to the structured approaches rooted in Frederick W. Taylor's historical principles of scientific management.[8]

An example of how adversarial relations can affect labor and management in the workplace is presented in Table 3.2, which shows actual comments of hourly maintenance employees of a transit company. Both columns of descriptive adjectives were provided by hourly employees to the director of maintenance education and development. The director, who later successfully developed an employee involvement program to reverse the attitudes, confirmed that the employees' perceptions of how hourly employees regarded management and how management regarded them were generally accurate. However, the contrast between the conditions viewed by the workers and the same conditions seen through the eyes of the managers is quite revealing. For example, managers frequently thought of the workers as ignorant (un-

Table 3.2 Perceived Labor Versus Management Attitudes

Hourly Employee Perceptions (related to company and management)	Management Perceptions (related to hourly employees)
Unionization	Labor agreement
Grievance procedures	Excuse makers
Job duties and assignments	Untrustworthy
Poor basic skill development	Ignorant
Poor training	Lazy
Poor working conditions	Stepchildren
Low morale	No team players
Untrained leadership	No goals
Suspicious (of management)	"Bus driver" orientation
No information (from management)	No sound basis for improvement

able to learn) or lazy, while the workers merely viewed themselves as having poor basic skills (math, reading, etc.) and poor training. When management acknowledged the truth in the workers' perceptions and instituted courses in basic skill development, job-related skills, and participative problem solving, employee attitudes quickly became more positive.[9] This illustration shows that training and employee involvement are important means of removing such barriers. We will discuss these issues in greater detail in Chapter 6.

Point 10: *Eliminate Exhortations* Posters, slogans, and motivational programs calling for Zero Defects, Do It Right the First Time, Improve Productivity and Quality, and so on, are directed at the wrong people. These motivational programs assume that all quality problems are due to human behavior and that workers can improve simply through motivational methods. Workers become frustrated when they cannot improve or are penalized for defects.

Motivational approaches overlook the source of many problems—the system. Common causes of variation stemming from the design of the system are management's problem, not the workers'. If anything, workers' attempts to fix problems only increase the variation. Improvement occurs by understanding the nature of special and common causes. Thus, statistical thinking and training, not slogans, are the best route to improving quality. Motivation can be better achieved from trust and leadership than from slogans and goals.

Point 11: *Eliminate Numerical Quotas and Management by Objective (MBO)* Measurement has been, and often still is, used punitively. Standards and quotas are born of short-term perspectives and create fear. They do not encourage improvement, particularly if rewards or performance appraisals are tied to meeting quotas. Workers may shortcut quality to reach the goal. Once a standard is reached, little incentive remains for workers to continue production or to improve quality; they will do no more than they are asked to do.

Arbitrary management goals, such as increasing sales by 5 percent next year or decreasing costs next quarter by 10 percent, have no meaning without a method to achieve them. Deming acknowledged that goals are useful, but numerical goals set for others without incorporating a method to reach the goal generate frustration and resentment. Further, variation in the system year to year or quarter to quarter—a

5 percent increase or a 6 percent decrease, for example—makes comparisons meaningless. Management must understand the system and continually try to improve it, rather than focus on short-term goals.

Point 12: *Remove Barriers to Pride in Workmanship* People on the factory floor and even in management have become, in Deming's words, "a commodity." Factory workers are given monotonous tasks, provided with inferior machines, tools, or materials, told to run defective items to meet sales pressures, and report to supervisors who know nothing about the job. Salaried employees are expected to work evenings and weekends to make up for cost-cutting measures that resulted in layoffs of their colleagues. Many are given the title of "management" so that overtime need not be paid. Even employees in the quality profession are not immune.[10] An inspection technician stated, "This profession always seems to end up being called the troublemakers." A quality engineer stated, "The managers over me now give little direction, are very resistant to change, and do little to advance their people." A quality supervisor said, "Someone less qualified could perform my job . . . for less money." How can these individuals take pride in their work? Many cannot be certain they will have a job next year.

Deming believed that one of the biggest barriers to pride in workmanship is performance appraisal. Performance appraisal destroys teamwork by promoting competition for limited resources, fosters mediocrity because objectives typically are driven by numbers and what the boss wants rather than by quality, focuses on the short term and discourages risk-taking, and confounds the "people resources" with other resources. If all individuals are working within the system, then they should not be singled out of the system to be ranked. Some people have to be "below average," which can only result in frustration if those individuals are working within the confines of the system. Deming sorted performance into three categories: the majority of performances that are within the system, performances outside the system on the superior side, and performances outside the system on the inferior side. Statistical methods provide the basis for these classifications. Superior performers should be compensated specially; inferior performers need extra training or replacement.

Although many companies will not eliminate performance appraisals completely, some have made substantial changes. The Xerox "Green Book" developed in 1983, their documentation of Leadership Through Quality (see the Quality in Practice case in Chapter 1), cites one example:

> *Xerox will separate performance appraisal from annual salary reviews. The primary focus of appraisal will be recognition of both the accomplishment of results and the use of the Quality Improvement Process. The current Merit Increase Planning (MIP) system requires a prescribed distribution of appraisal results, which leads to stack ranking. This makes people feel like "numbers" and leads to competition within the group. Separating pay from appraisal allows managers to evaluate individual performance more constructively and eliminates competition. Performance appraisals will be separated from annual salary reviews by a minimum of three months. In conjunction with corporate personnel, existing appraisal systems will be examined for their suitability to achieve the objective appraisals described here. Where necessary, they will be modified.*[11]

Point 13: *Encourage Education and Self-Improvement* The difference between this point and Point 6 is subtle. Point 6 refers to training in specific job skills; Point 13 refers to continuing, broad education for self-development. Organizations must invest in their people at all levels to ensure success in the long term. A fundamental mission of business is to provide jobs as stated in Point 1, but business and society also have the responsibility to improve the value of the individual. Developing the worth of the individual is a powerful motivation method.

Point 14: *Take Action* The transformation begins with top management and includes everyone. Applying the Deming philosophy launches a major cultural change that many firms find difficult, particularly when many of the traditional management practices Deming felt must be eliminated are deeply ingrained in the organization's culture. Ford Motor Company, for example, has embraced the Deming philosophy totally. Its experience is discussed in the Quality in Practice section later in this chapter.

Many people have criticized Deming because his philosophy is just that: a philosophy. It lacks specific direction and prescriptive approaches and does not fit into the traditional American business culture. Many behavioral scientists contend that Deming's ideas are contrary to research findings. Fueling this attitude is the almost cult-like fervor and devotion of "Deming's disciples" who believe that his is the only way to approach quality.

Deming did not propose specific methods for implementation because he wanted people to study his ideas and derive their own approaches. As he often stated, "There is no instant pudding." Despite the controversy, many firms have organized their quality approaches around Deming's philosophy. Some companies, such as 1991 Baldrige Award winner Zytec Corporation, now a part of Artesyn Technologies (see *Quality Profile*) have been successful. Chapter 14 discusses further the importance of considering other approaches to quality and adapting those that best fit a firm's indi-

Quality Profile

Zytec Corporation

Zytec Corporation designs and manufactures electronic power supplies and repairs power supplies and CRT monitors. Most of its customers are large multinational companies, and Zytec competes for business with Far East and European companies as well as approximately 400 U.S. companies. In 1991 Zytec won the Malcolm Baldrige National Quality Award.

Since its start, Zytec has used quality and reliability of its products and services as the key strategy to differentiate itself from its competition. To carry out its mission, Zytec's senior executives embraced Dr. Deming's 14 Points as the cornerstone of the company's quality improvement culture. They established the Deming Steering Committee to guide the Deming process and champion individual Deming points.

The results of Zytec's attention to Deming's philosophy are impressive. Product quality improved from 99 percent in 1988 to 99.7 percent in 1990. Product reliability—measured as mean time between failures in hours—improved by a magnitude of 10 in just five years and ranks among the world's leaders. In a two-year period, warranty costs fell 48 percent, repair cycle time was reduced 31 percent, product costs were cut 30 to 40 percent, internal yields improved 51 percent, manufacturing cycle time fell 26 percent, and scrap rate was cut in half. In an independent survey of power supply manufacturers, Zytec ranked number one against its competitors and exceeded the industry average in 21 of 22 attributes deemed important to its customers.

Source: Adapted from Zytec Malcolm Baldrige National Quality Award Application Summary.

vidual culture. Deming's legacy lives on through the W. Edwards Deming Institute (*http://www.deming.org*).

THE JURAN PHILOSOPHY

Joseph Juran was born in Romania in 1904 and came to the United States in 1912. He joined Western Electric in the 1920s as it pioneered the development of statistical methods for quality. He spent much of his time as a corporate industrial engineer and, in 1951, did most of the writing, editing, and publishing of the *Quality Control Handbook*. This book, one of the most comprehensive quality manuals ever written, has been revised several times and continues to be a popular reference.

Like Deming, Juran taught quality principles to the Japanese in the 1950s and was a principal force in their quality reorganization. Juran also echoed Deming's conclusion that U.S. businesses face a major crisis in quality due to the huge costs of poor quality and the loss of sales to foreign competition. Both men felt that the solution to this crisis depends on new thinking about quality that includes all levels of the managerial hierarchy. Upper management in particular requires training and experience in managing for quality.

Unlike Deming, however, Juran did not propose a major cultural change in the organization, but rather sought to improve quality by working within the system familiar to managers. Thus, his programs were designed to fit into a company's current strategic business planning with minimal risk of rejection. He argued that employees at different levels of an organization speak in their own "languages." (Deming, on the other hand, believed statistics should be the common language.) Juran stated that top management speaks in the language of dollars; workers speak in the language of things; and middle management must be able to speak both languages and translate between dollars and things. Thus, to get top management's attention, quality issues must be cast in the language they understand—dollars. Hence, Juran advocated the use of quality cost accounting and analysis to focus attention on quality problems. At the operational level, Juran focused on increasing conformance to specifications through elimination of defects, supported extensively by statistical tools for analysis. Thus, his philosophy fit well into existing management systems.

Juran proposed a simple definition of quality: "fitness for use." This definition suggests that quality be viewed from both external and internal perspectives; that is, quality is related to "(1) product performance that results in customer satisfaction; (2) freedom from product deficiencies, which avoids customer dissatisfaction." How products and services are designed, manufactured and delivered, and serviced in the field all contribute to fitness for use. Thus, the pursuit of quality is viewed on two levels: (1) The mission of the firm as a whole is to achieve high design quality; and (2) the mission of each department in the firm is to achieve high conformance quality. Like Deming, Juran advocated a never-ending spiral of activities that includes market research, product development, design, planning for manufacture, purchasing, production process control, inspection and testing, and sales, followed by customer feedback. The interdependency of these functions emphasizes the need for competent companywide quality management. Senior management must play an active and enthusiastic leadership role in the quality management process.

Juran's prescriptions focus on three major quality processes, called the **Quality Trilogy**:

1. Quality planning: the process of preparing to meet quality goals
2. Quality control: the process of meeting quality goals during operations
3. Quality improvement—the process of breaking through to unprecedented levels of performance.

Quality planning begins with identifying customers, both external and internal, determining their needs, translating customer needs into specifications, developing product features that respond to those needs, and developing the processes capable of producing the product or deliver the service. Thus, like Deming, Juran wanted employees to know who uses their products, whether in the next department or in another organization. Quality goals based on meeting the needs of customers and suppliers alike at a minimum combined cost are then established. Next, the process that can produce the product to satisfy customers' needs and meet quality goals under operating conditions must be designed. Strategic planning for quality—similar to the firm's financial planning process—determines short-term and long-term goals, sets priorities, compares results with previous plans, and meshes the plans with other corporate strategic objectives.

As a parallel to Deming's emphasis on identifying and reducing sources of variation, Juran stated that quality control involves determining what to control, establishing units of measurement to evaluate data objectively, establishing standards of performance, measuring actual performance, interpreting the difference between actual performance and the standard, and taking action on the difference.

Unlike Deming, however, Juran specified a detailed program for quality improvement. Such a program involves proving the need for improvement, identifying specific projects for improvement, organizing support for the projects, diagnosing the causes, providing remedies for the causes, proving that the remedies are effective under operating conditions, and providing control to maintain improvements. At any given point in time, hundreds or even thousands of quality improvement projects should be under way in all areas of the firm. In Chapter 10, we discuss the specifics of Juran's quality improvement approach.

Juran's assessment of most companies revealed that quality control receives top priority among the trilogy; most companies feel strong in this category. Quality planning and quality improvement, however, do not receive priority attention and are significantly weaker in most organizations. Juran felt that more effort should go into quality planning and, especially, quality improvement. Juran supported these conclusions with several case examples in which Japanese firms using technology, materials, and processes identical to those of U.S. firms had much higher levels of quality and productivity. Beginning about 1950, upper management in Japan took responsibility for managing quality, trained employees at every level of the firm, and added quality goals to their business plans. They implemented quality improvement projects at a far greater pace than their Western counterparts, and fully involved the entire workforce. As a result, both the quality of design and conformance surged ahead of Western manufacturers up through the 1970s and 1980s.

Many aspects of the Juran and Deming philosophies are similar. The focus on top management commitment, the need for improvement, the use of quality control techniques, and the importance of training are fundamental to both philosophies. However, they did not agree on all points. For instance, Juran believed that Deming was wrong to tell management to drive out fear. According to Juran, "Fear can bring out the best in people."[12] The Juran Institute, founded by Dr. Juran, provides substantial training in the form of seminars, videotapes, and other materials. Information about the Juran Institute can be found at *http://www.juran.com*.

THE CROSBY PHILOSOPHY

Philip B. Crosby was corporate vice president for quality at International Telephone and Telegraph (ITT) for 14 years after working his way up from line inspector. After leaving ITT, he established Philip Crosby Associates in 1979 to develop and offer training programs. He also authored several popular books. His first book, *Quality Is Free,* sold about one million copies. The essence of Crosby's quality philosophy is embodied in what he calls the "Absolutes of Quality Management" and the "Basic Elements of Improvement." Crosby's Absolutes of Quality Management include the following points:

- *Quality means conformance to requirements, not elegance.* Crosby quickly dispels the myth that quality follows the transcendent definition discussed in Chapter 1. Requirements must be clearly stated so that they cannot be misunderstood. Requirements act as communication devices and are ironclad. Once requirements are established, then one can take measurements to determine conformance to those requirements. The nonconformance detected is the absence of quality. Quality problems become nonconformance problems, that is, variation in output. Setting requirements is the responsibility of management. Crosby maintained that once the requirements were specified, quality is judged solely on whether they have been met. Therefore these requirements must be clearly defined by management and not left by default to front line personnel.

- *There is no such thing as a quality problem.* Problems must be identified by those individuals or departments that cause them. Thus, a firm may experience accounting problems, manufacturing problems, design problems, front-desk problems, and so on. In other words, quality originates in functional departments, not in the quality department, and therefore the burden of responsibility for such problems falls on these functional departments. The quality department should measure conformance, report results, and lead the drive to develop a positive attitude toward quality improvement. This Absolute is similar to Deming's third point.
- *There is no such thing as the economics of quality; doing the job right the first time is always cheaper.* Crosby supports the premise that "economics of quality" has no meaning. Quality is free. What costs money are all actions that involve not doing jobs right the first time. The Deming chain reaction sends a similar message.
- *The only performance measurement is the cost of quality, which is the expense of nonconformance.* Crosby notes that most companies spend 15 to 20 percent of their sales dollars on quality costs. A company with a well-run quality management program can achieve a cost of quality that is less than 2.5 percent of sales, primarily in the prevention and appraisal categories. Crosby's program calls for measuring and publicizing the cost of poor quality. Quality cost data are useful to call problems to management's attention, to select opportunities for corrective action, and to track quality improvement over time. Such data provide visible proof of improvement and recognition of achievement. Juran supported this approach.
- *The only performance standard is "Zero Defects (ZD)."* Crosby feels that the Zero Defects concept is widely misunderstood and resisted. Many thought it to be a motivational program. It is described as follows:

> *Zero Defects is a performance standard. It is the standard of the craftsperson regardless of his or her assignment. . . . The theme of ZD is do it right the first time. That means concentrating on preventing defects rather than just finding and fixing them.*
>
> *People are conditioned to believe that error is inevitable; thus they not only accept error, they anticipate it. It does not bother us to make a few errors in our work . . . to err is human. We all have our own standards in business or academic life—our own points at which errors begin to bother us. It is good to get an A in school, but it may be OK to pass with a C.*
>
> *We do not maintain these standards, however, when it comes to our personal life. If we did, we should expect to be shortchanged every now and then*

> *when we cash our paycheck; we should expect hospital nurses to drop a constant percentage of newborn babies. . . . We as individuals do not tolerate these things. We have a dual standard: one for ourselves and one for our work.*
>
> *Most human error is caused by lack of attention rather than lack of knowledge. Lack of attention is created when we assume that error is inevitable. If we consider this condition carefully, and pledge ourselves to make a constant conscious effort to do our jobs right the first time, we will take a giant step toward eliminating the waste of rework, scrap, and repair that increases cost and reduces individual opportunity.*[13]

Juran and Deming, on the other hand, would point out the uselessness, or even hypocrisy of exhorting a line worker to produce perfection because the overwhelming majority of imperfections stem from poorly designed manufacturing systems beyond the workers' control.

Crosby's Basic Elements of Improvement include determination, education, and implementation. Determination means that top management must take quality improvement seriously. Everyone should understand the Absolutes, which can be accomplished only through education. Finally, every member of the management team must understand the implementation process. Crosby's improvement process is discussed in Chapter 10.

Unlike Juran and Deming, Crosby's approach is primarily behavioral. He emphasizes using management and organizational processes rather than statistical techniques to change corporate culture and attitudes. Like Juran and unlike Deming however, his approach fits well within existing organizational structures.

Crosby's approach provides relatively few details about how firms should address the finer points of quality management. It focuses on managerial thinking rather than on organizational systems. By allowing managers to determine the best methods to apply in their own firm's situations, his approach tends to avoid some of the implementation problems experienced by firms that have adopted the Deming philosophy.

Crosby's philosophy has not earned the respect of his rivals.[14] Even though they agree that he is an entertaining speaker and a great motivator, they say his approach lacks substance in the methods of achieving quality improvement. Nevertheless, hundreds of thousands have taken his courses in-house or at his Quality College in Winter Park, Florida and his influence was a major contributor to the quality revolution in the United States Crosby's current business pursuits are described at his Web site, *http://www.philipcrosby.com.*

Comparisons of Quality Philosophies

In spite of the fact that they have significantly different approaches to implementing organizational change, the philosophies of Deming, Juran, and Crosby are more alike than different. Each views quality as imperative in the future competitiveness in global markets; makes top management commitment an absolute necessity; demonstrates that quality management practices will save, not cost money; places responsibility for quality on management, not the workers; stresses the need for continuous, never-ending improvement; acknowledges the importance of the customer and strong management—worker partnerships; and recognizes the need for and difficulties associated with changing the organizational culture.

The individual nature of business firms complicates the strict application of any one specific philosophy. Although each of these philosophies can be highly effective, a firm must first understand the nature and differences of the philosophies and then develop a quality management approach that is tailored to its individual organization. Any approach should include goals and objectives, allocation of responsibilities, a measurement system and description of tools to be employed, an outline of the management style that will be used, and a strategy for implementation. After taking these steps, the management team is responsible for leading the organization through successful execution. We address these issues further in the final chapter of this book.

OTHER QUALITY PHILOSOPHERS

Other notable figures in the quality arena include A. V. Feigenbaum and Kaoru Ishikawa. Feigenbaum and Ishikawa were both awarded the title of Honorary Members of the American Society for Quality in 1986.[15] At that time the society had only four living honorary members, two of whom were W. Edwards Deming and Joseph M. Juran. Obviously, the title of "Honorary Member" is not given lightly by the ASQ. In this section we briefly review the accomplishments that have made them part of this elite group, and also introduce another influential thinker in the quality movement, Genichi Taguchi.

A. V. Feigenbaum

A. V. Feigenbaum's career in quality began more than 40 years ago. For 10 years, he was the manager of worldwide manufacturing and quality control at General Electric. In 1968 he founded General Systems Company of Pittsfield, Massachusetts, and serves as its president. Feigenbaum has traveled and spoken to various audiences and groups around the world over the years. He was elected as the founding chairman of the board of the International Academy of Quality, which has attracted active participation from the European Organization for Quality Control, the Union of Japanese Scientists and Engineers (JUSE), as well as the American Society for Quality.

Feigenbaum is best known for coining the phrase *total quality control*, which he defined as ". . . an effective system for integrating the quality development, quality maintenance, and quality improvement efforts of the various groups in an organization so as to enable production and service at the most economical levels which allow full customer satisfaction." His book *Total Quality Control* was first published in 1951 under the title *Quality Control: Principles, Practice, and Administration*. He viewed quality as a strategic business tool that requires involvement from everyone in the organization, and promoted the use of quality costs as a measurement and evaluation tool.

Feigenbaum's philosophy is summarized in his Three Steps to Quality:

1. *Quality Leadership:* A continuous management emphasis is grounded on sound planning rather than reaction to failures. Management must maintain a constant focus and lead the quality effort.
2. *Modern Quality Technology:* The traditional quality department cannot resolve 80 to 90 percent of quality problems. This task requires the integration of office staff as well as engineers and shop-floor workers in the process who continually evaluate and implement new techniques to satisfy customers in the future.
3. *Organizational Commitment:* Continuous training and motivation of the entire workforce as well as an integration of quality in business planning indicate the importance of quality and provide the means for including it in all aspects of the firm's activities.

The Japanese latched on to this concept of total quality control as the foundation for their practice called **companywide quality control (CWQC)**, which began in the

1960s. Feigenbaum also popularized the term *hidden factory*, which described the portion of plant capacity wasted due to poor quality. Many of his ideas remain embedded in contemporary thinking, and have become important elements of the Malcolm Baldrige National Quality Award criteria. They include the principles that the customer is the judge of quality; quality and innovation are interrelated and mutually beneficial; managing quality is the same as managing the business; quality is a continuous process of improvement; and customers and suppliers should be involved the process.

Kaoru Ishikawa

An early pioneer in the quality revolution in Japan, Kaoru Ishikawa was the foremost figure in Japanese quality until his death in 1989. He was instrumental in the development of the broad outlines of Japanese quality strategy, and without his leadership, the Japanese quality movement would not enjoy the worldwide acclaim and success that it has today. Dr. Ishikawa was a professor of engineering at Tokyo University for many years. As a member of the editorial review board for the Japanese journal *Quality Control for Foremen*, founded in 1962, and later as the chief executive director of the QC Circle Headquarters at the Union of Japanese Scientists and Engineers (JUSE), Dr. Ishikawa influenced the development of a participative, bottom-up view of quality, which became the trademark of the Japanese approach to quality management. However, Ishikawa was also able to get the attention of top management and persuade them that a companywide approach to quality control was necessary for total success.

Ishikawa built on Feigenbaum's concept of total quality and promoted greater involvement by all employees, from the top management to the front-line staff, and reducing reliance on quality professionals and quality departments. He advocated collecting and analyzing factual data using simple visual tools, using statistical techniques, and teamwork as the foundations for implementing total quality. Like others, Ishikawa believed that quality begins with the customer and therefore, understanding customers needs is the basis for improvement, and that complaints should be actively sought. Some key elements of his philosophy are summarized here.

1. Quality begins with education and ends with education.
2. The first step in quality is to know the requirements of customers.
3. The ideal state of quality control occurs when inspection is no longer necessary.
4. Remove the root cause, not the symptoms.
5. Quality control is the responsibility of all workers and all divisions.
6. Do not confuse the means with the objectives.
7. Put quality first and set your sights on long-term profits.
8. Marketing is the entrance and exit of quality.
9. Top management must not show anger when facts are presented by subordinates.
10. Ninety-five percent of problems in a company can be solved with simple tools for analysis and problem solving.
11. Data without dispersion information (i.e., variability) are false data.

Genichi Taguchi

A Japanese engineer, Genichi Taguchi—whose philosophy was strongly advocated by Deming—explained the economic value of reducing variation. Taguchi maintained that the manufacturing-based definition of quality as conformance to specification limits is inherently flawed. For example, suppose that a specification for some quality characteristic is 0.500 ± 0.020. Using this definition, the actual value of the quality characteristic can fall anywhere in a range from 0.480 to 0.520. This approach assumes that the customer, either the consumer or the next department in the production process, would accept any value within the 0.480 to 0.520 range, but not be satisfied with a value outside this tolerance range. Also, this approach assumes that costs do not depend on the actual value of the quality characteristic as long as it falls within the tolerance specified (see Figure 3.4).

But what is the real difference between 0.479 and 0.481? The former would be considered as "out of specification" and either reworked or scrapped while the latter would be acceptable. Actually, the impact of either value on the performance characteristic of the product would be about the same. Neither value is close to the nominal specification 0.500. The nominal specification is the ideal target value for the critical quality characteristic. Taguchi's approach assumes that the smaller the variation about the nominal specification, the better is the quality. In turn, products are more consistent, and total costs are less. The following example supports this notion.

The Japanese newspaper *Ashai* published an example comparing the cost and quality of Sony televisions at two plants in Japan and San Diego.[16] The color density of all the units produced at the San Diego plant were within specifications, while some of those shipped from the Japanese plant were not (see Figure 3.5). However, the average loss per unit of the San Diego plant was $0.89 greater than that of the Japanese plant. This increased cost occurred because workers adjusted units that were out of specification at the San Diego plant, adding cost to the process. Furthermore, a unit adjusted to minimally meet specifications was more likely to generate customer complaints than a unit close to the original target value, therefore incurring higher field service costs. Figure 3.5 shows that fewer U.S.-produced sets met the tar-

Figure 3.4 Traditional Economic View of Conformance to Specifications

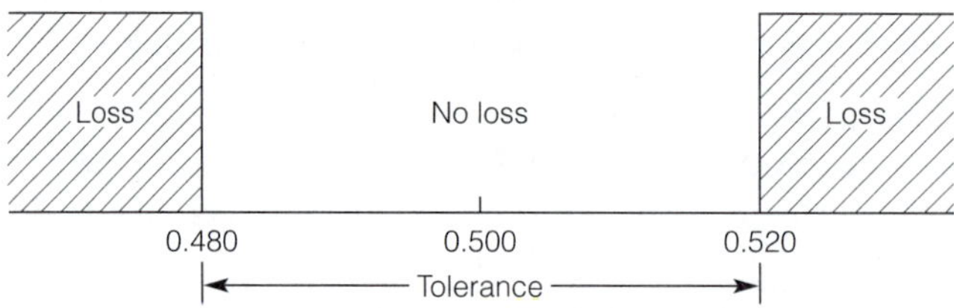

Figure 3.5 Variation in U.S.-Made Versus Japanese-Made Television Components

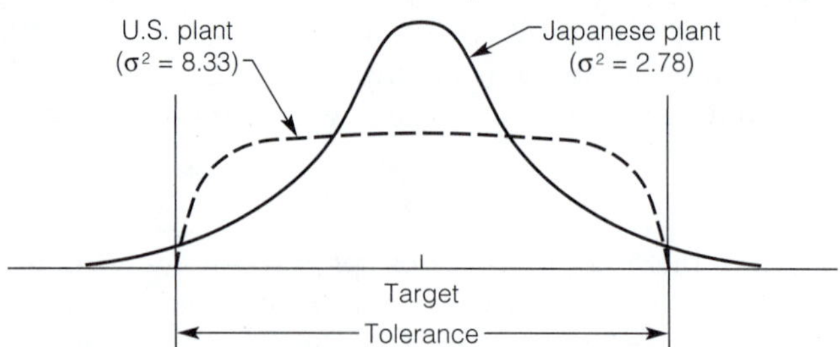

get value for color density. The distribution of quality in the Japanese plant was more uniform around the target value, and though some units were out of specification, the total cost was less. Taguchi measured quality as the variation from the target value of a design specification, and then translated that variation into an economic "loss function" that expresses the cost of variation in monetary terms. We will discuss the mathematics of this approach in Chapter 7.

Taguchi also contributed to improving engineering approaches to product design. By designing a product that is insensitive to variation in manufacture, specification limits become meaningless. He advocated certain techniques of experimental design to identify the most important design variables in order to minimize the effects of uncontrollable factors on product variation. Thus, his approaches attached quality problems early in the design stage rather than react to problems that might arise later in production.

QUALITY MANAGEMENT AWARD FRAMEWORKS

The philosophies of Deming, Juran, Crosby, and others have provided much guidance and wisdom in the form of "best practices" to managers around the world, and have led to the development of awards and award criteria for recognizing effective application of TQ principles. Although awards justifiably recognize only a select few, the award criteria provide frameworks for managing from which every organization can benefit. The two awards and criteria that have had the most impact on business practices worldwide are the Deming Prize and the Malcolm Baldrige National Quality Award.

The Deming Prize

The Deming Application Prize was instituted in 1951 by the Union of Japanese Scientists and Engineers (JUSE) in recognition and appreciation of W. Edwards Deming's achievements in statistical quality control and his friendship with the Japanese people. The Deming Prize has several categories, including prizes for individuals, factories, and small companies, and the Deming application prize, which is an annual award presented to a company or a division of a company that has achieved distinctive performance improvements through the application of companywide quality control. As defined by JUSE, CWQC is a system of activities to assure that quality products and services required by customers are economically designed, produced, and supplied while respecting the principle of customer orientation and the overall public well-being. These quality assurance activities involve market research, research and development, design, purchasing, production, inspection, and sales, as well as all other related activities inside and outside the company. Through everyone in the company understanding both statistical concepts and methods, through their application to all the aspects of quality assurance and through repeating the cycle of rational planning, implementation, evaluation, and action, CWQC aims to accomplish business objectives.[17]

The judging criteria consist of a checklist of 10 major categories as shown in Table 3.3. Each major category is divided into subcategories, or "checking points." For example, the policy category includes policies pursued for management, quality, and quality control; methods for establishing policies; appropriateness and consistency of policies; utilization of statistical methods; communication and dissemination of policies; checks of policies and the status of their achievement; and the relationship between policies and long- and short-term plans. Each category is weighted equally.

Table 3.3 The Deming Application Prize Checklist

Items	Checking Points
1. Policies	(1) Management, quality and quality control/management policies (2) Methods for establishing policies (3) Appropriateness and consistency of policies (4) Utilization of statistical methods (5) Communication and dissemination of policies (6) Checks on policies and status of their achievement (7) Their relationship to long- and short-term plans
2. The organization and its operations	(1) Clarity of authority and responsibility (2) Appropriateness of the delegation of authority (3) Interdepartmental coordination (4) Committee activities (5) Utilization of staff (6) Utilization of QC Circle activities (7) Quality control/management diagnosis
3. Education and dissemination	(1) Educational plan and results (2) Consciousness of quality and how it is managed, and understanding of quality control/management (3) Education on statistical concepts and methods and the degree to which they are disseminated (4) Grasp of effects (5) Education of associated companies (especially, group companies, vendors, contractors and distributors) (6) QC Circle activities (7) The system of improvement suggestions and its status
4. Information gathering, communication and its utilization	(1) Collection of external information (2) Interdepartmental communication (3) Speed of communication (utilization of computers) (4) Information processing, (statistical) analysis and utilization of information
5. Analysis	(1) Selection of important issues and improvement themes (2) Appropriateness of analytical methods (3) Utilization of statistical methods (4) Linkage with industry intrinsic technology (5) Quality analysis and process analysis (6) Utilization of analysis results (7) Action taken on improvement suggestions
6. Standardization	(1) System of standards (2) Methods of establishing, revising and abolishing standards (3) Actual performance in establishing, revising and abolishing standards (4) Contents of the standards (5) Utilization of statistical methods (6) Accumulation of technology (7) Utilization of standards
7. Control/management	(1) Management systems for quality and other related elements, such as cost and delivery (quantity) (2) Control points and control items (3) Utilization of statistical methods and concepts, such as control charts (4) Contributions of QC Circle activities (5) Status of control/management activities (6) In-control situations

Table 3.3 The Deming Application Prize Checklist *(continued)*

Items	Checking Points
8. Quality assurance	(1) New product and service development methods (quality deployment and analysis, reliability testing and design review) (2) Preventive activities for safety and product liability (3) Degree of customer satisfaction (4) Process design, process analysis and process control and improvement (5) Process capabilities (6) Instrumentation and inspection (7) Management of facilities, vendors, procurement and services (8) Quality assurance system and its diagnosis (9) Utilization of statistical methods (10) Quality evaluation and audit (11) Status of quality assurance
9. Effects	(1) Measurements of effects (2) Tangible effects such as quality, service, delivery, cost, profit, safety and environment (3) Intangible effects (4) Conformity of actual performance to planned effects
10. Future plans	(1) Concrete understanding of current situation (2) Measures for solving defect problems (3) Future promotion plans (4) Relationship between future plans and long-term plans

Source: Compiled by the Deming Application Prize Subcommittee, revised 1984. The Deming Prize Guide for Oversea Companies, Union of Japanese Scientists and Engineers, 1992.

Hundreds of companies apply for the award each year. After an initial application is accepted as eligible for the process, the company must submit a detailed description of its quality practices. Sorting through and evaluating a large number of applications is an extraordinary effort in itself. Based on review of the written descriptions, only a few companies believed to be successful in CWQC are selected for a site visit. The site visit consists of a company presentation, in-depth questioning by examiners, and an executive session with top managers. Examiners visit plants and are free to ask any worker any question. For example, at Florida Power and Light, the first non-Japanese company to win the Deming Prize, examiners asked questions of specific individuals such as, "What are your main accountabilities?" "What are the important priority issues for the corporation?" "What indicators do you have for your performance? For your target?" "How are you doing today compared to your target?" They request examples of inadequate performance. Documentation must be made available immediately. The preparation is extensive and sometimes frustrating.

The Deming Prize is awarded to all companies that meet the prescribed standard. However, the small number of awards given each year is an indication of the difficulty of achieving the standard. The objectives are to ensure that a company has so thoroughly deployed a quality process that it will continue to improve long after a prize is awarded. The application process has no "losers." For companies that do not qualify, the examination process is automatically extended up to two times over three years.

More than 150 companies have won a Deming Prize, including the seven largest Japanese industrial corporations. Some winners of the Deming Prize include Toyota

Motor Company, Ltd., NEC IC/Microcomputer Systems, Shimizu Construction Company, Ltd., and the Kansai Electric Power Company. Toyota has captured nearly 10 percent of the world's automotive market. NEC has earned a reputation for exceptional quality in a diverse set of electronics areas. Shimizu Construction is one of the top five construction firms in Japan and has entered the U.S. market by developing golf courses and condominium communities. Kansai Electric helped to bring recognition of total quality management into the service sector. Kansai offers electrical service at consistently low rates and has managed to shorten service interruptions significantly in comparison with other Japanese electric utilities. Kansai was the major benchmark firm for Florida Power and Light when it began to consider seriously making a bid for the prize. In addition to Florida Power and Light, three other firms outside of Japan have won the Deming prize: Sundaram-Clayton (see *Quality Profile*), AT&T's Power Systems Division (see the *Quality Profile* in Chapter 2), and Phillips Semiconductors in Taiwan.

Deming Prize winners are eligible for the Japan Quality Medal, which was established to encourage winners to continue practicing and enhancing their quality efforts. Since its inception in 1969, fewer than 20 companies have received it, as it demands sustained performance to rigorous standards over a five-year period. In 1998, Phillips Semiconductors in Taiwan was the first non-Japanese company to win the Japan Quality Medal.

Quality Profile

Sundaram-Clayton

Sundaram-Clayton (S-C) is a manufacturer of air-brake systems and castings, headquartered in Chennai, India, and is part of an Indian industrial group called TVS–Suzuki. S-C became India's first-ever winner of the Deming Prize for Overseas Companies. In discussing how and why S-C adopted a Japanese type of quality system, CEO Venu Srinivasan pointed to a long history of conformance to procedures, which was part of the culture of the firm. However, he also said that they developed their own unique approach, based on encouragement from their Japanese quality advisors. Srinivasan took over as CEO in 1977, after receiving his MBA from Purdue University. Applying his business school learning, he conducted an analysis of the company's strengths, weaknesses, opportunities, and threats, which revealed—to the company's horror—that a 90 percent market share was no insulation against top-class competition. Concluding that short-term tactics or defensive strategies could not deliver what a long-term transition to excellence could, Srinivasan set the company on the route to total quality.

The company identifies the critical issues three months ahead of each new financial year. The three most important issues are chosen and communicated to everyone in the company. Workers spend a minimum of 45 hours a year on classroom training, well above the industry average of 4 hours, starting with how and why to keep machines and the shop floor clean using the Japanese "5 Ss": seiri (clearing up), seiton (organizing), seiso (cleaning), seiketsu (standardizing), and shitsuke (training). They also learn to use quality problem-solving tools and implement them in small, self-managed teams. When S-C won the Deming Prize, sales per employee had increased three times over the prior year, and frame assembly line rejections had dropped from 12 percent to 0.5 percent over 10 years.

Source: India Today Web page, *http://www.india-today.com/btoday/22111998/cover.html.*

The Malcolm Baldrige National Quality Award

In Chapter 1 we noted that the Malcolm Baldrige National Quality Award has been one of the most powerful catalysts of total quality in the United States, and indeed, throughout the world. More importantly, the award's Criteria for Performance Excellence establish a framework for integrating total quality principles and practices in any organization. This framework provides the foundation for the next six chapters. In this section we present an overview of the Baldrige Award, its criteria, and the award process.

History and Purpose Recognizing that U.S. productivity was declining, President Reagan signed legislation mandating a national study and conference on productivity in October 1982. The American Productivity and Quality Center (formerly the American Productivity Center) sponsored seven computer networking conferences in 1983 to prepare for an upcoming White House Conference on Productivity. The final report on these conferences recommended that "a National Quality Award, similar to the Deming Prize in Japan, be awarded annually to those firms that successfully challenge and meet the award requirements. These requirements and the accompanying examination process should be very similar to the Deming Prize system to be effective." The Malcolm Baldrige National Quality Improvement Act was signed into law (Public Law 100-107) on August 20, 1987. The program focused on the following points:

- Helping to stimulate American companies to improve quality and productivity for the pride of recognition while obtaining a competitive edge through increased profits
- Recognizing the achievements of those companies that improve the quality of their goods and services and providing an example to others
- Establishing guidelines and criteria that can be used by business, industrial, governmental, and other enterprises in evaluating their own quality improvement efforts
- Providing specific guidance for other American enterprises that wish to learn how to manage for high quality by making available detailed information on how winning enterprises were able to change their cultures and achieve eminence.

The award is named after President Reagan's Secretary of Commerce, who was killed in an accident shortly before the Senate acted on the legislation. Malcolm Baldrige was highly regarded by world leaders, having played a major role in carrying out the administration's trade policy, resolving technology transfer differences with China and India, and holding the first Cabinet-level talks with the Soviet Union in seven years, which paved the way for increased access for U.S. firms in the Soviet market. Up to three companies can now receive an award in each of the original categories of manufacturing, small business, and service (prior to 1999, only two). Congress approved award categories in nonprofit education and health care in 1999. Table 3.4 shows the recipients through 2000.

The award has evolved into a comprehensive National Quality Program, administered through the National Institute of Standards and Technology in Gaithersburg, Maryland, of which the Baldrige Award is only one part. The National Quality Program is a public-private partnership, funded primarily through a private foundation. The program's Web site at *www.quality.nist.gov* provides current information about the award, the performance criteria, award winners, and a variety of other information.

The Criteria for Performance Excellence The award examination is based upon a rigorous set of criteria, called the *Criteria for Performance Excellence*, designed to

Table 3.4 Malcolm Baldrige Award Recipients

Year	Manufacturing	Small Business	Service
1988	Motorola, Inc. Westinghouse Commercial Nuclear Fuel Division	Globe Metallurgical, Inc.	
1989	Xerox Corp. Business Products and Systems Milliken & Co.		
1990	Cadillac Motor Car Division IBM Rochester	Wallace Co., Inc.	Federal Express (FedEx)
1991	Solectron Corp. Zytec Corp.	Marlow Industries	
1992	AT&T Network Systems Texas Instruments Defense Systems & Electronics Group	Granite Rock Co.	AT&T Universal Card Services The Ritz-Carlton Hotel Co.
1993	Eastman Chemical Co.	Ames Rubber Corp.	
1994		Wainwright Industries, Inc.	AT&T Consumer Communication Services GTE Directories, Inc.
1995	Armstrong World Industries Building Products Operations Corning Telecommunications Products Division		
1996	ADAC Laboratories	Custom Research Inc. Trident Precision Manufacturing, Inc.	Dana Commercial Credit Corp.
1997	3M Dental Products Division Solectron Corp.		Merrill Lynch Credit Corp. Xerox Business Services
1998	Boeing Airlift and Tanker Programs Solar Turbines, Inc.	Texas Nameplate Co.	
1999	STMicroelectronics, Inc.–Region Americas	Sunny Fresh Foods	BI The Ritz-Carlton Hotel Company, L.L.C.
2000	Dana Corporation–Spicer Driveshaft Division KARLEE Company	Los Alamos National Bank	Operations Management International, Inc.

encourage companies to enhance their competitiveness through an aligned approach to organizational performance management that results in:

1. Delivery of ever-improving value to customers, contributing to marketplace success
2. Improvement of overall organizational effectiveness and capabilities
3. Organizational and personal learning.

The criteria consist of a hierarchical set of categories, items, and areas to address. The seven categories are as follows:

1. *Leadership:* This category examines how an organization's senior leaders address values, direction, and performance expectations, as well as a focus on customers and other stakeholders, empowerment, innovation, and learning. Also examined is how an organization addresses its responsibilities to the public and supports its key communities.
2. *Strategic Planning:* This category examines how an organization develops strategic objectives and action plans. Also examined are how chosen strategic objectives and action plans are deployed and how progress is measured.
3. *Customer and Market Focus:* This category examines how an organization determines requirements, expectations, and preferences of customers and markets. Also examined is how the organization builds relationships with customers and determines the key factors that lead to customer acquisition, satisfaction, and retention and to business expansion.
4. *Information and Analysis:* This category examines an organization's information management and performance measurement systems and how the organization analyzes performance data and expansion.
5. *Human Resource Focus:* This category examines how an organization motivates and enables employees to develop and utilize their full potential in alignment with the organization's overall objectives and action plans. Also examined are the organization's efforts to build and maintain a work environment and an employee support climate conducive to performance excellence and to personal and organizational growth.
6. *Process Management:* This category examines the key aspects of an organization's process management, including customer-focused design, product and service delivery, key business, and support processes. This category encompasses all key processes and all work units.
7. *Business Results:* This category examines an organization's performance and improvement in key business areas—customer satisfaction, product and service performance, financial and marketplace performance, human resource results, and operational performance. Also examined are performance levels relative to those of competitors.

Both the 2000 and 2001 criteria can be found on the CD-rom accompanying this book; and they will be used in various cases and exercises in this book. We encourage you to read the entire document for clarifying notes and explanations. Also, slightly different versions of the criteria are written for education and health care, primarily to conform to unique language and practices in these sectors. Because the criteria are updated each year, we suggest that you obtain the current version. A single free copy of the criteria can be obtained from the National Institute of Standards and Technology. Write to the Baldrige National Quality Program, National Institute of Standards and Technology (NIST), Route 270 & Quince Orchard Road, Administration Building,

Room A635, 100 Bureau Drive, Stop 1020, Gaithersburg, MD 20899; call 301-975-2036, send a fax to 301-948-3716, e-mail to *nqp@nist.gov*; or download the criteria from the Web site (*http://www.quality.nist.gov/*).

The seven categories form an integrated management system as illustrated in Figure 3.6. The umbrella over the seven categories reflects the focus that organizations must have on customers through their strategy and action plans for all key decisions. Leadership, Strategic Planning, and Customer and Market Focus represent the "leadership triad," and suggest the importance of integrating these three functions. Human Resource Focus and Process Management represent how the work in an organization is accomplished and leads to Business Results. These functions are linked to the leadership triad. Finally, Information and Analysis supports the entire framework by providing the foundation for performance assessment and management by fact.

Each category consists of several *items* (numbered 1.1, 1.2, 2.1, etc.) that focus on major requirements on which businesses should focus. Each item, in turn, consists of a small number of *areas to address* (e.g., 6.1a, 6.1b) that seek specific information on approaches used to ensure and improve competitive performance, the deployment of these approaches, or results obtained from such deployment.

For example, the Leadership Category consists of two examination items and two areas to address (items with only one area to address have the same title):

1.1 Organizational Leadership
- *a. Senior Leadership Direction*
- *b. Organizational Performance Review*

Figure 3.6 Malcolm Baldrige National Quality Award Criteria Framework

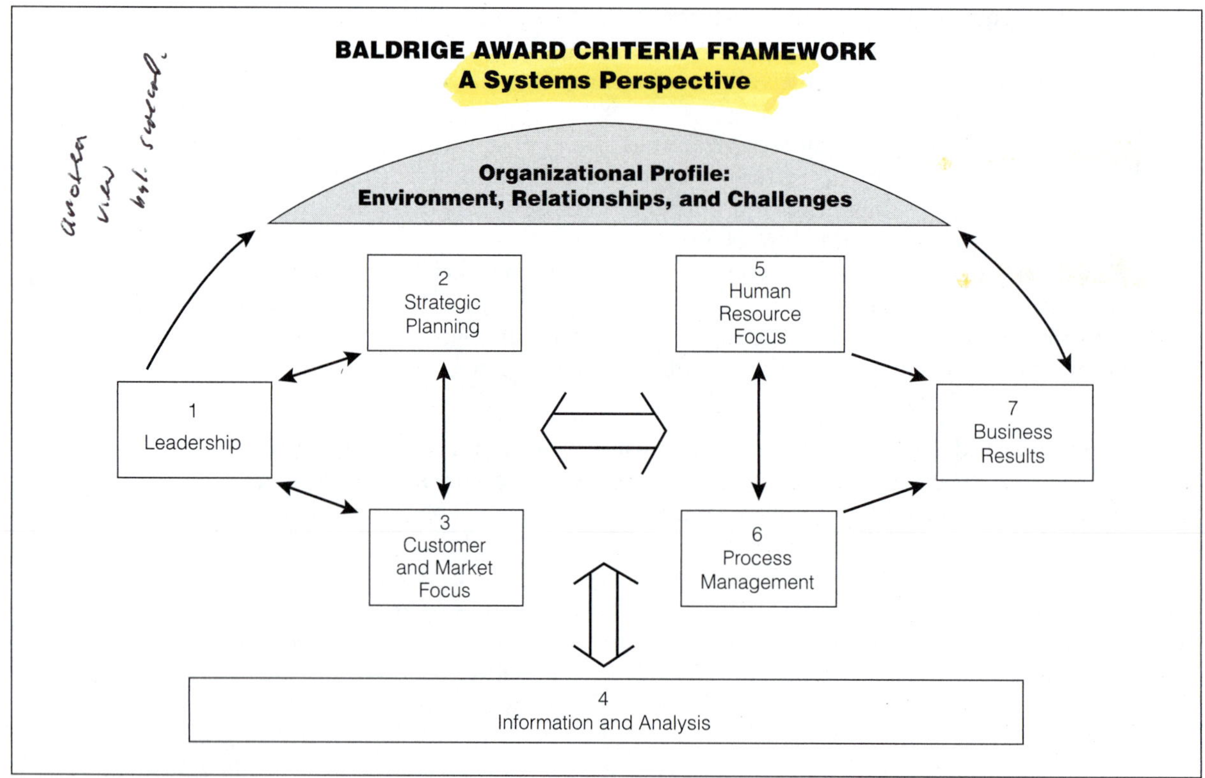

1.2 Public Responsibility and Citizenship
  a. Responsibilities to the Public
  b. Support of Key Communities

The Senior Leadership Direction area (2001 criteria) asks organizations to answer the following questions:

- How do senior leaders set and deploy organizational values, short- and longer-term directions, and performance expectations, including a focus on creating and balancing value for customers and other stakeholders? Include how senior leaders communicate values, directions, and expectations through your leadership system and to all employees.
- How do senior leaders create an environment for empowerment, innovation, organizational agility, and organizational and employee learning?

To illustrate how companies address these items in their applications, consider some of the information for the Leadership category provided by The Ritz-Carlton Hotel Company L.L.C. (see the *Quality in Practice* in Chapter 2 for basic information about the company) in its 1992 and 1999 applications (with a caveat that the scope of the criteria has changed substantially over the years).* When Horst Schulze became president in 1988, he and his leadership team personally took charge of managing for quality because they realized that managing for quality could not be delegated. They personally established the Gold Standards, which are the foundation of The Ritz-Carlton quality philosophy. The Gold Standards, in their simplicity, represent an easy-to-understand definition of service quality, and are aggressively communicated and internalized at all levels of the organization. The constant and continuous reinforcement techniques of the Gold Standards, led by senior leaders, include lectures at new employee orientation, developmental training, daily lineup meetings, administration of both positive and negative reinforcement, mission statements displayed, distribution of Credo cards, The Credo as first topic of internal meetings, and peer pressure. As a result, employees have an exceptional understanding and devotion to the company's vision, values, quality goals, and methods.

Since 1984, all members of senior leadership have personally ensured that each new hotel's goods and services are characteristic of The Ritz-Carlton on opening day. An important aspect of this quality practice takes place during the concentrated and intense "seven-day countdown" when senior leaders work side by side with new employees using a combination of hands-on behavior modeling and reinforcement. During these formative sessions, which all new employees must attend, the president and COO personally interacts with every new employee, both individually and in a group setting. The president personally creates the employee-guest interface image and facilitates each department's first vision statement. Throughout the entire process, the senior leaders monitor work areas for "start-up," instill Gold Standards, model the company's relationship management, insist upon 100 percent compliance to customers' requirements, and recognize outstanding achievement.

Senior leaders set direction through seven specific approaches:

10 Year Vision: To be The Premier Worldwide Provider of Luxury Travel and Hospitality Products and Services

*Adapted from The Ritz-Carlton Hotel Co. 1992 and 1999 Malcolm Baldrige National Quality Award application summaries. © 1992 The Ritz-Carlton Hotel Company. All rights reserved. Reprinted with the permission of The Ritz-Carlton Hotel Company, L.L.C.

5 Year Mission: Product and Profit Dominance
3 Year Objectives: The Vital Few Objectives
1 Year Tactics: Key Production and Business Processes
Strategy: Customer and Market Focus Strategy with Action Plans
Methods: TQM—Application of Quality Sciences; Malcolm Baldrige National Quality Award Criteria; *The GreenBook*—2d edition (the company's handbook of quality processes and tools)
Foundation: Values and Philosophy—The Gold Standards, Credo, Motto, Three Steps of Service, Basics, Employee Promise

Leadership effectiveness is evaluated on key questions of a semi-annual employee satisfaction survey and through audits on public responsibility. Gaps in leadership effectiveness are addressed with development and training plans and extensive use of developmental job assignments.

In the Baldrige criteria, areas to address that request information on approach or deployment begin with the word "how"; that is, they define a set of key actionable management practices. Thus, the Baldrige Award criteria define both an integrated infrastructure and a set of fundamental practices for a high-performance management system. One thing they do not do is prescribe specific quality tools, techniques, technologies, systems, or starting points, and are not associated with any one quality philosophy. Companies are encouraged to develop and demonstrate creative, adaptive, and flexible approaches to meeting basic requirements. Many innovative approaches have been developed by Baldrige winners and are now commonly used by many other companies. We will see many examples in the "Leading Practices" sections of subsequent chapters.

The Baldrige Award Evaluation Process Applicants for the award submit a 50-page application that addresses their management approaches in each category. Fictitious examples of applications written for examiner training are available on the book's CD-rom: Collin Technologies (1999), and Coyote Community College (2000), a case based on the education criteria.

The Baldrige evaluation process is rigorous, and designed to be objective and tamperproof against political pressures. In the first stage, each application is thoroughly reviewed by up to 10 examiners chosen from among leading quality professionals in business, academia, health care, and government (all of whom are volunteers). Examiners evaluate the applicant's response to each examination item, listing major "strengths" and "opportunities for improvement" relative to the criteria. Strengths demonstrate an effective and positive response to the criteria. Opportunities for improvement do not prescribe specific practices or examiners' opinions on what the company should be doing, but rather deficiencies in responding to the criteria. To help examiners understand the context of the organization, applicants are required to provide an *Organizational Profile*, which is basically a snapshot of the organization that describes the organizational environment; key relationships with customers, suppliers, and other partners; types of employees and technologies used; the competitive environment; key strategic challenges it faces; and its system for performance improvement. (Prior to 2001, this was called the Business or Organizational Overview.) The Organizational Profile helps the organization focus on key performance requirements and results, and helps examiners to understand the organization and what it considers important.

Based on the comments, a percentage score from 0 to 100 in increments of 10 is given to each item. Each examination item is evaluated on approach and deployment or results.

Approach refers to the methods the organization uses to achieve the requirements addressed in each category. The factors used to evaluate approaches include:

1. The appropriateness of the methods to the requirements
2. The effectiveness of methods, namely, the degree to which the approach is repeatable, integrated, and consistently applied; the degree to which the approach embodies evaluation/improvement/learning cycles; and is based on reliable information and data
3. Alignment with organizational needs
4. Evidence of innovation

Deployment refers to the extent to which the approaches are applied to all requirements of the item. The factors used to evaluate deployment include:

1. Use of the approach in addressing item requirements relevant to the organization
2. Use of the approach by all appropriate work units

Results refers to outcomes in achieving the purposes given in the item. The factors used to evaluate results include:

1. Current performance levels
2. Performance levels relative to appropriate comparisons and benchmarks
3. Rate and breadth of performance improvements
4. Linkage of results to important customer, market, process, and action plan performance requirements identified in the approach/deployment items and the Organizational Profile.

Table 3.5 summarizes the scoring guidelines.

Scores for each examination item are computed by multiplying the examiner's score by the maximum point value that can be earned (see Table 3.6). The scores are reviewed by a national panel of nine judges without knowledge of the specific companies. The higher scoring applications enter a *consensus stage* in which a selected group of examiners discuss variations in individual scores and arrive at consensus scores for each item. The panel of judges then reviews the scores and selects the highest scoring applicants for site visits. At this point, six or seven examiners visit the company for up to a week to verify information contained in the written application and resolve issues that are unclear. Final contenders each receive more than 1,000 hours of evaluation. The judges use the site visit reports to recommend award recipients to the Secretary of Commerce. All information is kept strictly confidential, and examiners are bound by conflict of interest rules and a code of conduct.

All applicants receive a feedback report that critically evaluates the company's strengths and areas for improvement relative to the award criteria. The feedback report, frequently 30 or more pages in length, contains the evaluation team's response to the written application. It includes a distribution of numerical scores of all applicants and a scoring summary of the individual applicant. This feedback is one of the most valuable aspects of applying for the award.

Criteria Evolution As the important management practices of any organization should be, the specific award criteria are evaluated and improved each year. Over the years, the criteria have been streamlined and simplified to make them more relevant and useful to organizations of all types and sizes. For example, the initial set of criteria in 1988 had 62 items with 278 areas to address. By 1991 the criteria had only 32 items and 99 areas to address. The 1995 criteria were reduced to 24 items and 54 areas

Table 3.5 Baldrige Award Scoring Guidelines

Score	Approach/Deployment
0%	• no systematic approach evident; anecdotal information
10% to 20%	• beginning of a systematic approach to the basic purposes of the Item • major gaps exist in deployment that would inhibit progress in achieving the basic purposes of the Item • early stages of a transition from reacting to problems to a general improvement orientation
30% to 40%	• a sound, systematic approach, responsive to the basic purposes of the Item • approach is deployed, although some areas or work units are in early stages of deployment • beginning of a systematic approach to evaluation and improvement of basic Item processes
50% to 60%	• a sound, systematic approach, responsive to the overall purposes of the Item • approach is well deployed, although deployment may vary in some areas or work units • a fact-based, systematic evaluation and improvement process is in place for basic Item processes • approach is aligned with basic organizational needs identified in the other Criteria Categories
70% to 80%	• a sound, systematic approach, responsive to the multiple requirements of the Item • approach is well deployed, with no significant gaps • a fact-based, systematic evaluation and improvement process and organizational learning/sharing are key management tools; clear evidence of refinement and improved integration as a result of organizational-level analysis and sharing • approach is well integrated with organizational needs identified in the other Criteria Categories
90% to 100%	• a sound, systematic approach, fully responsive to all the requirements of the Item • approach is fully deployed without significant weaknesses or gaps in any areas or work units • a very strong, fact-based, systematic evaluation and improvement process and extensive organizational learning/sharing are key manage ment tools; strong refinement and integration, backed by excellent organizational-level analysis and sharing • approach is fully integrated with organizational needs identified in the other Criteria Categories

to address. In 1997 further refinements to develop the shortest list of key requirements necessary to compete in today's marketplace, improve the linkage between process and results, and make the criteria more generic and user-friendly resulted in 20 items and 30 areas to address. In 1999, the criteria were reworded in a question format that managers can easily understand.

Most significantly, the word *quality* has been judiciously dropped in the mid-1990s. For example, prior to 1994, the Strategic Planning category had been titled "Strategic Quality Planning." The change to "Strategic Planning" signifies that qual-

Table 3.5 Baldrige Award Scoring Guidelines *(continued)*

Score	Results
0%	• no results or poor results in areas reported
10% to 20%	• some improvements *and/or* early good performance levels in a few areas • results not reported for many to most areas of importance to the organization's key business requirements
30% to 40%	• improvements *and/or* good performance levels in many areas of importance to the organization's key business requirements • early stages of developing trends and obtaining comparative information • results reported for many to most areas of importance to the organization's key business requirements
50% to 60%	• improvement trends *and/or* good performance levels reported for most areas of importance to the organization's key business requirements • no pattern of adverse trends and no poor performance levels in areas of importance to the organization's key business requirements • some trends *and/or* current performance levels—evaluated against relevant comparisons *and/or* benchmarks—show areas of strength *and/or* good to very good relative performance levels • business results address most key customer, market, and process requirements
70% to 80%	• current performance is good to excellent in areas of importance to the organization's key business requirements • most improvement trends *and/or* current performance levels are sustained • many to most trends *and/or* current performance levels—evaluated against relevant comparisons *and/or* benchmarks—show areas of leadership and very good relative performance levels • business results address most key customer, market, process, and action plan requirements
90% to 100%	• current performance is excellent in most areas of importance to the organization's key business requirements • excellent improvement trends *and/or* sustained excellent performance levels in most areas • evidence of industry and benchmark leadership demonstrated in many areas • business results fully address key customer, market, process, and action plan requirements

ity should be a part of business planning, not a separate issue. Throughout the document, the term *performance* has been substituted for *quality* as a conscious attempt to recognize that the principles of total quality are the foundation for a company's entire management system, not just the quality system. As Dr. Curt Reimann, former director and architect of the Baldrige Award Program noted, "The things you do to win a Baldrige Award are exactly the things you'd do to win in the marketplace. Our strategy is to have the Baldrige Award criteria be a useful daily tool that simulates real competition."

To this end, the most significant changes in the criteria reflect the maturity of business practices and total quality approaches. The criteria have evolved from a primary

Table 3.6 2001 Baldrige Award Items Point Values

2001 Categories/Items		Point Values
1	**Leadership**	**120**
	1.1 Organizational Leadership	80
	1.2 Public Responsibility and Citizenship	40
2	**Strategic Planning**	**85**
	2.1 Strategy Development	40
	2.2 Strategy Deployment	45
3	**Customer and Market Focus**	**85**
	3.1 Customer and Market Knowledge	40
	3.2 Customer Satisfaction and Relationships	45
4	**Information and Analysis**	**90**
	4.1 Measurement and Analysis of Organizational Performance	50
	4.2 Information Management	40
5	**Human Resource Focus**	**85**
	5.1 Work Systems	35
	5.2 Employee Education, Training, and Development	25
	5.3 Employee Well-Being and Satisfaction	25
6	**Process Management**	**85**
	6.1 Product and Service Processes	55
	6.2 Business Processes	15
	6.3 Support Processes	15
7	**Business Results**	**450**
	7.1 Customer Focused Results	125
	7.2 Financial and Market Results	125
	7.3 Human Resource Results	80
	7.4 Organizational Effectiveness Results	120
	Total Points	**1,000**

emphasis on product and service quality assurance in the late 1980s, to a broad focus on performance excellence in a global marketplace by the late 1990s. The improvements include the following shifts in emphasis:

- From quality assurance and strategic quality planning to a focus on process management and overall strategic planning
- From a focus on current customers to a focus on current and future customers and markets
- From human resource utilization to human resource development and management

- From supplier quality to supplier partnerships
- From individual quality improvement activities to cycles of evaluation and improvement in all key areas
- From data analysis of quality efforts to an aggregate, integrated organizational level review of key company data
- From results that focus on limited financial performance to a focus on a composite of business results, including customer satisfaction and financial, product, service, and strategic performance.

Using the Baldrige Criteria The Baldrige Award criteria form a model for business excellence in any organization—manufacturing or service, large or small. The former Texas Instruments Defense Systems & Electronics Group (see *Quality Profile*), for example, used the criteria to provide focus and coherence to the activities across the corporation.[18] They were able to tackle a part of total quality that previously had been unreachable: implementing quality efforts in staff, support, and nonmanufacturing areas. In 1989 TI asked every business unit to prepare a mock award application as a way of measuring its progress. This task represented a radical change for some operations because, until that time, most staff functions were not required to measure

Quality Profile

Texas Instruments Defense Systems & Electronics Group

Texas Instruments Defense Systems & Electronics Group (DSEG), now part of Raytheon Systems Co., achieved distinction in 1992 after receiving the Malcolm Baldrige National Quality Award. DSEG was a $2 billion Dallas-based maker of precision-guided weapons and other advanced defense technology. DSEG employed 15,000 people and operated 11 manufacturing, testing, research, and distribution facilities at sites located in North and Central Texas. The individuals who founded Texas Instruments created a culture in which people are valued and involved, ethics and integrity are more important than profit and loss, customer focus is stressed, individuals are recognized and rewarded, and technical innovators are prized as highly as skilled managers. Executives view quality as the best approach to accomplishing any objective—from increasing market share to controlling employee health care costs—and teams as the most effective means of executing the company's quality strategy. From a pilot group of four worker teams in 1983, a network of more than 1,900 DSEG teams had grown to link all units and levels, from top management to individual work teams.

Customers recognized the company's quality progress. A Navy evaluation of 17 missiles found TI-DSEG HARM and Shrike missiles to be the most reliable. Since 1986 more than 100 Texas Instrument processes and techniques were designated by the Navy as "best manufacturing practices," more than any other company. Formal customer complaints fell by 62 percent, and in an independent survey of 2,000 customers, the company topped its main competitors in all 11 customer satisfaction categories, ranging from cost-effective pricing and deployment of technology to product support. Since receiving the Baldrige Award, continuing quality efforts have reduced the number of in-process defects to one-tenth of their level in 1992. Processes that took four weeks now take only one week to perform, with cost improvements of 20 to 30 percent.

Sources: Malcolm Baldrige National Quality Award, Profiles of Winners, National Institute of Standards and Technology, Department of Commerce; Ann B. Rich, "Continuous Improvement: The Key to Future Success," *Quality Progress*, June 1997, 34.

their processes or their results. The Defense Systems & Electronics Group's self-assessment revealed that they were a long way from applying for and winning the Baldrige Award. But the group aggressively adopted the criteria as a blueprint for improving its business. Many executives did not believe that the criteria could be applied to defense contractors. Similarly, many executives today question whether small businesses can realistically meet the Baldrige Award criteria. TI discovered that all companies have one thing in common: customers. Focusing on customers to make the company more competitive provides meaning to the award. The Baldrige Award application process changed almost everything within the Defense Systems & Electronics Group. Before applying, the group had no way of systematically measuring how well it understood its customers' concerns, captured customers' feedback, or made improvements in interacting with customers. Mountains of data were being collected, but most of the data measured internal criteria, not customer satisfaction. The structured, hierarchical management environment made it difficult to adopt ideas from outside sources.

Many other types of organizations have used the criteria. For example, although the legal profession in general has not adopted quality management practices, the Trial Division of Nationwide Insurance, which operates 56 law offices in 20 states, uses the Baldrige model as a key component of its business plan. Senior leaders introduced it to the company's managing trial attorneys and encouraged individual offices to apply for local or state Baldrige-based awards.[19] The incorporation of education and health care as categories in the award program in 1999 was a reflection of the growing interest in these sectors. Many school districts, such as Hunterdon Central Regional School District and Brazosport Independent School District cited in Chapter 2 are using the criteria. One large Chicago-area hospital applied for the Baldrige-based Lincoln Award for Excellence and prepared for its accreditation visit by JCAHO at the same time, recognizing the synergy and overlap of Baldrige principles and JCAHO standards.

Many small businesses (defined as those with 500 or fewer employees) believe that the Baldrige criteria are too difficult to apply to their organizations because they cannot afford to implement the same types of practices as large companies. However, approaches to address the criteria requirements need not be formal or complex. For example, the ability to obtain customer and market knowledge through independent third party surveys, extensive interviews, and focus groups, which are common practices among large companies, may be limited by the resources of a small business. What is important, however, is whether the company is using appropriate mechanisms to gather information and use it to improve customer focus and satisfaction. Similarly, large corporations frequently have sophisticated computer information systems for data management, while small businesses may perform data and information management with a combination of manual methods and personal computers. Also, systems for employee involvement and process management may rely heavily on informal verbal communication and less on formal written documentation. Thus, the size or nature of a business does not affect the appropriateness of the criteria, but rather the context in which the criteria are applied.

Companies use the Baldrige criteria for self-assessment or internal recognition programs, even if they have no intention to apply for the award. The benefits of using the criteria for self-assessment include accelerating improvement efforts, energizing employees, and learning from feedback, particularly if external examiners are involved. For instance, Honeywell, Inc., uses it as a companywide framework for understanding, evaluating, and improving their business. Honeywell's mandate is to use the model for managing the business and engage senior management in an annual assessment process. This framework is used by general managers to exchange information, ask for help, and learn from each other.[20] Even the U.S. Postal Service has decided to use the Baldrige criteria as a basis to reestablish a quality system by identifying the areas that need the most improvement and providing a baseline to track progress. Using the award criteria as a self-assessment tool provides an objective framework, sets a high standard, and compares units that have different systems or organizations.

The approaches used for self-assessment vary. They may include simple questionnaires developed from the criteria, for which answers are compiled and used as a basis for an improvement plan; facilitated assessments in which key business leaders gather together to examine their organization against the criteria; and full written "applications" that are evaluated by trained internal and/or external examiners.[21] Assessments are often linked to the organization's strategic planning process, which serves as a means of implementing the opportunities for improvement that are identified through the process.

The Baldrige Criteria and the Deming Philosophy

It is no secret that W. Edwards Deming was not an advocate of the Baldrige Award.[22] (Joseph Juran, however, was highly influential in its development.) The competitive nature of the award is fundamentally at odds with Deming's teachings. However, many of Deming's principles are reflected directly or in spirit within the criteria. In fact, Zytec (see the *Quality Profile* earlier in this chapter), which implemented its total quality system around Deming's 14 Points, received a Baldrige Award.

Specific portions of the 2001 Baldrige Criteria that support each of Deming's 14 Points are summarized next.

1. *Statement of Purpose.* Strategy development requires a mission and vision. Commitment to aims and purposes by senior leaders is specifically addressed in the Leadership category and in enhancing customer satisfaction and relationships.
2. *Learn the New Philosophy.* Communication of values, expectations, customer focus, and learning is a key area of the Organizational Leadership item.
3. *Understand Inspection.* The Process Management category addresses the development of appropriate measurement plans. In the Support Process item, the criteria seek evidence of how a company aims to minimize the costs associated with inspection.
4. *End Price Tag Decisions.* This point is implicitly addressed throughout the Process Management category and in the criteria's emphasis on overall performance and linkages among processes and results.
5. *Improve Constantly.* Continuous improvement through organizational and personal learning and innovation are core values of the criteria. The criteria specifically seek "how do you keep your [processes for . . .] current with business needs and directions" throughout.
6. *Institute Training.* Item 5.2, Employee Education, Training, and Development, recognizes the importance of training and employee development in meeting performance objectives.
7. *Teach and Institute Leadership.* Category 1 is devoted exclusively to leadership, and it is recognized as the principal driver of the management system in Figure 3.6.
8. *Drive Out Fear and Innovate.* The Human Resource Focus, Customer and Market Focus, and Strategic Planning categories focus on work design, empowerment, and implementation issues that support this point.

9. *Optimize the Efforts of Teams and Staff.* The criteria have a significant focus on teamwork and customer knowledge in product/process design and process management, as well as in the Human Resource Focus category.
10. *Eliminate Exhortations.* While not directly addressed, the focus on work and job design as the driver of high performance makes it a moot point.
11. *Eliminate Quotas and MBO; Institute Improvement, and Understand Processes.* The Organizational Leadership and Strategy Development items, as well as the Information and Analysis and Process Management categories deal with fact-based management and understanding processes.
12. *Remove Barriers.* The Leadership and Human Resource Focus categories, as well as the Customer Satisfaction and the Relationships items support this goal.
13. *Encourage Education.* This point is addressed directly in the Employee Education, Training, and Development and Employee Well-Being and Satisfaction items.
14. *Take Action.* This role of leadership is addressed directly in the Leadership category.

The consistencies among Deming's 14 Points and the Baldrige Criteria attest to the universal nature of quality management principles.

Other Quality Award Programs

Most states in the United States, as well as the federal government, have developed award programs similar to the Baldrige Award. The President's Quality Award (PQA) program recognizes federal organizations for continuous improvement through the application of quality management principles. The PQA has two award levels:

- The Presidential Award for Quality is presented to organizations that demonstrate mature approaches to quality that are well-deployed, and have documented world-class results and sustained improvement.
- The Award for Quality Improvement is given to organizations that demonstrate beginnings of good approaches and early positive results.

From 1989 through 1999, only eight organizations have received the Presidential Award for Quality. Information about the program is available at *www.opm.gov/quality*.

State award programs generally are designed to promote an awareness of productivity and quality, foster an information exchange, encourage firms to adopt quality and productivity improvement strategies, recognize firms that have instituted successful strategies, provide role models for other businesses in the state, encourage new industry to locate in the state, and establish a quality-of-life culture that will benefit all residents of the state.[23] Each state is unique, however, and thus the specific objectives will vary. For instance, the primary objectives of Minnesota's quality award are to encourage all Minnesota organizations to examine their current state of quality and to become more involved in the movement toward continuous quality improvement, as well as to recognize outstanding quality achievements in the state. Missouri, on the other hand, has as its objectives to educate all Missourians in quality improvement, to foster the pursuit of quality in all aspects of Missouri life, and to recognize quality leadership. Other states, such as Tennessee and Ohio, use their award programs to provide developmental advice to organizations just starting on their quality journey. Information and links to state award programs can be found at the Baldrige Award Web site.

In addition, numerous countries and regions of the world have established awards and award criteria that are based on the Baldrige Award, as shown in Figure 3.7. We highlight some of them next.

Figure 3.7 Countries With Quality Awards Around the World

European Quality Award In October 1991 the European Foundation for Quality Management (EFQM) in partnership with the European Commission and the European Organization for Quality announced the creation of the European Quality Award. The award was designed to increase awareness throughout the European Community, and businesses in particular, of the growing importance of quality to their competitiveness in the increasingly global market and to their standards of life. The European Quality Award consists of two parts: the European Quality Prize, given to companies that demonstrate excellence in quality management practice by meeting the award criteria, and the European Quality Award, awarded to the most successful applicant. In 1992 four prizes and one award were granted for the first time.

Applicants must demonstrate that their TQ approach has contributed significantly to satisfying the expectations of customers, employees, and other constituencies. The award process is similar to the Deming Prize and Baldrige Award. The assessment is based on customer satisfaction, business results, processes, leadership, people satisfaction, resources, people management, policy and strategy, and impact on society. Figure 3.8 shows the integrated management framework for the European

Figure 3.8 European Quality Award Framework

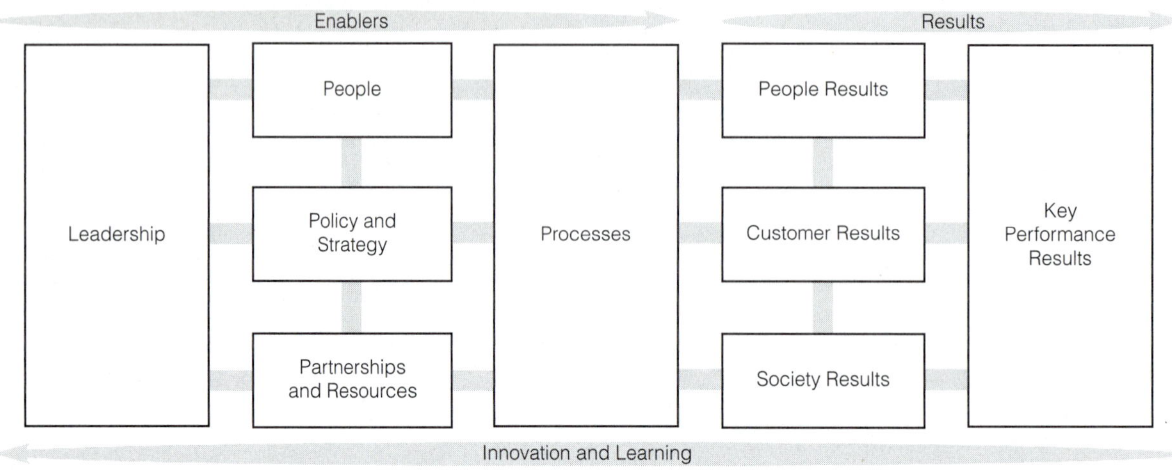

Source: Used with permission of EFQA. © EFQM, 1999. The EFQM Excellence Model is a registered trademark.

Quality Award, now known as the Business Excellence Model.[24] Like Baldrige, results—including customer, people (employee), and society results—constitute a high percentage of the total score. Results are driven by "Enablers," the means by which an organization approaches its business responsibilities, and a foundation of innovation and learning. The categories are roughly equivalent to those in Baldrige. However, the results criteria of people satisfaction, customer satisfaction, impact on society, and business results are somewhat different.[25] The impact on society results category focuses on the perceptions of the company by the community at large and the company's approach to the quality of life, the environment, and the preservation of global resources. The European Quality Award criteria place greater emphasis on this category than is placed on the public responsibility item in the Baldrige Award criteria. Sixteen countries participate in the award program. Recent winners include Yellow Pages (UK), Volvo Cars–Gent (Belgium), Danish International Continuing Education (Denmark), and Servitique Network Services (France).

Canadian Awards for Business Excellence Canada's National Quality Institute (NQI) recognizes Canada's foremost achievers of excellence through the prestigious Canada Awards for Excellence. NQI is a nonprofit organization designed to stimulate and support quality-driven innovation within all Canadian enterprises and institutions, including business, government, education, and health care. The Canadian Awards for Business Excellence quality criteria are similar in structure to the Baldrige Award criteria, with some key differences. The major categories and items within each category follow:

1. *Leadership:* strategic direction, leadership involvement, and outcomes
2. *Customer focus:* voice of the customer, management of customer relationships, measurement, and outcomes
3. *Planning for improvement:* development and content of improvement plan, assessment, and outcomes

4. *People focus:* human resource planning, participatory environment, continuous learning environment, employee satisfaction, and outcomes
5. *Process optimization:* process definition, process control, process improvement, and outcomes
6. *Supplier focus:* partnering and outcomes

These categories seek similar information to the Baldrige Award criteria. For example, the people focus category examines the development of human resource planning and implementation and operation of a strategy for achieving excellence through people. It also examines the organization's efforts to foster and support an environment that encourages and enables people to reach their full potential. Recipients of Canada's top quality award include Ford Electronics Manufacturing Corporation and the Toronto Manufacturing Plant of IBM Canada.

Australian Business Excellence Award The Australian Quality Awards (now called Business Excellence Award) were developed independently from the Baldrige Awards in 1988. The Awards are administered by the Australian Quality Awards Foundation, a subsidiary of the Australian Quality Council. Four levels of awards are given.

1. *The Business Improvement Level:* encouragement recognition for "Progress Toward Business Excellence" or "Foundation in Business Excellence"
2. *The Award Level:* representing Australian best practices; recognition as a Winner or Finalist
3. *The Award Gold Level:* open only to former Award winners; represents a revalidation and ongoing improvement
4. *The Australian Business Excellence Prize:* open only to former Award winners; represents international best practices evident throughout the organization

The assessment criteria address leadership, strategy and planning, information and knowledge, people, customer focus, processes, products and services, and busi-

Figure 3.9 Australian Business Excellence Model

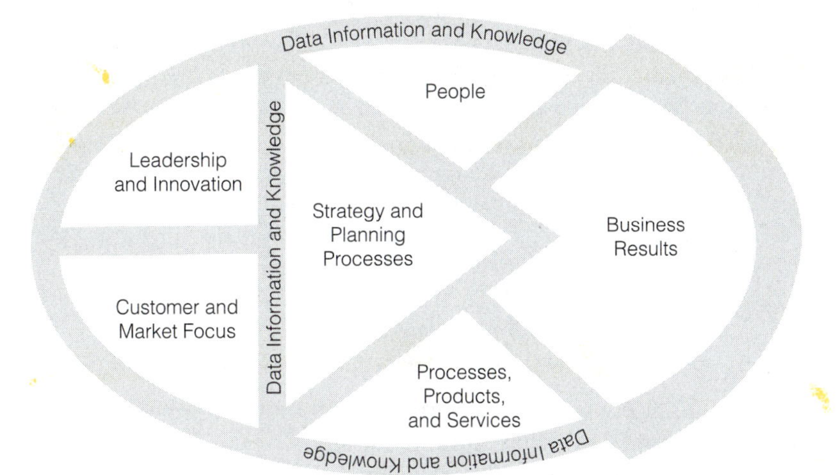

Source: The Australian Business Excellence Model is used with permission of the Australian Quality Council. *http://www.aqc.org.au.*

ness results within the framework shown in Figure 3.9. In this model, leadership and customer focus are the drivers of the management system and enablers of performance. Strategy, policy and planning, information and analysis, and people are the key internal components of the management system. Quality of process, product, and service is focused on how work is done to achieve the required results and obtain improvement. Business results are the outcome of the management system—a results category. As with Baldrige, the framework emphasizes the holistic and interconnected nature of the management process. The criteria are benchmarked with the Baldrige criteria and the European Business Excellence Model. One of the distinctive aspects of Australia's program is solid union support.

The 1999 winners were Britax Rainsfords of South Australia, an automotive parts manufacturer; Noyce Lawyers, a legal firm in a suburb of Sydney; and Southern Pathology. Previous recipients include Abbot International division of Abbot Australasia Pty Ltd., BHP Research, the Wesley Hospital, Ericcson Australia Pty Ltd., ICI Pharmaceuticals, Integral Energy, Ford Motor Company of Australia Limited, Avis Australia; Ford Motor Company Plastics Plant, the TVS Partnership Proprietary, Limited (see case study in Chapter 6) and Toyota Motor Corporation Australia Limited.

ISO 9000:2000

As quality became a major focus of businesses throughout the world, various organizations developed standards and guidelines. Terms such as *quality management*, *quality control*, *quality system*, and *quality assurance* acquired different, sometimes conflicting meanings from country to country, within a country, and even within an industry.[26] As the European Community moved toward the European free trade agreement, which went into effect at the end of 1992, quality management became a key strategic objective. To standardize quality requirements for European countries within the Common Market and those wishing to do business with those countries, a specialized agency for standardization, the International Organization for Standardization (ISO), founded in 1947 and composed of representatives from the national standards bodies of 130 nations, adopted a series of written quality standards in 1987. They were revised in 1994, and again (significantly) in 2000. The most recent version is called the **ISO 9000:2000** family of standards.

ISO took a unique approach in adopting the "ISO" prefix in naming the organization and standards. "ISO" is not an acronym; otherwise the organization would be called "IOS." *Iso* is a scientific term derived from the Greek *isos*, meaning equal (as in isotherm lines on a weather map, which show equal temperatures). Thus, organizations certified under the ISO 9000 standard are assured to have quality equal to their peers. The standards have been adopted in the United States by the American National Standards Institute (ANSI) with the endorsement and cooperation of the American Society for Quality (ASQ). The standards are recognized by about 100 countries, including Japan.

ISO 9000 defines *standards* as documented agreements containing technical specifications or other precise criteria to be used consistently as rules, guidelines, or definitions of characteristics, to ensure that materials, products, processes, and services are fit for their purpose. The standards were created to meet five objectives:

1. Achieve, maintain, and seek to continuously improve product quality (including services) in relationship to requirements.
2. Improve the quality of operations to continually meet customers' and stakeholders' stated and implied needs.
3. Provide confidence to internal management and other employees that quality requirements are being fulfilled and that improvement is taking place.

4. Provide confidence to customers and other stakeholders that quality requirements are being achieved in the delivered product.
5. Provide confidence that quality system requirements are fulfilled.

The standards prescribe documentation for all processes affecting quality and suggest that compliance through auditing leads to continuous improvement. The standards are intended to apply to all types of businesses, including electronics and chemicals, and to services such as health care, banking, and transportation. In some foreign markets, companies will not buy from suppliers who are not certified to the standards. For example, many products sold in Europe, such as telecommunication terminal equipment, medical devices, gas appliances, toys, and construction products require product certifications to assure safety. Often, ISO certification is necessary to obtain product certification. Thus, meeting these standards is becoming a requirement for international competitiveness.

Structure of the ISO 9000:2000 Standards

The ISO 9000:2000 standards consist of four primary standards:

- ISO 9000: Quality Management Systems—Fundamentals and Vocabulary
- ISO 9001: Quality Management Systems—Requirements
- ISO 9004: Quality Management Systems—Guidance for Performance Improvement
- ISO 19011: Guidelines on Quality and Environmental Auditing

ISO 9000 provides definitions of key terms. ISO 9001 provides a set of minimum requirements for a quality management system, and is intended to demonstrate compliance with recognized quality principles to customers and for third-party certification. ISO 9004 focuses on improving the quality management system beyond these minimum requirements.

The original ISO 9000:1994 series standards consisted of 20 elements of a quality system; the ISO 9000:2000 standards structure 21 elements into four major sections: Management Responsibility; Resource Management; Product Realization; and Measurement, Analysis, and Improvement, as shown in Table 3.7.[27] These four sections describe the four phases of a fundamental concept (based on the Quality Management Principles) for the new standards referred to as the *Process Model*.

To illustrate the changes in the scope of the ISO 9001 requirements, consider number 5, Management Responsibility, which was a component of the previous standards. The old standards used to simply require that:

- The company establishes, documents, and publicizes its policy, objectives, and commitment to quality. (Same as new items 5.1 and 5.3 in Table 3.7.)
- The company designates a representative with authority and responsibility for implementing and maintaining the requirements of the standard. (Same as new items 5.5.2 and 5.5.3.)
- The company provides adequate resources for managing, performing work, and verifying activities including internal quality audits. (Same as new item 5.4.)
- The company conducts in-house verification and review of the quality system. These reviews should consider the results of internal quality audits, management effectiveness, defects and irregularities, solutions to quality problems, implementation of past solutions, handling of nonconforming product, results of statistical scorekeeping tools, and the impact of quality methods on actual results. (Same as new items 5.5.4, 5.5.5, 5.5.6, 5.5.7, and 5.6.)

Table 3.7 ISO 9000:2000 Requirements

1 Scope
- 1.1 General
- 1.2 Permissible exclusions

2 Normative references

3 Terms and definitions

4 Quality management system
- 4.1 General requirements
- 4.2 General documentation requirements

5 Management responsibility
- 5.1 Management commitment
- 5.2 Customer focus
- 5.3 Quality policy
- 5.4 Planning
  - 5.4.1 Quality objectives
  - 5.4.2 Quality planning
- 5.5 Administration
  - 5.5.1 General
  - 5.5.2 Responsibility and authority
  - 5.5.3 Management representative
  - 5.5.4 Internal communication
  - 5.5.5 Quality Manual
  - 5.5.6 Control of documents
  - 5.5.7 Control of quality records
- 5.6 Management review
  - 5.6.1 Review input
  - 5.6.2 Review output

6 Resource management
- 6.1 Provision of resources
- 6.2 Human resources
  - 6.2.1 Assignment of personnel
  - 6.2.2 Training, awareness, and competency
- 6.3 Facilities
- 6.4 Work environment

7 Product realization
- 7.1 Planning of realization processes
- 7.2 Customer-related processes
  - 7.2.1 Identification of customer requirements
  - 7.2.2 Review of product requirements
  - 7.2.3 Customer communication
- 7.3 Design and/or development
  - 7.3.1 Design and/or development planning
  - 7.3.2 Design and/or development inputs
  - 7.3.3 Design and/or development outputs
  - 7.3.4 Design and/or development review
  - 7.3.5 Design and/or development verification
  - 7.3.6 Design and/or development validation
  - 7.3.7 Control of design and/or development changes
- 7.4 Purchasing
  - 7.4.1 Purchasing control
  - 7.4.2 Purchasing information
  - 7.4.3 Verification of purchased products
- 7.5 Production and service operations
  - 7.5.1 Operations control
  - 7.5.2 Identification and traceability
  - 7.5.3 Customer property
  - 7.5.4 Preservation of product
  - 7.5.5 Validation of processes
- 7.6 Control of measuring and monitoring devices

8 Measurement, analysis and improvement
- 8.1 Planning
- 8.2 Measurement and monitoring
  - 8.2.1 Customer satisfaction
  - 8.2.2 Internal audit
  - 8.2.3 Measurement and monitoring of processes
  - 8.2.4 Measurement and monitoring of product
- 8.3 Control of nonconformity
- 8.4 Analysis of data
- 8.5 Improvement
  - 8.5.1 Planning for continual improvement
  - 8.5.2 Corrective action
  - 8.5.3 Preventive action

Under the new standards, management has the responsibility for all of the above, plus several new responsibilities as listed in Table 3.7. In general, the revised standards place increased focus on top management commitment and customer satisfaction, organizational processes, and continual improvement.

Factors Leading to ISO 9000:2000

The original standards and the 1994 revision met with considerable controversy.[28] The standards only required that the organization have a documented, verifiable, process in place to ensure that it consistently produces what it says it will produce. A company could comply with the standards and still produce a poor-quality product—as long as it does so consistently! Dissatisfaction with ISO 9000 resulted in the European Union calling for a deemphasis of ISO 9000 registration, citing the fact that companies are more concerned with "passing a test" than on focusing their energies on quality processes. The Australian government stopped requiring ISO 9000 registration for government contracts. The Australian *Business Review Weekly* noted that "its reputation among small and medium businesses continues to deteriorate. Some small businesses have almost been destroyed by the endeavor to implement costly and officious quality assurance ISO 9000 systems that hold little relevance to their businesses."

The deficiencies in the old ISO 9000 standards led to a joint effort in 1994 by the Big Three automobile manufacturers—Ford, Chrysler, and General Motors—as well as several truck manufacturers, to develop QS-9000, an interpretation and extension of ISO 9000 for automotive suppliers. The goal was to develop fundamental quality systems that provide for continuous improvement, emphasizing defect prevention and the reduction of variation and waste in the supply chain. QS-9000 is based on ISO 9000 and includes all ISO requirements. However, QS-9000 goes well beyond the 1994 ISO 9000 standards by including additional requirements such as continuous improvement, manufacturing capability, and production part approval processes.

Many of the concepts in the Baldrige criteria are reflected in QS-9000.[29] For example, QS included requirements that suppliers have a formal, documented, comprehensive business plan and to develop both short- and longer-term goals and plans based on the analysis of competitive products and benchmarking information, and to revise and review the plan appropriately; methods to determine current and future customer expectations along with an objective and valid process to collect the information, and a process for determining customer satisfaction; and document trends in quality, customer satisfaction and dissatisfaction, operational performance (productivity, efficiency, and effectiveness, and current quality levels for key product and service features), and compare them with those of competitors and/or appropriate benchmarks to measure progress toward overall business objectives. The wording is almost identical to that found in the Baldrige Award criteria.

In addition, registration to QS-9000 requires demonstration of effectiveness in meeting the intent of the standards, rather than simply the "do it as you document it" philosophy. For instance, while ISO 9000 requires "suitable maintenance of equipment to ensure continuing process capability" under process control, QS-9000 requires suppliers to identify key process equipment and provide appropriate resources for maintenance, and to develop an effective, planned total preventive maintenance system. The system should include a procedure that describes the planned maintenance activities, scheduled maintenance, and predictive maintenance methods. Also, extensive requirements for documenting process monitoring, operator instructions, process capability, and performance requirements are built into the standards.

ISO 9000:2000 is a response to the widespread dissatisfaction that resulted from the old standards. The new standards have a completely new structure, based on eight principles—"comprehensive and fundamental rules or beliefs for leading and operating an organization" that reflect the basic principles of total quality that we introduced in Chapter 1, and many of the core values and concepts of the Baldrige and European Quality Award criteria. These eight principles were voted on, and overwhelmingly approved, at a conference in 1997 attended by 36 representatives of countries that have delegates in the TC 176 technical committee, charged with the responsibility of revising the ISO 9000 standards.[30] The principles and their explanations as defined by ISO are shown in Table 3.8, along with how they should be interpreted.

With this underlying philosophy, the ISO 9000:2000 revision aligns much closer to the performance excellence concept of Baldrige. For example,

Table 3.8 ISO 9000:2000 Quality Management Principles

Principle 1: Customer Focus
Organizations depend on their customers and therefore should understand current and future customer needs, should meet customer requirements, and strive to exceed customer expectations.

Principle 2: Leadership
Leaders establish unity of purpose and direction of the organization. They should create and maintain the internal environment in which people can become fully involved in achieving the organization's objectives.

Principle 3: Involvement of People
People at all levels are the essence of an organization and their full involvement enables their abilities to be used for the organization's benefit.

Principle 4: Process Approach
A desired result is achieved more efficiently when activities and related resources are managed as a process.

Principle 5: System Approach to Management
Identifying, understanding, and managing interrelated processes as a system contributes to the organization's effectiveness and efficiency in achieving its objectives.

Principle 6: Continual Improvement
Continual improvement of the organization's overall performance should be a permanent objective of the organization.

Principle 7: Factual Approach to Decision Making
Effective decisions are based on the analysis of data and information.

Principle 8: Mutually Beneficial Supplier Relationships
An organization and its suppliers are interdependent and a mutually beneficial relationship enhances the ability of both to create value.

Source: http://www.iso.ch/9000e/QMP.html. Used with permission.

- Organizations now need a process to determine customer needs and expectations, translate them in to internal requirements, and measure customer satisfaction and dissatisfaction.
- Managers must communicate the importance of meeting customer and regulatory requirements, integrate ISO 9000 into business plans, set measurable objectives, and conduct management reviews. No longer can top management delegate the program to people lower in the organization.
- Organizations now must view work as a process and manage a system of interrelated processes. This revision is significantly different from the "document what you do" requirements of earlier versions.
- Analysis now needs to be done to provide information about customer satisfaction and dissatisfaction, products, and processes with the focus on improvement.
- Evaluation of training effectiveness and making personnel aware of the importance of their activities in meeting quality objectives.
- In the previous standards, organizations were required to perform corrective and preventive action, but now must have a planned process for improvement.[31]

Implementation and Registration

Implementing ISO 9000 is not an easy task.[32] The ISO 9000 standards originally were intended to be advisory in nature and to be used for two-party contractual situations (between a customer and supplier) and for internal auditing. However, they quickly evolved into criteria for companies who wished to "certify" their quality management or achieve "registration" through a third-party auditor, usually a laboratory or some other accreditation agency (called a registrar). This process began in the United Kingdom. Rather than a supplier being audited for compliance to the standards by each customer, the registrar certifies the company, and this certification is accepted by all of the supplier's customers.

The registration process includes document review by the registrar of the quality system documents or quality manual; preassessment, which identifies potential noncompliance in the quality system or in the documentation; assessment by a team of two or three auditors of the quality system and its documentation; and surveillance, or periodic reaudits to verify conformity with the practices and systems registered. During the assessment, auditors might ask such questions as (using *Management responsibility* as an example): Does a documented policy on quality exist? Have management objectives for quality been defined? Have the policy and objectives been transmitted and explained to all levels of the organization? Have job descriptions for people who manage or perform work affecting quality been documented? Are descriptions of functions that affect quality available? Has management designated a person or group with the authority to prevent nonconformities in products, identify and record quality problems, and recommend solutions? What means are used to verify the solutions?[33]

Recertification is required every three years. Individual sites—not entire companies—must achieve registration individually. All costs are borne by the applicant, so the process can be quite expensive. A registration audit may cost anywhere from $10,000 to more than $40,000 while the internal cost for documentation and training may exceed $100,000.

Perspectives on ISO 9000

Although the 2000 revision of ISO 9000 has incorporated many of the principles that the Baldrige criteria have had since its inception, it still is not a comprehensive business performance framework. Meeting the standards provides no assurance that defective or unsafe products will be provided, as the Bridgestone/Firestone recall of 6.5 million tires in August 2000 showed—the tire manufacturing plant was QS-9000 certified. (The recall was a result of numerous injuries and fatalities that resulted from the tire tread separation, causing accidents or rollovers in many sport utility vehicles.) Certification only examines compliance to a quality management system, and registrars issue indemnification clauses as part of their contracts with QS-9000 customers to ensure they are not held liable for product outcomes. Nevertheless, ISO 9000 provides a set of good basic practices for initiating a quality system, and is an excellent starting point for companies with no formal quality assurance program. Organizations as diverse as schools, real estate agencies, blood centers, and ski resorts have achieved ISO certification. In fact, it provides more detailed guidance on process and product control than Baldrige. Thus, for companies in the early stages of developing a quality program, the standards enforce the discipline of control that is necessary before they can seriously pursue continuous improvement. The requirements of periodic audits reinforce the stated quality system until it becomes ingrained in the company.

Many organizations have realized significant benefits from ISO 9000. At DuPont, for example, ISO 9000 has been credited with increasing on-time delivery from 70 to

90 percent, decreasing cycle time from 15 days to 1.5 days, increasing first-pass yields from 72 to 92 percent, and reducing the number of test procedures by one-third. Sun Microsystems' Milpitas plant was certified in 1992, and managers believe that it has helped deliver improved quality and service to customers.[34] In Canada, Toronto Plastics, Ltd. reduced defects from 150,000 per million to 15,000 per million after one year of ISO implementation.[35] The first home builder to achieve registration, Michigan-based Delcor Homes, reduced its rate for correctable defects from 27.4 to 1.7 in two years and improved its building experience approval rating from the mid 60s to the mid 90s on a 100-point scale.[36] Thus, using ISO 9000 as a basis for a quality system can improve productivity, decrease costs, and increase customer satisfaction. Current information can be obtained from the following Web sites:

- The ISO Web site (*http://www.iso.ch*), which carries general information regarding the ISO 9001:2000 and ISO 9004:2000 revision program.
- ISO/TC176 Web site (*http://www.tc176.org*), which includes general information on the structure and work program of ISO/TC176 including links to related password-protected and public Web sites.
- ISO/TC176/SC 2 Web site (*http://www.bsi.org.uk/iso-tc176-sc2*), which carries detailed information on the ISO 9001/9004 revision program, updated on a regular basis.

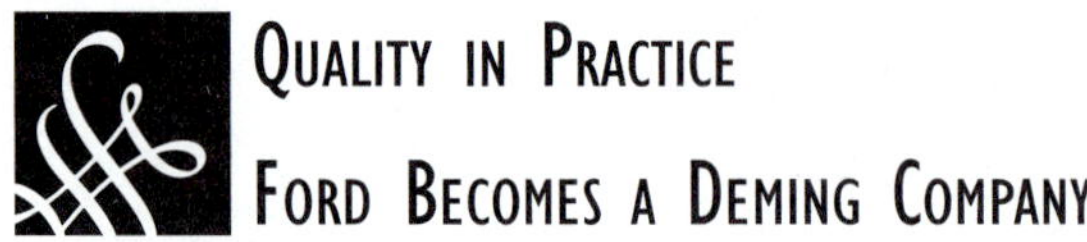

Quality in Practice

Ford Becomes a Deming Company

Ford Motor Company has been one of the leaders in adopting the Deming philosophy. Dr. Deming came to Ford in 1981 to meet with President Donald Petersen and other company officials, who were stimulated by NBC's program "If Japan Can . . . Why Can't We?" Actually, or so the story goes, Deming was first approached by one of Ford's vice presidents. Deming's response was that he would not come unless invited by the CEO as an indication of top management commitment.

Deming began by giving seminars for top executives and meeting with various employees, suggesting changes corresponding to his 14 Points. Ford managers visited Nashua Corporation to learn how statistical methods were used. Chief executives from many of Ford's major suppliers visited Japan. Petersen himself took a course on statistical methods. The 14 Points became the basis for a transformation of Ford's philosophy. Management commitment is evident in statements found in various annual reports:

> *Last year [1982] we pledged our efforts to continuous improvement. . . . We renew that pledge. In product, this means unqualified commitment to customer-response excellence worldwide . . . we made quality our No. 1 objective several years ago. We have achieved steady and substantial quality improvement in the United States, where Ford now leads its major domestic competition. . . . Ford's quality goals also include leadership in customer service. . . . Our key to continued success in the quest for product quality is establishing an effective long-term relationship with our suppliers. . . . Ford is involving suppliers far earlier in the design process. . . . This helps reduce engineering and production costs and ensures uninterrupted improvement in quality. Ford has instituted a system that makes quality considerations a critical factor in every supplier-selection decision and establishes formal quality ratings for every supplier. The Q1 Preferred Quality Award recognizes suppliers who achieve and maintain a consistently high level of quality and prove their commitment to continuing improvement. (Ford Motor Company 1983 Annual Report)*

Company Mission, Values, and Guiding Principles

Mission

Ford Motor Company is a worldwide leader in automotive and automotive-related products and services as well as in newer industries such as aerospace, communications, and financial services. Our mission is to improve continually our products and services to meet our customers' needs, allowing us to prosper as a business and to provide a reasonable return for our stockholders, the owners of our business.

Values

How we accomplish our mission is as important as the mission itself. Fundamental to success for the company are these basic values:

- *People. Our people are the source of our strength. They provide our corporate intelligence and determine our reputation and vitality. Involvement and teamwork are our core human values.*
- *Products. Our products are the end result of our efforts, and they should be the best in serving customers worldwide. As our products are viewed, so are we viewed.*
- *Profits. Profits are the ultimate measure of how efficiently we provide customers with the best products for their needs. Profits are required to survive and grow.*

Guiding Principles

- *Quality comes first. To achieve customer satisfaction, the quality of our products and services must be our number one priority.*
- *Customers are the focus of everything we do. Our work must be done with customers in mind, providing better products and services than our competition.*
- *Continuous improvement is essential to our success. We must strive for excellence in everything we do; in our products, in their safety and value—and in our services, our human relations, our competitiveness and our profitability.*
- *Employee involvement is our way of life. We are a team. We must treat each other with trust and respect.*
- *Dealers and suppliers are our partners. The Company must maintain mutually beneficial relationships with dealers, suppliers, and our other business associates.*
- *Integrity is never compromised. The conduct of our Company worldwide must be pursued in a manner that is socially responsible and commands respect for its integrity and for its positive contributions to society. Our doors are open to men and women alike without discrimination and without regard to ethnic origin or personal beliefs. (Ford Motor Company 1984 Annual Report)*

After the industrywide crisis at the turn of the decade, Ford embarked on an intensive quality improvement process. Results have been dramatic. Customer research shows that the quality of our 1986 cars and trucks is more than 50 percent better than that of our 1980 models. . . . We have explored new approaches to accelerate the rate of improvement. This led us to focus on strategic issues related to our quality effort. The strategy that evolved was to concentrate on developing and implementing fundamental changes in the overall quality/customer satisfaction process. . . . Quality includes every aspect of the vehicle that determines customer satisfaction and provides fundamental value. This means how well the vehicle is made, how well it performs, how well it lasts, and how well the customer is treated by both the Company and the dealer. There will be no compromise in our quest for quality. (Ford Motor Company 1985 Annual Report)

Ford's 1987 earnings were the highest for any company in automotive history, despite a 7 percent drop in U.S. car and truck industry sales, higher capital spending, and increased marketing costs. (Ford Motor Company 1987 Annual Report)

Ford has developed a policy of Total Quality Excellence that emphasizes the importance of quality in every action, operation, and product associated with Ford Motor Company. The fundamental precepts of this policy are:

- *Quality is defined by the customer; the customer wants products and services that, throughout their life, meet his or her needs and expectations at a cost that represents value.*
- *Quality excellence can best be achieved by preventing problems rather than by detecting and correcting them after they occur.*
- *All work that is done by Company employees, suppliers, and dealers is part of a process that creates a product or service for a customer. Each person can influence some part of that process and, therefore, affects the quality of its output and the ultimate customer's satisfaction with our products and services.*
- *Sustained quality excellence requires continuous process improvement. This means, regardless of how good present performance may be, it can become even better.*
- *People provide the intelligence and generate the actions that are necessary to realize these improvements.*
- *Each employee is a customer for work done by other employees or suppliers, with a right to expect good work from others and an obligation to contribute work of high caliber to those who, in turn, are his or her customers.*

The goal of Ford Total Quality Excellence is to achieve superior external and internal customer satisfaction levels. Each employee's commitment to the precepts of Ford Total Quality Excellence and management's further commitment to implementation of supporting managerial and operating systems is essential to realizing that goal.

Donald Petersen has stated:

> *The work of Dr. Deming has definitely helped change Ford's corporate leadership. It is management's responsibility to create the environment in which everyone can contribute to continuous improvement in processes and systems. We're making good progress along these lines with employee involvement and participative management. Real gains of the new management system are shared with employees through job security, recognition of contribution, and compensation.*
>
> *While employees have benefited, so has the Company and our customers. For example, we are running well over 60 percent better levels of quality in our products today. I dare say we would not have predicted that much improvement in that short a time. Dr. Deming has influenced my thinking in a variety of ways. What stands out is that he helped me crystallize my ideas concerning the value of teamwork, process improvement and the pervasive power of the concept of continuous improvement.*[37]

Key Issues for Discussion

1. Discuss specific themes in the Deming philosophy that are evident in statements made in Ford's annual reports.
2. Which definition of quality (see Chapter 1) is used in the 1985 Annual Report?
3. Review recent Ford annual reports and summarize their quality efforts. What changes, if any, are evident, either in their view of quality or approaches to achieve it?

QUALITY IN PRACTICE

FLORIDA POWER AND LIGHT[38]

Florida Power and Light (FPL) is one of the largest electric utilities in the United States. Its territory covers 27,650 square miles, about half of Florida, and services a population of 5.7 million people. FPL has about 15,000 employees, operates 13 plants, 397 substations, and more than 53,000 miles of transmission and distribution lines.

During the 1970s the company was forced to increase utility rates repeatedly because of increasing costs, slower sales growth, and stricter federal and state regulations. The company had become bureaucratic and inflexible. In 1981 Marshall McDonald, then chairman of the board, realized that the company had been concerned with keeping defects under control rather than improving quality. Due to his concern for quality, McDonald introduced quality improvement teams at FPL. Management knew this change was a step in the right direction, but such teams alone would not bring about the change needed for the company to survive. McDonald tried to convince other executives that a total quality improvement process was needed, but all the experts that FPL talked to were in manufacturing, while FPL was primarily a service company. In 1983, while in Japan, McDonald met a president of Kansai Electric Power Company, a Deming Prize winner, who told him about their total quality efforts. Company officials began to visit Kansai regularly, and with their help, FPL began its quality improvement program (QIP) in 1983.

"Policy deployment" was the driving force behind the QIP program. Policy deployment (see Chapter 5) is a method that takes corporate vision and determines priority issues that will make the vision a reality. For FPL, the issues involved improving reliability, customer satisfaction, and employee safety while keeping costs in control. Each department was then responsible for developing plans to improve in these areas. Once plans were determined, their status was checked regularly to make sure they were on schedule. Each department was limited to working on no more than three items that had the most influence on their department's performance, but the work on these was expected to be done in great detail.

"Quality in daily work" (QIDW) is the expression that FPL used for another concept for improving business systems quality. It involves standardizing work routines, removing waste from them, promoting the concept of internal customers, and enabling better practice to be replicated from one location to another. QIDW control systems consist of flowcharts, process and quality indicators, procedure standards, and computer systems. By examining and analyzing work over and over again, employees in every area contribute to simplifying their work and improving processes. They discover opportunities for computer systems to free line employees from repetitive tasks.

One illustration of how QIDW was used was the development of a computer system for processing customer trouble calls. In the system, the computer first checks to find out whether the customer has been disconnected for nonpayment, then begins to locate places and devices that may be malfunctioning, and routes the call through a dispatcher to a troubleshooter. A repairperson heading to the scene may have a diagnosis before arrival. The information is stored in a database to be used for future improvement planning.

FPL revamped a centralized suggestion system it had been using for many years. Only about 600 suggestions had been submitted annually and it usually took six months for evaluation. A new decentralized system was proposed with simplified procedures to improve the response time. Employees participated in the implementation of their own suggestions. In 1988, 9,000 suggestions were submitted; in 1989 this number increased to 25,000.

Training has played an important role in FPL's quality transformation. They found that training enhanced enthusiasm and participation. Supervisors are expected to train their employees and play a more active role as coaches and cheerleaders. As line employees have become more skilled in diagnosing and solving problems, issues that once required management attention are now handled by line employees. Problems are dealt with on a factual basis, not with intuition. All employees have developed a much broader view of the company and more flexibility in dealing with customers.

The management system has also changed. Customer satisfaction has become the focus of attention rather than cost control. Management reviews check on improvement progress monthly. Goals are now long term, but progress checks are frequent. Managers review progress with better statistical insight, recognizing that variation will exist, but seek to rid the system of common causes. Cross-functional teams are used to carry out large-scale improvement projects. Finally, the budget is integrated with quality improvement.

The influence of total quality control at FPL can be seen in Figure 3.10. The average length of service interruptions dropped from about 75 minutes in 1983 to about 47 minutes in 1989; the number of complaints per 1,000 customers fell to one-third of the 1983 level; safety has improved; and the price of electricity has stabilized.

After the Deming Prize[39]

Although winning the Deming Prize in 1989 was an honor of which the company and its employees were very proud, a number of employees were feeling that the quality improvement program, intensified by the Deming challenge, had become

Figure 3.10 Some of Florida Power and Light's Accomplishments

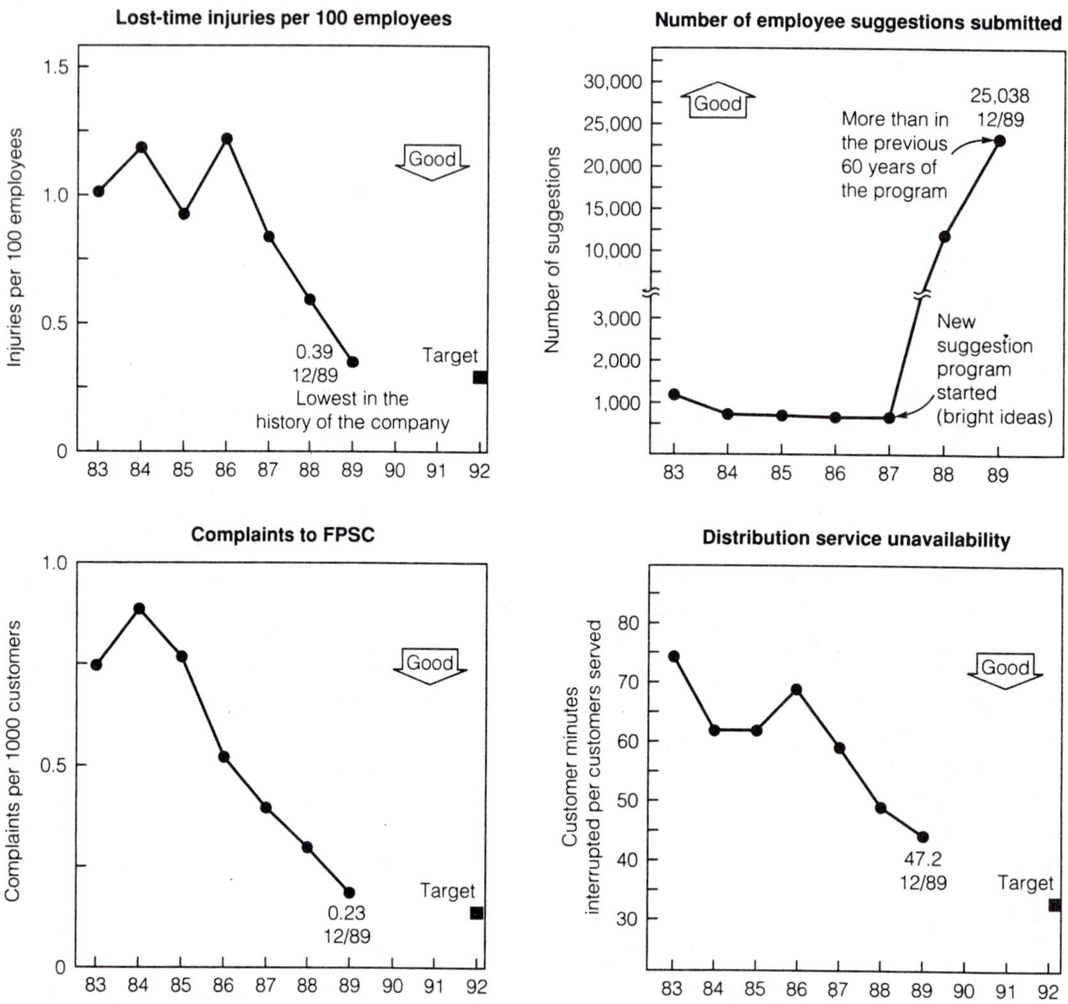

mechanical and inflexible. In fact, the bureaucratic features that had developed in the process were becoming barriers to continuous improvement in many instances.

At the same time, management had underestimated the speed and impact of the growing threat of deregulation and new competition in the electric utility industry. It was not preparing quickly enough to shift its structure and strategy to compete in this new environment, and needed to re-examine its vision and approach to the quality process. In 1990 the new chairman and CEO, James L. Broadhead, began to investigate both issues. He spoke personally to more than 500 employees in small groups and selected a team to make recommendations to address employees' concerns about the quality processes. The team suggested several changes, including retaining only those indicators, teams, and reports that contributed in a substantial way to achieving the objectives of the department and the company; eliminating many of the formal management reviews; no longer requiring a structured problem-solving process, but emphasizing continuous improvement and solutions that benefited the company and its customers; continuing to train all employees in the problem-solving process so they would have the appropriate tools and speak a common language; and dispersing the quality organizations within the company, making quality the responsibility of each business unit. In a letter to all employees, Mr. Broadhead reiterated management's commitment to continuous improvement in all aspects of FPL's business; nevertheless, some news media suggested that FPL was dismantling its quality efforts while attacking the quality movement. Although the current and future focus is on cost reduction in an increasingly competitive environment, Mr. Broadhead has stated emphatically that "it is unacceptable to reduce costs at the expense of quality."

Five years after winning the Deming Prize, FPL still had an unwavering commitment to quality initiatives, which was noted by Noriaki Kano of the Union of Japanese Scientists and Engineers, after observing presentations from 11 FPL business units. Dr. Kano, who had served as a counselor to FPL since 1986, was "pleasantly surprised" that FPL has simultaneously reduced costs and improved quality. Kano noted that recent improvements were based on skills developed through QIP practices. For example, one team improved service reliability by reducing transformer failures due to lightning. Before, an average of 23 transformers out of 761 on their worst-performing feeder failed each year. This number was reduced to zero failures, even though lightning strikes had increased 250 percent. Newly installed transformers incorporate the team's recommended changes, and existing transformers are modified as needed. The team leader stated that they found creative ways to use quality improvement tools and techniques to their best advantage without getting caught up in excessive paperwork or attending compulsory meetings. "Like most employees, we're so familiar with the quality processes that it's almost second nature."

Key Issues for Discussion

1. What makes FPL unique in the types of quality problems it encounters? How is its product similar to and different from oil being processed in a refinery? From water being delivered by a city water department?
2. How did FPL use policy deployment to improve quality?
3. What was the role of QIP teams at FPL in developing quality, which enabled them to win the Deming Prize?
4. What lessons did FPL learn after winning the Deming Prize? What can other companies learn about implementing quality from FPL's example?

Summary of Key Points

- W. Edwards Deming, Joseph Juran, and Philip Crosby are recognized as the top three international leaders of modern quality thinking. A. V. Feigenbaum, Kaoru Ishikawa, and Genichi Taguchi have also made significant contributions to modern quality management practices.
- Deming's philosophy is based on improving products and services by reducing uncertainty and variation. Systems thinking, statistical understanding of variation, the theory of knowledge, and psychology are the foundation of his philosophy. He advocates a radical cultural change in organizations, which is embodied in his 14 Points.
- The Deming chain reaction states that quality improvement reduces cost, increases productivity, increases market share, and allows firms to stay in business and provide jobs.
- Joseph Juran's philosophy seeks to provide change within the current American management system. Quality is defined as fitness for use. The Quality Trilogy—planning, control, and improvement—provides a direction for quality assurance in organizations.
- Philip Crosby's approach to quality is summarized in his Absolutes of Quality Management and Basic Elements of Improvement. He places more emphasis on behavioral change rather than on the use of statistical techniques as advocated by Deming and Juran.

- A. V. Feigenbaum views quality as a strategic business tool and coined the phrase *total quality control*. He promoted the importance of shifting quality responsibility to everyone in an organization and developing cost of quality approaches.
- Kaoru Ishikawa was instrumental in the Japanese quality movement, particularly in advocating a companywide quality control approach, the use of employee teams, and the use of problem-solving tools for quality improvement.
- Genichi Taguchi explained the economic value of reducing variation around a target value in production and proposed new engineering approaches for product design focused on quality improvement.
- Managers need to understand the differences and similarities in the leading quality philosophies and develop a quality management approach tailored to their organizations.
- The Deming Prize was established in 1951 to recognize companies that have achieved distinction through the application of companywide quality control approaches, supported by statistical methods and continuous improvement efforts.
- The Malcolm Baldrige National Quality Award recognizes U.S. companies that excel in quality management practices and business results that achieve the highest levels of customer satisfaction. The Baldrige Award criteria define key practices in categories of leadership, customer and market focus, strategic planning, human resource focus, information and analysis, process management, and business results. The Baldrige Award has generated a phenomenal amount of interest, and many companies use its criteria as a basis for internal assessment of their quality systems. Many state and international award programs are patterned after the Baldrige Award.
- ISO 9000 defines quality system standards, based on the premise that certain generic characteristics of management practices can be standardized, and that a well-designed, well-implemented, and carefully managed quality system provides confidence that the outputs will meet customer expectations and requirements. The eight principles that underlie the 2000 revision of the standards align the standards closer to the spirit of Baldrige and other international quality award frameworks that focus on performance excellence.

Review Questions

1. Explain the Deming Chain Reaction.
2. How does Deming's definition of quality compare with the definitions discussed in Chapter 1?
3. Summarize the four components of Profound Knowledge. How do they mutually support each other?
4. Explain the implications of not understanding the components of Profound Knowledge as suggested by Peter Scholtes.
5. Summarize Deming's 14 Points. How does each relate to the four components of Profound Knowledge?
6. Explain Juran's Quality Trilogy.
7. How is Juran's philosophy similar to or different from Deming's?
8. What are Crosby's Absolutes of Quality Management and Basic Elements of Improvement? How are they similar to or different from Deming's 14 Points?
9. Summarize the key contributions of Feigenbaum, Ishikawa, and Taguchi to modern quality thinking.

10. How does Taguchi's approach to measuring variation support the Deming philosophy?
11. What does JUSE mean by "companywide quality control"? How do the Deming Prize criteria relate to this concept?
12. Summarize the purposes of the Malcolm Baldrige National Quality Award.
13. Explain the Baldrige Award framework and why each element is important in any quality system.
14. Describe the key issues addressed in each of the seven categories of the criteria for performance excellence.
15. Describe the Baldrige Award scoring system. What do we mean by *approach* and *deployment*?
16. How are the Baldrige Award criteria commonly used by companies that do not apply for the award?
17. How do the Baldrige criteria support Deming's 14 Points?
18. Explain the differences between the Baldrige, European, Canadian, and Australian Quality Awards.
19. Briefly summarize the key elements of ISO 9000. Are they something that every company should be doing? Why or why not?
20. Explain the process of obtaining ISO 9000 registration. What is a registrar?
21. List the reasons companies pursue ISO 9000 registration. What benefits can registration provide?
22. Why has ISO 9000 been controversial? How has the 2000 revision addressed some of the controversial issues?

Discussion Questions

1. What implications might the Theory of Knowledge have for Wall Street analysts who react to quarterly earnings reports?
2. Discuss the interrelationships among Deming's 14 Points. How do they support each other? Why must they be viewed as a whole rather than separately?
3. The following themes form the basis for Deming's philosophy. Classify the 14 Points into these categories and discuss the commonalties within each category.
   a. Organizational purpose and mission
   b. Quantitative goals
   c. Revolution of management philosophy
   d. Elimination of seat-of-the-pants decisions
   e. Cooperation building
   f. Improvement of manager-worker relations
4. Think of a system with which you are familiar, such as your college, fraternity, or a student organization. What is the purpose of that system? What would it mean to optimize that system?
5. List some examples of variation that you observe in your daily life. How might they be reduced?
6. Suggest ways that management can recognize the existence of fear in an organization. What strategies might managers use to deal with and eliminate fear?
7. Discuss how Deming's 14 Points can apply to an academic environment. How can learning and classroom performance be improved by applying Deming's philosophy?

8. In a videotape made in 1993, Deming related a story of a woman executive who spent an entire day flying from city to city, changing planes several times, because her company's travel department received a cheaper fare than if she had taken a direct flight. How does this example violate the concepts of Profound Knowledge and the 14 Points, and what should the company do about it?
9. The original version of Deming's 14 Points (developed in the early 1980s) is given in Table 3.9. Contrast each of these points with the revised version in Table 3.1 early in the chapter. Explain the implications of the changes. Why might Deming have made these changes?

Table 3.9 Original Version of Deming's 14 Points

1. Create constancy of purpose toward improvement of product and service, with the aim of becoming competitive and to stay in business and to provide jobs.
2. Adopt the new philosophy. We are in a new economic age. Western management must awaken to the challenge, must learn their responsibilities, and take on leadership for change.
3. Cease dependence on inspection to achieve quality. Eliminate the need for inspection on a mass basis by building quality into the product in the first place.
4. End the practice of awarding business on the basis of price tag alone. Instead, minimize total cost. Move toward a single supplier for any one item, on a long-term relationship of loyalty and trust.
5. Improve constantly and forever the system of production and service to improve quality and productivity, and thus constantly decrease costs.
6. Institute training on the job.
7. Institute leadership. The aim of supervision should be to help people and machines and gadgets do a better job. Supervision of management is in need of overhaul, as well as the supervision of production workers.
8. Drive out fear so everyone can work effectively for the company.
9. Break down barriers between departments. People in research, design, sales, and production must work as a team, to foresee problems of production and those that may be encountered with the product or service.
10. Eliminate slogans, exhortations, and targets for the work force that ask for zero defects or new levels of productivity. Such exhortations only create adversarial relationships, as the bulk of the causes of low quality and low productivity belong to the system and thus lie beyond the power of the work force.

11a. Eliminate work standards (quotas) on the factory floor. Substitute leadership.

11b. Eliminate management by objective. Eliminate management by numbers, numerical goals. Substitute leadership.

12a. Remove barriers that rob hourly workers of their right to pride of workmanship. The responsibility of supervisors must be changed from sheer numbers to quality.

12b. Remove barriers that rob people in management and engineering of their right to pride in workmanship. This means, *inter alia*, abolishment of the annual or merit rating and of management by objective.

13. Institute a vigorous program of education and self-improvement.
14. Put everybody in the company to work to accomplish the transformation. The transformation is everybody's job.

Source: Reprinted from *Out of the Crisis* by W. Edwards Deming by permission of MIT and the W. Edwards Deming Institute. Published by MIT, Center for Advanced Educational Services, Cambridge, MA 02139. © 1986 by The W. Edwards Deming Institute.

10. Create a matrix diagram in which each row is a category of the Baldrige Award criteria and four columns correspond to a level of organizational maturity with respect to quality:
    - Traditional management practices
    - Growing awareness of the importance of quality
    - Development of a solid quality management system
    - Outstanding, world-class management practice

    In each cell of the matrix, list two to five characteristics that you would expect to see for a company in each of the four situations above for that criteria category. How might this matrix be used as a self-assessment tool to provide directions for improvement?
11. Contrast the categories of the Baldrige Award with the Deming Prize. How are they similar? Different?
12. Discuss the implications of the Baldrige criteria for e-commerce. What are the specific challenges that e-commerce companies face within each category of the criteria?
13. Map the elements of ISO 9000:2000 against the Baldrige Criteria. How are they similar? How are they different?

Projects, Etc.

1. Study the annual reports of some major companies issued over a period of several years. Do you see evidence of implementation of the quality philosophies discussed in this chapter?
2. Design a questionnaire or survey instrument to determine the degree to which an organization is "Demingized." Explain how you developed the questions.
3. Visit the National Quality Program Web site (*http://www.quality.nist.gov/*) and write a report on the information that can be found there.
4. From the National Quality Program Web site, download the current Baldrige Education criteria. Select a category, and interview your school administrators using the criteria questions as a basis for the interview. Write a report assessing your school against the criteria.
5. Does your state have a quality award program? If so, obtain some current information about the program and report on it. If not, contact your state representative to see why not.
6. Interview some managers at a local company that is pursuing or has pursued ISO 9000 or QS-9000 registration. Report on the reasons for achieving registration, the perceived benefits, and the problems the company encountered during the process. How has the recent ISO 9000:2000 revision affected their plans and progress?

Cases

I. The Reservation Clerk

Mary Matthews works for an airline as a reservation clerk. Her duties include answering the telephone, making reservations, and providing information to customers. Her supervisor told her to be courteous and not to rush callers. However, the supervisor also told her that she must answer 25 calls per hour so that the department's account manager can prepare an adequate budget. Mary comes home each day frustrated because the computer is slow in delivering information that she needs, and sometimes reports no information. Without information from the computer, she is forced to use printed directories and guides.

Discussion Questions

1. What is Mary's job? What might Deming say about this situation?
2. Drawing upon Deming's principles, outline a plan to improve this situation.

II. Modern Steel Technology[40]

Modern Steel Technology, Inc. (MST), is a supplier of custom-designed, hardened steel components and replacement parts to heavy industry worldwide. Steel mills and mining companies account for 75 percent of sales, while aluminum, paper, chemical, and cement industries account for the remaining 25 percent. The main product groups are gears, couplings, wheels, and rolls. MST operates three plants; two are located in Pennsylvania, and one is in Canada, with 374 people.

The MST mission is to "serve our customers by producing and delivering products of superior quality and value; maintain a commitment to continuous improvement, and provide long-term value to our shareholders." Each year the president and his staff meet off-site to develop and refine a plan for the next year; discuss goals, strategies, and objectives; and make capacity, personnel, and quality decisions. This plan is then passed down to middle management for review and suggestions. Middle management takes the yearly plan and determines monthly goals for sales, production, inventory, backlog, expenses, and revenues. All employees have access to these plans. Every three months, managers review their department's progress against the plan and present the results to the president. If the plan is not being met, suggestions for improvement are discussed.

MST is conscious of its community responsibilities at its Pennsylvania headquarters. The CEO is a board member of the United Way, the Fine Arts Council, and other local community efforts. Annually, MST employees are encouraged to contribute to these causes. MST complies with all EPA and OSHA regulations, and offers flu shots and other health-related seminars to its employees.

MST understands its customer requirements. In a highly competitive industry, failure to meet a customer need usually results in a lost customer. For example, European Community customers required ISO 9000 certification, which MST was able to obtain in June of 1995. Customer satisfaction is determined by on-time delivery and quality results. Each year, the roll product manager visits all customers and conducts a survey on product performance. Often, a latent customer need is determined, and MST seeks ways to fulfill this need.

MST uses a mainframe computer-based information system to track quotes, orders, inventory, schedules, and purchasing activities. Networked PCs within the company allow different departments to access the same information. Departments have access only to those databases they use. For example, the quality department monitors on-time delivery, cycle time, and cost. Several improvements have been made. For example, roll heat treat recipes were kept in duplicate books by both the metallurgy and heat treat departments, resulting in errors if only one book was updated. These data are now maintained in a common database, accessible to both departments.

MST compares its performance to competitors by examining product performance of rolls at steel mills. In addition, the company uses annual surveys of the gear industry published by a manufacturing association to compare its gears against others based on performance and production cost. The company also uses cost of quality indicators to measure performance. An external measure is defined as the cost to repair or replace a product after if fails, and an internal measure is the cost of rework and scrap. Each internal incident is traced back and charged to the budget of the responsible department. These data are analyzed in total to determine possible corrective actions.

Employee excellence is recognized through the use of annual employee appraisals. The employee and his or her immediate supervisor sit down and discuss the appraisal and the employee's score. Merit raises are based on the appraisal. The discussion also identifies any weaknesses the employee may have, and additional training may be suggested to strengthen the weak areas. Promotions are generally made when vacancies occur. Consequently, turnover of salaried employees in many positions is relatively high. MST has an employee stock ownership plan. In 1997 the last of the company stock was distributed, and new employees contribute to a base retirement plan and are unable to participate in company ownership.

Customer requirements are transmitted through blueprints. Blueprints are generated by the engineering department and contain product dimensions, specified hardness requirements, and other information necessary to manufacture the product.

Quality control measurement techniques are defined and vary by product. Key product characteristics, such as gear tooth thickness, are measured against tolerances. Inspection personnel are trained and certified in applicable testing techniques. If a dimension is out of tolerance, the inspector must call a technician who will decide whether immediate corrective action should be taken. A department manager makes the decision to take preventive action to stop an undesirable condition from recurring.

MST maintains an informal partnership with a supplier of forgings. MST meets periodically to convey its requirements. Currently, on-time delivery is above 90 percent for all product groups except gears, which is at a 60 percent level. Delivery dates for gears are difficult to determine because the product mix is constantly changing, cycle times vary, and machines used for production are common to several products, creating a challenge for capacity planners.

Assignment

1. Using the Baldrige Criteria, identify any key strengths and weaknesses or gaps in this company's management practices in each of the seven categories.
2. How well does the company address the principles of total quality described in Chapter 1?

III. Collin Technologies: Key Business Factors

The complete Collin Technologies case study, a fictitious example of a Baldrige application, can be found on the CD-rom accompanying this book and will also be used in later chapters. We will use the 2000 criteria to evaluate this case (written in 1999) because the changes to the 2001 criteria would make it inappropriate to use the 2001 criteria. However, the basic content of the criteria are similar so as not to affect learning from analyzing the case significantly. For this case, read the business overview that describes the company and its competitive environment.

Assignment

1. Summarize the important business factors of this company in each of the following categories:
   - *Basic description of the company:* nature of business; organizational culture; products and services; company size and location; major markets; principal customer types; employee base, including number, types, educational level, bargaining units; major equipment, facilities, technologies use; regulatory environment
   - *Customer and market requirements:* important requirements, and differences among customer groups and market segments
   - *Supplier and partnering relationships:* types and number of suppliers of goods and services; most important types; any limitations or special requirements that may exist with some or all suppliers and partners
   - *Competitive situation:* company's position in the industry; number and types of competitors; principal factors that determine competitive success; changes taking place that affect competition
   - *Business directions:* major new thrusts; new business alliances; introduction of new technologies; changes in strategy; other unique factors
2. Discuss how these business factors might influence Collin's approach to designing its total quality system. What specific *practices* might Collin use to support its infrastructure: customer focus, leadership, strategic planning, human resource, process management, and data and information management systems?

NOTES

1. John Hillkirk, "World-Famous Quality Expert Dead at 93," *USA Today*, December 21, 1993.

2. W. Edwards Deming, *The New Economics for Industry, Government, and Education* (Cambridge, MA: MIT Center for Advanced Engineering Study, 1993).

3. The quincunx simulator is contained in the Quality Gamebox, a registered trademark of Productivity-Quality Systems, Inc., 10468 Miamisburg-Springboro Road, Miamisburg, OH 45342; 937-885-2255; 800-777-3020. The Quality Gamebox software is distributed with this book with permission of PQ Systems, Inc.

4. Peter R. Scholtes, "Communities as Systems," *Quality Progress*, July 1997, 49–53. Used with the author's permission.

5. Edmund Faltermayer "Is This Layoff Necessary?" *Fortune*, June 1, 1992, 71–86.

6. Walter A. Shewhart, *Economic Control of Quality of a Manufactured Product* (New York: Van Nostrand, 1931).

7. Gervase R. Bushe, "Cultural Contradictions of Statistical Process Control in American Manufacturing Organizations," *Journal of Management* 14 (May 1988), 19–31.

8. "Detroit vs. the UAW: At Odds over Teamwork," *Business Week*, August 24, 1987, 54–55.

9. William M. Lindsay, Kent Curtis, and Ralph C. Hennie, "Houston Metropolitan Transit Authority: Where Cooperative Team Efforts Produce Measurable Results," Presentation at the IAQC Fall Conference, Orlando, FL, 1986.

10. Brad Stratton, "The Price Is Right: ASQC Annual Salary Survey," *Quality Progress* 21, no. 9 (September 1988), 24–29.

11. Xerox Quality Solutions, *A World of Quality: The Timeless Passport* (Milwaukee, WI: ASQC Quality Press, 1993), 54.

12. Jeremy Main, "Under the Spell of the Quality Gurus," *Fortune*, August 18, 1986, 30–34.

13. Philip B. Crosby, *Quality Is Free* (New York: McGraw-Hill, 1979), 200–201.

14. Main, see note 12.

15. Facts in this section were obtained from "Profile: the ASQC Honorary Members A. V. Feigenbaum and Kaoru Ishikawa," *Quality Progress* 19, no. 8 (August 1986), 43–45; and Bruce Brocka and M. Suzanne Brocka, *Quality Management: Implementing the Best Ideas of the Masters* (Homewood, IL: Business One Irwin, 1992).

16. April 17, 1979; cited in L. P. Sullivan, "Reducing Variability: A New Approach to Quality," *Quality Progress* 17, no. 7 (July 1984), 15–21.

17. JUSE, *The Deming Prize Guide for Oversea Companies* (Tokyo, 1992), 5.

18. Adapted from Jerry R. Junkins, "Insights of a Baldrige Award Winner," *Quality Progress* 27, no. 3 (March 1994), 57–58. Used with permission of Texas Instruments.

19. Nancy Blodgett, "Service Organizations Increasingly Adopt Baldrige Model," *Quality Progress*, December 1999, 74–78.

20. Paul W. DeBaylo, "Ten Reasons Why the Baldrige Model Works," *The Journal for Quality and Participation*, January/February 1999, 1–5.

21. DeBaylo, ibid.

22. Letter from W. Edwards Deming, *Harvard Business Review*, January/February 1992, 134.

23. Paul M. Bobrowski, and John H. Bantham, "State Quality Initiatives: Mini-Baldrige to Baldrige Plus," *National Productivity Review* 13, no. 3 (Summer 1994), 423–438.

24. Kevin Shergold and Deborah M. Reed, "Striving for Excellence: How Self-Assessment Using the Business Excellence Model Can Result in Step Improvements in All Areas of Business Activities," *TQM Magazine* 8, no. 6 (1996), 48–52.

25. B. Nakkai, and J. Neves, "The Deming, Baldrige, and European Quality Awards," *Quality Progress*, April 1994, 33–37.

26. Michael J. Timbers, "ISO 9000 and Europe's Attempts to Mandate Quality," *Journal of European Business* (March/April 1992), 14–25.

27. *http://www.bsi.org.uk/iso-tc176-sc2/*. Document: "Transition Planning Guidance for ISO/DIS 9001:2000," ISO/TC 176/SC 2/N 474, December 1999.

28. Amy Zuckerman, "ISO/QS-9000 Registration Issues Heating Up Worldwide," *The Quality Observer*, June 1997, 21–23.

29. See James R. Evans, "Beyond QS-9000," *Production and Inventory Management Journal* 38, no. 3 (Third Quarter 1997), 72–76, for a more complete discussion of this topic.

30. Amy Zuckerman and Rosalind McClymont, "Tracking the Ongoing ISO 9000 Revisions," *Business Standards*, 2, no. 2 (March/April 2000), 13–15. Jack West, with Charles A. Cianfrani, and Joseph J. Tsiakals, "A Breeze or a Breakthrough? Conforming to ISO 9000:2000," *Quality Progress*, March 2000,

41–44. See also by West et al., "Quality Management Principles: Foundation of ISO 9000:2000 Family, Part 5," *Quality Progress*, February 2000, 113–116; and "Quality Management Principles: Foundation of ISO 9000:2000 Family, Part 6," *Quality Progress*, March 2000, 79–81.

31. The 2000 standard requires fewer specific procedures and details. For instance, it requires documented procedures in only 6 places, versus 18 in the old standards. Although the 1994 document had more specific manufacturing language, the new standard is more flexible to meet the needs of service organizations.

32. Implementation guidelines are suggested by the case study by Steven E. Webster, "ISO 9000 Certification, A Success Story at Nu Visions Manufacturing," *IIE Solutions*, April 1997, 18–21.

33. AT&T Corporate Quality Office, *Using ISO 9000 to Improve Business Processes* (July 1994).

34. ISO 9000 Update, *Fortune*, September 30, 1996, 134[J].

35. Astrid L. H. Eckstein, and Jaydeep Balakrishnan, "The ISO 9000 Series: Quality Management Systems for the Global Economy," *Production and Inventory Management Journal* 34, no. 4 (Fourth Quarter 1993), 66–71.

36. "Home Builder Constructs Quality with ISO 9000," *Quality Digest*, February 2000, 13.

37. Donald R. Katz, "Coming Home" *Business Month*, October 1988, 58.

38. Brad Stratton, "A Beacon for the World," *Quality Progress* (May 1990), 60–65; Al Henderson and Target Staff, "For Florida Power and Light After the Deming Prize: The "Music Builds . . . And Builds . . . And Builds," *Target* (Summer 1990), 10–21.

39. The remainder of this Quality in Practice is adapted from "A Status Report on FPL's Improvement Activities Four Years After Receiving the Deming Prize," "Quality at Work," *FPL Today* 2, no. 1 (Spring 1993); and "Quality Effort Yields 'Impressive Results'," *INSIDEFPL* (May 1994). We gratefully acknowledge Alan E. Siebe, manager, quality services at FPL, for providing these materials.

40. Developed from a term paper by Ms. Debra Bergerhouse. Her contribution is gratefully acknowledged.

BIBLIOGRAPHY

Brocka, Bruce, and M. Suzanne Brocka. *Quality Management: Implementing the Best Ideas of the Masters*. Homewood, IL: Business One Irwin, 1992.

Bush, David, and Kevin Dooley."The Deming Prize and the Baldrige Award: How They Compare," *Quality Progress* 22, no. 1 (January 1989) 28–30.

Daniels, Susan E. "Tire Failures, SUV Rollovers, Put Quality on Trial," *Quality Progress* 33, no. 12 (December 2000), 30–46.

DeCarly, Neil J., and W. Kent Sterett. "History of the Malcolm Baldrige Award," *Quality Progress* 23, no. 3 (March 1990), 21–27.

Deming, W. Edwards. *The New Economics for Industry, Government, Education*. Cambridge, MA: MIT Center for Advanced Engineering Study, 1993.

———. *Out of the Crisis*. Cambridge, MA: MIT Center for Advanced Engineering Study, 1986.

Duncan, W. Jack, and Joseph G. Van Matre. "The Gospel According to Deming: Is It Really New?" *Business Horizons*, July/August 1990, 3–9.

Hunt, V. Daniel. *Managing for Quality*. Homewood, IL: Business One Irwin, 1993.

Juran, J. M. *Juran on Quality by Design*. New York: The Free Press, 1992.

———. "Product Quality—A Prescription for the West." *Management Review*, June/July 1981.

———. "The Quality Trilogy." *Quality Progress* 19 (August 1986), 19–24.

Kivenko, Ken. "Improve Performance by Driving Out Fear." *Quality Progress* 27, no. 10 (October 1994), 77–79.

Mehta, Pradip V. "President's Quality Program Honors Government Organizations," *Quality Progress*, 33, no. 8 (August 2000), 57–62.

Ohio Quality and Productivity Forum Roundtable. "Deming's Point Four: A Study." *Quality Progress* 21, no. 12 (December 1988), 31–35.

Raturi, A., and D. McCutcheon. "An Epistemological Framework for Quality Management," Working Paper. Cincinnati, OH: University of Cincinnati, Department of Quantitative Analysis and Information Systems, March 1990.

Reimann, Curt W. "The Baldrige Award: Leading the Way in Quality Initiatives," *Quality Progress* 22, no. 7 (July 1989), 35–39.

Scherkenbach, William W. *Deming's Road to Continual Improvement*. Knoxville, TN: SPC Press, 1991.

PART 2

THE MANAGEMENT SYSTEM

For quality to succeed in an organization, it must become a part of everyone's daily activities. A total quality system must be built on effective managerial practices that focus on customers; provide leadership to all employees; integrate quality into strategic business planning; involve and motivate everyone; build quality into all products and processes; and provide useful information to maintain high performance, continuously improve, and lead to sustainable competitive advantage. The Baldrige framework, introduced in Chapter 3, provides a structure for designing an organization around high-performance management practices. Part 2 of this book addresses the seven key criteria elements of the Baldrige criteria on which a total quality foundation should be built.

Chapter 4 examines the role and importance of customers and customer satisfaction in achieving strategic business objectives, and describes various approaches for acquiring customer knowledge and measuring satisfaction. Chapter 5 focuses on leadership and strategic planning activities, emphasizing the importance of leadership in driving quality throughout an organization, and the natural role that leaders play in strategic planning, as well as introducing useful tools that support strategic planning efforts. Chapter 6 examines the role of human resources in achieving total quality, including the design of high-performance work systems and effective management of human resources. Chapter 7 discusses process management, including approaches for controlling and improving design, production, delivery, and other key processes by which work gets accomplished. Finally, Chapter 8 deals with measurement and strategic information management, focusing on the importance of using a balanced set of performance measures and business results to guide organizational decisions and direction.

In each of these chapters, we describe "leading practices" that high-performance organizations, primarily Baldrige winners, use in deploying the principles of total quality. We also illustrate, via portions of a Baldrige training case study, how an organization might respond to the criteria and how their approaches might be assessed by experts in the field.

Chapter 4

Focusing on Customers

Outline

Deer Valley Resort in Park City, Utah, is viewed by many as the Ritz-Carlton of ski resorts, providing exceptional services and a superior ski vacation experience.[1] The resort offers curbside ski valet service to take equipment from vehicles, parking lot attendants to ensure efficient parking, and a shuttle to transport guests from the lot to Snow Park Lodge. Guests walk to the slopes on heated pavers that prevent the pavement from freezing and assist in snow removal. The central gathering area by the base lifts is wide and level, allowing plenty of room to put on equipment and easy access to the lifts. At the end of the day, guests can store their skis without charge at each lodge. The resort limits the number of skiers on the mountain to reduce lines and congestion, and offers complimentary mountain tours for both expert and intermediate skiers. Everyone is committed to ensuring that each guest has a wonderful experience, from "mountain hosts" stationed at the top of the lifts to answer questions and provide directions, to the friendly workers at the cafeterias and restaurants, whose food is consistently rated number one by ski enthusiast magazines. "Our goal is to make each guest feel like a winner," says Bob Wheaton, president and general manager. "We go the extra mile on the mountain, in our ski school, and throughout our food-service operation because we want our guests to know they come first."

In Japanese a single word—*okyakusama*—means both "customer" and "honorable guest." World-class organizations are obsessed with meeting and exceeding customer expectations. Many companies such as The Ritz-Carlton Hotel Company, Disney, and Nissan Motor Co.'s Infiniti division were built on the notion of satisfying the customer. Home Depot, cited by Wal-Mart's CEO as the best retail organization in the United States, has as its service philosophy: "Every customer has to be treated like your mother, your father, your sister, or your brother."[2]

Other firms have had to learn to be customer-focused, often in response to a competitive crisis. Motorola is one example. Like many innovative engineering firms, it created new markets by essentially telling customers what they wanted. But as customers became more sophisticated and competition increased, they told Motorola that the company needed to improve. As a consequence, Motorola changed its objectives from a product focus to a customer focus. In 1979 Motorola set total customer satisfaction as its fundamental goal. Less than 10 years later, it was one of the first winners of the Malcolm Baldrige National Quality Award.

A Deloitte and Touche research study noted that 83 percent of executives surveyed said that the quality of their customer relationships will be a critical factor to compete in the twenty-first century, yet only 56 percent of them felt they had strong capabilities in this area.[3] To create satisfied customers, the organization needs to identify customers' needs, design the production and service systems to meet those needs, and measure the results as the basis for improvement. The organization must also use customer focus as a key driver for its strategic planning activities. This chapter focuses on this concept of customer-driven quality.

THE IMPORTANCE OF CUSTOMER SATISFACTION AND LOYALTY

As we noted in Chapter 1, a strong competitive advantage is driven by customer wants and needs.[4] Growth in market share is strongly correlated with customer satisfaction. Avis, for instance, recognizes two main ways to increase market share in the rental car business: (1) by buying large volumes of corporate business with extremely low rates, and (2) by improving customer satisfaction levels, thereby increasing repurchase intent and repeat business. Avis stated that it will not buy business at low rates for the sole purpose of increasing market share. Avis's marketing department uses a full range of research and analysis to keep pace with changing market trends and develop programs that respond to customers' needs. Through information technology, Avis queries all customers at car return to monitor trends and levels of customer satisfaction. It also calls 1,500 customers each month to assess in detail satisfaction in each of nine service delivery areas.[5] Customer satisfaction is also an important factor for the bottom line. At IBM, for instance, each percentage point in improved customer satisfaction translates into $500 million more revenue over five years.[6] Another study found that companies with a 98 percent customer retention rate are twice as profitable as those at 94 percent. On the other hand, dissatisfied customers purchase from competitors. Studies have shown that dissatisfied customers tell at least twice as many friends about bad experiences as they tell about good ones.

Although satisfaction is important, modern firms need to look further. Achieving strong profitability and market share requires *loyal* customers—those who stay with a company and make positive referrals. Satisfaction and loyalty are different concepts. To quote Patrick Mehne, the chief quality officer at The Ritz-Carlton: "Satisfaction is an attitude; loyalty is a behavior." Customers who are merely satisfied may often purchase from competitors because of convenience, promotions, or other factors. Loyal customers place a priority on doing business with a particular organization, and will often go out of their way or pay a premium to stay with the company. Loyal customers spend more, are willing to pay higher prices, refer new clients, and are less costly to do business with. For instance, although Home Depot customers spend only about $38 each visit, they shop 30 times annually and spend more than $25,000 throughout a lifetime.[7] Carl Sewell, owner of Sewell Cadillac in Dallas, calculated that the average lifetime value of a loyal customer for his dealership was $332,000.[8] Statistics also show that the typical company gets 65 percent of its business from existing customers, and it costs five times more to find a new customer than to keep an existing one happy.[9]

A firm cannot create loyal customers without first creating satisfied customers. One study of a Tennessee commercial bank found that a one-tenth percentage point improvement in overall customer satisfaction translated into an increase in six-tenths of a percentage point in customer retention. Customer satisfaction occurs when products and services meet or exceed customer expectations—our principal definition of quality. To ensure satisfaction, an organization must deliver ever-improving value to its customers. Value, as defined in Chapter 1, is quality related to price. Consumers no longer buy solely on the basis of price. They compare the total package of products and services that a business offers (sometimes called the **consumer benefit package**) with the price and with competitive offerings. The consumer benefit package influences the perception of quality and includes the physical product and its quality dimensions; presale support, such as ease of ordering; rapid, on-time, and accurate delivery; and postsale support, such as field service, warranties, and technical support. If competitors offer better choices for a similar price, consumers will rationally select the package with the highest perceived quality. One example is Midwest Express Airlines, a Milwaukee-based operation that caters to business travelers. Midwest Express earned its reputation for providing the "best care in the air" by offering passengers luxury service at competitive coach or discounted fares. The airline offers free coffee and newspapers each morning at its gates, fresh-baked chocolate chip cookies on afternoon flights, and steak and shrimp at dinner, all in planes with wide leather seats, no more than two across. Such practices have produced a host of awards from travel magazines and consumer groups.

Likewise, if a competitor offers the same quality package of goods and services at a lower price, customers would generally choose the one having the lower price. Midwest Express outperforms its competitors both financially and in terms of the percentage of seats filled.[10] Thus, understanding exactly what customers want and their perception of value is absolutely crucial to competitive success. However, lower prices require lower costs if the firm is to continue to be profitable. Quality improvements in operations reduce costs. Therefore, businesses must focus on continually improving the consumer benefit package and improving the quality of its internal operations.

In addition to value, satisfaction and loyalty are influenced greatly by service quality, integrity, and the relationships that organizations build with customers.[11] One study found that customers are five times more likely to switch because of perceived service problems than for price concerns or product quality issues.[12] As one small business owner stated, "We build customer loyalty by telling our customers the truth, whether it is good or bad news."[13]

The American Customer Satisfaction Index[14]

In 1994 the University of Michigan Business School and the American Society for Quality (ASQ) released the first American Customer Satisfaction Index (ACSI), a new economic indicator that measures customer satisfaction at the national level. It was the first cross-industry benchmark in the United States to measure customer satisfaction. In January 1998 it was announced that the Arthur Andersen consulting firm would join the earlier sponsors in funding and marketing the index. Similar indexes had previously existed in Sweden and Germany.

The ACSI is based on customer evaluations of the quality of goods and services purchased in the United States and produced by both domestic firms and foreign firms with a substantial U.S. market share. The 1994 ACSI provides a baseline against which customer satisfaction levels can be tracked over time. It is designed to answer the questions: Are customer satisfaction and evaluations improving or declining for the nation's output of goods and services? Are they improving or declining for particular sectors of industry or specific industries? The index quantifies the value that customers place on products, and thus drives quality improvement. Companies can use the data to assess customer loyalty, identify potential barriers to entry within markets, predict return on investments, and pinpoint areas in which customer expectations are not being satisfied.

The index uses a tested, multi-equation, econometric model to produce four levels of indexes: a national customer satisfaction index and indexes for seven industrial sectors, 40 specific industries, and 203 companies and agencies within those industries. ACSI is based on results of telephone interviews conducted in a national sample of 46,000 consumers who have recently bought or used a company's product or service. The econometric model used to produce ACSI links customer satisfaction to its determinants: customer expectations, perceived quality, and perceived value. Customer satisfaction, in turn, is linked to customer loyalty, which has an impact on profitability. This model is summarized in Figure 4.1.

The initial 1994 results showed that nondurable manufacturing scored relatively high in customer satisfaction while public administration and government services scored relatively low. However, the overall national index declined continually until 1998, from 74.5 to 71.7, but has improved by a small amount through 2000 to a score of 72.8. These results suggest that quality improvements are not keeping pace with consumer expectations.

The ACSI is updated on a rolling basis with one to three sectors of the economy measured each quarter. Beginning in 2000, e-commerce companies have been included. In 2000, e-commerce companies scored higher than traditional retailers, and

Figure 4.1 ACSI Model

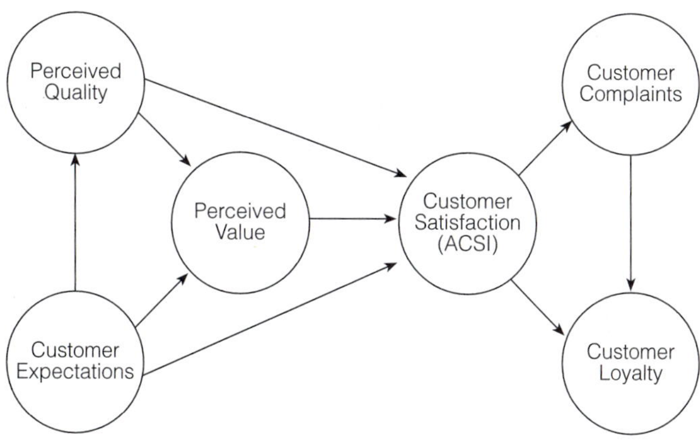

Source: Courtesy of National Quality Research Center (see note 14).

Amazon.com's index exceeded all other service companies in the ACSI. Magazines such as *Fortune* and *Business Week* generally report current ACSI results; a question later in this chapter will ask you to research recent trends. Company scores and other information are available at *http://acsi.asq.org*, *http://www.bus.umich.edu*, and *http://www.cfigroup. com*. Further information on ACSI methodology and results can be obtained from ASQ at 800-248-1946. Over time, attention to the index could potentially raise the public's perception and understanding of quality, as do the consumer price index and other economic indicators. This increased awareness will help to interpret price and productivity measures and promote customer-driven quality.

In April 2000, a similar European Customer Satisfaction Model was announced (see the Web site *http://www.efqm.org/pressrel/custsat.htm*). It is based on customer evaluations of the quality of goods and services that are purchased in Europe and produced by both European Community and non-European Community companies that have substantial European market share. It will provide both national and European indexes (ECSI). ECSI has been built to be compatible with ACSI to allow comparison of results outside Europe.

CREATING SATISFIED CUSTOMERS

Figure 4.2 provides a view of the process in which customer needs and expectations are translated into outputs during the design, production, and delivery processes. True customer needs and expectations are called **expected quality**. Expected quality is what the customer assumes will be received from the product. The producer identifies these needs and expectations and translates them into specifications for products and services. **Actual quality** is the outcome of the production process and what is delivered to the customer. Actual quality may differ considerably from expected quality. This difference happens when information gets lost or is misinterpreted from one step to the next. For instance, ineffective market research efforts may incorrectly assess the true customer needs and expectations. Designers of products and services may develop specifications that inadequately reflect these needs. Manufacturing operations or customer-contact personnel may not deliver according to the specifications. A further complication comes from the customer who sees and believes the

Figure 4.2 Customer-Driven Quality Cycle

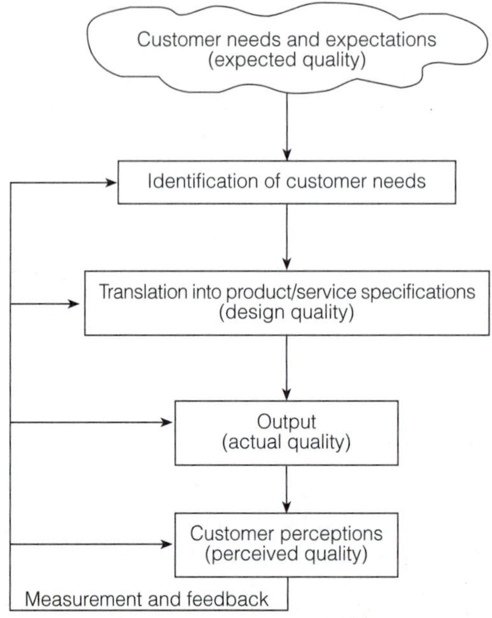

quality of the product (**perceived quality**) as considerably different from what he or she actually receives (actual quality). Because perceived quality drives consumer behavior, this area is where producers should really center their concerns.

These different levels of quality can be summarized by a fundamental equation:

Perceived quality = Actual quality – Expected quality

Any differences between the expected quality and actual quality can cause either unexpected satisfaction (actual quality is higher than expected quality) or dissatisfaction (actual quality is lower than expected quality). Understanding these relationships requires a system of customer satisfaction measurement and the ability to use customer feedback for improvement. This model suggests that producers must take great care to ensure that customer needs are met or exceeded both by the design and production process (discussed further in Chapter 7). Meeting or exceeding expectations requires looking at processes through the customers' eyes, not the organization's.

Leading Practices

Successful companies in every industry engage in a variety of customer-oriented practices that lead to profitability and market share. These generic practices, and some specific examples, are described in the following list.

1. *They clearly define key customer groups and markets, considering competitors and other potential customers, and segment their customers accordingly.* For example, Solectron selects its customers and markets based on current customer relationships, growth projections, emerging markets and companies, regional economics, supply relationships, and Solectron strengths versus competitor weaknesses. The Ritz-Carlton Hotel Company ranks potential and current customers

by volume, geography, and profit. GTE Directories (see *Quality Profile*) segments its customers into three distinct groups: advertisers, consumers, and companies that contract for Yellow Pages services. Such segmentation recognizes differences among customer groups and allows organizations to tailor their approaches to the unique needs of the groups.

2. *They understand both near-term and longer-term customer needs and expectations (the "voice of the customer") and employ systematic processes for listening and learning from customers.* Cadillac, for example, has a network of more than 1,600 dealers with primary responsibility for customer contact. The company collects customer information on new vehicle concepts in product and features clinics. Customer councils bring current vehicle owners and vehicle team members together to talk about product satisfaction and areas for improvement. At Whirlpool, when customers rate a competitor's product higher in satisfaction surveys, engineers take it apart to find out why. They also have hundreds of consumers fiddle with computer-simulated products while engineers record the users' reactions on videotape.[15] GTE Directories uses four basic approaches for identifying customer needs and monitoring satisfaction: (1) primary research, which includes focus groups, surveys, and interviews; (2) secondary research from monitoring competitors; (3) customer performance tracking that studies consumer behavior; and (4) customer feedback from sales representatives. At BI (see *Quality Profile*), each business unit manager is responsible for analyzing customer data to better understand customer needs and changing requirements. This information is systematically reviewed by the External Customer Satisfaction Team and other teams to form generalizations about service features, relative importance, and value.

Quality Profile
GTE Directories Corporation

GTE Directories Corporation, a 1994 winner of the Baldrige Award, publishes and sells advertising for telephone directories. It produces more than 1,200 directory titles in 45 states and 17 countries. More than 5,000 employees work at its Dallas–Ft. Worth headquarters and at dozens of other sites in North America and overseas.

In the 1980s GTE Directories faced increased competition from other publishers and other media. The company responded by transforming itself from an organization that relied on experience, enthusiasm, and gut instincts to one focused on anticipating and satisfying customer needs based on concrete, systematic customer input. The company introduced formal quality improvement techniques in 1986, supported with strong leadership from the company's executive management. Their vision is "100 Percent Customer Satisfaction Through Quality."

The results are impressive. In 1993 the published error ratio was just over 350 per million listings. In addition, it rates best-in-class in errors per thousand paid items. The number of advertisers handled by individual sales representatives has increased in each of the three years prior to 1994, and the number of sales hours spent with advertisers has jumped. Independent studies show that GTE directories are preferred in 271 of 274 primary markets, and the company has enjoyed sustained, increasing revenue growth.

Source: Malcolm Baldrige National Quality Award, Profiles of Winners, National Institute of Standards and Technology, Department of Commerce.

Quality Profile

BI

BI's business is helping other companies to achieve their own goals by enhancing the performance of the people who hold the keys to success—customers' employees, distributors, or consumers. As one of the three major players offering full-service business improvement and incentive programs across the country, BI employs more than 1,400 associates. Most are located at its headquarters in Minneapolis, Minnesota. Others are in Eden Valley, Minnesota; Sioux Falls, South Dakota; and in 21 U.S. sales offices. BI works behind the scenes to help customers succeed by integrating communications, training, measurement, and rewards to improve performance. Almost every BI account requires a customized product or service. Improvement efforts are driven by the goal of customer delight and grouped under a process management system known as the "BI Way," which includes training, problem-solving techniques, process improvement, incentives, and a focus on results. BI has identified five corporate objectives that are front-and-center at every decision made by the company: revenue, productivity, customer satisfaction, associate satisfaction, and added value. Every action at BI must support at least one of these objectives, and all plans, improvement teams, and measures that track progress and quantify the company's success are tied to these objectives. BI first began using the Baldrige approach to quality and performance improvement in 1990, and applied for 10 consecutive years before winning in 1999.

Company revenue has grown by a cumulative 47 percent over the second half of the 1990s. BI consistently has outperformed its two key competitors on customer-focused results. In 1998, for instance, a key measure of overall customer satisfaction scored 8.5 on a 10-point scale compared with competitor ratings of 7.9 and 7.6; on-time performance scored 8.1 compared to 7.9 and 7.7 for competitors; and a measure of accurate performance was 8.1 versus 7.8 and 7.7 for competitors. Associate retention was 83 percent, which was particularly strong in a tight Twin Cities labor market.

Source: Malcolm Baldrige National Quality Award, Profiles of Winners, National Institute of Standards and Technology, Department of Commerce.

3. *They understand the linkages between the voice of the customer and design, production, and delivery processes.* This practice ensures that no critical requirements fall through the cracks, and minimizes the potential gaps between expected quality and actual quality. Texas Instruments Defense Systems & Electronics Group translates key customer requirements, such as reducing the power demands, size, and weight of airborne radar systems, into clear improvement goals. Ames Rubber Corporation uses a closed-loop communication system, called Continuous Supplier and Customer Involvement. New products begin with a series of customer meetings to create a product brief, which outlines technical, material, and operational requirements. The product brief is then forwarded to internal departments to select materials, processes, and procedures as approved by the customer. The customer evaluates prototypes until completely satisfied. Finally, a trial production run is made. Not until the customer approves the results does full-scale production commence.
4. *They build relationships with customers through commitments that promote trust and confidence, provide easy accessibility to people and information, set effective service stan-*

dards, train customer contact employees, and effectively follow-up on products, services, and transactions. Eastman Chemical Company (see *Quality Profile*) has a no-fault return policy on its plastics products believed to be the only one of its kind in the chemical industry. A customer may return any plastics product for any reason for a full refund. This policy was a direct result of Eastman's customer surveys. Eastman also provides a toll-free number through which customers can contact virtually anyone in the company—including the president—24 hours a day, seven days a week. AT&T Transmission Systems offers risk-free trials of new products and 24-hour technical support. Their new 2000 family of products is supported by a five-year warranty, the most extensive in the industry. Customer relationship management includes attention to training and developing customer-contact employees, and empowering them to do whatever is necessary to satisfy the customer. All new Universal Card Services customer-contact associates attended an eight-week training program that emphasized empowerment, technical training, and customer delight, using an industry-leading instructional database that simulated the real customer-contact environment.

5. *They have effective complaint management processes by which customers can easily comment, complain, and receive prompt resolution of their concerns.* Every customer relations representative at GTE Directories tries to handle customer complaints on the first call. They are authorized to propose immediate solutions, including credit adjustments, free advertising, or even advertising in other media to offset omissions or misprints. If immediate resolution is not possible, they must resolve the complaint within 10 days. The Ritz-Carlton uses Guest Incident Action forms, which are aggregated on a monthly basis at each hotel, to ensure

Quality Profile

Eastman Chemical Company

Eastman Chemical Company, an outgrowth of Eastman Kodak, was founded in 1920 in Kingsport, Tennessee, to supply chemicals critical to photographic processes. Today Eastman employs approximately 18,000 people, marketing products in more than 80 countries and supplying the world with more than 400 chemicals, fibers, and plastics. Eastman works hard at continually improving its total quality management efforts to meet its Strategic Intent Vision: To Be the World's Preferred Chemical Company. As part of its Strategic Intent, Eastman leaders have established Major Improvement Opportunities, which are companywide areas of emphasis on improvement. They focus on exceeding customer expectations while achieving rapid globalization, superior return on assets, and aggressive sales revenue growth.

The achievements in supplying customers with products of consistently high quality are due to the use of statistical methods, focused breakthrough efforts, and continual improvements made by employees and teams. The company's shipping reliability has consistently performed near 100 percent for the past four years. Significant improvements have reduced energy utilization and waste emissions. Claims and returns due to product and service quality fell more than 35 percent (as measured by percent of sales dollars). More than 70 percent of Eastman's worldwide customers have ranked them as their number one supplier. Eastman received a Baldrige Award in 1993.

Source: Malcolm Baldrige National Quality Award, Profiles of Winners, National Institute of Standards and Technology, Department of Commerce.

that complaints were handled effectively and steps taken to eliminate the cause of the problem. Granite Rock (see *Quality in Practice* case at the end of this chapter) has a similar process by which complaints are reported through product-service discrepancy reports and analyzed to identify the cause.

6. *They measure customer satisfaction, compare the results relative to competitors, and use the information to evaluate and improve internal processes.* FedEx uses a 10-component service quality indicator that comprehensively describes how its performance is viewed by customers. Management meets daily to discuss the previous day's performance and tracks weekly, monthly, and annual trends. A cross-functional team for each service component supports the evaluation and improvement initiatives. BI uses three approaches to track customer satisfaction: a transactional customer satisfaction index for immediate feedback, an annual relationship customer satisfaction index to learn about specific attributes of satisfaction and intent for repeat business, and a competitive study to see how it performs relative to competitors.

The remainder of this chapter expands upon these important themes.

IDENTIFYING CUSTOMERS

To understand customer needs, a company must know who its customers are. Most employees think that "customers" are those people who ultimately purchase and use a company's products. These customers, or **consumers**, certainly are an important group. Identifying consumers is a top-management task related to the company's mission and vision. However, consumers are not the only customer group of concern to a business. The easiest way to identify customers is to think in terms of customer-supplier relationships.

AT&T uses a customer-supplier model as shown in Figure 4.3. Every process receives inputs from suppliers and creates outputs for customers. The feedback loops suggest that suppliers must also be considered as customers. They need appropriate information about the requirements they must meet. This model can be applied at the organization level, the process level, and the performer level (see the discussion of the "Three Levels of Quality" in Chapter 1).

At the organization level, a business has various external customers (organizations not part of the company, but impacted by the company's activities) that may fall between the organization and the consumer. For example, manufacturers of consumer products distribute to retail stores such as Wal-Mart and grocery stores. The retail stores are external customers of the manufacturers. They have specific needs for timely delivery, appropriate product displays, accurate invoicing, and so forth. These

Figure 4.3 AT&T's Customer-Supplier Model

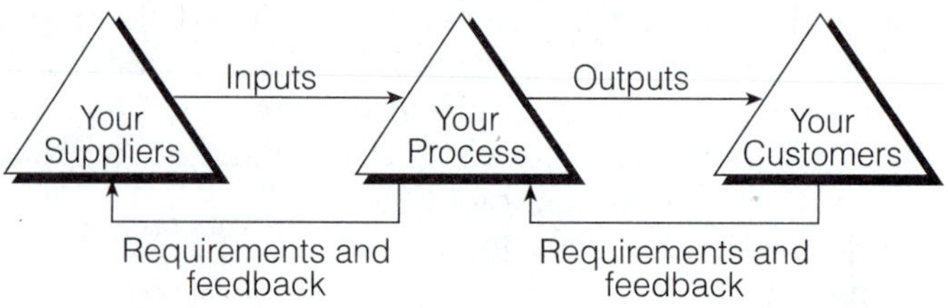

Source: Reproduced with permission from AT&T © 1988. All rights reserved.

stores allocate shelf space for the manufacturers' products, and therefore represent important customers. The manufacturers are customers of the chemical companies, printing companies, and other suppliers of such things as materials and packaging materials.

At the process level, individual departments and key cross-functional processes within a company have internal customers who contribute to the company's mission and depend on the department's or function's products or services to ultimately serve consumers and external customers. For instance, manufacturing is a customer of purchasing, a nursing unit is a customer of the hospital laundry, and reservations is a customer of the information systems department for an airline or hotel. Figure 2.1 in Chapter 2 is a good example of the internal customer-supplier relationships within a typical manufacturing firm.

At the performer level, each employee receives inputs from others and produces some output to internal customers. A customer may be the assembly line worker at the next station, an executive's secretary, the order taker who passes along orders to the food preparer at McDonald's, or an X-ray technician who must meet a physician's request.

Identifying customers begins with asking some fundamental questions:

1. What products or services are produced?
2. Who uses these products and services?
3. Who do employees call, write to, or answer questions for?
4. Who supplies the inputs to the process?

As individuals, departments, and functions develop their customer-supplier models, natural linkages become evident. These linkages build up the "chain of customers" throughout the company that connect every individual and function to the external customers and consumers. Eventually, everyone can better understand their role in satisfying not only their internal customers, but also the external customers.

If an organization remembers that its customers include its employees and the public, then it consciously maintains a work environment conducive to the well-being and growth of all employees. Efforts in this area should go beyond the expected training and job-related education. Health, safety, and ergonomics (the study of physical capabilities of people in the design of workplaces, tools, instruments, and so on) should be included in quality improvement activities. Many companies offer special services such as counseling, recreational and cultural activities, nonwork-related education, day care, flexible work hours, and outplacement to their employees. Texas Instruments, for instance, provides preventive health screenings at little or no cost to encourage personal involvement in health management. The company-sponsored employee association, called "Texins," uses fitness activities, recreational clubs, and family events to promote employee well-being.

The public is also an important customer of business. A company must look ahead to anticipate public concerns and assess possible impacts on society of its products, services, and operations. Business ethics, environmental concerns, and safety are important societal issues. Companies can have a powerful influence on communities as corporate citizens through their contributions to charitable activities and the personal involvement of their employees. Based on a company's actions in promoting education, health care, and ethical conduct, the public judges a company's community behavior, which, in turn, can impact sales and profitability. For example, AT&T announced in August 1989 that they would eliminate emissions of chlorofluorocarbons from all manufacturing processes by 1994, and the Texas Instruments Defense Systems & Electronics Group's waste management program began with scrap metals recycling and has expanded to include white paper, plastic, corrugated paper, and wood. It also encourages employees to participate in volunteer activities within local communities, particularly in helping schools prepare students to meet the technical and quality challenges of business.

Finally, everyone is his or her own customer. As we discussed in Chapter 1, quality must be personalized, or it will have little meaning at any other level. Robert Galvin, former CEO of Motorola, once told the Economic Club of Chicago, "Quality is a very personal obligation. If you can't talk about quality in the first person . . . then you have not moved to the level of involvement of quality that is absolutely essential."

Customer Segmentation

Customers generally have different requirements and expectations. A company usually cannot satisfy all customers with the same products or services. This issue is particularly important for companies that do business globally (just think of the differences in regulations for automobiles in various countries or the differences in electrical power systems in the United States versus Europe). Therefore, companies that segment customers into natural groups and customize the products or services are better able to respond to customers' needs. Juran suggests classifying customers into two main groups: the vital few and the useful many.[16] For example, organizers of conventions and meetings book large blocks of hotel rooms and have large catering needs. They represent the vital few and deserve special attention on an individual basis. Individual travelers and families are the useful many and typically need only standardized attention as a group.

Customer segmentation might be based on geography, demographic factors, ways in which products are used or purchased (e.g., retail store customers versus Internet customers), volumes, or expected levels of service. For example, telecommunications services might be segmented by

1. Residential customers, grouped according to dollar amount billed.
2. Business customers, grouped according to size of business, number of different services used, and volume of usage.
3. Third-party resellers, who purchase telecommunications capacity in bulk and manage their own customer groups.[17]

Such segmentation allows a company to prioritize customer groups. One way to prioritize segments is to consider, for each group, the benefits of satisfying their requirements and the consequences of failing to satisfy their requirements. This determination of benefits and consequences allows the company to align its internal processes according to the most important customer expectations.

Another way of segmenting customers with an eye toward business results is by profit potential, measured by the **net present value of the customer (NPVC)**.[18] NPVC is the total profits (revenues associated with a customer minus expenses needed to serve a customer) discounted over time. For instance, the profit associated with customers at an automobile dealer consist of the profit from the sale of a car plus the profit from service visits. The number of transactions associated with repeat customers can easily be estimated. For example, frequent fliers represent high NPVC customers to an airline. By segmenting them according to their frequency, an airline can determine the net value of offering increasing levels of benefits to fliers at higher frequency levels as a means of retaining current customers or enticing potential customers. Firms can also use NPVC to eliminate customers with low or negative values that represent a financial liability. For example, the Fleet Financial Group dropped its basic savings account interest rate, hoping to lose customers who had only savings accounts.[19]

UNDERSTANDING CUSTOMER NEEDS

David A. Garvin suggests that products and services have many dimensions of quality:[20]

1. *Performance:* a product's primary operating characteristics. Using an automobile as an example, these would include such things as acceleration, braking distance, steering, and handling.
2. *Features:* the "bells and whistles" of a product. A car may have power options, a tape or CD deck, antilock brakes, and reclining seats.
3. *Reliability:* the probability of a product's operating over a specified period of time under stated conditions of use. A car's ability to start on cold days and frequency of failures are reliability factors.
4. *Conformance:* the degree to which physical and performance characteristics of a product match pre-established standards. A car's fit and finish and freedom from noises and squeaks can reflect this dimension.
5. *Durability:* the amount of use one gets from a product before it physically deteriorates or until replacement is preferable. For a car it might include corrosion resistance and the long wear of upholstery fabric.
6. *Serviceability:* the speed, courtesy, and competence of repair work. An automobile owner might be concerned with access to spare parts, the number of miles between major maintenance services, and the expense of service.
7. *Aesthetics:* how a product looks, feels, sounds, tastes, or smells. A car's color, instrument panel design, control placement, and "feel of the road," for example, may make it aesthetically pleasing.

Table 4.1 gives some examples of these dimensions for both a manufactured product and a service product. They form the basis for what customers want. A driver seeking performance, for example, might look to BMW, while one who values reliability might prefer a Toyota. Others who want features might choose Chrysler or Lincoln. Therefore, companies need to focus on the key drivers of customer satisfaction that lead to business success. Considerable marketing efforts go into correctly identifying customer needs. Ford, for example, identified about 90 features that customers want in sales and service, including a ride to their next stop when they drop off a car for service and appointments within one day of a desired date. Ford then trimmed the

Table 4.1 Quality Dimensions of a Manufactured Product and Service

Quality Dimension	Manufactured Product (Stereo Amplifier)	Service Product (Checking Account)
Performance	Signal-to-noise ratio; power	Time to process customer requests
Features	Remote control	Automatic bill paying
Conformance	Workmanship	Accuracy
Reliability	Mean time to failure	Variability of time to process requests
Durability	Useful life	Keeping pace with industry trends
Serviceability	Ease of repair	Resolution of errors
Aesthetics	Oak cabinet	Appearance of bank lobby

Source: Adapted from Paul E. Pisek, "Defining Quality at the Marketing/Development Interface," *Quality Progress* 20, no. 6 (June 1987), 28–36.

list to seven service standards and six sales standards against which dealers have begun to measure themselves.[21]

For services, research has shown that five key dimensions of service quality contribute to customer perceptions:

1. *Reliability:* the ability to provide what was promised, dependably and accurately. Examples include customer service representatives responding in the promised time, following customer instructions, providing error-free invoices and statements, and making repairs correctly the first time.
2. *Assurance:* the knowledge and courtesy of employees, and their ability to convey trust and confidence. Examples include the ability to answer questions, having the capabilities to do the necessary work, monitoring credit card transactions to avoid possible fraud, and being polite and pleasant during customer transactions.
3. *Tangibles:* the physical facilities and equipment, and the appearance of personnel. Tangibles include attractive facilities, appropriately dressed employees, and well-designed forms that are easy to read and interpret.
4. *Empathy:* the degree of caring and individual attention provided to customers. Some examples might be the willingness to schedule deliveries at the customer's convenience, explaining technical jargon in layperson's language, and recognizing regular customers by name.
5. *Responsiveness:* the willingness to help customers and provide prompt service. Examples include acting quickly to resolve problems, promptly crediting returned merchandise, and rapidly replacing defective products.

AT&T Universal Card Services incorporated many of these factors in a life-cycle approach for its credit card product. They identified key customer expectations for four key activities:

1. Applying for an account: *accessible, responsive, do it right, and professional*
2. Using the card: *easy to use and hassle free, features, credit limit*
3. Billing: *accurate, timely, easy to understand*
4. Customer service: *accessible, responsive, do it right, and professional.*

A Japanese professor, Noriaki Kano, suggested three classes of customer requirements:

1. *Dissatisfiers:* requirements that are expected in a product or service. In an automobile, a radio, heater, and required safety features are examples, which are generally not stated by customers but assumed as given. If these features are not present, the customer is dissatisfied.
2. *Satisfiers:* requirements that customers say they want. Many car buyers want a sunroof, power windows, or antilock brakes. Although these requirements are generally not expected, fulfilling them creates satisfaction.
3. *Exciters/delighters:* new or innovative features that customers do not expect. The presence of unexpected features, such as the example shown in Figure 4.4, leads to high perceptions of quality. Collision avoidance systems, for example, may be an automotive exciter/delighter soon.

Meeting customer expectations (that is, providing satisfiers) is often considered the minimum required to stay in business. To be truly competitive, companies must surprise and delight customers by going beyond the expected. Teams at Custom Research, Inc. (see *Quality Profile*), all have the same goal of "surprising and delighting" their clients. Client requirements are determined during client interviews, and drive

Figure 4.4 An Example of an Exciter/Delighter in the Hotel Industry

MARRIOTT'S
Orlando World Center
RESORT AND CONVENTION CENTER

Room Number ________

Welcome to Marriott's Orlando World Center!

We hope your stay will be an enjoyable one. As an added convenience, we have provided this service card.

Please check the appropriate box and we will gladly service your room daily at the time you have requested throughout your stay.

☐ 8 - 10 a.m.	☐ 12 - 2 p.m.
☐ 10 - 12 a.m.	☐ 2 - 4 p.m.
☐ For today only ________	☐ After 4 p.m.
☐ For the remainder of my stay ________	☐ Do Not Disturb

Departure date ________________

Please hang outside your door before retiring.

Thank you very much,
Housekeeping Staff

Source: Courtesy of Marriott International, Inc.

account plans to ensure that each project meets or exceeds client requirements through clearly agreed-upon service standards, as well as longer-term process plans to improve the company's key processes. Feedback at the end of each project and annual interviews of major clients measure satisfaction and drive improvements. Thus, successful companies continually innovate and study customer perceptions to ensure that needs are being met.

As customers become familiar with them, exciters and delighters become satisfiers over time. Eventually, satisfiers become dissatisfiers. For instance, antilock brakes and airbags certainly were exciters or delighters when they were first introduced. Now,

Quality Profile
Custom Research, Inc.

Custom Research, Inc. (CRI) is a national marketing research firm based in Minneapolis. Employing only 100 people, in 1996 it became the smallest company to receive a Baldrige Award. CRI adopted a highly focused customer-as-partner approach in 1988, and leverages an intensive focus on customer satisfaction, a team-oriented workforce, and information technology to pursue individualized service and satisfied customers. More recently, senior management aimed for high levels of consistency and competence in delivering its services by organizing, systematizing, and measuring quality. Each research project is monitored on four essentials: accuracy, on time, on budget, and meeting or exceeding client expectations. CRI's business system is focused on a "Surprise and Delight" strategy, supported by five key business drivers: people, processes, requirements, relationships, and results.

In 1996 CRI had revenues over $21 million and met or exceeded clients' expectations on 97 percent of its projects. More impressive is the fact that 70 percent of its clients said that the company exceeded expectations. CRI is rated by 92 percent of clients as "better than competition" on the key dimension "overall level of service."

Source: Malcolm Baldrige National Quality Award, Profiles of Winners, National Institute of Standards and Technology, Department of Commerce.

most car buyers expect them. Satellite navigational systems for automobiles are a more recent example of exciters and delighters that are becoming more commonplace and may soon be viewed as satisfiers. As technology evolves, consumer expectations continually increase.

In the Kano classification system, dissatisfiers and satisfiers are relatively easy to determine through routine marketing research. For example, the hot-selling Ford F-150 pickup truck relied on extensive consumer research at the beginning of the redesign process. Perhaps one of the best examples of understanding customer needs and using this information to improve competitiveness is Frank Perdue's chicken business.[22] Perdue learned what customers' key purchase criteria were, which included a yellow bird, high meat-to-bone ratio, no pinfeathers, freshness, availability, and brand image. He also determined the relative importance of each criterion, and how well the company and its competitors were meeting each one. By systematically improving his ability to exceed customers' expectations relative to the competition, Perdue gained market share even though his chickens were premium-priced. Among Perdue's innovations was using a jet engine that dried the chickens after plucking, allowing the pinfeathers to be singed off.

However, traditional market research efforts may not be effective in understanding exciters and delighters, and may even backfire. For example, Ford listened to a sample of customers and asked if they wanted a fourth door on the Windstar minivan. Only about a third thought it was a great idea, so Ford scrapped the idea. Chrysler, on the other hand, spent a lot more time living with owners of vans and observing their behavior, watching them wrestle to get things in and out, noting all the occasions where a fourth door would really be convenient, and was very successful after introducing a fourth door.[23] Thus, a company must make special effort to identify exciters and delighters. Sony and Seiko, for instance, go beyond traditional market research and produce dozens, even hundreds, of Walkman audio products and wristwatches with a variety of features to help them understand what excites and delights the customer. Those models that do not sell are simply dropped from the product lines. To practice this strategy effectively, marketing efforts must be supported by highly flexible manufacturing systems that permit rapid setup and quick response. Producing breakthrough products or services often requires that companies ignore consumer feedback and take risks. As Steve Jobs of Apple Computer noted about the iMac, "That doesn't mean we don't listen to customers, but it's hard for them to tell you what they want when they've never seen anything remotely like it. Take desktop video editing. I never got one request from someone who wanted to edit movies on his computer. Yet now that people see it, they say, 'Oh my God, that's great!'"[24]

Besides consumers, companies must also pay attention to the needs of external customers. In designing its Icy Rider sled, Rubbermaid used a combination of field research, competitive product analysis, and consumer focus groups. It also listened to major retailers, such as Wal-Mart, who wanted such products to be stackable and save space.[25]

Understanding the needs of internal customers is as important as understanding those of external customers. This relationship is reflected in the AT&T customer-supplier model in Figure 4.3, which the company uses to help employees comprehend internal customer-supplier issues. For example, in many service industries, customer-contact employees depend on a variety of information and support from internal suppliers, such as the information systems department, warehousing and production scheduling, and engineering and design functions. Failure to meet the needs of customer-contact employees will have a detrimental effect on external customers. One company, GTE Supply, negotiates contracts, purchases products, and distributes goods for internal telephone operations customer groups at each GTE local telephone company (telco). In response to complaints from its internal customers, GTE Supply began to survey its internal customers to identify needs and information for improvement. This approach dramatically improved satisfaction levels, reduced costs, and decreased cycle times.[26]

GATHERING CUSTOMER INFORMATION

Customer requirements, as expressed in the customer's own terms, are called the **voice of the customer**. However, the customer's meaning is the crucial part of the message. As the vice president of marketing at Whirlpool stated, "The consumer speaks in code."[27] Whirlpool's research showed that customers wanted clean refrigerators, which could be interpreted to mean that they wanted easy-to-clean refrigerators. After analyzing the data and asking more questions, Whirlpool found out what most consumers actually wanted was refrigerators that looked clean with minimum fuss. As a result, Whirlpool developed models having stucco-like fronts and sides that hide fingerprints.

Companies use a variety of methods, or "listening posts," to collect information about customer needs and expectations, their importance, and customer satisfaction with the company's performance on these measures. Zytec Corporation relies on eight different processes to gather data and information from and about customers, as shown in Figure 4.5. Notice how the number and sophistication of these processes increased over the years, indicating cycles of learning and refinement. Some of the key approaches to gathering customer information include the following:

1. *Comment cards and formal surveys:* Comment cards and formal surveys are easy ways to solicit customer information. These approaches typically concentrate on measuring customer satisfaction, which is discussed later in this chapter,

Figure 4.5 Zytec Corporation's Processes for Determining Customer Requirements and Expectations

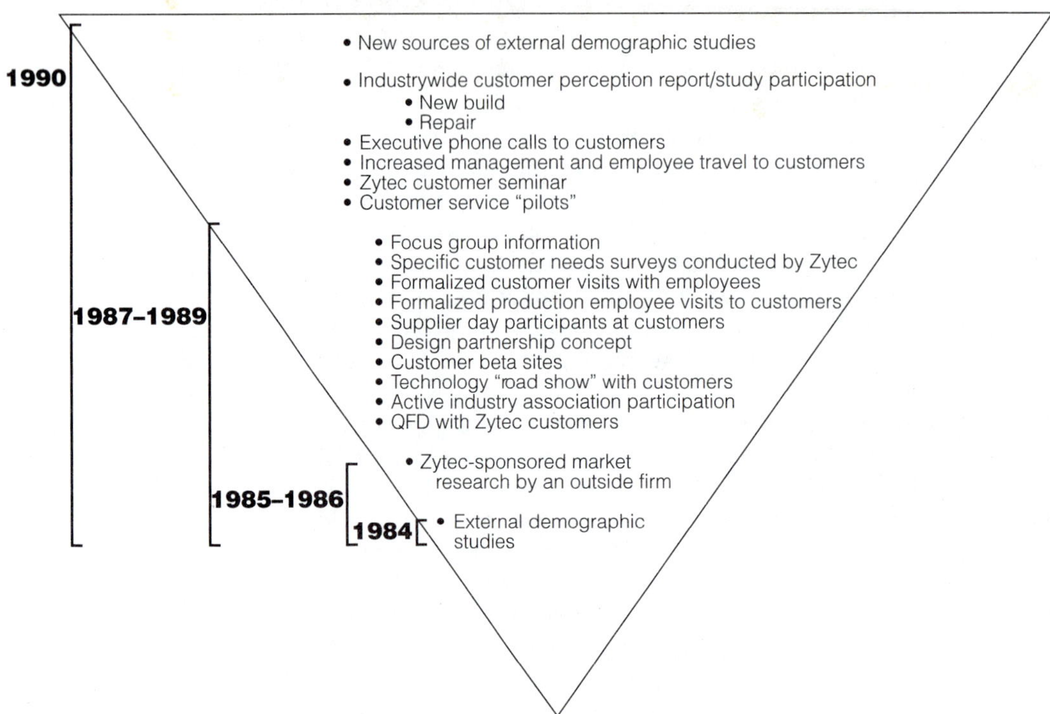

and often include questions pertaining to the customers' perception of the importance of particular quality dimensions as well as open-ended questions. Figure 4.6 shows one example; note that question 5 seeks ideas for improvements. However, few customers generally will respond to comment cards placed at restaurant tables or in hotel rooms, and those who do may not represent the typical customer.

Formal surveys can be designed to scientifically sample a customer base, but usually only a small proportion of customers respond. However, some companies find that they work well. USAA, a San Antonio financial services company, mails 500,000 surveys to customers from a base of 2.5 million to inquire about satisfaction, future needs, and ideas for new products, and gets a 60 percent return. BASF Corporation includes a self-addressed stamped card with each product shipment, asking customers if the shipment arrived on time, its condition and conformance to requirements, whether paperwork was included, if the correct fittings and equipment were on the truck, and if the truck driver was courteous and helpful.[28] Intel Corporation created the Vendor of Choice system to gather customer information. This survey asks customers what they want from a supplier and covers areas of service, price, delivery, quality, and technology. Formal surveys must be designed carefully to ensure that the right information is acquired, and that unclear questions, biased questions, and excessively long questionnaires are not used.

2. *Focus groups:* A focus group is a panel of individuals (customers or noncustomers) who answer questions about a company's products and services as well

Figure 4.6 Comment Card

BUSINESS REPLY MAIL
FIRST-CLASS PERMIT NO. 5972 ORLANDO, FL

POSTAGE WILL BE PAID BY ADDRESSEE

TRAINING & DEVELOPMENT
RED LOBSTER
1700 DIPLOMACY ROW
ORLANDO, FL 32809-9702

288

TELL US WHAT YOU THINK

1) During your visit were you called by name? Yes ☐ No ☐

2) Did a manager visit your table? Yes ☐ No ☐

3) How would you rate your service?

	Strongly Agree	Agree	Neutral	Disagree	Strongly Disagree
I felt welcome when I arrived					
The staff looked attractive, neat and clean					
The staff was warm & friendly					
The restaurant was adequately staffed					
My experience was pleasant & relaxed					
The staff was attentive to my needs					
My experience was a good value					
My meal was paced to my needs					

4) How would you rate your food?

	Excellent	Very Good	Good	Fair	Poor
Appearance					
Taste					
Temperature					
Portion Size					

5) Is there something we should work on improving? ______________

6) Your name and address (optional) ______________

Source: Courtesy of Red Lobster, Inc.

as those of competitors. This interview approach allows a company to carefully select the composition of the panel and probe panel members about important issues, with in-depth comparisons of experiences with expectations. Key questions that companies ask include: What do you like about the product or service? What pleases or delights you? What do you dislike? What problems have you encountered? If you had the ability, how would you change the product or service? Binney & Smith, maker of Crayolas, conducts focus groups with the ultimate customer: young children.

Although customers generally like to fill out surveys and comment cards, by doing so they are simply responding to the perspective of the people who designed the survey. Focus groups offer a substantial advantage by providing the direct voice of the customer to an organization. A disadvantage of focus groups is their higher cost of implementation compared to other approaches.

3. *Direct customer contact:* In customer-driven companies, top executives commonly visit with customers personally. Hearing issues and complaints firsthand is often an eye-opening experience. For example, top managers at Xerox spend one day each month answering customer service phones to interface with customers directly. Black & Decker executives go to homeowners' workshops to watch how customers use their tools, ask why they like or dislike certain ones, and even observe how they clean up their work space when they finish.[29] This approach also works well with rank-and-file employees. In 1992 Honda factory workers called more than 47,000 recent Accord buyers, about half of the owners who registered their cars with the company the previous spring, to find out whether customers were happy and to get ideas for improvements. Globe Metallurgical sends individual workers or teams to customers' facilities to find out which product characteristics are important to the customer and how customers use the products.
4. *Field intelligence:* Any employee who comes in direct contact with customers, such as salespeople, repair technicians, telephone operators, and receptionists, can obtain useful information simply by engaging in conversation and listening to customers. The effectiveness of this method depends upon a culture that encourages open communication with superiors. AT&T Universal Card Services, for example, received more than 1,000 customer comments per month. UCS had a well-defined process in which customer comments received by associates were submitted and reviewed by a manager, who then initiated any appropriate corrective action. All comments and suggestions were aggregated as a whole and used to improve existing products or for new product development activities.

   As another approach, employees simply observe customer behavior. One hotel noticed that customers did not use the complimentary bath crystals, so they eliminated the crystals (saving costs) and added other features that customers wanted. Honda frequently videotapes drivers as they test new cars.
5. *Complaint analysis:* Complaints, although undesirable from a service point of view, can be a key source of customer information. Complaints allow an organization to learn about product failures and service problems, particularly the gaps between expectations and performance. Hewlett-Packard, for example, assigns every piece of customer feedback to an "owner" in the company who must act on the information and report back to the person who called. If a customer complains about a printer, someone will check the company's database to see whether the complaint is widespread and what the company is doing about it. AT&T Transmission Systems uses cross-functional teams to address customer complaints and collect data for further analysis.

Studies indicate that approximately one out of 25 customers complains. Thus, to take full advantage of complaints, companies must make it easy for customers to complain. The Coca-Cola Company, for instance, was among the first in the soft drink industry to set up a toll-free consumer hotline number, which is printed on all product packages. Representatives log every contact into a computer system, which allows any quality problems to be tracked and resolved. Many companies use this practice today.

6. *Internet monitoring:*[30] In recent years, the growth of the Internet is offering companies a fertile arena for finding out what consumers think of their products. Internet users frequently seek advice from other users on strengths and weaknesses of products, share experiences on service quality, or pose specific problems they need to resolve. By monitoring the conversations on Usenet discussion groups, for example, managers can obtain valuable insights on customer perceptions and product or service quality problems. In open forums, customer comments can often be translated into creative product improvements. In addition, the Internet can be a good source of information about competitors' products. The cost of monitoring Internet conversations is minimal compared to the costs of other types of survey approaches, and customers are not biased by any questions that may be asked. However, the conversations may be considerably less structured and unfocused, and thus may contain less usable information. Also, unlike a focus group or telephone interview, inaccurate perceptions or factual errors cannot be corrected.

Some companies use unconventional and innovative approaches to understand customers. Texas Instruments created a simulated classroom to understand how mathematics teachers use calculators; and a manager at Levi Strauss used to talk with teens who were lined up to buy rock concert tickets. Other approaches for obtaining useful customer and market information might be rapid innovation and field trials of products and services to better link research and development with design to the market; close tracking of technological, competitive, societal, environmental, economic, and demographic factors that may affect customer requirements and expectations; and interviewing lost customers to determine the factors they use in their purchase decisions.

Tools for Classifying Customer Requirements

Throughout this book various graphical tools to help manage information for quality are introduced. These tools are simple to use and understand, and being graphical in nature, provide a visual means of communication, particularly when used by teams. This section presents affinity diagrams and tree diagrams. Although they are used to classify customer requirements, these tools can be applied in any setting that requires efficiently organized information. Other applications are described in later chapters.

The affinity diagram—a main ingredient of the KJ method, developed in the 1960s by Kawakita Jiro, a Japanese anthropologist—is a technique for gathering and organizing a large number of ideas or facts.[31] Its purpose is to allow teams to sift through large volumes of information efficiently and identify natural patterns or groupings in the information. With an affinity diagram, managers can more easily focus on the key issues and their elements rather than an unorganized collection of information. A tree diagram shows a hierarchical structure of facts and ideas. It is similar to an affinity diagram in that it categorizes concepts into natural groups. (Tree diagrams are also used in designing implementation plans for projects, which are shown in a later chapter.) Both affinity and tree diagrams are often used to organize customer requirements into logical categories, particularly after a variety of input is captured from interviews, field intelligence, and so on. For example, suppose that a banking team determined that the most important requirement for mortgage customers is timely closings.[32] Through focus groups and other customer interviews, customers listed the following as key elements of timely closings:

1. Expeditious processes
2. Reliability
3. Consistent and accurate information
4. Competitive rates
5. Notification of industry changes
6. Prior approvals
7. Innovation
8. Modem link between computers
9. Buyer orientation
10. Diversity of programs
11. Mutual job understanding
12. Flexibility
13. Professionalism
14. Timely and accurate status reports

The company's team would group these items into logical categories, and provide a descriptive title for each category. (For example, the use of Post-it® notes allow individual categorization in this process and can be easily moved around on a wall.) The result is an affinity diagram, shown in Figure 4.7, which indicates that the key customer requirements for timely closings are communication, effective service, and loan products. Through organization of an affinity diagram, information can be used to better design a company's products and processes to meet customer requirements. A tree diagram organizes the information in a slightly different fashion, as shown in Figure 4.8.

Figure 4.7 Affinity Diagram

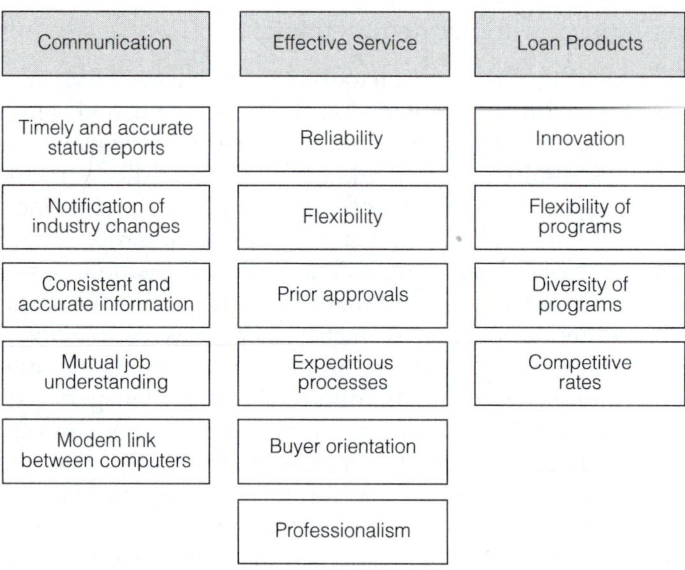

Figure 4.8 Tree Diagram

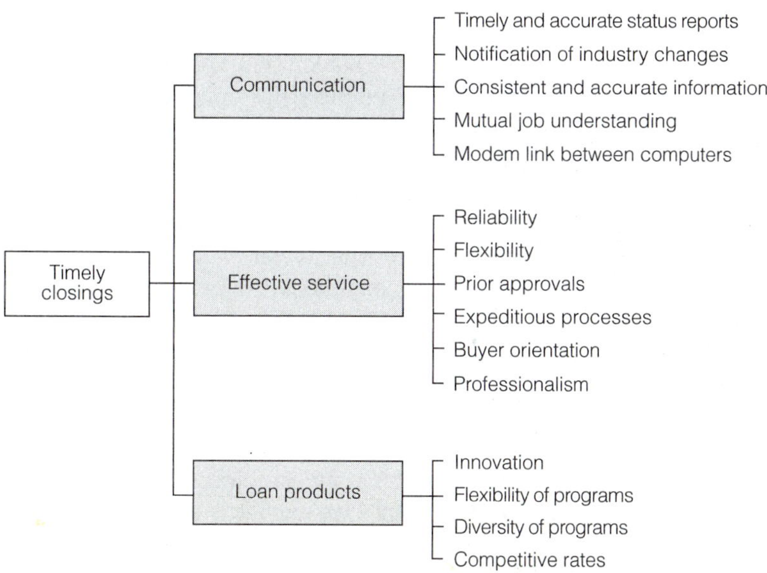

Affinity and tree diagrams are general tools that can be used for many other applications. For example, affinity diagrams can be used to organize any large group of complex ideas or issues, such as potential reasons for quality problems, or things a company must do to successfully market a product. A tree diagram can be used to map out sequences of activities that must be accomplished to meet a primary goal and related subgoals. We will present other examples in the next chapter.

CUSTOMER RELATIONSHIP MANAGEMENT

A company builds customer loyalty by developing trust, communicating with customers, and effectively managing the interactions and relationships with customers through approaches and its people. Truly excellent companies foster close relationships with customers that lead to loyalty. For example, Lexus owners who become accustomed to the at-home pickup of their vehicles for service, free loaners, and other special dealer touches may find it difficult to give up these services when it is time to purchase a new car. In Bank of Montreal's Private Client Services group, bankers provide services according to the preferences of their clients who value convenience and time, not the traditions of the bank. Such service might mean meeting in the client's home or office instead of the bank.[33] Dell Computer Corporation offers a variety of customer-friendly services that includes loading all the customer's software, even proprietary applications, at the factory and configuring it the way it is going to be used, saving hours of work by highly paid computer technicians.[34]

In services, customer satisfaction or dissatisfaction takes place during moments of truth—every instance in which a customer comes in contact with an employee of the company. Moments of truth may be direct contacts with customer representatives or service personnel, or when customers read letters, invoices, or other company correspondence. Problems result from unkept promises, failure to provide full service, service not provided when needed, incorrectly or incompletely performed service, or failure to convey the correct information. At moments of truth, customers form perceptions about the quality of the service by comparing their expectations with the actual outcomes.

Consider an airline, for example. (The phrase *moment of truth* was actually popularized by the CEO of Scandinavian Airlines System, Jan Carlzon.) Moments of truth occur when a customer makes a reservation, buys tickets, checks baggage, boards a flight, orders a beverage, requests a magazine, deplanes, and picks up baggage. Multiply these instances by the number of passengers and the number of daily flights, and it is easy to see that hundreds of thousands of moments of truth occur each day. Each occurrence influences a positive or negative image about the company. Southwest Airlines (see *Quality Profile*) recognizes the power of customer focus.[35] The company insists on capitalizing the word *Customer* in all its ads and brochures. Every one of the approximately 1,000 customers who write to the airline get a personal response (not a form letter) within four weeks, and frequent fliers get birthday cards. The airline even moved a flight up a quarter-hour when five medical students who commuted weekly to an out-of-state medical school complained that the flight got them to class 15 minutes late. To quote the CEO, "We dignify the Customer." Throughout the 1990s Southwest was more profitable than most major U.S. airlines.

Excellent customer relationship management depends on five aspects:

1. Accessibility and commitments
2. Selecting and developing customer contact employees
3. Relevant customer contact requirements
4. Effective complaint management
5. Strategic partnerships and alliances

Each aspect is addressed in the next sections.

Quality Profile

Southwest Airlines

Southwest Airlines began operations on June 18, 1971, with flights to Houston, Dallas, and San Antonio, and has grown to become the fifth largest U.S. airline in terms of domestic customers carried. The airline operates more than 2,150 flights daily with more than 23,000 employees. Known for its legendary service, the Southwest culture ensures that it serves the needs of its Customers (with a capital C) in a friendly, caring, and enthusiastic manner. This applies to internal customers also; it is not unusual to find pilots helping ground crews unload baggage. As executive vice president Colleen Barrett stated, "We are not an airline with great customer service. We are a great customer service organization that happens to be in the airline business."

As of 1996 Southwest had 23 years of consistent profitability, and was the only major carrier to make both net and operating profits in 1990, 1991, and 1992. From 1992–1995, Southwest was recognized for best baggage handling, fewest customer complaints, and best on-time performance of any major U.S. airline, and has been recognized with numerous honors, including one of America's Most Admired Corporations by *Fortune* magazine.

Sources: Southwest Airlines home page *http://iflyswa.com* and Kevin Freiberg and Jackie Freiberg, *NUTS! Southwest Airlines' Crazy Recipe for Business and Personal Success* (Austin, TX: Bard Press, 1996).

Accessibility and Commitments

Customer-focused organizations provide customers easy access to their employees. Procter & Gamble was the first company to install a toll-free number for its products in 1974. AT&T Universal Card Services, for instance, used an 800 number, fax, and access for the hearing impaired 24 hours every day throughout the year, translation services for 140 languages, and bilingual Spanish-English operators. Customers were also informed when they would have to wait more than a minute. Globe Metallurgical and Westinghouse allow customers to conduct quality audits of the company facilities. Customers of Ames Rubber Corporation have immediate access to top division management, manufacturing personnel, quality engineers, sales and service representatives, and technical support staff. Today, e-mail and Web site access are becoming the media of choice for many consumers.

Companies that truly believe in the quality of their products make strong commitments to their customers. Commitments address the principal concerns of customers, are free from conditions that might weaken customers' trust and confidence, and are communicated clearly and simply to customers. Many commitments take the form of explicit guarantees and warranties. FedEx is highly recognized for its guarantee, which refunds full charges if a shipment is even a minute late. Xerox replaces any product that a customer does not find satisfactory, for any reason, within three years of purchase. Xerox has also implemented a Check Performance Guarantee. This guarantee ensures that Xerox will pay all bank processing fees that result from any checks produced on a Xerox 4197 II laser printer being rejected by a bank due to printer or toner-related problems.[36] Texas Instruments Defense Systems & Electronics Group pioneered the first product warranty for a missile product in its HARM warranty that allowed customers to return any system that failed within the first year after delivery. This practice was unheard of in the defense industry at that time. Similarly, Zaring Homes, a Cincinnati-based builder, promises that its homes will be built on time, on budget, and within specified quality standards, or the home is free—an extremely bold step for the housing industry.

Extraordinary guarantees that promise exceptional, uncompromising quality and customer satisfaction, and back that promise with a payout intended to fully recapture the customer's goodwill with few if any strings attached are one of the strongest actions a company can take to improve itself.[37] L.L. Bean's guarantee is a good example: "Everything we sell is backed by a 100 percent unconditional guarantee. We do not want you to have anything from L.L. Bean that is not completely satisfactory. Return anything you buy from us at any time for any reason it proves otherwise." By translating every element of customer dissatisfaction into financial costs, such guarantees quickly alert the company to problems and direct priorities. Workers gain better knowledge of the business and quality improves, which, in turn, results in increased sales and higher profits.

Selecting and Developing Customer-Contact Employees

Customer-contact employees are particularly important. They are the people whose main responsibilities bring them into regular contact with customers—in person, by telephone, or through other means. Procter & Gamble calls its consumer relations department the "voice of the company." A staff of more than 250 employees handles in excess of 3 million contacts each year. Their mission is stated as "We are a world-class consumer response center. We provide superior service to consumers who contact Procter & Gamble, encourage product repurchase, and help build brand loyalty. We protect the Company's image and the reputation of our brands by resolving complaints before they are escalated to government agencies or the media. We capture and report consumer data to key Company functions, identify and share consumer insights, counsel product categories on consumer issues and trends, and manage consumer handling and interaction during crises." Today, companies rely on call centers—more than 60,000 in the United States and growing at 20 percent per year—as their primary means of customer contact. Call centers can be a means of competitive advantage by serving customers more efficiently and personalizing transactions to build relationships. However, they must be supported by appropriate technology, such as automating routine calls to minimize the necessity of answering the same questions over and over, and routing calls to people with appropriate skills. Inefficient processes can only lead to frustrated customers.

Companies must carefully select customer-contact employees, train them well, and empower them to meet and exceed customer expectations. Many companies begin with the recruiting process, selecting those employees who show the ability and desire to develop good customer relationships. Major companies such as Procter & Gamble seek people with excellent interpersonal and communication skills, strong problem-solving and analytical skills, assertiveness, stress tolerance, patience and empathy, accuracy and attention to detail, and computer literacy. Job applicants often go through rigorous screening processes. At AT&T Universal Card Services, for instance, every applicant completed a two-part general aptitude test. The company then invited successful candidates to participate in additional testing, which included a customer-service role-playing exercise. Each applicant was asked to handle simulated incoming and outgoing calls. After completing the initial screening test, each candidate had to pass a background check, credit check, and a medical evaluation, including drug testing, before being hired.

Companies committed to customer relationship management ensure that customer-contact employees understand the products and services well enough to answer any question, develop good listening and problem-recovery skills, and feel able to handle problems. Effective training not only increases employees' knowledge, but improves their self-esteem and loyalty to the organization. The Ritz-Carlton Hotel Company follows orientation training with on-the-job training and, subsequently, job certification. The company reinforces its values daily, recognizes extraordinary achievement, and appraises performance based on expectations explained during the orientation, training, and certification processes. For many organizations, customer relationship training involves every person who comes in contact with customers, including receptionists.

Customers dislike being transferred to a seemingly endless number of employees to obtain information or resolve a problem. Empowered employees are able to make decisions on their own to satisfy the customer. TQ-focused companies empower their front-line people to do whatever is necessary to satisfy the customer. At The Ritz-Carlton, all employees are empowered to do whatever it takes to provide "instant pacification." No matter what their normal duties are, other employees must assist if aid is requested by a fellow worker who is responding to a guest's complaint or wish. Universal Card Services customer-contact associates were empowered to award a customer a $10 service guarantee certificate to apply to their bill if they perceive that the company inconvenienced the customer. However, the actions of empowered employees should be guided by a common vision. That is, employees require a consistent understanding of what actions they may or should take.

Customer-contact employees also need access to the right technology and company information to do their jobs. FedEx, for example, furnishes employees with the information and technology they need to continually improve their performance.

The Digitally Assisted Dispatch System (DADS) communicates to all couriers through screens in their vans, enabling quick response to pickup and delivery dispatches; it allows couriers to manage their time and routes with high efficiency. Information technology improves productivity, increases communication, and allows customer contact employees to handle most customer issues.

Customer Contact Requirements

Front-line personnel who come in daily contact with customers have a significant amount of responsibility for customer satisfaction. **Customer contact requirements** are measurable performance levels or expectations that define the quality of customer contact with representatives of an organization. They might include technical requirements such as response time (answering the telephone within two rings), or behavioral requirements (using a customer's name whenever possible). Cadillac, for example, has well over 200 standards in its annual dealer service evaluation that measure dealer's customer satisfaction and service operation effectiveness. Customer needs and expectations form the basis of measurable contact requirements. For example, a customer need might be a rapid response to an inquiry. In this case, the contact requirement might be to return the customer's call within two hours with the information requested, even if the call is received near the end of the business day. The *Quality in Practice* case about Florida Power and Light later in this chapter provides a good example of how customer expectations determine contact requirements.

Companies need to communicate these requirements to all customer-contact employees. This communication often initially takes place during new employee orientations. However, to maintain the consistency and effectiveness of these standards, companies must continually reinforce their standards. Additionally, many customer-contact employees depend on internal customers for support, who also must understand the role they play in meeting the requirements. The key to satisfying external customers is to satisfy internal customers first. At Southwest Airlines, for example, the philosophy is that if employees can provide the same service to one another as they do to passengers, the airline will benefit.[38] Each operating division identifies an internal customer. Mechanics who service planes target the pilots who fly them, and marketers treat reservation agents as customers. Departments even provide free ice cream or pizza as tokens of customer appreciation or for a job well done. Use of the customer-supplier model approach effectively communicates the importance of these relationships.

Finally, a company should implement a process for tracking adherence to the requirements and providing feedback to the employees to improve their performance. Information technology supplies the data for effectively tracking conformance to customer contact requirements.

Effective Complaint Management

Despite all efforts to satisfy customers, every business experiences unhappy customers. Complaints can adversely affect business if not dealt with effectively. A company called TARP, formerly known as Technical Assistance Research Programs, Inc., conducted studies that revealed the following information:

1. The average company never hears from 96 percent of its unhappy customers. For every complaint received, the company has 26 more customers with problems, six of whose problems are serious.

2. Of the customers who make a complaint, more than half will again do business with that organization if their complaint is resolved. If the customer feels that the complaint was resolved quickly, the figure jumps to 95 percent.
3. The average customer who has had a problem will tell nine or ten others about it. Customers who have had complaints resolved satisfactorily will only tell about five others of the problem resolution.[39]
4. With the advent of the Internet, TARP also found that 4 percent of satisfied customers post their feelings on the Web, while 15 percent of unsatisfied customers do the same.[40]

Leading organizations consider complaints as opportunities for improvement. Encouraging customers to complain, making it easy for them to do so, and effectively resolving complaints increase customer loyalty and retention. Many customers do not complain because they feel it wouldn't do any good or they are uncomfortable with the process. Besides providing easy access to the company using toll-free telephone numbers (which should be adequately staffed and supported), many firms actively solicit complaints. Nissan, for instance, telephones each person who buys a new car or brings one in for significant warranty work. Its objective is to resolve all dissatisfaction within 24 hours.[41]

Companies involved in customer relationship management train customer-contact personnel to deal with angry customers. Customer service personnel need to listen carefully to determine the customer's feelings and then respond sympathetically, ensuring that the complaint is understood. They should make every effort to resolve the problem quickly. At The Ritz-Carlton Hotel Company, for example, employees can spend up to $2,000 to resolve complaints with no questions asked.

Many companies have well-defined processes for dealing with complaints. For example, at BI, all complaints, regardless of where they come from, are forwarded directly to the appropriate business unit manager.[42] The manager follows the Service Recovery Process (see Figure 4.9) and contacts the customer directly for clarification of the issue and additional information. Findings are then communicated to the account executive, sales manager, account manager, and all involved business unit associates via e-mail. This process enables the BI team to work in conjunction with the customer to address the failure and provide a solution that meets the customer's needs. A written follow-up of the resolution is shared with all BI team members working with the customer.

Complaints provide a source of product and process improvement ideas. Leading-edge companies encourage employees to bring complaints to the surface in a variety of formal and informal ways, such as a response center to encourage employees to call with ideas and process improvements as well as complaints, and rewards and recognition for employees involved in the processes. To improve products and processes effectively, companies must do more than simply fix the immediate problem. They need a systematic process for collecting and analyzing complaint data and then using that information for improvements. Typically, cross-functional teams study the information, determine the real source of the complaints, and make recommendations. Technology is often used to capture, analyze, and report complaint data. In addition, the complaint process itself needs to be monitored, evaluated, and improved. Companies typically track the percentage of customers who are satisfied with complaint resolution, the cost of resolving complaints, and the time required to resolve them.

Strategic Partnerships and Alliances

Today's suppliers are being asked to take on greater responsibilities to help their customers. As companies focus more on their core competencies—the things they do

Figure 4.9 BI Service Recovery Process

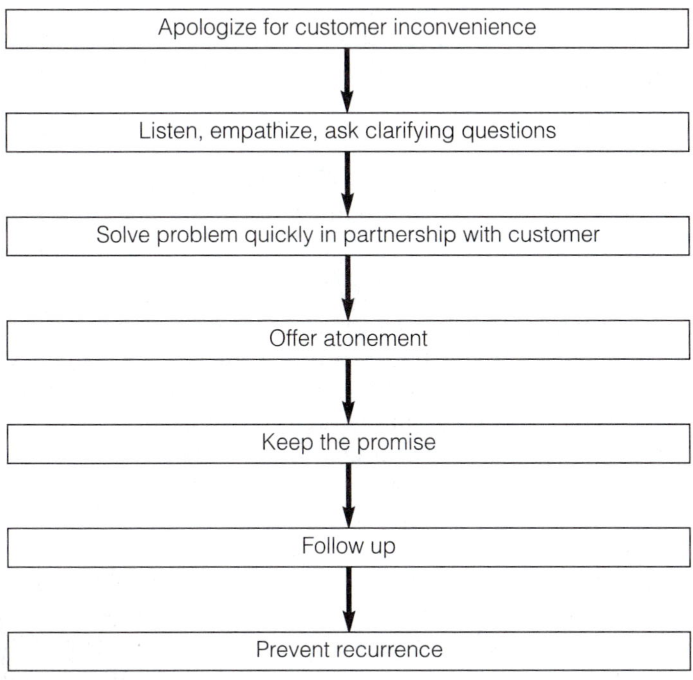

Source: Courtesy of Guy Schoenecker, president and chief quality officer.

best—they are looking outside their organizations for assistance with noncritical support processes. Customer-supplier partnerships represent an important strategic alliance in achieving excellence and business success. Benefits of such partnerships include access to technology or distribution channels not available internally, shared risks in new investments and product development, improved products through early design recommendations based on supplier capabilities, and reduced operations costs through better communications. For example, FedEx and Jostens formed a strategic partnership that enabled both to benefit from new sales of scholastic jewelry and yearbooks.[43] They took advantage of each other's strengths: Jostens provided a high-quality product with superior service, and FedEx provided reliable high-volume, short-interval delivery for these time-critical products.

Many companies work closely with suppliers that share common values. This close relationship improves supplier capabilities by teaching them quality-related tools and approaches. Although many companies have formal supplier certification programs (discussed in Chapter 7) in which they rate their suppliers, some companies such as Motorola, ask suppliers to rate *them* as customers. Motorola uses a 15-member council of suppliers that rates Motorola's practices and offers suggestions for improving, for example, the accuracy of production schedules or design layouts that Motorola provides.[44] Some typical questions that companies might ask of their suppliers might be[45] What expectations do you have that are not being met? What type of technical assistance would you like from us? What type of feedback would you like from us? What benefits are you looking for in a partnership? Better two-way communication can improve both products and relationships.

MEASURING CUSTOMER SATISFACTION

Customer feedback is vital to a business. Through feedback, a company learns how satisfied its customers are with its products and services and sometimes about competitors' products and services. Measurement of customer satisfaction completes the loop shown in Figure 4.2. Measures of customer satisfaction allow a business to do the following:

1. Discover customer perceptions of how well the business is doing in meeting customer needs.
2. Compare the company's performance relative to competitors.
3. Discover areas for improvement, both in the design and delivery of products and services.
4. Track trends to determine whether changes actually result in improvements.

An effective customer satisfaction measurement system results in reliable information about customer ratings of specific product and service features and about the relationship between these ratings and the customer's likely future market behavior. However, it is important to understand that customer satisfaction is a psychological attitude. It is not easy to measure and can only be observed indirectly. The ACSI model in Figure 4.1 shows that customer satisfaction is influenced by customer expectations and perceptions of quality and value. Thus, it is difficult to reduce these complex relationships into a single measure.

Customer satisfaction measures may include product attributes such as product quality, product performance, usability, and maintainability; service attributes such as attitude, lead time, on-time delivery, exception handling, accountability, and technical support; image attributes such as reliability and price; and overall satisfaction measures. At FedEx, customers are asked to rate everything from billing to the performance of couriers, package condition, tracking and tracing capabilities, complaint handling, and helpfulness of employees. Measurements are based on a bona fide customer requirement or need.

The most helpful customer data include comparisons with key competitors. Companies often rely on third parties to conduct blind surveys to determine who key competitors are and how their products and services compare. Competitive comparisons often clarify how improvements in quality can translate into better customer satisfaction or whether key quality characteristics are being overlooked.

Designing Satisfaction Surveys

The first step in developing a customer satisfaction survey is to determine its purpose. Surveys should be designed to clearly provide the users of the survey results with the information they need to make decisions. A critical question to consider is: Who is the customer? Managers, purchasing agents, end users, and others all may be affected by a company's products and services. Xerox, for instance, sends specific surveys to buyers, managers, and users. Buyers provide feedback on their perceptions of the sales processes, managers provide input on billing and other administrative processes, and users provide feedback on product performance and technical support. And customer satisfaction measurement should not be confined to external customers. Information from internal customers also contributes to the assessment of the organization's strengths and weaknesses. Often the problems that cause employee dissatisfaction are the same issues that cause dissatisfaction in external customers. Many companies use employee opinion surveys or similar vehicles to seek employee feedback on the work environment, benefits, compensation, management, team activities, rewards and recognition, and company plans and values. However, other indicators of employee satisfaction are absenteeism, turnover, grievances, and strikes, which can often supply better information than surveys that many employees may not take seriously.

The next question to address is who should conduct the survey. Independent third-party organizations often have more credibility to respondents and can ensure objectivity in the results. After these preliminary steps are completed, it is necessary to define the sample frame; that is, the target group from which a sample is chosen. Depending on the purpose of the survey, it might be the entire customer base or a specific segment. For example, a manufacturer of commercial lawn tractors might design different surveys for golf course superintendents who purchase the tractors and another for end users who ride them daily.

The next step is to select the appropriate survey instrument. Formal written surveys are the most common means of measuring customer satisfaction, although other techniques, such as face-to-face interviews, telephone interviews, and focus groups are used. Written surveys have the advantage of low data collection costs, self-administration, and ease of analysis; when used, they should be kept short and simple. In addition, they can probe deeply into the issues. However, they suffer from high nonresponse bias, require large sample sizes, and measure predetermined perceptions of what is important to customers, thus reducing the scope of qualitative information that can be obtained. Face-to-face interviews and focus groups, on the other hand, require much smaller sample sizes and can generate a significant amount of qualitative information, but incur high costs and participant time commitments. Telephone interviews fall somewhere in between these extremes. Telephone interviews appear to be the preferred approach for companies with a limited number of business customers; mail-based surveys are used to track routine transactions, where key attributes are stable over time. For example, Toyota uses mail surveys to identify unhappy customers and then telephones them for more details. This approach is cost-effective when the majority of customers are satisfied.[46]

The types of questions to ask must be properly worded to achieve actionable results. By actionable, we mean that responses are tied directly to key business processes, so that what needs to be improved is clear; and responses are translated into cost-revenue implications to support the setting of improvement priorities. One should avoid leading questions, compound questions that address more than one issue or idea, ambiguous questions, acronyms and jargon that the respondent may not understand, and double negatives. For example, the question "How would you rate our service?" is too ambiguous and provides little actionable information. A better question would be "How would you rate the response time of our technical support desk?" Another poor example is "Should Burger Mart increase its food portions at a higher price?" This question addresses two different issues. Open-ended questions such as "If this were your business, what would you do differently?" often lead to honest opinions. Most surveys also ask for basic demographic information to stratify the data.

A "Likert" scale is commonly used to measure the response (see Table 4.2). Likert scales allow customers to express their degree of opinion. Five-point scales have been shown to have good reliability and are often used. Responses in the "5" range tell a company what it is doing very well. Responses in the "4" range suggest that customer expectations are being met, but that the company may be vulnerable to competitors. Responses in the "3" range mean that the product or service barely meets customer expectations and that much room for improvement exists. Responses in the "1" or "2" range indicate serious problems. However, most scales like these exhibit response bias. That is, people tend to give either high or low values. If responses are clustered on the high side, it is difficult to discriminate among responses, and the resulting skewness in the distribution causes the mean value to be misleading.

Table 4.2 Examples of Likert Scales Used for Customer Satisfaction Measurement

Very Poor 1	Poor 2	Neither Poor nor Good 3	Good 4	Very Good 5
Strongly Disagree 1	Disagree 2	Neither Agree nor Disagree 3	Agree 4	Strongly Agree 5
Very Dissatisfied 1	Dissatisfied 2	Neither Satisfied nor Dissatisfied 3	Satisfied 4	Very Satisfied 5

Many customer satisfaction measures evaluate service characteristics. Developing measurable service quality characteristics can be difficult. For instance, a quality characteristic such as "availability" is ambiguous and not as easy to measure as the accuracy of order filling. Typically, such quality characteristics are translated into specific statements that clearly describe the concept. For example, any of the following statements could be used to describe "availability."

1. The doctor was available to schedule me at a good time.
2. I could get an appointment with the doctor at a time I desired.
3. My appointment was at a convenient time.

Customers are more likely to complete a survey if they understand how the company will use it. For example, the Marriott Corporation conducts extensive surveys of randomly selected hotel guests. The cover letter accompanying the survey, signed by J. W. Marriott, Jr., chairman of the board and president, includes the following:

> *I want to assure you, as a valued patron of Marriott Hotels and Resorts, we are committed to providing you a consistently high level of quality guest service at all our lodging products. To help us achieve our commitment, we are asking you, and other randomly selected Marriott guests, to participate in the enclosed guest survey. By your evaluating our hospitality—telling us what we do right as well as what we must improve—you will help us meet your expectations. I personally will review some of the comments as well as the results compiled from all of the surveys. Your comments will be shared with each hotel's General Manager, to ensure follow-up is taken on any service or product shortcomings.*

One example of a simple satisfaction survey for Hilton Hotels is shown in Figure 4.10. The survey asks direct and detailed questions about the guest bathroom, including such potential dissatisfiers as shower water pressure and temperature and bathtub-sink drainage, likelihood of future recommendation, and space for open-ended comments. A seven-point Likert scale is used in this example.

The final task is to design the reporting format and the data entry methods. Modern technology, such as computer databases in conjunction with a variety of statistical analysis tools, assists in tracking customer satisfaction and provides information for continuous improvement. As a final note, surveys should always be pretested to determine whether instructions are understood, to identify questions that may be misunderstood or poorly worded, to assess how long it takes to complete the survey, and to determine the level of customer interest.

Figure 4.10 Hilton Hotel Guest Survey

Completely fill in your response ● Correct **GUEST**Scope

Hilton

Please rate your satisfaction with the comfort level of your accommodations.

	Level of Satisfaction							
	Low			Avg.			High	N/A
	1	2	3	4	5	6	7	
Accommodations look and smell clean and fresh:	☐	☐	☐	☐	☐	☐	☐	☐
Clean and comfortable linens:	☐	☐	☐	☐	☐	☐	☐	☐
Comfort level of pillow:	☐	☐	☐	☐	☐	☐	☐	☐
Comfort level of mattress:	☐	☐	☐	☐	☐	☐	☐	☐
Easily regulated room temperature:	☐	☐	☐	☐	☐	☐	☐	☐
Housekeeping during stay:	☐	☐	☐	☐	☐	☐	☐	☐
Overall satisfaction with this Hilton:	☐	☐	☐	☐	☐	☐	☐	
Likelihood you would recommend Hilton:	☐	☐	☐	☐	☐	☐	☐	
Likelihood, **if returning to the area**, you would return to this Hilton:	☐	☐	☐	☐	☐	☐	☐	
Value of accommodations for price paid:	☐	☐	☐	☐	☐	☐	☐	

Primary purpose of visit? ☐ Individual business ☐ Convention/Meeting ☐ Pleasure

How many times have you been a guest at this Hilton? ☐ 1 ☐ 2 ☐ 3 ☐ 4 ☐ 5+

Did you have a hotel product or service problem during your stay? ☐ Yes ☐ No

If yes—did you report it to the staff? ☐ Yes ☐ No

If yes—was it resolved to your satisfaction? ☐ Yes ☐ No

If yes—what was the nature of the problem? ______________________

Please share any thoughts on any other aspects of your visit; including the names of any staff members who made your stay more enjoyable: ______________________

Name: *Daytime Phone:*

Date of Stay: PLEASE DO NOT WRITE BELOW THIS LINE FD2 *Room:*

Analyzing and Using Customer Feedback

Deming stressed the importance of using customer feedback to improve a company's products and processes (refer to Figure 1.3 in Chapter 1). By examining trends in customer satisfaction measures and linking satisfaction data to its internal processes, a business can see its progress and areas for improvement. As the next step, the company assigns to an employee or group of employees the responsibility and accountability for developing improvement plans based on customer satisfaction results. Many companies, for example, tie managers' annual bonuses to customer satisfaction results. This practice acts as an incentive for managers and a direction for their efforts.

Appropriate customer satisfaction measurement distinguishes between processes that have high impact on satisfaction and low performance and those that are performing well. One way to ensure that measurement is appropriate is to collect information on both the importance and the performance of key quality characteristics. For example, Figure 4.11 shows selected portions of the survey used by Marriott (the full survey consists of more than 30 multiple-section questions with additional space for comments). Question 8 asks about the overall efficiency (performance) of the hotel staff; part of question 13 seeks the respondent's perception of the importance of overall staff efficiency. Evaluation of such data can be accomplished using a grid similar to the one shown in Figure 4.12, on which mean performance and importance scores for individual attributes are plotted.[47] Results in the diagonal quadrants (the shaded areas) are good. A firm ideally wants high performance on important characteristics and not to waste resources on characteristics of low importance. Results off the diagonal indicate that the firm either is wasting resources to achieve high perfor-

Figure 4.11 Selected Portions of the Marriott Guest Survey

1. How would you rate our hotel on an overall basis?

EXCELLENT POOR
(10)(9)(8)(7)(6)(5)(4)(3)(2)(1)

7. How would you rate our hotel on:

	EXCELLENT — POOR
Check-in speed	(10)(9)(8)(7)(6)(5)(4)(3)(2)(1)
Cleanliness and servicing of your room during stay	(10)(9)(8)(7)(6)(5)(4)(3)(2)(1)
Check-out speed	(10)(9)(8)(7)(6)(5)(4)(3)(2)(1)
Value of room for price paid	(10)(9)(8)(7)(6)(5)(4)(3)(2)(1)
Service overall	(10)(9)(8)(7)(6)(5)(4)(3)(2)(1)
Overall staff attitude	(10)(9)(8)(7)(6)(5)(4)(3)(2)(1)

8. How would you rate the <u>efficiency</u> of our staff on an overall basis?

EXCELLENT POOR
(10)(9)(8)(7)(6)(5)(4)(3)(2)(1)

9. Please rate the following in terms of their friendly service.

	EXCELLENT — POOR
Reservation staff	(10)(9)(8)(7)(6)(5)(4)(3)(2)(1)
Front desk clerk	(10)(9)(8)(7)(6)(5)(4)(3)(2)(1)
Bellstaff	(10)(9)(8)(7)(6)(5)(4)(3)(2)(1)
Housekeeping staff	(10)(9)(8)(7)(6)(5)(4)(3)(2)(1)
Telephone operators	(10)(9)(8)(7)(6)(5)(4)(3)(2)(1)
Gift shop staff	(10)(9)(8)(7)(6)(5)(4)(3)(2)(1)
Engineering staff	(10)(9)(8)(7)(6)(5)(4)(3)(2)(1)
Front desk cashier	(10)(9)(8)(7)(6)(5)(4)(3)(2)(1)
Concierge staff:	
Concierge Level*	(10)(9)(8)(7)(6)(5)(4)(3)(2)(1)
Hotel lobby*	(10)(9)(8)(7)(6)(5)(4)(3)(2)(1)
Pool staff*	(10)(9)(8)(7)(6)(5)(4)(3)(2)(1)
Golf staff*	(10)(9)(8)(7)(6)(5)(4)(3)(2)(1)
Tennis staff*	(10)(9)(8)(7)(6)(5)(4)(3)(2)(1)
Valet parking staff*	(10)(9)(8)(7)(6)(5)(4)(3)(2)(1)

*(*Not available at all hotels)*

12. Was everything in your room in working order?

○ Yes ○ No

If "NO", which of the following items were not in working order?

○ Room air conditioning	○ Television reception
○ Room heating	○ Heat lamp
○ Bathtub drain	○ Door latch
○ Sink drain	○ Drapes
○ Water temperature	○ Telephone
○ Water pressure	○ TV in-room movies
○ Other bathroom plumbing	○ Light bulbs
○ Television	○ Clock/clock radio

○ Other (please specify)________________

____

13. How <u>important</u> were each of the following items in determining your overall satisfaction with your hotel stay?

	EXTREMELY IMPORTANT — NOT AT ALL IMPORTANT
Having correct reservation information	(10)(9)(8)(7)(6)(5)(4)(3)(2)(1)
Honoring your reservation	(10)(9)(8)(7)(6)(5)(4)(3)(2)(1)
Fulfilling any special room-type or location requests	(10)(9)(8)(7)(6)(5)(4)(3)(2)(1)
Check-in speed	(10)(9)(8)(7)(6)(5)(4)(3)(2)(1)
Cleanliness and servicing of your room during your stay	(10)(9)(8)(7)(6)(5)(4)(3)(2)(1)
Check-out speed	(10)(9)(8)(7)(6)(5)(4)(3)(2)(1)
Value of room for price paid	(10)(9)(8)(7)(6)(5)(4)(3)(2)(1)
Service overall	(10)(9)(8)(7)(6)(5)(4)(3)(2)(1)
Overall staff efficiency	(10)(9)(8)(7)(6)(5)(4)(3)(2)(1)
Overall staff attitude	(10)(9)(8)(7)(6)(5)(4)(3)(2)(1)
Overall maintenance and upkeep of hotel	(10)(9)(8)(7)(6)(5)(4)(3)(2)(1)
Having all items in your room in working order	(10)(9)(8)(7)(6)(5)(4)(3)(2)(1)

Source: Courtesy of Marriott International, Inc.

Figure 4.12 Performance-Importance Comparison

Importance	**Performance** Low	High
Low	Who cares?	Overkill
High	Vulnerable	Strengths

mance on unimportant customer attributes (overkill), or is not performing acceptably on important customer attributes, leaving the firm vulnerable to competition. The results of such an analysis can help target areas for improvement and cost savings, as well as provide useful input for strategic planning. Often, competitor data are also plotted, providing a comparison against the competition (see the *Quality in Practice* on Granite Rock at the end of this chapter).

Many companies have integrated customer feedback into their continuous improvement activities. For example, by listening to customers, Bank One opened nearly 60 percent of its 1,377 branches in Ohio and Texas on Saturdays, and 20 percent on Sundays. A 24-hour customer hotline is also available. Since the early 1980s, Xerox has surveyed tens of thousands of customers annually and tracked the results through its Customer Satisfaction Measurement System (CSMS).[48] The data guide continuous improvements within the corporation. For instance, the CSMS uncovered the fact that customers wanted one-call, one-person problem resolution. As a result, Xerox created six customer care centers, staffed by specially trained customer care representatives who handle some 1.2 million telephone calls and about 1 million written inquiries each year. Employees are cross-trained and empowered to adjust bills, correct forms, or take other steps to solve problems single-handedly. Any problems that cannot be resolved instantly are given a 10-day resolution deadline. The files remain open until customers confirm that they are totally satisfied with Xerox actions. CSMS data also showed that customer satisfaction is linked to cycle time—the elapsed time between the reporting phone call and the solution of the problem. The data also showed that simply knowing when a technician will arrive has a positive effect on customer satisfaction. Xerox modified the system to call customers shortly after problems are reported and give them an estimated time of arrival.

Wainwright Industries' external customer satisfaction index (CSI) process, shown in Figure 4.13, ties together survey data to an improvement process by which customer champions monitor the status of their customer feedback (visually using red and green flags in a central meeting room called "Mission Control"), and initiate corrective action plans for *any* score below 95 percent (on a scale in which A = 100, B = 90, C = 50, and D = 0). The use of such a systematic process ensures that all customer satisfaction data are handled consistently and that potential problems are addressed immediately.

Why Many Customer Satisfaction Efforts Fail[49]

Determining and using customer satisfaction information should be viewed as a key business process. Just going through the motions can often lead to failure. A. Blanton Godfrey, former CEO of the Juran Institute, suggests several reasons why customer satisfaction efforts fail to produce useful results.

Figure 4.13 Wainwright Industries Customer Satisfaction Process

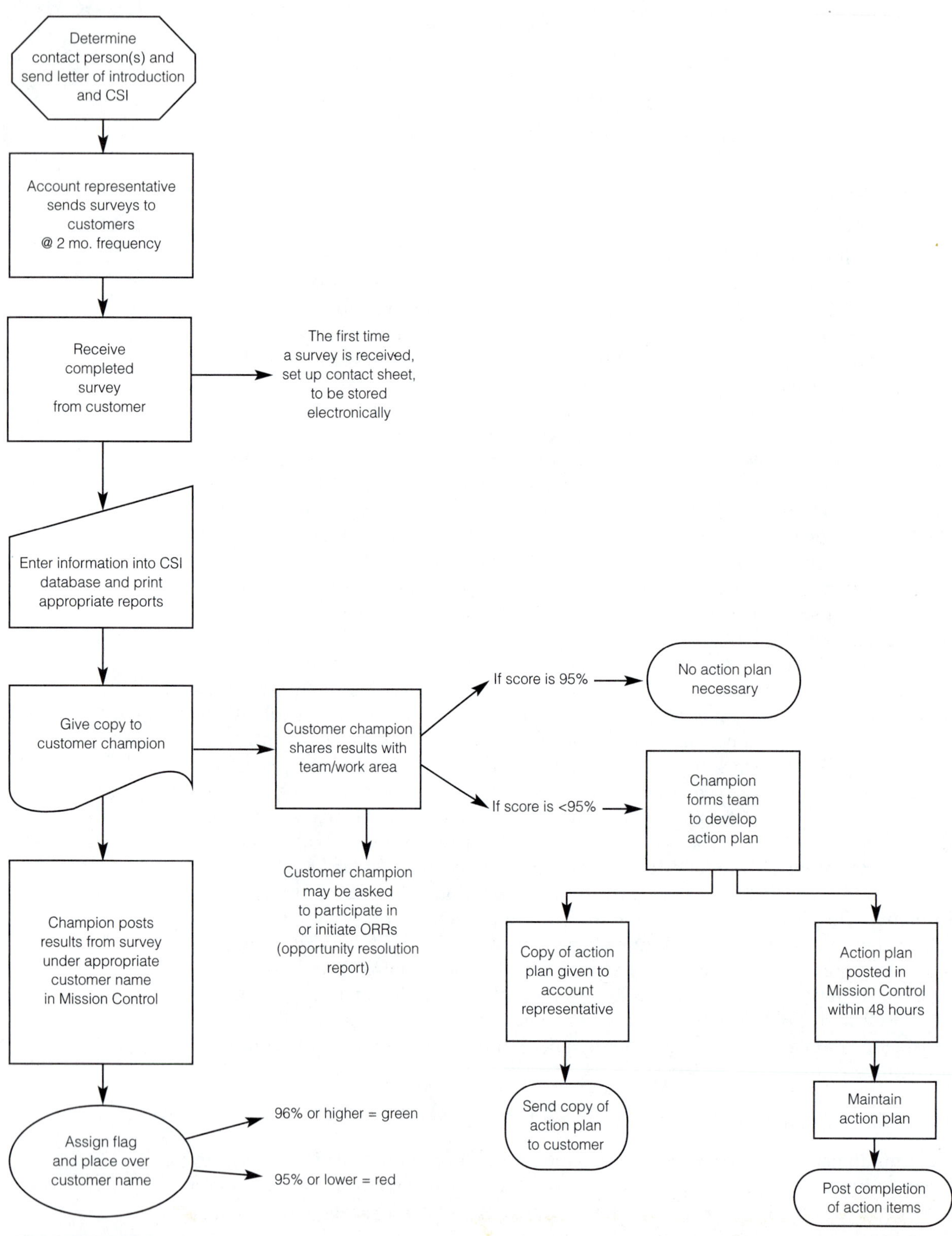

Source: Wainwright Industries, Inc.

1. *Poor measurement schemes.* Just tracking the percentage of "satisfied and very satisfied" customers on a 5-point Likert scale provides little actionable information. Many surveys provide biased results because dissatisfied customers do not respond, or the surveys lack adequate sample sizes or randomization. Survey designers need appropriate understanding of statistical concepts.
2. *Failure to identify appropriate quality dimensions.* Many surveys address issues the company thinks are important, not what customers think. This failure results from a lack of capturing reliable information about customer needs and expectations.
3. *Failure to weight dimensions appropriately.* Even if organizations measure the right things, they may not understand which dimensions are important. As a result, they spend too much effort on dimensions with the lowest scores that may not be important to the customers. Use of techniques such as importance-performance analysis can help focus attention to the key dimensions.
4. *Lack of comparison with leading competitors.* Quality and perception of quality is relative. Without appropriate comparative data, competitors may be improving much faster than an organization realizes.
5. *Failure to measure potential and former customers.* Without an understanding of why noncustomers do not do business with a company, or more importantly, why customers leave, an organization risks losing market share to competitors and may be headed for demise.
6. *Confusing loyalty with satisfaction*. As we noted at the beginning of this chapter, these two concepts are distinctly different. Customer retention and loyalty provide an indication of the organization's future.

CUSTOMER FOCUS IN THE BALDRIGE AWARD CRITERIA[50]

Category 3 of the 2001 Malcolm Baldrige National Quality Award Criteria for Performance Excellence (see the criteria on the CD-rom) is titled *Customer and Market Focus.* This category examines how a company determines requirements, expectations, and preferences for customers and markets, and how it builds relationships with customers and determines their satisfaction. Item 3.1, *Customer and Market Knowledge,* examines an organization's key processes for gaining knowledge about current and future customers and markets, with the aim of offering relevant products and services, understanding emerging customer requirements and expectations, and keeping pace with changing markets and changing ways of doing business. The criteria ask how an organization determines key customer groups and segments its markets, considers potential customers, including competitors' customers; key requirements and drivers of purchase decisions; and key product and service features. These factors are likely to differ for different customer groups and market segments. Knowledge of customer groups and market segments allows an organization to tailor listening and learning strategies and marketplace offerings, to support marketing strategies, and to develop new business. Finally, the criteria ask how an organization improves its customer listening and learning strategies so that it can keep current with changing business needs and directions.

In a rapidly changing competitive environment, many factors may affect customer preference and loyalty and an organization's interface with customers in the marketplace. The changing environment makes it necessary to listen and learn on a continuous basis. To be effective as an organization, listening and learning need to be closely linked with an organization's overall business strategy and strategy-setting process. A relationship strategy may be possible with some customers but not with others. Differing relationships may require different listening and learning strategies. The use of e-commerce is rapidly changing many marketplaces and may affect listening and learning strategies as well as definitions of customer groups and market segments. Some frequently used strategies include focus groups with key customers, close integration with key customers, interviews with lost customers about their purchase decisions, use of the customer complaint process to understand key product and service attributes, won-lost analysis relative to competitors, and survey-feedback information, including information collected on the Internet. These issues are captured in the criteria.

Item 3.2, *Customer Satisfaction and Relationships*, examines an organization's processes for determining customer satisfaction and building customer relationships, with the aim of acquiring new customers, retaining existing customers, and developing new opportunities. The criteria ask how an organization provides easy access for customers and potential customers to seek information or assistance and/or to comment and complain; how customer contact requirements are determined and deployed; how the organization aggregates, analyzes, and learns from complaint information; how relationships are built with customers; and how approaches to all aspects of customer relationships are kept current with changing business needs and directions, particularly when approaches to and bases for relationships may change quickly. The criteria also address an organization's satisfaction and dissatisfaction determination processes and how they differ for different customer groups, and how it follows up with customers regarding products, services, and recent transactions, and determines customers' satisfaction relative to competitors so that it may improve future performance.

The focus is on obtaining actionable information from customers. To be *actionable*, an organization should be able to tie the information to key business processes, and should be able to determine cost-revenue implications for improvement priority setting. Complaint aggregation, analysis, and root cause determination should lead to effective elimination of the causes of complaints and to priority setting for process, product, and service improvements. Successful outcomes require effective deployment of information throughout the organization.

A key aspect of customer satisfaction determination is satisfaction relative to competitors and competing or alternative offerings. Such information might be derived from comparative studies or from independent studies. The factors that lead to customer preference are of critical importance in understanding factors that drive markets and potentially affect longer-term competitiveness.

The following example shows how one company might respond to Item 3.1, Customer and Market Knowledge, and the feedback that a Baldrige examiner team might provide to the company. *You should read Case III in Chapter 3 first, which provides background about this fictitious company. Think about how the response addresses the questions asked in the 2000 criteria. The criteria are available on the CD-rom accompanying this book.*

Example 1: Collin Technologies

Response to Criteria Item 3.1: Customer and Market Knowledge

Collin currently serves four specialized segments in the overall printed circuit board market defined by product functionality and use, customer requirements, and benefits. Important functional characteristics of Collin's products are their multiple layers, advanced materials, high component density, and fine lines and spacing. Its products are typically used in demanding environments and are integrated into customers' products. Customers choose Collin because of its high quality and reliability, fast technical response, consistent just-in-time (JIT) delivery, and focus on customer service. For example, just-in-time delivery creates a "virtual warehouse" for customers at Collin's site. By working closely with customers from product design to reorder, Collin's experienced design and customer support staff become a "virtual workforce" to save customers money and to enhance relationships.

Segmentation is based on market data collected from current customers, customers of competitors, and potential customers and markets. Collin begins the segmentation process at the global level by determining the factors and trends that drive customer requirements. It uses market intelligence data gathered throughout the year as part of the Perennial Planning Process (PPP). Business segment managers use this information to forecast opportunities within each geographic area and to define segment requirements. Then they analyze existing customer data by segment using Collin's customer database and customer surveys. Results of these analyses are used as inputs to the PPP and to design product and service offerings.

Collin's business is organized to satisfy the needs of its four key segments (Figure 4.14): commercial (C), government (G), industrial products (I), and advanced technology (A). Government customers use Collin's products in defense and research programs that require small quantities of highly reliable products. Commercial customers integrate Collin's products into their products; they want fast turnaround and competitive prices. Advanced technology customers deploy Collin's products under extreme environmental conditions; they order smaller quantities of robust products for harsh environments. Industrial products customers use Collin's products in internal process control manufacturing applications; they want high reliability products for demanding conditions.

Collin determines customer requirements and expectations via multiple listening posts deployed at key points throughout the customer life cycle and information obtained through independent external sources. Employee owners (EOs) follow up

Figure 4.14 Collin Technologies Customer Requirements by Segment

Requirements	Segment			
High Quality	C	G	I	A
High Reliability		G	I	A
On-Time Delivery	C		I	
Short Delivery Time	C		I	
Competitive Price	C		I	
Rapid Response			I	
Cutting-Edge Technology	C	G		A
Stable Dimensions		G	I	A

with customers to verify performance on current orders, determine repurchase intentions, and seek new business opportunities. Collin deploys a variety of mechanisms that make it easy for customers to communicate with the company.

Customer satisfaction survey ratings generate quantitative measurements on product performance versus current requirements, relative importance, priorities, and relative level of interest in new offerings. Collin combines this posttransaction information with Baldrige self-assessments to overlay evolving customer needs against company capability assessments. It aggregates customer data by segment to discern segment trends, detect shifts in segmentation variables, and project future segment opportunities.

Customer focus groups verify the data gathered through Collin's field listening mechanisms and seek customer perspectives on changing requirements and potential customers by segment. These results are part of the inputs to the PPP. Collin reviews short- and long-term product strategies with customers to learn how well plans address current and emerging requirements.

Collin monitors competitor activities by studying how (buyer selection) and why (vendor preference) it is selected by customers over other vendors. Collin tracks the number of customers that leave, why they leave, where they go, and the amount of lost revenue to understand the strength of the competition. In addition, Collin uses data from a cross-section of noncustomers to understand why companies choose other vendors. These analyses enable Collin to offer broader product and service lines than competitors.

A cross-section of EOs participate in Collin's industry, supplier, and customer seminars, groups, and conferences to understand their industries and to obtain information on changing industry, segment, and customer requirements. At trade shows, Collin conducts market interest surveys to gather information from customers of competitors and other potential customers. Industry publications help Collin calibrate strategic direction, anticipate competitive responses, and identify evolving opportunities. It commissions independent market and segment studies and merges these data with internal accounting, marketing, preferred supplier, sales coordinator, customer satisfaction, and complaint data to create ongoing competitive scenarios.

Quarterly, business segment managers collect, analyze, and review the customer, competitive analysis, and industry data and incorporate these inputs in the PPP. Through reciprocal partnering agreements, Collin participates in customer strategic planning processes as key suppliers, just as customers participate in Collin's PPP. Most opportunities for innovation arise in the commercial and advanced technology segments, where there is significant participation by Collin in customer strategic planning and on customer design teams. Customer and supplier participation on Baldrige-based assessment teams provides ongoing customer input on the relative importance of product and service features and how Collin can best address these requirements.

The limit defining the slope of the learning (cost leadership) curve for addressing future customer requirements is the cycle time for incorporating technological advances in the design and manufacture of new products. Manufacturing technology innovators come to Collin to test, refine, and develop their ideas. As new technologies are studied, Collin uses customer requirement data to identify customers who would most likely benefit from incorporating these breakthroughs in their current and future products. Collin's reputation as the manufacturer of technically sophisticated products attracts demanding customers who seek its advice on how to address their advanced technical requirements and to create prototypes. Collin's process laboratory develops new technologies and runs prototypes for use in customers' research and development activities.

Annually, business segment managers review listening methods, their deployment, and the learning process. They assess and update survey instruments to ensure that questions address changing company capabilities and customer requirements. They review listening and learning data and analysis processes to determine procedural changes and select new data collection mechanisms to improve the effectiveness of the approach. These reviews have provided several refinements in Collin's approach. For example, satisfaction surveys are deployed throughout the year rather than once a year. This approach, implemented by benchmarking a similar-sized, mid-range computer distributor identified through the Consulting Best Practices Program, has improved efficiency, turnarounds, response rates, currency of data, and customer satisfaction with the satisfaction measurement process. Also, it has provided Collin with many program expansion capabilities.

Examiner Feedback

Strengths

- The company divides customers into four key business segments in the printed circuit board market: government, commercial, advanced technology, and industrial products. Customers are grouped based on product functionality and use, customer requirements, and benefits. Market data are collected from current customers, customers of competitors, and potential customers and markets to determine the segmentation and ensure responsiveness to specialized market needs.
- A variety of methods is used to learn from customers and potential customers, including employee follow-up on current orders, customer satisfaction surveys, customer focus groups, lost customer studies, trade show market interest studies, and participation in customer strategic planning. The use of multiple approaches provides a broad spectrum of information that helps the applicant stay current with changing customer requirements.
- Reciprocal partnering agreements have been established with customers for obtaining information on needs on an ongoing basis. Customers participate in the PPP, and, in return, the applicant is involved in the customers' planning and design processes. It is a particularly useful approach in the advanced technology and commercial market segments, because these markets "push" breakthrough technological development. Partnerships also include customer involvement in the company's internal Baldrige assessment, which provides another avenue for obtaining input on the importance of product and service features, enabling the company to understand how to best address these features.
- Business segment managers review listening methods, their deployment, and the learning process in order to make refinements. They assess and update surveys, review data and analysis processes to determine procedural changes, and select new approaches for gathering data. Evidence of refinements includes changing from an annual customer satisfaction survey process to a continuous process with improved efficiency, turnaround, and market awareness.
- Key competitor activities and lost business revenue are monitored to understand customer preference and the drivers of customer retention. Among the

methods used are the collection of data from a cross-section of noncustomers to determine drivers of vendor preference; employee data collection of information regarding changing industry, segment, and customer requirements; and surveys, reviews of industry publications, and market studies. The variety of methodologies and sources for gathering data provides a continuous, validated, and reliable flow of information about customers and competitors and allows the applicant to anticipate and respond to changing market needs in a timely manner.

Opportunities for Improvement

- Although participation in conferences, trade shows, and customer strategic planning is used to obtain information on changing requirements, how the applicant uses this participation to determine key product features and their relative importance to customers for the purposes of current and future marketing, product planning, or other business development is not described.
- It is not clear that the company assesses differences in market segments or customer groups with respect to the determination of key requirements and drivers of purchase decisions. For example, it is not defined how the applicant considers North American, Asian, and future European geographical market segments to determine what the unique needs of customers in these markets might be. Additionally, it is not clear that the company identifies the needs of end users as part of its analysis of customer requirements (e.g., in the commercial market segment, where the applicant's products are resold to other businesses). The lack of such identification hampers any assessment of whether the unique needs of all types of customers in different markets are being met.

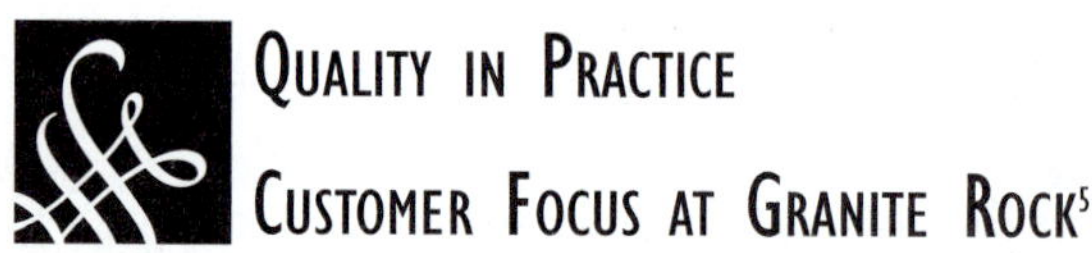

Quality in Practice

Customer Focus at Granite Rock[51]

Granite Rock Company is a California manufacturer of high-quality construction materials for road and highway construction and maintenance, and for residential and commercial building construction. Its major product lines include rock, sand and gravel aggregates, ready-mix concrete, blacktop, and other products. In an industry that typically buys from the lowest-bid supplier, Granite Rock is expanding the terms of competition to include high quality and speedy service. The strategy resulted in revenue earned per employee that is about 30 percent above the industry average. Granite Rock won the Malcolm Baldrige National Quality Award in the Small Business category in 1992.

Granite Rock began its total quality program in 1985, stressing 100 percent satisfaction of customers' needs. Granite Rock's key customers are the contractor, who normally makes the purchasing decisions, and the end customer, who ultimately pays for the buildings or roads made with the company's materials. By emphasizing the hidden costs associated with slow service and substandard construction materials, such as rework and premature deterioration, Granite Rock has convinced a growing number of contractors of the value of using their high-quality materials and unmatched service. One of the customer-focused innovations that Granite Rock introduced is GraniteXpress, an automatic loading system—similar to an automated teller machine—at the A. R. Wilson Quarry. A customer inserts a credit card and requests the specific material. The truck is rapidly, accurately, and automatically loaded over a scale and automatically billed. The facility is open 24 hours a day, seven days a week. The subsequent reductions in trucking time can save customers thousands of dollars on a single project. The company is so serious about satisfying customers that customers need not pay their invoice unless completely satisfied. Granite Rock regularly surveys its customers, tracks and responds promptly to customer complaints, and ensures that its products arrive on time.

Surveying its principal customer groups is one of the key approaches Granite Rock uses to improve customer satisfaction. The surveys ask respondents to rate factors in buying concrete, not only from Granite Rock, but from competitors as well. (Figure 4.15 shows such a survey.) Through information obtained from the surveys, Granite Rock determined that the most important factors to customers in order of importance are on-time delivery, product quality, scheduling (ability to deliver products on short notice), problem resolution, price, credit terms, and salespeople's skills. Annually, the company surveys customers and noncustomers to obtain a "report card" on their service (see Figure 4.16). Granite Rock repeats the survey every three or four years as priorities change, particularly if the economy changes. The results of the importance survey and competitive performance survey are summarized and plotted

Figure 4.15 Granite Rock Customer Importance Survey

What is important to *YOU*?

Please rate each of the following on a scale from 1 to 5 with 5 being most important in your decision to purchase from a supplier.

Importance	Concrete Least . . . Most	Building Materials Least . . . Most
Responsive to special needs	1 2 3 4 5	1 2 3 4 5
Easy to place orders	1 2 3 4 5	1 2 3 4 5
Consistent product quality	1 2 3 4 5	1 2 3 4 5
On-time delivery	1 2 3 4 5	1 2 3 4 5
Accurate invoices	1 2 3 4 5	1 2 3 4 5
Lowest prices	1 2 3 4 5	1 2 3 4 5
Attractive credit terms	1 2 3 4 5	1 2 3 4 5
Salespeople's skills	1 2 3 4 5	1 2 3 4 5
Helpful dispatchers	1 2 3 4 5	1 2 3 4 5
Courteous drivers	1 2 3 4 5	1 2 3 4 5
Supplier resolves problems fairly and quickly	1 2 3 4 5	1 2 3 4 5

Please write in any other items not listed above which are very important to you in making your purchase decision:

____

____

Figure 4.16 Granite Rock Customer Report Card

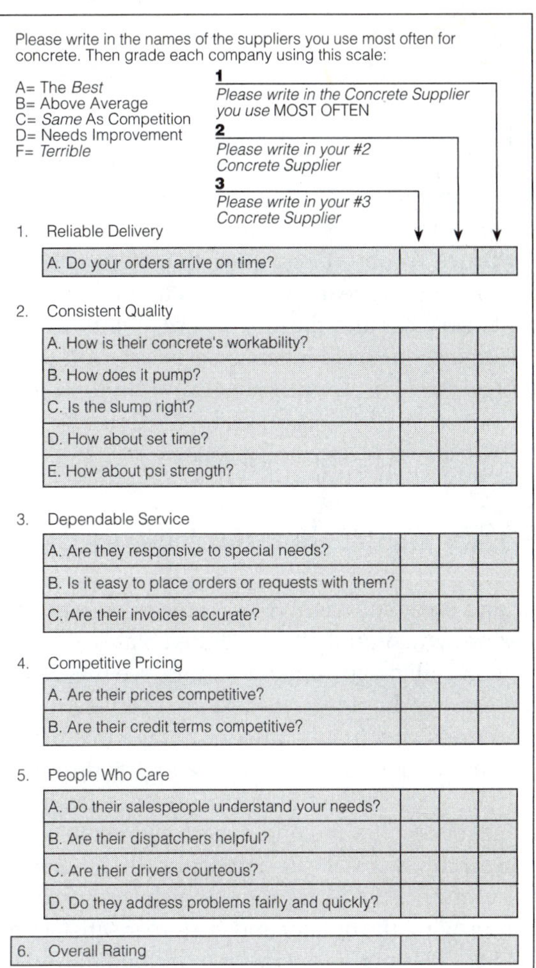

Please write in the names of the suppliers you use most often for concrete. Then grade each company using this scale:

A= The *Best*
B= Above Average
C= *Same* As Competition
D= Needs Improvement
F= *Terrible*

1 *Please write in the Concrete Supplier you use* MOST OFTEN
2 *Please write in your #2 Concrete Supplier*
3 *Please write in your #3 Concrete Supplier*

	1	2	3
1. Reliable Delivery			
A. Do your orders arrive on time?			
2. Consistent Quality			
A. How is their concrete's workability?			
B. How does it pump?			
C. Is the slump right?			
D. How about set time?			
E. How about psi strength?			
3. Dependable Service			
A. Are they responsive to special needs?			
B. Is it easy to place orders or requests with them?			
C. Are their invoices accurate?			
4. Competitive Pricing			
A. Are their prices competitive?			
B. Are their credit terms competitive?			
5. People Who Care			
A. Do their salespeople understand your needs?			
B. Are their dispatchers helpful?			
C. Are their drivers courteous?			
D. Do they address problems fairly and quickly?			
6. Overall Rating			

on an importance-performance graph to assess the strengths and vulnerabilities of the company and its competitors. The scales are chosen so that each axis represents the industry average. Granite Rock looks at the distance between its ratings and those of the competitors. If the ratings are close, customers cannot differentiate Granite Rock from its competitors on that particular measure. By posting these graphs on bulletin boards at each plant, the company ensures that all employees, particularly salespeople, are fully informed of the survey results. However, salespeople do not use the results to downgrade the competition, but rather to understand the difference that Granite Rock can make to a contractor.

The surveys also ask open-ended questions about what customers like and dislike. As marketing services manager Greg Diehl stated, "In the construction industry, people aren't afraid to tell you what they think. If we take the time to read what they have written, we have a feel for what is happening in the marketplace. Customers tell us about things they are not happy with, but frequently, they take the time to compliment us or they tell us why they do business with us." President Bruce Woolpert has noted that "Our customer surveys reveal a 100% correlation between quality services and the employees' ability to understand our products and services. That tells us the only thing stopping us from providing excellence is lack of knowledge." The results also help employees to align their priorities on improvements. Internal teams use the information to develop action plans to improve customer service.

Key Issues for Discussion

1. Explain the relationships between the customer importance survey and the customer report card. Do these surveys provide enough information to perform an importance-performance analysis? Explain why.
2. Discuss the benefit of plotting competitors' results along with one's own company results on an importance-performance graph. How can this information be used?

Quality in Practice

Waiting Time and Customer Satisfaction at Florida Power and Light[52]

Florida Power and Light (FPL) is the third-largest investor-owned utility in the United States, with about 3.4 million customer accounts (see the *Quality in Practice* in Chapter 3). Its customer service centers (call centers) are divided into four major business segments; each segment handles a logical bundle of call types. Depending on their experience, customer service representatives within each segment specialize in certain types of calls (see Figure 4.17). The Service Assurance Systems group, which is responsible for improving the quality and customer satisfaction levels of FPL's phone operations, decided to find out what customers expect when they call to conduct business. Using focus groups and survey instruments, FPL discovered that its customers desired a pleasant experience while on hold, order taking conducted in a timely manner, and treatment typically accorded to valued customers. FPL wanted to keep costs down without increasing staff size. A cross-functional team suggested that providing customers with an estimate of the time they could expect to wait before being connected to a representative would help meet FPL's needs and increase customer satisfaction. To determine whether this idea had merit, FPL needed quantitative answers to the following questions:

1. How long do customers expect to wait?
2. What is the impact of a wait time announcement on customers' tolerance for waiting?
3. At what point does the wait time result in a significant decrease in customer satisfaction?
4. What is the relationship between wait time and the customer's satisfaction with the call itself?
5. Does wait time vary by type of call?
6. Are customers' stated wait time expectations congruent with the time they are actually willing to wait?

On a busy Monday, a random sample of 150 customers was taken. Wait time announcements were made manually from a control center and actual wait times were monitored. The customers were interviewed that evening to assess their reactions to the proposed service. The surveys showed that the average time customers expected to wait, without knowing the length of wait, was 94 seconds. But when the customers knew the length of wait, they were willing to wait an average of 105 seconds longer (a total of 199 seconds). More than 90 percent of customers in the sample indicated that the announcement was helpful. Customers were also asked to rate their level of satisfaction with their wait times (without advance knowledge). The results showed that a significant decrease in satisfaction occurred at two minutes. These results implied that FPL could buy more time without decreasing satisfaction by offering

Figure 4.17 Florida Power and Light Customer Service Centers

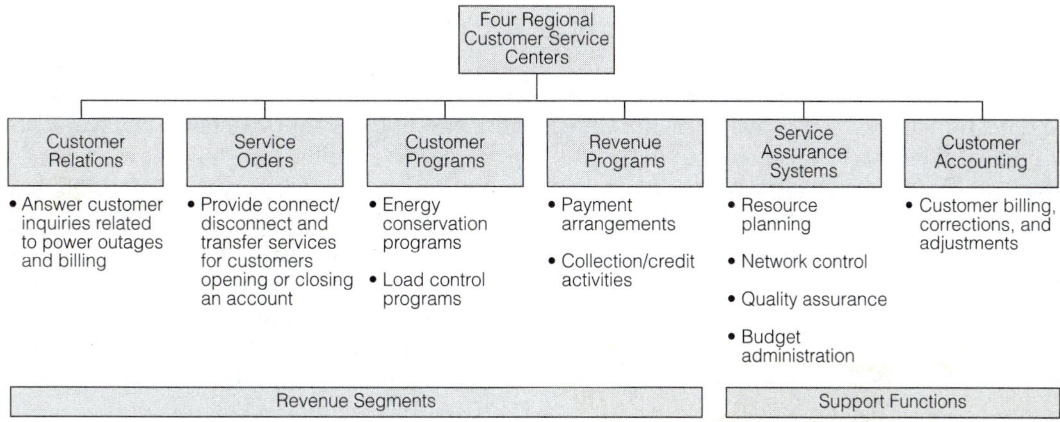

customers the choice of waiting for a predicted period or calling back later.

FPL knew that customer satisfaction relates directly to how callers perceive the quality of the phone representatives and wondered whether this perception might be negatively biased after a long wait. The survey revealed a 10 to 17 percent bias in customers' ratings of phone representatives caused by excessive waiting time. If this bias could be eliminated, FPL could more accurately measure customers' satisfaction with the phone contact experience.

FPL segmented calls into three broad categories:

1. Routine calls for connecting or disconnecting service
2. Nonroutine and more complex calls regarding high bills and power outages
3. Calls regarding account-related financial arrangements, such as payment extension requests

After asking customers how long they would expect to wait for each type of call, FPL found that customers expected to wait significantly longer for the third category than for the others. FPL now had evidence that customers calling for different services had different wait time requirements. Finally, FPL discovered that customers thought they waited longer than they actually did.

From this research, FPL developed a system called "Smartqueue," which continuously updates the number of callers waiting and indicates the longest time a caller has been waiting for each department. The system then stores the information and compares it with earlier updates. This adjusted time is increased by a multiplier to account for customers' perceptions of the length of the wait. When a caller is transferred to the appropriate business segment, the unit tells the caller an approximate wait time and how many callers are waiting ahead of him or her. A pilot test of the system in Miami found that customers overwhelmingly perceived Smartqueue to be reasonably accurate in predicting waiting time; virtually all customers thought it was helpful and took the frustration out of waiting.

Key Issues for Discussion

1. Have one of your friends time you while you wait for varying amounts of time between 30 seconds and 3 minutes. Try not to count the seconds! Estimate the amount of time you waited. Did you find that your actual waiting times were longer or shorter than your estimates? Compare these results with those of your classmates. What does this experiment mean for organizations that are trying to set service standards?
2. What key lessons can be learned by other organizations from FPL's experience?

Quality in Practice

Improving Customer Satisfaction at a Software Support Call Center[53]

In this case study, we describe how one company improved customer satisfaction statistics at a software support call center by 43 percent in one month in an industry where the monthly norm is a low single-digit percentage. The company, which provides technical support services to software publishing companies, had managed to slowly improve customer satisfaction figures over a three-year period. The improvement had occurred through efforts initiated by management to implement commonsense business practices such as consistent follow-up, better technical training, and improvement of what they call the personal factor. But the improvement had plateaued and a crisis emerged—a major customer, who accounted for 45 percent of revenues, threatened to pull the account unless further improvement was made.

Facing a potential disaster, management formed committees of technical support staff and asked them for suggestions. The results were initially discouraging. Suggestions only mirrored those already thought of by management. The logjam was broken when someone discovered the work of Gary Klein.[54] Klein specializes in the anatomy of expert decision making with the aim of developing ways to speed up the training process. He reasons that experts in high-pressure emergency occupations are often unable to explain how they arrive at a decision because the process by which decisions are made is mostly intuitive. Although incidents of help line support do not ordinarily qualify as emergencies, the company assumed that this use of intuition was the reason even expert staff members directly involved in customer service could not explain their success. The best support engineers, like experts in other fields, were usually unable to completely explain their reasons for success in making good instant decisions. The company carefully analyzed calls, looking for patterns that would explain the success of the most successful support engineers. Once they could effectively describe these patterns to the non-expert support engineers, they were able to improve their customer satisfaction ratings quickly.

They began by interviewing experts in a department that supported a popular word processing package. They could do no better than management in suggesting new approaches. They were, however, able to examine more closely the faulty assumptions implicit in the suggestions. The suggestions fell into two groups—more adequate training and more personalization with the customer.

The suggestions in the first group rested on one basic assumption: If the customer's objective is to get the right answer, technicians could produce satisfied customers by simply giving the right answer. This assumption seemed reasonable because all technicians could recall certain types of problems that could be resolved instantaneously, and customers were always satisfied with these calls. There were, however, three problems with this solution:

1. Some technicians of below average technical ability nevertheless consistently earned high customer satisfaction ratings. Even more puzzling, some technicians earned high ratings even when they could not supply the correct answer. Paul, for example, sometimes spent days on a problem before informing the customer that he could not supply a solution, yet customers usually gave him high satisfaction ratings.
2. Customers frequently gave low satisfaction ratings despite the fact that they received the correct answer. Take, for example, Joe, a technically competent support engineer who solved a customer's problem with a complex development software product in 10 minutes. This service was excellent for the level of complexity involved, yet the customer complained that the service was inadequate because "it took too long."
3. Even with the best training, most technicians need some experience with troubleshooting before they can give correct answers. Beginners, then, will always degrade the overall performance of the group. Performance averages can take a significant hit because turnover rates in the software support business are frequently high (almost 50 percent in this case), and some products may require up to six months of ramp time.

The company concluded that, although the correct answer could be important under certain conditions, another factor seemed to be involved—the personal factor. These suggestions assumed that the technician did something on a personal level; such as using a particular tone of voice or a friendly greeting that satisfied the customer. One successful technician said it was just a matter of "loving the customer to death." The company had already heavily emphasized the personal factor. Management had prominently displayed signs in the office that read, "Treat the customers as you would like to be treated," "Smile because a customer can hear your smile," and "Don't say no." These types of guidelines and suggestions comprised 60 percent of the procedures listed in the employee manual. Yet these apparently did little for customer satisfaction ratings.

In the ensuing research, 20 engineers responsible for supporting a well-known word-processing package were chosen out of 200. They were divided into two groups—experts and subexperts. The first group was comprised of those engineers who achieved an average customer satisfaction rating of greater than 74 percent during a six-month period. The second group achieved ratings below 75 percent during the same period. The company taped and analyzed two support calls per engineer. Because the engineers were not chosen randomly, the focus was not on gathering a statistically significant sample, but trying to discover what information would be most useful and effective for training support engineers. They compared and contrasted the two groups to seek out the distinctive factors that led to the higher satisfaction rates of the experts, and validated the initial results with interviews of supervisors and the support engineers themselves.

The greatest surprise was discovering how little the personal factor counted. They found that those experts who do establish a more personal relationship fare no better than those who do not. One engineer acted almost robotic while another took every opportunity to use the customer's name in an effort to be more personal. Yet these differences did not affect the ratings. It seemed that short of openly obnoxious behavior, the personal dimension was irrelevant. This result surprised the trainers until they thought about it further. It appears that the customer seeking help for a technical problem has no reason to expect someone who can or will display social skills. Rather, he or she simply wants a solution to a technical problem. That a solution is often not possible because of the current low quality of software support facilities only makes a correct answer even more appreciated. This idea led them to the central method that all experts used to solve problems whether they were personable or not, which they called the *transparency principle.*

When following the transparency principle, the expert support engineer signals throughout the call that he or she is constantly applying troubleshooting skills to the customer's problem. Some of these signals are obvious—restating the problem in the beginning, asking questions to clarify the problem, and giving explanations. Some are less obvious—admitting that a wrong course of action has been recommended, or simply grunting something like "uh-huh" instead of restating the entire problem initially. This method is simple but powerful, so powerful in fact, that when it is properly executed, the customer may walk away highly satisfied even after the engineer has failed to solve his or her problem because the customer believes that the engineer did everything possible to solve the problem. It is called the transparency principle because the expert gives the impression that he or she is not hiding any thoughts and actions from the customer.

Although simple in principle, this method is more complex in practice. Following is an example of how it works when the engineer must probe a moderate amount to find a solution for a caller.

Stage 1: Immediate establishment of status of engineer as a problem solver and expert. The expert engineer communicates that he or she understands the problem the customer is describing. The standard previously set by management was that the engineer should explicitly restate the problem. Only about half the experts in this study did this consistently. The other half simply issued a series of uh huhs. The important thing is for the engineer to issue audible signals as evidence of paying attention to the customer's words.

This technique may present a problem for the beginner who encounters a particularly complex situation. In this case, the engineer should act exactly as an expert who has encountered a difficult problem by asking the customer to describe the steps that led to the problem. The engineer should then explain that this exercise may lead to the discovery of a simple mistake that has a simple solution.

Stage 2: Initiating the troubleshooting. After completing Stage 1, the engineer must quickly show evidence of mental activity directed toward problem resolution. Several ways can be employed to indicate this activity, and the engineer may use any combination of them:

1. The engineer asks the customer to do a series of operations on his or her computer. The commands are issued rapidly and without hesitation. The implicit message is, "I want you to do x, y, and z to verify a hunch I have about what is wrong."
2. In a variation of strategy 1, the engineer offers an explicit diagnosis before issuing the commands, which sets the expectation that the engineer has a definite solution in mind.
3. In a variation of strategy 2, the engineer gives a hint that he or she is thinking of an as-yet ill-defined solution by talking to the customer almost as if he or she were thinking aloud. The engineer then issues the commands, which sets the expectation that he or she might have a solution.
4. The engineer cannot think of a way to attack the problem and must consult information databases or other technicians. He or she apprises the customer of this necessity so the customer understands the reason for the long silence. If Stage 2 leads to a solution, the call produces a satisfied customer. If not, Stage 3 begins.

Stage 3: Open admission of a wrong hypothesis. The engineer immediately shows he or she is working on finding another strategy by recycling through a variation of Stage 2.

The research showed that the difference between the expert and subexpert groups in terms of adherence to the transparency principle was large enough to suggest training. The effects of the training were immediate and dramatic—a 90 percent satisfaction rate one month after the training. It represented a 43 percent increase over the average and was 27 percent higher than ever before. The training brought a gratifying result and an unexpected surprise—the experts themselves also improved significantly. It seemed that once the high-performing experts realized the reasons for their success, they used this knowledge to do even better.

Joe, the support engineer mentioned previously, exemplified this improvement. Despite his expertise as an engineer, at least 20 percent of the surveyed customers gave him a low rating. After learning about transparency, he realized where he went wrong. Whenever Joe put a customer on hold to research a problem, he did not apprise him or her of his plans. The customer, therefore, had no idea why he or she was on hold, at times for as long as 10 minutes. From this point on Joe made sure always to describe his research plan before putting the customer on hold, and he found that the customer sounded more relaxed when he returned to the phone.

Key Issues for Discussion

1. What does this case suggest about the importance of understanding customers' true needs and expectations?
2. What are the implications of the transparency principle?
3. The concept of studying the best people in an organization as a method of learning to improve others' skills has long been advocated by Joseph Juran. How might the learning from this case be applied to other organizations?

Summary of Key Points

- Creating satisfied and loyal customers is perhaps the most important aspect for long-term competitive success. Customer satisfaction occurs when products or services meet or exceed customer expectations, and requires continual improvement of the consumer benefit package, improving the quality of internal operations, and building good relationships.
- The American Customer Satisfaction Index is a national measure of customer satisfaction, linking expectations, perceived quality, and perceived value to customer satisfaction, which in turn is linked to customer loyalty and profitability.

Results suggest that quality improvements are not keeping up with consumer expectations.

- Customers form perceptions of the quality of goods and services by comparing their expectations with actual outcomes. Positive differences can result in unexpected satisfaction while negative differences can lead to dissatisfaction. Thus, careful attention must be paid to design and production processes, as well as customer feedback.
- The leading practices for achieving customer satisfaction include defining key customer segments; understanding the voice of the customer; understanding the linkages between customer needs and design, production, and delivery processes; building relationships through commitments, accessibility, standards, customer contact employees, and effective follow-up; managing and resolving complaints effectively, and measuring customer satisfaction and acting on the results.
- The customer-supplier model advocated by AT&T facilitates the identification of customers at the organization, process, and performer levels. Customers include consumers, external customers, internal customers, the public, and oneself.
- Customer needs differ, requiring organizations to segment their customers into logical groups that have unique needs or value to the organization and must be managed differently.
- Customer needs revolve around many different dimensions of quality, such as performance, features, reliability, and so on. For services, five key dimensions are reliability, assurance, tangibles, empathy, and responsiveness. The Kano model segments customer requirements into dissatisfiers, satisfiers, and exciters and delighters. Most successful companies take special efforts to understand the last category and develop products and services that truly delight customers.
- Gathering customer information is accomplished by various methods, or "listening posts," including comment cards and formal surveys, focus groups, direct customer contact, field intelligence, complaint analysis, and Internet monitoring. Affinity diagrams and tree diagrams are helpful tools for classifying customer requirements and can be used for a variety of other applications.
- Customer relationship management includes providing access to the organization and its employees and establishing commitments, developing relevant customer contact requirements, training and empowering customer-contact employees, effectively dealing with complaints, and forming strategic partnerships and alliances with customers.
- A good customer satisfaction measurement process is scientifically designed, includes performance and importance measures, and provides actionable information to improve a company's operations and products to further satisfy its customers. Many customer satisfaction efforts fail because of poor measurement, useless questions, lack of proper focus, no comparative data, inattention to potential and former customers, and confusing satisfaction with loyalty.

Review Questions

1. Explain the difference between satisfaction and loyalty. Why is loyalty more important?
2. What is a *consumer benefit package*? Why is it important in understanding satisfaction and loyalty?
3. Describe the model used in computing the American Customer Satisfaction Index. How might a business use the information from the ACSI database?

4. Explain the customer-driven quality cycle. What are expected quality, actual quality, and perceived quality, and how do they relate to one another?
5. List and provide an example of the six leading practices of customer-focused quality.
6. Define the principal types of customers that an organization encounters.
7. Explain the AT&T customer-supplier model.
8. Why is it important to segment customers? Describe some ways of defining customer segments.
9. Explain the different dimensions of quality defined by David Garvin.
10. What is the Kano model, and what are its implications for quality management?
11. List the major approaches to gathering customer information. What are the advantages and disadvantages of each?
12. Describe how affinity diagrams and tree diagrams are used to organize and work with customer-related information.
13. Explain the concept of *moments of truth*.
14. Who are customer-contact employees? Why are they critical to an organization?
15. Explain the importance of accessibility and commitments to building customer relationships.
16. Define the term *customer contact requirements*. Why are they important?
17. Explain the role of training and empowerment of customer-contact employees in achieving customer satisfaction.
18. Why should a company make it easy for customers to complain? How should complaint information be used?
19. Why are strategic partnerships and alliances useful to an organization?
20. Why does an organization measure customer satisfaction?
21. Describe the key steps that must be addressed in designing customer satisfaction surveys.
22. Explain the concept of importance-performance analysis and its benefit to an organization.
23. Why do many customer satisfaction efforts fail?
24. What specific issues of customer focus are addressed in the Baldrige Award criteria?

Discussion Questions

1. Can you describe a customer-focused organization, similar to Deer Valley Resort, with which you have had personal experience? What aspects of the organization impressed you the most?
2. Why do you think that many firms fail to recognize the importance of customers until they are faced with a crisis?
3. How might a bank quantify the value of a loyal customer? Try to develop a quantitative model.
4. How might your school use the customer-driven quality cycle in Figure 4.2?
5. Consider a fraternity or other student organization and make a list of all of its customers.
6. How might a college or university segment its customers? What specific needs might each of these customer groups have?
7. For services, how do the quality dimensions defined by David Garvin relate to the five dimensions of reliability, assurance, tangibles, empathy, and responsiveness identified by other researchers? Do they all fit into one of these categories?

8. Which of the five key dimensions of service quality—reliability, assurance, tangibles, empathy, or responsiveness—would the following items from a retail banking customer survey address?
   a. Following through on promises
   b. Offering convenient banking hours
   c. Providing prompt customer service
   d. Properly handling any problems that arise
   e. Maintaining clean and pleasant branch office facilities
   f. Demonstrating knowledge of bank products and services
   g. Giving undivided attention to the customer
   h. Never being too busy to respond to customer requests
   i. Charging reasonable service fees
   j. Maintaining a professional appearance
   k. Providing error-free bank statements
   l. Keeping customer transactions confidential
9. Give several examples of dissatisfiers, satisfiers, and exciters and delighters in products or services that you have recently purchased. Why did you classify them into these categories?
10. Consider the following customer expectations for a fast-food restaurant. Would you classify them as dissatisfiers, satisfiers, or exciters and delighters?
    a. Special prices on certain days
    b. Food that is safe to eat
    c. Hot food served hot
    d. Friendly service
    e. Background music
    f. Playland for children
    g. Clean restaurant
    h. Fresh food
    i. A "one-bite" money-back guarantee
    j. Phone-in orders for pickup at a separate window
11. In the context of a fast-food restaurant, make a list of different characteristics that might describe "freshness." Classify them by means of an affinity diagram or tree diagram. What does your response mean for measuring satisfaction of this attribute?
12. Prepare a list of moments of truth that you encounter during a typical quarter or semester at your college or university.
13. If you were the manager of a small pizza restaurant (dine-in and limited delivery), what customer contact requirements might you specify for your employees who take phone orders, work the cash register, and wait tables? How would you train them?
14. Comment on the following items that you might see on customer satisfaction surveys. Discuss some of the problems with these items and how they might be improved.
    a. The staff is professional.
    b. ETAs are adequate.
    c. Waiting time was reasonable.
    d. Food safety is important to my purchase decision.
    e. The service representative was friendly and helpful.
15. A local franchise of a national car rental firm conducted a survey of customers to determine their perceptions of the importance of key product and service attributes as well as their perceptions of the company's performance.[55] The results are given in Tables 4.3 and 4.4. In Table 4.3, importance

Table 4.3 Importance Ratings of Product/Service Attributes

Mechanical condition of car	4.00
Cleanliness of vehicle	3.93
Friendliness of staff	3.86
Check-out speed/efficiency	3.80
Getting reserved car or better	3.80
Check-in speed/efficiency	3.79
Cleanliness of facility	3.66
Employee appearance	3.45
Getting nonsmoking car	3.45
Speed of coach service	3.24

Table 4.4 Customer Ratings of Performance

	Personal use	**Business use**
Mechanical condition of car	4.815	4.750
Cleanliness of vehicle	4.893	4.563
Friendliness of staff	4.929	4.688
Check-out speed/efficiency	4.759	4.688
Getting reserved car or better	96%	100%
Check-in speed/efficiency	4.821	4.750
Cleanliness of facility	4.893	4.500
Employee appearance	100%	100%
Getting nonsmoking car	86%	100%
Speed of coach service	100%	100%

was measured on a 4-point scale ranging from "not at all important" to "very important." Note that Table 4.4 is segmented by personal and business use, and that two different scales were used (the percentage values are based on the percentage of "yes" responses; all others are on a 5-point scale from "poor" to "excellent"). What conclusions might you make from these data? What possible improvements can you suggest?

16. Analyze the following customer satisfaction results (on a 5-point scale) for a fast-food restaurant. What recommendations would you make to the managers?

Attribute	**Importance**	**Performance**
Fresh buns	4.83	4.80
Cheese is melted	4.26	4.82
Drink is not watery	4.88	4.64
Fries are crisp	4.85	4.80
Fries are salty	4.12	4.48
Service is fast	4.93	4.61
Open 24 hours	3.91	4.81
Good variety of food	4.46	3.87
Nutritional data displayed	3.76	4.65
Children's menu available	4.80	3.97
Tables kept clean	4.91	4.89
Low-fat items available	3.62	4.55

17. How do the Baldrige criteria address the issues raised in the discussion of the reasons why many customer satisfaction efforts fail? Can addressing the criteria help to mitigate these reasons?
18. Suppose you received the examiner feedback in the Collin Technologies example. What would you do within the company to improve?
19. Contrast the requirements of Category 3 in the 2000 and 2001 Baldrige criteria. What are the key differences? What are the implications of the changes?

PROJECTS, ETC.

1. Perform some research to examine trends in the American Customer Satisfaction Index over the last three years. What economic sectors show improvement? Which don't? How has the overall index changed?
2. Determine whether your school implements any of the leading practices of customer focus in a systematic manner and write a report describing their approaches.
3. Based on the information in this chapter, propose new approaches for measuring customer satisfaction for your faculty and instructors that go beyond the traditional course evaluation processes that your school may use.
4. You may have visited or purchased items from large computer and software retail stores. In a group brainstorming session, identify those characteristics of such a store that would be most important to you, and design a customer survey to evaluate customers' importance and the store's performance.
5. Table 4.5 lists customer requirements as determined through a focus group conducted by Western America Airlines. Develop an affinity diagram and classify these requirements into appropriate categories, and design a questionnaire to survey customers. Be sure to address any other pertinent issues/questions as well as customer information that would be appropriate to include in the questionnaire.

Table 4.5 Airline Customer Requirements

- Quality food
- Ability to solve problems and answer questions during flight
- Efficient boarding procedures
- Appealing interior appearance
- Well-maintained seats
- Reservation calls answered promptly
- Timely and accurate communication of information prior to boarding
- Good selection of magazines and newspapers
- Efficient and attentive flight attendants
- Good beverage selection
- Clean lavatories
- Efficient ticket line and waiting procedures
- Convenient ground transportation
- Courteous reservations personnel
- Good quality audio/visual system
- Sufficient quantity of food
- Interesting in-flight magazine
- Courteous and efficient gate personnel
- In-flight telephone access
- Good variety of audio/visual programming
- Flight attendants knowledgeable of airline programs and policies
- Correct explanation of fares and schedules
- Efficient seat selection process
- Courteous and efficient sky cap
- Timely and accurate communication of flight information (in-flight)
- Convenient baggage check-in
- Timely baggage check-in
- Comfortable seating and leg room
- Assistance for passengers with special needs
- Courteous ticket counter personnel
- Convenient parking close to terminal
- Ability to solve baggage claim problems
- Ability of reservation agents to answer questions

6. Interview some managers of small businesses to determine how they respond to complaints and use complaint information in their organizations.
7. Gather several customer satisfaction surveys or comment cards from local establishments. Analyze them as to their ability to lead to actionable information that will help the organization, and propose any improvements or redesign you deem appropriate.

Cases

I. The Case of the Missing Reservation

Mark, Donna, and their children, along with another family, traditionally attended Easter brunch at a large downtown hotel. This year, as in the past, Donna called and made a reservation about three weeks prior to Easter. Because half the party consisted of small children, they arrived 20 minutes prior to the 11:30 reservation to ensure being seated early. When they arrived, however, the hostess said that they did not have a reservation. She explained that guests sometimes failed to show and that she would probably have a table available for them before long. Mark and Donna were quite upset and insisted that they had made a reservation and expected to be seated promptly. The hostess told them, "I believe that you made a reservation, but I can't seat you until all the people on the reservation list are seated. You are welcome to go to the lounge for complimentary coffee and punch while you wait." When Mark asked to see the manager, the hostess replied, "I am the manager," and turned to other duties. The party was eventually seated at 11:45, but was not at all happy with the experience.

The next day, Mark wrote a letter to the hotel manager explaining the entire incident. Mark was in the MBA program at the local university and taking a course on total quality management. In the class, they had just studied issues of customer focus and some of the approaches used at The Ritz-Carlton Hotel, a two-time Baldrige Award winner. Mark concluded his letter with the statement, "I doubt that we would have experienced this situation at a hotel that truly believes in quality." About a week later, he received the following letter:

> *We enjoy hearing from our valued guests, but wish you had experienced the level of service and accommodations that we strive to achieve here at our hotel. Our restaurant manager received your letter and asked me to respond as Total Quality Lead.*
>
> *Looking back at our records we did not show a reservation on the books for your family. I have addressed your comments with the appropriate department head so that others will not have to experience the same inconveniences that you did.*
>
> *Thank you once again for sharing your thoughts with us. We believe in a philosophy of "continuous improvement," and it is through feedback such as yours that we can continue to improve the service to our guests.*

Discussion Questions

1. Were the hostess's actions consistent with a customer-focused quality philosophy? What might she have done differently?
2. How would you have reacted to the letter that Mark received? Could the Total Quality Lead have responded differently? What does the fact that the hotel manager did not personally respond to the customer tell you?

II. Cincinnati Veterans Administration Medical Center[56]

The Cincinnati VA Medical Center (CVAMC) provides health care to eligible veterans in Ohio, southeast Indiana, and northern Kentucky. The CVAMC is an acute care, university-affiliated 220-bed facility. It is a part of the Veterans Healthcare Administration of the Department of Veterans Affairs. It comprises one of five medical centers within the Veterans Integrated Services Network

10 (VISN 10). The CVAMC works to provide a variety of services as needed across the continuum of care for veteran patients, as well as trainee education and the pursuit of new knowledge through research. The mission arises from federal mandates to support health care, education, and research.

CVAMC's vision is to "... shape our future by breaking the traditional VA mold, building on our strengths, and emerging as the health care center of choice for all Veterans. As pioneers of change we will:

1. Establish the patient at the core of all processes with the focus on continuity of care leading to optimal patient outcomes.
2. Develop a united team of competent, caring, empowered employees committed to providing service that exceeds expectations.
3. Foster unprecedented labor-management trust and cooperation.
4. Create a proactive organization that is responsive, streamlined, and personal.
5. Be recognized as an innovative, vital health care leader and educational resource in our VA system and the Greater Cincinnati community."

The CVAMC is able to offer a variety of inpatient and outpatient health care services. The Medical Service staff offers services in primary care, general internal medicine, and in multiple medical subspecialties such as cardiology, nephrology, pulmonary, and gastroenterology. The Surgery Service offers general surgical care and specialty care in such areas as urology, orthopedics, vascular surgery, and neurosurgery. The Mental Health Service provides psychiatric and psychological support care for patients with a variety of programs including care for patients with posttraumatic stress disorder, substance abuse, and serious mental illnesses. The Neurology Service cares for patients with disorders of the nervous system. It has special programs in epilepsy, neuromuscular disease, stroke, and movement disorders. Physical Medicine and Rehabilitation Service offers support for patients with acute and chronic debilitating conditions. It offers programs in occupational, physical, and speech therapy as well as chronic pain management and prostheses.

The CVAMC also provides specialty services in support of other medical centers within the VISN, including surgical, psychiatric, neurological, and medical specialty care to patients at Dayton, Chillicothe, and Columbus. Additionally, some specialized care is offered for veterans from other areas of the state and country, including the production of special limb prostheses.

The primary customer is the veteran patient. Highest priority is given to veterans with medical conditions or injuries related to their service in the military, and to those veterans with limited resources who otherwise would have difficulty obtaining the care they need. CVAMC offers a broad range of services to other eligible veterans as well. Other customers include the families of veteran patients, the veterans support organizations (VSO), the trainees including residents and medical students, and the staff at the other VISN facilities. It maintains a special relationship with the University of Cincinnati. This relationship involves all three major missions of this medical center. The majority of the staff physicians have joint appointments with the University. Some specialized care is provided through sharing agreements with the University, including radiation therapy, special radiological studies, and cardiac surgery. The CVAMC is a major teaching center for many of the University's residents and medical students. The CVAMC also supports researchers with joint appointments at the University. The unions and the Medical Center have formed a partnership. Finally, a partnership operates between the Medical Center and a local elementary school.

The 1,100 employees of the CVAMC include physicians, nurses, psychologists, dieticians, social workers, therapists, and other health care professionals. This number also includes those members of the services that support the delivery of care including environmental management, security, medical administration, finance, and acquisition personnel. Physicians represent approximately 10 percent of the full-time work force, while nursing personnel account for about one-third.

The main facility for the CVAMC includes the acute care bed services and clinic areas housed in one building in Cincinnati. The inpatient facilities include two intensive care units, acute medical and surgical services, and acute and intermediate term psychiatry services. Outpatient facilities include clinics on three floors and a patient evaluation area for patients with emergencies. Full-scale laboratory, clinical pathology, and radiological services are available on-site. There are facilities for computerized fabrication of artificial limbs for patients with amputations. Day treatment facilities are also available for patients with PTSD and substance abuse. The CVAMC operates a nursing home and a domiciliary for homeless veterans at its Fort Thomas location. The CVAMC also supports an outpatient facility in Bellevue, Kentucky, for easier access for veteran patients in northern Kentucky. The CVAMC also offers specialty services to other VAMCs in VISN 10 through outreach programs at those facilities. One major regulatory body is the Joint Commission for Accreditation of Healthcare Organizations. Other regulatory bodies that review the activities of the CVAMC include the Nuclear Regulatory Commission, the College of Pathology, the Environmental Protection Agency, and OSHA.

Veteran patients require accessibility to care, including the need to be seen at a location convenient to them. Additionally, they must be able to get an appointment with their clinicians within a reasonable period of time. A 30-day limit for specialty clinic consultation has been targeted as a key customer service standard. Patients do not want to have to wait for long periods on the day of their appointments. They need access to the latest technology and specialty skills as appropriate for their medical conditions. This access is important even if the CVAMC does not have the necessary equipment or personnel on site. The CVAMC must then contract for those services. Veteran patients need to have continuity of care. They want to see the same clinician each visit to develop rapport with someone who understands their particular needs. They want that provider to be aware of the results of any specialty consultations or hospitalizations. These patients deserve the availability of a range of services to meet their needs. They recognize the need for interdisciplinary approaches to solve some of their health problems. They demand to be heard during medical decision making and want their end-of-life wishes respected.

The families of veteran patients need to be informed about the care of their loved ones. They want to be able to participate in educational activities. They wish to be able to support the patient when treatment decisions are being made. They want convenient access to care for the veteran patients, because they are often responsible for getting the patient to the appointments.

The veterans services organizations play a key role in supporting veteran patients. They demand that the veterans' needs be met. To this end, they require access to top management of the CVAMC in order to discuss their concerns.

The trainees demand access to teaching facilities. They want to be able to assist in the care of patients with a variety of health conditions. They want to be able to discuss issues with experienced staff. They demand access to the latest technology and treatments. They want to be able to interact with researchers to gain a better understanding of their patients' conditions and options for care.

The staff at other VISN facilities needs to be able to take advantage of the expertise and equipment at the CVAMC when these services are not readily available at their own sites. They want access for their patients that is timely and convenient. They demand timely reports of these evaluations and wish to be included in medical decision making.

The University demands satisfaction of its teaching requirements for the trainees. The University requires regular monitoring of the trainees' progress. University staff also monitors the trainees' evaluation of their experience while at the CVAMC. The University requires payment for clinical services provided.

The CVAMC holds a special place in the competitive health care market in the region. It is the only hospital in its service area dedicated to veterans. Even though this focus limits the number of potential customers, CVAMC can use its focus in its pursuit of its targeted customers. It is relatively small compared to the area's major medical centers, but it can take advantage of its membership in the large chain of medical centers in the VHA when purchasing medications and equipment. It can also take advantage of its ties with the University and nationally funded research programs to lend an aura of quality. It also provides the most vertically integrated health care delivery system in the market, with a variety of services for its veteran patients across the continuum from outpatient to inpatient. It currently provides care to approximately 21,000 veteran patients, but this figure represents only about a 10 percent penetration of its target market. This limited penetration is due in part to years of restricted eligibility to receive care at this facility. Because of its role of supporting veterans with limited resources, it has been viewed at times as a provider of last resort. Federal regulations restrict the ability to advertise, limiting the ability to market its services. The CVAMC also faces a declining population of veterans in its service area.

The CVAMC has a number of competitors in the region, including all of the major medical facilities that provide inpatient or outpatient care. They compete with the CVAMC mostly for patients with insurance or Medicare coverage. Veteran patients with limited resources may also go to places other than the CVAMC, because some support for indigent care is available. Additionally, the other VA medical centers in the state can compete with the CVAMC for veteran patients. Funding of these centers depends in part on the number of veteran patients served. The CVAMC must be ready to compete with these other facilities, inside and outside of the VHA, if it is to succeed.

Several factors are important when competing in this health care market. The reputation for quality may be a critical factor for some patients. Cost is a major factor for many veteran patients, because they have little or no out-of-pocket expenses for care provided at the CVAMC. Accessibility is critical, because patients are often unwilling to tolerate long waits for appointments or long delays on the day of their visits. Many patients show strong preferences for local access to care, the ability to avoid bridge or downtown traffic, and ease of parking. Continuity of care is important to many patients. Many patients want their providers to be able to coordinate their visits and tests, with good communication of results among their providers. Staff courtesy, empathy, and efforts to educate the patients may also be factors of importance to health care customers.

Change continues to affect the health care market. Recent changes in federal reimbursement of medical facilities under the Balanced Budget Act have caused financial strain among health care providers. The VHA is funded separately but is not immune to budget cutting activities in Congress. The insurance companies have also been aggressively trying to reduce their expenses, impacting the revenues of medical facilities. The aging of the population has increased the demand for services. The costs of pharmaceuticals and medical technology continue to rise. Changes in coverage of medications have forced some patients to consider different sources for their health care. CVAMC must attend to these changes if it is to prosper in this changing health care environment.

The major new initiative for the CVAMC is to improve access to care by the placement of outpatient facilities at sites more convenient to veteran patients. This process started with the planning for and implementation of the community-based outpatient clinic (CBOC) in Bellevue, Kentucky. Analysis of zip code information for eligible veterans in the region showed a high concentration of patients in the three counties of northern Kentucky. Focus groups were held with patients from this area that showed that these patients strongly disliked having to cross the Ohio River for their health care. An adequate site was found for a clinic in northern Kentucky. Since its opening, enrollment with patients new to the system has occurred rapidly. In view of this success, the demographic data was reviewed for consideration of two more veterans service centers. Sites in southeast Indiana and Clermont County have been approved. These centers should help the CVAMC to meet its targets of increased patient enrollment as well as improved access to care.

The Mental Health Service has undertaken an initiative to improve access to its targeted group of veteran patients in the northern suburbs of Hamilton County. This initiative will also improve access to care and utilization of CVAMC resources as these patients begin to use other services.

The CVAMC has taken part in a new VISN case management program. It involves assigning a nurse to patients in certain high-risk categories. The categories of risk were determined by review of resource utilization including days of hospitalization. The case manager is trained to improve coordination of care and assure appropriate preventative measures are taken to improve the health state of the patient, limiting the use of scarce resources.

Major research programs are helping the CVAMC achieve its missions. The medical center is one of three sites funded nationally as a Patient Safety Center of Inquiry to look at how mistakes occur and how they can be limited in the delivery of health care. The Mental Health Service has recently received further funding from the National Institutes of Health to study substance abuse management. These programs help to fund staff positions while improving the quality of care offered to veteran patients.

The computerized system for automated production of prostheses represents a new service that is not available elsewhere in the VISN. Additionally, it is far superior in cycle time to any system available anywhere else in the region. This system allows the CVAMC to offer unparalleled service to its patients with amputations. The shorter cycle time increases the chances that the veteran patient will be able to ambulate well after an amputation procedure. The system allows us to provide similar service for veteran patients at other facilities within the VISN and beyond, without the need for these patients to travel to Cincinnati.

Another area receiving great attention at this time is achieving increasingly strict customer service standards. Standards help focus attention of all employees on the issues of importance to veteran patients. These standards have associated monitors and measures, with benchmarks from health care systems nationally.

The major unique factor at the CVAMC is the strategic planning process. This process occurs at the Quorum, a quarterly meeting of managers from all services as well as representatives of major customer groups. Results of prior initiatives are reviewed. The group decides whether the resources should continue to be assigned to those projects. New initiatives are considered in view of changes in the environment and customer needs. The large size of the group improves organizational buy-in for initiatives. The monitoring activities of this group have allowed the elimination of some committees including the Quality Assurance Committee. The size and nature of this strategic planning group is unusual for a health care organization. The quarterly meetings allow the medical center to respond more quickly to change. This process will be important in the future success of the CVAMC.

Discussion Questions

1. Based on this background information about the CVAMC, propose a set of approaches that the medical center might pursue to help achieve its vision and truly be customer-focused. Focus on the types of customers the CVAMC has identified, their needs, and the organization's role in the community and with respect to its competition.
2. The file VAsurvey.doc on the CD-rom accompanying this book shows a patient satisfaction survey used at the CVAMC (each page is also saved as a jpeg image, vasurvey 1.jpg, etc.). Classify the questions according to the key dimensions of service quality described in this chapter. Analyze the questions as to their ability to provide actionable information for improvement, address key patient needs and expectations, and assess satisfaction and loyalty. Write a summary report of your conclusions.

III. Collin Technologies: Customer Satisfaction and Relationships

Read Item 3.2, Customer Satisfaction and Relationships, in the Collin Technologies case study on the CD-rom accompanying this book. Using the 2000 Baldrige criteria, develop a list of strengths and opportunities for improvement similar to the style in Example 1. Strengths should focus on things the company is doing exceptionally well and that support their vision and strategy. (Read the business overview section of the case first to identify specific factors that are important to customer satisfaction and relationships.) Opportunities for improvement should highlight issues in its approach or deployment that can better meet the requirements of the Baldrige criteria. Your comments should include a reason why a strength or opportunity for improvement is important, that is, provide some insight to upper-level managers that they might not have otherwise realized. Use the wording in the scoring guidelines in Table 3.5 to help you structure your comments.

IV. Gold Star Chili: Customer and Market Knowledge[57]

Gold Star Chili has hired you as a consultant to help them improve their approach to focusing on customers. They have prepared a Baldrige-like application for their state award program (portions of which follow), and they want some specific advice, including useful tools and techniques that might help them. What would you tell them? Base your response on the 2000 criteria.

Company Background

Gold Star Chili, Inc., based in Cincinnati, Ohio, was founded in 1965 as a family-owned system of franchised and company-owned restaurants. Gold Star currently operates 118 regional locations (99 of which are franchised; the remaining are company restaurants or are co-owned). The Gold Star menu is based on a unique "Cincinnati-style" chili recipe, flavored with a proprietary blend of spices from around the world. The chili is prepared in a central commissary designed to reduce equipment needs at individual restaurants, promote consistency, and reduce labor costs.

Gold Star operates in a highly competitive market against other multilocation chili firms and traditional fast-food competitors such as McDonald's, Taco Bell, and KFC. It trails its major competitor, Skyline, which has a larger advertising campaign, in market share. In the late 1980s Gold Star recruited a nonfamily member to serve as CEO in order to expand the number of restaurants and geographic coverage. In early 1997 Gold Star launched a total quality initiative, "The Gold Star Way."

3.1a Customer and Market Knowledge

Gold Star is committed to achieving exceptional customer satisfaction through the creation of lasting relationships and by offering a consistently high-caliber set of products and services that customers perceive as an excellent value. Through the effective application of the "one customer at a time" philosophy, each associate strives to provide the level of customer service that permits the company to create and keep customers for life. Through attention to each customer's needs at each "moment of truth," the company focus is on not only satisfying, but delighting each customer. Through careful implementation and adherence to the "Gold Star Way," the company seeks to develop an enhanced understanding of customers and markets.

(1) Gold Star Chili defines two key customer groups: direct customers who use Gold Star products and services, and indirect customers with whom Gold Star has other relationships. Direct customers are categorized into six customer segments, determined by product use: restaurant customers, franchisees, franchise applicants, retail customers, retail wholesalers, and mail-order customers. Indirect customers include product suppliers, service suppliers, co-packers, brokers and consultants, shareholders, and regulatory agencies.

(2) To learn from customers, Gold Star uses multiple listening posts, including market research, focus groups, customer comment cards, satisfaction surveys, and roundtable meetings, advisory council group meetings, and one-on-one meetings. In determining the restaurant consumer requirements, market research is conducted every two to three years. Gold Star benchmarks consumer preferences in eating habits, consumer loyalty, product awareness, and attribute ratings for quality, service and value of its restaurants and competitors. Focus groups determine consumer preferences against the competition. Customers expect product consistency, a clean and pleasant atmosphere, and consistent service. Each restaurant has postage-paid comment cards (see Figure 4.18) available at counters and tables. Monthly,

Figure 4.18 Customer Comment Card

We would like to have your comments.
NO POSTAGE NECESSARY! Please Mail:
DATE: _____ TIME: _____ AM/PM LOCATION: _____
Servers Name: _____
What Did You Order: _____

QUALITY	👍	👎		👍	👎
Good value	☐	☐	Taste	☐	☐
Quality of food	☐	☐	Portion	☐	☐
Temperature of food	☐	☐	Appearance of food	☐	☐
SERVICE					
Speed	☐	☐	Hospitality	☐	☐
Accuracy	☐	☐	Appearance of server	☐	☐
CLEANLINESS					
Inside store	☐	☐			
Outside store	☐	☐			
Rest rooms	☐	☐			

What radio station(s) do you listen to most often?
_____

How would you rate your overall dining experience?
1 2 3 4 5 6 7 8 9 10
POOR GOOD EXCELLENT
COMMENTS: _____

OPTIONAL: Name: _____
Address: _____
Phone: _____

Gold Star receives an average of 200–300 comment cards. Customer service representatives enter each comment into a database and produce monthly reports on consumer satisfaction of each restaurant. From time to time, consumers will call direct to Gold Star offices to make a formal complaint; these contacts are also tabulated into the monthly customer comment report. The primary communication with restaurant customers occurs at the customer-server interface. In addition, store managers are encouraged to talk with guests regularly. An 800 number is also available to consumers of retail products.

Franchisees are attracted by the relatively low investment required to join the Gold Star family of restaurants, as well as the opportunity to operate a profitable business and to profit from the strong brand equity built into the Gold Star name. They expect consistency in chili product, effective corporate direction in the form of advice, market feedback, and promotional activities. Prior to the addition of a new restaurant, a geodemographic analysis of potential locations is performed to ensure that any new facility will not take more than 10 percent of its business from another Gold Star location. Gold Star's franchisee service representatives (FSRs) take product orders from individual franchisees by telephone on daily and weekly bases. These frequent interactions create a continuous dialog between the franchisee and the FSR as well as the delivery person who delivers product.

Numerous opportunities are created to listen and learn from franchisees, including a Franchise Advisor Council consisting of elected owners who meet monthly to review and determine business decisions that affect the chain. The council members are also assigned to committee groups that meet with department heads to review business practices in areas of marketing, purchasing, menu pricing, operational costs, and gross profit analysis. Gold Star also conducts quarterly business meetings with restaurant owners and key managers. These meetings cover operations issues affecting the chain; outside suppliers are welcome to attend the meetings also. In 1996 a comprehensive survey of franchisees was initiated. Many complained that the survey was too long and not anonymous. Consequently, the survey was redesigned in 1997 into a short, five-question "Franchise Satisfaction Survey" and sent to all locations on a quarterly basis (see Figure 4.19).

(3) Through the data received from market research and focus group studies, Gold Star can determine consumer awareness, preferences, and dislikes. Feedback from advisory council meetings and quarterly business meetings help guide the company in designing training for management development of franchisees and their staff. Satisfaction survey results help target areas of opportunity and create action plans. The relative importance of product and service features to franchisees is tracked through the quarterly meetings, as well as through learning from daily and weekly phone calls to FSRs and face-to-face discussions with delivery personnel.

More than 70 percent of customers eat in a Gold Star restaurant at least once a month, and 20 to 30 percent eat at least once per week. The loyalty of the customer base permits servers and store managers to get to know customers personally and learn much about consumer needs. Marketing consultants perform an annual telephone survey of 300 "heavy chili users" to learn more about what consumers seek in chili products.

(4) Gold Star Chili is an active participant in roundtable events sponsored by the Greater Cincinnati Chamber of Commerce. The organization also participates with the Cincinnati Restaurant Association and the National Restaurant Association. These associations help maintain awareness of business trends and advances in new technology. Changing business needs are assessed by reviewing the annual reports of competing restaurants and through an annual market research study, which permits benchmarking against the restaurant and convenience food industry in general. Gold Star also reviews market research questions and redesign questions to gain better feedback. Mystery shoppers of Gold Star and competing restaurants provide a cross-check of the results obtained from survey and focus groups. Service industry trade literature is read regularly. In some instances, store operators have developed their own set of customer satisfaction tracking tools, for example, tracking tip amounts.

3.2 Customer Satisfaction and Relationships

Gold Star uses several interlinked approaches to determine customer satisfaction and to strengthen relationships.

(1) A comment card program and toll-free

Figure 4.19 Franchisee Satisfaction Survey

Gold Star Chili

Franchisee Satisfaction Survey

Franchisee: ____________________

Please complete this survey and mail by return date.
Rating and comments should pertain to all departments.

RATING SCALE	
A	TOTALLY SATISFIED
B	GENERALLY SATISFIED
C	GENERALLY DISSATISFIED
D	TOTALLY DISSATISFIED

	Rating
Communication Staff effectively communicates to you and listens to your needs and makes you feel important; Is easy to contact.	
Quality Quality food and products; Consistent and accurate services provided.	
Timeliness On-time deliveries; Handles emergencies; Speedy solutions.	
Dependability Promises kept; Trust in overall direction of the company.	
Cooperativeness Responds to needs; Flexible; Courteous; Sensitive to franchisee's needs.	

Please help us continuously improve by providing comments when a grade of "B" or less is given.

How does Gold Star Chili rate against other companies that you work with:
Please circle one: A B C D

Comments:

____

Suggestions:

____

number makes it easy for the consumer to provide feedback. The operations department has two directors of operations, each overseeing half of the franchise community. Restaurant owners are given the director's phone number, pagers, cell phone numbers, e-mail addresses, and home phone numbers. All potential franchise owners meet with the executive staff prior to purchasing a franchise to establish a relationship.

(2) Every worker is trained to ask customers about their experience and see whether the worker can do anything to make it better. Comment cards are responded to within 24 hours of receipt. A follow-up letter apologizing for an error or thanking them for a compliment is sent. All department heads are asked to respond to franchise needs within 24 hours of a call. If a franchisee reports a problem with product quality, a hand-delivered replacement product the same day is a typical response.

(3) Restaurant customers with complaints most often present them directly to the server or manager. Usually the manager will attempt to recover from the service incident by offering partial or total credit, or a coupon redeemable for free food. Gold Star Chili has a formal Customer Response System. All complaints are channeled to Gold Star's customer service representative (CSR). All complaints, verbal or written, are logged onto a Comment Action Form. If the comment is determined to be critical, then a call is made to the customer. The CSR must make two attempts to contact the customer within 24 hours. If the CSR cannot make contact, then a letter is sent to the customer along with free coupons. Afterwards, the CSR will telephone the outcome directly to the franchisee. Occasionally, a three-way conference is conducted between the CSR, the franchisee, and the customer. The Comment Action Form is

logged into the database and forwarded to the appropriate department for review and signature. The CSR prepares a monthly complaint log highlighting all comments, which are reviewed by senior management.

(4) Gold Star's mission is to create lasting relationships based upon respect, trust, and support of its customers. Many franchisees build relationships through local store marketing. Many owners-managers are active in the community with sponsorships of teams or school programs. Gold Star provides owners with school achievement awards they can distribute to local schools.

(5) Gold Star keeps its approaches to customer access and relationships current through benchmarking Baldrige Award winners and attending regional and national conference to learn best practices.

3.2b Customer Satisfaction Determination

(1) Gold Star measures customer satisfaction for each of the major customer groups, consumers, franchise operators, associates, and suppliers, using comment cards and satisfaction surveys. Consumer comment cards rates key attributes as "thumbs up" or "thumbs down," and the overall dining experience on a scale from 1–10. The other satisfaction surveys use a score of A, B, C, or D for five attributes, and have a section for open comments. Action plans are set for any scores that fall below A. The franchise operator and supplier surveys also seek ratings against other companies they deal with. The associate survey asks for specific likes and dislikes about working for Gold Star Chili.

(2) The majority of follow-up with dine-in customers is done face-to-face. At each restaurant, the server visits the table two to three times to ensure that everything is acceptable and to see whether customer needs are being met.

(3) Through various meetings between corporate and franchisees, Gold Star obtains information about satisfaction relative to competitors. The franchise satisfaction survey gives specific and reliable information from stores. For consumers, satisfaction relative to competitors is obtained from focus groups.

(4) As with other approaches to customer relationships, Gold Star keeps its approaches to satisfaction determination current through benchmarking Baldrige Award winners and best practice research. For example, Gold Star was able to implement changes to its satisfaction survey process by following the method used by a past winner.

NOTES

1. Courtesy of Deer Valley Resort.

2. Patricia Sellers, "Companies That Serve You Best," *Fortune*, May 31, 1993, 6.

3. "Making Customer Loyalty Real: Lessons from Leading Manufacturers," Special Advertising Section, *Fortune*, June 21, 1999.

4. S. C. Wheelwright, "Competing Through Manufacturing," in *International Handbook of Production and Operations Management*, Ray Wild, ed. (London: Cassell Educational, Ltd., 1989), 15–32.

5. AVIS 1992 Annual Report and Quality Review.

6. David Kirkpatrick, "Breaking Up IBM," *Fortune*, July 27, 1992, 44–58.

7. "Companies That Serve You Best," see note 2.

8. Carl Sewell and Paul B. Brown, *Customers for Life* (New York: Doubleday-Currency, 1990).

9. Jane Norman, "Royal Treatment Keeps Customers Loyal," *Cincinnati Enquirer*, May 31, 1998, E3, E5.

10. David Leonhardt, "Big Airlines Should Follow Midwest's Recipe," *Business Week*, June 28, 1999.

11. J. M. Juran, *Juran on Quality by Design* (New York: The Free Press, 1992), 7.

12. The Forum Corporation, Customer Focus Research, executive briefing, Boston, 1988.

13. "Companies That Serve You Best," see note 2.

14. Model developed by National Quality Research Center, University of Michigan Business School for the American Customer Satisfaction Index, (ACSI). Cosponsored with American Society for Quality Control, 1994.

15. "How to Listen to Consumers," *Fortune*, January 11, 1993, 77.

16. J. M. Juran, *Juran on Quality by Design* (New York: The Free Press, 1992), chap. 3.

17. AT&T Quality Steering Committee, Achieving Customer Satisfaction, AT&T Bell Laboratories, 1990.

18. Michael J. Stahl, et al., "Customer-Value Analysis Helps Hone Strategy," *Quality Progress*, April 1999, 53–58.

19. "Time to Put Away the Checkbook: Now Fleet Needs to Bring Order to Its Furious Expansion," *Business Week*, June 10, 1996, 100.

20. David A. Garvin, "What Does Product Quality Really Mean?" *Sloan Management Review* 26, no. 1 (1984), 25–43.

21. Rahul Jacob, "Why Some Customers Are More Equal Than Others," *Fortune*, September 19, 1994, 215–224.

22. Robert D. Buzzell and Bradley T. Gale, *The PIMS Principles: Linking Strategy to Performance* (New York: The Free Press, 1987).

23. "Getting an Edge," *Across the Board*, February 2000, 43–48.

24. "Apple's One-Dollar-a-Year Man," *Fortune*, January 24, 2000, 71–76.

25. Bruce Nussbaum, "Designs for Living," *Business Week*, June 2, 1997, 99.

26. James H. Drew and Tye R. Fussell, "Becoming Partners with Internal Customers," *Quality Progress* 29, no. 10 (October 1996), 51–54.

27. "How to Listen to Consumers," *Fortune*, January 11, 1993, 77.

28. Manfred Buller, "Quality Improvement Process at BASF Polymers Group," in *When America Does It Right*, Jay Spechler, ed. (Norcross, GA: Industrial Engineering and Management Press, 1988), 55–63.

29. Susan Caminiti, "A Star Is Born," *Fortune*, Autumn/Winter 1993, 44–47.

30. Byron J. Finch, "A New Way to Listen to the Customer," *Quality Progress* 30, no. 5 (May 1997), 73–76.

31. "KJ" is a registered trademark of the Kawayoshida Research Center.

32. This example is adapted from Donald L. McLaurin and Shareen Bell, "Making Customer Service More Than Just a Slogan," *Quality Progress* 26, no. 11 (November 1993), 35–39.

33. Jane Carroll, "Mickey's Not for Everybody," *Across the Board*, February 2000, 11.

34. See note 3, "Making Customer Loyalty Real."

35. Richard S. Teitelbaum, "Where Service Flies Right," *Fortune*, August 24, 1992, 117–118.

36. "Xerox Guarantee Pays for Bank Processing Fees of Rejected Checks," *Quality Progress* 28, no. 12 (December 1995), 16.

37. Christopher Hart, "What Is an Extraordinary Guarantee?" *The Quality Observer* 3, no. 5 (March 1994), 15.

38. Teitelbaum, see note 35.

39. Karl Albrecht and Ronald E. Zemke, *Service America* (Homewood, IL: Dow Jones-Irwin, 1985).

40. John Goodman, Pat O'Brien and Eden Segal, "Turning CFOs Into Quality Champions—Show Link to Enhanced Revenue and Higher Margins," *Quality Progress* 33, no. 3 (March 2000), 47–56.

41. "Focusing on the Customer," *Fortune*, June 5, 1989, 226.

42. BI 1999 Malcolm Baldrige National Quality Award Application Summary.

43. AT&T Corporate Quality Office, *Supplier Quality Management: Foundations* (1994), 52.

44. Myron Magnet, "The New Golden Rule of Business," *Fortune*, February 21, 1994, 60–64.

45. Patricia C. La Londe, "Surveys as Supplier Relationship Tool," ASQ's 54th Annual Quality Congress Proceedings, Indianapolis, IN (2000), 684–686.

46. John Goodman, David DePalma, and Scott Breetzmann, "Maximizing the Value of Customer Feedback," *Quality Progress* 29, no. 12 (December 1996), 35–39.

47. Importance-performance analysis was first introduced by J. A. Martilla and J. C. James, "Importance-Performance Analysis," *Journal of Marketing* 41, 1977, 77–79.

48. "Quality '93: Empowering People With Technology," advertisement, *Fortune*, September, 1993.

49. A. Blanton Godfrey, "Beyond Satisfaction," *Quality Digest*, January 1996, 15. Reprinted by kind permission of A. Blanton Godfrey and *Quality Digest*.

50. Adapted from 2000 Malcolm Baldrige National Quality Award Criteria for Performance Excellence, Item Descriptions and Comments.

51. Adapted from Malcolm Baldrige National Quality Award Profiles of Winners, 1988–1993, and materials provided by Granite Rock, including the 1992 Malcolm Baldrige Application Summary; Edward O. Welles, "How're We Doing?" *Inc.*, May 1991; Martha Heine, "Using Customer Report Cards Ups Service," undated reprint from Concrete Trader, and "Customer Report Cards at Granite Rock," exhibit at *http://www.baldrigeplus.com*.

52. Adapted from Bob Graessel and Pete Zeidler, "Using Quality Function Deployment to Improve Customer Service," *Quality Progress* 26, no. 11 (November 1993), 59–63.

53. Adapted from Charles Palson and Dale Seidlitz, "Customer Satisfaction at a Software Support Call Center," *Quality Progress*, June 2000, 71–75. © 2000. American Society for Quality (ASQ). Reprinted with permission.

54. Gary Klein, *Sources of Power: How People Make Decisions* (Cambridge, MA: MIT Press, 1990).

55. Adapted from Ralph F. Altman and Marilyn M. Helms, "Quantifying Service Quality: A Case Study of a Rental Car Agency," *Production and Inventory Management* 36, no. 2 (Second Quarter 1995), 45–50. Reprinted with permission of APICS—The Educational Society for Resource Management, Falls Church, VA.

56. We thank our student team, William Cahill, Troy Hall, and Rachel Whitaker, and the Cincinnati Veterans Administration Medical Center for providing this case information.

57. We thank our student team, Sudipta Bhattacharya, Terry Fitzpatrick, Gordon Jamieson, and Jeremy Smith, for their work on the initial version of this case for the fourth edition of this book; Kim Olden of Gold Star Chili for providing current information; and Gold Star Chili, Inc. for granting permission to use this material.

BIBLIOGRAPHY

AT&T Quality Steering Committee. *Achieving Customer Satisfaction*. Quality Technology Center, AT&T Bell Laboratories, 1990.

Fierman, Jaqclyn. "Americans Can't Get No Satisfaction." *Fortune*, December 11, 1995, 186–194.

Hayes, Bob E. *Measuring Customer Satisfaction*. Milwaukee, WI: ASQC Quality Press, 1990.

"How Ford's F-150 Lapped the Competition." *Business Week*, July 29, 1996, 74–75.

King, R. "Listening to the Voice of the Customer." *National Productivity Review* 6, no. 3 (1987), 277–281.

Malcolm Baldrige National Quality Award, 1998 Criteria for Performance Excellence.

Nogami, Glenda Y. "Eight Points for More Useful Surveys." *Quality Progress* 29, no. 10 (October 1996), 93–96.

Rosenberg, Jarrett. "Five Myths about Customer Satisfaction." *Quality Progress* 29, no. 12 (December 1996), 57–60.

Sanes, Christina. "Customer Complaints = Golden Opportunities." 1993 ASQC Quality Congress Transactions, Boston, 45–51.

Toxell, Joseph R. "Service Time Quality Standards." *Quality Progress* 14, no. 9 (September 1981), 35–37.

Whitely, Richard C. *The Customer-Driven Company*. Reading, MA: Addison-Wesley, 1991.

Zeithaml, A. Parasuraman, and Leonard L. Berry. *Delivering Quality Service*. New York: The Free Press, 1990.

Zimmerman, Richard E., Linda Steinmann, and Vince Schueler. "Designing Customer Surveys that Work." *Quality Digest*, October 1996, 22–28.

LEADERSHIP AND STRATEGIC PLANNING

OUTLINE

Jack Welch, CEO of General Electric, is probably the most admired CEO of his generation. The following dialog about General Electric's Six-Sigma quality initiative (see Chapter 9) took place between a *Fortune* magazine reporter and Welch:[1]

> Fortune: *Jack, you're doing a total-quality thing ten or fifteen years after the rest of corporate America did it. Why are you doing it, and why now?*
>
> Welch: *There was only one guy in the whole country who hated quality more than me. I always believed quality would come from just operating well and fast, and all these slogans were nonsense.*
>
> *The guy who hated quality more was Larry Bossidy. He hated quality totally. Then he left GE and went to AlliedSignal. In order to resurrect AlliedSignal, Larry went out, saw Motorola, and did some stuff on Six-Sigma. And he called me one day and he said, "Jack, this ain't b.s.—this is real stuff, this is really great stuff."*
>
> *We poll 10,000 employees every year. In '95 they came back and said, we desperately need a quality issue. So Six-Sigma was something we adopted then. The results are fantastic. We're going to get $1.2 billion of gain this year. For years our operating margin was never over ten. It's been improving, and it's going to be 16.7 this year. Our working-capital turns were four for 35 years. It will be nine this year.*

The one thing that all quality experts agree on is that strong leadership, especially from senior managers, is absolutely necessary to develop and sustain a TQ culture. **Leadership** is the ability to positively influence people and systems under one's authority to have a meaningful impact and achieve important results. Leaders may seek to motivate employees and develop enthusiasm for quality with rhetoric, but actions often speak louder than words, as seen in Welch's behavior. The former CEO of Motorola, Robert Galvin, made a habit of making quality the first item on the agenda of executive staff meetings—and then leaving the meeting before the discussion of financial issues. His leadership guided Motorola to become one of the first winners of the Malcolm Baldrige National Quality Award.

Leaders create clear and visible quality values, and integrate these values into the organization's strategy. **Strategy** is the pattern of decisions that determines and reveals a company's goals, policies, and plans to meet the needs of its stakeholders. Through an effective strategy, a business creates a sustainable competitive advantage. This process of envisioning the organization's future and developing the necessary procedures and operations to achieve that future is called **strategic planning**. In today's business environment, quality is a key element of strategic planning. This chapter describes the role of leadership and strategic planning for quality and performance excellence, with an emphasis on the application of leadership concepts in a TQ environment and the process of formulating and implementing TQ-based strategies.

LEADERSHIP FOR QUALITY

Despite the countless articles and books written about it, leadership is one of the least-understood concepts in business. Even though many theories of leadership have been developed, no single approach adequately captures the essence of the concept. Most definitions of leadership reflect an assortment of behaviors; some examples follow:

- Vision that stimulates hope and mission that transforms hope into reality
- Radical servanthood that saturates the organization
- Stewardship that shepherds its resources
- Integration that drives its economy

- Courage to sacrifice personal or team goals for the greater community good
- Communication that coordinates its efforts
- Consensus that drives unity of purpose
- Empowerment that grants permission to make mistakes, encourages the honesty to admit them, and gives the opportunity to learn from them
- Conviction that provides the stamina to continually strive toward business excellence.[2]

In practice, the notion of leadership can be as elusive as the notion of quality itself. This section briefly summarizes the principal concepts of leadership and prominent leadership practices in quality management.

When we think of leadership, we generally think of *executive leadership*, which focuses on the roles of senior managers in guiding an organization to fulfill its mission and meet its goals. The critical importance of senior managers' roles in business excellence is affirmed by numerous research studies and from practitioners' perspectives. In the Baldrige Criteria, as well as other frameworks such as the European Quality Award, Australian Quality Award, and Japan's Deming Prize, leadership is the first category. Among the many activities that senior executives perform are

1. Defining and communicating business directions.
2. Ensuring that goals and expectations are met.
3. Reviewing business performance and taking appropriate action.
4. Creating an enjoyable work environment that promotes creativity, innovation, and continual improvement.
5. Soliciting input and feedback from customers.
6. Ensuring that employees are effective contributors to the business.
7. Motivating, inspiring, and energizing employees.
8. Recognizing employee contributions.
9. Providing honest feedback.

As we move further into the new economy, some of the cherished views about leadership being centered at the top of the organization are being seriously challenged. Today's fluid, "de-jobbed" organizations—in which parts of the work are being done by traditional departments, parts are being done by temporary project teams, parts are being done by business partners in another organization, and parts are being done by external contract employees who are indistinguishable from the company's own workers—require a broader view of leadership:

- The formal organizational leadership that is responsible for integrating, resourcing, and orchestrating the activities of the various project teams
- The ad hoc leadership required within project teams
- Leadership in every member of every project team that incorporates the initiative, the self-management capacity, the readiness to make hard decisions, the embodiment of organizational values, and the sense of business responsibility that in the traditional organization were limited to the top people in the organization.[3]

For example, formal organizational leadership is manifested in developing clear values, creating a competitive advantage, defining customer and market focus, and encouraging continual learning. Ad hoc leadership within project teams is seen by observing the leader working to make those on the team successful, removing barriers to team performance, establishing good lines of communication, and resolving problems. Individual leadership is revealed through people maintaining the focus and discipline to consistently complete jobs, being proactive in identifying and solving problems, working for win-win agreements, and making continuous learning a personal habit.

Effective leadership requires five core leadership skills: *vision, empowerment, intuition, self-understanding,* and *value congruence.*[4] Leaders are visionaries; they manage for the future, not the past (think back to the first of Deming's 14 Points). Vision is crucial at every level during times of change. Leaders recognize the radical organizational changes taking place today as opportunities to move closer to total quality. Jack Welch, for example, began pushing GE to become a leader among traditional old-economy companies in embracing the Internet after noticing his wife Christmas shopping on the Web. "I realized that if I didn't watch it, I would retire as a Neanderthal," he was reported as saying. "So I just started reading everything I could about it." He began by pairing 1,000 Web-savvy mentors with senior people to get his top teams up to Internet speed quickly.[5] Visionary leaders create mental and verbal pictures of desirable future states and share these visions with their organizational partners, including customers, suppliers, and employees.

Leaders empower employees to assume ownership of problems or opportunities, and to be proactive in implementing improvements and making decisions in the best interests of the organization. At Motorola, for example, every department has Participative Management Process teams consisting of eight to twelve members who set objectives to support corporate goals. Individual employees develop goals and plans, track progress, and receive bonuses based on successful and timely achievement of goals. The philosophy at GTE Directories Corporation summarizes this facet of leadership nicely: *Put a stake in the ground, get out of the way, and stay the course.* Empowerment threatens many managers who are accustomed to wielding their power, often coercively through fear of punishment or sanctions.[6] True power is not based upon formal position and authority, but rather aids in spreading power downward and outward and developing leadership at lower levels of the organization. It is this notion that Deming was trying to convey in one of his 14 Points: Institute Leadership.

Leaders are not afraid to follow their intuition. Even in the face of uncertainty and change, they must anticipate the future and must be prepared to make difficult decisions that will help the organization to be successful. When he was appointed CEO of Xerox in 1982, David Kearns had already witnessed firsthand the implementation of TQM at Fuji Xerox. On his return from Japan, he listed the factors that made the Japanese better than their American counterparts. After eliminating those factors he felt were insignificant, three elements remained: cost, quality, and expectations.[7] His intuition in this case led him to develop the Leadership Through Quality initiative at Xerox.

Self-understanding requires the ability to look at one's self and then identify relationships with employees and within the organization. It requires an examination of one's weaknesses as well as strengths. One manager told Roger Milliken, chairman and CEO of Milliken & Co. (see *Quality Profile*), "There are only five managers [out of 400] in this room who know how to listen." Milliken recognized the need to do something. At the end of the meeting, Milliken stood up on a banquet chair, and raising his right arm, asked all of the assembled executives to repeat after him: "I will listen. I will not shoot the messenger. I recognize that management is the problem."[8] Many leaders have an insatiable appetite for knowledge and self-learning as well as a drive to develop their skills and use them effectively.

Finally, value congruence occurs when leaders integrate their values into the company's management system. Values are basic assumptions and beliefs about the nature of the business, mission, people, and relationships of an organization. Specifically, values include trust and respect for individuals, openness, teamwork, integrity, and commitment to quality. They become standards by which choices are made, and create an organizational structure in which quality is a routine part of activities and decisions. Employees quickly recognize leaders who do not apply the values they es-

Quality Profile
Milliken & Company

Milliken is a major textile manufacturer headquartered in Spartanburg, South Carolina. It is privately held and employs more than 14,000 associates at 47 facilities in the United States, with annual sales exceeding $1 billion. Its 28 businesses produce more than 48,000 different textile and chemical products, ranging from apparel fabrics to specialty chemicals and floor coverings. In the late 1970s the company recognized that Japanese competitors were achieving higher quality, less waste, greater productivity, and fewer customer complaints despite less advanced technology. This realization led to the conclusion that the company's management approaches and personnel practices were to blame. In 1981 senior management launched the Pursuit of Excellence process to focus on customer satisfaction throughout the company. This process led to a flatter management structure and a commitment to teamwork and human resources.

From 1984 to 1988, Milliken improved on-time delivery from 75 percent to an industry best of 99 percent. As a result, it received numerous customer awards, including a record number of General Motors' Mark of Excellence manufacturing awards. After winning the Malcolm Baldrige National Quality Award in 1989, Milliken set its sights on "Ten-Four" objectives—to achieve a tenfold improvement in key customer-focused quality measures over four years. Its long-range goal is to be fully responsive to customer needs, providing "products that customers want, in the quantity they want, when they want them."

Source: Malcolm Baldrige National Quality Award, Profiles of Winners, National Institute of Standards and Technology, Department of Commerce. Courtesy Milliken & Company.

pouse or who do so inconsistently. This incongruence causes employees to constantly doubt management's message. For instance, the founder and first CEO of Solectron Corporation (see *Quality Profile*), Winston Chen, developed the Solectron Beliefs, a set of basic values to use as the model for behavior of all employees: Customer First, Respect for the Individual, Quality, Supplier Partnership, Business Ethics, Shareholder Value, and Social Responsibility. His successor, Ko Nishimura, continues to reaffirm the Solectron Beliefs year after year, and personally coaches the leadership team to live them. He has stated that if the company's behavior does not reflect the Beliefs, then the behavior—not the Beliefs—has to change. His leadership led Solectron to become the first two-time Baldrige award winner.

These core skills of vision, empowerment, intuition, self-understanding, and value congruence are reflected in the practices of quality leaders in organizations throughout the world.

Leading Practices for Leadership

In firms committed to total quality, various leadership practices share common elements. True leaders promote quality and business performance excellence in several ways.

- *They create a customer-focused strategic vision and clear quality values that serve as a basis for business decisions at all levels of the organization.* An organization's vision and values emanate from senior leaders, as seen from the previous discussion of Solectron, and often revolve around customers, both external and internal. For

Quality Profile

Solectron Corporation

Solectron Corporation of Milpitas, California, was founded in 1977 as a small-assembly job shop. Today it is a worldwide provider of electronics design and manufacturing services to original equipment manufacturers with 1997 revenues of $3.7 billion. To ensure quality performance and on-time delivery, two teams work with each customer: a project planning team that plans, schedules, and defines material requirements and product lead times, and a total quality control team that monitors and evaluates production in order to anticipate potential problems and improve process yields. All customers are surveyed weekly, and the results are compiled in a customer satisfaction index, which senior executives review at one of their three weekly meetings on quality-related issues. Most of the employees, representing more than 20 different cultures, are trained in statistical tools and problem solving and are empowered to improve processes and take corrective action when necessary. Average turnover rates are between 1.5 and 4 percent, compared to an industry average of 21 percent.

By 1991 Solectron's total quality efforts had reduced its defect rates to 233 parts per million, and its on-time delivery rate was greater than 97 percent. In 1991 Solectron received the Malcolm Baldrige National Quality Award. From 1992 through 1997, market share doubled, customer satisfaction on quality, delivery, and service remained at a 90 percent level on a rating scale in which a C receives a zero and a D a score of –100. In 1997 Solectron became the first company to win the Baldrige Award a second time, against more stringent criteria, indicating its continued focus on improvement and performance excellence.

Sources: Karen Bemowski, "Three Electronics Firms Win 1991 Baldrige Award," *Quality Progress* 24, no. 11 (November 1991), 39–41. 1997 Malcolm Baldrige Award winners press release.

example, FedEx's concise motto of *People, Service, Profits* conveys that commitment to the people—the employees of FedEx—come first. Employees who are treated with respect and have empathetic leaders will provide exceptional service to customers, and profits will follow. BI (see *Quality Profile* in Chapter 4) has developed a three-pronged approach to business excellence: a pervasive customer focus, strong employee focus, and its internal quality management philosophy called the "BI Way." This philosophy, which includes training, problem-solving techniques, process improvement, incentives, and a focus on results, brings TQ principles into the fabric of the company. Rhetoric cannot stand alone; leaders must demonstrate commitment to the vision and values. At FedEx, every business decision is evaluated against the People-Service-Profits hierarchy, in that order. At BI, every associate takes part in the improvement process, but the company's leaders drive the process and give it priority and energy.

- *They create and sustain a leadership system and environment for empowerment, innovation, and organizational learning.* Leaders provide an environment with few bureaucratic rules and procedures. Such an environment encourages managers to experiment and take risks, permits employees to talk openly about problems, supports teamwork, and promotes employees' understanding of their responsibilities for quality. Solectron managers, for example, foster teamwork and give workers responsibility for meeting quality goals. They encourage a strong family atmosphere, promote clear and effective communications, and recognize and reward groups for exceptional performance. Besides monetary awards, Solectron often buys lunch for an entire division or brings in ice cream for the whole corporation. At Custom Research, Inc., the four senior leaders ensure that employees have the responsibility, training, and information they need to do their jobs through empowering everyone to do whatever it takes to serve clients, working with nine other senior people to set strategy, and making middle managers the real leaders.

Organizational learning requires leaders to assess organizational performance, identify opportunities for improvement and innovation, and evaluate their own leadership effectiveness. For instance, senior leaders at Solectron review surveys of all customers on a weekly basis, and Ko Nishimura travels to each site every quarter to review performance in detail. Critical issues are integrated into action plans. FedEx managers meet daily to discuss the previous day's performance and track longer-term trends. FedEx executives also conduct surveys in which their leadership is evaluated by their employees. They then develop action plans to address weaknesses revealed by the surveys and are held accountable for the leadership they provide.

- *They set high expectations and demonstrate substantial personal commitment and involvement in quality, often with a missionary-like enthusiasm.* A leader can inspire people to do things they do not believe they can do. Motorola set aggressive goals of reducing defects per unit of output in every operation by 100-fold in four years and reducing cycle time by 50 percent each year. The 3M Company seeks to generate 25 percent of sales from products less than two years old. To promote such "stretch goals," leaders provide the resources and support necessary to meet them, especially training.

  Leaders, like Jack Welch in this chapter's opening quotation, display a passion about quality and actively live the values. By "walking the walk," leaders serve as role models for the whole organization. Many CEOs lead quality training sessions, serve on quality improvement teams, work on projects that do not usually require top-level input, and personally visit customers. Senior managers at Texas Instruments Defense Systems & Electronics Group led 150 of 1,900 cross-functional teams. The president and CEO of AT&T Universal Card Services and his business team listened to customers' calls, reviewed daily process measures, met with suppliers, co-chaired monthly customer listening post meetings, hosted team sharing rallies, led associate focus groups, and held all-associate meetings quarterly. In small businesses, such as Marlow Industries (see *Quality Profile*), CEO and president Raymond Marlow chairs the TQM Council and has daily responsibility for quality-related matters.

- *They integrate quality values into daily leadership and management and communicate extensively through the leadership structure and to all employees.* At Zytec Corporation, senior executives formed a Deming Steering Committee to promote Deming's 14 Points. Members serve as advisors to Deming implementation teams. Leaders apply quality tools to improve their management processes. The chairman of Westinghouse (see *Quality Profile*) invited the Westinghouse Productivity and Quality Center to conduct a quality audit of the executive office, believing that if it was good enough for the rest of the company, it was good enough for him. General Electric redefined its promotion standards around quality. Managers will not be considered for promotions, but will face dismissal, unless they visibly demonstrate support for the company's Six-Sigma quality strategy.[9]

  Successful leaders continually promote their vision throughout the organization using many forms of communication: personal interaction, talks, newsletters,

Quality Profile
Marlow Industries

Marlow Industries received a Baldrige Award in 1991 in the small business category. Marlow Industries, based in Dallas, Texas, produces customized thermoelectric coolers, which are small, solid-state electronic devices that heat, cool, or stabilize the temperature of electronic equipment. In 1991 the company employed 160 people and had annual sales of $12 million. Its quality initiative dates back to 1987, when the company set out to improve a manufacturing and service operation that did not seem to need fixing, challenging itself to exceed its already demanding customer requirements. Since 1987 employee productivity has increased at an average annual rate of 10 percent, the time between new product design and manufactured product has been trimmed, and the cost of scrap, rework, and other nonconformance errors has been cut nearly in half. Customers benefit with improved on-time deliveries, extended warranties, and stable or decreasing prices.

Marlow describes its TQ system as a "top to bottom" approach to continuous improvement, led by the CEO and president. All workers, from CEO to hourly employee, have taken Marlow's voluntary "Quality Pledge," committing to "Do it right today, better tomorrow." Extensive training, supplier partnerships, and information support contribute to meeting customer satisfaction objectives. Marlow has won numerous quality awards from customers, and in 1990, its top 10 customers rated the quality of Marlow products at 100 percent.

Source: Malcolm Baldrige National Quality Award, Profiles of Winners, National Institute of Standards and Technology, Department of Commerce. Courtesy of Marlow Industries.

seminars, e-mail, and video. For example, senior managers at Eastman Chemical use every opportunity, including personal visits to teams, in-plant television broadcasts, and bimonthly quality management forums, to communicate the company's vision, values, and goals. Communication is often enhanced by flattening the organizational structure. Texas Instruments Defense Systems & Electronics Group reduced the number of organizational layers from eight to five and increased the number of employees per supervisor.

- *They integrate public responsibilities and community support into their business practices.* Leadership responsibilities include promoting ethical behavior among all employees and the protection of public health, safety, and the environment that may be affected by a company's products and services. For example, among GTE Directories' standard operating procedures and personnel practices are 11 that address business practices and ethics, 15 that address public health and safety, and 9 that address the environment and/or waste management. Eastman Chemical Company helped to develop the Chemical Manufacturers Association's Responsible Care principles, which require member companies to assume responsibility for public health, safety, and environmental protection in everything they do. Solectron France was the first French company to have its environmental management and audit system certified by the European Economic Community, and sites in Malaysia and China helped to train local governments in best practices for recycling, hazardous material handling, and auditing.

Support of key communities, such as education, health care, professional organizations, and community services, are important roles for companies and a

Quality Profile

Westinghouse Electric Commercial Nuclear Fuel Division

The Westinghouse Electric Corporation (now CBS) Commercial Nuclear Fuel Division (CNFD) employs about 2,000 people at three sites. The Specialty Metals Plant near Pittsburgh produces zircalloy tubes that encase pellets of uranium dioxide fuel processed at CNFD's plant in Columbia, South Carolina. CNFD uses state-of-the-art technology such as robots and other automated processing equipment, supercomputer simulations, and laser welding. Management, however, attributes substantial improvements in quality and efficiency not so much to advanced technology as to its workforce and to CNFD's total quality approach to operations. A quality council of managers sets policies, plans, and strategies, and directs the quality improvement process. Quality is fully integrated into all design, production, and customer service activities. Progress is measured by a unique system called Pulse Points, which tracks improvements in more than 60 key performance areas and determines measurable goals within each unit of CNFD, down to the jobs of the hourly workers.

Although its eye is on the bottom line, CNFD management deliberately did not include cost concerns in its quality improvement program, believing that gains in quality would spawn cost reductions through increases in efficiency. Between 1984 and 1987, first-time-through yields in the manufacture of fuel rods increased from below 50 percent to 87 percent, substantially reducing scrap, rework, and manufacturing cycle time. This accomplishment helped CNFD to achieve three consecutive years of 100 percent on-time delivery. The division was one of the first winners of the Malcolm Baldrige National Quality Award in 1988.

Source: Malcolm Baldrige National Quality Award, Profiles of Winners, National Institute of Standards and Technology, Department of Commerce. Courtesy of Westinghouse Productivity and Quality Center.

leadership responsibility. BI, for instance, emphasizes education and direct volunteer efforts. Its associates designed and teach a "School to Work" curriculum in the local school district. BI donates a consistent percentage of its profits to the community each year, and matches funds raised by its associates for charitable causes. GTE Directories' community activities include corporate philanthropy, and a volunteer initiatives program that provides funding to nonprofit organizations based on employee volunteer time.

From all these examples, we see that leadership is the "driver" of the entire quality system. Without leadership, a total quality initiative simply becomes the "flavor of the month," which is the major reason that total quality efforts fail in many organizations. Effective leadership practice, however, is built upon a sound foundation of organization structure and theory.

LEADERSHIP THEORY AND PRACTICE

Leadership involves both people and measurement and control systems, thus it has both a "soft" side and a "hard" side. To understand how leadership is developed and practiced, it is important to understand its foundations in management theory. Dozens of leadership theories have been derived from literally thousands of leadership studies. Unlike some areas of quality management that are only a few decades old, leadership theories can often be traced back 50–75 years or more.

Table 5.1 Classification of Leadership Theories

Leadership Theory	Pioneer/Developer	Type of Theory
"Great man" model[10]	Ralph Stogdill	Trait
Ohio State Studies[11]	E. A. Fleishman, E. F. Harris et al.	Leader Behavior
Michigan Studies[12]	Rensis Likert	
Theory X-Theory Y model[13]	Douglas MacGregor	
Managerial Grid model[14]	Robert Blake and Jane S. Mouton	
Leadership effectiveness model[15]	Fred E. Fiedler	Contingency (Situational)
Supervisory contingency decision model[16]	V. H. Vroom and P. W. Yetton V. H. Vroom and A. G. Jago	
Managerial roles[17]	Henry Mintzberg	Role approach
Charismatic theory[18]	R. J. House; J. A. Conger	Emerging theories
Transformational theory[19]	James M. Burns; N. M. Tichy and D. O. Ulrich; B. M. Bass	
Substitutes for leadership[20]	Jon P. Howell et al.	
Emotional intelligence[21]	Daniel Goleman	

The purpose of leadership theories is to explain differences in leadership styles and contexts. A comprehensive review of these theories is well beyond the scope of this text. However, the theories are quite important within the context of TQ; therefore, this section provides a brief summary of the most popular leadership approaches and discusses their implications in a TQ environment. The well-informed manager, engineer, or technician should be aware of such approaches and use them to broaden his or her understanding of how leadership can affect behavior in the workplace and lead to the successful adoption of TQ. Table 5.1 summarizes some of the key theories that have influenced today's leadership styles.

Traditional Leadership Theories

Leadership theory can be studied from at least five perspectives: the trait approach, the behavioral approach, contingency (situational) approaches, the role approach, and emerging theories.[22] The first four represent traditional theories and are discussed in this section.

The **trait approach** involves discovering how to be a leader by examining the characteristics and methods of recognized leaders. Pioneering studies were performed several years ago;[23] however, academicians have discredited these studies to some extent. A more recent empirical study of 200 European CEOs and more than 1,000 key subordinates identified five key leadership styles that support TQ.[24] These styles and their key traits, in decreasing order of impact on success factors, are

- *Team builder:* tolerant, motivational, inspirational, supportive
- *Captain:* respectful, trusting, reliable, fair
- *Strategist:* trustworthy
- *Creative:* innovative, visionary, courageous, inspirational, confident
- *Impulsive:* obsessed with new ideas, curious, energetic, participative.

The leadership profile of any individual is a composite of multiple styles; however, the predominance of some styles over others will influence the success of that individual.

The **behavioral approach** attempts to determine the types of leadership behaviors that lead to successful task performance and employee satisfaction. Researchers at Ohio State University performed an extensive series of leadership studies in developing this theory.[25] Work done independently at the University of Michigan on leader behavior came to similar conclusions. Both groups of researchers showed that effective leadership depends on a proper blending of an employee relationship-centered approach to employees' needs with a production-centered approach to getting work done. A more recent study by Zenger-Miller, an international consulting and training firm, analyzed 1,871 examples of good and bad leadership, and used them to develop a list of 17 competencies that people most often associate with leadership:[26]

1. Setting or sharing a vision
2. Managing a change
3. Focusing on the customer
4. Dealing with individuals
5. Supporting teams and groups
6. Sharing information
7. Solving problems, making decisions
8. Managing business processes
9. Managing projects
10. Displaying technical skills
11. Managing time and resources
12. Taking responsibility
13. Taking initiative beyond job requirements
14. Handling emotions
15. Displaying professional ethics
16. Showing compassion
17. Making credible presentations.

The 17 leadership competencies identified in the Zenger-Miller study suggest that today's leaders are embodying many TQ principles in their routine leadership activities. Table 5.2 compares traditional management practice with true quality leadership. Traditional management all too often relies on mechanistic planning and organizing, reacting to events, pushing products, and controlling people.

Other well-known behavioral leadership models include Douglas McGregor's *Theory X–Theory Y model*[27] and the Blake-Mouton *Managerial Grid model*.[28] McGregor explicitly defined contrasting assumptions that managers hold about workers and how those assumptions tend to influence the manager's behavior. Blake and Mouton defined five managerial styles that combined varying degrees of production-oriented and people-oriented concerns. Their contribution was to suggest that a high concern for both production and people was needed and that effective managers could be trained to develop a balanced concern for both.

Table 5.2 TQ Leadership Contrasts

Managers	Leaders
Plan Projects	**Practice**
• Make plans for the future (on paper)	• Envision the future
• Organize materials and methods	• Optimize materials and methods
• Preach management by objective	• Use participative management
Push Products	**Produce**
• Give "lip-service" to quality	• Exemplary quality
• Sell to customers	• Service to their customers
• Cut costs	• Less waste through better processes
• Perform R&D	• Innovative products and services
Control People	**Motivate People**
• Control people and things through systems	• Develop people's talents, control things with systems
• Reward conformance, punish deviation	• Reward effort, skill development, and innovation; empower employees
• Maintain status quo	• Look to the future through continuous improvement

McGregor's Theory X-Y model, suggests that the Theory X manager assumes subordinates must be coerced and controlled in order to prevent quality problems and to obtain high productivity. McGregor's Theory Y manager assumes work is a natural activity, and people who are led well can be expected to be self-motivated to perform their best work if given the opportunity. Much of Deming's philosophy follows the principles in Theory Y and agrees with Blake and Mouton that balanced concern for people and production is essential for organizational effectiveness. From the standpoint of the Baldrige criteria (discussed later in this chapter), it is important for senior leaders who adopt a TQ philosophy to set, communicate, and deploy organizational values, performance expectations, and to balance value for customers and stakeholders. Attention to the Theory X-Y and Managerial Grid values can help accomplish this goal.

The **contingency** or **situational approach** holds that no universal approach to leadership exists; rather, effective leadership behavior depends on situational factors that may change over time. Current leadership theory is based heavily on this approach, which states that effective leadership depends on three variables: the leader, the led, and the situation. Frederick E. Fiedler, a participant in the Ohio State research, developed one of the pioneering contingency theories of leadership.[29] Fiedler's model, which is included in most principles of management texts, shows the effect of leadership styles on leader performance according to situational contingencies.

Victor H. Vroom and Phillip W. Yetton developed a supervisory contingency model that was based in part on leadership propositions that follow from Vroom's VIE motivation theory[30] (see Chapter 6 for more discussion of motivation). The model, later updated and modified by Vroom and Jago,[31] prescribes an appropriate leadership style based on various contingencies in a decision-making situation. The model centers on the problem-solving function of leadership, and is based on the theory that the three major concerns of a leader in solving problems are (1) the quality of the decision, (2) the degree of acceptance of the decision by the subordinate(s), and (3) the time frame within which the decision must be made.

Two other contingency models of leadership—House's *Path-Goal model* and Hershey and Blanchard's *Situational Leadership model*—deserve special mention. Robert House developed his Path-Goal Leadership model based on expectancy theory.[32] Thus, the model bears some resemblance to the Vroom-Jago model. House's model states that the appropriate path to high performance and high job satisfaction is dependent on employee needs and abilities, the degree of structure of tasks to be performed, and the leadership style that is selected by the leader. Effective leaders choose one of four styles (achievement-oriented, directive, participative, or supportive) that matches the situational contingencies and helps team members along the path to their highest-value goals. The Hershey and Blanchard model relates the requirement for directive or supportive behavior of the leader to team members' readiness (relative maturity) to take responsibility and participate in decision making.[33]

According to the various contingency leadership theories, quality can be enhanced by a TQ-oriented leader with the correct mix of the leader's style of management, the characteristics of those who are led, and the situation. Emery Air Freight, for example, found that when the leader (supervisor) emphasized daily performance measures and used positive reinforcement, quality benefits resulted within that organization.[34] However, for a leader in an R&D laboratory—an entirely different situation—such an approach probably would not work. In fact, current leadership research suggests that the same outcome is unlikely. The R&D leader would probably be more effective by using a participative approach, taking into consideration the situation of the high technical skills and professional expertise of the employees. This approach is in agreement with the contingency model developed by Fiedler and others.

The **role approach** suggests that leaders perform certain roles in order to be effective. The role approach is similar to the trait and behavioral approaches, but also takes into account situational factors. Thus, according to the theory, leaders at upper levels of the organization, or in large firms, may frequently be called upon to play the role of figurehead or liaison person between the firm and its outside environment. At a lower level, where spans of control extend widely, motivational, coordinative, or disturbance handling roles may be needed for effective leadership. Henry Mintzberg's various texts and articles provide the basis for this approach.[35]

Mintzberg's role theory also suggests that appropriate roles for managers also depend on situational factors. For example, a line manager in an insurance firm, who is abandoning a command and control management style in order to take a TQ approach to reorganizing, would want to change some of the roles previously used successfully in management. Some of the changes might involve a move away from the highly structuring roles of decision maker, disturbance handler, and entrepreneur, toward the more facilitating roles that assist subordinates, such as motivator, liaison, and spokesperson. The subordinates, in turn, would be expected to perform some of the former managerial roles of making decisions, taking care of conflicts, and finding opportunities for improvement (an entrepreneurial activity) as part of self-managed teams.

Contemporary Concepts and Emerging Theories

Traditional leadership theories were largely based on an assumption of rational thinking. *Emerging leadership theories* build on or enlarge traditional theory by attempting to answer questions raised, but not answered, by earlier approaches. According to the various contemporary leadership theories developed over the last 20 or 30 years, leadership effectiveness can be improved with the correct mix of the leader's style of management, the characteristics of those who are led, and the situation. Some of the new and emerging theories include *attributional*, *transactional*, and *emotional intelligence* theories, which enter the realm of human emotions to explain how good leaders seem to succeed, and where mediocre ones show mixed results or fail to accomplish their goals.

Attributional theory states that leaders' judgment on how to deal with subordinates in a specific situation is based on their attributions of the internal or external causes of the behaviors of their followers. For example, if a leader observes an employee producing poor quality material, the leader may attribute the problem to internal factors within the person's control, such as poor effort, commitment, or lack of ability. Alternately, the leader could attribute the problem to external factors, such as bad material or defective equipment. Depending on these attributions (and how/whether they are justified), the leader will decide whether to use punishment (reprimand, demotion, firing) or corrective solutions (problem-finding, job redesign, training) to resolve the problem. Readers who are interested in learning more about this approach are referred to Hellriegel et al.[36]

Transactional (charismatic) theory assumes that certain leaders may develop the ability to inspire their subordinates to exert extraordinary efforts to achieve organizational goals, owing to the leader's vision and understanding of how to tap into the developmental needs of the subordinates. An emerging leadership theory that falls within the transactional category shows potential for dealing with the leadership needs of organizations that want to develop a total quality management process. This approach, called **transformational leadership theory,** can help to explain the impact of leadership in a TQ environment.[37] According to this model, leaders adopt many of the behaviors discussed earlier in this chapter. They take a long-term perspective, focus on customers, promote a shared vision and values, work to stimulate their organizations intellectually, invest in training, take some risks, and treat employees as individuals. The CEOs and executive team members of nearly every Malcolm Baldrige Award recipient have modelled this leadership behavior. Some empirical evidence found in research suggests that transformational leadership is strongly correlated with lower turnover, higher productivity and quality, and higher employee satisfaction than other approaches.

Not all managers in TQ organizations ought to be transformational leaders, however. The charismatic transformational leader, such as a Jack Welch, is rare, and most effective at the top. An organization pursuing TQ needs both those who establish visions and those who are effective at the day-to-day tasks needed to achieve them[38]

Another emerging concept of leadership is called the **substitutes for leadership theory.**[39] This research takes the intriguing view that in many organizations, if characteristics of subordinates (team members), the nature of the tasks that they perform, and the guidance and incentives provided by the organization are aligned, then formal leadership tends to be unproductive or counterproductive. It is suggested that this leadership approach may be useful in cases of low leadership effectiveness where the leader cannot be removed for various political or other reasons (the owner's incompetent son or daughter is the "leader"), or on teams that have high member training or competence (a surgical team), or where the situation is very dynamic (battling oil well fires in the desert). In such situations, self-management, professional education, or even computer technology can be developed or "built in" to substitute for leadership. The implication for a TQ-focused organization is that each situation calls for just the right amount of leadership (not too much and not too little) in order to attain high quality results.

One of the newest of the emerging leadership theories is called the **emotional intelligence theory.**[40] Goleman defined five components of emotionally intelligent leaders: (1) self-awareness, (2) self-regulation, (3) motivation, (4) empathy, and (5) social skill. His premise is that too much reliance has been placed on the rational side of leadership in leadership research studies and training done over the years. He argues that expectations for emotional intelligence are generally not captured in performance evaluation systems, but that the self-management (components 1 through 3) and interpersonal skills (components 4 and 5) represented by the five components are as essential for executive-level leaders as "traditional" intelligence (measured by IQ tests) and technical competence. The significance of emotional intelligence for effective total quality lies in translating the "vision" of an integrated leadership system and long-range planning process into action. Without credible self-management, represented by the first three components, it is difficult for subordinates within the organization to "buy into" the vision of the leader. Without mature empathy and social skills, represented by the last two components, it is difficult for the leader to work effectively with customers, suppliers, and others outside the organization in order to build rapport needed for long-term enterprise effectiveness, which is critical for a TQ-focused organization.

Applying Leadership Theory at The Ritz-Carlton

Chapter 3 described how senior leadership at The Ritz-Carlton Hotel Company has modeled many of the behaviors of effective leaders as developed within existing leadership theories. By examining characteristics of several of the emerging leadership theories, we can see how they are applied in practice at The Ritz-Carlton.

Horst Schultz, the CEO of The Ritz-Carlton, and his senior leadership team take care that leaders' judgments on how to deal with subordinates in a specific situation are based on positive attributions (attribution theory). The assumption of worker competency is a given at The Ritz-Carlton, even extending to the company motto of "Ladies and gentlemen serving ladies and gentlemen."

Aspects of transformational leadership theory are evident during the new hotel start-up process, when senior leaders are visible, doing what transformational leaders do. These activities include taking a long-term perspective, focusing on customers, promoting a shared vision and values, working to stimulate their organizations intellectually, investing in training, taking some risks, and treating employees as individuals.

Can it be that The Ritz-Carlton's staff is expected to be like a team of oil-well firefighters? The substitutes for leadership theory provides some support for this notion. As outlined earlier, if characteristics of subordinates (team members), the nature of the tasks that they perform, and the guidance and incentives provided by the organization are aligned, then formal leadership tends to be unproductive or counterproductive. In The Ritz-Carlton's leadership model, high levels of team member training (focusing on the Gold Standards) and competence (often seen in highly professional jobs, such as surgical teams) are required for the situations that are often dynamic. Thus, workers must often be self-led. They "substitute for leadership" and must be empowered to take action without waiting for supervisory approval.

By empowering employees as leaders at every level, The Ritz-Carlton provides an environment that will lead to the development and use of greater emotional intelligence, as outlined in emotional intelligence theory. Thus, the employee-guest interface and relationship management approaches that Ritz-Carlton teaches every employee, provide interpersonal skills and supplement self-management. The components of emotionally intelligent leaders—self-awareness, self-regulation, motivation, empathy, and social skill—are regularly seen in employees' ability to be self-managed (self-awareness, self-regulation, and motivation) and in their use of interpersonal skills (empathy and social skills).

CREATING THE LEADERSHIP SYSTEM

The **leadership system** refers to how leadership is exercised throughout a company. This system includes how key decisions are made, communicated, and carried out at all levels. It includes the formal and informal mechanisms for leadership development used to select leaders and managers, to develop their leadership skills, and to provide guidance and examples regarding behaviors and practices. An effective leadership system creates clear values that reflect the requirements of company stakeholders, and sets high expectations for performance and performance improvements. It builds loyalties and teamwork based upon these shared values, encourages initiative and risk taking, and subordinates organization to purpose and function. It includes mechanisms for leaders' self-examination and improvement. Finally, it ties the values of the organization, the leaders' vision, and the organizational strategy to the performance measurement and improvement system.

To illustrate these themes, the leadership system at Solar Turbines, Inc. (see *Quality Profile*), shown in Figure 5.1, operates in three distinct, yet highly integrated modes. First, through a functional organizational structure led by the president's staff ("1" in Figure 5.1), Solar maintains a focus on functional excellence through the recruitment, hiring, development of critical skills, and the application of tools and common processes to continuously improve functional effectiveness. Secondly, three cross-functional leadership structures ("2" in the figure), comprised of managers and technical experts selected from multiple levels of the organization, facilitate companywide teamwork and decision making. This expanded leadership team, consisting of the operations council (74 leaders from across the business) and the expanded

QUALITY PROFILE

SOLAR TURBINES, INC.

San Diego-based Solar Turbines, Inc., a wholly owned subsidiary of Caterpillar Inc. since 1981, is the world's largest supplier of midrange industrial gas turbine systems, with more than 10,000 systems installed throughout the world. Following its six "strategies to win," the company has increased its share of the worldwide market for new turbine equipment to a position of strong market leadership since 1992. Five of Solar's strategies focus on meeting customer requirements, building the performance capabilities necessary to quickly deliver superior products, and engaging the full potential of its workforce. Sustained progress in these areas has enabled the company to realize its sixth strategy, delivering investor-grade returns in a low-margin industry. Teams at every level, from executive leadership to shop-floor work teams, are effectively linked to others, ensuring that decisions and actions do not occur in isolation or without understanding of businesswide impacts.

From 1994 to 1998, the year Solar received a Baldrige Award, new product development cycle time was reduced from 39 to 22 months, warranty claims have decreased significantly, and nonrecoverable commissioning costs have been cut. Because of its quality gains, maintenance costs for customers are 42 percent lower than the average for all suppliers. Revenues generated per employee increased 61 percent between 1993 and 1997.

Source: Malcolm Baldrige National Quality Award Profiles of Winners, National Institute of Standards and Technology, Department of Commerce.

Figure 5.1 Solar Turbines, Inc. Leadership System

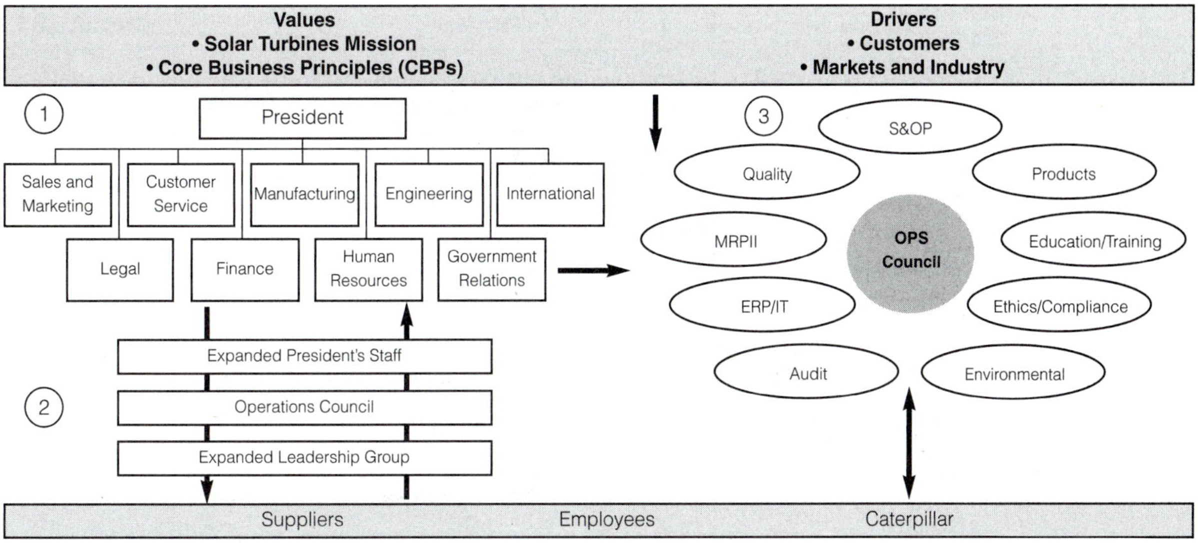

Values
- **Solar Turbines Mission**
- **Core Business Principles (CBPs)**

Drivers
- **Customers**
- **Markets and Industry**

(1) President — Sales and Marketing, Customer Service, Manufacturing, Engineering, International, Legal, Finance, Human Resources, Government Relations

(2) Expanded President's Staff — Operations Council — Expanded Leadership Group

(3) OPS Council — S&OP, Quality, Products, MRPII, Education/Training, ERP/IT, Ethics/Compliance, Audit, Environmental

Suppliers — Employees — Caterpillar

Source: Authorization by Solar Turbines, Incorporated.

leadership group (more than 400 managers and supervisors), enable Solar to develop the next generation of business leaders. It also promotes rapid, effective communication among employees with cross-functional teaming occurring at all levels of the organization. The third leadership structure is the set of 10 interlocking committees ("3" in the figure) that coordinate and integrate all business areas. These committees, listed in Table 5.3, provide a mechanism to strengthen organizational learning through cross-functional sharing, companywide communication, and strategic direction setting. Members of the president's staff chair key committees and, along with other senior business leaders, actively participate to provide guidance, learn, share, and support each other's decisions as a leadership team.[41]

In contrast to the large manufacturing environment at Solar, the small service company of Custom Research Inc. (see the *Quality Profile* in Chapter 4) has a four-person steering committee as the center of the leadership system (see Figure 5.2). The senior leaders developed the company vision, exemplified by the CRI Star shown in Figure 5.3. The Star defines the five driving forces of the business:

1. Developing competent and empowered people
2. Managing work through technology-driven processes
3. Meeting or exceeding unique client requirements and expectations
4. Building partnering relationships with major clients and suppliers
5. Producing growth and profit results.

The steering committee sets the company directions, integrates performance excellence goals, and promotes the development of all employees. Committee members have frequent interaction with associates, and review overall company performance daily. They meet formally each month to evaluate performance and identify areas for improvement.

The use of steering teams of senior managers is prevalent in TQ organizations. Such teams assume many responsibilities such as incorporating total quality principles

Table 5.3 Solar Turbines, Inc., Committee Structure

Committee	Purpose	Conducted
Operations Council	Communicate business status, develop strategies and business plans	Biannually
Quality Council	Customer satisfaction, operational quality	Monthly
Sales and Operations Planning	Current and future performance to plan, supplier performance	Monthly
MRP II Steering Committee	Process improvement, benchmarking, teams, employee satisfaction, internal Baldrige assessments	Monthly
Products Committee	New product development, product strategy	Monthly
Education Steering Committee	Training and education, human resource development	Quarterly
Environmental Council	Environmental health, and safety, products and processes	Quarterly
ERP/IT Council	Information technology planning and deployment, enterprise resource planning	Monthly
Audit Committee	Internal/external policy, regulatory compliance, and business controls	Quarterly
Ethics and Compliance Committee	Contract review, ethics, legal compliance, and oversight	Quarterly

Source: Authorization by Solar Turbines, Incorporated.

Figure 5.2 Custom Research Inc. Leadership System

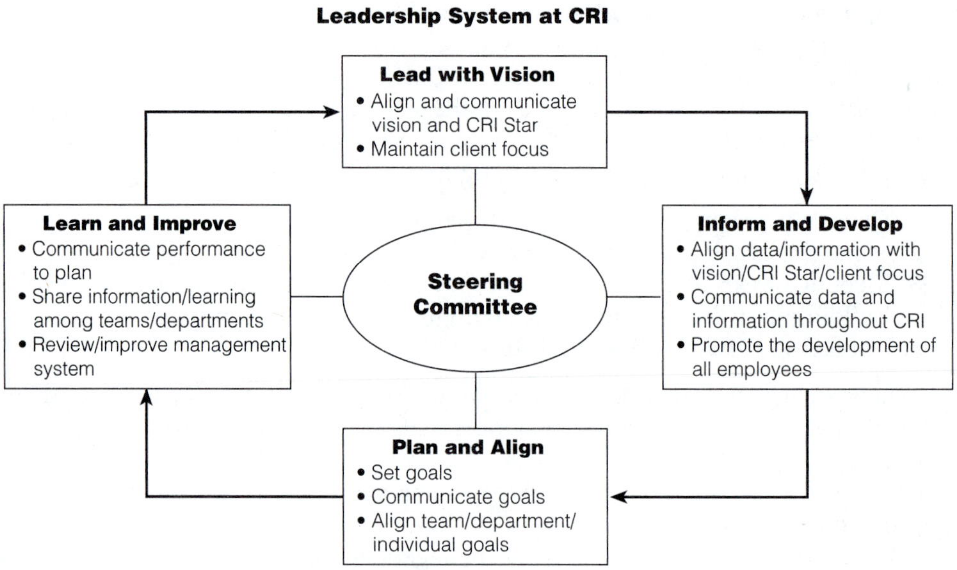

Source: Courtesy of CRI.

Figure 5.3 CRI Star

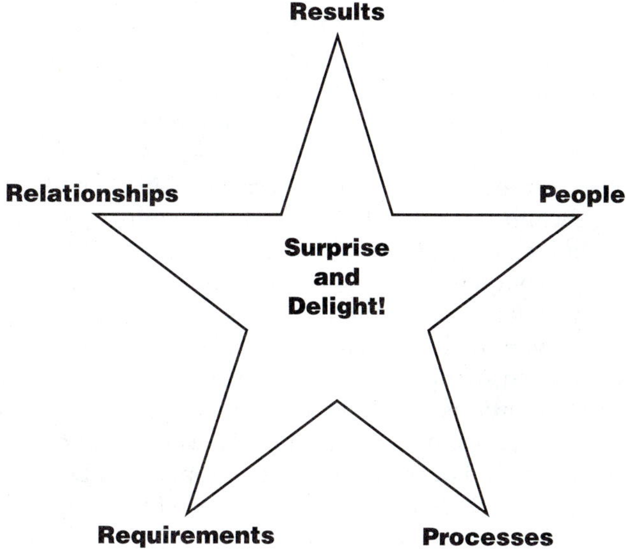

Source: Courtesy of CRI.

into the company's strategic planning process and coordinating the overall effort. At AT&T, the steering team is characterized by several essential elements.[42]

- *Leadership*: promoting and articulating the quality vision, communicating responsibilities and expectations for management action, aligning the business management process with the quality approach, maintaining high visibility for commitment and involvement, and ensuring that businesswide support is available in the form of education, consulting, methods, and tools
- *Planning*: planning strategic quality goals, understanding basic customer needs and business capabilities, developing long-term goals and near-term priorities, formulating human resource goals and policies, understanding employees' perceptions about quality and work, ensuring that all employees have the opportunity and skills to participate, and aligning reward and recognition systems to support the quality approach
- *Implementation*: forming key business process teams, chartering teams to manage and improve these processes, reviewing improvement plans, providing resources for improvement, enlisting all managers in the process, reviewing quality plans of major organizational units, and working with suppliers and business partners in joint quality planning
- *Review*: tracking progress through customer satisfaction and internal measures of quality, monitoring progress in attaining improvement objectives, celebrating successes, improving the quality system through auditing and identifying improvement opportunities, planning improvements, and validating the impact of improvements.

Leadership and Public Responsibilities

An important aspect of an organization's leadership is its responsibility to the public and practice of good citizenship, which includes ethics and protection of public health, safety, and the environment. Planning activities, such as product design (see Chapter 7) should anticipate adverse impacts from production, distribution, transportation, use, and disposal of a company's products. It is the responsibility of senior leaders to ensure that problems are prevented, forthright responses are made should problems occur, and that information is made available to maintain public awareness, safety, and confidence. Organizations should not only meet all local, state, and federal laws and regulatory requirements, but should treat these regulations as opportunities for continuous improvement beyond mere compliance.

At Solar Turbines, for example, its Social Responsibility Core Business Principle and Environmental, Health and Safety Policy guide the company's responsibility and citizenship actions. Solar's environmental health and safety strategy for its internal operation is to surpass compliance and strive for industry leadership. Products and services must comply with local, state, and federal standards in each locale as well as country-specific and governing body standards for emissions and effluent discharge. Solar's strategy has yielded significant reduction in the use of hazardous raw materials and production of hazardous waste, increased recycling and reuse, improved energy efficiency, and reduced water consumption. An example of commitment to the community was demonstrated dramatically by the response of Los Alamos National Bank (see *Quality Profile*) to the May 2000 Cerro Grande fire in the Los Alamos area, which burned nearly 50,000 acres, destroyed over 280 homes, and forced the evacuation of 20,000 Los Alamos and White Rock residents. While the primary location in Los Alamos and its branch office in White Rock were forced to close, bank employees moved its entire operation overnight to the Santa Fe branch. As a result, customers received uninterrupted service. In addition, the bank took extensive measures to support the people and businesses of Los Alamos, including:

- Offering zero interest loans to anyone in the community (not just customers) who was affected by the fire
- Eliminating overdraft charges and late fees
- Negotiating with Fannie Mae to suspend mortgage payments on lost homes
- Providing free day care on bank premises to employees
- Paying full salary to employees during evacuation days plus double time to employees who worked during evacuation
- Providing counseling, bonuses, and cash grants to employees affected by the fire.

Practicing good citizenship refers to leadership and support—within the limits of an organization's resources—of publicly important purposes, including improving education, community health, environmental excellence, resource conservation, community service, and professional practices. Good citizenship might entail leading efforts to help define the obligations of the industry to its communities.

STRATEGIC PLANNING

One of the critical aspects of any organization that requires the attention of senior leadership is strategic planning. Through strategic planning, leaders mold an organization's future and manage change by focusing on an ideal vision of what the organization should and could be three, five, or more years in the future. The objective of strategic planning is to build a posture that is so strong in selective ways that the organization can achieve its goals despite unforeseeable external forces.

The concept of strategy has different meanings to different people. James Quinn characterizes strategy this way:

Quality Profile

Los Alamos National Bank

Los Alamos National Bank (LANB) is an independent community bank that provides a full range of financial services to the consumer, commercial, and government markets in northern and central New Mexico. With assets of $650 million, LANB has 167 employees and locations in Los Alamos, White Rock, and Santa Fe. LANB is the primary financial institution for 66 percent of Los Alamos County residents and is the largest Guaranteed Rural Housing lender in New Mexico and the leading originator of Fannie Mae loans in northern New Mexico. Because of streamlined procedures, LANB approves home equity loans in two days or fewer while its competitors take from one to six weeks.

LANB has a high level of customer loyalty. One-third of bank customers have five or more banking relationships with the bank, an industry benchmark at more than five times the national average. In a recent survey, 80 percent of the bank's customers said they were "very satisfied" with the service they received. This is considerably higher than the levels received by its primary competitors (52 percent and 40 percent) and the national average for banks (55 percent). Returns on key financial indicators exceed local competitors and the national average. For example, the bank's net income has increased by more than 60 percent over the five years between 1995 and 1999; annual return on stock exceeded the S&P 500 by 50 percent; return on average assets has exceeded the national average every year since 1995; earnings per share increased from $1.20 in 1995 to nearly $2.00 in 1999; dividends per share increased from $.50 in 1995 to nearly $.80 per share in 1999. Employee satisfaction results have been well above those of banks its size in five of eight key indicators of employee satisfaction, and has exceeded the norm for banks of its size in six of 12 dimensions important to its mission and culture. LANB received a Baldrige Award in the Small Business Category in 2000.

Source: Malcolm Baldrige National Quality Award 2000 Award Recipients Press Release.

> *A strategy is a pattern or plan that integrates an organization's major goals, policies, and action sequences into a cohesive whole. A well-formulated strategy helps to marshal and allocate an organization's resources into a unique and viable posture based on its relative internal competencies and shortcomings, anticipated changes in the environment, and contingent moves by intelligent opponents.*[43]

A focus on both customer-driven quality and operational performance excellence, as opposed to traditional financial and marketing goals, is essential to an effective strategy. To be competitive and profitable, an organization must focus on the drivers of customer satisfaction, customer retention, and market share; building operational capability through increasing speed, responsiveness, and flexibility contributes to short- and longer-term productivity growth and cost-price competitiveness. For many firms, quality has been an essential element of business strategy. Consider the Xerox Corporation, which was profiled in a *Quality in Practice* case in Chapter 1. The Xerox *Leadership Through Quality* strategy is built on three elements:

1. **Quality Principles**
   - Quality as the basic business principle for Xerox in its leadership position
   - An understanding of customers' existing and latent requirements

- Products and services that meet the requirements of all external and internal customers
- Employee involvement, through participative problem solving, in improving quality
- Error-free work as the most cost-effective way to improve quality

2. **Management Actions and Behaviors**
   - Assure strategic clarity and consistency
   - Provide visible supportive management practices, commitment, and leadership
   - Set quality objectives and measurement standards
   - Establish and reinforce a management style of openness, trust, respect, patience, and discipline
   - Develop an environment in which each person can be responsible for quality
3. **Quality Tools**
   - The Xerox quality policy
   - Competitive benchmarking and goal setting
   - Systematic defect-detection and error-prevention processes
   - Training for leadership through quality
   - Communication and recognition programs that reinforce leadership through quality
   - A measure for the cost of quality (or its lack)

Following the formation of this strategy, senior executives at Xerox defined the goals they would strive to achieve and the activities necessary to implement these goals over the next five years.

Leading Practices for Strategic Planning

Effective organizations share several common approaches in their strategic planning efforts.

- *Top management, employees, and even customers or suppliers actively participate in the planning process*. Strong leadership is necessary to establish the credibility of a total quality focus and integrate quality principles into the business planning process. At The Ritz-Carlton Hotel Company, for example, senior leadership also serves as the senior quality group. Similarly, senior executives at AT&T Transmission Systems comprise the company's quality council. This council prioritizes quality objectives and reviews the progress of quality improvement efforts. Each member of the council chairs a separate steering committee responsible for the deployment of quality objectives.

  Employees represent an important resource in strategic planning. Not only can the company capitalize on employee knowledge of customers and processes, but employee involvement greatly enhances the effectiveness of strategy implementation. Such "bottom-up" planning facilitates better understanding and assessment of customer needs. At The Ritz-Carlton, teams at all levels—corporate, management, and employee—set objectives and devise action plans. Each hotel has a quality leader who serves as a resource and advisor to teams for developing and implementing plans. At Solar Turbines, Inc., the strategy development process involves people from all parts of its worldwide organization, customers, and suppliers. Sales, marketing, service, engineering, and manufacturing people in functional and cross-functional teams perform information gathering, analysis, and conclusions. This information is carried forward to the leadership system committees and the Operations Council where they are integrated and synthesized into strategies and critical success factor goals.

It is not unusual for customers and/or suppliers to be involved in strategic planning efforts because of their importance in the supply chain. For example, suppliers to the Wallace Company, as well as customers, participated directly in the annual revision of the company's strategic plan.

- *They have systematic planning systems for strategy development and deployment, including measurement, feedback, and review.* Using a systematic process helps to optimize the use of resources, ensure the availability of trained employees, and ensure bridging between short-term and longer-term requirements that may entail capital expenditures or supplier development. For example, Figure 5.4 shows the strategic planning process for Eastman Chemical Company. Eastman's approach is driven by its mission, vision, Major Improvement Opportunities (MIOs), and other critical planning inputs. These lead to the development of an overall strategy and the MIOs and key initiatives for each organizational unit. Deployment is achieved by a project management focus and cycles of review and improvement.

The strategic planning process at Corning Telecommunications Products Division (TPD) (see *Quality Profile*) consists of a four-stage planning system shown in Figure 5.5. Components of the system are *strategy development,* in which new or updated strategy is determined; *planning,* in which strategy is translated into key strategic initiatives and associated critical success factors, as well as three-year

Figure 5.4 Strategic Quality Planning Process at Eastman Chemical Company

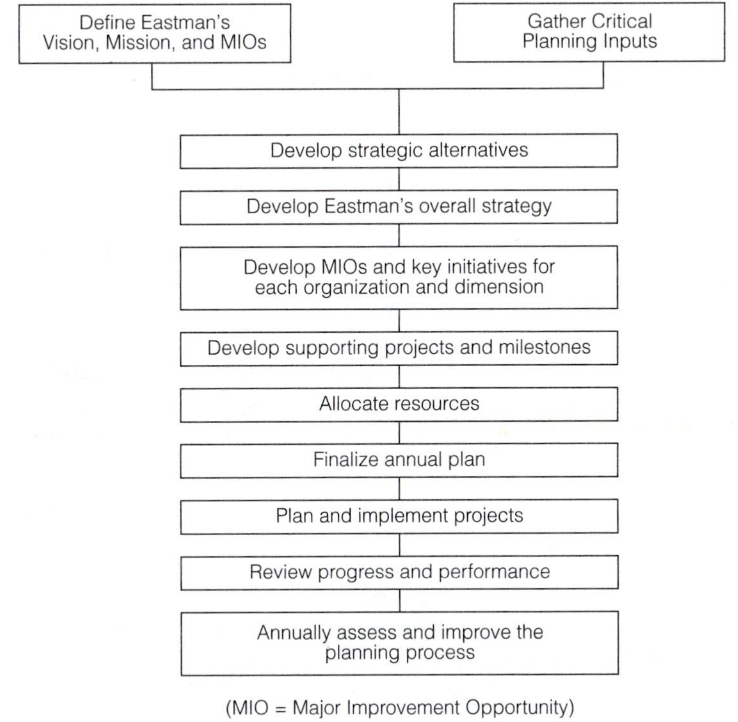

Source: Used with permission of Eastman Chemical Company.

Quality Profile

Corning Telecommunications Products Division

The Telecommunications Products Division (TPD) of Corning, Inc. produces hair-thin optical fiber used to transmit large amounts of data over long distances for three distinct customer groups (cable manufacturers, end users, and joint-venture fiber-making companies) in more than 30 countries. In a highly competitive industry, the division's executive leadership team has integrated the principles of total quality into its "Plan to Win," which embodies six fundamental components: strategic direction, customer focus, formalized systems of process management, a culture of continuous improvement, measurement of progress using the Baldrige criteria, and foundation values of people, processes, and technology. The approach develops strategic direction by carefully linking vision, mission, strategy, plans, goals, and individual employee objectives. Customer focus is ensured through their Customer Response System, which is used to gather customer inputs, establish priorities, and initiate action plans to increase customer satisfaction. Processes are designed to be formalized, closed-loop, systems, ensuring that short-term plans, goals, and individual employee contributions contribute to meeting long-term strategic aims. TPD uses surveys and other feedback mechanisms to ensure that individual employees understand how their personal work objectives contribute to meeting the division's key strategic objectives.

In 1994, 98 percent of customers rated the quality of TPD products as "very good" or "excellent" and 99 percent of end-user customers viewed TPD as the industry and technological leader. These ratings stem from many internal improvements. For example, returns of unsatisfactory products were reduced by a factor greater than 24 over a 10-year period, while performance in meeting customer shipping requirements improved tenfold. TPD also reduced hazardous waste levels by six times in the seven years preceding its winning the Baldrige Award in 1995. TPD achieved these results even as the price of optical fiber dropped by almost 50 percent.

Source: Malcolm Baldrige National Quality Award, Profiles of Winners, National Institute of Standards and Technology, Department of Commerce.

and one-year plans to deploy the strategy; and *strategy deployment*, in which the company develops goals and objectives in alignment with the key strategic initiatives for units, workgroups, and individuals. The fourth stage, *business priority process*, provides review and feedback to ensure that planning remains effective despite changes in customer requirements and in the competitive environment.

- *They gather and analyze a variety of data about external and internal factors as part of the strategic planning process.* Effective strategic planning depends upon a clear understanding of customer and market needs and expectations, competitive environment and capabilities, financial and societal risks, human resource and other operational capabilities and needs, and supplier and partner capabilities and needs. The Ritz-Carlton, for instance, evaluates all action plans on how effectively they address customer requirements. A key goal is to become the first hospitality company with 100 percent customer retention; all plans must address this goal. The approaches for gathering customer information described in Chapter 4 are used in the annual planning processes. Similarly, AT&T Consumer Communications Services (see *Quality Profile*) identified five key determinants of customer satisfaction: call quality, customer service, billing, price,

Figure 5.5 Strategic Planning Process at Corning Telecommunications Products Division

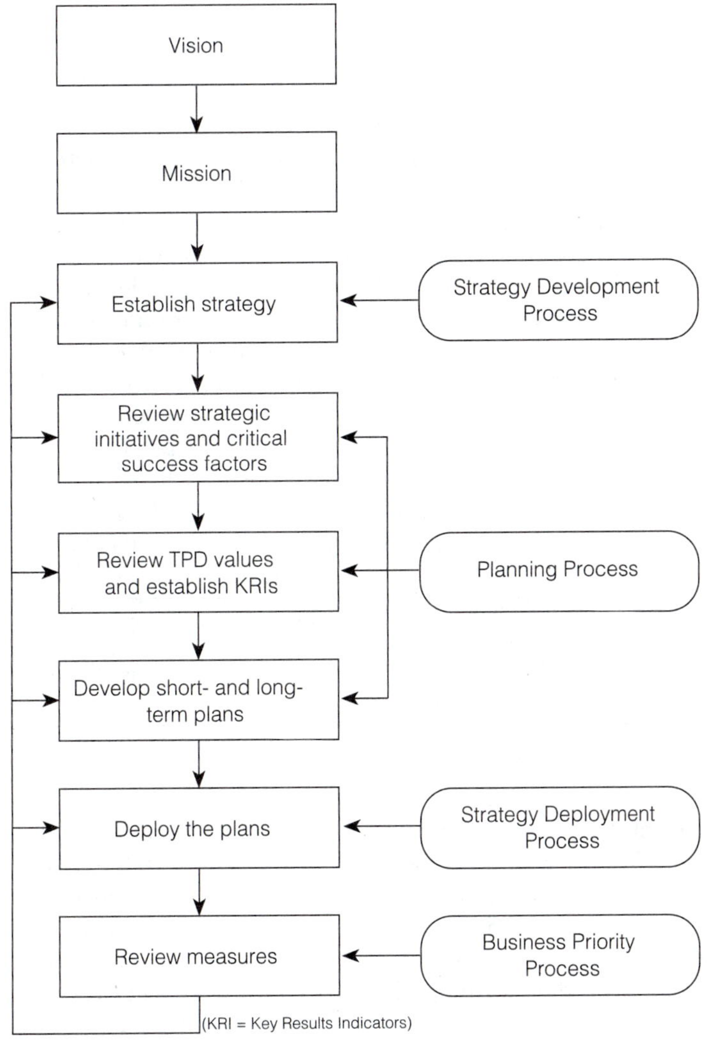

Source: 1995 Malcolm Baldrige National Quality Award Application Summary. Courtesy of Telecommunications Products Division, Corning, Incorporated.

and company reputation. Company goals are directly aligned with these requirements and used to set targets for process improvements and new services. Solar Turbines, Inc., looks at six external factors that affect its business: customer needs and wants, market trends and opportunity, industry trends, competitive dynamics, governmental and regulatory issues, and technological innovations that can change the nature of products and services.

- *They align short-term action plans with long-term strategic objectives and communicate them throughout the organization, using measurements to track progress.* This practice ensures that strategies will be deployed effectively at the "three levels of quality"—the organization level, process level, and individual job level. At

Quality Profile

AT&T Consumer Communications Services

AT&T Consumer Communications Services (CCS), the largest of 22 AT&T units, provides long-distance communications services to more than 80 million residential customers. CCS operates in an intensely competitive, technology-driven industry that today includes more than 500 long-distance companies. CCS employs 44,000 associates at more than 900 sites throughout the United States.

With the aim of enhancing existing services, developing new ones, and distinguishing itself from competitors, CCS invests heavily in new technology, which has enabled it to expand the capabilities and increase the reliability of its Worldwide Intelligent Network. CCS has developed a highly automated system (FASTAR) that restores calling capacity within 10 minutes of a major facility outage. Real-time network monitoring and other technologies have strengthened CCS's ability to anticipate and prevent service disruptions.

In its 185 million daily interactions with customers, CCS measures its progress against the company's chief goal of achieving a perfect connection and contact for each customer, every time. Customer satisfaction levels have shown a steady upward trend, and more than 90 percent of customers rate the overall quality of the company's service as good or excellent. To deepen its understanding of customer needs, CCS revamped its customer-focused measurement system to provide greater detail and yield clearer targets for improvement. In 1994 CCS received the Malcolm Baldrige National Quality Award in the service category.

Source: Malcolm Baldrige National Quality Award, Profiles of Winners, National Institute of Standards and Technology, Department of Commerce.

BI, for example, the strategic business and quality plan (SBQP) is communicated to all BI leaders and then each vice president facilitates division planning with their teams. The result is a divisional SBQP with measurable objectives and action plans, which is communicated to all associates within the division. Each director, regional sales manager, and team leader then facilitates a planning session with their individual teams, which results in a department, region, or team plan with objectives and action plans of its own. The strategic planning team meets quarterly to report progress of each action plan against its timeline and reviews results measurements against corporate objectives.

Strategy Development

Henry Mintzberg, an unconventional thinker when it comes to management and organizational structures, argued that competitive success requires strategic thinking by senior leaders in the organization.[44] He describes strategy development as

> *. . . capturing what the manager learns from all sources (both soft insights from his or her personal experiences and the experiences of others throughout the organization and the hard data from market research and the like) and then synthesizing that learning into a vision of the direction that the business should pursue.*

In many organizations, strategy development is nothing more than a group of managers sitting around in a room and generating ideas. Effective strategy development requires a systematic process. Although specific approaches vary from one company to another (as evidenced by our examples from Eastman and Corning), all generally follow the basic model shown in Figure 5.6. The organization's leaders first explore and agree upon (or reaffirm) the mission, vision, and guiding principles of the organization, which form the foundation for the strategic plan.

The **mission** of a firm defines its reason for existence; it asks the question "Why are we in business?" It might include a definition of products and services the organization provides, technologies used to provide these products and services, types of markets, important customer needs, and distinctive competencies—the expertise that sets the firm apart from others. The mission of Solectron is ". . . to provide worldwide responsiveness to our customers by offering the highest quality, lowest total cost, customized, integrated, design, supply chain and manufacturing solutions through long-term partnerships based on integrity and ethical business practices." The mission of the Cadillac Motor Car Company is stated in a similar fashion: "[T]o engineer, produce, and market the world's finest automobiles, known for uncompromised levels of distinctiveness, comfort, convenience, and refined performance."

A firm's mission guides the development of strategies by different groups within the firm. It establishes the context within which daily operating decisions are made and sets limits on available strategic options. In addition, it governs the trade-offs among the various performance measures and between short- and long-term goals. Finally, it can inspire employees to focus their efforts toward the overall purpose of the organization.

The **vision** describes where the organization is headed and what it intends to be; it is a statement of the future that would not happen by itself. It articulates the basic characteristics that shape the organization's strategy. A vision should be brief, focused, clear, and inspirational to an organization's employees. It should be linked to customers' needs and convey a general strategy for achieving the mission. For example, PepsiCo states, "We will be an outstanding company by exceeding customer expectations through empowered people, guided by shared values." Texas Instrument's vision is stated as ". . . to become a premier electronics company providing world leadership in digital solutions for the networked society—a society transformed by personalized electronics, all speaking the same digital language, all able to communicate anytime, anywhere." Solectron's is simple: "Be the best and continuously improve."

Figure 5.6 Strategic Planning Process

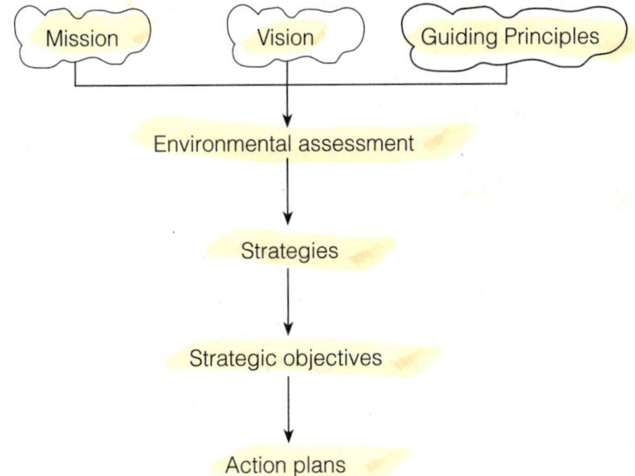

A vision must be consistent with the culture and values of the organization. **Values**, or **guiding principles**, guide the journey to that vision by defining attitudes and policies for all employees, which are reinforced through conscious and subconscious behavior at all levels of the organization. PepsiCo's shared values are diversity (respecting individual differences), integrity (doing what we say), honesty (speaking openly and working hard to understand and resolve issues), teamwork (working on real customer needs), accountability (committing fully to meeting expectations), and balance (respecting individual decisions to achieve professional and personal balance in life).

The mission, vision, and guiding principles serve as the foundation for strategic planning. They must be articulated by top management and others who lead, especially the CEO. They also have to be transmitted, practiced, and reinforced through symbolic and real action before they become "real" to the employees and the people, groups, and organizations in the external environment that do business with the firm.

Although an organization's mission, vision, and values rarely change, the environment in which the organization exists usually does. Thus, strategy development requires an **environmental assessment** of key factors noted in the Leading Practices section: customer and market requirements and expectations; the competitive environment; financial, societal, and other risks; and human resource, operational, and supplier and partner capabilities. This information is usually gathered and maintained as inputs to the planning process. Such environmental assessments are often accompanied by SWOT (strengths, weaknesses, opportunities, threats) analyses, and help identify critical success factors on which a strategy must focus.

From the environmental assessment, an organization develops strategies, objectives, and action plans. **Strategies** are broad statements that set the direction for the organization to take in realizing its mission and vision. A strategy might be directed toward becoming a preferred supplier, a low-cost producer, a market innovator, or a high-end or customized service provider. **Strategic objectives** are what an organization must change or improve to remain or become competitive. Strategic objectives set an organization's longer-term directions and guide resource allocation decisions. For example, a strategic objective might be to increase the number of patents by 50 percent in two years. **Action plans** are things that an organization must do to meet its strategic objectives. Strategic objectives and action plans often require significant changes in human resource requirements, such as redesigning the work organization or jobs to increase employee empowerment and decision making, promoting greater labor-management cooperation, modifying compensation and recognition systems, or developing new education and training initiatives. For example, to increase the number of patents, an organization's action plans might include hiring more engineers, developing a creativity training program, and changing its financial incentive approaches. Finally, organizations need performance measures or indicators for tracking progress relative to action plans.

An increasingly important part of strategic planning is projecting the competitive environment. This practice helps to detect and reduce competitive threats, to shorten reaction time, and to identify opportunities. Organizations might use a variety of modeling, scenario, or other techniques and judgments to project the competitive environment. Projections of key performance measures and comparisons with competitors, benchmarks, and past performance help an organization evaluate its performance in achieving its objectives, strategies, and ultimately, its vision.

Despite the importance of an effective strategic planning process, many organizations fail to execute one. According to Patrick Schaefer, principal at Ernst & Young, some key issues include the following:[45]

- Lack of understanding important causal relationships, such as business drivers and outcomes.
- The wrong information serving as the informational basis. Much of the knowledge that organizations create does not focus on real strategic needs.
- Inability to connect strategic objectives to everyday operating activities. One way of connecting strategic objectives is through performance measurement systems, which we address in Chapter 8.
- Dormant learning processes often result from inadequate analytical tools, lack of employee inputs (in favor of a top-down approach), and failure to define what gives the organization a dynamic character, that is, what differentiates it from others.

To address these issues, organizations should ask three basic questions:

1. What is the fundamental logic of the strategic planning process? Is it comprehensive, objective, timely, and broad-based in terms of inputs from key parts of the organization?
2. How is the strategic plan linked to everyday operations to ensure effective implementation?
3. How is the process supported through a learning and information process that is focused on the strategic objectives?

Strategy Deployment

Top management requires a method to ensure that its plans and strategies are executed successfully within the organization. **Deployment** refers to developing detailed action plans, defining resource requirements and performance measures, and aligning work unit, supplier, and partner plans with overall strategic objectives. The traditional approach to deploying strategy is top-down. From a TQ perspective, subordinates are both customers and suppliers, and therefore their input is necessary. An iterative process in which senior management asks what lower levels of the organization can do, what they need, and what conflicts may arise can avoid many of the implementation problems that managers typically face.

The Japanese deploy strategy through a process known as *hoshin kanri*, or *hoshin planning*. In the United States, this process is often referred to as *policy deployment*, or *management by planning*. Many companies, notably Florida Power and Light, Hewlett-Packard, and AT&T among many others, have adopted this process. The literal Japanese translation of hoshin kanri is "pointing direction."[46] The idea is to point, or align, the entire organization in a common direction. Florida Power and Light defines policy deployment as "the executive deployment of selected policy-driven priorities and the necessary resources to achieve performance breakthroughs." Hewlett-Packard calls it "a process for annual planning and implementation which focuses on areas needing significant improvement." AT&T's definition is "an organization-wide and customer-focused management approach aimed at planning and executing breakthrough improvements in business performance." Regardless of the particular definition, policy deployment emphasizes organization-wide planning and setting of priorities, provides resources to meet objectives, and measures performance as a basis for improvement.

Policy deployment is essentially a TQ-based approach to executing a strategy by ensuring that all employees understand the business direction and are working according to a plan to make the vision a reality.

M. Imai provides an example of policy deployment:

> *To illustrate the need for policy deployment, let us consider the following case: The president of an airline company proclaims that he believes in safety and that his corporate goal is to make sure that safety is maintained throughout the company. This proclamation is prominently featured in the company's quarterly report and its advertising. Let us further suppose that the department managers also swear a firm belief in safety. The catering manager says he believes in safety. The pilots say they believe in safety. The flight crews say they believe in safety. Everyone in the company practices safety. True? Or might everyone simply be paying lip-service to the idea of safety?*
>
> *On the other hand, if the president states that safety is company policy and works with his division managers to develop a plan for safety that defines their responsibilities, everyone will have a very specific subject to discuss. Safety will become a real concern. For the manager in charge of catering services, safety might mean maintaining the quality of food to avoid customer dissatisfaction or illness.*
>
> *In that case, how does he ensure that the food is of top quality? What sorts of control points and checkpoints does he establish? How does he ensure that there is no deterioration of food quality in flight? Who checks the temperature of the refrigerators or the condition of the oven while the plane is in the air?*
>
> *Only when safety is translated into specific actions with specific control and checkpoints established for each employee's job may safety be said to have been truly deployed as a policy. Policy deployment calls for everyone to interpret policy in light of his own responsibilities and for everyone to work out criteria to check his success in carrying out the policy.*[47]

Figure 5.7 provides a simplified description of the policy deployment process.[48] With policy deployment, top management is responsible for developing and communicating a vision, then building organization-wide commitment to its achievement.[49] The long-term strategic plan forms the basis for shorter-term planning. This vision is deployed through the development and execution of annual objectives and plans. All levels of employees actively participate in generating strategy and action plans to attain the vision. At each level, progressively more detailed and concrete means to accomplish the objectives are determined. Objectives should be challenging, but people should feel that they are attainable. To this end, middle management negotiates with senior management regarding the objectives that will achieve the strategies, and what process changes and resources might be required to achieve those objectives. Middle management then negotiates with the implementation teams the final short-term objectives and the performance measures that are used to indicate progress toward accomplishing the objectives.

Management reviews at specific checkpoints ensure the effectiveness of individual elements of the strategy. The implementation teams are empowered to manage actions and schedule their activities. Periodic reviews (monthly or quarterly) track progress and diagnose problems. Management may modify objectives on the basis of these reviews, as evidenced by the feedback loop in the figure. Top management evaluates results as well as the deployment process itself through annual reviews, which serve as a basis for the next planning cycle.

Figure 5.7 The Policy Deployment Process

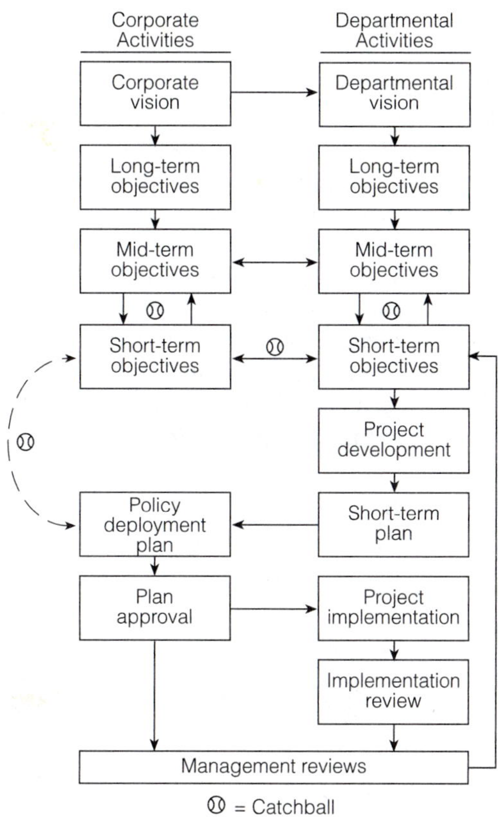

Source: Kersi F. Munshi, "Policy Deployment: A Key to Long-Term TQM Success," *ASQC Quality Congress Transactions* (Boston, 1993), 236–244.

Note, however, that top management does not develop action plans; it sets overall guidelines and strategies. Departments and functional units develop specific implementation plans. Hence, the process in Figure 5.7 includes both corporate and departmental activities. In practice, policy deployment entails a high degree of detail, including the anticipation of possible problems during implementation. The emphasis is on the improvement of the process, as opposed to a results-only orientation.

The negotiation process is called *catchball* (represented by the baseball symbol in Figure 5.7). Leaders communicate midterm objectives and measures to middle managers who develop short-term objectives and recommend necessary resources, targets, and roles and responsibilities. These issues are discussed and debated until agreement is reached. The objectives then cascade to lower levels of the organization where short-term plans are developed. Catchball is an up, down, and sideways communication process as opposed to an autocratic, top-down management style. It marshals the collective expertise of the whole organization and results in realistic and achievable objectives that do not conflict. In the spirit of Deming, the process focuses on optimizing the system rather than on individual goals and objectives. Clearly, this process can only occur in a TQ culture that nourishes open communication.

THE SEVEN MANAGEMENT AND PLANNING TOOLS

Managers may use a variety of tools and techniques, known as the *seven management and planning tools*, to implement policy deployment. These tools are particularly useful in structuring unstructured ideas, making strategic plans, and organizing and controlling large, complex projects. Thus, they can benefit all employees involved in quality planning and implementation. These tools had their roots in post–World War II operations research developments in the United States, but were combined and refined by several Japanese companies over the past several decades as part of their planning processes. They were popularized in the United States by the consulting firm GOAL/QPC and have been used by a number of firms since 1984 to improve their quality planning and improvement efforts. Many companies formally integrated these tools into policy deployment activities. Two of them—affinity diagrams and tree diagrams—were introduced in the previous chapter. The next section briefly describes the management and planning tools, and shows how they can be used in policy deployment. The text presents a hypothetical high-technology consumer electronics company, MicroTech, to illustrate the application of these tools. MicroTech's mission is

> *to design and manufacture miniature electronics products utilizing radio frequency technologies, digital signal processing technologies, and state-of-the-art surface mount manufacturing techniques.*

Affinity Diagrams

The affinity diagram, introduced in the previous chapter, is a tool for organizing a large number of ideas, opinions, and facts relating to a broad problem or subject area. In developing a vision statement, for example, senior management might conduct a brainstorming session to develop a list of ideas to incorporate into the vision. This list might include

Low product maintenance
Satisfied employees
Courteous order entry
Low price
Quick delivery
Growth in shareholder value
Teamwork
Responsive technical support
Personal employee growth
Low production costs
Innovative product features
High return on investment
Constant technology innovation
High quality
Motivated employees
Unique products
Small, lightweight designs

Once a large number of ideas have been generated, they can be grouped according to their "affinity" or relationship to each other. An affinity diagram for the preceding list is shown in Figure 5.8.

Interrelationship Digraph

An interrelationship digraph identifies and explores causal relationships among related concepts or ideas. It shows that every idea can be logically linked with more than one other idea at a time, and allows for "lateral thinking" rather than "linear thinking." This technique is often used after the affinity diagram has clarified issues and problems. Figure 5.9 shows an example of how the key strategic factors for MicroTech relate to one another. The elements having the most net outward-pointing arrows (number out minus number in) represent the primary drivers of the com-

Figure 5.8 Affinity Diagram for MicroTech

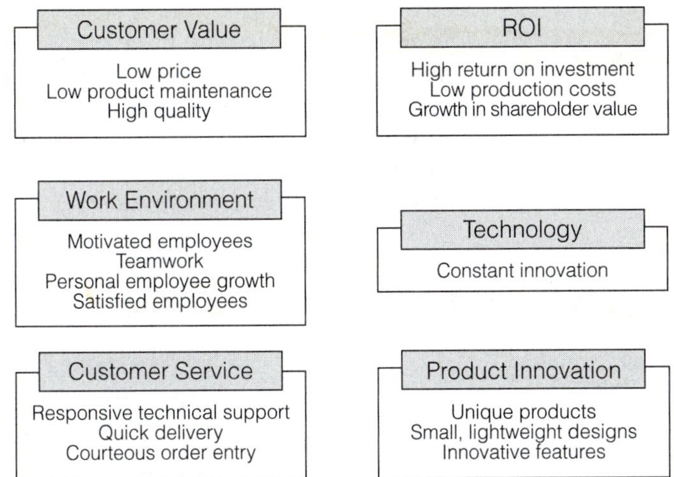

pany's vision: in this case, work environment and customer service. As a result, MicroTech might develop the following vision statement:

> *We will provide exceptional value to our customers in terms of cost-effective products and services of the highest quality, leading to superior value to our shareholders. We will provide a supportive work environment that promotes personal growth and the pursuit of excellence and allows each employee to achieve his or her full potential. We are committed to advancing the state-of-the-art in electronics miniaturization and related technologies and to developing market opportunities that are built upon our unique technical expertise.*

Tree Diagrams

A tree diagram maps out the paths and tasks necessary to complete a specific project or reach a specified goal. Thus, the planner uses this technique to seek answers to

Figure 5.9 Interrelationship Digraph of MicroTech's Strategic Factors

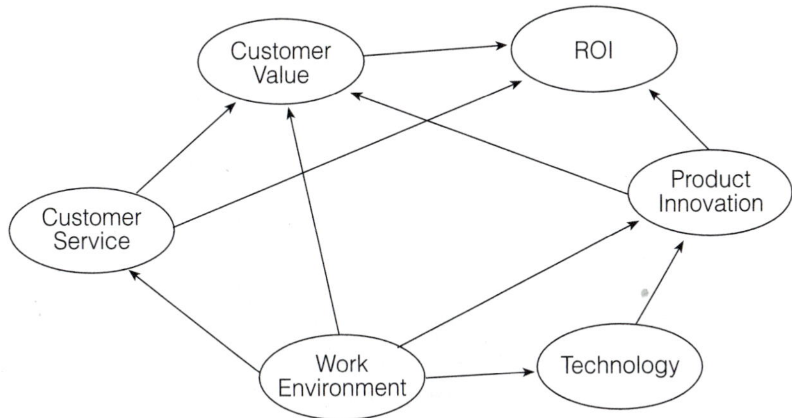

such questions as "What sequence of tasks will address the issue?" or "What factors contribute to the existence of the key problem?"

A tree diagram brings the issues and problems revealed by the affinity diagram and the interrelationship digraph down to the operational planning stage. A clear statement specifies problem or process. From this general statement, a team can be established to recommend steps to solve the problem or implement the plan. The "product" produced by this group would be a tree diagram with activities and perhaps recommendations for timing the activities. Figure 5.10 shows an example of how a tree diagram can be used to map out key goals and strategies for MicroTech.

Figure 5.10 Tree Diagram of MicroTech Goals and Strategies

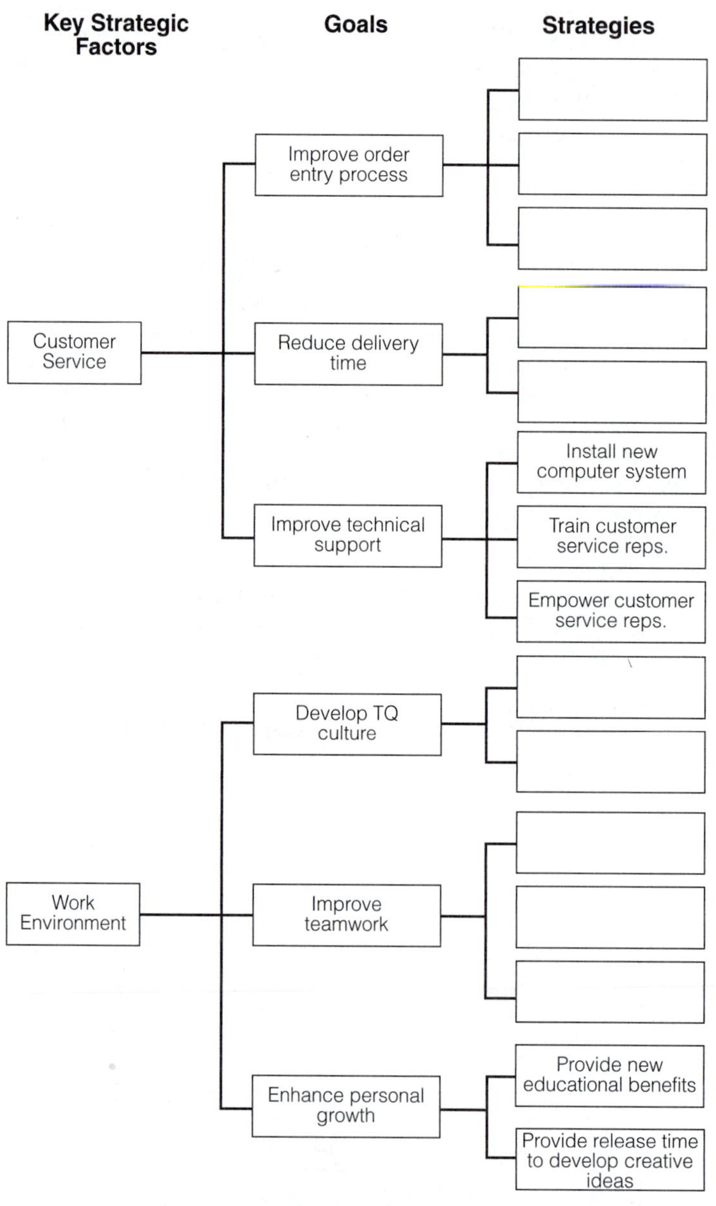

Matrix Diagrams

Matrix diagrams are "spreadsheets" that graphically display relationships between ideas, activities, or other dimensions in such a way as to provide logical connecting points between each item. A matrix diagram is one of the most versatile tools in quality planning. One example is shown in Figure 5.11. Here, we have listed the three principal goals articulated in MicroTech's vision statement along the rows, and the key strategies along the columns. Typically, symbols such as ●, ○, and △ are used to denote strong, medium, and weak relationships. Matrix diagrams provide a picture of how well two sets of objects or issues are related, and can identify missing pieces in the thought process. For instance, a row without many relationships might indicate that the actions proposed will not meet the company's goals. In Figure 5.11, we see that focused attention to these three strategies should meet MicroTech's goals. Other matrixes might relate short-term plans to medium-term objectives, or individual actions to short-term plans. These visual depictions can help managers set priorities on plans and actions.

Matrix Data Analysis

Matrix data analysis takes data and arranges them to display quantitative relationships among variables to make them more easily understood and analyzed. In its original form used in Japan, matrix data analysis is a rigorous, statistically based "factor analysis" technique. Many feel that this method, while worthwhile for many applications, is too quantitative to be used on a daily basis and have developed alternative tools that are easier to understand and implement. Some of these alternatives are similar to decision analysis matrixes that you may have studied in a quantitative methods course.

A small example of matrix data analysis is shown in Figure 5.12. In this example, MicroTech market researchers determined that the four most important consumer requirements are price, reliability, delivery, and technical support. Through market research, an importance weighting was developed for each. They also determined

Figure 5.11 Matrix Diagram for MicroTech's Goals and Strategies

Goals \ Actions	Improve Work Environment	Improve Manufacturing Technology	Develop New Products
Cost Effectiveness	●	○	
High Quality	●	●	
Shareholder Value		△	●

● = Strong relationship
○ = Medium relationship
△ = Weak relationship

Figure 5.12 Matrix Data Analysis of Customer Requirements for MicroTech

Requirement	Importance Weight	Best Competitor Evaluation	MicroTech Evaluation	Difference*
Price	.2	6	8	+2
Reliability	.4	7	8	+1
Delivery	.1	8	5	−3
Technical support	.3	7	5	−2

*MicroTech Evaluation – Best Competitor Evaluation

numerical ratings for the company and their best competitor. Such an analysis provides information as to which actions the company should deploy to better meet key customer requirements. For example, in Figure 5.12, reliability is the highest in importance, and MicroTech has a narrow lead over its best competitor; thus, it should continue to strive for improving product reliability. Also, technical support is of relatively high importance, but MicroTech is perceived to be inferior to its best competitor in this category. Thus, improving the quality of support services should be a major objective.

Process Decision Program Charts

A process decision program chart (PDPC) is a method for mapping out every conceivable event and contingency that can occur when moving from a problem statement to possible solutions. A PDPC takes each branch of a tree diagram, anticipates possible problems, and provides countermeasures that will (1) prevent the deviation from occurring, or (2) be in place if the deviation does occur. Figure 5.13 shows one example for implementing a strategy to educate and train all employees to use a new computer system.

Arrow Diagrams

For years, construction planners have used arrow diagrams in the form of CPM and PERT project planning techniques. Arrow diagramming has also been taught extensively in quantitative methods, operations management, and other business and engineering courses in the United States for a number of years. Unfortunately, its use has generally been confined to technical experts. Adding arrow diagramming to the "quality toolbox" has made it more widely available to general managers and other nontechnical personnel. Figure 5.14 shows an example. Time estimates can easily be added to each activity in order to schedule and control the project.

These seven tools provide managers with improved capability to make better decisions and facilitate the implementation process. With proper planning, managers can use their time more effectively to continuously improve and innovate.

LEADERSHIP, STRATEGY, AND ORGANIZATIONAL STRUCTURE

The effectiveness of both the leadership system and the strategic planning system depends in part on **organizational structure**—the clarification of authority, responsibil-

Figure 5.13 A Process Decision Program Chart

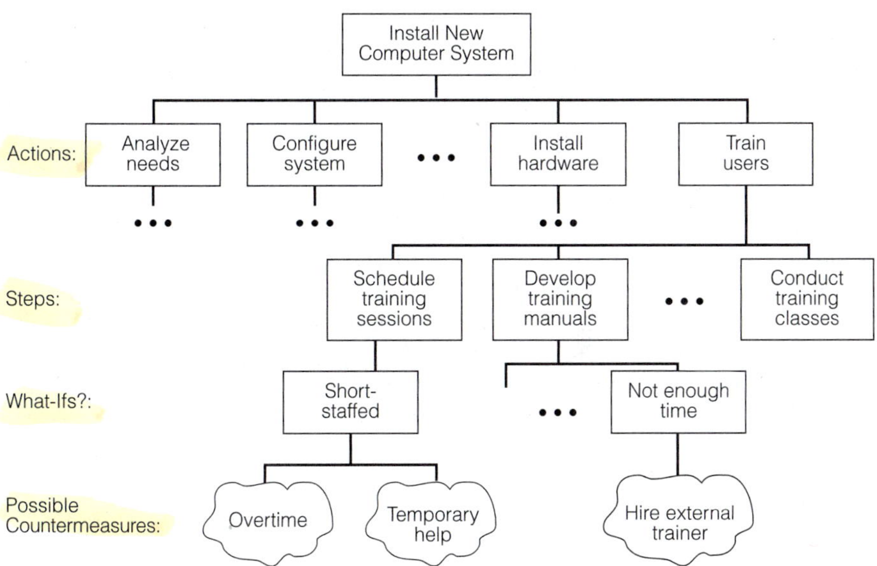

ity, reporting lines, and performance standards among individuals at each level of the organization. It is also true that effective strategy deployment is also dependent on, and tends to shape, organizational structure.

Traditional organizations tend to develop structures that help them to maintain stability. They tend to be highly structured, both in terms of rules and regulations, as well as the height of the "corporate ladder," with seven or more layers of managers between the CEO and the first-line worker. In contrast, organizations in the rapidly changing environments characteristic of modern organizations have to build flexibility into their organization structures. Hence, they tend to have fewer written rules and regulations and flatter organizational structures.

Several factors having to do with the context of the organization have an impact on how work is organized.[50]

Figure 5.14 An Arrow Diagram for Project Planning

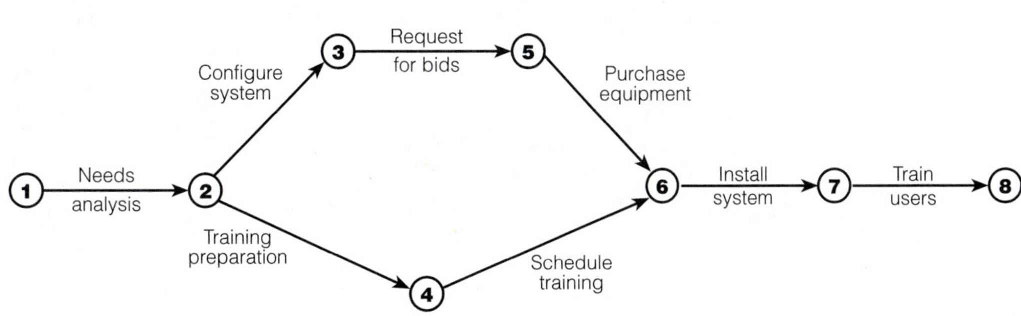

1. *Company operational and organizational guidelines.* Standard practices that have developed over the firm's history often dictate how a company organizes and operates.
2. *Management style.* The management team operates in a manner unique to a given company. For example, management style might be formal or informal, or democratic or autocratic. If the organization operates in a highly structured, formal atmosphere, organizing a quality effort around informal meetings would probably meet with little success.
3. *Customer influences.* Formal specifications or administrative controls may be required by customers, particularly governmental agencies. Thus, the organization needs to understand and respond to these requirements.
4. *Company size.* Large companies have the ability to maintain formal systems and records, whereas smaller companies may not.
5. *Diversity and complexity of product line.* An organization suitable for the manufacture of a small number of highly sophisticated products may differ dramatically from an organization that produces a high volume of standard goods.
6. *Stability of the product line.* Stable product lines generate economies of scale that influence supervision, corrective action, and other quality-related issues. Frequent changes in products necessitate more control and commensurate changes to the quality system.
7. *Financial stability.* Quality managers need to recognize that their efforts must fit within the overall budget of the firm.
8. *Availability of personnel.* The lack of certain skills may require other personnel, such as supervisors, to assume duties they ordinarily would not be assigned.

An organization chart shows the apparent structure of the formal organization. However, some organizations refuse to be tied down by a conventional organization chart, even to the extent that employees make a running joke of titles. For example, Semco, Inc., a radically unconventional manufacturer of industrial equipment (mixers, washers, air conditioners, bakery plant units) located in São Paulo, Brazil, has what is called a "circular" organization chart with four concentric circles (they avoid the use of the term *levels*). The titles that go with these are counselors (CEO and the equivalent of vice presidents), partners (business unit heads), coordinators (supervisory specialists and functional leaders), and associates (everyone else). If anyone desires, he or she can think up a title for external use that describes their area or job responsibility. As owner and CEO Ricardo Simler explains:

> *Consistent with this philosophy, when a promotion takes place now at Semco we simply supply blank business cards and tell the newly elevated individual: "Think of a title that signals externally your area of operation and responsibility and have it printed." If the person likes "Procurement Manager," fine. If he wants something more elegant, he can print up cards saying, "First Pharaoh in Charge of Royal Supplies." Whatever he wants. But inside the company, there are only four options. (Anyway, almost all choose to print only their name.)*[51]

Although many different organizational structures exist, most are variations or combinations of three basic types: (1) the line organization, (2) the line and staff organization, and (3) the matrix organization.

The line organization is a functional form, with departments that are responsible for marketing, finance, and operations. In the traditional organization, the quality department ("Quality Control," "Quality Assurance," or some similar name) is generally distinct from other departments. In a TQ organization, the role of quality is invisible in the organization chart, because quality planning and assurance are part of the responsibility of each operating manager and employee at every level. In theory, this organizational form could exist in a fairly large organization if all employees were thoroughly indoctrinated in the philosophy of quality and could be counted on to place quality as the top priority in all aspects of their daily work. In practice, this particular structure is not generally successful except when used in small firms.

The line and staff organization is the most prevalent type of structure for medium-sized to large firms. In such organizations, line departments carry out the functions of marketing, finance, and production for the organization. Staff personnel, including quality managers and technical specialists, assist the line managers in carrying out their jobs by providing technical assistance and advice. Variations on the basic line and staff organization can include geographic or customer organizations. In this traditional form of organization structure, instead of technical experts who assist line managers and workers in attaining quality, quality managers and inspectors may take on the role of guardians of quality. This guardian-type role also happens when the quality assurance function is placed too low in the organization or when pressure from higher levels of the organization forces quality inspectors to ease up on quality so that more products can be shipped. The major cause of this problem is too much responsibility with insufficient authority.

The matrix type of organization was developed for use in situations where large, complex projects are designed and carried out, such as defense weapons systems or large construction projects. Firms that do such work have a basic need to develop an organizational structure that will permit the efficient use of human resources while maintaining control over the many facets of the project being developed. In a matrix-type organization, each project has a project manager and each department that is providing personnel to work on the various projects has a technical or administrative manager. Thus, a quality assurance technician might be assigned to the quality assurance department for technical and administrative activities but would be attached to Project A for day-to-day job assignments. The technician would report to the project manager of Project A and to his or her "technical boss" in the quality assurance department. When Project A is completed, the technician might be reassigned to Project B under a new project manager. He or she would still be reporting to the "technical boss" in quality assurance, however.

The matrix type of organization for project work has a number of advantages. It generally improves the coordination of complex project work as well as improving the efficiency of personnel use. Its major drawback is that it requires split loyalty for people who report to two supervisors. This division of loyalty can be especially troublesome or even dangerous in a quality assurance area. For example, in a nuclear power plant project, a project manager who is under pressure to complete a project by a certain deadline might try to influence quality assurance personnel to take shortcuts in completing the inspection phase of the project. The quality manager, who might be hundreds of miles away from the site, would often not have the influence over the inspectors that the project manager would have.

As more and more companies accept the process view of organizations, they are structuring the quality organization around functional or cross-functional teams. The organizational structures of many organizations are built around high-performance, cross-functional teams as shown in Figure 5.15. A specific example is that of GTE Directories, which is shown in Figure 5.16. In this organizational structure, the management board leads the quality effort, meeting twice each month to discuss and review management and quality issues. Quality is implemented through various teams: core business process team, cross-functional coordinating committee, regional management councils, major business process management teams (PMTs), Malcolm Baldrige

Figure 5.15 Team-Based Organizational Chart

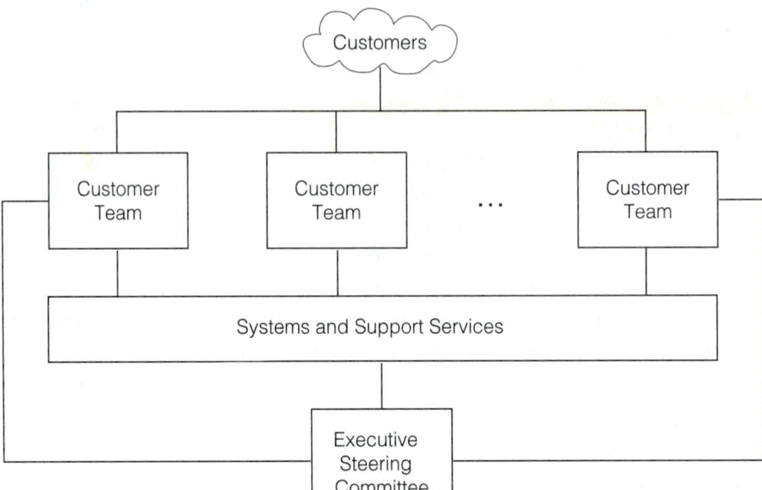

National Quality Award teams, and quality improvement teams. The regional management councils identify and address key regional issues; the cross-functional coordinating committee reviews major proposals for consistency with the strategic plan and business priorities. Such team-based organization structures spread the ownership and the accountability for quality throughout the organization. The "quality department" serves as an internal consulting group, providing advice, training, and organizational development to the teams.

Figure 5.16 GTE Directories Management Structure

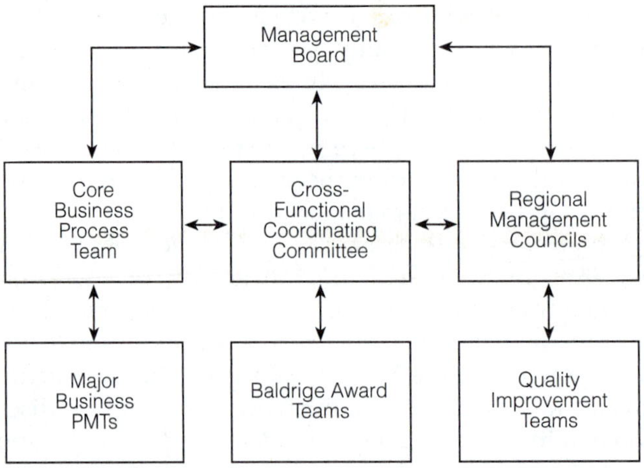

Source: Courtesy of GTE Directories Corporation.

We see that a "one-size fits all" quality organization is inappropriate. The organization must be tailored to reflect individual company differences and provide the flexibility and the ability to change. What is important, however, is that senior leaders drive quality and performance excellence concepts throughout the organization through effective communication and as role models, and ensure that strategic planning focuses all key stakeholders in achieving the organization's mission and vision.

LEADERSHIP AND STRATEGIC PLANNING IN THE BALDRIGE CRITERIA

Category 1 of the 2001 Malcolm Baldrige National Quality Award Criteria for Performance Excellence is *Leadership*. As the first of the seven categories, it signifies the critical importance of leadership to business success. The criteria focus on an organization's leadership and the roles of senior leaders, with the aim of creating and sustaining a high performance organization. Item 1.1, *Organizational Leadership*, examines how senior leaders address values, directions, and performance expectations taking into account the expectations of customers and other stakeholders; and create an environment for empowerment, innovation, learning, and agility. The criteria also ask how senior leaders review organizational performance and use review findings to drive improvement and change. Reviewing company performance is a crucial aspect of leadership, because reviews help to build consistency behind goals and allocation of resources.

Item 1.2, *Public Responsibility and Citizenship*, addresses how an organization addresses its public responsibilities and encourages, supports, and practices good citizenship. It includes how the organization addresses impacts on society of its products, services, and operations in a proactive manner; how it ensures ethical business practices in all stakeholder transactions and interactions; and how the organization, its senior leaders, and employees actively support, and strengthen key communities as part of good citizenship practices.

Category 2, *Strategic Planning* stresses that customer-driven quality and operational performance excellence are key strategic issues that need to be an integral part of overall planning. Item 2.1, *Strategy Development*, examines how an organization develops strategic objectives, with the aim of strengthening overall performance and competitiveness. It includes how strategic planning is carried out, and how key external and internal influences, risks, and challenges affect the development of strategic plans. The emphasis is on a future-oriented, thorough, and realistic context for the development of a customer- and market-focused strategy to guide ongoing decision making, resource allocation, and overall management.

Item 2.2, *Strategy Deployment*, looks at how an organization translates strategic objectives into action plans and to enable assessment of progress. Particular attention is given to product and services, customers and markets, human resource plans, and resource allocations. The criteria seek information on key measures and indicators for tracing progress and how the organization aligns strategic objectives, action plans, and performance. It also seeks short- and long-term projections of key performance measures as a basis for comparing past performance and performance relative to competitors and benchmarks.

The following example shows how one company might respond to Area to Address 1.2, Public Responsibility and Citizenship, and the feedback that a Baldrige examiner team might provide to the company. *You should read Case III in Chapter 3 first, which provides background about this fictitious company. Think about how the response addresses the questions asked in the 2000 criteria. The criteria are available on the CD-rom accompanying this book.*

Example 1: Collin Technologies—Public Responsibility and Citizenship

Response to Criteria Item 1.2, Public Responsibility and Citizenship

At Collin, one of the core values is to become better at improving the community. To meet this goal, the company does more than just comply with regulatory and legal requirements associated with the manufacturing of products. It strives to set the precedent for excellence. Collin advances its business and relationships with regulatory agencies so that the goals of both are met to serve the community.

1.2a Collin's processes and products, if not properly controlled, could have a major impact on the current and future state of the community. These impacts relate to:

1. Public Health (workplace and community risks)
2. The Environment (air and water pollution)
3. Waste Management (landfill, control of solid waste, and recycling)
4. Energy Management.

Because of these potential impacts, the circuit board manufacturing business is highly regulated and subject to frequent audits by the EPA, OSHA, Air Quality Management District, and HazMat Affairs Office, as well as many other city, county, and state agencies and their equivalents in Japan. Over the last 10 years, no violations, fines, or sanctions have been imposed on the company. To maintain this perfect record and address future societal impacts, Collin has set up specific public health, environmental improvement, waste management, and energy conservation risk management teams. It is the responsibility of these teams to identify potential exposures, define control practices, establish measures, and set stretch targets to drive proactive improvement, not only within the company, but also with the regulatory agencies. Table 5.4 identifies some of the risks, practices, measures, and targets associated with these areas.

The public health team (led by Shirley Ogrysko, director of Health, Safety, and Security Services) is chartered to work with OSHA and all public health organizations in the community. Her team personally audits all facilities for maintenance of "Material Safety Data Sheets," hazardous material exposures, and potential safety or health

Table 5.4 Collin Technologies Risk Management Practices, Measures, and Targets

Area	Risk	Practices	Measures	Targets/Goals
Public Health	Lead exposure	Quarterly EO blood testing	% lead in blood	< 0.2% of legal limit
	Chemicals in air	Monthly monitoring	% hazardous chemicals in air	0.00% induced chemicals
	Chemical handling	Daily audits	Number of violations	0.00% handling violations
Environmental	VOCs	VOC filtering	% VOCs in air	0.00%
	Water contamination	Reclamation process	Purity of water	99.9%
Waste Management	Landfill	Recycle process	Tons of recycled material	95% of all waste material
Energy Conservation	Global warming	Minimize usage	Equipment use efficiency	90% used when on

violations. The team also works closely with the Tennessee regulatory board and many insurance carriers, often accompanying them on routine audits. Improvement goals are set in conjunction with the local fire department and emergency planning committee. Shirley is an active member of the local emergency planning committee and serves as a consulting member to the state Department of Emergency Planning. In this role, she not only becomes aware of future criteria, but also has a major part in setting the future direction of public health and workplace safety requirements. Within Collin, Shirley oversees the activities of the safety committee, hazmat team, and emergency response team (ERT). The Red Cross certifies every ERT member to administer first aid and handle workplace trauma incidents.

Fred Fischer, Ph.D., director of Production Engineering, and chief environmental officer, leads the environmental control team. He and his team have set the standard for excellence in the area of workplace environmental controls. Fred Fischer is no stranger to environmental programs. He has been an active member of "A Green Society" for the last three years and currently chairs the regional "Better Air for Factories" subcommittee for the state Air Quality Management District. The team's approach used technology to advance Collin's position in the area of environmental compliance. Its first objective was to make all Collin operations free of volatile organic compounds (VOCs).

This goal was accomplished through the development of a class I microfilter that, when attached to emission-producing equipment, captured and eliminated all VOCs being released into the air. The filter automatically created, separated, and catalogued emission reports daily. In 1997, Collin received a patent for this technology and currently offers the Microfilter process to its customer and supplier base. The team also works with the EPA to set up licensing agreements to offer the technology as a "best available technology" (BAI) to the general business public. To anticipate future requirements, Fred Fischer assigned members of his team to sit as active members on environmental boards, at both state and national levels.

Andy Waterman, director of Support Contracts, leads both the waste management team and the energy conservation team. In 1987, Collin set a goal to eliminate solid waste from its manufacturing operations, which was accomplished by changing the handling and de-trash processes and in-plant reclamation and recycling programs. Suppliers who have reached Step 3 (see Figure 6.1-2 in the full case study on the CD-rom) are now required to supply material only in recyclable or reusable containers. In-house, solid waste recycle bins have been strategically placed throughout all buildings, and the waste management team monitors the tonnage reports monthly to ensure no drop-off occurs in the material being recycled. Because the business requires a tremendous amount of water usage, Collin has installed a building-wide reverse osmosis system and reclaims more than 90% of all process water. This water reclamation process has been certified by the Tennessee Water Utilities Board and is tested by the board on a quarterly basis. Water quality measurements are taken, and reports are submitted to the board each month. Collin has been recognized by the state as a "Model System," and the state encourages other companies to visit one of Collin's facilities.

Energy conservation is also key to Collin's success. To this end, all heavy energy use equipment is monitored for nonuse time, which is called the energy dead time indicator. Through monthly reviews, the energy conservation team identifies equipment displaying a high-energy dead time. It works with operations to automatically shut down or suspend this equipment, thus reducing the dead time. Building lights are on timers and motion sensors. Since 1995, Collin has been able to reduce wasted energy by more than 75 percent. A software program is currently being evaluated that would automatically sample the activity of all PCs in the company and selectively suspend their power based on nonactivity, much like a screen saver program for monitors. The program can be installed on the LAN and administered by CAIN. When implemented, this program reduces power consumption of personal computers by an estimated 60 percent.

Business ethics is another area in which Collin does not compromise. All EOs are trained for four hours on this subject. Also included in this training is a review of the Collin business conduct procedure. At the end of the session, each EO takes a test and signs a condition of understanding and practice statement regarding company ethics. The Business Conduct Procedure covers customer interactions, gifts, outside work, competitors, harassment, supplier relations, and software use. In addition, CAIN software has built-in polling and licensing checks. Daily, it scans all computers for unlicensed software and flags the information systems (IS) group when strange or unlicensed software is found.

1.2b Collin provides support and works to strengthen the community in four specific areas: education, government, health, and general community activities. It allows each EO up to one paid day per month to participate in related community activities.

In the area of education, EOs work with the local community and state colleges to bring business and learning closer. Many senior executives conduct presentations on circuit board technology at Peak State University, University of Koga, and community colleges. In the engineering department of Peak State, Collin set up a working lab for students to design and fabricate circuit boards. A similar lab is being constructed in the University of Koga in Japan. Collin has donated valuable equipment to the universities. Fred Fischer teaches evening classes on environmental controls in a business operation as part of the Peak State University MBA curriculum. Every summer, Collin supports both the community and state colleges by hiring co-op students. These students are asked to return each summer until they graduate. Students who remain in the program are immediately eligible for hire upon graduation. The Collin computer training center is open and staffed for use by the local K–12 schools. Classes are conducted in basic computer training for K–12 students who desire to learn or further their skills. Instruction is given on word processing, spreadsheets, graphics, and the Internet. These classes, which run from 9:00 A.M. to 1:00 P.M. on Saturdays, include lunch for the students. Between 1:00 P.M. and 6:00 P.M., the computer center is open for students to complete assignments or conduct research on the Internet.

In the area of government support, as mentioned previously, Collin works with regulatory agencies to better align the needs of the agencies to the business processes. In addition, Collin works with permit agencies to streamline processes that will facilitate the construction of new plants. Collin also is active in the Tennessee Valley Government and Business Joint Venture (IVG-BJV) program, chaired by the mayor of Nashville, and whose initiatives are designed to make the Tennessee Valley a model for integration of business and government.

The public health team has identified a number of programs to train and enhance the community. In addition, the ERT offers tornado survival classes each month, and the ERT in Koga conducts similar classes for earthquake readiness.

Many EOs volunteer at local health organizations. Shirley Ogrysko maintains a list of EOs who offer room in their homes for victims of natural disasters. This list is also on file at the local emergency planning committees. The Collin quality video has been distributed to more than 50 companies and is available through the Institute of Industrial Engineers (IIE) catalog. Some other key community support activities in which EOs and leaders are involved are listed in Table 5.5.

Table 5.5 Collin Technologies Community Support Activities

Community Area	EOs	Description of Activity Involvement
Education	EOs	Quality learning and application at K–12 schools
	Executive staff	MBA presentations at regional and state universities (United States and Japan)
	Managers, executives	Principal replacement day
	IS EOs	Wired local grade schools and high schools for Internet access
Government	CEO	Presentation on application of TQM in government
	Quality Manager (Japan)	Worked with local government to repair roads around city of Koga
Health	EOs	United Way, Red Cross, Food for Needy, Koga Disaster Relief
	EOs	Free flu shots for community, free body fat analysis for community
General Support	CEO	Member, Board of Directors of the Institute of Printed Circuits
	Executives and EOs	Speakers and participants in the annual Tennessee Quality Expo
	Executives and EOs	Participated in the Consortium Quality Interchange
	EOs	Provided gifts for holiday programs

Examiner Feedback

Strengths

- Teams proactively address future societal impacts in the areas of public health, environmental improvement, waste management, and energy conservation risk management. The company has a sustained history of no violations, fines, or sanctions from any regulatory agency. The teams identify risks, define applicable practices and measures, establish targets and goals in key areas, and share these practices with suppliers.
- In support of the strategy to apply technology to solve problems, the company has developed a class I microfilter technology addressing volatile organic compounds (VOCs). This process is acknowledged by the Environmental Protection Agency as the "best available technology" for reducing VOC emissions. The company is sharing this patented technology with its customer and supplier base.
- All employees are required to attend a four-hour class on business ethics and the Business Conduct Procedure. The review of the Business Conduct Procedure covers policy related to customer interactions, gifts, outside work, competitors, harassment, supplier relations, and software use. An example of an action that the company has taken to ensure the ethical use of software throughout the

business is use of its information technology system to scan for unlicensed software in its computer network.

- The company provides support and works to strengthen the community in four key community areas: education, government, health, and the general community. EOs ranging from senior managers to individual contributors are actively encouraged to strengthen the community. The company demonstrates strong commitment to the community by giving each EO up to one paid day per month to support activities related to the four key community areas.
- The company demonstrates strong support for local educational efforts. In partnership with community and state colleges, senior executives conduct presentations on circuit board technology at Peak State University and the University of Koga. The company provides learning opportunities for co-op students who are hired each summer. The computer center is open to local kindergarten through 12th-grade students for computer training by EOs; the company lab is open for students' use in designing and fabricating circuit boards.

Opportunities for Improvement

- Other than the one-time training event on the Business Conduct Procedure, it is not clear how the company systematically and consistently communicates, reinforces, and ensures compliance with ethical requirements in all business practices worldwide.
- It is not clear how the applicant addresses public concerns associated with the future development of products, services, and operations, especially those associated with future growth in Europe. Without a description of how future risks are managed, it is difficult to assess the effectiveness of the company in responding to a rapidly changing industry within a highly regulated environment.
- Although one of its core values focuses on improving the community, it is not evident that a systematic process is used by the leadership team to evaluate and improve community involvement, making it difficult to assess how these activities are consistent with company goal and values. Also, it is unclear how stakeholder teams address community activities. How community needs are determined for the Nashville and Koga communities is not described.

Quality in Practice

Leadership in the Virgin Group[52]

One has to look hard for the application of systematic quality principles in an organization like Virgin Enterprises, whose major product lines include music CDs, videos, clothing, financial services, national and international air travel, Internet car sales in Britain, and national train travel services. Here is an organization—actually, a loose conglomeration of separate, stand-alone companies—that "grew like Topsy" with only the vision of its charismatic founder and guru, Richard Branson (now "Sir Richard," after being knighted in March 2000), to guide it. Yet, principles and practices behind the apparent organizational chaos have helped to make this global British firm a competitor.

Sir Richard, founder and CEO of the Virgin Group, is one of the new breed of global leaders that business researchers Manfred Kets de Vries and Elizabeth Florent-Treacy[53] use as an example. The Group is headquartered in a suburb of London in the United Kingdom, but has an increasing presence in the United States and Asia, as well as Europe. Something of the philosophy and structure of the firms can be seen in the following excerpt from the group's Web site.

> *Having successfully run a student magazine in London in the late 1960s, Richard Branson and his colleagues decided to set up a record company. After days of argument and discussion they settled on the name Virgin. It sounded trendy and, as Richard said at the time, "We thought it was good because we could apply it to other businesses, not just music."*
>
> *Today, 96% of British consumers have heard of Virgin and it is one of the world's top 50 brands. Sometimes it appears in the list of well-known brands in countries where it doesn't even trade.*
>
> *Virgin has achieved all this in a unique way. The group's origins date back to the original mail-order record company, record shops and recording studio, which were all founded in the early 1970s. As Richard Branson grew the businesses during that decade, he followed [British economist] Schumacher's 'small is beautiful' philosophy and always set up new businesses, rather than managing Virgin as one big conglomerate. When he set up Virgin Atlantic Airways in 1984, this philosophy continued, as it did with all the new businesses of the 1990s [until the present]. So today Virgin is not really a group at all. Financial results are not aggregated centrally and each business runs its own affairs, but there is a collection of shared ownership, shared leadership and shared values. In many respects Virgin resembles a mixture of a branded venture capital organisation and a Japanese keiretsu (or society of business). The Japanese seem to think so anyway!*
>
> *What ties all the businesses together are the values of the brand and the philosophy of management. In the eyes of consumers, Virgin stands for value, quality, innovation, fun, and a sense of competitive challenge. Not all of [their] new businesses can achieve these values, especially when they grow out of old companies in need of rejuvenation (or Virginisation!). It is then that the organisation brings its management skills to bear.*

Management believe passionately in Virgin values and in what they are doing, and are convinced that together they can create the first global British brand name of the twenty-first century. Realizing this ambition is a highly motivating challenge and has already seen the creation of 200 companies worldwide that currently employ more than 25,000 people. Total revenues around the world in 1999 exceeded £3 billion (US$5 billion) in a variety of business areas.

Richard was born in 1950 of middle-class professional parents (his father was a lawyer, his mother, an actress and airline flight attendant), and was a teenage entrepreneur and "ordinary" student in the elite Stowe school. He quit without taking his final senior examinations in order to start a magazine called *Student*. There he was editor, publisher, and advertising manager. The venture was not an outstanding financial success, so in 1970, Branson advertised recordings of alternative music at a 15 percent discount over record stores in his magazine, thus beginning what was soon to be called Virgin Records. In 1984, after several ups and downs, Virgin Records was solidly successful. Branson then took another risk and started a unique, low-fare trans-Atlantic airline called Virgin Atlantic. In 1986, the company went public, but after a financial market downturn in 1987, Branson again took the company private, in 1988. Other ventures followed throughout the 1990s to bring the company to its present level of prominence.

Branson attributed his early success in the record company to the fact that they created independent, stand-lone companies. The difference was that other record companies at this time were selling rights to recordings to other companies. As Branson pointed out in an interview,[54]

> *Actually, a lot of companies evolved out of the record company. If you needed a record company, you needed shops to sell your products; you needed an export company to export your records; you needed foreign companies to distribute your records abroad and market them as well; you needed editing suites to edit your videos, and so on.*

The independent Virgin firms were developing, growing, and signing local groups to make recordings in Germany, France, Japan, and the United States.

In starting and growing Virgin Atlantic, Branson's friends and advisors thought he had gone crazy. In 1984, it was not economically feasible to make a profit in an airline. However, Branson felt that part of the problem was that airlines were managed abysmally at that time. He said:

> *Their way of doing business was really terrible. As far as service quality was concerned, the airline business was perhaps the worst run of almost any business I can think of. The big airlines tried to get away with as much as they could. They were either national airlines or just ex-national airlines. They charged as much as they could. Their costs had gone through the roof. They offered the customers the minimum because they could afford to do so, being monopolies or duopolies. We decided to get in there and compete and offer good-quality service. Looking back on that decision, the past ten years have been exhilarating, great fun.*

The fact that Virgin Atlantic has remained in business for more than 16 years is a tribute to the tenacity of Branson and the firm's management. Table 5.6 summarizes the essence of Virgin's competitive advantage.

Table 5.6 Key Points of Virgin's Unique Competitive Advantage

The key to Virgin's competitive advantage is the creative talents of individual employees, which is made apparent in the following areas:

Corporate Culture

- Putting the world "right"
- The notion of "family"; "People are our greatest asset."
- Cultural glue based on sense of community, bonds of group, not codified
- Friendly, egalitarian, nonhierarchical atmosphere
- Anybody with a crazy idea gets a hearing
- Empowerment: "We're in the business of making millionaires."
- Motivating people is key to organization's success: "If your staff is enjoying their work, they will perform well. Consequently, customers will enjoy their experience with your company."
- Staff should have happy memories of their time in the organization

Leadership Style

- Reassuring contact with followers
- Social worker, both with followers and in vision for new products (e.g., Mates condoms)
- Pragmatic idealist
- Extremely competitive
- Counterbalanced by strong executive role constellation
- Top person should enjoy himself so that others will feel free to have fun
- "Renaissance entrepreneur": 100 percent involvement in startup of new ventures, then delegate

Organizational Design

- Truly entrepreneurial and intrapreneurial organization; organic growth rather than acquisition
- "Small is beautiful"; small, autonomous units, small head office
- Work as an exciting adventure, challenging the status quo
- "If you do something for fun and create the best possible product, then the profit will come."
- No formal board meetings; employees encouraged to contact Branson directly with ideas, problems
- "Communication from bottom to top"; lateral communication
- Speed: employees get a quick response directly from Branson, or just "go ahead and do it"

Continuous Transformation and Change

- Share the wealth with people who have new ideas; create a sense of ownership
- Attract and develop mavericks
- Environment offers high degree of freedom and encourages original ideas; "Drive for change."
- "Creative adaptation"; avoiding the not-invented-here syndrome

Building a Global Organization

- *Keiretsu-like* system: more than 500 small companies around the world operating quasi-independently

Source: "An Interview with Richard Branson," in *The New Global Leaders* (San Francisco: Jossey-Bass, 1999), 56–57.

Key Issues for Discussion

1. Given the free-wheeling style of Branson and his managers, do you think that the Virgin enterprises can be classified as a TQ organization? Why or why not?
2. How well do you think that Branson and his managers perform the strategic planning process? What are some indications that they do, or do not do, strategic planning?
3. How well do you think that Branson and his managers perform managerial and leadership tasks? How might these tasks be better balanced?
4. What leadership theory do you think best fits the senior leadership of the Virgin Group? What theory would best fit Branson as leader? Why might they differ?

QUALITY IN PRACTICE

STRATEGIC PLANNING AND DEPLOYMENT AT SOLECTRON[55]

Solectron Corporation uses a three-pronged strategic planning process to keep pace with the rapidly changing electronic environment and the equally rapid growth of the company. The planning process includes a three-year strategic plan (called their long-range plan, or LRP) that is updated annually, an annual operating plan (AOP), and an annual improvement plan that sets specific goals and stretch targets for all units and processes within the company. Figure 5.17 summarizes their strategic planning process (SPP).

The first step in the SPP is a review of the company's mission, vision, values, and strategy. This process is led by the CEO, Ko Nishimura, and includes site general managers, senior VPs, and the corporate staff. They review current projected performance; previous years' mission, vision, strategy, and plans; and long-range technological,

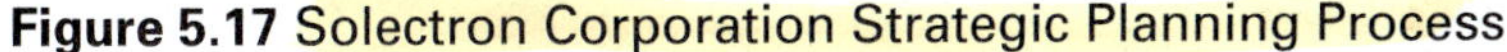

Figure 5.17 Solectron Corporation Strategic Planning Process

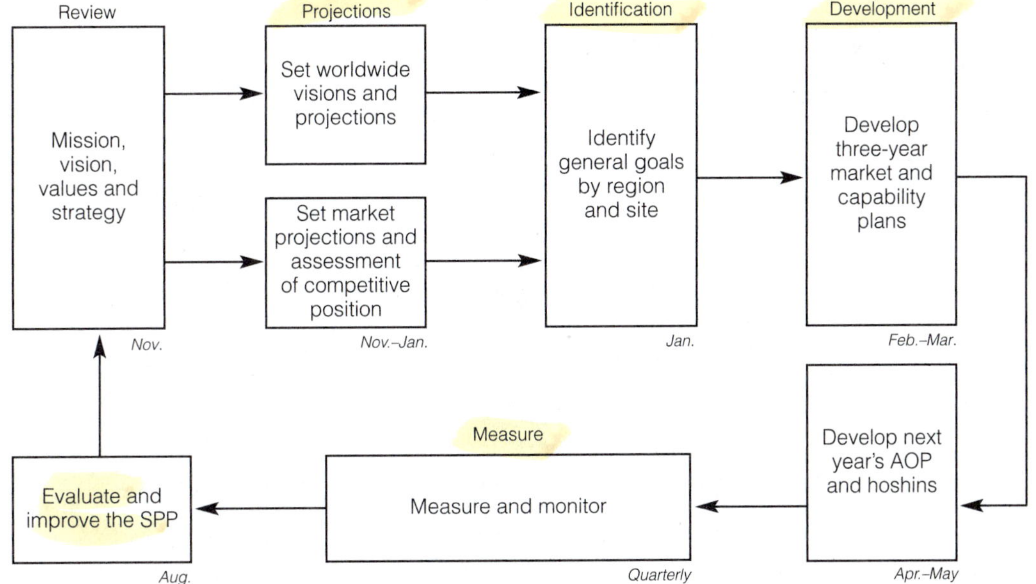

economic, and societal trends and risks to identify markets and services to be served, establish mid- to long-range financial targets, update the mission and vision as appropriate, and understand company capabilities. In developing market projections regional and site leaders and corporate staff develop their visions, business projections, and capability requirements. Account plans are developed for all customers. The corporate marketing group uses market and competitor information to assess risks. Information sources include industry tracking organizations, Solectron management and staff as well as the 10-k reports of publicly held competitors. The marketing group also distills competitor data into a quarterly report to senior management. This general information is used to fine-tune projections for local markets.

The inputs to the goal-setting process for regions and sites include the corporate mission, vision, and strategy, the worldwide market and competitor trends, and customer requirements. The output of this process is the strategies, market targets and financial targets for the regions and sites. Capability maps are also developed and the mission, vision, and strategies for the regions and sites are aligned with those of the corporation as a whole. Three-year market plans are developed based on local and regional projections. Plans for all regions are reviewed for alignment, and plans to fill capability gaps are also finalized.

Figure 5.18 shows the process for developing one-year action plans based on the three-year plan. The AOP is the first year of the LRP and represents the annual business plan. Solectron uses a hoshin planning process to deploy its strategic plan and define the annual improvement plan. Figure 5.19 shows the detailed process for developing the hoshin plan. Regional executives and the general managers at each production site determine their targets on the basis of their knowledge of customer requirements. Individual plans for each account and each site support Solectron's strategic objectives; however, managers still have considerable freedom in determining how to achieve goals for financial performance, customer satisfaction, and employee satisfaction.

Key Issues for Discussion

1. Compare Solectron's approach to the generic strategic planning process described in this chapter. What are some of its unique features?
2. Explain how the hoshin planning process

Figure 5.18 Solectron Corporation Action Plan Development Process

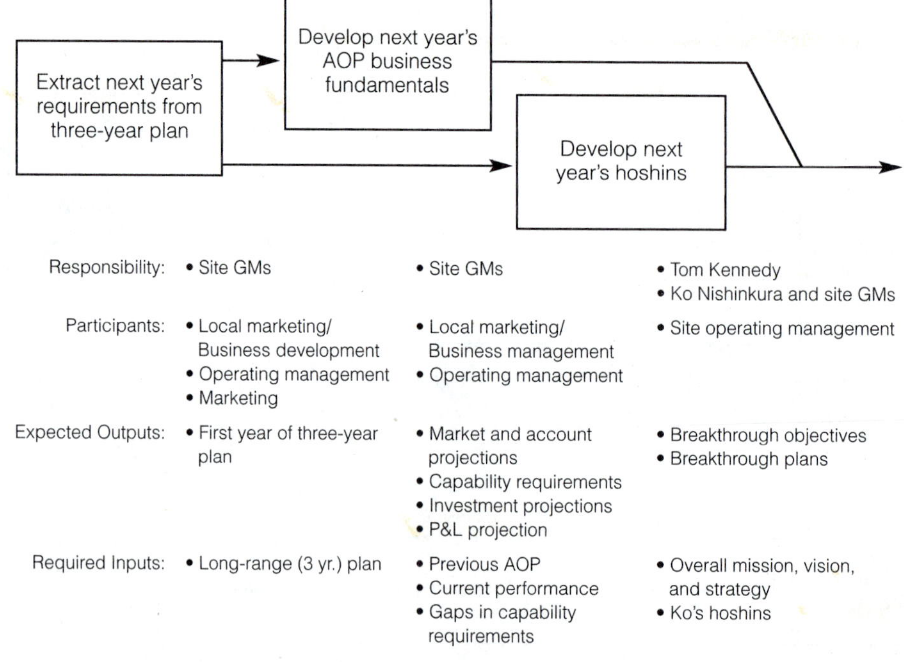

Figure 5.19 Solectron Corporation Hoshin Planning Process

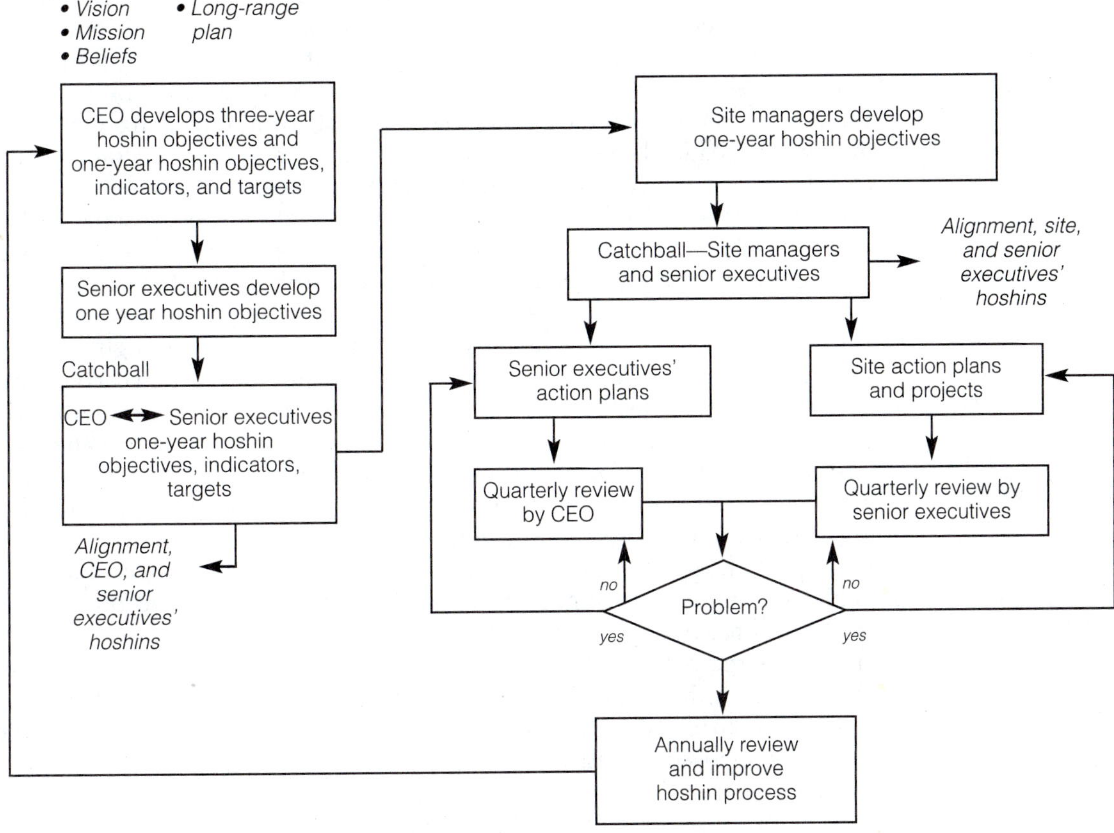

aligns site plans with corporate strategies. Why is this alignment especially important for a company such as Solectron? (You may wish to refer to the *Quality Profile* information in this chapter).

Summary of Key Points

- Leadership is the ability to positively influence people and systems under one's authority to have a meaningful impact and achieve important results. Leaders create clear and visible quality values and integrate these into the organization's strategy.
- Although we often equate leadership with the executive level of an organization, leadership is critical for the organization as a whole, among teams, and for individuals in their daily work.
- Five core leadership skills are vision, empowerment, intuition, self-understanding, and value congruence. These skills help true leaders to promote and practice total quality by creating a customer-driven vision, setting high expectations,

demonstrating personal involvement, integrating quality into daily management, and sustaining an environment for quality excellence.

- Leading practices for leadership include creating a customer-focused strategic vision and clear quality values that serve as a basis for business decisions, sustaining a leadership system and environment for empowerment, innovation, and organizational learning, setting high expectations and demonstrating substantial personal commitment and involvement in quality, integrating quality values into daily leadership and management, communicating extensively through the leadership structure and to all employees, and integrating public responsibilities and community support into business practices.
- Leadership has been studied from at least five major perspectives: the trait approach, the behavioral view, the contingency approach, and the role approach. Some of the new and emerging theories include attributional, transactional, and emotional intelligence theories.
- The leadership system refers to how leadership is exercised throughout a company, including how key decisions are made, communicated, and carried out at all levels; mechanisms for leadership development; and guidance regarding behaviors and practices. An effective leadership system creates clear values, and sets high expectations for performance and performance improvements, builds loyalties and teamwork, encourages initiative and risk taking, and subordinates organization to purpose and function.
- An important aspect of an organization's leadership is its responsibility to the public and its practice of good citizenship, including ethics and protection of public health, safety, and the environment.
- Strategy is the pattern of decisions that determines and reveals a company's goals, policies, and plans, and is determined through strategic planning. A focus on both customer-driven quality and operational performance excellence—as opposed to traditional financial and marketing goals—is essential to an effective strategy.
- Leading practices for effective strategic planning include active participation by top management, employees, and even customers or suppliers in the planning process; systematic planning systems for strategy development and deployment, including measurement, feedback, and review; gathering and analyzing a variety of data about external and internal factors; aligning short-term action plans with long-term strategic objectives and communicating them throughout the organization; and using measurements to track progress.
- Strategy development begins with determining the organization's mission, vision, and guiding principles; conducting an environmental assessment of customer and market requirements and expectations; evaluating the competitive environment; financial, societal, and other risks; and weighing human resource, operational, and supplier and partner capabilities. These aspects lead to strategies, strategic objectives, and action plans that set the direction for achieving the mission.
- Deployment refers to developing detailed action plans, defining resource requirements and performance measures, and aligning work unit, supplier, and partner plans with overall strategic objectives. Deploying strategy effectively is often done through a process called hoshin kanri. Hoshin kanri emphasizes organization-wide planning and setting of priorities, providing resources to meet objectives, and measuring performance as a basis for improving it. It is essentially a total quality approach to executing a strategy.

- The seven management and planning tools help managers to implement policy deployment and are useful in other areas of quality planning. These tools are the affinity diagram, interrelationship digraph, tree diagram, matrix diagram, matrix data analysis, process decision program chart, and arrow diagram.
- Common organizational structures are the line, line and staff, and matrix organization. Organizational structures for quality must reflect individual company differences and provide the flexibility and ability to change. Companies must understand that processes, rather than hierarchical reporting relationships, drive quality within the organization.
- Leadership and Strategic Planning are two of the seven categories of the Malcolm Baldrige National Quality Award Criteria for Performance Excellence. These categories address Organizational Leadership, Public Responsibility and Citizenship, Strategy Development, and Strategy Deployment.

REVIEW QUESTIONS

1. Define leadership. Why is it necessary for successful total quality management?
2. How does leadership relate to strategic planning?
3. List the key roles that senior executives play as leaders of their organizations.
4. List the five core leadership skills. Of what value are these skills in TQ?
5. What are the leading leadership practices of top managers in TQ-based organizations? Provide some examples of each.
6. Explain the traditional theories of leadership and their implications for total quality.
7. How do emerging theories differ from traditional theories? What implications do they have for TQ?
8. What is key concept of the theory of emotional maturity? How does it explain leadership in a TQ environment?
9. Define the term *leadership system*. What elements should an effective leadership system have?
10. What is the role of steering teams in many leadership systems?
11. Why are public responsibility and community support important elements of leadership?
12. What is a strategy? What elements do most strategies contain?
13. What are the leading practices for effective strategic planning?
14. Explain the basic strategic planning process.
15. Define mission, vision, and guiding principles. What is the purpose of each?
16. What is hoshin kanri? Provide a simplified description of this process.
17. How does catchball play an important role in policy deployment?
18. List and explain the major uses for the seven management and planning tools.
19. Describe the key contextual factors that affect organizational structure. What implications do they have for quality?
20. Describe the types of organization structure commonly used. What are the advantages or disadvantages of each?
21. What types of organization structures are common in TQ-based organizations today?
22. Explain how leadership and strategic planning are addressed in the Baldrige criteria.

Discussion Questions

1. We stated that leadership is the "driver" of a total quality system. What does this statement imply and what implications does it have for future CEOs? Middle managers? Supervisors?
2. Provide examples from your own experiences in which leaders (not necessarily company managers—consider academic unit heads, presidents of student organizations, and even family members) exhibited one or more of the five core leadership skills described in this chapter. What impacts did these skills have on the organization?
3. State some examples in which leaders you have worked for have exhibited some of the leading practices described in this chapter. Can you provide examples for which they have not?
4. Discuss the 17 leadership competencies identified in the Zenger-Miller study. Do you feel that they describe leadership or simply management? Why?
5. Review Deming's 14 Points in Chapter 3. What aspects of leadership theories are evident in them, either individually or as a holistic philosophy?
6. Give examples of different "situational conditions" that would affect leadership styles according to Fiedler's model. As a company moves from a little to a high degree of TQ adoption, how do the situational conditions change? What do these changes mean for leadership?
7. How does the Xerox Leadership Through Quality strategy support TQ?
8. How can TQ principles improve the process of strategic planning?
9. The Johnson & Johnson credo was written in 1943 by its chairman Robert Wood Johnson: "We believe our first responsibility is to the doctors, nurses and patients, to mothers and fathers and all others who use our products and services. In meeting their needs, everything we do must be of high quality." What would you expect to see in Johnson & Johnson's leadership and strategic planning approaches that reflect this philosophy?
10. Examine the following mission statements. Do you think they have a true purpose or are they merely cosmetic devices because someone felt that no major company can be seen without one?[56]
    a. Our single focus will continue to be helping customers all over the world succeed in their businesses. When we do that—when we make them winners—then employees, dealers, and stockholders win as well.
    b. XYZ strives to understand and fulfill the needs of all our customers by providing the highest level of reliability and service at all times.
    c. XYZ creates value by providing transportation-related products and services with superior quality, safety, and environmental care to demanding customers in selected segments.
    d. We are dedicated to being the world's best at bringing people together—giving them easy access to each other and to the information and services they want and need—anytime, anywhere.
11. Try to match the following companies with their actual mission statement in question 10. Could you think of more appropriate mission statements for any of these organizations?
    a. Volvo
    b. AT&T
    c. Caterpillar
    d. DHL Worldwide Express

12. Contrast the following vision statements in terms of their usefulness to an organization.
    a. To become the industry leader and achieve superior growth and market share.
    b. To become the best-managed electric utility in the United States and an excellent company overall and be recognized as such.
    c. Being the best at everything we do, exceeding customer expectations; growing our business to increase its value to customers, employees, shareowners, and communities in which we work.
13. Propose three applications for each of the seven management and planning tools discussed in the chapter. You might consider some applications around school, such as in the classroom, studying for exams, and so on.
14. Discuss how each of the following quality values, which are the core values and concepts underlying the Baldrige criteria, are reflected in each item of the Baldrige criteria for strategic planning (i.e., 2.1 Strategy Development, and 2.2 Strategy Deployment): customer-driven excellence, visionary leadership, organizational and personal learning, valuing employees and partners, agility, managing for innovation, focus on the future, management by fact, public responsibility and citizenship, focus on results and creating value, and systems perspective.
15. Suppose you received the examiner feedback for the Collin Technologies example. What would you do in response to the feedback?
16. Compare and contrast the 2000 and 2001 Baldrige business criteria for the Leadership and Strategic Planning categories (available on CD-rom). What are the key differences and management implications?

Problems

1. "Let's plan a graduation party for our seniors," suggested Jim Teacher, president of the Delta Mu Zeta fraternity at State U. Everyone on the fraternity council thought that it was a good idea, so they agreed to brainstorm ideas for the party.

   "First, we have to pick a date," suggested Joe. "It'll have to be after final exams are over, but before graduation."

   "That narrows it down pretty quickly to June 8, 9, or 10. The 11th is a Sunday and the 12th is graduation day," said Jim. "I propose that we try for Thursday the 8th, with the alternate date of Friday, the 9th. We'll have to take a vote at the fraternity meeting tomorrow."

   "Now, let's list things that have to be done in order to get ready for the party," suggested Amber. They quickly produced the following list (not in any order).

   Pick date
   Plan menu
   Get food delivered
   Estimate costs
   Locate and book a hall
   Determine budget
   Select music
   Hire a DJ
   Plan decorations
   Setup, decorate hall

Determine how much can be paid from treasury and what the cost of the special assessment will be for each member
Design and print invitations
Set up mailing list
Dress rehearsal (day before party) "dummy activity"
Mail invitations
Plan ceremony for seniors
Rehearse ceremony
Plan after-party cleanup and bill-paying
Have the party
Clean up and pay bills

Next, they selected Joe as the "project manager" because he had fraternity party planning experience and was taking a quality management course where he was exposed to the seven management and planning tools.

a. Put yourself in Joe's position. Develop an interrelationship digraph for the party planners. Draw arrows from one activity to the next one that must occur. Note that the activities that have the most arrows going into them will tend to be the long-range results. Activities having the most arrows originating from them will tend to be the initial activities.
b. What can you conclude from the graph? How would this digraph help make the job of organizing the party easier for the project team?

2. Creative Design Group (CDG) designs brochures for companies, trade groups and associations. Their emphasis on customer service is based on speed, quality, creativity, and value. They want each brochure to "wow" the customer in its design, meet or exceed the preparation deadline, and be of superior quality at a reasonable price. Value is emphasized over price, because the president, Trendy Art, believes that CDG's experienced staff should emphasize high quality and creativity instead of price. They accomplish their primary objectives 97 percent of the time.

To carry out their objectives, the small company has four designers, a customer service estimator (CSE), and Trendy, who is the creative director and strategic visionary. The work environment, in a converted garage behind Trendy's house, features modern (though not always state-of-the-art) computer hardware and software, excellent lighting, and modern communications for sending design documents to clients and printers. Designers generally work independently of each other, consulting with the CSE when status updates or client-initiated changes are requested. They also consult with Trendy, who signs off on the creative design, after consultation with each client. A casual dress code and work policies, and a number of perks for workers, such as health insurance, flextime, generous vacation and sick leave benefits, a 401K retirement plan, competitive wages, and so on, have, in the past, made it easy to attract and retain talented people. However, with fewer talented people graduating from design schools in the area, and more competitive firms bidding up salaries, turnover has become an issue.

The CSE, Green Ishied, is the contact point for all projects, of which there may be 10 to 20 active at any one time. He must ensure that projects are carefully estimated and prepare proposals, track progress of each project, and communicate with clients on status and change requests. He is also responsible for advertising and promotion of the firm.

Trendy's husband, Hy, is a CPA and part-time accountant for the company. He has noticed recently that costs are increasing, the percentage of bids accepted is decreasing, and the ROI is slipping.

Develop an affinity diagram that captures the major organizational features and issues. How could this diagram help Trendy develop a three- to five-year strategic plan for CDG?

3. Given the situation in problem 2, Trendy has determined several long-range objectives, among which are outdistancing the competition so as to grow the business by 10 percent per year for each of the next five years (a 61 percent compound growth rate), and adding a new designer every two years. These goals are key ingredients for increasing her profitability by 10 percent per year. To accomplish her objectives, she must deal with the two major issues of the increasing competition and employee recruitment and retention in order to develop effective action plans to support her long-range plan. Develop a tree diagram, starting with "Develop action plans" as the main theme. At the next level, include the two main issues. One, for example is, "Develop a plan to meet competition." Then break each of the issues into two or three feasible proposals, such as "Make advertising more effective," under the previous item of "Develop a plan to meet competition." Finally, add another level of specificity with two to four items, such as "Place ads in business newspaper," "Redesign Web page," and so on under the "Make advertising more effective" item.
4. Jim Teacher (see problem 1) was able to get some estimating information from the president of another fraternity that had planned and carried out a similar party for graduating seniors last year. They had not kept financial information, but they did have the actual hours that it took to complete each activity. From these data, Jim obtained the following time estimates for Delta Mu Zeta.

Activity	*Time Estimate (days)*
Pick date	1
Plan menu	2
Get food delivered	1
Estimate costs	3
Locate and book a hall	5
Determine budget	3
Select music	2
Select and hire a DJ	3
Plan decorations	2
Setup, decorate hall	1
Dress rehearsal (day before party) "dummy activity"	0
Determine how much can be paid from treasury and what the cost of the special assessment will be for each member	1
Design and print invitations	3
Set up mailing list	5
Mail invitations	1
Plan ceremony for seniors	2
Rehearse ceremony	1
Plan after-party cleanup and bill-paying	2
Have the party	1
Cleanup and pay bills	1

a. You are Joe, the project manager. Use the interrelationship digraph developed in problem 1 to draw an arrow diagram, making sure that activities are sequenced in the correct order.

b. If you are familiar with PERT/CPM through other courses, use the preceding data to calculate the minimum time that the project will take, that is, compute the critical path.

5. Given Creative Design Group's (CDG) situation in problem 2 and Trendy's development of strategic objectives in problem 3, she decided that, along with improving her recruiting processes for new and replacement hiring, it was time to replace the computer system with state-of-the-art hardware and software. Knowing that she and her staff did not have the expertise to design the type of system that they needed, Trendy looked around, analyzed three competing firms' proposals, and finally settled on Creative Computer Group (CCG) to act as consultants and system integrators. Before signing the contract, Trendy decided to ask Hy and Green Ishied (the CSE) to meet with her and the CEO of CCG to clarify the system design requirements and the wording of the contract.

Trendy, Hy, and Green all agreed that the system needed to be completely integrated, with the capability to gather cost and scheduling data directly from the designers, and to produce all necessary business reports, as well as having graphics capability. Both cost and design information would have to be available to everyone in the firm. Therefore, the network should be capable of interfacing Macintosh and PC desktops via USB connections, with common printers. It should also provide for high bandwidth Internet access and capability to send and receive graphic and text data files. Charlie Nerd, the president of CCG, said that all of those requirements could be met by the system that he would design. This project was so important for his company that he would personally be the project manager for the installation and testing of the new system. After outlining the plans for the system, Charlie asked if they had any questions. Trendy, High, and Green had no immediate questions, but promised to get back to Charlie within three days.

a. Given the following information, perform a matrix data analysis to determine why, or if, CCG should get the contract to install the computer system. Justify your analysis.

Supplier Characteristics	Weights	Rating for CCG	Rating for COG	Rating for COW	Weighted Value CCG	Weighted Value COG	Weighted Value COW
System design reliability	0.3	8	6	5			
Delivery timeliness	0.2	7	4	9			
Cost	0.2	5	7	6			
System service	0.2	9	6	4			
Experience	0.1	4	9	6			
Totals	1.0						

Note: Independent ratings on a scale of 1–10 (where 10 is best) were performed by the Small Business Council of Qualdale, where CDG is located.

Suppliers: CCG = Creative Computer Group
COG = Computer Organizational Group
COW = Computer Operations Workgroup

b. What questions would you suggest that Trendy, Hy, and Green ask Charlie?
c. Construct a process decision program chart, similar to Figure 5.13 in the chapter, but closely reflecting CCG's training needs. What special considerations would need to be included in training graphic designers with little business knowledge and business-oriented people (such as Hy and Green) with little artistic design knowledge, about each other's areas of work in order to use an integrated system?

Projects, Etc.

1. Using the information in this chapter, design a questionnaire that might be used to understand leadership effectiveness in an organization.
2. Interview someone you know about the leadership characteristics of their supervisor. What leadership style does he or she appear to reflect?
3. Interview managers at some local organizations to determine whether they have well-defined missions, visions, and guiding principles. If they do, how are they translated into strategy? If not, what steps should they take?
4. Find several examples of mission and vision statements for *Fortune* 500 companies. Critique these statements with respect to their usefulness, relevance to the organization, and ability to inspire and motivate employees.
5. Does your university or college have a mission and strategy? How might policy deployment be used in a university setting? Discuss with a senior executive administrator at your college or university (such as the VP of Administration or the VP of Academic Affairs) how policy deployment is, or might be, done.
6. Research the leadership and strategic planning practices of recent Baldrige Award winners. Discuss different approaches that these firms use and why they seem appropriate for their organizations. How do they reflect the leading practices described in this chapter?
7. In your role as a student, develop your own statements of mission, vision, and guiding principles. How would you create a strategy to achieve your mission and vision?
8. Compare the organizational structures of several companies. What differences are reflected in their quality approaches and results?

Cases

I. Teaching the Buffalo to Fly: Johnsonville Foods[57]

Ralph C. Stayer, owner and CEO of Johnsonville Foods Co. in Sheboygan Falls, Wisconsin, has been profiled by Tom Peters in his book *Thriving on Chaos* and the PBS video program, *The Leadership Alliance.*[58] Stayer revealed his leadership secrets in the book that he coauthored with James A. Belasco under the intriguing title of *Flight of the Buffalo.*[59] Stayer was responsible for initiating the process that transformed a sleepy, family-owned sausage-making company into a nationally recognized firm that is using an innovative self-management process to remain healthy in an increasingly competitive industry. In the first chapter of his book, Stayer compares his company to a herd of buffalo that follows a single leader wherever the leader wants them to go. In the old West when buffalo hunters wanted to kill a lot of buffalo, they just killed the lead buffalo. The rest of the herd was easily cut down, because they would stop and mill around the fallen leader, waiting for him to lead them to safety.

Stayer wanted to change the leadership paradigm to encourage his employees to become responsible, interdependent workers, more like a flock of wild geese. Geese fly in their typical "V" formation, with different birds taking the lead at different points in time. Essentially, they share the leadership load. He stated that the leadership principles for the new paradigm include the following points:

1. Leaders transfer ownership of the work to those who execute the work.
2. Leaders create the environment for ownership where each person wants to be responsible.
3. Leaders coach the development of personal capabilities.
4. Leaders learn fast themselves and encourage others also to learn quickly.[60]

Ralph Stayer began to transform Johnsonville in the early 1980s before the firm reached a point of crisis. It was a small regional meat packer that was strong in Wisconsin and beginning to make some inroads into surrounding states. Over the next 10 years, through his efforts and those of the company's "associates," their return on assets doubled, sales increased nine times, and product and quality levels improved significantly, even though the company was in a mature and declining industry.

Stayer tried the "prescriptions" of job descriptions, MBO, communication improvement methods, and even an early version of quality circles to transform the company's culture. None stood the test of time nor his gut feel for what changes were needed in the company. He felt that his small entrepreneurial firm had the potential to be great, but was only performing up to the average measures in the industry.

The Palmer Sausage decision, detailed in a 1985 Harvard Business School case, was the turning point for employee learning and empowerment.[61] Palmer Sausage Co., a larger regional competitor, had a product that it wanted to distribute, but the firm was consolidating plants and contacted Johnsonville about the possibility of providing some extra capacity. Although this "golden opportunity" would help the company grow, Johnsonville would have to build a new plant, hire additional workers, and make other improvements. Meanwhile, if Palmer didn't like Johnsonville's product it could cancel the contract with a 30-day notice, leaving Johnsonville in a vulnerable position with unused plant capacity and too many workers on the payroll. Instead of making an executive decision, Ralph Stayer empowered his workers and managers to study the problem and decide whether to accept Palmer's offer. Many small groups met and discussed the decision and decided to accept the offer.

The employees rose to the challenge. Initially, they worked six or seven days per week while the new plant was being built. The new employees were brought on board and trained, and the old employees rapidly learned new skills. The quality levels for both Johnsonville and Palmer products rose, despite the strain of high production. The new plant was successfully brought on line in 1987.

A result that is perhaps even more significant is the degree to which employees have taken over both strategic and operating management responsibilities at Johnsonville Foods. In Stayer's words:

> *Profoundly, Johnsonville people learned what they needed to do. They learned to be responsible for more of the strategic decisions at Johnsonville. They changed the career tracking system and set new team performance standards. Then they went on transforming themselves from buffalo into geese.*

Capital budgeting, new product development, scheduling, hiring and firing, quality and productivity measurement, and a number of other strategic and operating decisions are now made by teams of line employees at Johnsonville.

In summary, Stayer sees the key to leadership success as doing the job of changing the leadership paradigm, owning up to being part of the problem as a traditional manager, empowering employees to do the jobs that they are capable of doing and growing into, coaching and rewarding performance in multiple ways, and learning, learning, learning.

Discussion Questions

1. From a strategic management standpoint, does Ralph Stayer provide sufficient planning and control to keep the company on track?
2. What type of management style does he seem to follow? Does it fit any of the leadership theories that were developed in the chapter?
3. How easy or difficult would it be for other companies to duplicate the leadership style of Stayer and the organizational systems practiced at Johnsonville Foods?

II. Corryville Foundry Company[62]

Corryville Foundry Company (CFC) was founded in the mid-1940s in a 3,000-square-foot building with nine people as a small family business to produce castings. In the 1960s, as business grew, the company expanded its facilities and its capability to develop its own tooling patterns, eventually moving into a 40,000-square-foot building. Over this time period, the foundry industry declined from more than 12,000 companies to about 4,000.

With such a shrinking market, CFC began to listen more to its customers. They discovered that customers were not happy with the quality of the products they had been receiving. In 1989 CFC made a commitment to quality by hiring a quality assurance manager, Ronald Chalmer. Chalmer felt that upper management was committed to quality and saw an opportunity to change the company's culture. He also firmly believed in Deming's philosophy. One of the first things he did was to work with upper management in developing a mission statement:

> *Our mission at CFC is to improve the return on investment. We can accomplish this by changing attitudes and incorporating a quality/team environment. This will improve the quality of our products, enhance our productivity (which in turn will allow us to quote competitive prices) and elevate our service and response level to our customers. There are several factors which make positive change imperative.*
>
> *The standards for competitive levels of quality and service are becoming more demanding. The emergence of the "World Market" has brought on new challenges. We are in a low-growth, mature market. In order for CFC to improve return on investment, we must develop a strategy to improve quality and responsiveness in all areas of the company. We need to have all employees recognize the importance of product quality and service and move toward more favorable pricing. We need to change thinking throughout the organization to get employees involved, to encourage teamwork, to develop a more flexible workforce and adaptable organization. We need to instill pride in the workplace and the product.*
>
> *We believe that we can best achieve the desired future state by study of and adherence to the teachings of W. Edwards Deming.*

Under Chalmer's direction, CFC made some substantial improvements in the quality of castings, particularly reducing scrap and reject rates. He worked closely with the factory workers directly responsible for the products, asking them what they needed to get the job done and ensuring management commitment to provide the necessary resources. For example, CFC invested in a new controller for the furnaces that provided a digital readout of temperature. With this technology, workers were able to categorize the metal temperatures needed for each casting type and were able to adjust the process as needed. The success of this project led the company to empower employees to control many other aspects of the system.

Three years later, the president and CEO retired. The new CEO, who had been a vice president of a major manufacturing company, did not feel that the mission statement provided a clear and vivid direction. Consequently, he set up a planning retreat for senior management (including Chalmer) to develop a new strategic vision.

Discussion Questions

1. Comment on the current mission statement. Does it provide the strategic direction necessary for success for this company?
2. How can the mission statement be improved? Suggest a better statement of mission, vision, and guiding principles.

III. Collin Technologies: Organizational Leadership

Read Item 1.1, Organizational Leadership, in the Collin Technologies case study on the CD-rom accompanying this book. Using the 2000 Baldrige criteria, develop a list of strengths and opportunities for improvement similar to the style in Example 1. Strengths should focus on things the company is doing exceptionally well and support their vision and strategy. (Read the Business Overview section of the case first to identify specific factors that are important to customer satisfaction and relationships.) Opportunities for improvement should highlight issues in its approach or deployment that that can better meet the requirements of the Baldrige criteria. Your comments should include a reason for why a strength or opportunity for improvement is important; that is, provide some insight to upper-level managers that they might not have otherwise realized. Use the wording in the scoring guidelines in Table 3.6 to help you structure your comments.

IV. Collin Technologies: Strategic Planning

Read Category 2, Strategic Planning, in the Collin Technologies case study on the CD-rom accompanying this book. Using the 2000 Baldrige Criteria and the other instructions in Case III, develop a list of strengths and opportunities for improvement similar to the style in Example 1 and the additional instructions in Case III.

NOTES

1. Jack Welch, Herb Kelleher, Geoffrey Colvin, and John Huey, "How to Create Great Companies and Keep Them That Way," *Fortune* 139, no. 1 (1999), 163.
2. Rick Edgeman, Su Mi Park Dahigaard, Jens J. Dalhgaard, and Franz Scherer, "On Leaders and Leadership," *Quality Progress,* October 1999, 49–54.
3. William Bridges "Leading the De-Jobbed Organization," in *The Leader of the Future,* Frances Hesselbein, Marshall Goldsmith, and Richard Beckhard, eds. (San Francisco: Jossey-Bass, 1996), 16–17.
4. R. E. Byrd, "Corporate Leadership Skills: A New Synthesis," *Organizational Dynamics,* Summer 1987, 34–43.
5. Award, The Newsletter of Baldrigeplus, May 7, 2000. *http://www.baldrigeplus.com.*
6. J. R. P. French, Jr., and B. H. Raven, "The Bases of Social Power," in *Group Dynamics: Research and Theory*, D. Cartwright and A. Zanders, eds., 2d ed. (New York: Harper & Row, 1960), 607–623.
7. Xerox Quality Solutions, *A World of Quality: The Timeless Passport* (Milwaukee, WI: ASQC Quality Press, 1993), 5.
8. Robert Haavind and the editors of *Electronic Business, The Road to the Baldrige Award* (Boston: Butterworth-Heinemann, 1992), 50–51.
9. Robert Slater, *Jack Welch and the GE Way* (New York: McGraw-Hill, 1999), 219.
10. R. M. Stogdill, *Handbook of Leadership* (New York: The Free Press, 1974).
11. E. A. Fleishman and E. F. Harris "Patterns of Leadership Behavior Related to Employee Grievances and Turnover," *Personnel Psychology* (1962), 15, 43–56.
12. Rensis Likert, *The Human Organization: Its Management and Value* (New York: McGraw-Hill, 1967).
13. Douglas McGregor, *The Human Side of Enterprise* (New York: McGraw-Hill, 1960).
14. R. R. Blake and J. S. Mouton, *The Managerial Grid* (Houston: Gulf Publishing, 1965).
15. Frederick E. Fiedler, *A Theory of Leadership Effectiveness* (New York: McGraw-Hill, 1967).
16. V. H. Vroom and A. G. Jago, *The New Leadership* (Englewood Cliffs, NJ: Prentice Hall, 1988).
17. Henry Mintzberg, *Mintzberg on Management: Inside Our Strange World of Organizations* (New York: The Free Press, 1989). Also, *The Nature of Managerial Work* (New York: Harper & Row, 1973); "The Manager's Job: Folklore and Fact," *Harvard Business Review*, July/August 1975.
18. R. J. House "A 1976 Theory of Charismatic Leadership" in *Leadership: The Cutting Edge,* J. G. Hunt and L. L. Larson, eds. (Carbondale, IL: Southern Illinois University Press, 1977), 189–207. Also, J. A. Conger, *The Charismatic Leader: Behind the Mystique of Exceptional Leadership* (San Francisco: Jossey-Bass, 1989).
19. Op cit. James M. Burns; N. M. Tichy and D. O. Ulrich, etc. See note 9.
20. Op cit. Jon P. Howell et al. See note 10.
21. Op cit. Daniel Goleman. See note 11.
22. Judith R. Gordon, *A Diagnostic Approach to Organizational Behavior,* 3d ed. (Boston: Allyn and Bacon, 1991), 341–370.
23. R. M. Stogdill, *Handbook of Leadership* (New York: The Free Press, 1974).
24. J. J. Dahlgaard, A. Norgaard, and S. Jakobsen, "Styles of Success," *European Quality,* November/December 1997, 36–39; and J. J. Dahlgaard, A. Norgaard, and S. Jakobsen, "Profile of Success," *European Quality,* January/February 1998, 30–33. Cited in Edgeman et al. (see note 2).

25. R. M. Stogdill, see note 15; R. House and M. Baetz, "Leadership: Some Generalizations and New Research Directions," in *Research in Organizational Behavior*, B. M. Staw, ed. (Greenwich, CT: JAI Press, 1979), 359.

26. "Customer Focus: One of Seventeen Core Leadership Competencies" excerpted from "An Essay from Zenger-Miller: Updating the Meaning of Leadership: A Grass-Roots Model for the Workplace" (no other citation given), *The Quality Observer*, January 1997, 28–29.

27. Douglas McGregor, *The Human Side of Enterprise* (New York: McGraw-Hill, 1960).

28. R. R. Blake and J. S. Mouton, *The Managerial Grid* (Houston: Gulf Publishing, 1965).

29. Op cit. note 20.

30. Victor H. Vroom and Phillip W. Yetton, *Leadership and Decision Making* (Pittsburgh, PA: University of Pittsburgh Press, 1973).

31. V. H. Vroom and A. G. Jago, *The New Leadership* (Englewood Cliffs, NJ: Prentice Hall, 1988).

32. Robert J. House, "A Path-Goal Theory of Leadership Effectiveness," *Administrative Science Quarterly* 16 (1971), 321–328; R. J. House and T. R. Mitchell, "Path-Goal Theory of Leadership," *Journal of Contemporary Business* (Autumn 1974), 81–98.

33. P. Hershey and K. H. Blanchard, *Management of Organizational Behavior*, 5th ed. (Englewood Cliffs, NJ: Prentice Hall, 1988).

34. Edward J. Feeney, "At Emery Air Freight: Positive Reinforcement Boosts Performance," *Organizational Dynamics* 1, no. 3 (1973), 41–50.

35. Op cit. note 22.

36. Reprinted by permission from Don Hellriegel, John W. Slocum, Jr., and Richard W. Woodman, *Organizational Behavior*, 6th ed. (St. Paul, MN: West, 1992), 413–414. All rights reserved.

37. The term *transformational leadership* has been attributed to James M. Burns. See his book, *Leadership* (New York: Harper & Row, 1978). N. M. Tichy and D. O. Ulrich, "The Leadership Challenge: A Call For the Transformational Leader," *Sloan Management Review* 26 (1984), 59–68; N. M. Tichy and M. A. Devanna, *The Transformational Leader* (New York: John Wiley, 1986); B. M. Bass, *Leadership and Performance Beyond Expectations* (New York: The Free Press, 1985).

38. Philip Atkinson, "Leadership, Total Quality and Cultural Change," *Management Services* (June 1991), 16–19.

39. Jon P. Howell et al., "Substitutes for Leadership: Effective Alternatives for Ineffective Leadership," *Organizational Dynamics* (Summer 1990). Also see Steve Kerr and John Jermier, "Substitutes for Leadership: Their Meaning and Measurement," *Organizational Behavior and Human Performance*, December 1978, and Jon P. Howell, Peter W. Dorfman, and Steven Kerr, "Moderator Variables in Leadership Research," *Academy of Management Review*, March 1986.

40. Daniel Goleman, "What Makes a Leader?" *Harvard Business Review*, November/December, 1998, 93-–02. and Daniel Goleman, *Working With Emotional Intelligence* (New York: Bantam Books, 1998).

41. Solar Turbines, Inc., *Malcolm Baldrige National Quality Award Application Summary*, 1999, 4.

42. AT&T Quality Steering Committee, *Leading the Quality Initiative*, AT&T Bell Laboratories, 1990, 13–14.

43. James Brian Quinn, *Strategies for Change: Logical Incrementalism* (Homewood, IL: Richard D. Irwin, 1980).

44. Henry Mintzberg, "The Fall and Rise of Strategic Planning," *Harvard Business Review*, January/February 1994, 107–114.

45. "Strategic Planning: What Works . . . And What Doesn't," based on APQC's Third Knowledge Symposium, 1999. *http://www.apqc.org*.

46. Bob King, *Hoshin Planning: The Developmental Approach* (Methuen, MA: GOAL/QPC, 1989).

47. M. Imai, *Kaizen: The Key to Japan's Competitive Success* (New York: McGraw-Hill, 1986), 144–145.

48. Adapted from Kersi F. Munshi, "Policy Deployment: A Key to Long-Term TQM Success," *ASQC Quality Congress Transactions* (Boston, 1993), 236-–244.

49. The Ernst & Young Quality Improvement Consulting Group, *Total Quality: An Executive's Guide for the 1990s* (Homewood, IL: Dow Jones-Irwin, 1990).

50. Kermit F. Wasmuth, "Organization and Planning," in *Quality Management Handbook*, Loren Walsh, Ralph Wurster, and Raymond J. Kimber, eds. (Wheaton, IL: Hitchcock Publishing Company, 1986), 9–34.

51. Ricardo Simler, *Maverick* (New York: Warner Books, 1993), 196.

52. Adapted from Manfred F. R. Kets de Vries, "Charisma in Action: The Transformational Abilities of Virgin's Richard Branson and ABB's Percy Barnevik," *Organizational Dynamics* 26, no. 3 (January 1, 1998), 6.

53. Manfred F.R. Kets de Vries and Elizabeth Florent-Treacy, *The New Global Leaders: Richard Branson, Percy Barnevik, and David Simon* (San Francisco: Jossey-Bass Publishers, 1999), xiii–xiv. © 1999. Reprinted by permission of Jossey-Bass, Inc. A subsidiary of John Wiley & Sons, Inc.

54. Ibid., "An Interview with Richard Branson," in *The New Global Leaders* (San Francisco: Jossey-Bass Publishers, 1999), 40. Reprinted by permission of Jossey-Bass, Inc. a subsidiary of John Wiley & Sons, Inc.

55. Information extracted from Solectron Corporation, Malcolm Baldrige National Quality Award Application Summary, 1997.

56. "Missions for All Seasons," Across the Board, April 2000, 12.

57. Information for this case study was adapted from several sources, including Ralph Stayer, "How I Learned to Let My Workers Lead," *Harvard Business Review,* November/December 1990, 66–83; James A. Belasco and Ralph C. Stayer, *Flight of the Buffalo: Soaring to Excellence, Learning to Let Employees Lead* (New York: Warner Books, Inc., 1993); Tom Peters, *Thriving on Chaos: Handbook for a Management Revolution* (New York: Alfred A. Knopf, 1987). Additional information is also available in the Harvard cases by M. J. Roberts, Johnsonville Sausage Co. (A), [#9-387-103]; Johnsonville Sausage Co. (B), [#9-393-063]; HBR Videotape [9-888-517].

58. Tom Peters, *Thriving on Chaos: Handbook for a Management Revolution* (New York: Alfred A. Knopf, 1987); Tom Peters, "The Leadership Alliance," videotape, Video Publishing House, Inc., 1988.

59. James A. Belasco and Ralph C. Stayer, *Flight of the Buffalo: Soaring to Excellence, Learning to Let Employees Lead* (New York: Warner Books, 1993).

60. Ibid., 19.

61. Johnsonville Sausage, Harvard Business School (1985), Cases #9-387-103 and #9-393-063.

62. This fictitious case stems from a real company. We thank our students John P. Rosiello and David Seilkop for contributing the research.

BIBLIOGRAPHY

AT&T Quality Steering Committee. *Batting 1000: Using Baldrige Feedback to Improve Your Business.* AT&T Bell Laboratories, 1992.

AT&T Quality Steering Committee. *Policy Deployment.* AT&T Bell Laboratories, 1992.

Bass, B. M. *Leadership and Performance Beyond Expectations.* New York: The Free Press, 1985.

Bennis, Warren, and Burt Nanus, *Leaders: The Strategies for Taking Charge.* New York: Harper & Row, 1985, 15.

Brager, Joan. "The Customer-Focused Quality Leader." *Quality Progress* 25, no. 5 (May 1992), 51–53.

Conger, J., and R. Kanugo. "Toward a Behavioral Theory of Charismatic Leadership in Organizational Settings." *Academy of Management Review* (October 1987), 637–647.

Coud, Dana M. "The Function of Organizational Principles and Process," in *Quality Control and Reliability Management,* ASQC Education and Training Institute. Milwaukee: ASQC, 1969, 6-1 to 6-3.

Emery, F. E., E. L. Trist, and J. Woodward. *Management and Technology.* London: Her Majesty's Stationery Office, 1958.

Evans, James R., and James W. Dean, Jr. *Total Quality: Management, Organization, and Strategy,* 2d ed. Cincinnati, OH: South-Western, 2000.

Hart, Christopher W. L., and Christopher E. Bogan. *The Baldrige.* New York: McGraw-Hill, 1992.

Juran, J. M. *Juran on Quality by Design.* New York: The Free Press, 1992.

Kenyon, David A. "Strategic Planning with the Hoshin Process," *Quality Digest,* May 1997, 55–63.

Kukla, R. E. "Organizing a Manufacturing Improvement Program." *Quality Progress,* November 1983, 28.

Lawrence, P. R., and J. W. Lorsch. *Organization and Environment.* Boston: Harvard University, Division of Research, Graduate School of Business Administration, 1967.

"Learning to Compete Through Quality," *The Quality Observer,* January 1997, 10–24.

Profiles of Malcolm Baldrige Award Winners. Boston: Allyn & Bacon, 1992.

Rue, L. W., and L. Byars. *Management Theory and Application,* 9th ed. New York: McGraw-Hill/Irwin, 1999.

St. Lawrence, Dennis, and Bob Stinnett. "Powerful Planning With Simple Techniques." *Quality Progress* 27, no. 7 (July 1994), 57–64.

Taylor, Glenn L., and Martha N. Morgan, "The Reverse Appraisal: A Tool for Leadership Development," *Quality Progress* 28, 12, (December 1995), 81–87.

Tedesco, Frank M. "Building Quality Goals into the Business Plan." *The Total Quality Review* 4, no. 1 (March/April 1994), 31–34.

U.S. Department of Commerce and Booz-Allen & Hamilton, Inc. Total Quality Management (TQM): Implementer's Workshop, May 1990.

Waldman, David A. "A Theoretical Consideration of Leadership and Total Quality Management." *Leadership Quarterly* 4 (1993), 65–79.

Whiteley, Richard C. *The Customer Driven Company.* Reading, MA: Addison-Wesley, 1991.

Chapter 6

Human Resource Practices

Outline

Toyota's Georgetown, Kentucky, plant has been a three-time winner of the J. D. Power Gold Plant Quality Award. When asked about the "secret" behind the superior Toyota paint finishes, one manager replied "We've got nothing, technology-wise, that anyone else can't have. There's no secret Toyota Quality Machine out there. The quality machine is the workforce—the team members on the paint line, the suppliers, the engineers—everybody who has a hand in production here takes the attitude that we're making world-class vehicles."[1] The human resource is the *only* one that competitors cannot copy, and the *only* one that can synergize, that is, produce output whose value is greater than the sum of its parts. Deming emphasized that no organization can survive without good people, people who are improving.

Businesses in the United States are beginning to learn that to satisfy customers, they must first satisfy employees. FedEx, for instance, has found direct statistical correlation between customer and employee satisfaction; a drop in employee satisfaction scores precedes a drop in customer satisfaction by about two months. Heskett, Sasser, and Schlesinger of the Harvard Business School have conducted research in a number of service operations in industries ranging from communications to banking to fast food, and observed similar relationships.[2] They found that as employee satisfaction increased, so did customer satisfaction and loyalty to the organization. If employees were satisfied with their working conditions and jobs, they stayed with the company, became familiar with customers and their needs, had the opportunity to correct errors because the customers knew and trusted them, and had outcomes of higher productivity and high service quality. Customers of these firms became more loyal, thus providing more repeat business, were willing to complain about service problems so that employees could fix them, and benefited from the relationship by seeing lower costs and better service, thus leading to a new cycle of increased customer satisfaction. Satisfying employees, however, can go well beyond simple job security. As *Fortune* magazine noted,

> *Welcome to the brave new workplace, as revealed by* Fortune's *third annual survey to determine the 100 Best Companies to Work For in America. In an ultratight labor market, companies primp to woo and retain talent. They offer perks and amenities like concierge services, unheard of until recently. They listen to employee input, adjust schedules to suit family obligations, provide training, and cut workers into stock-purchase, stock-option, and stock-award programs formerly reserved for the management elite.*[3]

The role of human beings at work has certainly changed as business and technology have evolved over the years. Prior to the Industrial Revolution, skilled craftspeople had a major stake in the quality of their products because their families' livelihoods depended on the sale of those products. They were motivated by pride in their work as well as the need for survival. The departure from the craftsmanship concept was promulgated by Frederick W. Taylor. Taylor concluded that a factory should be managed on a scientific basis. So he focused on work methods design, the establishment of standards for daily work, selection and training of workers, and piecework incentives. Taylor separated planning from execution, concluding that foremen and workers of those days lacked the education necessary to plan their work. The foreman's role was to ensure that the workforce met productivity standards. Other pioneers of scientific management, such as Frank and Lilian Gilbreth and Henry Gantt, further refined the Taylor system through motion study, methods improvement, ergonomics, scheduling, and wage incentive systems.

The Taylor system dramatically improved productivity. However, it also changed many manufacturing jobs into a series of mundane and mindless tasks. Without a systems perspective and a focus on the customer, the responsibility for quality shifted from workers to inspectors, and as a result, quality eroded. The Taylor philosophy also contributed to the development of labor unions and established an adversarial relationship between labor and management that has yet to be completely overcome. Nevertheless, the Taylor system was the key force behind the explosive economic development of the twentieth century "old economy." Peter Drucker, arguably the most respected and influential writer on management, observed:

> *Whatever his limitations and shortcomings—and he had many—no other American, not even Henry Ford (1863–1947), had anything like Taylor's impact. "Scientific Management" (and its successor, "Industrial Engineering") is the one American philosophy that has swept the world—more so even than the Constitution and the Federalist Papers. In the last century there has been only one worldwide philosophy that could compete with Taylor's: Marxism. And in the end Taylor has triumphed over Marx.*[4]

Perhaps the most significant drawback of the Taylor system was that it failed to make use of an organization's most important asset—the knowledge and creativity of the workforce. As executives at The Ritz-Carlton Hotel Company have stated, human beings don't serve a function, they have a purpose, and the role of the human resources function is to unleash the power of the workforce to achieve the goals of the organization.[5] In their postwar rebuilding years, Japanese manufacturers clearly demonstrated that attention to the human resource can improve quality and productivity far more than technology alone, and led to new thinking about the role of human resources. The Taylor system philosophy assumed that (1) people are part of the process; (2) the process needs to be controlled externally to be productive; and (3) managers have to control carefully what people do. Modern thinking is that (1) people design and improve the process; (2) workers who run the process must control it; and (3) managers must obtain the commitment of people to design, control, and improve processes so that they can remain productive. Studies have shown that this new philosophy results in higher quality, lower costs, less waste, better utilization, increased capacity, reduced turnover and absenteeism, faster implementation of change, greater human skill development, and better individual self-esteem.[6] It also requires more attention to the psychological aspects of work—one of the key principles of the Deming philosophy.

The revolution in industrial psychology and human relations began at the Hawthorne Works of the Western Electric Company in the late 1920s and was set alight by a Harvard team of researchers. Both Deming and Juran were working for Western Electric at the time, which may have influenced their views on quality and the workforce. A few years later, the work of such behavioral scientists as Abraham Maslow, Douglas McGregor, and Frederick Herzberg helped to develop new concepts of motivation, employee development, and individual and group approaches to job design. The total quality movement has caused business to look more closely at the human side of work. The focus on customer satisfaction and flexibility to meet ever-changing customer demands has brought new approaches to work design and employee development. In this chapter, we address human resource management within a total quality environment, focusing on the design and management of high-performance work systems.

THE SCOPE OF HUMAN RESOURCE MANAGEMENT

Human resource management (HRM) consists of those activities designed to provide for and coordinate the people of an organization.[7] These activities include determining the organization's human resource needs; assisting in the design of work systems; recruiting, selecting, training and developing, counseling, motivating, and rewarding employees; acting as a liaison with unions and government organizations; and handling other matters of employee well-being. HRM seeks to build a high-performance workplace and maintain an environment for quality excellence to enable employees and the organization to achieve its strategic objectives and adapt to change.

HRM is a modern term for what has been traditionally referred to as *personnel administration* or *personnel management*. In their traditional role, personnel managers in a business organization interviewed job applicants, negotiated contracts with the union, kept time cards on hourly workers, and occasionally taught a training course. Today their role has changed dramatically. Human resource managers may still perform the traditional tasks of personnel managers, but the scope and importance of their area of responsibility have altered significantly. Instead of being corporate watchdogs, human resource managers now take on a strategic leadership role in their organizations. They must view human resource requirements in an integrated way, that is, aligned with the organization's strategic directions, and at the same time, oversee day-to-day operations and maintenance of the HRM system. For example, the importance of human resources at a company like BI (see *Quality Profile* in Chapter 4) is reflected in the fact that HR is led by a senior vice president within the office of the president.

Just as all managers are responsible for quality even though their organizations may have quality professionals, all managers have a responsibility for human resources, even if the formal organizational structure has HRM professionals. Developing skills through training and coaching, promoting teamwork and participation, motivating and recognizing employees, and providing meaningful communication are important human resource skills that all managers must embrace for total quality to succeed. At Xerox, for instance, managers are directly accountable for the development and implementation of human resource plans that support the quality goals of the company. Thus, understanding HRM practices is necessary for a total quality environment and a critical task for all managers.

Leading companies have revolutionized all (or nearly all) of their major human resource policies and procedures.[8] Table 6.1 contrasts traditional HRM policies with those supporting a total quality perspective. In traditional organizations, HRM functions identify, prepare, direct, and reward employees for following rather narrow objectives. In TQ organizations, HRM units develop policies and procedures to ensure that employees can perform multiple roles, improvise when necessary, and direct themselves toward continuous improvement of both product quality and customer service. The new HRM paradigm has been used successfully by many companies to develop a more cooperative, productive, flexible, and innovative work environment that recognizes the value of the human resources in meeting customer needs and achieving strategic business objectives.

Leading Practices

TQ-based HRM practices work to accomplish the following tasks:

1. Communicate the importance of each employee's contribution to total quality.
2. Stress quality-related synergies available through teamwork.

Table 6.1 Traditional Versus Total Quality Human Resource Paradigms

Corporate Context Dimension	Traditional Paradigm	Total Quality Paradigm
Corporate Culture	Individualism Differentiation Autocratic leadership Profits Productivity	Collective efforts Cross-functional work Coaching/enabling Customer satisfaction Quality
Human Resource Characteristics	**Traditional Paradigm**	**Total Quality Paradigm**
Communications	Top-down	Top-down Horizontal, lateral Multidirectional
Voice and involvement	Employment-at-will Suggestion systems	Due process Quality circles Attitude surveys
Job design	Efficiency Productivity Standard procedures Narrow span of control Specific job descriptions	Quality Customization Innovation Wide span of control Autonomous work teams Empowerment
Training	Job related skills Functional, technical Productivity	Broad range of skills Cross-functional Diagnostic, problem solving Productive and quality
Performance measurement and evaluation	Individual goals Supervisory review Emphasize financial performance	Team goals Customer, peer, and supervisory review Emphasize quality and service
Rewards	Competition for individual merit increases and benefits	Team/group-based rewards Financial rewards, financial and nonfinancial recognition
Health and safety	Treat problems	Prevent problems Safety programs Wellness programs Employee assistance
Selection/promotion career development	Selected by manager Narrow job skills Promotion based on individual accomplishment Linear career path	Selected by peers Problem-solving skills Promotion based on group facilitation Horizontal career path

Source: Blackburn and Rosen, "Total Quality and Human Resources Management: Lessons Learned from Baldrige Award-Winning Companies," *The Academy of Management Executive* 7, no. 3 (1993), 49–66.

3. Empower employees to "make a difference."
4. Reinforce individual and team commitment to quality with a wide range of rewards and reinforcements.[9]

These goals are realized by leading companies through the following practices:

- *They integrate human resource plans with strategic objectives and action plans to fully address the needs and development of the entire workforce.* Anything an organization needs to do differently will inevitably impact people. Thus, overall strategic plans should drive human resource plans. AT&T, for instance, links its training and education to strategic plans to establish current and future competencies for both the organization and the individual. The Consumer Communications Services division develops long-term and short-term plans in four areas: competencies, organization effectiveness, performance, and people. Short-term plans in the first area include strengthening the linkage among identification, assessment, employee development, and business needs, and refining roles and responsibilities to increase employee empowerment. Long-term plans center around the continuous learning environment and formulating new systems for empowering and developing employees.[10] Granite Rock has an employee evaluation system called an individual professional development plan for integrating the company's human resource needs and quality objectives with the individual's aspirations and abilities. Policy deployment, discussed in Chapter 5, provides a vehicle for ensuring that human resource plans are aligned with the overall strategic plans of the organization.
- *They design work and jobs to promote organizational learning, innovation, and flexibility for changing business needs.* Sunny Fresh Foods (see *Quality Profile*), for example, designs its work systems to emphasize safety, quality, compensation and recognition, and employee development in support of individual development and SFF's long-term goals. Many of its work systems are unique to the industry. Examples are a "ramp-in" schedule in which new employees are allowed to work for only a specified number of hours to learn their jobs and minimize the potential for repetitive stress injuries; and a rotation system by which employees rotate to another work station every 20 minutes. This practice ensures that workers can understand internal customers as well as respond to product quality issues at any stage of the process; it fights boredom, reduces repetitive stress injuries, and promotes learning. In addition, SFF uses a "buddy" system in which new employees are matched with high-performing experienced employees who serve as role models for operational excellence and behavioral competencies. Merrill Lynch Credit Corporation uses a wide variety of approaches to promote learning and flexibility. Partners are cross-trained and may "float" to other jobs to address areas of increased volume; MLCC's approach to data analysis and problem solving requires lessons learned and countermeasures to be shared with all other areas. Best practices workshops are used to share approaches and techniques used by the best performers for critical process steps.

  Innovation is frequently promoted through suggestion systems. General Motors established a suggestion system more than 50 years ago, and Cadillac believes that it is one of the secrets to its quality success. Cadillac commits to answering all suggestions within 24 hours; 70 percent of the suggestions received involve quality issues. Milliken either implements or rejects every suggestion within three days. Although no specific rewards are offered, employees still submit suggestions. In 1989 Milliken implemented 87 percent of the more than 262,000 suggestions submitted.

Quality Profile
Sunny Fresh Foods

Sunny Fresh Foods (SFF) manufactures and distributes more than 160 different types of egg-based food products to more than 1,200 U.S. food service operations, such as quick service restaurants, schools, hospitals, convenience stores, and food processors. A subsidiary of Cargill, Inc., SFF operates three manufacturing facilities with a total of 380 employees. At SFF, a satisfied, motivated workforce is a vital ingredient of the company's successful operational and business performance. As measured in annual surveys, employees' rising level of satisfaction and their nearly complete awareness of how their jobs affect customers correlate directly with increasing customer satisfaction. SFF refers to its workers as "stakeholders" and ensures that they share in the benefits of continuous improvement. For example, although the base pay is set slight below the industry midpoint for salaried workers, incentives can increase earnings above the 75th percentile. In addition, extensive reward and recognition systems, including monetary rewards for exemplary safety performance to extra vacation days for quality achievements, also help to motivate employees to contribute to the company's progress toward its improvement goals.

Innovations and a near-perfect record for on-time delivery have helped SFF earn sole-supplier status from several major national restaurant chains. In its 1999 customer survey, SFF earned scores of 100 percent on three of its five key indicators of satisfaction: on-time delivery, technical support, and customer service access. Scores on the other two—product performance and product freshness—topped 90 percent. SFF ranks second in its industry market share, up from 14th in 1988. SFF was a 1999 Baldrige Award recipient.

Source: Malcolm Baldrige National Quality Award, Profiles of Winners, National Institute of Standards and Technology, Department of Commerce.

- *They develop effective performance management systems, compensation, and reward and recognition approaches to support high performance and motivate employees.* At Sunny Fresh Foods, the performance management process (PMP) is an ongoing process of setting expectations, coaching, and reviewing performance. Inputs include key results areas, behavioral competencies, and skill development. BI's process involves associates setting annual goals and objectives that link to division and department objectives, developing action plans, and measuring their performance. The process includes internal customer feedback from peers, a self-evaluation, and director feedback. At FedEx, performance management involves upward, downward, and peer feedback and focuses on goals rather than numbers. At STMicroelectronics, peer evaluations account for 40 percent of team members' performance; the remainder is based on attendance and team leader review. Annual development plans are included in each employee's performance review and progress and performance are reviewed quarterly by their teams. ST's compensation system supports its job design by rewarding employees through pay increases and promotions as skills are developed and demonstrated. A variable pay program encourages individual, team, unit, and company goal achievement for all employees.

Leading companies also recognize and reward employee contributions beyond monetary compensation. Solectron has employee and team recognition processes at each site, including family-oriented Employee Appreciation Days. In 1995 Trident Precision Manufacturing (see *Quality Profile*) recognized or rewarded employees more than 1,200 times. Westinghouse Electric Corporation tailors rewards to what is valued by employees. Each site within the division customizes its awards; some give mall gift certificates to use at local malls, while others give cash or other awards. Figure 6.1 shows the wide scope of recognition approaches used by Merrill Lynch Credit Corporation (see *Quality Profile*).

- *They promote cooperation and collaboration through teamwork.* Teams encourage free-flowing participation and interaction among its members. FedEx has more than 4,000 quality action teams; Boeing Airlift and Tanker Division has more than 100 integrated product teams (IPTs) that are typically made up of engineering, work-team, customer, and supplier representatives. Granite Rock, with fewer than 400 employees, has about 100 functioning teams, ranging from 10 corporate quality teams to project teams, purchasing teams, task forces, and function teams composed of people who do the same job at different locations. Special efforts keep the teams relevant and make sure that no teams exist just for the sake of having them. Texas Nameplate Company (see *Quality Profile*) builds its leadership system upon a team framework that includes a senior leadership team (business excellence leadership team), a daily operations and innovation team, teams within each production and support service department for daily work activities, corrective action teams, and various other teams such as the Recognition Committee.
- *They empower individuals and teams to make decisions that affect quality and customer satisfaction.* Many companies talk about empowerment, but few truly practice it. At AT&T, design engineers have the authority to stop a design, and line operators can stop the production line if they detect a quality problem. At The Ritz-Carlton Hotel Co., each employee can "move heaven and earth" and spend up

Quality Profile

Trident Precision Manufacturing, Inc.

Founded in 1979 with only three people, privately held Trident manufactures precision sheet metal components, electromechanical assemblies, and custom products, mostly in the office-equipment, medical-supply, computer, and defense industries with a workforce of about 170. Its 1995 revenues totaled $14.5 million. Trident has established quality as its basic business plan to accomplish short- and long-term goals for five key business drivers: customer satisfaction, employee satisfaction, shareholder value, operational performance, and supplier partnerships. Trident's human resource strategies emphasize training, involvement through teams, empowerment, and reward and recognition. Since 1989 Trident has invested 4.4 percent of its payroll in training and education, two to three times the average for all U.S. industry and an especially large amount for a small firm.

Employee turnover has declined dramatically, from 41 percent in 1988 to 5 percent in 1994 and 1995. Defect rates have fallen so much that Trident offers a full guarantee against defects in its custom products. On-time delivery performance has increased from 87 percent in 1990 to 99.94 percent in 1995. Trident was a 1996 recipient of the Baldrige Award.

Source: Malcolm Baldrige National Quality Award, Profiles of Winners, National Institute of Standards and Technology, Department of Commerce.

Figure 6.1 Recognition Approaches at Merrill Lynch Credit Corporation

Types of Recognition	Partner Category			
President's Award			3	4
Special Recognition Award			3	4
Partner Suggestion Program	1	2	3	4
Partner-of-the-Month Program			3	4
Honor Roll Program		2		
Partner-to-Partner Notes	1	2	3	4
Service Recognition Award	1	2	3	4
VICP/EIP Bonus Pool	1	2	3	4
ML&Co/MLCC Gifts	1	2	3	4
Perfect Attendance			3	4
Partner Appreciation Week	1	2	3	4
Partner Birthday Gifts	1	2	3	4
Summer/Holiday Parties	1	2	3	4

Legend: 1 = Senior management 2 = Management
3 = Supervisor 4 = All other partners

Source: From "The 1997 Malcolm Baldrige National Quality Award Application Summary," a publication of Merrill Lynch Credit Corporation. Any further reproduction or redistribution is strictly prohibited.

to $2,000 to satisfy a customer. To foster innovation at Trident Precision Manufacturing, employees "own" specific processes and are given the responsibility for identifying problems and opportunities for improvement. In addition, they have the authority to modify their processes using the company's documented process improvement procedure. Because of the high level of empowerment given to individuals and teams at Texas Nameplate, the company disbanded its quality control department, assigning its activities to various people who do the work.

- *They make extensive investments in training and education.* At Wainwright Industries, associates are fully engaged in quality training efforts beginning with their first day on the job. During new associate orientation, senior managers explain the importance of quality and customer satisfaction and outline the company's approaches to continuous improvement. Follow-up sessions are held 24 and 72 days after the start of employment. The company invests up to 7 percent of its payroll in training and education. All associates take courses on quality values, communication techniques, problem solving, statistical process control, and synchronous manufacturing. Because almost 13 percent of its workforce represent minorities, Sunny Fresh Foods has translated training materials into Spanish and uses interpreters to facilitate understanding; it offers English as a second language during work hours. At Dana Commercial Credit (see *Quality Profile*), training and education needs and effectiveness are reviewed monthly, focusing on skill enhancement of those people, including senior managers, who

Quality Profile
Merrill Lynch Credit Corporation

Merrill Lynch Credit Corporation (MLCC) provides a wide variety of liability management services including home financing, personal credit, and investment and business financing. MLCC's 830 employees, known as partners, market and sell all its products through a nationwide network of more than 14,000 financial consultants at Merrill Lynch Private Client sales offices. MLCC considers partner empowerment critical to its success. Partners are encouraged to take initiative and responsibility, especially in areas such as flexibility, cooperation, rapid response, and learning. Cross- and just-in-time training, cross-functional teams, and flow reengineering teams help partners achieve success. MLCC strives to be the employer of choice and offers multiple methods of improving partner satisfaction, including alternative work arrangements.

MLCC emphasizes process management and measurement systems to link every partner to company objectives, and makes heavy use of technology to enable partners to meet the ever-increasing expectations of clients and the company's financial consultants. Using process improvement techniques, the percentage of legal submissions returned late was reduced from 20 percent in the first half of 1995 to zero percent in the second half of 1996. Net income rose 100 percent from 1994 to 1996 and exceeds the industry group average. Return on equity increased approximately 74 percent and return on assets increased by about 36 percent during the same period. Partner satisfaction with the company's recognition programs improved from 42 percent in 1994 to 70 percent in 1996.

Source: Malcolm Baldrige National Quality Award, Profiles of Winners, National Institute of Standards and Technology, Department of Commerce. Portions of "The 1997 Malcolm Baldrige National Quality Award Summary" are reprinted by permission of Merrill Lynch Credit Corporation. Copyright © 1997.

have direct contact with customers. AT&T uses a systematic methodology called the *Instructional Technology Approach* to assess, analyze, and develop curricula to identify and address skill and development gaps.

- *They maintain a work environment conducive to the well-being and growth of all employees.* Satisfied employees are productive employees. Leading-edge firms include well-being factors such as health, safety, and ergonomics in their improvement activities. Ames Rubber Corporation, for example, has nine major long-range plans in effect, covering such areas as affirmative action, health benefits and safety, and accident reduction. FedEx teaches employees how to handle dangerous goods, lift heavy packages correctly, and drive safely. Leading companies also perform audits to identify risks and prevent accidents, focusing on root cause analysis. Texas Instruments, for example, uses safety, environmental, and ergonomic experts to institute preventive actions, investigate accidents, and provide training. At The Ritz-Carlton, project teams configure the best combination of technology and procedures to eliminate causes of safety and security problems.

Employee satisfaction is enhanced by such special services as counseling, recreational or cultural activities, nonwork-related education, day care, flexible working hours, and outplacement activities. Texas Instruments, for example, has a company-sponsored employee association called "Texins" that provides fitness activities, recreational clubs, and family events; the company also offers free counseling for personal and relationship problems. Granite Rock sponsors company picnics and parties at regular intervals. Solectron provides American

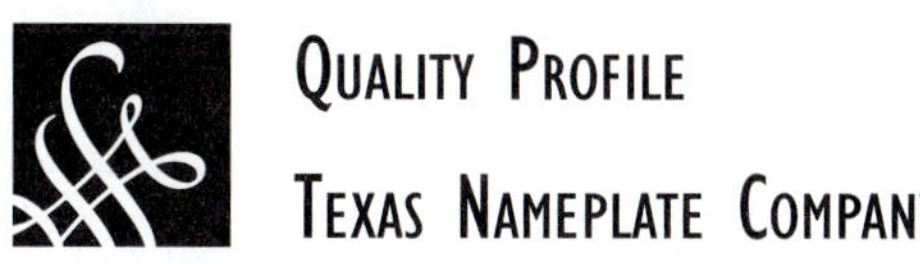

Quality Profile

Texas Nameplate Company

Founded in 1946, Texas Nameplate Company, Inc. (TNC), manufactures and sells identification and information labels that are affixed to refrigerators, oil-field equipment, high-pressure valves, trucks, computer equipment and other products made by more than 1,000 customers throughout the United States and in nine foreign countries. With only 66 employees, it was the smallest company to receive a Baldrige Award when it did so in 1998. Customer contact employees are empowered to resolve customer complaints without consulting management, and production workers are responsible for tailoring processes to optimize contributions to company goals and to meet team-set standards. To help workers identify opportunities for improvement, each process is mapped using a flow chart. The average employee receives 75 hours of training in the first two years of employment, much of it delivered on a just-in-time basis. About one in 10 workers is a multipurpose employee, trained in three or more jobs, allowing them to be moved to any area of the company that needs assistance to meet fluctuating customer and market demands. Profit sharing and gain-sharing incentives, along with higher-than-industry-average pay scales, serve to reinforce the workforce's commitment to quality and foster company loyalty.

In its 1997 employee survey, satisfaction rates ranged from 72 to 88 percent in five areas that employees say are the most important: fair pay, job content satisfaction, recognition, fairness and respect, and career development, as compared to rates of 50 to 57 percent nationally. Gross profit as a percentage of sales increased from 50.5 percent in 1994 to 59 percent in 1998, and net profit as a percentage of sales more than doubled. TNC reduced its defects from 3.65 percent to about 1 percent in four years. Customers consistently give the company an "excellent" rating (5 to 6 on a scale of 6) in 12 key business areas, including product quality, reliable performance, on-time delivery, and overall satisfaction.

Source: Malcolm Baldrige National Quality Award, Profiles of Winners, National Institute of Standards and Technology, Department of Commerce.

culture and citizenship classes, wellness committees to communicate health information programs, employee assistance programs, sports and recreation programs, and tuition reimbursement.

- *They monitor the extent and effectiveness of human resource practices and measure employee satisfaction as a means of continuous improvement.* Employee surveys and measurement of key HRM indicators monitor employee satisfaction and identify problem areas. These surveys frequently ask employees to rate their supervisors on leadership, communication, and support. For instance, Merrill Lynch Credit Corporation surveys a subset of employees quarterly on 15 drivers of partner satisfaction. AT&T conducts an opinion survey every two years to measure employee attitudes and the effect of improvement efforts. Management compares the results within AT&T and with benchmarks of other high-performance companies. GTE Directories chartered a team to determine how the company should measure quality improvement team effectiveness. The team discovered that inconsistent evaluation guidelines made it difficult to manage the process, so they developed specific and measurable guidelines emphasizing customer satisfaction, measurable results, cross-functional involvement, and ini-

Quality Profile

Dana Commercial Credit Corporation

Dana Commercial Credit Corporation (DCC) is a provider of leasing and financing to a broad range of commercial customers. Since 1992, when the company embarked on an effort to improve teamwork and organizational communications, the company has scored gains in the quality of its performance, customer satisfaction, and the percentage of repeat business. In 1996 the company received a Baldrige Award. To achieve its objective of being the preferred financial services provider in selected markets, DCC relies on the skills and innovativeness of its people and through its quality improvement system. A "just do it" policy empowers DCC's people to act on their ideas for improvement without prior approval. An education group develops and teaches courses in interpersonal communications, quality, and marketing, as well as in technical areas. Each DCC person receives an average of 48 hours of formal training and education, almost three times the leasing industry average.

Rates of return on equity and assets have increased more than 45 percent since 1991. The Dealer Products Group has reduced the time to approve a transaction from about 7 hours in 1992 to an hour or less in 1996. Since 1994 this group has received customer satisfaction ratings of between 8 and 9 on a 10-point scale, nearly 3 points higher than the industry average. Since 1991 the dollar volume of DCC leases has more than tripled, topping $1 billion.

Source: Malcolm Baldrige National Quality Award, Profiles of Winners, National Institute of Standards and Technology, Department of Commerce.

tiative. Sunny Fresh Foods identifies its key factors for employee well-being from performance reviews, exit interviews, and individual discussions. Results are segmented and analyzed by plant and employee groups, these practices allow management at each plant to tailor initiatives for their employees.

Indicators such as the number of teams, rate of growth, percentage of employees involved, number of suggestions implemented, time taken to respond to suggestions, team activities, absenteeism, turnover rates, and grievances provide a basis for evaluation and improvement. Texas Instruments has a training council that uses a computerized system to monitor individualized training plans. This process, along with employee surveys, customer surveys, suggestions, and so on, helps to identify needs.

LINKING HUMAN RESOURCE PLANS AND BUSINESS STRATEGY

Prior to developing a TQ focus, most organizations neglected the strategic aspects of human resource management, relegating HRM to a support function. TQ-focused firms, such as Armstrong Building Products Operations (BPO), recognize that HRM plays a key role in overall strategic planning. BPO's overall HR strategy is

- To provide the opportunity for employees to reach their full potential by developing a high performance organization which supports the operation's Vision, Mission, and Goal. The behavior in deploying the strategy will be consistent with our corporate Operating Principles.

- To attract, develop, challenge and retain a diverse work force to assure we have the skills and organization to build our business.
- To involve and empower employees to improve processes and participate in decisions that affect the business.
- To recognize and reward performance that contributes to the business strategy and goals.
- To continuously improve those elements of the work environment that enhance employees' well being, satisfaction, and productivity.[11]

At Armstrong BPO, the translation of business needs to HR plans is performed by the same team that is accountable for business results, thus helping to ensure focus, alignment, and proper allocation of resources.

Managers must make choices in five traditional areas of the HRM system: planning, staffing, appraising, compensating, and training and development. Each of these five areas has dimensions that can be viewed on a continuum from a structured environment with rigid practices to an unstructured environment with flexible practices, as shown in Table 6.2. Conventional HRM practices generally fall on the left side of each continuum. HRM choices that support a TQ environment are listed on the right-hand side of the table. In addition to these traditional areas of an HRM system, strategic human resource plans often include one or more of the following:

- Redesign of the work organization to increase empowerment and decision making or team-based participation
- Initiatives for promoting greater labor-management cooperation, such as union partnerships
- Initiatives to foster knowledge sharing and organizational learning
- Partnerships with educational institutions to help ensure the future supply of well-prepared employees

Whatever the choices, it is vital that they support the organization's overall strategy. Without proper alignment, the work that people do can be focused in a direction entirely different from the way the organization intends to go.

DESIGNING HIGH-PERFORMANCE WORK SYSTEMS

High-performance work refers to work approaches used to systematically pursue ever-higher levels of overall organizational and human performance. High-performance work systems are characterized by flexibility, innovation, knowledge and skill sharing, alignment with organizational directions, customer focus, and rapid response to changing business needs and marketplace requirements. As we noted in Chapter 1, organizations may be viewed at three levels: the individual level, the process level, and the organizational level. The design of high-performance work systems can be addressed using this framework. At the individual level, work systems should enable effective accomplishment of work activities and promote flexibility and individual initiative in managing and improving work processes. It requires extensive employee involvement, empowerment, and training and education. At the process level, cooperation, teamwork, and communication are key ingredients. At the organizational level, compensation and recognition, and attention to employee well-being through health, safety, and support services are major factors for outstanding performance. The entire system must be managed effectively through sound motivational principles and practices such as recruitment and career development, performance appraisal, and continual evaluation and improvement of HRM practices.

Table 6.2 Human Resource Management Practice Continuums

	Planning Choices	
Informal	....	Formal
Short term	....	Long term
Explicit job analysis	....	Implicit job analysis
Job simplification	....	Job enrichment
Low employee involvement	....	High employee involvement
	Staffing Choices	
Internal sources	....	External sources
Narrow paths	....	Broad paths
Single ladder	....	Multiple ladders
Explicit criteria	....	Implicit criteria
Limited socialization	....	Extensive socialization
Closed procedures	....	Open procedures
	Appraising Choices	
Behavioral criteria	....	Results criteria
	Purposes: Development, Remedial, Maintenance	
Low Employee participation	....	High employee participation
Short-term criteria	....	Long-term criteria
Individual criteria	....	Group criteria
	Compensating Choices	
Low base salaries	....	High base salaries
Internal equity	....	External equity
Few perks	....	Many perks
Standard, fixed package	....	Flexible package
Low participation	....	High participation
No incentives	....	Many incentives
Short-term incentives	....	Long-term incentives
No employment security	....	High employment security
Hierarchical	....	High participation
	Training and Development Choices	
Short term	....	Long term
Narrow application	....	Broad application
Productivity emphasis	....	Quality-of-work-life emphasis
Spontaneous, unplanned	....	Planned, systematic
Individual orientation	....	Group orientation
Low participation	....	High participation

Source: Adapted from R. S. Schuler, "Human Resource Management Practice Choices," in *Readings in Personnel and Human Resource Management*, 3d ed., R. S. Schuler, S. A. Youngblood, and V. L. Huber, eds. (St. Paul, MN: West Publishing Company, 1988).

Thus, high-performance work systems require attention to work structures, management processes, and HR practices. In this section we address the most important elements in designing high-performance work systems that support a total quality focus.

Work and Job Design

Work design refers to how employees are organized in formal and informal units, such as departments and teams. **Job design** refers to responsibilities and tasks assigned to individuals. Both work and job design are vital to organizational effectiveness and personal job satisfaction. The design of work should provide individuals with both the intrinsic and extrinsic motivation to achieve quality and operational performance objectives. Unfortunately, managers often do not understand workers' needs. One research study found that the top five employee needs in the workplace are (1) interesting work, (2) recognition, (3) feeling "in" on things, (4) security, and (5) pay. Managers, however, believed pay to be number one.

An integrating theory that helps us understand how job design impacts motivation, satisfaction, and organizational effectiveness was proposed by Hackman and Oldham.[12] Their model, which has been validated in numerous organizational settings, is shown in Figure 6.2. The model contains four major segments:

1. Critical psychological states
2. Core job characteristics
3. Moderating variables
4. Outcomes

Three critical psychological states drive the model. *Experienced meaningfulness* is the psychological need of workers to have the feeling that their work is a significant contribution to the organization and society. *Experienced responsibility* indicates the need

Figure 6.2 Hackman and Oldham Work Design Model

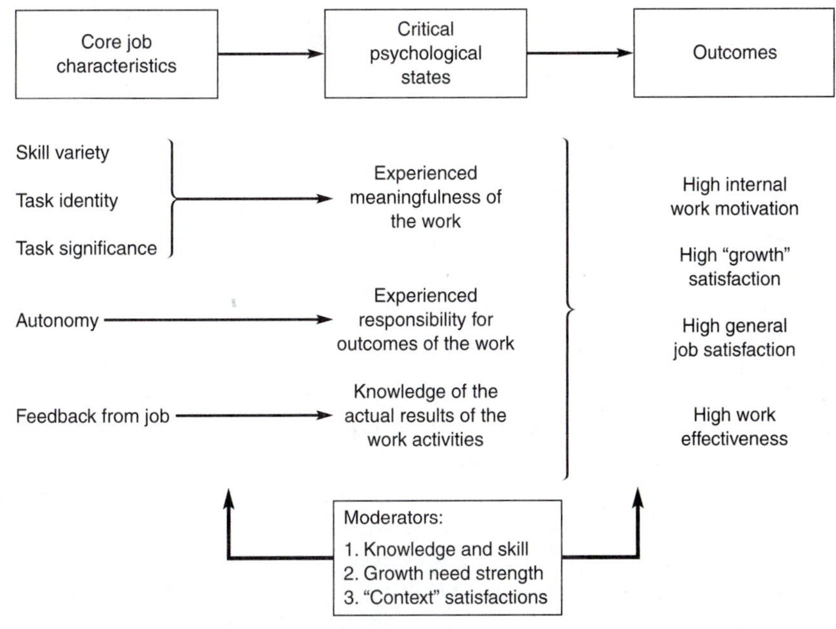

Source: J. Richard Hackman and Greg R. Oldham, WORK REDESIGN (figure 4.6 from page 90). © 1980 by Addison-Wesley Publishing Co., Inc. Reprinted by permission of Addison Wesley Longman.

of workers to be accountable for the quality and quantity of work produced. *Knowledge of results* implies that all workers feel the need to know how their work is evaluated and what the results of the evaluation are.

Five core job characteristics have been identified as having an impact on the critical psychological states:

1. *Task significance:* the degree to which the job gives the participant the feeling that it has a substantial impact on the organization or the world.
2. *Task identity:* the degree to which the worker can perceive the task as a whole, identifiable piece of work from start to finish.
3. *Skill variety:* the degree to which the job requires the worker to use a variety of skills and talents.
4. *Autonomy:* the degree to which the task permits freedom, independence, and personal control to be exercised over the work.
5. *Feedback from the job:* the degree to which clear, timely information about the effectiveness of performance of the individual is available.

Quality is related in a primary or secondary sense to all five of these core job characteristics. Quality of a product or service is undoubtedly increased by a worker's dedicated application of skills, which is enhanced by task identity and a feeling of task significance. More directly, quality of work is enhanced by a job design that incorporates autonomy and feedback relating to quality characteristics. The key outcomes of high general job satisfaction and high work effectiveness can then be seen as results that define and reinforce excellent quality.

As an example illustrating characteristics of the Hackman and Oldham model, consider the case of workers in a small Delaware firm that produces spacesuits for astronauts. The work requires a great deal of handcrafting, using conventional sewing machinery as well as high technology in testing the suits for proper functioning. Task significance and task identity are evident in the workers' ability to see the job's extreme importance and its fit into the complete unit (a spacesuit for an individual astronaut). Skill variety and autonomy are somewhat limited since conventional sewing techniques must be used and rigid specifications must be precisely followed. However, other motivating aspects of the job may compensate for the lack of these characteristics. Feedback on results is timely and individualized. Comprehensive testing and inspection of the spacesuits is performed to assure that no defective units are produced.

Several common approaches to work design—job enlargement, job rotation, and job enrichment—are supported by this model. IBM was apparently the first user of *job enlargement*, in which workers' jobs were expanded to include several tasks rather than one single, low-level task. This approach reduced fragmentation of jobs and generally resulted in lower production costs, greater worker satisfaction, and higher quality, but it required higher wage rates and the purchase of more inspection equipment. *Job rotation* is a technique by which individual workers learn several tasks by rotating from one to another. The purpose of job rotation is to renew interest or motivation of the individual and to increase his or her complement of skills. However, several studies show that the main benefit was to increase workers' skills but that little, if any, motivational benefit could be expected.[13] Finally, *job enrichment* entails "vertical job loading" in which workers are given more authority, responsibility, and autonomy rather than simply more or different work to do. Job enrichment has been used successfully in a number of firms, notably AT&T, which experienced better employee attitudes and performance, as well as Texas Instruments, IBM, and General Foods.

Employee Involvement

Tom Peters suggested involving everyone in everything, in such activities as quality and productivity improvement, measuring and monitoring results, budget development, new technology assessment, recruiting and hiring, making customer calls, and participating in customer visits.[14] **Employee involvement (EI)** refers to any activity by which employees participate in work-related decisions and improvement activities, with the objectives of tapping the creative energies of all employees and improving their motivation. Pete Coors, CEO of Coors Brewing, explained it simply: "We're moving from an environment where the supervisor says, 'This is the way it is going to be done and if you don't like it, go someplace else,' to an environment where the supervisor can grow with the changes, get his troops together and say, 'Look, you guys are operating the equipment, what do you think we ought to do?'"[15]

EI approaches can range from simple sharing of information or providing input on work-related issues and making suggestions to self-directed responsibilities such as setting goals, making business decisions, and solving problems, often in cross-functional teams. This continuum is summarized in Table 6.3. As total quality matures in an organization, higher levels of employee involvement are evident. One of the most prominent employee involvement processes has been GE's "Work-Out" program.[16] Employees are encouraged to get together in a series of meetings to discuss reports, meetings, measurements, and approvals in their work area or department. The meetings are facilitated by an outside leader, but supervisors are forbidden to attend, except for a brief opening appearance, until the last day of a three-day session. At the final Work-Out session, the supervisor, and often, his or her boss, is at the

Table 6.3 Levels of Employee Involvement

Level	Action	Primary Outcome
1. Information sharing	Managers decide, then inform employees	Conformance
2. Dialogue	Managers get employee input, then decide	Acceptance
3. Special problem solving	Managers assign a one-time problem to selected employees	Contribution
4. Intragroup problem solving	Intact groups meet weekly to solve local problems	Commitment
5. Intergroup problem solving	Cross-functional groups meet to solve mutual problems	Cooperation
6. Focused problem solving	Intact groups deepen daily involvement in a specific issue	Concentration
7. Limited self-direction	Teams at selected sites function full time with minimum supervision	Accountability
8. Total self-direction	Executives facilitate self-management in an all-team company	Ownership

Source: Copyright © Jack D. Orsburn, Linda Moran, Ed Musselwhite, and John H. Zenger, *Self-Directed Work Teams* (Burr Ridge, IL: Business One Irwin, 1990), 34. Reproduced with permission of The McGraw-Hill Companies.

front of the room, having no idea what has been discussed during the previous two days. The supervisor can only respond to items that the employees recommend in one of three ways:

1. Agree on the spot to implement the proposal.
2. Say no to the proposal.
3. Ask for more information.

Typically, more than 80 percent of the Work-Out recommendations have received an immediate answer. For example, Armand Lauzon, head of plant services at GE Aircraft Engines factory in Lynn, Massachusetts, was confronted with 108 proposals at the end of a Work-Out session by his employees. He said yes to 100 recommendations on the spot, including one in which an employee had sketched a design for protective shields for machines on a brown paper bag. The employee asked if his group could bid on the work. They got the bid when they quoted a cost of $16,000 versus an outside vendor's proposed cost of $96,000!

A number of different labels have been applied to various EI approaches used in organizations. Some of the broad behavioral management approaches for individual participation include "quality of worklife (QWL)," "humanization of work," "work reform," "work restructuring," "work design," and "sociotechnical systems." Terms used to designate team approaches include QWL teams, productivity action teams (PATs), quality circles, and self-managed work teams (SMWTs).

EI initiatives are by no means new.[17] Many programs and experiments have been implemented over more than 100 years by industrial engineers, statisticians, and behavioral scientists. Early attempts influenced modern practices considerably. Unfortunately, these approaches lacked the complementary elements of TQ, such as a customer orientation, top management leadership and support, and a common set of tools for problem solving and continuous improvement.

Early work improvement activities at the Zeiss Company in Germany in the 1890s involved workers in work planning, design of precision machinery, and group problem solving.[18] In 1913 the Lincoln Electric Company began to develop its unique mix of work improvement and employee incentive plans, including an employee advisory board, employee stock ownership, year-end bonuses, and a benefit package.[19] Lincoln Electric still boasts outstanding productivity, quality, and employee loyalty, some 85 years after beginning its experiment. Other productivity and quality improvement initiatives, such as work simplification and planned methods change, relied on some form of employee involvement.

During the 1940s and through the 1960s, a number of work innovation experiments that focused on worker motivation and productivity took place. These behavioral experiments frequently, though not exclusively, relied on the use of group participation at the operating level to achieve organizational change. Firms that were leaders in work innovation experiments included General Motors, Procter & Gamble, Exxon, General Foods, TRW, Cummins Engine, Butler Manufacturing, Mars, Inc., Citibank, Prudential Insurance, Donnelly Mirrors, and Eaton Corporation.[20]

EI is rooted in the psychology of human needs and supported by the motivation models of Maslow, Herzberg, and McGregor, which are discussed later in this chapter. Employees are motivated through exciting work, responsibility, and recognition. EI provides a powerful means of achieving the highest order individual needs of self-realization and fulfillment. EI offers many advantages over traditional management practices:

- Replaces the adversarial mentality with trust and cooperation
- Develops the skills and leadership capability of individuals, creating a sense of mission and fostering trust
- Increases employee morale and commitment to the organization
- Fosters creativity and innovation, the source of competitive advantage
- Helps people understand quality principles and instilling these principles into the corporate culture
- Allows employees to solve problems at the source immediately
- Improves quality and productivity.[21]

Employee involvement should begin with a personal commitment to quality, as discussed in Chapter 1. If employees accept and commit to a quality philosophy, they are more apt to learn quality tools and techniques and use them in their daily work. As they begin to see the benefits of a commitment to quality, they will then be more receptive to working in teams. This team interaction, in turn, reinforces personal commitment, driving a never-ending cycle of improvement. Employee involvement also depends on the amount and type of information shared with employees, training, compensation and rewards, and the empowerment practices of the firms.[22] Thus, HRM practices must be designed to support and facilitate EI.

One of the easiest ways to involve employees on an individual basis is the **suggestion system.** An employee suggestion system is a management tool for the submission, evaluation, and implementation of an employee's idea to save cost, increase quality, or improve other elements of work such as safety. Companies typically reward employees for implemented suggestions. At Toyota, for instance, employees generate nearly three million ideas each year—an average of 60 per employee—of which 85 percent are implemented by management. Cadillac asked teams of employees to tear apart the Seville and put it back together; they returned with 330 suggestions on how to improve it. Suggestion systems are often tied to incentives. For instance, at Wainwright Industries, a 1994 Baldrige recipient, employees fill out a short form describing their idea (which may be as simple as repairing a frayed extension cord before an accident occurs), and obtain a supervisor's approval. The employee's name is entered in a weekly drawing (a safety idea counts as three entries, and all members of a team idea receive an entry); the winner receives a gift certificate for whatever they want. The process is run entirely by employees without management involvement; they even set the program's annual budget. Wainwright set a benchmark for annual implemented suggestions—more than 50 per employee!

Fostering such employee creativity has many benefits. Thinking about solutions to problems at work makes even routine work enjoyable; writing down the suggestions improves workers' reasoning ability and writing skills. Satisfaction is the byproduct of an implemented idea and a job made easier, safer, or better. Recognition for suggestions leads to higher levels of motivation, peer recognition, and possible monetary rewards. Workers gain an increased understanding of their work, which may lead to promotions and better interpersonal relationships in the workplace. Table 6.4 summarizes strategies that can foster the success of suggestion systems.

Resistance to EI Many individuals resist change to cooperative efforts. Traditional labor managers, like their corporate management counterparts, prefer to adhere to the structured approaches that have their roots in the Taylor system.[23] Workers may resist because of past management credibility problems and the "fad of the month" syndrome. Unions naturally resist such efforts, reading in ulterior motives of making

Table 6.4 Success Factors for Suggestion Systems

1. Ensure that management, first and foremost, is involved in the program. Involvement should begin at the top and filter down through all levels until all employees participate.
2. Push decision making regarding suggestion evaluation to lower levels.
3. Gain union support by pledging no layoffs due to productivity gains from adopted suggestions.
4. Train everyone in all facets of the suggestion system. Improve problem-solving capability by promoting creative problem solving through the use of the seven basic statistical tools.
5. Resolve all suggestions within one month.
6. Encourage all suggestors to personally describe their idea to a supervisor, engineer, or manager.
7. Promote pride in work, and quality and productivity gains from suggestions, rather than the big cash awards if possible.
8. Remove ceilings on intangible suggestion awards. Revise evaluations of intangible suggestions to value them more on par with tangible suggestions.
9. Eliminate restrictions prohibiting suggestions regarding a worker's immediate work area.
10. Continuously promote the suggestion program, especially through supervisor support.
11. Trust employees enough to make allowances for generation, discussion, and submittal of suggestions during work hours.
12. Keep the program simple.

Source: Muse and Finster, "A Comparison of Employee Suggestion Systems in Japan and the USA," University of Wisconsin Working Paper (1989).

employees work harder and trying to break up the union. Resistance is driven by fear as reflected in one of Deming's 14 Points. Thus, EI is often viewed as a threat to old ways of working and could undermine managerial and union control. If approached incorrectly by management, it could fail miserably. Fortunately, such attitudes have changed considerably in the last few decades. Employee involvement has gained increased acceptance as an important component of modern quality management. Nevertheless, considerable opportunity still exists in many organizations.

Keys to overcoming resistance are early involvement by all parties, open and honest dialogue, and good planning. Management holds the key, however. As the organizational leaders, they must believe in workers and their ability to contribute. As leaders, managers must also show commitment and support by providing the right training, rewards, and recognition. Some specific suggestions include the following:

- Design the change process to include significant management involvement in its implementation.
- Create significant dissatisfaction with the status quo, stimulating a need for change. (For many companies, the crisis is usually there.)
- Provide support to raise comfort levels with the new concepts.
- Be consistent in the pursuit of participative management, continuously modeling the desired behavior.
- Be intolerant of insubordination, and deal immediately and decisively with flagrant resisters.[24]

Empowerment

Empowerment simply means giving people authority to make decisions based on what they feel is right, to have control over their work, to take risks and learn from mistakes, and to promote change. Empowerment requires, as the management philosophy of Wainwright Industries states, *a sincere belief and trust in people.* A survey by Annandale, Virginia-based MasteryWorks Inc. concluded that employees leave their organizations because of trust, observing that "Lack of trust was an issue with almost every person who had left an organization."[25]

Examples of empowerment abound. Workers in the Coors Brewery container operation give each other performance evaluations, and even screen, interview, and hire new people for the line. At Motorola, sales representatives have the authority to replace defective products up to six years after purchase, a decision that used to require top management approval. A Corning Glass plant replaced 21 different jobs with one "specialist" job and gave employee teams broad authority over production scheduling and division of labor. Hourly employees at GM's antilock brake system plant in Dayton, Ohio, can call in suppliers to help solve problems, and manage scrap, machine downtime, absences, and rework.

The need to empower the entire workforce in order for quality to succeed has long been recognized, even if only recently put into practice. Juran wrote that "ideally, quality control should be delegated to the workforce to the maximum extent possible."[26] Empowerment resembles Juran's concept of "self-control." Five of Deming's 14 Points relate directly to the notion of empowerment:

Point 6: Institute training.
Point 7: Teach and institute leadership.
Point 8: Drive out fear. Create trust. Create a climate for innovation.
Point 10: Eliminate exhortations for the workforce.
Point 13: Encourage education and self-improvement for everyone.[27]

These points suggest involving employees more directly in decision-making processes, giving them the security and confidence to make decisions, and providing them with the necessary tools and training.

Empowered employees must have the wisdom to know what to do and when to do it, the motivation to do it, and the right tools to accomplish the task.[28] It requires significant changes in work systems, specifically, that

- Employees be provided education, resources, and encouragement.
- Policies and procedures be examined for needless restrictions on the ability of employees to serve customers.
- An atmosphere of trust be fostered rather than resentment and punishment for failure.
- Information be shared freely rather than closely guarded as a source of control and power.
- Workers feel their efforts are desired and needed for the success of the organization.
- Managers be given the required support and training to adopt a "hands-off" leadership style.
- Employees be trained in the amount of latitude they are allowed to take. Formulating decision rules and providing role-playing scenarios are excellent ways of teaching employees.[29]

Empowerment also means that leaders and managers must relinquish some of the power that they previously held. This power shift often creates management fears that workers will abuse this privilege. However, experience shows that front-line workers generally are more conservative than managers. For example, companies that have empowered employee groups to evaluate performance and grant pay raises to their peers have found that they are much tougher than managers were.

Empowerment gives managers new responsibilities. They must hire and develop people capable of handling empowerment, encourage risk-taking, and recognize achievements. Giving employees information about company finances and the financial implications of empowered decisions is also important. At DuPont's Delaware River plant, management shares cost figures with all workers.[30] By sharing this information, management believes that workers will think more for themselves and identify with company goals. Globe Metallurgical regularly conducts small group meetings with its employees to review financial performance. To help employees make decisions on issues affecting production, a department manager at the Eastman Chemical plant in Texas supplied operators with a daily financial report that showed how their decisions affected the bottom line. As a result, department profits doubled in four months and quality improved by 50 percent as employees began suggesting cost-saving improvements.[31]

Empowerment can be viewed as vertical teamwork between managerial and nonmanagerial personnel. It builds confidence in workers by showing them that the company has confidence in their ability to make decisions on their own. It generates commitment and pride. It also gives employees better experience and an opportunity to advance their careers. It benefits customers who buy the organization's products and services. For instance, empowered employees can often reduce bureaucratic red tape that customers encounter, such as seeking a supervisor's signature, which makes customer transactions speedier and more pleasant. John Akers, former chairman of IBM, said, "Empowering our employees and inculcating a sense that everyone owns his or her piece of the business not only unleashes the talent and energy of our people, but also flattens the organization and reduces stifling bureaucracy."[32]

Although many workers prefer an empowered workplace to the old style of narrowly defined tasks, empowerment is not for everyone.[33] One worker at Eaton Corporation hated the idea of being her own boss and its associated responsibilities such as fixing broken machines and having to learn a wide variety of jobs, and left after nine months. This example suggests that selecting the right people for a particular work environment is an important task. We will discuss this issue later in this chapter.

Training and Education

Companies committed to TQ invest heavily in training and education. Xerox Business Products and Systems invested more than $125 million in quality training. Cadillac sent more than 1,400 employees to a four-day Deming seminar at a cost of nearly $1 million. Operations Management International, Inc. (see *Quality Profile*) provides a broad array of training opportunities for its workforce, including a six-day Obsessed with Quality orientation program, OMI University for management and leadership development, on-the-job training, and mentoring. Customer service representatives at FedEx receive five weeks of training before they ever speak unsupervised with a customer.

Training is one of the largest initial costs in a total quality initiative. Not surprisingly, it is one in which many companies are reluctant to invest. Even if companies make the investment, they often take great pains to measure the benefits against the

Quality Profile

Operations Management International, Inc.

Headquartered in Greenwood Village, Colorado, Operations Management International, Inc. (OMI) operates and maintains more than 160 public- and private-sector wastewater and water treatment facilities in 29 states and facilities in Brazil, Canada, Egypt, Israel, Malaysia, New Zealand, Philippines, and Thailand. OMI's primary services are processing raw wastewater to produce clean, environmentally safe effluent and processing raw groundwater and surface water to produce clean, safe drinking water. OMI's "E3" motto, "Exceed our customers' expectations, empower our employees, enhance the environment," is the foundation for its Quality as a Business Strategy leadership system. The leadership team communicates organizational priorities and strategic direction to all of its sites, which develop business and action plans that are consistent with its overall strategy, yet are specific to a particular site. Four strategic objectives—customer focus, business growth, innovation, and market leadership—enable OMI to design management systems and processes that consistently achieve high performance, reduce operating costs, and satisfy customers and associates.

OMI's annual average revenue per associate improved since 1997 from $92,600 to almost $108,00 in 2000. OMI's total revenue has grown from about $80 million in 1996 to about $145 million in 2000. This is an average annual growth rate of 15 percent, while top competitor revenues dropped by 4.5 percent. A survey of OMI's 19 industrial clients in 1999 found that OMI never fails to meet expectations and 88 percent say the company exceeds expectations. OMI's client satisfaction rating increased by 13.5 percent between 1992 and 1998 to a level of 5.47, on a scale of 1 (very poor) to 7 (outstanding). Satisfaction for its major competitor increased only 10 percent to a level of 5.05. OMI received a 2000 Baldrige Award.

Source: Malcolm Baldrige National Quality Award 2000 Recipients Press Release.

costs. Motorola used to do this assessment, but no longer. Its management *knows* that the benefits of quality-based training outweigh the costs by at least 30 to 1. Training and education have become an essential responsibility of HRM departments in TQ organizations, particularly as empowered employees require new knowledge and skills, which should not have to be cost-justified.

The leaders in quality—Deming, Juran, and Crosby—actively promoted quality training and education. Two of Deming's 14 Points, for example, are devoted to these issues. The approaches of quality leaders are not based on sophisticated statistics or new technologies. Rather, they are focused on the philosophical importance of quality and simple tools and techniques that are easily applied and understood. Once the basics are in place, more advanced statistical methods can be taught and applied.

Training generally includes quality awareness, leadership, project management, communications, teamwork, problem solving, interpreting and using data, meeting customer requirements, process analysis, process simplification, waste reduction, cycle time reduction, error-proofing, and other issues that affect employee effectiveness, efficiency, and safety. For instance, employees at Xerox learn a range of techniques, from the basic quality improvement tools introduced in Chapter 10 through benchmarking. Motorola employees learn statistical methods and defect reduction approaches. Other companies, such as FedEx and Wallace, train workers in team development and people issues. Solectron Corporation, with a large multicultural workforce in its U.S. facilities, offers English as a second language, and training in communications, interpersonal skills, and technical manufacturing skills, all with bilingual trainers.

In a total quality environment, employees need to understand the goal of customer satisfaction, to be given the training and responsibilities to achieve this goal, and to feel that they do indeed make a difference. For example, at the Coors Brewing Company in Golden, Colorado, the customer satisfaction improvement program is focused on giving employees the appropriate skills, and on creating the environment in which employees have one responsibility and one hoped-for result: to satisfy and delight their customers, especially internal customers. Coors engaged in a massive training program to learn TQ principles, and then restructured its organization systems (compensation, evaluation, and so on) to support the new effort. The company succeeded in developing in its employees a passion for their jobs and pride in their work, which translated into measurable improvements in productivity, a remarkably low turnover rate, and the delivery of quality product and service throughout the system.[34]

Training plans should be based upon job skill requirements and strategic initiatives of the company. For example, customer-contact personnel typically need a higher level of training in behavioral topics than manufacturing engineers, who may need advanced statistical skills. Customer needs should always drive training strategies. At IBM Rochester, for example, managers tell the education department what they need, and programs are designed to meet those needs. By treating the training function as an internal supplier, the time taken to deliver training programs has been reduced from five days to two.

Leading companies have formal training departments, whose systems and approaches evolved along with their overall quality systems. Specific approaches vary by company. In some, managers train their workers directly in a top-down fashion; this approach was pioneered by Xerox, beginning with the CEO, David Kearns himself, during their transition to total quality. Others have used self-paced methods employing advanced technology. The FedEx Quality Academy, established in 1991, uses a television network that broadcasts courses in a "just-in-time" fashion at the employees' work site. It also has a network of interactive video instruction, consisting of 1,200 workstations at 700 locations. More than 2,000 course titles are available for self-paced instruction. The Quality Academy tracks test scores, pass rates, and time spent online.[35] Honda of America uses interactive computer-based training modules on dedicated workstations in the plant.[36] Smaller companies often use outside consultants.

Training content should be customized to the company's needs; "packaged" seminars are often a waste of time. For example, AT&T developed a three-day training course for every manager.[37] The first day was aimed at creating an awareness of quality and productivity programs and progress throughout the world. Outside speakers reviewed the challenges to U.S. industry and the reasons for Japanese success. Company vice presidents discussed the challenges facing their lines of business. Other speakers talked about the methods used by other companies to manage quality and productivity. The second day focused on Juran's approach to quality and productivity improvement and how to organize and manage an annual improvement program. The final day dealt with tools, such as statistical methods, software, and project management. In addition, AT&T developed a number of courses specifically for product and process designers: a statistical reliability workshop, a reliability prediction workshop, an experimental design workshop, and a product and process design optimization workshop.

Continual reinforcement of lessons learned in training programs is essential. Many companies send employees to courses, but then allow the knowledge to slip away. New knowledge can be reinforced in several ways. Motorola uses on-the-job coaching to reinforce training; The Ritz-Carlton has follow-up sessions to monitor instructional effectiveness. The Ritz-Carlton holds a "quality lineup" briefing session each day in every work area. During these sessions, employees receive instructions on achieving quality certification within the company. Work area teams set the quality certification performance standards of each position. Finally, companies need an approach for evaluating training effectiveness. The Ritz-Carlton requires employees to pass written and skill demonstration tests. Other companies use on-the-job evaluation or tests in simulated work environments. Many measure behavior and attitude changes. However, the true test of training effectiveness is results. By establishing a linkage between training and results (see the discussion of interlinking in Chapter 8), companies can show the impact on customer satisfaction and also identify gaps in training.

Teamwork and Cooperation

Traditionally, human resource management has focused on individuals. This mindset is built into the management system by such practices as management by objectives, individual performance evaluation, professional status and privileges, and individual promotion. Focusing on individuals contributes to rivalries, competition, favoritism, and self-centeredness, which collectively work against accomplishing the true mission of an organization: serving customers. Alfie Kohn, who studied issues of cooperation and competition among employees over five years, concluded that the ideal amount of competition in any company is none at all. Any informal competition that may develop is best discouraged; management should go out of the way to design cooperative work groups and incentive systems.[38] Research has shown that the effectiveness of supervisors and subordinates alike is positively related to cooperation and negatively related to competitiveness. Even at the organizational level, cooperation between such departments as design and manufacturing, doctors and hospital administrators, and business managers and orchestra conductors is not the norm.

A single person rarely has enough knowledge or experience to understand all aspects of the most important work processes; thus, team approaches are essential for process improvement. Teamwork breaks down barriers between individuals, departments, and line and staff functions, an action prescribed by one of Deming's 14 Points. A **team** is a small number of people with complementary skills who are committed to a common purpose, set of performance goals, and an approach for which they hold themselves mutually accountable.[39] Although organizations have traditionally been formed around task or work groups, the concept of teams and teamwork has taken on a new meaning in a TQ environment. Teams provide opportunities to individuals to solve problems that they may not be able to solve on their own. Teams may perform a variety of problem-solving activities, such as determining customer needs, developing a flowchart to study a process, brainstorming to discover opportunities for improvement, selecting projects, recommending corrective actions, and tracking the effectiveness of solutions. Teams may also assume many traditional managerial functions. For example, an assembly team at GM's Saturn plant interviews and hires its own workers, approves parts from suppliers, chooses its equipment, and handles its own budget. Many special teams, programs, and committees support KARLEE Company's (see *Quality Profile*) culture of mutual trust, honesty, respect, and team member well-being. The company encourages such initiative as the KARLEE Cares Team that supports team members during stressful times such as a serious illness or death in the family.

Quality Profile
KARLEE Company

KARLEE Company is a contract manufacturer of precision sheet metal and machined components for the telecommunications, semiconductor, and medical equipment industries. It provides a full range of manufacturing services from initial component design to assembled, integrated products. Located in Garland, Texas, KARLEE's 550 team members have met or exceeded sales growth goals every year since 1994, while continuing to improve customer satisfaction and operational performance. Through the year 2000, sales growth rate has averaged more than 25 percent per year. Serving four major customers in the telecommunications, semiconductor, and medical equipment industries, KARLEE's customer focus is exemplified by constant, scheduled communications. Each primary customer is assigned a three-person customer service team to provide ongoing and proactive support. KARLEE leadership and team members actively support the community. Activities include tutoring at a local elementary school, coaching a high school team for a national robotics competition, and adopting needy families in the Garland community.

To improve the work environment and production processes, KARLEE uses manufacturing cells, consisting of state-of-the-art Computer Numerical Control equipment, machining centers, and robotic loading systems as well as concepts, such as lean manufacturing principles and statistical process control, which often are not used by smaller companies. In 2000, KARLEE went from lead-time assemblies of two to three weeks to quick-turn assemblies of one to two days. These increased turns have remained consistent in the presence of sales growth of 49 percent for these products. Results from KARLEE's Overall Customer Satisfaction Surveys since 1996 indicate that customer satisfaction ratings have improved 32.2 percent, while production volumes have more than tripled. KARLEE was recognized as a 2000 Baldrige Award recipient.

Source: Malcolm Baldrige National Quality Award 2000 Award Recipients Press Release.

Effective teams are goal-centered, independent, open, supportive, and empowered. The central role of teams, and the need for such team skills as cooperation, interpersonal communications, cross-training, and group decision making, represents a fundamental shift in how the work of public and private organizations is performed in the United States and most countries in the Western world. Employees who participate in team activities or who work in organizations that have formal quality improvement initiatives feel more empowered, are more satisfied with the rate of improvement in quality in their companies, and are far more likely to have received training on job-related, problem-solving, and team-building skills.

Many types of teams exist in different companies and industries. Among the most common are the following:

- *Quality Circles:* teams of workers and supervisors that meet regularly to address workplace problems involving quality and productivity.
- *Problem-Solving Teams:* teams whose members gather to solve a specific problem and then disband.
- *Management Teams:* teams consisting mainly of managers from various functions like sales and production that coordinate work among teams.

- *Work Teams:* teams organized to perform entire jobs, rather than specialized, assembly line-type work. When work teams are empowered, they are called *self-managed teams (SMTs)*. SMTs are complex and vary a great deal in how they are structured and how they function.
- *Project Teams:* teams with a specific mission to develop something new or to accomplish a complex task.
- *Virtual Teams:* relatively new, these team members communicate by computer, take turns as leaders, and jump in and out as necessary.[40]

Work teams and quality circles typically are intraorganizational; that is, members usually come from the same department or function. Management teams, problem-solving teams, project teams, and virtual teams are usually *cross-functional*; they work on specific tasks or processes that cut across boundaries of several different departments regardless of their organizational home. An example is the platform team approach to automotive vehicle development introduced by Chrysler.[41] This cross-functional team approach brings together professionals from engineering, design, quality, manufacturing, business planning, program management, purchasing, sales, marketing, and finance to work together to get a new vehicle to market. This idea, brought to Chrysler by its merger with smaller, more innovative AMC/Jeep was not accepted at Chrysler without significant upheaval and struggles. "You talk about internal strife," recalls one Chrysler loyalist. "This was war!"[42] Nevertheless, the concept was just what was needed to pull the company from bankruptcy and near collapse. The Dodge Viper, introduced in 1992, and the 1993 Jeep Grand Cherokee tested this approach, which led to the development of the Chrysler Concorde, Dodge Intrepid, and Eagle Vision in just 39 months, not only on time and under budget, but exceeding 230 product excellence targets. Today, all automobile manufacturers develop products using cross-functional teams.

Problem solving drives the team concept. Figure 6.3 illustrates the process by which teams commonly operate. The three basic functions are to identify, analyze, and solve quality and productivity problems. The methodology is a process of creative problem solving as discussed in Chapter 10. Problem-solving tools are taught to members by team leaders with the assistance of a facilitator, who is a full-time or part-time resource person. To illustrate how this process works, an information systems (IS) team for a manufacturing company faced a serious problem with internal customer satisfaction about its response to requests for application changes and help with using new software.[43] The team asked several internal customers to attend a meeting where the group brainstormed what the problem was. They agreed on the statement "Our response time to fix people's PCs is 24 hours, and the customer needs a response of eight hours or less." The team decided to collect data on cycle time and responsiveness to understand why delays were occurring. As they shared this information, they realized they had not known many of the facts. After analyzing the data, they decided to try a solution that assigned each person on the IS team as an account manager for each department. Their responsibility was to coordinate and communicate with accounts to monitor response time and customer satisfaction. If response time was not within the goal, the account manager was responsible for working with the IS team and department to handle the situation. As a means of control, they prompted the organization every two months for feedback about the solution and the process.

One example of the power of teamwork is New York Life.[44] Throughout the New York Life organization, teams with such innovative names as Hot Pursuit, Watch Dogs, Just the Fax, French Connection, and Raiders of the Lost Transactions are streamlining operations. One of the most successful efforts was the work of an 18-person team

Figure 6.3 Functions of Teams

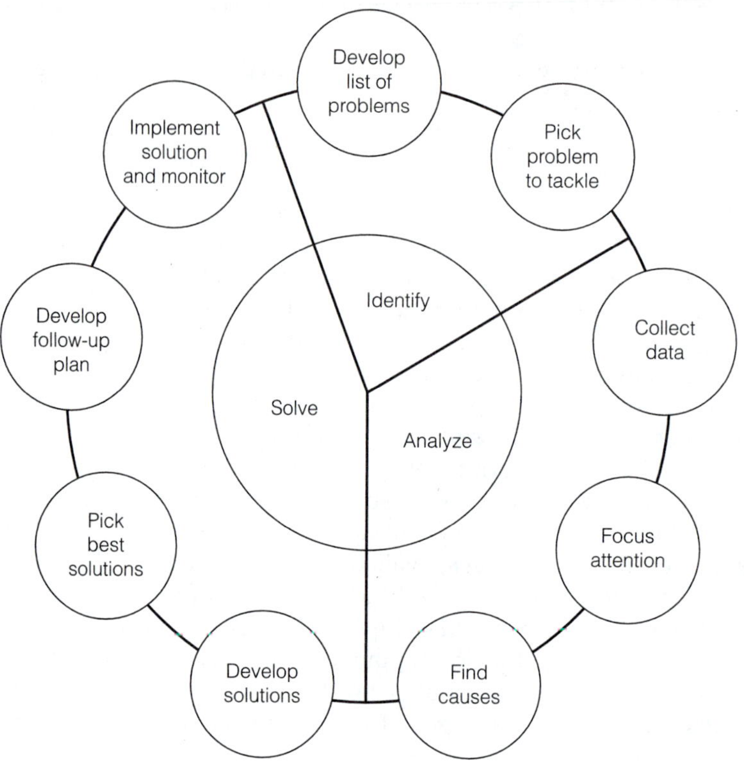

formed to determine why 7,000 letters a week—primarily premium notices—were being returned by the Post Office as "undeliverable." Called the Gravediggers because of their purpose of digging up addresses, the team, composed of employees from around the country, met weekly via teleconferences. Using problem-solving approaches, they discovered root causes such as policyholders moving and forgetting to notify the company; addresses that did not fit into the mailing envelope windows; addresses on applications that were difficult to read; and inadequate procedures for locating more accurate addresses. After implementing a variety of corrective measures, the volume of returned mail was reduced by more than 20 percent and saved more than $600,000 through bar coding and sorting.

Quality Circles A **quality circle** is a small group of employees from the same work area who meet regularly and voluntarily to identify, solve, and implement solutions to work-related problems.[45] The concept is attributed to Dr. Kaoru Ishikawa, of the University of Tokyo. The initial growth of quality circles in Japan was phenomenal. The Union of Japanese Scientists and Engineers (JUSE) estimated that registration in quality circles grew from 400 members in 1962 to 200,000 members in 1968 to more than 700,000 members in 1978. Today, millions of workers are involved. Toyota, for example, uses the problem-solving skills of circles and engineers to their advantage. When the firm found that 50 percent of its warranty losses were caused by 120 large problems and 4,000 small problems, the set of large problems were assigned to their engineers. The set of small problems was given to their quality circles.[46]

Quality circle concepts were not only known but also used by some U.S. firms in the late 1960s, according to existing evidence.[47] However, the concept received widespread publicity when a team of managers for Lockheed Missiles and Space Division in California made a trip to Japan in 1973 to view quality circles in action, and subsequently established them at Lockheed. After the success of the Lockheed program became known, many other manufacturing firms—including Westinghouse, General Electric, Cincinnati Milacron, Ford Motor Company, Dover Corporation, and Coors Brewing Company—established quality circle programs or began using similar team problem-solving approaches. Later, service organizations such as hospitals, school systems, and state and federal governmental units started quality circle programs.[48] After about five or six years of use in the United States, however, quality circles were labeled a "fad." Much of the feeling of disappointment in their promise resulted from management's failure to understand how to implement and manage them successfully. Still, they represented a starting point for many U.S. companies to develop and test out ideas on teamwork and participative management, and many are still active today. More importantly, they paved the way for more progressive kinds of teams.

Self-Managed Teams Many companies have now adopted the self-managed team (or self-directed work team) concept. A **self-managed team (SMT)** is defined as "a highly trained group of employees, from 6 to 18, on average, fully responsible for turning out a well-defined segment of finished work. The segment could be a final product, like a refrigerator or ball bearing; or a service, like a fully processed insurance claim. It could also be a complete but intermediate product or service, like a finished refrigerator motor, an aircraft fuselage, or the circuit plans for a television set."[49] SMTs are empowered to take corrective action and resolve day-to-day problems; they also have direct access to information that allows them to plan, control, and improve their operations. In short, employees in SMTs manage themselves.[50] SMTs offer a way to put the concepts of job enrichment and job enlargement into active operation.

The SMT concept was developed in Britain and Sweden in the 1950s. One of the early companies to adopt it was Volvo, the Swedish auto manufacturer. Pioneering efforts in SMT development were made by Procter & Gamble in 1962 and by General Motors in 1975. These U.S. developments were concurrent with the Japanese quality team developments which, in many cases, cannot be classified as true SMTs because of their limited autonomy. SMTs began to gain popularity in the United States in the late 1980s and are currently used in many industries, including food processing, auto-related businesses, petrochemicals, glassmaking, and other miscellaneous industries.[51] In 1994 3M Corporation designed and built a new facility in Canada entirely based on the SMT concept.

SMTs have the following characteristics:

- They are empowered to share various management and leadership functions.
- They plan, control, and improve their own work processes.
- They set their own goals and inspect their own work.
- They often create their own schedules and review their performance as a group.
- They may prepare their own budgets and coordinate their work with other departments.
- They usually order materials, keep inventories, and deal with suppliers.
- They frequently are responsible for acquiring any new training they might need.
- They may hire their own replacements or assume responsibility for disciplining their own members.
- They take responsibility for the quality of their products and services.[52]

A good example of an SMT in action is found at AT&T Credit Corporation, which was established in 1985 to provide financing for customers who lease equipment.[53] In most financial companies, the jobs in the back offices consist of processing applications, claims, and customer accounts—tasks that are similar to manufacturing assembly lines: dull and repetitive. The division of labor into small tasks and the organization of work by function are characteristic of many service organizations. One department handled applications and checked the customer's credit standing, a second drew up contracts, and a third collected payments. No one person had responsibility for providing full service to a customer. Recognizing these drawbacks, the company president decided to hire his own employees and give them ownership of the process and accountability for it. Although his first concern was to increase efficiency, his approach had the additional benefit of providing more rewarding jobs. In 1986 the company set up 11 teams of 10 to 15 newly hired workers in a high-volume division serving small businesses. The three major lease-processing functions were combined in each team. The company also divided its national staff of field agents into seven regions and assigned two or three teams to handle business from each one. In this way, the same teams always worked with the same sales staff, establishing a personal relationship with both them and their customers. Above all, team members took responsibility for solving customers' problems. Their slogan became, "Whoever gets the call owns the problem." Members make most decisions on how to deal with customers, schedule their own time off, reassign work when people are absent, and interview prospective new employees. The teams process up to 800 lease applications daily versus half that amount under the old system, and they have reduced the time for final credit approvals from several days to 24 to 48 hours.

SMTs have many benefits. They facilitate continuous improvement, provide greater flexibility and faster response, offer employees a higher level of involvement and job satisfaction, increase organizational commitment, and help to attract and retain the best people. They have also achieved many positive results. Experts estimate that SMTs are 30 to 50 percent more productive than conventional teams. FedEx, for instance, reduced service errors by 13 percent; one 3M facility increased production by 300 percent; in a Mercedes-Benz plant, defects were reduced by 50 percent. A study of 22 manufacturing plants using SMTs found that more than half of them made improvements in quality and productivity, removed at least one layer of management or supervision, and decreased their levels of grievances, absenteeism, and turnover.[54]

Developing Successful Teams Jumping into team approaches without adequate planning is an invitation to disaster. A period of investigation, reflection, and soul searching is necessary before plunging into any team initiatives. Many companies rush out and form the wrong kind of teams for a specific job. For example, quality circle-type teams cannot achieve the same type of results as a cross-functional problem-solving team or a self-managed team. Managers should examine their organization's goals, objectives, and culture to evaluate its readiness to develop and support team-based initiatives. This step may be the most difficult portion of the process, because it demands a hard self-appraisal of the organization as a whole. One enthusiastic manager can often get teams going, but solid support at a number of managerial levels is necessary to keep them going. Managers should then analyze the work required. Teams take a lot of maintenance, and if the work can be done faster and better by a single person, a team should not be used.

Peter Scholtes, a leading authority on teams for quality improvement, has suggested 10 ingredients for a successful team:

1. *Clarity in team goals.* As a sound basis, a team agrees on a mission, purpose, and goals.
2. *An improvement plan.* A plan guides the team in determining schedules and mileposts by helping the team decide what advice, assistance, training, materials, and other resources it may need.
3. *Clearly defined roles.* All members must understand their duties and know who is responsible for what issues and tasks.
4. *Clear communication.* Team members should speak with clarity, listen actively, and share information.
5. *Beneficial team behaviors.* Teams should encourage members to use effective skills and practices to facilitate discussions and meetings.
6. *Well-defined decision procedures.* Teams should use data as the basis for decisions and learn to reach consensus on important issues.
7. *Balanced participation.* Everyone should participate, contribute their talents, and share commitment to the team's success.
8. *Established ground rules.* The group outlines acceptable and unacceptable behaviors.
9. *Awareness of group process.* Team members exhibit sensitivity to nonverbal communication, understand group dynamics, and work on group process issues.
10. *Use of the scientific approach.* With structured problem-solving processes, teams can more easily find root causes of problems.[55]

Self-managed teams represent the greatest challenge because the teams are empowered. Organizations that have SMTs have typically arrived at them through one of two routes—organizational start up with SMTs in place, or transformations from more limited team structures. The second is often a next logical step after other types of employee involvement programs have reached maturity. Figure 6.4 shows the approach used by Boeing Airlift and Tanker Programs to develop self-managed teams, a result of an historic agreement between the company and union to support employee participation and empowerment.

A process for moving from quality circle-type teams to SMTs involves the following:[56]

1. *Creating a work unit responsible for an entire task.* This step requires defining a whole work unit based on identifying a customer, establishing a means of contact between the team and customer, and establishing the standard for the product or service.
2. *Establishing specific measures of the work unit's output.* It includes defining standards for outputs in terms of quality, quantity, cost, and timeliness, together with accountability and a feedback system.
3. *Designing multiskilled jobs.* A systematic study of workflow functions and variances is followed by redesign of the jobs to enhance the development of multiple skills.
4. *Creating internal management and coordination tasks.* The coordination of the work team's tasks, typically handled by managers in a conventional organization, is handled by the team and covers items such as scheduling, task assignments, hiring of new members, and cross-functional training, which must be addressed by designers as well as by the team itself.
5. *Creating boundary management tasks.* Processes and procedures must be established to coordinate with managers, other departments, suppliers, and customers outside the group.

Figure 6.4 Boeing A&T Team Development Process

Stage 1* Team Formation	Stage 2* Team Building	Stage 3* Empowerment	Stage 4* Self-Direction/ High Performance
Amount of Empowerment at Team Level →			
• Plan team tasks • Develop team communication	• Define measures • Develop team milestones • Improve quality, cost, and cycle time • Schedule and hold team meetings	• Attack larger problems • Review team measures • Control inventory • Schedule team training • Perform equipment maintenance	• Manage team performance • Continually improve quality, cost, and cycle time • Identify own jobs • Perform to team budget; track costs and take accountability • Select team members
Directs Team—Builds Trust • Identify goals, outcomes, timelines • Provide direction • Lead in solving problems, making decisions • Control budget and some scheduling • Give frequent follow-up	**Coaches Team—Shares Information** • Involve team in problem solving • Control team budget • Provide support • Work with team to define performance and how measured	**Supports Team—Creates Autonomy** • Help in problem solving • Share budget responsibility • Ask team to lead in solving problems	**Delegates Authority—Provide Support** • Support multiple teams
Transition from Manager to Leader →			

* Stages may overlap under certain conditions. Team maturity and level of process improvement already in place may impact stage application.

Source: Courtesy of Boeing Airlift and Tanker Programs.

6. *Establishing access to information.* The group defines the information needed and the design of the processes, hardware, and software necessary to obtain direct, accurate, and timely performance-related feedback and information.
7. *Establishing support systems.* The work team must consider how the teams are to be supported, which involves the "hows" of training, career progression (based on skills developed and used), team interfacing with management, and payments and rewards.

A study conducted by Development Dimensions International, the Association for Quality and Participation, and *Industry Week* identified four key factors associated with successful SMTs.[57] First, the longer teams have been in place, the more positive are the reported results. This observation suggests that higher benefits occur with time, and that companies need to be patient. Second, a direct positive correlation could be made between the extent of job rotation and the reported results, which suggests that teams with a more complete understanding of their processes and business have a greater impact on quality and productivity. Third, the effective leadership of supervisors and group leaders in providing direction, resources, and business information; coaching teams; and recognizing contributions led to increased member satisfaction, quality, and productivity. Finally, teams that had responsibility for both production and personnel tasks reported the most positive results. These factors provide important guidelines for organizations that plan on using SMTs.

Compensation and Recognition

Without willing, sustained, individual effort and coordinated teamwork focused on meeting organizational goals, TQ is an impossible dream. However, when organizations ask employees to assume new challenges and responsibilities, the question "What's in it for me?" ultimately gets asked. Extrinsic and intrinsic rewards are the key to sustained individual efforts. *Compensation and recognition* refer to all aspects of pay and reward, including promotions, bonuses, and recognition, either monetary and nonmonetary or individual and group.

Compensation Compensation is always a sticky issue, closely tied to the subject of motivation and employee satisfaction. Money is a motivator when people are at the bottom of Maslow's hierarchy (discussed later in this chapter). Pay for performance can diminish intrinsic motivation. It causes most employees to believe they are being treated unfairly, and forces managers to deliver negative messages. Eventually, it creates win-lose situations. The objectives of a good compensation system should be to attract, retain, and not demotivate employees. Other objectives include reducing unexplainable variation in pay (think about Deming's principles) and encouraging internal cooperation rather than competition. Most companies still use traditional financial measures, such as revenue growth, profitability, and cost management, as a basis for compensation; more progressive organizations use quality measures such as customer satisfaction, defect prevention, and cycle-time reduction to make compensation decisions.

Many TQ-focused companies now base compensation on the market rate for an individual with proven capabilities, and then make adjustments as capabilities are increased, along with enhanced responsibilities, seniority, and business results. For example, General Motors' Powertrain Division, influenced strongly by Deming, decoupled compensation from performance appraisals. Compensation is determined from a "maturity curve" that considers an individual's seniority, level of expertise, and market for his or her services. Peers and subordinates have input as to an individual's rating on this curve. Distinctions based on contributions are limited to truly exceptional individuals. This exception is found in few companies; most have not eliminated merit ratings from their salary systems.

Many companies link compensation to company track records, unit performance, team success, or individual achievement.[58] At Kaiser Aluminum, such performance-based compensation incentives led to an 80 percent improvement in productivity and 70 percent decrease in poor quality costs over five years.[59] Team-based pay and *gainsharing*, an approach in which all employees share savings equally, are gaining in popularity and importance. Xerox and Texas Nameplate, for example, use gainsharing plans. Compensation for individuals is sometimes tied to the acquisition of new skills, often within the context of a continuous improvement program in which all employees are given opportunities to broaden their work-related competencies. However, legal restrictions in federal wage and hour laws make it difficult to implement some of these approaches. At a 1999 hearing of a subcommittee of the House Committee on Education and the Workforce, Pam Farr, a management consultant with the Cabot Advisory Group who had previously worked for Marriott Corporation as a human resources executive, testified:

> *A recent survey by William M. Mercer indicated that just 24% of large and midsize companies use team-based incentive pay. For companies that have chosen to implement team incentive pay programs, however, the results are overwhelmingly positive. A recent study by the Hay Group indicated that team-based and gainsharing plans are the most effective programs to help*

> *improve employee performance and satisfaction. A General Accounting Office study indicated that such programs significantly improve employer-employee relations, and reduce grievances, absenteeism and turnover. By removing the impediments to team-based pay systems, Congress will facilitate employee pay increases, employee work satisfaction and encourage productivity increases.*[60]

Nucor Corporation, one of the nation's largest steel producers, is well-known for having succeeded in attacking quality, productivity, participation, and compensation issues.[61] Nucor has more than 6,000 employees in plants in the United States and had annualized sales exceeding $4 billion in mid-1997. All employees, from the president on down, have the same benefits; the only differences in individual pay are related to responsibilities. Workers at Nucor's five nonunion steel mills earn base hourly rates that are less than half of the going rate for unionized steelworkers. Nucor uses pay incentives designed around groups of 40 to 50 workers, including secretaries and senior managers. They offer four basic compensation plans:

1. *Production Incentive Plan.* Employees involved directly in manufacturing are paid weekly bonuses on the basis of production of their work groups, which range from 20 to 40 workers each. These productivity and quality bonuses are based on the number of tons of steel of acceptable quality produced by a given production team. The formulas are nondiscretionary, based upon established production goals, and can average 80–150 percent of the base wage. This plan creates pressure for each individual to perform well, and in some facilities, is tied to attendance and tardiness standards. No bonus is paid if equipment is not operating, thus creating a strong emphasis on maintaining equipment in top operational condition at all times. The bonuses are paid every week to reinforce motivation. The average worker at Nucor earns several thousand dollars per year more than the average worker in the industry, while the company is able to sell its steel at competitive worldwide market prices.
2. *Department Manager Incentive Plan.* Department managers earn incentive bonuses paid annually based primarily on the return on assets of their facility.
3. *Nonproduction and Nondepartment Manager Incentive Plan.* Participants include accountants, engineers, secretaries, and other employees. The bonus is based on the facility's return on assets. Each month every operation receives a report showing progress, which is posted in the employee cafeteria or break area to keep employees informed of their expected bonus levels throughout the year.
4. *Senior Officers Incentive Plan.* Senior officers do not receive profit sharing, pension, discretionary bonuses, or retirement plans. A significant part of their compensation is based upon Nucor's return on stockholder's equity above a certain minimum earnings. If Nucor does well, compensation is well above average, as much as several times base salary. If the company does poorly, compensation is limited to base salary, which is below the average pay at comparable companies.

The company was producing a ton of steel for less than half the average costs of a U.S. steel company.[62] For example, in September 1997, when other steel companies were attempting to raise prices for steel, Nucor announced that it was cutting the price of cold-rolled steel, one of the most widely used product lines, by 7 percent.[63] Nucor required fewer than four hours of labor per ton, Japanese companies required about five hours per ton, and other U.S. mills averaged more than six hours per ton. This comparison illustrates the use and benefits of team-based pay policies.

During downturns, managers at Nucor frequently find that their bonuses are cut, even while hourly workers continue to receive theirs, based on production rates. One difficult year, Nucor cut salaries for its 12 top executives by 5 percent and froze wages for its 3,500 employees. However, despite the tough times, it maintained their policy of no layoffs as it had throughout the history of the current company. The next year, when the United Steelworkers Union signed a contract to reduce wages and benefits in order to improve the competitiveness of the basic steel industry, Nucor announced a 5 percent wage increase. More about the Nucor story can be found on its Internet site at *http://www.nucor.com.*

Special Recognition and Rewards Special recognition and rewards can be monetary or nonmonetary, formal or informal, individual or group. They might include trips, promotional gifts, clothing, time off, or special company-sponsored awards and events. Awards provide a visible means of promoting quality efforts and telling employees that the organization values their efforts, which stimulates their motivation to improve. Most importantly, rewards should lead to behaviors that increase customer satisfaction. A Conference Board study found that a combination of cash and noncash recognition works better for clerical and hourly workers than for managers and professional or technical employees; for these groups, compensation-based incentives such as stock options are more successful.[64] As an example, in October 1994, Continental Airlines new CEO Gordon Bethune calculated that late and canceled flights were costing the company $6 million per month to put passengers on rival airlines or send them to hotels. He declared that if Continental ranked among the top three airlines for on-time performance in any month, he would split half the savings (about $65 per person) with all nonexecutive employees. Within two months, Continental was first. To ensure that the bonuses made a vivid impression, Bethune issued the checks separately and traveled around the country to distribute thousands of them personally. The behavioral changes are best illustrated by a story executives like to retell. A catering truck pulls up to a plane but is 10 meals short. In the old days, the flight attendant would have told the driver to get the extra meals while the plane sat at the gate for 40 minutes. The newly gung ho flight attendant, however, crisply tells the catering guy not to screw up again and shuts the cabin door. The plane pushes back on schedule, and she finds a bunch of investment bankers and offers them free liquor in place of the meal.[65]

Employees should contribute to the company's performance and recognition approaches. L.L. Bean, for example (see the *Quality in Practice* case at the end of this chapter), gives dinners or certificates exchangeable for merchandise. Winners of "Bean's Best Awards" are selected by cross-functional teams based on innovative ideas, exceptional customer service, role modeling, expertise at their jobs, and exceptional management ability.[66]

Certain key practices lead to effective employee recognition and rewards:

- *Giving both individual and team awards.* At The Ritz-Carlton, individual awards include verbal and written praise and the most desirable job assignments. Team awards include bonus pools and sharing in the gratuity system. Many companies have formal corporate recognition programs, such as IBM's Market Driven Quality Award for outstanding individual and team achievements in quality improvement, or the Xerox President's Award and Team Excellence Award.
- *Involving everyone.* Recognition programs involve both front-line employees and senior management. Westinghouse has a Wall of Fame to recognize quality achievers at each site. Solectron rewards groups by buying lunch for entire divisions and bringing in ice cream for everyone in the plant. A Monsanto Company chemical plant ties worker bonuses to results at individual units and rewards

workers for helping to prevent accidents.[67] What is particularly interesting is that different programs exist in different Monsanto plants—all developed with the participation of workers. Bonus plans that failed had been ones decreed by corporate headquarters, rather than those formulated in cooperation with employees.

- *Tying rewards to quality based on measurable objectives.* Leading companies recognize and reward behavior, not just results. Zytec rewards employees for participating in the suggestion program by providing cash awards for each implemented suggestion. A group of peers selects the best improvement ideas each month, which are also rewarded with cash. Many rewards are linked to customer satisfaction measures. Awards that conflict with quality values are modified or eliminated. Continuous feedback reinforces good performance and identifies areas for improvement. When Custom Research, Inc., attains a specific corporate goal, the entire company is taken on a trip to destinations such as San Francisco and Disney World!
- *Allowing peers and customers to nominate and recognize superior performance.* Texas Instruments, for example, has a Site Quality Award to recognize the top 2 percent on the basis of peer nomination. Employees at FedEx who receive favorable comments from a customer are automatically nominated for the Golden Falcon Award. Recipients chosen by a review committee receive a gold pin, a congratulatory call from the CEO, recognition in the company newsletter, and 10 shares of company stock. AT&T Universal Card Services' World of Thanks award consists of a globe-shaped pad of colored paper with "Thank You" written in different languages. Anyone in the company can write a message of thanks to someone else. In four years, employees have used over 130,000 of them![68]
- *Publicizing extensively.* Many companies recognize employees through newsletters, certificates and pins, special breakfasts or luncheons, and annual events such as competitions. Motorola, for example, developed a worldwide total customer satisfaction (TCS) team competition. Approximately half of Motorola's 142,000 employees are on teams that compete locally, regionally, and internationally to attend the final one-day, corporatewide competition that is held at a resort each year. The 1996 competition included 24 teams from eight countries. Teams were scored on such criteria as project selection, teamwork, analysis techniques, remedies, results, institutionalization (permanence, deployment, and team growth from the project), and presentation. Corporatewide results over eight years have been impressive, with an estimated savings of $2.4 billion per year.[69]
- *Making recognition fun.* Domino's Pizza stages a national Olympics, in which teams from the company's three regions compete in 15 events based on 15 job categories, such as doughmaking, driving, answering the telephone, and delivery. Winners, standing on platforms while the Olympic theme is played, receive medals, checks, and other forms of recognition. The finals are broadcast live to commissaries around the country. Domino's Olympics provides an excellent way to benchmark efforts throughout the corporation; winners attend three days of discussion with upper management to discuss what's good about the company, what needs improvement, and how those improvements can be made.[70]

Health, Safety, and Employee Well-Being

Because employees are key stakeholders of any organization, their health, safety, and overall well-being are important factors in the work environment. Health and safety have always been priorities in most companies, but working conditions now extend beyond basic issues of keeping the work area safe and clean. For example, as we learn more about ergonomic-related disorders such as carpal tunnel syndrome, employers have an even greater responsibility to incorporate health and safety factors into human resource plans. And there are other responsibilities, such as providing reasonable accommodations for workers with disabilities or ensuring that employees are protected from sexual harassment from fellow workers and others.

Most companies have many opportunities to contribute to the quality of working life. They can provide personal and career counseling, career development and employability services, recreational or cultural activities, daycare, special leave for family responsibilities or for community services, flexible work hours, outplacement services, and extended health care for retirees. Johnson & Johnson's Ethicon Endo-surgery Division, in Blue Ash, Ohio, has a wellness center with exercise rooms and equipment to support employees in their manufacturing and R&D facility. Employees can use the center before or after working hours or during their breaks. In addition, those workers who are assembling products get regular, programmed "ergonomic" breaks every few hours, where they are required to do exercises designed to prevent repetitive motion injuries. All of these opportunities contribute to creating a more productive, safer, and more enjoyable work environment.

SAS Institute, Inc., one of *Fortune*'s "100 Best Companies to Work For" (number two in the 2000 poll), is a high-tech software development company based in Cary, North Carolina. SAS has a people-focused founder and CEO in the person of James Goodnight. Perhaps the most eye-opening policy of the firm is its mandated seven-hour work day. No "all-nighters" are expected of SAS employees. The multi-billionaire, Goodnight, sets the example by leaving the office at 5 P.M., sharp. Many of the lavish employee perks at the sprawling corporate campus are family- and lifestyle-oriented, from daycare centers, lactation rooms, a Montessori school, and a college prep private high school, to a 55,000-square-foot athletic facility, free massages, free car washes, and end-of-year bonuses. The payoff? SAS has about 4 percent turnover in an industry where 20 percent is the norm.[71]

MANAGING HUMAN RESOURCES IN A TOTAL QUALITY ENVIRONMENT

Even though management can do much to design a high-performance workplace, the day-to-day management activities, which includes how employees are selected and developed, how they are motivated at work, and how their performance is evaluated can have a major impact on the success or failure of total quality efforts in an organization.

Recruitment and Career Development

Meeting and exceeding customer expectations begins with hiring the right people whose skills and attitudes will support and enhance the organization's objectives. For example, some companies are finding that not all people are successful in an empowered workplace.[72] Motorola ties recruitment and selection activities to results in order to gauge the quality of its recruiting efforts as it strives for TQ at every level.[73] The recruiting department is measured by a new quality-oriented criterion: success of recruits on the job. Instead of using the old measure of how much it costs to hire each recruit, recruiters are now measured on whether new hires were well trained coming into the company, brought in at the right salary level, or left the company after the first six months for a better job. Based on these and other data, the department decided it had to increase, rather than decrease, the amount spent on each recruit. Thus, in recruiting activities, Motorola plans and sets objectives for recruiting, charts progress over time in order to reduce "defects" in the hiring process, and determines whether the "output" of the process (excellent employees) is under control, rather than simply measuring inputs (dollars per recruit). Other major companies such as Procter & Gamble seek entry-level college graduates who understand total quality principles. They specifically want their new employees to think in terms of creating quality and value for consumers, to understand their customers and needs, and to work toward results despite obstacles.

Customer-contact employees make up one of the fastest-growing segments of the workforce. Limited availability of people with the skills to perform complex, rapidly changing jobs is forcing HRM managers to rethink their selection strategies. Traditional hiring practices have been based on cognitive or technical rather than interpersonal skills. The criterion is now shifting to attributes such as enthusiasm, resourcefulness, creativity, and the flexibility to learn new skills rapidly. The internal customer concept suggests that every employee needs good interpersonal skills. Even technical skill requirements are changing; to apply quality principles on the job, all workers must have basic mathematics and logical-thinking abilities.

Customer-focused employees should exhibit certain characteristics:[74]

- The ability to remain calm under stressful situations
- Optimism, initiative, and a "people orientation"
- The ability to listen well
- An orientation toward analysis and prevention
- The ability to solve problems

To ensure that job candidates have the requisite skills, new approaches, such as psychological testing and situational role playing, are now being used in the hiring process.

Cisco Systems, one of the most successful Silicon Valley companies, provides a good example of how far recruiting processes have recently evolved.[75] "Cisco has an overall goal of getting the top 10 percent to 15 percent of people in our industry," says CEO John Chambers. It has proven to be a major challenge for recruiters for Cisco as the job market for technically trained people has become increasingly tight in the United States. Cisco has developed several recruiting innovations to help cope with the challenge. The company has targeted what it terms "passive job seekers." These are excellent employees who have survived layoffs in their current firms and who are not actively seeking opportunities to change jobs. To get them to come to Cisco, the firm found that it had to analyze the characteristics of its target job seekers, as well as reengineer its own recruiting procedures.

The company assembled focus groups of typical recruiting targets, such as experienced engineers and marketing personnel. They determined what they did in their spare time, which Web sites they visited most frequently, and how they felt about job hunting. A significant finding was that the target population hated job hunting. Cisco then began to develop a nontraditional recruiting strategy to make prospects aware of opportunities at the firm and also make hiring them a more comfortable process.

Recruiters went to locations where job prospects might be found, such as local festivals and home shows. They took out newspaper ads that listed general job categories rather than specific jobs, and asked prospects to apply directly from Cisco's home page on the Web (*http://www.cisco.com*). They also developed a "Friends at Cisco" program, whereby volunteer Cisco employees make themselves available to talk to prospects who want to know what it's like to work at Cisco, and even advertised this program at area movie houses, a favorite hangout for relaxing "techies."

As a last resort, Cisco has also gained new, talented employees by acquiring firms. It acquired 12 firms in 1996, and kept almost all of those firms' employees. To keep pace with growth that is faster than Cisco has office space for, the new employees are often permitted to telecommute.

Career development is also changing because of TQ. As managerial roles shift from directing and controlling to coaching and facilitating, managers who must deal with cross-functional problems benefit more from horizontal movement than from upward movement in narrow functional areas. Flatter organizations limit promotion opportunities. Thus, career development expands learning opportunities and creates more challenging assignments rather than increasing spans of managerial control.

Motivation

Motivation and human behavior are major elements of Deming's Profound Knowledge discussed in Chapter 3. Deming spoke of motivation as being primarily intrinsic (internal), and was suspicious of external forms of motivation, such as incentives and bonuses. Managers must understand that there is no such thing as an unmotivated employee. The system within which employees work can seriously affect motivation. Although thousands of studies have been performed over the years on human and animal subjects in attempts to define and refine the concept of motivation, it remains an extremely complex phenomenon that still is not fully understood.

As managers in a TQ environment take on new roles as coaches and facilitators, their skills in motivating employees become even more crucial. If managers and workers are to be successful in organizational design, teamwork, and improvement activities, then simplistic knowledge and understanding of motivation are insufficient. To aid them in job design and organizational processes, managers and workers can apply some appropriate motivational tools that are available. This section briefly reviews the major theories, models, and approaches, and their implications for TQ.

Saul W. Gellerman defined **motivation** as "the art of creating conditions that allow every one of us, warts and all, to get his work done at his own peak level of efficiency."[76] A more formal definition of motivation is *an individual's response to a felt need*. Thus, some stimulus, or activating event, must spur the need to respond to that stimulus, generating the response itself. For example, an individual worker given the goal or quality task of achieving zero defects on the parts that he or she produces may feel a need to keep his or her job. Consequently, the worker is motivated by the stimulus of fear and responds by carefully producing parts to achieve the goal. Another less insecure worker may feel the need for approval of his or her work by peers or superiors and be motivated by the stimulus of pride. The worker then responds to that need and that stimulus by producing high-quality parts.

Researchers have proposed many theories and models to describe how and why people are motivated. A theory is a way to describe, predict, and control what is observed in the world. Models graphically or symbolically show what a theory is saying in words. Often a model is so closely associated with a theory that the terms are used interchangeably. Theories and models are often classified according to common themes. James L. Bowditch and Anthony F. Buono categorize motivation theories as *content*, *process*, and *environmentally based* theories.[77] These theories are often studied in traditional management courses and are summarized in Table 6.5. In the behavioral sciences, as well as in the pure sciences, the originator of a theory is becoming more and more difficult to determine because many researchers' ideas often overlap.

Table 6.5 A Classification of Motivation Theories

Motivation Theory	Pioneer/Developer	Type of Theory
Content Theories		
Hierarchy of Needs	Abraham Maslow	Need
Motivation and Maintenance	Frederick Herzberg	Need/satisfaction
Theory X-Y	Douglas McGregor	Managerial expectations
n-Ach, n-Aff, n-Pow	David McClelland	Acquired need
Process Theories		
Preference–Expectancy	Victor H. Vroom	Expectancy
Contingency	Porter and Lawler	Expectancy/reward
Goal Setting	Edward Locke	Goal
Path–Goal Theory of Leadership	Robert J. House	Goal
Environmentally Based Theories		
Operant Conditioning	B. F. Skinner	Reinforcement
Equity	J. Stacy Adams	Equity
Social Learning/Self-Efficacy	A. Bandura Snyder and Williams	Social Learning/Self-Efficacy

Thus, the information in Table 6.5 is merely suggestive of one or more names that have been associated with the development of the theory. Although we will review some fundamental ideas, a complete discussion of motivation is beyond the scope of this text.

Content Theories Many of the theories of motivation developed by behavioral scientists over the past 75 years use simple content models that describe how and why people are motivated to work. Four of the best-known content models are those developed by Abraham Maslow, Douglas McGregor, Frederick Herzberg, and David McClelland.[78]

Content models provide for a static "snapshot" of how people are motivated to perform certain activities. For example, Herzberg's two-factor theory describes two categories of factors, called "maintenance" and "motivational" factors. Maintenance factors are conditions that employees have come to expect, such as a safe working environment, a reasonable level of job security, supervision, and even adequate pay. Workers in a situation with these conditions will not be dissatisfied, but maintenance factors generally do not provide any motivation to work harder. Motivational factors, such as recognition, advancement, achievement, and the nature of the work itself are less tangible, but do motivate people to be more committed to and satisfied with their work. From Herzberg's theory arose the concept of job enrichment, defined earlier in this chapter. With job enrichment, employees gain a sense of fulfillment (satisfaction) from completion of every cycle of a task. Acquiring cross-functional skills, working in teams, and increased empowerment are forms of job enrichment.

Garvin presents an interesting example of how Japanese managers in the air-conditioning industry view job enrichment as important to quality.[79] In Japan, newly hired workers are trained so that they can do every job on the line before eventually being assigned to only one job. Training frequently requires six to twelve months, in contrast to the standard training time of one to two days for newly hired production workers in U.S. air-conditioning companies. The advantage of this "enriched" training is that workers are better able to track a defect to its source and can frequently suggest remedies to problems because they understand the entire process from start to finish.

Process Theories The second major thrust in motivation theories was the development of *process models*. Process theories and their models explain the dynamic process (as opposed to the static "snapshots" of content theories) of how people make choices under certain types of processes or situations in an effort to obtain desired rewards. The most influential theories were developed by Victor H. Vroom, Lyman Porter and Edward Lawler, Edward Locke, and Robert J. House.

Vroom proposed his preference-expectancy theory in 1964.[80] Vroom's work formed the basis for one of the better known process theories, the Porter and Lawler model, which is one of the most widely accepted process models of motivation available today. Porter and Lawler extended Vroom's work by examining more closely the traits and perceptions of the individual and the nature and impact of rewards on motivation. The Porter and Lawler model is a process model that explains the conditions and processes (contingencies) by which motivation to work takes place.[81] A contingency model defines the variables of a process, the interactions between those variables, and the dynamic conditions under which those variables work.

The Porter and Lawler model is shown in Figure 6.5. The flow of this model indicates that effort (Box 3) is dependent on value of reward (Box 1) and perceived effort-reward probability (Box 2). Effort leads to performance (Box 6), which is affected by the abilities and traits (Box 4) and the role perceptions (Box 5) of the individual. Performance (Box 6), in turn, influences actual rewards—intrinsic (Box 7A) or extrinsic (Box 7B)—as well as perceived equitable rewards (Box 8), and exerts a long-term influence (feedback) on perceived effort-reward probability. The rewards (Boxes 7A and 7B) and their perceived equity (Box 8) then influence satisfaction (Box 9), which has a long-term influence (feedback) on the value of reward (Box 1).

Figure 6.5 Porter and Lawler Expectancy Model

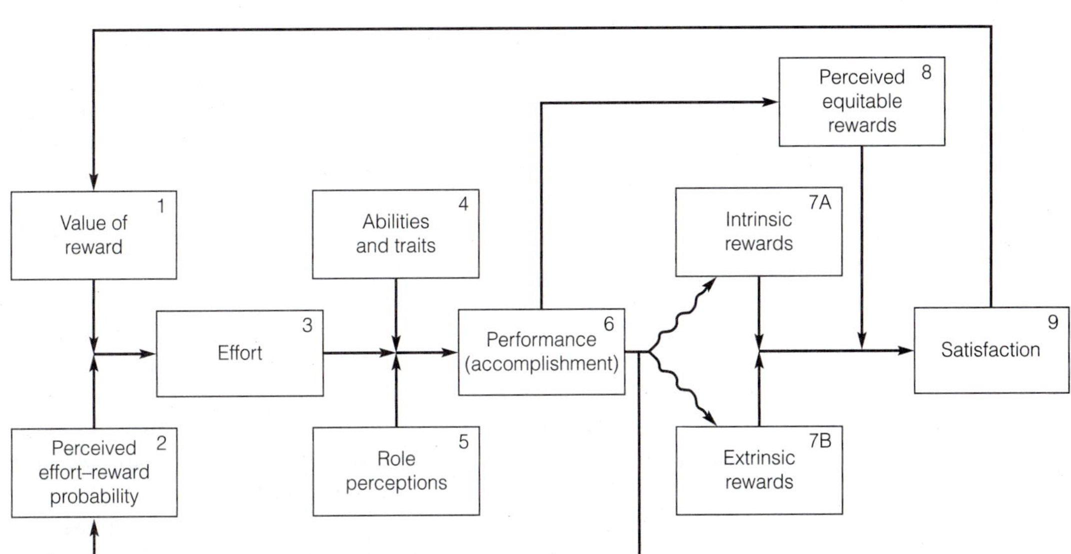

Source: L. W. Porter and Edward E. Lawler, *Managerial Attitudes and Performance* (Burr Ridge, IL: Irwin, 1968); used with permission.

Components of the model are *expectancy* (which includes performance-outcome expectancy and effort-performance expectancy), *instrumentality* (the combination of abilities, traits, and role perceptions), and *valence* (preference for anticipated outcomes). Valence is represented by the value of reward. Expectancy is included in the perceived effort-reward probability and is also related to perceived equitable rewards. Instrumentality is the linking of effort to performance (accomplishment), moderated by abilities and traits and role perceptions. Successful performance then results in intrinsic rewards (a feeling of accomplishment) and extrinsic rewards (raises or bonuses). Given that rewards are equitable, employees experience satisfaction, which in turn contributes to renewal of the motivation cycle. The model states that, depending on the actions of management, the expectations of employees, and the actual outcomes, a certain quantity and quality of employee motivation is present in an organization. Porter and Lawler's model, while more complex than content models, accounts for the process dynamics that content models lack.

Both opportunities and questions surround the issue of how certain aspects of motivation theories, such as goals and performance targets, may be applied in a TQ environment.[82] Obviously, continuous improvement activities suggest that managers and workers set challenging goals and try to reach them. At the same time, if quality is a "race without a finish line," then no clear path of goal attainment can be determined. Without that clear path, managers cannot assist their workers in setting and reaching ever-higher goals toward improvement.

The debate between process and content theories of motivation centers on which theory is a more accurate representation of human motivation. Obviously, they represent two views of the same reality. The content approach provides a simple, static representation of components of motivation. The process approach focuses on the dynamic interaction between the components of effort, ability, rewards, and performance as perceived by individuals in the work environment. Understanding both content and process views can aid managers as they attempt to design work to enhance motivation for quality.

Environmentally Based and Other Motivation Theories Other theories of motivation are being developed and may have implications for motivating employees to make quality products and quality decisions. Some of the categories for these theories include environmentally based theories (such as Skinner's operant conditioning[83]), Adams' equity theory,[84] and social learning and self-efficacy theories.[85] The latter category holds promise because these theories attempt to integrate earlier approaches to controlling behavior and actions by managing the immediate environment with the more individualistic theories that say that people will exercise self-control and will have self-confidence in their abilities to perform well on the job, if given the chance. Goleman's "emotional intelligence" theory[86] is one of the newest social learning and self-efficacy theories now under development.

A TQ-based model that provides some interesting insights was presented by Thomas and Tymon.[87] Their theory is designed to systematically develop the underlying reasoning in support of Deming's idea of intrinsic (internal) motivation. Based on their research, they developed four components of internal motivation: (1) a sense of choice, (2) a sense of meaningfulness, (3) a sense of competence, and (4) a sense of progress. *Choice* is the opportunity one feels to select task activities that make sense and to perform them in ways that seem appropriate; *meaningfulness* is the opportunity one feels to pursue a worthy task purpose; *competence* is the accomplishment one feels in skillfully performing task activities; and *progress* is the accomplishment one feels in achieving the task purpose. The authors suggest ways to enhance these characteristics by building them into the job design of employees in a manner similar to the Hackman-Oldham job design model.

Applying Motivation Theories to TQ The motivation theories reviewed here can be applied to support TQ in an organization. Motivating factors such as achievement recognition and responsibility lead to personal satisfaction and sustained motivation for continuous improvement. But as noted earlier, applying motivation theories to management practices in a TQ environment has both advantages and drawbacks. On one hand, efforts to empower employees may appeal to individuals who have a high need for power, because they are likely to feel that management is correcting a long-standing problem of not giving most employees sufficient power to influence conditions on the job. On the other hand, empowerment may be fruitless or even dangerous if it is not carried out properly. For example, Herzberg's simple theory suggests that ignoring maintenance factors such as supervision, working conditions, salary, peer relations, status, and security will produce dissatisfaction. Thus, to talk TQ without addressing these issues can easily result in failure. Understanding this point is certainly a prerequisite to implementation.

As an example of how the Porter and Lawler model might apply in TQ, suppose that a bank decides to install a statistical process control system in its check-clearing department. It performs the activities of planning the new system, organizing the workforce, and training employees to use the new system. The bank even trains clerical workers in the details of recording information clearly and accurately. However, the bank emphasizes the detection of errors, the penalties for being caught making an error, and the advantages to the bank in reducing the costs of correcting errors. No positive reinforcement is built into the system for making improvements in the process, reducing errors, or recording and using information. A few weeks after the system is installed, turnover and absentee rates have increased, new types of errors are being made, old error rates are increasing, and morale in the department is generally low.

For this situation, the Herzberg model would indicate that the motivating factors of status and the work (content) itself are missing. The Porter and Lawler model could be used to trace out the flaws in the motivating process. The model shows that the bank's system has a deficiency in perceived effort-reward probability and, perhaps, value of reward as well. Thus, if employees do not perceive a high effort-reward probability or do not see a high value in the rewards that are given, they will not apply their best efforts to the task. Their abilities and traits will not be exercised to the fullest, and their perceptions of their role in the firm will be either negative or confused. These factors combine to result in low performance, which, in turn, will have a negative impact on extrinsic (tangible) rewards and intrinsic (intangible) rewards and on the perception of equitable (fair) rewards and overall satisfaction with accomplishment of the task. The negative cycle and its consequences are renewed each time the task is performed. To turn the situation around, companies must introduce an upward rather than a downward spiral of motivation by providing a positive combination of expectancy, effort, and accomplishment.

In this example, the value of the reward (Box 1 in the Porter and Lawler model in Figure 6.5), and the perceived effort-reward probability (Box 2) work in conjunction with intrinsic rewards, extrinsic rewards, and perceived equitable rewards (Boxes 7A, 7B, and 8) to produce motivated effort (Box 3), performance (Box 6), and satisfaction (Box 9). Thus, the attention to the details of job design can have a significant impact on the quality level in a work setting.

Bowditch and Buono suggested that an integrated theory of motivation, such as that under development with social learning and self-efficacy theories, could be developed by considering the behaviors in a group of people that are of interest to management.[88] Not all motivation theories are equally good in predicting a wide range of behavior, therefore managers may need to consider situational factors and to apply the correct motivational tools to the specific situation in order to improve results (as suggested in Thomas and Tymon's intrinsic motivation model). Table 6.6 shows a set of common management situations, with examples relating to TQ, and gives suggestions for the type of motivation theory that could be applied to understand individual motivation and to shape it to meet individual and organizational goals.

Performance Appraisal

Considerable truth can be found in the statement, "How one is evaluated determines how one performs." It can be a dangerous truth. Analog Devices, a successful Massachusetts analog and digital equipment manufacturer, embraced TQ but found its stock price steadily declining. One of its key measures (on which managers were rewarded) was new product introduction time, with an objective of reducing it from 36 to 6 months. The product development team focused on this objective; as a result, engineers turned away from riskier new products and designed mundane derivatives of old products that no longer met customers' needs. The company subsequently scrapped that goal.[89]

A TQ organization requires a closely monitored performance appraisal process that is oriented toward "best practices" and continuous improvement of quality. However, performance appraisal is an exceedingly difficult HRM activity. Organizations typically use performance appraisals for a number of reasons: to provide feedback to employees who can then recognize and build on their strengths and work on

Table 6.6 Applying Motivation Theories to TQ

Situation	TQ Example	Applicable Motivation Theories
Choice of employees	Decisions to join employee involvement groups	Expectancy
Prediction of choices	Management desires employee "buy-in" for reengineering	Equity, goal-setting
Effort exerted on a task	Group members' responses in performing a process improvement project	Reinforcement, equity
Work satisfaction	Responses to a survey on how well employees are responding to empowerment initiatives encouraged by management	Need, equity
On-the-job performance	Reduction of customer complaints in a hospital billing department, due to reduction of errors	Reinforcement, equity, goal-setting
Withdrawal from the job	Absenteeism, turnover	Reinforcement, equity, or expectancy (often related to rewards/goals)

their weaknesses, to determine salary increases, to identify people for promotion, and to deal with human resource legalities. As such, they can provide a paper trail to fight wrongful-discharge suits and act as a formal warning system to marginal employees.[90] Many leading organizations use performance appraisal for changing corporate culture.

Conventional appraisal processes typically involve setting objectives for a certain period of time (typically for the year ahead), either unilaterally or jointly by the manager with his or her subordinate. This initial goal-setting is followed by a supervisory review of accomplishments, strengths and weaknesses, and/or personal characteristics of the subordinate related to the job at the end of the review period. Often, the form used for performance rating has 10 to 15 tangible and intangible categories, such as quantity of work, quality of work, works well with others, takes initiative, and so on, to be rated on a five- or seven-point scale from "excellent" to "unsatisfactory" or "poor." The performance appraisal interview may be accompanied by announcements of raises, bonuses, and/or promotions. In some cases, company policy dictates a certain distribution of results, such as "no more than 10 percent of any department's employees may be rated as excellent" or "merit raises or bonuses will only be paid to employees who are rated as excellent or very good."

Dissatisfaction with conventional performance appraisal systems is common among both managers, who are the appraisers, and workers, who are appraised. General Motors, for example, discovered that 90 percent of its people believed they were in the top 10 percent. How discouraging is it to be rated lower? Many managers are inclined to give higher ratings because of potential negative impacts. Numerous research studies over the past several decades have pointed out the problems and pitfalls of performance appraisals.[91] Many legitimate objections can be made:[92]

- They tend to foster mediocrity and discourage risk taking.
- They focus on short-term and measurable results, thereby discouraging long-term planning or thinking and ignoring important behaviors that are more difficult to measure.
- They focus on the individual and therefore tend to discourage or destroy teamwork within and between departments.
- The process is detection-oriented rather than prevention-oriented.
- They are often unfair, because managers frequently do not possess observational accuracy.
- They fail to distinguish between factors that are within the employees' control and system-determined factors that are beyond their control.

W. Edwards Deming strongly condemned the performance appraisal process because of this last point.[93] For example, many salespersons' compensation is based on a sales quota. However, sales depends on more than the individual's contribution. Factors such as the economy, competition, customer interaction with other aspects of the company, and prior relationships all affect sales. These system factors are outside the control of the individual salesperson. Thus, Deming would point out that sales (y) is a function of both system (S) and individual (I) performance factors.

$$y = f(S, I)$$

Solving one equation with two unknowns is impossible. Yet this impossible task is precisely what traditional performance appraisal systems attempt to do.

Performance appraisals are most effective when they are based on the objectives of the work teams that support the organization.[94] In this respect, they act as a diagnostic tool and review process for individual, team, and organizational development and achievement. The performance appraisal can also be a motivator when it is developed and used by the work team itself. Team efforts are harnessed when team members are empowered to monitor their own workplace activities. In a TQ culture, quality improvement is one of the major dimensions on which employees are evaluated. Xerox, for instance, changed its performance review criteria by replacing traditional measures such as "follows procedures" and "meets standards" to evaluating employees on the basis of quality improvement, problem solving, and team contributions. Many companies use peer review, customer evaluations, and self-assessments as a part of the appraisal process.

One approach that has been gaining increasing acceptance and overcomes many of the objections cited earlier is called **360-degree feedback**.[95] In an ideal 360-degree approach, a group of individuals who interact with the employee (or team) on a frequent basis participates in both the goal-setting process and the performance appraisal process. This group might include suppliers, clients, peers, internal customers, managers, and subordinates. The process involves two-way communication in which both parties discuss such needs as service levels, response times, accuracy of work and so on, which are often expressed as written service contracts. At the end of the performance period, selected representatives who participated in the goal setting evaluate how well the goals of the service contracts have been met, and provide feedback. The final performance appraisal consists of discussing an aggregation of the comments and ratings with the employee, and serves as a process for setting goals for the next period and for employee development. Because the approach is new, little systematic research has been performed on its effectiveness; however, user feedback has been positive.

In the spirit of Deming, many companies are replacing performance evaluation altogether with personal planning and development systems. Cadillac, for instance, replaced its traditional performance review with a personnel development planning process in which managers meet with employees to set future expectations, identify training needs, provide coaching, and reward continuous improvement. Eastman Chemical Company eliminated employee labeling, improved the focus on individual development planning, and encouraged employee involvement and ownership. Granite Rock does not emphasize past performance, but sets professional development goals in conjunction with the company's needs. No stigma is attached to failure; the thrust of the process is to develop each individual to the fullest.

Today, many leading organizations are focusing on identifying a small number of *core competencies* that are critical to the organization's success.[96] These behaviors, skills, and attributes are expected in every member. They also use **mastery descriptions**, narratives of behavior that one who has mastered it would likely engage in. For example, a mastery description of *customer focus* might be:

> *Dedicated to meeting the expectations and requirements of internal and external customers. Knows who every one of his/her customers is and can state what that individual's expectations are. Gets first-hand customer information and uses it for improvements in products and services. Speaks and acts with customers in mind. Takes the client's side in well-founded complaints. Is skilled at managing customer expectations. Establishes and maintains effective relationships with customers and gains their trust and respect. Actively seeks customers' feedback on the quality of service he/she provides.*

A behavioral frequency scale, in which appraisers indicate how frequently the appraisee does the things listed in the mastery descriptions (rarely, occasionally, frequently, or regularly, for example) is often used. This assessment avoids numerical judgments of performance, defensive reactions, and provides a guide of what to do to improve.

Measuring Employee Satisfaction and HRM Effectiveness

Measurement of employee satisfaction and HRM effectiveness is useful to assess the linkages with company strategy and to provide a foundation for improvement. In fact, research has suggested that organizations that use people measures as part of a balanced set of measures to manage the business have significantly higher return on investment and return on assets than those who don't. HR measures allow companies to predict customer satisfaction, identify those issues that have the greatest impact on business performance. and allocate appropriate resources. The same holds true for organizations that say their employee surveys provide valuable information to guide decision making. Nevertheless, few organizations have well-defined people measures or use them to predict key business outcomes.[97]

Both outcome and process measures provide data by which to assess HRM effectiveness. Outcome measures might include "hard" measures of cost savings, productivity improvements, defect rate reduction, customer satisfaction improvements, cycle time reductions, and employee turnover, as well as "soft" measures of teamwork and management effectiveness, employee commitment, employee satisfaction, and empowerment. Typical process measures of success include the number of suggestions that employees make, the numbers of participants in project teams, and participation in educational programs. Team process effectiveness can be assessed by tracking the average time it takes to complete a process improvement project, and determining whether teams are getting better, smarter, and faster at performing improvements. Facilitators and program coordinators should also look for other indicators of success, such as improvements in team selection and planning processes, frequency of use of quality improvement tools by employees, employee understanding of problem-solving approaches, and senior management involvement. Employee surveys can also help in providing this information.

Questions in a typical survey might be grouped into such basic categories as quality of worklife, teamwork, communications, opportunities and training, facilities, leadership, compensation, benefits, and the company. Surveys might also address important team and individual behaviors, such as unity for a common purpose, listening effectively and acknowledging others' contributions, obtaining the participation of all members of the team, gathering and analyzing relevant data and information, sharing responsibility, using problem-solving processes and tools, and meeting company objectives for quality improvement. Many commercial survey instruments are available.[98] Like customer satisfaction surveys we discussed in Chapter 4, many employee surveys also seek feedback on the importance of key issues.

Employee surveys also help organizations better understand the "voice of the employee," particularly with regard to employee satisfaction, management policies, and their internal customers and suppliers. Such feedback helps organizations improve their human resource management practices. For example, Marlow Industries uses a survey that addresses a broad variety of issues, including management support, the company's total quality system, organizational effectiveness, training, and continuous improvement. Table 6.7 shows most of the questions included in their survey. All responses are made on a five-item scale ranging from *totally disagree* to *very much agree*. Xerox produces its survey in 25 languages. Fifty-four questions are grouped into eight categories: directions/communications, valuing people, trust, learning, feedback, recognition, participation/involvement, and teamwork. Xerox compares results against similar companies such as Allied Signal, Honeywell, Sun Microsystems, Texas Instruments, and others.

In evaluating results, trends and long-term consequences should be emphasized, and they should be communicated to employees. A good system should report results

Table 6.7 Employee Quality Survey—Marlow Industries

Management Support

1. The president is an active supporter of quality at Marlow Industries.
2. Senior management (VPs) are active supporters of quality at Marlow Industries.
3. My supervisor is an active supporter of quality at Marlow Industries.
4. My supervisor is concerned more about the quality of my work than the quantity of my work.
5. My supervisor can help me to do my job better.
6. My supervisor encourages good housekeeping efforts.
7. I receive recognition for a top quality job done.

Total Quality System

1. Marlow Industries' Total Quality System is not a fad. It will be active long into the future.
2. The Total Quality system has made an improvement in the performance of my work.
3. The Total Quality system has made an improvement in my ability to do my job right the first time.
4. I understand the meaning of the Quality Policy.
5. I believe in the meaning of the Quality Policy.
6. I understand the meaning of the Quality Pledge.
7. I believe in the meaning of the Quality Pledge.
8. All departments within Marlow Industries support the Total Quality system.
9. My co-workers support quality first.
10. My co-workers believe in the Quality Pledge.
11. My "supplier" co-worker treats me as his/her "customer" and meets my needs.
12. I know who my internal "customer" is.
13. I am able to meet the requirements of my internal customer.
14. I believe that improving quality is the key to maintaining Marlow Industries' success.

Organizational Effectiveness

1. I receive feedback that helps me perform my job better.
2. I am encouraged to stop and ask questions if something does not seem right.
3. There is a high level of quality in the products we ship to our external customers.
4. Marlow Industries provides reliable processes and equipment so that I can do my job right the first time.
5. I do not use defective materials.
6. I am provided proper procedures to do my job right.
7. My fellow workers have a high level of enthusiasm about Marlow Industries' quality.
8. I believe control charts will help us improve quality.
9. I believe Marlow Industries offers a high quality working environment.
10. I enjoy my job.

Training

1. I have received training to be able to do my job right the first time.
2. I have received training on how to determine if the work I do conforms to Marlow Industries' workmanship standards, and other requirements of the customer.
3. I receive adequate safety training so that I am aware of the safety and health requirements of my job.
4. My supervisor has received adequate training to be able to do his/her job right the first time.
5. My co-worker has received adequate training to be able to do his/her job right the first time.
6. I have received ongoing training.
7. The training I have received has been very helpful to me in my job.

Job Satisfaction and Morale

1. I have a high level of personal job satisfaction.
2. My morale is high.
3. The morale of my work group is high.

Involvement

1. I feel involved at Marlow Industries.
2. I would like to be more involved at Marlow Industries.

Source: Courtesy Marlow Industries.

on a regular basis, perhaps monthly or quarterly, with a summary year-end report, using graphical aids wherever possible. Detailed reports should go to lower-level managers, showing results at their level. Summary reports should go to higher management levels. Specific action, such as training, changes in reward or recognition, or improvements to support employee well-being should be taken based on results.

Labor Relations Issues

In the rapidly changing business environment, both managers and union leaders experience varying degrees of difficulty with sharing power with workers at every level. However, a TQ environment requires that unions and management cooperate in new and innovative ways if they are to survive. Union leaders and labor-relations managers have traditionally emphasized collective bargaining, work rules, grievance procedures, and management and worker domains. Many of these procedures and work rules are legally binding on the company and have arisen through years of negotiation and policy making.

To move toward a TQ culture, labor and management must first agree that a new paradigm is desirable, and then work cooperatively.[99] This activity requires that union members and leaders (1) take new approaches toward dispute resolution, (2) develop flexible work rules and means for accommodation to such rules by union stewards, (3) initiate peer performance feedback methods designed to improve work operations, and (4) establish new contract language and ongoing labor-management negotiation. Management will also be required to adjust through the following actions:

- Work with union representatives on how—or whether—new work systems will be adopted.
- Examine values within a joint framework and adopt new ones to guide the transformed organization.
- Include labor representation at every level at which process and job transformations are taking place.
- Fill key training and employee involvement (EI) facilitator positions with both union and management representatives. (For instance, Ford Motor Company has a parallel EI structure of union-management facilitators from the plant level up to corporate headquarters.)
- Recognize union strengths, such as the ability to take the pulse of its membership on various issues.

Many organizations have taken significant strides to improve labor-management cooperation. For example, at a Midwestern steel plant, 40 company officials and union members developed a set of jointly held and shared values and principles that served as the foundation for a number of cooperative efforts. Meetings between labor and management at Raytheon Systems Company focused on how to integrate a new philosophy with some of their currently existing joint programs. At Air Canada headquarters in Montreal, union officials and technical operations managers met in one- to two-day sessions every two to three months over a year to build stronger partnerships to improve performance and grow the business. They jointly developed a five-year plan, defined short-term goals, clarified roles of the parties for making the partnership work, and defined joint decision-making boundaries and responsibilities.[100]

The National Labor Relations Board (NLRB) ruled on two cases in 1993 and 1994 that complicate a company's determination of how far it can go legally to set up and use employee participation programs (EPPs) to make improvements in the workplace. These case decisions by a five-person board were based on interpretations of the 58-year-old National Labor Relations Act (NLRA, or Wagner Act) that prohibits unfair labor practices. The two cases involved a small, nonunion company, Electromation, and a large company, DuPont. The rulings are found in the NLRB proceedings as *Electromation v. International Brotherhood of Teamsters* (309 NLRB-No. 163), and *E. I. duPont de Nemours and Company v. Chemical Workers Association, Inc.* (311 NLRB-No. 88). In the *Electromation* case, the nonunion company's management set up five employee action committees to deal with policies concerning absenteeism, smoking, communications, pay for premium positions, and attendance bonuses. In DuPont's case, management unilaterally (without bargaining with the union) changed the composition of safety and fitness committees to include nonmanagerial employees (where the committees had previously been composed only of management) at a unionized New Jersey plant. Stated briefly, the cases specified that "employer-dominated labor organizations" are prohibited. In both cases, the employee teams/committees were ruled to be "labor organizations" and to be "management dominated." Fink et al. discussed the implications of the rulings for employee participation and labor-management cooperation.[101] They made four major points:

- Most small to large U.S. companies fall under NLRB jurisdiction, and many employee participation programs would be declared labor organizations that were dominated by employers, if tested by the NLRB-established guidelines.
- Companies with labor unions could probably establish "legal" EPPs by bargaining with the union and signing an agreement on how they would be structured and operated.
- As long as unions see the EPP to be in accordance with their self-interest, management could probably get them to agree to the program.
- Without the rulings of the NLRB being overturned in the courts, or legislation being passed to amend the NLRA, many nonunion companies could not withstand a challenge to their EPPs.

In summary, changes in union-management relations are critical where new work structures are considered vital to corporate survival or competitiveness. Good relations aid quality improvement and productivity at every level. On the other hand, poor relations produce changes that are cosmetic in nature, and guarantee that quality efforts will suffer.

A bill, entitled the Teamwork for Employees and Managers Act of 1997 (TEAM Act), was introduced as H.R. 634 in the House of Representatives by Representative Fawell and as S. 295 in the Senate by Senator Jeffords. The TEAM Act was designed to amend the National Labor Relations Act of 1937 and would allow employees and management in nonunion workplaces to meet and address issues such as safety, production, and benefits, while protecting the right of the employees to choose union representation. Despite passage of an earlier bill by both the House and the Senate in the 104th Congress in 1996, it was vetoed by President Clinton. Many of the laws regarding workplace practices were made in another era, when modern organization structures and communications were not even dreamed of. As the politics of the TEAM Act suggests, it is difficult to change entrenched practices and to modify the positions of interest groups in order to make it less complicated to do business in our increasingly decentralized, team-oriented workplaces.

HRM in the Internet Age

Has the information age changed what organizations need to know about HRM? The answer is surprisingly, no. Workers want to be treated with respect, have their basic needs addressed, understand the goals of their work, and have managers to recognize their unique individual differences. They want to be given challenging, meaningful work in which they can experience pride of ownership, personal learning and growth, and be rewarded fairly and equitably when they perform.

However, things have certainly changed in the fast-paced Internet age. Managers who don't recognize these changes and keep up with trends in job design, motivation, and leadership do so at their own peril. Take virtual teams, for example.[102] These types of teams use a combination of Internet, e-mail, phone, fax, video conferencing, PC-to-PC connections, and shared computer screen technologies to get their jobs done. Virtual teams are often given a distinct Web site for posting charts, meeting minutes, statistics, and other shared documents. Virtual teaming requires special attention to communication, technology, sponsorship, and leadership issues. For example, the team leader needs to be able to tackle issues that he or she might not have encountered with traditional teams. One of the biggest disadvantages is the lack of experience members have working with one another. They are not aware of each other's work standards and cannot scrutinize these ethics as consistently as traditional teams. This disadvantage can be overcome by developing operating agreements by all team members, spelling out what they commit to do or not to do. Another factor is that communication is more complex because body language, voice inflection, and other communication cues are eliminated. Thus, virtual team members must be able to excel in relating their own ideas, and also understand the information others are trying to convey.

Today's organizations are characterized by much less employee loyalty, much more organizational uncertainty (and paradoxically, much more individual opportunity), and much more dependence of the organization on its human capital than ever before. As one writer put it: "We are all temps [temporary workers]!" HRM practices in the Internet age will increasingly require employers to take nontraditional approaches to attract and retain high-skilled employees. These approaches may include special perks, increased levels of responsibility early in the employees' careers, and understanding of the effects of changes brought about by new technologies and new realities of employee lifestyles in the twenty-first century.

HUMAN RESOURCE MANAGEMENT IN THE BALDRIGE CRITERIA

Category 5 of the 2001 Malcolm Baldrige National Quality Award Criteria for Performance Excellence is *Human Resource Focus.* This category examines how an organization enables employees to develop and utilize their full potential, aligned with the company's objectives, and how the organization builds and maintains a work environment and employee support climate conducive to performance excellence and to personal and organizational growth. Item 5.1, *Work Systems*, focuses on organizational systems for work and job design, compensation, employee performance management, motivation, recognition, communication, succession planning, diversity, and hiring, all with the aim of enabling and encouraging all employees to contribute effectively and to the best of their ability.

Item 5.2, *Employee Education, Training, and Development*, examines an organization's workforce education, training, and on-the-job reinforcement of knowledge and skills, with the aim of meeting ongoing needs of employees and a high-performance workplace. Specifically, the emphasis is on how education and training are designed, delivered, and evaluated, with special emphasis on meeting individual career progression and organizational business needs. The criteria ask how employees and their supervisors participate in needs determination, design, and evaluation, because these individuals frequently are best able to identify critical needs and evaluate success.

Item 5.3, *Employee Well-Being and Satisfaction*, examines how an organization ensures a safe and healthful work environment and support climate for all employees, taking into account their differing work environments and associated requirements. It includes identifying appropriate measures and targets for key environmental factors so that status and progress can be tracked. The criteria also ask how the organization enhances employee well-being, satisfaction, and motivation and satisfies a diverse workforce with differing needs and expectations; and how it assesses these factors and relates findings to key business results to set improvement priorities.

The following example shows how one company might respond to Area to Address 5.2, *Employee Education, Training, and Development*, and the feedback that a Baldrige examiner team might provide to the company. *You should read Case III in Chapter 3 first, which provides background about this fictitious company. Think about how the response addresses the questions asked in the 2000 criteria. The criteria are available on the CD-rom accompanying this book.*

Example 1: Collin Technologies—Human Resource Focus

Response to Criteria Item 5.2, Employee Education, Training, and Development

Employee development is a key component of Collin's Invest-in-People strategy, which recognizes the critical influence, impact, and power of Collin EOs on the company's current and future success.

5.2a Collin's people development philosophy is competency-based, assessment-driven, and business-focused. It is designed to align employee development with the company's strategic goals so that employee development helps drive Collin from being skill-oriented to knowledge-oriented. Collin's people development program is individually tailored to build on the strengths of its EOs and enhance their competencies.

Vincent Daubert conducts the human resource capabilities assessment annually to identify the capabilities necessary in Collin's advancing industry. These capabilities are a specific element of the strategic (long-range) and action (short-term) plans resulting from the perennial planning process (PPP—see Category 2 in the full case). These plans identify the subjects and skills necessary to educate and train EOs to satisfy upcoming technical and leadership requirements.

Future needs of both the organization and EOs are addressed in succession planning. Succession management activities are included in the human resource capabilities assessment. Using the Attribute Model and the assessment procedure described in Area 5.1a, core competencies for team and functional responsibilities are identified, and individuals are assessed against this Competency Model. Figure 6.6 shows the process that Collin uses to identify high potential EOs for leadership positions.

Historically, a primary driver of Collin's success has been the innovation and commitment of its EOs. Recognizing this fact, Collin implemented formal career paths for technical, managerial, operations, quality, and administrative positions—all of which are necessary to make Collin successful. The technical career paths provide a clear career road map for all technically oriented EOs as well as an advanced growth roadmap for key technical positions. The other career paths, which are designed to provide development for managerial, operations, quality, and administrative careers, follow a similar outline. The education and training program that integrates these road maps and the EO development process enhance Collin's ability to match employment needs with recruitment and retention efforts for a high-quality

Figure 6.6 Collin Technologies Leadership Identification Process

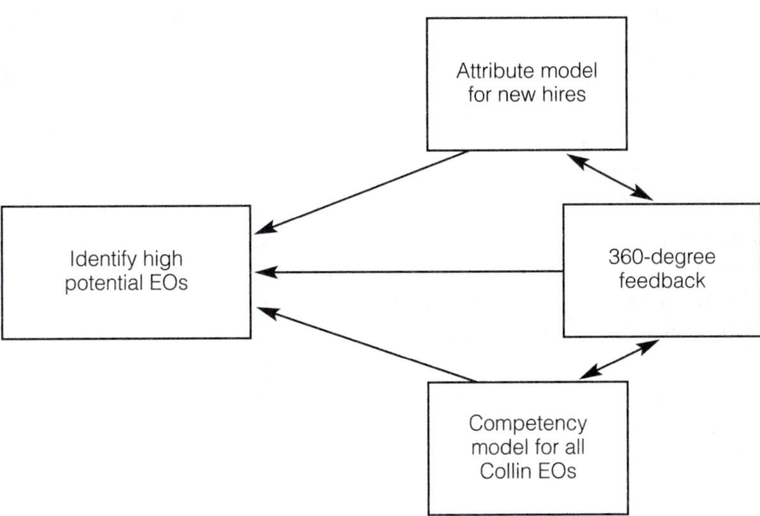

workforce. The career paths are subjected to an annual review by the HRC. This program ensures that Collin develops the talent and skills that the company needs.

Several sources are used as input for the PPP and provide Collin with valuable information about education and training needs. Baldrige self-assessments give all EOs the opportunity to share education and training needs, and inputs are supplemented with Baldrige inputs from preferred suppliers and customers. This internal input is complemented by external sources, including market surveys, customer surveys, government and industry sources, and third-party assessments. Human resource capabilities input is then compiled in CAIN, and collected and distributed for the resulting long- and short-range plans.

All Collin EOs attend a new-employee orientation class during their first week of work. Orientation helps new EOs become familiar with Collin's products, strategy, and leadership team, as well as employee benefits and opportunities. The orientation materials are also available on the company's Web site for reference.

Collin's training programs can be divided into five different areas:

1. Technical, including information systems
2. Managerial, including leadership and organizational dynamics, innovation, ethical behavior, and team development
3. Operations, including manufacturing and customer contact management
4. Quality management, including statistical process control (SPC), process improvement, and customer support relationship
5. Administrative, including CAIN and EHS&S.

Collin offers an abundance of training classes in each of these areas, as well as event-based training driven by business needs. Collin strongly believes that people development is more than just training. People development includes on-the-job experience, self-directed learning, special projects, assignments to teams, and coaching from managers and other team members.

Collin relies on the local educational institutions to satisfy some of its educational needs. Peak State University and Koga University provide most of the technical and managerial courses needed by the EOs. At least three managers at each site teach classes at the universities in their technical specialties. In addition, community colleges provide educational benefits to Collin's EOs. Collin uses distance learning to offer this valuable training to both the Nashville and Koga workforces. Twice in the last year, Collin has sponsored a professor from Japan to teach short-term courses in Nashville and vice versa in Japan; this practice has yielded educational and cultural benefits.

Training is also provided by Interskill and vocational centers in the Nashville and Koga communities. Computer-based training has been a valuable and time-saving method to deliver training, especially in the manufacturing, information systems administration, and office administration specialties.

Informal training is provided by EOs who have special skills that are in high demand throughout the workforce. This type of training is conducted in company training facilities at both plants and is often videotaped so that other EOs can view the sessions. Collin transfers technical specialists between plants to conduct short-term informal training.

Before any formal education and training approach is made available, it is piloted or tested with a representative sample of the target audience. In addition, course evaluation forms are completed at the end of training, and the results are tabulated and evaluated to determine effectiveness. Modifications are made to both the training content and approach, based upon the feedback. Finally, post-training assessments are also conducted three and six months after the training has been completed to determine the benefit the course has had on the job and its impact on actual job performance.

The utilization of quality standards, including metrics, performance standards, continuing improvement efforts, and quality controls, is a part of new employee orientation training. "Quality Leading the Way to Tomorrow" is the program that sets the stage for Collin EOs to embrace and utilize quality management in every aspect of their lives. Three levels of SPC are taught in local institutions; a basic level is taught at the Central Community College in downtown Nashville and in Hai Community College in Koga. Both undergraduate and graduate-level college courses are taught in Koga University and Peak State University. To increase Collin's level of awareness and understanding of the techniques involved with benchmarking, the company invites speakers from best-in-class companies, as well as those known for conducting benchmarking studies, to address all EOs.

As part of creating their own development plans, EOs participate in self-assessment sessions. These sessions are designed to allow individuals to point out areas in which they may need additional knowledge. The use of assessments and the incorporation of "Quality Leading the Way to Tomorrow" into every business level and function provide a consistent path to success for Collin as a growing company.

Examiner Feedback

Strengths

- Education, training, and EO development programs are based on an annual human resource capabilities assessment and the Baldrige assessment and are supplemented by external inputs from preferred suppliers, customers, market surveys, the government, industry, and third-party sources. Short- and longer-term needs for acquiring specific knowledge and capabilities are integrated into the PPP, ensuring that education and training programs align to the core values and support the company's move from a skill-oriented to a knowledge-oriented workforce.

- Functional career path structures have been developed for five employee categories: technical, managerial, operations, quality management, and administrative. Employee development and education and training programs, which are linked to career path design, enable the applicant to more effectively match employment needs with recruitment and retention efforts.
- Several approaches are used to deliver education and training. In addition to company classes aligned to the five career paths, the company provides coaching, self-directed learning, on-the-job training, computer-based training, special projects, and team assignments. In order to support the geographic challenges of a multinational workforce, these programs are supplemented by offerings at local colleges, third-party and vocational centers, and distance learning opportunities.
- The company has developed and implemented a training development program called "Quality Leading the Way to Tomorrow." From new-employee orientation through progressive course work, emphasis is placed on learning statistical process control, metrics, and quality management and benchmarking techniques to ensure rapid response to changing business requirements.
- A systematic and comprehensive approach is used to ensure that internally delivered education and training support the needs of EOs and to achieve the shift from a skill-based to a knowledge-based workforce. Pilots are conducted on formal programs, and post-course and post-training feedback is used to improve the quality of the programs.

Opportunities for Improvement

- A description of how the company designs education and training is not provided, which makes it difficult to determine how input from external sources and needs identified in various assessments are incorporated into course designs to ensure that company goals and EO career development are achieved.
- A plan identifying proficiency requirements for each employee category and the training required to develop a workforce capable of meeting future market needs is not provided. Without a clear understanding of competency and training requirements, it is difficult to understand how the company plans to achieve its mission to provide leadership excellence to all stakeholders.

QUALITY IN PRACTICE

TD INDUSTRIES[103]

TD Industries is an employee-owned firm that provides mechanical, refrigeration, electrical, plumbing, building controls, and energy services to customers in Texas and the Southwest. Headquartered in Dallas, the company expanded rapidly in the 1990s, due to the tremendous growth rate of the area. In the early 1990s the company employed about 600 people and had revenues of approximately $75 million per year. By the end of 1998, employment had grown to 1,050 employees, with revenues of $182 million. It is interesting to note that the company added 98 jobs over the 1997–98 timeframe, but had about 1,000 applications for those jobs! Why were these positions so sought after in an industry where the norm is hard physical work, highly cyclical demand, and typically has a high employee turnover rate? To help answer this question, consider the company's vision:

> *We are committed to providing outstanding career opportunities by exceeding our customers' expectations through continuous aggressive improvement.*

Note the focus on its people as reflected in the goal of providing outstanding career opportunities. A list of some of the awards it has won attests to its ability to achieve this vision:

- No. 4 on *Fortune*'s "The 100 Best Companies to Work for in America," for 1999; no. 2 in 1998; and no. 5 in 1997
- Texas Quality Award (based on the Malcolm Baldrige criteria) in 1998
- National Member of the Year Associated Builders and Contractors in 1996
- Jack Lowe, CEO, earned the Crystal Achievement Award National Association of Women in Construction in 1996
- National Carrier Distinguished Dealer Award in 1996
- *Contracting Business*'s, Commercial Contractor of the Year in 1995
- United Way Pacesetter/Elite Company for 1995, 1996, and 1997

In testifying to the members of the U.S. House of Representatives Committee on Education and the Workforce (*http://edworkforce.house.gov/*) on May 20, 1998, regarding "The American Worker at a Crossroads Project," Ben Houston, president of TD Industries shared the company philosophy:

> *We have humbly accepted the above awards on behalf of all Partners of TD Industries because we believe our culture is founded upon having fun while we accomplish the following: Trust, Servant Leadership, Quality, Sharing. To have fun, every meeting agenda item begins with Item #1—HUMOR. Our entire culture is based on a trusting relationship between all of our stakeholders—our clients, our communities, our partners, and our suppliers. We believe in the value of the individual, and attempt, in our culture, to recognize this value.*
>
> *TD Industries believes in Robert Greenleaf's philosophy as indicated in his book entitled,* "The Servant Leader." *We believe that all individuals within TD Industries, regardless of their jobs, are leaders and managers of their own jobs. We also believe that in order to lead one must first serve those that are to be led.*
>
> *We believe everything we do must strive towards meeting our stakeholders needs—our clients, our communities, our partners, and our suppliers. In order to ensure quality teamwork among all TD Partners, our clients, and suppliers is essential. Most opportunities for improvement are accomplished through quality work teams. We avoid the term "buy in" because it implies someone has the correct answer and must sell it to others. We prefer to have the best solution created by equal input from all participants.*

In order to ensure improvement, TD Industries measures many items on an ongoing basis and the information is available to all TD Partners, but especially the work group that can affect the improvement. These measurements include the following:

1. *Partner Satisfaction:* This goal is accomplished through an annual confidential questionnaire that is compared with national groups, benchmarked against TD's own performance year by year to ensure that improvement is being made in all areas.
2. *Supervisors Survey:* Supervisors are confidentially rated annually by the partners who work with them, and the reports are given to the supervisors to be reviewed with their supervisor within three weeks.
3. *Customer Surveys:* Every area of customer contact is surveyed on a regular basis depending on the type of business. A goal of 9 out of 10 has been set, and all scores below 7 are reviewed with the client and the responsible manager and reviewed for lessons learned.
4. *One-with-One's:* One-with-one reviews are required yearly with each partner and his or her supervisor and not at the same time as pay evaluations.
5. *Pay Evaluations:* Pay evaluations are done twice annually with training records and career paths being a portion of the review.
6. *Productivity Reports:* Reports are sent to the partners doing the work.

7. *Safety Reports:* These reports are also sent to the partners doing the work.
8. *Continuous Improvement:* All partners, regardless of their position in the company, are asked to obtain a minimum of 32 hours of training in order to sharpen the skills of the individual, and assist in ensuring the continuous improvement of TD's greatest resource—its people.

In addition, safety orientation, mentors, 90-day orientation, 6-months benefit orientation, 1-year TD opportunities, second year quality and year 3 through 6 leadership training on diversity, team work, leadership and seven habits make up the formal leader training. Associated Builders and Contractors Wheels of Learning craft courses are offered as well as technical and management courses.

TD Industries provides many benefits to its employees: medical, dental, group term life, long-term disability, insurance, employee stock ownership plan (ESOP)/401(k)—30% of the profits go to partners in the ESOP and 40l(k) plans—paid personal time, holidays, sick pay, job injury pay, jury duty, wellness program, funeral pay, continuing education program that is fully paid for by TD Industries, prescription safety glasses, and partner grant requests, with up to $100 for a community service in which the partner works. Partners are encouraged to participate in many associations such as Associated Builders and Contractors and United Way in order to give back to the industry and community. Financial incentives are paid to virtually every partner based on improvements in the partner's own operation, if partner satisfaction, supervisor scores, and customer satisfaction are acceptable. Thirty percent of all pretax profits are distributed to the partners in the ESOP and 401(k) plans. As Houston noted, "These items of SHARING close the loop of TRUST due to the sharing that TD Industries practices with all Partners."

Key Issues for Discussion

1. Explain how human resource activities at TD Industries work toward achieving the company's vision statement.
2. How do HRM processes at TD Industries support the fundamental principles of TQ: customer focus, participation and teamwork, and continuous improvement?

Source: Courtesy of TD Industries, Ben Houston, president.

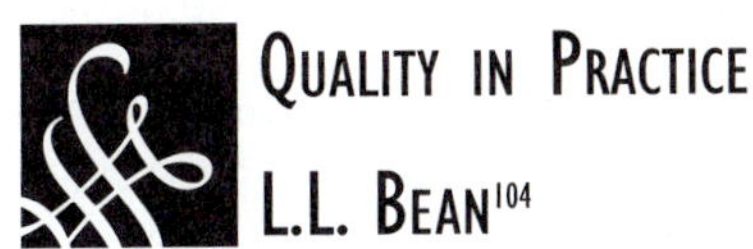

Quality in Practice

L.L. Bean[104]

L.L. Bean Co., a sporting goods and apparel mail-order distributor and retailer headquartered in Freeport, Maine, has been known for quality and a focus on the customer since it was founded in 1912 by Leon Leonwood Bean, a Maine outdoorsman. "L.L.," as he was called, grew tired of coming home with wet, sore feet from the heavy leather woodsman's boots of his day. He invented a new kind of boot that combined lightweight leather tops with waterproof rubber bottoms, incorporating the best features of both materials. The practical advantages of his new L.L. Bean Boots were readily apparent, and he soon sold 100 pairs to fellow sportsmen through the mail. Unfortunately, 90 pairs were sent back when the stitching gave way. But L.L. was true to his word, refunded his customers' money, and started over with an improved boot.

L.L. Bean operated his business based on the following belief: "Sell good merchandise at a reasonable profit, treat your customers like human beings, and they will always come back for more." The company now sells more than 16,000 outdoor products, and even has eight stores in Japan. The Freeport flagship store is one of the most popular tourist destinations in Maine, receiving more than 3.5 million visitors a year. The company also has nine factory outlet stores: six in New England, one in Delaware, and two in Oregon. L.L.'s products were originally sold only through the mail. But so many people dropped by his Freeport workshop to purchase items that he opened a showroom in 1917. Over the years, the company kept growing as L.L. added casual and sports apparel, gear and other footwear to his line. By 1951, people were dropping in by day and night on their way to hunt and fish in Maine, and L.L. announced he had "thrown away the keys," deciding to keep the retail store open continuously. It has been open to the public 24 hours a day, 365 days a year, ever since.

Legendary stories are told of commitment to quality and service in its catalogs and inside and around the company. One such story was told of a customer service representative who was informed of a late shipment, loaded a canoe on his car, and drove from Freeport to New York City (a distance of almost 300 miles, or 475 km) so that the customer could go hunting the next morning. Bean backs up its reputation for quality and customer focus with a "Guarantee of 100% Satisfaction," on all products.

For 30 years, Bean had enjoyed 20–25 percent annual growth in sales. Recently, the firm has been caught in a major industry downturn, with rising costs and shrinking demand. To deal with these realities, Bean launched a TQ and HR effort in the mid-1990s. The focus on quality was led by an 85-person total quality and human resources (TQHR) unit, composed of HR generalists, some HR specialists, and process-improvement consultants.

Bean, a people-focused organization, resisted massive layoffs as a viable cost-cutting option. Bob Peixotto, vice president of total quality and human resources stated: "People are the solution, not the problem." Traditionally, the company has paid an average of 15 percent of salary as a profit-sharing bonus each year. In a recent year, no bonus was paid, for the first time in more than 50 years. Limited voluntary retirements and staff reductions were carried out, but TQHR saw that the solution was to "work smarter, not harder."

As a mail-order and retail business, large-scale complexity and dependence on world-class business logistics put people, total quality, and customer service at the heart of the company. To save time and meet customer needs, continual process review and improvement were essential. L.L. Bean began to rethink each of these elements.

L.L. Bean already had an intense customer focus, so the two key drivers of the total quality effort were people (their involvement in the business) and processes (business process management and improvement). A new people-process model helped to integrate TQ into the HR department. Total quality was defined by Bean employees as "managing an enterprise to maximize customer satisfaction in the most efficient and effective way by totally involving people in improving the way work is done." TQHR's mission was to support the company TQ mission by acting as a catalyst for total quality and superior performance.

For a retail organization such as L.L. Bean, quality is not a production-line issue. As Peixotto said, "It happens every time a customer representative receives a call in the telephone center. That interaction is where quality really happens, so a third goal was to change the infrastructure to support such customer interaction. This eventually meant a redesigned TQHR department."

To accomplish their TQ goals, departmental leadership decided to focus its own efforts on five operational themes:

1. Servicing line managers to meet employee needs, role revision for managers, and management learning.
2. Practicing what it preached, with its own performance improvement and management being one example.
3. Acting as one unified department with a portfolio of products and services.
4. Regarding itself as a business, with regular feedback from internal customers as critical evidence of performance.
5. Continually reviewing and rethinking the TQHR process.

When TQHR reviewed its work to identify the types of business in which it should be involved, almost 50 different kinds emerged, including business-process improvement, publishing, facilitation, management consulting, report management, legal-care management, physical therapy, learning-center operations, and career counseling.

Next, the department devised a portfolio of TQHR products or services for internal customers for which resources were needed. The final list of 109 included career assessment, ergonomic workstation design, quality assessments, and change-management counseling. Six core processes were identified for delivering these products and services to other parts of the business, including recruiting and orienting people, developing people, separating people, organizational-development planning, product and service development, and delivering products and services.

Peixotto explains, "These changes helped us to create a new TQHR paradigm, where departmental staff worked directly in customer areas and therefore at the front end of the business and total quality. Our role here was to act as consultants, not order takers for HR products or services." As a result of the rethinking, the new TQHR organization was divided into two sections: the resource center and the service teams that work in internal-customer areas across all L.L. Bean's operations.

The resource center acts as a strategic HR think-tank, deciding what TQHR should be offering and examining the strategic needs of internal customers in relation to employee performance, productivity, and continuous improvement. The service teams are business partners, delivering products and services directly for internal customers, working away from their own operational area.

To accomplish work across departmental units, TQHR teams called "pods," were also introduced. These short-life teams of rapidly and flexibly deployed process-improvement consultants are "the catalysts for change who go after costs," in Peixotto's words. These pods are expert teams that address needs such as training and development, recruitment, and compensation, and can assume both strategic and operational roles for their work. For example, the compensation pod is investigating new, major TQHR approaches such as team-based rewards and recognition.

Broadly skilled business people are assigned to work in TQHR. Their skills include both traditional HR competencies, such as training and recruitment, and specific process-improvement skills such as systems, information technology, and industrial engineering. Thus, they can be deployed across the resource center, pods, or service teams.

Peixotto's unit also does not hesitate to use talent from elsewhere within the organization. For example, any L.L. Bean employee with appropriate skills is invited to attend the annual training courses in facilitation and process improvement. In return, these "outside" individuals guarantee TQHR 52 days of personal input a year to support its activities. He says, "They act as skilled personnel and change or process-improvement missionaries. Broad and interrelated consultancy skills will always be TQHR's critical capability. But, as internal consultants, we never tell any part of the organization what it should be doing: our job is to listen first and then recommend action or tools for getting things done effectively."

Peixotto uses the TQHR unit as a test laboratory for the organization's HR tools or techniques to support its work in continuous-improvement process. TQHR then must anticipate internal customer requirements or how their needs might change with new business priorities. They test out the tools and techniques that range from the basics—pay, incentives, training, competencies, performance measures, employee relations and so on—to more complex approaches, including job redesign and process improvement. They may be applied in one of two scenarios: (1) as tested templates for managers to use to save on their own time and resources and avoid reinventing the wheel; or (2) for service teams, where they have been invited to help in a function or business area. "The invitation is important," explains Peixotto, "because our role is to act as facilitators and enablers." TQHR also benchmarks itself with any organization that has proven best practices. Recently, performance management, leadership development, idea-generation systems, compensation issues, and workplace safety have been benchmarked.

TQHR departmental productivity savings have reduced operating expenses by $500,000. Additional direct savings from TQHR-driven initiatives in one year were $5.6 million from business-process improvement projects, $2.75 million less in health costs because of better working practices, and $2.1 million through workforce planning.

With a renewed focus on high customer service and quality standards, Peixotto's reengineered process is receiving high marks for internal customer satisfaction. The highest rated attributes of the TQHR unit are customer responsiveness, "easy to do business with," accessibility, and flexibility. Previously, these qualities were among those the original HR department performed less well in, which contributed to a loss of organizational credibility. Peixotto now feels that the redesigned and repositioned TQHR unit is well placed (and expert enough) to work in partnership with other support areas in the company. They are now beginning to have a substantial impact on quality problems through the use of process-improvement projects and, where appropriate, by reengineering processes or by specific departmental activities.

TQHR is now a kind of "amoebic unit," which Peixotto describes as teams separating and forming as required, continuously learning and operating as if every day is a new pilot project. He comments, "Change is the organization's constant. TQHR's job is to increase its own effectiveness first, to help people to understand their processes and to cope with the level of change we're creating. The big name of the game for the late 1990s will be managing change."

Bob Peixotto says that L.L. Bean's traditional HR department, the forerunner of the total quality and human resources unit, was viewed as "the necessary organizational stepchild and extra business cost." The reengineered, customer-focused department, in contrast, is "easy to do business with," accessible, and flexible. If the name of the game for the turn of the century is to be managing change, the TQHR unit at L.L. Bean will surely be at the forefront.

Key Issues for Discussion

1. Discuss L.L. Bean's approach to blending human resource management with total quality. What lessons can be applied to other organizations?
2. How has the TQHR department modeled the characteristics of teams given in Scholtes's list of successful team characteristics?
3. Because L.L. Bean is primarily a service firm, what special challenges does it face as it attempts to emphasize quality to its employees?

Summary of Key Points

- The Taylor system, upon which much of modern manufacturing is designed, failed to exploit the knowledge and creativity of the workforce. TQ and many of Deming's principles have provided a renewed focus on the role of people in work. In addition, research and practice have demonstrated that employee satisfaction leads to customer satisfaction and good business performance.
- Human resource management (HRM) consists of activities designed to provide for and coordinate all the people of an organization. These activities include determining the organization's human resource needs; recruiting, selecting, developing, counseling, and rewarding employees; acting as a liaison between unions and government organizations; and handling other matters concerning employee well-being. HRM seeks to build a high-performance workplace and maintain an environment for quality excellence.
- Leading practices include integrating HR plans with strategic business objectives; designing work and jobs to promote organizational learning, innovation, and flexibility; developing effective performance management systems, compensation, and reward and recognition approaches; promoting cooperation and collaboration through teamwork; empowering individuals and teams; investing in training and education; maintaining a work environment conducive to the well-being and growth of all employees; and monitoring the effectiveness of HR practices along with measuring employee satisfaction.
- HR plans should be aligned with action plans derived from company strategy. Such alignment requires making strategic choices in planning, staffing, appraising, compensating, and training and development, as well as possible redesign of work, better cooperation and knowledge sharing, and partnerships with external organizations.
- High-performance work refers to work approaches used to systematically pursue ever-higher levels of overall organizational and human performance. Work design refers to how employees are organized in formal and informal units, such as departments and teams. Job design refers to responsibilities and tasks assigned to individuals. Work and job design affect motivation, satisfaction, and organizational effectiveness. Approaches such as job enlargement, job rotation, and job enrichment support TQ principles.

- Employee involvement (EI) refers to any activity by which employees participate in work-related decisions and improvement activities. Although not new, EI approaches support TQ principles by developing trust, encouraging cooperation, and developing leadership abilities.
- Empowerment—giving employees authority and autonomy to make decisions—has been advocated by quality gurus such as Juran and Deming. However, it requires significant changes in work systems, and requires managers to view work much differently. Empowerment often requires a substantial commitment to training and education, one of the hallmarks of TQ organizations.
- A team is a small number of people with complementary skills who are committed to a common purpose, set of performance goals, and approach for which they hold themselves mutually accountable. Common types of teams include quality circles, problem-solving teams, management teams, work teams, project teams, and virtual teams. Developing successful teams requires solid management support and good planning. Self-managed teams present additional challenges because of the high level of maturity required.
- Compensation and recognition refer to all aspects of pay and reward, including promotions, bonuses, and both monetary and nonmonetary forms of recognition. Extrinsic and intrinsic rewards are important to sustaining employee motivation. Team-based pay and gainsharing are prevalent in TQ organizations, as are a variety of nonmonetary recognition approaches.
- Managing human resources in a TQ environment requires increased attention to recruitment and career development, particularly for customer-contact employees, motivation, and performance appraisal. Many longstanding theories of motivation have important implications in TQ organizations, and need to be understood by all levels of managers. Content, process, and environmentally based theories and models provide a theoretical basis for managerial leadership.
- Traditional performance appraisal processes often are at odds with a TQ philosophy. Performance appraisal should be based on quality-related issues, problem identification, coaching, and continuous improvement rather than being tied to compensation and merit-rating systems. A relatively new approach, 360-degree feedback, focuses on two-way communication between employees and customers, suppliers, managers, subordinates, and peers. Many companies are now replacing performance appraisal with planning and development systems.
- To assess the linkages with strategy and to provide a foundation for improvement, measurement of employee satisfaction and HRM effectiveness is necessary. Typical measures include outcomes such as productivity improvement, defect reduction, employee turnover, and perceptions of behavioral performance, and process measures, such as suggestion rates and problem-solving effectiveness. Employee perceptions are usually measured through surveys.
- HRM practices in the Internet age often require employers to take nontraditional approaches to attract and retain high-skilled employees. These approaches may include special perks, increased levels of responsibility early in the employees' careers, and understanding of the effects of changes brought about by new technologies and new realities of employee lifestyles in the twenty-first century.
- The Baldrige criteria in the Human Resource Focus category address the design of high-performance work systems; education, training, and development; and employee well-being and satisfaction. The criteria focus on alignment with company objectives, and how these build and maintain an environment conducive to performance excellence, participation, and organizational growth.

Review Questions

1. Discuss the impact of the Taylor system on quality, productivity, and human resource management. How has TQ changed business thinking about Taylor?
2. Define *human resource management*. Contrast it with the traditional role of personnel management.
3. Contrast traditional HRM approaches with the approaches required in a TQ environment.
4. Summarize the leading HRM practices encountered in TQ organizations.
5. What role does HRM play in supporting strategic business plans? Discuss the strategic choices that HR managers must consider.
6. What is *high-performance work*? What types of HR practices contribute to a high performance work environment?
7. Explain the difference between *work design* and *job design*. How does the Hackman and Oldham model enhance understanding of how job design affects motivation, satisfaction, and organizational effectiveness?
8. What is *employee involvement*? Discuss some of the early developments of EI approaches. What are the advantages of EI over traditional management practices?
9. How can managers overcome resistance to EI initiatives?
10. What is *empowerment*? Discuss the changes that empowerment brings to organizations.
11. Discuss the role of training and education in supporting total quality.
12. What is a *team*? Define the major types of teams found in organizations today.
13. Contrast the differences between quality circles and self-managed teams. What are the key characteristics of self-managed teams not found in quality circles?
14. Explain the important issues an organization must consider in developing successful teams. What steps must organizations take to make the transition from quality circles to self-managed teams?
15. What types of compensation practices support total quality?
16. What are the key practices that lead to effective recognition and reward approaches?
17. What issues must organizations consider with respect to health, safety, and employee well-being in the work environment?
18. In a TQ-based organization, what is the role of recruitment and career development? What challenges does TQ pose in these areas?
19. Define the term *motivation*. Why is motivation critical in a TQ environment?
20. Outline the differences between process, content, and environmentally based theories of motivation. Which type is essential to quality managers?
21. What insights are provided by the Porter and Lawler model of motivation?
22. Briefly summarize traditional performance appraisal processes. Within a TQ perspective, what objections have been raised concerning these processes? What steps can be taken to make performance appraisal more consistent with TQ principles?
23. What is *360-degree feedback*? How does it differ from traditional performance appraisal approaches? How does it addresses the major criticisms of traditional performance appraisal processes and support TQ efforts?

24. Why is it important to measure employee satisfaction and HRM effectiveness? Describe some common approaches.
25. How has TQ changed labor-management relations? What impacts have recent NLRB rulings had on HRM practices in a TQ environment?
26. Summarize the HRM issues addressed in the Malcolm Baldrige National Quality Award criteria.

Discussion Questions

1. What is your reaction to *Fortune's* statements about "the brave new workplace" in the chapter introduction? Do you believe that managers can continue to escalate the perks in order to attract top technotalent? What affect might this escalation have on other employees?
2. Comment on Drucker's observations about the Taylor system. Do you agree with his statement about Taylor versus Marx? Why or why not?
3. How easily can a company shift from the traditional HRM approach to the TQ-based approach? Which of the areas—philosophy, business objectives, quality objectives, business information sharing, inclusion of constituencies, or employee involvement—might be the most difficult for companies to change? Why?
4. How can a fraternity or student organization use leading HRM practices of companies to develop its own strategic HRM plans? If you are involved in such an organization, develop a strategic HRM plan that supports total quality.
5. Think of a job you have had. Apply the Hackman and Oldham model to evaluate how the job design impacted your motivation and satisfaction, as well as organizational effectiveness.
6. Cite some examples of empowerment or lack of empowerment from your own experiences.
7. How might the concept of empowerment be employed in a classroom?
8. Many companies today seek the best available applicants and train them in TQ principles. What implications does this have for designing college curricula and choosing elective courses in a given program?
9. How might a jazz quartet be viewed as a metaphor for a team in a business situation?
10. Students in early grades often receive many kinds of recognition: stickers, candy, and simple rewards, for good work. As we have discussed, similar forms of recognition are common in the workplace. Yet little daily recognition is given at the high school and college level. Discuss possible reasons for this difference, and design a recognition program that might be appropriate in your class.
11. Consider the statement "How one is evaluated determines how one performs." What does it mean for your classes? Would your performance change if grades were abolished (as Deming strongly advocated)?
12. Discuss the controversy over performance appraisal. Do you agree with Deming's approach, or do you take the more traditional viewpoint toward performance review? Why?
13. Most colleges and universities use a course-instructor evaluation system. If your school has one, how is it used? Does it support continuous improvement

or is it used strictly for performance appraisal? How might the evaluation instrument or process be modified to better reflect TQ principles?

14. The Xerox training strategy is summarized as follows:
    a. The training is uniform—common tools and processes are taught across all of Xerox, to all employees, creating a "common language within Xerox" that fosters cohesive team functioning.
    b. Training is conducted in family groups, with all members starting and finishing training at the same time to facilitate the change process.
    c. Training starts at the top of the organization with the CEO and cascades downward to all employees.[105]

    What advantages does such strategy have? Do you see any possible disadvantages? Would this approach work in any business?
15. Discuss the conditions under which team incentives, gainsharing, and "pay for increased skills" reward systems may work. When is it a poor idea to install such systems?
16. What motivates *you* to study and perform in the classroom? How do motivation theories apply to you personally? Discuss how these theories might lead to new ways of teaching and learning.
17. When simple theories such as Maslow's, Herzberg's, and McGregor's explain motivation, why does the search continue for more complex ones or for ones that integrate several different theories, such as Porter and Lawler's theory? What implications do they have for quality?
18. Suppose that someone told you that she was just promoted to manager of a department with several "star" employees that are constantly getting new job offers. Aside from compensation issues (assume they are well paid), what might you suggest as means of ensuring that these employees remain loyal to the company?
19. Compare and contrast the Human Resource Focus category for the 2000 and 2001 Baldrige business criteria (available on the CD-rom). What are the key differences and implications for an organization's management system?

Projects, Etc.

1. Briefly review the history of HRM. Conduct a thorough literature search of one of the "branches" of HRM and relate it to current quality management issues. Search some current business periodicals, such as *Fortune* and *Business Week*, for articles dealing with HRM issues. Explain how they relate to the material in this chapter. Are any new approaches emerging?
2. Interview managers at a local organization about their HRM practices, focusing on work and job design issues. Report on your perceptions of how well their practices support a high-performance workplace.
3. Survey local companies to determine if and how they use suggestion systems. What levels of participation do they have? Are suggestions tied to rewards and recognitions?
4. Investigate the extent of team participation at some local companies. What kinds of teams do you find? Do managers believe these teams are effective?
5. Survey several managers in one or two companies on the topic of motivation for quality. Try to find managers at each of the following levels to interview:
    a. Quality control/assurance
    b. Manufacturing or industrial engineering

c. Upper-level management
d. First-line supervision
e. Line employees (perhaps a union steward or officer)

6. Research the impacts of the Internet age on human resource practices in an actual firm. One possible approach would be to interview an HR manager at a company that is changing from a "bricks and mortar" to an Internet-based organization (such as a telephone company that is shifting to a broad-based communications firm). Another approach might be to visit the Web sites of several firms, examine HR practices that may be described , and compare and contrast your findings.
7. If you were a HRM manager at a nonunion TQ-oriented firm that had employee participation teams, what would you recommend to top management in light of the recent NLRB rulings? Read the sources listed in the text, and any others you may find and write a brief position paper justifying your answer.

Cases

I. The Hopeful Telecommuter

Jennifer Smith was pregnant, and she was happy about it. She and her husband, Jim, had been planning to start a family for some time. However, she was concerned about her job as a Northeast zone supply chain manager for health and beauty products for Big Bear Stores. Big Bear was a large, multibillion dollar foodstore chain that had stores in 47 states. It was a conventionally organized retailer divided into three geographic regions (Atlantic, Mid-American, and Western) with 12 zones (four per region).

Zone supply chain managers, such as Jennifer, were the link between the store managers and their product-line suppliers. Jennifer had been ranked number one in customer and in supplier satisfaction surveys for health and beauty product lines for the last two years. She knew that she was eligible for six month's maternity leave under the federal Family Leave Act, and that the company would have to provide a job for her upon her return. What she didn't like was the thought that they did not have to, and probably would not, give her the same job that she was now holding so well.

Jennifer had talked with Jim, at length, about what to do. They agreed that she should approach her regional manager, Sarah Strong, the zone VP, about the possibility of "telecommuting" to her job after the baby came. Jennifer thought that she could do 85 to 90 percent of the job at home on her own schedule. A large part of her job consisted of verbal and fax contacts with store managers and suppliers, as well as extensive use of a computer for manipulating databases, preparing spreadsheet reports, and sending and responding to e-mail. The other 10 to 15 percent of the time, when she had to be in the office for face-to-face meetings or had to take brief trips, her parents and Jim could keep the baby and cover for her at home.

When Jennifer approached Sarah Strong, she was interested, but would not commit herself to supporting Jennifer's request to telecommute. She said that the company had never done that before, and it might pose a number of difficulties. She did say that she would take her request forward to the two VPs who could approve or disapprove it. Both senior managers would have to approve Jennifer's request, however. Sarah asked Jennifer to prepare some "talking points" concerning the benefits versus the limitations of the arrangement that she could present to the vice president of human resources, and the senior vice president of operations, Sarah's manager. She also asked her to prepare a cost estimate, in consultation with the zone information systems manager.

Jennifer prepared the following estimated costs:

Laptop computer and docking station	$3,500
Setup DSL dedicated phone line	250
Fax machine	250
Computer desk and chair	375
Telephone line charges (6 months)	240
Total	$4,615

Discussion Questions

1. As Jennifer, what "talking points" would you prepare to support your case? Include both the strengths and limitations of telecommuting. Keep in mind the needs of your "customers," the human resources VP, as well as Sarah, and the VP of operations.
2. What issues do you think that the VP of human resources might raise? What issues do you think the senior VP of operations might raise?
3. How does your answer demonstrate the principles of empowerment? How might it fit the components of the Hackman-Oldham job characteristics model?

II. TVS Partnership Proprietary, Limited, Brisbane, Australia[106]

The environment of property development and the need for architectural services has been volatile in Australia. In the middle 1990s the development of commercial properties, such as resorts, office buildings, hotels, and apartment complexes, went through a rapid boom and bust cycle. Many developers eventually declared bankruptcy, and as a result, numerous architectural and property development firms either shrank in size or went bankrupt also.

TVS Partnership Proprietary, Ltd.,[107] is a small, closely held professional partnership that in 1990 had a staff of 12, and grew to about 22 people in the parent organization, plus approximately 55 others in subsidiary firms. From 1990 until 1997, TVS won numerous design profession awards, as well as the Australian Quality Award in 1993, the first time a small business in Australia won the award.

To smooth out business cycles, TVS has diversified into other services, such as interior design, environmental design, landscape architecture, and hotel property management. It invested in research, developing the first solar house (Solar I) in Australia, and pioneered in efforts to use "environmentally friendly" building design and management processes. During the period between 1990 and 1997, the firm grew by more than 50 percent in number of employees. Annual turnover (revenue) increased by approximately 50 percent per year for the last several years.

TVS was first introduced to formal concepts of TQ in 1989. All five directors who lead the organization are involved in, and responsible for, promoting quality, motivation, improvement, plan review, competitive performance, goals and objectives, education and training, and customer and supplier relations. Individual directors are responsible for overview and improvement of specific areas of activity, such as finance and administration, office facilities, operations, research and development, human resources, public relations, and quality processes. They are proud of their leadership style.

The vision of TVS focuses on three areas: self, customers, and community. "Success through service" was developed as a company slogan in 1990. The firm broadened its perspective to a customer focus by 1992. In 1993 it added a community focus. The I-CARE philosophy, an acronym for "Improvement that is continuous and relentless," extends across the TVS organization. It expresses values, goals, and aspirations, and provides a practical and tangible work guide for individuals within the firm. It is also, of course, a marketing tool that ensures customers are aware of the philosophy and implies quality that they can expect to receive from the firm. The TVS philosophy can be summarized by:

- Improvement that is continuous and relentless
- The power of teams
- The importance of its individual members
- The long-term focus
- Understanding and satisfying client needs
- Creative cost-effective and efficient solutions that give more with less
- The integration of the specialist design disciplines: architecture (the built environment), interior design (the human interface), and landscape design (the natural environment)
- The value of efficient and appropriate supporting processes and technology
- Management by measurement, data, and analysis
- A long-term commitment to the local and global environment
- The encouragement of honesty, trust, integrity, and responsibility
- Innovation

Recruiting is based primarily on referral with little advertising. In addition, TVS extends offers to students who have worked at the firm through a cooperative student program at Queensland University of Technology, and selects the best interns who graduate from various university hospitality programs (for its hotel division). During the four-month employment probation period, the company assesses and retains new employees who are high achievers and people with good values.

Clarity of induction, through use of an induction manual, helps to ensure that all divisions and new employees are aligned with company goals. The I-CARE philosophy and principles are stressed for new hires. TVS enjoys low turnover; average retention is about seven years. TVS's induction process allows the managing director to walk into any division and immediately feel comfortable. The values emphasized are honesty and integrity, customer focus, the concept of customer service, service to the community, fire and enthusiasm, commitment to grow, commitment to change, support of a dynamic theory of the firm, and understanding of the need for continuously changing processes.

Some weaknesses are apparent in the induction process, especially as it relates to transmission of the TQ philosophy. Employees who were at TVS at the time of receiving the AQA are probably the most enthusiastic about TQ. Even the veteran drafters could explain the quality process and its components. However, this knowledge and enthusiasm seems to be lacking in newer employees. The induction manual was written just prior to receipt of the AQA Award and has not been revised since that date. In it, the current corporate philosophy, culture, teamwork, and the reward and recognition process are mentioned only in passing. The nature of the employee mix is now quite varied, compared to 1992. The firm now has technical staff, administrative staff, service staff, and professionals that include architects, designers, and managers. They need to have general knowledge about the firm and its everyday procedures, but also specialized knowledge pertaining to their division.

TVS experienced a serious drop in morale in 1994, which was later attributed to three factors: (1) an external environmental slump, with many property developers going bankrupt, (2) a shift of the firm's offices to temporary quarters for six months while a new office was being built, and (3) new offshore expansion projects. At that point TVS developed a new strategic planning approach. The leadership team (five directors, two associates, and the quality manager) reorganized the management of the firm into teams, and dropped centralized job controls. Job costing was shifted to the teams, and an administrative team became facilitators. Quality control was also made a team responsibility.

Prior to setting up the teams, weekly alignment meetings for the whole office had been held to coordinate employee and company efforts. Everyone had to speak or pass at the meetings, which had no meeting facilitators. As the firm grew, less input was offered because the less-articulate staff became reluctant to speak in a large group setting. Eventually, these weekly meetings were discontinued because they were becoming too unproductive.

Weekly meetings of smaller teams were used as a substitute for the alignment meetings. However, weekly meetings were sometimes problematic because of travel schedules and urgent tasks of directors and team leaders. Of 12 planned monthly meetings, the directors might make it to only 8 or 9. Teams sometimes became jealous of each other's territories. Although these team meetings produced cohesion among group members, the level of interteam coordination suffered. When more people were needed on a team, some were moved, sometimes grudgingly, to the team needing resources.

TVS is currently finalizing another team reorganization to improve interteam coordination. Two people from each team will now meet weekly. Full office meetings will be held monthly. The cost coordination will fall on the shoulders of the project leader.

Compensation is an area where the directors of TVS have struggled. Before 1993 they set aside 10 percent of profit for salary increases and bonuses. They would meet annually and debate how much each person should get at each level. They came up with several elaborate schemes for allocating the amounts to each person systematically. In the end, this arrangement did not work well. After winning the AQA, they went back to the old allocation method.

TVS has tried to diversify the types of reward and recognition systems. One such program, the Eagle Card, was a motivational system developed by an American management consultant. For outstanding performance, employees received Eagle Cards and various rewards associated with them. However, TVS determined that such approaches have a short life cycle, after which they must be replaced by a new scheme.

TVS's directors are flexible about the type of rewards and recognition used. They like to reward employees for outstanding performance as close to the event as possible. For example, they have done such things as paid for an employee's wedding, paid the deposit for a person's house, given an employee time off and paid for a trip to Bangladesh for humanitarian purposes, and bought a set of tires for an employee who needed them. They will give time off for a sabbatical, time to sort out family life, and so on. The downside is that employees occasionally feel that they did not receive a reward when they deserved one. Although the directors complied with the AQA criteria, which suggest a consistent, repeatable process for rewarding people, they struggled with the notion, feeling it was not right for their organization. The final success of many projects cannot be measured for a year or more after commencement.

TVS tried an employee shareholding plan in 1990. Many employees were not especially interested and did not appreciate the value of shares. The plan was reviewed and the company directors eventually bought back the employees' shares. Problems arose with the valuation and transfer of shares between employees. Recently they have begun to issue shares to senior managers. It is now being proposed that the company will issue and sell shares to senior managers and associates on an invitation basis.

Discussion Questions

1. How may changes in the organizational structure have affected human resource policies? What were the strengths and weaknesses in the human resources management approaches that TVS adopted?
2. Why has the HR function undergone so many changes in a short period of time? What approach might you recommend?
3. Creative and operations-oriented parts of an organization often view quality from different points of view. How could managers from the different divisions be encouraged to share their perspectives and knowledge to benefit the whole organization?

III. Collin Technologies: Work Systems

Read Item 5.1, Work Systems, in the Collin Technologies case study on the CD-rom accompanying this book. Using the 2000 Baldrige criteria, develop a list of strengths and opportunities for improvement similar to the style in Example 1. Strengths should focus on things the company is doing exceptionally well and support their vision and strategy. (Read the Business Overview section of the case first to identify specific factors that are important to customer satisfaction and relationships.) Opportunities for improvement should highlight issues in its approach or deployment that that can better meet the requirements of the Baldrige criteria. Your comments should include a reason for why a strength or opportunity for improvement is important; that is, provide some insight to upper-level managers that they might not have otherwise realized. Use the wording in the scoring guidelines in Table 3.5 to help you structure your comments.

IV. Collin Technologies: Employee Well-Being and Satisfaction

Read Item 5.3, Employee Well-Being and Satisfaction, in the Collin Technologies case study on the CD-rom accompanying this book. Using the 2000 Baldrige criteria and the other instructions in Case III, develop a list of strengths and opportunities for improvement similar to the style in Example 1.

NOTES

1. Robin Yale Bergstrom, "People, Process, Paint," *Production*, April 1995, 48–51.
2. James L. Heskett, W. Earl Sasser, Jr., and Leonard A. Schlesinger, *The Service Profit Chain*. (New York: The Free Press, 1997), 101.
3. Robert Levering and Milton Moskowitz

(with Reporter Associates: Feliciano Garcia; Karen Vella-Zarb), "The 100 Best Companies to Work For," *Fortune* 141, no. 1 (January 10, 2000), 82.

4. Peter F. Drucker, *Management Challenges for the 21st Century* (New York: HarperBusiness, 1999), 139.

5. Town Hall discussion at the Quest for Excellence Conference, Washington, D.C., March 2000.

6. Richard E. Walton, "From Control to Commitment in the Workplace," *Harvard Business Review* 63, no. 2 (March/April 1985), 77–84.

7. Lloyd L. Byars and Leslie W. Rue, *Human Resource Management*, 6th ed. (New York: Irwin/McGraw-Hill, 2000), 6.

8. Richard Blackburn and Benson Rosen, "Total Quality and Human Resources Management: Lessons Learned from Baldrige Award-Winning Companies," *Academy of Management Executive* 7, no. 3 (1993), 49–66.

9. Blackburn and Rosen, see note 8.

10. AT&T Consumer Communication Services, Summary of 1994 Application for the Malcolm Baldrige National Quality Award.

11 Armstrong Building Products Operations Malcolm Baldrige National Quality Award Application Summary, 1996.

12. Portions adapted from Chapter 4, "Motivation Through the Design of Work," in J. R. Hackman and G. R. Oldham, *Work Redesign* (Reading, MA: Addison-Wesley, 1980).

13. Hackman and Oldham, 25, see note 2.

14. Tom J. Peters, *Thriving on Chaos: Handbook for a Management Revolution* (New York: Alfred A. Knopf, 1988).

15. Alan Wolf, "Golden Opportunities," *Beverage World*, February 1991.

16. Robert Slater, *Jack Welch and the GE Way* (New York: McGraw-Hill, 1999), 153–155, 158–159.

17. A more comprehensive review of history and the forerunners of quality circles from the early 1900s can be found in William M. Lindsay, "Quality Circles and Participative Work Improvement: A Cross-Disciplinary History," in *Southern Management Association Proceedings*, Dennis F. Ray, ed. (Mississippi State, MS: Mississippi State University, 1987), 220–222.

18. Sud Ingle, *Quality Circles Master Guide: Increasing Productivity with People Power* (Englewood Cliffs, NJ: Prentice Hall, 1982), 7.

19. Leslie W. Rue and Lloyd L. Byars, *Management Theory and Application*, 9th ed. (New York: Irwin/McGraw-Hill, 2000), 45.

20. Richard E. Walton, "Work Innovations in the U.S.," *Harvard Business Review*, July/August 1979, 88, 91.

21. Joseph J. Gufreda, Larry A. Maynard, and Lucy N. Lytle, "Employee Involvement in the Quality Process," in *Total Quality!: An Executive's Guide for the 1990s*, The Ernst & Young Quality Improvement Consulting Group (Homewood, IL: Richard D. Irwin, 1990).

22. Edward E. Lawler, III, Susan Albers Mohrman, and Gerald E. Ledford, Jr., *Employee Involvement and Total Quality Management: Practices and Results in Fortune 1000 Corporations* (San Francisco: Jossey-Bass, 1992), 33–36.

23. "Detroit vs. the UAW: At Odds Over Teamwork," *Business Week*, August 24, 1987, 54–55.

24. Peter B. Grazier, *Before It's Too Late* (Chadds Ford, PA: Teambuilding, Inc., 1989).

25. "It's My Manager, Stupid," *Across the Board*, January 2000, 9.

26. J. M. Juran, *Juran on Leadership for Quality: An Executive Handbook* (New York: The Free Press, 1989), 264.

27. Phillip A. Smith, William D. Anderson, and Stanley A. Brooking, "Employee Empowerment: A Case Study," *Production and Inventory Management* 34, no. 3 (1993), 45–50.

28. John Troyer, "Empowerment," Guest Editorial, *Quality Digest*, October 1996, 64.

29. AT&T Quality Steering Committee, *Great Performances* (AT&T Bell Laboratories 1991), 39; and William Smitley and David Scott, "Empowerment: Unlocking the Potential of Your Work Force," *Quality Digest* 14, no. 8 (August 1994), 40–46.

30. "Changing a Culture: DuPont Tries to Make Sure That Its Research Wizardry Serves the Bottom Line," *Wall Street Journal*, March 27, 1992, A5.

31 Robert S. Kaplan, "Texas Eastman Company," Harvard Business School Case, No. 9-190-039.

32. John F. Akers, "World-Class Quality: Nothing Else Will Do," *Quality Progress* 24, no. 10 (October 1991), 26–27.

33. Timothy Aeppel, "Not All Workers Find Idea of Empowerment as Neat as It Sounds," *Wall Street Journal*, September 8, 1997, A1.

34. Alan Wolf, "Coors' Customer Focus," *Beverage World*, March 1991.

35. Bill Wilson, "Quality Training At FedEx," *Quality Digest* 15, no. 1 (January 1995), 40–43.

36. "Honda of America Launches Computerized Quality Assurance Training," *Quality Progress* 30, no. 10 (October 1997), 19–20.

37. A. Blanton Godfrey, "Training and Education in Quality and Reliability—A Modern Approach," *Communications in Statistics—Theory and Methods* 14 (1985), 2621–2638.

38. Alfie Kohn, *No Contest: The Case Against Competition* (Boston: Houghton Mifflin, 1986).

39. Jon R. Katzenback and Douglas K. Smith, "The Discipline of Teams," *Harvard Business Review*, March/April 1993, 111–120.

40. Brian Dumaine, "The Trouble With Teams," *Fortune*, September 5, 1994, 86–92.

41. "Platform Approach at Chrysler," *Quality '93: Empowering People With Technology, Fortune* Advertisement, (September 20, 1993).

42. Brock Yates, *The Critical Path* (Boston: Little, Brown and Co., 1996), 76.

43. Helene F. Uhlfelder, "It's All About Improving Performance," *Quality Progress*, February 2000, 47–52.

44. "Gravedigging at New York Life," *Quality '92: Leading the World-Class Company, Fortune* Advertisement (September 21, 1992).

45. Much of the brief history in this section has been adapted from J. M. Juran, "The QC Circle Phenomenon," *Industrial Quality Control*, January 1967, 329–336.

46. Jeremy Main, *Quality Wars* (New York: The Free Press, 1994), 62.

47. Sidney P. Rubinstein, "QC Circles and U.S. Participative Movements," *1972 ASQC Technical Conference Transactions*, Washington, DC, 391–396.

48. For more about the history and impact of quality circles in the early 1980s in the United States, see William M. Lindsay, *Measurement of Quality Circle Effectiveness: A Survey and Critique*, unpublished M.S. thesis, University of Cincinnati, College of Engineering (May 1986), 72, 117–120.

49. Jack D. Orsburn, Linda Moran, Ed Musselwhite, and John H. Zenger, *Self-Directed Work Teams* (Homewood, IL: Business One-Irwin, 1990), 8.

50. Ron Williams, "Self-Directed Work Teams: A Competitive Advantage," *Quality Digest*, November 1995, 50–55.

51. Peter Lazes and Marty Falkenberg, "Workgroups in America Today," *The Journal for Quality and Participation* 14, no. 3 (June 1991), 58–69.

52. Richard S. Wellins, William C. Byham, and Jeanne M. Wilson, *Empowered Teams* (San Francisco: Jossey-Bass, 1991).

53. Adapted from "Benefits for the Back Office, Too," *Business Week*, July 10, 1989, 59.

54. Lazes and Falkenberg, see note 51.

55. Peter R. Scholtes, et al., *The Team Handbook: How to Use Teams to Improve Quality* (Madison, WI: Joiner Associates, Inc., 1988), 6-10–6-22.

56. J. Michael Donovan, "Self-Managing Work Teams: Extending the Quality Circle Concept," *Quality Circles Journal* (now *The Journal for Quality and Participation*) 9, no. 3 (March 1986), 15–20.

57. Richard S. Wellins, Jeanne Wilson, Amy J. Katz, Patricia Laughlin, Charles R. Day, Jr., and Doreen Price, *Self Directed Teams: A Study of Current Practice* (Cincinnati: AQP, 1990).

58. "Bonus Pay: Buzzword or Bonanza?" *Business Week*, November 14, 1994, 62–64.

59. Woodrumm Imberman, "Pay for Performance Boosts Quality Output," *IIE Solutions*, October 1996, 34–36.

60. Quoted from "Statement of Pam Farr, President & COO, The Cabot Advisory Group on behalf of Cabot Advisory Group, LLC on the Rewarding Performance in Compensation Act before The House Committee on Education and the Workforce Subcommittee On Workforce Protections—April 13, 1999."

61. Nancy J. Perry, "Here Come Richer, Riskier Pay Plans," *Fortune*, December 19, 1988, 50–58; "The Nucor Story," Nucor Corporation Web site, *http://www.nucor.com*.

62. Frank C. Barnes, "Nucor (A)," in *Managing Productivity and Change*, Robert R. Bell and John M. Burnham, (Cincinnati, OH: South-Western Publishing Company, 1991), 507.

63. Chris Adams, "Nucor Slashes Its Hot-Rolled Steel Prices by 7%," *Wall Street Journal*, September 30, 1997, A3.

64. Bruce N. Pfau and Steven E. Gross, *Innovative Reward and Recognition Strategies in TQM*, The Conference Board, Report Number 1051, 1993.

65. Brian O'Reilly, "The Mechanic Who Fixed Continental," *Fortune*, December 20, 1999, 176–186.

66. Dawn Anfuso, "L.L. Bean's TQM Efforts Put People Before Processes," *Personnel Journal*, July 1994, 73–83.

67. "Bonus Pay: Buzzword or Bonanza?" *Business Week*, November 14, 1994, 62–64.

68. Bob Nelson, "Secrets of Successful Employee Recognition," *Quality Digest*, August 1996, 26–30.

69. Leigh Ann Klaus. "Motorola Brings Fairy Tales to Life," *Quality Progress*, June 1997, 25–28.

70. "Domino's Pizza, Inc." *Profiles in Quality* (Boston: Allyn and Bacon, 1991), 90–93.

71. Michelle Conlin and Kathy Moore. "Photo Essay—SAS," *Business Week*, June 19, 2000, 192–202.

72. Timothy Aeppel, "Not All Workers Find Idea of Empowerment as Neat as It Sounds," *Wall Street Journal*, September 8, 1997, A1, A13.

73. Ronald Henkoff, "Make Your Office More Productive," *Fortune*, February 25, 1991, 76.

74. *Great Performances*, see note 29.

75. Adapted from Patricia Nakache, "Cisco's Recruiting Edge," *Fortune*, September 29, 1997, 275–276.

76. Saul W. Gellerman, *Motivation in the Real World* (New York: Dutton, 1992).

77. James L. Bowditch and Anthony F. Buono, *A Primer on Organizational Behavior*, 2d ed. (New York: John Wiley & Sons, 1990), 52.

78. See, for example, Abraham Maslow, "A Theory of Human Motivation," *Psychological Review* 50, no. 4 (July 1943), 370–396; Abraham Maslow, *Motivation and Personality* (New York: Harper & Row, 1954); F. Herzberg, B. Mausner, and B. Snyderman, *The Motivation to Work*, 2d ed. (New York: John Wiley and Sons, 1959); Douglas McGregor, *The Human Side of Enterprise* (New York: McGraw-Hill, 1960); and D. C. McClelland, *Assessing Human Motivation* (Morristown, NJ: General Learning Press, 1971).

79. David A Garvin, *Managing Quality* (New York: The Free Press, 1988), 202–203.

80. Victor H. Vroom, *Work and Motivation* (New York: John Wiley and Sons, 1964).

81. L. W. Porter and Edward E. Lawler, *Managerial Attitudes and Performance* (Homewood, IL: Richard D. Irwin, 1968).

82. James R. Evans and James W. Dean, Jr., *Total Quality: Management Organization and Strategy*, 2d ed. (Cincinnati, OH: South-Western, 2000), 270–271.

83. B. F. Skinner, *Science and Human Behavior* (New York: The Free Press, 1953). See also *Beyond Freedom and Dignity* (New York: Bantam Books, 1971).

84. J. S. Adams, "Toward an Understanding of Equity," *Journal of Abnormal and Social Psychology* 67 (1963), 422–436. See also J. S. Adams and W. E. Rosenbaum, "The Relationship of Worker Productivity and Cognitive Dissonance About Wage Inequities," *Journal of Applied Psychology* 55, no. 1 (1971), 161–164.

85. A. Bandura, *Social Learning Theory* (Englewood Cliffs, NJ: Prentice Hall, 1977). See also Marilyn Gist and Terence R. Mitchell, "Self-Efficacy: A Theoretical Analysis of Its Determinants and Malleability," *Academy of Management Review* 17, no. 2, (1992), 183–211; and R. Kreitner and F. Luthans, "A Social Learning Approach to Behavioral Management: Radical Behaviorists 'Mellowing Out'," *Organizational Dynamics* 13, no. 2 (1984), 47–65. Also see R. A. Snyder and Ronald R. Williams, "Self Theory: An Integrative Theory of Work Motivation," *Journal of Occupational Psychology* 55 (1982), 257–267.

86. Daniel Goleman, "What Makes a Leader?" *Harvard Business Review*, November/December 1998, 93–102; and Daniel Goleman, *Working With Emotional Intelligence* (New York: Bantam Books, 1998).

87. Kenneth W. Thomas and Walter G. Tymon, Jr.. "Bridging the Motivation Gap With Total Quality," *Quality Management Journal* 4, no. 2 (1997), 80–96. See also, Kenneth W. Thomas. *Intrinsic Motivation at Work* (San Francisco: Berrett-Koehler Publishers, Inc., 2000).

88. Bowditch and Buono, 73–74, see note 82.

89. Jeremy Main, *Quality Wars* (New York: The Free Press, 1994), 130.

90. George Eckes, "Practical Alternatives to Performance Appraisals," *Quality Progress* 27, no. 11 (November 1994), 57–60.

91. Douglas McGregor, "An Uneasy Look at Performance Appraisal," *Harvard Business Review*, September/October 1972; Herbert H. Meyer, Emanuel Kay, and John R. P. French, Jr., "Split Roles in Performance Appraisal," *Harvard Business Review*, January/February 1965; Harry Levinson, "Appraisal of What Performance?" *Harvard Business Review*, January/February 1965; A. M. Mohrman, *Deming Versus Performance Appraisal: Is There a Resolution?* (Los Angeles: Center for Effective Organizations, University of Southern California, 1989).

92. John F. Milliman and Fred R. McFadden, "Toward Changing Performance Appraisal to Address TQM Concerns: The 360-Degree Feedback Process," *Quality Management Journal* 4, no. 3 (1997), 44–64.

93. W. Edwards Deming, *Out of the Crisis* (Cambridge, MA: MIT Center for Advanced Engineering Study, 1986).

94. Stanley M. Moss, "Appraise Your Performance Appraisal Process," *Quality Progress*, November 1989, 60.

95. Milliman and McFadden, see note 92.

96. Dick Grote, "The Secrets of Performance Appraisal: Best Practices from the Masters," *Across the Board*, May 2000, 14–20.

97. Brian S. Morgan and William A. Schiemann, "Measuring People and Performance: Closing the Gaps," *Quality Progress*, January 1999, 47–53.

98. Dale Henderson and Fess Green, "Measuring Self-Managed Workteams," *Journal for Quality and Participation*, January/February 1997, 52–56.

99. Robert B. Leventhal, "Union Involvement in New Work Systems," *Journal for Quality and Participation*, June 1991, 36–39.

100. Hill Kemp and Bob Stump, "Getting Unions and Management Together," *Journal for Quality and Participation*, May/June 1999, 42–44.

101. Ross L. Fink, Robert K. Robinson, and Ann Canty, "DuPont v. Chemical Workers Association: Further Limits on Employee Participation Programs," *Industrial Management*, March/April 1994, 3–5; Robert K. Robinson, Ross L. Fink, and Edward L. Gillenwater, "Do Employee Participation Programs Violate U.S. Labor Laws?" *Industrial Management*, May/June 1993, 3–5.

102. Mark R. Hagen, "Teams Expand into Cyberspace," *Quality Progress*, June 1999, 90–93.

103. Courtesy of TD Industries, Ben Houston, president.

104. Adapted from the L.L. Bean Web site, *http://www.llbean.com* and from Chris Ashton, " HR at the Forefront of Change Management at L.L. Bean," *International Journal of Retail & Distribution Management* 26, no. 4–5 (April 1998), 192; ISSN: 0959-0552, Copyright 1998 MCB University Press Ltd. (UK). Further permission courtesy of L.L. Bean, Inc.

105. Xerox Business Products and Systems, Malcolm Baldrige National Quality Award submission document (1989).

106. By William M. Lindsay and Arthur Preston, Senior Research Fellow, Queensland University of Technology. See William M. Lindsay and Arthur Preston. "Maintaining Quality Through Evolving Strategy: The TVS Partnership" *Industrial Management and Data Systems* 100, no. 4 (2000), 164–171, for further details. Appreciation is expressed to the TVS Partnership Proprietary, Limited, and especially to directors Laurie Truce and Mark Thomson, as well as Penny Pinkham, Quality Manager and Administrative Team Leader, for their hospitality and cooperation in preparation of this case.

107. Adapted from Application of The TVS Partnership—Architects to the Australian Quality Award Foundation, Australian Quality Award, Small Enterprise, 1993.

BIBLIOGRAPHY

AT&T Quality Steering Committee. *Batting 1000: Using Baldrige Feedback to Improve Your Business.* AT&T Bell Laboratories (1992).

Great Performances! AT&T Bell Laboratories (1991).

Blackburn, Richard, and Benjamin Rosen. "Total Quality and Human Resources Management: Lessons Learned from Baldrige Award-Winning Companies." *Academy of Management Executive* 7, no. 3 (1993), 49–66.

Christison, William L. "Financial Information Is Key to Empowerment." *Quality Progress* 27, no. 7 (July 1994), 47–48.

Chung, Kae H., and Margaret Ann Gray. "Can We Adopt Japanese Methods of Human Resources Management?" *Personnel Administrator* 27 (May 1982), 43.

Dowling, William F. "Job Redesign on the Assembly Line: Farewell to the Blue-Collar Blues?" *Organizational Dynamics* 2, no. 2 (1973), 61.

General Motors Powertrain. "Application of Dr. Deming's Teachings to People Systems." Presentation slides (undated).

Griffin, R. W. "Toward an Integrated Theory of Task Design." In *Research in Organizational Behavior,* L. L. Cummings and B. W. Staw, eds. Greenwich, CT: JAI Press, 1987, 79–120.

Hart, Christopher W. L., and Christopher E. Bogan. *The Baldrige.* New York: McGraw-Hill, 1992.

Herzberg, Frederick. *Work and the Nature of Man.* Cleveland, OH: World, 1966.

———."One More Time: How Do You Motivate Employees?" *Harvard Business Review* 46 (January/February 1968), 53–62.

Kanfer, Ruth. "Motivation Theory in Industrial and Organizational Psychology." In *Handbook of Industrial and Organizational Psychology,* 2d ed., vol. 1, eds. Marvin D. Dunnette and Leaeta M. Hough. Palo Alto, CA: Consulting Psychologists Press, Inc., 1990, 75–170.

Kern, Jill P., John J. Riley, and Louis N. Jones, eds. *Human Resources Management.* Quality and Reliability Series, sponsored by the ASQC Human Resources Division. New York: Marcel Dekker, Inc., and Milwaukee: ASQC Quality Press, 1987.

Kilman, R. H., and T. J. Covin and Associates. *Corporate Transformation: Revitalizing Organizations for a Competitive World.* San Francisco: Jossey-Bass, 1988.

Lewin, Kurt. *A Dynamic Theory of Personality.* New York: McGraw-Hill, 1935.

Lindsay, William M., and Joseph A. Petrick. *Total Quality and Organization Development.* Boca Raton, FL: CRC/St. Lucie Press, 1997.

Locke, E. A., and G. P. Latham. *Goal Setting: A Motivational Technique that Works!* Englewood Cliffs, NJ: Prentice Hall, 1984.

Mayo, Elton. *The Human Problems of Industrial Civilization.* Cambridge, MA: Harvard Graduate School of Business, 1946.

Messmer, Max. "Rightsizing, Not Downsizing: How to Maintain Quality Through Strategic Staffing." *Industry Week* 3 (August, 1993), 23–26.

Miner, John B. *Theories of Organizational Behavior*. Hinsdale, IL: Dryden Press, 1980.

Olian, Judy D., and Sara L. Rynes. "Making Total Quality Work: Aligning Organizational Processes, Performance Measures, and Stakeholders." *Human Resource Management,* Fall 1991, 303–333.

Palmer, Brian, and Mike Ziemlanski, "Tapping Into People." *Quality Progress,* April 2000, 74–79.

Pierce, J. L., and R. B. Dunham. "The Measurement of Perceived Job Characteristics: The Job Diagnostic Survey Versus the Job Characteristics Inventory." *Academy of Management Journal* 21 (1978), 123–128.

Pierce, Jon L. "Job Design in Perspective." *Personnel Administrator* 25, no. 12 (1980), 67.

Powell, Cash, Jr. "Empowerment, the Stake in the Ground for ABS." *Target* (January/February 1992).

Rubinstein, Sidney P. "Quality and Democracy in the Workplace." *Quality Progress* 21, no. 4 (April 1988), 25–28.

Ryan, John. "Labor/Management Participation: The A. O. Smith Experience." *Quality Progress* 21, no. 4 (April 1988), 36–40.

Semerad, James M. "Create a New Learning Environment." *APICS—The Performance Advantage,* April 1993, 34–37.

Snell, Scott A., and James W. Dean. "Integrated Manufacturing and Human Resource Management: A Human Capital Perspective." *Academy of Management Journal* 35, no. 3 (1992), 467–504.

Steers, Richard M., Lyman W. Porter, and Gregory A. Bigley. *Motivation and Leadership at Work,* 6th ed., New York: McGraw-Hill, 1996.

Taylor, Frederick W. *The Principles of Scientific Management.* New York: Harper & Row, 1911.

Teel, Kenneth S. "Performance Appraisal: Current Trends, Persistent Progress." *Personnel Journal* 59, no. 4 (April 1980), 296–301.

Wagel, William H. "Corning Zeros in on Total Quality." *Personnel,* July 1987.

Walton, Richard E. "From Control to Commitment in the Workplace." *Harvard Business Review* 63, no. 2 (March/April 1985), 77–85.

Yee, William, and Ed Musselwhite. "Living TQM With Workforce 2000." 1993 ASQC *Quality Congress Transactions.* Boston, 141–146.

Yukl, Gary *A. Leadership in Organizations,* 2d ed. Englewood Cliffs, NJ: Prentice Hall, 1989.

Chapter 7

Process Management

Outline

The "New Economy," as many call it, is revolutionizing business. For example, between Thanksgiving and Christmas in 1999, some 22 million shoppers spent more than $5 billion shopping on-line.[1] Traffic on sites such as Yahoo and Kbkids.com grew by 500 percent. Outpost.com, a computer and electronics retailer, sold $2 million of merchandise in one day. However, it wasn't long before Internet message boards were filled with comments like "I doubt I will ever shop again online for Christmas." and other comments unfit to print here. As *Fortune* magazine noted ". . . it takes much more than a logo and a Web site to run an e-tailing operation. Online retailers aren't so different from brick and mortar stores. They run out of stock, sell damaged merchandise, and hire rude sales help. . . . Hordes of companies flooded the market. Trouble is, many of them spent heavily to market and promote their brands but scrimped on infrastructure—the unglamorous side of the business, which focuses on delivering products to customers. The results were often disastrous." Amazon.com, for example, initially tried to have suppliers maintain inventory, but has found that it needed to build traditional distribution centers around the country to improve customer service and control over the product.[2] A. Blanton Godfrey notes that many organizations are "wired for failure"; that is, their processes are not designed effectively or aligned with each other.[3] He cites other examples in addition to the problems that confronted e-retailers. One example is overscheduling at airports. During the 4:15 to 4:30 P.M. time slot, 35 arrivals are scheduled in Atlanta, even though in optimal weather conditions the airport can handle only 25 in 15 minutes; with bad weather, this level drops to 17. Another company celebrated its largest sales contract in history only to discover that all qualified suppliers for critical materials were at capacity. A third example is the unwillingness of departments to work together. For example, when products fail in the plant or in service, it isn't because designers choose components they know will fail; they often have insufficient information about the problems that result from their choices.

These observations point to the importance of designing and managing effective processes—such as product design, order entry, manufacturing, distribution, and customer service—throughout the supply chain. Deming and Juran observed that the overwhelming majority of quality problems are associated with processes; few are caused by the workers themselves. Rather, management is responsible—actually, it shares responsibility with the workforce—to design and continuously improve the processes with which individuals work. The president of Texas Instruments Defense Systems & Electronics Group (now Raytheon-TI Systems) had a sign in his office that sums up these issues nicely: "Unless you change the process, why would you expect the results to change?"

Process management involves planning and administering the activities necessary to achieve a high level of performance in a process, and identifying opportunities for improving quality and operational performance, and ultimately, customer satisfaction. It involves the *design*, *control*, and *improvement* of key business processes. Design focuses on the prevention of poor quality by ensuring that products meet customer requirements and that production and delivery processes are capable of achieving high levels of performance. The distinction between control and improvement is illustrated in Figure 7.1. Any process performance measure naturally fluctuates around some average level. Abnormal conditions cause an unusual deviation from this pattern. Removing the causes of such abnormal conditions and maintaining level performance is the essence of control. Improvement, on the other hand, means changing the performance to a new level. Process management activities help to prevent defects and errors, eliminate waste and redundancy, and thereby lead to better

Figure 7.1 Control Versus Improvement

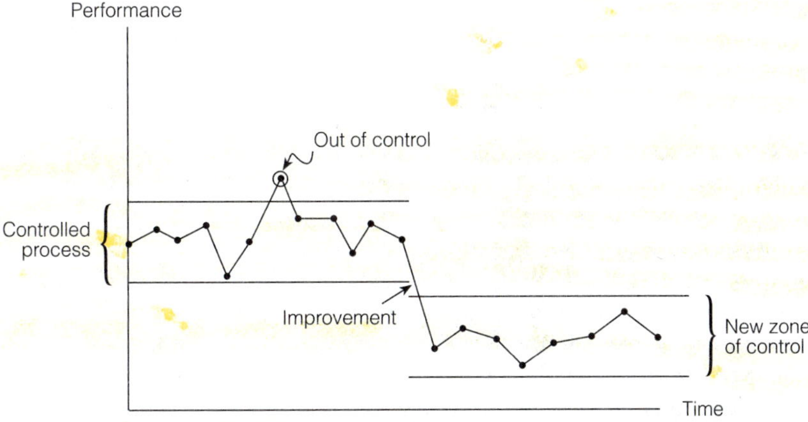

quality and improved company performance through shorter cycle times, improved flexibility, and faster customer responsiveness.

Nearly every leading company has a well-defined methodology for process management. AT&T, for example, bases its methodology on the following principles:

- Process quality improvement focuses on the end-to-end process.
- The mindset of quality is one of prevention and continuous improvement.
- Everyone manages a process at some level and is simultaneously a customer and a supplier.
- Customer needs drive process quality improvement.
- Corrective action focuses on removing the root cause of the problem rather than on treating its symptoms.
- Process simplification reduces opportunities for errors and rework.
- Process quality improvement results from a disciplined and structured application of the quality management principles.[4]

This chapter discusses philosophies and approaches for managing business processes, with a principal focus on the design of these processes. In Chapters 10 through 12, we will discuss specific tools and techniques for controlling and improving processes.

THE SCOPE OF PROCESS MANAGEMENT

As we noted in Chapter 1, essentially all work in an organization is performed by some process. This precept is conveyed by the AT&T customer-supplier model introduced in Chapter 4. Common business processes include acquiring customer and market knowledge, strategic planning, research and development, purchasing, developing new products or services, fulfilling customer orders, managing information, measuring and analyzing performance, and training employees, to name just a few. Individuals or groups, known as **process owners**, are accountable for process performance and have the authority to manage and improve their process. Process owners may range from high-level executives who manage cross-functional processes to workers who run machinery on the shop floor. Assigning process owners ensures that someone is responsible to manage the process and optimize its effectiveness.

Leading companies identify important business processes throughout the supply chain that affect customer satisfaction. These typically fall into four categories:

1. Design processes
2. Production/delivery processes
3. Support processes
4. Supplier and partner processes

Design processes involve all activities that are performed to incorporate customer requirements, new technology, and past learning into the functional specifications of a product (i.e., a manufactured good or service), and thus define its fitness for use. **Production/delivery processes** create or deliver the actual product; examples are manufacturing, assembly, dispensing medications, teaching a class, and so on. These processes must be designed to ensure that the product will conform to specifications (the manufacturing definition of quality) and also be produced economically and efficiently. Product design greatly influences the efficiency of manufacture as well as the flexibility of service strategies, and therefore must be coordinated with production/delivery processes. The ultimate value of the product and, hence, the perceived quality to the consumer depend on both types of processes.

Design and production/delivery processes that drive the creation of products and services, are critical to customer satisfaction, and have a major impact on the strategic goals of an organization are generally considered **core processes** of a business. **Support processes** provide infrastructure for core processes, and though essential to the survival of the business, generally do not add value directly to the product or service. Table 7.1 shows the core processes defined by Merrill Lynch Credit Corporation (see *Quality Profile* in Chapter 6). Their support processes include technology information systems, human resources, administrative services, legal, business services such as quality assurance, and finance. A process such as order entry that might be considered a core process for one company, such as a direct mail distributor, might be considered as a support process for another, for instance, a custom manufacturer. In general, core processes are driven by external customer needs while support processes are driven by internal customer needs. Because core processes do add value to products and services, they require a higher level of attention than do support processes.

For many businesses, goods and services provided by suppliers or partners account for a significant portion of the cost and value of the final product. Suppliers include not only companies that provide materials and components, but also distributors, transportation companies, and information, health care, and education providers. Key suppliers might provide unique design, integration, or marketing capabilities that are not available within the business, and therefore can be critical to achieving strategic objectives. Partners for a company might include educational institutions that collaborate on research and training. (Conversely, a company might be viewed as a partner for an educational institution.) **Supplier and partner processes** describe how supplier and partner relationships are managed, for instance, how performance requirements are communicated and ensured, mutual assistance and training, and so on.

We may view process management according to the three levels of quality discussed in Chapter 1. Major core and support processes are generally defined at the organizational level and require attention by senior managers. Each major process consists of many subprocesses that are managed by functional managers or cross-functional teams. Finally, each subprocess consists of many specific work steps performed by individuals at the performer level. Boeing Airlift and Tanker (A&T) Programs (see *Quality Profile*) has developed an "enterprise process model" that views the entire business as eight interconnected process families. These major

Table 7.1 Core Processes at Merrill Lynch Credit Corporation

Process	Owner	Description	Principal Requirements
1.0 Design	Business Development	Design and enhance credit products and services to meet market and client needs in a timely manner	• Design innovative, high-value products and services tailored for high net worth clients and/or customized for individual needs
2.0 Market	Marketing	Develop communication information tools in a timely and cost-efficient manner	• Provide easy-to-understand information that educates and assists clients in selecting most suitable credit products and services
3.0 Pre-Origination	Client Services	Provide personalized product expertise on mortgage and credit products in a timely manner	• Fast and simple access to information • Knowledgeable and responsive representatives • Personalized information and advice to help select best credit products and services
4.0 Order	Lending Support Services	Process orders quickly at low cost and ensure a high percentage of client satisfaction with appraisers; monitor supplier relationships	• Provide highly accurate and complete products and services at competitive prices in a timely manner
5.0 Under-write	Under-writing	Review loans to determine risk and marketability (resale value) by verifying accuracy and completeness in a timely manner	• Knowledgeable and responsive representatives • Low loan delinquency/foreclosure rate • Process loans quickly
6.0 Approve	RLOs/ Lending Services	Bring loans to a closing status within projected time frame by ensuring that required documents are complete, communicating with clients, and making product recommendations	• Knowledgeable and responsive representatives • High approval rate • Make product and service recommendations as needed • Process loans within projected time frame
7.0 Audit/ Fund	Post-Closing Secondary Marketing	Audit files to prepare loans for secondary market resale; resolve audit issues in a timely manner; fund loans on time; sell loans and make physical delivery to investors	• Fund loans accurately and in a timely manner • Identify errors accurately and promptly • Provide feedback to RLOs to reduce processing errors • Ensure data integrity for setup and resale
8.0 Setup Service	Loan Admini-stration	Setup loan quickly and accurately and ensure that clients are satisfied with the servicing of the loan by responding to client requests and complaints; release liens quickly	• Setup account accurately and quickly • Provide personalized, responsive service and product expertise • Notify client of servicing issues quickly • Provide clear, helpful statements and annual summaries • Provide prompt lien release at loan payoff

Note: RLO = Regional Lending Officer.

Source: "The 1997 Malcolm Baldrige National Quality Award," a publication of Merrill Lynch Credit Corporation.

Quality Profile

Boeing Airlift and Tanker Programs

Boeing Airlift and Tanker (A&T) Programs designs, develops, and produces the C-17 Globemaster 111 airlifter, which is capable of carrying 170,000 pounds and is used by the U.S. Air Force to transport large, heavy cargo to sites around the world. In 1996, A&T signed a $14.2 billion agreement to deliver 80 C-17s to the Air Force. A few years earlier, the Defense Department had threatened to cancel the C-17 program because of technical problems, cost overruns, and late deliveries. A&T overhauled its operations to become "process-focused and customer-driven," initiating partnerships with customers, unions, and suppliers, and replacing manager-controlled teams with empowered teams of workers. To help it perform to plan, A&T developed a seven-step approach to defining, managing, stabilizing, and improving processes and established performance measures that are indicators of efficiency and the chief drivers of customer satisfaction: quality, timeliness, and cycle time. Using this process, one team developed a dry sealant to precoat the 1.4 million fasteners used to assemble a C-17 to replace a wet sealant that was difficult to apply and cost more to dispose of than to buy. The innovation reduced rework, improved airframe quality, reduced structural fatigue, and enabled mechanics to work "faster, cleaner, and better."

Between 1995 and its winning a Baldrige Award in 1998, A&T has maintained an on-time delivery record of 100 percent. Productivity increased from $200,000 per employee in 1994 to more than $300,000 in 1998. Performance on key quality measures has improved by 50 percent from 1994 to 1998, cycle time was cut by more than 80 percent, and supplier on-time delivery increased from 75.9 percent to 99.8 percent. The C-17's 1997 level of performance was nearly four times better than that of the next best competitor's aircraft, and return on net assets was nearly seven times better than the next best competitor.

Source: Malcolm Baldrige National Quality Award, Profiles of Winners, National Institute of Standards and Technology, Department of Commerce.

groupings range from enterprise leadership and new business development to production and postdelivery product support. Each family encompasses up to 10 major processes, which, in turn, are made up of several tiers of supporting subprocesses. A&T manages cross-cutting relationships as "mega-processes" that extend to suppliers and customers.

To apply the techniques of process management, processes must be (1) repeatable, and (2) measurable. Repeatability means that the process must recur over time. The cycle may be long, as with product development processes or patent applications; or it may be short, as with a manufacturing operation or an order entry process. Measurement provides the ability to capture important quality and performance indicators to reveal patterns about process performance. Meeting these two conditions ensures that sufficient data can be collected to reveal useful information for evaluation and learning that lead to improvement and maturity.

Leading Practices

Process management requires a disciplined effort involving all managers and workers in an organization. Companies that are recognized world leaders in quality and customer satisfaction share some common practices.

- *They translate customer requirements into product and service design requirements early in the design process, taking into account linkages between product design requirements and manufacturing process requirements, supplier capabilities, and legal and environmental issues.* Product development must be driven by customer needs. At Ames Rubber Corporation, for example, customers work directly with design engineers on new product development teams. Leading companies coordinate design and production/delivery processes. AT&T Transmission Systems has a new product introduction center that evaluates designs based on manufacturing capabilities, recognizing that good designs both reduce the risk of manufacturing defects and improve productivity. The Bell Laboratories engineering research center supports the introduction of new processes by simulating the manufacturing environment needed to evaluate new technologies. An operational policy developed at Eastman Chemical encourages employees to maximize product value by operating the process at target levels, not just within some specification limits, thus better meeting design performance requirements.

  At Cadillac, product development and improvement teams include assembly operators and supplier representatives. AT&T Universal Card Services (now part of Citibank) evaluated possible new services against screening criteria before beginning its formal development process. This practice ensured that service designs meet consumer needs, strategic and financial objectives, risk parameters and legal requirements, and core competencies. The criteria were designed by the strategic planning group and coordinated with the company's strategic plan. Eastman Chemical reviews designs for safety, reliability, waste minimization, patent position, toxicity information, environmental risks, product disposal, and other customer needs. It also conducts a market analysis of key suppliers' abilities to manage costs, obtain materials, maintain production, and ship reliably.
- *They ensure that quality is built into products and services and use appropriate engineering and quantitative tools and approaches during the development process.* Eastman Chemical, for instance, uses laboratory modeling of processes, computer simulation, designed statistical experiments, and evaluation in customers' plants to assess the quality of its products prior to production. Texas Instruments locates its design centers strategically throughout its facilities. These centers offer expertise and systems with extensive capability for electrical and mechanical computer-aided design, system engineering, and manufacturing, and allow the evaluation of parts that have the best quality history, producibility, reliability, and other special engineering requirements. AT&T Universal Card Services used qualitative and quantitative research and testing to verify how accurately it understood customer needs. Before it introduced new products or services, market trials were conducted to determine whether they met customer and business requirements. The company's program management process had guidelines for deliverables, which addressed all quality requirements. Each phase of the process fulfilled specific requirements, which must be completed, reviewed, and approved before the next phase of development begins. IBM Rochester (see *Quality Profile*) uses statistical techniques to study customers' priorities and trade-offs; validates this information with customer councils, satisfaction surveys, and other forms of feedback; and maintains a Software Partner Laboratory in which customers can certify that requirements are being met and that programs will operate correctly on their systems.
- *They manage the product development process to enhance cross-functional communication, reduce product development time, and ensure trouble-free introduction of products and services.* Leading companies use cross-functional teams to coordinate all phases

QUALITY PROFILE

IBM ROCHESTER, MINNESOTA

The Malcolm Baldrige National Quality Award can be awarded to entire corporations or to individual business units and divisions. Despite the ups and downs that IBM Corporation has experienced in recent history, a shining star is IBM Rochester, a 1990 Baldrige Award recipient. IBM Rochester manufactures and develops AS 400 intermediate computer systems and develops hard disk drives for PS2, RISC/6000, and AS 400 computers in Rochester, Minnesota. In 1995 the facility employed 5,100 people. Its strategic quality initiatives are based on six critical success factors: (1) improved product and service requirements definition, (2) an enhanced product strategy, (3) a defect elimination strategy, (4) cycle time reductions, (5) improved education, and (6) increased employee involvement and ownership. The Rochester quality process is a continuous loop that begins, ends, and begins again with the customer. Of approximately 40 data sources analyzed to guide improvement efforts, most either provide information on customers' product and service requirements or guide steps to refine these expectations into detailed specifications for new IBM offerings.

Between 1986 and 1989, IBM invested more than $300 million in improving its processes and information systems, and focused on improving problem-solving capabilities to prevent rather than detect defects. During that period productivity improved 30 percent, product development time declined by more than half, manufacturing cycle time increased 60 percent, and product reliability rose threefold.

Source: Malcolm Baldrige National Quality Award, Profiles of Winners, National Institute of Standards and Technology, Department of Commerce, and IBM Corporation.

of product development and reduce development times. Boeing A&T has more than 100 integrated product teams (IPTs) that oversee the design, production, and delivery of C-17 aircraft's more than 125,000 parts and supporting services. AT&T established nine expert breakthrough teams—called Achieving Process Excellence Teams—that identify process improvements for developing and deploying products faster in the market. They establish standards, procedures, and training for cross-functional communication that prevents problems from occurring. At The Ritz-Carlton Hotel Company, for instance, the interface of all design, marketing, operations, and legal functions throughout each project allows the company to anticipate requirements and evaluate progress. Customized hotel products and services, such as meetings and banquet events, receive the full attention of local hotel cross-functional teams. These teams involve all internal and external suppliers, verify production and delivery capabilities before each event, critique samples, and assess results. At Globe Metallurgical, a team consisting of employees from customer service, engineering, and quality assurance works together before product development even begins. Afterward, a team of customers and employees from purchasing, engineering, and quality assurance works with the first team to manage the development process. To ensure a trouble-free launch of its products, Solar Turbines uses advanced computerized design and analytical tools that ensure collaboration and sharing of data between manufacturing and key suppliers. Other tools, such as predictive modeling and rapid prototyping are used to validate function, performance, and manufacturability.

- *They define and document important production/delivery and support processes, and manage them as important business processes.* Armstrong Building Products Operations (see *Quality Profile*) has two main production processes: forming and finishing. These processes are documented with written specifications and processing procedures. The documentation also includes a measurement plan for in-process and finished-product quality attributes, testing methods, standard operating conditions, equipment settings, and product formulas. Logistics processes also are documented and linked with other processes, using process flow diagrams. Corning Telecommunications Products Division (TPD) has identified and documented more than 800 processes in all areas of its business, of which 50 are designated as core business processes that merit special emphasis in continuous improvement efforts. Each core process is owned and managed by a key business leader. Although every project at Custom Research, Inc., is unique, the company has documented seven key processes that are common to all projects: identification of client requirements and expectations, questionnaire design, programming, sampling, data collection, data tabulation, and reporting and analysis, plus two support processes of internal communication and client communication. GTE Directories uses a series of cross-functional teams that manage each individual core business process. These teams also conduct appropriate process reviews, review process performance objectives, translate strategic quality plans into process requirements, and communicate new product designs throughout the company.
- *They define performance requirements for suppliers, ensure that requirements are met, and develop partnering relationships with key suppliers and other organizations.* At Dana Commercial Credit, strategic suppliers include financial institutions and

Quality Profile

Armstrong World Industries Building Products Operations

Armstrong World Industries Building Products Operations (BPO), headquartered in Lancaster, Pennsylvania, manufactures acoustical ceilings and wall panels and employs about 2,400 people, 85 percent of whom work at seven manufacturing plants in six states. All quality-focused changes, from redesigning jobs and operations to reorganizing its salesforce, are driven by thoroughly evaluated expectations of increases in customer value. More than half of the BPO workforce participates in its 250-plus improvement teams operating at any given time. The team objectives range from correcting specific operational problems at a plant to improving key business processes across the organization. All quality improvement teams are required to develop specific action plans and set goals that will have a measurable impact on one of the company's key business drivers: customer satisfaction, sales growth, operating profit, asset management, and high performance organization (human resource capabilities).

Across eight market segments, at least 97 percent of customers gave BPO an overall rating of good or better in 1994. Scrap was cut by 38 percent, and manufacturing output per employee rose 39 percent between 1991 and 1995. A supplier quality management process was established in 1985. From 1992 to 1994, notices of nonconformance sent to suppliers fell 32 percent and on-time delivery improved from 93 percent to 97.3 percent, despite reducing the delivery window from 4 hours to 30 minutes.

Source: Malcolm Baldrige National Quality Award, Profiles of Winners, National Institute of Standards and Technology, Department of Commerce.

law firms. Legal requirements are communicated at the early stages of a relationship; feedback from customers determines whether requirements are being met. Corning TPD classifies its suppliers in a hierarchy: Level 1 suppliers have a direct impact on customer satisfaction; Level 2 suppliers are important, but do not have direct linkage to customer satisfaction; Level 3 suppliers provide commodity-like products. Level 1 suppliers are supported by cross-functional teams and integrated into development activities. Armstrong conducts site visits and has a five-level scale to help suppliers understand where they stand in meeting the company's expectations. STMicroelectronics (see *Quality Profile*) develops an annual Supplier Quality & Service plan, which sets goals for suppliers and specifies how ST will review performance, share data, and carry out other responsibilities in the relationship. Long-term partnerships with quality-minded suppliers have enabled Texas Nameplate Company to nearly eliminate inspections of incoming materials. These "ship-direct-to-stock" suppliers are required to be defect-free for at least two years and meet all requirements specified on purchase orders.

- *They control the quality and operational performance of key processes and use systematic methods to identify significant variations in operational performance and output quality, determine root causes, make corrections, and verify results.* Leading companies establish measures and indicators to track quality and operational perfor-

Quality Profile

STMicroelectronics, Inc., Region Americas

Headquartered in Carrollton, Texas, STMicroelectronics, Inc., Region Americas (ST), a wholly owned subsidiary of a French firm, ranks among the world's top manufacturers of semiconductor integrated circuits, supplying consumer-electronics, automotive, medical, telecommunications, and computer equipment markets. ST competes against approximately 20 semiconductor manufacturers with broad product lines as well as hundreds of smaller rivals that serve niche markets. In this industry, missteps in planning and execution quickly translate into competitive disadvantages. ST cultivates long-term relationships that enable it to acquire detailed knowledge of customers' technology and service requirements. ST aims to distinguish itself through advances in technological innovation, increases in the breadth of its product and service offerings, and continuous improvement in just-in-time delivery, fast prototyping, rapid problem resolution, and other areas responsive to customers' high-priority requirements. In 1998, ST initiated a "gung ho" program to promote teaming and employee empowerment, resulting in the redesign of manufacturing work systems and jobs—all with the aim of encouraging and enabling employees to take control of their work.

ST is tightly aligned with its parent corporation's quest to become the world leader in environmental compliance. The company's "Ten Environmental Commandments" commit ST to meeting or exceeding the most rigid requirements set in any of the locations where ST or its parent company operates. In the two years following 1997, energy used to manufacture silicon wafers declined by 20 percent. Employee satisfaction levels in 1999 exceed the industry composite in 8 of 10 categories, and its supplier management program earned "best in class" rating in an independent evaluation of performance in 19 benchmark areas. ST was a 1999 Baldrige Award winner.

Source: Malcolm Baldrige National Quality Award, Profiles of Winners, National Institute of Standards and Technology, Department of Commerce.

mance, and use them as a basis for controlling the processes and consistently meeting specifications and standards. At Eastman Chemical, manufacturing processes are monitored and controlled by collecting millions of pieces of process data each day. In the chemical business, equipment maintenance is crucial to safety, environmental protection, and quality. Eastman maintains a staff of highly qualified maintenance personnel who are trained to prevent and react to equipment breakdowns. Cadillac assesses in-process quality at every stage of the product development process. At the preproduction stage, prototype build checks are used to evaluate the assembly of the product; match checks verify the fit of sheet metal components and interior trim; engine tests ensure that the assembly plants are supplied with high-quality finished engines. Similar controls are used during and after assembly. Leading companies use statistical tools for understanding and controlling processes. Granite Rock, for instance, was the first in the construction materials industry to apply statistical process control in the management of production of aggregates, concrete, and asphalt products. Leading companies identify, analyze, and solve quality problems using formal problem-solving processes described in Chapter 10.

An important aspect of control is empowering employees to stop production whenever significant variations are found. Not long ago this type of employee control was unthinkable in many industries. Today employees at the lowest level of the organization (who are most familiar with the process) have the responsibilities to identify and resolve process upsets. The Ritz-Carlton Hotel Company has a policy by which the first person who detects a problem is empowered to break away from routine duties, investigate and correct the problem immediately, document the incident, and then return to their routine.

AT&T Universal Card Services employed meetings, training, and a variety of media such as methods and procedures documents, newsletters, and electronic mail to prevent problems from occurring once root causes are identified. It verified corrective actions by reviewing measurement trends and increasing sampling efforts, by developing new measures targeting inconsistent processes, system changes, or enhancements, and by comparing internal results with customer-contact survey results.

- *They continuously improve processes to achieve better quality, cycle time, and overall operational performance*. Leading companies employ systematic approaches for analyzing data and identifying improvements. Figure 7.2, for example, shows the process used at Ames Rubber Corporation. Note that this process relies heavily on the analysis of a variety of measurements and information. Leading companies use proven techniques such as process analysis and simplification and advanced technologies. Cycle time for new product development at 3M Dental Products Division (see *Quality Profile*) was reduced from three years in 1984 to 10 months for the six new products introduced in 1994. At IBM Rochester, cross-functional teams examine all elements of production and support processes, from order entry to delivery and installation. The teams evaluate and remove, change, and improve steps in these processes. The Ritz-Carlton has eight mechanisms devoted solely to the improvement of process, product, and service quality:

1. New hotel start-up improvement process: a cross-sectional team from the entire company that works together to identify and correct problem areas
2. Comprehensive performance evaluation process: the work area team mechanism that empowers people who perform a job to develop the job procedures and performance standards

Figure 7.2 Data Analysis and Improvement Planning Process at Ames Rubber Corporation

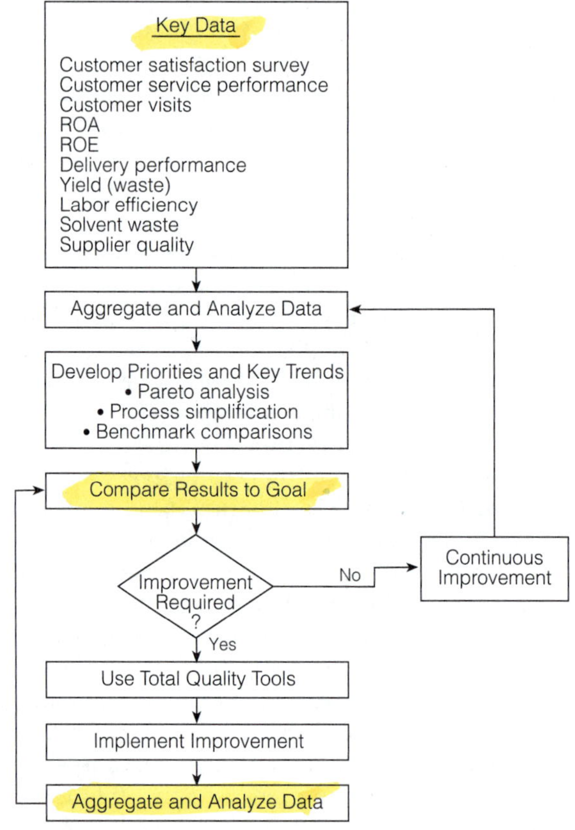

Source: Courtesy Ames Rubber Corporation.

3. Quality network: a mechanism of peer approval through which an individual employee can advance a good idea
4. Standing problem-solving team: a standing work area team that addresses any problem it chooses
5. Quality improvement team: special teams assembled to solve an assigned problem identified by an individual employee or leaders
6. Strategic quality planning: annual work area teams that identify their missions, primary supplier objectives and action plans, internal objectives and action plans, and progress reviews
7. Streamlining process: the annual hotel evaluation of processes, products, or services that are no longer valuable to the customer
8. Process improvement: the team mechanism for corporate leaders, managers, and employees to improve the most critical processes.

- *They innovate to achieve breakthrough performance using such approaches as benchmarking and reengineering.* We will discuss these approaches in greater detail

Quality Profile
3M Dental Products Division

Launched in 1964, 3M Dental Products Division (DPD), a Baldrige winner in 1997, is a business unit of 3M Corporation, manufacturing and marketing more than 1,300 products used by dentists around the world, including restorative and crown and bridge materials and dental adhesive and infection control products. Innovation is a key success factor enabling the company to be a leader in the competitive dental products marketplace. The company's Business Performance Management Matrix provides a systematic and comprehensive tool for aligning key business drivers and goals down, through, and across all business and functional units. This approach also provides critical data and information during design, production, and delivery of products and services. More than 40 cross-functional teams arrange new product introduction, solve problems, and manage and improve business processes.

In 1997 new product sales accounted for 45 percent of total sales, accelerating from 12 percent in 1992. Additionally, the number of patents per employee, an indicator of innovation, is better than twice the rate of its closest competitor. 3M DPD has been the industry leader in overall satisfaction of its U.S. distributors since 1989 and in overall satisfaction of dentists since 1987.

Source: Malcolm Baldrige National Quality Award, Profiles of Winners, National Institute of Standards and Technology, Department of Commerce.

later. Briefly, benchmarking is the search for best practices, in any company, in any industry, anywhere in the world; and reengineering is the radical redesign of business processes to achieve significant improvements in performance. As an example of benchmarking, when Granite Rock could not find any company that was measuring on-time delivery of concrete, it talked with Domino's Pizza, a worldwide leader in on-time delivery of a rapidly perishable product (a characteristic shared with freshly mixed concrete) to acquire new ideas for measuring and improving its processes. AT&T has a corporate database to share benchmarking information among its business units. The database contains data from more than 100 companies and 250 benchmarking activities for key processes such as hardware and software development, manufacturing, financial planning and budgeting, international billing, and service delivery. AT&T obtains this information from customers, visits to other companies, trade shows and journals, professional societies, product brochures, and outside consultants.

To illustrate the concept of reengineering, Intel Corporation previously used a 91-step process costing thousands of dollars to purchase ballpoint pens—the same process that was used to purchase forklift trucks! The improved process was reduced to eight steps. In rethinking its purpose as a customer-driven, retail service company rather than a manufacturing company, Taco Bell eliminated the kitchen from its restaurants. Meat and beans are cooked outside the restaurant at central commissaries and reheated. Other food items such as diced tomatoes, onions, and olives are prepared off-site. This innovation saved about 11 million hours of work and $7 million per year over the entire chain.[5]

PRODUCT DESIGN PROCESSES

Companies today face incredible pressures to continually improve the quality of their products while simultaneously reducing costs, to meet ever-increasing legal and environmental requirements, and to shorten product life cycles to meet changing consumer needs and remain competitive. The ability to achieve these goals depends, to a large extent, on product design. The complexity of today's products makes design a difficult activity; a single state-of-the-art integrated circuit may contain millions of transistors and involve hundreds of manufacturing steps. Nevertheless, improved designs not only reduce costs, but increase quality. For example, a network interface card from 1990 contained about 40 chips; five years later, the entire system board of a Macintosh Performa 5200 had just 19. Fewer components typically mean fewer points of failure and less chance of assembly error.[6]

Most companies have some type of structured product development process. Dana Corporation's Spicer Driveshaft division (see *Quality Profile*) uses an Advanced Product Quality Planning (APQP) process for designing new, similar, or existing products and services and their related production and delivery processes. The APQP process is implemented by a cross-functional team that includes customers and representatives from sales, engineering, quality, and purchasing departments as

QUALITY PROFILE

DANA CORPORATION—SPICER DRIVESHAFT DIVISION

Dana Corporation—Spicer Driveshaft Division is North America's largest, independent manufacturer of driveshafts and related components for light, medium, heavy duty, and off-highway vehicles. Spicer Driveshaft has 17 manufacturing, assembly, and administrative facilities around the United States, employing more than 3,400 people. The company uses Customer Platform Teams as one of the focal points for identifying customer requirements and building and maintaining new business, product offerings, and customer relationships. These teams include sales, engineering, quality, and warranty personnel that use a variety of formal and informal methods to listen and learn from customers. All senior leaders are involved in a two-phase strategic planning process that addresses long-term direction and short-term objectives, which are linked and aligned from headquarters to the individual manufacturing plants. A comprehensive diversity plan is used to help develop candidates for promotion from within the organization, improve community involvement efforts, and establish a mentoring program.

From 1997 to 1999, sales have increased by nearly 10 percent; economic value added has increased from $15 million to $35 million; inventory as a percentage of sales has decreased from 6.8 percent to 6.3 percent; and working capital has decreased from 13 percent to 10.2 percent of sales. Internal defect rates have decreased more than 75 percent from 1996 to 2000 and are approaching best-in class levels. Employees are encouraged to develop and implement changes and innovative ideas and evaluate their results. Ideas submitted by employees average about three per month, which is approaching best-in-class. In 1999, almost 80 percent of ideas were implemented. Employee turnover rate is below 1 percent, which is better than the best competitor; and the attendance rate has remained above 98 percent for the last six years. The division received a Baldrige Award in 2000.

Source: Malcolm Baldrige National Quality Award 2000 Award Recipients Press Release.

well as from manufacturing and assembly plants. The team establishes a project plan that sets design, development, validation, reliability goals, and a timeline. The company also works closely with its supplier base to ensure a high level of quality and productivity and to control costs. Although we tend to equate product development with manufactured goods, it is important to realize that design processes apply to services as well. For example, in the late 1980s, Citibank designed a new mortgage approval procedure that reduced turnaround times from 45 to fewer than 15 days; FedEx has consistently developed new variations of its package delivery services.[7]

The typical product development process, shown in Figure 7.3, consists of six phases:

1. *Idea Generation*. As emphasized in Chapter 4, new or redesigned product ideas should incorporate customer needs and expectations. However, true innovations often transcend customers' expressed desires, simply because customers may not know what they like until they have it. A good example is Chrysler's decision to develop the minivan, despite research that showed that people balked at such an odd-looking vehicle.[8]
2. *Preliminary Concept Development.* In this phase, new ideas are studied for feasibility, addressing such questions as: Will the product meet customers' requirements? Can it be manufactured economically with high quality? Objective criteria are required for measuring and testing the attributes associated with these questions. One tool for assisting in this and subsequent steps is quality function deployment, which will be described later in this chapter.
3. *Product/Process Development.* If an idea survives the concept stage—and many do not—the actual design process begins by evaluating design alternatives and determining engineering specifications for all materials, components, and parts. This phase usually includes prototype testing in which a model, real or simulated, is constructed to test the product's physical properties or use under actual operating conditions, as well as consumer reactions to the prototypes. For example, in developing the user interface for an automobile navigation system, BMW conducted extensive consumer tests with a keyboard, a rotating push button, and a joystick, ultimately selecting the push button.[9] Boeing's 777 jet was built using digital prototypes. Design reviews are frequently conducted to identify and eliminate possible causes for manufacturing and marketing problems. In addition to the actual product design, companies develop, test,

Figure 7.3 Structured Product Development Process

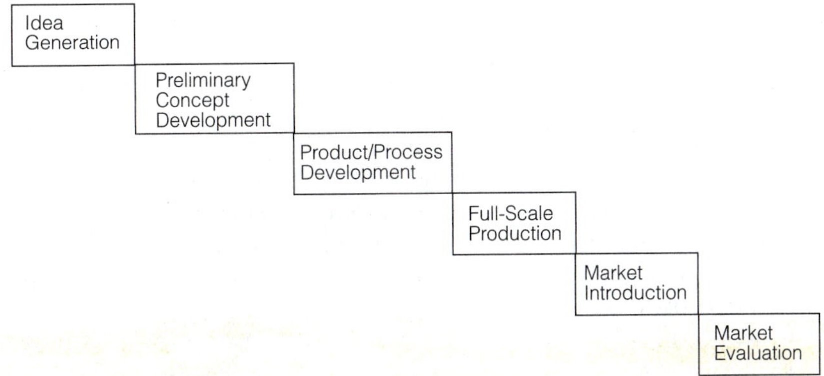

and standardize the processes used in manufacturing, which includes selecting the appropriate technology, tooling, and suppliers, and performing pilot runs to verify results.

4. *Full-Scale Production.* If no serious problems are found, the company releases the product to manufacturing or service delivery teams.
5. *Market Introduction*. The product is distributed to customers.
6. *Market Evaluation*. Deming and Juran both advocated an ongoing product development process that relies on market evaluation and customer feedback to initiate continuous improvements. In fact, Deming's introductory lecture to Japanese managers in 1950 contrasted the "old way" of product design—design it, make it, and try to sell it—with a "new way":
   - Design the product (with appropriate tests).
   - Make it and test it in the production line and in the laboratory.
   - Put it on the market.
   - Test it in service through market research; find out what the user thinks of it, and why the nonuser has not bought it.
   - Redesign the product, in light of consumer reactions to quality and price.[10]

   This philosophy is one of the key ingredients in a successful TQ culture.

Many companies view customers as significant partners in product development, thus integrating market evaluation throughout the process. Ames Rubber Company, for example, uses a four-step approach to product development that maintains close communication with the customer.[11] Typically, Ames Rubber initiates a new product through a series of meetings with the customer and its sales and marketing or technical services group. From these meetings, management prepares a product brief listing all technical, material, and operational requirements. The brief is forwarded to internal departments, such as engineering, quality, and manufacturing. The technical staff then selects materials, processes, and procedures, and submits its selections to the customer. Upon the customer's approval, a prototype is made. Ames delivers the prototype to the customer, who evaluates and tests it and reports results to the company. Ames makes the requested modifications and returns the prototype for further testing. This process continues until the customer is completely satisfied. Next, Ames makes a limited preproduction run. Data collected during the run are analyzed and shared with the customer. Upon approval, full-scale production commences.

Design approaches often differ depending on the nature of products or services. For example, approaches to designing entirely new products will be unlike those that address minor changes and improvements. Design approaches might consider factors such as functional performance, cost, manufacturability, safety, and environmental impacts. We address some of these issues next.

Quality Engineering

Product design requires some basic engineering to establish the functional performance of the product to meet customer requirements, and be produced economically and efficiently with high quality. This requirement is the role of quality engineering. Many modern approaches to quality engineering stem from the work of Genichi Taguchi. Taguchi views quality engineering as composed of three elements: *system design*, *parameter design*, and *tolerance design*. We will focus our attention on manufactured goods, although similar considerations apply to services and will be discussed in the context of process design.

System design is the process of applying scientific and engineering knowledge to produce a basic functional design that meets both customer needs and manufacturing requirements. The first question a designer must ask is: What is the product intended to do? A product's function must be driven by customer requirements. For example, consumers expect a camera to take good pictures. In developing a new camera, Japanese engineers studied pictures developed at photo labs and talked with customers to determine the major causes of poor pictures. The three biggest problems were underexposures, out-of-focus, and out-of-film (attempting to take pictures past the end of the roll). They developed the first camera that included a built-in flash to prevent underexposure, an autofocus lens, and an automatic rewind feature. Today, most popular models have these features to meet customer requirements. Other design considerations include the product's weight, size, appearance, safety, life, serviceability, and maintainability. When decisions about these factors are dominated by engineering considerations rather than by customer requirements, poor designs that fail in the market are often the result.

Developing a basic functional design involves translating customer requirements into measurable technical requirements and, subsequently, into design specifications. Technical requirements, sometimes called design characteristics, translate the voice of the customer into technical language, specifically into engineering measures of product performance. For example, consumers might want portable stereos with "good sound quality." Technical aspects of a stereo system that affect sound quality include the frequency response, flutter (the wavering in pitch), and the speed accuracy (inconsistency affects the pitch and tempo of the sound). Technical requirements are actionable; they lead to design specifications such as the dimensions of all parts in a stereo system. Developing such specifications is the task of parameter and tolerance design.

Parameter design establishes nominal specifications, which represent the transition from a designer's concept to a producible design. Manufacturing specifications consist of *nominal dimensions* and *tolerances*. Nominal refers to the ideal dimension or the target value that manufacturing seeks to meet; tolerance is the permissible variation, recognizing the difficulty of meeting a target consistently. To illustrate these concepts, consider a microprocessor. The drawing in Figure 7.4 shows some of the critical dimensions and tolerances for the microprocessor. The "ratio" notation (0.514/0.588) denotes the permissible range of the dimension. Unless otherwise stated, the nominal dimension is the midpoint. Thus, the specification of 0.514/0.588 may be interpreted as a nominal dimension of 0.551 with a tolerance of plus or minus

Figure 7.4 Microprocessor

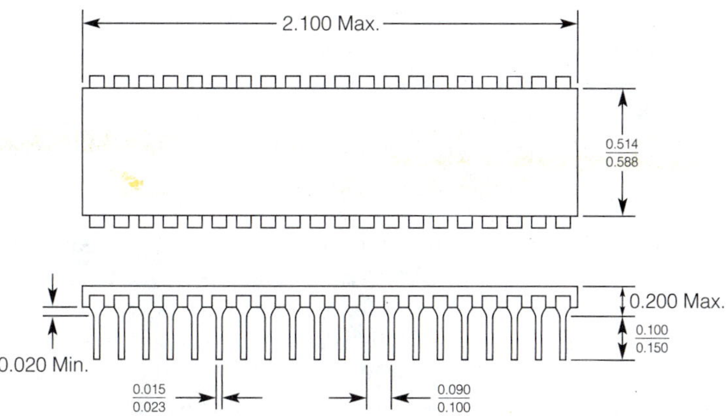

0.037. Usually, this specification is written as 0.551 ± 0.037. The manufacturing-based definition of quality conformance to specifications is based on such tolerances.

Specifications apply to services as well. At Starbucks, the national chain of coffeehouses, milk must be steamed to at least 150 degrees Fahrenheit but never more than 170 degrees, and every espresso shot must be pulled within 23 seconds of service or tossed.[12] Government regulations often determine specifications for food and pharmaceutical products. For example, the U.S. Food and Drug Administration (FDA) sets quality standards regarding the number of unsavory items that find their way into food products.[13] Packaged mushrooms are allowed to contain up to 20 maggots of any size per 100 grams of drained mushrooms or 15 grams of dried mushrooms, while 100 grams of peanut butter may have an average of 30 insect fragments and one rodent hair. (Need we say more?)

Tolerances are necessary because not all parts can be produced exactly to nominal specifications because of natural variations (common causes) in production processes due to the "5 Ms": men and women, materials, machines, methods, and measurement. Common cause variation cannot be reduced unless the production technology (at least one of the 5 Ms) is changed. If a process is incapable of producing within design specifications, management must weigh the cost of acquiring new technology against the consequences and related cost of allowing nonconformities in production. These costs may include, among others, 100 percent inspection, allowing nonconforming parts further in the production process, and possible loss of present and future customers.

Tolerance design involves determining the permissible variation in a dimension. To design tolerances effectively, engineers must understand the necessary trade-offs. Narrow tolerances tend to raise manufacturing costs but they also increase the interchangeability of parts within the plant and in the field, product performance, durability, and appearance. Also, a tolerance reserve or factor of safety is needed to account for engineering uncertainty regarding the maximum variation allowable and compatibility with satisfactory product performance. Wide tolerances, on the other hand, increase material utilization, machine throughput, and labor productivity, but have a negative impact on product characteristics, as previously mentioned. Thus, factors operating to enlarge tolerances include production planning requirements; tool design, fabrication, and setup; tool adjustment and replacement; process yield; inspection and gauge control and maintenance; and labor and supervision requirements.

Traditionally, tolerances are set by convention rather than scientifically. A designer might use the tolerances specified on previous designs or base a design decision on judgment from past experience. Setting inappropriate tolerances can be costly. For instance, in one company, a bearing seat had to be machined on a large part, costing more than $1,000. Because of the precision tolerance specified by design engineers, one or two parts per month had to be scrapped when the tolerance was exceeded. A study revealed that the bearings being used did not require such precise tolerances. When the tolerance was relaxed, the problem disappeared. This one design change resulted in approximately $20,000 in savings per year.

All too often, tolerance settings fail to account for the impact of variation on product functionality, manufacturability, or economic consequences. In a review of Audi's TT Coupe when it was first introduced, automobile columnist Alan Vonderhaar noted "There was apparently some problem with the second-gear synchronizer, a device that is supposed to ease shifts. As a result, on full-power upshifts from first to second, I frequently got gear clashes." He observed others with the same problem from Internet newsgroups and concluded "It appears to be an issue that surfaces just now and again, here and there throughout the production mix, suggesting it may be a tolerance issue—sometimes the associated parts are close enough to specifications to get along well, other times they're at the outer ranges of manufacturing tolerance and cause problems."[14]

The Taguchi Loss Function

A scientific approach to tolerance design uses the Taguchi loss function, the concept of which was introduced in Chapter 3. Taguchi assumed that losses can be approximated by a quadratic function so that larger deviations from target cause increasingly larger losses. For the case in which a specific target value is best and quality deteriorates as the value moves away from the target on either side (called "nominal is best"), the loss function is represented by

$$L(x) = k(x - T)^2$$

where x is any value of the quality characteristic, T is the target value, and k is some constant. Figure 7.5 illustrates this function.

The constant k is estimated by determining the cost of repair or replacement if a certain deviation from the target occurs, as the following example illustrates.

Example 1: Estimating the Taguchi Loss Function. Assume that a certain quality characteristic has a specification of 0.500 ± 0.020. An analysis of company records reveals that if the value of the quality characteristic exceeds the target of 0.500 by the tolerance of 0.020 on either side, the product is likely to fail during the warranty period and costs $50 for repair. Then,

$$50 = k(0.020)^2$$

$$k = 50/0.0004 = 125{,}000$$

Therefore, the loss function is

$$L(x) = 125{,}000(x - T)^2$$

Thus, if the deviation is only 0.010, the estimated loss is

$$L(0.010) = 125{,}000(0.010)^2 = \$12.50$$

Figure 7.5 Nominal-Is-Best Loss Function

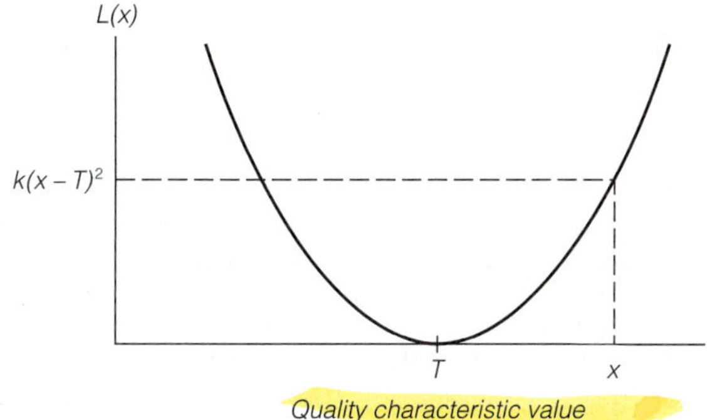

If the distribution of the variation about the target value is known, the average loss per unit can be computed by statistically averaging the loss associated with possible values of the quality characteristic. In statistical terminology, this average loss per unit is simply the expected value of the loss. To keep the mathematics simple, consider Example 2.

Example 2: Computing Expected Loss with the Taguchi Loss Function. Suppose that two processes, A and B, have the following distributions of a quality characteristic with specification 0.50 ± 0.02. In process A, the output of the process has values ranging from 0.48 to 0.52, all of which are equally likely. For process B, 60 percent of the output is expected to have a value of 0.50, 15 percent has a value of 0.49, and so on.

Value	Process A Probability	Process B Probability
0.47	0	0.02
0.48	0.20	0.03
0.49	0.20	0.15
0.50	0.20	0.60
0.51	0.20	0.15
0.52	0.20	0.03
0.53	0	0.02

Notice that the output from process A is spread equally over the range from 0.48 to 0.52 and lies entirely within specifications. In process B, output is concentrated near the target value, but does not entirely lie within specifications. Using the loss function

$$L(x) = 125{,}000(x - 0.50)^2$$

the expected loss for each process can be computed as follows:

Value, x	Loss	Process A Probability	Weighted Loss	Process B Probability	Weighted Loss
0.47	112.5	0.00	0	0.02	2.25
0.48	50.0	0.20	10	0.03	1.50
0.49	12.5	0.20	2.5	0.15	1.875
0.50	0.0	0.20	0	0.60	0
0.51	12.5	0.20	2.5	0.15	1.875
0.52	50.0	0.20	10	0.03	1.50
0.53	112.5	0.00	0	0.02	2.25
		Expected loss	25.0		11.25

Clearly process B incurs a smaller total expected loss even though some output falls outside specifications.

The expected loss is computed using a simple formula that involves the variance of the quality characteristic, σ^2, and the square of the deviation of the mean value from the target $D^2 = (\bar{x} - T)^2$. The expected loss is

$$EL(x) = k(\sigma^2 + D^2)$$

For instance, in process A, the variance of the quality characteristic is 0.0002 and $D^2 = 0$ since the mean value is equal to the target. Thus,

$$EL(x) = 125{,}000(0.0002 + 0) = 25$$

A similar computation can be used to determine the expected loss for process B.

To relate this analysis to the Sony television example cited in Chapter 3, k was determined to be 0.16. The mean of both distributions of color density fell on the target value and therefore $D^2 = 0$ for both the U.S. and the Japanese plants. However, the variance of the distributions differed. For the San Diego plant, $\sigma^2 = 8.33$ and for the Japanese plant, $\sigma^2 = 2.78$. Thus the average loss per unit was computed to be

San Diego plant: 0.16(8.33) = \$1.33
Japanese plant: 0.16(2.78) = \$0.44

or a difference of \$0.89 per unit.

The expected loss provides a measure of variation that is independent of specification limits. Such a measure stresses continuous improvement rather than acceptance of the status quo simply because a product "conforms to specifications."

Not all quality characteristics have nominal targets with tolerances on either side. In some cases, such as impurities in a chemical process or fuel consumption, "smaller is better." In other cases, "larger is better" as with breaking strength or product life. The loss function for the smaller-is-better case is

$$L(x) = kx^2$$

and for the larger-is-better case is

$$L(x) = k(1/x^2)$$

These formulas can be applied in a manner similar to the previous examples. The following example shows how the Taguchi loss function may be used to set tolerances.

Example 3: Using the Taguchi Loss Function for Tolerance Design. The desired speed of a cassette tape is 1.875 inches per second. Any deviation from this value causes a change in pitch and tempo and thus poor sound quality. Suppose that adjusting the tape speed under warranty when a customer complains and returns a cassette player costs a manufacturer \$20. (This repair expense does not include other costs due to customer dissatisfaction and therefore is at best a lower bound on the actual loss.) Based on past information, the company knows the average customer will return a player if the tape speed is off the target by at least 0.15 inch per second. The loss function constant is computed as

$$20 = k(0.15)^2$$
$$k = 888.9$$

and thus the loss function is

$$L(x) = 888.9(x - 1.875)^2$$

At the factory, the adjustment can be made at a much lower cost of \$3, which consists of the labor to make the adjustment and additional testing. What should the tolerance be before an adjustment is made at the factory?

To use the loss function, set $L(x) = \$3$ and solve for the tolerance:

$$3 = 888.9 \text{ (one-half tolerance)}^2$$

$$\text{tolerance} = \pm \sqrt{3/888.9} = \pm 0.058$$

Therefore, if the tape speed is off by more than 0.058 inches per second, adjusting it at the factory is more economical. Thus, the specifications should be 1.875 ± 0.058 or 1.817 to 1.933.

Cost, Manufacturability, and Quality

Product design affects the costs of manufacturing (direct and indirect labor, materials, and overhead), the costs of warranty and field repair, and the amount of redesign activities. General Electric, for example, found that 75 percent of its manufacturing costs are determined by design. With products in which parts alone represent 65 to 80 percent of the manufacturing cost, design may account for 90 percent or more of the total manufacturing cost. Other companies exhibit similar figures. For Rolls Royce, design determines 80 percent of the final production costs.

Simplifying the design can often improve cost. By cutting the number of parts, material costs generally go down, inventory levels fall, the number of suppliers shrinks, and production time can be shortened. Back in the days of dot matrix printers, IBM, for example, realized many benefits of design simplification. IBM had been buying its dot matrix printers from Seiko Epson Corporation, then the world's low-cost producer. When IBM developed a printer with 65 percent fewer parts that was designed to snap together during final assembly without the use of fasteners, the result was a 90 percent reduction in assembly time and major cost reductions.

Many aspects of product design can adversely affect manufacturability and, hence, quality.[15] Some parts may be designed with features difficult to fabricate repeatedly or with unnecessarily tight tolerances. Some parts may lack details for self-alignment or features for correct insertion. In other cases, parts so fragile or so susceptible to corrosion or contamination may be damaged in shipping or by internal handling. Sometimes a design simply has more parts than are needed to perform the desired functions, which increases the chance of assembly error. Thus, problems of poor design may show up as errors, poor yield, damage, or functional failure in fabrication, assembly, test, transport, and end use.

A product's design affects quality at the supplier's plant and in the manufacturer's own plant. A frequent cause of supplier quality problems is incomplete or inaccurate specification of the item they are to supply. This problem often occurs with custom parts and is caused by weakness in the design process, engineers who do not follow set procedures, or sloppiness in the procurement and purchasing process. The greater the number of different parts and the more suppliers involved, the more likely a supplier is to receive an inaccurate or incomplete parts specification. Such problems can be reduced by designing a product around preferred parts (those already approved based on their reliability and qualified source of supply), minimizing the number of parts in the design, and procuring parts from a minimum number of vendors.

In manufacturing and assembly, many of the same problems described in the preceding paragraph can occur, as well as problems in assembly and testing. For instance, designs with numerous parts increase the incidence of part mixups, missing parts, and test failures. Parts that are similar but not identical create the possibility that an assembler will use the wrong part. Parts without details to prevent insertion in the wrong orientation lead to more frequent improper assembly. Complicated assembly steps or tricky joining processes can cause incorrect, incomplete, unreliable, or otherwise faulty assemblies. Finally, the designer's failure to consider conditions to which parts will be exposed during assembly such as temperature, humidity, vibration, static electricity, and dust, may result in failures during testing or use.

Design for manufacturability (DFM) is the process of designing a product for efficient production at the highest level of quality. DFM is intended to prevent product designs that simplify assembly operations but require more complex and expensive components, designs that simplify component manufacture while complicating the assembly process, and designs that are simple and inexpensive to produce but difficult or expensive to service or support.

Table 7.2 summarizes important design guidelines for improving manufacturability and thus improving quality and reducing costs. Many industries have developed more specific guidelines. For example, guidelines for designing printed circuit boards include the following:

- Placing all components on the top side of the board
- Grouping similar components whenever possible
- Maintaining a 0.60-inch clearance for insertable components.

Design and Public Responsibilities

Safety in consumer products represents a major issue in design, and certainly an important part of a company's public responsibilities. Balancing safety with customer quality expectations is not always easy. For example, an analysis of the issues surrounding the Bridgestone/Firestone tire recall in 2000 (briefly discussed in Chapter 3) suggested that improved tire designs—that would help hold tires together when the tread peels off—produce a bouncier ride, which few drivers want. This leads to interesting ethical issues and the role of government regulation that have no easy answers. Liability concerns cause many companies to forego certain product development activities. For example, Unison Industries, Inc., of Rockford, Illinois, developed a new solid-state electronic ignition system for piston-engine aircraft. The company dropped the product after prototype testing. Unison says it was sued over crashes involving aircraft on which its products were not even installed. Getting removed from the lawsuits proved costly in itself.[16] In a survey of more than 500 chief executives, more than one-third worked for firms that have canceled introduction of products because of liability concerns. Many companies have closed plants and laid off workers, and more than 20 percent of the executives believe their companies have lost market share to foreign competitors because of product liability costs.

All parties responsible for design, manufacture, sales, and service of a defective product are now liable for damages. According to the theory of strict liability, anyone who sells a product that is defective or unreasonably dangerous is subject to liability for any physical harm caused to the user, the consumer, or the property of either.[17] This law applies when the seller is in the business of selling the product, and the product reaches the consumer without a substantial change in condition even if the

Table 7.2 Design Guidelines for Quality Assurance

Guideline	Result
Minimize Number of Parts	
• Fewer parts and assembly drawings	→ Lower volume of drawings and instructions to control
• Less complicated assemblies	→ Lower assembly error rate
• Fewer parts to hold to required quality characteristics	→ Higher consistency of part quality
• Fewer parts to fail	→ Higher reliability
Minimize Number of Part Numbers	
• Fewer variations of like parts	→ Lower assembly error rate
Design for Robustness (Taguchi method)	
• Low sensitivity to component variability	→ Higher first-pass yield; less degradation of performance with time
Eliminate Adjustments	
• No assembly adjustment errors	→ Higher first-pass yield
• Eliminates adjustable components with high failure rates	→ Lower failure rate
Make Assembly Easy and Foolproof	
• Parts cannot be assembled wrong	→ Lower assembly error rate
• Obvious when parts are missing	→ Lower assembly error rate
• Assembly tooling designed into part	→ Lower assembly error rate
• Parts are self-securing	→ Lower assembly error rate
• No "force fitting" of parts	→ Less damage to parts; better serviceability
Use Repeatable, Well-Understood Processes	
• Part quality easy to control	→ Higher part yield
• Assembly quality easy to control	→ Higher assembly yield
Choose Parts that Can Survive Process Operations	
• Less damage to parts	→ Higher yield
• Less degradation of parts	→ Higher reliability
Design for Efficient and Adequate Testing	
• Less mistaking "good" for "bad" product and vice versa	→ Truer assessment of quality; less unnecessary rework
Lay Out Parts for Reliable Process Completion	
• Less damage to parts during handling and assembly	→ Higher yield; higher reliability
Eliminate Engineering Changes on Released Products	
• Fewer errors due to changeovers and multiple revisions/versions	→ Lower assembly error rate

Source: D. Daetz, "The Effect of Product Design on Product Quality and Product Cost," *Quality Progress* 20, no. 6 (June 1987), 63–67.

seller has exercised all possible care in the preparation and sale of the product. The principal issue is whether a defect, direct or indirect, exists. If the existence of a defect can be established, the manufacturer usually will be held liable. A plaintiff need prove only that (1) the product was defective; (2) the defect was present when the product changed ownership; and (3) the defect resulted in injury.

Strict liability was used as a basis for the 1978 ruling against Ford in the Pinto automobile case. In the initial product liability case, the plaintiff was awarded $125 million in punitive damages. Based on Ford's own engineering documents, the plaintiff's lawyers established evidence that the company had determined that changing the fuel tank design was more expensive than paying a few product liability claims.

In 1997 Chrysler was ordered to pay $262.5 million in a case involving defective latches on minivans; thus, the economic consequences can be significant.

With the doctrine of strict liability, the manufacturer is required to prove innocence. That is, the manufacturer must prove that it would be highly unlikely a product would be shipped in defective condition. Defective condition could mean a design defect, poor design implementation, inadequate warnings, improper instructions, failure to anticipate misuse, improper materials, assembly errors, inadequate testing, or failure to take corrective action. Thus, we see that liability extends throughout all production stages.

Attention to design quality can greatly reduce the possibility of product liability claims as well as provide supporting evidence in defense arguments. Liability makes documentation of quality assurance procedures a necessity. A firm should record all evidence that shows the designer has established test and monitoring procedures of critical product characteristics. Feedback on test and inspection results along with corrective actions taken must also be documented. Even adequate packaging and handling procedures are not immune to examination in liability suits, because packaging is still within the manufacturer's span of control. Managers should address the following questions:[18]

- Is the product reasonably safe for the end user?
- What could possibly go wrong with it?
- Are any needed safety devices absent?
- What kind of warning labels or instructions should be included?
- What would attorneys call "reasonable foreseeable use"?
- What are some extreme climatic or environmental conditions for which the product should be tested?
- What similarities does the product have with others that may have had previous problems?

In addition to legal issues, environmental concerns have an unprecedented impact on product and process designs. An estimated 350 million home and office appliances were disposed of in 1993 and has certainly increased since then. Personal care appliances such as hair dryers are discarded at the rate of 50 million per year.[19] The problem of what to do with obsolete computers is a growing design and technological waste problem today.[20] A monitor contains eight pounds of lead; a CPU has another three to five pounds, as well as other hazardous metals, such as mercury. According to a 1997 Carnegie Mellon University study, 150 million dead but not decaying PCs will be buried in U.S. landfills by 2005. In Europe, the European Commission has proposed a ban on materials such as lead-based solder in PCs and the imposition of recycling responsibilities on manufacturers beginning in January 2004. Pressures from environmental groups clamoring for "socially responsive" designs, states and municipalities that are running out of space for landfills, and consumers who want the most for their money have caused designers and managers to look carefully at the concept of **design-for-environment**, or **DfE.**[21] DfE offers the potential to create more desirable products at lower costs by reducing disposal and regulatory costs, increasing the end-of-life value of products, reducing material use, and minimizing liabilities.

DfE is the explicit consideration of environmental concerns during the design of products and processes, and includes such practices as designing for recyclability and disassembly. Recyclable products are designed to be taken apart and their components repaired, refurbished, melted down, or otherwise salvaged for reuse. Although 20.6 million PCs fell into disuse in 1998, only 11 percent were recycled. It can cost as much as $35 per CPU, monitor or printer, for companies such as Technology

Recycling to collect and disassemble the PCs. Once extracted, the precious metals and hazardous materials are processed by EPA-approved facilities and eventually sold in the spot-metal market.

The recyclability feature appeals to environmentalists as well as city and state officials, both of whom are fighting the effects of waste disposal. At the same time, however, it creates new issues for designers and consumers. For example, designers strive to use fewer types of materials, such as plastics, with certain characteristics, such as thermal properties, that allow for reuse. *Business Week* cites several U.S. firms already working on or marketing such products, including Whirlpool, Digital Equipment, 3M, and General Electric.[22] The latter's plastics division, which serves the durable goods market, uses only thermoplastics in its products. Unlike many other varieties of plastics, thermoplastics can be melted down and recast into other shapes and products, thus making them recyclable. Designers must also refrain from using certain methods of fastening, such as glues and screws, in favor of quick connect-disconnect bolts or other such fasteners. These changes in design will have an impact on tolerances, durability, and quality of products. Such design changes affect consumers who will be asked to recycle products (perhaps to recover a deposit), in spite of inconveniences such as transporting them to a recycling center.

Repairable products are not a new idea, but the concept lost favor when, in the 1960s and 1970s, the United States became known as the "throwaway society." Many products are discarded simply because the cost of maintenance or repair is too high when compared with the cost of a new item. Now design for disassembly promises to bring back easy, affordable product repair. For example, Whirlpool Corporation is developing a new appliance designed for repairability, with its parts sorted for easy coding. Thus, repairability has the potential of pleasing customers, who frequently find it easier and less costly to repair a product rather than discard it. At the same time, companies are challenged to consider fresh approaches to design that build both cost-effectiveness and quality into the product. For instance, even though it is more efficient to assemble an item using rivets instead of screws, this approach is contrary to a design-for-disassembly philosophy. An alternative might be an entirely new design that eliminates the need for fasteners in the first place.

These issues need not be viewed as hindrances to manufacturers. On the contrary, design for recyclability and repairability can improve manufacturability, resulting in a win-win situation for consumers and producers alike. Xerox and IBM are two companies that have integrated DfE specialists directly into design teams; by 1996 more than 75 percent of design teams had adopted DfE. Some of the product changes they have made as a result of DfE in addition to designs for disassembly include the use of snap-fits on IBM PC housings and reusable Xerox toner cartridges and bottles.

Streamlining the Product Development Process

The importance of speed in product development cannot be overemphasized. To succeed in highly competitive markets, companies must churn out new products quickly. Whereas automakers once took four to six years to develop new models, most are striving to do it within 24 months. In fact, Toyota's goal is just 18 months! GM has planned to introduce a new or overhauled vehicle about every 28 days. Boeing took 54 months to design its 777 airplane; yet the company would like to reduce it to 10 because the market changes so quickly. The product development process can be improved with various advanced technologies, such as computer-aided design (CAD), computer-aided manufacturing (CAM), flexible manufacturing systems (FMS), and computer-integrated manufacturing (CIM). These technologies automate and link design and manufacturing processes, reducing cycle times as well as removing opportunities for human error, thus improving quality. Such automation is a significant factor at Toyota.[23]

One of the most significant barriers to efficient product development is poor intraorganizational cooperation. Successful product development demands the involvement and cooperation of many different functional groups within an organization to identify and solve design problems and try to reduce product development and introduction times. All departments play crucial roles in the design process. The designer's objective is to design a product that achieves the desired functional requirements. The manufacturing engineer's objective is to produce it efficiently. The salesperson's goal is to sell the product, and the finance person's goal is to make a profit. Purchasing seeks parts that meet quality requirements. Packaging and distribution deliver the product to the customer in good operating condition. Clearly, all business functions have a stake in the product; therefore, all should work together.

Unfortunately, the product development process often is performed without such cooperation. In many large firms product development is accomplished in a serial fashion, as suggested in Figure 7.3. In the early stages of development, design engineers dominate the process. Later, the prototype is transferred to manufacturing for production. Finally, marketing and sales personnel are brought into the process. This approach has several disadvantages. First, product development time is long. Second, up to 90 percent of manufacturing costs may be committed before manufacturing engineers have any input to the design. Third, the final product may not be the best one for market conditions at the time of introduction.

An approach that alleviates these problems is called **concurrent engineering,** or **simultaneous engineering.** Concurrent engineering is a process in which all major functions involved with bringing a product to market continuously participate in product development from conception through sales. Such an approach not only helps achieve trouble-free introduction of products and services, but also results in improved quality, lower costs, and shorter product development cycles. Typical benefits include 30 to 70 percent less development time, 65 to 90 percent fewer engineering changes, 20 to 90 percent less time to market, 200 to 600 percent improvement in quality, 20 to 110 percent improvement in white collar productivity, and 20 to 120 percent higher return on assets.[24]

Concurrent engineering involves multifunctional teams, usually consisting of 4 to 20 members and including every specialty in the company. The functions of such teams are to determine the character of the product and decide what design and production methods are appropriate; analyze product functions so that all design decisions can be made with full knowledge of how the item is supposed to work; perform a design for manufacturability study to determine whether the design can be improved without affecting performance; formulate an assembly sequence; and design a factory system that fully involves workers.

Concurrent engineering has been a major force behind the resurgence of U.S. automobile companies by enabling them to dramatically reduce product development time. In the past, automobile development followed a sequential process in which styling engineers dreamed up a concept and sent the concept to product engineers to design components. They in turn would send the designs to manufacturing and suppliers. This process was costly and inefficient; each handoff lost something in time and money. What appeared feasible for one group often proved impossible for another to accomplish. By the time the vehicle was finally produced, marketing was faced with selling a product for which they had no input. Often the vehicle was priced incorrectly for the target market.

In 1980 Ford launched Team Taurus, modeled after program management concepts in the aerospace industry. Program managers headed product teams that included representatives from design, engineering, purchasing, marketing, quality assurance, sales, and service. Cadillac adopted simultaneous engineering in 1985. Vehicle teams, composed of disciplines from every area of the organization, were responsible for managing all steps of product development. They defined the target market and the overall vehicle goals, and managed the timing, profitability, and continuous improvement of the vehicle's quality, reliability, durability, and performance. Chrysler's adaptation of simultaneous engineering enabled it to develop and introduce the celebrated Viper sports car in just two years. Among U.S. automakers Chrysler is the leader in fast product development.[25]

One approach often used to facilitate product development is the **design review**. The purpose of a design review is to stimulate discussion, raise questions, and generate new ideas and solutions to help designers anticipate problems before they occur. Generally, a design review is conducted in three major stages: preliminary, intermediate, and final. The preliminary design review establishes early communication between marketing, engineering, manufacturing, and purchasing personnel and provides better coordination of their activities. It usually involves higher levels of management and concentrates on strategic issues in design that relate to customer requirements and thus the ultimate quality of the product. A preliminary design review evaluates such issues as the function of the product, conformance to customer's needs, completeness of specifications, manufacturing costs, and liability issues.

After the design is well established, an intermediate review takes place to study the design in greater detail to identify potential problems and suggest corrective action. Personnel at lower levels of the organization are more heavily involved at this stage. Finally, just before release to production, a final review is held. Materials lists, drawings, and other detailed design information are studied with the purpose of preventing costly changes after production setup.

In summary, a total approach to product development and process design involves the following activities:

1. Constantly thinking in terms of how one can design or manufacture products better, not just solving or preventing problems
2. Focusing on "things done right" rather than "things gone wrong"
3. Defining customer expectations and going beyond them, not just barely meeting them or just matching the competition
4. Optimizing desirable features or results, not just incorporating them
5. Minimizing the overall cost without compromising quality of function.

Quality engineering, quality function deployment (QFD), and other techniques discussed next chapter all contribute to achieving these objectives.[26]

QUALITY FUNCTION DEPLOYMENT

A major problem with the traditional product development process is that customers and engineers speak different languages. A customer might express a desire to own a car that is easy to start. The translation of this requirement into technical language might be "car will start within 3 seconds of continuous cranking." Or, a requirement that "soap leaves my skin feeling soft" demands translation into pH or hardness specifications for the bar of soap. The actual intended message can be lost in the translation and subsequent interpretation by design or production personnel.

The Japanese developed an approach called **quality function deployment (QFD)** to meet customers' requirements throughout the design process and also in the design of production systems. The term, a translation of the Kanji characters used to describe the process, can sound confusing. QFD is a customer-driven planning process to guide the design, manufacturing, and marketing of goods. Through QFD, every design, manufacturing, and control decision is made to meet the expressed needs of customers. It uses a type of matrix diagram (described in Chapter 5) to present data and information.

QFD originated in 1972 at Mitsubishi's Kobe shipyard. Toyota began to develop the concept shortly thereafter, and has used it since 1977 with impressive results. Between January 1977 and October 1979, Toyota realized a 20 percent reduction in start-up costs on the launch of a new van. By 1982, start-up costs had fallen 38 percent from the 1977 baseline, and by 1984, were reduced by 61 percent. In addition, development time fell by one-third at the same time quality improved. Xerox and Ford initiated the use of QFD in the United States in 1986. Today, QFD is used successfully by manufacturers of electronics, appliances, clothing, and construction equipment, by firms such as General Motors, Ford, Mazda, Motorola, Xerox, Kodak, IBM, Procter & Gamble, Hewlett-Packard, and AT&T. The 1992 model Cadillac was planned and designed entirely with QFD. Two organizations, the American Supplier Institute, Inc., a nonprofit organization, and GOAL/QPC, a Massachusetts consulting firm, have publicized and developed the concept in the United States.

At the strategic level, QFD presents a challenge and the opportunity for top management to break out of its traditional narrow focus on results, which can only be measured after the fact, and to view the broader process of how results are obtained. Under QFD, all operations of a company are driven by the voice of the customer, rather than by edicts of top management or the opinions or desires of design engineers. At the tactical and operational levels, QFD departs from the traditional product planning process in which product concepts are originated by design teams or research and development groups, tested and refined, produced, and marketed. A considerable amount of wasted effort and time is spent redesigning products and production systems until customer needs are met. If customer needs can be identified properly in the first place, then such wasteful effort is eliminated, which is the principal focus of QFD.

QFD benefits companies through improved communication and teamwork between all constituencies in the production process, such as between marketing and design, between design and manufacturing, and between purchasing and suppliers. Product objectives are better understood and interpreted during the production process. Use of QFD determines the causes of customer dissatisfaction, making it a useful tool for competitive analysis of product quality by top management. Productivity as well as quality improvements generally follow QFD. Perhaps most significant, though, QFD reduces the time for new product development. QFD allows companies to simulate the effects of new design ideas and concepts. Through this benefit, companies can reduce product development time and bring new products into the market sooner, thus gaining competitive advantage. Details of the QFD process and its use are presented next.

The Quality Function Deployment Process

A set of matrixes is used to relate the voice of the customer to a product's technical requirements, component requirements, process control plans, and manufacturing operations. The first matrix, the customer requirement planning matrix shown in Figure 7.6,

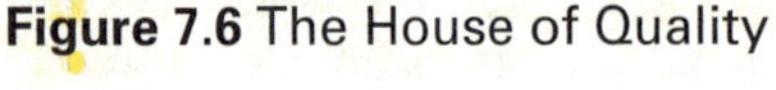

Figure 7.6 The House of Quality

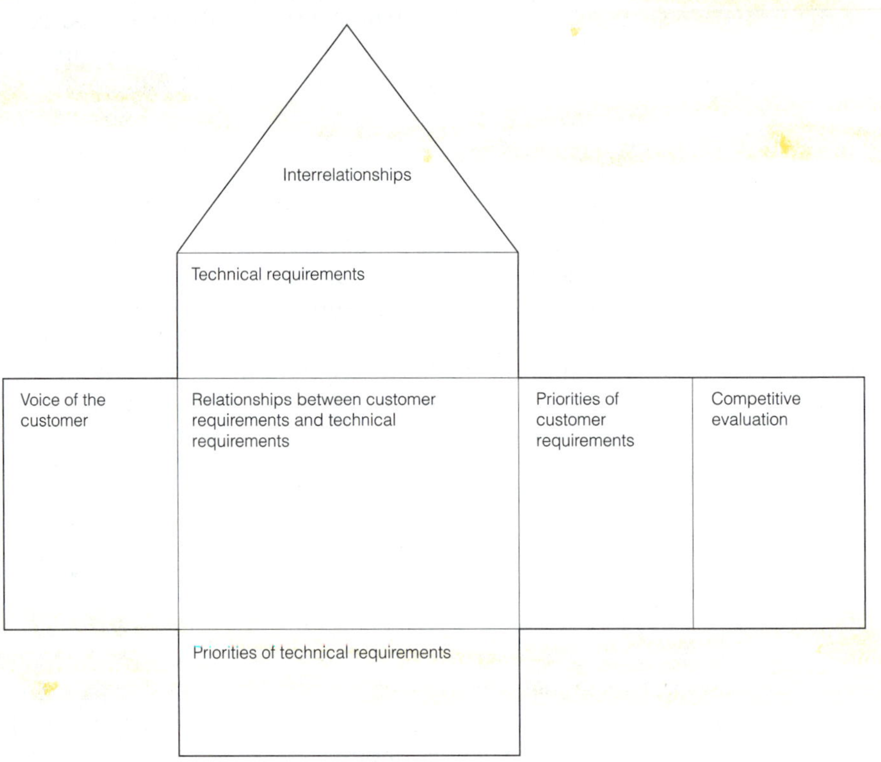

provides the basis for the QFD concept. The figure demonstrates why this matrix is often called the **House of Quality**.

Building the House of Quality consists of six basic steps:

1. Identify customer requirements.
2. Identify technical requirements.
3. Relate the customer requirements to the technical requirements.
4. Conduct an evaluation of competing products or services.
5. Evaluate technical requirements and develop targets.
6. Determine which technical requirements to deploy in the remainder of the production/delivery process.

To illustrate the development of the House of Quality and the QFD process, the task of designing a new fitness center in a community with two other competing organizations is presented.

Step 1: Identify customer requirements. The voice of the customer is the primary input to the QFD process. As discussed in Chapter 4, many methods can be used to gather valid customer information. The most critical and most difficult step of the process is to capture the essence of the customer's needs and expectations. The customer's own words are vitally important in preventing misinterpretation by designers and engineers. Figure 7.7 shows the voice of the customer in the House of Quality for the fitness center, perhaps based on a telephone survey or focus groups. Their needs and expectations are grouped

Figure 7.7 Voice of the Customer

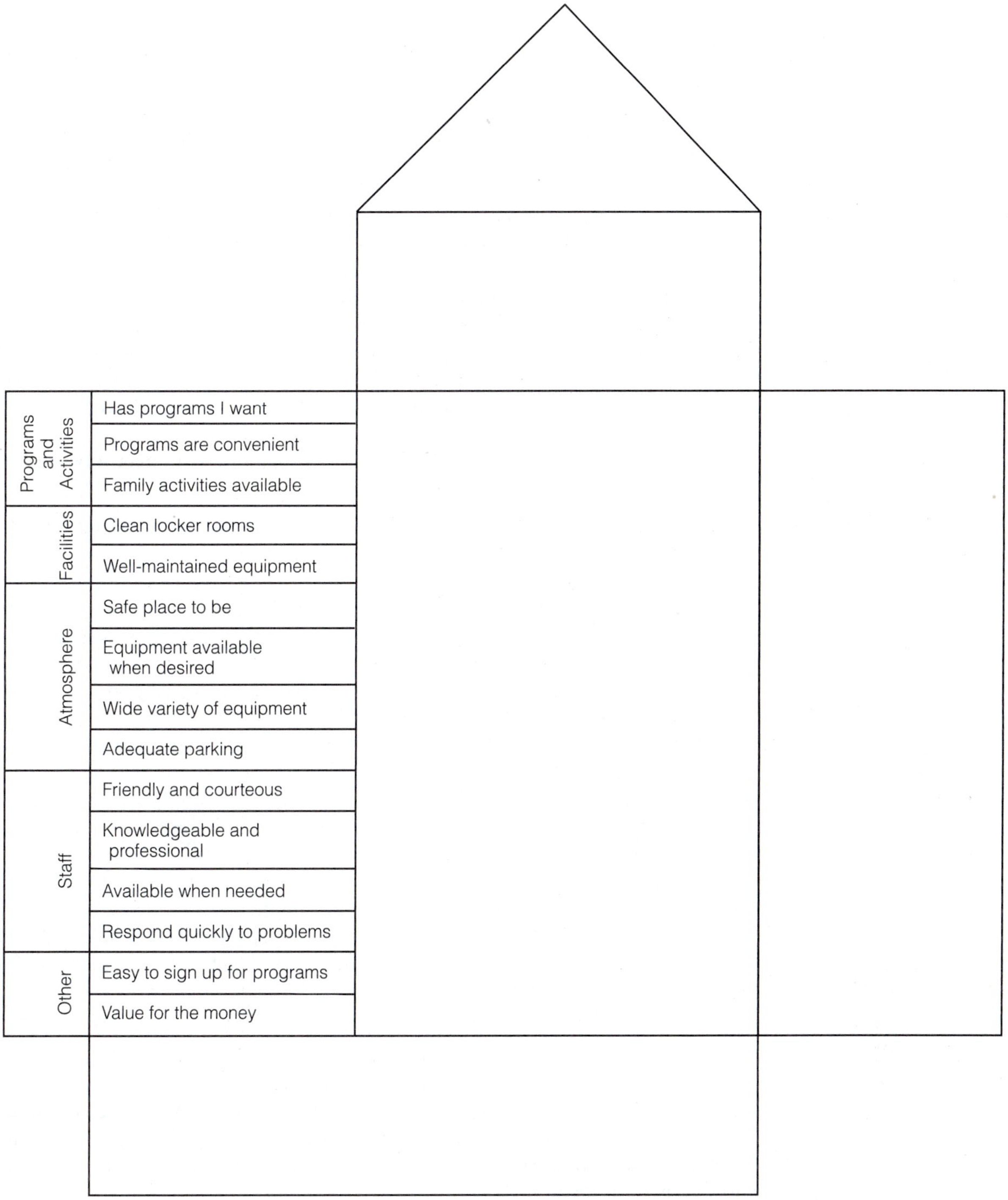

Programs and Activities	Has programs I want
	Programs are convenient
	Family activities available
Facilities	Clean locker rooms
	Well-maintained equipment
Atmosphere	Safe place to be
	Equipment available when desired
	Wide variety of equipment
	Adequate parking
Staff	Friendly and courteous
	Knowledgeable and professional
	Available when needed
	Respond quickly to problems
Other	Easy to sign up for programs
	Value for the money

into five categories: programs and activities, facilities, atmosphere, staff, and other. This grouping can easily be done using affinity diagrams, for example.

Step 2: List the technical requirements that provide the foundation for the product or service design. Technical requirements are design characteristics that describe the customer requirements as expressed in the language of the designer or engineer. Essentially, they are the "hows" by which the company will respond to the "whats,"or customer requirements. They must be measurable, because output is controlled and compared to objective targets. For the fitness center, they include the number and type of program offerings and equipment, times, staffing requirements, facility characteristics and maintenance, fee structure, and so on. Figure 7.8 adds this information to the House of Quality.

The roof of the House of Quality shows the interrelationships between any pair of technical requirements. Various symbols denote these relationships. A typical scheme uses the symbol ● to denote a very strong relationship, ○ for a strong relationship, and △ to denote a weak relationship. These relationships indicate answers to questions such as "How does a change in a technical characteristic affect others?" For example, increasing program offerings will probably require more staff, a larger facility, expanded hours, and higher costs; hiring more maintenance staff, building a larger facility, and buying more equipment will probably result in a higher membership fee. Thus, design decisions cannot be viewed in isolation. This relationship matrix helps to assess trade-offs.

Step 3: Develop a relationship matrix between the customer requirements and the technical requirements. Customer requirements are listed down the left column; technical requirements are written across the top. In the matrix itself, symbols indicate the degree of relationship in a manner similar to that used in the roof of the House of Quality. The purpose of the relationship matrix is to show whether the final technical requirements adequately address customer requirements. This assessment is usually based on expert experience, customer responses, or controlled experiments.

The lack of a strong relationship between a customer requirement and any technical requirement shows that the customer needs either are not addressed or that the final design will have difficulty in meeting them. Similarly, if a technical requirement does not affect any customer requirement, it may be redundant or the designers may have missed some important customer need. For example, the customer requirement "clean locker rooms" bears a very strong relationship to the maintenance schedule and only a strong relationship to the number of maintenance staff. "Easy to sign up for programs" would probably bear a very strong relationship to Internet access and only a weak relationship to the hours the facility is open. Figure 7.9 shows an example of these relationships.

Step 4: Add competitor evaluation and key selling points. This step identifies importance ratings for each customer requirement and evaluates competitors' existing products or services for each of them (see Figure 7.10). Customer importance ratings represent the areas of greatest interest and highest expectations as expressed by the customer. Competitive evaluation highlights the absolute strengths and weaknesses in competing products. By using this step, designers can discover opportunities for improvement. It also links QFD to a company's strategic vision and indicates priorities for the design process. For example, if an important customer requirement receives a low evaluation on all competitors' products (for instance, "family activities available"), then by focusing on

Figure 7.8 Technical Requirements

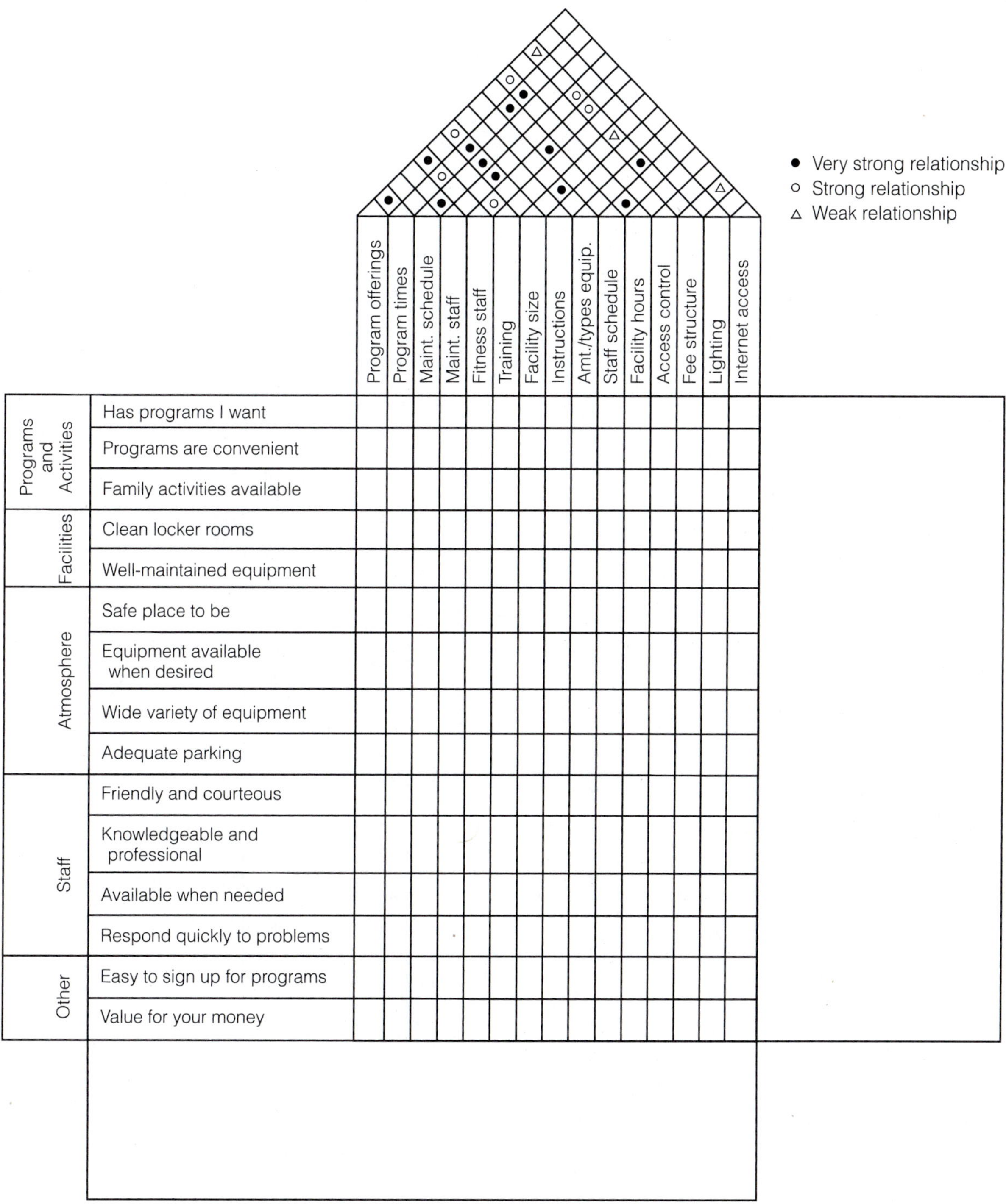

Figure 7.9 Relationship Matrix

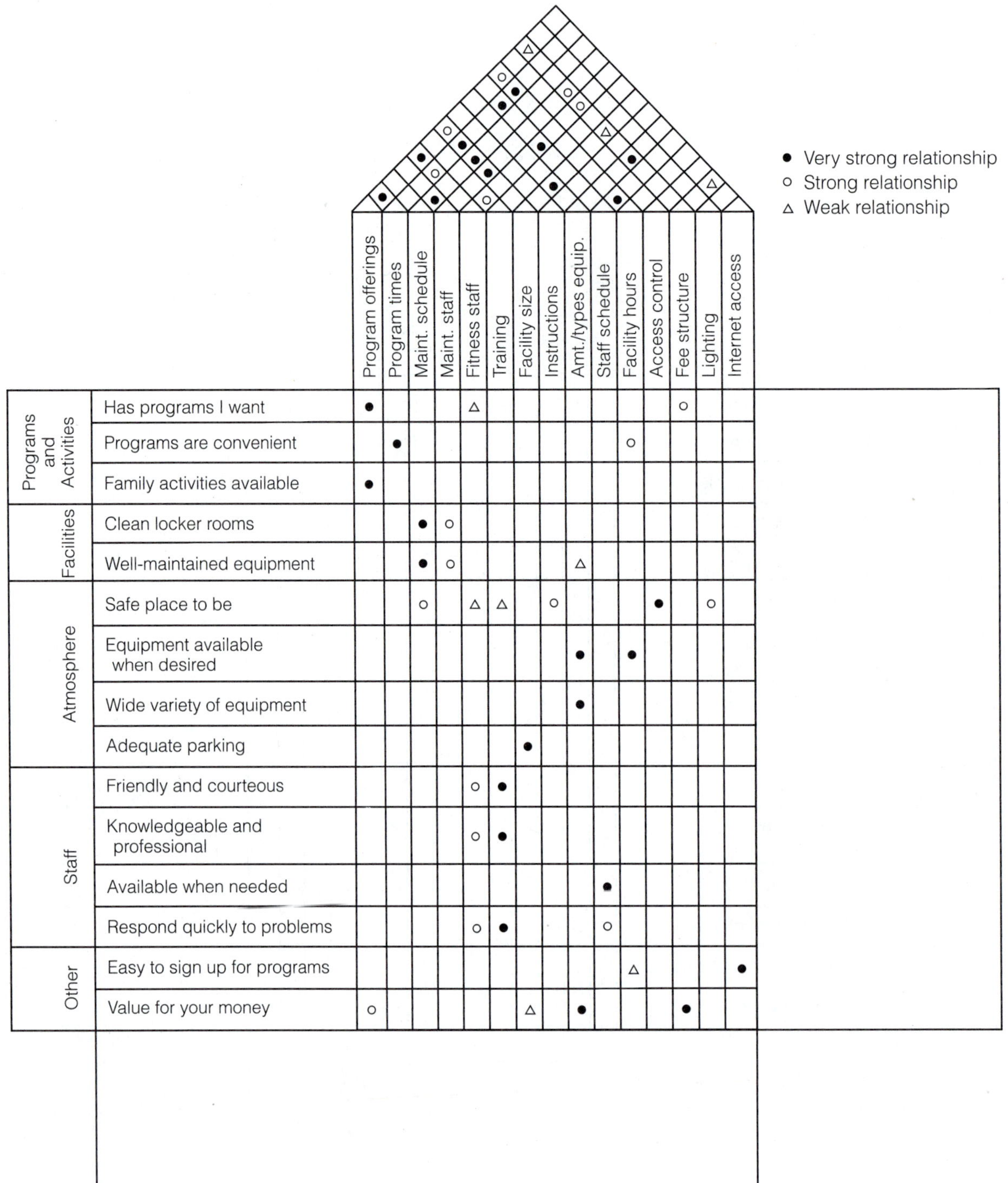

Figure 7.10 Competitive Evaluation

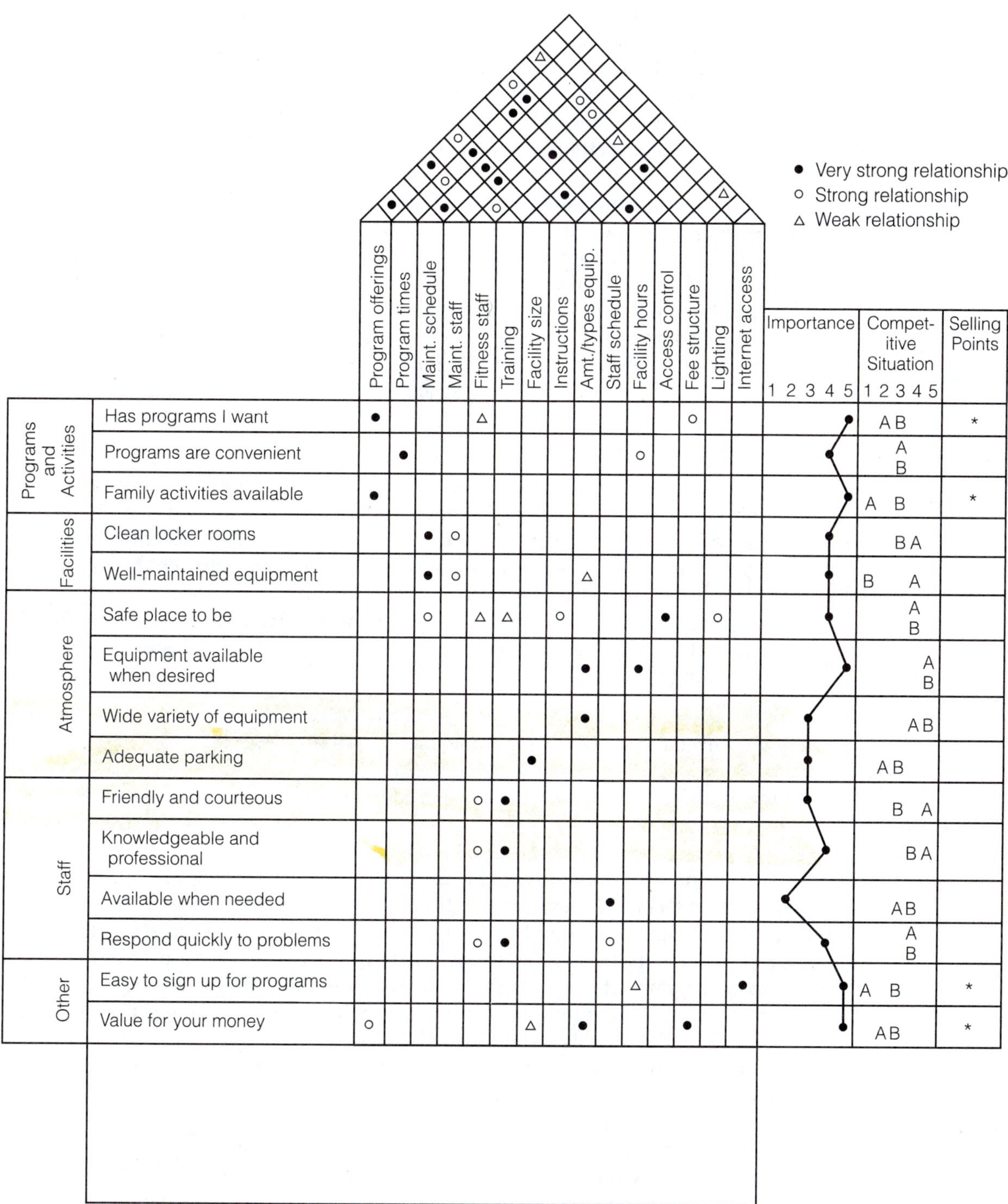

this need a company might gain a competitive advantage. Such requirements become key selling points and the basis for formulating marketing strategies.

Step 5: Evaluate technical requirements of competitive products and services and develop targets. This step is usually accomplished through intelligence gathering or product testing and then translated into measurable terms. These evaluations are compared with the competitive evaluation of customer requirements to determine inconsistencies between customer requirements and technical requirements. If a competing product is found to best satisfy a customer requirement but the evaluation of the related technical requirements indicates otherwise, then either the measures used are faulty or the product has an image difference (either positive toward the competitor or negative toward the company's product) that affects customer perceptions. On the basis of customer importance ratings and existing product strengths and weaknesses, targets for each technical requirement are set, as shown in Figure 7.11. For example, customers have rated programs and family activities of high importance while competitive evaluation shows them to be quite low. Setting a higher target for these requirements will help to meet this critical need and be a source of competitive advantage.

Step 6: Select technical requirements to be deployed in the remainder of the process. The technical requirements that have a strong relationship to customer needs, have poor competitive performance, or are strong selling points are identified during this step. These characteristics have the highest priority and need to be "deployed" throughout the remainder of the design and production process to maintain responsiveness to the voice of the customer. Those characteristics not identified as critical do not need such rigorous attention. For example, program offerings, amount and types of equipment, facility hours, fee structure, and Internet access have been identified in Figure 7.11 as the key issues to address in designing the fitness center.

The House of Quality provides marketing with an important tool to understand customer needs and gives top management strategic direction. However, it is only the first step in the QFD process. The voice of the customer must be carried throughout the production/delivery process. Three other "houses of quality" are used to deploy the voice to the customer to (in a manufacturing setting) component parts characteristics, process plans, and quality control.

The second house is similar to the first house but applies to subsystems and components. The technical requirements from the first house are related to detailed requirements of subsystems and components (see Figure 7.12). At this stage, target values representing the best values for fit, function, and appearance are determined. For example, program offerings might be broken down into fitness programs, children programs, family programs, and so on, each with its own unique set of design requirements, and hence, its own House of Quality.

In manufacturing, most of the QFD activities represented by the first two houses of quality are performed by product development and engineering functions. At the next stage, the planning activities involve supervisors and production line operators. In the third house, the process plan relates the component characteristics to key process operations, the transition from planning to execution. (For the fitness center, this activity might involve creating a project plan for selecting, designing, and evaluating programs.) Key process operations are the basis for a *control point*. A control point forms the basis for a quality control plan delivering those characteristics that are crucial to achieving customer satisfaction, as specified in the last house of quality.

Figure 7.11 Completed House of Quality

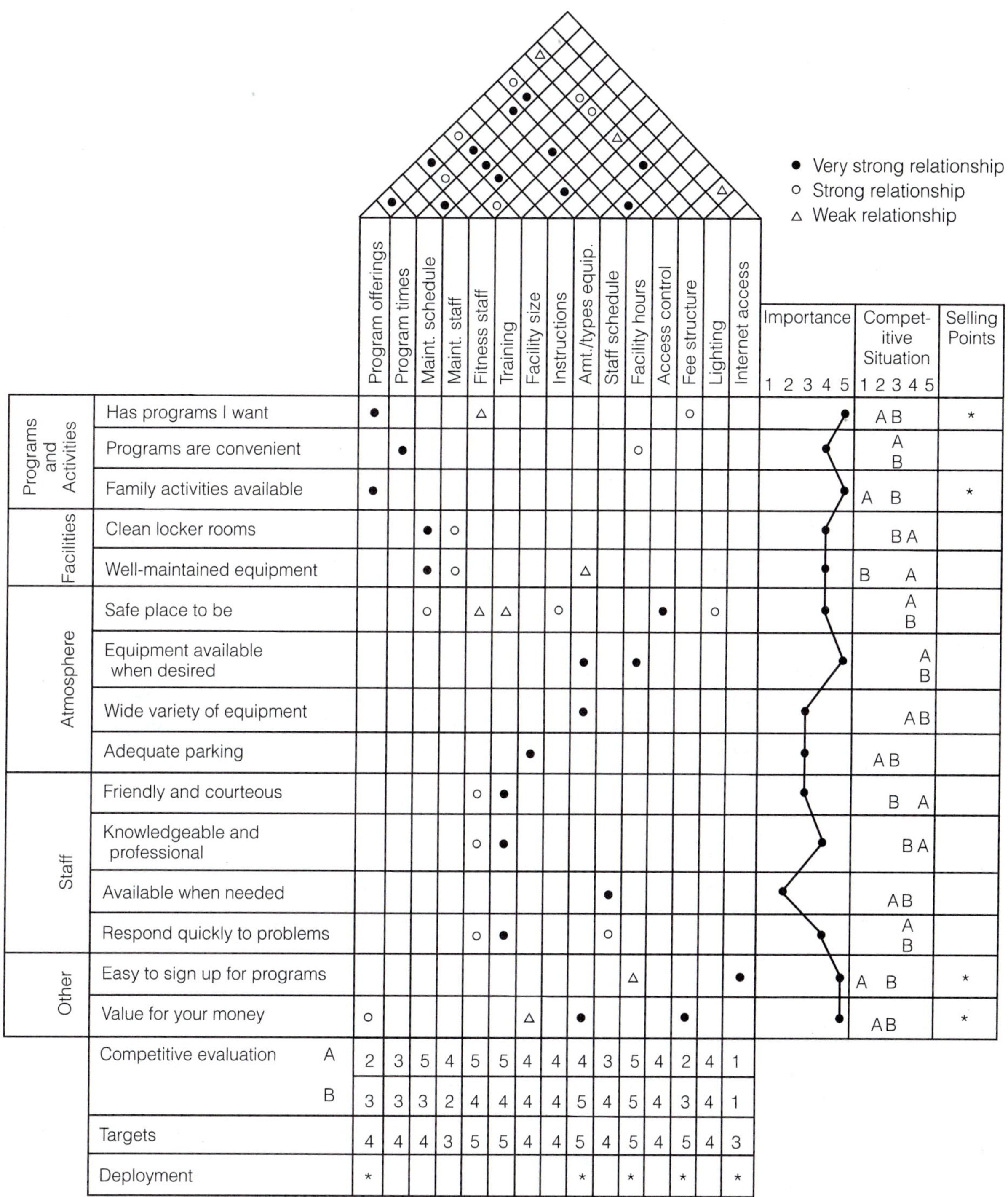

Figure 7.12 The Four Houses of Quality

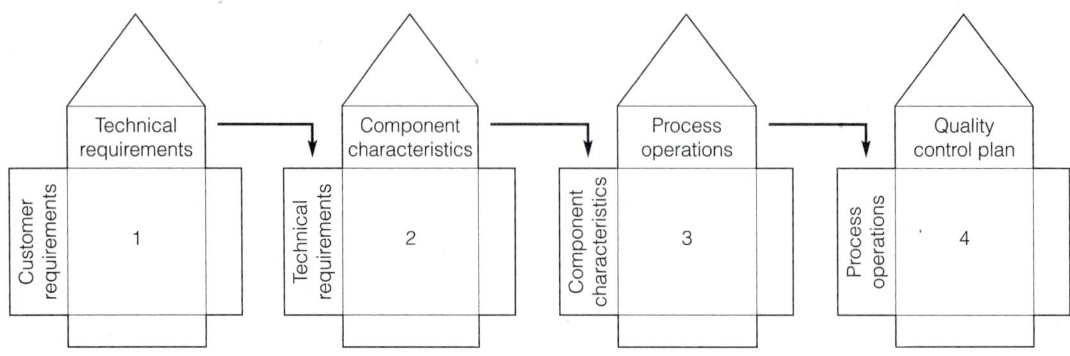

At this point, for example, the fitness center might design membership surveys for evaluating programs, checklists for maintenance, performance appraisal approaches for the staff, and measures of equipment failures and problems. These things must be measured and evaluated on a continuous basis to ensure that processes continue to meet the important customer requirements defined in the first House of Quality. Thus, the QFD process provides a thread from the voice of the customer, through design and production/delivery activities, to daily management and control.

The vast majority of applications of QFD in the United States concentrate on the first and, to a lesser extent, the second houses of quality. Lawrence Sullivan, who brought QFD to the West, suggested that the third and fourth houses of quality offer far more significant benefits, especially in the United States.[27] In Japan, managers, engineers, and workers are more naturally cross-functional and tend to promote group effort and consensus thinking. In the United States, workers and managers are more vertically oriented and tend to suboptimize for individual and/or departmental achievements. Companies in the United States tend to promote breakthrough achievements, which often inhibits cross-functional interaction. If a U.S. company can maintain the breakthrough culture with emphasis on continuous improvement through more effective cross-functional interactions as supported by QFD, it can establish a competitive advantage over foreign competitors. The third and fourth houses of quality utilize the knowledge of about 80 percent of a company's employees, its supervisors and operators. If their knowledge goes unused, this potential is wasted.

PRODUCTION/DELIVERY AND SUPPORT PROCESSES

The design of the processes that produce and deliver goods and services can have a significant impact on cost (and hence profitability), flexibility (the ability to produce the right types and amounts of products according to customer demand or preferences), and the quality of the output. Standardized processes establish consistency of output. The typical Japanese company spends about two-thirds of its research and development funds on process design. In producing a new, compact CD player, Sony had to develop entirely new manufacturing processes, because no process in existence was able to make this product as small and as accurate as the design required. FedEx uses a wireless data collection system that employs laser scanners to manage millions of packages daily through its six main hubs, improving not only customer service, but saving labor costs as well.[28]

Today, many companies use a strategy of **mass customization**—providing personalized, custom-designed products to meet individual preferences at prices comparable to mass-produced items. Motorola, for instance, produces one-of-a-kind pagers from more than 29 million combinations of options in a mass assembly process at a low cost. Dell Computer configures each computer system to customer specifications. At Levi Strauss, customers are measured for custom-fit jeans at local stores; the jeans are produced at a central factory and delivered to the customer's store. Mass customization requires significant changes to traditional manufacturing processes that focus on either customized, crafted products or mass-produced, standardized products.[29] These processes include flexible manufacturing technologies, just-in-time systems, information technology, and an emphasis on cycle time reduction.

The design of a process begins with the process owner: an individual, a team, a department, or some cross-functional group. The goal of process design is simple: to develop an efficient procedure to satisfy both internal and external customer requirements. A basic approach to process design is suggested by Motorola:

1. *Identify the product or service:* What work do I do?
2. *Identify the customer:* Who is the work for?
3. *Identify the supplier:* What do I need and from whom do I get it?
4. *Identify the process:* What steps or tasks are performed? What are the inputs and outputs for each step?
5. *Mistake-proof the process:* How can I eliminate or simplify tasks? What "poka-yoke" (i.e., mistake-proofing) devices (see Chapter 10) can I use?
6. *Develop measurements and controls, and improvement goals:* How do I evaluate the process? How can I improve further?

Steps 1 through 3 address such questions as "What is the purpose of the process?" "How does the process create customer satisfaction?" and "What are the essential inputs and outputs of the process?" Step 4 focuses on the actual process design, by defining the specific tasks performed in transforming the inputs to outputs. Step 5 focuses on making the process efficient and capable of delivering high quality. Step 6 ensures that the process will be monitored and controlled to the level of required performance by gathering in-process measurements and/or customer feedback on a regular basis and using this information to control and improve the process.

The actual process design is the specification of how the process works. The first phase is to list in detail the sequence of steps—value-adding activities and specific tasks—involved in producing a product or delivering a service, usually depicted as a flowchart. Such a graphical representation provides an excellent communication device for visualizing and understanding the process. Flowcharts can become the basis for job descriptions, employee-training programs, and performance measurement. They help managers to estimate human resources, information systems, equipment, and facilities requirements. As design tools, they enable management to study and analyze processes prior to implementation in order to improve quality and operational performance. Figure 7.13 shows The Ritz-Carlton's Three Steps of Service process. The process is highly structured and defines the procedures for anticipating and complying with customer needs. All employees who come in contact with customers are trained to follow this process.

The AT&T customer-supplier model introduced in Chapter 4 provides a way of building a detailed process flowchart. Start with the outputs—customer requirements—and move backward through the process to identify the key steps needed to produce each output; stop when the process reaches the supplier input stage. AT&T calls this technique **backward chaining.**[30] AT&T suggests the following steps:

Figure 7.13 The Ritz-Carlton Hotel Company: Three Steps of Service Process

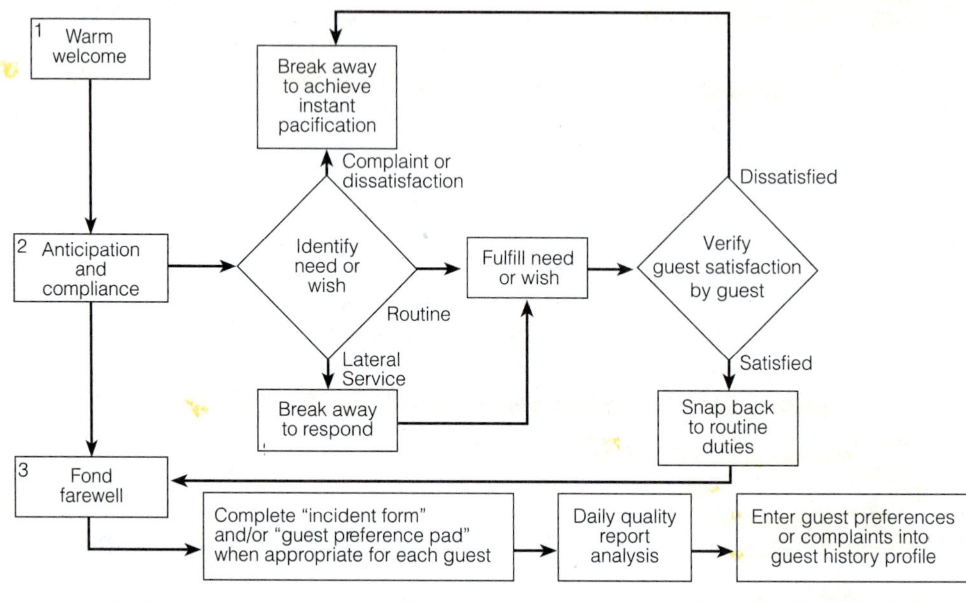

1. Begin with the process output and ask, "What is the last essential subprocess that produces the output of the process?"
2. For that subprocess, ask, "What input does it need to produce the process output?" For each input, test its value to ensure that it is required.
3. For each input, identify its source. In many cases, the input will be the output of the previous subprocess. In some cases, the input may come from external suppliers.
4. Continue backward, one subprocess at a time, until each input comes from an external supplier.

This technique can be applied to each subprocess to create a more detailed process description.

Once a process is designed, several fundamental questions arise that assist in completing steps 5 and 6 of Motorola's process design approach:

- Are the steps in the process arranged in logical sequence?
- Do all steps add value? Can some steps be eliminated and should others be added in order to improve quality or operational performance? Can some be combined? Should some be reordered?
- Are capacities of each step in balance, that is, do bottlenecks exist for which customers will incur excessive waiting time?
- What skills, equipment, and tools are required at each step of the process? Should some steps be automated?
- At which points in the system might errors occur that would result in customer dissatisfaction, and how might these errors be corrected?
- At which point or points should quality be measured?
- Where interaction with the customer occurs, what procedures and guidelines should employees follow that will present a positive image?

In many companies, core production/delivery processes take the form of **projects**, which are temporary work structures that start up, produce products or services, and then shut down.[31] As opposed to repetitive processes, projects produce unique outputs, generally using specialized teams of people. Examples include performing clinical trials for pharmaceutical companies, market research studies, consulting, and systems installation. The following steps can summarize the typical project management process:

1. *Project initiation:* define directions, priorities, limitations, and constraints.
2. *Project plan:* create a blueprint for the scope of the project and resources needed to accomplish it.
3. *Execution:* produce the deliverables for the customer.
4. *Close out:* evaluate customer satisfaction and assess success and failures that provide learning for future projects.

Traditional project management methodologies were developed before the advent of total quality, and hence, TQ approaches are often not incorporated. Approaches such as identifying customer requirements and using a customer-supplier model, teamwork principles, cycle time reduction, and in-process measurements can improve the quality of the result. For example, although each project is unique, many projects have similar underlying processes. As an illustration, consider Custom Research Incorporated, which conducts unique market research studies for many different organizations. A cycle time task force identified nine common processes for all marketing research studies: identification of client requirements/expectations, questionnaire design, questionnaire programming, sampling, data collection, data tabulation, report and analysis, internal communication, and client communication. A process task force was formed to map and improve each process. For example, CRI developed a "one-entry system" that eliminates the need to enter data into its computer system more than once, allows questionnaires to be tested for validity and reliability, eliminates several programming steps, and helps reduce cycle time. An account team is in charge of every research project. Project-related problems anywhere in the process are recognized and reported by the team. Team members use their problem-solving skills to determine whether the variation is due to common or special causes, analyze the reasons for the occurrence, and implement changes that will prevent it from occurring. When each project is completed, the account team completes a Project Quality Recap documenting problems and solutions and rating the performance of internal departments. Teams refer to the Recaps on file when they have similar projects or subsequent projects from the same client.[32]

Special Considerations in Service Process Design

The fundamental differences between manufacturing and service processes, including support processes, deserve special attention. Some common examples of service processes are preparing an invoice, taking a telephone order, processing a credit card, and checking out of a hotel. First, the outputs of service processes are not as well defined as are manufactured products. For example, even though all banks offer similar tangible goods such as checking, loans, automatic tellers, and so forth, the real differentiating factor among banks is the service they provide. Second, most service processes involve a greater interaction with the customer, often making it easier to identify needs and expectations. On the other hand, customers often cannot define their needs for service until after they have some point of reference or comparison.

Service process designers must concentrate on doing things right the first time, minimizing process complexities, and making the process immune to inadvertent human errors, particularly during customer interactions. Fast-food restaurants, for example, have carefully designed their processes for high degree of accuracy and fast response time.[33] New hands-free intercom systems, better microphones that reduce ambient kitchen noise, and screens that display a customer's order are all focused on these requirements. Timers at Wendy's count every segment of the order completion process to help managers identify problem areas. Kitchen workers wear headsets to hear orders as they are placed. Even the use of photos on drive-through order boards make it more likely for customers to select these items; less variety means faster order fulfillment.

Service processes often involve both internal and external activities, a factor that complicates quality design. In a bank, for example, poor service can result from the way that tellers treat customers and from poor quality of computers and communications equipment beyond the control of the tellers. Internal activities are primarily concerned with efficiency (quality of conformance), while external activities with direct customer interaction require attention to effectiveness (quality of design). All too often, workers involved in internal operations do not understand how their performance affects the customers they do not see. The success of the process depends on workers involved in both internal as well as external activities, so that everyone understands that they add value to the customer.

Researchers have suggested that services have three basic components: (1) physical facilities, processes, and procedures, (2) employees' behavior, and (3) employees' professional judgment.[34] Designing a service essentially involves determining an effective balance of these components. The goal then is to provide a service whose elements are internally consistent and directed at meeting the needs of a specific target market segment. Too much or too little emphasis on one component will lead to problems and poor customer perceptions. For example, too much emphasis on procedures might result in timely and efficient service, but might also suggest insensitivity and apathy toward the customer. Too much emphasis on behavior might provide a friendly and personable environment at the expense of slow, inconsistent, or chaotic service. Too much emphasis on professional judgment might lead to good solutions to customer problems but also to slow, inconsistent, or insensitive service.

A useful approach to designing effective services is first to recognize that services differ in the degree of customer contact and interaction, the degree of labor intensity, and the degree of customization. For example, a railroad is low in all three dimensions. On the other hand, an interior design service would be high in all three dimensions. A fast-food restaurant would be high in customer contact and labor intensity, but low in customization.

Services low in all three dimensions of this classification are more similar to manufacturing organizations. The emphasis on quality should be focused on physical facilities and procedures; behavior and professional judgment are relatively unimportant. As contact and interaction between the customer and the service system increases, two factors must be taken into account. In services low in labor intensity, the customer's impression of physical facilities, processes, and procedures is important. Service organizations must exercise special care in choosing and maintaining reliable and easy-to-use equipment. With higher levels of contact and interaction, appropriate staff behavior becomes increasingly important.

As labor intensity increases, variations between individuals become more important; however, the elements of personal behavior and professional judgment will remain relatively unimportant as long as the degrees of customization and contact and interaction remain low. As customization increases, professional judgment becomes a bigger factor in the customer's perception of service quality. In services that are high in all three dimensions, facilities, behavior, and professional judgment must be equally balanced.

In services, quality standards take the place of the dimensions and tolerances applicable in manufacturing. Examples of service quality standards might include the following:

- Ninety percent of calls are answered within 3 rings.
- Customers receive a response to a complaint within 24 hours.
- Customer service representatives greet each customer with eye contact and a smile.

However, service standards are inherently more difficult to define and measure than manufacturing specifications. They require extensive research into customer needs and attitudes regarding timeliness, consistency, accuracy, and other service requirements, as discussed in previous chapters. Although many product specifications developed for manufactured products are focused on meeting a target, such as a product dimension, service targets typically are "smaller is better." Thus, the true service standard is zero defects, and any other standards should be construed as interim standards and targets only.

In designing high-quality service processes, some questions to consider are[35] What service standards are already in place? Which of these standards have been clearly communicated to all service personnel? Have these standards been communicated to the public? Which standards require refinement? What is the final result of the service provided? What should it ideally be? What is the maximum access time that a patron will tolerate without feeling inconvenienced? How long should it take to perform the service itself? What is the maximum time for completion of service before the customer's view of the service is negatively affected? At what point does service begin, and what indicator signals the completion of the service? How many different people must the consumer deal with in completing the service? What components of the service are essential? Desirable? Superfluous? What components or aspects of service must be controlled in order to deliver a service encounter of equal quality each time one occurs? Which components can differ from encounter to encounter while still leading to a total service encounter that meets standards? What products that affect its service performance does a service organization obtain from other sources?

As you can see, service process design is not a trivial exercise.

Controlling Production/Delivery and Support Processes

A principal responsibility of process owners is to ensure that process outputs meet operational and customer requirements. **Control** is the continuing process of evaluating process performance and taking corrective action when necessary. Control is necessary for two reasons. First, companies need to maintain performance of their processes. Second, a company must bring processes under control before any improvements can be made. The effect of potential improvements is impossible to measure if the process is in a continual state of flux.

The need for control arises because of the inherent variation in any system or process. Walter Shewhart is credited with recognizing the distinction between *common* and *special causes* of variation at Bell Laboratories in the 1920s. A process governed only by common causes, although exhibiting variation, is stable and remains essentially constant over time. The variation is predictable within established statistical limits. Prediction was the key idea in Shewhart's definition of control:

> *A phenomenon will be said to be controlled when, through the use of past experience, we can predict, at least within limits, how the phenomenon may be expected to vary in the future.*[36]

Special causes occur sporadically and change the stable pattern of variation, throwing the process out of control. Controlling a process, therefore, is tantamount to identifying and removing special causes of variation. These ideas are discussed further in Chapter 9.

Any control system has three components: (1) *a standard or goal*, (2) *a means of measuring accomplishment*, and (3) *comparison of actual results with the standard, along with feedback to form the basis for corrective action*. Goals and standards are defined during planning and design processes. They establish what is supposed to be accomplished. These goals and standards are reflected by measurable quality characteristics, such as dimensions of machined parts, numbers of defectives, customer complaints, or waiting times. Methods for measuring these quality characteristics may be automated or performed manually by the workforce. Measurements supply the information concerning what has actually been accomplished. Workers, supervisors, or managers then assess whether the actual results meet the goals and standards. If not, then remedial action must be taken. For example, workers might check the first few parts after a new production setup (called setup verification) to determine whether they conform to specifications. If not, the worker adjusts the setup. Sometimes this process occurs automatically. For instance, in the production of plastic sheet stock, thickness depends on temperature. Sensors monitor the sheet thickness; if it begins to go out of tolerance, the system can adjust the temperature in order to change the thickness.

In manufacturing, control is usually applied to incoming materials (often done by the supplier and not the customer), key processes (by the process owners), and final products and services. As an example of the last case, automobile manufacturers perform extensive inspection and tests of cars at the end of assembly, and dealers often ask customers to evaluate the process of receiving delivery of a new car.

An example of a structured quality control process in the service industry is the "10-Step Monitoring and Evaluation Process" set forth by the Joint Commission on Accrediting Health Care Organizations. This process, shown in Table 7.3, provides a detailed sequence of activities for monitoring and evaluating the quality of health care in an effort to identify problems and improve care. Standards and goals are defined in steps 2 through 5; measurement is accomplished in step 6; and comparison and feedback is performed in the remaining steps.

Short-term remedial action often can be taken by process owners themselves. Long-term remedial action is the responsibility of management. The responsibility for control can be determined by checking the three components of control systems. A process owner must have the means of knowing what is expected (the standard or goal) through clear instructions and specifications; they must have the means of determining their actual performance, typically through inspection and measurement; and they must have a means of making corrections if they discover a variance between what is expected of them and their actual performance. If any of these criteria is not met, then the process is the responsibility of management, not the process owner.

Both Juran and Deming made this important distinction. If process owners are held accountable for or expected to act on problems beyond their control, they become frustrated and end up playing games with management. Juran and Deming stated that the majority of quality problems are management-controllable, or the result of common cause variation. For the smaller proportion of problems resulting from special causes, process owners must be given the tools to identify them and the authority to take action. This philosophy has shifted the burden of assuring quality from inspection departments and quality control personnel to workers on the shop floor and in customer-contact positions.

Table 7.3 10-Step Monitoring and Evaluation Process for Health Care Organizations

- *Step 1: Assign Responsibility.* The emergency department director is responsible for, and actively participates in, monitoring and evaluation. The director assigns responsibility for the specific duties related to monitoring and evaluation.
- *Step 2: Delineate Scope of Care.* The department considers the scope of care provided within emergency services to establish a basis for identifying important aspects of care to monitor and evaluate. The scope of care is a complete inventory of what the emergency department does.
- *Step 3: Identify Important Aspects of Care.* Important aspects of care are those that are high-risk, high-volume, and/or problem-prone. Staff identify important aspects of care so that monitoring and evaluation focuses on emergency department activities with the greatest impact on patient care.
- *Step 4: Identify Indicators.* Indicators of quality are identified for each important aspect of care. An indicator is a measurable variable related to a structure, process, or outcome of care. Examples of possible indicators (all of which would need to be further defined) include insufficient staffing for sudden surges in patient volume (structure), delays in physicians reporting to the emergency room (process), and transfusion errors (outcome).
- *Step 5: Establish Thresholds for Evaluation.* A threshold for evaluation is the level or point at which intensive evaluation of care is triggered. A threshold may be 0% or 100% or any other appropriate level. Emergency department staff should establish a threshold for each indicator.
- *Step 6: Collect and Organize Data.* Appropriate emergency department staff should collect data pertaining to the indicators. Data are organized to facilitate comparison with the thresholds for evaluation.
- *Step 7: Evaluate Care.* When the cumulative data related to an indicator reach the threshold for evaluation, appropriate emergency department staff evaluate the care provided to determine whether a problem exists. This evaluation, which in many cases will take the form of peer review, should focus on possible trends and performance patterns. The evaluation is designed to identify causes of any problems or methods by which care or performance may be improved.
- *Step 8: Take Actions to Solve Problems.* When problems are identified, action plans are developed, approved at appropriate levels, and enacted to solve the problem or take the opportunity to improve care.
- *Step 9: Assess Actions and Document Improvement.* The effectiveness of any actions taken is assessed and documented. Further actions necessary to solve a problem are taken and their effectiveness is assessed.
- *Step 10: Communicate Relevant Information to the Organization-wide Quality Assurance Program.* Findings from and conclusions of monitoring and evaluation, including actions taken to solve problems and improve care, are documented and reported monthly through the hospital's established channels of communication.

Source: "Medical Staff Monitoring and Evaluation—Departmental Review," Chicago. Copyright by the Joint Commission on Accreditation of Health Care Organizations, Oakbrook Terrace, IL. Reprinted with permission (undated).

Control should be the foundation for organizational learning. Many companies are adopting an approach that has been used in the U.S. military, called **after action review.** This review asks four basic questions:

1. What was supposed to happen?
2. What actually happened?

3. Why was there a difference?
4. What can we learn?

Thus, rather than simply correcting unacceptable events, the focus is on preventing them from occurring again in the future.

SUPPLIER AND PARTNERING PROCESSES

In business today, operations are often highly decentralized and dispersed around the world. Consequently, managing a complex network of suppliers becomes a critical interorganizational issue. Suppliers play a vital role throughout the product development process, from design through distribution. Suppliers can provide technology or production processes not internally available, early design advice, and increased capacity, which can result in lower costs, faster time-to-market, and improved quality for their customers. In turn, they are assured of stable and long-term business. At Daimler-Chrysler, for example, suppliers are involved early in the design process.[37] As a result, Daimler-Chrysler often finds out about new materials, parts, and technologies before other automakers.

Increasingly, suppliers are viewed as partners with customers, because of the codependent relationship that develops between them. A powerful example of supplier partnerships is the response that occurred when a fire destroyed the main source of a crucial $5 brake valve for Toyota.[38] Without it, Toyota had to shut down its 20 plants in Japan. Within hours of the disaster, other suppliers began taking blueprints, improvising tooling systems, and setting up makeshift production lines. Within days, the 36 suppliers, aided by more than 150 other subcontractors, had almost 50 production lines making small batches of the valve. Even a sewing-machine company that had never made car parts spent 500 labor-hours refitting a milling machine to make just 40 valves a day. Toyota promised the suppliers a bonus of about $100 million "as a token of our appreciation."

Successful suppliers have a culture in which employees and managers share in customers' goals, commitments, and risks to promote such long-term relationships (recall one of Deming's 14 Points about supplier relationships—not purchasing solely on the basis of price). Strong customer-supplier relationships are based on three guiding principles:

1. Recognizing the strategic importance of suppliers in accomplishing business objectives, particularly minimizing the total cost of ownership
2. Developing win-win relationships through partnerships rather than as adversaries
3. Establishing trust through openness and honesty, thus leading to mutual advantages.

Joseph Juran has described the evolution of supplier relationships from an adversarial approach to one of teamwork and partnership, as shown in Table 7.4. One example is the Baldwin Piano & Organ Company, which set up a 10-year agreement with Southland Marketing Inc. for piano plates to get "higher quality, more consistent supply, and lower cost."[39] Baldwin helped finance the purchase of the equipment needed to finish the plates. The contract is expected to save Baldwin 10 percent a year on its plate costs.

In many companies, suppliers are treated as if they were actually a part of the organization. For example, functions such as cafeteria service, mailroom operations, and information processing are being performed by suppliers at their customers' fa-

Table 7.4 Juran's Trends in Supplier Relations

Element	Adversarial Focus	Teamwork Focus
Number of suppliers	Multiple; often many	Few; often single source
Duration of supply contracts	Annual	Three years or more
Criteria for quality	Conformance to specifications	Fitness for use
Emphasis on surveys	Procedures; data systems	Process capability; quality improvement
Quality planning	Separate	Joint
Pattern of collaboration	Arms length; secrecy; mutual supervision	Mutual visits; disclosures; assistance

Source: Adapted with the permission of The Free Press, a Division of Simon & Schuster, Inc. from JURAN ON LEADERSHIP FOR QUALITY: An Executive Handbook by J. M. Juran. Copyright © 1989 by The Juran Institute, Inc.

cilities. As more and more of this type of outsourcing is done, the lines between the customer and the supplier become increasingly blurred.

To ensure that suppliers can provide high quality and reduce costs associated with incoming inspection or testing, many companies provide various types of assistance to their suppliers in developing quality assurance programs or solving quality problems. Joint conferences, training, incentives, recognition, and long-term agreements help to improve suppliers' abilities to meet key quality requirements. The Delco Moraine Division, a manufacturer of automotive brake controls, uses an awareness program that includes a videotape presentation emphasizing quality, which is shown at supplier plants. After viewing the tape, supplier employees have been better able to relate their work to Delco. Similarly, Daimler-Chrysler instituted a program with its suppliers to identify cost reduction ideas; both parties benefit from the lower costs.

Many companies segment suppliers into categories based on their importance to the business and manage them accordingly. For example, at Corning, Level 1 suppliers, who provide raw materials, cases, and hardware, are deemed critical to business success and are managed by teams that include representatives from engineering, materials control, purchasing, and the supplier company. Level 2 suppliers provide specialty materials, equipment, and services, and are managed by internal customers. Level 3 suppliers provide commodity items and are centrally managed by purchasing.[40]

Measurement plays an important role in supplier management. Texas Instruments measures suppliers' quality performance by parts per million defective, percentage of on-time deliveries, and cost of ownership.[41] An electronic requisitioning system permits a paperless procurement process. More than 800 suppliers are linked to Texas Instruments through an information exchange system. Integrated data systems track the incoming quality and timeliness of deliveries as materials are received. Analytical reports and on-line data are used to identify material defect trends. Performance reports are sent each month to key suppliers. Joint customer-supplier teams are formed to communicate and improve performance. A supplier management task force of top managers directs current and strategic approaches to improving supplier management practices.

Finally, communication, feedback, and recognition or awards are important practices in supplier and partnering processes. For instance, the Fastener Supply Corporation, which distributes fasteners, electronic hardware, and other products to more than 300 customers makes frequent contact with its 250 suppliers, invites them to company functions and shares such information as customers' forecasted requirements.[42] Feedback should provide timely and actionable information to suppliers to lead to improvement and ensure that suppliers meet the organization's performance requirements. At Fastener, any potential performance problems are brought to attention with prompt notice and immediate feedback. An annual award dinner recognizes outstanding suppliers for quality and continuous improvement. Many companies such as Bethlehem Steel, Miller Brewing, and Honda, make a point of delivering supplier awards not only to upper management at a fancy banquet, but also to the workers on the shop floor. "It's one thing for the boss to say that quality is important, but another thing entirely for the customer to come out and say it," says Jerry Schiedt, corporate purchasing director for Miller Brewing Company in Milwaukee. "When we actually visit a plant to present an award to the folks who made the award possible, then we build a relationship with the company and the folks on the floor who do the work to ensure the quality of the products we buy."[43]

Supplier Certification Systems

Supplier certification is used by many companies as the focal point of their supplier management system. Formal programs typically are established to rate and certify suppliers who provide quality materials in a cost-effective and timely manner. The Pharmaceutical Manufacturers Association defines a **certified supplier** as one that, after extensive investigation, is found to supply material of such quality that routine testing on each lot received is unnecessary. Certification provides recognition for high-quality suppliers, which motivates them to improve continuously, which in turn attracts more business.

The American Society for Quality's customer-supplier technical committee developed specific criteria for supplier certification.[44]

- Certified suppliers experience virtually no product-related lot rejections for a significant time period, usually for 12 months, or in some cases two years.
- Certified suppliers have no nonproduct-related rejections for a stated period of time. "Nonproduct-related" means mismarkings on a container, for example. Nonproduct-related problems require different types of corrective action than product-related problems. Typically, nonproduct-related problems can be corrected faster and easier.
- Certified suppliers precipitate no production-related negative incidents for a stated period of time, usually six months. While incoming inspections determine conformance to specifications, specifications cannot possibly define every aspect of a product. Production-related problems are not always detectable by inspection and can result in latent defects that only become apparent later in the product's life.
- Certified suppliers successfully pass an on-site quality system evaluation (audit), conducted within the past year.
- Certified suppliers operate according to an agreed-on specification. Documentation should not contain ambiguous phrases such as "free of flash" or "no characteristic odor."
- Certified suppliers have a fully documented process and quality system, which should include the use of statistical process control and a program for continuous improvement.
- Certified suppliers furnish timely copies of certificates of analysis, inspection data, and test results.

The details of supplier certification processes vary by company. For instance, Florida Power and Light has a three-tier certification program.[45] Vendors (another term for suppliers) can be certified as a "Quality Vendor," "Certified Vendor," and "Excellent Vendor." To become a Quality Vendor, a supplier's products or services must meet basic requirements of quality, cost, delivery, and safety. In addition, the supplier must have a quality improvement process in place and be able to demonstrate that it has achieved significant improvements. It must also have an audit system to certify the process and the results. To become a Certified Vendor, the supplier must have demonstrated the use of statistical process control and prove that its processes can meet FPL's specification requirements. It must also be able to document capability and have a plan for continuous quality improvement. To achieve Excellent Vendor status, suppliers must demonstrate the ability to exceed FPL's specification requirements, employ reliability assurance techniques, and show that quality improvement is a central part of their management system.

At the Gillette Company, the supplier certification program begins with Gillette identifying those suppliers with a proven ability to meet its specifications.[46] Once a supplier is selected to participate, Gillette expects them to establish a preproduction planning system to assess the capability of their process to meet Gillette's specifications. Feedback is offered in the form of recommended changes that will improve quality, reduce cost, or facilitate ease of manufacture. The responsibilities of Gillette's certified suppliers include the following:

1. To control production processes during manufacture to prevent nonconformities.
2. To control product and measure conformance against acceptance criteria to ensure that the product shipped will meet Gillette's requirements.
3. To provide suitable quantitative and/or qualitative inspection data with each lot.
4. To maintain the integrity of the production lot as well as the traceability of inspection data to a specific lot.
5. To develop internal and external feedback systems to provide prompt and effective corrective actions when required.

Companies that have many suppliers spend large amounts of resources to certify every one of them. One approach to avoiding unnecessary audit costs and helping to assure buyers that specified practices are being followed is to create a uniform set of standards—an independent and transportable supplier qualification system. This system is the major focus of ISO 9000 and QS-9000, which were discussed in Chapter 3.

Supplier certification programs can be time-consuming and expensive to administer. Nevertheless, they are an important means of controlling incoming materials, particularly in a "just-in-time" environment.

PROCESS IMPROVEMENT

Prior to the total quality movement, most U.S. managers simply maintained products and processes until they could be replaced by new technology. Japanese managers, on the other hand, focused on continually improving products and processes. The MIT Commission on Industrial Productivity observed this difference and stated:

> *Another area in which U.S. firms have often lagged behind their overseas competitors is in exploiting the potential for continuous improvement in the quality and reliability of their products and processes. The cumulative effect of successive incremental improvements and modifications to established products and processes can be very large and may outpace efforts to achieve technological breakthroughs.*[47]

Improvement should be a proactive task of management, not simply a reaction to problems and competitive threats. A good illustration is Dell Computer. Although it has had some of the highest quality ratings in the PC industry, Michael Dell became obsessed with finding ways to reduce machine failure rates. He concluded that failures were related to the number of times a hard drive was handled during assembly, and insisted that the number of "touches" be reduced from an existing level of more than 30 per drive. Production lines were revamped and the number was reduced to fewer than 15. Soon after, the reject rate of hard drives fell by 40 percent and the overall failure rated dropped by 20 percent.[48] Another example is Microsoft. In 1996, Gates noticed that Microsoft was printing 350,000 sales reports per year, and that there were 114 different forms used in procurement alone.[49] After many discussions with other top managers and employees, a directive was issued that basically stated that all paper forms and reports must be eliminated unless a compelling reason could be made for their use. The results included the following:

- The total number of paper forms at Microsoft was reduced from 1,000 to 60; of these, 10 are required by law, 40 are required by outside parties, and 10 are seldom used.
- Only one procurement form now exists.
- Savings for the first year (1997–98) were estimated at $40 million.
- Studies by accounting firms suggest that the average form costs $145 to process, and that the average cost of a similar average electronic transaction, as verified by Microsoft, is $5.

Microsoft accomplished this process improvement by using the company intranet, "frequently asked questions" (FAQ), search capabilities, and links to related pages for each electronic form; scanning outside documents and putting them into the internal system; and developing a self-service approach so that individuals could handle 90 percent of their administrative information processing needs on their own desktop PCs.

Many opportunities for improvement exist, including the obvious reductions in manufacturing defects and cycle times. Organizations should also consider improving employee morale, satisfaction, and cooperation; improving managerial practices; improving the design of products with features that better meet customers' needs, and that can achieve higher performance, higher reliability, and other market-driven dimensions of quality; and improving the efficiency of manufacturing systems by reducing workers' idle time and unnecessary motions, and by eliminating unnecessary inventory, unnecessary transportation and material handling, and scrap and rework.

Historical Perspective

The concept of continuous improvement was conceived and developed in the United States, yet it is often cited as the most important difference between Japanese and Western management.[50] One of the earliest examples in the United States was at National Cash Register Company (NCR). After a shipment of defective cash registers was returned in 1894, the company's founder discovered unpleasant and unsafe working conditions. He made many changes, including better lighting, new safety devices, ventilation, lounges, and lockers. The company offered extensive evening classes to improve employees' education and skills, and instituted a program for soliciting suggestions from factory workers. Workers received cash prizes and other recognitions for their best ideas; by the 1940s the company was receiving an average of 3,000 suggestions each year.

The Lincoln Electric Company, another early pioneer in continuous improvement, designed an "incentive management" system to promote continuous improvement.

Workers were rewarded with compensation proportional to output and given increased status and publicity for their contributions. They were not penalized for finding more efficient ways to produce, but rather were rewarded for their ingenuity and increased productivity. The company profited because fixed overhead could be spread over the increased production. Workers had full responsibility for their work stations and were held accountable for quality. An employee advisory board elected by the workforce met regularly with top management to discuss ideas and to identify problems.

While the experiences at NCR and Lincoln Electric were isolated, productivity improvement has always been the focal point of the profession of industrial engineering (IE). One productivity improvement program, called *work simplification*, was developed by Allan Mogensen. Mogensen believed that workers know their jobs better than anyone else. Therefore, if they are trained in the simple steps necessary to analyze and challenge the work they are doing, they are more likely to be able to make improvements. In work simplification programs, workers receive training in the use of basic analytical techniques such as methods analysis, flowcharting, and diagramming to analyze work procedures for improvement. This concept greatly helped the production effort during World War II. Maytag and Texas Instruments were among the first companies to use work simplification.

Another approach, pioneered by Procter & Gamble, is called *planned methods change*. Although work simplification emphasized continuous improvement, planned methods change went one step further, seeking not only to improve, but also to replace or eliminate unnecessary operations. This approach relied on forming teams of employees to study operations, establishing specific dollar goals as to how much of their cost they would try to eliminate through planned change, and providing positive recognition for success.

Traditional improvement programs focused almost exclusively on productivity and cost. A focus on quality improvement, on the other hand, is relatively recent, stimulated by the success of the Japanese. During the rebuilding years after World War II in Japan, U.S. consultants taught the Japanese how to generate methods improvement ideas, and how to make sure they were implemented. At the same time, Japanese executives toured the United States and returned with numerous ideas. Many companies developed continuous improvement programs; some of the early ones included Toshiba in 1946, Matsushita Electric in 1950, and Toyota in 1951. Toyota, in particular, pioneered just-in-time (JIT). JIT showed that companies could make products with virtually zero defects, and reversed the thinking that achieving zero defects was a costly practice. In fact, JIT proved that producing extremely low defect levels typically saved money. Most importantly, JIT established a philosophy of improvement, which the Japanese call **kaizen** (pronounced kī-zen).

Kaizen[51]

Kaizen, which is a Japanese word that means gradual and orderly continuous improvement, is a philosophy that subsumes all business activities and everyone in an organization. Kaizen strategy has been called "the single most important concept in Japanese management—the key to Japanese competitive success." Often in the West, quality improvement is viewed simply as making improvements in product quality. In the kaizen philosophy, improvement in all areas of business—cost, meeting delivery schedules, employee safety and skill development, supplier relations, new product development, or productivity—serve to enhance the quality of the firm. Thus, any activity directed toward improvement falls under the kaizen umbrella. Activities to establish traditional quality control systems, install robotics and advanced technology, institute employee suggestion systems, maintain equipment, and implement just-in-time production systems all lead to improvement.

Kaizen focuses on small, gradual, and frequent improvements over the long term. Financial investment is minimal. Everyone participates in the process; many improvements result from the know-how and experience of workers. At Nissan Motor Co., Ltd., for instance, any suggestion that saves at least 0.6 seconds in a production process is seriously considered by management. The concept of kaizen is so deeply ingrained in the minds of both managers and workers that they often do not even realize they are thinking in terms of improvement. The Kaizen Institute (*http://www.kaizen-institute.com*) suggests some basic tips for implementing kaizen. These include discarding conventional fixed ideas; thinking of how to do something, not why it cannot be done; not seeking perfection; not making excuses, but questioning current practices; and seeking the wisdom of 10 people rather than the knowledge of one.

The first and foremost concern of the kaizen philosophy is the quality of people. If quality of people is improved, then the quality of products will follow. By instilling kaizen into people and training them in basic quality improvement tools, workers can build this philosophy into their work and continually seek improvement in their jobs. This process-oriented approach to improvement encourages constant communication among workers and managers.

Three things are required for a successful kaizen program: operating practices, total involvement, and training.[52] First, operating practices expose new improvement opportunities. Practices such as just-in-time reveal waste and inefficiency as well as poor quality. Second, in kaizen, every employee strives for improvement. Top management, for example, views improvement as an inherent component of corporate strategy and provides support to improvement activities by allocating resources effectively and providing reward structures that are conducive to improvement. Middle management can implement top management's improvement goals by establishing, upgrading, and maintaining operating standards that reflect those goals; by improving cooperation between departments; and by making employees conscious of their responsibility for improvement and developing their problem-solving skills through training. Supervisors can direct more of their attention to improvement rather than "supervision," which, in turn, facilitates communication and offers better guidance to workers. Finally, workers can engage in improvement through suggestion systems and small group activities, self-development programs that teach practical problem-solving techniques, and enhanced job performance skills. All these activities require significant training, both in the philosophy and in tools and techniques.

The kaizen philosophy has been widely adopted and is used by many firms in the United States and around the world. For example, at ENBI Corporation, a New York manufacturer of precision metal shafts and roller assemblies for the printer, copier, and fax machine markets, kaizen projects have resulted in a 48 percent increase in productivity, a 30 percent reduction in cycle time, and a 73 percent reduction in inventory.[53] Kaizen has been successfully applied in the Mercedes-Benz truck factory in Brazil, resulting in reductions of 30 percent in manufacturing space, 45 percent in inventory, 70 percent in lead time, and 70 percent in setup time over a three-year period. Sixteen employees have full-time responsibility for kaizen activities.[54]

Flexibility and Cycle Time Reduction

Success in globally competitive markets requires a capacity for rapid change and flexibility. Electronic commerce, for instance, requires more rapid, flexible, and customized responses than traditional market outlets. **Flexibility** refers to the ability to adapt quickly and effectively to changing requirements. It might mean rapid changeover from one product to another, rapid response to changing demands, or the ability to produce a wide range of customized services. Flexibility might demand special strategies such as modular designs, sharing components, sharing manufacturing lines, and specialized training for employees. It also involves outsourcing decisions, agreements with key suppliers, and innovative partnering arrangements.

One important business metric that complements flexibility is cycle time. **Cycle time** refers to the time it takes to accomplish one cycle of a process—for instance, the time a customer orders a product to the time that it is delivered, or the time to introduce a new product. Reductions in cycle time serve two purposes. First, they speed up work processes so that customer response is improved. Second, reductions in cycle time can only be accomplished by streamlining and simplifying processes to eliminate non-value-added steps such as rework. They force improvements in quality by reducing the potential for mistakes and errors. By reducing non-value-added steps, costs are reduced as well. Thus, cycle time reductions often drive simultaneous improvements in organization, quality, cost, and productivity. Significant reductions in cycle time cannot be achieved simply by focusing on individual subprocesses; cross-functional processes must be examined all across the organization. Through this examination, the company can better understand work at the organizational level and engage in cooperative behaviors.

One example of cycle time reduction is Procter & Gamble's over-the-counter (OTC) clinical division, which conducts clinical studies that involve testing drugs, health care products, or treatments in humans.[55] Such testing follows rigorous design, conduct, analysis, and summary of the data collected. P&G had at least four different ways to perform a clinical study and needed to find the best way to meet its research and development needs. In their evaluation, they focused on cycle time reduction. Their approach built on fundamental TQ principles: focusing on the customer, fact-based decisions, continual improvement, empowerment, the right leadership structure, and an understanding of work processes. An example is shown in Figure 7.14. The team found that final reports took months to prepare. Only by mapping the existing process did they fully understand the causes of long production times and the amount of rework and recycling during review and sign-off. By restructuring the activities form sequential to parallel work and identifying critical measurements to monitor the process, they were able to reduce the time to less than four weeks.

Agility is a term that is commonly used to characterize flexibility and short cycle times. Agility is crucial to such customer-focused strategies as mass customization, which requires rapid response and flexibility to changing consumer demand. Enablers of agility include close relationships with customers to understand their emerging needs and requirements (see Chapter 4), empowering employees as decision makers (see Chapter 6), effective manufacturing and information technology, close supplier and partner relationships, and breakthrough improvement.

Breakthrough Improvement

Breakthrough improvement refers to discontinuous change, as opposed to the gradual, continuous improvement philosophy of kaizen. Breakthrough improvements result from innovative and creative thinking; often these are motivated by **stretch goals,** or **breakthrough objectives.** Stretch goals force an organization to think in a radically different way, and to encourage major improvements as well as incremental ones. When a goal of 10 percent improvement is set, managers or engineers can usually meet it with some minor improvements. However, when the goal is 1,000 percent

Figure 7.14 Final Report "Is" and "Should" Process Map Example

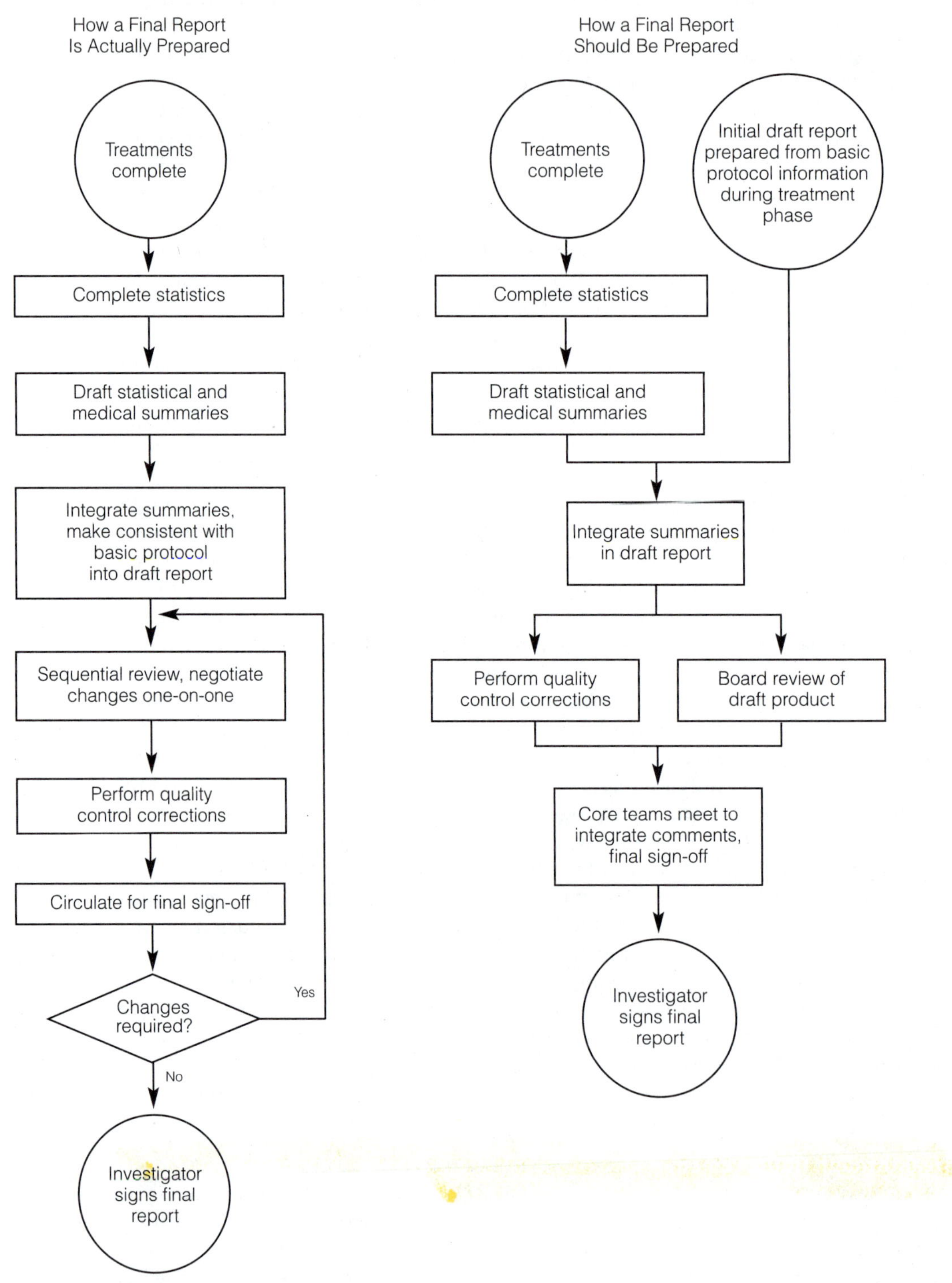

Source: David A. McCamey, Robert W. Bogs, and Linda M. Bayuk, "More, Better, Faster From Total Quality Effort," *Quality Progress,* August 1999, 43–50. © 1999. American Society for Quality. Reprinted with permission.

improvement, employees must be creative and think "out of the box." The seemingly impossible is often achieved, yielding dramatic improvements and boosting morale. A widely publicized example is Motorola. Motorola uses *defects per unit* as a quality measure throughout the company. A unit is any output of work, such as a line of computer code, a solder connection, or a page of a document. A **defect** is any failure to meet customer requirements. Motorola developed a concept called "six-sigma" quality, which refers to allowing, at most, 3.4 defects per million units. (The statistical reasoning for six-sigma and implementation approaches are explained in Chapter 10.) In 1987, Motorola set the following goal:

> *Improve product and services quality ten times by 1989, and at least one hundred fold by 1991. Achieve six-sigma capability by 1992. With a deep sense of urgency, spread dedication to quality to every facet of the corporation, and achieve a culture of continuous improvement to assure total customer satisfaction. There is only one ultimate goal: zero defects—in everything we do.*

Throughout the 1990s, Motorola has continued to set challenging goals. These ambitious goals apply to all areas of the company, including order entry, sales, purchasing, manufacturing, and design. For stretch goals to be successful, they must derive unambiguously from corporate strategy. Organizations must not set goals that result in unreasonable stress to employees or punish failure. In addition, they must provide appropriate help and tools to accomplish the task. Two approaches for breakthrough improvement that help companies achieve stretch goals are *benchmarking* and *reengineering*.

Benchmarking The development and realization of improvement objectives, particularly stretch objectives, is often aided through a process known as benchmarking. **Benchmarking** is defined as "measuring your performance against that of best-in-class companies, determining how the best-in-class achieve those performance levels, and using the information as a basis for your own company's targets, strategies, and implementation."[56] Or more simply, it can be thought of as "the search of industry best practices that lead to superior performance."[57] The term **best practices** refers to approaches that produce exceptional results, are usually innovative in terms of the use of technology or human resources, and are recognized by customers or industry experts.

Through benchmarking, a company discovers its strengths and weaknesses and those of other industrial leaders and learns how to incorporate the best practices into its own operations. Benchmarking can provide motivation to achieve stretch goals by helping employees to see what others can accomplish. For example, to meet a stretch target of reducing the time to build new 747 and 767 airplanes at Boeing from 18 months (in 1992) to 8 months, teams studied the world's best producers of everything from computers to ships. By 1996 the time had been reduced to 10 months.[58]

The concept of benchmarking is not new.[59] In the early 1800s Francis Lowell, a New England industrialist, traveled to England to study manufacturing techniques at the best British mill factories. Henry Ford created the assembly line after taking a tour of a Chicago slaughterhouse and watching carcasses, hung on hooks mounted on a monorail, move from one work station to another. Toyota's just-in-time production system was influenced by the replenishment practices of U.S. supermarkets. Modern benchmarking was initiated by Xerox—an eventual winner of the Malcolm Baldrige National Quality Award (see the *Quality in Practice* in Chapter 1)—and has since become a common practice among leading firms.

Three major types of benchmarking have emerged in business. **Competitive benchmarking** involves studying products, processes, or business performance of competitors in the same industry to compare pricing, quality, technical features, and other quality or performance characteristics of products and services. For example, a television cable company might compare its customer satisfaction rating or service response time to other cable companies; a manufacturer of televisions might compare its unit production costs or field failure rates against competitors. Significant gaps suggest key opportunities for improvement. Competitive benchmarking was refined into a science by Xerox during the 1970s and 1980s. **Process benchmarking** emerged soon after. It centers on key work processes such as distribution, order entry, or employee training. This type of benchmarking identifies the most effective practices in companies that perform similar functions, no matter in what industry. For example, the warehousing and distribution practices of L.L. Bean were adapted by Xerox for its spare parts distribution system. Texas Instruments studied the kitting (order preparation) practices of six companies, including Mary Kay Cosmetics, and designed a process that captured the best practices of each of them, cutting kitting cycle time in half. A General Mills plant in Lodi, California, had an average machine changeover time of three hours. Then somebody said, "From three hours to 10 minutes!" Employees went to a NASCAR track and videotaped the pit crews, and studied the process to identify how the principles could be applied to the production changeover processes. Several months later, the average time fell to 17 minutes.[60] Thus, companies should not aim benchmarking solely at direct competitors; in fact, they would be mistaken to do so. If a company simply benchmarks within its own industry, it may be competitive and have an edge in those areas in which it is the industry leader. However, if benchmarks are adopted from outside the industry, a company may learn ideas and processes as well as new applications that allow it to surpass the best within its own industry and to achieve distinctive superiority. Finally, **strategic benchmarking** examines how companies compete and seeks the winning strategies that have led to competitive advantage and market success.

The typical benchmarking process can be described by the process used at AT&T.

1. *Project conception:* identify the need and decide to benchmark.
2. *Planning:* determine the scope and objectives, and develop a benchmarking plan.
3. *Preliminary data collection:* collect data on industry companies and similar processes as well as detailed data on the organization's own processes.
4. *Best-in-class selection:* select companies with best-in-class processes.
5. *Best-in-class collection:* collect detailed data from companies with best-in-class processes.
6. *Assessment:* compare the organization's and best-in-class processes and develop recommendations.
7. *Implementation planning:* develop operational improvement plans to attain superior performance.
8. *Implementation:* enact operational plans and monitor process improvements.
9. *Recalibration:* update benchmark findings and assess improvements in processes.[61]

Benchmarking has many benefits.[62] The best practices from any industry may be creatively incorporated into a company's operations. Benchmarking is a motivating activity. It provides targets that have been achieved by others. Resistance to change may be lessened when ideas for improvement come from other industries. Technical breakthroughs from other industries that may be useful can be identified early on. Benchmarking broadens people's experience base and increases organizational learning and knowledge. To be effective, it must be applied to all facets of a business. For example, Motorola encourages everyone in the organization to ask, "Who is the best person in my own field and how might I use some of their techniques and characteristics to improve my own performance in order to be the best (executive, machine operator, chef, purchasing agent) in my 'class'?" Used in this fashion, benchmarking becomes a tool for improvement.

Reengineering Reengineering has been defined as "the fundamental rethinking and radical redesign of business processes to achieve dramatic improvements in critical, contemporary measures of performance, such as cost, quality, service, and speed."[63] Reengineering involves asking basic questions about business processes: Why do we do it? and Why is it done this way? Such questioning often uncovers obsolete, erroneous, or inappropriate assumptions. Radical redesign involves tossing out existing procedures and reinventing the process, not just incrementally improving it. The goal is to achieve quantum leaps in performance. For example, IBM Credit Corporation cut the process of financing IBM computers, software, and services from seven days to four hours by rethinking the process. Originally, the process was designed to handle difficult applications and required four highly trained specialists and a series of handoffs. The actual work took only about 1.5 hours; the rest of the time was spent in transit or delay. By questioning the assumption that every application was unique and difficult to process, IBM Credit Corporation was able to replace the specialists by a single individual supported by a user-friendly computer system that provided access to all the data and tools that the specialists would use.

Successful reengineering requires fundamental understanding of processes, creative thinking to break away from old traditions and assumptions, and effective use of information technology. PepsiCo has embarked on a program to reengineer all of its key business processes, such as selling and delivery, equipment service and repair, procurement, and financial reporting. In the selling and delivery of its products, for example, customer reps typically experience stockouts of as much as 25 percent of product by the end of the day, resulting in late-day stops not getting full deliveries and the need to return to those accounts. Many other routes return with overstock of other products, increasing handling costs. By redesigning the system to include hand-held computers, customer reps can confirm and deliver that day's order and also take a future order for the next delivery to that customer.[64]

Benchmarking can greatly assist reengineering efforts. Reengineering without benchmarking probably will produce 5 to 10 percent improvements; benchmarking can increase this percentage to 50 or 75 percent. When GTE reengineered eight core processes of its telephone operations, it examined the best practices of some 84 companies from diverse industries. By studying outside best practices, a company can identify and import new technology, skills, structures, training, and capabilities.[65]

Contrary to the suggestions of many authors and consultants, reengineering is not completely different from total quality principles. The issue is not kaizen versus breakthrough improvement. In fact, Juran talked about breakthrough improvement long before Hammer and Champy popularized the term *reengineering* in their book. Incremental and breakthrough improvement are complementary approaches that fall under the total quality umbrella; both are necessary to remain competitive. In fact, some suggest that reengineering requires total quality support in order to be successful.[66] Reengineering alone is often driven by upper management without the full support or understanding of the rest of the organization, and radical innovations may end up as failures. A total quality philosophy encourages participation and systematic study, measurement, and verification of results that support reengineering efforts, thus helping to ensure its success.

PROCESS MANAGEMENT IN THE BALDRIGE CRITERIA

Category 6 of the 2001 Malcolm Baldrige National Quality Award Criteria for Performance Excellence is *Process Management*. The focus of this category is on how key business processes are designed, effectively managed, and improved to achieve better performance. The criteria cover the management of product and service processes, specifically, design processes, production/delivery processes, support processes, and other business processes such as supplier/partnering processes. Built into the criteria are the central requirements for efficient and effective process management, which include effective design, a prevention orientation, linkage to suppliers and partners, operational performance, cycle time, and evaluation, continuous improvement, and organizational learning.

Item 6.1, *Product and Service Processes*, examines an organization's key product and service design and delivery processes, with the aim of improving marketplace and organizational performance. The criteria address how an organization incorporates customer and market requirements and new technology; key factors in design effectiveness such as cost control, cycle time, and past learning; how all important operational performance requirements are met in designs; and how coordination among all appropriate groups such as marketing, design, engineering, production, and testing ensure effective launch of new products and services. This criteria item also seeks to understand how key performance measures are used for controlling and improving products, services, and processes to meet day-to-day performance requirements. Finally, it calls for information on how processes are improved to achieve better performance, which might include sharing successful strategies across the organization, process analysis and research, benchmarking, and reengineering.

Item 6.2, *Business Processes*, which was added in the 2001 criteria, asks an organization to identify nonproduct/nonservice processes that are considered most important to business growth and success—such as research and development, knowledge management, supply chain management, or project management—and to describe how it manages and improves these processes. Finally, Item 6.3, *Support Processes*, calls for similar information about key support processes, particularly on how they are designed to meet appropriate internal and external customer requirements, and how they are controlled and improved.

The following example shows how Collin Technologies might respond to Item 6.1, *Product and Service Processes*, and the feedback that a Baldrige examiner team might provide. *You should read Case III in Chapter 3 for background information, if you have not already done so, and review the 2000 Baldrige criteria for this item on the CD rom accompanying this book.* References to other Baldrige categories or items can be found in the full case study on the CD-rom.

Example 4: Collin Technologies—Product and Service Processes

Response to Criteria Item 6.1, Product and Service Processes

Collin has documented all product and service processes throughout the organization. Both facilities have been verified to comply with ISO 9001. To meet the ISO 9001 certification, Collin took an integrated approach, meeting with its selected ISO registering agency and presenting a proposal that included all key elements required by ISO in Collin's internal assessment process. Because Collin regularly conducts internal assessments to the Baldrige Criteria (including ISO requirements) with published results, actions, and follow-up, it entered into an agreement with the ISO registrar that, with minor additions, these reviews would suffice and satisfy the requirements for ongoing ISO surveillance assessments. During most of these assessments, a participating member from the ISO registering agency is assigned.

6.1a The Product Development Process (PDP) is shown in Figure 7.15. This process is followed for all new circuit boards developed. Collin has created four boilerplate Product Requirements Documents (PRD) that address basic requirements by business segment. Specific customer requirements are then added during the PDR. The Plan of Record (POR) is created after prototype verification and in conjunction with the Marketing Requirements Document (MRD) that defines specific customer and manufacturing specifications. These are shown with an asterisk in Figure 7.15.

Figure 7.16 shows how the PDP is integrated into Collin's overall five-step product life cycle process that includes customers, suppliers, Integrated Product Development Teams (IPDTs), the Collin production process, and product certification.

Multilayer boards are designed to uniform rules that specify areas such as fine widths and spacing with standard hole sizes and locations. These rules are adapted

Figure 7.15 Product Development Process (PDP)

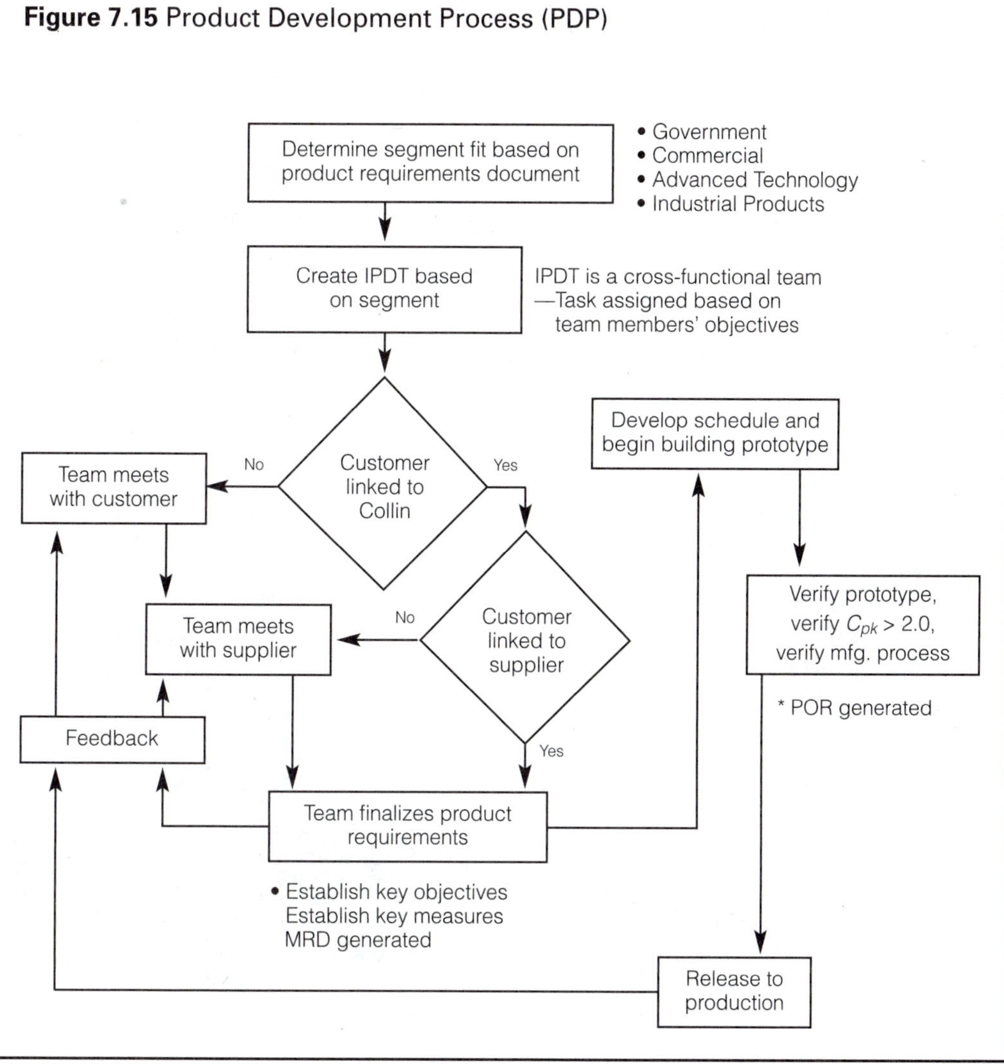

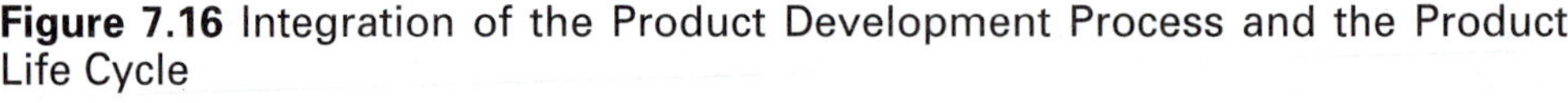

Figure 7.16 Integration of the Product Development Process and the Product Life Cycle

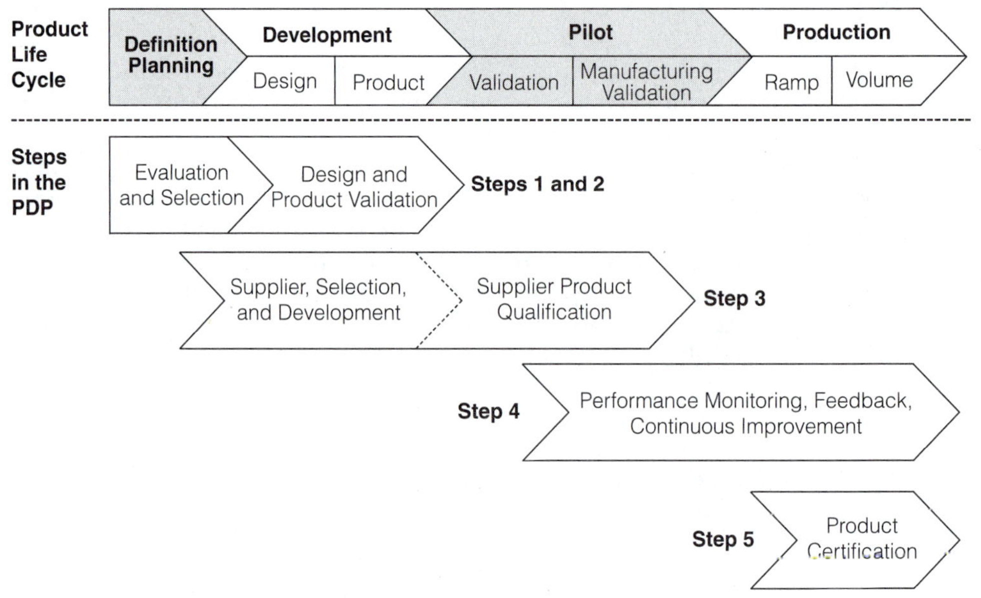

to individual customer requirements. In Figure 7.16, standard quality techniques, including failure mode and effect analysis as well as quality function deployment, are utilized in design and product validation (Step 2) and in verification processes (Step 3).

The design and production processes are maintained within the CAIN system, and changes to both are automatically included in the overall process. The automated production delivery system, controlled by CAIN, is designed to deliver prototypes overnight and production quantities within five calendar days for new orders or design changes. (The plants operate seven days per week.)

Key customers have a direct input to the CAIN system (Item 4.2) and are able to make changes to their products. Collin engineers enter changes for other customers. These changes may be the result of evolving requirements or conditions, or they may be the result of new technology that results in products of higher value.

Collin IPDTs and Process Support Teams (PSTs) also make changes to product design and processes. If modifications are required, the process laboratory ensures that the changes do not affect the capability of the process. These determinations are finalized in an eight-hour time period.

New technology is a constant driver, and the IPDTs and PSTs are continually involved in the loop of process and product design modifications. An example of how new technology is being applied in producing multilayer boards is the Chemically Bonded Deposition Process (CBDP). This proprietary process was developed for the advanced technology segment that requires applications for low current densities, and a high number of lines are present. It uses a deposition process on bare substrates and does not utilize copper etching techniques. This new process results in fewer layers, smaller and lighter boards, and improved reliability. Production quantities are being produced in the process laboratory, and the volume is increasing.

This process will be expanded to other customer segments as the need becomes applicable.

Board production is totally automated with tightly controlled processes to assure customer satisfaction. When a change in process is indicated, the IPDTs and PSTs review all characteristics, concentrating on any necessary changes from the established process.

These teams are responsible for maintaining and modifying all processes to reflect customer needs and the needs of maintaining the process capabilities for their range of responsibilities.

The design process is maintained and improved through the use of the design guidelines that are continually updated through knowledge and application of updated techniques and learning experiences. All information is contained within CAIN, which distributes information to all locations. The best prevention tool to improve quality and reduce cycle time and costs is control through robust process capability studies and ongoing process control. The IPDTs work closely with customers and suppliers and maintain the production processes. All processes are designed to operate within a minimum C_{pk} of 2 (see Chapter 10 for a discussion of C_{pk}). Changes in any parameter must meet the minimum C_{pk} requirement. This specification has resulted in quality defects measured in parts per billion. PSTs follow the same criteria but remain more internally focused. The results of aggressive process design and control are shown in Category 7 for both production processes and support processes.

The process laboratory is used by both the IPDTs and PSTs to facilitate the design validation and product verification processes. It is also used to improve product C_{pk} levels and meet Collin's target goal of C_{pk} of 2 prior to production release.

All inner and outer layers of boards are automatically bar coded when released into the production process, therefore all units have unique identifying numbers that are continually tracked throughout the process with historical records established in CAIN. The bar coding on the boards automatically alerts the production process for any changes as an individual order proceeds through production.

6.1b The production/delivery processes and their key performance characteristics are listed in Table 7.5 All deliveries are made by air with a carrier that tracks location to minimize the time in transit.

Production processes are precisely controlled by CAIN with a process capability designed to operate with a minimum C_{pk} of 2. Some individual processes are de-

Table 7.5 Production/Delivery Process

Production Process	Key Performance Characteristics
Material preparation	Dimensions, cleanliness, no surface imperfections
Exposing and development	Dimensions of lines and spacing, no shorts or opens
Laminating	Dimensions, cleanliness, no delamination of layers
Drilling	Hole size and locations, cleanliness of holes
Plating	Thickness and adhesion of plating
Delivery	Minimized time in transit

signed and controlled with C_{pk}s as high as 10. The processes are sampled with an in-process sampling plan that ensures that they remain "in control" and the mean values are maintained. The results of these samples are tracked for preventive purposes. An example of an in-process sampling audit is shown in Category 7.

Test coupon holes are automatically designed in all boards to provide test-plated holes for process verification and assurance that the production process performs as designed.

By utilizing a process design that is well within the design tolerances and maintained by an adequate sampling plan, Collin ensures that products meet customer requirements. Table 7.6 shows some of the characteristics sampled to ensure process control.

Collin products are designed to operate in extreme environments. To ensure performance on a sample basis, boards are subjected to extreme environmental conditions to verify compliance with customer requirements and to ensure reliable lifetime operation. These tests are performed in the process laboratory.

The PSTs are responsible for all production processes and are constantly looking for ways to improve processes as new technology becomes available. Improvements in production and design capability also help to reduce cycle time and cost and enhance quality.

A prime customer need, cycle time reduction is constantly monitored when improvements are implemented. Cycle time results are shown in Category 7. IPDTs and PSTs benchmark other companies' processes in the multilayer printed circuit board business and utilize the University of Koga and the Peak State University, which perform extensive research work in new board processes. Through the continuous improvement process (Figure 7.17), Collin maintains control of key processes while identifying opportunities for improvement. When opportunities are identified, the "five-step" analysis process is used to verify that improvements are warranted. Improvements are made using the improvement matrix shown in Figure 7.17. To ensure that processes are maintained in a preventive manner, the data are continuously analyzed using the "five-step" approach described in Item 4.2. Customers and suppliers also provide valuable information to aid in process improvements. Many changes have been made in response to their suggestions.

The facilities in Nashville and Koga are nearly identical When equipment is purchased for one facility, a duplicate is purchased for the second. In addition, CAIN facilitates sharing and updating of information on an ongoing basis. This constant updating ensures the consistency of products and processes, learning, and production flexibility.

Table 7.6 Process Verification

Characteristic	Frequency	Product or Process
Copper surface	1%	Product
Layer thickness	1%	Product
Plating characteristics	4×/shift	Process
Hole cross-section	1/panel	Process
Environmental testing	1/production lot	Process/product

Figure 7.17 Continuous Improvement Process

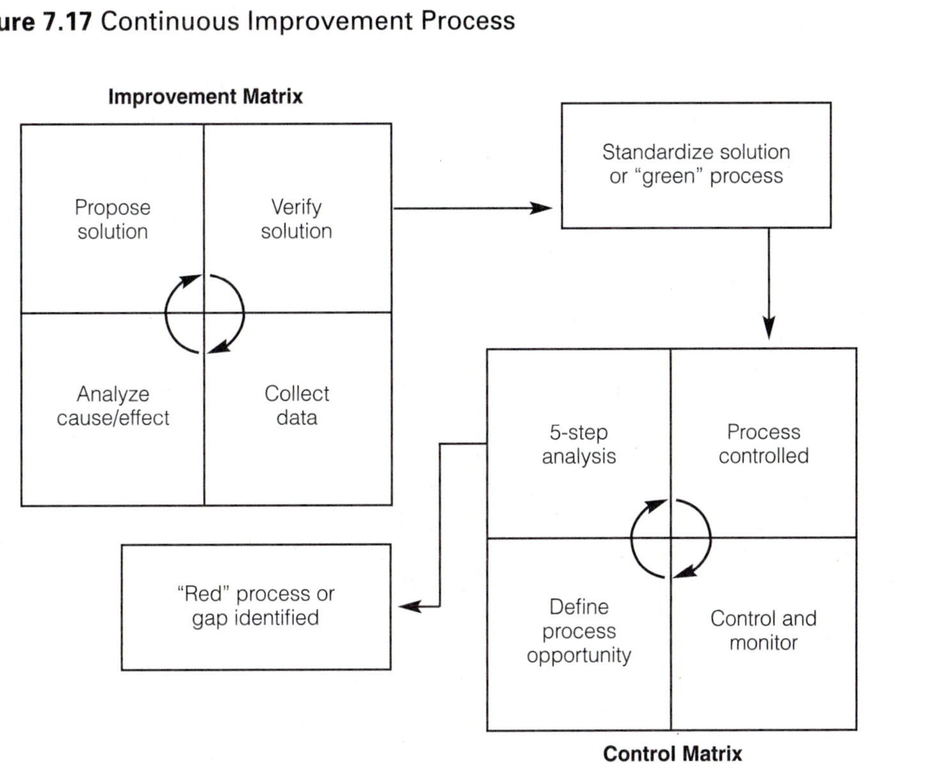

Examiner Feedback

Strengths

- A systematic Product Development Process (PDP) is used to meet customer requirements for cutting-edge technology products while reducing cycle time. This process identifies requirements by business and customer segment and verifies customer, supplier, and manufacturing specifications through the Marketing Requirements Document (MRD) process. Dedicated Integrated Product Development Teams (IPDTs) integrate the PDP with the five-step product life cycle process. During all phases of development, input from customers and suppliers are supported by analyses such as failure mode and effect analysis as well as quality function deployment.
- All information collected during design and production is maintained on the CAIN system. The system is capable of producing prototypes overnight and producing orders within five days based on changes made directly into the system by customers, company engineers, and IPDTs, and PSTs. Deployment of information via CAIN ensures timeliness of information transfer across the organization and supports the company goal for a paperless environment.
- Technology plays a key role in the management of production and delivery processes such as multilayer board production, a proprietary chemically bonded deposition process (CBDP), C_{pk} process control, analytical testing, and bar coding for inventory control and shipping. Through the innovation of the CBDP, the new design results in a lighter, more reliable circuit board for the advanced technology customers, thereby meeting key requirements for that business segment.

- All processes are designed to control limits of a minimum C_{pk} of 2.0. By utilizing a process design that is better than or within the design tolerances, the applicant ensures that products meet customer requirements.
- A continuous improvement process controls production processes while allowing for continuous improvements through the use of a five-step analysis process. The CAIN system helps control processes while allowing for reliable and timely information sharing between the Nashville and Koga facilities.

Opportunities for Improvement

- Although the CBDP is an example of how new technology resulted in a product specifically designed to meet the advanced technology customer requirements, the process for how new technology is developed and used in product and production system design is not sufficiently described. Without a clear description, it is difficult to determine whether a systematic approach for identifying, developing, and introducing new technology is in place, which is a key factor in achieving the company's strategic objectives.
- While examples of design and process improvements are described, it is not clear how the applicant systematically evaluates and improves the effectiveness of its overall approach for product and process design. For example, information concerning improvements and "lessons learned" is available via CAIN; however, it is unclear how the applicant uses this information to drive improvement and whether the applicant evaluates the effectiveness of the approach.
- It is not clear how the company selects key performance characteristics for its production processes to ensure that product performance meets customer requirements. It is also unclear how the applicant establishes limits for those production processes that it considers critical.

Quality in Practice

Applying Quality Function Deployment to a University Support Service[67]

Most applications of QFD have focused on manufacturing firms or the needs of the external customer. However, QFD can be applied effectively in service organization, taking into account the needs of internal customers. Tennessee Technological University applied QFD to their Research Resources Center (RRC), an internal service system. Originally created as a support facility for faculty and student research, the RRC has grown to offer many more services, including test preparation, manuscript preparation, resumes, flyers, brochures, faxing, copying, typing, and computer applications. The RRC is staffed weekdays from 7:30 A.M. to 4:30 P.M. with highly experienced support personnel. Jody, the head coordinator of the RRC, is proficient in specialty computer applications. She has a work station at her disposal loaded with word-processing, graphics, and desktop publishing software. Peripherals such as a laser printer, color printer, and a full-page scanner allow her to generate high-quality output. Candy specializes in word processing, and Marie specializes in copying, collating, and stapling or binding. All three are proficient in most of the RRC functions.

Jobs can be classified as student, teacher, or rush. Most jobs are single-task oriented and can be completed by one RRC professional. The professional may be dependent on student workers to process job orders accurately and place them in the appropriate incoming-jobs bin. Some jobs, however, are dependent on the other employees' functions. For instance, Candy types the tests, and Marie makes the copies and packages the final product. In these instances, Marie functions as an internal customer. She becomes dependent on another professional employee to accomplish her job.

Students involved in scholarship and work study programs are also employed part time to support RRC personnel. The RRC, functioning as a unit of the College of Business, is bound by the same regulations as other university offices: It has little control over the student employment selection process.

The responsibilities of the students include taking work orders and assisting customers in low tech functions, such as making copies and finding research materials. No formal training is given. The student workers are briefly informed of the RRC's functions and told to be courteous to customers. When student workers have questions, they ask one of the professionals. The student workers are primarily used as an interface between RRC professionals and customers.

With some of the documents that the RRC processes, security presents an issue. Some faculty members choose to have the RRC type and print their tests. In these instances, student workers cannot be involved in any process regarding the test. The order is taken by one of the professionals, the job is executed, and the final product is locked in file cabinets in a room where student workers are not allowed. Additionally, some student documents may not be handled by student workers. Project papers submitted for typing should not be viewed by a student worker who, by chance, may be in the same class and have the same assignment.

Because of limited space in the RRC, little distinction separates the back office from the front office. A counter is set up to the right as the customer walks in. All workers are stationed behind this counter. As customers need assistance, they are met at the counter by student workers. The student workers assist the customers. If a customer requires a job, then the appropriate work-order forms are filled out. During this time, the customer is in full view of the operations. Some frequent customers prefer to relay their job orders directly to the professionals. Due to the customized nature of many of the jobs, this direct interaction is sometimes appropriate. Therefore the RRC professionals will occasionally have to leave the work they are doing to serve the customer.

The area to the left of the counter is available for customer use (see Figure 7.18). Four large tables are centrally located for faculty members and students

Figure 7.18 RRC Old Layout

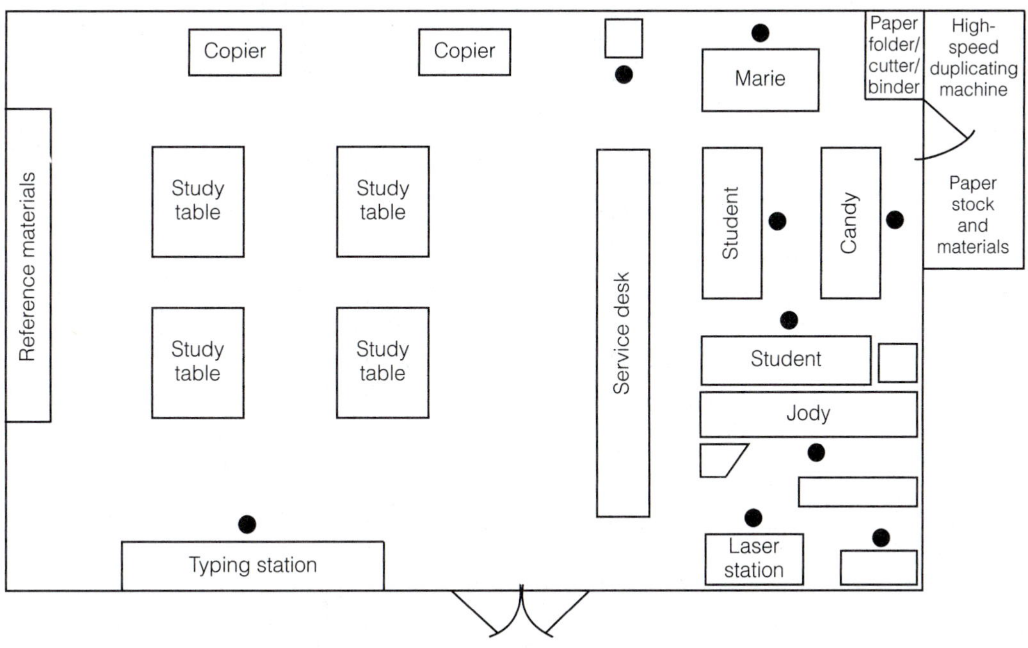

Source: R. Natarajan, et al. (see note 67). © 1999 American Society for Quality. Reprinted with permission.

to use for study purposes. The waiting area is merely the area between the counter and these tables. No structured service line is set up, and service personnel attempt to serve customers on a first-come, first-served basis. When customers have work orders that can be completed quickly, they may choose to wait at the counter. Occasionally, a queue develops in front of the service counter.

QFD was used to analyze where a concerted effort may increase the RRC's quality level as perceived by the customer. Customer requirements were grouped along the five dimensions of service quality (in rank order of importance): reliability, responsiveness, assurance, empathy, and tangibles. These categories were further broken down into secondary requirements as shown in the House of Quality (Figure 7.19). Existing operations in the RRC were observed internally over a three-month period and the following components were identified:

- *Planning:* layout, resources equipment, resources personnel, and system capacity
- *Procedures:* housekeeping, customer handling, documents handling, information handling, nonroutine situations, inventory, and job and personnel scheduling
- *Personnel:* selection, skills training, and attitude and morale

The roof of the House of Quality illustrates the relationships between these service components. An expert from the RRC was used to assess these relationships. The completed House of Quality

Figure 7.19 RRC House of Quality

■ Strong ● Medium ▲ Weak

What? Customer quality criteria / Service facility facets How?

			Planning				Procedures							Personnel		
Primary	Secondary	Relative importance	Layout	Resources (equipment)	Resources (personnel)	System capacity	Housekeeping	Customer handling	Documents handling	Information handling	Nonroutine situations	Inventory	Job/personnel scheduling	Selection	Skills/training	Attitudes/morals
Reliability	Accuracy	5			■				■	■						
	Dependability	5		■	■					■	■	●	■		●	
Responsiveness	Willingness to help	4			■			■		●						■
	Prompt service	4	▲		■	■		■	■	■			●			■
Assurance	Knowledge and courtesy of employees	3			■			●		▲	■				●	●
	Ability to convey trust and assurance	3			●			●								●
Empathy	Caring of and attention to customers	2			●	■	▲	■		▲	■				■	■
Tangibles	Appearance of physical facility, equipment, personnel, and materials	1	●	■								▲	●			

Source: R. Natarajan, et al. (see note 67).

reveals that three service components—resource personnel, documents handling, and information handling—are the most important design issues related to customer perceptions of service quality, In redesigning the current process, the primary focus should be on these issues.

The study resulted in a number of recommendations that will enable the RRC to deliver a higher level of service. One recommendation is to incorporate a better document-handling procedure. Currently the RRC takes the documents (resumes, tests, papers, and so on) and places them in one incoming-work bin. Staff members are good at sorting through the work orders and almost always identify the high-priority orders and complete them in plenty of time. But occasionally a work order is not noticed until it is almost too late. These orders are rushed and tend to be more prone to errors.

To prevent errors, procedures can be established that will separate the work orders into separate bins for high-priority jobs and normal jobs. Bins can also be placed at each person's work station so employees don't have to sort through everyone else's work. Thus, employees would have a better idea of the work they have to do and may better allocate their time.

As mentioned earlier, the RRC has no formal training program. Even though it may not be feasible for such a small organization to have a formal training program, some training procedures should be considered. Employees should be thoroughly trained on documenting and routing work orders. An error in the work order will inevitably result in an error in the final document. For instance, if a worker is not familiar with the work orders, he or she may document margin size in the wrong location. The professional, accustomed to seeing that information in a particular location, may not notice the correct margin settings, resulting in a flawed document.

Another improvement is the facility layout. Currently, many self-serve machines and resources are scattered around the room (see Figure 7.18). If machines and resources were centrally located, a customer could immediately target his or her needs upon entering the facility. Also, the service counter has no identifiable queuing system. If customers met the service counter head-on when entering the facility and key personnel were strategically positioned behind the counter, a quasi-service queue could be created as customers would direct themselves to specific service personnel. A proposed layout is suggested in Figure 7.20.

Figure 7.20 RRC Proposed Layout

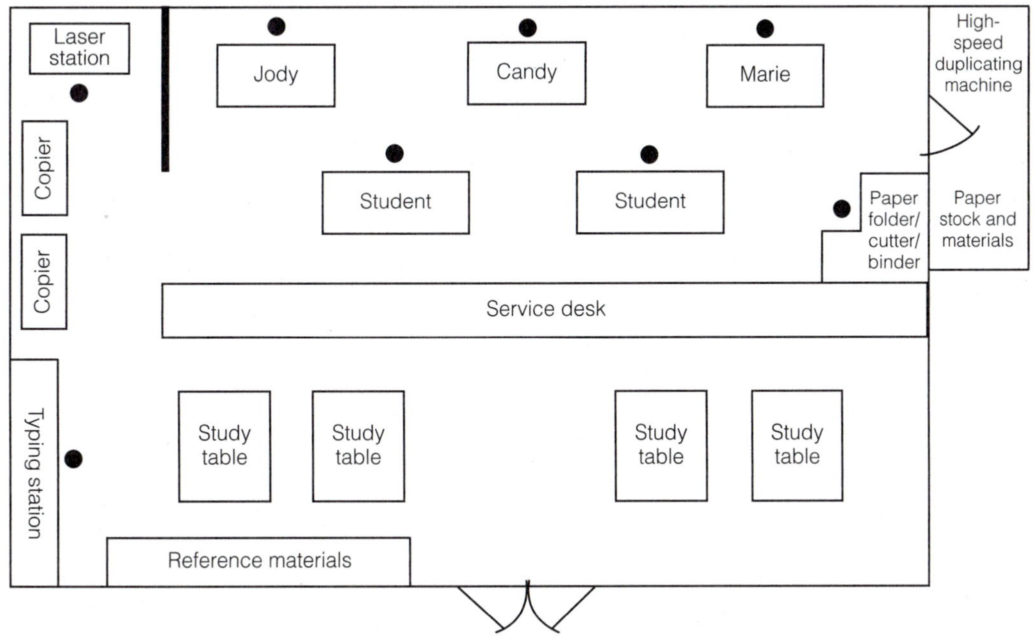

Source: R. Natarajan, et al. (see note 67). © 1999 American Society for Quality. Reprinted with permission.

This layout would also facilitate document flow with Jody's design, Candy's typing, and Marie's copying and folding, cutting, and binding in the same area.

These recommendations resulted in changes that were within the control of RRC personnel and therefore considered feasible. For instance, the layout was changed to facilitate smoother traffic flow and improve customer contact with service providers. Self-serve equipment, such as copiers, computers, and printers were grouped in the new layout for easy access.

Key Issues for Discussion

1. Do you agree with the relative importance measures of the voice of the customer in Figure 7.19? Explain why these rankings are reasonable, or provide counter arguments for a different ranking.
2. Using the relative importance ratings of the customer attributes and setting a scale of 1 = weak, 3 = medium, and 5 = strong for the relationship matrix, compute a weighted score for each of the technical requirements in Figure 7.19. Do your scores support the conclusions of the study in terms of the key service components to deploy in the QFD process?
3. What other recommendations might you suggest based on the information provided in this case?

(We encourage you to read the Gold Star Chili case in Chapter 4 first for background information about the company.) Gold Star Chili, a chain of chili restaurants in the greater Cincinnati area, views process management activities as critical to its business success. Quality improvement teams, technology, and strong relationships with suppliers ensure that its chili is produced in a consistent fashion with respect to taste, viscosity, and general quality.

Figure 7.21 shows a process-based organization of the company. Three major core processes link the operation of the company to its customers and other stakeholders:

1. Franchising
2. Restaurant operations
3. Manufacturing/distribution.

Sustaining these core processes are various support processes, such as research and development, human resources, accounting, purchasing, operations, training, marketing, and customer satisfaction, as well as design processes for new products, menus, and facilities. Production/delivery processes are coordinated at the corporate office and documented in manuals provided to each store. Internal customer needs are addressed in quality improvement team meetings.

The franchising process, outlined in Figure 7.22, is designed to ensure a smooth and successful start-up that meets company objectives. The process has been refined over time and includes extensive interaction with prospective and approved franchisees. New technology has been introduced to facilitate the process. For example, a site-selection software package is used to evaluate market potential using a variety of demographic data. Computer-aided design is also used for site development. Because franchise process delays are costly, the process helps to eliminate variability, reduce cycle time, and cut down on problems that might occur during development and introduction. Procedure manuals have been developed to provide each store with the necessary information and training to ensure that they operate efficiently.

Restaurant processes include cash register, steam table, drive-thru, tables, bussers, and management. These processes are designed to ensure that the principal requirements of all customers, such as being served in a timely manner and receiving their order accurately, are met. Prior to the opening of each restaurant, training sessions ensure that these processes are performed correctly and according to company standards. Each employee is cross-trained to perform each function.

Figure 7.21 Gold Star Chili, Inc. Organization

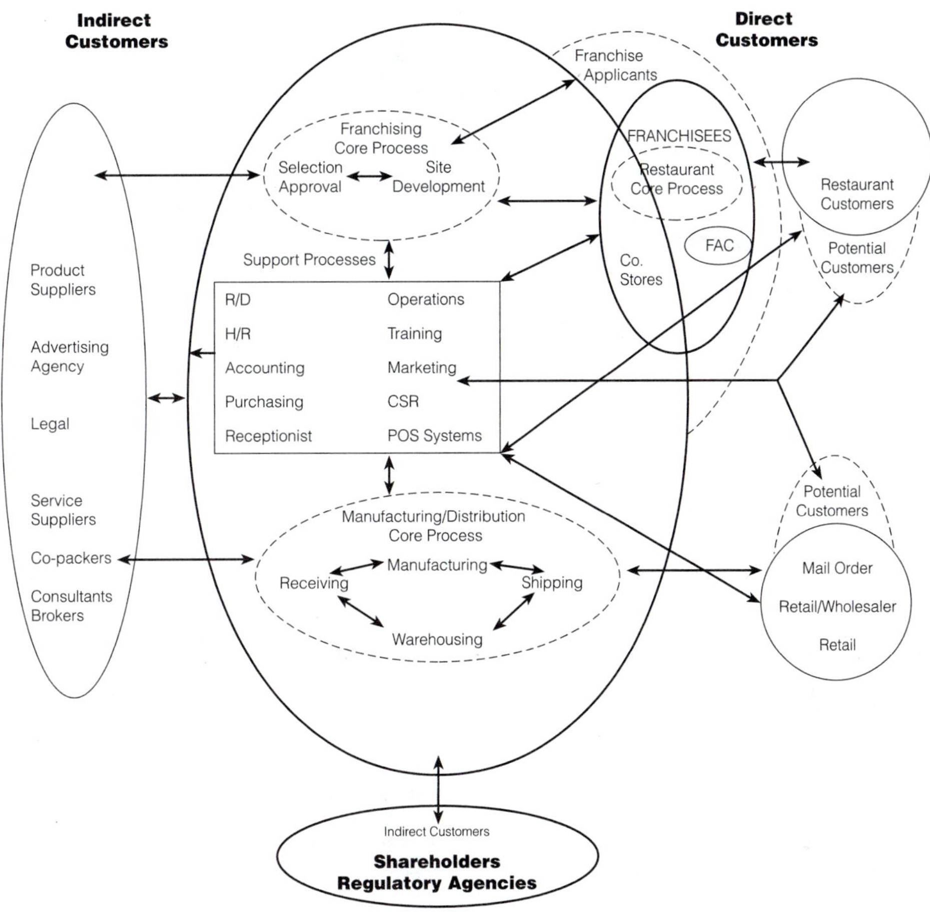

Source: Courtesy of Gold Star Chili. Used with permission.

Chili production is performed at the Gold Star Commissary. A nine-member team, cross-trained to perform each process, is responsible for adding beef, spices, tomatoes, and water during production. The chili must pass a series of strict tests before being shipped to restaurants. Control of chili production is assisted by various pieces of equipment for precise measurement. For example, a Bostwick viscosity meter determines the consistency of the chili, determining whether it is too thick or thin, and a flow meter adds the proper amount of water. Other equipment analyzes the fat content of the ground beef used in the chili. The final test, taste, is performed by members of the commissary to ensure that each batch meets established standards.

The commissary team also serves as a quality improvement team. Since July of 1996, they have met informally on a daily basis to discuss processes and feedback from internal and external customers; they use a formal improvement process in reporting their activities. They use information from customer comment cards, measurements of waiting time for drive-through service, and feedback from restaurant managers to analyze and adjust processes as necessary. Store performance and quality are measured quarterly through visits by corporate employees. Monthly meetings of key process leaders and daily team meetings analyze processes for improvement opportunities, such as changes in procedures or the introduction of new technology. For example, several restaurants

Figure 7.22 Gold Star Chili Franchising Process

GOLD STAR CHILI, INC.

5204 Beechmont Avenue
Cincinnati, Ohio 45230
(513) 231-4541

Steps to a Gold Star Chili Franchise

1. Submit a fully completed franchise application. We will respond to you within 15 business days on your applications.
2. You will receive for your review our Uniform Franchise Offering Circular and Exhibits. At this time you will sign and date the Receipt of Offering Circular.
3. Ten days after we receive your Receipt of Offering Circular, you will be sent a Confidentiality Agreement which you must hold for 5 days, then sign, date, and return to us.
4. Schedule and complete a meeting with support staff of Gold Star Chili in our Cincinnati location.
5. Attend a two-day orientation in Cincinnati. You will work with our Operations and Training personnel who will review your qualifications and objectives.
6. You will then be notified of your approval or disapproval of your request to become a Gold Star Chili Franchisee.
7. Gold Star personnel will begin the process of identifying and approving a restaurant location. A scope of work per Gold Star standards will be completed.
8. Sign Gold Star Chili Franchise Agreement and pay initial fee.
9. Begin construction.
10. Complete the training program.
11. Develop an opening plan.
12. Open your Gold Star Chili Restaurant.

Source: Courtesy of Gold Star Chili. Used with permission.

discovered large clumps of beef in the chili. The team determined that a new beef pump was not grinding the meat correctly.

The selection of suppliers is driven by two criteria: quality and price. Gold Star partners with key product suppliers for restaurant equipment and food products. They seek out local companies and educate them in their business needs and practices. For example, they have invited suppliers to attend a seminar on the Gold Star Chili total quality philosophy and suppliers' role in the process. To ensure that raw materials meet Gold Star specifications, potential and current suppliers visit the commissary to be informed about what

Gold Star requires and what technologies the company expects them to have. Suppliers are required to meet or exceed quality standards and provide products at reasonable prices.

Gold Star attempts to establish long-term relationships with its suppliers. Company managers visit suppliers' facilities on a regular basis to solicit comments and complaints, and to discuss areas for improvement. During these discussions, suppliers often provide Gold Star with information about new technologies, suggestions for process improvements, and other helpful knowledge. For example, by sharing information with one key paper supplier, the supplier was able to redesign Gold Star's purchasing process, enabling the supplier to increase minimum order levels for deliveries, which reduced Gold Star's overall costs. The company conducts annual cost audits to determine whether costs might be lowered without sacrificing quality. If an alternative supplier is found with similar quality, service, and lower costs, Gold Star will approach its current supplier with the opportunity to lower costs.

Key Issues for Discussion

1. How does the organization structure in Figure 7.21 reflect Deming's view of a production system as discussed in Chapter 1?
2. As a small, privately held company, Gold Star is relatively new at applying total quality management approaches to its process management. Based on the information provided here, what suggestions might you provide in the process management area as the company matures in its journey to total quality?

Summary of Key Points

- Process management involves design, control, and improvement of key business processes, which include design, production/delivery, support, and supplier/partnering processes. To apply process management techniques, processes must be repeatable and measurable.
- Leading process management practices include translating customer requirements into product and service design requirements; ensuring that quality is built into products using appropriate engineering and statistical tools; effective management of the product development process; defining and documenting important production/delivery and support processes; managing supplier and partnering relationships; controlling quality and operational performance of all key business processes; continuously improving processes using systematic problem-solving approaches; and innovating to achieve breakthrough performance.
- The product development process consists of idea generation, preliminary concept development, product/process development, full-scale production, product introduction, and market evaluation.
- Good product design relies on sound quality engineering to produce a functional design that meets customer requirements, and establish specifications and tolerances for production or service delivery. The Taguchi loss function is a way of quantifying the costs due to variation from a target specification and has been used to demonstrate the economic value of being on target.
- Improvements in cost and quality often result from simplifying designs and employing techniques such as design for manufacturability.
- Public responsibilities in the design process include product safety and environmental concerns, which have made design for environment (DfE) an important feature of products, because it permits easy removal of components for recycling or repair and eliminates other environmental hazards.

- Concurrent, or simultaneous, engineering is an effective approach for managing the product development process by using multifunctional teams to help remove organizational barriers between departments and therefore reduce product development time.
- Customers, engineers, and designers speak different languages. Quality function deployment (QFD) is a technique used to carry the voice of the customer through the design and production process. The major planning document in QFD is called the House of Quality. It provides a planning structure for relating customers' needs to technical specifications and confirming that key specifications are identified and deployed throughout the subsequent production process.
- Flowcharts and backward chaining are useful tools for designing processes. A basic approach involves identifying the product or service, customers, suppliers, and process steps; mistake-proofing the process; and controlling and improving the process using measurements.
- In designing services, one must consider physical facilities, processes, and procedures; behavior; and professional judgment. Classification of services along dimensions of customer contact and interaction, labor intensity, and degree of customization directs attention to the proper balance of these design elements.
- Control is the continuing process of evaluating performance, comparing outputs to goals or standards, and taking corrective action when necessary. Any control system has three components: (1) a standard or goal, (2) a means of measuring accomplishment, and (3) comparison of actual results with the standard to provide feedback for corrective action.
- Strong customer-supplier relationships are based on recognizing the strategic importance of suppliers in accomplishing business objectives, developing win-win relationships through partnerships, and establishing trust through openness and honesty. Supplier certification systems are often used to manage supplier relationships.
- Process improvement has been approached in various ways, including work simplification, planned methods change, and more recently, kaizen. Kaizen, the Japanese term for improvement, is a philosophy of quality improvement in all areas of business using small, frequent, and gradual improvements over the long term.
- Stretch goals force an organization to think in a radically different way and to encourage breakthrough improvements. Benchmarking and reengineering often facilitate breakthrough thinking. Benchmarking is the search for best practices in any industry and reengineering is the fundamental rethinking and radical redesign of business processes to achieve dramatic improvements in performance. Both approaches complement continuous improvement efforts in a TQ culture.

Review Questions

1. Define process management and its three key components. Why is it important to any business?
2. Summarize the principles on which AT&T bases its process management methodology.
3. Define the four principal categories of processes.
4. Why must processes be repeatable and measurable?

5. Summarize the leading practices in process management.
6. Describe the product design and development process.
7. Explain the role of system, parameter, and tolerance design in quality engineering.
8. Explain how the Taguchi loss function differs from the traditional loss function assumed from specifications and tolerances.
9. How can product design affect manufacturability? Explain the concept and importance of design for manufacturability.
10. Summarize the key design practices for high quality in manufacturing and assembly.
11. Discuss the public responsibility issues relating to product design facing businesses today.
12. Discuss the importance of and impediments to reducing the time for product development.
13. Explain the basic principles of quality function deployment. How is it implemented in an organization?
14. What are the principal benefits of QFD?
15. Outline the process of building the House of Quality. What departments and functions within the company should be involved in each step of the process?
16. Describe the basic approach used for designing production/delivery and support processes. How can flowcharts and backward chaining assist in this approach?
17. Explain the differences between designing manufactured products and services. How should the design of services be approached?
18. Describe the three components of any control system.
19. How can one check whether process owners have true responsibility for controlling a process?
20. Explain the concept of after-action review.
21. Why is it important to establish strong relationships with suppliers? What are some good supplier management practices?
22. What is the purpose of supplier certification? Explain some of the common practices for supplier certification.
23. Describe some of the early approaches to process improvement.
24. Explain the Japanese concept of kaizen. How does it differ from traditional Western approaches to improvement?
25. What is flexibility and why is it important to a modern organization?
26. What are the key impacts of cycle time reduction?
27. What is a stretch goal? How can stretch goals help an organization?
28. Define benchmarking and list its benefits. How does it differ from competitive comparison?
29. What is reengineering? How does it relate to TQ practices?
30. Discuss how process management is addressed in the Baldrige criteria.

Discussion Questions

1. Provide some examples of processes that are repeatable and measurable and some that are not.
2. List some of the common processes that a student performs. How can these processes be improved?

3. Are classroom examinations a means of control or improvement? What should they be?
4. Why are modern products more difficult to manufacture than traditional products such as bicycles or hand tools?
5. How can kaizen be applied in a classroom?
6. The kaizen philosophy seeks to encourage suggestions, not to find excuses for failing to improve. Typical excuses are "If it's not broken, don't fix it," "I'm too busy to work on it," and "It's not in the budget." Think of at least five other excuses why people don't try to improve.
7. What is the product development process that a school might use for designing and introducing a new course? How might it be improved to reduce "time-to-market"?
8. How can a manager effectively balance the three key components of a service system design?
9. In a true story related by our colleague Prof. James W. Dean, Jr., the general manager of an elevator company was frustrated with the lack of cooperation between the mechanical engineers who designed new elevators and the manufacturing engineers who determined how to produce them.[69] The mechanical engineers would often completely design a new elevator without any consulting with the manufacturing engineers, and then expect the factory to somehow figure out how to build it. Often the new products were difficult or nearly impossible to build, and their quality and cost suffered as a result. The designs were sent back to the mechanical engineers (often more than once) for engineering changes to improve their manufacturability, and customers sometimes waited for months for deliveries. The general manager believed that if the two groups of engineers communicated early in the design process, many of the problems would be solved. At his wits' end, he found a large empty room in the plant and had both groups moved into it. The manager relaxed a bit, but a few weeks later he returned to a surprise. The two groups of engineers had finally learned to cooperate—by building a wall of bookcases and file cabinets right down the middle of the room, separating them from each other! What would you do in this situation?
10. Legal Sea Foods operates several restaurants and fish markets in the Boston area. The company's standards of excellence mandate that it serves only the freshest, highest-quality seafood. It guarantees the quality by buying only the "top of the catch" fish daily. Although Legal Sea Foods tries to make available the widest variety every day, certain species of fish are subject to migratory patterns and are not always present in New England waters. Weather conditions may also prevent local fishermen from fishing in certain areas.

    Freshly caught fish are rushed to the company's quality control center where they are cut and filleted in an environmentally controlled state-of-the-art facility. All shellfish come from government-certified beds and are tested in an in-house microbiology laboratory for wholesomeness and purity. Special lobster storage tanks hold all lobsters under optimum conditions, in clean, pollution-free water. Every seafood item is inspected for quality eight separate times before it reaches the table.

    At Legal Sea Foods' restaurants, each meal is cooked to order. Although servers make every effort to deliver all meals within minutes of each other, they will not jeopardize the quality of an item by holding it beneath a heat lamp until the entire order is ready. The service staff is trained to work as a team for better service. More than one service person frequently delivers food to a table. When any item is ready, the closest available person serves it. Customer questions can be directed to any employee, not just the person who took the initial order.

a. What are the major processes performed by Legal Sea Foods? How does the process design support its goal of serving only the freshest, highest-quality seafood?
b. Where would Legal Sea Foods fall on the three-dimensional classification of service organizations? Is its process design consistent with this classification?

11. The president of Circle H has assigned you to perform a complete investigation to determine the causes of certain quality problems and to recommend appropriate corrective action. You have authority to talk to any other person within the company.

    The early stages of your investigation establish that the three reasons most often cited by customers are symptomatic of some major quality problems in the company's operations. In proceeding with the audit, you decide to review all available data, which may yield indications of the root causes of these problems.

    Further investigation reveals that, over a recent four-month period, a procedural change was made in the order approval process. You wish to find out whether this change caused a significant difference in the amount of time required to process an order from field sales through shipping. You therefore decide to investigate this particular situation.

    On completion of your investigation into the problems with order processing, you determine that the change in procedures for order approval has led to an increase in the amount of time required to restock goods in the customers' stores. You want to recommend corrective action for this problem, but you first do additional investigation as to why the change was made. You learn that, because of large losses on delinquent accounts receivable, the change was made to require that the credit manager approve all restock orders. This requirement added an average of three hours to the amount of internal processing time needed for a restock order.

    On review of your report, the president of Circle H takes note of administrative problems whose existence he had never suspected. To assure that corrective action will be effective and sustained, the president assigns you to take charge of the corrective action program.[70]

    a. What types of data would be most useful to review for clues as to why the three major customer complaints occurred?
    b. How would you investigate whether the change in the order approval process had a significant effect on order processing time?
    c. Given your knowledge of problems in both order processing and accounts receivable, what should you do?

12. Compare and contrast the process management categories in the 2000 and 2001 Baldrige business criteria (available on the CD-rom). What are the key differences and implications for managers who use the criteria?

Projects, Etc.

1. Identify some of the major processes a student encounters in a college or university. What types of noneducational institutions perform similar processes and might be candidates for benchmarking?
2. Write down *your* process for preparing for an exam. How could this process be improved to make it shorter and/or more effective? Compare your process to those of your classmates? How might you collectively develop an improved process?
3. Interview a plant manager at a local factory to determine his or her philosophy on meeting specifications. Is the manager familiar with the Taguchi loss function? Does he or she buy into the concept?
4. Investigate design-for-environment practices in some of your local industries. Describe company policies and the methods and techniques that they use to address environmental concerns in product design.
5. Design a process for
   a. Preparing for a job interview
   b. Writing a term paper
   c. Planning a vacation
   d. Making breakfast for your family
   e. Washing your car

   Draw a flowchart for each process and discuss how ways in which both quality and cycle time might be improved.
6. Using whatever "market research" techniques are appropriate, define a set of customer attributes for
   a. Purchasing books at your college bookstore
   b. A college registration process
   c. A hotel room used for business
   d. A hotel room used for family leisure vacations

   For each case, determine a set of technical requirements, and construct the relationship matrix for the House of Quality.
7. *(This exercise would best be performed in a group.)* Suppose that you were developing a small pizza restaurant with a dining area and local delivery. Develop a list of customer requirements and technical requirements and try to complete a House of Quality. What service standards might such an operation have?
8. Most children (and many adults) like to assemble and fly balsa-wood gliders. From your own experiences or from interviews with other students, define a set of customer requirements for a good glider. (Even better, buy one and test it to determine these requirements yourself.) If you were to design and manufacture such a product, how would you define a set of technical requirements for the design? Using your results, construct a relationship matrix for a House of Quality.
9. Fill in the following House of Quality relationship matrix for a screwdriver. By sampling your classmates, develop priorities for the customer attributes and use these and the relationships to identify key technical requirements to deploy.

	Price	Interchangeable bits	Steel shaft	Rubber grip	Ratchet capability	Plastic handle
Easy to use						
Does not rust						
Durable						
Comfortable						
Versatile						
Inexpensive						
Priority						

PROBLEMS

1. A specification for the length of an auto part is 5.0 ± 0.025 centimeters (cm). It costs $15 to scrap a part that is outside the specifications. Determine the Taguchi loss function for this situation.
2. A blueprint specification for the thickness of a dishwasher part is 0.300 ± 0.022 centimeters (cm). It costs $3 to scrap a part that is outside the specifications. Determine the Taguchi loss function for this situation.
3. A team was formed to study the auto part described in Problem 1. While continuing to work to find the root cause of scrap, the team found a way to reduce the scrap cost to $10 per part.
   a. Determine the Taguchi loss function for this situation.
   b. If the process deviation from target can be held at 0.020 cm, what is the Taguchi loss?
4. A team was formed to study the dishwasher part described in Problem 2. While continuing to work to find the root cause of scrap, they found a way to reduce the scrap cost to $2 per part.
   a. Determine the Taguchi loss function for this situation.
   b. If the process deviation from target can be held at 0.018 cm, what is the Taguchi loss?
5. Ruido Unlimited makes electronic soundboards for car stereos. Output voltage to a certain component on the board must be 10 + 0.0 / – 0.2 volts. Any value on the high side is unacceptable, because it will destroy the board. Exceeding the limits results in an estimated loss of $50. Determine the Taguchi loss function.

6. An electronic component has a specification of 150 ± 5 ohms. Scrapping the component results in a $100 loss.
   a. What is the value of k in the Taguchi loss function?
   b. If the process is centered on the target specification with a standard deviation of 2 ohms, what is the expected loss per unit?
7. An automatic cookie machine must deposit a specified amount of 30 ± 0.3 grams (g) of dough for each cookie on a conveyor belt. If the machine either over- or underdeposits the mixture, it costs $0.04 to scrap the defective cookie.
   a. What is the value of k in the Taguchi loss function?
   b. If the process is centered on the target specification with a standard deviation of 0.1 g, what is the expected loss per unit?
8. A computer chip is designed so that the distance between two adjacent pins has a specification of 2.000 ± 0.002 millimeters (mm). The loss due to a defective chip is $4. A sample of 25 chips was drawn from the production process resulting in the following measurements.

2.001	2.000	2.001	1.998	1.999
2.000	2.000	2.002	1.999	2.000
1.998	1.999	2.001	2.000	2.000
2.000	1.999	2.001	2.001	2.000
2.000	2.002	2.000	2.000	2.001

   a. Compute the value of k in the Taguchi loss function.
   b. What is the expected loss from this process based on the sample data?
9. The average time to handle a call in a call processing center has a specification of 6 ± 1.5 minutes. The loss due to a mishandled call is $10. A sample of 25 calls was drawn from the process and the results, in minutes, follow.

6.5	6.0	6.5	5.0	5.5
7.3	6.6	6.2	4.3	6.7
5.5	4.8	7.2	6.9	6.4
5.1	5.6	7.4	6.1	6.3
5.9	7.1	4.6	4.7	6.2

   a. Compute the value of k in the Taguchi loss function.
   b. What is the expected loss from this process based on the sample data?
10. In the production of transformers, any output voltage that exceeds (25 volts is unacceptable to the customer. Exceeding these limits results in an estimated loss of $400. However, the manufacturer can adjust the voltage in the plant by changing a resistor that costs $1.50.
   a. Determine the Taguchi loss function.
   b. Suppose the nominal specification is 120 volts. At what tolerance should the transformer be manufactured?
11. In the transformer business mentioned in Problem 10, managers gathered data from a customer focus group and found that any output voltage that exceeds 20 volts was unacceptable to the customer. Exceeding these limits results in an estimated loss of $450. However, the manufacturer can still adjust the voltage in the plant by changing a resistor that costs $1.50.
   a. Determine the Taguchi loss function.
   b. Suppose the nominal specification remains at 120 volts. At what tolerance should the transformer be manufactured?
12. Two processes, P and Q, are used by a supplier to produce the same component, Z, which is a critical part in the engine of a new airplane. The specifica-

tion for Z calls for a dimension of 0.24 mm (0.03. The probabilities of achieving the dimensions for each process based on their inherent variability are shown in the following table.

Dimension Value (mm) – x	Process P Probability	Process Q Probability
0.20		0.02
0.21	0.14	0.03
0.22	0.14	0.15
0.23	0.14	0.15
0.24	0.16	0.30
0.25	0.14	0.15
0.26	0.14	0.15
0.27	0.14	0.03
0.28		0.02

If $k = 100{,}000$, what is the expected loss for each process? Which would be the best process to use, based on minimizing the expected loss?

13. The *Hillsdale Observer*, a small-town newspaper in Hillsdale, Ohio, recently hired a quality consultant to conduct a study of the six mortgage lending institutions in town. The *Observer* then published it in the business section of the paper. Data from the study are listed in Table 7.7. A sample of customers who had obtained mortgages from each of the institutions was surveyed. Each person in the customer sample was asked to rate the importance of various quality factors that influenced the decision to get their mortgage loan from a particular institution. Weighting factors were calculated and appear

Table 7.7 Hillsdale Mortgage Institutions Comparative Data

	Lending Institutions					
Customer Service Factors	**National Mortgage**	**Sunset FSB**	**Local Bankcorp**	**Investor's Trust**	**Cities' Service FSB**	**Dewey, Cheatham Lenders**
1. Competitive rates (1.10)	10	9	6	7	8	5
2. Accurate processing (1.05)	9	7	8	9	7	4
3. Timely completion (1.01)	8	6	7	7	8	7
4. Single point of contact* (0.95)	5	5	6	5	6	9
5. Courteous, knowledgeable personnel (0.89)	9	8	8	8	7	3
Total (weighted)	8.26	7.04	6.98	6.80	7.23	5.24

*Based on number of institutional representatives that customers had to deal with.

in parentheses in the left column of the table. Another survey was then taken involving area realtors, who typically worked with all of the mortgage institutions. Realtors were asked to rate each institution on each of the "customer" dimensions, using a scale of 0 to 10. The ratings (rounded) on each dimension are shown in the body of the table for the six institutions.

a. What information contained in the survey data applies to the quality function deployment process?
b. Develop a House of Quality matrix using this information. What further information is needed?
c. How could this information be used to develop a competing mortgage loan service?

14. Bob's Big Burgers has conducted consumer surveys and focus groups and has identified the most important customer expectations as
    - Healthy food
    - Speedy service
    - Easy-to-read menu board
    - Accurate order filling
    - Perceived value

    Develop a set of technical requirements to incorporate into the design of a new facility and a House of Quality relationship matrix to assess how well your requirements address these expectations. Refine your design as necessary, based upon the initial assessment.
15. Bob's Big Burgers (Problem 14) has acquired some additional information. It found that consumers placed the highest importance on healthy food, followed by value, followed by order accuracy and service. The menu board was only casually noted as an important attribute in the surveys. Bob faces three major competitors in this market: Grabby's, Queenburger, and Sandy's. Studies of their products have yielded the information shown in Table 7.8. Results of the consumer panel ratings for each of these competitors are shown in Table 7.9 (a scale of 1 to 5 with 5 being the best). Using this information, modify and extend your House of Quality from Problem 14 and de-

Table 7.8 Competitors' Product Information

Company	Price	Size (oz.)	Calories	Sodium (mg)	Fat (%)
Grabby's	1.55	5.5	440	75	13
Queenburger	2.25	7.5	640	95	23
Sandy's	1.75	6.0	540	80	16

Table 7.9 Consumer Panel Ratings

Attribute	Grabby's	Queenburger	Sandy's
Menu board	4	4	5
Order accuracy	4	5	3
Healthy food	4	2	3
Speedy service	3	5	4
Taste appeal	2	4	3
Visual appeal	3	4	3
Value	5	3	4

velop a deployment plan for a new burger. On what attributes should the company focus its marketing efforts?

16. Fingerspring, Inc., is working on a design for a new personal digital assistant (PDA). Marketing staff members have conducted extensive surveys and focus groups with potential customers to determine the characteristics that the customers want and expect in a PDA. Fingerspring's studies have identified the most important customer expectations as
    - Initial cost
    - Reliability
    - Ease of use
    - Features
    - Operating cost
    - Compactness

    Develop a set of technical requirements to incorporate into a House of Quality relationship matrix to assess how well your requirements address these expectations. Refine your design as necessary, based upon the initial assessment.
17. Fingerspring, Inc., (Problem 16), faces three major competitors in this market: Harespring, Springbok, and Greenspring. It found that potential consumers placed the highest importance on reliability (measured by such things as freedom from operating system crashes and battery life), followed by compactness (weight/bulkiness), followed by flexibility (features, ease of use, and types of program modules available). The operating cost was only occasionally noted as an important attribute in the surveys. Studies of their products have yielded the information shown in Table 7.10. Results of the consumer panel ratings for these competitors are shown in Table 7.11 on a scale of 1 to 5 with 5 being the best.

Table 7.10 Competitors' Product Information

Company	Price	Wt. (oz.)	Size (In.)	Features	Operating Program	Battery life (hrs)	Opr. Cpsts (Batt./Prg/)
Harespring	575	4.0	4.8 x 3.2	15	Win CE®	50	High
Springbok	195	7.5	5.1 x 3.3	9	Hardmark*	12	Low
Greenspring	450	8.8	5.3 x 3.3	12	Easyware**	25	Moderately high

Note: Win CE® is one of the most recognized operating software programs for PDAs.
*New unproven software, unique to Springbok
**Well-received proprietary software, used on many PDAs for several years

Table 7.11 Consumer Panel Ratings

Attribute	Harespring	Springbok	Greenspring
Initial cost	3	5	4
Reliability	5	2	3
Ease of use	4	1	3
Features	4	2	3
Operating cost	5	3	4
Weight	5	3	3
Size	4	4	4

Using this information, modify and extend your House of Quality from Problem 18 and develop a deployment plan for a new PDA. On what attributes should the company focus its marketing efforts?

CASES

I. THE STATE UNIVERSITY EXPERIENCE

Wow! That State University video was really cool. It has lots of majors; it's close to home so I can keep my job; and Mom and Dad loved it when they visited. I wish I could know what it's really like to be a student at State. Hmmm, I think I'll ask Mom and Dad to take a campus tour with me. . . .

I'm sure that we took our tour on the hottest day of the summer. The campus is huge—it took us about two hours to complete the tour and we didn't even see everything! I wasn't sure that the tour guide knew what he was doing. We went into a gigantic lecture hall and the lights weren't even on. Our tour guide couldn't find them so we had to hold the doors open so the sunlight could come in. About three-fourths of the way through the tour, our guide said, "State University isn't really a bad place to go to school; you just have to learn the system." I wonder what he meant by that? . . .

This application is really confusing. How do I let the admissions office know that I am interested in physics, mechanical engineering, and industrial design? Even my parents can't figure it out. I guess I'll call the admissions office for some help. . . .

I'm so excited! Mom just handed me a letter from State! Maybe they've already accepted me. What? What's this? They say I need to send my transcript. I did that when I mailed in my application two weeks ago. What's going on? I hope it won't affect my application. I'd better check with Admissions. . . .

You can't find my file? I thought you were only missing my transcript. I asked my counselor if she had sent it in yet. She told me that she sent it last week. Oh, you'll call me back when you locate my file? O.K. . . .

Finally, I've been accepted! Wait a minute. I didn't apply to University College; that's a two-year program. I wanted physics, M.E., or industrial design. Well, since my only choice is U. College and I really want to go to State, I guess I'll send in the confirmation form. It really looks a lot like the application. In fact, I know I gave them a lot of the same information. I wonder why they need it again? Seems like a waste of time. . . .

Orientation was a lot of fun. I'm glad they straightened out my acceptance at U. College. I think I will enjoy State after all. I met lots of other students. I saw my advisor and I signed up for classes. All I have left to do is pay my tuition bill. Whoops. None of my financial aid is on this bill. I know I filled out all of the forms because I got an award letter from State. There is no way my parents and I can pay for this without financial aid. It says at the bottom, I'll lose all of my classes if I don't pay the bill on time. . . .

I'm not confirmed on the computer? I sent in my form and the fee a long time ago. What am I going to do? I don't want to lose all of my classes. I have to go to the admissions office or my college office and get a letter that says I am a confirmed student. O.K. If I do that tomorrow, will I still have all of my classes? . . .

I can't sleep; I'm so nervous about my first day. . . .

Discussion Questions

1. What breakdowns in service processes has this student experienced?
2. What types of process management activities should State University administrators undertake?

II. A CASE OF FAILURE IN PRODUCT DEVELOPMENT[71]

In 1981 market share and profits in General Electric's appliance division were falling. The company's technology was antiquated compared to that of foreign competitors. For example, making a refrigerator compressor required 65 minutes of labor in comparison with just 25 minutes by competitors in Japan and Italy. Moreover, their labor costs were lower. The alternatives were obvious: Either purchase compressors from Japan or Italy or design and build a better model. By 1983 the decision to build a new rotary compressor in-house was made, along with a commitment for a new $120 million factory. GE was not a novice in rotary compressor technology; they had invented it and had been using it in air conditioners for many years. A rotary compressor weighed less, had one-third fewer parts, and was more energy-efficient than the current reciprocating compressors. Also, it took up less space, thus providing more room inside the refrigerators and therefore helped meet customer requirements better.

However, some engineers had argued against the change. Rotary compressors run hotter. In most air conditioners, this is not a problem since the coolant cools the compressor. In a refrigerator, the coolant flows only one-tenth as fast, and the unit runs about four times longer in one year than in an air conditioner. GE had problems with the early rotary compressors in air conditioners. Although the bugs had been eliminated in smaller units, GE quit using rotaries in larger units after frequent breakdowns in hot climates.

GE managers and design engineers were concerned about other issues. Rotary compressors make a high-pitched whine, and managers were afraid that this would adversely affect consumer acceptance. Many hours were spent by managers and consumer test panels on this issue. The new design also required key parts to work together with a tolerance of only 50 millionths of an inch. Nothing had been mass produced with such precision before, but manufacturing engineers felt sure that they could do it.

The compressor they finally designed was nearly identical to that used in air conditioners, with one change. Two small parts inside the compressor were made out of powdered metal, rather than the hardened steel and cast iron used in air conditioners. This material was chosen because it could be machined to much closer tolerances and reduced machining costs. It was tried a decade earlier on air conditioners and did not work. This fact was told to the design engineers who were new to designing compressors, and they did not pay attention.

A consultant suggested that GE consider a joint venture with a Japanese company who had a rotary refrigerator compressor already on the market. This idea was rejected by management. The original designer of the air conditioning rotary compressor, who had left GE, had offered his services as a consultant. GE declined this offer, writing to him that they had sufficient technical expertise.

About 600 compressors were tested in 1983 without a single failure. They were run continuously for two months under elevated temperatures and pressures that were supposed to simulate five years of operation. GE normally conducts extensive field testing of new products; their original plan to test models in the field for two years was reduced to nine months to meet time pressures to complete the project.

After testing, the technician who disassembled and inspect the parts thought they did not look right. Parts of the motor were discolored, a sign of excessive heat. Bearings were worn, and it appeared that high heat was breaking down the lubricating oil. The technician's supervisors discounted these findings and did not relay them to upper levels of management. Another consultant who evaluated the test results believed that something was wrong because only one failure was found in two years, and he recommended that test conditions be intensified. This advice too was rejected by management.

By 1986, only 2.5 years after board approval, the new factory was producing compressors at a rate of 10 per minute. By the end of the year, more than 1 million had been produced. Market share rose and the new refrigerator appeared to be a success. In July 1987 the first compressor failed. Soon after, reports of other failures in Puerto Rico arrived. By September, the appliance division knew it had a major problem. By December, the plant stopped making the compressor. It was not until 1988 that the problem was diagnosed as excessive wear in the two powdered-metal parts that burned up the oil. The cost in 1989 alone was $450 million. By mid-1990 GE had voluntarily replaced nearly 1.1 million compressors with new ones purchased from six suppliers, five of them foreign.

Discussion Questions

1. What factors in the product development process caused this disaster? Which individuals were responsible?
2. Discuss how techniques of quality engineering might have improved the product development process for the compressor.
3. What lessons did GE probably learn for the future?

III. Collin Technologies: Support Processes

Read Item 6.2, *Support Processes*, in the Collin Technologies case study on the CD-rom accompanying this book. Using the 2000 Baldrige Criteria, develop a list of strengths and opportunities for improvement similar to the style in Example 4. Strengths should focus on things the company is doing exceptionally well and support their vision and strategy. (Read the business overview section of the case first to identify specific factors that are important to this item.) Opportunities for improvement should highlight issues in its approach or deployment that can better meet the requirements of the Baldrige criteria. Your comments should include a reason for why a strength or opportunity for improvement is important; that is, provide some insight to upper-level managers that they might not have otherwise realized. Use the wording in the scoring guidelines in Table 3.6 to help you structure your comments.

IV. Collin Technologies: Supplier and Partnering Processes

Read Item 6.3, *Supplier and Partnering Processes*, in the Collin Technologies case study on the CD-rom accompanying this book. Using the 2000 Baldrige Criteria, develop a list of strengths and opportunities for improvement similar to the style in Example 4, following the guidelines suggested in Case III.

NOTES

1. Adapted from Katrina Brooker, "The Nightmare Before Christmas," *Fortune*, January 24, 2000. 24–25.
2. Robert Hof, Debra Sparks, Ellen Neuborne, and Wendy Zellner, "Can Amazon Make It?" *Business Week*, July 10, 2000, 38–43.
3. A. Blanton Godfrey, "Planned Failures," *Quality Digest*, March 2000, 16.
4. AT&T Quality Steering Committee, *Process Quality Management & Improvement Guidelines*, AT&T Publication Center, AT&T Bell Laboratories (1987).
5. Michael Hammer and James Champy, *Reengineering the Corporation* (New York: HarperBusiness, 1993), 177–178.
6. Steven H. Wildstrom, "Price Wars Power Up Quality," *Business Week*, September 18, 1995, 26.
7. Philip A. Himmelfarb, "Fast New-Product Development at Service Sector Companies," *Quality Digest*, April 1996, 41–44.
8. Justin Martin, "Ignore Your Customer," *Fortune*, May 1, 1995, 121–126.
9. Wolfgang Schneider, "Test Drive Into the Future," *BMW Magazine* 2 (1997), 74–77.
10. Peter J. Kolesar, "What Deming Told the Japanese in 1950," *Quality Management Journal* 2, no. 1 (Fall 1994), 9–24.
11. Ames Rubber Corporation, Application Summary for the 1993 Malcolm Baldrige National Quality Award.
12. Jennifer Reese, "Starbucks: Inside the Coffee Cult,"*Fortune*, December 9, 1996, 190–200.
13. Susan Dillingham, "A Little Gross Stuff in Food Is OK by FDA," *Insight*, May 22, 1989, 25.
14. Alan Vonderhaar, "Audi's TT Coupe's Ever So Close," *Cincinnati Enquirer*, November 27, 1999, F1, F2.
15. Adapted from Douglas Daetz, "The Effect of Product Design on Product Quality and Product Cost," *Quality Progress*, June 1987, 63–67. Copyright © 1987, Hewlett-Packard Co. All rights reserved. Reprinted with permission.
16. Carolyn Lochhead, "Liability's Creative Clamp Holds Firms to the Status Quo," *Insight*, August 29, 1988, 38–40.
17. John H. Farrow, "Product Liability Requirements," *Quality Progress*, May 1980, 34–36; Mick Birmingham, "Product Liability: An Issue for Quality," *Quality*, February 1983, 41–42.
18. Randall Goodden, "Quality and Product Liability," *Quality Digest*, October 1995, 35–41.
19. Peter Dewhurst, "Product Design for Manufacture: Design for Disassembly," *Industrial Engineering*, September 1993, 26–28.
20. David Pescovitz, "Dumping Old Computers—Please Dispose of Properly" *Scientific American* 282, no. 2 (February 2000), 29; *http://www.sciam.com/2000/0200issue/0200techbus2.html.*
21. Early discussions of this topic can be found in Bruce Nussbaum and John Templeton, "Built to

Last—Until It's Time to Take It Apart," *Business Week*, September 17, 1990, 102–106. A more recent reference is Michael Lenox, Andrew King, and John Ehrenfeld, "An Assessment of Design-for-Environment Practices in Leading U.S. Electronics Firms," *Interfaces* 30, no. 3, May/June 2000, 83–94.

22. Nussbaum and Templeton, see note 21.

23. Valerie Reitman and Robert L. Simison, "Japanese Car Makers Speed Up Car Making," *Wall Street Journal*, December 29, 1995, 17.

24. Don Clausing and Bruce H. Simpson, "Quality by Design," *Quality Progress*, January 1990, 41–44.

25. For the fascinating story of how Chrysler redesigned itself, along with their design process, see Brock Yates, *The Critical Path* (Boston: Little, Brown and Co., 1996).

26. "A Smarter Way to Manufacture," *Business Week*, April 30, 1990.

27. L. P. Sullivan, "Quality Function Deployment: The Latent Potential of Phases III and IV," in *A TQM Approach to Achieving Manufacturing Excellence*, A. Richard Shores, ed. (Milwaukee, WI: ASQC Quality Press, 1990), 265–279.

28. Kelly Scott, "How Federal Express Delivers Customer Service," *APICS—The Performance Advantage*, November 1999, 44–46.

29. Rebecca Duray and Glenn W. Milligan, "Improving Customers Satisfaction Through Mass Customization, *Quality Progress*, August 1999, 60–66.

30. AT&T Quality Steering Committee, *Reengineering Handbook*, AT&T Bell Laboratories (1991), 45.

31. Paula K. Martin and Karen Tate, "Projects That Get Quality Treatment," *Journal for Quality and Participation*, November/December 1998, 58–61.

32. Custom Research Incorporated, "Highlights of CRI's Best Practices," 1996 Baldrige Application Abstract, 13–14.

33. Sarah Anne Wright, "Putting Fast-Food to the Test," *Cincinnati Enquirer*, July 9, 2000, F1, 2.

34. John Haywood-Farmer, "A Conceptual Model of Service Quality," *International Journal of Operations and Production Management* 8, no. 6 (1988), 19–29.

35. Charles D. Zimmerman, III, and John W. Enell, "Service Industries," Sec. 33 in *Juran's Quality Control Handbook*, 4th ed., J. M. Juran, ed. (New York: McGraw-Hill, 1988).

36. Walter A. Shewhart, *Economic Control of Quality of Manufactured Product* (New York: Van Nostrand, 1931).

37. Justin Martin, "Are You as Good as You Think You Are?" *Fortune*, September 30, 1996, 142–152.

38. Valerie Reitman, "Toyota's Fast Rebound After Fire at Supplier Shows Why It's Tough," *Wall Street Journal*, May 8, 1997, 1.

39. Ursula Miller, "Baldwin Finds New Supplier," *Cincinnati Enquirer*, February 9, 1999, B10.

40. Larry Kishpaugh, "Process Management and Business Results," presentation at the 1996 Regional Malcolm Baldrige Award Conference, Boston, Massachusetts.

41. Texas Instruments Defense Systems & Electronics Group, Malcolm Baldrige Application Summary (1992).

42. Hokey Min, "A World-Class Continuous Quality Improvement Program: The Fastener Supply Corporation Case," *Production and Inventory Management Journal*, Fourth Quarter 1998, 10–14.

43. Elizabeth Baatz, "Are Supplier Awards Really Worth It?" *Purchasing Magazine*, 1998, 58. Cahners Business Information, a division of Reed Elsevier Inc.

44. Richard A. Maass, "Supplier Certification—A Positive Response to Just-in-Time," *Quality Progress* 21, no. 9 (September 1988), 75–80.

45. John J. Hudiburg, *Winning With Quality: The FPL Story* (White Plains, NY: Quality Resources, 1991).

46. Mike Lovitt, "Responsive Suppliers Are Smart Suppliers," *Quality Progress* (June 1989), 50–53.

47. M. L. Dertouzos, R. K. Lester, R. M. Solow, and the MIT Commission on Industrial Productivity, *Made in America* (Cambridge, MA: MIT Press, 1989), 74.

48. Andrew E. Serwer, "Michael Dell Turns the PC World Inside Out," *Fortune*, September 8, 1997, 76–86.

49. Bill Gates with Collins Hemingway. *Business @ the Speed of Thought* (New York: Warner Books, 1999).

50. Dean M. Schroeder and Alan G. Robinson, "America's Most Successful Export to Japan: Continuous Improvement Programs," *Sloan Management Review* 32, no. 2 (Spring 1991), 67–81.

51. Masaaki Imai, *KAIZEN—The Key to Japan's Competitive Success* (New York: McGraw-Hill, 1986).

52. Alan Robinson, ed., *Continuous Improvement in Operations* (Cambridge, MA: Productivity Press, 1991).

53. Lea A. P. Tonkin, "Kaizen Blitz: Bottleneck-Bashing Comes to Rochester, New York," *Target* 12, no. 4 (September/October 1996), 41–43.

54. Mark Oakeson, "Makes Dollars & Sense for Mercedes-Benz in Brazil," *IIE Solutions* (April 1997), 32–35.

55. David A. McCamey, Robert W. Bogs, and Linda M. Bayuk, "More, Better, Faster From Total Quality Effort," *Quality Progress*, August 1999, 43–50.

56. Lawrence S. Pryor, "Benchmarking: A Self-Improvement Strategy," *Journal of Business Strategy*, November/December 1989, 28–32.

57. Robert C. Camp, *Benchmarking: The Search for Industry Best Practices That Lead to Superior Performance* (Milwaukee, WI: ASQC Quality Press and UNIPUB/Quality Resources, 1989).

58. Shawn Tully, "Why to Go for Stretch Targets," *Fortune*, November 14, 1994, 45–58.

59. Christopher E. Bogan and Michael J. English, "Benchmarking for Best Practices: Winning Through Innovative Adaptation," *Quality Digest*, August 1994, 52–62.

60. John Hackl, "New Beginnings: Change Is Here to Stay," editorial comment, *Quality Progress*, February 1998, 5.

61. AT&T Consumer Communication Services Summary of 1994 Application for the Malcolm Baldrige National Quality Award.

62. Robert C. Camp, see note 57.

63. Hammer and Champy, see note 5.

64. P. Kay Coleman, "Reengineering Pepsi's Road to the 'Right Side Up' Company," *Insights Quarterly* 5, no. 3 (Winter 1993), 18–35.

65. Bogan and English, see note 59.

66. Gerhard Plenert, "Process Re-Engineering: The Latest Fad Toward Failure," *APICS—The Performance Advantage* 4, no. 6 (June 1994), 22–24.

67. Adapted from R. Nat Natarajan, Ralph E. Martz, and Kyosuke Kurosaka, "Applying QFD To Internal Service System Design," *Quality Progress*, February 1999, 65–70. © 1999. American Society for Quality. Reprinted with permission.

68. We wish to thank Andy Assaley, Scott Atkinson, Frank Cornell, and Eugene Wulsin for their work on which this case is based. Courtesy Gold Star Chili, Inc.

69. James R. Evans and James W. Dean, Jr., *Total Quality: Management, Organization, and Strategy*, 2d ed. (Cincinnati, OH: South-Western, 2000).

70. Adapted from ASQ Quality Auditor Certification Brochure (July 1989).

71. Thomas F. O'Boyle, "GE Refrigerator Woes Illustrate the Hazards in Changing a Product." Reprinted by permission of *The Wall Street Journal*, May 7, 1990, A1, A6. © 1990 Dow-Jones & Company, Inc. All Rights Reserved Worldwide.

BIBLIOGRAPHY

Ahmed, Pervaiz K., and Mohammed Rafiq. "Integrated Benchmarking: A Holistic Examination of Select Techniques for Benchmarking Analysis." *Benchmarking for Quality Management & Technology* 5, 3 (1998), 225–242.

AT&T Quality Steering Committee. *Batting 1000*. AT&T Bell Laboratories, 1992.

———. *Process Quality Management & Improvement Guidelines*. AT&T Bell Laboratories, 1987.

Box, G. E. P., and S. Bisgaard. "The Scientific Context of Quality Improvement." *Quality Progress* 20, no. 6 (June 1987), 54–61.

Brassard, Michael. *The Memory Jogger Plus+*. Methuen, MA: GOAL/QPC, 1989.

Burke, Charles J. "10 Steps to Best-Practices Benchmarking," *Quality Digest* (February 1996), 23–28.

"Chrysler Is Told to Pay $262.5 Million by Jurors in Minivan-Accident Trial," *Wall Street Journal*, October 9, 1997, A-3, A-4.

Cross, Kelvin, John Feather, and Richard Lynch. "TQM vs. Reengineering? There Should Be No Argument." *Quality Digest* (May 1994), 53–54.

DeToro, Irving, and Thomas McCabe. "How to Stay Flexible and Elude Fads." *Quality Progress* (March 1997), 55–60.

Donnell, Augustus, and Margaret Dellinger. *Analyzing Business Process Data: The Looking Glass*. AT&T Bell Laboratories, 1990.

Freeman, N. B. "Quality on the Mend." *American Machinist and Automated Manufacturing*, April 1986, 102–112.

Gitlow, H., S. Gitlow, A. Oppenheim, and R. Oppenheim. *Tools and Methods for the Improvement of Quality*. Homewood, IL: Irwin, 1989.

Godfrey, Blan, "Future Trends: Expansion of Quality Management Concepts, Methods and Tools to All Industries." *Quality Observer* 6, no. 9 (September 1997), 40–43, 46.

Hradesky, John L. *Productivity and Quality Improvement*. New York: McGraw-Hill, 1988.

Hurley, Heather, "Cycle-Time Reduction: Your Key to a Better Bottom Line." *Quality Digest*, April 1996, 28–32.

Melan, E. H. "Process Management in Service and Administrative Operations." *Quality Progress* 18, no. 6 (June 1985), 52–59.

Melan, Eugene H. *Process Management, A Systems Approach to Total Quality*. Portland, OR: Productivity Press, 1995.

Mizuno, Shigeru. *Management for Quality Improvement: The 7 New QC Tools*. Cambridge MA: Productivity Press, 1988.

Rosenfeld, Manny, "Only the Questions That Are Asked Can Be Answered." *Quality Progress*, April 1994, 71–73.

Sherman, Strat, "Stretch Goals: The Dark Side of Asking for Miracles." *Fortune*, November 13, 1995, 231–232.

Performance Measurement and Strategic Information Management

Outline

Robert Kaplan and David Norton pose the following scenario:[1]

> *Imagine entering the cockpit of a modern jet airplane and seeing only a single instrument there. How would you feel about boarding the plane after the following conversation with the pilot?*
>
> ***Q:** I'm surprised to see you operating the plane with only a single instrument. What does it measure?*
>
> ***A:** Airspeed. I'm really working on airspeed this flight.*
>
> ***Q:** That's good. Airspeed certainly seems important. But what about altitude? Wouldn't an altimeter be helpful?*
>
> ***A:** I worked on altitude for the last few flights and I've gotten pretty good on it. Now I have to concentrate on proper air speed.*
>
> ***Q:** But I notice you don't even have a fuel gauge. Wouldn't that be useful?*
>
> ***A:** You're right; fuel is significant, but I can't concentrate on doing too many things well at the same time. So on this flight I'm focusing on air speed. Once I get to be excellent at air speed, as well as altitude, I intend to concentrate on fuel consumption on the next set of flights.*

Clearly, you would be a bit uneasy about taking this flight. However, the analogy with business is not that far-fetched. Many companies still manage their organizations by primarily concentrating on financial measures. To make decisions that further the overall organizational goals of meeting, or exceeding, customer expectations and making productive use of limited resources, companies need good data about customers and markets, financial performance, human resource effectiveness, supplier performance, product and service quality, and other key factors. A supply of consistent, accurate, and timely information across all functional areas of business provides real-time information for the evaluation, control, and improvement of processes, products, and services to meet both business objectives and rapidly changing customer needs. "In God we trust; all others use data" is a phrase one often hears.

Information is derived from the analysis of data. Data, in turn, come from measurement. **Measurement** is the act of quantifying the performance dimensions of products, services, processes, and other business activities. **Measures** and **indicators** refer to the numerical information that results from measurement. For example, the presence or absence of surface defects for a brass sink fixture might be assessed by visual inspection. A useful measure of quality might be the percentage of fixtures that have surface defects. As another example, the diameter of machined ball bearings might be measured by a micrometer. Statistics such as the mean diameter and standard deviation provide information to evaluate the ability of the production process to meet specifications. For services, examples of measurements would be the percentage of orders filled accurately and the time taken to fill a customer's order. The term *indicator* is often used for measurements that are not a direct or exclusive measure of performance. For instance, you cannot directly measure dissatisfaction, but you can use the number of complaints or lost customers as indicators of dissatisfaction. Measurements and indicators provide a scorecard of business performance that can be used at all levels of the organization.

Good information allows managers to make decisions on the basis of facts, not opinions. When Dr. Noriaki Kano consulted with Florida Power and Light (FPL), the company told him that lightning was the principal cause of service interruptions. Kano asked why groundings or arresters had not prevented the interruptions; FPL replied that these would not work with Florida's severe lightning. Kano asked for the data to back up this conclusion, but FPL could not produce any. About 18 months later, when Kano next visited the company, they had collected data and found that interruptions occurred even when strong lightning was not present. In addition, they discovered that many utility poles did not have sufficient groundings, a situation they had not recognized until they collected the data.[2]

However, having too much data can be as bad as not having any. It is important to gather the right information. When Ford studied Mazda's management approaches, former CEO Donald Peterson observed, "Perhaps, most important, Mazda had been able to identify the types of information and records that were truly useful. It didn't bother with any other data. [At Ford] we were burdened with mountains of useless data and stifled by far too many levels of control over them."[3]

Although Deming believed in using data as a basis for problem solving, he was highly critical of overemphasizing measurement. He often stated that the most important figures, such as the value of a loyal customer, are unknown and unknowable. Although this statement is certainly true, considerable value lies in using objective data for planning and decision making. Osborne and Gaebler make three insightful observations:

1. If you don't measure results, you can't tell success from failure.
2. If you can't see success, you can't reward it—and if you can't reward success, you are probably rewarding failure.
3. If you can't recognize failure, you can't correct it.[4]

Despite the fact that more than half of the workforce in the United States is engaged in the generation, processing, or dissemination of data and/or information, many companies do a poor job of systematically collecting appropriate data, getting it to the right people, and analyzing it properly. Bill Gates, for example, notes that middle mangers need as much business data as top managers, but often have no way to get it. He also says that that face-to-face meetings devoted to status updates are a symptom of poor information flow, because that type of information could be handled much more effectively using electronic transfer of data and e-mail.[5] Dealing with data and information should be addressed from a process perspective, and TQ concepts can be applied to the generation, analysis, and use of data and information. This chapter introduces basic concepts of performance measurement and strategic information management.

THE STRATEGIC VALUE OF INFORMATION

Organizations need performance measures for three reasons:

1. To lead the entire organization in a particular direction; that is, to drive strategies and organizational change.
2. To manage the resources needed to travel in this direction by evaluating the effectiveness of action plans.
3. To operate the processes that make the organization work and continuously improve.[6]

Many managers and quality professionals view measurement activities only in terms of outputs from the production system. This interpretation is a mistake because a broad base of measurements, tied together by strong information systems, can help to align a company's operations with its strategic directions. A good analogy for information systems within an organization might be the central nervous system in the body (Bill Gates, in fact, refers to information as the "digital nervous system" of an organization). The central nervous system sends messages to and from the brain to various points in the body where the work gets done, such as lifting, walking, thinking, or digesting food. Effective information systems provide the right information to the right people at the right time. By having a central source of information accessible to everyone, individuals in manufacturing can have input on product design and sales; designers can obtain immediate feedback about manufacturing and financial implications of decisions; and everyone can share information for solving problems. Empowered individuals with the right information can make more timely decisions and can take action to better serve customers.

Data and information support analysis at the "three levels of quality"—performer/job, process, and organization—as discussed in Chapter 1. At each of these levels the primary focus of data and information is control, diagnosis, and planning, respectively. The types of information and how it is disseminated and aligned with organizational levels are equally vital to success. At the performer/job level, data provide real-time information to identify assignable causes for variation, determine root causes, and take corrective action as needed. These activities require lean communication channels consisting of bulletins, computerized quality reports, and digital readouts of part dimensions to provide immediate information on what is happening and how things are progressing. At the process level, operational performance data such as yields, cycle times, and productivity measures help managers determine whether they are doing the right job, using resources effectively, and improving. Information at this level generally is aggregated: for example, daily or weekly scrap reports, customer complaint data obtained from customer service representatives, or monthly sales and cost figures faxed in from field offices. At the organization level, quality and operational performance data from all areas of the firm, along with relevant financial, market, human resource, and supplier data, form the basis for strategic planning and decision making. Such information is highly aggregated and obtained from many different sources throughout the organization.

Good data and information management provide many benefits:

- They help the company know that customers are receiving appropriate levels of service because indicators are used to measure service attributes.
- They provide concrete feedback to workers to verify their progress.
- They establish a basis for reward and recognition.
- They provide a means of assessing progress and signaling the need for corrective action.
- They reduce the costs of operations through better planning and improvement actions.

A survey conducted by William Schiemann & Associates found that measurement-managed companies are more likely to be in the top third of their industry financially, complete organizational changes more successfully, reach clear agreement on strategy among senior managers, enjoy favorable levels of cooperation and teamwork among management, undertake greater self-monitoring of performance by employees, and have a greater willingness by employees to take risks.[7]

Leading Practices

Successful companies recognize the importance of reliable and appropriate data and information in strategic planning and daily customer-focused decision making. Data and information are the forces that drive quality excellence and improve operational and competitive performance. Some of the key practices are summarized here.

- *They develop a comprehensive set of performance indicators that reflect internal and external customer requirements and the key factors that drive the business.* Performance indicators span the entire business operation, from suppliers to customers, and from front-line workers to top levels of management. Wainwright Industries (see *Quality Profile*) aligns the company's business objectives with customers' critical success factors: price, line defects, delivery, and partnership. This alignment process has prompted the development of five key strategic indicator categories: safety, internal customer satisfaction, external customer satisfaction, defect rate, and business performance. Within each category, Wainwright has developed specific indicators and goals. For instance, for external customer satisfaction, they measure a satisfaction index and compile complaints each month; for business performance, they track sales, capital expenditures, and market share for drawn housings. Boeing Airlift and Tanker Programs defines performance measurements in five key categories that support company goals: customer satisfaction, program performance, workforce effectiveness, operational and process performance, and financial results. Even the IRS Restructuring and Reform Act of 1998 has proposed a new measurement system that includes customer satisfaction, employee satisfaction, and business results (quality and quantity) measures.

Collecting data that no one uses or wants, however, wastes valuable time and resources. Leading companies select appropriate measures and indicators using well-defined criteria. Boeing A&T uses five criteria to select data: important to customers, effective in measuring performance, effective in forecasting results, actionable, and easily collected with integrity.

Quality Profile

Wainwright Industries, Inc.

Wainwright Industries, Inc., headquartered in St. Peters, Missouri, is a family-owned business that manufactures stamped and machined parts for U.S. and foreign customers in the automotive, aerospace, home security, and information processing industries. Annual sales total $30 million, and the company employs 275 associates. Craftsmanship, teamwork, and innovation have been commitments at Wainwright since its inception in 1947. Delivering products and services of unequaled quality that generate total customer satisfaction is Wainwright's principal objective. This commitment led the company to a Malcolm Baldrige National Quality Award in the small business category in 1994.

Wainwright constantly looks for ways to improve, searching inside and outside the organization for ideas and examples on how to streamline processes, cut delivery times, make training programs more effective, or enhance any other facet of its customer-focused operations. Its empowered workforce provides a rich source of ideas; each associate averages more than one implemented improvement per week. From 1992 to 1994, overall customer satisfaction increased from 84 to 95 percent. Simultaneously, defect and scrap rates, manufacturing cycle time, and quality costs fell. Ninety-five percent of all purchase orders are processed within 24 hours. The lead time for making one of Wainwright's principal products—drawn housings for electric motors—was reduced to 15 minutes from its former level of 8.75 days. Since initiating continuous improvement processes in 1991, the company reports steadily growing market share for its major products, productivity gains exceeding industry averages, and increasing profit margins.

Source: Malcolm Baldrige National Quality Award, Profiles of Winners, National Institute of Standards and Technology, Department of Commerce.

- *They use comparative information and data to improve overall performance and competitive position.* Comparative information includes comparisons relative to direct competitors as well as best-practices benchmarking, either inside or outside one's industry (see Chapter 7). Such information allows organizations to know where they stand in relation to competitors and other leading companies, provides the impetus for breakthrough improvement, and helps them understand their own processes before they compare performance levels. For example, Corning Telecommunications Products Division (TPD) uses a competitive analysis process to gather publicly available data to analyze competitors' intentions and capabilities, including manufacturing capacity, cost, and cost of incremental capacity, and determines product capability and quality through direct evaluation of competitors' products. The steering committee at Custom Research, Inc. (CRI), uses a benchmarking matrix to identify areas where benchmarking could benefit the company most; it is targeted on five key processes. All employees are encouraged to informally benchmark through industry and other organizations, conferences, and seminars, and bring back what they learn to CRI. Xerox Business Services (see *Quality Profile*) identifies companies with best practices by relying on its own employees and customers, as well as user groups, advisory boards, partnerships, and joint ventures.
- *They involve everyone in measurement activities and ensure that performance information is widely visible throughout the organization.* No longer do "quality control" departments perform inspection and measurement activities. Instead, organizations expect all process owners to collect and analyze data from their individual processes as a basis for problem solving and improvement activities. Motorola, for instance, strives to measure every task performed by every one of its 120,000 employees. At GTE Directories, functional and cross-functional teams through-

Quality Profile

Xerox Business Services

Xerox Business Services (XBS) provides document outsourcing services and consulting, including on-site management of mailrooms and print shops and the creation, production, and management of documents. XBS has 14,000 people, 80 percent of whom are located at customer sites throughout the world. XBS puts heavy emphasis on benchmarking throughout its organization, gathering comparative information from companies that are large, small, tenured, new, inside or outside their industry. XBS uses a process called Managing for Results that cascades action plans into challenging and aligned objectives for each manager, supervisor, and front-line associate. Key performance measures are deployed to all teams and individuals in the company, and the process enables them to design work systems more rapidly and with greater flexibility.

When XBS received the Baldrige Award in 1997, its U.S. market share was increasing while its two leading competitors were experiencing flat or declining market shares. Revenue per employee increased from about $78,000 in 1992 to $106,000 in 1996. Its customer satisfaction rating of 95 percent is higher than those of its two main competitors. To obtain as much customer satisfaction data as possible, XBS plants a tree in national forests for each customer who completes the evaluation form.

Source: Malcolm Baldrige National Quality Award, Profiles of Winners, National Institute of Standards and Technology, Department of Commerce.

out the company work to maintain up-to-date scope, management, and quality of key operational measurement data. The owner of data at Texas Nameplate Company is the person who has access to the data and responsibility to use them.

Performance information can quickly pinpoint areas that need improvement; but just knowing that one is doing a good job can also be a powerful motivator. Thus, organizations need to share performance information with all employees. For example, The Ritz-Carlton disseminates its Service Quality Indicator statistics to the workforce on a daily basis. Solar Turbines shares comparative data in its leadership and all-employee meetings showing projected comparisons with each of its "top tier measures."

- *They ensure that data are reliable and accessible to all who need them.* The instruments used to capture data must be reliable; that is, they must measure the true value consistently. Therefore, workers must give careful attention to instrument calibration and maintenance, as well as to the human factors associated with inspection and measurement activity. Most companies now rely on computer-based information systems for data processing and analysis. Texas Instruments, for instance, has a state-of-the art, on-line computer network that serves as the backbone of a comprehensive set of systems supplemented by local processing capabilities. The accuracy and reliability of support software is crucial in these systems. Texas Instruments uses standard formats and interfaces, a central group to conduct system performance review, and extensive training for developers and users. STMicroelectronics designs its systems to bypass human data entry whenever possible and performs validity checks at the database level.

  Leading companies provide rapid access to data and information to all employees who need the information. Xerox, for example, maintains one of the most extensive computer networks in the world, linking hundreds of sites on four continents to provide information 24 hours a day, seven days a week. At Milliken and STMicroelectronics, for example, databases and on-line reports are available to every associate to support daily operations and empower employees to take appropriate action.
- *They use sound analytical methods to conduct analyses and use the results to support strategic planning and daily decision making.* Strong analytical capability is the necessary precursor of good analysis. Leading companies employ a variety of statistical tools and structured approaches for analyzing data and turning them into useful information. Fuji-Xerox, a Japanese subsidiary of Xerox, uses a variety of statistical techniques such as regression and analysis of variance to develop mathematical models relating such factors as copy quality, machine malfunctions, and maintenance time to customer satisfaction results.

  Data can provide an indication of important cause-and-effect relationships. FedEx, for example, collects a lot of data using its automated systems and aggregates the material into an internal process quality index and an external service quality index. It strives for internal measures to predict external measures. Companies need to ask the key question: How do overall improvements in product and service quality and operational performance relate to changes in company financial performance and customer satisfaction? Corning Telecommunications Products Division aggregates data and information into key financial and business level analyses that quantify the impact of decisions on financial and market performance. Its data researchers examine relationships among quality, price, and image as they relate to the attraction and retention of customers. They also quantify the relationships between process capability, people and process productivity, and unit costs. Trident Precision Manufacturing correlates quality, cost, delivery, and service data with customer satisfaction data to verify their understanding of their customers. GTE Directories uses a proprietary third-party model and software to perform similar analyses. Texas Nameplate analyzes overall and segmented profit figures and compares them to sales and operations expenses to determine overall efficiency, and analyzes in-house and customer rejects relative to throughput, cycle time, and expedite volume to determine causes of rejects.

- *They continually refine information sources and their uses within the organization.* Poor data and analysis lead to poor decisions. Leading companies continually improve their analysis capabilities and training, staying abreast of new techniques. They conduct ongoing review and update their sources and uses of data, shorten the cycle time from data gathering to access, and broaden access to everyone who requires data for management and improvement. At quarterly "measurement summits" at ADAC Laboratories (see *Quality Profile*), representatives from all departments review the types of data collected according to three criteria: whether the data support key business drivers; address one of the "five evils" (waste, defects, delays, accidents, or mistakes); or support objective analysis for improvement. Xerox developed a data systems quality assurance approach for the design, development, and major upgrade of each data system. Teams at Corning TPD brainstorm and research new measurements, consult with experts, and test the measurements for three to six months before full implementation.

All of these practices encourage "management by fact," one of the key elements of total quality.

Quality Profile
ADAC Laboratories

ADAC Laboratories is a 710-person Silicon Valley-based maker of high-technology healthcare products such as diagnostic imaging and healthcare information systems. ADAC used quality management principles to change the company culture after successfully coming out of a turnaround in the mid-1980s. ADAC replaced its executive-driven quality council with two weekly meetings open to all employees as well as customers and suppliers. During these meetings, numerous employees present data on key measures of customer satisfaction, quality, productivity, and operational and financial performance. The company has made significant investments in data collection systems targeted to key needs and activities, such as tracking design defects and customer calls for support.

ADAC consistently brings products to market faster than its larger competitors. From 1990 to 1996, company revenues have tripled; defect rates measured at final inspection have fallen by about 40 percent. If a system breaks down, ADAC technicians will have it back in operation within an average of 17 hours after receiving the call, less than a third of the time it took in 1990. On eight measures of service satisfaction, ADAC was the sole leader in five categories and tied for the top spot in the remaining ones.

Source: Malcolm Baldrige National Quality Award, Profiles of Winners, National Institute of Standards and Technology, Department of Commerce.

THE SCOPE OF PERFORMANCE MEASUREMENT

Most businesses have traditionally relied on organizational performance data based almost solely on financial or accounting-based factory productivity considerations, such as return on investment, earnings per share, direct labor efficiency, and machine utilization.[8] Unfortunately, many of these indicators are inaccurate and stress quantity over quality.[9] They reward the wrong behavior; lack predictive power; do not capture key business changes until it is too late; reflect functions, not cross-functional processes; and give inadequate consideration to difficult-to-quantify resources such as intellectual capital.[10] For example, financial measures reflect past decisions; they do not focus on factors that create value and predict financial success. Measurements such as direct labor efficiency promote building unnecessary inventory and overcontrol direct labor. This focus prevents workers from assuming responsibility for control and from focusing on process improvement. Focusing on machine utilization encourages having fewer, but larger, general purpose machines, which results in more complex material flows and increased inventory and throughput time. In traditional manufacturing and service operations, cost was the key measure of performance, particularly in highly competitive markets. Today, however, quality drives key decisions. This approach requires a much broader set of performance measures that are aligned to an organization's strategy.

The Balanced Scorecard

The term *balanced scorecard* was coined by Robert Kaplan and David Norton of the Harvard Business School in response to the limitations of traditional accounting measures. Its purpose is "to translate strategy into measures that uniquely communicate your vision to the organization." Their version of the balanced scorecard consists of four perspectives:

1. *Financial perspective* measures the ultimate results that the business provides to its shareholders, including profitability, revenue growth, return on investment, economic value added (EVA), and shareholder value.
2. *Internal perspective* focuses attention on the performance of the key internal processes that drive the business, including such measures as quality levels, productivity, cycle time, and cost.
3. *Customer perspective* focuses on customer needs and satisfaction as well as market share, including service levels, satisfaction ratings, and repeat business.
4. *Innovation and learning perspective* directs attention to the basis of a future success—the organization's people and infrastructure. Key measures might include intellectual assets, employee satisfaction, market innovation, and skills development.

A good balanced scorecard contains both leading and lagging measures and indicators. *Lagging measures* (outcomes) tell what has happened; *leading measures* (performance drivers) predict what will happen. For example, customer survey results about recent transactions might be a leading indicator for customer retention (a lagging indicator); employee satisfaction might be a leading indicator for turnover, and so on. These measures and indicators should also establish cause-and-effect relationships across perspectives. For example, Figure 8.1 shows a causal relationships among the key measures in IBM Rochester's balanced scorecard (see the *Quality in Practice* case later in this chapter). This model suggests that improving internal capabilities such as people skills, product/service quality, and products and channels, will lead to improved customer satisfaction and loyalty, which in turn, lead to improved

Figure 8.1 Causal Relationships Among Categories of IBM Rochester's Balanced Scorecard

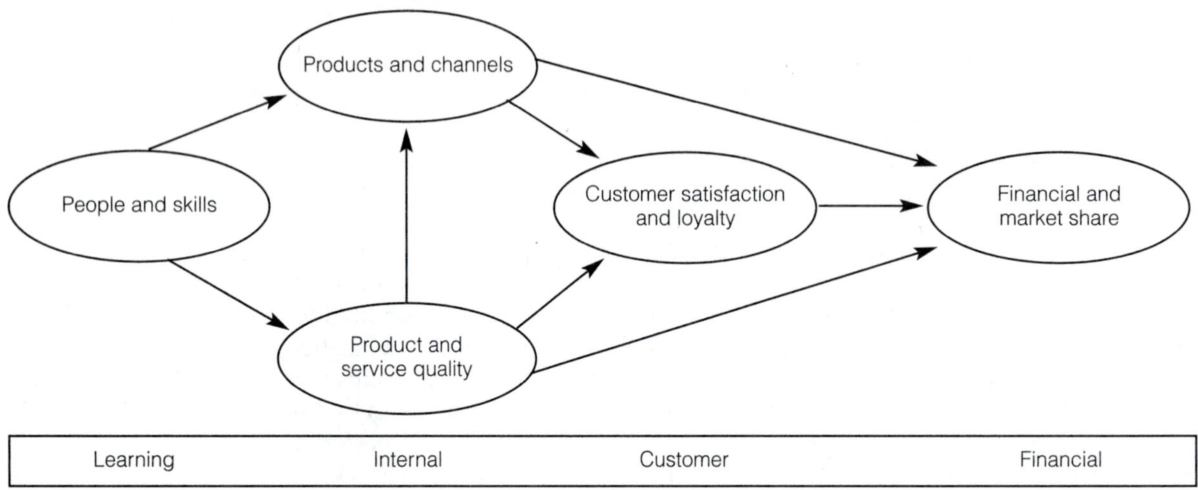

Source: Courtesy of IBM Rochester, MN.

financial and market share performance. Understanding such relationships is important in using data and information for strategic and operational decisions.

Kaplan and Norton's balanced scorecard is only one version of performance measurement systems that have emerged as companies recognize the need for a broad set of performance measures that provide a comprehensive view of business performance. Raytheon's version defines customer, shareholder, process, and people perspectives. The Malcolm Baldrige Criteria for Performance Excellence Results category groups performance measures into five sets (groups 4 and 5 were combined in the 2001 critera):

1. Customer
2. Financial and market
3. Human resource
4. Supplier and partner performance
5. Organizational effectiveness

These measures are summarized in Figure 8.2, along with examples of measures in each category. Table 8.1 illustrates some of the key measurements taken by Texas Instruments. This set is quite similar to the balanced scorecard, and in fact, any measure in the balanced scorecard can easily be assigned to one of these categories. We will briefly discuss each of these categories. As we describe specific examples, note that the specific measures an organization chooses are tied to the key factors that make it competitive in its industry.

Customer-Focused Measures

We discussed the importance of measuring customer satisfaction in Chapter 4. Relevant measures and indicators of an organization's performance as viewed by customers include direct measures of customer satisfaction and dissatisfaction, customer retention, gains and losses of customers and customer accounts, customer complaints and warranty claims. Other indicators of customer satisfaction include measures of

Figure 8.2 Business Performance Measures and Indicators

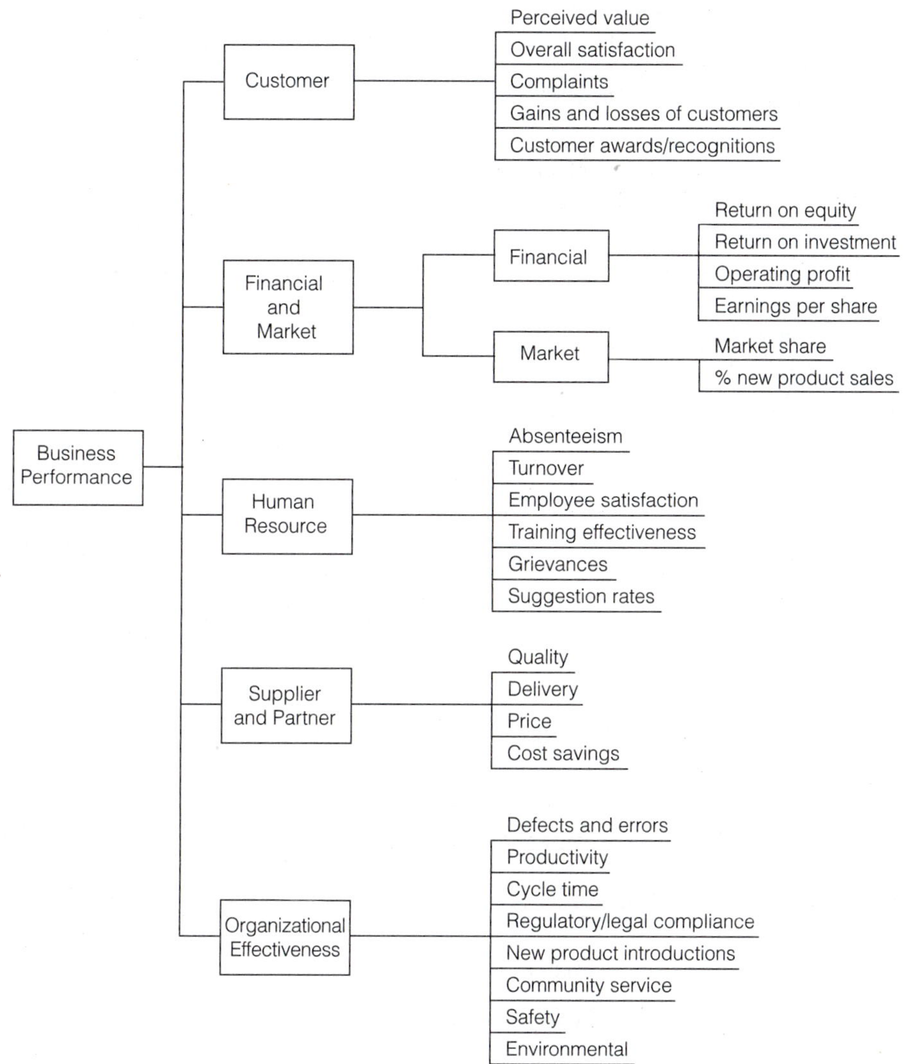

perceived value, loyalty, positive referral, and customer relationship building. Customer satisfaction should be measured over three areas at a minimum: product quality, service quality, and cycle times. For example, 3M's automotive trades business has as its direct customers automotive distributors, while end users are the secondary group. Service quality and cycle times are key satisfaction measures for distributors, while product quality is the principal satisfaction indicator for end users. 3M's measurements include the following:

- In-stock service levels
- On-time delivery
- Order completeness
- Emergency response time

Table 8.1 Key Quality Measurements at Texas Instruments

Customer-Related Measures
- Percent shipping performance
- Warehouse errors
- Returned material cycle time

Product Quality Measures
- Parts per million defective, electrical
- Parts per million defective, visual/mechanical
- Operating life test

Process Quality Measures
- Cycle time
- Rework at various stages
- Final test yield

Supplier Performance Measures
- Parts per million defective
- Purity level
- Functional test results

Organizational Effectiveness Performance Measures
- Cost of conformance
- Cost of nonconformance
- Total cost of quality

Source: Adapted with the permission of The Free Press, a Division of Simon & Schuster, from JURAN ON QUALITY BY DESIGN: The New Steps for Planning Quality into Goods and Services by J. M. Juran. Copyright © 1992 by The Juran Institute, Inc.

- Ease of dealing with supplier
- Ease of contact with customer service department
- Complaint handling
- Accuracy of shipment
- Order cycle time
- Product quality and performance[11]

In addition, measures and indicators of product and service performance that have a strong correlation with customer satisfaction are appropriate to monitor. STMicroelectronics, for example, tracks the number of nonconforming production lots, which play a significant role in complaints received by their customers. They also track different measures for different customer segments. For instance, the telecommunications industry has a short cycle-to-market requirement; key measures that address this requirement are delivery time, flexibility, response delay, early warning, quality and reliability, and response quality.

Financial and Market Measures

Financial measures are generally tracked by senior leadership to gauge overall company performance and are often used to determine incentive compensation for senior executives. Measures of financial performance might include revenue, return on equity, return on investment, operating profit, pretax profit margin, asset utilization, earnings per share, and other liquidity measures. In a capital-intensive industry such as airline production, key financial measures at Boeing Airlift and Tanker Programs are return on sales, return on net assets, and net asset turnover. The Ritz-Carlton Hotel Company, on the other hand, monitors earnings before taxes, depreciation, and amortization, administrative costs, and gross profit among its key financial indicators. A useful financial performance indicator is the *cost of quality*, which managers use to prioritize improvement projects and gauge the effectiveness of total quality efforts and which we will discuss this later in this chapter. It is one of Solar Turbine's key measures.

Marketplace performance indicators could include market share, measures of business growth, new product and geographic markets entered, and percentage of new product sales as appropriate. In a commodity market in which Sunny Fresh Foods competes, its performance drivers include the U.S. share of market and total pounds of egg products sold. In the highly competitive semiconductor industry, STMicroelectronics looks not only at sales growth, but at differentiated product sales.

Human Resource Measures

Many companies do not measure human resource results, despite the critical importance of human resources in achieving quality and performance objectives. We addressed this issue in Chapter 6. HR measures can relate to employee well-being, satisfaction, training and development, work system performance, and effectiveness. Examples include safety, absenteeism, turnover, and employee satisfaction. Other measures might include the extent of training, training effectiveness, and measures of improvement in job effectiveness. Texas Nameplate Company measures the percent on net earnings for its risk-based compensation (gain sharing) program, because it significantly impacts employee productivity, motivation, and satisfaction. Boeing Airlift and Tanker Programs tracks grievance backlog reduction as a way of quantifying improving relationships with its unions. The Ritz-Carlton tracks percent turnover closely as a key indicator of employee satisfaction and the effectiveness of their selection and training processes.

Supplier and Partner Performance Measures

We discussed the importance of suppliers and partnerships in Chapter 7. Key measures of supplier performance are quality, delivery and service, and price. Quality might be measured by defect rates, complaints, functional performance, reliability, and maintainability. For example, STMicroelectronics measures the number of complaints suppliers receive from them, and the mean time between failures for critical equipment. Delivery and service performance data often include timeliness, responsiveness, dependability, and technical support. The Ritz-Carlton monitors the number of suppliers who achieve an 80 percent or better rating on all attributes of the supplier certification survey. With the increased focus on supply chain management, many companies are including cost savings; total supply chain management costs; reductions in waste, inventory, and cycle time; and indicators of better communication, such as achieved via electronic commerce. Solar Turbines, for example, monitors supplier lead times for two critical components—forgings and castings.

Organizational Effectiveness Measures

This category includes measures and indicators of design, production, delivery, and support process performance. Examples of common measures are cycle times, product and service quality, production flexibility, lead times, setup times, time to market, product/process yields, and delivery performance. Boeing A&T, for instance, tracks the mean time between corrective maintenance of its aircraft; increasing this time indicates improved quality of the aircraft systems.

Product and service quality indicators focus on the outcomes of manufacturing and service processes. A common indicator of manufacturing quality is the number of **nonconformities per unit,** or **defects per unit**. Because of the negative connotation of "defect" and its potential implications in liability suits, many organizations use the term *nonconformity*; however, quite a few still use defect. In this text, both terms are used interchangeably to be consistent with current literature and practice. In services, a measure of quality analogous to defects per unit is **errors per opportunity**. Each customer transaction provides an opportunity for many different types of errors.

Nonconformities per unit or errors per opportunity are often reported as rates per thousand or million. A common measure is **defects per million opportunities (dpmo)**. Thus, a defect rate of 2 per thousand is equivalent to 2,000 dpmo. At some Motorola factories, quality is so good that they measure defects per billion!

Many companies classify defects into three categories:

1. *Critical defect:* A critical defect is one that judgment and experience indicate will surely result in hazardous or unsafe conditions for individuals using, maintaining, or depending on the product and will prevent proper performance of the product.
2. *Major defect:* A major defect is one not critical but likely to result in failure or to materially reduce the usability of the unit for its intended purpose.
3. *Minor defect:* A minor defect is one not likely to materially reduce the usability of the item for its intended purpose, nor to have any bearing on the effective use or operation of the unit.[12]

Critical defects may lead to serious consequences or product liability suits; thus, they should be monitored and carefully controlled. On the other hand, minor defects might not be monitored as closely, because they do not affect fitness for use. For many products, however, even minor defects can lead to customer dissatisfaction. To account for each category, many companies create a composite index in which major and critical defects are weighted more heavily than minor defects. For example, FedEx has an extensive quality measurement system that includes a composite measure, called the service quality indicator (SQI), which is a weighted sum of 10 factors that reflect customers' expectations of company performance. FedEx's SQI is shown in Table 8.2. Different weights reflect the importance of each failure; losing a package, for instance, is more serious that delivering it a few minutes late. The index is reported weekly and summarized on a monthly basis.

Many organizational effectiveness measures focus on process (both core and support) performance. Process data can reflect defect and error rates of intermediate operations, and also efficiency measures such as cost, cycle time, productivity, schedule performance, machine downtime, preventive maintenance activity, rates of problem resolution, energy efficiency, and raw material usage. For example, Motorola measures nearly every process in the company, both in terms of defects and errors and time. One of its key business objectives is to reduce total cycle time—the time from the point a customer expresses a need until the customer happily pays the company. All processes within the company, including design, order entry, manufacturing, and marketing, are measured for improvements in error rates and cycle times. American Express analysts monitor telephone conversations for politeness, tone of voice, accuracy of the transaction, and other customer service aspects. Comparisons between judgments of the analysts and judgments of customers in posttransaction interviews determine the relevance of specific internal measurements. When differences arise

Table 8.2 FedEx Service Quality Indicator and Factors

Error Type	Description	Weight
1.	*Complaints reopened*—customer complaints (on traces, invoices, missed pickups, etc.) reopened after an unsatisfactory resolution	3
2.	*Damaged packages*—packages with visible or concealed damage or spoilage due to weather or water damage, missed pickup, or late delivery	10
3.	*International*—a composite score of performance measures of international operations	
4	*Invoice adjustments*—customer requests for credit or refunds for real or perceived failures	1
5.	*Late pickup stops*—packages that were picked up later than the stated pickup time	3
6.	*Lost packages*—claims for missing packages or with contents missing	10
7.	*Missed proof of delivery*—invoices that lack written proof of delivery information	1
8.	*Right date late*—delivery past promised time on the right day	1
9.	*Traces*—package status and proof of delivery requests not in the COSMOS IIB computer system (the FedEx "real time" tracking system)	3
10.	*Wrong day late*—delivery on the wrong day	5

Source: Service Quality Indicators at FedEx (internal company document).

between customer satisfaction and internal measures of performance—for instance, when internal measures seem good yet customer satisfaction is low—the company takes it as an indication that it is measuring the wrong things. Thus, companies need to compare external data with internal data.

Organizational effectiveness measures may also include such measures of regulatory or legal compliance and public responsibility as reduced emission levels, waste stream reductions, and recycling; and measures of accomplishment of organizational strategy, such as R&D investment, or number of patents granted—two of STMicroelectronics key indicators. Texas Nameplate uses toxic chemicals in its etching process; thus, it monitors the pH level and amount of suspended metals in water discharge to meet local regulations. Because of the importance of hiring skilled people, The Ritz-Carlton embarked on a major project to improve the cycle time from when a potential new-hire walks in the door and a job offer is tendered; it became one of their key measures in this category.

The Role of Comparative Data

Looking at data without a basis for comparison can easily lead to a false sense of achievement. Organizations need comparative data, such as industry averages, best competitor performance, and world-class benchmarks to gain an accurate assessment of performance. For example, a performance measure may be improving, but at a rate slower than its competition. Without that information, it would be difficult for an organization to recognize the need for further improvements or an accelerated pace of change to close the gap. Comparative and benchmark information also provides the motivation to seek breakthrough improvements.

Comparative data should be driven by an organization's needs and priorities, and focus on areas most critical to competitive strategy. Comparative data can be obtained in a variety of ways. They include third-party surveys and benchmarking approaches. The Ritz-Carlton Hotel Company, for instance, uses ratings and awards from travel industry publications and salesforce reports to assess its competitive status. Boeing A&T seeks information from three sources:

1. *Best-in-Boeing:* high-performing processes identified through various company-level councils
2. *Best-in-Industry:* companies identified through various benchmarking centers, the International Benchmarking Clearinghouse, and their internal Business Environmental Assessment group
3. *World Class:* leading edge companies, winners of national awards, or those cited by customers, suppliers, and industry experts`

Figure 8.3 shows the performance of lead time from order placement until delivery for Texas Nameplate Company. TNC's results are compared against two major competitors and industry averages from a third-party survey. The results show that TNC has consistently maintained a position of leadership in this measure. A good source of comparative benchmarks is the performance of Baldrige-winning organizations.

DESIGNING EFFECTIVE PERFORMANCE MEASUREMENT SYSTEMS

In designing a performance measurement system, organizations must consider two things. First, how will the measures support senior executive performance review and organizational planning to address the overall health of the organization? Second, how will the measures support daily operations and decision making? Answering these questions requires an organization to align its measurement system to its vision and strategy and select meaningful process-level measurements. Many organizations make

Figure 8.3 Texas Nameplate Performance Results for Delivery Lead TIme

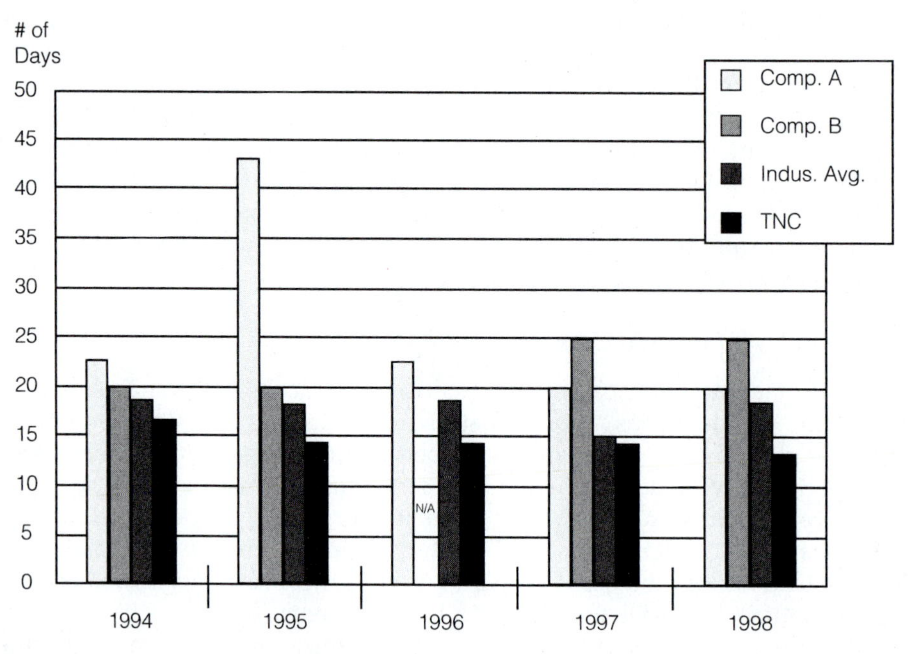

Source: Courtesy of Texas Nameplate Company.

two fundamental mistakes: (1) not measuring key characteristics critical to company performance or customer satisfaction, and (2) taking irrelevant or inappropriate measurements. In the first case, the organization often fails to meet customer expectations or performance goals. In the second, the measurement system directs attention to areas that are not important to customers, thus wasting time and resources. The number of performance indicators seems to grow with the size and complexity of the organization. In many organizations, performance indicators have been around for a long time, and few managers can probably say where, when, and why they developed. In most cases, somebody just decided they were good to have. For example, IDS Financial Services, a subsidiary of American Express, used to measure more than 4,000 individual tasks: functions like phone calls, mail coding, and application acceptance. Many of these tasks were subject to 100 percent inspection. Now, after redesigning its information management system, IDS measures 80 service processes and uses statistical sampling.

Linking Measures to Strategy

A balanced scorecard approach helps in identifying the right measures by aligning them with the organization's vision and strategy. It provides a means of setting targets and allocating resources for short-term planning, communicating strategies, aligning departmental and personal goals to strategies, linking rewards to performance, and supplying feedback for organizational learning.

Effective performance measures that are aligned with business strategy are driven by factors that determine what is important to the success of the business. They include the following:

- The nature of a company's products and services
- Major markets
- Principal customers and their key quality and performance requirements
- Organizational culture; its purpose, mission, and vision
- Capabilities and core competencies, such as facilities and technologies
- Supplier and partnering relationships
- Regulatory environment
- Position in market and competitive environment
- Principal factors that determine competitive success, such as product innovation, cost reduction, or productivity growth
- Current business directions, such as new product and market changes and new business alliances.

For example, the First National Bank of Chicago asked its customers what they considered as good-quality features of a product and the delivery of those features.[13] Responses included timeliness, accuracy, operations efficiency, economics, and customer responsiveness. These responses initiated the development of quality indicators such as lockbox processing time, bill keying accuracy, customer service inquiry resolution time, and money transfer timeliness. A computer software company might not need to collect extensive data on environmental quality issues whereas a chemical company certainly would. A pizza franchise that delivers bulk orders to fraternities and parties around a college campus would have a different set of performance measures and indicators than one in a quiet suburban residential neighborhood. Thus, an organization first needs to understand its competitive environment, market requirements, and internal capabilities.

The things an organization needs to do well to accomplish its vision are often called **key business drivers** or **key success factors.** They represent things that separate an organization from its competition and define strengths to exploit or weaknesses to correct.

Measures should logically be tied to these factors. MBNA, the Wilmington, Delaware, credit card company that markets custom cards to "affinity groups" such as professional associations, universities, and sports team fans, views speed of service as one of its key business drivers. Thus, it measures the time to process customer address changes, the percentage of times phones are picked up within two rings, and the time taken to transfer calls from the switchboard.[14] Similarly, Armstrong Building Products Operations has identified five components of value that drive its business strategy: customer satisfaction, sales growth, operating profit, asset management, and high-performance organization. Each of these components is supported by key measurements and analysis approaches. For example, product, a key driver of customer satisfaction, is measured by dimensions and squareness, fire performance, acoustics and color, dimensional stability, competitor product quality analysis, and claims. Likewise, service quality is measured by on-time delivery and missed-item promises, pricing and billing, and information support for customers. Another key business driver, operating profit, is measured by process effectiveness, units per employee, scrap and downtime, and cost of quality. Organizational performance measures include recordable injury rate, number of improvements/work orders, percentage of employees recognized, gainsharing savings, and employee satisfaction trends and turnover rate.

Key performance measures should be aligned with strategies and action plans. Setting targets for each measure provides the basis for strategy deployment as discussed in Chapter 5. Figure 8.4 shows an example from Merrill Lynch Credit Corporation (MLCC), a 1997 Baldrige Award recipient. MLCC defines its critical few objectives from its long-term focused strategies: client satisfaction, partner satisfaction, business growth, and shareholder value. For each of these objectives, they define key performance measures and targets by which to evaluate progress toward meeting these objectives. They also align each of the objectives with eight core processes described in Chapter 7 (Table 7.1). Such an approach ensures that process owners focus on the right measurements that support the company's strategy.

Many organizations have adopted the term *dashboard* as an alternative to a balanced scorecard. This reference stems from the analogy to an automobile's dashboard—a collection of indicators (speed, RPM, oil pressure, temperature, etc.) that summarize performance. IBM Rochester's quality dashboard groups 19 key performance measures into seven areas of customer satisfaction, software performance, hardware performance, service, delivery, administration, and image. Each is reported quarterly as a single index, with color-coded "quality" and "status" columns. In the quality column, red indicates an adverse trend, yellow a flat trend, and green an improving trend; in the status column, red means "not on track to attain plan," yellow means "plan attainment at risk," and green means "tracking to plan." It provides a concise, visual summary of overall organizational performance.

Process-Level Measurements

What makes a good performance measurement system? Many organizations define specific criteria for selecting measures and indicators. IBM Rochester, for example, asks the following questions:

- Does the measurement support our mission?
- Will the measurement be used to manage change?
- Is it important to our customers?
- Is it effective in measuring performance?
- Is it effective in forecasting results?
- Is it easy to understand/simple?

Figure 8.4 Merrill Lynch Credit Corporation's Alignment of Measures With Strategies and Processes

* Proprietary Information Deleted

Long-Term Focus	MLCC Critical Few Objective Requirements (Form 1)	Resources ($)	Key Performance Measures	Targets *	Targets *	1.0	2.0	3.0	4.0	5.0	6.0	7.0	8.0
1.0 Client Satisfaction	1.1 Increase end-user satisfaction	*	% Good to excellent/Excellent	*	*	●	●	●	●	○	●		●
	1.2 Increase field/FC satisfaction		% Good to excellent/Excellent	*	*	○	○		●		●		
	1.3 Increase internal client satisfaction		% Good to excellent/Excellent	*	*	○	○	●	●	●	●	●	●
2.0 Partner Satisfaction	2.1 Increase partner satisfaction	*	% Overall partner satisfaction	*	*	●	●	●	●	●	●	●	●
	2.2 Reduce partner turnover		% Turnover	*	*	○	○			●	●	○	
	2.3 Develop managerial skills/capability model		Determine leadership req'mnts	*	*	●	●		○		●	●	●
	2.4 Deploy partner productivity measurement standards		% Partners reviewed	*	*	○	○				●	●	●
	2.5 Ensure proper staffing levels		% Budget vs. actual	*	*	○	○	●			●		●
3.0 Business Growth	3.1 Increase origination volume	*	Overall units/$ Volume (billions)	*	*	●	●	●			●		●
	3.2 Increase FC effectiveness		% Approval ratio	*	*	●	●	●					
	3.3 Institutionalize liability management		# of client impressions # of FC impressions	*	*	●	●	●					
4.0 Shareholder Value	4.1 Reduce operating expenses	*	% Revenue/Expense ratio	*	*	●	●	●	○		●		●
	4.2 Increase process productivity		Application approval cycle time	*	*	●	●		○	○	●	●	●
	4.3 Develop MLCC-wide compliance program		% Approved compliance procedures in place	*	*					●	●	●	○

Column groups: Business Priority Matrix (Long-Term Focus through Targets); Support Process Alignment — Core Process No.* (1.0–8.0).

Legend: ● = High Impact ○ = Medium Impact Blank = Low or No Impact

*(Refer to Table 7.1 for Core Process Names)

Source: From "The 1997 Malcolm Baldrige National Quality Award Application Summary," a publication of Merrill Lynch Credit Corporation. Any further reproduction or redistribution is strictly prohibited.

- Are the data easy/cost-efficient to collect?
- Does the measurement have validity, integrity, and timeliness?
- Does the measure have an owner?

Good measures and indicators are **actionable**; that is, they provide the basis for decisions at the level at which they are applied. To generate useful performance measures a systematic process is required.[15]

1. Identify all customers of the system and determine their requirements and expectations. Organizations need answers to key questions: Who are my customers? and What do they expect? Many of the tools introduced in Chapter 4 can be used in this step, including customer surveys, focus groups, and user panels. Customer expectations change over time; thus, regular feedback must be obtained.
2. Define the work process that provides the product or service. Key questions include: What do I do that impacts customer needs? and What is my process? The use of flowcharts for process mapping can stimulate the definition of work processes and internal customer-supplier relationships.
3. Define the value-adding activities and outputs that compose the process. This step—identifying each part in the system in which value is added and an intermediate output is produced—weeds out activities that do not add value to the process and contribute to waste and inefficiency. Analysis performed in this step identifies the internal customers within the process along with their needs and expectations.
4. Develop specific performance measures or indicators. Each key activity identified in step 3 represents a critical point where value is added to the output for the next (internal) customer until the final output is produced. At these checkpoints, performance can be measured. Key questions include: What factors determine how well the process is producing according to customer requirements? What deviations can occur? What sources of variability can occur?
5. Evaluate the performance measures to ensure their usefulness. Questions to consider include: Are measurements taken at critical points where value-adding activities occur? Are measurements controllable? Is it feasible to obtain the data needed for each measure? Have operational definitions for each measurement been established? Operational definitions are precise definitions of measurements that have no ambiguities. For example, when measuring "invoice errors," a precise definition of what is an error and what is not is needed. Does an error include an omission of information, wrong information, or misspelling? Operational definitions provide a common understanding and enhance communication throughout the organization.

To illustrate this approach, consider the process of placing and filling a pizza order. Customer expectations include a quick response and a fair price. The process that provides this service is shown in Figure 8.5. To begin, the order taker is an internal customer of the caller who provides the pizza order. Later, the caller is a customer of the deliverer either at the pickup window or the caller's home. Also, the cook is a customer of the order taker who prepares the documentation for the ordered pizza.

Some possible performance measures include the following:

- Number of pizzas, by type per hour. If this number is high relative to the kitchen's capacity, then perhaps cooking time and/or preparation is being short-cut or delivery times are stretched out.
- Order accuracy (as transmitted to the kitchen). This measure can indicate a lack of attention or knowledge on the part of the order taker.

Figure 8.5 Example of a Pizza Ordering and Filling Process (Home Delivery)

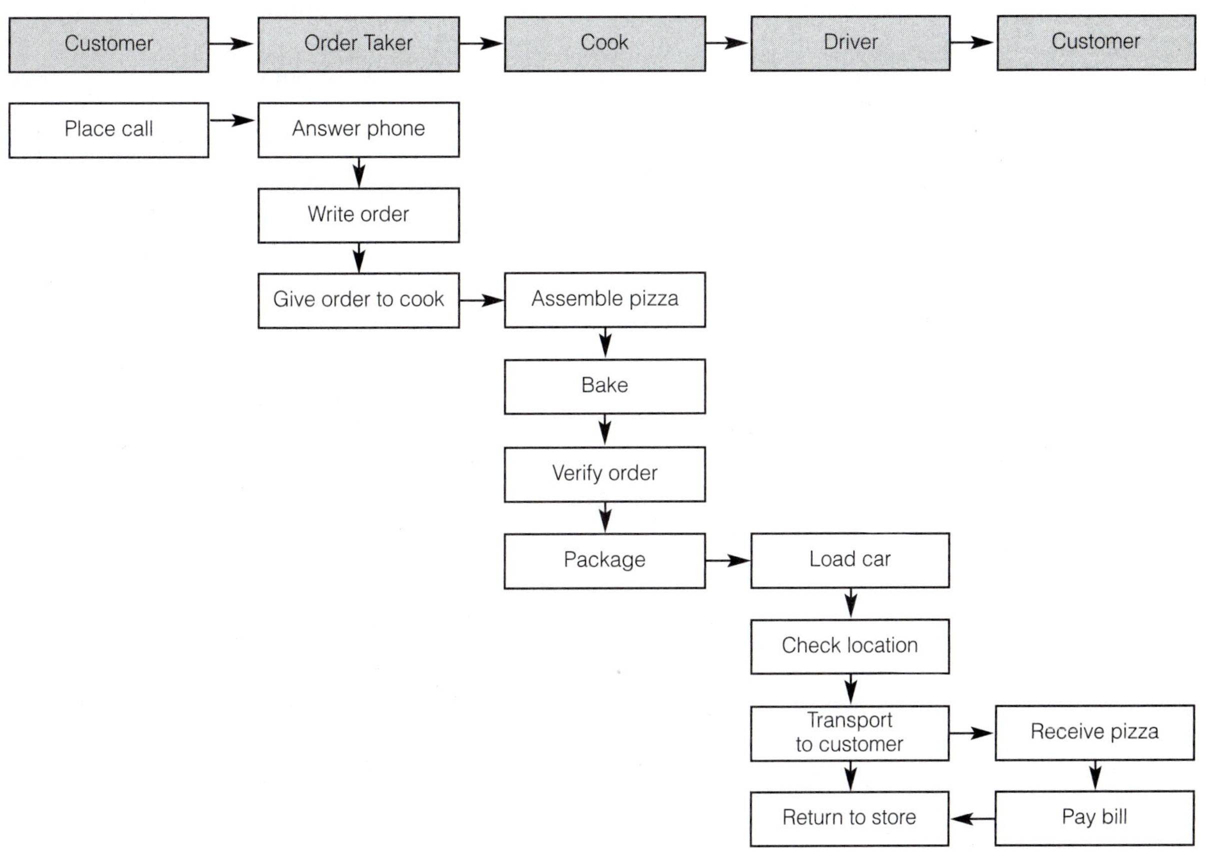

- Number of pizzas rejected per number prepared. A high number for this measure can indicate a lack of proper training of cooks, resulting in poor products and customer complaints.
- Time to delivery. This measure might indicate a problem within the restaurant or inadequate training of the driver. (Of course, as happened with Domino's, measuring delivery time could encourage drivers to drive too fast and lead to safety problems.)
- Number of errors in collections. Errors here can result in lost profits and higher prices.
- Raw materials (dough, etc.) or finished pizzas inventory. A high number might result in spoilage and excess costs. Low inventory might result in lost orders or excessive customer waiting time.

Notice that these measures—only a few among many possible measures—are related to the customer expectations and business performance.

Aligning Strategic and Process-Level Measurements[16]

It is possible that all work processes could be meeting their requirements while the organization is not achieving its longer-term goals. Thus, aligning strategic and process-level measurements is vital to a high-performing organization, and can be viewed as an approach for strategy deployment (see Chapter 5). Figure 8.6 illustrates how goals and measures might be aligned for a hypothetical retail manufacturer. Alignment might even go further, down to the team and individual levels. Note that alignment is tied fundamentally to the performance goals; the measures support goal attainment. The organization does not have to have one set of performance measures that everyone produces and reports, but rather, measures are used where they are most appropriate. Production line data, for example, might be reviewed only at the line level for daily operations control, while some data might be integrated at the next level for process improvement. Information that supports review of organizational-level performance is passed on to the corporate level.

THE COST OF QUALITY

In most firms cost accounting has been an important function. All organizations measure and report costs as a basis for control and improvement. The concept of the **cost of quality (COQ)** emerged in the 1950s. Traditionally, the reporting of quality-related costs had been limited to inspection and testing; other costs were accumulated in overhead accounts. As managers began to define and isolate the full range of quality-related costs, a number of surprising facts emerged.[17] First, quality-related costs were

Figure 8.6 An Example of Aligning Strategic and Process-Level Performance Measures

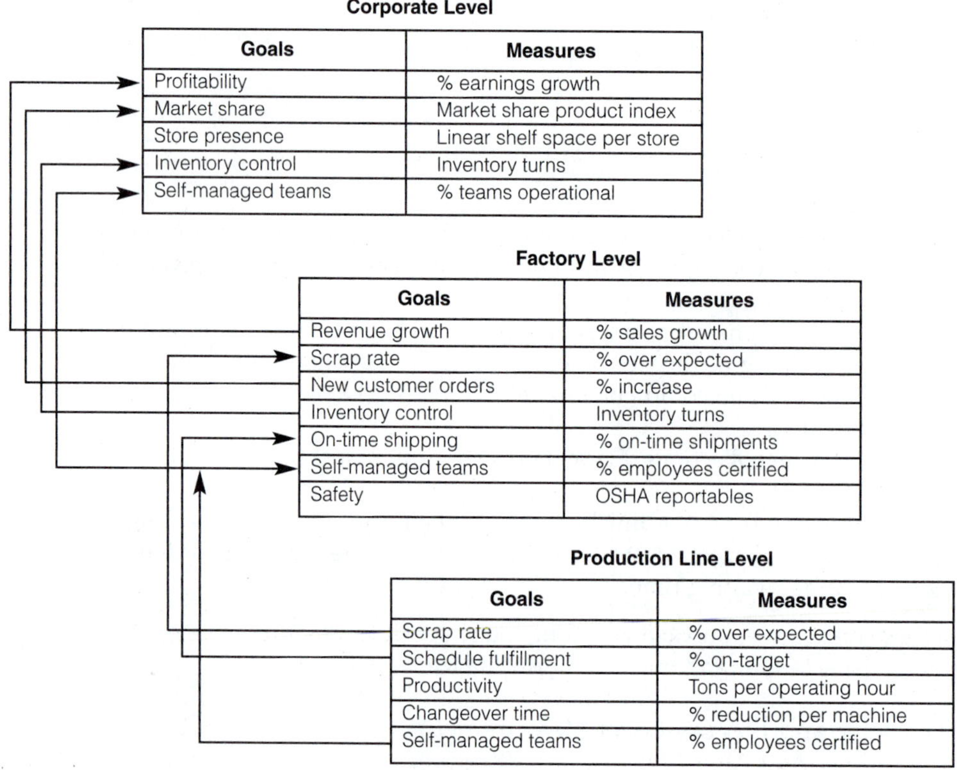

Source: R. I. Wise, "A Method for Aligning Process-Level and Strategy-Level Performance Metrics," *The Quality Management Forum*, Vol. 25, No. 1. Spring 1999, pp. 4–6. American Society for Quality, 11th Annual Quality Management Conference.

much larger than previously reported, generally in the range of 20 to 40 percent of sales. Second, quality-related costs were not only related to manufacturing operations, but to ancillary services such as purchasing and customer service departments as well. Third, most of the costs resulted from poor quality and were avoidable. Finally, while the costs of poor quality were avoidable, no clear responsibility for action to reduce them was assigned, nor was any structured approach formulated to do so. As a result, many companies began to develop cost of quality programs. The "costs of quality"—or more specifically, the costs of *poor* quality—were associated with avoiding poor quality or incurred as a result of poor quality.

COQ approaches have numerous objectives. Perhaps the most important objective is to translate quality problems into the "language" of upper management—the language of money. Juran noted that workers and supervisors speak in the "language of things," which includes units, defects, and so on. Unfortunately, quality problems expressed as the number of defects typically have little impact on top managers who are generally more concerned with financial performance. But if the magnitude of quality problems can be translated into monetary terms, such as "How much would it cost us to run this business if there were no quality problems?" the eyes of upper managers are opened. Dollar figures can be added meaningfully across departments or products, and compared to other dollar measures. Middle managers who must deal with both workers and supervisors as well as top management must have the ability to speak in both languages. Quality cost information serves a variety of other purposes, too. It helps management evaluate the relative importance of quality problems and thus identify major opportunities for cost reduction. It can aid in budgeting and cost control activities. Finally, it can serve as a scoreboard to evaluate the organization's success in achieving quality objectives.

To establish a cost of quality approach, one must identify the activities that generate cost, measure them, report them in a way that is meaningful to managers, and analyze them to identify areas for improvement. The following sections discuss these activities in greater detail.

Quality Cost Classification

Quality costs can be organized into four major categories: prevention costs, appraisal costs, internal failure costs, and external failure costs. **Prevention costs** are investments made to keep nonconforming products from occurring and reaching the customer, including the following specific costs:

- *Quality planning costs,* such as salaries of individuals associated with quality planning and problem-solving teams, the development of new procedures, new equipment design, and reliability studies
- *Process control costs,* which include costs spent on analyzing production processes and implementing process control plans
- *Information systems costs* expended to develop data requirements and measurements
- *Training and general management costs,* including internal and external training programs, clerical staff expenses, and miscellaneous supplies.

Appraisal costs are those associated with efforts to ensure conformance to requirements, generally through measurement and analysis of data to detect nonconformances. Categories of appraisal costs include the following:

- *Test and inspection costs* associated with incoming materials, work-in-process, and finished goods, including equipment costs and salaries

- *Instrument maintenance costs*, arising from calibration and repair of measuring instruments
- *Process measurement and control costs*, which involve the time spent by workers to gather and analyze quality measurements.

Internal failure costs are incurred as a result of unsatisfactory quality found before the delivery of a product to the customer. Some examples include the following:

- *Scrap and rework costs*, including material, labor, and overhead
- *Costs of corrective action*, arising from time spent determining the causes of failure and correcting production problems
- *Downgrading costs*, such as revenue lost when selling a product at a lower price because it does not meet specifications
- *Process failures*, such as unplanned machine downtime or unplanned equipment repair.

External failure costs occur after poor-quality products reach the customer, specifically

- *Costs due to customer complaints and returns*, including rework on returned items, cancelled orders, and freight premiums
- *Product recall costs* and *warranty claims*, including the cost of repair or replacement as well as associated administrative costs
- *Product liability costs*, resulting from legal actions and settlements.

Experts estimate that 60 to 90 percent of total quality costs are the result of internal and external failure and are the responsibility of, but not easily controllable by management. In the past, managers reacted to high failure costs by increasing inspection. Such actions, however, only increase appraisal costs. The overall result is little, if any, improvement in quality or profitability. In practice, an increase in prevention usually generates larger savings in all other cost categories. In a typical scenario, the cost of replacing a poor-quality component in the field might be $500; the cost of replacement after assembly might be $50; the cost of testing and replacement during assembly might be $5; and the cost of changing the design to avoid the problem might be only 50 cents.

Better prevention of poor quality clearly reduces internal failure costs, as fewer defective items are made. External failure costs also decrease. In addition, less appraisal is required, because the products are made correctly the first time. However, because production is usually viewed in the short term, many managers fail to understand or implement these ideas.

A convenient way of reporting quality costs is through a breakdown by organizational function as shown in Figure 8.7. This matrix serves several purposes. First, it allows all departments to recognize their contributions to the cost of quality and participate in a cost of quality program. Second, it pinpoints areas of high quality cost and turns attention toward improvement efforts. Such a report can be implemented easily on a spreadsheet.

Quality costs are often reported as an *index*; that is, the ratio of the current value to a base period. Index numbers increase managers' understanding of the data, particularly how conditions in one period compare with those in other periods. A simple type of index is called a relative index, computed by dividing a current value by a base period value. Sometimes the result is multiplied by 100 to express it as a percentage. As an example, consider the following direct labor costs per quarter for a manufactured product:

Quarter	Cost
1	$1,500
2	1,800
3	1,700
4	1,750

If the first quarter is the base period, the cost relative indexes expressed as percentages are computed as

Quarter	Cost Relative Index		%
1	(1,500/1,500)(100)	=	100
2	(1,700/1,500)(100)	=	120
3	(1,700/1,500)(100)	=	113.33
4	(1,750/1,500)(100)	=	116.67

Costs and prices are often sensitive to changes in the firm. For example, if the number of units produced in each quarter differs, comparisons of direct labor costs are meaningless. However, a measure such as cost per unit would provide useful information for managers.

Quality costs themselves provide little information, because they may vary due to such factors as production volume or seasonality. Thus, index numbers can more effectively analyze quality cost data. Some common measurement bases are labor, manufacturing cost, sales, and units of product. Each is described here.

- *Labor-Based Index* Quality cost per direct labor-hour represents a typical quality cost index that is easily understood by managers. Accounting departments can

Figure 8.7 Cost of Quality Matrix

	Design Engineering	Purchasing	Production	. . .	Finance	. . .	Accounting	Totals
Prevention costs Quality planning Training . . .								
Appraisal costs Test and inspection Instruments . . .								
Internal failure costs Scrap Rework . . .								
External failure costs Returns Recall costs . . .								
Totals								

usually provide direct labor data, either in total labor-hours or standard labor-hours. Standard hours often provide a better measure than total labor-hours because they represent planned rather than actual production. Labor-based indexes are drastically influenced by automation and other changes in technology, however, so one must be careful in using them over long periods of time. Often quality cost per direct labor-dollar is used to eliminate the effects of inflation.

- *Cost-Based Index* Quality cost per manufacturing cost dollar is a common index in this category. Manufacturing cost includes direct labor, material, and overhead costs that are usually available from accounting departments. Cost-based indexes are more stable than labor-based indexes, because they are not affected by price fluctuations or by changes in the level of automation.
- *Sales-Based Index* Quality cost per sales dollar is a popular index that appeals to top management. However, this measure is rather poor for short-term analysis, because sales usually lag behind production and are subject to seasonal variations. In addition, a sales-based index is affected by changes in the selling price.
- *Unit-Based Index* A common measure in this category is quality costs per unit of production. This simple index is acceptable if the output of production lines is similar; however, it is a poor measure if many different products are made. In such a case, an alternative index of quality costs per equivalent unit of output is often used. To obtain this index, different product lines are weighted to approximate a standard or "average" product that is used as a common base.

All these indexes, although used extensively in practice, have a fundamental problem. A change in the denominator can appear to be a change in the level of quality or productivity alone. For instance, if direct labor is decreased through managerial improvements, the direct labor-based index will increase even if quality does not change. Also, the common inclusion of overhead in manufacturing cost is certain to distort results. Nevertheless, use of such indexes is widespread and helpful for comparing quality costs over time. Generally, sales bases are the most popular, followed by cost, labor, and unit bases.[18]

Quality cost data can be broken down by product line, process, department, work center, time, or cost category. This categorization makes data analysis more convenient and useful to management. For example, a company might collect quality costs by cost category and product for each time period, say one month. An example is given in the following table:

	January		February	
Cost Category	**Product A**	**Product B**	**Product A**	**Product B**
Prevention	$ 2,000	$ 4,000	$ 2,000	$ 4,000
Appraisal	10,000	20,000	13,000	21,000
Internal failure	19,000	106,000	16,000	107,000
External failure	54,000	146,000	52,000	156,000
Total	$85,000	$276,000	$83,000	$288,000
Standard direct labor costs	$35,000	$ 90,000	$28,000	$ 86,000

A total quality cost index is

Total quality cost index = Total quality costs/Direct labor costs

Alternatively, individual indexes can be computed by category, product, and time period, and are summarized in the following table:

	January		February	
Cost Category	**Product A**	**Product B**	**Product A**	**Product B**
Prevention	0.057	0.044	0.071	0.047
Appraisal	0.286	0.222	0.464	0.244
Internal failure	0.543	1.178	0.571	1.244
External failure	1.543	1.622	1.857	1.814
Total	2.429	3.067	2.964	3.349

Such information can be used to identify trends or areas that require significant attention. Of course, such information can only signal areas for improvement; it cannot tell managers what the specific problems are. Teams of workers are responsible for uncovering the sources of problems and determining appropriate corrective action. For example, a steady rise in internal failure costs and decline in appraisal costs might indicate a problem in assembly, maintenance of testing equipment, or a lack of proper control of purchased parts.

A useful analysis tool that we will study formally in Chapter 10 is Pareto analysis. In the context of quality costs, the sources of cost are rarely uniformly distributed. Pareto analysis consists of ordering cost categories from largest to smallest. For example, chances are that 70 or 80 percent of all internal failure costs are due to only one or two manufacturing problems. Identifying these "vital few," as they are called, leads to corrective action that has a high return for a low dollar input.

For most companies embarking on a quality cost program, management typically finds that the highest costs occur in the external failure category, followed by internal failure, appraisal, and prevention, in that order. Clearly, the order should be reversed; that is, the bulk of quality costs should be found in prevention, some in appraisal, perhaps a few in internal failure, and virtually none in external failure. Thus, companies should first attempt to reduce external failure costs to zero by investing in appraisal activities to discover the sources of failure and take corrective action. As quality improves, failure costs will decrease, and the amount of appraisal can be reduced with the shift of emphasis to prevention activities.

Quality Costs in Service Organizations

The nature of quality costs differs between service and manufacturing organizations. In manufacturing, quality costs are primarily product-oriented; for services, however, they are generally labor-dependent, because labor often accounts for as much as 75 percent of total costs. Traditional external failure costs such as warranty and field support are less relevant to services than to manufacturing. Process-related costs, such as customer service and complaint-handling staff and lost customers are more critical.

Internal failure costs might not be as evident in services as in manufacturing. For example, a small distributor focused a great deal of attention on minimizing inventories while trying to improve service. The company knew that backorders existed, but believed that it was simply the nature of the business. But further analysis revealed nearly one backorder for every five orders. After examining the process, the cost of backorders was determined to be $30 per transaction, for an annual cost of $200,000. The reasons were found to include suppliers not meeting delivery dates, errors in sales orders, and other non-value-added operations.[19] Internal failure costs tend to be much lower for service organizations with high customer contact, which have little opportunity to correct an error before it reaches the customer. By that time, the error becomes an external failure.

Work measurement and sampling techniques are often used extensively to gather quality costs in service organizations. For example, work measurement can be used to determine how much time an employee spends on various quality-related activities. The proportion of time spent multiplied by the individual's salary represents an estimate of the quality cost for that activity. Consumer surveys and other means of customer feedback are also used to determine quality costs for services. In general, however, the intangible nature of the output makes quality cost accounting for services difficult.

Capturing Quality Costs Through Activity-Based Costing[20]

The importance of quality has had a major impact on the role of accounting systems in business. Standard accounting systems are generally able to provide quality cost data for direct labor, overhead, scrap, warranty expenses, product liability costs, and maintenance, repair, and calibration of test equipment. However, most accounting systems are not structured to capture important cost-of-quality information. Costs such as service effort, product design, remedial engineering effort, rework, in-process inspection, and engineering change losses must usually be estimated or collected through special efforts. Some costs due to external failure, such as customer dissatisfaction and future lost revenues, are impossible to estimate accurately. Although prevention costs are the most important, appraisal costs, internal failure, external failure, and prevention costs (in that order) are usually easier to collect.

Traditional accounting systems focused on promoting the efficiency of mass production, particularly production with few standard products and high direct labor. Traditional systems accurately measure the resources that are consumed in proportion to the number of units produced of individual products. Today's products are characterized by much lower direct labor, and many activities that consume resources are unrelated to the volume of units produced. As a result of automation, direct labor typically is only 15 percent of manufacturing cost and can be as low as 5 percent in high-tech industries. Meanwhile, overhead costs have grown to 55 percent or more, and are spread across all products using the same formula. Because of these changes, traditional accounting systems present an inadequate picture of manufacturing efficiency and effectiveness and do a poor job of allocating the expenses of these support resources to individual products. Moreover, they attach no value to such elements as rework or bottlenecks that impede processing. Because these costs are hidden, managers typically have little incentive to cut them.

Activity-based costing organizes information about the work (or activity) that consumes resources and delivers value in a business. People consuming resources in work ultimately achieve the value that customers pay for. Examples of activities might be moving, inspecting, receiving, shipping, and order processing. To get a handle on these activities, cross-functional teams of workers, managers, and even secretaries map each step of every business process using flowcharts. These flowcharts pinpoint the operations that add value and reveal the ones that do not.

Activity-based costing allocates overhead costs to the products and services that use them. Knowing the costs of activities supports efforts to improve processes. Once activities can be traced to individual products or services, then additional strategic information is made available. The effects of delays and inefficiencies become readily apparent. The company can then focus on reducing these hidden costs.

With the new information provided by activity-based costing, managers can make better decisions about product designs, process improvements, pricing, and product mix. Other benefits include the facilitation of continuous improvement activities to reduce overhead costs, and the ease with which relevant costs can be determined. For instance, Caterpillar Inc. used activity-based costing to determine the value of intangibles such as better quality and faster time-to-market to persuade the board to approve a $2 billion modernization effort in 1987. LTV has incorporated activity-based costing into its Integrated Process Management Methodology.[21] The accounting department supports the manufacturing and other departments by providing information on product costing and operating activities to evaluate performance, identify deficiencies, and assess quality costs arising from internal and external failure of products and customer product requirements. The system helps managers to integrate customer requirements with product improvement strategies.

MEASURING THE RETURN ON QUALITY

Total quality efforts should lead to the achievement of outstanding business results. However, a successful quality initiative does not guarantee financial success. (Many argue that without it, however, a company will eventually be doomed to failure.) Many companies fail to pay enough attention to the financial returns on quality-related investments. Financial returns not only demonstrate when the efforts are going in the right direction, but can help identify changes and improvements that need to be made before staying on the wrong path too long. For example, AT&T's chairman receives a quarterly report from each business unit that describes quality improvements and their financial impacts.

Traditionally, measuring reductions in quality-related costs through COQ was the principal method of documenting the benefits of quality. However, this approach only focuses on the internal view of quality. Attention must also be paid to the external view and accounting for increases in revenues associated with improved customer satisfaction. Measuring expected revenue gains against costs associated with quality efforts has become known as **return on quality,** or **ROQ**. ROQ is based on four main principles:[22]

1. Quality is an investment.
2. Quality efforts must be made financially accountable.
3. It is possible to spend too much on quality.
4. Not all quality expenditures are equally valid.

The foundation for the approach stems from the model in Chapter 1 (Figure 1.4), relating quality to profitability, which proposes that quality improvement leads to financial returns through improvements in customer satisfaction and loyalty. Sophisticated statistical methods are often used to estimate these effects and the financial implications.

A prescription for implementing ROQ was described in *Business Week*:

1. *Start with an effective quality approach.* Companies that don't have the basics, such as process and inventory controls and other building blocks, will find a healthy return on quality elusive.
2. *Calculate the cost of current quality initiatives.* Cost of warranties, problem prevention, and monitoring activities all count. Measure these against the returns for delivering a product or service to the customer.
3. *Determine what key factors retain customers and what drives them away.* Conduct detailed surveys. Forecast market changes, especially quality and new-product initiatives of competitors.

4. *Focus on quality efforts most likely to improve customer satisfaction at a reasonable cost.* Figure the link between each dollar spent on quality and its effect on customer retention and market share.
5. *Roll out successful approaches after pilot-testing the most promising efforts and cutting the ones that don't have a big impact.* Closely monitor results. Build word of mouth by publicizing success stories.
6. *Improve quality efforts continually.* Measure results against anticipated gains. Beware of the competition's initiative and don't hesitate to revamp approaches accordingly. Quality never rests.[23]

The ROQ approach was applied to evaluating a training program to improve customer service skills of branch staff at Chase Manhattan Bank.[24] The intended outcomes of the program included the ability of the branch staff to identify behavior that creates a positive memorable customer experience, analyze interactions with customers, identify what customers want, and understand the nature of caring customer service. Test and control groups were used. The net present value of the loss avoided from customers not becoming dissatisfied as a result of the training program was then estimated at $471,000 and compared to a $326,000 net present value of training costs. The resulting return on investment was computed to be 44.4 percent. This evaluation showed that a systemwide training program would likely be profitable. Results were circulated among Chase managers, and the company moved forward with expansion of the training program.

MANAGING AND USING PERFORMANCE DATA

Simply collecting data is not enough. Companies must ensure that data are reliable and accessible to all who need them and analyze the data to transform them into useful information.

Data Validity and Reliability

The familiar computer cliché, "Garbage in, garbage out," applies equally well to quality-related data. Data used for planning and decision making need to be complete and accurate, particularly with the increasing use of electronic data transfer. Like any business process, information creation should be managed with total quality principles.[25] The quality of information can be improved by capturing data only once, and as close to the origin of the data as possible; eliminating human error by capturing data electronically where possible; using a single database whenever feasible; eliminating all unnecessary handling of data by intermediaries, such as data entry clerks; placing accountability on the creators of data and information; ensuring proper training; and defining targets and measures of data quality.

Any measurement is subject to error, and, as a result, the credibility of data can be suspect. A measure is **valid** if it measures what it says it measures. **Reliability** of a measurement refers to how well the measuring instrument—manual instruments, automated equipment, or surveys and questionnaires—consistently measures the "true value" of the characteristic. Measurement reliability in manufacturing demands careful attention to metrology, the science of measurement (discussed in Chapter 11).

In services, a useful approach to ensuring data reliability is periodic audits of the processes used to collect the data, conducted by internal cross-functional teams or external auditors, who assess the reliability of a company's data. Standardized forms, clear instructions, and adequate training lead to more consistent performance in data collection. AT&T Universal Card Services, for example, used standard data entry templates and procedures to facilitate the consistency and uniform editing of manually input data. Data collected automatically from interfaces with other systems use standard record formats and edits, and are reconciled at each handoff. Also, a central data dictionary defines critical data elements according to source, meaning, format, and valid content of each. AT&T follows stringent guidelines and standards for developing, maintaining, documenting, and managing data systems.

Data Accessibility

A company's efforts are wasted if collected data are not available to the right employees when needed. In most companies, data are accessible to top managers and others on a need-to-know basis. In TQ-focused companies, quality-related data are accessible to everyone. A customer service representative who tells a customer that the rep needs to find some information and will call back the next day cannot satisfy that customer in a timely fashion. At Milliken, all databases, including product specifications, process data, supplier data, customer requirements, and environmental data are available to every associate throughout the computer network. Electronic charts displayed throughout the plant and in business support departments show key quality measures and trends. Salespeople at the Wallace Company can check inventory available at any district office. Data accessibility empowers employees and encourages their participation in quality improvement efforts.

Modern information technology plays a critical role in data accessibility. Many companies have state-of-the-art on-line computer networks supplemented by local processing capabilities. Prudential Insurance Company agents take portable computers to customer's homes or places of business.[26] This practice reduces the time needed to answer a client's questions and increases the accuracy and reliability of the answers. Sales and service offices are connected electronically. Each can obtain information about the current status of contracts being serviced by another office, and thus can be of assistance to customers who contact them directly. They can also electronically forward requests for action to the appropriate office.

Analyzing and Using Performance Data

Data related to quality, customers, and operational performance support both operational-level decision making and strategic planning. Data can be analyzed using many different types of descriptive statistical techniques and charts to identify trends over time, compare performance among business units, and show comparisons with key benchmarks. The capabilities of today's spreadsheet and database software, such as Microsoft Excel® and Access®, make it simple for nearly any employee. However, volumes of data acquired at the process level, while useful for daily operations, generally are not appropriate for senior executive review. Organizations need a process for transforming data, usually in some integrated fashion, into information that top management can understand and work with. For instance, some companies develop an aggregate customer satisfaction index (CSI) by weighting satisfaction results, market share, and gains or losses of customers. As discussed earlier, FedEx aggregates different quality components into a single index.

Simply reporting statistical measures or graphs and charts is not enough. As we noted in our discussion of the balanced scorecard, managers must also understand the linkages between key measures of business performance. Establishing a clear cause-and-effect linkage between external lagging results and internal leading measures provides a visible and obvious direction for improvement. Examples of such analyses include the following:

- How product and service quality improvement correlates with key customer indicators such as customer satisfaction, customer retention, and market share
- Financial benefits derived from improvements in employee safety, absenteeism, and turnover
- Benefits and costs associated with education and training
- Relationships between product and service quality, operational performance indicators, and overall financial performance
- Profit impacts of customer satisfaction and retention
- Market share changes as a result of changes in customer satisfaction
- Impacts of employee satisfaction on customer satisfaction

Numerous aggregate studies have demonstrated positive cause-and-effect relationships between employee satisfaction, customer satisfaction, and financial or market share results. However, companies need to establish specific relationships using their own data. For example, FedEx correlates the 10 quality components with customer satisfaction through extensive market research. Additionally, it conducts focus groups and other surveys to validate these relationships.

Interlinking is a term that describes the quantitative modeling of cause-and-effect relationships between external and internal performance measures, such as the relationship of customer satisfaction measures to internal process measures of product quality or employee performance.[27] A simple interlinking model was developed by Florida Power and Light.[28] In studying the telephone operation of its customer service centers, FPL sampled customers to determine their level of satisfaction with waiting times on the telephone. Satisfaction began to fall significantly at about two minutes (see Figure 8.8). FPL also found that customer satisfaction is directly related to how callers perceive the competence of the phone representatives. Research showed that excessive waiting times caused a bias in the ratings. Eliminating this bias

Figure 8.8 Interlinking Model of Customer Satisfaction and Time on Hold

Customer Satisfaction Rating	Time on Hold
1.32	<30 sec.
1.57	30–60 sec.
1.67	1–2 min.
2.14	2–3 min.

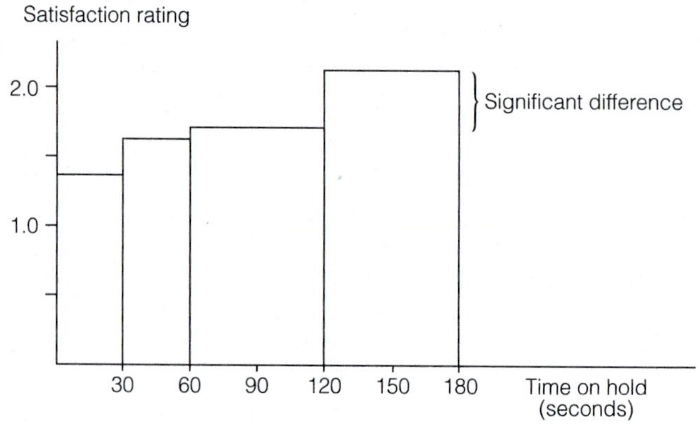

made a substantial contribution toward accurately measuring customer satisfaction with the phone contact experience. To improve customer satisfaction, FPL developed a system to notify customers of the anticipated wait and give them a choice of holding or deferring the call to a later time. Customers were actually willing to wait longer on hold without being dissatisfied if they knew the length of the wait, which improved customer satisfaction even when call traffic was heavy.

Another example is Sears Roebuck.[29] Sears provided a consulting group with 13 financial measures, hundreds of thousands of employee satisfaction data points, and millions of data points on customer satisfaction. Using advanced statistical modeling, the analysts discovered that employee attitudes about the job and the company are key factors that predict their behavior with customers, which, in turn, predicts the likelihood of customer retention and recommendations, which in turn predict financial performance. Sears can now predict that if a store increases its employee satisfaction score by 5 units, customer satisfaction scores will go up by 2 units, and revenue growth will beat the stores' national average by 0.5 percent.

Not all interlinking models need to be based on sophisticated statistical and computer models. Ames Rubber Corporation, for example, has shown that simple graphs establish important correlations among measures that impact business decisions and strategy. For example, it has found that internal yields increase as employee turnover decreases, and that lost time accidents decrease with increasing training hours, leading to new initiatives for training and HR policies.

By using such interlinking models, managers can determine objectively the effects of additional resources or changes in the system to reduce waiting time. Improving the process is only appropriate once a linkage to customer satisfaction is established. This practice is "management by fact"; without it, it is only "management by guess." The objectives and benefits of interlinking include the following:

- Screening out weak or misleading performance measures
- Focusing management attention on key performance measures that do make a difference
- Predicting performance such as customer satisfaction levels
- Setting target standards for performance
- Requiring areas such as marketing and operations to coordinate their data analysis efforts
- Making wise decisions faster than competitors do
- Seeing relationships among performance variables that competitors miss
- Enhancing communication within the organization based on good data analysis and management by fact.[30]

Recently, interlinking is being supported by new software technology for analyzing data, particularly data mining. **Data mining** is the process of searching large databases to find hidden patterns in data, using various analytical approaches and technologies such as cluster analysis, neural networks, and fuzzy logic. Data mining computer programs can sort through millions of pieces of information and identify subtle correlations between many variables, which is far more than the human mind is capable of doing. For example, data mining might discover that a particular supplier has a higher defect rate on parts costing less than $5, or that consumers who purchase a backup disk drive also tend to purchase a software utility package. Using data mining, MCI has developed a set of 22 detailed and highly secret statistical profiles to identify potential customers who might leave for a rival company.[31] Data mining is relatively inexpensive and can provide new competitive knowledge. However, it requires clean data and although it establishes correlations among variables, it cannot necessarily establish cause and effect. Also, it can easily lead to useless insights or overlook insights that are important. Nevertheless, the technology holds considerable promise.

INFORMATION AND ANALYSIS IN THE BALDRIGE CRITERIA

Category 4 of the 2001 Malcolm Baldrige National Quality Award Criteria for Performance Excellence is titled *Information and Analysis.* This category examines an organization's performance management system and how the organization analyzes performance data and information. Item 4.1, *Measurement and Analysis of Organizational Performance*, examines how an organization designs its performance management system for measuring, analyzing, aligning, and improving performance across the organization. The criteria ask how an organization gathers and integrates data and selects appropriate measures and indicators for use in daily operations and decision making; how it selects and uses comparative information and data; and how it keeps its performance measurement system current. It also looks at how an organization analyzes performance data to support senior executive review and organizational planning, how results are communicated to work-group and functional-level operations to support decision making, and how the results of analysis align with strategic objectives and action plans. The aim of analysis is to guide an organization's process management activities toward the achievement of key business results and strategic objectives. Organizations have a critical need for effective analytical capability because resources are limited and cause-and-effect connections are often unclear.

Item 4.2, *Information Management*, addresses how an organization ensures the quality and availability of data for employees, suppliers or partners, and customers. It addresses issues of information integrity and accuracy, and the reliability of hardware and software systems.

The following example shows how Collin Technologies might respond to Item 4.2, and the feedback that a Baldrige examiner team might provide. *You should read Case III in Chapter 3 first if you have not already done so. Think about how the response addresses the questions asked in the 2000 criteria. The criteria are available on the CD-rom accompanying this book along with the complete case study.*

Example 1: Collin Technologies—Information and Analysis

Response to Criteria Item 4.2, Analysis of Organizational Performance

The leadership team uses the subset of the leading and lagging indicators of a balanced scorecard (BSC) to evaluate the overall health of the organization. Analysis of these (BSC) indicators is key to providing the leadership team with a clear picture of the overall health of the company and short-term company performance. It supports Collins core values of becoming "better" at serving customers, employee-owners (EOs), and suppliers, reinvestment and use of profits, and the community. As noted in Area 1.1a, stakeholder teams are designated with the responsibility to make this improvement happen. They are also responsible for analyzing relevant leading and lagging measures. Then they present both positive and negative results affecting the BSC measures to Candice Trobaugh and the leadership team during bimonthly performance review meetings. The process used to analyze BSC measures (Figure 8.9) is also used to analyze all results. It is a key element of Collin's Continuous Improvement Process described in Category 6. The analysis process follows a "five-step"

Figure 8.9 Collin's Five-Step Analysis Process

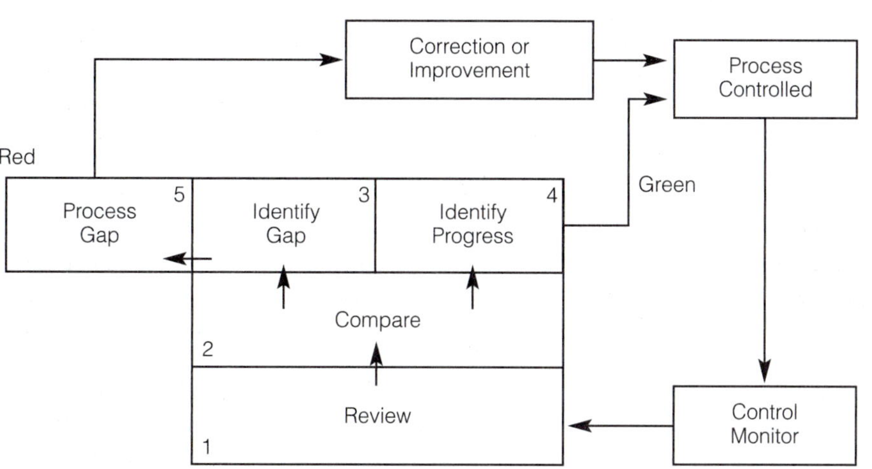

analysis approach (center block of Figure 8.9). This process as applied to the BSC measures is as follows:

1. Both leading and lagging information measurement results are reviewed.
2. BSC output results (OPR) measures are compared to known comparisons provided by the Benchmark Team.
3. Gaps to short-term goals are identified.
4. PDR (predictive results) measures that are on track and that allow BSC OPRs to close short-term gaps are noted and labeled as "Green."
5. PDR measures that are not on track and inhibit BSC OPRs from closing short-term gaps are noted and labeled as "Red."

Collin's Continuous Improvement Process is then utilized to identify actions for all "Red" PDR measures and bring them back to "Green" status. The same process is used for long-term or strategic goals. By depicting information in this way, areas that are operating well are clear as well as those needing additional support. As identified in Area 4.1a, lagging data and their associated measures are also used to control organizational-level performance. Their analysis is based on a combination of daily trend analysis by Collin EOs and automatic "action-requesting" exception reports triggered by the CAIN system. When trigger settings are exceeded, a flag message is sent to the managers or team leaders responsible for the measure. This linkage of result to process ensures that functional-level decisions are based on factual data and trends. One example of how trend data are analyzed and translated into useful information at the operational level is described in the following paragraphs.

One of Collin's BSC indicators is the leading PDR measure of shipment linearity deviation, or Collin's ability to produce a product in a systematic way throughout the month to ensure that customers receive the product on time. The related OPR result tracked is on-time delivery performance. The PDR measure tracked identifies the deviation from planned shipment. At the operational level, Collin tracks this measure as a leading indicator; but as a BSC indicator, it is sampled weekly and plotted as a monthly average. A trigger point is set within CAIN to notify management if the drift from plan exceeds 10 percent. (The trigger limit is based on one half of the allowable upside capacity of 20 percent.) This signal allows decision-makers to use the excess capacity as a method to catch up when schedules slip. This exception flag warning system is a last resort process because the information provided daily is predictive and, when watched, helps to prevent major drifts. Even when unexpected problems occur that trigger the system, Collin has a plan to get back on track before delivery schedules are impacted. A results figure in Item 7.5 shows Collin's ability to plan and execute to a planned schedule for the last five years. As noted previously, most lagging (OPR) measures are not BSC indicators, but are aligned with leading PDR measures. All BSC measures are aligned with OPR measures (see Category 1), thus showing what drives performance toward meeting plans and goals. In this way, they provide a direct path from processes to benchmarks to leadership team reviews. The predictive type BSC measures are aligned to the plans and objectives of the company. They are then linked to appropriate OPR measures and helps determine Collin's strategic position relative to the industry and the business community. Figure 8.10 shows this alignment.

As Collin increased its emphasis on process management and customers increased pressure to decrease product prices, the importance of the cost of each step in each key process also increased. As the process support teams (PSTs) continued their investigations of manufacturing processes, the activities and resulting costs associated with each purchased part were found to represent the input cost prior to productive work by Collin's teams. The work that these teams add to the price of the finished product represents additional costs to be incorporated into the final price of each product. When this incremental production cost is added to the cost of purchased parts, and the sum is subtracted from the final price for which the product is sold to the customer, the resulting figure represents the value that Collin has added to the product.

Collin is just beginning to formulate an overall program for monitoring this value. However, three years' worth of data have been collected for products supplied to key market segments, and this information is available from CAIN. The results for

Figure 8.10 BSC Measure Alignment

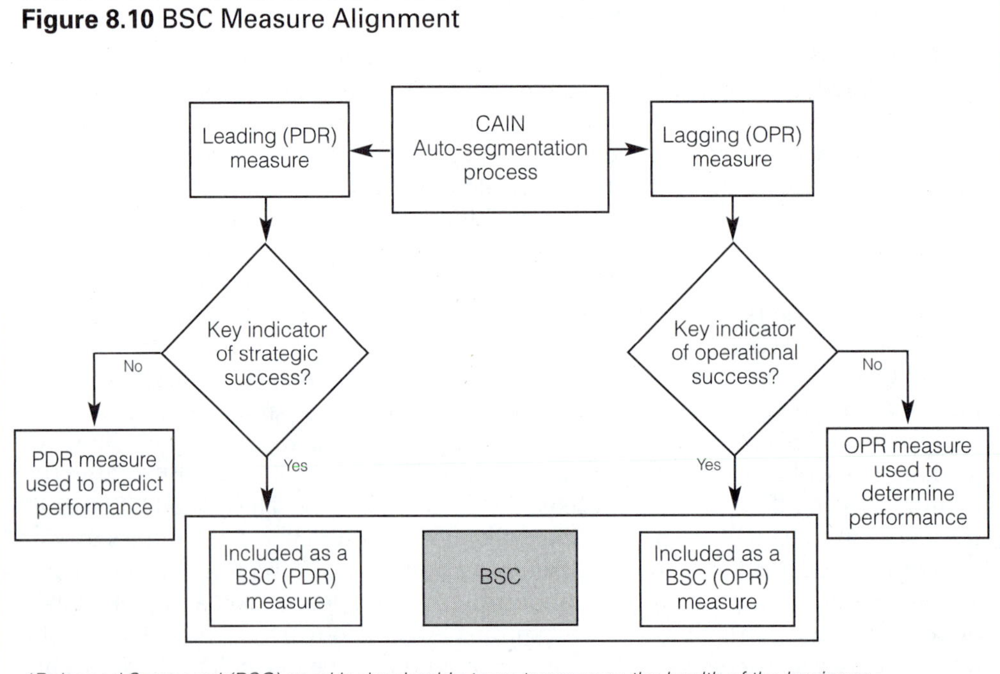

**Balanced Scorecard (BSC) used by leadership team to measure the health of the business.*

typical boards for the advanced technologies and commercial markets are shown in Item 7.2. The *Strategic Direction* element of the PPP requires completion of this value-added initiative by midyear.

Examiner Feedback

Strengths

- A five-step process is used by stakeholder teams to analyze BSC measures prior to the bimonthly performance review conducted by the leadership team. The process includes data review, comparative and gap analysis, and identification of opportunities to improve performance against short- and longer-term goals. This approach ensures that both strategic goals and short-term performance objectives, including competitive performance position, are regularly monitored and tracked.
- EOs analyze and trend organizational performance data on a daily and exception basis. For example, delivery schedules are proactively managed as a result of the exception-flag warning system that triggers an alert on emerging delivery problems. When trigger settings are exceeded, "action-requesting" exception reports are generated in the CAIN system to ensure timely deployment of a corrective action.
- Alignment of action plans to strategies is maintained by linking output measures directly to leading BSC indicators. This linkage provides a direct path between process performance results and comparisons against the BSC indicators. As the BSC measures are aligned with strategic goals and objectives, the applicant is able to determine current relative position to industry, competition, and benchmarks and also to evaluate its position relative to longer-term goals and objectives.

Opportunities for Improvement

- Even though BSC measures are reviewed regularly by the stakeholder teams and the leadership team, how the applicant systematically evaluates and assesses operational performance against plan using measures that are tracked below the BSC level is unclear.
- The applicant has stated that a key capability for achieving the strategic objective of product cost reduction is the ability to analyze the cost of opportunities and operational processes. Although some data are collected, the company appears to be in the early stages of developing this decision-making capability.

QUALITY IN PRACTICE

MEASUREMENT AND DATA MANAGEMENT AT XEROX[32]

In Chapter 1, the *Quality in Practice* feature described the quality transformation at Xerox. Measurement and data analysis is the cornerstone of its total quality effort. In 1989 Xerox had more than 375 major information systems supporting the business. Of these, 175 related specifically to the management, evaluation, and planning of quality, and were used to support more than 300 specific applications of these tasks. Figure 8.11 illustrates the scope and depth of the data used to support a prevention-based approach to quality improvement.

The Xerox quality measurement system extends from suppliers to customers. Metrics are specified at key measurement points of the Xerox Delivery Process. The answer to the question "What information can help us meet both internal

Figure 8.11 Scope and Depth of Xerox Quality-Related Data

134 Data Uses to *EVALUATE* the Quality of All Xerox Work Processes

SCOPE ▶ / ▼ DEPTH	CUSTOMER 17	SUPPLIER 13	INTERNAL OPS 23	PRODUCT/ SERVICES 20	EMPLOYEES 17	COMPETI-TION 10	BENCH-MARK 15	SAFETY 18	ENVIRON-MENTAL 1
PLANNING 15	• Cust. sat. data	• Local cont validation	• L-T-Q assess • PDP phase	• Reliability data	• Employee attitude	• Prod assess • Dealer dist	• TQC benchmark-	• Occup illness data	
DESIGN 26									
MANUFAC-TURING 34									
SALES 12									
SERVICE 18									
ADMIN 14									
SUPPORT 15									

79 Data Uses to Enable *MANAGEMENT* Decisions for Continuous Improvement

SCOPE ▶ / ▼	CUSTOMER	SUPPLIER 9	INTERNAL OPS 28	PRODUCT/ SERVICES 17	EMPLOYEES 10	COMPETI-TION 3	BENCH-MARK	SAFETY
10	• Cust. sat. data	• Site and sourcing data	• L-T-Q assess • Team tracking	• Xerox Dev process	• Mgmt. styles scores	• Competitive news flash	• Org plng	• UL data
DESIGN 18								
MANUFAC-TURING 16								
SALES 10								
SERVICE 9								
ADMIN 8								
SUPPORT 8								

92 Data Uses to *PLAN* for Continuous Quality Improvement

SCOPE ▶ / ▼ DEPTH	CUSTOMER 12	SUPPLIER 17	INTERNAL OPS 14	PRODUCT/ SERVICES 17	EMPLOYEES 14	COMPETI-TION 9	BENCH-MARK 9
PLANNING 27	• Customer requirements • Focus Group findings • Market research findings	• Supplier base • Technical plans • Product Array data • Quality history data	• Team excellence reports • Leadership through quality assessments	• Product - Quality - Reliability - Operability - Productivity - Planning • BRMS	• Training stats • Human resource data	• Trade assoc. reports • Trade show reports • Competitive scenarios	• Benc nws • Benc ref • Benc data
DESIGN 15	• Customer visits data • Problem ID data	• Commodity mix • Build site(s) • Technology data	• Cost of quality data • PDP test data	• Reliability • FMEA • Product life data • Config. data	• Mgmt. styles scores • Employee attitude survey	• Competitive support practices data	• Benc prac data
MANUFAC-TURING 12	• Customer visits data	• Commodity team surveys • Proc. capa-bility data • Source verif. data	• Suggestion system • Production line quality data	• Product quality data • In-line quality data	• Mgmt. styles scores • Employee attitude survey	• Competitive support practices data	• Benc prac data
SALES 10	• Customer sat. data • Problem ID data	N/A	• Establishment pinc info sys • Int. mktg sys • Copy vol sys	• Demo skills profile	• Mgmt. styles scores • Employee attitude survey	• Competitive support practices data	• Benc prac data
SERVICE 11	• Customer sat. data	• Spares Demand Data	• Field service suggestions • Cancels data	• Serv call data • Field rel • Field perf data	• Mgmt. styles scores • Employee attitude survey	• Competitive support practices data	• Benc prac data
ADMIN 9	• Customer sat. data • Order-to-invoice data • Billing quality data	N/A	• Audit results	• Performance data	• Mgmt. styles scores • Employee attitude survey scores	• Competitive support practices data	• Benc prac data
SUPPORT 8	N/A	• Education - Total Quality Control - Stat Process Control	• Quality Team Results • Cost of Quality Data	• Grievance system reports	• Xerox employee assist prog. • Reward & recog. data	• Competitive support practices data	• Benc prac data

and external customer requirements?" determines which information the company includes in its quality-related information systems. Each major operation, such as the U.S. marketing group or development and manufacturing, has a system review board composed of senior managers with the responsibility of validating customer requirements and overseeing the process by which those requirements are transformed into detailed specifications. As requirements develop, line and MIS groups work closely together to meet any needs within the information/data system.

Xerox structures its data management system to enhance data accuracy, validity, timeliness, consistency, standardization, and easy access. It formulates procedures for the improved collection, retention, and security of data. Users—internal customers—work closely with the data management organizations to define requirements for the timely use, dissemination, and presentation of data and information. Validity, accuracy, and timeliness are emphasized by the data systems quality assurance steps, shown in Figure 8.12, during the design, construction, and major upgrade of each data system. The accessibility of one of the most extensive computer networks in the world provides an average end-to-end response time of 2.5 seconds (better than the industry average), linking hundreds of Xerox sites on four continents and supplying information 24 hours a day, seven days a week.

Xerox has several major systems for collecting, tracking, analyzing, and integrating data needed to make specific decisions. One, the Automated Installation Quality Report system, contains data on the installation and initial performance of every machine at a customer location anywhere in the United States. This database can be accessed from anywhere for quality analysis and action from the customer interface back to design. A second, called Technology Readiness, is a conceptual framework for bringing together all the technological information required for development of a new product. It prescribes data and data analysis requirements regarding failure modes, critical parameters, subsystem interactions, achievable manufacturing variances, and system performance against goals that reflect both internal and external customer satisfaction requirements.

The primary measure of product quality is defects per machine, defined as any variance from customer requirements. In the early 1980s Xerox tracked only those defects attributable to internal operations. After the total quality effort, defects arising from all causes were given equal attention. Product teams use statistical tools and cost of quality analysis to track improvements. Beginning in

Figure 8.12 Data Systems Quality Assurance Steps

No.	Data Systems Quality Assurance Steps	Validity	
		Data Accuracy	**Data Timeliness**
1	Is the specific data definition consistent with today's need?	Requirement check	
2	Is the process flow from data input to ultimate use defined and disciplined?	Process check	Timing check
3	Is the data integrity maintained under all possible test conditions?	Accuracy standard check	
4	Is there a mechanism for introducing change in the process flow without disrupting the system?		Improvement check
5	Is there a process for users to correct errors in the data?	Error correction check	
6	Is there a process for evaluating data errors for root cause and correction?	Root cause check	
7	Is a set of integrated performance standards and measurements in place for data input, processing, and output?	Performance check	Performance check
8	Is there a system in place to improve the validity of, or eliminate the need for, these data?	Continuous improvement check	Continuous improvement check

1985 Xerox manufacturing quality measurements became a mirror image of customer requirements. After a new machine is installed, quality results for product reliability are monitored via customer reports. To verify internal results, early unscheduled maintenance calls act as a key indicator. Other measures the company tracks include product development and delivery lead times, repair response time and efficiency, operability and productivity, total cost of ownership, billing accuracy, delivery of supplies, order entry, professionalism, sales representative attention, and administrative competence.

Key Issues for Discussion

1. Discuss how data captured by Xerox span the entire scope of company performance.
2. This description of Xerox's data and information approaches was written before the concept of interlinking. What approaches might Xerox now employ based on the information presented here?
3. "Operability" means expanded features that are simple and easy to use, such as auto jam clearance, document handling, and easy-load paper and toner cartridges. Describe some methods to measure operability.

Quality in Practice

Modeling Cause-and-Effect Relationships at IBM Rochester[33]

IBM's AS/400 Division in Rochester, Minnesota, winner of the 1990 Malcolm Baldrige National Quality Award, struggled with the dilemma of having a wealth of information and a plethora of measurements without understanding which factors have the greatest impact on overall business performance. To better ascertain which factors were most critical, IBM initiated a study to determine whether any relationships existed among the numerous measurements. Interviews with division managers identified measurements they felt were most important. A list of more than 50 key measurements was considered. This list included traditional measurements such as market share, overall customer satisfaction, employee morale, job satisfaction, warranty costs, inventory costs, product scrap, and productivity.

The key measurements were defined in three general areas: business-related, such as revenue and productivity; quality-related, such as customer satisfaction and warranty costs; and people-related, such as employee satisfaction and morale. Customer satisfaction data were derived from customer satisfaction surveys of AS/4000 customers and measured the percentage of customers responding *satisfied* or *very satisfied* on five-point-scale surveys. Employee satisfaction data were derived from an annual survey of AS/400 division employees. An unweighted index represented the percentage of employees responding favorably to a set of survey questions. These survey questions, among other things, addressed employees' satisfaction with their job, their immediate manager, and their level of skills. Productivity was computed as the measurement of revenue produced per number of employees, calculated on an annual basis. Quality is reflected by the cost of quality. Although numerous measurements of the cost of quality included scrap and rework expenses, warranty costs (expenses) had the highest correlation to the other measurements used in this study. Warranty costs include labor, parts, and service expended during the warranty period of an AS/400. An aggregate of both hardware and software maintenance and service was used in this calculation to represent the total required costs associated with servicing an AS/400 at a customer's location, including replacement costs. Warranty cost per employee is calculated on an annual basis.

Using 10 years of data, the researchers identified a strong correlation among market share, customer satisfaction, productivity, warranty cost, and employee satisfaction. Table 8.3 shows those measurements that have a correlation equal to or greater than 0.7. Figure 8.13 shows a model that describes the cause-and-effect relationship among the factors (only those measurements with a correlation factor equal to or greater than 0.7 are shown). This model suggests that to improve employee satisfaction, a manager must focus on improving job satisfaction, satisfaction with management, and satisfaction with having the right skills for the job.

Table 8.3 IBM AS/400 Division Data 1984–1994

	Market Share	Customer Satisfaction	Productivity	Cost of Quality	Employee Satisfaction	Job Satisfaction	Manager	Satisfaction with Right Skills
Market Share	1.00	0.71	0.97	–0.86	0.84	0.84	—	0.97
Customer Satisfaction	0.71	1.00	—	–0.79	0.70	—	—	0.72
Productivity	0.97	—	1.00	—	0.93	0.92	0.86	0.98
Cost of Quality	–0.86	–0.79	—	1.00	—	—	—	—
Employee Satisfaction	0.84	0.70	0.93	—	1.00	0.92	0.92	0.86
Job Satisfaction	0.84	—	0.92	—	0.92	1.00	0.70	0.84
Satisfaction with Manager	—	—	0.86	—	0.92	0.70	1.00	0.92
Right Skills	0.97	0.72	0.98	—	0.86	0.84	0.92	1.00

Figure 8.13 The Relationship Between Market Share, Customer Satisfaction, Productivity, Cost of Quality, and Employee Satisfaction

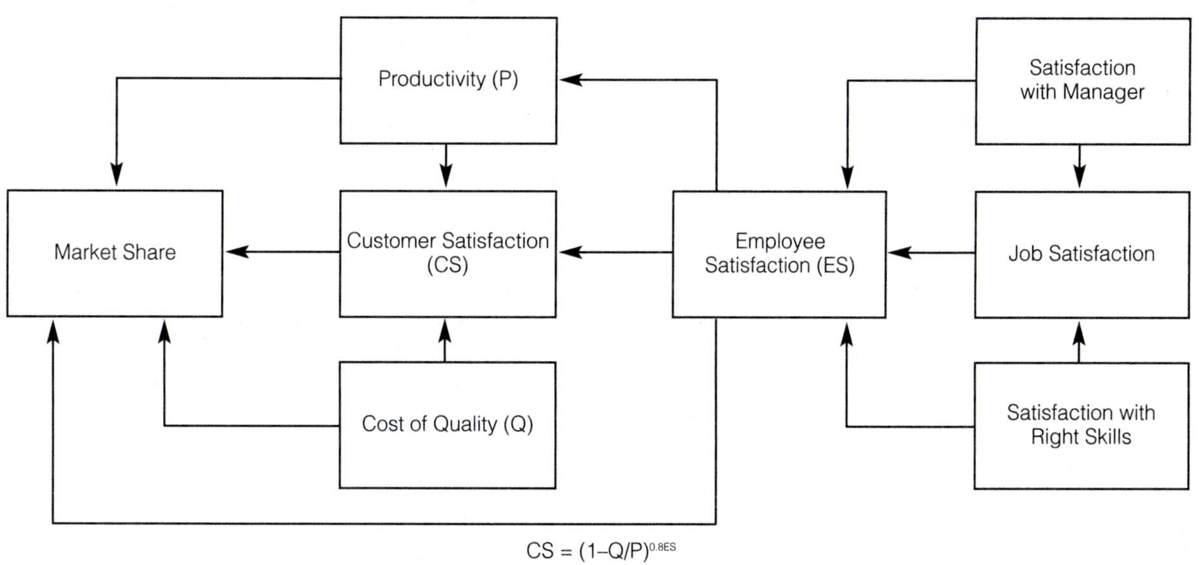

$CS = (1-Q/P)^{0.8ES}$

To improve job satisfaction, a manager must focus on improving satisfaction with management and satisfaction with having the right skills for the job. Improving satisfaction with having the right skills for the job will improve employee satisfaction and job satisfaction and will positively impact productivity, market share, and customer satisfaction. Improving employee satisfaction will directly impact productivity and customer satisfaction and will decrease warranty costs. Decreasing warranty costs will directly impact customer satisfaction and market share. Improving customer satisfaction will directly impact market share.

The study was not meant to explore every possible impact or relationship between operational measurements. However, it does suggest the need to take an enterprise view of measurements and understand the impact of one measurement on another. Most organizations are hierarchical and functionally oriented. Typically, customer satisfaction, employee satisfaction, quality, and productivity are each managed by a different group. Therefore, analyses and decisions are generally performed by each separate group without consideration for overall integration among these measurements. Additionally, reviews of these measurements are typically done through separate meetings or reports. A company needs to understand these relationships and review the measurements in aggregate. Otherwise, actions may be taken that have the opposite desired outcome on upstream results. For instance, if an action is taken that impacts employee satisfaction such as a layoff, the company must consider counteractions to prevent a decline in productivity, customer satisfaction, and market share.

Key Issues for Discussion

1. Explain why the relationships shown in Figure 8.13 make sense in theory.
2. Can these results apply to other businesses? Why or why not?

Summary of Key Points

- Measurement is the act of quantifying the performance dimensions of products, services, processes, and other business activities. Measures and indicators refer to the numerical information that results from measurement. Organizations need performance measures to drive strategies and organizational change, to manage resources, and to operate processes effectively and continuously improve.
- Data and information support control, diagnosis, and planning at the three levels of quality. Benefits include better knowledge of product and service quality, worker feedback, a basis for reward and recognition, means of assessing progress, and reduced costs through better planning.
- Leading practices for information management include developing a set of performance indicators that reflect customer requirements and key business drivers, using comparative information and data to improve performance, involving everyone and ensuring that information is widely visible throughout the organization, ensuring that data are reliable and accessible, using sound analytical methods that support strategic planning and daily decision making, and continually refining information sources and practices.
- The balanced scorecard consists of four perspectives: financial, internal, customer, and innovation and learning perspectives. A good balanced scorecard contains both leading and lagging measures and links them through logical cause-and-effect relationships.
- The Baldrige criteria provides a slightly different view of a balanced scorecard, and focuses on five categories of performance measurements and indicators: customer, financial and market, human resource, supplier and partner, and or-

ganizational effectiveness measures. Although many specific measures and indicators can be defined in each category, the ones an organization chooses should be tied to those factors that make it competitive in its industry.

- Comparative and benchmark data on which to evaluate performance results are needed to gain an accurate assessment of performance. Such data can be acquired through third parties and benchmarking leading organizations, such as Baldrige winners.
- Performance measures and indicators used by senior leaders should be aligned with company strategy and be actionable. Process-level measures are derived through close examination of the processes that create products and services. Strategic and process measures should be aligned in order to drive strategic goals through the organization.
- Quality cost programs translate quality problems into the language of upper management—money. Through the use of quality cost information, management identifies opportunities for quality improvement. Quality cost information also aids in budgeting and cost control and serves as a scoreboard to evaluate an organization's success.
- Quality costs generally are categorized into prevention, appraisal, internal failure, and external failure costs. These costs are often expressed as indexes using labor, manufacturing cost, sales, or unit measurement bases. Pareto analysis identifies quality problems that account for a large percentage of costs and that, if solved, result in high returns on investment.
- Activity-based costing allocates overhead cost to the products and services that use them. This practice can capture many quality costs that traditional accounting systems are unable to capture, and provides more useful information for quality improvement.
- Some organizations measure the return on quality (ROQ) as a means of justifying quality expenditures and demonstrating their value to senior management. This approach requires statistical techniques to measures the effects of changes in customer satisfaction, loyalty, and other factors on profitability.
- Organizations must ensure that data are valid and reliable; that is, they measure what they are supposed to consistently, and that employees have access to the data they need to do their jobs. Effective analysis capabilities ensure that managers can understand the meaning of data, particularly cause and effect linkages between external lagging results and internal leading indicators.
- Interlinking is the quantitative modeling of cause-and-effect relationships between external and internal performance measures. Interlinking allows managers to determine objectively the effects of internal variables under their control upon external measures, and hence to make better managerial decisions.
- The Baldrige criteria address an organization's performance measurement system, focusing on how measures and indicators are selected and aligned, how comparative information and data are used, and how all information is analyzed and used to support senior executive review, organizational planning, and daily operations.

Review Questions

1. Define measurement.
2. Explain the difference between measures and indicators.
3. Why do organizations need performance measures?

4. Explain the use of data and information at the three levels of quality in an organization.
5. What are the benefits of good data and information systems?
6. Summarize the leading practices related to data and information management.
7. What is the balanced scorecard? Describe its four components.
8. Explain the difference between leading and lagging measures. How are they used within a balanced scorecard?
9. What are the five key categories of results measures in the Malcolm Baldrige Criteria? Provide examples of measurements and indicators in each category.
10. Explain the types of measures commonly used for product and service quality.
11. What is the role of comparative data in a performance measurement system?
12. What two fundamental mistakes do organizations frequently make about measurement?
13. Explain the importance and utility of linking performance measures to strategy.
14. What do we mean by the term *actionable* in reference to measures and indicators?
15. Describe the process of defining process-level measurements.
16. Why are cost of quality programs valuable to managers?
17. List and explain the four major categories of quality costs. Give examples of each.
18. Discuss how index numbers are often used to analyze quality cost data.
19. How do quality costs differ between service and manufacturing organizations?
20. How does activity-based costing facilitate the acquisition of quality cost data?
21. What do we mean by validity and reliability of data? Why are these concepts important?
22. What is return on quality, or ROQ? Why is it a useful approach for organizations?
23. Why is accessibility of data important? How does information technology improve accessibility?
24. Describe ways by which data can be analyzed to generate useful managerial information?
25. What is interlinking? Provide an example.
26. How is information and analysis addressed in the Baldrige criteria?

Discussion Questions

1. Classify the measurements described in Figure 8.2 into one of the three levels of quality: organization, process, and performer/job level.
2. Under which perspective of the balanced scorecard would you classify each of the following measurements?
   a. On-time delivery to customers
   b. Time to develop the next generation of products
   c. Manufacturing yield
   d. Engineering efficiency
   e. Quarterly sales growth
   f. Percent of products that equals 70 percent of sales
   g. Cash flow
   h. Number of customer partnerships
   i. Increase in market share
   j. Unit cost of products

3. Many "course and instructor evaluation" systems consist of inappropriate or ineffective measurements. Discuss how the principles in this chapter can be used to develop an effective measurement system for instructor performance.
4. How can measurement be used to control and improve the daily operations of your college or university?
5. What types of performance measurements might be used by a fraternity or student organization?
6. In the making of cheese, companies test milk for somatic cell count to prevent diseases. They also test for bacteria to determine how clean the milk is, and perform a freezing-point test to see whether the milk was diluted with water (milk with water in it freezes at a lower temperature, which increases production costs because all the excess water must be extracted). Final cheese products are subjected to tests for weight, presence of foreign elements or chemicals, and for taste and smell. What customer-related measures might interlink with these internal measures?
7. What information would you need to fully answer the questions that IBM Rochester uses for selecting measures and indicators? Where would you get this information?
8. Discuss what the different categories of quality costs might mean to your college and university? How can they be measured?
9. Many quality experts like Joseph Juran and Philip Crosby advocate cost-of-quality evaluations. Deming, however, states that "the most important figures are unknown and unknowable." How can these conflicting opinions be resolved?
10. Should a quality department have to cost-justify an expensive piece of measuring equipment based on a return-on-quality argument, or should the department manager simply point to "increased competition" as justification?
11. Using information you learned in prior courses in statistics or quantitative methods, discuss some analytical approaches that organizations can use for analyzing performance data.
12. Compare and contrast the Information and Analyses and Results categories in the 2000 and 2001 Baldrige business criteria (available on the CD-rom). What are the key differences and implications for managing a business?

Projects, Etc.

1. Interview managers at a local airline, hospital, governmental agency, or police department to determine what types of performance measures or indicators they use. Can you construct a balanced scorecard for them?
2. Many restaurants and hotels use "tabletop" customer satisfaction surveys. Find several of these from local businesses. What internal performance indicators might be good leading indicators for the customer satisfaction items in the surveys?
3. Interview managers at a local company to identify the key factors that drive their business. What performance measures or indicators does the company use? Are these indicators consistent with their business factors?
4. Interview managers at a local company to determine which, if any, of the leading practices described in this chapter they follow. What advice would you give them?
5. Using as many measures in Figure 8.2 as you can, draw a diagram similar (but with more detail) to the IBM Rochester model in Figure 8.1 showing leading and lagging indicators and cause-and-effect relationships among these measures.

6. Interview some local quality or production managers to determine whether their companies conduct cost-of-quality evaluations. If they do, how do they use the information? What types of quality costs do they measure?
7. Design a spreadsheet template for conducting quality cost analyses and apply it to problems in this chapter.

PROBLEMS

1. The percentage of total quality costs in a firm are distributed as follows:

Prevention	11%
Appraisal	29%
Internal failure	38%
External failure	22%

What conclusions can you reach from these data?

2. Analyze the following cost data. What are the implications of these data for management?

	Product A	Product B	Product C
Total sales	$1,537,280	$933,600	$1,397,120
External failure	**35%**	**25%**	**13%**
Internal failure	**52%**	**30%**	**37%**
Appraisal	**12%**	**42%**	**35%**
Prevention	**1%**	**3%**	**15%**

(Bold figures represent percentages of quality costs by product.)

3. Analyze the following cost data. What are the implications of these data for management? How do these data differ from those given in Problem 2?

	Product A	Product B	Product C
Total sales	$1,000,000	$900,000	$1,200,000
External failure	**45%**	**37%**	**20%**
Internal failure	**40%**	**35%**	**50%**
Appraisal	**12%**	**20%**	**15%**
Prevention	**3%**	**8%**	**15%**
Total quality costs	$250,000	$180,000	$180,000

(Bold figures represent percentages of quality costs by product.)

4. Compute a sales dollar-based index for Midwest Sales, Inc., to analyze the following quality cost information, and prepare a memo to management.

	Quarterly Costs (in thousands of dollars)			
	1	2	3	4
Total sales	$4,120	$4,206	$4,454	$4,106
External failure	280.8	208.2	142.8	128.6
Internal failure	468.2	372.4	284.4	166.4
Appraisal	194.2	227.7	274.4	266.2
Prevention	28.4	29.2	50.2	80.2
Total quality costs	$ 971.6	$ 837.5	$ 751.8	$ 641.4

5. What conclusions can be drawn from the following data?

Cost Category	Amount
Equipment design	$ 20,000
Scrap	300,000
Reinspection and retest	360,000
Loss	90,000
Supplier quality surveys	8,000
Repair	80,000

6. Analyze the following cost data. What are the implications of these data for management? How do these data differ from those in problem 3?

	Product A	Product B	Product C
Total sales	$2,500,000	$1,800,000	$2,600,000
Quality cost as a % of sales	**35%**	**25%**	**18%**
External failure	**42%**	**20%**	**15%**
Internal failure	**45%**	**25%**	**30%**
Appraisal	**12%**	**52%**	**40%**
Prevention	**1%**	**3%**	**15%**

(Bold figures represent percentages of quality costs by product.)

7. Compute a labor-based index for Miami Valley Steel Co. to analyze the following quality cost information and prepare a memo to management.

	Quarterly Costs (in thousands of dollars)			
	1	2	3	4
Total sales	$6,000.0	$6,600.0	$7,260.0	$7,986.0
External failure	1,000.8	1,063.2	962.7	855.6
Internal failure	3,240.2	3,265.4	3,000.0	2,240.1
Appraisal	950.2	1,100.0	1,135.5	966.2
Prevention	420.4	480.3	550.6	900.2
Total quality costs	$5,611.6	$5,908.3	$5,648.8	$4,962.1

8. Prepare a graph or chart showing the different quality cost categories and percentages for a printing company.

Cost Element	Amount
Customer complaint remakes	$ 28,000
Printing plate revisions	28,000
Quality improvement projects	14,000
Other waste	39,000
Correction of typographical errors	210,000
Proofreading	500,000
Quality planning	7,000
Press downtime	285,000
Bindery waste	53,000
Checking and inspection	42,000

9. Jeans Are Us, Inc., has a distribution center in Cincinnati where it receives and breaks down bulk orders from suppliers' factories, and ships out products to retail customers. Prepare a graph or chart showing the different quality cost categories and percentages for the company's quality costs that were incurred over the past year.

Cost Element	Amount
Checking outbound boxes for errors	$710,000
Quality planning	10,000
Downtime due to conveyor/computer problems	405,000
Packaging waste	75,000
Incoming product inspection	60,000
Customer complaint rework	40,000
Correcting erroneous orders before shipping	40,000
Quality training of associates	30,000
Quality improvement projects	20,000
Other waste	55,000
Correction of typographical errors (pick tickets)	10,000

10. The following cost-of-quality data were collected at the installment loan department of the Hamilton Bank. Classify these data into the appropriate cost of quality categories and analyze the results. What suggestions would you make to management?

Loan Processing	
1. Run credit check	$ 26.13
2. Review documents	3,021.62
3. Make document corrections; gather additional information	1,013.65
4. Prepare tickler file; review and follow up on titles, insurance, second meetings	156.75
5. Review all output	2,244.14
6. Correct rejects and incorrect output	425.84
7. Reconcile incomplete collateral report	78.34
8. Respond to dealer calls; address associate problems; research and communicate information	2,418.88
9. Compensate for system downtime	519.38
10. Conduct training	1,366.94
Loan Payment	
1. Receive and process payments	1,045.00
2. Respond to inquiries when no coupon is presented with payments	783.64
Loan Payoff	
1. Receive and process payoff and release documents	13.92
2. Research payoff problems	14.34

11. Given the following cost elements, determine the total percentage in each of the four major quality cost categories for the HiTeck Tool Company.

Cost Element	Amount
Incoming test and inspection	$ 7,500
Scrap	35,000
Quality training	0
Inspection	25,000
Test	5,000
Adjustment cost of complaints	21,250
Quality audits	2,500
Maintenance of tools and dies	9,200
Quality control administration	5,000
Laboratory testing	1,250
Design of quality assurance equipment	1,250
Material testing and inspection	1,250
Rework	70,000
Quality problem solving by product engineers	11,250
Inspection equipment calibration	2,500
Writing procedures and instructions	2,500
Laboratory services	2,500
Rework due to vendor faults	17,500
Correcting imperfections	6,250
Setup for test and inspection	10,750
Formal complaints to vendors	10,000

12. Use Pareto analysis to investigate the following quality losses at Oakton Paper Mill. What conclusions do you reach?

Category	Annual Loss
Downtime	$ 28,000
Testing costs	14,000
Rejected paper	427,000
Odd lot	63,000
Excess inspection	21,000
Customer complaints	98,000
High material costs	49,000

13. Use Pareto analysis to investigate the following quality losses at Beecom Software Corp. What conclusions do you reach?

Category	Annual Loss
Rework costs	$ 30,000
Rejected disks (loaded)	360,000
Rejected disks (blank)	89,000
Inspection costs (extra), incoming	18,000
Inspection costs (extra), outgoing	28,000
Customer returns	185,000
Training and system improvement costs	67,000
System downtime	138,000

14. National Computer Repairs, Inc., has a thriving business repairing and upgrading computers. The following are costs of quality collected over the past year. Use Pareto analysis to investigate their quality losses and to suggest which areas they should address first in an effort to improve their quality.

Category	Annual Loss
Customer returns	$160,000
Inspection costs, outgoing	31,000
Inspection costs, incoming	15,000
Workstation downtime	80,000
Training/system improvement	27,000
Rework costs	40,000

15. Excelsior Inn, a medium-sized hotel (approximately 450 rooms) has gathered a considerable amount of data and is trying to estimate its return on quality. The site manager is interested in determining what the return would be if she invested in additional service. She has evidence that additional effort in making sure that rooms (in particular, the bathroom) are clean will result in increases in market share, which can easily be translated into dollars of profit. In the following table are data taken from a pilot study where various amounts of additional labor, above the present standard, were applied to

room cleaning. These measurements have been expressed in annual dollar amounts, based on wages and fringe benefits of current employees servicing the rooms. Customers who stayed in those rooms were then surveyed to determine their levels of satisfaction/dissatisfaction. Percentages of dissatisfied customers have been matched with the annual dollars of improvement efforts from the study.

a. Using linear regression (for example, the Data Analysis tool or Add Trendline option in Excel), determine the equation that can be used to estimate the reduction in customer dissatisfaction, based on additional cleaning effort. What would be the appropriate level of effort to apply, based on your calculations?
b. Suppose that each point of market share increase brings in approximately $600,000 of profit per year, and the cost per year is your suggested investment in improvement (from part a). What would be the return on quality (improvement), based on a three-year discounted cash flow at 10 percent of the investment costs, if the site manager estimated that she could realize a 2.5 percent increase in market share?

Excelsior Inn Return on Quality

Service Improvement Investment (in thousands of dollars)	Percent of Dissatisfied Customers
0	0.200
50	0.150
150	0.100
260	0.076
290	0.067
300	0.059
450	0.052
600	0.045
750	0.040
900	0.035
1050	0.031
1200	0.027
1350	0.024
1500	0.021
1650	0.017
1800	0.014
1950	0.010
2100	0.007

16. A company has collected information about customer behavior and lost sales as a result of service problems. They estimate that, given the current level of service and historical data on complaints, the company will lose a total of 940,020 sales from customers who experience problems over a five-year period.
    a. At an average of $20 profit per sale, what is the average lost profit per year?
    b. Suppose the company can reduce its annual number of lost sales by 5 percent by investing $85,000 per year to enhance its service through training and better technology. How much profit can be earned as a result? What is the return on this quality investment?

Cases

I. Ultra-Productivity Fasteners, Part I

The Ultra-Productivity Fasteners Company was founded in 1959 to supply a variety of fasteners—rivets, clips, and screws—to appliance manufacturers. These fasteners are used in the assembly of major appliances, including dishwashers, washing machines, clothes dryers, and ranges. In 1985 Ultra-Productivity successfully penetrated the automotive market. Currently, the appliance market with three major OEM customers represents 60 percent of the annual sales. Two automotive customers account for approximately 30 percent of the sales; the remaining 10 percent of sales are made to a variety of smaller customers.

In the design phase, appliance manufacturers expect rapid response in the design and manufacture of special fasteners, and technical assistance in properly applying existing fastener designs. In the production and warranty phases, appliance manufacturers expect just-in-time delivery; fasteners that consistently meet specifications; fasteners that can be used on the product line without difficulty, and frequently with automated equipment; and fasteners that will not break during handling, shipping, or repair.

Requirements of the automotive customers are similar, but the need for fasteners that will not break is more critical because of the additional vibration and safety considerations. Just-in-time delivery is a primary requirement for automotive customers because a lack of fasteners may hold up assembly of an automobile.

Ultra-Productivity is one of three major manufacturers in the fastener market, in addition to a large number of small regional manufacturers. The market for fasteners is extremely competitive; price is a key consideration in the purchase decision.

Ultra-Productivity is headquartered in Louisville, Kentucky, with a major manufacturing plant at that location. Two other manufacturing plants are located at Lansing, Michigan, and Atlanta, Georgia. The Louisville and Lansing plants are of comparable size, with approximately 300 production workers each. The Atlanta plant is only one-third the size of other plants with approximately 100 production employees. Although quality has always been an important consideration, a formal, companywide quality improvement program was initiated in 1995 after a major automotive contract was lost.

Assignment

Summarize the key factors that drive this company's business and define a set of quality performance indicators that would be consistent with these factors.

II. Ultra-Productivity Fasteners, Part II

In this case, you are to play the role of a Malcolm Baldrige National Quality Award examiner and evaluate the company's response to item 7.5—*Organizational Effectiveness Results*. Please review this item in the Baldrige Criteria first. Note that this item asks for results, not approach and deployment. Some additional information from Award Criteria about reporting and interpreting results is provided in Figure 8.14.

Assignment

Two versions of the company's response are provided. Read Version A first and identify the strengths and areas for improvement relative to the criteria. Strengths should reflect positive responses to the Areas to Address in the criteria. Areas for improvement should highlight issues that do not respond adequately to the Areas to Address. Then, using the scoring guidelines in Chapter 3, Table 3.6 (results section), assign a score to this item. Repeat this process for Version B. What differences do you find? Why did your scores differ between versions?

Version A

7.5 Organizational Effectiveness Results
Based on extensive regression analysis, the key internal measure of product quality which predicts customer satisfaction is "Lots Accepted at Test"

Figure 8.14 Baldrige Guidelines for Responding to Results Items

The Criteria place the greatest emphasis on results. The following information, guidelines, and example relate to effective and complete reporting of results.

1. **Focus on the most critical business results.**

   Results reported should cover the most important requirements for your business success, highlighted in your Business Overview, and in the Strategic Planning and Process Management Categories.

2. **Note the meaning of the four key requirements from the Scoring Guidelines for effective reporting of results data.**

   - *trends* to show directions of results and rates of change;
   - *performance levels* on a meaningful measurement scale;
   - *comparisons* to show how results compare with those of other, appropriately selected organizations; and
   - *breadth and importance of results* to show that all important results are included.

3. **Include trend data covering actual periods for tracking trends.**

   No minimum period of time is specified for trend data. Trends might span five years or more for some results. However, for important results, new data should be included even if trends and comparisons are not yet well established.

4. **Use a compact format—graphs and tables.**

   Many results can be reported compactly by using graphs and tables. Graphs and tables should be labeled for easy interpretation. Results over time or compared with others should be "normalized"—presented in a way (such as use of ratios) that takes into account various size factors. For example, reporting safety trends in terms of lost workdays per 100 employees would be more meaningful than total lost workdays, if the number of employees has varied over the time period, or if you are comparing your results to organizations varying in size.

5. **Integrate results into the body of the text.**

   Discussion of results and the results themselves should be close together in an Award application. *Trends that show a significant positive or negative change should be explained.* Use figure numbers that correspond to Items. For example, the third figure for Item 7.1 would be Figure 7.1-3. (See the example in the figure that follows.)

The following graph illustrates data an organization might present as part of a response to Item 7.1, Customer Focused Results. In the Business Overview, the organization has indicated on-time delivery as a key customer requirement.

Figure 7.1-3 On-Time Delivery Performance

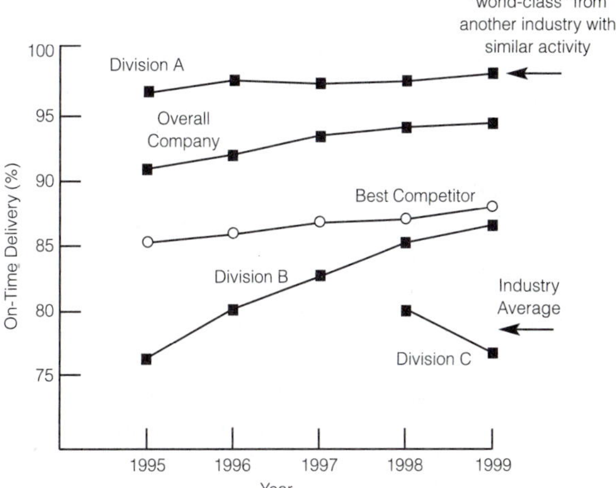

Using the graph, the following characteristics of clear and effective data reporting are illustrated:

- A figure number is provided for reference to the graph in the text.
- Both axes and units of measure are clearly labeled.
- Trend lines report data for a key customer requirement—on-time delivery.
- Results are presented for several years.
- Appropriate comparisons are clearly shown.
- The company shows, using a single graph, that its three divisions separately track on-time delivery.

To help interpret the Scoring Guidelines, the following comments on the graphed results would be appropriate:

- The current overall company performance level is excellent. This conclusion is supported by the comparison with competitors and with a "world-class" level.
- The company shows excellent improvement trends.
- Division A is the current performance leader—showing sustained high performance and a slightly positive trend. Division B shows rapid improvement. Its current performance is near that of the best industry competitor but trails the "world-class" level.
- Division C—a new division—is having early problems with on-time delivery. (The company briefly should explain these early problems.)

the first time submitted. This measure has shown a steady, favorable trend (see Figure 8.15) and has exceeded the target set by the production VP, who has more than 40 years of experience in this type of manufacturing.

Two key service quality measures for just-in-time customers are Shipments Reliability Index and Delivery Satisfaction Index. The Shipments Reliability Index (see Figure 8.16) tracks delivery against the original promised date established at the monthly "three-month schedule projection" meeting with the customer. Trends have been favorable and show Ultra-Productivity to be highly competitive with the two competitors tracked through feedback from automotive customers.

With the high-volume customers served, frequent last-minute changes occur in production model schedules, which generate last-minute changes in delivery schedules. The Delivery Satisfaction Index (see Figure 8.17) tracks shipments against original promised dates or changes made by customer request. This index reflects the ability to respond to customers' last-minute changes. It is much more rigorous than the Shipment Reliability Index and has shown a positive trend that reflects Ultra-Productivity's "customer first" quality value.

The improvements in both the Shipments Reliability Index and the Delivery Satisfaction Index are directly related to the ability to measure and improve the performance of the process contributing to order fulfillment. The quality improvement team responsible for improvement of these two indices found that the major contributor to orders not shipped on time was order entry errors. A tracking system for "Order Entry Error Rate" was put in place in 1997 and has provided dramatic improvement (see Figure 8.18).

The measure of "Complaints Resolved on First Contact" (see Figure 8.19) has shown a dramatic improvement since the Customer Service Associ-

Figure 8.15 Lots Accepted at Test

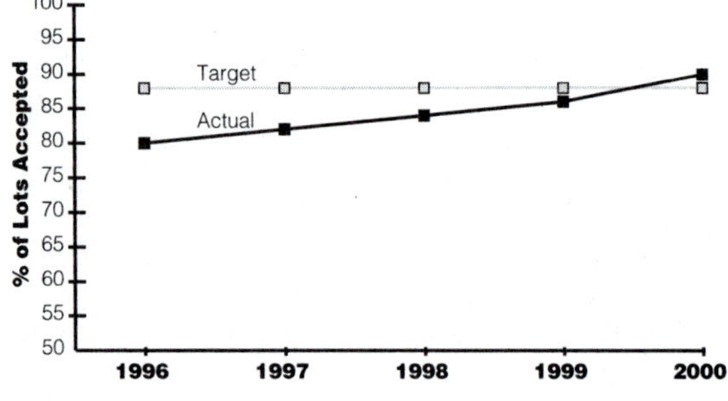

Figure 8.16 Shipments Reliability Index

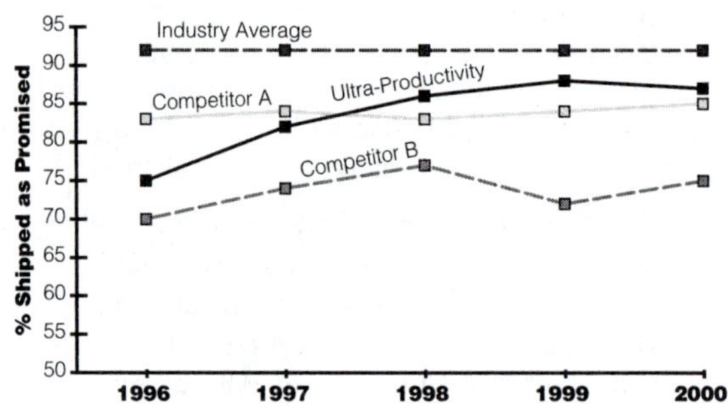

Figure 8.17 Delivery Satisfaction Index

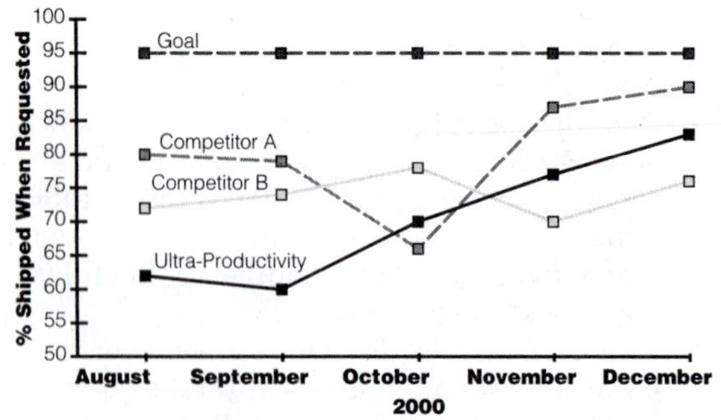

Figure 8.18 Order Entry Error Rates

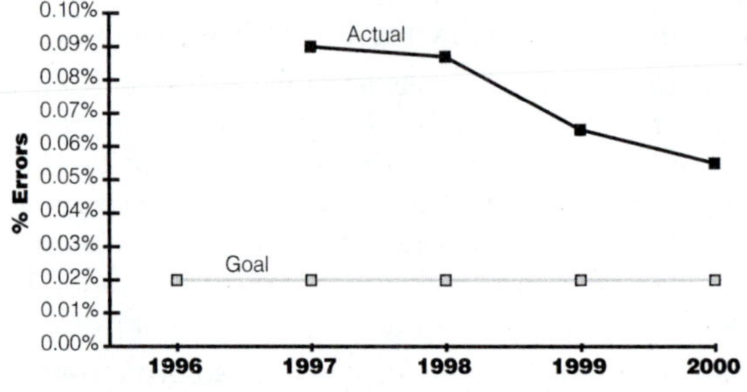

ate training program was introduced in 1996. This improvement, coupled with a reduction in overall complaints, has been a major contributor to improved customer satisfaction.

The percentage of "Invoice Errors" is another internal measure of Ultra-Productivity's ability to deliver outstanding products and services that meet customers' requirements and expectations. Figure 8.20 shows real improvement in this area since 1998. A longer-range objective is to be equal to "world-class" companies that are down to 0.2 percent invoice errors.

Version B

7.5 Company-Specific Results

Extensive regression analysis has shown that the level of product quality as perceived by the customer is actually a function of meeting both dimensional characteristics and meeting hardness specifications. Therefore, levels of compliance are tracked separately for these two important characteristics. "Lots Accepted at Test—Dimensional" first-time-submitted trends are shown in Figure 8.21. A positive trend is shown and compares well with the best-manufacturer-benchmark level established by the Automated Machines Council, which represents manufacturers using equipment similar to that installed in Ultra-Productivity shops.

"Lots Accepted at Test—Hardness" data are shown in Figure 8.22. Data plotted by plant for each of the three plants proved to be a real revelation, showing the Louisville plant to be an obviously poor performer. Investigation showed that the hardening furnaces installed when the Louisville plant opened required excessive maintenance and lacked the sophisticated temperature control systems used in the other plants. In 1998, a major capital investment was made to replace the Louisville hardening furnaces with state-of-the-art

Figure 8.19 Complaints Resolved on First Contact

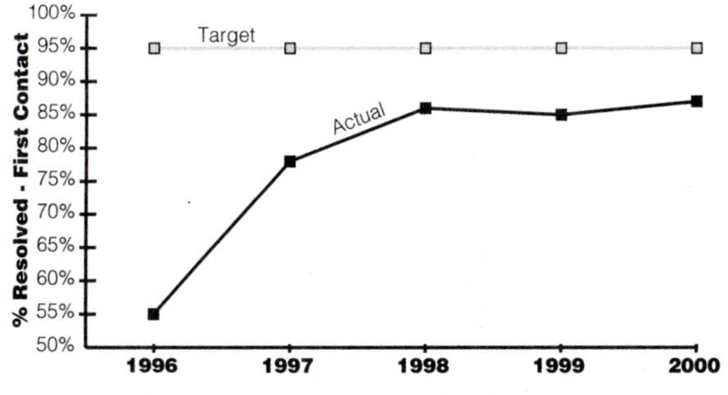

Figure 8.20 Invoice Errors

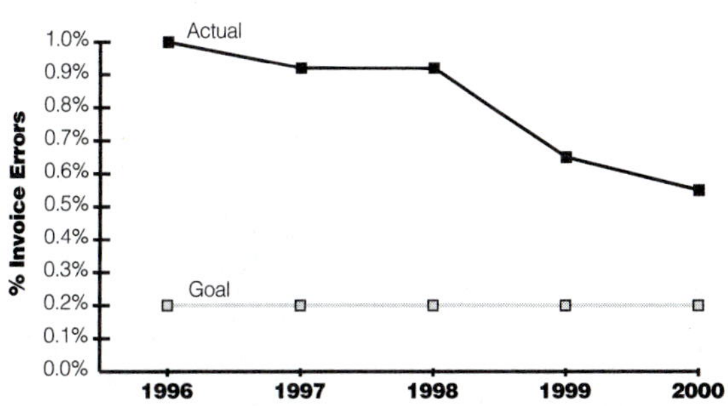

Figure 8.21 Lots Accepted at Test—Dimensional

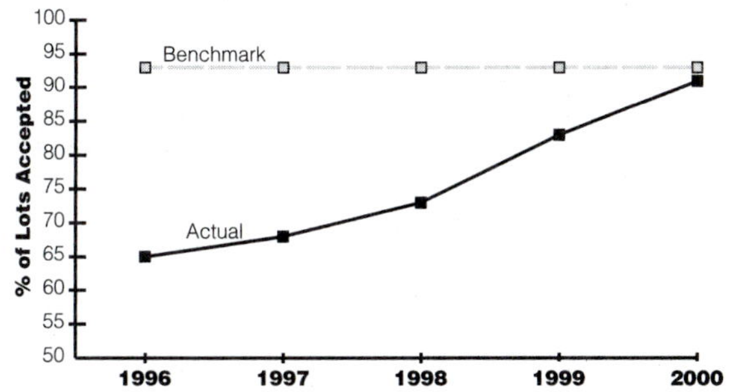

Figure 8.22 Lots Accepted at Test—Hardness

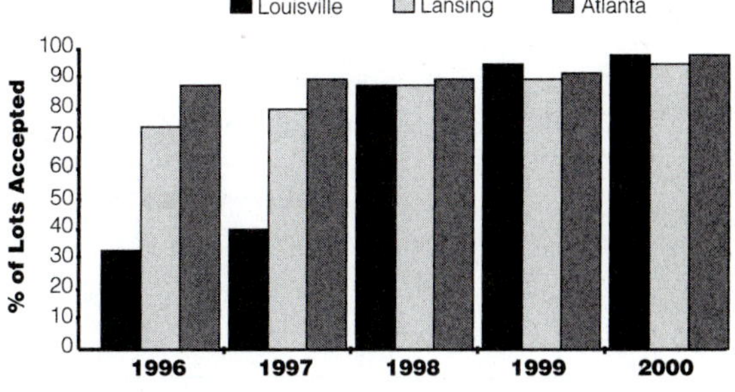

equipment. Data in Figure 8.22 show the dramatic improvement achieved. No benchmarks have been found for this hardness control characteristic, so work has been initiated through the Automated Machines Council to identify best manufacturers for benchmarking.

Two key service quality measures for just-in-time customers are the Shipments Reliability Index and the Delivery Satisfaction Index. The Shipments Reliability Index (see Figure 8.23) tracks delivery against the original promised date established at the monthly three-month schedule projection meeting with the customer. Trends have been favorable and show Ultra-Productivity to be highly competitive with the two best competitors tracked through feedback from one automotive and one major appliance customer.

With the high-volume customers served, frequent last-minute changes occur in production model schedules, which generate last-minute changes in delivery schedules. The Delivery Satisfaction Index (see Figure 8.24) tracks shipments against original promised dates or changes made by customer request. This index reflects our ability to respond to customers' last-minute changes. It is much more rigorous than the Shipments Reliability Index and has shown a positive trend, which reflects a "customer first" quality value.

The improvements in both Shipments Reliability Index and Delivery Satisfaction Index are directly related to our ability to measure and improve the performance of the process contributing to order fulfillment. The quality improvement team responsible for improvement of these two indexes found that the major contributor to orders not shipped on time was order entry errors. A tracking system for "Order Entry Error Rates" was put in place in 1997 and has provided dramatic improvement (see Figure 8.25).

The measure of "Complaints Resolved on First Contact" (see Figure 8.26) has shown a dramatic improvement since the Customer Service Associate training program was introduced in 1996. This improvement, coupled with a reduction in overall

Figure 8.23 Shipments Reliability Index

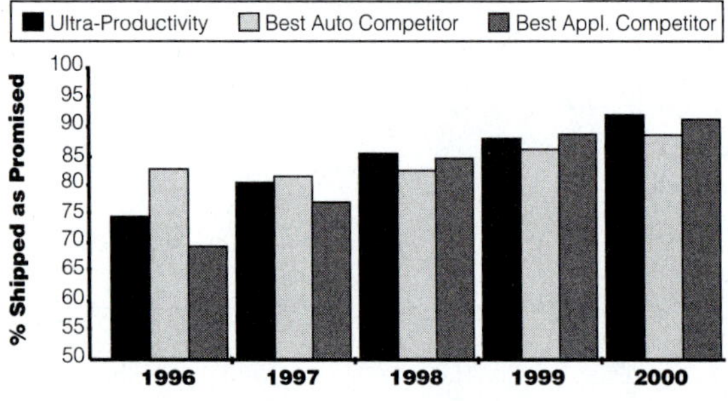

Figure 8.24 Delivery Satisfaction Index

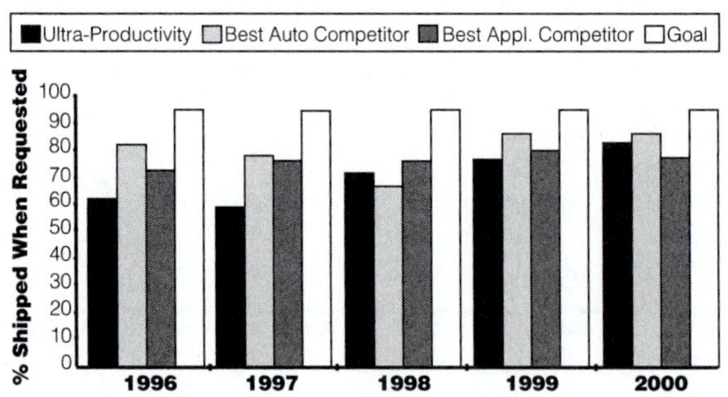

Figure 8.25 Order Entry Error Rates

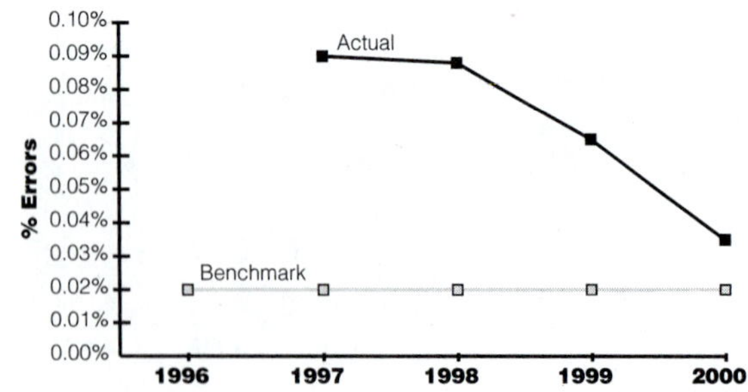

Figure 8.26 Complaints Resolved on First Contact

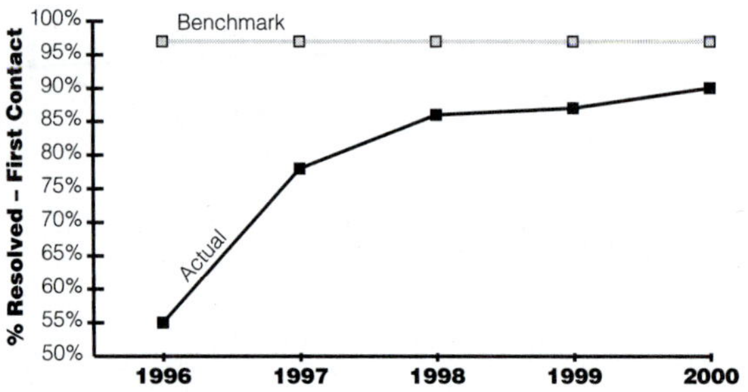

complaints, has been a major contributor to improved customer satisfaction. A benchmark of 96 percent for best performance in similar customer-supplied companies was established.

The percentage of "Invoice Errors" is another internal measure of Ultra-Productivity's ability to deliver outstanding products and services that meet customers' requirements and expectations. Figure 8.27 shows real improvement in this area since 1998. A longer-range objective is to be equal to "world-class" companies that have 2,000 ppm (parts per million) invoice error rates.

Figure 8.27 Invoice Errors

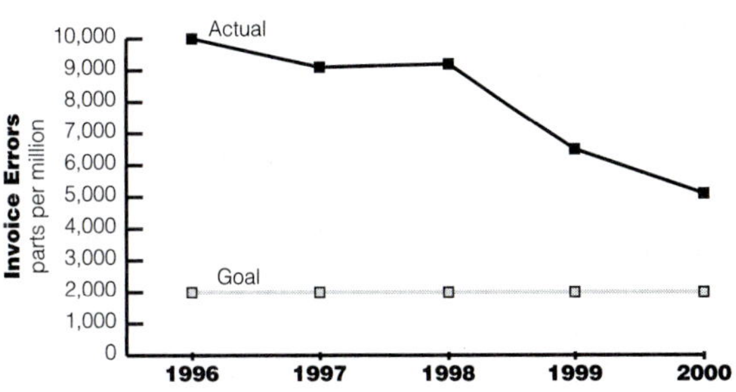

III. Collin Technologies: Measurement of Organizational Performance

Read Item 4.1, *Measurement of Organizational Performance,* in the Collin Technologies case study on the CD-rom accompanying this book. Using the 2000 Baldrige Criteria, on which this case is based, develop a list of strengths and opportunities for improvement similar to the style in Example 1. Strengths should focus on things the company is doing exceptionally well and support their vision and strategy. (Read the business overview section of the case first to identify specific factors that are important to this item.) Opportunities for improvement should highlight issues in its approach or deployment that can better meet the requirements of the Baldrige criteria. Your comments should include a reason why a strength or opportunity for improvement is important, that is, provide some insight to upper-level managers that they might not have otherwise realized. Use the wording in the scoring guidelines in Table 3.5 to help you structure your comments.

NOTES

1. Robert S. Kaplan and David P. Norton, *The Balanced Scorecard* (Boston, MA: Harvard Business School Press, 1996), 1.
2. Noriaki Kano, "A Perspective on Quality Activities in American Firms," *California Management Review* (Spring 1993), 12–31.
3. Blan Godfrey, "Future Trends: Expansion of Quality Management Concepts, Methods, and Tools to All Industries," *Quality Observer* 6, no. 9 (September 1997), 40–43, 46.
4. D. Osborne and T. Gaebler, *Reinventing Government: How the Entrepreneurial Spirit Is Transforming the Public Sector* (Reading, MA: Addison-Wesley Publishing Co., 1992).
5. Bill Gates with Collins Hemingway. *Business @ the Speed of Thought* (New York: Warner Books, 1999).
6. Kicab Casteñeda-Méndez, "Performance Measurement in Health Care," *Quality Digest*, May 199, 33–36.
7. Laura Struebing, "Measuring for Excellence," *Quality Progress*, December 1996, 25–28.
8. Robert S. Kaplan and David P. Norton, "The Balanced Scorecard—Measures That Drive Performance," *Harvard Business Review*, January/February 1992, 71–79.
9. Ernest C. Huge, "Measuring and Rewarding Performance," in Total Quality: An Executive's Guide for the 1990s, Ernst & Young Quality Consulting Group (Homewood IL: Irwin, 1990).
10. New Corporate Performance Measures, A Research Report, Report Number 1118-95-RR (New York: The Conference Board, 1995).
11. John Geanuracos and Ian Meiklejohn, *Performance Measurement: The New Agenda; Using Non-Financial Indicators to Improve Profitability* (London: Business Intelligence, 1993).
12. Glenn E. Hayes and Harry G. Romig, *Modern Quality Control* (Encino, CA: Benziger, Bruce & Glencoe, Inc., 1977).
13. "First National Bank of Chicago," *Profiles in Quality* (Boston, MA: Allyn and Bacon, 1991).
14. Justin Martin, "Are You as Good as You Think You Are?" *Fortune*, September 30, 1996, 142–152.
15. U.S. Office of Management and Budget, "How to Develop Quality Measures That Are

Useful in Day-to-Day Measurement," U.S. Department of Commerce, National Technical Information Service (January 1989).

16. Robert I. Wise, "A Method for Aligning Process Level and Strategy Level Performance Metrics," *American Society for Quality*, 11th Annual Quality Management Conference. See also Robert I. Wise, "A Method for Aligning Process-Level and Strategy-Level Performance Metrics," *The Quality Management Forum* 25, no. 1 (Spring 1999), 4–6.

17. Frank M. Gryna, "Quality Costs," *Juran's Quality Control Handbook*, 4th ed. (New York: McGraw-Hill, 1988).

18. Edward Sullivan and Debra A. Owens, "Catching A Glimpse of Quality Costs Today," *Quality Progress* 16, no. 12 (December 1983), 21–24.

19. ASQ Quality Costs Committee, "Profiting from Quality in the Service Arena," *Quality Progress*, May 1999, 81–84.

20. The reader is referred to the text by Cooper and Kaplan (1991) cited in the bibliography for a thorough treatment of this topic.

21. L. Reid, "Continuous Improvement Through Process Management," *Management Accounting*, September 1992, 37–44.

22. Rust, R. T., Zahorik, A. J., and Keiningham, T. L., "Return on Quality (ROQ): Making Service Quality Financially Accountable," *Journal of Marketing* 59, no. 2 (April 1995), 58–70.

23. "Quality: How to Make It Pay," *Business Week*, August 8, 1994, 54–59.

24. Roland T. Rust, Timothy Keiningham, Stephen Clemens, and Anthony Zahorik, "Return on Quality at Chase Manhattan Bank," *Interfaces* 29, 2 (March/April 1999), 62–72.

25. Larry English, "Data Quality: Meeting Customer Needs," *Data Management Review*, November 1996, 44–51, 86.

26. Ethan I. Davis, "Quality Service at The Prudential," *When America Does It Right*, Jay W. Spechler (Norcross, GA: Industrial Engineering and Management Press, 1988), 224–232.

27. David A. Collier, *The Service/Quality Solution* (Milwaukee, WI: ASQC Quality Press, and Burr Ridge, IL: Richard D. Irwin, 1994).

28. Bob Graessel and Pete Zeidler, "Using Quality Function Deployment to Improve Customer Service," *Quality Progress* 26, no. 11 (November 1993), 59–63.

29. "Bringing Sears Into the New World," *Fortune*, October 13, 1997, 183–184.

30. Collier, 235–236, see note 7.

31. "Coaxing Meaning Out of Raw Data," *Business Week*, February 3, 1997, 134–138.

32. Adapted from Xerox 1989 Malcolm Baldrige National Quality Award Application, Xerox Corporation, 1993.

33. Adapted from Steven H. Hoisington and Tse-His Huang, "Customer Satisfaction and Market Share: An Empirical Case Study of IBM's AS/400 Division," in *Customer Centered Six Sigma*, Earl Naumann and Steven H. Hoisington (Milwaukee, WI: ASQ Quality Press, 2001). Reprinted with permission of ASQ Quality Press.

BIBLIOGRAPHY

American National Standard: Guide to Inspection Planning, ANSI/ASQC E-2-1984. Milwaukee, WI: American Society for Quality Control, 1984.

AT&T Quality Steering Committee. *Process Quality Management & Improvement Guidelines*. AT&T Bell Laboratories, 1987.

Case, Kenneth E., and Lynn L. Jones. *Profit Through Quality: Quality Assurance Programs for Manufacturers*. Norcross, GA: American Institute of Industrial Engineers, 1978.

Cooper, Robin, and Robert S. Kaplan. *The Design of Cost Management Systems: Text, Cases, and Readings*. New York: Prentice Hall, 1991.

Cupello, James M. "A New Paradigm for Measuring TQM Progress." *Quality Progress* 27, no. 5 (May 1994), 79–82.

Davidow, William H., and Bro Uttal. *Total Customer Service*. New York: Harper & Row, 1989.

Donnell, Augustus, and Margaret Dellinger. *Analyzing Business Process Data: The Looking Glass*. AT&T Bell Laboratories, 1990.

Ferdeber, Charles J. "Measuring Quality and Productivity in a Service Environment." *Industrial Engineering*, July 1981, 193–201.

Haavind, Robert. *The Road to the Baldrige Award*. Boston: Butterworth-Heinemann, 1992.

Hart, Christopher W. L., and Christopher E. Bogan. *The Baldrige*. New York: McGraw-Hill, 1992.

Holm, Richard A. "Fulfilling the New Role of Inspection." *Manufacturing Engineering*, May 1988, 43–46.

Johnson, H. Thomas. "Activity-Based Information: A Blueprint for World-Class Management Accounting." *Management Accounting*, June 1988, 23–30.

Juran, Joseph M. *Juran on Quality By Design*. New York: The Free Press, 1992.

Kaplan, Robert S. "Yesterday's Accounting Undermines Production." *Harvard Business Review*, July/August, 1984.

Kaplan, Robert S., and David P. Norton. *The Balanced Scorecard*. Boston: Harvard Business School Press, 1996.

Puma, Maurice. "Quality Technology in Manufacturing." *Quality Progress* 13, no. 8 (August 1980), 16–19.

Rice, George O. "Metrology." In *Quality Management Handbook*, Loren Walsh, Ralph Wurster, and Raymond J. Kimber, eds. New York: Marcel Dekker, 1986, 517–530.

Rosander, A. C. *The Quest for Quality in Services*. Milwaukee, WI: ASQC Quality Press, 1989.

Strong, Carol. "Measuring Performance Improves Service—If You Measure and Reward the Right Behaviors." *The Service Edge Newsletter*, October 1989.

Troxell, Joseph R. "Service Time Quality Standards." *Quality Progress* 14, no. 9 (September 1981), 35–37.

———. "Standards for Quality Control in Service Industries." *Quality Progress* 12, no. 1 (January 1979), 32–34.

Whitley, Richard C. *The Customer Driven Company*. Reading, MA: Addison-Wesley, 1991.

Wilkerson, David, and Clifton Cooksey. *Customer Service Measurement*. Arlington, VA: Coopers & Lybrand, 1994.

Yakhou, Mehenna, and Boubekeur Rahali. "Integration of Business Functions: Roles of Cross-Functional Information Systems." *APICS—The Performance Advantage* 2, no. 12 (December 1992), 35–37.

PART 3

TECHNICAL ISSUES IN QUALITY

Even though a strong foundation of managerial practices is absolutely essential for success, quality is made on the factory floor and on the front lines of service systems. Assuring quality of products and services is assisted by the appropriate use of effective analytical tools and techniques for analyzing data, solving problems, improving and controlling processes, and reducing the potential for failure. In this part of the book, we focus on these issues.

Chapter 9 builds upon the Deming philosophy, introduced in Chapter 3, particularly the role of statistics and statistical thinking in evaluating process effectiveness and making informed decisions. In Chapter 10, we present a variety of approaches and tools for quality improvement—a key component of process management. Our principal focus in this chapter is on the Six-Sigma philosophy that has gained increasing popularity in recent years among large companies, such as General Electric. Chapter 11 focuses on quality control and addresses the design of a quality assurance infrastructure that supports the basic elements of the ISO 9000 standards that were described in Chapter 3, as well as technical issues related to measurement. In Chapter 12, we address statistical process control, focusing on the construction and use of the most common types of control charts. The last chapter in this section, Chapter 13 provides an introduction to reliability, focusing on the quantitative tools and approaches used in design and production. Each chapter in this section of the book provides numerous problems for practice in developing these technical skills.

Statistical Thinking and Applications

Outline

Brian Joiner, a noted quality management consultant, relates the following case:

> *Ed was a regional VP for a service company that had facilities around the world. He was determined that the facilities in his region would get the highest customer satisfaction ratings in the company. If he noticed that a facility had a major drop in satisfaction ratings in one month or had "below average" ratings for three months in a row, he would call the manager and ask what had happened—and make it clear that next month's rating had better improve. And most of the time, it did!*

As the average satisfaction score dropped from 65 to 60 between February and March, Ed's memo to his managers read:

Bad news! We dropped five points! We should all focus on improving these scores right away! I realize that our usage rates have increased faster than anticipated, so you've really got to hustle to give our customers great service. I know you can do it![1]

As Joiner observed, "Do you look at data this way? This month versus last month? This month versus the same month last year? Do you sometimes look at the latest data point? The last two data points? ". . . I couldn't understand why people would only want to look at two data points. Finally, it became clear to me. With any two data points, it's easy to compute a trend: 'Things are down 2% this month from last month. This month is 30% above the same month last year.' Unfortunately, we learn nothing of importance by comparing two results when they both come from a stable process . . . and most data of importance to management are from stable processes."

Many managers who do not understand how to use statistics effectively make similar mistakes. Statistical concepts are crucial to good quality management and are the key in dealing with processes and their inherent variation. In this chapter we discuss the importance of statistical thinking in managing for quality, and provide an overview of key statistical concepts and tools useful in quality-related analyses.

STATISTICAL THINKING

Statistics is a science concerned with "the collection, organization, analysis, interpretation, and presentation of data."[2] Measurement processes provide data. The data may be dimensions of bolts being produced on a production line, order entry errors per day in an order entry department, or numbers of flight delays per week at an airport. Raw data such as the individual lengths of bolts do not provide the information necessary for quality control or improvement. Data must be organized, analyzed, and interpreted. Statistics provide an efficient and effective way of obtaining meaningful information from data, allowing managers and workers to control and improve processes.

The importance of statistical concepts in quality management cannot be overemphasized. Indeed, statistics is essential in implementing a continuous improvement philosophy. **Statistical thinking** is a philosophy of learning and action based on the following principles:

1. All work occurs in a system of interconnected processes.
2. Variation exists in all processes.
3. Understanding and reducing variation are keys to success.[3]

Understanding processes provides the context for determining the effects of variation and the proper type of managerial action to be taken. By viewing work as a process, we can apply statistical tools to establish consistent, predictable processes, study them, and improve them. While variation exists everywhere, many business decisions do not often account for it, and managers frequently confuse common and special causes of variation. We must understand the nature of variation, before we can focus on reducing it.

Any production process contains many sources of variation, as illustrated in Figure 9.1. Different lots of material vary in strength, thickness, or moisture content, for example. Cutting tools have inherent variation in their strength and composition. During manufacturing, tools experience wear, vibrations cause changes in machine settings, and electrical fluctuations cause variations in power. Operators do not position parts on fixtures consistently, and physical and emotional stress affect operators' consistency. In addition, measurement gauges and human inspection capabilities are

Figure 9.1 Sources of Variation in Production Processes

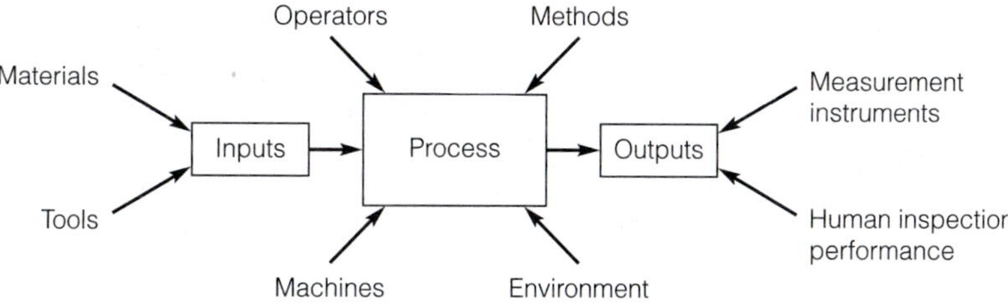

not uniform. Even when measurements of several items by the same instrument are the same, it is due to a lack of precision in the measurement instrument; extremely precise instruments always reveal slight differences.

The complex interactions of these variations in materials, tools, machines, operators, and the environment are not easily understood. Variation due to any of these individual sources appears at random; individual sources cannot be identified or explained. However, their combined effect is stable and can usually be predicted statistically. These factors that are present as a natural part of a process are referred to as **common causes** of variation. Common causes of variation generally account for about 80 to 95 percent of the observed variation in a production process. Common causes are a result of the design of the system—as management has designed it. For instance, suppose that boards are to be cut to the precise length of 55 inches. If the worker is provided with only a handsaw, a table, and a 12-inch ruler, it will be virtually impossible for him or her to cut lengths of this precision consistently, and a significant amount of measurable variation will exist. A reduction in common cause variation can only be achieved if better technology and training is provided. For this example, suppose that a 60-inch metal tape measure, a fixture for holding the boards, and an electric saw are available. Clearly, the output from this system will have less variability and more consistent quality.

The remaining variation in a production process is the result of **special causes**, often called **assignable causes** of variation. Special causes arise from external sources that are not inherent in the process. They appear sporadically and disrupt the random pattern of common causes. Hence, they tend to be easily detectable using statistical methods, and are usually economical to correct. For instance, the worker cutting boards may be distracted by a supervisor and mark the boards incorrectly before cutting, resulting in several pieces that may be an inch too short. Common factors that lead to special causes are a bad batch of material from a supplier, a poorly trained substitute machine operator, a broken or worn tool, or miscalibration of measuring instruments. Unusual variation that results from such isolated incidents can be explained or corrected.

A system governed only by common causes is labeled a **stable system**. Understanding a stable system and the differences between special and common causes of variation is essential for managing any system. If we do not understand the variation in a system, we cannot predict its future performance. Management can make two fundamental mistakes in attempting to improve a process:

1. To treat as a special cause any fault, complaint, mistake, breakdown, accident, or shortage when it actually is due to common causes.
2. To attribute to common causes any fault, complaint, mistake, breakdown, accident, or shortage when it actually is due to a special cause.

In the first case, tampering with a stable system can increase the variation in the system. In the second case, the opportunity to reduce variation is missed because the amount of variation is mistakenly assumed to be uncontrollable.

How often do managers make decisions based on a single data point or two, seeing trends when they don't exist, or manipulating financial figures they cannot truly control? The lack of broad and sustained use of statistical thinking in many organizations is due to two reasons.[4] First, statisticians historically have functioned as problem solvers in manufacturing, research, and development, and thereby focused on individual clients rather than on organizations. Second, statisticians have focused primarily on technical aspects of statistics rather than emphasizing process definition, measurement, control, and improvement—the key activities that lead to bottom-line results.

Senior management needs to champion the use of statistical thinking by defining the strategy and goals of the approach, clearly and consistently communicating the benefits and results, providing the necessary resources, coaching others, and recognizing and rewarding the desired behavior. To help managers work in this fashion, many organizations are creating core groups of highly trained professionals who are skilled in statistical thinking tools and can help others to use them effectively. It requires an environment conducive to learning new behaviors and concepts.

Statistical thinking can be applied at all levels of an organization.[5] At the organizational level, it helps executives to understand the business system and its core processes, use data from the entire organization to assess performance, develop useful measurement systems, and encourage employees to experiment to improve their work. At the process level, it can motivate managers to develop and assess standardized project management systems, set realistic goals, keep employees better informed, and focus on the process without blaming employees for variation. Finally, at the individual or personal level, statistical thinking can help employees to be knowledgeable about variation, to analyze work data better, and to identify important measures and improvement opportunities. Thus, every manager and employee can benefit from statistical thinking and using total quality tools. Technology that includes today's powerful PCs and user-friendly software for data analysis and visualization, such as Microsoft Excel and other spreadsheet packages, has facilitated greatly the ability to use statistics and quality tools in daily work.

Deming's Red Bead and Funnel Experiments[6]

Statistical thinking is at the heart of the Deming philosophy and his principles of Profound Knowledge (see Chapter 3). Frank H. Squires, a well-known expert on quality, has credited W. Edwards Deming with keeping statistics in the forefront of the worldwide quality improvement movement. Squires stated:

> *The triumph of statistics is the triumph of Dr. Deming. When others have wavered or been lukewarm in their support for statistics, Dr. Deming has stood firm in his conviction that statistics is the heart of quality control. Indeed, he goes further and makes statistical principles central to the whole production process.*[7]

In his four-day management seminars, Deming used two simple, yet powerful experiments to educate his audience about statistical thinking. The first is the Red Bead experiment, which proceeds as follows. A Foreman (usually Deming) selects several volunteers from the audience: six Willing Workers, a Recorder, two Inspectors, and a Chief Inspector. The materials for the experiment include 4,000 wooden beads—800 red and 3,200 white—and two Tupperware boxes, one slightly smaller than the other. Also, a paddle with 50 holes or depressions is used to scoop up 50 beads, which is the prescribed workload. In this experiment, the company is "producing" beads for a new customer who needs only white beads and will not take red beads. The Foreman explains that everyone will be an apprentice for three days to learn the job. During apprenticeship, the workers may ask questions. Once production starts, however, no questions are allowed. The procedures are rigid; no departures from procedures are permitted so that no variation in performance will occur. The Foreman explains to the Willing Workers that their jobs depend on their performance and if they are dismissed, many others are willing to replace them. Furthermore, no resignations are allowed.

The company's work standard, the Foreman explains, is 50 beads per day. The production process is simple: Mix the raw material and pour it into the smaller box. Repeat this procedure, returning the beads from the smaller box to the larger one. Grasp the paddle and insert it into the bead mixture. Raise the paddle at a 44-degree angle so that every depression will hold a bead. The two Inspectors count the beads independently and record the counts. The Chief Inspector checks the counts and announces the results, which are written down by the Recorder. The Chief Inspector then dismisses the worker. When all six Willing Workers have produced the day's quota, the Foreman evaluates the results.

Figure 9.2 shows the results of the first day's production generated with the Quality Gamebox computer simulation software. The Foreman is disappointed. He reminds the Willing Workers that their job is to make white beads, not red ones. The company is on a merit system, and it rewards only good performance. Marty only made 7 red beads and deserves a pay increase. The data do not lie; he is the best worker. Dennis made 14 red beads. Everyone likes him, but he must be placed on probation. The Foreman announces that management has set a goal of no more than 7 red beads per day per worker, and sees no reason why everyone cannot be as good as Marty.

Figure 9.3 shows the cumulative results for the second day. We see that after two days, Jeff had produced 23 red beads, Dave 23, Tom 20, Dennis 21, Marty 17, and Ann 23. (The second day's results can be found by subtraction: Jeff produces 13 beads, Dave 13, Tom 9, Dennis 7, Marty 10, and Ann 12.) The overall performance was not good. Management is watching carefully. The Foreman reminds them again that their

Figure 9.2 First Day's Production (The paddle shows the result of the last Willing Worker, Ann.)

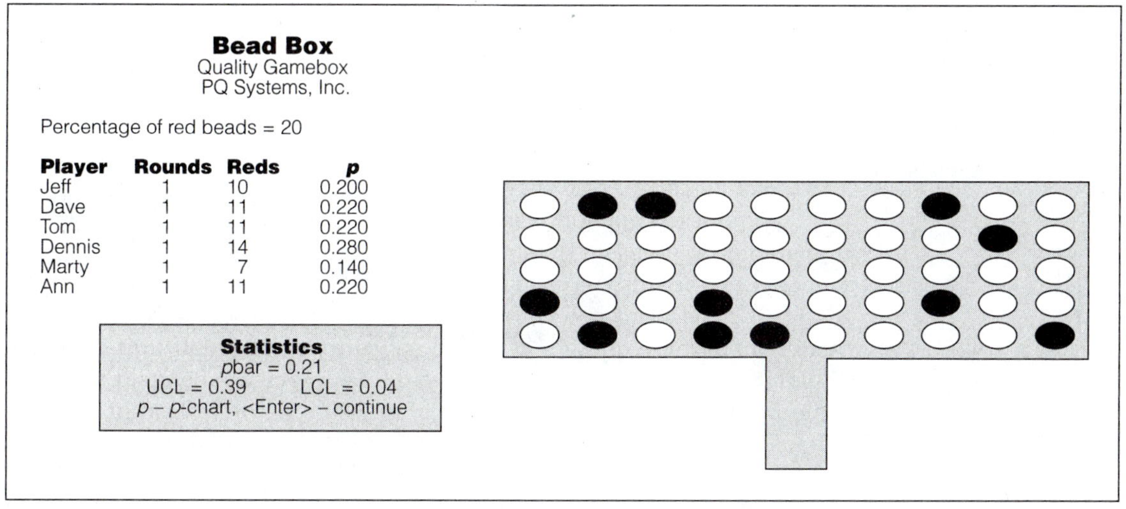

Figure 9.3 Second Day's Cumulative Results

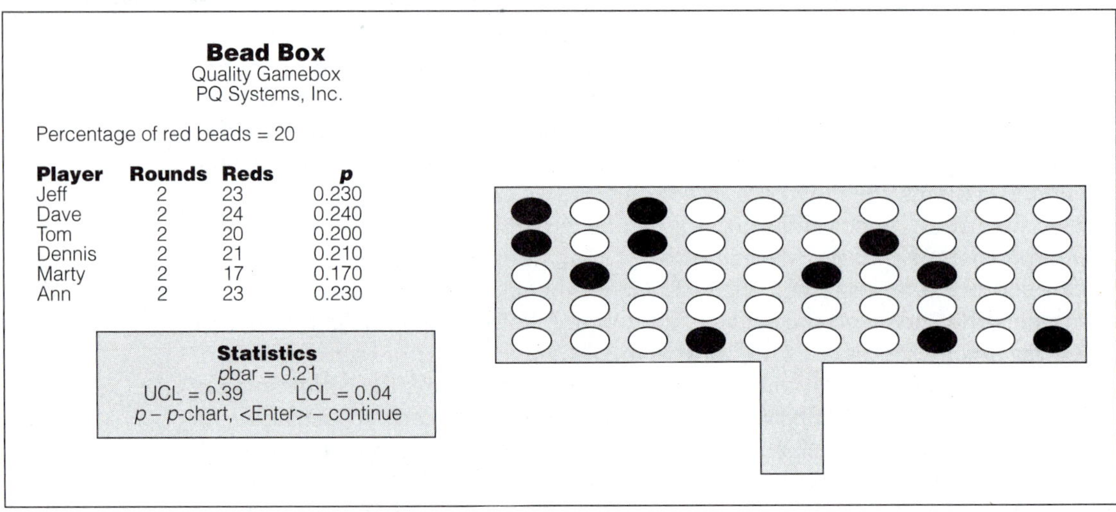

jobs depend on performance. Marty is a big disappointment. The merit increase obviously went to his head. The Foreman chastises him in front of the other workers. Dennis, on the other hand, showed remarkable improvement; probation and the threat of losing his job made him a better worker—only 7 red beads—a 50 percent reduction in defects! He met the goal; if he can do it, anyone can. Dennis gets a special commendation from the plant manager.

At the beginning of the third day, management announces a Zero Defects Day. Everyone will do their best on this last day of the apprenticeship program. The Foreman is desperate and he tells the Willing Workers again that their jobs are their own responsibility. From Figure 9.4, production figures can be determined (by computing

Figure 9.4 Third Day's Cumulative Results

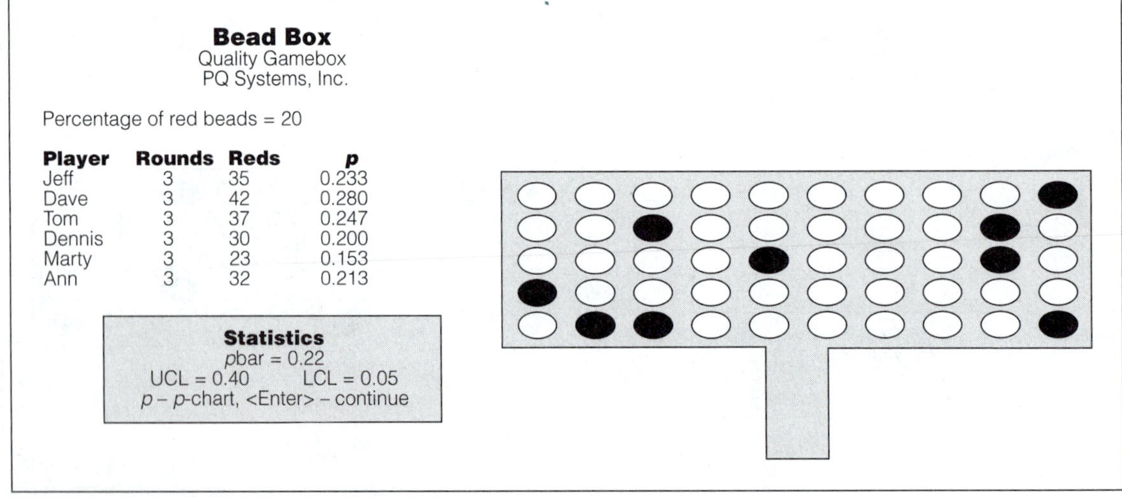

the difference between the cumulative output of day 3 and day 2), and shows that Jeff produces 12 red beads, Dave 18, Tom 17, Dennis 9, Marty 6, and Ann 11. Clearly, Marty learned a lesson the day before, but the group's overall performance is not good. Management is bitterly disappointed at the results. The Zero Defect Day program did not improve quality substantially; in fact, more red beads were produced today than ever before. Costs are getting out of control, and there is talk of shutting down the entire plant. Dave and Tom receive pink slips informing them that tomorrow will be their last day; their work is clearly much worse than the others. But the Foreman is optimistic. He puts up a poster saying "Be a Quality Worker!" to encourage the others to reach the goal.

On the fourth day (see Figure 9.5), we find that the number of red beads produced by the six Willing Workers is 8, 11, 8, 9, 8, and 9. The production is still not good enough. The Foreman announces that management has decided to close the plant after all.

The Red Bead experiment offers several important lessons for managers:

- *Variation exists in systems and, if stable, can be predicted.* If we plot the fraction of red beads produced by each worker each day, we can observe this variation easily. Figure 9.6 is a plot of the fraction of red beads produced over time. All points fluctuate about the overall average, which is 0.21, falling roughly between 0.10 and 0.40. In Chapter 12 we will learn to calculate *statistical limits of variation* (0.04 and 0.38)—limits between which we would expect results from a stable system to fall. These results show that the system of production is indeed stable; that is, the variation arises from common causes. Although the exact number of red beads in any particular paddle is not predictable, we can describe statistically what we expect from the system.
- *All the variation in the production of red beads, and the variation from day to day of any Willing Worker, came entirely from the process itself.* In this experiment, Deming deliberately eliminated the source of variability that managers usually believe is the most significant: people. Each worker was basically identical, and no evidence showed that any one of them was better than another. They could not control the number of red beads produced, and could do no better than the

Figure 9.5 Fourth Day's Cumulative Results

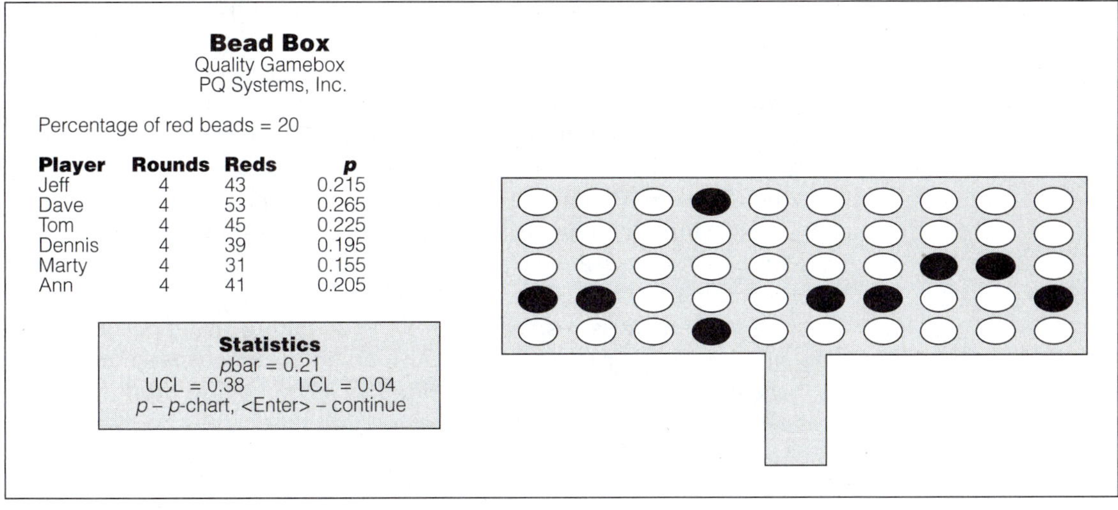

Figure 9.6 Run Chart of Fraction of Red Beads Produced

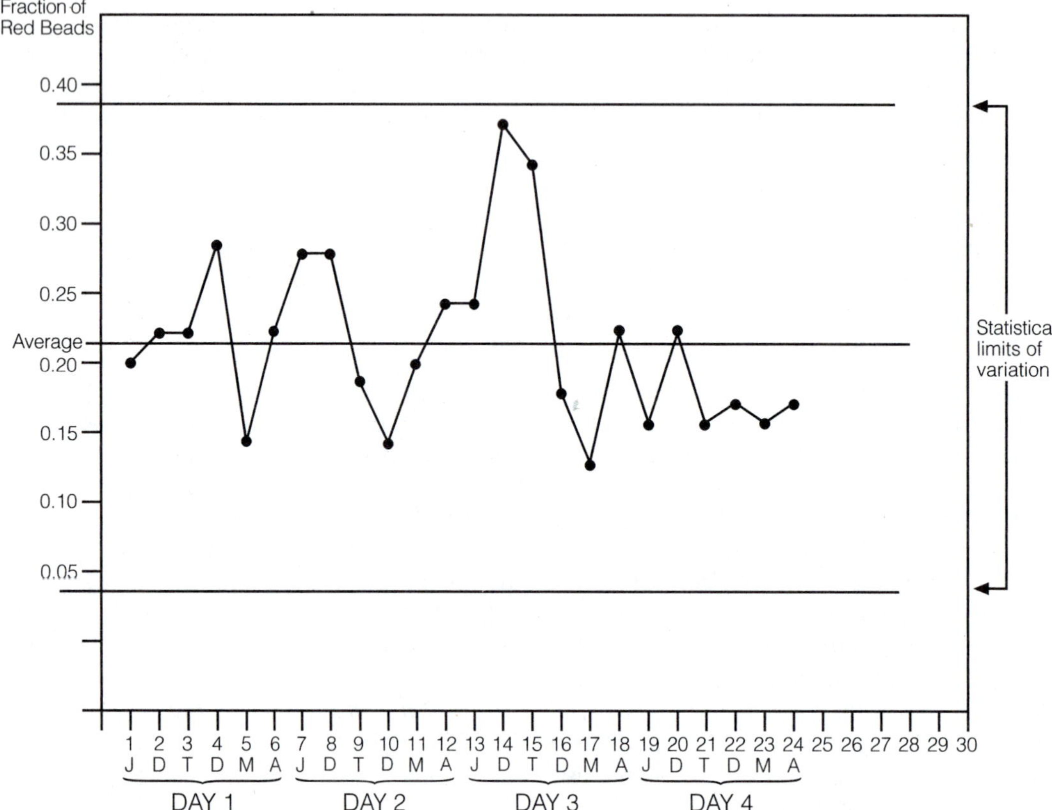

system would allow. Neither motivation nor threats had any influence. Unfortunately, many managers believe that all variation is controllable and place blame on those who cannot do anything about it.

- *Numerical goals are often meaningless.* A Foreman who gives out merit pay and puts people on probation, supposedly as rewards and punishment of performance, actually rewards and punishes the performance of the process, not the Willing Workers. To rank or appraise people arbitrarily is demoralizing, especially when workers cannot influence the outcomes. No matter what the goal is, it has no effect on the actual number of red beads produced. Exhorting workers to "Do their best" only leads to frustration. Management has no basis to assume that the best Willing Workers of the past will be the best in the future.
- *Management is responsible for the system.* The experiment shows bad management. Procedures are rigid. The Willing Workers have no say in improving the process. Management is responsible for the incoming material, but does not work with the supplier to improve the inputs to the system. Management designed the production system and decided to rely on inspection to control the process. These decisions have far more influence on the outcomes than the efforts of the workers. Three inspectors are probably as costly as the six workers and add practically no value to the output.

Deming's second experiment is the Funnel Experiment. Its purpose is to show that people can and do affect the outcomes of many processes and create unwanted variation by "tampering" with the process, or indiscriminately trying to remove common causes of variation. In this experiment, a funnel is suspended above a table with a target drawn on a tablecloth. The goal is to hit the target. Participants drop a marble through the funnel and mark the place where the marble eventually lands. Rarely will the marble rest on the target. This variation is due to common causes in the process. One strategy is to simply leave the funnel alone, which creates some variation of points around the target, which may be called Rule 1. However, many people believe they can improve the results by adjusting the location of the funnel. Three possible rules for adjusting the funnel are:

Rule 2. Measure the deviation from the point at which the marble comes to rest and the target. Move the funnel an equal distance in the opposite direction from its current position. See Figure 9.7(a).

Rule 3. Measure the deviation from the point at which the marble comes to rest and the target. Set the funnel an equal distance in the opposite direction of the error from the target. See Figure 9.7(b).

Rule 4. Place the funnel over the spot where the marble last came to rest.

Figure 9.8 shows a computer simulation of these strategies using the Quality Gamebox. Clearly the first rule—leave the funnel alone—results in the least variation.

People use these rules inappropriately all the time, causing more variation than would normally occur. An amateur golfer who hits a bad shot tends to make an immediate adjustment. If the last manufactured part is off-specification, adjust the machine. If a schedule was not met last month, change the process. If the last quarter's earnings report was less than expected, dump the stock. If an employee's performance last week was subpar (or exceptional), punish (or reward) the employee. In all these cases, the error is usually compounded by an inappropriate reaction. These policies stem from a lack of understanding of variation, which originates from not understanding the process.

STATISTICAL METHODS IN QUALITY MANAGEMENT

Statistical methods have applications in many areas of quality management, including product and market analysis, product and process design, process control, testing and inspection, identification and verification of process improvements, and reliability analysis. All managers, supervisors, and production and clerical workers should have some knowledge of the technical aspects of statistical methods. Readers of this

Figure 9.7 Two Rules for Adjusting the Funnel

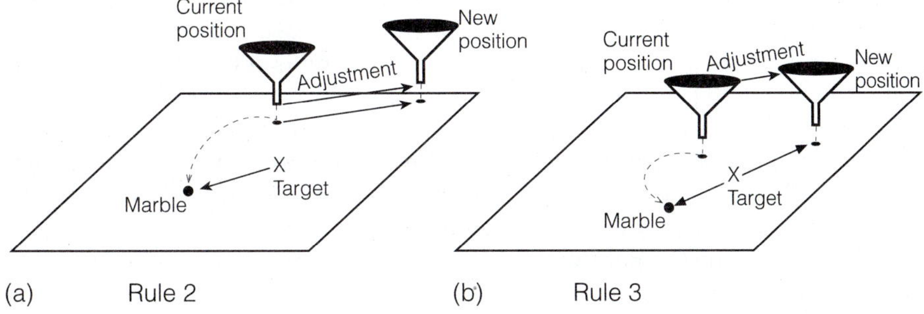

Figure 9.8 Results of the Funnel Experiment

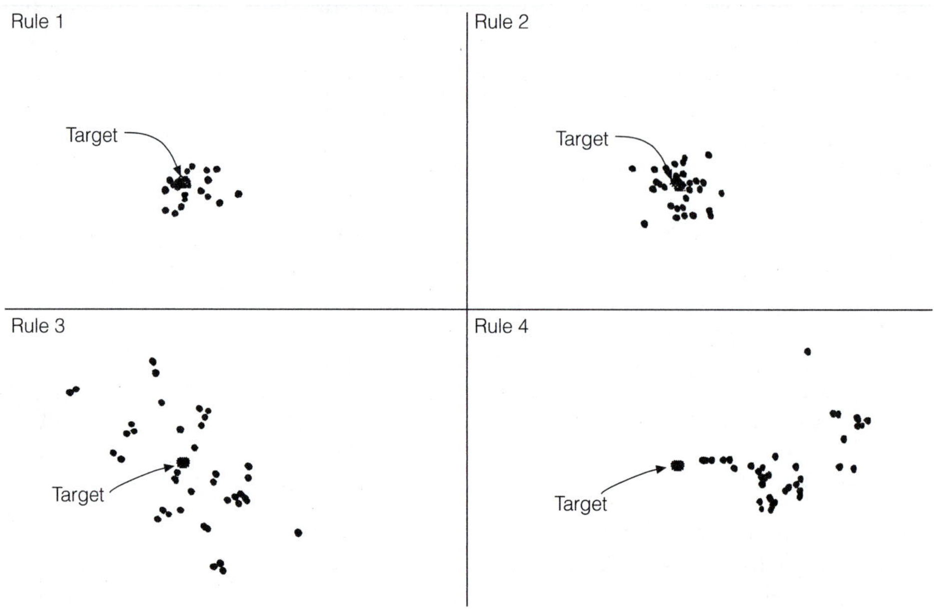

text are assumed to have prior knowledge of elementary statistics. This section provides a brief review of some important statistical concepts used in quality control and improvement.

Basic Statistical Methodology

The first major component of statistical methodology is the efficient collection, organization, and description of data, commonly referred to as **descriptive statistics**. Frequency distributions and histograms are used to organize and present data. Measures of central tendency (means, medians, proportions) and measures of dispersion (range, standard deviation, variance) provide important quantitative information about the nature of the data. For example, an airline might investigate the problem of lost baggage and determine that the major causes of the problem are lost or damaged identification tags, incorrect tags on the bags, and misrouting to baggage claim areas. An examination of frequencies for each of these categories might show that lost or damaged bags accounted for 50 percent of the problems, incorrect bags for 30 percent, and misrouting for only 20 percent. The airline might also compute the average number of baggage errors per 1,000 passengers each month. Such information is useful in identifying quality problems and as a means of measuring improvement.

The second component of statistical problem solving is **statistical inference**. Statistical inference is the process of drawing conclusions about unknown characteristics of a population from which data were taken. Techniques used in this phase include hypothesis testing and experimental design. For example, a chemical manufacturer might be interested in determining the effect of temperature on the yield of a new manufacturing process. In a controlled experiment, the manufacturer might test the hypothesis that the temperature has an effect on the yield against the alternative hypothesis that temperature has no effect. If the temperature is, in fact, a critical variable, steps will be required to maintain the temperature at the proper level and to draw inferences as to whether the process remains under control, based on samples taken from it. Experimental design is important for helping to understand the effects of process factors on output quality and for optimizing systems.

The third component in statistical methodology is **predictive statistics**, the purpose of which is to develop predictions of future values based on historical data. Correlation analysis and regression analysis are two useful techniques. Frequently, these techniques can clarify the characteristics of a process as well as predict future results. For example, in quality assurance, correlation is frequently used in test instrument calibration studies. In such studies, an instrument is used to measure a standard test sample that has known characteristics. The actual results are compared to standard results, and adjustments are made to compensate for errors. Figure 9.9 summarizes statistical processes and methods commonly used in quality assurance.

Random Variables and Probability Distributions

The collectively exhaustive set of outcomes from an experiment makes up a **sample space**. A mathematical function that assigns numerical values to every possible outcome in a sample space is called a **random variable**. A random variable can be either discrete or continuous, depending on the specific numerical values it may assume. A *discrete random variable* can take on only finite values. An example would be the number of defects observed in a sample. A *continuous random variable* can take on any real value over a specified interval of real numbers. An example would be the

Figure 9.9 Statistical Methodology in Quality Assurance

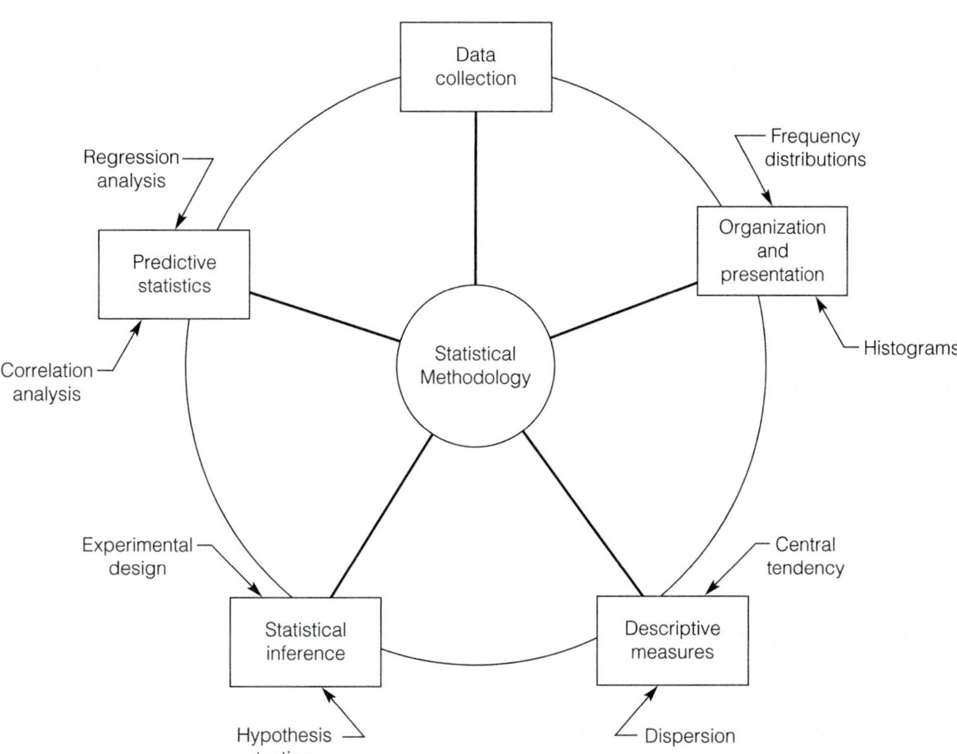

diameters of bearings being manufactured in a factory. Of course, the actual observed values for the variable are limited by the precision of the measuring device. Hence, only a finite number of actual observations would occur. In theory, this result would still be a continuous random variable. Random variables are the key component used in the development of probability distributions.

A **probability distribution** represents a theoretical model of the relative frequency of a random variable. Relating probability distributions to the random variables that they represent allows a classification of the distributions as either discrete or continuous. The appendix to this chapter provides a review of the more useful probability distributions in quality assurance and control. You are undoubtedly quite familiar with the normal distribution and its use as a common assumption in statistical models. Unfortunately, most business processes do not produce normal distributions.[8] The lack of normal distributions often results from the tendency to control processes tightly, which eliminates many sources of natural variation, as well as from human behavior, physical laws, and inspection practices. For example, data on the number of days customers take to pay bills typically show that many customers like to prepay; others send payments that arrive just after the due date. This behavior causes spikes in the distribution that do not conform to normality. In a hot-dip galvanizing process, a zinc layer forms when the base material reaches the temperature of molten zinc. However, if the part is removed before the critical temperature is reached, no zinc will adhere at all. Thus, all parts will have some minimum zinc thickness and the left side of the distribution will not tail off gradually as does a normal distribution. Measuring perpendicularity as the absolute deviation from 90 degrees instead of the actual angle can easily lead to nonnormality. Therefore, it is important to fully understand the nature of particular data before applying statistical theory that depends on normality assumptions.

Sampling Theory and Distributions

Sampling techniques are essential in quality control. A **population** is a complete set or collection of objects of interest; a **sample** is a subset of objects taken from the population. The purpose of sampling is to gain knowledge about the characteristics of the population from the information contained in a sample. Characteristics of a population, such as the mean μ, standard deviation σ, or proportion π, are generally known as parameters of the population. In statistical notation, they are written as follows:

$$\text{Population mean: } \mu = \frac{1}{N}\sum_{i=1}^{N} x_i$$

$$\text{Population standard deviation: } \sigma = \sqrt{\frac{\sum_{i=1}^{N}(x_i - \mu)^2}{N}}$$

$$\text{Population proportion: } \pi = \frac{Q}{N}$$

where x_i is the value of the ith observation, N is the number of items in a population, and Q is the number of items exhibiting a criterion of interest, such as manufacturing defects or on-time departures of aircraft.

The sample mean, sample standard deviation, and sample proportion are computed as follows:

$$\text{Sample mean: } \bar{x} = \frac{1}{n}\sum_{i=1}^{n} x_i$$

$$\text{Sample standard deviation: } s = \sqrt{\frac{\sum_{i=1}^{n}(x_i - \bar{x})^2}{n-1}}$$

$$\text{Sample proportion: } p = \frac{q}{n}$$

where n is the number of items in a sample, and q is the number of items in a sample exhibiting a criterion of interest.

Statistical theory is devoted to exploring the relationship between such sample statistics ($\bar{x}$, s, and p) and their corresponding population parameters (μ, σ, and π). For instance, the sample statistic $\bar{x}$ is generally used as a point estimator for the population parameter μ, and s as a point estimator for σ. The actual numerical values of $\bar{x}$ and s, which represent the single "best guess" for each unknown population parameter, are called point estimates.

Different samples will produce different estimates of the population parameters. Therefore, sample statistics such as $\bar{x}$, s, and p are random variables that have their own probability distribution, mean, and variance. These probability distributions are called **sampling distributions**. Knowledge of these sampling distributions will help in making probability statements about the relationship between sample statistics and population parameters. In quality control, the sampling distributions of $\bar{x}$ and p are of the most interest.

When using simple random sampling, the expected value of $\bar{x}$ is the population mean μ, or

$$E(\bar{x}) = \mu$$

The standard deviation of the sampling distribution of $\bar{x}$ (often called the **standard error of the mean**) is given by the formula

$$\sigma_{\bar{x}} = \frac{\sigma}{\sqrt{n}}$$ for infinite populations or sampling with replacement from an infinite population, and

$$\sigma_{\bar{x}} = \sqrt{\frac{N-n}{N-1}}\frac{\sigma}{\sqrt{n}}$$ for finite populations.

When $n/N \leq 0.05$, $\sigma_{\bar{x}} = \sigma/\sqrt{n}$ provides a good approximation for finite populations.

The last step is to develop the form of the probability distribution of $\bar{x}$. If the true population distribution is unknown, the **central limit theorem** can provide some useful insights. The central limit theorem (CLT) is stated as follows:

> *If simple random samples of size* n *are taken from any population having a mean* μ *and a standard deviation of* σ*, the probability distribution of the sample mean approaches a normal distribution with mean* μ *and standard deviation (standard error)* $\sigma_{\bar{x}} = \sigma/\sqrt{n}$ *as* n *becomes very large. In more precise mathematical terms: As* $n \to \infty$ *the distribution of the random variable* $z = (\bar{x} - \mu)/(\sigma/\sqrt{n})$ *approaches that of a standard normal distribution.*

The power of the central limit theorem can be seen through computer simulation using the *Quality Gamebox* software that is included on the CD-rom accompanying this text. Figure 9.10 shows the results of sampling from a triangular distribution for sample sizes of 1, 2, 5, and 10. For samples as small as size 5, the sampling distribution begins to develop into the symmetric bell-shaped form of a normal distribution. Also observe that the variance decreases as the sample size increases. The approximation to a normal distribution can be assumed for sample sizes of 30 or more. If the population is *known* to be normal, the sampling distribution of $\bar{x}$ is normal for any sample size.

Next, consider the sampling distribution of p, in which the expected value of p, $E(p) = \pi$. Here π is used as the population parameter and is not related to the *number* $\pi = 3.14159$. The standard deviation of p is

$$s_p = \sqrt{\frac{\pi(1-\pi)}{n}}$$

for infinite populations.

For finite populations, or when $n/N > 0.05$, modify s_p by

$$s_p = \sqrt{\frac{N-n}{N-1}}\sqrt{\frac{\pi(1-\pi)}{n}}$$

In applying the central limit theorem (CLT) to p, the sampling distribution of p can be approximated by a normal distribution for large sample sizes (see the chapter appendix).

This and subsequent chapters explore various applications of the CLT to statistical quality control in the areas of process capability determination and control charting. The following example illustrates an application of sampling distributions.

Figure 9.10 Illustration of Central Limit Theorem

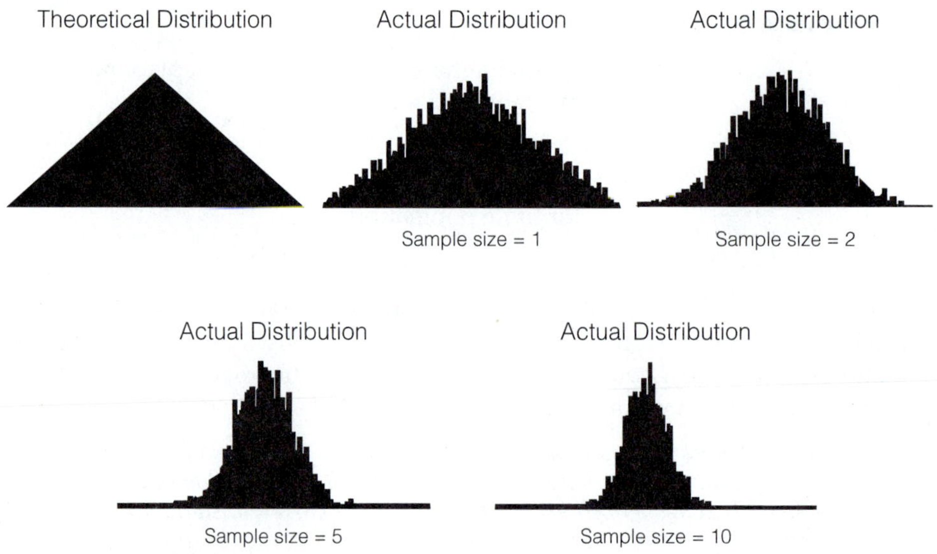

Theoretical Distribution

Actual Distribution

Sample size = 1

Actual Distribution

Sample size = 2

Actual Distribution

Sample size = 5

Actual Distribution

Sample size = 10

Source: Courtesy of P–Q Systems, Inc.

Example 1: Sampling Distribution of Shaft Lengths. The mean length of shafts produced on a lathe has historically been 50 inches, with a standard deviation of 0.12 inch. If a sample of 36 shafts is taken, what is the probability that the sample mean would be greater than 50.04 inches?

The sampling distribution of the mean is approximately normal with mean 50 and standard deviation of $0.12/\sqrt{36}$. Thus,

$$z = \frac{\bar{x} - \mu}{\sigma/\sqrt{n}} = \frac{50.04 - 50}{0.12/\sqrt{36}} = 2.0$$

In the standard normal table, the value of 2.0 yields the probability of 0.4772 between the mean and this value. The area for $z \geq 2.0$ then is found by

$$P(z \geq 2.0) = 0.5000 - 0.4772 = 0.0228$$

Thus, the probability of a value equal to or greater than 50.04 inches as the mean of a sample of 36 items is only 0.0228 if the population mean is 50 inches. The applicability of sampling distributions to statistical quality is that "shifts" in the population mean can quickly be detected using small representative samples to monitor the process.

Similarly, if a sample size of 64 is used, $\sigma/\sqrt{n} = 0.12/8 = 0.015$ and

$$z = \frac{\bar{x} - \mu}{\sigma/\sqrt{n}} = \frac{50.04 - 50}{0.015} = 2.67$$

and $P(z \geq 2.67) = 0.5000 - 0.4962 = 0.0038$. As the sample size increases, it is less likely that a mean value of at least 50.04 will be observed purely by chance. If it did, some special cause would likely be present.

Sampling Techniques

Suppose that you worked in a 1,000-bed hospital and wanted to determine the attitudes of a certain group of patients about the quality of care they received while in the hospital. Several factors should be considered before making this study:

1. What is the objective of the study?
2. What type of sample should be used?
3. What possible error might result from sampling?
4. What will the study cost?

One approach to tackling this problem would be to take a complete census—a survey of every person in the entire population. However, the objective of the study will dictate which method should be used to perform the study in the most effective and efficient manner. This decision requires sensitivity to the needs of the user and an understanding of the strengths and weaknesses of the specific techniques being used. Would sampling work just as well? If the user needs the results next week to make a decision involving the expenditure of $1,000, the study will require a different design from one in which the results influence a decision that will be made in six months and has a $1 million expenditure. Sampling provides a distinct advantage over a complete census in that much less time and cost are required to gather the data. In many cases, such as inspection, sampling may be more accurate than 100 percent inspection because of reduction of inspection errors. However, sampling is frequently subject to a higher degree of error.

The second issue relates to different methods of sampling. The following are some of the most common:

1. *Simple random sampling:* Every item in the population has an equal probability of being selected.
2. *Stratified sampling:* The population is partitioned into groups, or strata, and a sample is selected from each stratum.
3. *Systematic sampling:* Every *n*th (4th, 5th, . . .) item is selected.
4. *Cluster sampling:* A typical group (division of the company, for example) is selected, and a random sample is taken from within the group.
5. *Judgment sampling:* Expert opinion is used to determine the location and characteristics of a definable sample group.

In choosing the appropriate type of sampling method, an analyst must consider what the sample is designed to do. A sampling study has a goal of selecting a sample at the lowest cost that will provide the best possible representation of the population, consistent with the objectives of precision and reliability that have been determined for the study.

Suppose that your objective is to provide a report to top management of the hospital to help them decide whether to expand the use of quality control measures within the hospital. Some issues that would have to be considered before choosing a sample would be the time frame for completing the study, the size and cost limitations of the sample, the accessibility of the population of patients, and the desired accuracy. Assume that you have six weeks to complete the study, a limited operating budget of $1,500, and a population of 800 maternity patients (the category in which you are interested) who could be involved in the quality study. Further assume that the accuracy of your study requires a sample of at least 400 patients and that the cost of each response would vary from $2 to $4, depending on how the survey is administered. Obviously, you would have to select a sample, because a complete census of all patients would not be feasible within the budget limitation. Time limitations would make travel to conduct face-to-face interviews virtually impossible. Thus, the only feasible alternatives would be mailed questionnaires, telephone interviews, or a combination of the two.

Given this information, what type of sample should be chosen? Each type has advantages and disadvantages. A simple random sample would be easy to select but might not include sufficient representation by floor or ward. If a list of the patients, perhaps in alphabetical order, was available, a systematic sample of every fourth name could be easily selected. It would have the same disadvantages as the random sample, however. On the other hand, a cluster sample or judgment sample could be selected to include more representatives from floors or wards. However, cluster and judgment samples frequently take more time to identify and select appropriate sampling units. Also, because more subjective judgment is involved, a biased, nonrepresentative sampling plan is more likely to be developed.

The third issue in sampling relates to error. Errors in sampling generally stem from two causes: **sampling error** and **systematic error** (often called **nonsampling error**). Sampling error occurs naturally and results from samples that may not always be representative of the population, no matter how carefully they are selected. The only way to reduce sampling error is to take a larger sample from the population. Systematic errors, however, can be reduced or eliminated by design.

Sources of systematic error include the following:

1. *Bias:* the tendency to see problems and solutions from one's own viewpoint.

2. *Noncomparable data:* data that come from two populations but are erroneously considered to have come from one.
3. *Uncritical projection of trends:* the assumption that what has happened in the past will continue into the future.
4. *Causation:* the assumption that because two variables are related, one must be the cause of changes in the other.
5. *Improper sampling:* the use of an erroneous method for gathering data, thus biasing results (for example, using electronic mail surveys to get opinions from a population having few individuals with electronic mail services).

These sources of error can be overcome through careful planning of the sampling study. Bias can be reduced by frequent interaction with end users of the study as well as cross-checking research designs with knowledgeable analysts. Noncomparable data can be avoided by a sensitivity to conditions that could contribute to development of dissimilar population segments. In the hospital example, data gathered from different floors, wards, or shifts could prove to be noncomparable. In production firms, different shifts, machines, or products may define different populations, even though the characteristics being measured are the same for each. Uncritical projection of trends can be avoided by analysis of the underlying causes of trends and a constant questioning of the assumption that tomorrow's population will be the same as yesterday's. Reasons for causation must be investigated. Relationships between variables alone is not sufficient to conclude that causality exists. Causation can often be tested by holding one variable constant while changing the other to determine effects of the change. Finally, improper sampling can be avoided by a thorough understanding of sampling techniques and a determination of whether the method being used is capable of reaching any unit in the population in an unbiased fashion. This section concludes with some examples of sampling applications in quality control.

Simple Random Sampling A simple random sample is a small sample of size n drawn from a large population of size N in such a way that every possible sample of size n has an equal chance of being selected. For example, if a box of 1,000 plastic components for electrical connectors is thoroughly mixed and 25 parts are selected randomly without replacement, the random aspect of this definition has been satisfied. Simple random sampling forms the basis for most scientific statistical surveys, such as auditing, and is a useful tool for quality assurance studies. Many statistical procedures depend on taking random samples. If random samples are not used, bias may be introduced. For instance, if the items are rolled in coils, sampling only from the exposed end of the coil (a convenience sample) can easily result in bias if the production process that produced the coils varies over time.

Simple random samples can be selected by using a table of random numbers (see Appendix C). For example, a unique number may be assigned to each element of the population by using serial numbers or by placing the items in racks or trays with unique row and column numbering, or by associating with each item a physical distance (such as depth in a file drawer). Numbers are then chosen from the table in a systematic fashion. A sample is formed by selecting the items that correspond to the chosen random numbers. The selection may begin at any point in the table and move in any direction, using any set of digits that serves the sampler's purpose. An illustration of the use of the random number table for simple random sampling follows.

Example 2: Sampling Medical Patient Records. A particular nursing unit has 30 patients. Five patient records are to be sampled to verify the correctness of a medical procedure. To determine which patients to select, assign numbers 1 through 30 to the 30 patients. Select, for example, the first row in Appendix C and examine consecutive two-digit integers until five different numbers between 01 and 30 are found. (Any two-digit number greater than 30 is rejected because it does not correspond to an item in the given population.) Thus, the following sequence of random numbers and decisions occurs.

Number	Decision
63	reject
27	select
15	select
99	reject
86	reject
71	reject
74	reject
45	reject
11	select
02	select
15	duplicate
14	select

Based on the preceding sequence, 2, 11, 14, 15, and 27 are selected.

Simple random sampling is generally used to estimate population parameters such as means, proportions, and variances. When using $\bar{x}$ to estimate a population mean, for example, one also needs to know how close the estimate is to the true population mean. The error due to sampling variability is given by the standard error of the mean, which is used to construct a confidence interval on the true population mean. The amount of error is determined by the sample size and is a crucial issue in sampling.

First, consider the sample size when using $\bar{x}$ to provide a point estimate of the population mean for variables data. A $100(1 - \alpha)$ percent confidence interval on $\bar{x}$ is given by

$$\bar{x} \pm z_{\alpha/2}\sigma/\sqrt{n}$$

Thus, a $1 - \alpha$ probability exists that the value of the sample mean will provide a sampling error of $z_{\alpha/2}\sigma/\sqrt{n}$ or less. This sampling error is denoted by E. Solving the equation

$$E = z_{\alpha/2}\sigma/\sqrt{n}$$

for n, we find

$$n = (z_{\alpha/2})^2\sigma^2/E^2$$

This sample size will provide a point estimate having a sampling error of E or less at a confidence level of $100(1 - \alpha)$ percent.

To use this formula, specify the confidence level (from which $z_{\alpha/2}$ is obtained), the maximum sampling error E, and the standard deviation σ. If σ is unknown, at least a preliminary value is needed in order to compute n. A preliminary sample or a good guess based on prior data or similar studies can be used to estimate σ.

Example 3: Sample Size Determination for Variables Data. A firm conducting a process capability study on a critical quality dimension wishes to determine the sample size required to estimate the process mean with a sampling error of at most 0.1 at a 95 percent confidence level. From control chart data, an estimate of the standard deviation of the process was found to be 0.47. To find the appropriate sample size, the following calculations are used.

$$\begin{aligned} n &= (z_{\alpha/2})^2\sigma^2/E^2 \\ &= (1.96)^2(0.47)^2/(0.1)^2 \\ &= 84.86 \text{ or } 85 \text{ units} \end{aligned}$$

The next task is to determine the sample size for estimating a population proportion for attributes data. A point estimate of the population proportion, π, is given by the sample proportion p. The standard error of the proportion is

$$\sigma_p = \sqrt{p(1-p)/n}$$

Thus, a $100(1-\alpha)$ percent confidence interval for the population proportion is

$$p \pm z_{\alpha/2}\sqrt{p(1-p)/n}$$

The sampling error is given by

$$E = z_{\alpha/2}\sqrt{p(1-p)/n}$$

Solving this equation for n provides the following formula for the sample size:

$$n = (z_{\alpha/2})^2 p(1-p)/E^2$$

If a good value of p is not known, use $p = 0.5$; this value provides the minimum sample size recommendation that guarantees the required level of precision.

Example 4: Sample Size Determination for Attributes Data. Suppose a sample from a large finished goods inventory is needed to determine the proportion of nonconforming product. Historically, about 0.5 percent level of nonconformance has been observed. A 90 percent confidence level with an allowable error of 0.25 percent is desired. Thus, $E = 0.0025$, $p = 0.005$, $z_{0.05} = 1.645$. The required sample size is

$$n = (1.645)^2 0.005(1-0.005)/(0.0025)^2 = 2{,}154$$

In some situations, certain activities are so critical that only a small number of nonconformances is tolerable. A typical example is in health care; compliance with rigorous procedures must be adhered to 100 percent of the time. A nursing manager, for instance, will need to determine a sample size necessary to reveal at least one error in the sample if the population occurrence rate is equal to or greater than a specified critical rate of occurrence.

A technique used in such situations is called **discovery sampling**. Discovery sampling is a statistical sampling plan used for attributes in which the expected rate of occurrence in most cases is zero, and the maximum tolerable rate of occurrence is critical and thus very small. Discovery sampling tables have been published for selecting the appropriate sample size.[9] An example is shown in Table 9.1. One must know the population size and critical rate of occurrence and must specify the desired confidence level. The table gives the probability of finding at least one occurrence in the sample.

Example 5: An Application of Discovery Sampling. Suppose that a nursing manager wants to be 95 percent confident of finding at least one incident in which nursing personnel have failed to comply with a critical procedure. If 1,000 patient charts were prepared during the period under consideration and the critical rate of occurrence is 2 percent, Table 9.1 shows that 200 charts must be examined. If one occurrence is found in this random sample, the manager can conclude with 98.9 percent confidence that the quality of patient care in this area is unacceptable.

Table 9.1 Discovery Sampling Table

	Critical Occurrence Rate						
	0.05%	0.1%	0.5%	1%	2%	5%	10%
Sample Size	*Probability of Finding at Least One Occurrence*						
	Population Size: 1,000						
10		1.0%	4.9%	9.6%	18.4%	40.3%	65.3%
25		2.5	11.9	22.5	40.0	72.7	93.1
50		5.0	22.7	40.3	64.5	92.8	99.6
100		10.0	41.0	65.3	88.1	99.6	100.0
200		20.0	67.3	89.4	98.9	100.0	100.0
400		40.0	92.3	99.4	100.0	100.0	100.0
	Population Size: 2,000						
10	0.5%	1.0%	4.9%	9.6%	18.3%	40.2%	65.2%
50	2.5	4.9	22.4	39.9	64.0	92.6	99.5
100	5.0	9.8	40.2	64.3	87.4	99.5	100.0
200	10.0	19.0	65.2	88.0	98.6	100.0	100.0
400	20.0	36.0	89.3	98.9	100.0	100.0	100.0
600	30.0	51.0	97.2	99.9	100.0	100.0	100.0

Source: Adapted from H. P. Hill, J. L. Roth and H. Arkin, *Sampling in Auditing: A Simplified Guide and Statistical Tables* (New York: Ronald Press, 1962).

Other Types of Sampling Procedures Alternatives to simple random sampling are available and are discussed briefly here. These methods have distinct advantages over simple random sampling in many situations.

1. **Stratified random sampling:** A stratified random sample is obtained by separating the population into nonoverlapping groups, and then selecting a simple random sample from each group. The groups might be different machines, wards in a hospital, departments, and so on. For example, suppose a population of 28,000 items is produced on three different machines:

Machine	Group Size
1	20,000
2	5,000
3	3,000

   Assume that a specific confidence level requires a sample of 525 units in this case. One could draw these units randomly from the entire population. Under stratified random sampling, a simple random sample of 250 units from machine 1, 150 units from machine 2, and 125 units from machine 3 might be taken. Formulas are available for combining the results of individual samples into an overall estimate of the population parameter of interest. This technique will demonstrate quality differences that may exist between machines.

   Stratified random sampling will provide results similar to simple random sampling but with a smaller total sample size. It produces a smaller bound on the error of the estimation than would be produced by a simple random sample of the same size. These statements are particularly true if measurements within each group are homogeneous, that is, if the units within strata are alike.
2. **Systematic sampling:** In some situations, particularly with large populations, selecting a simple random sample using random number tables and searching through the population for the corresponding element is impractical. With systematic sampling, the population size is divided by the sample size required, yielding a value for n. The first item is chosen at random from among the first n items. Thereafter, every nth item is selected. For example, suppose that a population has 4,000 units and a sample of size 50 is required. Select the first unit randomly from among the first 80 units. Every 80th (4,000/50) item after that would be selected.

   Systematic sampling is based on the assumption that if the first element is chosen at random, the entire sample will have the properties of a simple random sample. This method should be used with caution because quality characteristics may vary in some periodic fashion with the length of the sampling interval and thus bias the results.
3. **Cluster sampling:** In cluster sampling, the population is first partitioned into groups of elements called clusters. A simple random sample of the clusters is selected. The elements within the clusters selected constitute the sample. For example, suppose that products are boxed in groups of 50. Each box can be regarded as a cluster. We would draw a sample of boxes and inspect all units in the boxes selected.

   Cluster sampling tends to provide good results when the elements within the clusters are not alike (heterogeneous). In this case, each cluster would be representative of the entire population.

4. **Judgment sampling:** With judgment sampling, an arbitrary sample of pertinent data is examined and the percentage of nonconformances is calculated. Because judgment sampling is not random, the risks associated with making an incorrect conclusion cannot be quantified. Thus, it is not a preferred method of sampling.

Experimental Design

Design of experiments (DOE), developed by R. A. Fisher in England, dates back to the 1920s. A designed experiment is a test or series of tests that enable the experimenter to compare two or more methods to determine which is better, or determine levels of controllable factors to optimize the yield of a process or minimize the variability of a response variable.[10] For example, a paint company might be interested in determining whether different additives have an effect on the drying time of paint in order to select the additive that results in the shortest drying time. As another example, suppose that two machines produce the same part. The material used in processing can be loaded onto the machines either manually or with an automatic device. The experimenter might wish to determine whether the type of machine and the type of loading process affect the number of defectives and then to select the machine type and loading process combination that minimizes the number of defectives.

As a practical tool for quality improvement, experimental design methods have achieved considerable success in many industries. In a celebrated case, the Ina Tile Company, a Japanese ceramic tile manufacturer, had purchased a $2 million kiln from West Germany in 1953.[11] Tiles were stacked inside the kiln and baked. Tiles toward the outside of the stack tended to have a different average and more variation in dimensions than those further inside the stack. The obvious cause was the uneven temperatures inside the kiln. Temperature was an uncontrollable factor, a noise factor. To try to eliminate the effects of temperature would require redesign of the kiln itself, a very costly alternative. A group of engineers, chemists, and others who were familiar with the manufacturing process brainstormed and identified seven major controllable variables that could affect the tile dimensions:

1. Limestone content
2. Fineness of additive
3. Content of agalmatolite
4. Type of agalmatolite
5. Raw material quantity
6. Content of waste return
7. Content of feldspar

The group designed and conducted an experiment using these factors. The experiment showed that the first factor, the limestone content, was the most significant factor; the other factors had smaller effects. By increasing the limestone content from 1 percent to 5 percent and choosing better levels for other factors, the percentage of size defects was reduced from 30 percent to less than 1 percent. Limestone was the cheapest material in the tile. In addition, the experiment revealed that a smaller amount of agalmatolite, the most expensive material in the tile, could be used without adversely affecting the tile dimension. Both the effect of the noise factor and the cost of the product were reduced at the same time! This discovery was a breakthrough in the ceramic tile industry.

As another example, ITT Avionics Division, a leading producer of electronic warfare systems, experienced a high defect rate when using a wave solder machine to solder assemblies on printed circuit boards.[12] The wave solder machine, developed to eliminate hand soldering, transports printed circuit boards through a wave of solder under computer control. A brainstorming session identified 14 process variables. From three sets of designed experiments the subsequent data results in decisions that lowered the defect rate from seven or eight to 1.5 per board. With 2,500 solder connections per board, the defect rate now translates to 600 defects per million connections, a rate being constantly improved. ITT's Suprenant Company, an electrical wire and cable manufacturer and a supplier to Ford, saved an estimated $100,000 per year in scrap, reduced product variability by a factor of 10, and improved the run rate of an extruding operation by 30 percent.

Historically, experimental design was not widely used in industrial quality improvement studies because engineers had trouble working with the large number of variables and their interactions on many different levels in industrial problems. However, improved computer software and more sophisticated training have made experimental design an important tool for quality improvement.

Factorial Experiments One of the most common types of experimental designs is called a **factorial experiment**. In a factorial experiment, all combinations of levels of each factor are considered. For example, suppose that temperature and reaction time are identified as important factors in the yield of a chemical process. An experiment designed to analyze the effect of two levels of each factor (for instance, temperature at 100 and 120 degrees, and time at 60 and 75 minutes) then would have $2^2 = 4$ possible combinations to test:

Temperature	Time
100 degrees	60 minutes
100 degrees	75 minutes
120 degrees	60 minutes
120 degrees	75 minutes

In general, an experiment with m factors at k levels would have m^k combinations. Each combination should be performed in a random fashion to eliminate any potential systematic bias.

The purpose of a factorial experiment is to estimate the effects of each factor. For example, what is the effect of a 20-degree change in temperature? Of a 15-minute change in reaction time? These questions are answered easily by finding the differences of the averages at each level. For instance, suppose we obtained the following results:

Temperature	Time	Yield (%)
100 degrees	60 minutes	85
100 degrees	75 minutes	88
120 degrees	60 minutes	90
120 degrees	75 minutes	80

The average yield for a temperature of 100 degrees is $(85 + 88)/2 = 86.5$. The average yield for a temperature of 120 degrees is $(80 + 90)/2 = 85$. Thus, the average difference in yield from increasing the temperature from 100 to 120 degrees is 85 – 86.5 = –1.5 percent. Similarly, the average difference in increasing the time from 60 to 75 minutes is [(88 + 80)/2] – [(85 + 90)/2] = 84 – 87.5 = – 3.5 percent. These differences—how the change in the level of one factor affects the response—are called **main effects**. Thus, we might conclude that increasing temperature or time decreases the yield of the process.

However, in many situations, the effect of changing one factor depends on the level of other factors. For example, the effect of temperature may depend on the reaction time. In this example, we see that if the temperature is held constant at 100 degrees, an increase in reaction time results in a higher yield. However, when the temperature is 120 degrees, an increase in reaction time decreases the yield, and is called an *interaction*. Interaction is easy to determine by graphing the results as shown in Figure 9.11. If the lines are nearly parallel, then no interaction exists. In this case, we see an interaction. We may quantify the interaction by taking the average of difference of the yield when the temperature is increased from 100 to 120 degrees at a constant reaction time of 60, and subtracting the average of difference of the yield when the temperature is increased from 100 to 120 degrees at a constant reaction time of 75:

$$\text{Temperature} \times \text{Time} = [(90 - 85)/2] - [(80 - 88)/2] = 6.5 \text{ percent}$$

The closer this quantity is to zero, the smaller the interaction effect. In this case, a significant interaction is evident. When interactions are present, main effects have little meaning; individual factors must be interpreted relative to levels of the other factors. We see that higher temperature and lower time appear to optimize the yield.

The following example shows a simple application of a three-factor experiment not unlike those used in industrial and business settings.

Figure 9.11 Interaction Effects

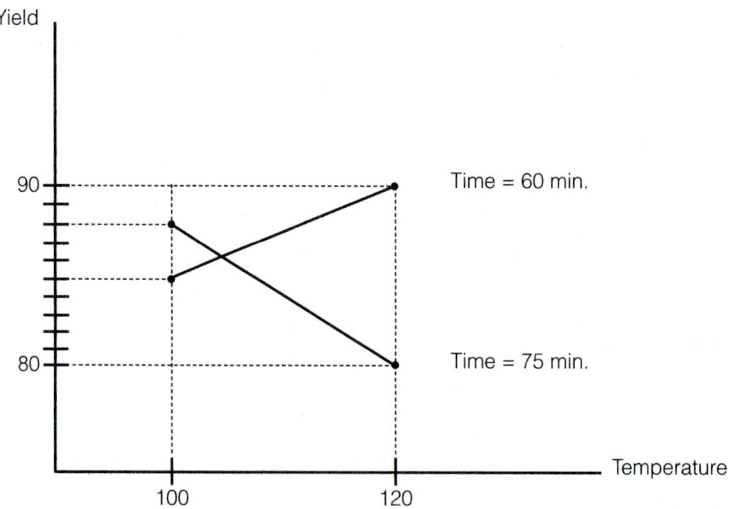

Example 6: Using DOE to Determine Battery Life.[13] Many one-tenth scale remote control (RC) model car racing enthusiasts believe that spending more money on high-quality batteries, using expensive gold-plated connectors, and storing batteries at low temperatures will improve battery life performance in a race. To test this hypothesis, an electrical test circuit was constructed to measure battery discharge under different configurations. Each factor (battery type, connector type, and temperature) was evaluated at two levels, resulting in $2^3 = 8$ experimental conditions shown in Table 9.2.

Calculations of the main effects are as follows:

Battery cost
- Low = (72 + 93 + 75 + 94)/4 = 83.5 minutes
- High = (612 + 490 + 493 + 489)/4 = 521 minutes
- Main effect = High – Low = 437.5 minutes

Connector type
- Gold-plated = (94 + 75 + 490 + 493)/4 = 288 minutes
- Standard = (72 + 93 + 612 + 489)/4 = 316.5 minutes
- Main effect = Standard – Gold-plated = 28.5 minutes

Temperature
- Cold = (72 + 75 + 490 + 612)/4 = 312.25 minutes
- Ambient = (93 + 489 + 493 + 94)/4 = 292.25 minutes
- Main effect = Ambient – Cold = 20 minutes

These results suggest that high cost batteries do have a longer life, but that the impact of gold plating or battery temperature do not appear to be significant. Because only one factor appears to be significant, calculation of interaction effects are not required. These conclusions can be tested more rigorously using analysis of variance, which can be found in most statistics textbooks. Indeed, an analysis of variance confirms that the battery cost factor is statistically significant while the other factors are indistinguishable from experimental error.

Table 9.2 Experimental Design for Testing Battery Performance

Experimental Run	Battery Type	Connector Type	Battery Temperature	Discharge Time (minutes)
1	High cost	Gold-plated	Ambient	493
2	High cost	Gold-plated	Cold	490
3	High cost	Standard	Ambient	489
4	High cost	Standard	Cold	612
5	Low cost	Gold-plated	Ambient	94
6	Low cost	Gold-plated	Cold	75
7	Low cost	Standard	Ambient	93
8	Low cost	Standard	Cold	72

Much more can be said about experimental design, and we encourage you to consult more complete statistics books. It is important to understand that DOE is a powerful tool for understanding the effects of numerous process variables and improving quality.

Classical experimental design can require many, often costly, experimental runs to estimate all main effects and interactions. Another approach to experimental design was proposed by a Japanese engineer, Dr. Genichi Taguchi. He developed an approach to designing experiments that focused on the critical factors while deemphasizing their interactions, which greatly reduced the number of required experiments. However, Taguchi's approach to experimental design violates some traditional statistical principles and has been criticized by the statistical community.[14] To add to the shortcomings of his approach, Taguchi introduced some statistically invalid and misleading analyses, ignored modern graphical approaches to data analysis, and failed to advocate randomization in performing the experiments. Even though many of these issues are subject to debate, Taguchi's approaches have been used effectively by numerous companies.

STATISTICAL ANALYSIS OF PROCESS VARIATION

Statistics provides the basis for quantifying the variation in processes. For example, Table 9.3 shows a random sample of 120 measurements (accurate to 0.05 centimeter) of the inside distance (a critical dimension in auto assembly) between the ends of a U-bolt (illustrated in Figure 9.12) having a design specification of 10.70 ± 0.20. Important questions to consider are: What is the inherent variability of the process that produces these parts? What percentage of parts might we expect to be defective, that is,

Table 9.3 Measurements of U-Bolts

10.65	10.70	10.65	10.65	10.85
10.75	10.85	10.75	10.85	10.65
10.75	10.80	10.80	10.70	10.75
10.60	10.70	10.70	10.75	10.65
10.70	10.75	10.65	10.85	10.80
10.60	10.75	10.75	10.85	10.70
10.60	10.80	10.70	10.75	10.75
10.75	10.80	10.65	10.75	10.70
10.65	10.80	10.85	10.85	10.75
10.60	10.70	10.60	10.80	10.65
10.80	10.75	10.90	10.50	10.85
10.85	10.75	10.85	10.65	10.70
10.70	10.70	10.75	10.75	10.70
10.65	10.70	10.85	10.75	10.60
10.75	10.80	10.75	10.80	10.65
10.90	10.80	10.80	10.75	10.85
10.75	10.70	10.85	10.70	10.80
10.75	10.70	10.60	10.70	10.60
10.65	10.65	10.85	10.65	10.70
10.60	10.60	10.65	10.55	10.65
10.50	10.55	10.65	10.80	10.80
10.80	10.65	10.75	10.65	10.65
10.65	10.60	10.65	10.60	10.70
10.65	10.70	10.70	10.60	10.65

Figure 9.12 U-Bolt

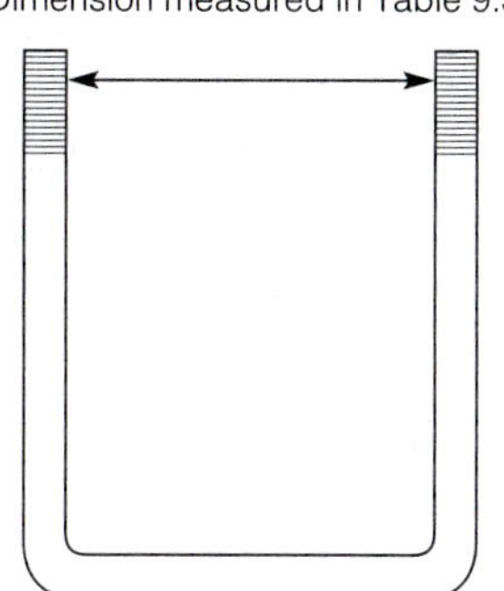

fall outside of specifications? How must we improve the process to ensure nearly defect-free product? These questions may be answered using statistical techniques. In this book we will use spreadsheets to perform statistical analyses.

Statistical Analysis with Microsoft Excel

Spreadsheets have replaced the calculator as one of the most useful tools for managers and analysts. In this part of the book, we will use Microsoft Excel whenever appropriate to perform statistical calculations and display graphs or charts. The disk accompanying this book contains all of the major spreadsheets used in examples in this book, which will help you in working many end-of-chapter problems. The files available on the disk are identified by their name (NAME.XLS) in the text. Please see the README file on the disk for further information.

Microsoft Excel provides a set of data analysis tools—called the *Analysis ToolPak*—that are useful in complex statistical analyses. You provide the data and parameters for each analysis; the tool uses the appropriate statistical functions and then displays the results in an output table. Some tools generate charts in addition to output tables. To view a list of available analysis tools, click *Data Analysis* on the *Tools* menu. If the *Data Analysis* command is not on the *Tools* menu, run the Setup program to install the Analysis ToolPak. After you install the Analysis ToolPak, you must select it in the *Add-In Manager*. Excel also provides many other statistical worksheet functions. To see a list of available functions, click *Edit Formula* on the formula bar, and then click the down-arrow in *Insert Function*. We strongly encourage you to learn how to use the capabilities of Excel for quality assurance applications. Much more information can be found in the Help files available with Excel.

Example 7: Descriptive Statistics with Excel. We will assume that the sample of U-bolt measurements in Table 9.3 is representative of the population from which they were drawn. These data were entered into an Excel spreadsheet in the range A2:A121. Figure 9.13 shows the Descriptive Statistics dialog box that is displayed after choosing "Descriptive Statistics" from the *Tools/Data Analysis* options. An explanation of the items in this dialog box follows. (This information can also be obtained from the Help files in Excel.)

Input Range Enter the cell reference for the range of data you want to analyze. The reference must consist of two or more adjacent ranges of data arranged in columns or rows. Excel will compute individual statistics for each row or column; thus, all data in Table 9.3 are entered in a single column.

Grouped By To indicate whether the data in the input range are arranged in rows or in columns, click *Rows* or *Columns.*

Labels in First Row/Labels in First Column If the first row of the input range contains labels, select the Labels in First Row check box. If the labels are in the first column of the input range, select the Labels in First Column check box. This check box is clear if the input range has no labels; Microsoft Excel generates appropriate data labels for the output table.

Confidence Level for Mean Select this option to include a row in the output table for the confidence level of the mean. In the box, enter the desired confidence level. For example, a value of 95 percent calculates the confidence level of the mean at a significance of 5 percent.

K*th Largest* Select this option to include a row in the output table for the *k*th largest value for each range of data. In the box, enter the number to use for *k*. If you enter 1, this row contains the maximum of the data set.

K*th Smallest* Select this option to include a row in the output table for the *k*th smallest value for each range of data. In the box, enter the number to use for *k*. Enter 1 and this row will contain the minimum of the data set.

Figure 9.13 Microsoft Excel Descriptive Statistics Dialog Box

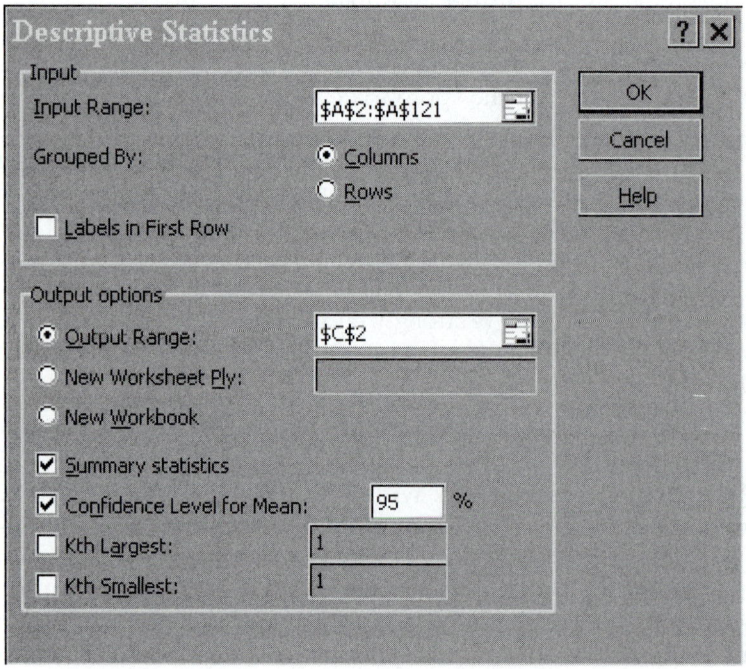

Output Range Enter the reference for the upper-left cell of the output table. This tool produces two columns of information for each data set. The left column contains statistics labels, and the right column contains the statistics. Microsoft Excel writes a two-column table of statistics for each column or row in the input range, depending on the Grouped By option selected.

New Worksheet Ply Click to insert a new worksheet in the current workbook and paste the results starting at cell A1 of the new worksheet. To name the new worksheet, type a name in the box.

New Workbook Click to create a new workbook and paste the results on a new worksheet in the new workbook.

Summary Statistics This option commands Microsoft Excel to produce one field for each of the following statistics in the output table: Mean, Standard Error (of the mean), Median, Mode, Standard Deviation, Variance, Kurtosis, Skewness, Range, Minimum, Maximum, Sum, Count, Largest (#), Smallest (#), and Confidence Level. Figure 9.14 shows the results obtained.

A second useful data analysis tool is the *histogram*, which is described as follows. Figure 9.15 shows the Excel dialog box for this option.

Input Range Enter the reference for the range of data to be analyzed.

Bin Range (optional) Enter the cell reference to a range that contains an optional set of boundary values that define bin ranges. These values should be in ascending order. Microsoft Excel counts the number of data points between the current bin number and the adjoining higher bin, if any. A number is counted in a particular bin if it is

Figure 9.14 Microsoft Excel Descriptive Statistics Results

	A	B	C	D
1	**Measurements of U-Bolts**			
2	10.65		*Column1*	
3	10.75			
4	10.75		Mean	10.71708333
5	10.60		Standard Error	0.007927716
6	10.70		Median	10.7
7	10.60		Mode	10.65
8	10.60		Standard Deviation	0.086843778
9	10.75		Sample Variance	0.007541842
10	10.65		Kurtosis	-0.53752485
11	10.60		Skewness	-0.0420018
12	10.80		Range	0.4
13	10.85		Minimum	10.5
14	10.70		Maximum	10.9
15	10.65		Sum	1286.05
16	10.75		Count	120
17	10.90		Confidence Level(95.0%)	0.015697649
18	10.75			

Figure 9.15 Microsoft Excel Histogram Dialog Box

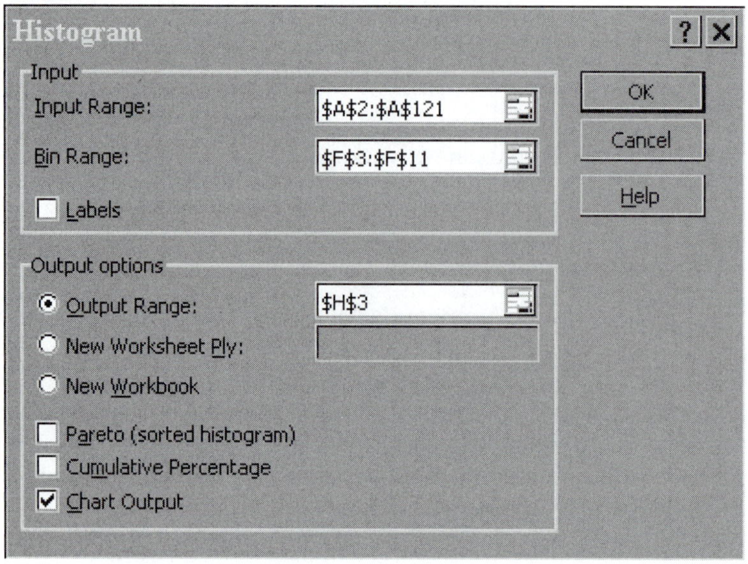

equal to or less than the bin number down to the last bin. All values below the first bin value are counted together, as are the values above the last bin value. If the bin range is omitted, Microsoft Excel creates a set of evenly distributed bins between the data's minimum and maximum values. In this example, we defined the bin range in cells F3:F11.

Labels Select if the first row or column of the input range contains labels. Clear this check box if the input range has no labels; Microsoft Excel generates appropriate data labels for the output table.

Output Range Enter the reference for the upper-left cell of the output table. Microsoft Excel automatically determines the size of the output area and displays a message if the output table will replace existing data.

Pareto (sorted histogram) Select to present data in the output table in descending order of frequency. If this check box is cleared, Microsoft Excel presents the data in ascending order and omits the three rightmost columns that contain the sorted data.

Cumulative Percentage Select to generate an output table column for cumulative percentages and to include a cumulative percentage line in the histogram chart. Clear to omit the cumulative percentages.

Chart Output Select to generate an embedded histogram chart with the output table.

Figure 9.16 shows the frequency distribution and histogram generated. We will use these results in another example later in this chapter.

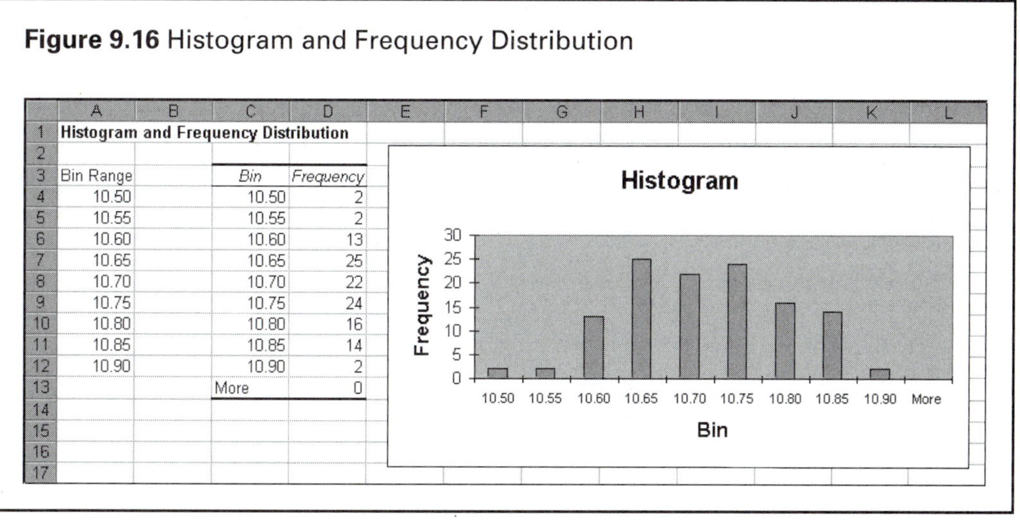

Histogram and Frequency Distribution

Bin Range		Bin	Frequency
10.50		10.50	2
10.55		10.55	2
10.60		10.60	13
10.65		10.65	25
10.70		10.70	22
10.75		10.75	24
10.80		10.80	16
10.85		10.85	14
10.90		10.90	2
		More	0

Figure 9.16 Histogram and Frequency Distribution

Process Capability

Process capability is the range over which the natural variation of a process occurs as determined by the system of common causes, that is, what the process can achieve under stable conditions. Process capability is important to both product designers and manufacturing engineers. Knowing process capability allows one to predict, quantitatively, how well a process will meet specifications and to specify equipment requirements and the level of control necessary. For example, suppose that the inside diameter of a bushing that supports a steel shaft must be between 1.498 and 1.510 inches for an acceptable fit. If the diameter is too small, it can be enlarged through a rework process. However if it is too large, the part must be scrapped. If the variation in the machining process results in diameters that typically range from 1.495 and 1.515 inches, we would say that the process is not capable of meeting the specifications. Management then faces three possible decisions: (1) measure each piece and either rework or scrap nonconforming parts; (2) develop a better process by investing in new technology; or (3) change the design specifications.

Such decisions are usually based on economics. Scrap and rework are poor strategies, because labor and materials have already been invested in a bad product. Also, inspection errors will probably allow some nonconforming products to leave the production facility. New technology might require substantial investment the firm cannot afford. Changes in design may sacrifice fitness-for-use requirements and result in a lower-quality product. Thus, these factors demonstrate the need to consider process capability in product design and acceptance of new contracts. Many firms now require process capability data from their suppliers.

Unfortunately, product design often takes place in isolation, with inexperienced designers applying tolerances to parts or products while having little awareness of the capabilities of the production process to meet these design requirements. Even experienced designers may be hard-pressed to remain up-to-date on the capabilities of processes that involve constant equipment changes, shifting technology, and difficult-to-measure variations in methods at scores of plants located hundreds or thousands of miles away from a centralized product design department. Process capability should be carefully considered in determining design specifications and is an important part of the design for manufacturability (DFM) concept discussed in

Chapter 7. Process capability information also aids in planning production schedules and inspection strategies.

Process Capability Studies A **process capability study** is a carefully planned study designed to yield specific information about the performance of a process under specified operating conditions. Typical questions that are asked in a process capability study include the following:

1. Where is the process centered?
2. How much variability exists in the process?
3. Is the performance relative to specifications acceptable?
4. What proportion of output will be expected to meet specifications?
5. What factors contribute to variability?

Many reasons exist for conducting a capability study. Manufacturing may wish to determine a performance baseline for a process, to prioritize projects for quality improvement, or to provide statistical evidence of quality for customers. Purchasing might conduct a study at a supplier plant to evaluate a new piece of equipment or to compare different suppliers. Engineering might conduct a study to determine the adequacy of R&D pilot facilities or to evaluate new processes.

Three types of studies are often conducted. A *peak performance study* determines how a process performs under ideal conditions. A *process characterization study* is designed to determine how a process performs under actual operating conditions. A *component variability study* assesses the relative contribution of different sources of total variation. The methods by which each study is conducted vary. A peak performance study is conducted under carefully controlled conditions over a short time interval to ensure that no special causes can affect variation. A process characterization study is performed over a longer time interval under actual operating conditions to capture the variations in materials and operators. A component variability study uses a designed experiment to control the sources of variability. Although this section considers a process characterization study, the general approach applies to a peak performance study with appropriate modifications.

The six steps in a process capability study are similar to those of any systematic study and include the following:

1. Choose a representative machine or segment of the process.
2. Define the process conditions.
3. Select a representative operator.
4. Provide materials that are of standard grade, with sufficient materials for uninterrupted study.
5. Specify the gauging or measurement method to be used.
6. Provide for a method of recording measurements and conditions, in order, on the units produced.

To obtain useful information, the sample size should be fairly large, generally at least 100. Process capability only makes sense if all special causes of variation have been eliminated and the process is in a state of statistical control (we will discuss this requirement further in Chapter 12). For this discussion, we assume that the process is in control.

Two statistical techniques are commonly used to evaluate process capability. One is the frequency distribution and histogram, the other is the control chart. The use of frequency distributions and histograms is covered in this section, but the discussion of control charts is deferred to a later chapter.

Example 8: Process Capability Analysis of U-Bolt Data. We may determine the process capability for the U-bolt dimensions shown in Table 9.3. From the descriptive statistics computed in Figure 9.14, we see that the mean is $\bar{x} = 10.7171$, and the sample standard deviation is $s = 0.0868$. The histogram shown in Figure 9.16 might suggest that the data are normally distributed. If we can verify this result, we may estimate the yield of conforming product for various manufacturing specifications analytically. Testing for normality can be done in several ways. The simplest and most practical method is to use normal probability paper. Normal probability paper is a special type of graph paper scaled so that the plot of a cumulative normal distribution will be a straight line. Usually the "straightness" of the line can be determined by visual inspection, and one can reach valid conclusions most of the time. Many computer packages have the ability to draw normal probability plots.

To test whether a frequency distribution is normal, first convert the data to a cumulative frequency distribution, that is, the number of observations less than or equal to a specified value. These cumulative frequencies are next converted to relative frequencies or probabilities by dividing the cumulative frequencies by the number of observations (120). From Figure 9.16 relative frequencies are as follows:

Dimensional Value	Frequency	Cumulative Frequency	Cumulative Relative Frequency
10.50	2	2	0.017
10.55	2	4	0.033
10.60	13	17	0.142
10.65	25	42	0.350
10.70	22	64	0.533
10.75	24	88	0.733
10.80	16	104	0.867
10.85	14	118	0.983
10.90	2	120	1.000

A plot of the cumulative relative frequencies on normal probability paper is shown in Figure 9.17. The result of an approximately straight line allows the reasonable conclusion that the process output follows a normal distribution.[16]

One of the properties of a normal distribution is that 99.73 percent of the observations will fall within three standard deviations from the mean. Thus, a process that is in control can be expected to produce a large percentage of output between $\mu - 3\sigma$ and $\mu + 3\sigma$, where μ is the process average. Therefore, the *natural tolerance limits* of the process are $\mu \pm 3\sigma$. A six standard deviation spread is used as a measure of process capability.

For the example, use the sample statistics $\bar{x} = 10.7171$ and $s = 0.0868$ as estimates of the population parameters μ and σ. Nearly all U-bolt dimensions are expected to fall between $10.7171 - 3(0.868) = 10.4566$ and $10.7171 + 3(0.0868) = 10.9766$. These calculations tell the production manager that if the design specifications are between 10.45 and 11.00, for instance, the process will be capable of producing nearly 100 percent conforming product. Suppose, however, that design specifications are such that the dimension must lie between 10.55 and 10.90. Calculate the expected percentage of nonconforming U-bolts by computing the area under a normal distribution having a mean of 10.7171 and standard deviation 0.0868 to the left and right of these specifications, as illustrated in Figure 9.18.

Figure 9.17 Normal Probability Plot

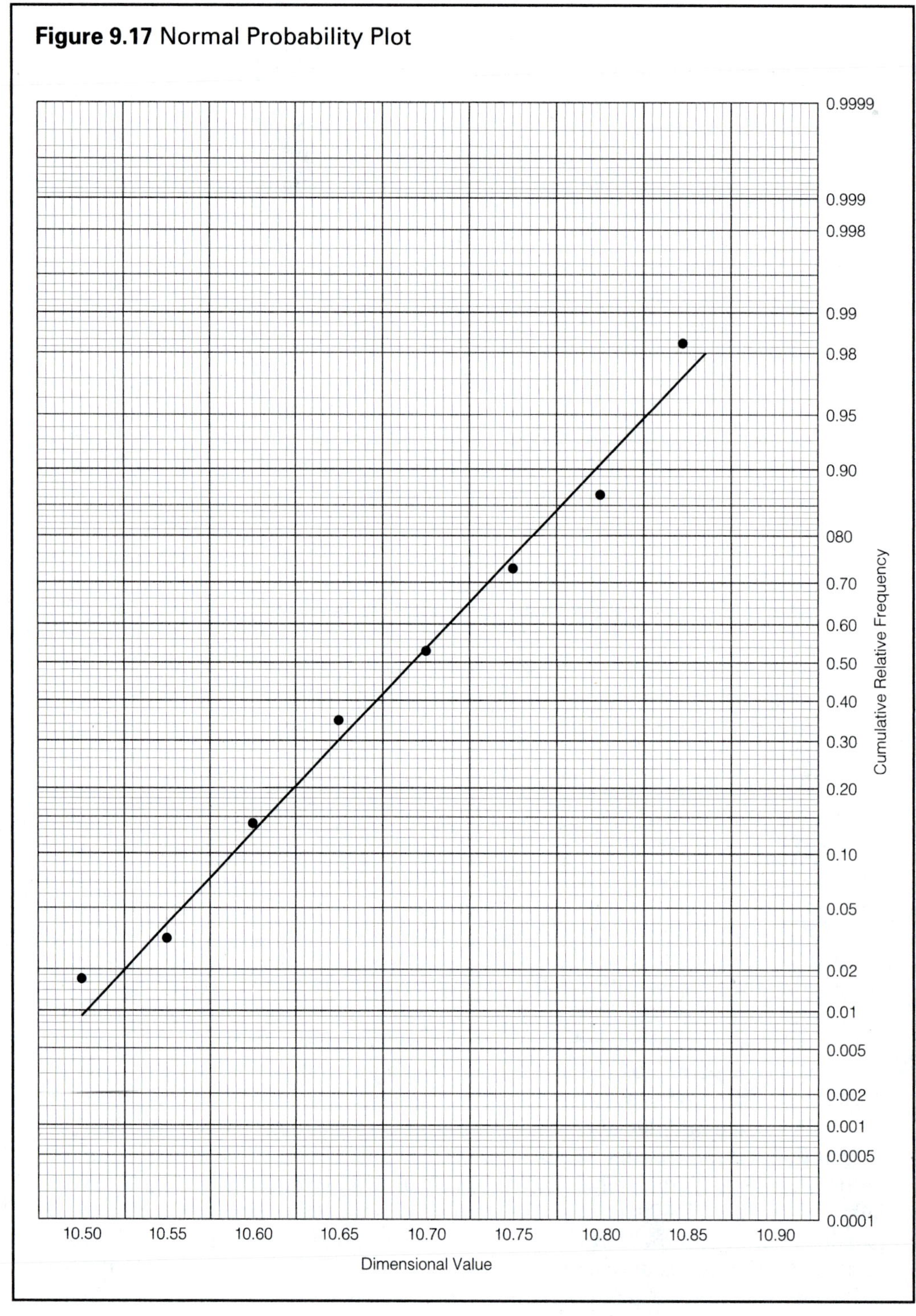

Figure 9.18 Probability of Nonconforming Product with Specifications of 10.55 to 10.90

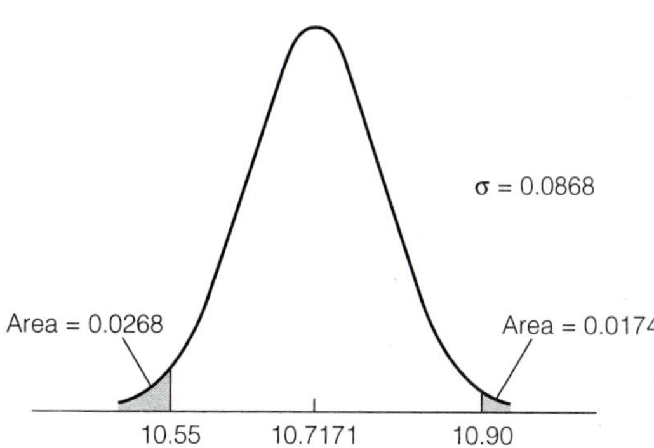

Converting 10.55 to a standard normal value yields $z = (10.55 - 10.7171)/0.0868 = -1.93$. Appendix A at the end of the book gives a value for the area to the *left* of $z = -1.93$ as $0.5000 - 0.4732 = 0.0268$. Similarly, the z value corresponding to 10.90 is $z = (10.90 - 10.7171)/0.0868 = 2.11$. The area to the *right* of $z = 2.11$ is $0.5000 - 0.4826 = 0.0174$. Therefore, the probability that a part will not meet specifications is $0.0268 + 0.0174 = 0.0442$ or, expressed as a percentage, is 4.42 percent. Similar computations can be used to estimate the percentage of nonconforming parts for other tolerances. This information can be used to help management determine scrap and rework policies, new equipment justification, and so on.

Not all process output will fit neatly to a normal curve; one can usually obtain important capability information directly from the histogram. Figure 9.19 shows some typical examples of process variation histograms that might result from a capability study. Figure 9.19(a) shows an ideal situation in which the natural variation is well within the specified tolerance limits. In Figure 9.19(b), the variation and tolerance limits are about equal; any shift of the distribution will result in nonconformances. The histogram in 9.19(c) shows a distribution with a natural variation greater than the specification limits; in this case, the process is not capable of meeting specifications. The histograms in Figures 9.19(d), (e), and (f) correspond to those in Figures 9.19(a), (b), and (c), except that the process is off-center from the specified tolerance limits. The capability of each is the same as in Figures 9.19(a), (b), and (c), but the shift in the mean of the distribution results in a higher level of nonconformance. Thus, in Figure 9.19(d), the process is capable; it is simply not adjusted correctly to the center of the specifications. In 9.19(g), the bimodal shape suggests that perhaps the data were drawn from two different machines or that two different materials or products were involved. The small distribution to the right in 9.19(h) may be the result of including pieces from a trial setup run while the machine was being adjusted. The strange distribution in 9.19(i) might be the result of the measurement process, such as inadequate gauging or rounding of data, and not inherent in the process itself. Finally, the truncated distribution in 9.19(j) is generally the result of sorting nonconforming parts; one would expect a smoother tail of the distribution on the left.

Figure 9.19 Examples of Process Variation Histograms and Specifications

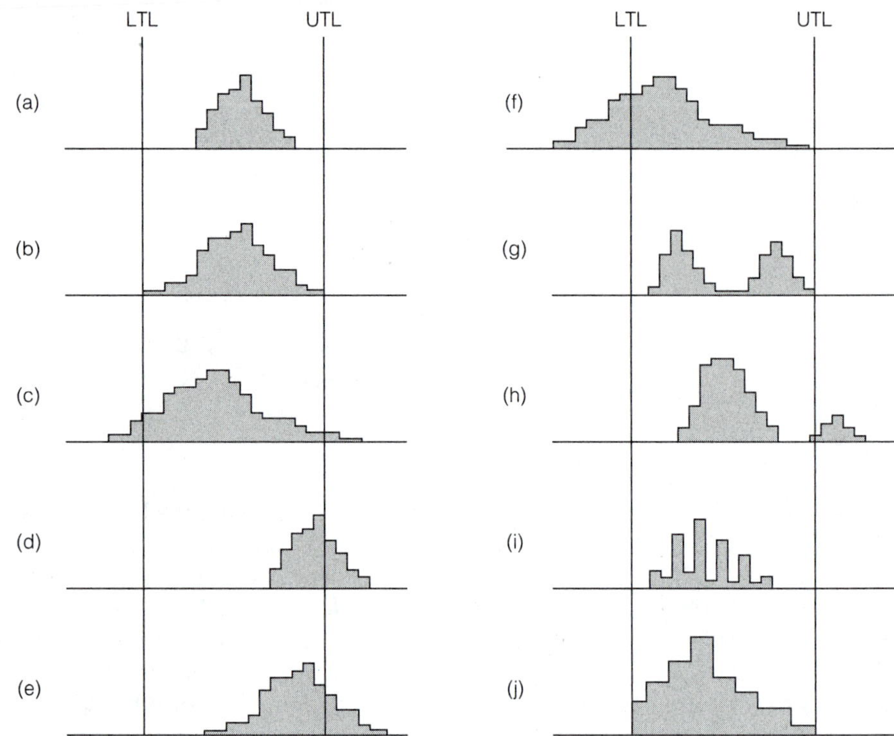

Therefore, one must be careful to ensure that observed variation comes from the process itself, not from external influences. A good control system is a necessity, because a histogram alone will not provide complete information.

An important issue that is often ignored in process capability studies is the error resulting from using the sample standard deviation, s, rather than the true standard deviation, σ. A simple table (see Table 9.4) can be constructed to find confidence intervals on the true value for σ for a given sample size. For a given sample size, σ will be less than or equal to s times the factor in that row with probability p, where p is the column heading. Thus, for a sample size of 30, $\sigma \leq 0.744s$ with probability 0.005; $\sigma \leq 1.280s$ occurs 95 percent of the time; and so on. A 90 percent confidence interval for σ can be found by using the factors in the columns corresponding to $p = 0.050$ and $p = 0.950$. Thus, for a sample size of 30, a 95 percent confidence interval would be ($0.825s$, $1.280s$). The interpretation of process capability information should be tempered by such an analysis.

Process Capability Indexes In Figure 9.19 we saw that the distribution of process output can differ in both location and spread relative to the specifications. The relationship between the natural variation and specifications is often quantified by a measure known as the **process capability index**. The process capability index, C_p (sometimes called the *process potential index*), is defined as the ratio of the specification width to the natural tolerance of the process. C_p relates the natural variation of the process with the design specifications in a single, quantitative measure.

Table 9.4 Ratio of Population to Sample Standard Deviation

Number of Samples	0.005	0.010	0.025	0.050	0.100	0.950	0.975	0.995
	Fraction of Population Less Than or Equal to Value in Table							
2	0.356	0.388	0.446	0.510	0.608	15.952	31.911	159.516
3	0.434	0.466	0.521	0.578	0.659	4.407	6.287	14.142
4	0.483	0.514	0.567	0.620	0.693	2.919	3.727	6.468
5	0.519	0.549	0.599	0.649	0.717	2.372	2.875	4.396
6	0.546	0.576	0.624	0.672	0.736	2.090	2.453	3.484
7	0.569	0.597	0.644	0.690	0.751	1.918	2.202	2.979
8	0.588	0.616	0.661	0.705	0.763	1.797	2.035	2.660
9	0.604	0.631	0.675	0.718	0.774	1.711	1.916	2.440
10	0.618	0.645	0.688	0.729	0.783	1.645	1.826	2.278
11	0.630	0.656	0.699	0.739	0.791	1.593	1.755	2.154
12	0.641	0.667	0.708	0.748	0.798	1.551	1.698	2.056
13	0.651	0.677	0.717	0.755	0.804	1.515	1.651	1.976
14	0.660	0.685	0.725	0.762	0.810	1.485	1.611	1.910
15	0.669	0.693	0.732	0.769	0.815	1.460	1.577	1.854
16	0.676	0.700	0.739	0.775	0.820	1.437	1.548	1.806
17	0.683	0.707	0.745	0.780	0.824	1.418	1.522	1.764
18	0.690	0.713	0.750	0.785	0.828	1.400	1.499	1.727
19	0.696	0.719	0.756	0.790	0.832	1.385	1.479	1.695
20	0.702	0.725	0.760	0.794	0.836	1.370	1.461	1.666
21	0.707	0.730	0.765	0.798	0.839	1.358	1.444	1.640
22	0.712	0.734	0.769	0.802	0.842	1.346	1.429	1.617
23	0.717	0.739	0.773	0.805	0.845	1.335	1.415	1.595
24	0.722	0.743	0.777	0.809	0.848	1.325	1.403	1.576
25	0.726	0.747	0.781	0.812	0.850	1.316	1.391	1.558
26	0.730	0.751	0.784	0.815	0.853	1.308	1.380	1.542
27	0.734	0.755	0.788	0.818	0.855	1.300	1.370	1.526
28	0.737	0.758	0.791	0.820	0.857	1.293	1.361	1.512
29	0.741	0.762	0.794	0.823	0.859	1.286	1.352	1.499
30	0.744	0.765	0.796	0.825	0.861	1.280	1.344	1.487
31	0.748	0.768	0.799	0.828	0.863	1.274	1.337	1.475
36	0.762	0.781	0.811	0.838	0.872	1.248	1.304	1.427
41	0.774	0.792	0.821	0.847	0.879	1.228	1.280	1.390
46	0.784	0.802	0.829	0.854	0.885	1.212	1.260	1.361
51	0.793	0.810	0.837	0.861	0.890	1.199	1.243	1.337
61	0.808	0.824	0.849	0.871	0.898	1.179	1.217	1.299
71	0.820	0.835	0.858	0.879	0.905	1.163	1.198	1.272
81	0.829	0.844	0.866	0.886	0.910	1.151	1.183	1.250
91	0.838	0.852	0.873	0.892	0.915	1.141	1.171	1.233
101	0.845	0.858	0.879	0.897	0.919	1.133	1.161	1.219

Source: Thomas D. Hall, "How Close Is s to σ? *Quality,* December 1991, 45. *Note:* The table published in this article was incorrect. An error notice was published in a subsequent issue and the correct table was made available by *Quality* magazine, and is shown here.

In numerical terms, the formula is

$$C_p = \frac{UTL - LTL}{6\sigma}$$

where

UTL = upper tolerance limit

LTL = lower tolerance limit

σ = standard deviation of the process

The process capability index can be used for setting objectives and improving processes. Suppose that a quality manager in a firm has a process with a standard deviation of 1 and a tolerance spread of 8. The value of C_p for this situation is 1.33. The manager realizes that the natural spread is within specifications at this time, but new contracts call for increasing the value of the capability index. Targets are set for increasing the index to 1.66 within three months, to 2.00 within six months, and to 2.33 within a year. Given that the tolerance spread (UTL – LTL) is held at the previous level of 8, the following table shows the required process standard deviation for each phase of the project.

C_p	UTL – LTL	6σ	σ
1.33	8	6	1
1.66	8	4.8	0.8
2.00	8	4	0.67
2.33	8	3.43	0.57

Operationally, this task involves reducing the variability in the process from a standard deviation of 1.000 to 0.57, which results in the desired increase of C_p from the current level of 1.33 to the final level of 2.33, which might be accomplished using process improvement and technology upgrades.

Two important facts about the C_p index should be pointed out. One relates to process conditions and the other relates to interpretation of the values that have been calculated. First, the calculation of the C_p has no meaning if the process is not under statistical control. The natural spread (6σ) should be calculated using a sufficiently large sample to get a meaningful estimate of the population standard deviation (σ). Second, a C_p of 1.00 would require that the process be perfectly centered on the mean of the tolerance spread to prevent some units from being produced outside the limits. The goal of all units being produced within specifications with a C_p of 1.33 is much easier to achieve, and still easier with a C_p of 2.00. Based on the experience of a number of practitioners, they have suggested a "safe" lower limit C_p of 1.5. A value above this level will practically guarantee that all units produced by a controlled process will be within specifications. Many firms require C_p values of 1.66 or greater from their suppliers.

The previous discussion assumed that the process was centered; clearly the value of C_p does not depend on the mean of the process. To include information on process centering, one-sided indexes are often used. One-sided process capability indexes are as follows:

$$C_{pu} = \frac{\text{UTL} - \mu}{3\sigma} \quad \text{(upper one-sided index)}$$

$$C_{pl} = \frac{\mu - \text{LTL}}{3\sigma} \quad \text{(lower one-sided index)}$$

$$C_{pk} = \min(C_{pl}, C_{pu})$$

To illustrate these computations for the U-bolt example, we found a mean of 10.7171. Thus,

$$C_{pl} = \frac{10.7171 - 10.50}{3(.0868)} = .83$$

$$C_{pu} = \frac{11.0 - 10.7171}{3(.0868)} = 1.086$$

$$C_{pk} = \min\{.83, 1.086\} = .83$$

We see that the process is more capable of satisfying the upper specification limit than the lower specification limit. The low value of C_{pk} indicates that the worst case is unacceptable. This index is often used in specifying quality requirements in purchasing contracts. Figure 9.20 shows a spreadsheet, available on the disk accompanying this book, designed to compute these indexes.

Some controversy exists over C_p and C_{pk} as measures of process capability, particularly with respect to the economic loss function philosophy of Taguchi.[15] For example, a process may have a high C_{pk} even when its mean is off target and close to the

Figure 9.20 Spreadsheet for Process Capability Calculations (PROCESS_CAPABILITY.XLS)

	A	B	C	D	E	F	G	H	I	J	K	L	M	N	O	P	Q
1	**Process Capability Analysis**																
2																	
3	This spreadsheet is designed to handle up to 150 observations. Enter data ONLY in yellow-shaded cells.																
4																	
5	**Nominal specification**				10.75		**Average**			10.7171			**Cp**	0.96			
6	**Upper tolerance limit**				11		**Standard deviation**			0.0868			**Cpl**	0.833			
7	**Lower tolerance limit**				10.5								**Cpu**	1.086			
8													**Cpk**	0.833			
9																	
10	**DATA**	**1**	**2**	**3**	**4**	**5**	**6**	**7**	**8**	**9**	**10**	**11**	**12**	**13**	**14**	**15**	
11	**1**	10.650	10.800	10.500	10.800	10.700	10.800	10.750	10.650	10.850	10.650	10.800	10.650				
12	**2**	10.750	10.850	10.800	10.800	10.700	10.700	10.850	10.700	10.800	10.550	10.700	10.850				
13	**3**	10.750	10.700	10.650	10.800	10.650	10.650	10.750	10.650	10.500	10.800	10.750	10.800				
14	**4**	10.600	10.650	10.650	10.700	10.600	10.750	10.800	10.850	10.650	10.650	10.700	10.600				
15	**5**	10.700	10.750	10.700	10.750	10.550	10.700	10.850	10.700	10.750	10.600	10.750	10.700				
16	**6**	10.600	10.900	10.850	10.750	10.650	10.650	10.600	10.750	10.750	10.600	10.650	10.650				
17	**7**	10.600	10.750	10.800	10.700	10.600	10.850	10.850	10.850	10.800	10.850	10.850	10.800				
18	**8**	10.750	10.750	10.700	10.700	10.700	10.600	10.650	10.850	10.750	10.650	10.700	10.650				
19	**9**	10.650	10.650	10.750	10.800	10.650	10.900	10.650	10.750	10.700	10.750	10.700	10.700				
20	**10**	10.600	10.600	10.750	10.800	10.750	10.850	10.750	10.750	10.700	10.650	10.600	10.650				
21																	

specification limits, as long as the process spread is small.[16] Several alternative measures have been proposed. One is to adjust C_p by a factor $(1 - k)$ as follows:

$$C_{pk} = C_p(1 - k)$$

where $k = 2\,|\text{mean} - \text{target}|\,/\text{tolerance}$. (Note: $|\text{mean} - \text{target}|$ signifies the absolute value of the difference.) When the sample mean is equal to the target, $k = 0$ and $C_{pk} = C_p$. As the sample mean deviates from the target, the absolute difference between them increases and k increases. Specification limits are used only to determine the tolerance; thus the focus of this measure is on the target value rather than on acceptable specification limits.

Another index that has been proposed is

$$C_{pm} = C_p / \sqrt{1 + (\text{mean} - \text{target})^2/\sigma^2}$$

This measure also accounts for deviations from the target value in a quadratic loss fashion based on the Taguchi loss function (see Chapter 7).

Example 9: Comparing Process Capability Indexes.[17] Suppose that UTL = 8, LTL = –8, target = 0, $\mu = 3$, and $\sigma = 1$ (see Figure 9.21). Then,

$$C_p = \frac{8 - (-8)}{6(1)} = 2.66$$

$$C_{pk} = \min\left\{\frac{8 - 3}{3(1)}, \frac{3 - (-8)}{3(1)}\right\} = 1.66$$

$$C_{pm} = \frac{2.66}{\sqrt{1 + (3 - 0)^2/1^2}} = .84$$

Although C_p and C_{pk} suggest that the process is highly capable, the value of C_{pm} indicates that the process is not. Because C_{pm} weights deviations of the process mean from the target rather heavily, the anomaly is explained.

Now consider another case. Suppose that UTL = 2.7, LTL = –2.7, target = μ = 0, and $\sigma = 1$ (see Figure 9.22). Then

$$C_p = \frac{2.7 - (-2.7)}{6(1)} = 0.9$$

$$C_{pk} = \min\left\{\frac{2.7 - 0}{3}, \frac{0 - (-2.7)}{3}\right\} = 0.9$$

$$C_{pm} = \frac{.9}{\sqrt{1 + (0 - 0)^2/1^2}} = 0.9$$

When the process is on target, these indexes have the same value. Although C_{pm} is higher, most customers would probably prefer the first case because a much higher proportion of products would be produced within the specifications. Thus, C_{pm} is only useful when the deviation from the target is the major concern.

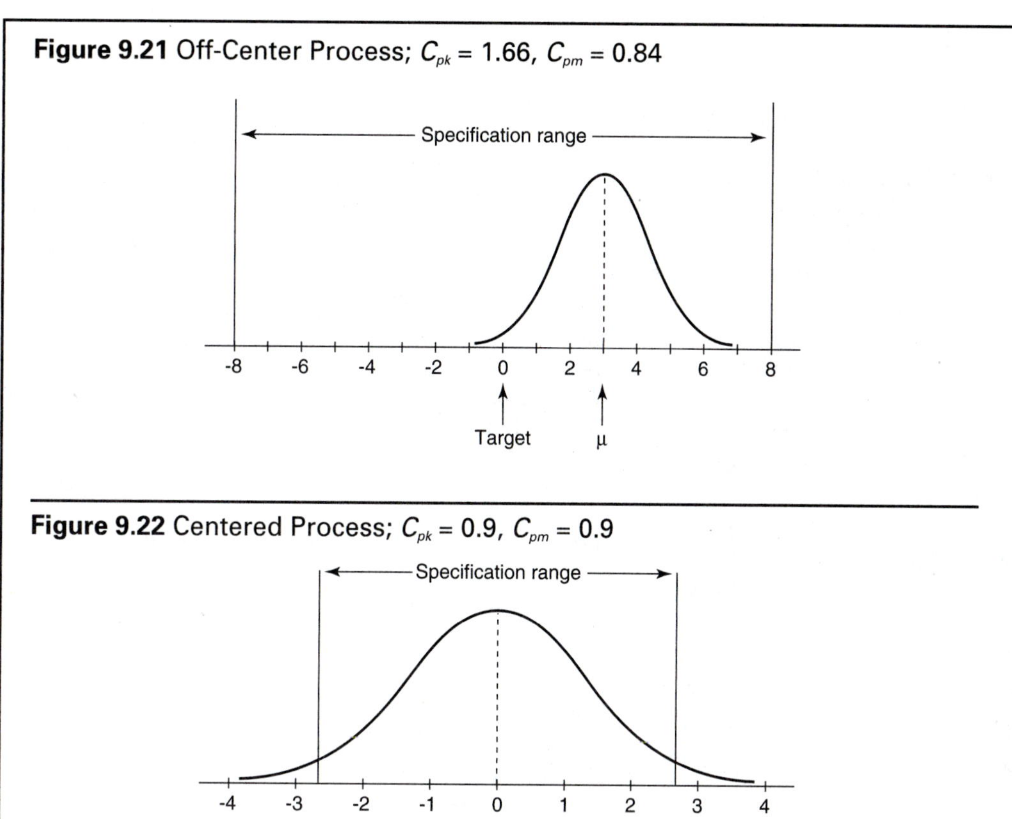

Figure 9.21 Off-Center Process; $C_{pk} = 1.66$, $C_{pm} = 0.84$

Figure 9.22 Centered Process; $C_{pk} = 0.9$, $C_{pm} = 0.9$

It is important to remember that C_p and C_{pk} are simply point estimates from some unknown distribution because they are based on samples. A confidence interval for C_{pk} can be expressed as[18]

$$C_{pk} \pm z_{\alpha/2}\sqrt{\frac{1}{9n} + \frac{C_{pk}^2}{2n-2}}$$

For example, suppose the point estimate is 1.15 and the sample size $n = 45$. Using this formula, a 95% confidence interval is (0.89, 1.41). While 1.15 may seem good, it is quite possible that the true population parameter is less than one because of sampling error. If a sample size of 400 were used instead to obtain the same point estimate, the confidence interval would be (1.06, 1.24), providing a better indication that the capability is indeed good.

Process capability indexes depend on the assumption that the distribution of output is normally distributed. When output is not normally distributed, such as in the chemical industry, when suppliers often pick and choose material that will meet the specifications of customers (which often results in a uniform distribution), or when output is affected by tool wear and exhibits a highly skewed distribution, process capability indexes can be below 1 even though all measurements are within specification limits. Finally, process capability may be affected by measurement error, which we will discuss in Chapter 11. If the measurement error is large, then process capability indexes must be viewed with caution.

Quality in Practice

Improving Quality of a Wave Soldering Process Through Design of Experiments[19]

A printed circuit assembly–encoder (PCA-Encoder) is a critical component for the base carriage assembly for a printer. The PCA-Encoder is produced by putting the electronic components on printed circuit boards (panels), which contain eight small boards, and then soldering the components using a wave soldering process. Any defect in any of the solder joints will lead to the failure of the circuit. Thus, it is important to ensure that soldering is defect-free. Typical soldering defects are blowholes (insufficient solder) and bridges (solder between two joints). At a Hewlett-Packard India Ltd. plant in Bangalore, India, a high level of soldering defects was observed, necessitating 100 percent inspection for all circuit boards. Any defects identified required manual rework, which consumed much time.

A study was undertaken to optimize the wave soldering process for reducing defects and thereby eliminating the inspection stage after the process. The quality engineers conducted a detailed study on the solder defects that identified the following aspects of the wave soldering process that might affect the resulting quality:

1. Conveyor speed
2. Conveyor angle
3. Solder bath temperature
4. Solder wave height
5. Vibration of wave
6. Preheater temperature
7. Air knife
8. Acid number (solid content in the flux), which is difficult to control because of environmental conditions

The engineers decided to use experimental design because of the long time frame required to adjust process parameters by trial and error, and the lack of insight into the possible joint effects of different parameters. Based on discussions with technical personnel, seven factors at three levels were selected for the experiment, as shown in Table 9.5. Conveyor speed and conveyor angle were fixed. A full factorial experiment would take 1,458 trials to conduct, which was not deemed to be practical. From statistical theory in the design of experiments, the seven main effects could be estimated by conducting only 18 trials as shown in Table 9.6.

Table 9.5 Factors and Levels for Experimentation

Factor	Code	Level 1	Level 2	Level 3
Bath temperature (°C)	A	248[a]	252	
Wave height[b]	B	4.38	4.40[a]	4.42
Overheated preheater (OH-PH) (PH-1)	C	340	360[a]	380
Preheater-1 (PH-1) (°C)	D	340	360[a]	380
Preheater (PH-2) (°C)	E	340	360[a]	380
Air Knife	F	0	3[a]	6
Omega[c]	G	0	2[a]	4

[a]Existing level

[b]The wave height is measured as the rpm of the motor pumping the solder.

[c]Omega refers to the vibration of the solder wave.

The experimental outcome (response) was the number of defective solder joints in a frame (352 joints). Each experiment was repeated three times.

Using analysis of variance, it was observed that bath temperature, wave height, and omega have a significant effect on the soldering defects. By setting the factors at the optimum levels identified through the experiments, the predicted defect level was 1,670 ppm as opposed to the current rate of greater than 6,000 ppm. However, the predicted average and the result of a confirmatory experiment were not sufficient to eliminate inspection completely, so additional experimental designs were conducted to reduce defects.

The next experiment considered the results of the first experiment and some of the uncontrollable factors. However, the different levels of the significant factors from the first experiment were selected in such a way that the new levels were allowed to vary around the optimum level of the first experiment. Based on the results of these additional experiments, new optimum levels of factors were identified and implemented with significant improvements. Figure 9.23 shows the ppm

Table 9.6 Data Corresponding to the First Experiment

Exp. No.	(1) Bath Temp. (°C)	(2) Wave Height	(3) OH-PH (°C)	(4) PH-2 (°C)	(5) PH-1 (°C)	(6) Air Knife	(7) Omega	Response 1	Response 2	Response 3
1	248	4.38	340	340	340	0	0	1	2	1
2	248	4.38	360	360	360	3	2	0	2	0
3	248	4.38	380	380	380	6	4	0	1	0
4	248	4.4	340	340	360	3	4	1	0	1
5	248	4.4	360	360	380	6	0	4	2	0
6	248	4.4	380	380	340	0	2	8	1	6
7	248	4.42	340	360	340	6	2	2	4	3
8	248	4.42	360	380	360	0	4	4	1	0
9	248	4.42	380	340	380	3	0	2	2	4
10	252	4.38	340	380	380	3	2	1	3	1
11	252	4.38	360	340	340	6	4	1	2	1
12	252	4.38	380	360	360	0	0	6	3	2
13	252	4.4	340	360	380	0	4	3	3	4
14	252	4.4	360	380	340	3	0	4	3	8
15	252	4.4	380	340	360	6	2	2	1	1
16	252	4.42	340	380	360	6	0	2	7	3
17	252	4.42	360	340	380	0	2	2	1	3
18	252	4.42	380	360	340	3	4	4	2	1

Figure 9.23 Solder Defects After Experimental Design Optimization

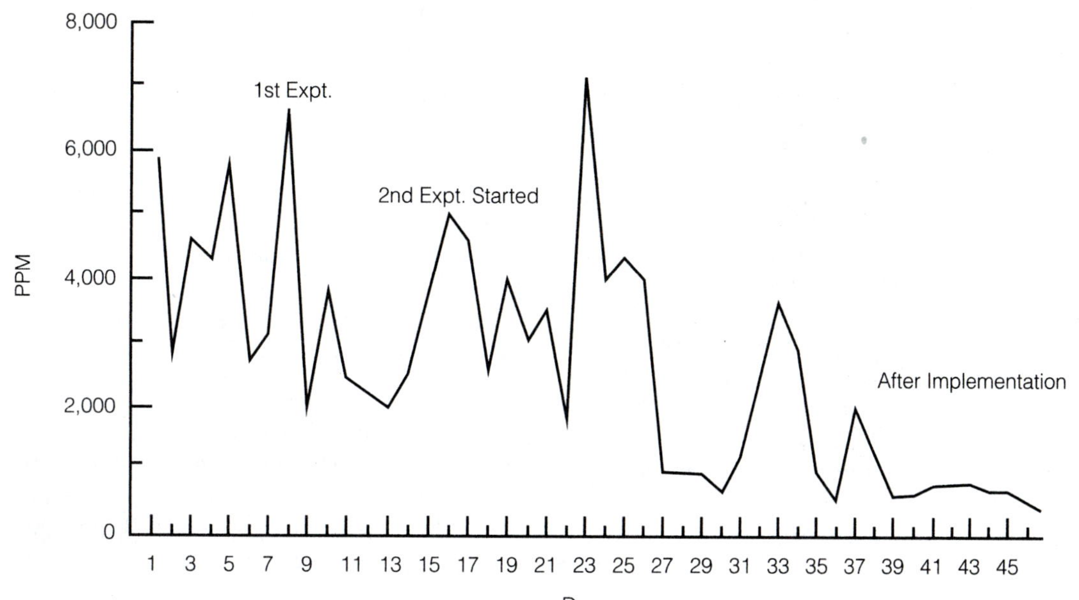

level during the course of the experimentation, which took only 45 days.

Key Issues for Discussion

1. Why did the first experimental design not find the true optimum combination of factors to achieve the maximum reduction of defects?
2. What were some of the advantages in using experimental design over a traditional trial-and-error approach?

Quality in Practice

Improving Process Capability Through Statistical Thinking at Alcoa[20]

Alcoa's Warrick Operations in Newburgh, Indiana, produces a metal product that is sold in coil form, and supplies this product to several major customers each with different mechanical, chemical, dimensional, and visual requirements. Each of these customers expects the product to meet all the requirements all the time; less than 1 percent of the coils shipped had been returned for quality problems. The company has been producing and selling this product for more than 30 years and is considered the leader in the industry. The demand for this product in the marketplace is increasing, and while the plant operates 24 hours a day, seven days a week, it can only meet 65 percent of the total market demand.

During one month, however, one customer had returned nearly 2 percent of the product. The primary reason for the returns was that the product was out of specification due to width (too wide). The customer specification for width is 34.8100 ± 0.0100 inches. This customer had told the organization that unless the quality of the product improved significantly and the returned coils replaced with good coils within the next two weeks, they would be forced to switch suppliers. With production yields that can barely meet current delivery needs, the need to replace nonconforming coils cause serious concern with management. After some discussion, the management team decided to form a quality improvement team to determine whether the customer was correct about the recent decline in quality, find the root cause, and implement a solution to eliminate the problem.

The team began to review the situation and discovered the following:

- The return rate in the past for width had been less than 1 percent.
- In-process sampling and testing for width had been going on for several years, and statistical control charts for the past two years were available.
- Nothing indicated a change to the process, systems, raw materials, etc.
- Within the past six months several operators had retired and were replaced with new operators.
- No major change had occurred with the equipment nor had a preventive maintenance (PM) check been done during the past month.
- The problem started within the past six months.

They decided to review and evaluate data from the past two years. The results of the analysis revealed the following:

1. The process was stable and in control during the past two years.
2. The width results followed a normal distribution.
3. The average width result was 34.8117 inches with a standard deviation of 0.0035 inches.
4. Process capability appeared good.
5. The process was not capable of meeting the desired tolerance of ± 0.0100 inches.

Further analysis revealed a difference between years. The average and standard deviation for 1997 was 34.8113 and 0.0029 respectively, and 34.8119 and 0.0038 respectively for 1998. The average had moved farther from the target of 34.8100 and the variability increased between the two years.

After the past performance was evaluated, the team knew that the following expression needed to be explored if the variability was to be understood and thus reduced:

$$S_{\text{product}} = \sqrt{S^2_{\text{process}} + S^2_{\text{measuring}}}$$

where S_{product} = the variability (standard deviation) of the produced product; S_{process} = the variability of the manufacturing process, and $S_{\text{measuring}}$ = the variability of the measuring system.

The team listed the interconnected processes that could influence the quality characteristic width. These processes were threading the coil, setting the equipment up, running the equipment, leveling the sheet, sampling the product, measuring the product, and reacting to the results. Next, the team brainstormed and listed several variables that could cause the process/product variability to increase (the increase in average was due to a setup issue that was easily addressed). These variables were line speed, unwind tension, leveler elongation, coil temperature, dancer roll, ambient temperature, operator, equipment setup, within coil variation, between coil variation, use of measuring system, and operator training/experience.

After much discussion, the team decided the measuring system should be investigated because it is located off line, and with new operators, could be a source of misuse, thus causing the higher overall product variation for 1998. They conducted a gage capability study (see Chapter 11 for a full description of this concept) that involved five operators and six specimens. Each operator measured each specimen twice on four different days. The analysis of this data revealed the following:

- The overall variability of the measuring system ($S_{\text{measuring}}$) was 0.0026 inches.
- The repeatability component ($S_{\text{repeatability}}$) was equal to 0.0012 inches or 23 percent of the overall variability of the measuring system.
- The reproducibility component ($S_{\text{reproducibility}}$) was equal to 0.0022 inches or 77 percent of the overall variability of the measuring system.
- The contribution of the overall measuring system variability to the total product variability was 43 percent.

Analysis of variance of these data indicated a significant difference in results between some of the operators and a significant difference in results between days for several operators. The average results for one operator (this operator was new to the job) were lower than the other four operators. It was decided to train or retrain all the operators in the proper use of the test equipment. After the additional training was completed, the gage capability study was repeated. The analysis of the second study resulted in the following:

- The overall variability of the measuring system was reduced to 0.0018 inches.
- The repeatability component was reduced to 0.0011 inches or 38 percent of the overall variability of the measuring system.
- The reproducibility component was reduced to 0.0014 inches or 62 percent of the overall variability of the measuring system.
- The contribution of the overall measuring system variability to the total product variability was reduced to 22 percent.

Analysis of variance of these data now indicated that the significant difference between some of the operators was reduced, and no significant difference appeared between days per operator. Next, the team turned its attention to the process.

The team decided to conduct an experimental design using three variables to see whether the overall process variability could be reduced. The three variables (identified by the earlier brainstorming) were leveler elongation, unwind tension, and equipment setup. Each variable was evaluated at two levels. Samples were taken from two coils within each run, and three samples were taken from within each coil (at the beginning, middle, and end of each run). Each sample was measured twice. It should be noted that only one operator was used during the study. Analysis of variance was used to analyze the data and showed that only the main effect setup was statistically significant. The average width decreased 0.005 inches when going from setup 1 to setup 2. The average width increased only 0.001 inches when going from tension 1 to tension 2 or from elongation 1 to elongation 2.

Because the purpose of the experiment was to gain knowledge about the sources of variation in order to reduce variation, the variability due to each effect was estimated. The overall variability observed during the study was 0.0038. The team realized that the major source of the variability was not due to the measuring system, but was coming from the process, in particular, setup issues between runs and between coils within runs. This variability was attributed to the fact that not all individuals were doing the job the same way, even though they had been given a well-written work instruction. As a result, the team then undertook the following activities:

- The team met with the production supervisors and the production crews to present the results and to reinforce how important it was for everyone to follow the setup and running practices. Operators were asked to set up to the customer's target.
- Training was completed for all new individuals and refresher training was given to some of the experienced workers.
- The measuring device and standard bars were checked and recalibrated.
- Two coils were cut up and the width was checked in numerous places to see whether the width was consistent within the coils.
- A procedure was implemented to measure every coil. The operators were asked to control chart the results and follow the reaction plan when an out-of-control or out-of-specification issue arose.

Today, the process is operating in a state of control and is capable of meeting the customer's requirements; in fact, the return rate decreased to under 0.1 percent.

Key Issues for Discussion

1. How was statistical thinking applied to the problem Alcoa faced?
2. Explain the relationships between the results of the statistical analyses and the actions the team took.
3. The team estimated the following *standard deviations* associated with individual effects. If all these contribute to the variability of the product, what is the standard deviation of the product?

Effect	Standard Deviations
Setup	0.0034
Tension	0.0007
Elongation	0.0006
Between coils	0.0018
Within coils	0.0001
Measuring	0.0008

Summary of Key Points

- Statistics is concerned with the collection, organization, analysis, interpretation, and presentation of data and has extensive applications in quality assurance. The three basic components of statistical methodology are descriptive statistics, statistical inference, and predictive statistics. Statistical methods are used in many areas of quality assurance.
- Statistical thinking is a philosophy of learning based on principles of understanding that all work occurs in a system of interconnected processes, variation exists in all processes, and variation must be understood and reduced.
- Common causes of variation are inherent to a process, generally account for most observed variation, and cannot be identified or controlled on an individual basis. Special causes of variation are sporadic in nature and result from external disturbances that can usually be identified statistically and either explained or corrected. A system governed only by common causes is called a stable system.
- Not understanding the differences between common and special causes can result in increasing the variation through tampering with stable systems, or missing opportunities to reduce special cause variation when it exists. Deming's Red Bead and Funnel experiments can help clarify the differences between common and special causes and improve managers' abilities to make effective decisions.
- Statistical methodology includes descriptive statistics, statistical inference, and predictive statistics. These techniques are commonly used in quality assurance, and a basic understanding is important for any modern manager. Spreadsheet

software such as Microsoft Excel enables one to easily perform statistical calculations on personal computers.

- Sample statistics are used to obtain estimates of population parameters. To make probability statements about sample statistics, we need to know the sampling distribution and its standard deviation, called the standard error.
- Several types of sampling techniques exist. They include simple random sampling, stratified sampling, systematic sampling, cluster sampling, and judgment sampling. Understanding the purpose of sampling and the statistical issues underlying each technique is important in choosing the appropriate one to use.
- Experimental design, or design of experiments (DOE), is a practical tool for drawing conclusions regarding the comparison of different methods or the determination of optimal levels of controllable factors. Simple factorial experiments allow one to identify the main effects and interaction effects associated with controllable factors.
- Process capability is the range over which the natural variation of a process occurs as determined by the system of common causes. It is determined through statistical analysis of variation in a production process and measured relative to specifications by process capability indexes.

Review Questions

1. What is statistical thinking? Why is it important to managers and workers at all levels of an organization?
2. Explain the difference between common and special causes of variation.
3. Explain the two fundamental mistakes that managers make when attempting to improve a process. Can you cite any examples in your personal experience in which such mistakes were made?
4. What are the lessons of the Red Bead and Funnel experiments? Can you cite any examples in your experience where someone acted counter to these lessons?
5. Discuss the differences between the three major components of statistical methodology (descriptive statistics, statistical inference, and predictive statistics). Why might the distinctions be important to a manager?
6. Provide some examples of discrete and continuous random variables in a quality management context.
7. Define a population and a sample. What are their major characteristics?
8. Explain the difference between the standard deviation and the standard error of the mean. How are they related?
9. State the meaning of the central limit theorem in your own words. How important is it in developing and using statistical quality control techniques?
10. What two factors influence sampling procedures?
11. Discuss the basic questions that must be addressed in a sampling study.
12. Describe the different methods of sample selection and provide an example in which each would be most appropriate.
13. What are the sources of systematic error in sampling? How can systematic error be overcome?
14. What is the purpose of design of experiments?
15. Describe a factorial experiment. Provide some examples of factorial experiments that you might use to solve some type of quality-related problem.
16. Explain the term *process capability*. How can process capability generally be improved?

17. What are the three major types of process capability studies? Describe the methodology of conducting a process capability study.
18. Define the process capability indexes, C_p, C_{pl}, and C_{pu}, and explain how they may be used to establish or improve quality policies in operating areas or with suppliers.
19. What are the advantages and disadvantages of the C_{pm} capability index?

PROBLEMS

1. Apply the Descriptive Statistics and Histogram tools in Excel to compute the mean, standard deviation and other relevant statistics, as well as a frequency distribution and histogram for the following data. From what type of distribution might you suspect the data are drawn?

8	8	2	88	13	106	56	47	51	28
30	14	25	37	62	23	2	16	3	15
1	80	45	35	2	14	22	52	71	3
37	63	15	100	115	2	7	13	25	8
88	12	39	32	23	16	41	47	80	15
18	39	4	99	34	21	6	9	37	49
42	11	23	19	26	70	2	3	42	65
47	101	28	43	1	35	176	12	5	58
37	12	1	1	8	73	1	58	24	17
18	11	22	14	15	2	34	152	17	13

2. Apply the Descriptive Statistics and Histogram analysis tools in Excel to compute the mean, standard deviation, and other relevant statistics, as well as a frequency distribution and histogram for the following data. From what type of distribution might you suspect the data are drawn?

2.9	3.6	3.4	4.7	3	3.6	3.1	4.1	2.9	2.3
4.7	4.7	3.6	4	2.4	4	2.4	4.1	3.7	3.5
3.6	3.6	2.9	4.2	3.1	4.1	5	1.9	3.3	4.3
4.3	3.1	3.6	2.9	5	3.7	3.1	4.3	3.8	3.8
1.9	2.7	3.8	4	2.6	4.9	4.1	4.7	2.6	4.3
3.9	3.7	4	3.5	3.4	3	3.8	3.2	2.5	4.2
3.2	3.6	3.2	4.5	5	2.9	3.2	3.1	3	3.4
4	3.7	3.3	5	3.9	3.4	3.5	3.1	4.3	2.3
3.1	4.8	2.6	3.5	3.5	2.8	4.3	2.6	3.4	4.6
3.4	3.6	3.7	3.2	5.3	2.5	3.2	3.4	3.8	4.1

3. Jamaican Punch is sold in 14-ounce cans. The mean number of ounces placed in a can is 13.77 with a standard deviation of 0.1 ounce. Assuming a normal distri-

bution, what is the probability that the filling machine will cause an overflow in a can, that is, the probability that more than 14 ounces will be placed in the can?

4. Georgia Tea is sold in 2-liter (2,000 milliliter) bottles. The mean volume of tea in the bottle is 2 liters and the standard deviation is 20 milliliters. If the process requires that there be only a 1 percent (total) probability of over- or underfilling, what should the upper and lower fill limits be?
5. Tasmanian Blend is sold in 700 milliliter (ml) cans. The mean volume of juice placed in a can is 675 ml with a standard deviation of 15 ml. Assuming a normal distribution, what is the probability that the filling machine will cause an overflow in a can, that is, the probability that more than 700 ml will be placed in the can?
6. The standard deviation of the weight of filled containers is 0.6 ounce. If 2 percent of the containers contain less than 16 ounces, what is the mean filling weight of the containers?
7. Outback Beer bottles have been found to have a standard deviation of 5 ml. If 5 percent of the bottles contain less than 622 ml, what is the average filling volume of the bottles?
8. In filling bottles of L & E Cola, the average amount of overfilling should be kept as low as possible. If the mean fill volume is 12.05 ounces and the standard deviation is 0.02 ounce, what percentage of bottles will have less than 12 ounces? More than 12.10 ounces (assuming no overflow)?
9. In a filling line at E & L Foods, Ltd., the mean fill volume for rice bubbles is 450 grams and the standard deviation is 3 grams. What percentage of containers will have less than 443 grams? More than 456 grams (assuming no overflow)?
10. The following data represent the weight of castings (in kilograms) being made in the Harrison Metalwork foundry. Based on this sample of 100 castings, find the mean and standard deviation of the sample. Use an Excel spreadsheet if possible to plot the histogram for the data. Plot the data on normal probability paper to determine whether the distribution of the data is approximately normal. (Note: The Regression tool in Excel has a normal probability plot that may be used here.)

Frequency Distribution

	Upper Cell Boundaries*	Frequencies	Cumulative %
Cell 1	37.5	1	1.00%
Cell 2	37.8	3	4.00%
Cell 3	38.1	8	12.00%
Cell 4	38.4	26	38.00%
Cell 5	38.7	29	67.00%
Cell 6	39.0	15	82.00%
Cell 7	39.3	13	95.00%
Cell 8	39.6	4	99.00%
Cell 9	39.9	1	100.00%

*Called "bins" in Excel.

11. The following data show the weight of castings (in kilograms) being made in the Harrison Metalwork foundry after process changes took place. Plot a histogram of the data. Based on this sample of 100 castings, find the

mean and standard deviation of the sample. Plot the data on normal probability paper to determine whether the distribution of the data is approximately normal.

Frequency Table

	Upper Cell Boundaries*	Frequencies	Cumulative %
Cell 1	37.5	1	1.00%
Cell 2	37.8	3	4.00%
Cell 3	38.1	8	12.00%
Cell 4	38.4	23	35.00%
Cell 5	38.7	25	60.00%
Cell 6	39.0	23	83.00%
Cell 7	39.3	10	93.00%
Cell 8	39.6	6	99.00%
Cell 9	39.9	1	100.00%

*Called "bins" in Excel.

12. Refer to Problem 10. If the upper tolerance limit (UTL) of the process is 41.1 and the lower tolerance limit (LTL) is 36.3, calculate the process capability index, C_p. Is it within satisfactory limits? How much reduction in the sample standard deviation would be required to bring the process capability index up to 2.5?
13. Refer to Problem 11. If the upper tolerance limit (UTL) of the process is 40.0 and the lower tolerance limit (LTL) is 38.5, calculate the process capability index, C_p. Is it within satisfactory limits? How much reduction in the sample standard deviation would be required to bring the process capability index up to 3.00?
14. A machining process has a required dimension on a part of 0.575 ± 0.007 inch. Twenty-five parts were measured as follow. What is its capability for producing within acceptable limits?

Sample Number

1	2	3	4	5
0.557	0.576	0.577	0.564	0.580
0.566	0.578	0.574	0.573	0.584
0.587	0.577	0.573	0.579	0.580
0.578	0.582	0.575	0.573	0.578
0.565	0.576	0.576	0.572	0.574

15. Adjustments were made in the process discussed in Problem 14 and 25 more samples were taken. The results are as follows. What can you observe about the process? What is its capability for producing within acceptable limits now?

Sample Number

1	2	3	4	5
0.573	0.578	0.576	0.579	0.574
0.575	0.575	0.573	0.577	0.576
0.573	0.574	0.576	0.575	0.579
0.576	0.577	0.577	0.574	0.575
0.576	0.574	0.575	0.575	0.576

16. For the following data, construct a histogram and estimate the process capability. If the specifications are 24 ± 0.03, estimate the percentage of parts that will be nonconforming. Finally, compute C_p, C_{pu}, and C_{pl}.

24.029	23.991	24.008	23.984	23.994
24.003	24.008	23.996	24.001	24.010
24.020	24.015	24.010	23.996	23.988
23.991	23.990	24.002	24.013	24.003
24.008	24.013	24.005	23.999	24.009
23.996	24.010	23.999	23.984	24.005
23.991	23.995	24.000	24.000	24.009
24.000	23.997	23.991	23.994	24.018
24.005	23.988	24.007	23.971	24.003
24.011	23.996	23.992	24.008	23.998
23.989	23.995	23.994	24.011	23.983
24.023	24.004	23.997	24.015	24.001
24.020	23.994	23.995	23.998	24.003
24.004	24.001	23.994	23.997	24.006
24.004	24.006	24.001	24.009	23.996
24.002	23.986	24.000	23.995	24.000
23.998	24.001	24.001	23.999	24.013
23.993	23.995	24.007	24.005	24.009
24.016	24.013	23.995	23.985	24.019
24.010	23.990	24.000	24.002	24.007

17. Samples for three parts were taken as follows. Data set 1 is for part 1, data set 2 is for part 2, and data set 3 is for part 3.

Data Set 1	Data Set 2	Data Set 3
1.74831	2.01144	1.25426
1.75740	2.00448	1.24775
1.75134	2.01492	1.24558
1.73316	2.00448	1.24992
1.75134	2.00448	1.23907
1.71498	2.00100	1.25860
1.75437	2.00796	1.25643
1.73619	2.00100	1.25209
1.73922	1.98708	1.25426
1.73619	1.99752	1.24341
1.74528	1.99752	1.25643
1.74831	2.00100	1.24775
1.76346	1.99404	1.24341
1.74528	2.00796	1.24558
1.76952	2.00448	1.23907
1.70892	2.00448	1.24124
1.75134	2.00100	1.24558
1.71195	1.99752	1.24992
1.74831	2.00100	1.25209
1.77861	2.00100	1.24992
1.75740	1.98708	1.24992
1.73619	1.99404	1.24558
1.74225	1.98708	1.24992
1.74528	1.98360	1.24775
1.73922	2.00100	1.24775

a. Calculate the mean and standard deviations for each part and compare them to the following specification limits:

Part	Nominal	Tolerance
1	1.750	±0.045
2	2.000	±0.060
3	1.250	±0.030

b. Will the production process permit an acceptable fit of all parts into a slot with a specification of 5 ± 0.081 at least 99.73 percent of the time?

18. Omega Parts Ltd. (OPL) is a small manufacturing company that produces various parts for tool manufacturers. One of OPL's production processes involves producing a Teflon® spacer plate that has a tolerance of 0.05 to 0.100 cm in thickness. On the recommendation of the quality assurance (QA) department and over objections of the plant manager, OPL had just purchased some new equipment to make these parts. Recently, the production manager was receiving complaints from customers about high levels of nonconforming parts. He suspected the new equipment, but neither QA nor plant management would listen.

The manager discussed the issue with one of his production supervisors who mentioned that she had just collected some process data for a study that the quality assurance department was undertaking. The manager decided that he would prove his point by showing that the new equipment was not capable of meeting the specifications. The data provided by the supervisor follow.

0.078	0.082	0.069	0.077
0.102	0.079	0.080	0.074
0.085	0.080	0.076	0.080
0.070	0.079	0.092	0.067
0.093	0.065	0.083	0.083
0.054	0.077	0.079	0.077
0.075	0.067	0.066	0.076
0.064	0.066	0.075	0.068
0.077	0.049	0.072	0.065
0.095	0.078	0.070	0.074
0.104	0.086	0.091	0.082
0.083	0.082	0.090	0.074
0.068	0.064	0.062	0.072
0.090	0.077	0.078	0.079
0.061	0.075	0.070	0.078

Perform a process capability study on these data and interpret your results.

19. Suppose that a process with a normally distributed output has a mean of 55.0 and a variance of 4.0.

a. If the specifications are 55.0 ± 4.00, compute C_p, C_{pk}, and C_{pm}.

b. Suppose the mean shifts to 53.0 but the variance remains unchanged. Recompute and interpret these process capability indexes.
c. If the variance can be reduced to 40 percent of its original value, how do the process capability indexes change (using the original mean of 55.0)?

20. A process has upper and lower tolerance limits of 5.60 and 5.20, respectively. If the customer requires a demonstrated C_p of 2.0, what must the process capability be? If both C_{pu} and C_{pl} must also be 2.0, determine the mean and standard deviation of the process, assuming a normal distribution of output.
21. A utility requires service operators to answer telephone calls from customers in an average time of 0.1 minute, with a tolerance of +0.04 and –0.06 minute. A sample of 50 actual operator times was drawn, and the results are given in the following table. In addition, operators are expected to ascertain customer needs and either respond to them or refer the customer to the proper department within 0.5 minute with a tolerance of +0.20 and –0.30 minute. Another sample of 50 times was taken for this activity and is also given in the table. If these variables can be considered to be independent, how often can the total time be expected to vary from 0.6 minute, with a tolerance of +0.24 and –0.36 minute?

Component	Mean Time	Standard Deviation
Answer	0.1023	0.0183
Service	0.5044	0.0902

22. Determine the appropriate sample size to estimate the proportion of sorting errors at a post office at a 95 percent confidence level. Historically, the error rate is 0.022, and you wish to have an allowable error of 0.01.
23. You are asked by a motel owner to develop a customer satisfaction survey to determine the percentage of customers who are dissatisfied with service. Based on the 21,000 customers who were serviced in the past year, he desires a 95 percent level of confidence with an allowable error of ±0.02. From past estimates, the manager believes that about 10 percent of customers have expressed dissatisfaction. What sample size should you use for this survey?
24. A local telephone company interviewed 150 customers to determine their satisfaction with service. Twenty-seven expressed dissatisfaction. Compute a 90 percent confidence interval for the proportion satisfied with an allowable error of 0.05.
25. A management engineer at Country Squire Hospital has determined that she needs to take a work sampling study to see whether the proportion of idle time in the diagnostic imaging department has changed since being measured in a previous study several years ago. At that time, the percentage of idle time was 12 percent. If the engineer can only take a sample of 600 observations due to cost factors, and can tolerate an allowable error of 0.03, what percent confidence level can be obtained from the study?
26. Using Table 9.1, suppose that the population consists of 2,000 units. The critical rate of occurrence is 1 percent, and you wish to be 99 percent confident of finding at least one nonconformity. What sample size should you select?
27. A process engineer is trying to determine whether a newer, more costly design involving a gold alloy in a computer chip is more effective than the present, less expensive silicon design. She wants to obtain an effective output voltage at both high and low temperatures, when tested with high and low signal strength. She hypothesizes that high signal strength will result in

higher voltage output, low temperature will result in higher output, and the gold alloy will result in higher output than the silicon material. She hopes that the main and interaction effects with the expensive gold will be minimal. The following data were gathered in testing of all 2^3 combinations. What recommendation would you make based on these data?

Signal	Material	Temperature	Output Voltage
High	Gold	Low	18
High	Gold	High	12
High	Silicon	Low	16
High	Silicon	High	10
Low	Gold	Low	8
Low	Gold	High	11
Low	Silicon	Low	7
Low	Silicon	High	14

CASES

I. THE DISCIPLINARY CITATION[21]

A local delivery service has 40 drivers who deliver packages throughout the metropolitan area. Occasionally, drivers make mistakes, such as entering the wrong package number on a shipping document, failing to get a signature, and so on. A total of 240 mistakes were made in one year as shown in Table 9.7. The manager in charge of this operation has issued a disciplinary citation to drivers for each mistake.

Discussion Questions

1. What is your opinion of the manager's approach? How does it compare with the Deming philosophy?
2. How might the analysis of these data help the manager to understand the variation in the system? (Plot the data to obtain some insight.) How can the data help the manager to improve the performance of this system?

II. THE QUARTERLY SALES REPORT[22]

Ron Hagler, the vice president of sales for Selit Corp., had just gotten a report on the past five years of quarterly sales data for the regions under his authority (see Table 9.8). Not happy with the results, he got on the phone to his secretary.

"Marsha, tell the regional managers I need to speak with them this afternoon. Everyone must attend."

Marsha had been Hagler's secretary for almost a decade. She knew by the tone in his voice that he meant business, so she contacted the regional

Table 9.7 Delivery Driver Citations

Driver No.	1	2	3	4	5	6	7	8	9	10	11	12	13	14
Mistakes	6	1	0	14	0	2	18	2	5	13	1	4	6	5
Driver No.	15	16	17	18	19	20	21	22	23	24	25	26	27	28
Mistakes	0	0	1	3	15	24	3	4	1	2	3	22	4	8
Driver No.	29	30	31	32	33	34	35	36	37	38	39	40		
Mistakes	2	6	8	0	9	20	9	0	3	14	1	1		

managers about the impromptu meeting at 2 P.M. At 1:55 P.M., the regional managers filed into the room. The only time they were called into a meeting together was when Hagler was unhappy.

Hagler wasted no time. "I just received the quarterly sales report. Northeast sales were fantastic. Steve, you not only improved 17.6% in the fourth quarter, but you also increased sales a whopping 20.6% over the previous year. I don't know how you do it!" Steve smiled. His philosophy of ending the year with a bang by getting customers to stockpile units paid off again. Hagler had failed to notice that Steve's first quarter sales were always sluggish.

Hagler continued: "Terry, Southwest sales were also superb You showed an 11.7% increase in the fourth quarter and an 11.8% increase over the previous year." Terry also smiled. She wasn't sure how she did so well, but she sure wasn't going to change anything.

"Jan, Northwest sales were up 17.2% in the fourth quarter, but down 8.2% from the previous year," said Hagler. "You need to find out what you did previously to make your sales go through the roof. Even so, your performance in the fourth quarter was good." Jan tried to hide his puzzlement. Although he had received a big order in November, it was the first big order he had received in a long time. Overall, sales for the Northwest were declining.

Hagler was now ready to deal with the "problem" regions. "Leslie, North Central sales were down 5.5% in the fourth quarter, but up 4.7% from the previous year. I don't understand how your sales vary so much. Do you need more incentive?" Leslie looked down. She had been working very hard the past five years and had acquired numerous new accounts. In fact, she received a bonus for acquiring the most new business in 1996.

"Kim, Mid-Atlantic sales were down 3.2% in the fourth quarter and down 2.6% from the previous year. I'm very disappointed in your performance. You were once my best sales representative. I had high expectations for you. Now, I can only hope that your first quarter results show some sign of life." Kim felt her face get red. She knew she sold more units in 1998 than in 1997. "What does Hagler know anyway," she thought to herself. "He's just an empty suit."

Hagler turned to Dave, who felt a surge of adrenaline. "Dave, South Central sales were the worst of all! Sales were down 19.7% in the fourth quarter and down 22.3% from the previous year. How can you explain this? Do you value your job? I want to see a dramatic improvement in this quarter's results or else!" Dave felt numb. This was a tough region, with a lot of competition. Sure, accounts were lost over the years, but those lost were always replaced with new ones. How could he be doing so badly?

Discussion Question

1. How can Hagler improve his approach by applying principles of statistical thinking? Use any analyses of the data that you feel are appropriate to fully explain your thinking and help him.

III. The HMO Pharmacy Crisis[23]

John Dover just completed an intensive course, "Statistical Thinking for Continuous Improvement," that was offered to all employees of a large health maintenance organization (HMO). He had no time to celebrate, however, because he was already under a lot of pressure. Dover worked as a pharmacy assistant in the HMO's pharmacy, and his manager, Juan de Pacotilla, was about to be fired. Pacotilla's dismissal appeared imminent because of numerous complaints and even a few lawsuits over inaccurate prescriptions. Pacotilla now was asking Dover for his assistance in trying to resolve the problem.

"John, I really need your help," said Pacotilla. "If I can't show some major improvement or at least a solid plan by next month, I'm history."

"I'll be glad to help," replied Dover, "but what can I do? I'm just a pharmacy assistant."

"Your job title isn't important. I think you're just the person who can get this done," said Pacotilla. "I realize that I've been too far removed from day-to-day operations in the pharmacy, but you work there every day. You're in a much better position to find out how to fix the problem. Just tell me what to do, and I'll do it."

Table 9.8 Five Years of Sales Data by Region (Data in thousands)

1996 Sales

Region	*First Quarter*	*Second Quarter*	*Third Quarter*	*Fourth Quarter*
Northeast	$ 924	$ 928	$ 956	$1,222
Southwest	1,056	1,048	1,129	1,073
Northwest	1,412	1,280	1,129	1,181
North Central	431	470	439	431
Mid-Atlantic	539	558	591	556
South Central	397	391	414	407

1997 Sales

Region	*First Quarter*	*Second Quarter*	*Third Quarter*	*Fourth Quarter*
Northeast	$ 748	$ 962	$ 983	$1,024
Southwest	1,157	1,146	1,064	1,213
Northwest	1,149	1,248	1,103	1,021
North Central	471	496	506	573
Mid-Atlantic	540	590	606	643
South Central	415	442	384	448

1998 Sales

Region	*First Quarter*	*Second Quarter*	*Third Quarter*	*Fourth Quarter*
Northeast	$ 991	978	1,040	$1,295
Southwest	1,088	4,322	1,256	1,132
Northwest	1,085	1,125	910	999
North Central	403	440	371	405
Mid-Atlantic	657	602	596	640
South Central	441	366	470	426

1999 Sales

Region	*First Quarter*	*Second Quarter*	*Third Quarter*	*Fourth Quarter*
Northeast	$ 756	$1,008	$1,038	$ 952
Southwest	4,352	1,353	1,466	1,196
Northwest	883	851	997	878
North Central	466	536	551	670
Mid-Atlantic	691	723	701	802
South Central	445	455	363	462

2000 Sales

Region	*First Quarter*	*Second Quarter*	*Third Quarter*	*Fourth Quarter*
Northeast	$1,041	$1,020	$ 976	$1,148
Southwest	1,330	1,003	1,197	1,337
Northwest	939	834	688	806
North Central	588	699	743	702
Mid-Atlantic	749	762	807	781
South Central	420	454	447	359

"But what about the statistical consultant you hired to analyze the data on inaccurate prescriptions?" asked Dover.

"To be honest, I'm really disappointed with that guy. He has spent two weeks trying to come up with a new modeling approach to predict weekly inaccurate prescriptions. I tried to explain to him that I don't want to predict the mistakes, I want to eliminate them. I don't think I got through, however, because he said we need a month of additional data to verify the model before he can apply a new method he just read about in a journal to identify 'change points in the time series,' whatever that means. But get this, he will only identify the change points and send me a list. He says it's my job to figure out what they mean and how to respond. I don't know much about statistics. The only thing I remember from my course in college is that it was the worst course I ever took. I'm becoming convinced that statistics really doesn't have much to offer in solving real problems. Since you've just gone through the statistical thinking course, maybe you can see something I can't. I realize it's a long shot, but I was hoping you could use this as the project you need to officially complete the course."

"I used to feel the same way about statistics, too," replied Dover. "But the statistical thinking course was interesting because it didn't focus on crunching numbers. I have some ideas about how we can approach making improvements in prescription accuracy. I think it would be a great project. But we might not be able to solve this problem ourselves. As you know, a lot of finger pointing is going on. Pharmacists blame the doctors' sloppy handwriting and incomplete instructions for the problem. Doctors blame the pharmacy assistants, who do most of the computer entry of the prescriptions, claiming that they are incompetent. Pharmacy assistants blame the pharmacists for assuming too much about their knowledge of medical terminology, brand names, known drug interactions, and so on."

"It sounds like there's no hope," said Pacotilla.

"I wouldn't say that at all," replied Dover. "It's just that there might be no quick fix we can do by ourselves in the pharmacy. Let me explain what I'm thinking about doing and how I would propose attacking the problem using what I just learned in the statistical thinking course."

How do you think Dover should approach this problem, using what he has just learned? Assume that he really did pick up a solid understanding of the concepts and tools of statistical thinking in the course.

IV. Hydraulic Lift Co.

The Hydraulic Lift Company (HLC) manufactures freight elevators and automotive lifts used in garages and service stations. Figure 9.24 shows a simplified diagram of a hydraulic lift. The check valve is an important component in the system. Its purpose is to control the flow of hydraulic oil from the oil reservoir to the cylinder when the elevator is rising. As the elevator descends, the rate at which oil flows from the cylinder back to the reservoir is also controlled by the check valve.

One of the most important parts of the check valve is the piston, which moves within the valve body as the valve is opened or closed. The quality manager at HLC noticed that scrap rates on the piston had been high over the past three years. Two models (part numbers 117227 and 117228) of check valve pistons are being manufactured. Because of extremely critical tolerances, these parts are among the most difficult ones produced in the machine shop.

A study to determine the magnitude of the problem revealed that approximately $2,200 per month worth of parts had been scrapped over the past three years (see Figure 9.25). This amount translates to about 14 percent of total production of the parts, a scrap rate that is considered unacceptable. About half of the defective items were scrapped due to inability of the process to hold a 0.4985–0.4990-inch tolerance on the valve stem (see Figure 9.26). The machining operation used to shape the valve stem is performed on a grinding machine, which should have the capability of holding a tolerance within 0.001–0.002 inch under standard operating conditions. Manufacturing engineers and the quality manager decided to do a process capability study on one part (no. 117227) to gather statistical data on the stem problem and make a recommendation for improvements.

For the first step, an operator ran 100 parts using the standard production methods. Results of

Figure 9.24 Simplified Diagram of a Hydraulic Lift

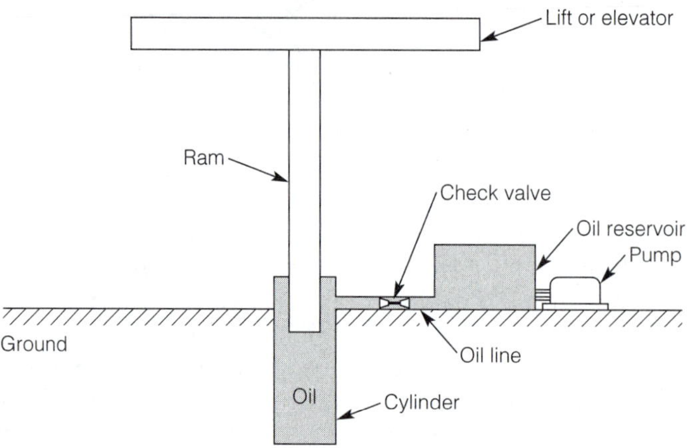

the study as shown in Figure 9.27(a) revealed that a machine problem existed. The data showed that a few parts were being produced outside the specifications. In addition, the strange shape of the histogram for dimensions within the specification limits prompted an investigation into the possibility of instability of the process. The study team observed that the operator was constantly adjusting the machine setting to try to hold to the specified tolerance.

Figure 9.25 Average Scrap Cost per Month

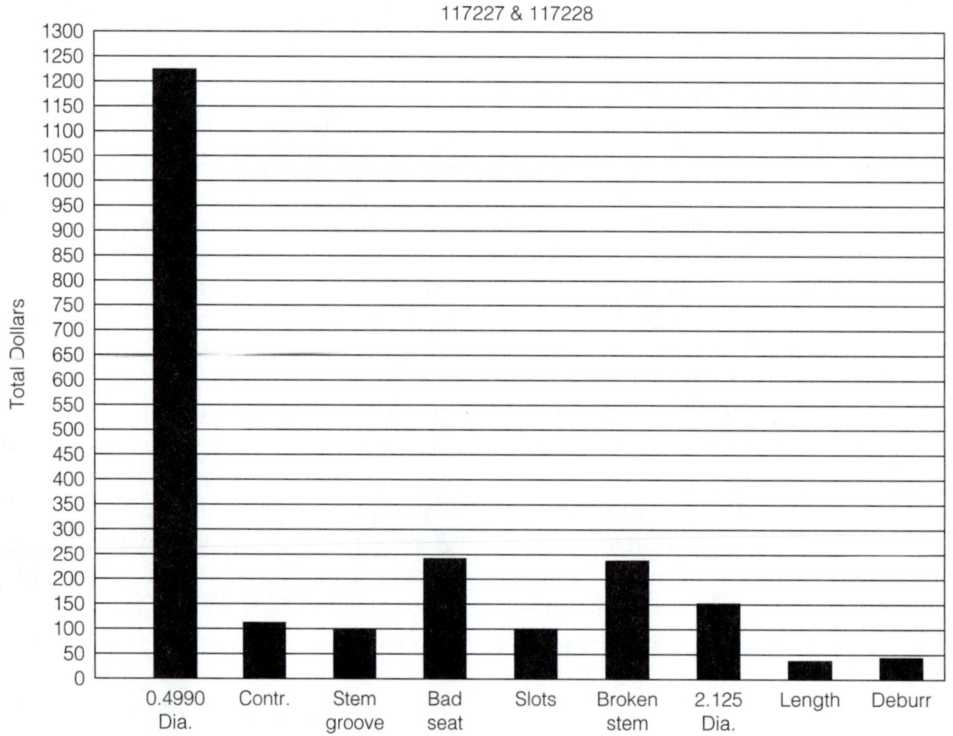

Figure 9.26 Part No. 117227 Check Valve Piston

6.312 ± 0.008
4 7/32
2.135 / 2.140
3/16
0.4990 / 0.4985 D
3/8
2.124 / 2.123 D
2 5/16 D
Valve stem

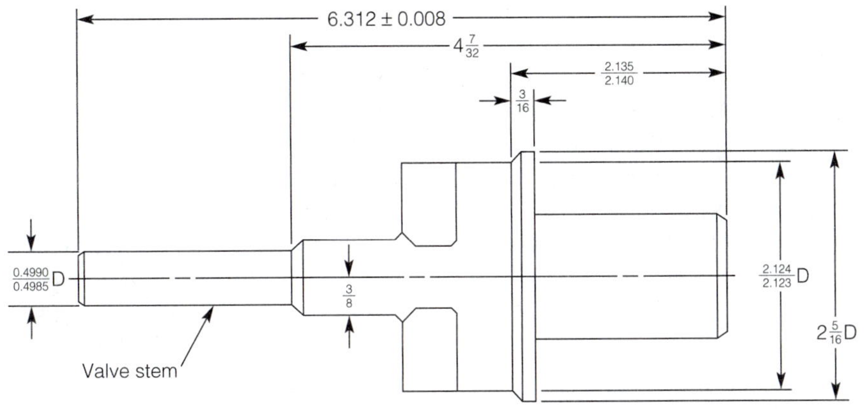

Figure 9.27 Process Capability for the Hydraulic Lift Company

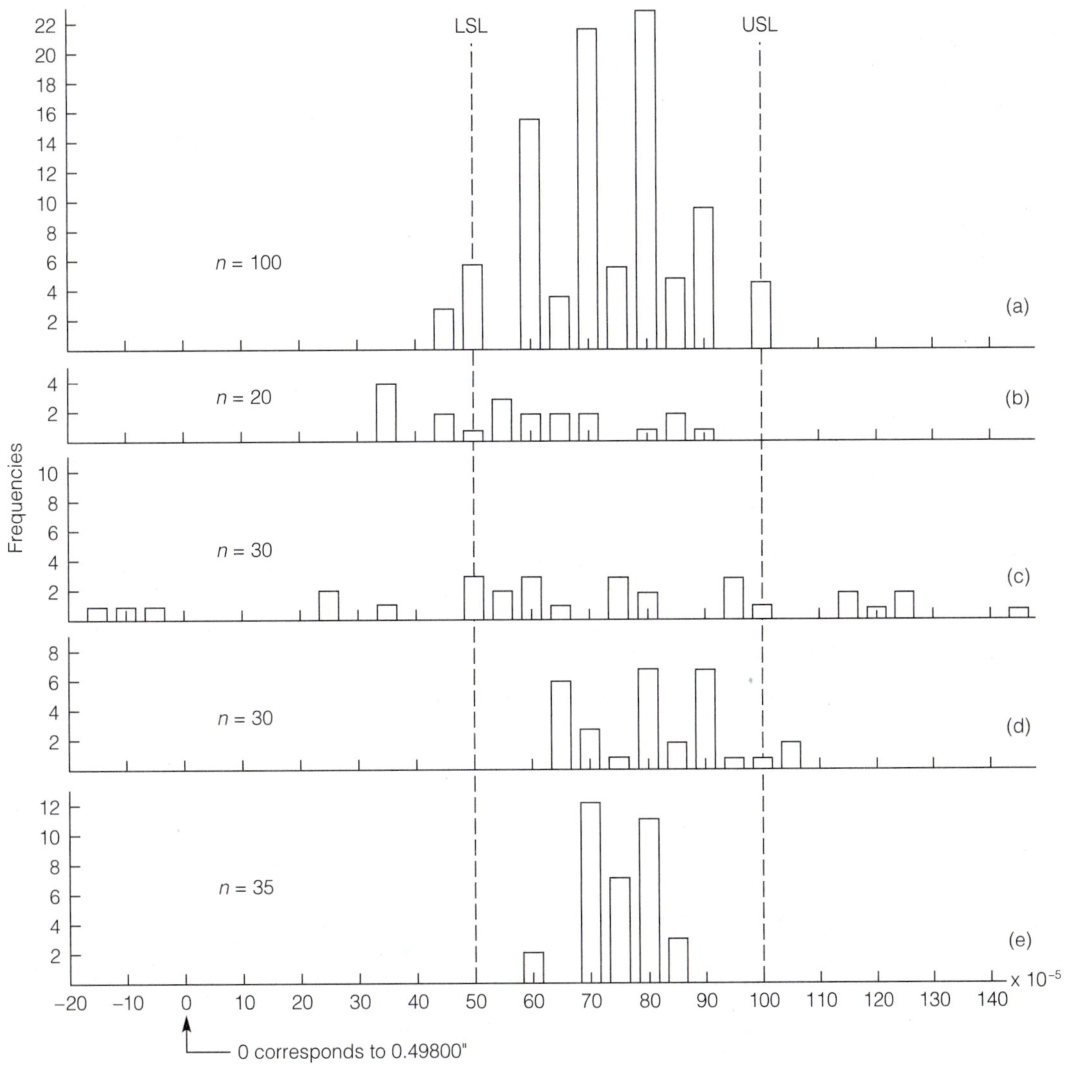

LSL
USL
Frequencies
n = 100
(a)
n = 20
(b)
n = 30
(c)
n = 30
(d)
n = 35
(e)
–20 –10 0 10 20 30 40 50 60 70 80 90 100 110 120 130 140
x 10⁻⁵
0 corresponds to 0.49800"

As a check on machine capability, the team asked the operator to run 20 parts without adjusting the machine, which results in scrapping six of 20 parts, a 30 percent scrap rate as shown in Figure 9.27(b). This test verified that the machine needed some major adjustments.

The machine manufacturer was contacted and a technician was dispatched to the plant. A run of 30 parts was made to show how the machine operated. Twelve of the 30 pieces were defective, with the stem dimension out of tolerance as indicated in Figure 9.27(c). The technician made the following adjustments:

- Installed new gaskets.
- Cleaned machine, adding oil and coolant.
- Loaded hand wheel bearing for more positive control.
- Reset retard pressure on grind wheel.
- Adjusted stone dresser mechanism.
- Reset dwell time (time the grindstone stays on the workpiece after reaching final diameter).

The results of these adjustments were significant. Another 30 parts were run, with only two falling outside the tolerance limits, shown in Figure 9.27(d). The team still did not consider the process to be fully satisfactory. The manufacturer's technician said that the grinder "ways" (channels on which the machine head travels) would have to be reground and that some parts in the machine would have to be replaced. This recommendation was made to management, who agreed to have the machine overhauled as required.

After the work was completed, a run of 35 parts was made. The results, shown in Figure 9.27(e), showed that all parts were well within tolerance limits. As a final step, operators and maintenance personnel were instructed on the proper use and care of the machine.

Assignment

1. Using the histograms in Figure 9.26, estimate the process capability indexes for each situation.
2. What lessons can be learned in terms of performing process capability studies and interpreting the results?

Chapter 9 Appendix

Important Probability Distributions

Certain discrete distributions describe many natural phenomena and have broad applications in statistical process control. Two of them are the binomial distribution and the Poisson distribution, discussed next. Later, some important continuous probability distributions are introduced.

Binomial Distribution

The **binomial distribution** describes the probability of obtaining exactly x "successes" in a sequence of n identical experiments, called trials. A *success* can be any one of two possible outcomes of each experiment. In some situations, it might represent a defective item, in others, a good item. The probability of success in each trial is a constant value p. The binomial probability function is given by the following formula:

$$f(x) = \binom{n}{x} p^x (1-p)^{n-x}$$

$$= \frac{n!}{x!(n-x)!} p^x (1-p)^{n-x} \qquad x = 0, 1, 2, \ldots, n$$

where p is the probability of a success, n is the number of items in the sample, and x is the number of items for which the probability is desired $(0, 1, 2, \ldots, n)$. The expected value, variance, and standard deviation of the binomial distribution are

$$E(p) = \mu = np$$
$$\sigma^2 = np(1-p)$$
$$\sigma = \sqrt{np(1-p)}$$

Binomial probabilities for selected values of p and n have been tabulated in Appendix D. Naturally, computer programs and Excel functions are also available to make binomial computations easier.

Example A1: Silicon Chip Defectives. To illustrate the use of the binomial distribution, suppose that a new process for producing silicon chips is averaging 40 percent defective items. If a quality supervisor takes a sample of five items to test for defectives, what is the probability of finding 0, 1, 2, 3, 4, or 5 defectives in the sample, and what is the expected number of defectives? For this problem, $n = 5$ and $p = 0.4$. Therefore, the binomial distribution for this experiment is

$$f(x) = \binom{5}{x}(0.4)^x(1-0.4)^{5-x}$$
$$= \frac{5!}{x!(5-x)!}(0.4)^x(0.6)^{5-x}$$

Table 9A.1 shows the detailed calculations required to compute individual probabilities. (You may wish to check the binomial probability table in Appendix D to verify these answers.)

Thus, the probability of finding exactly zero defectives in the sample of five is 0.0778, the probability of finding one defective is 0.2592, and so on. The expected number of defectives and the variance are given by

$$\mu = np = 5(0.4) = 2.0$$
$$\sigma^2 = np(1-p) = 2.0(0.6) = 1.2$$

Figure 9A.1 shows a graph of this probability distribution.

Table 9A.1 Binomial Probability Values

x	$\frac{5!}{x!(5-x)!}$	$(0.4)^x(0.6)^{5-x}$	$f(x)$
0	1	0.07776	0.0778
1	5	0.05184	0.2592
2	10	0.03456	0.3456
3	10	0.02304	0.2304
4	5	0.01536	0.0768
5	1	0.01024	0.0102
			1.0000

Figure 9A.1 Binomial Probability Distribution

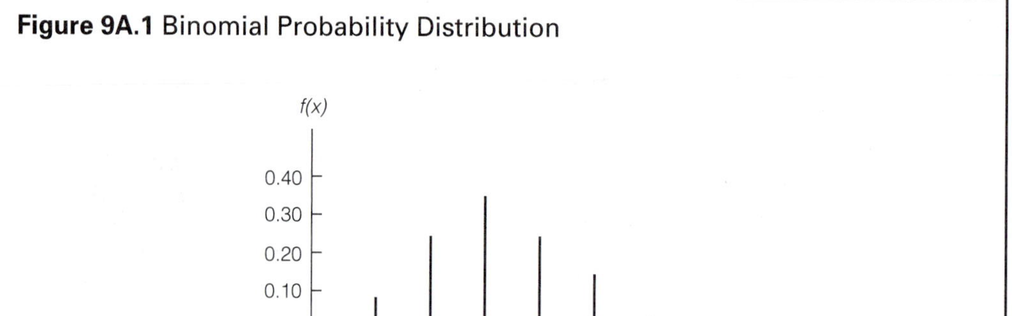

Poisson Distribution

The second discrete distribution often used in quality control is the **Poisson distribution**. The Poisson probability distribution is given by

$$f(x) = \frac{e^{-\mu}\mu^x}{x!}$$

where μ = expected value or average number of occurrences, $x = 0, 1, 2, 3, \ldots$, and $e \approx 2.71828$, a constant.

The Poisson distribution is closely related to the binomial distribution. It is derived by allowing the sample size (n) to become very large (approaching infinity) and the probability of success or failure (p) to become very small (approaching zero) while the expected value (np) remains constant. Thus, when n is large relative to p, the Poisson distribution can be used as an approximation to the binomial. A common rule of thumb is if $p \leq 0.05$ and $n \geq 20$, the Poisson will be a good approximation with $\mu = np$. It is also used to calculate the number of occurrences of an event over a specified interval of time or space, such as the number of scratches per square inch on a polished surface.

Example A2: Using the Poisson Distribution. Example 1 can be extended to show how the Poisson distribution can be used in quality control problems. Suppose that improvements are made in the production process, which bring the average level of defects down to 5 percent from the previous level of 40 percent. The quality supervisor now decides to use a sample size of 30 parts to detect changes in the quality level of the process with a much longer time period between samples. What is the probability of finding five or fewer defective items in any randomly selected sample of 30 parts?

Because the task requires finding discrete probabilities of 0, 1, 2, 3, 4, or 5 defectives, calculate each probability and add the results:

$$P\,(x \leq 5) = P(x = 0) + P(x = 1) + P(x = 2) + P(x = 3) + P(x = 4) + P(x = 5)$$

As an approximation to the binomial, the relationship to $\mu = np = 30(0.05) = 1.5$ can be used. This relationship then becomes the parameter μ for the Poisson distribution. The computations are given in Table 9A.2.

Thus, if the average value is 5 percent defectives, five or fewer defectives are likely to occur in a sample of 30 parts. In fact, this case carries a 0.99552 probability.

The probability of finding *more* than five defectives is small. It would be only

$$1 - P\,(x \leq 5) = 1 - 0.99552 = 0.00448$$

Table 9A.2 Poisson Probability Values

x	$e^{-1.5}$	$\frac{(1.5)^x}{x!}$	$f(x) = \frac{e^{-1.5}(1.5)^x}{x!}$
0	0.22313	1.00000	0.22313
1	0.22313	1.50000	0.33467
2	0.22313	1.12500	0.25102
3	0.22313	0.56250	0.12551
4	0.22313	0.21094	0.04707
5	0.22313	0.06328	0.01412
			0.99552

Note that the previously stated conditions under which the Poisson distribution is a good approximation of the binomial have been met; that is, $n \geq 20$ and $p \leq 0.05$. Table 9A.3 compares these probability values to the true values using the binomial distribution. The results show that the Poisson distribution does provide a good approximation to the binomial probabilities when the specified conditions are met. If the conditions for the Poisson approximation cannot be met, a normal approximation to the binomial, discussed in the next section, may be of use.

Two of the most frequently used continuous probability distributions are the normal distribution and the exponential distribution. They form the basis for many of the statistical analyses performed in quality assurance today.

Normal Distribution

The probability density function of the **normal distribution** is represented graphically by the familiar bell-shaped curve. However, not every symmetric, unimodal curve is a normal distribution, nor can all data from a sample or population be assumed to fit a normal distribution. However, data are often assumed to be normally distributed to simplify certain calculations. In most cases, this assumption makes little difference in the results but is important from a theoretical perspective.

The probability density function for the normal distribution is as follows:

$$f(x) = \frac{1}{\sqrt{2\pi\sigma^2}}\, e^{-(x-\mu)^2/2\sigma^2} \qquad -\infty < x < \infty$$

Table 9A.3 Binomial versus Poisson Probability Values

x	Binomial Probability	Poisson Probability
0	0.21464	0.22313
1	0.33890	0.33467
2	0.25864	0.25102
3	0.12705	0.12551
4	0.04514	0.04707
5	0.01235	0.01412
	0.99672	0.99552

where

μ = the mean of the random variable x

σ^2 = the variance of x

e = 2.71828 . . .

π = 3.14159 . . .

If a normal random variable has a mean $\mu = 0$ and a standard deviation $\sigma = 1$, it is called a **standard normal distribution**. The letter z is usually used to represent this particular random variable. By using the constants 0 and 1 for the mean and standard deviation, respectively, the probability density function for the normal distribution can be simplified as

$$f(z) = \frac{1}{\sqrt{2\pi}} e^{-z^2/2}$$

This standard normal distribution function is shown in Figure 9A.2. Because $\sigma = 1$, the scale on the z axis is given in units of standard deviations. Special tables of areas under the normal curve have been developed as an aid in computing probabilities. Such a table is given in Appendix A.

Fortunately, *any* normal distribution involving a random variable x with a known (or estimated) mean and standard deviation is easily transformed into a standard normal distribution using the following formula:

$$z = \frac{x - \mu}{\sigma}$$

This formula takes the value of the variable of interest (x), subtracts the mean value (μ), and divides by the standard deviation (σ). This calculation yields a random variable z, which has a standard normal distribution. Probabilities for this variable can then be found in the table in Appendix A.

The area under the curve that corresponds to one standard deviation from the mean is 0.3413; therefore, the probability that the value of a normal random variable falls within one standard deviation ($\pm 1\sigma$) from the mean is 0.6826. The corresponding x-values are often called *1-sigma limits* in statistical quality control terminology. Two standard deviations on one side of the mean correspond to 0.4772 area under the curve, so the probability that a normal random variable falls within a *2-sigma limit* is twice that figure, or 0.9544. Three standard deviations encompass 0.4986 area under the curve on either side of the mean, or a total area of 0.9972. Hence, the *3-sigma limit* encompasses nearly all of the normal distribution. These concepts form the basis for control charts discussed in Chapter 12.

Figure 9A.2 Standard Normal Distribution

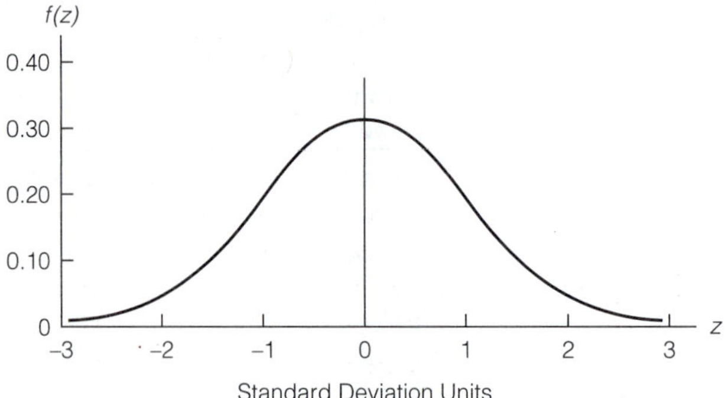

Example A3: Normal Probability Calculations. Randomly selected temperatures from a drying oven in an enamel wire manufacturing process exhibit a normal distribution with $\mu = 49$ and $\sigma = 7$. Given this information, calculate three probabilities [shown in Figures 9A.3(a), (b), and (c), respectively]: (1) that a sample value x will fall between 42 and 49, (2) that it will be less than 42, and (3) that it will fall between 50 and 57.

Referring to Figure 9A.3(a), to compute the probability that the random variable x will fall between 42 and 49, convert these values to standard normal values (z values):

$$z_1 = \frac{x - \mu}{\sigma} = \frac{42 - 49}{7} = -1.0 \text{ and } z_2 = \frac{49 - 49}{7} = 0$$

Because this case is bounded on the right by the mean of the distribution, simply read the normal table for the z_1 value and obtain the probability without further calculations. The table indicates that the area under the curve between –1.0 and 0 is 0.3413. This number means 34.13 percent of the values taken from this population would be expected to fall in the specified interval, and that a 34.13 percent probability of obtaining a value within that interval exists, given a random observation of the oven temperature.

To compute the probability that x is less than 42 for the second case, find the area under the normal curve from minus infinity to:

$$z_2 = \frac{42 - 49}{7} = -1.0$$

This value is 0.5 minus the area from –1.0 to 0, which is 0.3413 as found in Appendix A. Thus, the probability of obtaining a temperature reading of less than 42 degrees C is 0.5 – 0.3413 = 0.1587. This result is shown in Figure 9A.3(b).

Finally, for the third case, transform $x = 50$ and $x = 57$ to standard normal values and obtain:

$$z_1 = \frac{x - \mu}{\sigma} = \frac{50 - 49}{7} = 0.14 \text{ and } z_2 = \frac{57 - 49}{7} = 1.14$$

Figure 9A.3(a) Calculation of Probabilities from the Standard Normal Distribution

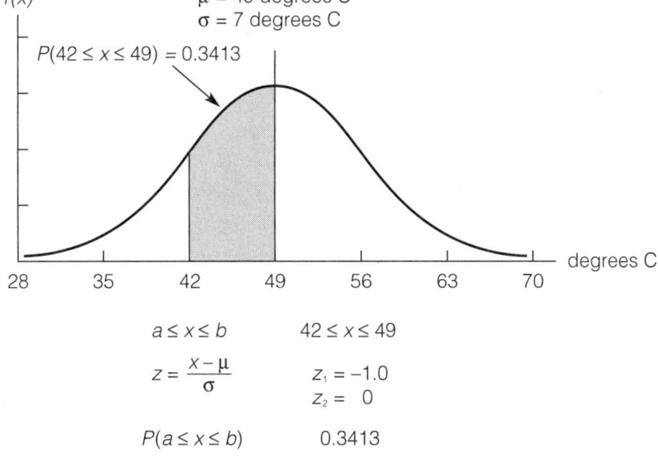

Figure 9A.3(b) Calculation of Probabilities from the Standard Normal Distribution

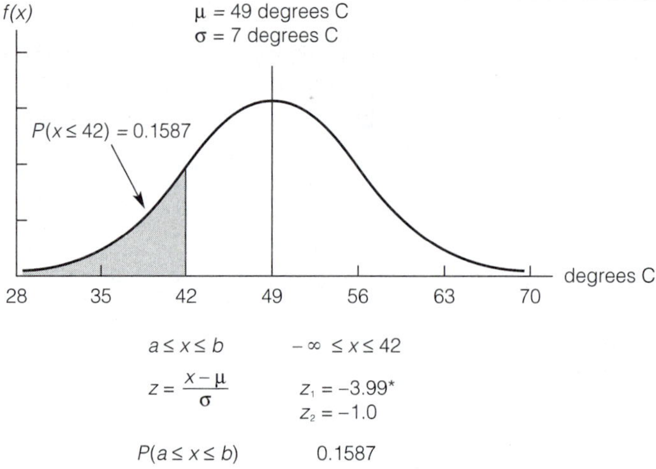

$a \le x \le b$	$-\infty \le x \le 42$
$z = \frac{x-\mu}{\sigma}$	$z_1 = -3.99$* $z_2 = -1.0$
$P(a \le x \le b)$	0.1587

*The left (lower most) limit of the distribution using the standard normal table in Appendix A is a z value of –3.99. Actually, the lower limit of the distribution extends to $-\infty$.

The area from 0 to $z_2 = 1.14$ can be read from the table as 0.3729. The area from 0 to $z_1 = 0.14$ is 0.0557. Then subtract the smaller area from the larger to obtain 0.3729 – 0.0557 = 0.3172, the area of interest. Thus, a probability of 0.3172 exists for observing an oven temperature between 50 and 57 degrees C. These calculations are summarized in Figure 9A.3(c).

Figure 9A.3(c) Calculation of Probabilities from the Standard Normal Distribution

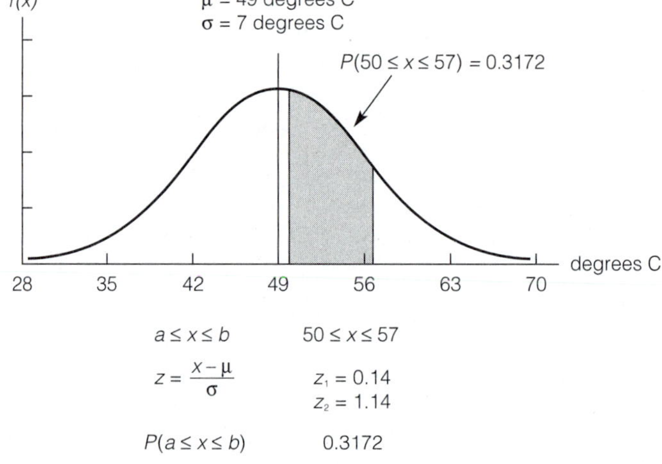

$a \le x \le b$	$50 \le x \le 57$
$z = \frac{x-\mu}{\sigma}$	$z_1 = 0.14$ $z_2 = 1.14$
$P(a \le x \le b)$	0.3172

Normal Approximation to the Binomial Although the binomial distribution is extremely useful, it has a serious limitation when dealing with either small probabilities or large sample sizes—it is tedious to calculate. The discussion of the Poisson approximation to the binomial showed that when the probability of success or failure becomes small, the Poisson distribution permits calculation of similar probability values more easily than the binomial. Also, as the sample size gets large (approaches infinity), the binomial distribution approaches the normal distribution as a limit. Hence, for large sample sizes, good approximations of probabilities that would have been calculated using the binomial distribution can be obtained by using the normal distribution. The normal approximation holds well when $np \geq 5$ and $n(1-p) \geq 5$.

Example A4: Normal Approximation. To illustrate, two changes in assumptions are made in the silicon chip example. Suppose, instead of using a small sample size, the sample size is 50. The probability of finding a defective item is still 0.40. To determine the probability of finding between 15 and 20 defective items in the sample, use the binomial distribution to calculate the probabilities.

$$f(x) = \binom{50}{x}(0.4)^x(1-0.4)^{50-x}$$

$$= \frac{50!}{x!(50-x)!}(0.4)^x(0.6)^{50-x}$$

This equation would have to be evaluated for $x = 15, 16, 17, 18$ 19 and 20, since

$$P(15 \leq x \leq 20) = P(x=15) + P(x=16) + P(x=17) + P(x=18) + P(x=19) + P(x=20)$$

These calculations would be difficult and time-consuming, even with a good electronic calculator!

By using the normal approximation, a reasonably accurate estimate of the probability is obtained. The calculations are as follows:

$$\mu = np = 50(0.40) = 20$$

$$\sigma_p^2 = np(1-p) = 20(0.60) = 12$$

$$\sigma_p = \sqrt{12} = 3.46$$

$$z_1 = \frac{x-\mu}{\sigma_p} = \frac{15-20}{3.46} = -1.45 \quad z_2 = \frac{20-20}{3.46} = 0$$

Using the table in Appendix A, the value for $P(-1.45 \leq z \leq 0) = 0.4265$. Thus, the probability of obtaining between 15 and 20 defectives in a sample of 50 parts is 0.4265. This result is shown in Figure 9A.4.

Figure 9A.4 Normal Approximation to the Binomial

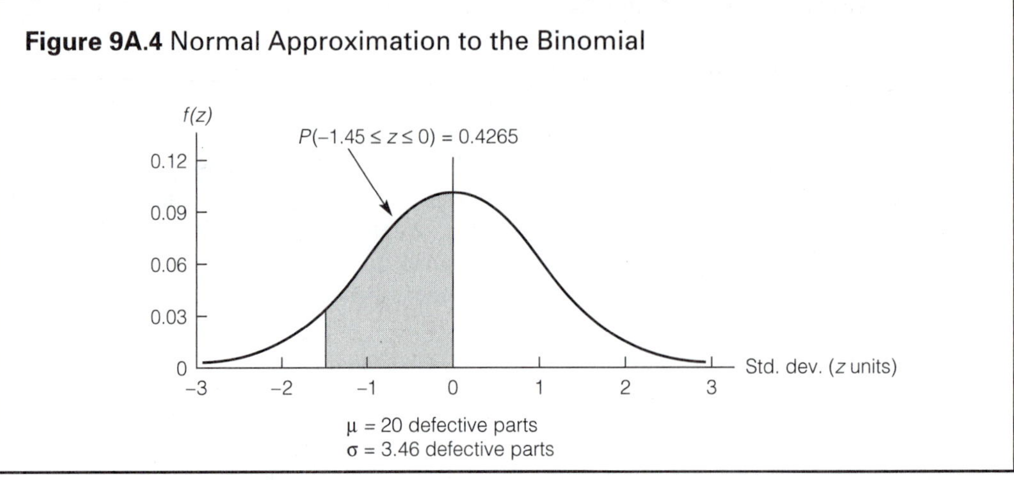

Exponential Distribution

Another continuous distribution commonly used in quality assurance is the **exponential distribution**. The exponential distribution is used extensively in reliability estimation, discussed in Chapter 13. The probability density function for the exponential distribution is much simpler than the one for the normal distribution. Therefore, direct evaluation is easier, although tabulated values for the exponential distribution are also readily available (see Appendix F). The formula for the exponential probability density function is

$$f(x) = \frac{1}{\mu} e^{-x/\mu}, \quad x \geq 0$$

where

μ = mean value for the distribution

x = time or distance over which the variable extends

e = 2.71828 . . .

The cumulative distribution function is

$$F(x) = 1 - e^{-x/\mu}$$

Example A5: Distribution of Light Bulb Failure Times. To illustrate an application of the exponential distribution, suppose that the maintenance manager of an office building is trying to schedule the maintenance crew that changes floodlights used to illuminate the exterior of the building. The manager is told by the light bulb supplier that the mean time between failure for the bulbs being used is 1,000 hours. What is the probability that the actual time between any two successive failures will be 750 hours or less? For this example, $\mu = 1000$ and $x = 750$. Thus,

$$F(x) = 1 - e^{-x/\mu} = 1 - e^{-0.75} = 1 - 0.4724 = 0.5276$$

Therefore, the probability is 0.5276 that the time between two successive failures will be 750 hours or less. The problem is shown graphically in Figure 9A.6.

Figure 9A.5 summarizes the four important distributions reviewed in this appendix.

Figure 9A.5 Summary of Common Probability Distributions Used in Quality Assurance

Distribution	Form	Probability Function	Comments on Application
Normal	μ	$y = \frac{1}{\sigma\sqrt{2\pi}} e^{-\frac{(x-\mu)^2}{2\sigma^2}}$ μ = Mean σ = Standard deviation	Applicable when a concentration of observations falls about the average and when observations are equally likely to occur above and below the average. Variation in observations is usually the result of many small causes.
Exponential	μ	$y = \frac{1}{\mu} e^{-\frac{x}{\mu}}$	Applicable when more observations are likely to occur below the average than above.
Poisson	$p = 0.1$, $p = 0.3$, $p = 0.5$, x	$y = \frac{e^{-\mu}\mu^x}{x!}$ n = Number of trials p = Probability of occurrence x = Number of occurrences $\mu = np$	Same as binomial but particularly applicable when many opportunities for occurrence of an event are possible but have a low probability (less than 0.10) on each trial.
Binomial	$p = 0.1$, $p = 0.3$, $p = 0.5$, x	$y = \frac{n!}{x!(n-x)!} p^x q^{n-x}$ n = Number of trials x = Probability of occurrence p = Number of occurrences $q = 1 - p$	Applicable in defining the probability of x occurrences in n trials of an event that has a constant probability of occurrence on each independent trial.

Source: Adapted from J. M. Juran and F. M. Gryna, Jr., Instructor's Manual to accompany *Quality Planning and Analysis* (New York: McGraw-Hill, 1980), 125. © 1980 by McGraw-Hill, Inc. Used with permission.

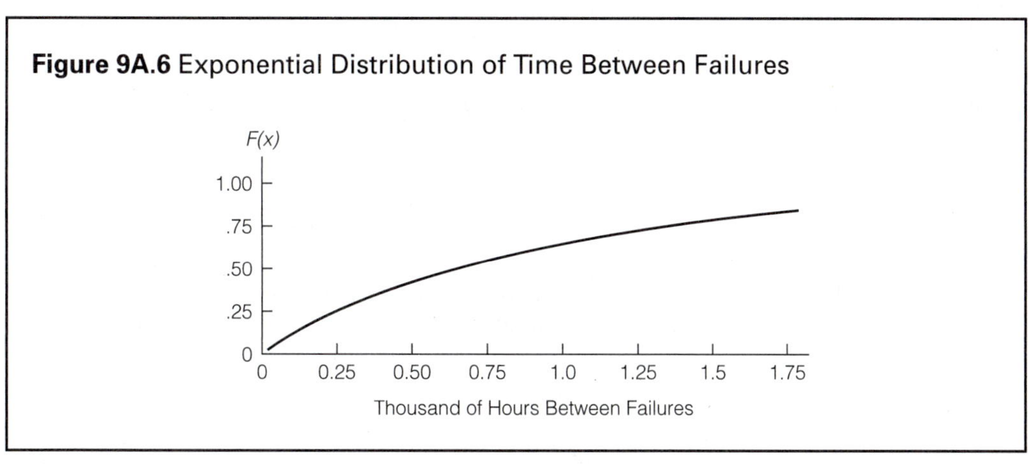

Figure 9A.6 Exponential Distribution of Time Between Failures

NOTES

1. Adapted from Brian L. Joiner, *Fourth Generation Management* (New York: McGraw-Hill, 1994), 129.

2. J. M. Juran and Frank M. Gryna, Jr., *Quality Planning and Analysis*, 2d ed. (New York: McGraw-Hill, 1980), 35.

3. Adapted from Galen Britz, Don Emerling, Lynne Hare, Roger Hoerl, and Janice Shade, "How to Teach Others to Apply Statistical Thinking," *Quality Progress*, June 1997, 67–79. © 1997. American Society for Quality. Reprinted with permission.

4. Ronald D. Snee, "Getting Better Business Results: Using Statistical Thinking and Methods to Shape the Bottom Line," *Quality Progress*, June 1998, 102–106.

5. Britz et al., see note 3.

6. Based on descriptions given in W. Edwards Deming, *The New Economics For Industry, Government, Education* (Cambridge, MA: MIT Center For Advanced Engineering Study, 1993).

7. Frank H. Squires, "The Triumph of Statistics," *Quality*, February 1982, 75.

8. Thomas Pyzdek, "Non-Normal Distributions in the Real World," *Quality Digest*, December 1999, 36–41.

9. H. P. Hill, J. L. Roth, and H. Arkin, *Sampling in Auditing: A Simplified Guide and Statistical Tables* (New York: Ronald Press, 1962). Reprinted by permission of John Wiley & Sons, Inc.

10. Johannes Ledolter and Claude W. Burrill, *Statistical Quality Control* (New York: John Wiley & Sons, 1999).

11. N. Raghu Kackar, "Off-Line Quality Control, Parameter Design, and the Taguchi Method," *Journal of Quality Technology* 17, no. 4 (October 1985), 176–188.

12. Bruce D. Nordwall, "ITT Uses Process Control Methods to Increase Plant Productivity," *Aviation Week & Space Technology*, May 11, 1987, 69–74.

13. Eric Wasiloff and Curtis Hargitt, "Using DOE to Determine AA Battery Life," *Quality Progress*, March 1999, 67–71. © 1999. American Society for Quality. Reprinted with permission.

14. Joseph J. Pignatiello, Jr., and John S. Ramberg, "The Top 10 Triumphs and Tragedies of Genichi Taguchi," presented at the 35th ASQC/ASA Fall Technical Conference, Lexington, KY, 1991.

15. Paul F. McCoy, "Using Performance Indexes to Monitor Production Processes," *Quality Progress* 24, no. 2 (February 1991), 49–55; see also Fred A. Spring, "The Cpm Index," *Quality Progress* 24, no. 2 (February 1991), 57–61.

16. Helmut Schneider, James Pruett, and Cliff Lagrange, "Uses of Process Capability Indices in the Supplier Certification Process," *Quality Engineering* 8, no. 2 (1995–1996), 225–235.

17. Adapted from Schneider et al., see note 16.

18. Mark L. Crossley, "Size Matters. How Good Is Your Cpk, Really?" *Quality Digest*, May 2000, 71–72.

19. Kalyan Kumar Chowdhury, E. V. Gigo, and R. Raghavan, "Quality Improvement Through Design of Experiments: A Case Study," *Quality Engineering* 12, no. 3 (2000), 407–416. Reprinted from *Quality Engineers*, courtesy of Marcel Dekker, Inc.

20. Adapted from Michael J. Mazu, "Using Statistical Thinking to Meet the Challenge," ASQ's 54th Annual Quality Congress Proceedings, 443–449. Reprinted with permission by the American Society for Quality, Inc. (ASQ), 611 East Wisconsin Ave., Milwaukee, WI 53201.

21. Based on an anecdote in W. Edwards Deming, *Out of the Crisis* (Cambridge, MA: MIT Center for Advanced Engineering Study, 1986).

22. Adapted from Britz et al. See note 3.

23. Adapted from Britz et al. See note 3.

BIBLIOGRAPHY

Boser, Robert B., and Cheryl L. Christ. "Whys, Whens, and Hows of Conducting a Process Capability Study." Presentation at the ASQC/ASA 35th Annual Fall Technical Conference, Lexington, Kentucky, 1991.

Chatfield, Christopher. *Statistics for*

Technology: A Course in Applied Statistics. New York: Halstead Press, division of John Wiley & Sons, 1978.

Deming, W. Edwards. *The New Economics for Industry, Government, Education.* Cambridge, MA: MIT Center for Advanced Engineering Study, 1993.

———. *Out of the Crisis.* Cambridge, MA: MIT Center for Advanced Engineering Study, 1986.

Duncan, Acheson J. *Quality Control and Industrial Statistics,* 5th ed. Homewood, IL: Richard D. Irwin, 1986.

Griffith, Gary. *Quality Technician's Handbook.* New York: John Wiley, 1986.

Gunter, Bert. "Process Capability Studies Part I: What Is a Process Capability Study?" *Quality Progress* 24, no. 2 (February 1991), 97–99.

Robbins, C. L., and W. A. Robbins. "What Nurse Managers Should Know about Sampling Techniques." *Nursing Management* 20, no. 6 (June 1989), 46–48.

Scherkenbach, William W. *Deming's Road to Continual Improvement.* Knoxville, TN: SPC Press, 1991.

Scholtes, Peter R. "Communities as Systems," *ASQC 50th Annual Quality Congress Proceedings* (1996), 258–65.

Tedaldi, Michael, Fred Seaglione, and Vincent Russotti. *A Beginner's Guide to Quality in Manufacturing.* Milwaukee, WI: ASQC Quality Press, 1992.

Chapter 10

Quality Improvement

Outline

A "Black Belt" means one thing to karate students; at General Electric, Black Belts (along with Green Belts and Master Black Belts), all highly trained in quality improvement principles and techniques, roam manufacturing plants to improve quality as a part of a major initiative introduced by CEO Jack Welch in 1996. This "Six-Sigma" initiative, which was benchmarked from Motorola, includes many TQ principles such as a better focus on customers, data-driven decisions, improved design and manufacturing capabilities, and individual rewards for process improvements. The effort aims to reduce defect levels to only a few parts per million for strategic products and processes.

Accomplishing such a daunting task requires effective implementation of statistical principles and various tools for diagnosing quality problems and facilitating improvement. Although not every company has the resources to do what General Electric has attempted, every organization should use basic statistical and problem-solving tools to help them make effective decisions and to continuously improve their processes. In this chapter we describe common management models for implementing quality improvement and present useful tools for supporting Six-Sigma efforts and improving the quality of any process.

THE ECONOMIC CASE FOR IMPROVEMENT

One of the biggest misconceptions that many managers have is that an inherent trade-off must be made between the cost of providing high quality and the costs resulting from poor quality, and that some level of nonconformance is not only acceptable, but economically "optimum," suggesting that continuous improvement is unjustified. Because this viewpoint can be dangerously misleading, and is still used in some literature, a brief discussion of it follows here.

Each activity devoted to meeting quality requirements incurs some cost. For example, receiving might inspect incoming materials; tool engineering maintains tools and gauges in proper condition; and workers measure the quality work in process. These costs are generally referred to as the *costs of quality assurance*. On the other hand, failure to conform to specifications will result in losses due to poor quality such as scrap, rework, and warranty adjustments. These costs are called *costs due to nonconformance*. Figure 10.1, the traditional economic model, illustrates the classic relationship between the costs of quality assurance and the costs due to nonconformance. As the quality of conformance (measured by the percentage of defective products manufactured) improves as a result of more effective quality assurance, the quality assurance costs increase and the costs due to nonconformance decrease. From a strict economic viewpoint, one seeks the optimal level of conformance that minimizes the total costs to the organization. This level shows the point that minimizes the total cost curve in Figure 10.1. This model has been used to justify operating at a conformance level less than 100 percent.

It is clear that if one is operating to the left of the optimum point, a significant opportunity to improve quality through increased control is evident. For example, if nonconformance costs greatly exceed quality assurance costs (to the left of the optimum), then the most sensible activity is to identify specific improvement projects that improve the quality of conformance and reduce the costs of poor quality. To the

Figure 10.1 Classic Economic Model of Quality of Conformance

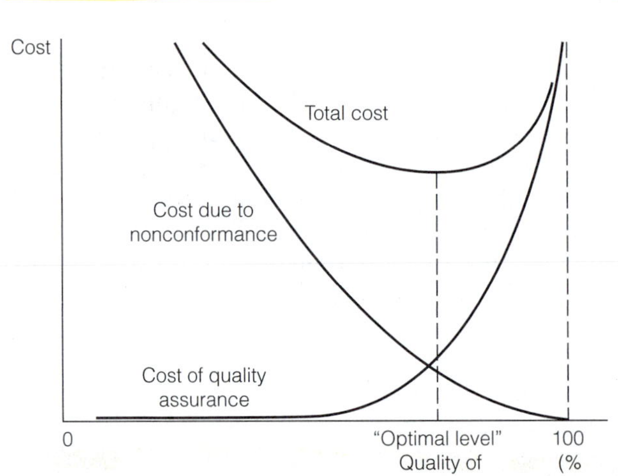

right, however, the cost of quality assurance seemingly outweighs the savings generated. However, in such situations, it may be possible to reduce the costs of quality assurance *without* sacrificing the level of conformance. This reduction in costs might be achieved by improving technology, reducing inspection through more appropriate control mechanisms, or relaxing unnecessarily tight quality standards relative to fitness-for-use criteria. The net effect of these activities is a continued shift of the "optimum" point to the right.

Hsiang and Lee have looked at this model more formally, and argued that it ignores several important realities.[1] First, the model assumes that sales of the product are constant. Evidence shows, however, that quality improvement or degradation can significantly alter the demand for the product. Dissatisfied customers are less likely to be repeat purchasers than are satisfied customers. Word-of-mouth reputation can be significant in maintaining market share. Under the assumption that the firm seeks to maximize revenue, Hsiang and Lee show mathematically that the optimal level of conformance should be higher than that shown in Figure 10.1 when the revenue effect is considered. Second, as prevention of poor quality becomes a focus, the inherent failure rates of materials and products are lowered through new technologies, and improvements in automation reduce human error during production and appraisal. Thus, companies now have the ability to achieve perfection in quality at a finite cost; the cost of assuring quality does not extend to infinity as 100 percent conformance is reached. The total quality cost curve reaches its minimum at 100 percent conformance as shown in Figure 10.2. Although this new model does not necessarily apply in every situation, such as when automation cannot be justified or used, these arguments suggest that continuous improvement efforts make good economic sense.

MANAGEMENT MODELS FOR QUALITY IMPROVEMENT

Successful quality improvement depends on the ability to identify and solve problems. According to Kepner and Tregoe, a **problem** is a deviation between what should be happening and what actually is happening that is important enough to make someone think the deviation ought to be corrected.[2] **Problem solving** is the activity associated with changing the state of what is actually happening to what should be happening.

Figure 10.2 Modern Economic Model of Quality of Conformance

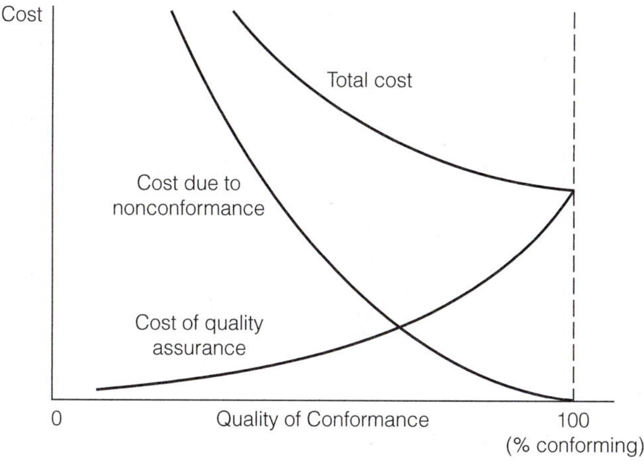

Classifying Quality Problems

Problems can usually be categorized in one of three ways: *structured, semistructured,* or *ill-structured*. This classification is determined by the amount of information available about the problem. For structured problems, complete information about the problem—what is happening, what should be happening, and how to get there—is available. Ill-structured problems, on the other hand, are characterized by a high degree of fuzziness or vagueness. Semistructured problems fall somewhere in between. The usefulness of these classifications lies in their ability to prescribe a problem-solving approach. Structured problems generally can be solved using routine, programmed decision-making techniques. Ill-structured and semistructured problems require more creative solutions and hence, a systematic process to find these solutions.

An example of a structured problem situation would be the case in which the diameter of a machined hole is smaller than the desired specification. The operator might be instructed to check the cutting tool for wear and replace it when necessary. Little problem-solving ability would be necessary to remedy this problem.

An example of a semistructured problem might be the case of determining what quality control actions to take when a new production setup on the shop floor has been initiated. A solution to this problem might be to employ the following rules: Run the first five parts after the setup and compute the average dimension. If it is within one standard deviation of the target based on historical data, continue production. If it is between one and two standard deviations of the target, take another sample. If it is beyond two standard deviations, stop and adjust the setup. Such problems can generally be solved using routine decision aids, although more creative effort may be needed to develop an acceptable solution.

Finally, an example of an ill-structured problem would be the situation in which 35 percent of final assemblies do not meet performance requirements. Here, considerably more ambiguity about the problem and how to go about solving it is involved than in either of the two previous cases. Simple, programmed decision rules cannot be developed. Such problems must be addressed individually using a systematic problem-solving methodology.

The following example shows how Hewlett-Packard dealt with a problem involving one of its suppliers.

Example 1: Solving a Supplier Reject Problem.[3] A supplier to Hewlett-Packard's Computer Division, in Cupertino, California, provided a unique assembly at a reasonable price but could not deliver the part without a high number of rejects. Management's first reaction was to consider a new supplier. However, since the original supplier had been difficult to find, management made the decision to help the supplier do a better job.

A project team, headed by the procurement engineer and aided by the buyer and incoming inspection supervisor, was formed. Its goals were to eliminate incoming inspection and establish direct shipment of the supplier's assemblies into stock. The project team developed a three-stage plan to achieve these goals: investigation of why rejects occur, elimination of causes to gain quality confidence, and implementation of a plan to eliminate incoming inspection. Investigation was initiated by analyzing the vendor's production and quality assurance capabilities. HP had to make sure the supplier had correct information on the product specifications required. It was found that the supplier's interpretation of the specification did not agree with

HP's expectations for the part specified. The specification was therefore modified to better meet the objectives of both the supplier and HP.

Next, HP needed to ensure that the supplier's production process was capable of meeting HP's requirements. The supplier outlined the production process and noted several improvements it could make to improve quality. HP and its supplier established the same quality-measuring methods, materials, and equipment at the supplier's facility that were used at the HP plant. HP also videotaped the supplier's process for better communication and as a reference for future audits, and performed on-site inspections on production runs prior to shipment.

To gain confidence, HP closely monitored its own data and supplier data to confirm that the quality methods, materials, and equipment established earlier were being used. The supplier was encouraged to make corrections to its production processes. Communications improved and control charts verified that the processes were producing at an acceptable quality level.

Two of the major problems that were uncovered involved a disparity in specifications and measurement. The brightness specification for computer monitors was 47 foot lamberts (F.L.). For customers other than HP, the supplier's average brightness level was 38.25 F.L., with a minimum of 35 F.L. The supplier apparently misread or misunderstood HP's specification of 47. Also, a check revealed that measuring equipment and the adjustment instructions in the supplier's assembly stations were incompatible. The problems were corrected.

Eventually, HP stopped routine incoming inspection. HP monitored product quality by using control charts and by making yearly visits to the supplier's plant. When the charts indicated a quality problem, HP and the supplier made special inspections and took corrective measures. The benefits of this planning and action included a reduction in supplier appraisal costs and average lead times and the elimination of 100 percent inspection and rework returns.

The problem faced by Hewlett-Packard probably falls into the ill-structured category due to its complexity and lack of clear information, which is characteristic of many important quality problems. This case reveals some important aspects of problem solving. First, the number-of-rejects problem was not specific enough to be solved; it was a symptom of other problems, but not the problem in itself. This type of situation is often called a "mess." HP and the supplier first had to identify specific problems, such as the misinterpretation of specifications, in order to correct the situation. Second, a project team was formed to address the problem. Third, the "gaining confidence" phase of the project relied on a significant amount of data collection and analysis, which enabled the problem-solving team to generate ideas for possible solutions. Fourth, both companies monitored and controlled the implementation of solutions.

Another way of classifying quality problems is by the *type* of problem.[4] Research using more than 1,000 published cases describing quality problem-solving activities suggests that virtually every instance of quality problem-solving falls into one of five categories:

1. *Conformance problems* are defined by unsatisfactory performance by a well-specified system. Users are not happy with the system outputs, such as quality or customer service levels. The system has worked before, but for some reason it is not performing acceptably. Problem solving is a matter of finding the causes of deviations and restoring the system to its intended mode of

functioning, which requires good diagnostic efforts to determine the causes of poor conformance.

2. *Unstructured performance problems* result from unsatisfactory performance by a poorly specified system. That is, the task is nonstandardized and not fully specified by procedures and requirements. An example would be poor sales. No one right way of selling a product means the problem cannot be cured by enforcing standards that do not exist. As we saw earlier, unstructured problems require more creative approaches to solving them.
3. *Efficiency problems* result from unsatisfactory performance from the standpoint of stakeholders other than customers. Typical examples are cost and productivity issues. Even though the quality of the outputs may be acceptable, the system's performance does not achieve internal organizational goals. Identification of solutions often involves tapping the knowledge and creativity of the workforce to streamline processes.
4. *Product design problems* involve designing new products that satisfy user needs. These issues were discussed thoroughly in Chapter 7. Quality function deployment (QFD) is a useful tool to tie customer needs into the design process.
5. *Process design problems* involve designing new processes or substantially revising existing processes. The challenge here is determining process requirements, generating new process alternatives, and linking these processes to customer needs. Techniques discussed in Chapter 7, such as benchmarking and reengineering, are useful tools for process design.

Understanding different problem types helps direct attention to past experiences and select appropriate problem-solving techniques.

Messy problems require a systematic process to develop and implement solutions. Any problem-solving process has four major components:[5]

1. *Redefining and analyzing the problem:* collect and organize information, analyze the data and underlying assumptions, and reexamine the problem for new perspectives, with the goal of achieving a workable problem definition.
2. *Generating ideas:* "brainstorm" to develop potential solutions.
3. *Evaluating and selecting ideas:* determine whether the ideas have merit and will achieve the problem-solver's goal.
4. *Implementing ideas:* sell the solution and gain acceptance by those who must use them.

A structured process provides all employees with a common language and a set of tools to communicate with each other, particularly as members of cross-functional teams. "Speaking the same language" builds confidence and assures that solutions are developed objectively, rather than by intuition. Leaders in the quality revolution—Deming, Juran, and Crosby (see Chapter 3)—have proposed specific methodologies for quality improvement. Each methodology is distinctive in its own right, yet they share many common themes. Most leading companies have adopted one of these methodologies or have developed their own unique version. This section reviews their approaches and then introduces a generic process for problem solving based on principles of creative thinking.

The Deming Cycle

Chapter 3 discussed W. Edwards Deming's 14 Points for management and his emphasis on the reduction of variation for quality improvement. The **Deming cycle** is a simple methodology for improvement. It was originally called the *Shewhart cycle* after its founder, Walter Shewhart, but was renamed the Deming cycle by the Japanese in 1950. The Deming cycle is composed of four stages: *plan, do, study,* and *act* (PDSA) as illustrated in Figure 10.3. (The third stage—study—was formerly called *check*, and the Deming cycle was known as the *PDCA cycle*. Deming made the change in 1990. "Study" is more appropriate; with only a "check," one might miss something. However, many people still use "check.")

Much of the focus of the Deming cycle is on implementation and learning. The *plan* stage consists of studying the current situation and describing the process: its inputs, outputs, customers, and suppliers; understanding customer expectations; gathering data; identifying problems; testing theories of causes; and developing solutions and action plans. In the *do* stage, the plan is implemented on a trial basis, for example, in a laboratory, pilot production process, or with a small group of customers, to evaluate a proposed solution and provide objective data. Data from the experiment are collected and documented. The *study* stage determines whether the trial plan is working correctly by evaluating the results, recording the learning, and determining whether any further issues or opportunities need be addressed. Often, the first solution must be modified or scrapped. New solutions are proposed and evaluated by returning to the *do* stage. In the last stage, *act*, the improvements become standardized and the final plan is implemented as a "current best practice" and communicated throughout the organization. This process then leads back to the *plan* stage for identification of other improvement opportunities. As Figure 10.3 suggests, the cycle is never-ending; that is, it is focused on continuous improvement. With this philosophy, one can easily see why the Deming cycle has been an essential element of Japanese quality improvement programs.

The Deming cycle is based on the premise that improvement comes from the application of knowledge.[6] This knowledge may be knowledge of engineering, management, or how a process operates, which can make a job easier, more accurate, faster, less costly, safer, or better able to meet customer needs. Consider the following three fundamental questions:

Figure 10.3 The Deming Cycle

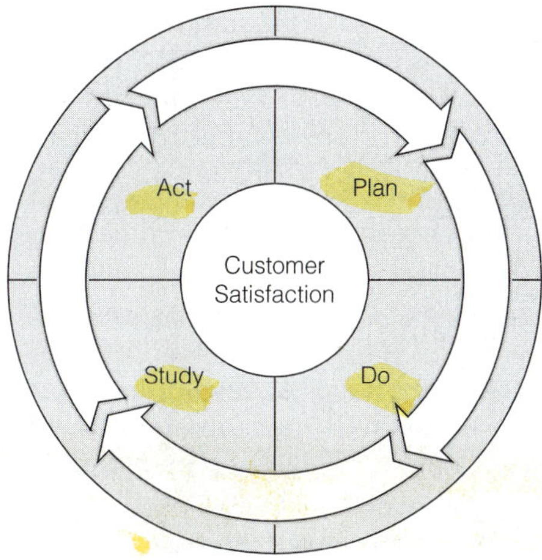

1. What are we trying to accomplish?
2. What changes can we make that will result in improvement?
3. How will we know that a change is an improvement?

Through a process of learning, knowledge is developed.

The following example demonstrates how the Deming cycle can be applied in practice.

Example 2: Improving Service at a Restaurant.[7] The co-owners of a luncheonette decided to do something about the long lines that occurred every day in their place of business. After discussions with their employees, several important facts came to light:

- Customers waited in line for up to 15 minutes.
- Usually, tables were available.
- Many of their customers were regulars.
- People taking orders and preparing food were getting in each other's way.

To measure the improvement that might result from any change they made, they decided to collect data on the number of customers in line, the number of empty tables, and the time until a customer received the food ordered.

In the plan stage, the owners wanted to test a few changes. They decided on three changes:

1. Provide a way for customers to fax their orders in ahead of time (rent a fax machine for one month).
2. Construct a preparation table in the kitchen with ample room for fax orders.
3. Devote one of their two cash registers to handling fax orders.

Both the length of the line and the number of empty tables were measured every 15 minutes during the lunch hour by one of the owners. In addition, when the 15-minute line check was done, she noted the last person in line and measured the time until that person got served.

In the do phase, the owners observed the results of the three measures for three weeks. In the study phase, they detected several improvements. Time in line went down from 15 minutes to an average of five minutes. The line length was cut to a peak average of 12 people, and the number of empty tables decreased slightly. In the act phase, the owners held a meeting with all employees to discuss the results. They decided to purchase the fax machine, prepare phone orders in the kitchen with the fax orders, and use both cash registers to handle walk-up and fax orders.

Juran's Improvement Program

Joseph Juran emphasized the importance of developing a habit of making annual improvements in quality and annual reductions in quality-related costs. Juran defined **breakthrough** as the accomplishment of any improvement that takes an organization to unprecedented levels of performance. Breakthrough attacks chronic losses or, in Deming's terminology, common causes of variation.

Example 3: Breakthrough at INCO, Ltd. An example of breakthrough was reported by the Manitoba Division of INCO Limited.[8] The data entry department employed a staff of six operators and a full-time working supervisor, yet still averaged 100 hours of overtime to handle the workload. After studying the processes and reviewing the needs with customers, the company simplified data entry procedures, employees cross-trained themselves in different skills, and workloads were smoothed. As a result, overtime was virtually eliminated (see Figure 10.4) and the supervisor, who was an integral part of the improvement, was transferred to a more challenging and rewarding position in another department.

Figure 10.4 Data Entry Overtime Hours

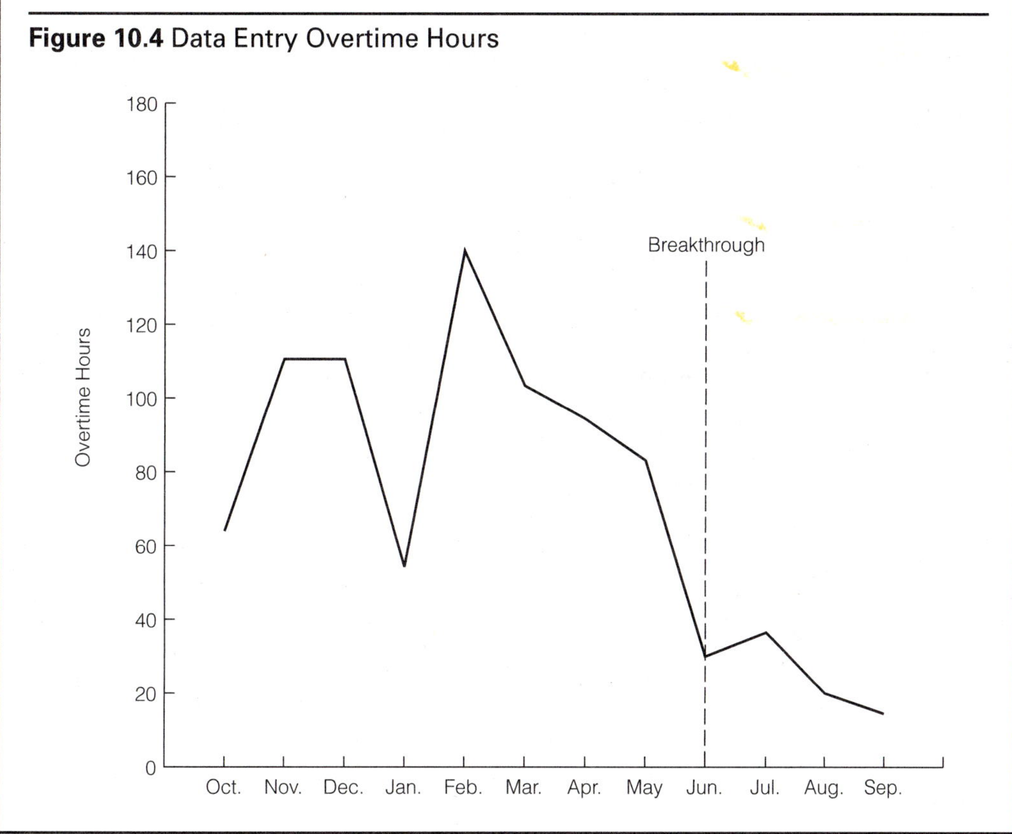

According to Juran, all breakthroughs follow a commonsense sequence of discovery, organization, diagnosis, corrective action, and control, which he formalized as the "breakthrough sequence." This breakthrough sequence can be summarized by the following points:

- *Proof of the need:* Managers, especially top managers, need to be convinced that quality improvements are simply good economics. Through data collection efforts, information on poor quality, low productivity, or poor service can be translated into the language of money—the universal language of top management—to justify a request for resources to implement a quality improvement program.
- *Project identification:* All breakthroughs are achieved project by project, and in no other way. By taking a project approach (see Chapter 7), management pro-

vides a forum for converting an atmosphere of defensiveness or blame into one of constructive action. Participation in a project increases the likelihood that the participant will act on the results.

- *Organization for breakthrough:* Organization for improvement requires a clear responsibility for guiding the project. The responsibility for the project may be as broad as an entire division with formal committee structures or as narrow as a small group of workers at one production operation. These groups provide the definition and agreement as to the specific aims of the project, the authority to conduct experiments, and implementation strategies. The path from problem to solution consists of two journeys: one from symptom to cause (the diagnostic journey) and the other from cause to remedy (the remedial journey), which must be performed by different individuals with the appropriate skills.
- *Diagnostic journey:* Diagnosticians skilled in data collection, statistics, and other problem-solving tools are needed at this stage. Some projects will require full-time, specialized experts while others can be performed by the workforce. Management-controllable and operator-controllable problems require different methods of diagnosis and remedy.
- *Remedial journey:* The remedial journey consists of several phases: choosing an alternative that optimizes total cost (similar to one of Deming's points), implementing remedial action, and dealing with resistance to change.
- *Holding the gains:* This final step involves establishing the new standards and procedures, training the workforce, and instituting controls to make sure that the breakthrough does not die over time.

Many companies have followed Juran's program religiously. A Xerox plant in Mitcheldean, England, for example, cut quality losses by 30 percent to 40 percent and won a national prize in Britain in 1984 for quality improvement using the Juran system.[9]

The Crosby Program

Philip Crosby proposed a 14-step program for quality improvement:

1. *Management commitment:* The program begins with obtaining commitment from management for quality improvement with an emphasis on the need for defect prevention. The personal commitment of management raises the visibility of a quality improvement program and encourages everyone's cooperation.
2. *Quality improvement team:* A quality improvement team is formed with representatives from each department. The team is oriented to the content and purpose of the program.
3. *Quality measurement:* Measurement for each activity must either be reviewed or established to show where improvement is possible, where corrective action is necessary, and to document actual improvement later.
4. *Cost of quality evaluation:* Accurate figures obtained on the cost of quality indicate where corrective action will be profitable. This step provides a companywide measurement of quality management performance.
5. *Quality awareness:* Share with employees the measurements of what a lack of quality is costing. This step gets supervisors and employees in the habit of talking positively about quality and changing existing attitudes.
6. *Corrective action:* As people are encouraged to talk about their problems, opportunities for correction come to light, particularly from the workers them-

selves. These problems must be brought to the attention of managers and resolved. As employees see that their problems are being corrected, they will get in the habit of identifying further problems.

7. *Establish an ad hoc committee for the zero defects program:* Three or four members of the team are selected to investigate the "zero defects" concept and ways to implement the program. It is not a motivation program, but a program to communicate the meaning of "zero defects" and the concept of doing it right the first time.
8. *Supervisor training:* All managers must understand each step well enough to explain it to their people. Training helps supervisors to understand the program and realize its value for themselves.
9. *Zero defects day:* The establishment of zero defects as the performance standard of the company should be done in one day so that everyone understands it the same way. It provides an emphasis and a long-lasting memory.
10. *Goal setting:* Each supervisor should establish goals that are specific and capable of being measured.
11. *Error cause removal:* Individual are asked to describe any problem that keeps them from performing error-free work on a simple, one-page form. The appropriate functional group develops the answer. Problems should be acknowledged quickly. People need to know that problems will be heard and develop trust in management.
12. *Recognition:* Establish award programs to recognize those who meet their goals or perform outstanding acts. The prizes or awards should not be financial; recognition is what is important. People appreciate recognition of performance, which increases support of the program.
13. *Quality councils:* The quality professionals and team chairpersons meet regularly to discuss and determine actions necessary to upgrade and improve the quality program.
14. *Do it over again:* The typical program takes one year to 18 months. Changes in the organization require new organization efforts. Quality must be ingrained in the organization.

The quality improvement philosophies of Deming, Juran, and Crosby differ considerably. The Deming cycle is purposefully simple—to be understood and performed by individuals and groups at all levels of an organization. However, it concentrates more on verifying solutions rather than developing them. Juran's approach, like the Deming cycle, is structured at the project level, but with a heavy emphasis on organizational issues and the use of specific techniques and methods for implementing each step. Crosby's program is a formal companywide program with a heavy emphasis on motivation and behavior change.

Creative Problem Solving

Solving quality problems often involves a great deal of creativity. In Japanese, the word *creativity* has a literal translation as *dangerous opportunity.* In the Toyota production system, which has become the benchmark for world-class efficiency, a key concept is *soikufu*—creative thinking or inventive ideas, which means capitalizing on worker suggestions. The chairman of Toyota once observed: "One of the features of Japanese workers is that they use their brains as well as their hands. Our workers provide 1.5 million suggestions a year, and 95 percent of them are put to practical use. There is an almost tangible concern for improvement in the air at Toyota."[10]

An effective problem-solving process that can easily be adapted to quality improvement stems from creative problem-solving (CPS) concepts advocated by Osborn and by Parnes.[11] This strategy consists of the following steps:

- Understanding the "mess"
- Finding facts
- Identifying specific problems
- Generating ideas
- Developing solutions
- Implementation

Notice that the *plan* stage in the Deming cycle, for example, actually consists of the first five steps; the *do*, *study*, and *act* stages deal more with implementation. In Juran's program, the "diagnostic and remedial journeys" are essentially the same as this process. Thus, understanding these steps will help improve the application of other problem-solving models.

Mess Finding Russell Ackoff, a noted authority on problem solving, defines a **mess** as a "system of external conditions that produces dissatisfaction."[12] Ackoff carefully distinguishes problems from messes. Managers in any organization generally deal with messes; problems must be identified and extracted from the mess. Quality messes are often characterized by high costs, excessive defects, a rash of customer complaints, or low customer satisfaction. These symptoms can arise from several sources:

- A lack of knowledge about how a process works, which is particularly critical if the process is performed by different people. Such lack of knowledge results in inconsistency and increased variation in outputs.
- A lack of knowledge about how a process *should* work, including understanding customer expectations and the goal of the process.
- A lack of control of materials and equipment used in a process.
- Inadvertent errors in performing work.
- Waste and complexity, which manifest themselves in many ways, such as unnecessary steps in a process and excess inventories.
- Hasty design and production of parts and assemblies; poor design specifications; inadequate testing of incoming materials and prototypes.
- Failure to understand the capability of a process to meet specifications.
- Lack of training.
- Poor instrument calibration and testing.
- Inadequate environmental characteristics such as light, temperature, and noise.

A mess represents a gold mine of opportunity for improvement; however, many managers fail to seeks the true causes of the symptoms.

Fact Finding Understanding a mess depends on collecting good data, observation, and careful listening—the focus of fact finding. As in the Hewlett-Packard example given earlier in this chapter, data from existing production processes and practices often provide important information, as does feedback from supervisors, workers, customers and field service employees.

Data collection should not be performed blindly. One must first ask some basic questions:

- What questions are we trying to answer?
- What type of data will we need to answer the question?

- Where can we find the data?
- Who can provide the data?
- How can we collect the data with minimum effort and with minimum chance of error?

The first step in any data collection effort is to develop **operational definitions** for all quality measures that will be used. For example, what does it mean to have "on-time delivery"? Does it mean within one day of the promised time? One week? One hour? What is an error? Is it wrong information on an invoice, a typographical mistake, or either? Clearly, any data are meaningless unless they are well defined and understood without ambiguity.

The Juran Institute suggests 10 important considerations for data collection:

1. Formulate good questions that relate to the specific information needs of the project.
2. Use appropriate data analysis tools and be certain the necessary data are being collected.
3. Define comprehensive data collections points so that job flows suffer minimum interruption.
4. Select an unbiased collector who has the easiest and most immediate access to the relevant facts.
5. Understand the environment and make sure that data collectors have the proper experience.
6. Design simple data collection forms.
7. Prepare instructions for collecting the data.
8. Test the data collection forms and the instructions and make sure they are filled out properly.
9. Train the data collectors as to the purpose of the study, what the data will be used for, how to fill out the forms, and the importance of remaining unbiased.
10. Audit the data collection process and validate the results.[13]

These guidelines can greatly improve the process of uncovering relevant facts necessary to identify and solve problems.

Problem Finding An old proverb says that a problem clearly stated is half solved. The purpose of problem finding is to separate the true problem from the "mess." Solving the wrong problem can be more detrimental than not solving any. A major flaw in many problem-solving approaches is a lack of emphasis on problem finding. Too often, we want to jump to a solution without fully understanding the nature of the problem and identifying the source, or root cause, of the problem. NCR Corporation defines **root cause** as "that condition (or interrelated set of conditions) having allowed or caused a defect to occur, which once corrected properly, permanently prevents recurrence of the defect in the same, or subsequent, product or service generated by the process."[14] As with a medical analogy, eliminating symptoms of problems usually provides only temporary relief; eliminating root causes provides long-term relief.

A useful approach for identifying the root cause is the "5 Why" technique.[15] This approach forces one to redefine a problem statement as a chain of causes and effects to identify the source of the symptoms by asking why, ideally five times. In a classic example at Toyota, a machine failed because a fuse blew. Replacing the fuse would have been the obvious solution; however, this action would have only addressed the symptom of the real problem. Why did the fuse blow? Because the bearing did not have adequate lubrication. Why? Because the lubrication pump was not working properly. Why? Because the pump axle was worn. Why? Because sludge seeped into the pump axle, which was the root cause. Toyota attached a strainer to the lubricating pump to eliminate the sludge, thus correcting the problem of the machine failure.

Idea Finding The purpose of the idea-finding step is to generate ideas for removing or resolving the problem. One of the difficulties in this task is the natural instinct to prejudge ideas before thoroughly evaluating them. Most people have a natural fear of proposing a "silly" idea or looking foolish. However, such ideas may actually form the basis for a creative and useful solution. Effective problem solvers must learn to defer judgment and develop the ability to generate a large number of ideas at this stage of the process. A number of processes and tools to facilitate idea generation can be used. One of the most popular is brainstorming.

Brainstorming, a useful group problem-solving procedure for generating ideas, was proposed by Alex Osborn[16] "for the sole purpose of producing checklists of ideas" that can be used in developing a solution to a problem. With brainstorming, no criticism is permitted, and people are encouraged to generate a large number of ideas through combination and enhancement of existing ideas. Wild ideas are encouraged and frequently trigger other good ideas from somewhere else.

The process often works in the following manner. Each individual in the group suggests an idea relating to the problem at hand, working in a round-robin fashion. If a person cannot think of anything, he or she passes. A facilitator writes down all ideas on a blackboard or easel so that everyone can see them. Only one idea is presented at a time by each individual. The process is repeated until no further ideas can be generated. By writing down the ideas in plain view of the group, new ideas are usually built from old ones by combining or extending previous suggestions.

For example, suppose that a group is examining the problem of the reasons for damage in the course of parts handling. The first individual might suggest "lack of storage"; the second, "poor placement of machines"; the third, "poor design of racks." The next individual might combine the previous two ideas and suggest "poor placement of parts on racks." In this fashion, one individual's idea might spawn a new idea from someone else.

Checklists are often used as a guide for generating ideas. Osborn proposed about 75 fundamental questions based on the following principles:

- Put to other uses?
- Adapt?
- Modify?
- Magnify?
- Minify?
- Substitute?
- Rearrange?
- Reverse?
- Combine?

By consciously seeking ideas based on this list, one can generate many unusual and often useful ideas.

Several other methods for generating ideas have been suggested. One is to change the wording of a problem statement. Simple modification of a single word can dramatically change the meaning. For example, consider this statement: "In what ways might this company reduce quality costs by 30 percent?" Dropping the qualifier "by 30 percent" broadens the problem and potential solutions. Relaxing the "by 30 percent" to "by 5 percent" produces a similar effect. Changing the action verb or goal can also change the problem perspective. Turning a negative statement into a positive one leads to different ideas, such as "reducing quality costs" to "increasing quality value." Reversing the focus of the problem is another technique. For instance, "how to reduce costs due to scrap" can be reversed to "how to use scrap to reduce costs" (by recycling, for example).

Solution Finding The purpose of solution finding is to evaluate ideas that have been proposed and select one. Often some sort of decision or scoring model is used to assess possible solutions against important criteria like cost, time, quality improvement potential, resources required, effects on supervisors and workers, and barriers to implementation.

Implementation To implement a solution effectively, responsibility must be assigned to a person or a group who will follow through on what must be done, where it will be done, when it will be done, and how it will be done. Implementation might entail designing and training the workforce in a new procedure or installing a new piece of equipment. Goals and milestones for evaluating the solution and, as Juran suggests, "holding the gains" should be established. The seven management and planning tools discussed in Chapter 5 are helpful in implementation planning.

How one approaches problem solving is not as critical as doing it in a systematic fashion, whether one uses the Deming cycle, Juran's approach, Crosby's steps, CPS, or some hybrid variation. For example, at the Bethesda Hospitals of Cincinnati, Ohio, both the Juran and Deming approaches are integrated as shown in Figure 10.5. The left side of the figure incorporates the essential elements of Juran's diagnostic/remedial journeys. Once a solution is proposed, the Deming cycle is then used to evaluate the solution's effectiveness prior to implementation. Not every approach is appropriate for all organizations; one must be chosen or designed to fit the organization's culture and people.

SIX-SIGMA

Motorola pioneered the concept of **Six-Sigma**—an approach to measuring and improving product and service quality. The late Bill Smith, a reliability engineer at Motorola, is credited with originating the concept during the mid-1980s and selling it to Motorola's CEO, Robert Galvin. Smith noted that system failure rates were substantially higher than predicted by final product test, and suggested several causes, including higher system complexity that resulted in more opportunities for failure, and a fundamental flaw in traditional quality thinking. He concluded that a much higher level of internal quality was required and convinced Galvin of its importance.[17] As a result, Motorola set the following goal in 1987:

> *Improve product and services quality ten times by 1989, and at least one hundred fold by 1991. Achieve six-sigma capability by 1992. With a deep sense of urgency, spread dedication to quality to every facet of the corporation, and achieve a culture of continual improvement to assure total customer satisfaction. There is only one ultimate goal: zero defects—in everything we do.*

Figure 10.5 Bethesda Hospital Process Improvement Model

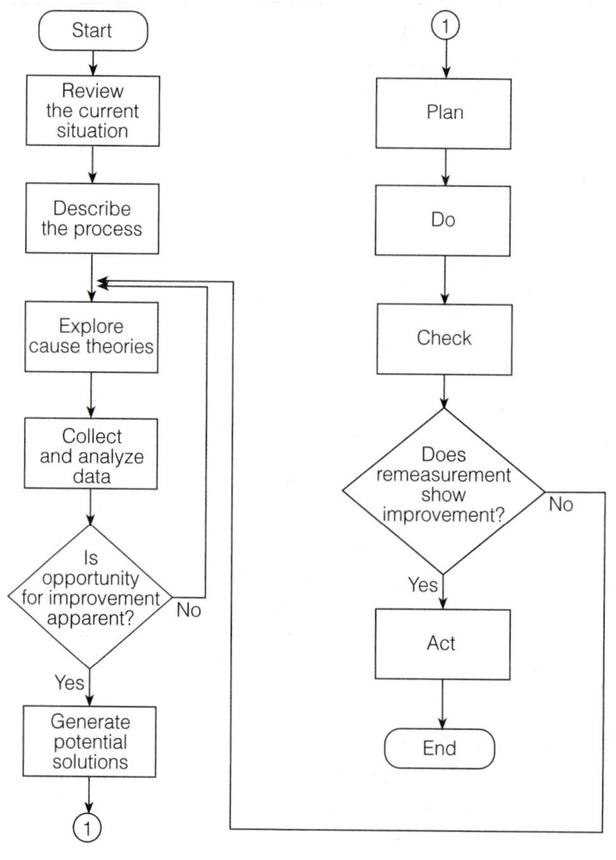

Source: Reprinted with permission of Bethesda Hospital, Inc., 619 Oak Street, Cincinnati, OH 45241.

Six-Sigma Metrics

Six-Sigma began by stressing a common measure for quality for products that an organization produces. In Six-Sigma terminology, a defect is any mistake or error that is passed on to the customer (many people also use the term ***nonconformance***). A unit of work is the output of a process or an individual process step. We can measure output quality by **defects per unit (DPU)**:

Defects per unit = Number of defects discovered/Number of units produced

However, such an output measure tends to focus on the final product, not the process that produces the product. In addition, it is difficult to use for processes of varying complexity, particularly service activities. Two different processes might have significantly different numbers of opportunities for error, making appropriate comparisons difficult. The Six-Sigma concept redefines quality performance as **defects per million opportunities (dpmo)**:

dpmo = DPU × 1,000,000/opportunities for error

For example, suppose that an airline wishes to measure the effectiveness of its baggage handling system. A DPU measure might be lost bags per customer. However, customers may have different numbers of bags; thus the number of opportunities for error is the average number of bags per customer. Thus, if the average number of bags per customer is 1.6, and the airline recorded 3 lost bags for 8,000 passengers in one month, then

$$\text{dpmo} = \frac{3}{(8{,}000)(1.6)} \times 1{,}000{,}000 = 234.375$$

The use of dpmo allows us to define quality broadly. In the airline case, a broad definition might mean every opportunity for a failure to meet customer expectations from initial ticketing until bags are retrieved.

Six-Sigma represents a quality level of at most *3.4 defects per million opportunities*. The theoretical basis for Six-Sigma is explained by Figure 10.6 in the context of manufacturing specifications. A six-sigma quality level corresponds to a process variation equal to half of the design tolerance (in terms of the process capability index, C_p = 2.0), while allowing the mean to shift as much as 1.5 standard deviations from the target. This figure was chosen by Motorola because field failure data suggested that Motorola's processes drifted by this amount on average. The allowance of a shift in the distribution is important, because no process can be maintained in perfect control. As discussed in the next chapter, many common statistical process control plans are based on sample sizes that only allow detection of shifts of about two standard deviations. Thus, it would not be unusual for a process to drift this much and not be noticed. The area under the shifted curves *beyond* the six-sigma ranges (the tolerance limits) is only 0.0000034, or 3.4 parts per million. Thus, if the process mean can be controlled to within 1.5 standard deviations of the target, a maximum of 3.4 defects per million can be expected. If it is held exactly on target (the shaded distribution in Figure 10.6), only 2.0 defects per billion would be expected!

In a similar fashion we could define three-sigma quality, five-sigma quality, and so on. The easiest way to understand this concept is to think of the distance from the target to the upper or lower specification (half the tolerance), measured in terms of standard deviations of the inherent variation, as the sigma level. A k-sigma quality level satisfies the equation:

Figure 10.6 Six-Sigma Quality

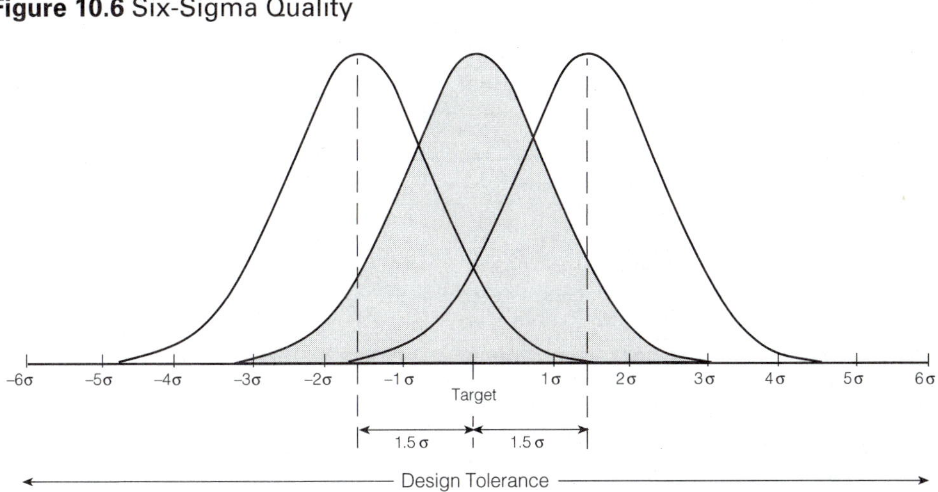

$$k * \text{process standard deviation} = \text{tolerance}/2$$

For a k-sigma quality level, the process capability index would be $2k\sigma/6\sigma = k/3$. For example, a four-sigma quality level corresponds to $C_p = 1.33$, while a three-sigma level corresponds to $C_p = 1.0$. Note that in Figure 10.6, if the design specification limits were only 4 standard deviations away from the target, the tails of the shifted distributions begin to exceed the specification limits by a significant amount.

Table 10.1 shows the number of defects per million for different sigma quality levels and different amounts of off-centering. Note that a quality level of 3.4 defects per million can be achieved in several ways:

- With 0.5-sigma off-centering and 5-sigma quality
- With 1.0-sigma off-centering and 5.5-sigma quality
- With 1.5-sigma off-centering and 6-sigma quality[18]

In many cases, controlling the process to the target is less expensive than reducing the process variability. This table can help assess these trade-offs.

Although originally developed for manufacturing in the context of tolerance-based specifications, the Six-Sigma concept has been operationalized to any process and has come to signify a generic quality level of at most 3.4 defects per million opportunities. It has been applied in product development, new business acquisition, customer service, accounting, and many other business functions. For example, suppose that a bank tracks the number of errors reported in customers' checking account statements. Finding 12 errors in 1,000 statements is equivalent to an error rate of 12,000 per million, somewhere between 3.5- and four-sigma levels. The difference between a four- and six-sigma quality level can be surprising. Put in practical terms, if your telephone system operated at a four-sigma level, you would be without service for more than four hours each month, whereas at six-sigma, it would only be about 9

Table 10.1 Number of Defectives (Parts per Million) for Specified Off-Centering of the Process and Quality Levels

	Quality Level						
Off-Centering	**3-sigma**	**3.5-sigma**	**4-sigma**	**4.5-sigma**	**5-sigma**	**5.5-sigma**	**6-sigma**
0	2,700	465	63	6.8	0.57	0.034	0.002
0.25-sigma	3,577	666	99	12.8	1.02	0.1056	0.0063
0.5-sigma	6,440	1,382	236	32	**3.4**	0.71	0.019
0.75-sigma	12,288	3,011	665	88.5	11	1.02	0.1
1-sigma	22,832	6,433	1,350	233	32	**3.4**	0.39
1.25-sigma	40,111	12,201	3,000	577	88.5	10.7	1
1.5-sigma	66,803	22,800	6,200	1,350	233	32	**3.4**
1.75-sigma	105,601	40,100	12,200	3,000	577	88.4	11
2-sigma	158,700	66,800	22,800	6,200	1,300	233	32

Source: Reprinted with permission of Pandu R. Tadikamalla (see note 18).

seconds a month; a four-sigma process would result in one nonconforming package for every three truckloads while a six-sigma process would have only one nonconforming package in more than 5,000 truckloads. And, if you play 100 rounds of golf each year, you would only miss one putt every 163 years at a six-sigma level! What may be more surprising to realize is that a change from three- to four-sigma represents a tenfold improvement; from four- to five-sigma, a 30-fold improvement; and from five- to six-sigma, a 70-fold improvement—difficult challenges for any organization.

At Motorola, Six-Sigma became part of the common language of all employees. To them, it means near perfection, even if they do not understand the statistical details. (Some tell their coworkers, "Have a six-sigma weekend!") Since stating its goal, Motorola has made great strides in meeting this goal, achieving six-sigma capability in many processes and four- or five-sigma levels in most others. Even in those departments that have reached the goal, Motorola employees continue their improvement efforts in order to reach the ultimate goal of zero defects.

Many companies have adopted this standard to challenge their own improvement efforts. The efforts by General Electric in particular, driven by CEO Jack Welch, have brought significant media attention to the concept and have made Six-Sigma a popular approach to quality improvement. Many other organizations such as Texas Instruments, Allied Signal (which merged with Honeywell), Boeing, Caterpillar, IBM, Xerox, Citibank, Raytheon, and the U.S. Air Force Air Combat Command have developed quality improvement approaches designed around the Six-Sigma concept.

From 1996 to 1998, GE has increased the number of Six-Sigma projects from 200 to 6,000. From all these efforts, GE hopes to save $7 to $10 billion over a decade. For example, GE credits the Six-Sigma concept with a tenfold increase in the life of CT scanner X-ray tubes, a 400 percent improvement in return on investment in its industrial diamond business, a 62 percent reduction in turnaround time at railcar repair shops, and $400 million in savings in its plastics business.[19] Other companies also report significant results. Between 1995 and the first quarter of 1997, Allied Signal reported cost savings exceeding $800 million from its Six-Sigma initiative. Citibank groups have reduced internal callbacks by 80 percent, credit process time by 50 percent, and cycle times of processing statements from 28 days to 15 days.[20]

Implementing Six-Sigma

Six-Sigma has developed from simply a way of measuring quality to an overall strategy to accelerate improvements and achieve unprecedented performance levels within an organization by finding and eliminating causes of errors or defects in processes by focusing on characteristics that are critical to customers.[21] The core philosophy of Six-Sigma is based on some key concepts:[22]

1. Emphasizing dpmo as a standard metric that can be applied to all parts of an organization: manufacturing, engineering, administrative, software, and so on
2. Providing extensive training followed by project team deployment to improve profitability, reduce non-value-added activities, and achieve cycle time reduction
3. Focusing on corporate sponsors responsible for supporting team activities, helping to overcome resistance to change, obtain resources, and focus the teams on overall strategic objectives
4. Creating highly qualified process improvement experts ("green belts," "black belts," and "master black belts") who can apply improvement tools and lead teams
5. Ensuring that appropriate metrics are identified early in the process and that they focus on business results
6. Setting stretch objectives for improvement

The recognized benchmark for Six-Sigma implementation is General Electric. GE's Six-Sigma problem solving approach (DMAIC) employs five phases:

1. *Define (D)*
   - Identify customers and their priorities.
   - Identify a project suitable for Six-Sigma efforts based on business objectives as well as customer needs and feedback.
   - Identify CTQs (critical-to-quality characteristics) that the customer considers to have the most impact on quality.
2. *Measure (M)*
   - Determine how to measure the process and how is it performing.
   - Identify the key internal processes that influence CTQs and measure the defects currently generated relative to those processes.
3. *Analyze (A)*
   - Determine the most likely causes of defects.
   - Understand why defects are generated by identifying the key variables that are most likely to create process variation.
4. *Improve (I)*
   - Identify means to remove the causes of the defects.
   - Confirms the key variables and quantify their effects on the CTQs.
   - Identify the maximum acceptable ranges of the key variables and a system for measuring deviations of the variables.
   - Modify the process to stay within the acceptable range.
5. *Control (C)*
   - Determine how to maintain the improvements.
   - Put tools in place to ensure that the key variables remain within the maximum acceptable ranges under the modified process.

Note that this approach is similar to the other quality improvement approaches we discussed and incorporates many of the same ideas. The key difference is the emphasis placed on customer requirements and the use of statistical tools and methodologies.

Example 4: Applying DMAIC at American Express[23] (In this example, data have been masked to protect confidentiality.)

Define and Measure: On average in 1999, American Express received 1,000 returned renewal cards each month. Of these, 65 percent are due to the fact that the card members changed their addresses and did not tell the company. The U.S. Post Office calls these forwardable addresses. Amex does not currently notify a card member when they receive a returned plastic card.

Analyze: Analysis of the data noted significant differences in the causes of returned plastics between product types. Optima, the revolving card product, had the highest incidence of defects, but was not significantly different from other card types in the percentage of defects. Renewals had by far the highest defect rate among the three areas of replacement, renewal, and new accounts. After additional testing, returns with forwardable addresses were overwhelmingly the largest percentage and quantity of returns.

Improve: An experimental pilot was run on all renewal files issued, comparing records against the National Change of Address database. As a result, they were able to reduce the dpmo rate by 44.5 percent, from 13,500 to 6,036 defects per million opportunities. This action enabled more than 1,200 card members who would not have automatically received their credit cards to receive them, increasing revenue and customer satisfaction.

Control: Amex began tracking the proportion of returns over time as a means of monitoring the new process to ensure that it remains in control.

In many ways, Six-Sigma is the realization of many fundamental concepts of "total quality management," notably, the integration of human and process elements of improvement.[24] Human issues include management leadership, a sense of urgency, focus on results and customers, team processes, and culture change; process issues include the use of process management techniques, analysis of variation and statistical methods, a disciplined problem-solving approach, and management by fact.

Several key principles are necessary for effective implementation of Six-Sigma:[25]

- *Committed leadership from top management.* Motorola's former CEO Bob Galvin passionately led the Six-Sigma effort with aggressive goals: tenfold reduction in defects in the first three years, and hundredfold improvement in the next three years. In addition to Welch's support at GE, other upper management (up to and including presidents and CEOs of GE divisions) participate in hands-on approaches:
    - Personally spending time in every Six-Sigma training wave, speaking and answering questions for students
    - Dropping in (usually unannounced) on weekly and monthly Six-Sigma reviews
    - Making site visits at the manufacturing and call-taking operations to observe firsthand the degree to which Six-Sigma in ingrained in the culture
    - Monitoring Six-Sigma project progress weekly through summary reports from the tracking database and monthly reviews with the master black belt team
- *Integration with existing initiatives, business strategy, and performance measurement.* In its 1998 annual report, General Electric CEO Jack Welch described three initiatives that are "fueling powerful growth in your Company and transforming its culture and soul"—globalization, services, and Six-Sigma. At companies such as GE and Allied Signal, Six-Sigma has been extended to all areas of the company, including product development and financial services. For example, GE first identifies all critical customer performance features and subjects these features to a rigorous statistical design process, thus designing products for six-sigma levels.
- *Process thinking.* Because process thinking is a foundation principle of total quality, it is not surprising that a process focus is a necessary prerequisite. Mapping all business processes is one of the key activities in Six-Sigma efforts, as is a disciplined approach to information gathering, analysis, and problem solving.
- *Disciplined customer and market intelligence gathering.* The ultimate goal is to improve those characteristics that are most important to customers; thus, knowledge of customer needs is vital.
- *A bottom-line orientation.* Six-Sigma projects must produce real savings or revenues in both the short term and long term. Most Six-Sigma projects are designed to be completed within 3–6 months.
- *Leadership in the trenches.* Within GE, Six-Sigma includes a diverse population of technical and nontechnical people, managers, and others from key business areas.
    - *Champions* are fully trained business leaders who promote and lead the deployment of Six-Sigma in a significant area of the business.

  - *Master black belts* are fully trained quality leaders responsible for Six-Sigma strategy, training, mentoring, deployment, and results.
  - *Black belts* are fully trained Six-Sigma experts who lead improvement teams, work projects across the business, and mentor green belts
  - *Green belts* are full-time teachers with quantitative skills as well as teaching and leadership ability; they are fully trained quality leaders responsible for Six-Sigma strategy, training, mentoring, deployment, and results.
  - *Team members* are individuals who support specific projects in their area.
- *Training.* Six-Sigma depends heavily on training. Many companies that embraced total quality provided employees with only basic awareness training, whereas Six-Sigma companies train nearly everyone in rigorous statistical and problem solving tools. GE has condensed its green belt training to 10 days. This training is delivered to all GE employees and is available in strategic locations across the world. It is typically rolled out over a four-month period and is scheduled to help facilitate the trainee in leading a "green belt project" to not only yield savings but also practice in a real-life situation what is being learned in the training.
- *Continuous reinforcement and rewards.* Companies get what they measure and reward. Six-Sigma companies have changed significantly performance measurement and reward systems. At GE, Jack Welch made it clear that Six-Sigma is not optional. Forty percent of executive incentives are tied to Six-Sigma goals and progress. Before any savings are credited to an individual, the black belt overseeing the project must show that the problems are fixed permanently. All employees, even executives, who want to be considered for promotion must be trained in Six-Sigma and complete a project.

TOOLS FOR SIX-SIGMA AND QUALITY IMPROVEMENT

The tools used in Six-Sigma efforts have been around for a long time. What is unique about Six-Sigma is the integration of the tools and methodology into management systems across the organization.[26] Figure 10.7 shows a typical Six-Sigma black belt training curriculum at General Electric. The topics covered may be categorized into seven general groups:

- *Elementary statistical tools:* basic statistics, statistical thinking, hypothesis testing, correlation, simple regression
- *Advanced statistical tools:* design of experiments, analysis of variance, multiple regression
- *Product design and reliability:* quality function deployment, failure mode and effects analysis
- *Measurement:* process capability, measurement systems analysis
- *Process control:* control plans, statistical process control
- *Process improvement:* process improvement planning, process mapping, mistake proofing
- *Implementation and teamwork:* organizational effectiveness, team assessment, facilitation tools, team development

Most of these topics are addressed in other chapters of this book. In this section we focus on elementary process improvement tools that are useful in almost any quality improvement effort. However, most organizations rarely go beyond these basic process improvement tools and fail to recognize the benefits of more sophisticated statistical tools such as design of experiments. As you can see, Six-Sigma has greatly expanded the requisite knowledge for true performance breakthroughs.

Figure 10.7 Six-Sigma Black Belt Training

Week 1	Week 2	Week 3	Week 4
• Overview • Process improvement planning • Process mapping • Quality function deployment • Failure mode and effects analysis • Organizational effectiveness concepts • Basic statistics • Process capability • Measurement systems analysis	• Statistical thinking • Hypothesis testing • Correlation • Simple regression • Team assessment	• Design of experiments • Analysis of variance • Multiple regression • Facilitation tools	• Control plans • Statistical process control • Mistake-proofing • Team development

Source: Roger W. Hoerl, "Six Sigma and the Future of the Quality Profession," *Quality Progress*, June 1998, 35–48.

The Original Seven QC Tools

Seven simple tools—flowcharts, check sheets, histograms, Pareto diagrams, cause-and-effect diagrams, scatter diagrams, and control charts—termed the **Seven QC** (quality control) **Tools** by the Japanese, support quality improvement problem solving efforts. Table 10.2 shows the primary applications of each tool in the problem-solving process. They are designed simply so that workers at all levels can use them easily. We will briefly review each of these tools to explain their role in quality improvement.

Table 10.2 Applications of the Seven QC Tools

Tool	Application
Flowcharts	Understanding the mess; establishing control procedures
Check sheets	Finding facts
Histograms	Identifying problems
Cause-and-effect diagrams	Generating ideas
Pareto diagrams	Understanding the mess; identifying problems
Scatter diagrams	Developing solutions
Control charts	Understanding the mess; holding the gains

Flowcharts To understand a process, one must first determine how it works and what it is supposed to do. Flowcharting, or **process mapping**, identifies the sequence of activities or the flow of materials and information in a process. Flowcharts help the people who are involved in the process understand it much better and more objectively. Understanding how a process works enables a team to pinpoint obvious problems, error-proof the process, streamline it by eliminating non-value-added steps, and reduce variation.

Flowcharts are best developed by having the people involved in the process—employees, supervisors, managers, and customers—construct the flowchart. A facilitator provides objectivity in resolving conflicts. The facilitator can guide the discussion through questions such as "What happens next?" "Who makes the decision at this point?" and "What operation is performed at this point?" Quite often, the group does not universally agree on the answers to these questions due to misconceptions about the process itself or a lack of awareness of the "big picture."

Flowcharts help all employees understand how they fit into a process and who are their suppliers and customers. This realization then leads to improved communication among all parties. By participating in the development of a flowchart, workers feel a sense of ownership in the process, and hence become more willing to work on improving it. If flowcharts are used in training employees, more consistency will be achieved. Flowcharts also help to pinpoint places where quality-related measurements should be taken. Once a flowchart is constructed, it can be used to identify quality problems as well as areas for productivity improvement. Questions such as "How does this operation affect the customer?" "Can we improve or even eliminate this operation?" or "Should we control a critical quality characteristic at this point?" trigger the identification of opportunities.

Example 5: Process Flowcharting at Boise Cascade[27] The Timber and Wood Products Division of Boise Cascade formed a team of 11 people with diverse backgrounds from manufacturing, administration, and marketing to improve a customer claims processing and tracking system that affected all areas and customers in the six regions of the division. Although external customer surveys indicated that the company was not doing badly, internal opinions of the operation were far more critical.

The first eye-opener came when the process was flowcharted and the group discovered more than 70 steps were performed for each claim. Figure 10.8 shows the original flowchart from the marketing and sales department. Combined division tasks numbered in the hundreds for a single claim; the marketing and sales portion of the flowchart alone consisted of as many as 20 separate tasks and seven decisions, which sometimes took months to complete. Most of these steps added no value to the settlement outcome. The flowchart accomplished much more than just plotting Boise Cascade's time and efforts; it also helped build team members' confidence in each other and foster mutual respect. When they saw how each member was able to chart his or her part of the process and state individual concerns, everyone's reason for being on the team was validated. The group eliminated 70 percent of the steps for small claims in the original flowchart as shown in Figure 10.9.

Run Charts and Control Charts A **run chart** is a line graph in which data are plotted over time. The vertical axis represents a measurement; the horizontal axis is the time scale. The daily newspaper usually has several examples of run charts, such as the

Figure 10.8 Original Flowchart from the Marketing and Sales Department

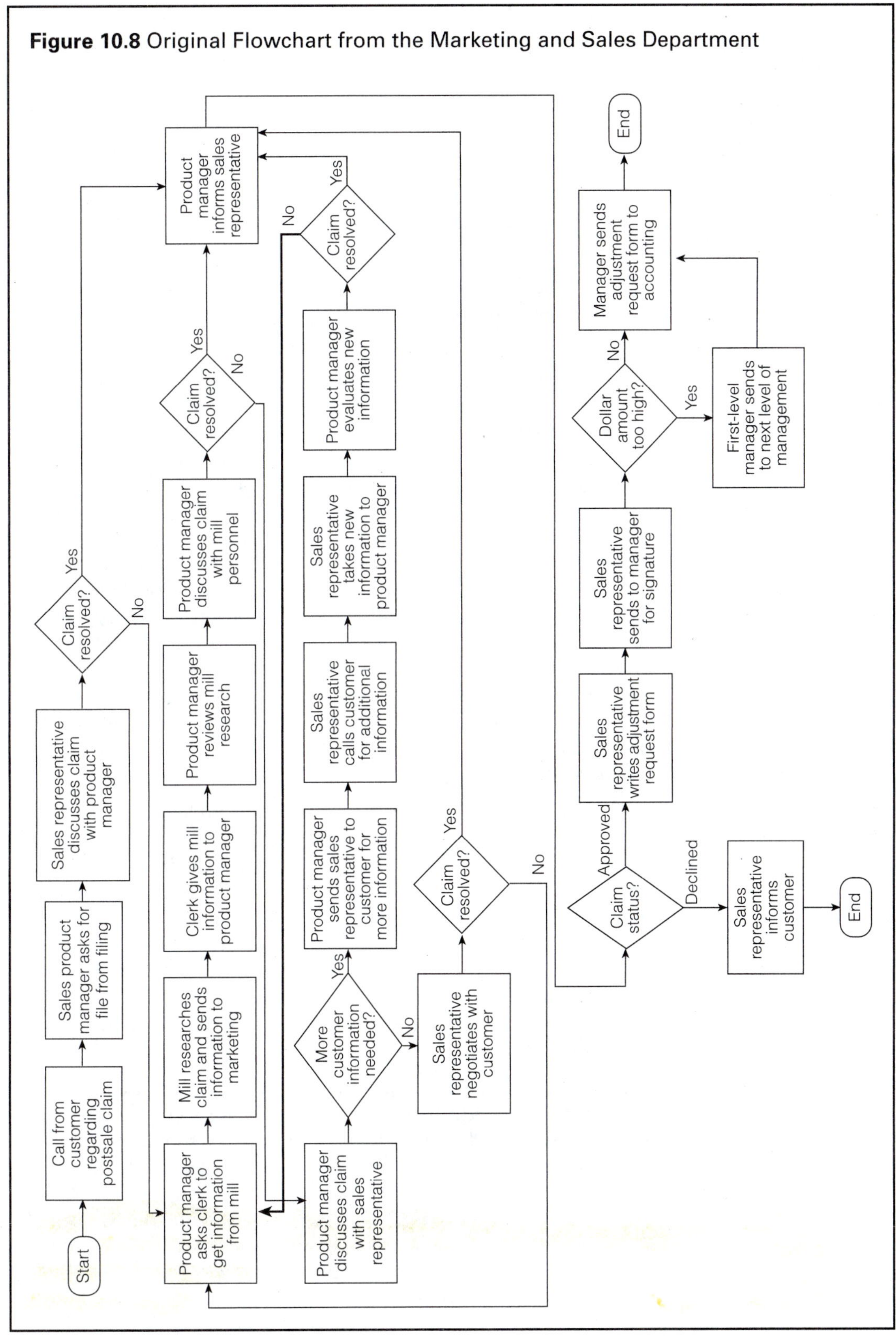

Figure 10.9 New Small Adjustment Request Form Process Flowchart for Marketing and Sales Department

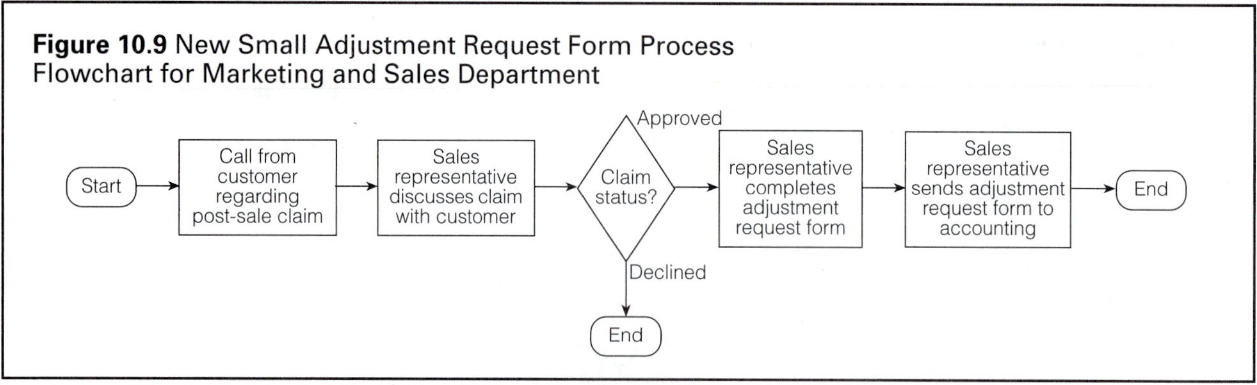

Dow Jones Industrial Average. Run charts show the performance and the variation of a process or some quality or productivity indicator over time. They can be used to track such things as production volume, costs, and customer satisfaction indexes. Run charts summarize data in a graphical fashion that is easy to understand and interpret, identify process changes and trends over time, and show the effects of corrective actions.

The first step in constructing a run chart is to identify the measurement or indicator to be monitored. In some situations, one might measure the quality characteristics for each individual unit of process output. For low-volume processes, such as chemical production or surgeries, this measurement would be appropriate. However, for high-volume production processes or services with large numbers of customers or transactions, it would be impractical. Instead, samples taken on a periodic basis provide the data for computing basic statistical measures such as the mean, range or standard deviation, proportion of items that do not conform to specifications, or number of nonconformances per unit.

Constructing the chart consists of the following steps:

Step 1. Collect the data. If samples are chosen, compute the relevant statistic for each sample, such as the average or proportion.

Step 2. Examine the range of the data. Scale the chart so that all data can be plotted on the vertical axis. Provide some additional room for new data as they are collected.

Step 3. Plot the points on the chart and connect them. Use graph paper if the chart is constructed by hand; a spreadsheet program is preferable.

Step 4. Compute the average of all plotted points and draw it as a horizontal line through the data. This line denoting the average is called the center line (CL) of the chart.

If the plotted points fluctuate in a stable pattern around the center line, with no large spikes, trends, or shifts, they indicate that the process is apparently under control. If unusual patterns exist, then the cause for lack of stability should be investigated and corrective action should be taken. Thus, run charts can identify messes caused by lack of control.

A **control chart** is simply a run chart to which two horizontal lines, called *control limits* are added: the *upper control limit (UCL)* and *lower control limit (LCL)*, as illustrated in Figure 10.10. Control charts were first proposed by Walter Shewhart at Bell Laboratories in the 1920s and were strongly advocated by Deming. Control limits are

Figure 10.10 The Structure of a Control Chart

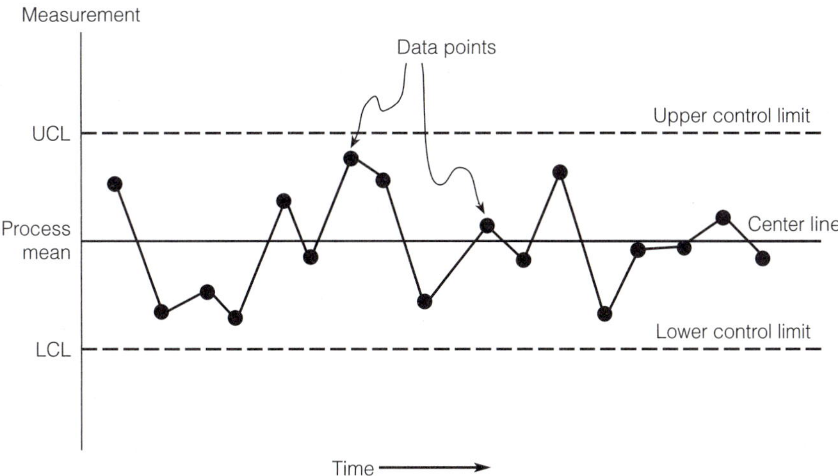

chosen statistically to provide a high probability (generally greater than 0.99) that points will fall between these limits if the process is in control. Control limits make it easier to interpret patterns in a run chart and draw conclusions about the state of control. These issues will be discussed in greater detail in Chapter 12.

If sample values fall outside the control limits or if nonrandom patterns occur in the chart, then special causes may be affecting the process; the process is not stable. The process should be examined and corrective action taken as appropriate. If evaluation and correction are done in real time, then the chance of producing nonconforming product is minimized. Thus, as a problem-solving tool, control charts allow operators to identify quality problems as they occur. Of course, control charts alone cannot determine the source of the problem. Operators, supervisors, and engineers may have to resort to other problem-solving tools to seek the root cause.

Example 6: Monitoring Surgery Infections. The Joint Commission Accreditation of Health Care Organizations (JCAHO) monitors and evaluates health care providers according to strict standards and guidelines. Improvement in the quality of care is a principal concern. Hospitals are required to identify and monitor important quality indicators that affect patient care and establish "thresholds for evaluation" (TFEs), which are levels at which special investigation of problems should occur. TFEs provide a means of focusing attention on nonrandom errors (that is, special causes of variation). A logical way to set TFEs is through control charts.

For instance, a hospital collects monthly data on the number of infections after surgeries. These data are shown in Table 10.3. Hospital administrators are concerned about whether the high percentages of infections (such as 1.76 percent in month 12) are caused by factors other than randomness. A control chart constructed from these data is shown in Figure 10.11. (Note that if the control limits are removed, it becomes a simple run chart.) The average percentage of infections is 55/7995 = 0.688 percent. Using formulas described in Chapter 12, the upper control limit is computed to be

Table 10.3 Monthly Data on Infections After Surgery

Month	Surgeries	Infections	Percent
1	208	1	0.48
2	225	3	1.33
3	201	3	1.49
4	236	1	0.42
5	220	3	1.36
6	244	1	0.41
7	247	1	0.40
8	245	1	0.41
9	250	1	0.40
10	227	0	0.00
11	234	2	0.85
12	227	4	1.76
13	213	2	0.94
14	212	1	0.47
15	193	2	1.04
16	182	0	0.00
17	140	1	0.71
18	230	1	0.43
19	187	1	0.53
20	252	2	0.79
21	201	1	0.50
22	226	0	0.00
23	222	2	0.90
24	212	2	0.94
25	219	1	0.46
26	223	2	0.90
27	191	1	0.52
28	222	0	0.00
29	231	3	1.30
30	239	1	0.42
31	217	2	0.92
32	241	1	0.41
33	220	3	1.36
34	278	1	0.36
35	255	3	1.18
36	225	1	0.44
	7,995	55	

2.35 percent. None of the data points falls above the upper control limit, indicating that the variation each month is due purely to chance and that the process is stable. To reduce the infection rate, management would have to attack the common causes in the process. The upper control limit would be a logical TFE to use, because any value beyond this limit is unlikely to occur by chance. Management can continue to use this chart to monitor future data.

Figure 10.11 Control Chart for Surgery Infections

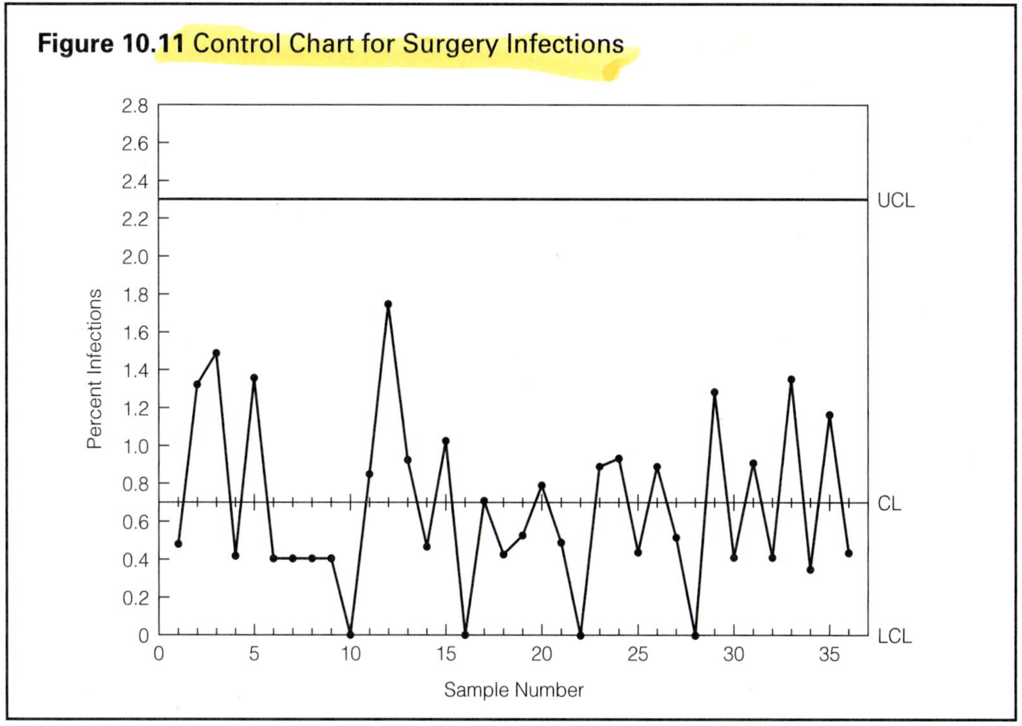

Check Sheets Check sheets are simple tools for data collection. Nearly any kind of form may be used to collect data. *Data sheets* are simple columnar or tabular forms used to record data. However, to generate useful information from raw data, further processing generally is necessary. Check sheets are special types of data collection forms in which the results may be interpreted on the form directly without additional processing.

In manufacturing, check sheets similar to Figure 10.12 are simple to use and easily interpreted by shop personnel. Including information such as specification limits makes the number of nonconforming items easily observable and provides an immediate indication of the quality of the process. For example, in Figure 10.12 a significant proportion of dimensions is clearly out of specification, with a larger number on the high side than the low side.

A second type of check sheet for defective items is illustrated in Figure 10.13, which shows the type of defect and a tally in a resin production plant. Such a check sheet can be extended to include a time dimension so that data can be monitored and analyzed over time, and trends and patterns, if any, can be detected.

Figure 10.14 shows an example of a defect location check sheet. Kaoru Ishikawa relates how this check sheet was used to eliminate bubbles in laminated automobile windshield glass.[28] The location and form of bubbles were indicated on the check sheet; most of the bubbles occurred on the right side. Upon investigation, workers discovered that the pressure applied in laminating was off balance—the right side was receiving less pressure. The machine was adjusted, and the formation of bubbles was eliminated almost completely.

Histograms A histogram is a basic statistical tool that graphically shows the frequency or number of observations of a particular value or within a specified group.

Figure 10.12 Check Sheet for Data Collection

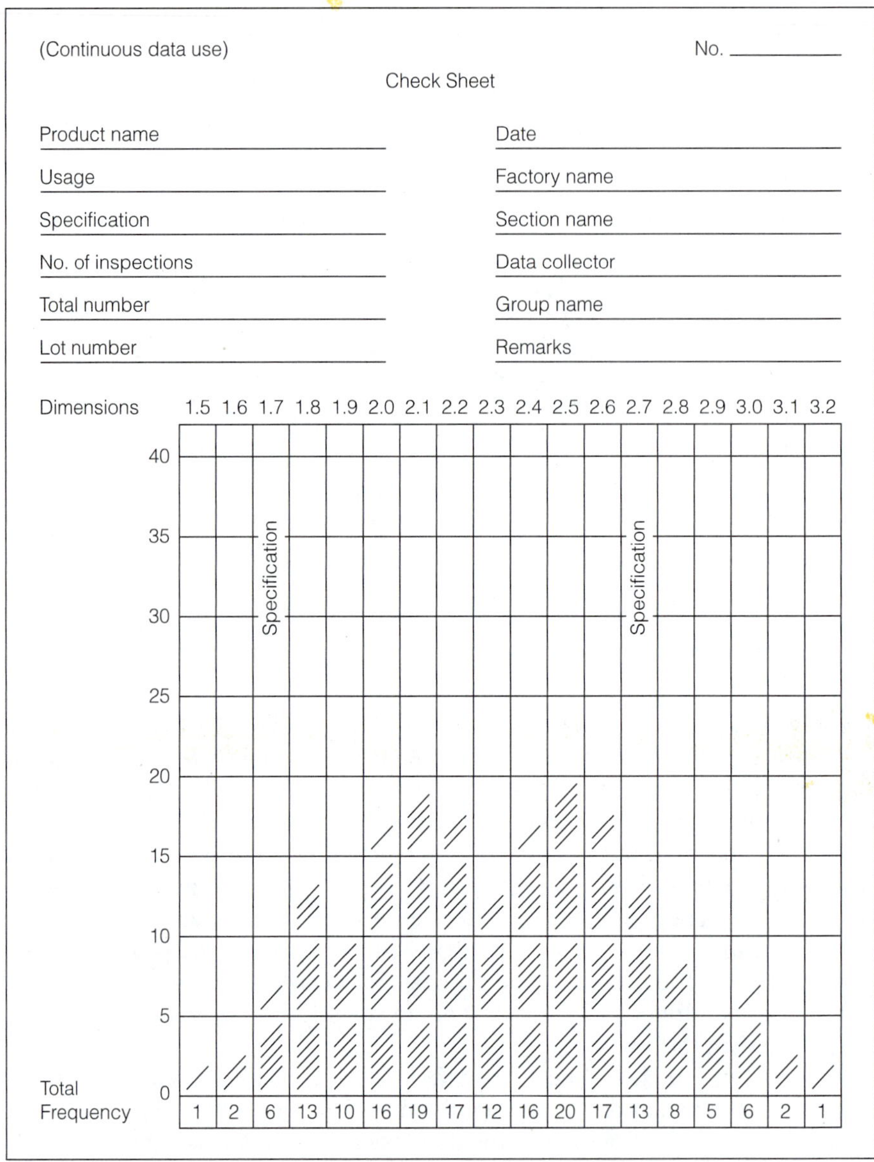
(Continuous data use) No. ______

Check Sheet

Product name ______ Date ______
Usage ______ Factory name ______
Specification ______ Section name ______
No. of inspections ______ Data collector ______
Total number ______ Group name ______
Lot number ______ Remarks ______

Dimensions	1.5	1.6	1.7	1.8	1.9	2.0	2.1	2.2	2.3	2.4	2.5	2.6	2.7	2.8	2.9	3.0	3.1	3.2
Total Frequency	1	2	6	13	10	16	19	17	12	16	20	17	13	8	5	6	2	1

Source: K. Ishikawa, *Guide to Quality Control* (Tokyo: Asian Productivity Organization, 1982), 31.

Histograms provide clues about the characteristics of the parent population from which a sample is taken. Patterns that would be difficult to see in an ordinary table of numbers become apparent. Histograms are extremely useful in process capability analysis to help understand variation in a process, as we saw in Chapter 9. The check sheet in Figure 10.12, for example, was designed to provide the visual appeal of a histogram as the data are tallied. For these data, one can easily determine the proportion of observations that fall outside the specification limits.

Figure 10.13 Defective Item Check Sheet

Check Sheet

Product:

Date:

Factory:

Manufacturing stage: final insp.

Section:

Inspector's name:

Type of defect: scar, incomplete, misshapen

Lot no.

Order no.

Total no. inspected: 2530

Remarks: all items inspected

Type	Check	Subtotal
Surface scars	### ### ### ### ### ### //	32
Cracks	### ### ### ### ///	23
Incomplete	### ### ### ### ### ### ### ### ### ///	48
Misshapen	////	4
Others	### ///	8
	Grand total	115
Total rejects	### ### ### ### ### ### ### ### ### ### ### ### ### ### ### ### ### /	86

Source: K. Ishikawa, *Guide to Quality Control* (Tokyo: Asian Productivity Organization, 1982), 33.

Some caution should be exercised when interpreting histograms. First, the data should be representative of typical process conditions. If a new employee is now operating the equipment, or the equipment, material, or method have changed, then new data should be collected. Second, the sample size should be large enough to provide good conclusions; the larger, the better. Various guidelines exist, but a suggested minimum of at least 50 observations should be drawn. Finally, any conclusions drawn should be confirmed through further study and analysis.

Pareto Diagrams The *Pareto principle* was observed by Joseph Juran in 1950. Juran found that most effects resulted from only a few causes. He named this technique after Vilfredo Pareto (1848–1923), an Italian economist who determined that 85 percent of the wealth in Milan was owned by only 15 percent of the people. For instance, in analyzing costs in a paper mill, Juran found that 61 percent of total quality costs were attributable to one category, "broke," which is paper mill terminology for paper so defective that it is returned for reprocessing. In an analysis of 200 types of field failures of automotive engines, only five accounted for one-third of all failures; the top 25 accounted for two-thirds of the failures. In a textile mill, three of fifteen weavers were found to account for 74 percent of the defective cloth produced. Pareto analysis clearly separates the vital few from the trivial many and provides direction for selecting projects for improvement.

Pareto analysis is often used to analyze data collected in check sheets. A **Pareto distribution** is one in which the characteristics observed are ordered from largest frequency

Figure 10.14 Defect Location Check Sheet

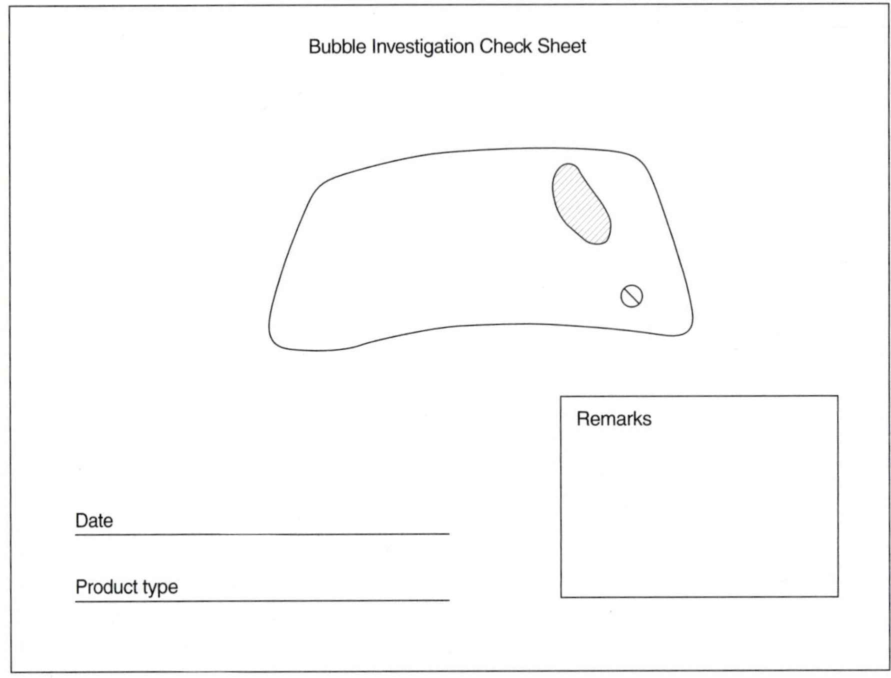

Source: K. Ishikawa, *Guide to Quality Control* (Tokyo: Asian Productivity Organization, 1982), 34.

to smallest. A **Pareto diagram** is a histogram of the data from the largest frequency to the smallest. Often one also draws a cumulative frequency curve on the histogram, as shown in Figure 10.15. Such a visual aid clearly shows the relative magnitude of defects and can be used to identify opportunities for improvement. The most costly or significant problems stand out. Pareto diagrams can also show the results of improvement programs over time. They are less intimidating to employees who are fearful of statistics.

Example 7: Pareto Analysis at Rotor Clip.[29] Rotor Clip Company, Inc., of Somerset, New Jersey, is a major manufacturer of retaining rings and self-tightening hose clamps, and a believer in the use of simple quality improvement tools. An application involved the use of a Pareto diagram to study rising premium freight charges for shipping retaining rings. The study covered three months in order to collect enough data to draw conclusions. The Pareto diagram is shown in Figure 10.16. The results were startling. The most frequent cause of higher freight charges was customer requests. The decision was made to continue the study to identify which customers consistently expedited their shipments and to work closely with them to find ways of reducing costs. The second largest contributor was the lack of available machine time. Once a die was installed in a stamping press, it ran until it produced the maximum number of parts (usually a million) before it was removed for routine maintenance. While this policy resulted in efficient utilization of tooling, it tied up the press and ultimately accounted for rush shipments. The policy was revised to limit die runs to fill orders more efficiently.

Figure 10.15 Pareto Diagram

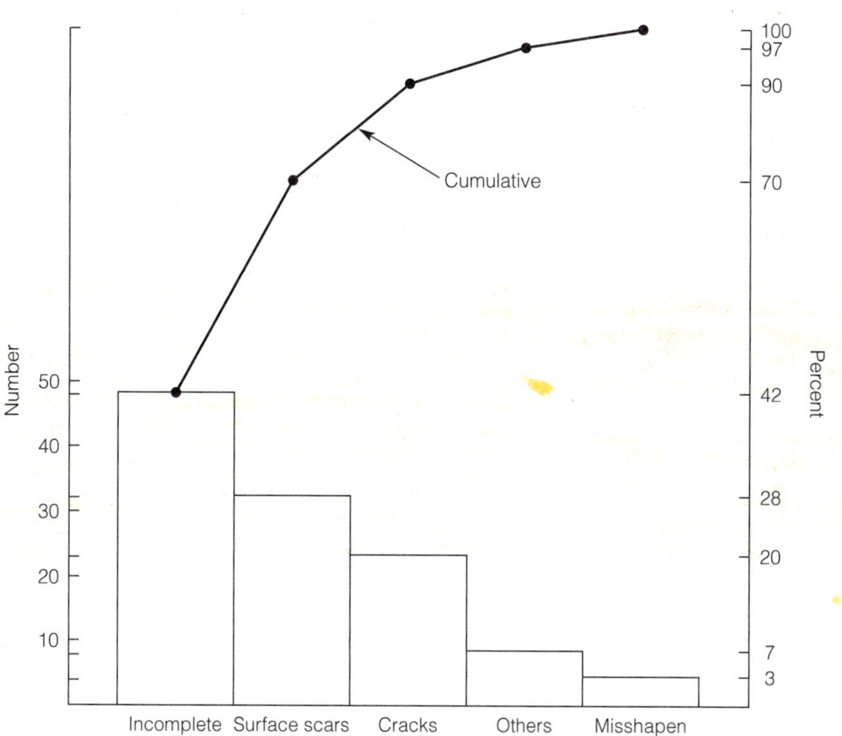

Figure 10.16 Pareto Diagram of Customer Calls

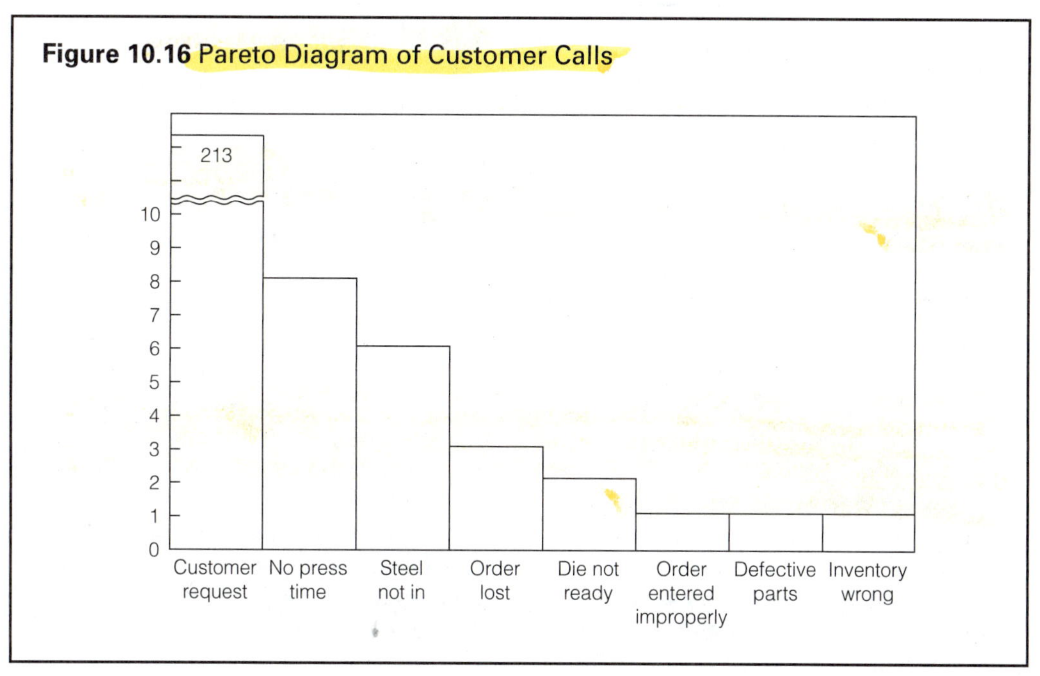

Pareto diagrams are used to progressively analyze specific problems. Figure 10.17 shows one example. At each step, the Pareto diagram stratifies the data to more detailed levels (or it may require additional data collection), eventually isolating the most significant issues.

Cause-and-Effect Diagrams Variation in process output and other quality problems can occur for a variety of reasons, such as materials, machines, methods, people, and measurement. The goal of problem solving is to identify the causes of problems in order to correct them. The cause-and-effect diagram is an important tool in this task; it assists in the generation of ideas for problem causes and, in turn, serves as a basis for solution finding.

The cause-and-effect diagram was introduced in Japan by Kaoru Ishikawa. It is a simple, graphical method for presenting a chain of causes and effects and for sorting out causes and organizing relationships between variables. Because of its structure, it is often called a *fishbone diagram*. The general structure of a cause-and-effect diagram is shown in Figure 10.18. At the end of the horizontal line, a problem is listed. Each branch pointing into the main stem represents a possible cause. Branches pointing to the causes are contributors to those causes. The diagram identifies the most likely causes of a problem so that further data collection and analysis can be carried out.

Cause-and-effect diagrams are constructed in a brainstorming type of atmosphere. Everyone can get involved and feel they are an important part of the problem-solving process. Usually small groups drawn from manufacturing or management work with a trained and experienced facilitator. The facilitator guides attention to discussion of the problem and its causes, not opinions. As a group technique, the cause-and-effect method requires significant interaction between group members. The facilitator who listens carefully to the participants can capture the important ideas. A group can often be more effective by thinking of the problem broadly and considering environmental factors, political factors, employee issues, and even government policies, if appropriate.

Example 8: A Cause-and-Effect Diagram for Hospital Emergency Department Admissions. A major hospital was concerned about the length of time required to get a patient from the emergency department to an inpatient bed. Significant delays appeared to be caused by beds not being available. A quality improvement team tackled this problem by developing a cause-and-effect diagram. They identified four major causes: environmental services, emergency department, medical/surgery unit, and admitting. Figure 10.19 shows the diagram with several potential causes in each category. It served as a basis for further investigations of contributing factors and data analysis to find the root cause of the problem.

Scatter Diagrams Scatter diagrams are the graphical component of regression analysis. Although they do not provide rigorous statistical analysis, they often point to important relationships between variables, such as the percentage of an ingredient in an alloy and the hardness of the alloy. Typically, the variables in question represent possible causes and effects obtained from Ishikawa diagrams. For example, if a manufacturer suspects that the percentage of an ingredient in an alloy is causing quality problems in meeting hardness specifications, an employee group might collect data from samples on the amount of ingredient and hardness and plot the data on a scatter diagram.

Figure 10.17 Use of Pareto Diagrams for Progressive Analysis

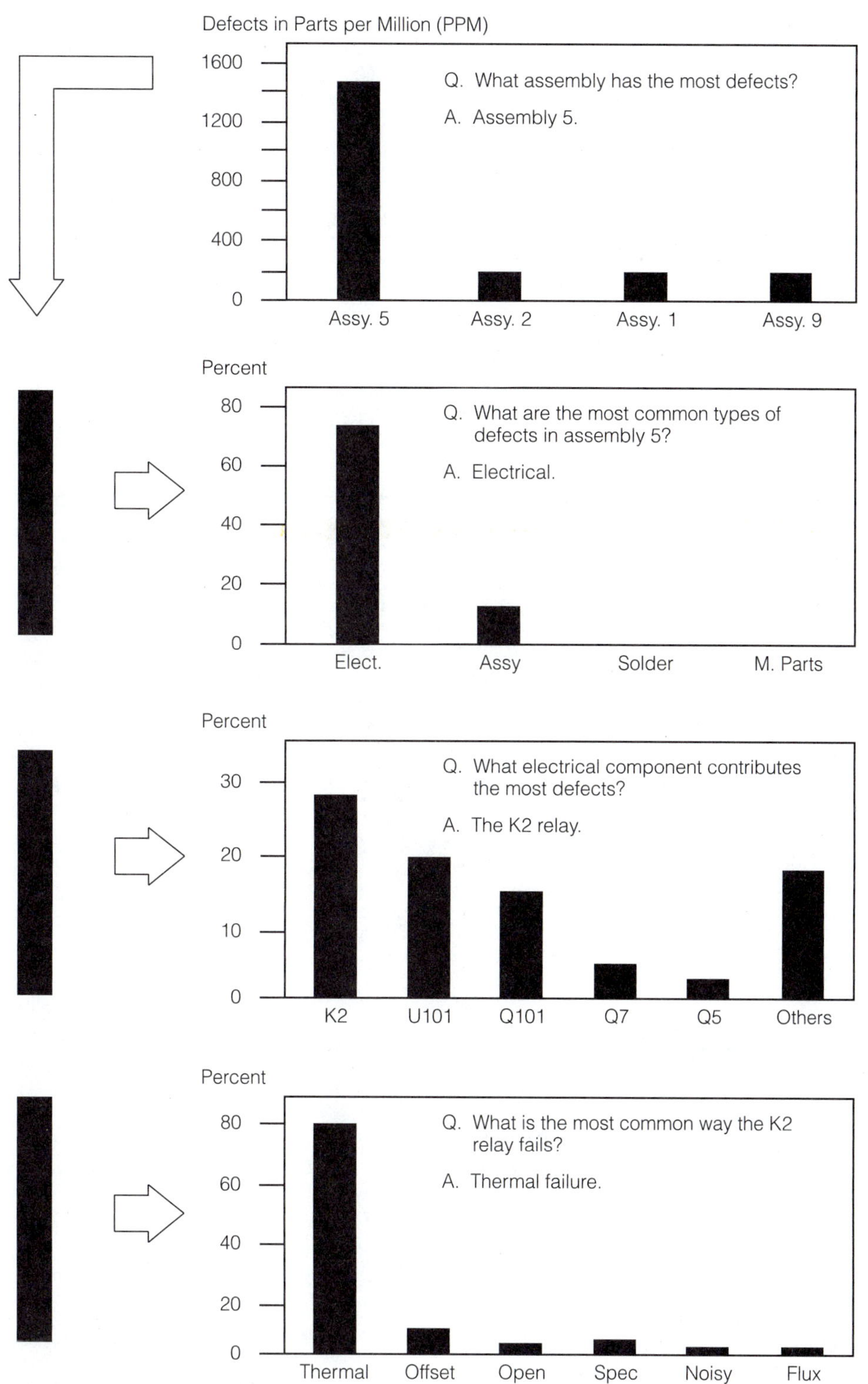

Source: Small Business Guidebook to Quality Management, Office of the Secretary of Defense, Quality Management Office, Washington, D.C.

Figure 10.18 General Structure of Cause-and-Effect Diagram

Cause
Cause
Contributor to cause
Problem
Cause

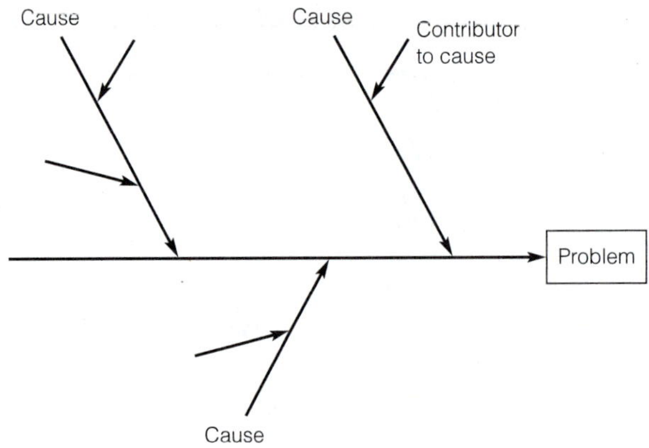

Figure 10.19 Cause-and-Effect Diagram for Hospital Emergency Admission

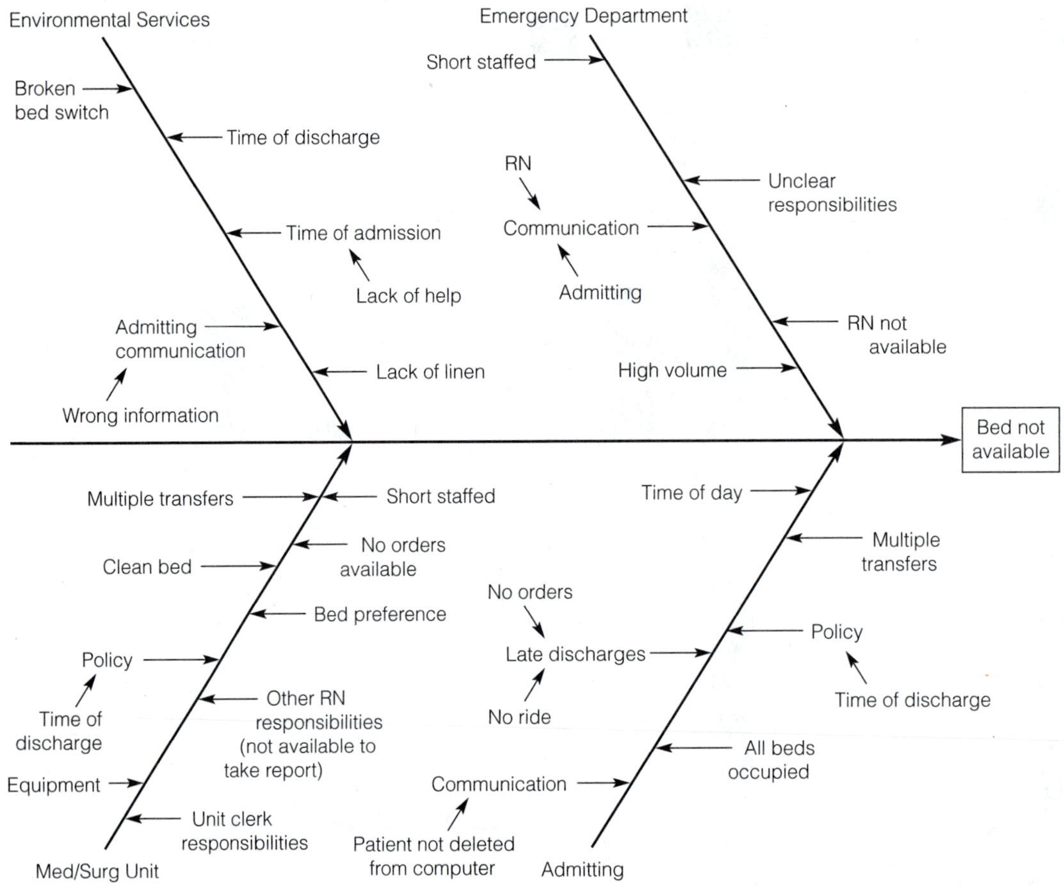

Environmental Services
Broken bed switch
Time of discharge
Time of admission
Lack of help
Admitting communication
Wrong information
Lack of linen
Emergency Department
Short staffed
RN
Communication
Admitting
Unclear responsibilities
RN not available
High volume
Bed not available
Multiple transfers
Short staffed
Clean bed
No orders available
Bed preference
Policy
Time of discharge
Other RN responsibilities (not available to take report)
Equipment
Unit clerk responsibilities
Med/Surg Unit
Time of day
Multiple transfers
No orders
Late discharges
No ride
Policy
Time of discharge
All beds occupied
Communication
Patient not deleted from computer
Admitting

Statistical correlation analysis is used to interpret scatter diagrams. Figure 10.20 shows three types of correlation. If the correlation is positive, an increase in variable x is related to an increase in variable y; if the correlation is negative, an increase in x is related to a decrease in y; and if the correlation is close to zero, the variables have no linear relationship.

Example 9: Understanding the Effect of Advertising Using Scatter Diagrams.[30] At Rotor Clip (see Example 7), the effect of advertising expenditures on the bottom line had been difficult to assess. Management wanted to learn whether the number of advertising dollars spent correlated with the number of new customers gained in a given year. Advertising dollars spent by quarter were plotted against the number of new customers added for the same period for three consecutive years (see Figure 10.21). The positive correlation showed that heavy advertising was related to new customers. The results were fairly consistent from year to year except for the second quarter of the third year, in which an outlier clearly stood out from the rest. Advertising checked the media schedule and discovered that experimental image ads dominated that particular period. This discovery prompted the advertising department to eliminate image ads from its schedule.

Poka-Yoke (Mistake-Proofing)

Human beings tend to make mistakes inadvertently. Errors can arise for a number of reasons:

- Forgetfulness due to lack of concentration
- Misunderstanding because of the lack of familiarity with a process or procedures
- Poor identification associated with lack of proper attention
- Lack of experience
- Absentmindedness
- Delays in judgment when a process is automated
- Equipment malfunctions.

Figure 10.20 Three Types of Correlation

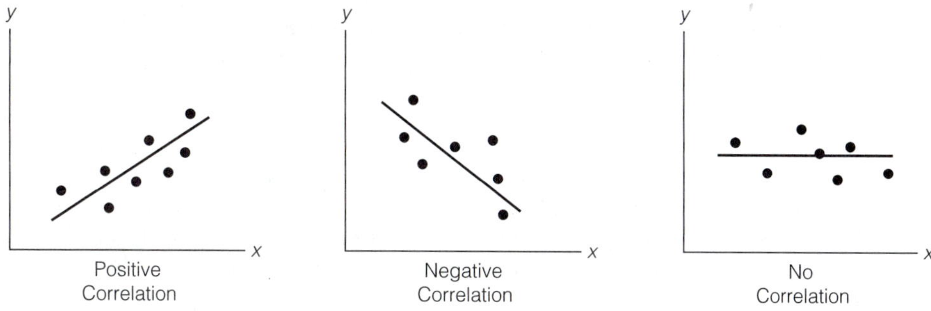

Figure 10.21 Scatter Diagram of New Customers versus Advertising Dollars

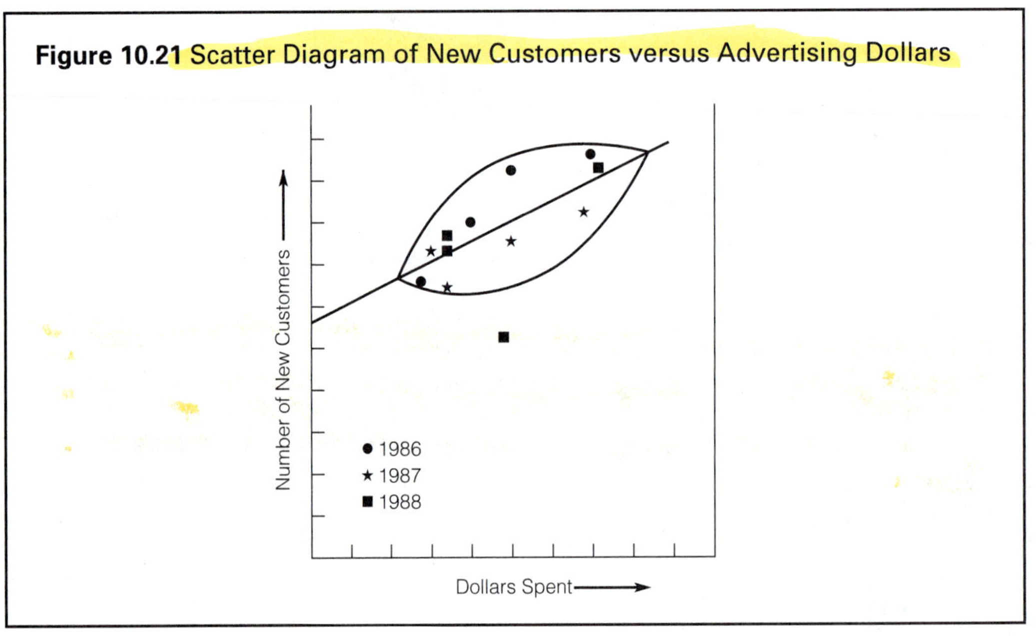

Typical mistakes in production are omitted processing, processing errors, setup errors, missing parts, wrong parts, and adjustment errors. Blaming workers not only discourages them and lowers morale, but does not solve the problem. **Poka-yoke** (POH-kah YOH-kay) is an approach for mistake-proofing processes using automatic devices or methods to avoid simple human or machine error. The poka-yoke concept was developed and refined in the early 1960s by the late Shigeo Shingo, a Japanese manufacturing engineer who developed the Toyota production system.[31]

Poka-yoke is focused on two aspects: prediction, or recognizing that a defect is about to occur and providing a warning, and detection, or recognizing that a defect has occurred and stopping the process. Many applications of poka-yoke are deceptively simple, yet creative. Usually, they are inexpensive to implement. One of Shingo's first poka-yoke devices involved a process at the Yamada Electric plant in which workers assemble a switch having two push buttons supported by two springs.[32] Occasionally, the worker would forget to insert a spring under each button, which led to a costly and embarrassing repair at the customer's facility. In the old method, the worker would take two springs out of a large parts box and then assemble the switch. To prevent this mistake, the worker was instructed first to place two springs in a small dish in front of the parts box, and then assemble the switch. If a spring remained in the dish, the operator knew immediately that an error had occurred. The solution was simple, cheap, and provided immediate feedback to the operator.

Many other examples can be cited:

- Machines have limit switches connected to warning lights that tell the operator when parts are positioned improperly on the machine.
- A device on a drill counts the number of holes drilled in a workpiece; a buzzer sounds if the workpiece is removed before the correct number of holes has been drilled.

- Cassette covers were frequently scratched when the screwdriver slipped out of the screw slot and slid against the plastic covers. The screw design was changed as shown in Figure 10.22 to prevent the screwdriver from slipping.
- A metal roller used to laminate two surfaces bonded with hot melted glue frequently causes defects in the laminate surface when glue stuck to the roller. An investigation showed that if the roller were dampened the glue would not stick. A secondary roller was added to dampen the steel roller during the process, preventing the glue from sticking.
- One production step at Motorola involves putting alphabetic characters on a keyboard, then checking to make sure each key is placed correctly. A group of workers designed a clear template with the letters positioned slightly off center. By holding the template over the keyboard, assemblers can quickly spot mistakes.
- Computer programs display a warning message if a file that has not been saved is to be closed.
- A 3.5-inch diskette is designed so that it cannot be inserted unless the disk is oriented correctly (try it!). These disks are not perfectly square, and the bevelled right corner of the disk allows a stop in the disk drive to be pushed away if it is inserted correctly.
- Power lawn mowers now have a safety bar on the handle that must be engaged in order to start the engine.
- A proxy ballot for an investment fund will not fit into the return envelope unless a small strip is detached. The strip asks the respondent to check if the ballot is signed and dated.

Richard B. Chase and Douglas M. Stewart suggest that the same concepts can be applied to services.[33] The major differences are that service mistake-proofing must account for the customers' activities as well as those of the producer, and fail-safe methods must be set up for interactions conducted directly or by phone, mail, or other technologies, such as ATM. Chase and Stewart classify service poka-yokes by the type of error they are designed to prevent: server errors and customer errors. Server errors result from the task, treatment, or tangibles of the service. Customer errors occur during preparation, the service encounter, or during resolution.

Task errors include doing work incorrectly, work not requested, work in the wrong order, or working too slowly. Some examples of poka-yoke devices for task errors are computer prompts, color-coded cash register keys, measuring tools such as McDonald's french-fry scoop, and signaling devices. Hospitals use trays for surgical instruments that have indentations for each instrument, preventing the surgeon from leaving one of them in the patient.

Figure 10.22 A Poka-Yoke Example of Screw Redesign

Old Design

New Design

Treatment errors arise in the contact between the server and the customer, such as lack of courteous behavior, and failure to acknowledge, listen, or react appropriately to the customer. A bank encourages eye contact by requiring tellers to record the customer's eye color on a checklist as they start the transaction. To promote friendliness at a fast-food restaurant, trainers provide the four specific cues for when to smile: when greeting the customer, when taking the order, when telling about the dessert special, and when giving the customer change. They encourage employees to observe whether the customer smiled back, a natural reinforcer for smiling.

Tangible errors are those in physical elements of the service, such as unclean facilities, dirty uniforms, inappropriate temperature, and document errors. Hotels wrap paper strips around towels to help the housekeeping staff identify clean linen and show which ones should be replaced. Spell-checkers in word-processing software eliminate document misspellings.

Customer errors in preparation include the failure to bring necessary materials to the encounter, to understand their role in the service transaction, and to engage the correct service. Digital Equipment provides a flowchart to specify how to place a service call. By guiding the customers through three yes-or-no questions, the flowchart prompts them to have the necessary information before calling.

Customer errors during an encounter can be due to inattention, misunderstanding, or simply a memory lapse, and include failure to remember steps in the process or to follow instructions. Poka-yoke examples include height bars at amusement rides that indicate rider size requirements, beepers that signal customers to remove cards from ATM machines, and locks on airplane lavatory doors that must be closed to turn on the lights. Some cashiers at restaurants fold back the top edge of credit card receipts, holding together the restaurant's copies while revealing the customer's copy.

Customer errors at the resolution stage of a service encounter include failure to signal service inadequacies, to learn from experience, to adjust expectations, and to execute appropriate post-encounter actions. Hotels might enclose a small gift certificate to encourage guests to provide feedback. Strategically placed tray-return stands and trash receptacles remind customers to return trays in fast-food facilities.

Mistake-proofing a service process requires identifying when and where failures generally occur. Once a failure is identified, the source must be found. The final step is to prevent the mistake from occurring through source inspection, self-inspection, or sequential checks.

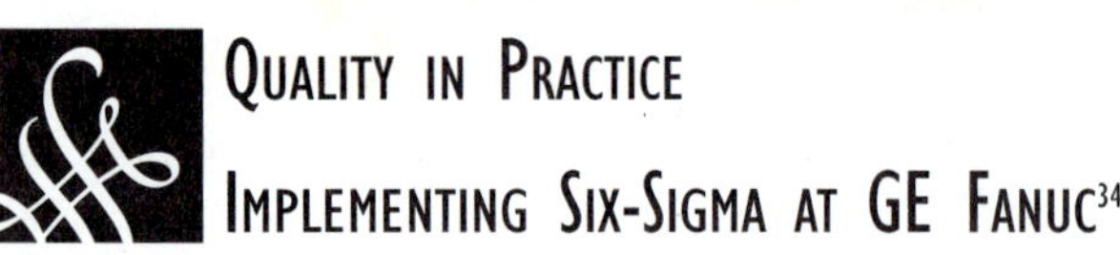

Quality in Practice

Implementing Six-Sigma at GE Fanuc[34]

GE Fanuc Automation in Charlottesville, Virginia, is a joint venture between General Electric and Fanuc Ltd. of Japan, a company that specializes in computer numerical control (CNC) and robotic technology. The division has annual sales of about $700 million from the manufacture and sale of factory automation products, which serve the automotive, food processing and packaging, paper, pharmaceutical, robotics, chemical, and energy markets. The headquarters and main manufacturing plant is at its Charlottesville facility, and includes more than 500,000 square feet of floor space divided among seven buildings on 50 acres of land. GE Fanuc implemented their Six-Sigma program in 1996, shortly after Jack Welch announced the quality initiative for the entire company. The program required a major cultural and attitude change at GE Fanuc and around the world at GE sites, but it has resulted in a stronger, quality-driven company.

The Six-Sigma way of thinking is ingrained in everything the company and its employees do. "From our corporate decisions all the way out to the factory floor, Six Sigma has raised our employees' mindset to look at data instead of emotion," says Sheila O'Donnell-Good, GE Fanuc's Six-Sigma business leader. "If you go out on the floor and visit each line, you're going to see a lot of good data driving decision making. . . . We have ingrained our tool sets within our people, so Six Sigma is a philosophy and an outlook that allows us to examine a broken process, get to a solution, and put controls on in the end. We also see it as a business strategy that helps us gain a competitive edge because it's a differentiator between us and our competitors.

"At one time, GE was a Three Sigma company and the cost of failure was estimated at 15% of sales. But achieving Six-Sigma represents a $4 billion cost-reduction opportunity through reduced cost of failure," says O'Donnell-Good. She adds that the savings are "really greater if you think about it because there have been significant improvements through this program other than the cost-of-failure reduction."

Six-Sigma teams are established to improve or correct processes. Don Splaun, manager of advanced manufacturing technology, headed a Six-Sigma team that wanted to eliminate the Environmental Stress Screen (ESS) test on circuit boards. Splaun felt the test was costly and unnecessary because the ESS was followed by a second and final test. The test was designed to eliminate premature failure in the boards, but required running the boards through a high-temperature oven for seven hours.

Initially, Splaun estimated that GE Fanuc was paying about $12,000 to $18,000 in electricity plus $2,000 to $70,000 a year in maintenance costs per oven and labor costs for loading and unloading the ovens. Concentrating on the field-control product line, team members collected and analyzed data to determine whether the final test was as effective as the ESS. Operators filled out data sheets with information such as board name, date, and whether the board passed or failed the ESS test and subsequent tests. These data helped team members determine whether boards that failed were false failures or dead on arrivals (DOAs), which aren't related to the ESS. Of 7,703 boards that were tested, 311 failed in the first pass. Of these, 284 (91.3%) were false failures and 26 (8.4%) were dead on arrival (DOA). Only 1 board (0.3%) actually failed during the ESS. DOAs were also found bad at the final test, indicating that the final test is an effective screen. Thus, Splaun and his team found only 1 failure out of 7,703 units, which was equivalent to 130 defects per million observations (DPMO), a yield of 99.99%, and a sigma level of 5.15.

This analysis indicated that the final test captured the same failures as the ESS in a more time- and cost-effective manner, so the ESS and the ovens used for the test could be eliminated. To control the improvement, the company began to track the number of failures and defective boards put on the line to ensure that product quality remained high after elimination of ESS. The actual benefits that resulted from the project are summarized here.[35]

Direct labor and materials savings	$ 84,742
Inventory reduction	48,400
Energy/maintenance	16,000
Total hard savings	$149,142
Labor cost avoidance	18,000
Total savings	$167,142

Removing the test from the manufacturing process also reduced the cycle time by a day.

GE Fanuc is only one example of the application of Six-Sigma within General Electric. The impact of Six-Sigma across the GE corporation is clearly described in the company's 1999 Annual Report:[36]

> *In 1999, the Six Sigma initiative was in its fifth year—its fifth trip through the operating system. From a standing start in 1996, with no financial benefit to the Company, it flourished to the point where it produced more than $2 billion in benefits in 1999.*
>
> *Jack Welch, CEO of GE stated: "We want being a product/services customer of GE to be analogous to bringing your car in for a 50,000-mile check and driving out with 100 more horsepower, better gas mileage and lower emissions."*
>
> *In the initial stages of Six Sigma, the company's effort consisted of training*

more than 100,000 people in its science and methodology and focusing thousands of "projects" on improving efficiency and reducing variance in internal operations—from industrial factories to financial services back rooms. From there, the firm's operating system steered the initiative into design engineering to prepare future generations of "Design for Six Sigma" products—and drove it rapidly across the customer-interactive processes of the financial services businesses. Medical Systems used it to open up a commanding technology lead in several diagnostic platforms and achieve dramatic sales increases and customer satisfaction improvements. Every GE product business and financial service activity [now] uses Six Sigma in its product design and fulfillment processes.

Welch concluded: "Today, Six Sigma is focused squarely where it must be—on helping our customers win. A growing proportion of Six Sigma projects now under way are done on customer processes, many on customer premises. The objective is not to deliver flawless products and services that we think the customer wants when we promise them—but rather what customers really want when they want them."

Key Issues for Discussion

1. How was GE's corporate-level vision of Six-Sigma put into practice at the GE Fanuc manufacturing site?
2. What is the difference between direct labor savings and labor cost avoidance savings from a managerial perspective?
3. Verify that the number of defective boards found in the first test gives a dpmo of 130.
4. If you were Splaun and were asked to make a presentation to other team leaders and managers (which, in fact, happened), what conclusions would you draw that might be useful to future teams about the way that the project was conducted?

Quality in Practice

Process Improvement on the Free-Throw Line[37]

Timothy Clark observed that in basketball games, his son Andrew's free-throw percentage averaged between 45 and 50 percent. Andrew's process was simple: Go to the free-throw line, bounce the ball four times, aim, and shoot. To confirm these observations, Andrew shot five sets of 10 free throws with an average of 42 percent, showing little variation among the five sets. Timothy developed a cause-and-effect diagram (Figure 10.23) to identify the principal causes. After analyzing the diagram and observing his son's process, he believed that the main causes were not standing in the same place on the free-throw line every time and having an inconsistent focal point. They developed a new process in which Andrew stood at the center of the line and focused on the middle of the front part of the rim. The new process resulted in a 36 percent improvement in practice (Figure 10.24). Toward the end of the 1994 season, he improved his average to 69 percent in the last three games.

During the 1995 season, Andrew averaged 60 percent. A control chart (Figure 10.25) showed that the process was quite stable. In the summer of 1995, Andrew attended a basketball camp where he was advised to change his shooting technique. This process reduced his shooting percentage during the 1996 season to 50 percent. However, his father helped him to reinstall his old process, and his percentage returned to its former level, also improving his confidence.

Key Issues for Discussion

1. How does this application conform to Deming's PDSA cycle?
2. Design a check sheet that might be useful to collect data for this analysis. How might Pareto diagrams be useful to enhance the analysis?

Figure 10.23 Free-Throwing Cause-and-Effect Diagram

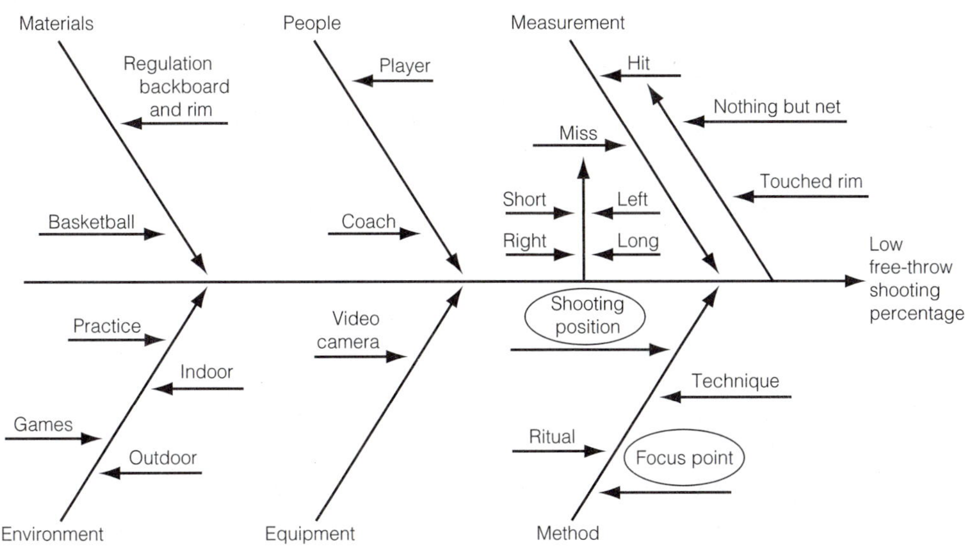

Source: Adapted from Timothy Clark and Andrew Clark, "Continuous Improvement at the Free-Throw Line," *Quality Progress,* October 1997, 78–80. © 1997. American Society for Quality. Reprinted with permission.

Figure 10.24 Free-Throwing Shots Made Before and After Implementing the Improvement (3/17/94–11/23/94)

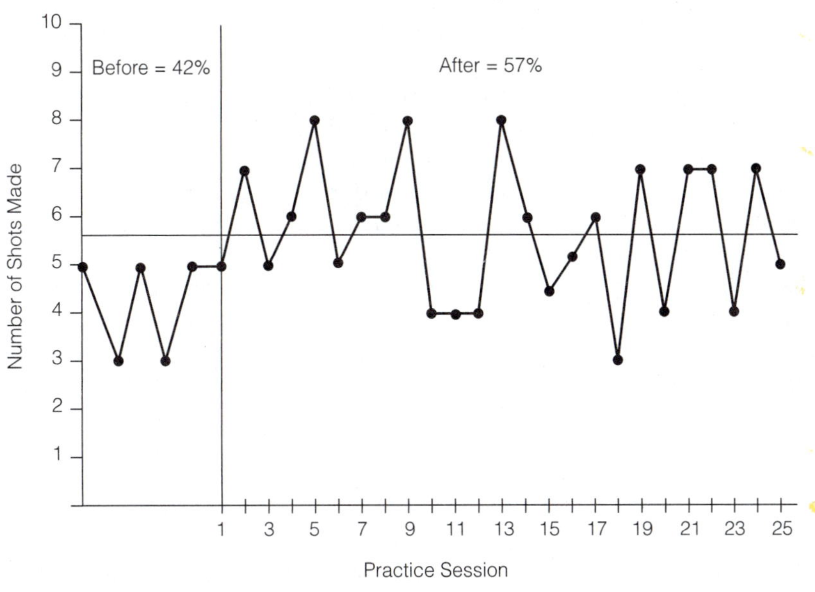

Source: Adapted from Timothy Clark and Andrew Clark, "Continuous Improvement at the Free-Throw Line," *Quality Progress,* October 1997, 78–80. © 1997. American Society for Quality. Reprinted with permission.

Figure 10.25 Determining Whether the Free-Throw Process Is Stable (3/17/94–11/23/94)

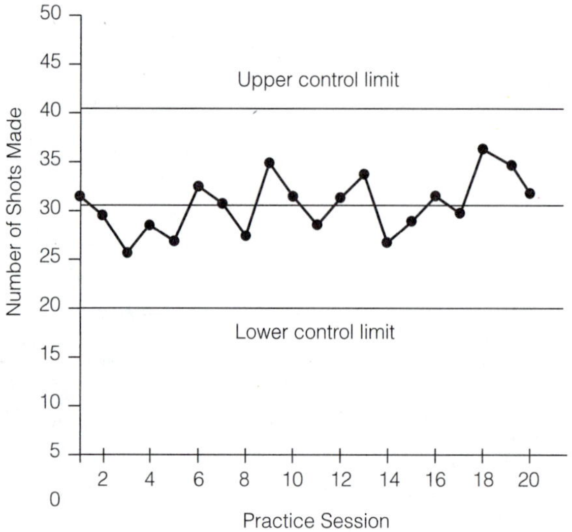

Source: Adapted from Timothy Clark and Andrew Clark, "Continuous Improvement at the Free-Throw Line," *Quality Progress,* October 1997, 78–80. © 1997. American Society for Quality. Reprinted with permission.

Summary of Key Points

- A problem is a deviation between what is actually happening and what should be happening. Problem solving is a highly creative effort at the heart of quality improvement that encompasses problem redefinition and analysis, idea generation, evaluation and selection of ideas, and implementation.
- The Deming cycle is a problem-solving methodology that consists of four elements: plan, do, study, and act. It is based on management by fact and continuous improvement principles and has been the foundation of most Japanese quality improvement efforts.
- Juran's quality improvement approach is based on breakthrough—improvement that takes an organization to unprecedented levels of performance. Juran's breakthrough sequence consists of proof of the need, project identification, organization for breakthrough, the diagnostic journey, the remedial journey, and holding the gains.
- Crosby proposed a 14-step program for quality improvement based more on a managerial/behavioral approach than on the use of analytical tools.
- The creative problem-solving process consists of mess finding, fact finding, problem finding, idea finding, solution finding, and implementation. The emphasis on finding root causes and separating idea generation from evaluation of solutions distinguishes this approach from traditional problem-solving techniques.
- Six-Sigma represents a quality level of at most 3.4 defects per million opportunities. It is a way of measuring quality levels and a comprehensive methodology for breakthrough improvement that relies heavily on statistical and other

analytical tools. Companies such as Motorola, General Electric, and Allied Signal have significant bottom-line results from Six-Sigma initiatives.

- The Seven QC Tools for quality improvement are flowcharts, run charts and control charts, check sheets, histograms, Pareto diagrams, cause-and-effect diagrams, and scatter diagrams. These tools support quality improvement processes and problem-solving efforts.
- Poka-yoke is an approach to mistake-proofing a process by using simple inexpensive devices or procedures to reduce inadvertent errors in performing work. Poka-yokes may be applied to both manufacturing and service delivery processes.

Review Questions

1. What is Kepner and Tregoe's definition of a problem? How does this definition apply to quality issues? Provide some examples.
2. Explain the difference between structured, semistructured, and ill-structured problems. What implications do these classifications have for solving problems?
3. What are the four major components of problem solving? Why is it important to have some type of systematic problem-solving methodology in an organization?
4. What is the Deming cycle? Explain the four steps.
5. What is breakthrough? Describe Juran's breakthrough sequence for quality improvement.
6. Explain Crosby's program for quality improvement. How does it differ from the Deming cycle and Juran's breakthrough sequence?
7. List and explain the six steps of the creative problem-solving (CPS) process.
8. How do the Deming cycle and Juran's breakthrough sequence relate to the creative problem-solving process?
9. Why do messes arise in organizations?
10. Describe the key issues that organizations face in the fact-finding phase of the CPS process.
11. What is a root cause? How does the "5 Why" technique help uncover the root cause?
12. Describe some techniques used to generate ideas.
13. What issues must be addressed in the solution-finding and implementation phases of the CPS process?
14. What is a defect? Explain how to compute defects per million opportunities (dpmo).
15. Explain the theoretical basis for Six-Sigma quality. How does it relate to the process capability index C_p?
16. Describe the Six-Sigma problem-solving approach (DIMAIC). How is it similar to or different from the other problem-solving approaches discussed in this chapter?
17. What are the key principles for effective implementation of Six-Sigma?
18. What are the major types of tools used in Six-Sigma projects?
19. List and explain the original Seven QC Tools. In what phases of the CPS process might each be most useful?
20. What types of questions might one ask to identify opportunities for improvement with a process flowchart?
21. Describe a control chart. How does it differ from a run chart?

22. Describe different types of check sheets that are useful in quality improvement.
23. Explain the difference between a histogram and a Pareto diagram. Do they apply to the same types of data?
24. Describe the structure of a cause-and-effect diagram.
25. How do scatter diagrams assist in finding solutions to quality problems?
26. Why do people make inadvertent mistakes? How does poka-yoke help prevent such mistakes?
27. Describe the types of errors that service poka-yokes are designed to prevent.

Discussion Questions

1. Describe a personal problem you face and how you might use the Deming cycle and the seven QC tools to address it.
2. A flowchart for a fast-food drive-through window is shown in Figure 10.26. Discuss the important quality characteristics inherent in this process and suggest possible improvements.
3. Develop a flowchart of the process you use to study for an exam. How might you improve this process?
4. Figure 10.27 shows the Pepsi-Cola Company's three-step method for customer-valued process improvement. Discuss its differences and similarities to the Deming cycle and Juran's breakthrough sequence.

Figure 10.26 Flowchart for Question 2

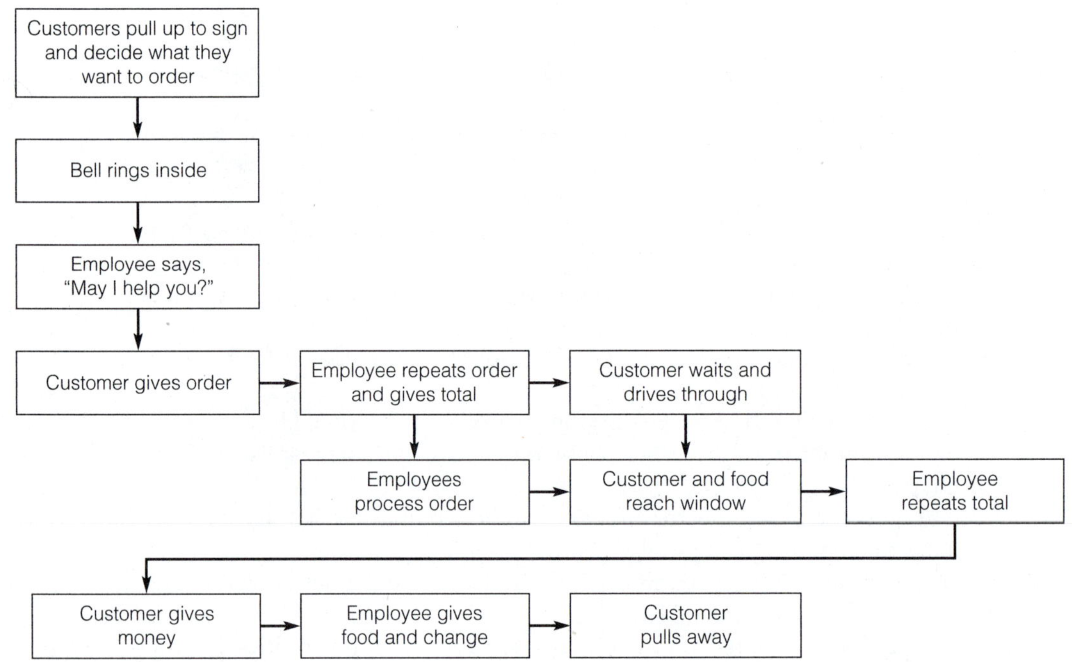

Figure 10.27 Pepsi-Cola Process Improvement Methodology

Steps	Actions
1. Start with the customer	a. Understand and prioritize customer needs b. Establish customer measures and success criteria c. Select a process with most impact on customer needs
2. Understand ourselves and plan improvements	a. Analyze the current process involving the performers in each step b. Design improved process c. Establish process measures
3. Do it	a. Pilot-test improved process b. Implement improved process c. Stabilize process d. Go to Step 1 (continuously improve)

Source: Courtesy of Pepsi-Cola Co. Reprinted with permission of The Forum Corporation.

5. What types of defects might the following organizations measure and improve as part of a Six-Sigma initiative?
   a. A metropolitan bus company
   b. A local department store
   c. An electric power company
   d. Walt Disney World or a regional amusement park such as Paramount or Six Flags
   e. Your college or university
6. Discuss what would be the most appropriate tool to use to attack each of the following quality issues:
   a. A copy machine suffers frequent paper jams, and users are often confused as to how to fix the problem.
   b. The publication team for an engineering department wants to improve the accuracy of their user documentation but is unsure of why documents are not error-free.
   c. An office manager has experienced numerous problems with a laser printer: double-spaced lines, garbled text, lost text, and blank pages. She is trying to figure out which is the most significant problem.
   d. A military agency wants to evaluate the weight of personnel at a certain facility.
   e. A contracting agency wants to investigate why they had so many changes in their contracts. They believe that the number of changes may be related to the dollar value of the original contract or the days between the request for proposal and the contract award.

f. A travel agency is interested in gaining a better understanding of how call volume varies by time of year in order to adjust staffing schedules.

7. A catalog order-filling process for personalized printed products can be described as follows:[38] Telephone orders are taken over a 12-hour period each day. Orders are collected from each person at the end of the day and checked for errors by the supervisor of the phone department, usually the following morning. The supervisor does not send each one-day batch of orders to the data processing department until after 1:00 P.M. In the next step—data processing—orders are invoiced in the one-day batches. Then they are printed and matched back to the original orders. At this point, if the order is from a new customer, it is sent to the person who did the customer verification and setup of new customer accounts. This process must be completed before the order can be invoiced. The next step—order verification and proofreading—occurs after invoicing is completed. The orders, with invoices attached, are given to a person who verifies that all required information is present and correct to permit typesetting. If the verifier has any questions, they are checked by computer or by calling the customer. Finally, the completed orders are sent to the typesetting department of the printshop.
   a. Develop a flowchart for this process.
   b. Discuss opportunities for improving the quality of service in this situation.

8. An independent outplacement service helps unemployed executives find jobs. One of the major activities of the service is preparing resumes. Three word processors work at the service typing resumes and cover letters. They are assigned to individual clients, currently about 120. Turnaround time for typing is expected to be 24 hours. The word-processing operation begins with clients placing work in the assigned word processor's bin. When the word processor picks up the work (in batches), it is logged in using a time clock stamp, and the work is typed and printed. After the batch is completed, the word processor returns the documents to the clients' bins, logs in the time delivered, and picks up new work. A supervisor tries to balance the workload for the three word processors. Lately, many of the clients have been complaining about errors in their documents—misspellings, missing lines, wrong formatting, and so on. The supervisor has told the word processors to be more careful, but the errors still persist.
   a. Develop a cause-and-effect diagram that might clarify the source of errors.
   b. What tools might the supervisor use to study ways to reduce the amount of errors?

9. Rick Hensley owns an automotive dealership. Service is a major part of the operation. Rick and his service team have spent considerable time in analyzing the service process and have developed a flowchart, shown in Figure 10.28, that describes the typical activities in servicing a customer's automobile. Rick wants to ensure that customers receive superior service and are highly satisfied; thus, he wants to establish poka-yokes for any possible failures that may occur. Your assignment is to identify any possible failure in the service process that may be detrimental to customer satisfaction and suggest poka-yokes to eliminate these failures.

10. Figure 10.29 shows a medication administration process in a hospital.[39] The administrative staff of the hospital is concerned about frequent medication errors. By examining this flowchart, discuss possible sources of errors, the types of individuals responsible (e.g., physicians, nurses, pharmacists, other), and poka-yokes that might be used to mitigate these errors.

Figure 10.28 Automobile Service Flowchart

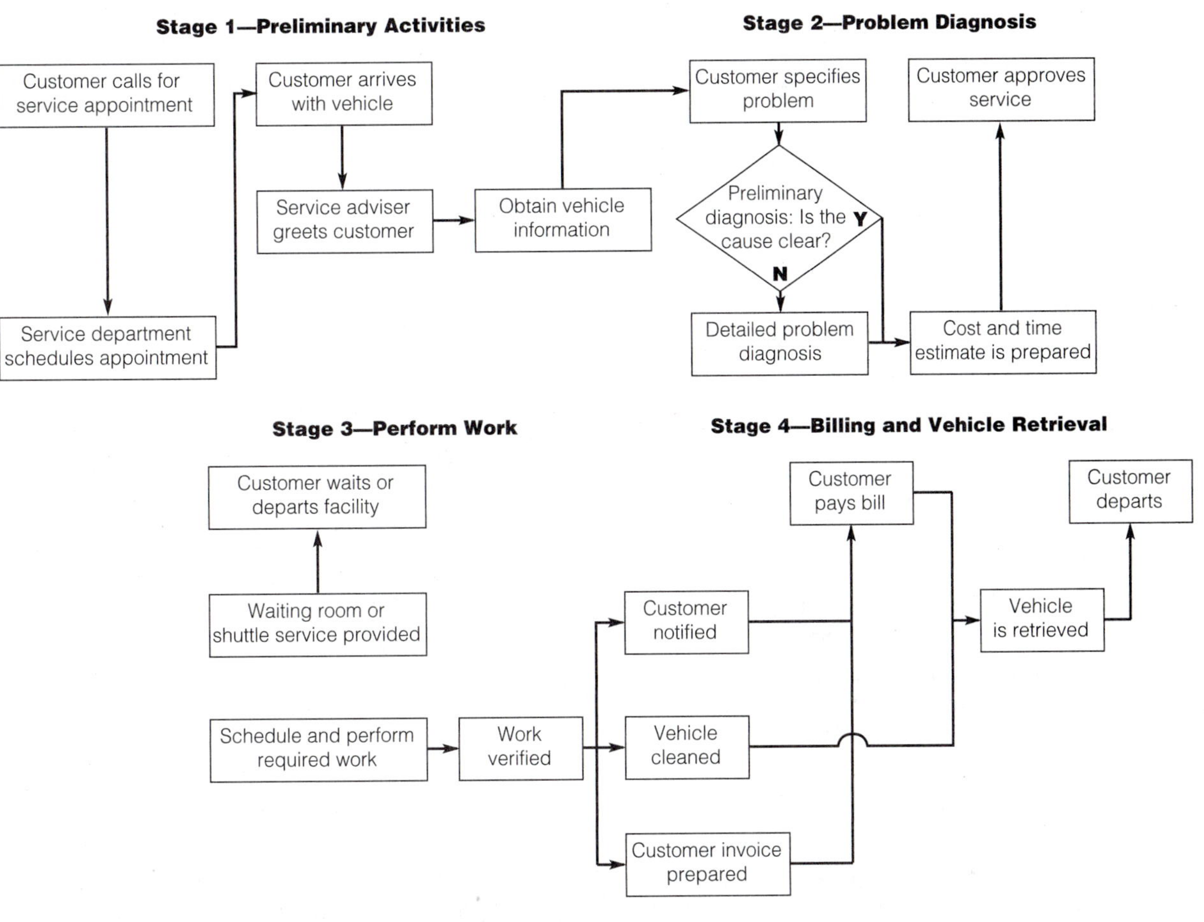

Source: Reprinted from "Make Your Service Fail-Safe," by Richard B. Chase and Douglas M. Stewart, *Sloan Management Review,* 40–41, by permission of the publisher.

11. The following two reports summarizing quality improvement projects performed by employee teams at Siemens Energy and Automation and Lucas Sumitomo Brakes, Inc. were presented in the 1997 Ohio Manufacturers' Association Case Studies in Team Excellence competition. Discuss how each case can be viewed in the context of (a) the Deming cycle, and (b) the creative problem-solving process.

Siemens Energy and Automation: Makin' Waves[40]

The Makin' Waves team is a continuous improvement team from the Siemens facility located in Urbana, Ohio. The Urbana facility is a supplier plant to the Siemens plant in Bellefontaine. It supplies molded plastic, stamping, and plating support to the Bellefontaine plant. The Makin' Waves team is from the Plastics Department. The team has been functioning for four years and has completed many highly successful projects. The team consists of two press

Figure 10.29 Medical Administration Process

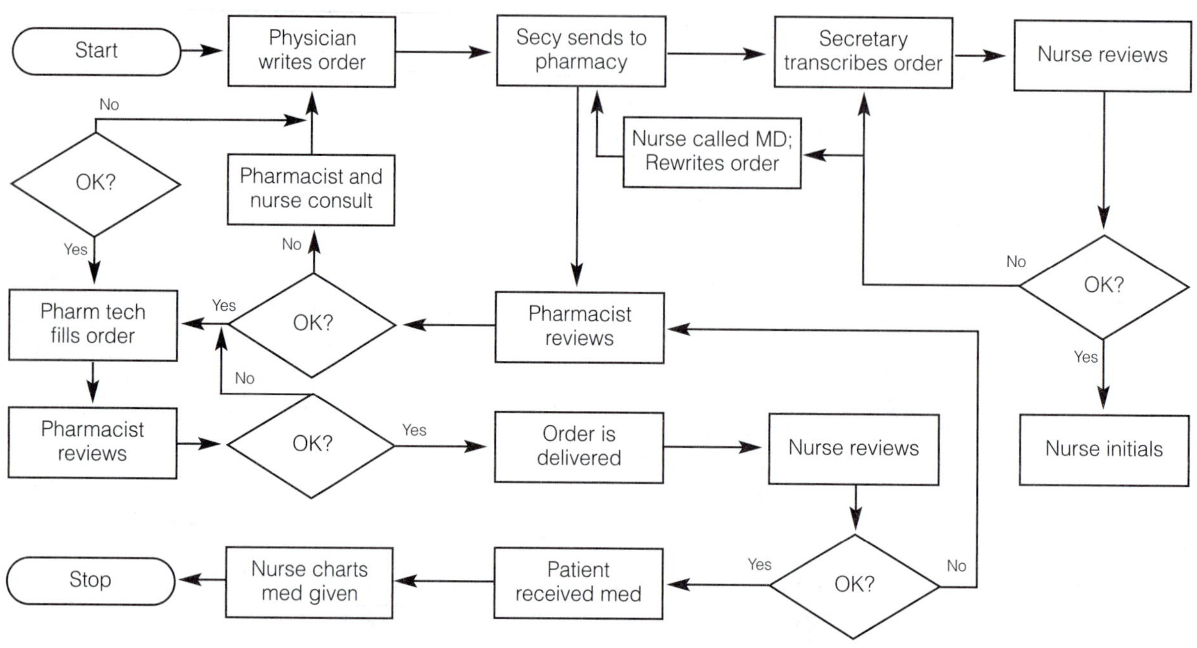

Source: Ellen Williams and Ray Tailey, "The Use of Failure Mode Effect and Criticality Analysis in a Medication Error Subcommittee," *ASQC Health Care Division Newsletter,* Winter 1996, 4.

operators, one product repair person, one janitor, and one quality assurance person, all from the Plastics Department. It also includes a supervisor from the E-Frame circuit breaker line in Bellefontaine who was added at the beginning of this project as a representative of stakeholders and to provide valuable input.

The team began this project by looking into ideas for a project from the Corrective Action System and the Value Improvement Program. The project started out as a way to reduce the negative effect caused by the poor appearance of the E-Frame breaker. Upon investigating the problem the team discovered that the operation causing the negative appearance could be eliminated. The team decided to focus on the elimination of the washing operation station in the production of the E-Frame plastic case.

The E-Frame breaker case is molded in a compression press. The problem begins during the trimming and filing processes that are done after the part is removed from the mold. The plastic contains fiberglass, which becomes a fine dust that adheres to the part. To eliminate the dust, the parts are put through a washing operation. This process uses a conveyor system to carry the parts through a water spray cleaning system. The problem with this process is that the finish comes out looking spotty and with some fiberglass particles still adhering to the parts themselves.

Customers on the E-Frame breaker line had written corrective actions against this procedure because of the poor appearance and the dust still present on the parts. They were experiencing problems with the fiberglass and were having to wear gloves to protect their hands.

Through data collection we realized that this operation takes 6,831 labor-hours a year at a cost of more than $96,000. Yet after the washing process the parts still were not clean and had an unacceptable negative appearance. The team took the top five part numbers and charted the clean versus the dirty parts. The results indicated that 97 percent of the parts did not meet customer standards and that customers were having to add a rework operation to keep the E-Frame line going!

The team set a goal to eliminate the washing operation by May 1997 and replace it with a better process. The team did a fishbone analysis to outline the causes of the problem, and followed up with a root cause analysis to eliminate any causes that did not pertain.

The team brainstormed for possible solutions, producing five possible alternatives to the washing operation:

- Constant air flow
- Shop vacuum
- Deflashing parts
- Ionizer (mouse trap)
- Air hose at press

Each solution was tested and evaluated with the help of both the operators in the Plastics department and customers on the breaker line. As a result of the evaluation, the team found that an air hose at the press was the best solution. Operators were trained to file the parts, and then blow them free of all fiber particles. Not being washed with water would eliminate the spotty appearance of the parts. The team set up direct communication with customers to make sure that this process was eliminating the problem permanently. Their feedback showed satisfaction with the new process, which addressed the problem with the fiberglass and the appearance of the parts. Based on the findings, the team recommended that the washing operation be eliminated and replaced by an air hose at the press. The team also suggested updating job instructions to reflect the new process, and supervisors and operators were trained on the new process at the end of their safety meetings. The scheduler eliminated the washing process from the system. After ongoing favorable feedback from the customers, the plug was pulled on the washing operation altogether.

The goal for the team had been to eliminate the washing operation. Not only did it accomplish this goal, but it realized other benefits attached to the project:

- A $98,000 cost reduction in labor and maintenance
- Additional 136 square feet of valuable floor space freed up
- Improved delivery to customer
- Improved teamwork between customer and supplier
- Open communication with customer
- Elimination of a rework operation
- Improved quality to the consumer
- Improved safety and health of operators

Lucas Sumitomo Brakes, Inc.: Easy Money[41]

Lucas Sumitomo Brakes, Inc., has been manufacturing front disc brake calipers at its plant in Lebanon, Ohio, since 1989. As a result of this manufacturing facility's success and worldwide reputation for quality, an expansion into manufacturing antilock braking system (ABS) components took place in early 1996. This expansion, and the subsequent start-up of production, created new challenges for the company and its employees.

The company's basic philosophy is that employees are involved in the development and growth of the company and are encouraged to focus on the continuous improvement of processes to meet company goals. As soon as the ABS unit began production, some significant problem areas appeared, one of which was the large amount of downtime throughout the factory. In keeping with the company philosophy, the employees in the Maintenance Department formed a continuous improvement team to address the downtime issue, and moved quickly to gather data. For a period of three months, each time a call for maintenance assistance was answered within the factory, team members completed a maintenance response report that indicated the machine associated with the downtime, the duration of the downtime, and the root cause of the production delay. The information from these reports was entered into a computer database, and a Pareto chart was generated to indicate downtime by machine. This chart clarified that machines located on the housing machining lines accounted for the majority of factory downtime; more specifically, two identical high-pressure washing machines were causing approximately 80 percent of the machining line downtime. The team established a goal of reducing downtime associated with the high-pressure washers by 40 percent in the short term, and by 70 percent over the long term.

Using the data collected, the team members brainstormed possible causes for the excessive washer downtime. The results pointed to the following three major recurring problems that, according to the data taken from the maintenance response reports, accounted for approximately 99 percent of the downtime.

- Proximity switch replacement and adjustments
- Repairing or replacing jig clamps or dryer clamps
- High pressure drops within the machine associated with the erosion of O-rings inside the rotary joints

Utilizing more brainstorming sessions, the fishbone diagram technique, and asking the five Whys, the team identified some possible solutions to these recurring problems. As a result, it was able to present specific ideas for improvement to engineering and manufacturing, which enabled these departments to assist in communicating with the machine manufacturer, give the project the support needed to implement the countermeasures identified by the team, and allow for scheduling of machine line downtime to perform trials, which were essential during a time when the machine lines were running production six days a week to meet customers' schedules in a just-in-time system. With this support, the team implemented the following corrective actions related to the problems associated with high-pressure washer downtime:

- The proximity switches and wires were relocated outside the washing machines to eliminate melted switches, and to prevent switches from being destroyed by the high-pressure water blast.
- High-temperature-resistant O-rings and seals were installed in the machines, and air tubing was changed to a larger size to eliminate machine clamping problems.
- A preventive maintenance program was implemented to rebuild rotary joints during scheduled downtime to eliminate unscheduled downtime due to worn O-rings.

Following implementation of these improvements, the team tracked downtime associated with the washing machines for a period of three months, and found that the results exceeded their expectations. A 45 percent decrease in downtime associated with the problems identified by the team was achieved, and average downtime per month was improved from 507 minutes to 276 minutes, saving more than a week of production time each year. Washer downtime associated with the improvements continued to improve as production levels increased.

PROJECTS, ETC.

1. Research several companies to identify the type of problem-solving approach they use in their improvement efforts. Compare and contrast their approaches. Which, if any, of the approaches described in the chapter are they most similar to?
2. Work with your school administrators to identify an important quality-related problem they face. Outline a plan for improvement. If time permits, apply some of the problem-solving tools to collect data, identify the root cause, and generate ideas for solving the problem or improving the situation.
3. Find some current information on Six-Sigma implementation efforts and results. Because many consulting firms now train and consult in this area, you should find quite a bit of information on the Internet.
4. In small teams, develop cause-and-effect diagrams for the following problems:
   - Poor exam grade
   - No job offers
   - Late for work or school
5. Work with teachers at a local high school or grade school to identify some students who are having difficulties in school. Apply quality tools to help find the source of the problems and create an improvement plan.
6. Identify several sources of errors as a student or in your personal life. Develop some poka-yokes that might prevent them.
7. Interview a plant manager or quality professionals at one or more local companies to see whether they have used any poka-yoke approaches to mistake-proof their operations.

PROBLEMS

1. A bank has set a standard that mortgage applications be processed within eight days of filing. If, out of a sample of 1,000 applications, 75 fail to meet this requirement, at what sigma level is this process operating?
2. During one month, 42 preflight inspections were performed on a military aircraft. Twenty-one nonconformances were noted. Each inspection checks 67 items. What sigma level does this correspond to?
3. Over the last year, 965 injections were administered at a clinic. Quality is measured by the proper amount of dosage as well as the correct drug. In two instances, the incorrect amount was given, and in one case, the wrong drug was given. At what sigma level is this process?
4. The *Wall Street Journal* reported on February 15, 2000, that about 750,000 airplane components are manufactured, machined, or assembled for Boeing Co. by workers from the Seattle Lighthouse for the Blind. A Boeing spokeswoman noted that the parts have an "exceptionally low" rejection rate of one per 1,000. At what sigma level is this process operating?

5. The times required for trainees in an electronics course to assemble a component used in a computer were measured. The results are shown in the following table. Construct a histogram to graphically show the data. What recommendations for improvement would you give the course instructor, based on your findings?

Student	Time (minutes)	Student	Time (minutes)
1	15	21	10
2	10	22	11
3	11	23	15
4	13	24	10
5	12	25	9
6	14	26	12
7	17	27	16
8	11	28	15
9	16	29	12
10	9	30	18
11	11	31	16
12	16	32	12
13	11	33	17
14	14	34	12
15	11	35	16
16	12	36	17
17	15	37	15
18	14	38	18
19	18	39	14
20	17	40	16

6. The following data were gathered from a process used to make plastic gears for a computer printer. The gears were designed to be 2.5 ± 0.05 centimeters (cm) in diameter. Construct a histogram based on the data given. What can you observe about the shape of the distribution? What would you recommend to the production manager, based on your analysis?

2.56	2.51	2.50	2.48	2.46
2.49	2.47	2.52	2.53	2.51
2.52	2.54	2.53	2.51	2.51
2.46	2.52	2.53	2.51	2.52
2.48	2.56	2.47	2.43	2.54
2.47	2.49	2.51	2.49	2.51
2.57	2.55	2.52	2.48	2.47
2.54	2.57	2.51	2.56	2.48
2.44	2.52	2.51	2.53	2.51
2.46	2.54	2.50	2.56	2.57
2.54	2.51	2.49	2.50	2.55
2.52	2.50	2.54	2.56	2.57
2.49	2.49	2.52	2.51	2.51
2.49	2.46	2.55	2.43	2.49
2.45	2.50	2.47	2.45	2.50
2.45	2.54	2.54	2.51	2.54
2.52	2.47	2.45	2.53	2.53
2.51	2.56	2.58	2.49	2.51

2.46	2.56	2.50	2.59	2.48
2.51	2.52	2.56	2.45	2.52
2.53	2.52	2.54	2.50	2.48
2.51	2.51	2.55	2.51	2.51
2.50	2.49	2.50	2.47	2.51
2.54	2.51	2.51	2.51	2.49
2.55	2.51	2.50	2.50	2.52

7. The times required to prepare standard-size packages for shipping were measured, and are given in the following table. Construct a scatter diagram for these data. What recommendations for improvement would you give the section leader, based on your findings?

Packer	Time (minutes)	Packer	Time (minutes)
1	12	21	12
2	7	22	13
3	8	23	15
4	10	24	14
5	9	25	16
6	11	26	19
7	14	27	11
8	10	28	18
9	13	29	11
10	6	30	13
11	9	31	18
12	12	32	13
13	9	33	16
14	12	34	13
15	11	35	14
16	10	36	17
17	11	37	16
18	12	38	19
19	16	39	18
20	15	40	16

8. In a manufacturing process, the production rate (parts/hour) was thought to affect the number of defectives found during a subsequent inspection. To test this theory, the production rate was varied and the number of defects were collected for the same batch sizes. The results follow:

Production rate	Number of defectives
10	21
20	16
30	14
40	12
45	13
60	8

Construct a scatter diagram for these data. What conclusions can you reach?

9. Ace Printing Company realized that they were losing customers and orders due to various delays and errors. In order to determine the root cause of the problem,

they decided to track problems that might be contributing to customer dissatisfaction. The following list indicates the problems that they found and their frequencies of occurrence over a six-month period. What technique might you use to graphically show the causes of customer dissatisfaction? What recommendations could you make to reduce errors and increase customer satisfaction?

Error/Delay Cause	Frequency
Customer change delays	15
Lack of press time	178
Design department delays	76
Paper not in stock	85
Lack of proper order information	32
Lost order	9
Press setup delays	205

10. Analysis of customer complaints for a large dot-com apparel house revealed the following:

Billing errors	537
Shipping errors	2,460
Electronic charge errors	650
Long delay	5,372
Delivery error	752

Construct a Pareto diagram for these data. What conclusions would you reach?

11. The number of defects found in 25 samples of 100 machine screws taken on a daily basis from a production line over a five-week period follows. Plot these data on a run chart, computing the average value (center line), but ignoring the control limits. Do you suspect that any special causes are present? Why?

0	5	4	4	3	1	0	0	3	6
0	1	1	7	6	6	15	12	6	3
3	2	2	4	6					

12. A pharmaceutical company that manufactures individual syringes is conducting a process capability study (see Chapter 9). The following data (in columns) represent the lengths of 35 consecutive samples.[42] Plot these data on a run chart. Do the data appear to come from a stable system so that a process capability study may be conducted appropriately?

4.95888	4.95385	4.95941
4.95533	4.96014	4.94539
4.94294	4.95252	4.96238
4.95422	4.96633	4.94337
4.96679	4.96255	4.95550
4.94487	4.95287	4.95482
4.95775	4.93541	4.96230
4.95710	4.94840	4.96175
4.96543	4.96114	4.96016
4.95603	4.93901	4.94626
4.96210	4.95966	4.95904
4.95311	4.93667	

Cases

I. Welz Business Machines[43]

Welz Business Machines sells and services a variety of copiers, computers, and other office equipment. The company receives many calls each day for service, sales, accounting, and other departments. All calls are handled centrally through customer service representatives and routed to other individuals as appropriate. A number of customers complained about long waits when calling for service, prompting a market research study that found that customers became irritated if the call was not answered within five rings. Scott Welz, the company president, authorized the customer service department manager, Tim, to study this problem and find a method to shorten the call waiting time for its customers. Tim met with the service representatives who answered the calls to attempt to determine the reasons for long waiting times. The following conversation ensued:

Tim: *This is a serious problem; how a customer phone inquiry is answered is the first impression the customer has of us. As you know, this company was founded on efficient and friendly service to all our customers. It's obvious why customers have to wait: you're on the phone with another customer. Can you think of any reasons that might keep you on the phone for an unnecessarily long time?*

Robin: *I've noticed that quite often that the party to whom I need to route the call is not present. It takes time to transfer the call and wait to see whether it is answered. If the party is not there, I end up apologizing and transferring the call to another extension.*

Tim: *You're right, Robin. Sales personnel often are out of the office for sales calls, absent on trips to preview new products, or not at their desks for a variety of reasons. What else might cause this problem?*

Ravi: *I get irritated at some customers who spend a great deal of time complaining about a problem that I cannot do anything about except to refer to someone else. Of course, I listen and sympathize with them, but this eats up a lot of time.*

LaMarr: *Some customers call so often that they think we're long lost friends and strike up a personal conversation.*

Tim: *That's not always a bad thing, you realize.*

LaMarr: *Sure, but it delays my answering other calls.*

Nancy: *It's not always the customer's fault. During lunch times, we're not all available to answer the phone.*

Ravi: *Right after we open at 9:00 A.M., we get a rush of calls. I think that many of the delays are caused by these peak periods.*

Robin: *I've notice the same thing between 4 and 5 P.M.*

Tim: *I've had a few comments from department managers that they were routed calls that didn't fall in their areas of responsibility and had to be transferred again.*

Mark: *But that doesn't cause delays at our end.*

Nancy: *That's right, Mark, but I just realized that sometimes I simply don't understand what the customer's problem really is. I spend a lot of time trying to get him or her to explain it better. Often, I have to route it to someone because other calls are waiting.*

Ravi: *Perhaps we need to have more knowledge of our products.*

Tim: *Well, I think we've covered most of the major reasons as to why many customers have to wait. It seems to me that we have four major reasons: the phones are short-staffed, the receiving party is not present, the customer dominates the conversation, and you may not understand the customer's problem. Next, we need to collect some information about these possible causes. I will set up a data collection sheet that you can use to track some of these things. Mark, would you help me on this?*

Assignment:

1. From the conversation between Tim and his staff, draw a cause-and-effect diagram.

2. Over the next two weeks, the staff collected data on the frequency of reasons why some callers had to wait. Their results are summarized in the following table.

Reasons	Total Number
Operators short-staffed	172
Receiving party not present	73
Customer dominates conversation	19
Lack of operator understanding	61
Other reasons	10

Perform a Pareto analysis of the data collected.

3. Discuss some actions the company might take to improve the situation.

II. Readilunch Restaurant

The owner of the Readilunch Restaurant, a downtown, quick service restaurant, was concerned about the loss of several regular customers. She measured the number of empty lunch tables from 11 A.M. until 2 P.M. over a four-week period as shown in Table 10.4. To better understand the reasons for the loss of customers, long lines, and dissatisfied patrons, Carol Read, owner of Readilunch, talked to several regular customers. She found that they liked the food and atmosphere of the restaurant, but felt that were opportunities for improvement based on the lack of capability to quickly handle take-out orders (they had to be phoned in, not faxed), excessive time spent waiting for tables, inefficient service, surly waiters on certain days, and long lines at the cash register. She puzzled over how to sort out possible causes that led to these perceived problems. Carol also decided to design a checksheet to systematically gather data and determine which of these were the most significant problems.

Assignment:

1. Plot the average number of empty tables on a run chart, computing the average value (center line), but ignoring the control limits. What do these data show?
2. Analyze the check sheet data in Table 10.5. What conclusions do you reach?
3. Use one of the seven QC tools to come up with a more detailed explanation of possible causes to explain customer dissatisfaction, based on the reasons described in the case.
4. What do you recommend that Carol do to overcome these problems?

Table 10.4 Vacant Tables During the Readilunch Restaurant Rush Hours

Monday	11:00	11:15	11:30	11:45	12:00	12:15	12:30	12:45	1:00	1:15	1:30	1:45	2:00
Wk. 1	10	8	4	3	0	1	1	2	2	2	5	6	9
Wk. 2	9	5	2	1	1	0	3	2	5	3	4	4	7
Wk. 3	6	3	1	0	2	0	4	4	4	3	6	3	8
Wk. 4	11	7	0	1	0	2	2	1	1	5	3	5	6
Tuesday													
Wk. 1	9	2	1	2	3	2	3	2	3	4	7	3	10
Wk. 2	7	0	0	1	2	1	5	1	2	3	6	6	7
Wk. 3	8	4	0	1	1	0	2	3	4	5	9	2	11
Wk. 4	3	1	2	0	4	1	3	1	5	6	8	4	8
Wednesday													
Wk. 1	9	5	2	1	1	1	3	2	4	3	4	5	7
Wk. 2	4	1	2	1	4	3	3	4	3	7	0	2	2
Wk. 3	11	7	0	2	0	2	2	3	2	5	3	4	6
Wk. 4	10	8	4	3	0	0	1	5	2	2	5	5	9

Table 10.4 Vacant Tables During the Readilunch Restaurant Rush Hours *(continued)*

Thursday													
Wk. 1	10	8	3	0	2	0	5	3	1	2	5	7	12
Wk. 2	6	3	1	2	2	2	4	5	3	3	6	3	8
Wk. 3	6	1	3	2	0	4	7	2	2	3	6	1	4
Wk. 4	11	7	1	0	0	1	1	0	3	2	8	4	6
Friday													
Wk. 1	2	2	4	0	0	0	1	3	4	5	7	3	9
Wk. 2	3	2	2	1	1	1	3	4	2	6	5	2	7
Wk. 3	6	0	1	2	2	0	0	4	0	6	6	4	8
Wk. 4	4	0	0	1	0	1	2	2	3	8	4	5	6

Table 10.5 Check Sheet Data for Customer Concerns During Readilunch Restaurant Rush Hours

Monday	11:00	11:30	12:00	12:30	1:00	1:30	2:00
Take-out problems	2	2	1	4	3	1	2
Long table wait	0	2	4	7	5	4	1
Inefficient service	1	3	6	4	5	8	3
Surly waiters	0	1	2	3	1	3	6
Long lines	0	1	3	5	4	2	1
Tuesday							
Take-out problems	1	1	3	3	3	6	3
Long table wait	3	0	2	5	2	6	7
Inefficient service	2	0	1	2	4	2	1
Surly waiters	1	2	4	3	5	4	3
Long lines	0	1	5	4	6	2	1
Wednesday							
Take-out problems	1	2	1	1	4	3	7
Long table wait	2	2	4	3	3	0	2
Inefficient service	0	0	0	2	2	3	6
Surly waiters	2	4	0	1	2	5	6
Long lines	0	2	6	4	5	6	1
Thursday							
Take-out problems	1	1	2	3	2	5	6
Long table wait	0	1	2	4	3	4	8
Inefficient service	2	3	0	3	4	2	4
Surly waiters	1	1	3	2	3	5	3
Long lines	0	4	5	3	3	2	1
Friday							
Take-out problems	1	4	0	1	4	6	1
Long table wait	2	2	1	3	2	5	7
Inefficient service	2	1	2	2	6	3	4
Surly waiters	1	0	1	2	2	1	2
Long lines	1	3	5	8	6	3	1
Totals by time	26	43	63	82	89	91	87

NOTES

1. C. Hsiang and L. Lee, "Zero Defects: A Quality Costs Approach," *Communications in Statistics-Theory and Methods* 14, no. 11 (1985), 2641–2655.

2. Charles H. Kepner and Benjamin B. Tregoe, *The Rational Manager* (New York: McGraw-Hill, 1965).

3. Adapted from John Flares and Constantine Pavsidis, "Help Your Supplier." Reprinted with permission from *Quality* 23 (September 1984), 42–43; a publication of Hitchcock Publishing, a Capital Cities/ABC, Inc. company.

4. Gerald F. Smith, "Too Many Types of Quality Problems," *Quality Progress*, April 2000, 43–49.

5. A. VanGundy, "Comparing 'Little Known' Creative Problem-Solving Techniques," in *Creativity Week III, 1980 Proceedings* (Greensboro, NC: Center for Creative Leadership, 1981). The reader is also referred to James R. Evans, *Creative Thinking in the Decision and Management Sciences* (Cincinnati, OH: South-Western Publishing Co., 1991), for a thorough treatment of creative problem solving.

6. Gerald Langley, Kevin Nolan, and Thomas Nolan, "The Foundation of Improvement," Sixth Annual International Deming User's Group Conference, Cincinnati, OH (August 1992).

7. Langley et al., see note 6.

8. Ames and W. D. Harwood, "People, Quality, and Process Improvement," Manitoba Division, INCO Limited (undated).

9. Jeremy Main, "Under the Spell of the Quality Gurus," *Fortune*, August 18, 1986, 31.

10. Masaaki Imai, *Kaizen: The Key to Japan's Competitive Success* (New York: McGraw-Hill, 1986), 15.

11. A. F. Osborn, *Applied Imagination*, 3d ed. (New York: Scribner's, 1963); S. J. Parnes, R. B. Noller, and A. M. Biondi, eds., *Guide to Creative Action* (New York: Scribner's, 1977).

12. Russell Ackoff, "Beyond Problem Solving," presented at the Fifth Annual Meeting of the American Institute for Decision Sciences (now the Decision Sciences Institute), Boston (16 November, 1973).

13. "The Tools of Quality Part V: Check Sheets," *Quality Progress* 23, no. 10 (October 1990), 53.

14. "NCR Corporation," in *Profiles in Quality* (Needham Heights, MA: Allyn and Bacon, 1991).

15. Howard H. Bailie, "Organize Your Thinking with a Why-Why Diagram," *Quality Progress* 18, no. 12 (December 1985), 22–24.

16. A. F. Osborn, see note 11.

17. "Origin of Six Sigma: Designing for Performance Excellence," *Quality Digest*, May 2000, 30.

18. Pandu R. Tadikamalla, "The Confusion over Six-Sigma Quality," *Quality Progress* 27, no. 11 (November 1994), 83–85. Reprinted with permission of Pandu R. Tadikamalla and *Quality Progress*.

19. "GE Reports Record Earnings With Six Sigma," *Quality Digest*, December 1999, 14.

20. Rochelle Rucker, "Six Sigma at Citibank," *Quality Digest*, December 1999, 28–32.

21. Ronald D. Snee, "Why Should Statisticians Pay Attention to Six Sigma?" *Quality Progress*, September 1999, 100–103.

22. Adapted from Stanley A. Marash, "Six Sigma: Business Results Through Innovation," ASQ's 54th Annual Quality Congress Proceedings, 2000, 627–630. Reprinted with permission by the American Society for Quality, Inc. (ASQ), 611 E. Wisconsin Ave., Milwaukee, WI 53201.

23. Adapted from Chris Bott, Elizabeth Keim, Sai Kim, and Lisa Palser, "Service Quality Six Sigma Case Studies," ASQ's 54th Annual Congress Proceedings, 2000, 225–231. Reprinted with permission by the American Society for Quality, Inc. (ASQ), 611 E. Wisconsin Ave., Milwaukee, WI 53201.

24. Ronald D. Snee, "Guest Editorial: Impact of Six Sigma on Quality Engineering," *Quality Engineering*, 12, no. 3, 2000, ix–xiv.

25. Jerome A. Blakeslee, Jr., "Implementing the Six Sigma Solution," *Quality Progress*, July 1999, 77–85. © 1999. American Society for Quality. Reprinted with permission. See also Kim M. Henderson and James R. Evans, "Successful Implementation of Six Sigma: Benchmarking General Electric Company," *Benchmarking: An International Journal* (2000), 260–281.

26. A. Blanton Godfrey, "Six Sigma Quality," *Quality Digest*, May 1999, 22.

27. Adapted from Dwight Kirscht and Jennifer M. Tunnell, "Boise Cascade Stakes a Claim on Quality," *Quality Progress* 26, no. 11 (November 1993), 91–96. With permission of Dwight M. Kirscht, Timber and Wood Products Division, Boise Cascade Corporation.

28. Kaoru Ishikawa, *Guide to Quality Control*, 2d rev. ed., edited for clarity (Tokyo: Asian Productivity Organization, 1986). Available from UNIPUB/Quality Resources, One Water Street, White Plains, NY 10601.

29. Adapted from Bruce Rudin, "Simple Tools Solve Complex Problems." Reprinted with permission from *Quality* (April 1990), 50–51; a publication of Hitchcock Publishing, a Capital Cities/ABC, Inc. company.

30. Adapted from Bruce Rudin, see note 29.

31. From *Poka-yoke: Improving Product Quality by Preventing Defects*. Edited by NKS/Factory Magazine, English translation copyright (1988 by Productivity Press, Inc., P.O. Box 3007, Cambridge, MA 02140, 800-394-6868. Reprinted by permission.

32. Harry Robinson, "Using Poka Yoke Techniques for Early Defect Detection," Paper presented at the Sixth International Conference on Software Testing and Analysis and Review (STAR '97).

33. Excerpts reprinted from Richard B. Chase and Douglas M. Stewart, "Make Your Service Fail-Safe," *Sloan Management Review* 35, no. 3 (Spring 1994), 35–44. Copyright © 1994 by the Sloan Management Review Association. All rights reserved.

34. Excerpted and reprinted by permission from an article in *Industrial Maintenance and Plant Operations*, October 2000. Copyright © 2000 Cahners Business Information, from their Web site *http:// www.impomag.com*, and materials supplied by Don Splaun, manager of advanced manufacturing technology at GE Fanuc, Charlottesville, VA.

35. Final figures provided at the end of the project by Don Splaun.

36. Adapted from the GE 1999 Annual Report.

37. Adapted from Timothy Clark and Andrew Clark, "Continuous Improvement on the Free-Throw Line," *Quality Progress*, October 1997, 78–80. © 1997. American Society for Quality. Reprinted with permission.

38. Adapted from Ronald G. Conant, "JIT in a Mail Order Operation Reduces Processing Time from Four Days to Four Hours," *Industrial Engineering* 20, no. 9 (September 1988), 34–37.

39. Ellen Williams and Ray Tailey, "The Use of Failure Mode Effect and Criticality Analysis in a Medication Error Subcommittee," *ASQ Health Care Division Newsletter*, Winter 1996, 4. Used with permission.

40. Courtesy of Siemens Energy and Automation Distribution Products Division.

41. Courtesy of Lucas Sumitomo Brakes, Inc., and "Easy Money" team members Ron Gogan, Darren Brown, Jeff Carroll, Mike Watkins, Denis Muse, Marte Wolfensperzjer, and Sean Miller.

42. Leroy A. Franklin and Samar N. Mukherjee, "An SPC Case Study on Stabilizing Syringe Lengths," *Quality Engineering* 12, no. 1 (1999–2000), 65–71.

43. This problem was developed from a classic example published in "The Quest for Higher Quality: The Deming Prize and Quality Control," by RICOH of America, Inc.

BIBLIOGRAPHY

AT&T Quality Steering Committee. *Batting 1000*. AT&T Bell Laboratories, 1992.

———. *Process Quality Management & Improvement Guidelines*. AT&T Bell Laboratories, 1987.

Box, G. E. P., and S. Bisgaard. "The Scientific Context of Quality Improvement." *Quality Progress* 20, no. 6 (June 1987), 54–61.

Brassard, Michael. *The Memory Jogger Plus+*. Methuen, MA: GOAL/QPC, 1989.

Gitlow, H., S. Gitlow, A. Oppenheim, and R. Oppenheim. *Tools and Methods for the Improvement of Quality*. Homewood, IL: Irwin, 1989.

Godfrey, Blan, "Future Trends: Expansion of Quality Management Concepts, Methods and Tools to All Industries," *Quality Observer* 6, no. 9 (September 1997), 40–43, 46.

Hradesky, John L. *Productivity and Quality Improvement*. New York: McGraw-Hill, 1988.

Tomas, Sam. "Six Sigma: Motorola's Quest for Zero Defects," *APICS, The Performance Advantage* (July 1991), 36–41.

———. "What Is Motorola's Six Sigma Product Quality?" *American Production and Inventory Control Society 1990 Conference Proceedings*. Falls Church, VA: *APICS*, 27–31.

CHAPTER 11

QUALITY CONTROL

OUTLINE

An international study by Landor & Associates, an independent design and image firm, showed conclusively that Coca-Cola is the number one brand in the minds of soft-drink consumers around the world, and affirmed that the company is totally committed to quality. Coca-Cola has stated "Our commitment to quality is something for which we will never lose our taste."[1] However, in early June 1999 quite a few people in Europe did after almost 100 Belgian children fell ill after drinking Coca-Cola. This incident caused the Belgian Health Ministry to require Coke to recall millions of cans of product in Belgium and to cease product distribution. Later, France and the Netherlands also halted distribution of Coke products as the contamination scare spread. It was quickly determined that contaminated carbon dioxide had been used during the carbonation process at the Antwerp bottling facility. According to the official statement from Coca-Cola, "Independent laboratory testing showed that the cause of the off-taste in the bottled products was carbon dioxide. That carbon dioxide was replaced and all bottles with off-taste have been removed from the market. The issue affects the taste of the soft drinks only. . . . The second issue involves an external odor on some canned products. In the case of the Belgian distribution system, a substance used in wood treatment has caused an offensive odor on the outside bottom of the can. Independent analysis determined that the product is safe. The Company, in conjunction with its bottling partner in Belgium, is taking all necessary steps to eliminate this offensive odor."[2] After two weeks, the company was allowed to begin producing and distributing products in the three countries. As if that wasn't enough of a problem, at the end of June, Coca-Cola Beverages Poland found that 1,500 bottles of its Bonaqua water product contained mold. This resulted in 246,000 glass bottles being withdrawn from the market in Poland, and replaced with plastic containers.

Although the Coca-Cola Company acted swiftly to resolve the problems and recover its image and reputation, this case demonstrates the importance of *quality control*. **Control** is the activity of ensuring conformance to requirements and taking corrective action when necessary to correct problems. Quality control is important for two reasons. First, quality control methods are the basis for effective daily management of processes. Second, longer-term improvements cannot be made to a process unless the process is first brought under control.

In this chapter we focus on two key issues: first, the essential elements of an effective quality control system; and second, the importance of maintaining accurate and calibrated measurement equipment and procedures for doing so. Having a good basic quality control system is essential for any company, particularly manufacturing organizations, and is the first step before moving toward more comprehensive quality management frameworks like the Baldrige criteria.

QUALITY CONTROL SYSTEMS

The need for control arises because of the inherent variation in any system or process as discussed in Chapter 9 when we introduced the concepts of common and special causes of variation. Not recognizing when contamination occurs in a bottling process—an example of a special cause of variation—for instance, signifies a lack of control and, as in Coca-Cola's case, can be devastating. Control charts, which will be discussed thoroughly in the next chapter, are an important tool for identifying special causes of variation in a process.

As we noted in Chapter 7, any control system has three components: (1) a standard or goal, (2) a means of measuring accomplishment, and (3) comparison of actual results with the standard, along with feedback to form the basis for corrective action. Measurements supply the information concerning what has actually been accomplished. Workers, supervisors, or managers then assess whether the actual results meet the goals and standards (using statistical methods discussed in Chapter 9). If not, then remedial action must be taken. For example, workers might check the first few parts after a new production setup (called setup verification) to determine whether they conform to specifications. If not, the worker adjusts the setup. Sometimes this process occurs automatically. For instance, in the production of plastic sheet stock, thickness depends on temperature. Sensors monitor the sheet thickness; if it begins to go out of tolerance, the system can adjust the temperature in order to change the thickness.

As one practical example of quality control, golf balls must meet five standards to conform to the Rules of Golf: minimum size, maximum weight, spherical symmetry, maximum initial velocity, and overall distance.[4] Methods for measuring such quality characteristics may be automated or performed manually by the workforce. For instance golf balls are measured for size by trying to drop it through a metal ring—a conforming ball sticks to the ring while a nonconforming ball falls through; digital scales measures weight to one-thousandth of a gram; and initial velocity is measured in a special machine by finding the time it takes a ball struck at 98 mph to break a ballistic screen at the end of a tube exactly 6.28 feet away. As another example, DaimlerChrysler manufactures the PT Cruiser at the company's Toluca Assembly Plant in Mexico. To ensure quality, the Toluca plant verifies parts, processes, fit, and finish every step of the way—from stamping and body to paint and final assembly. The quality control practices include visual management through quality alert systems, which are designed to call immediate attention to abnormal conditions. The system provides visual and audible signals for each station for tooling, production, maintenance, and material flow.[5]

DESIGNING THE QUALITY CONTROL SYSTEM

The basic elements of an effective quality control system include a **quality policy** and procedures for such key activities as specification and design control; process control, inspection, and testing; controlling nonconforming product and corrective action; controlling inspection, measuring, and test equipment; and control of essential records and documentation.

Typically, a quality policy identifies key objectives of products and services such as fitness for use, performance, safety, and dependability. We will illustrate these objectives with the quality policy of the former U.S. Machine Tool Group of Milacron Manufacturing Technologies. Milacron, headquartered in Cincinnati, Ohio, is a global leader in industrial processes, products, and services, including plastics and metal-working technology. It divested its machine tools division 1998. In 1996 its U.S. machine tool manufacturing plants had achieved ISO 9001 registration, joining its Birmingham, England, Machine Tool Group; Plastics Machinery Group located in Ohio, Germany, and Austria; Industrial Products Group, both in the United States and in Europe; and corporate R&D Metrology Services, who had all also achieved ISO 9000 registration.[6] Their quality policy is stated as follows:

> ***Total Quality Leadership is the business philosophy and guiding objective of the Machine Tool Group.*** *Our goal is to satisfy our internal and external customers, clearly define and meet our operating requirements, and continuously improve our operations. The following policies guide us in achieving this goal:*
>
> - ***Customer Satisfaction****—Our Policy is to meet our customers' requirements, and to strive to exceed their expectations by providing prompt and effective communications, services, and timely delivery of reliable, maintainable and durable products and services.*
> - ***Conformance to Requirements****—Our Policy is to clearly define and conform to requirements at each and every step of our work processes.*
> - ***Continuous Improvement****—Our Policy is to actively seek feedback on our performance and continuously work to improve our products, services, and operational processes.*
>
> *The quality management system is fully described in our quality manual, operating procedures, work instructions and related documents, the requirements of which are followed by all employees at all times.*[7]

Management must also identify and provide appropriate resources to achieve the objectives set forth in their quality policy. These resources might include people with special skills, manufacturing equipment, inspection technology, and computer software. Individuals must be given the responsibility to initiate actions to prevent the occurrence of defects and errors, to identify and solve quality-related problems, and to verify the implementation of solutions. The system should also include an audit program to determine whether the activities and results of the quality system comply with plans.

Contract Management, Design Control, and Purchasing

Because the ultimate objective of quality assurance is to provide goods and services that meet customer requirements, the quality system should provide for contract review to ensure that customer requirements are adequately defined and documented and that the company has the capability to meet these requirements. For companies that design products, the quality system should clearly delineate responsibilities for design and development activities, the organizational and technical interfaces between groups, product requirements, and any legal or regulatory requirements. For example, if the sales and marketing or engineering departments work directly with customers in establishing designs, then the process of how this design work is done and communicated should be defined. In addition, processes for design review and for verifying design outputs against input requirements should be defined. In some service organizations, such as retail sales, health care, or insurance, establishing a contract and providing the service occur simultaneously. This process would require appropriate training to ensure that requirements are met.

The purchasing function is critical because designs often require components or materials supplied by other firms. The purchasing function should include processes for evaluating and selecting suppliers on the basis of their ability to meet requirements, appropriate methods for controlling supplier quality, and means of verifying that purchased product conforms to requirements.

Process Control, Inspection, and Testing

Process control begins with understanding how a process works: what material, equipment, and other resources are needed; what steps and activities occur during the process; who makes decisions at various stages in the process and what information is needed to make those decisions; and if things go wrong, what needs to be done to correct the situation. Quality control systems include documented procedures for all key processes; a clear understanding of the appropriate equipment and working environment; methods for monitoring and controlling critical quality characteristics; approval processes for equipment; criteria for workmanship, such as written standards, samples, or illustrations; and maintenance activities. For example, Cincinnati Fiberglass, a small manufacturer of fiberglass parts for trucks, has a control plan for each production process that includes the process name, tool used, standard operating procedure, tolerance, inspection frequency, sample size, person responsible, reporting document, and reaction plan. Of particular importance is the ability to trace all components of a product back to key process equipment and operators and to the original material from which it was made. Process control also includes monitoring the accuracy and variability of equipment, operator knowledge and skills, the accuracy of measurement results and data used, and environmental factors such as time and temperature.

Data for process control generally come from some type of measurement or inspection. Whenever the term inspection is used in the quality vernacular, controversy inevitably arises. An early version of one of Deming's 14 Points was "eliminate mass inspection." What Deming was trying to convey was the need to eliminate quality assurance solely through final inspection, as was common industrial practice at that time. Heavy reliance on inspection proliferated because of the industrial revolution and the division of labor. The task of the inspection department was to seek out defective items in production and remove them prior to shipment.

What is the role of the inspector? Inspectors typically walk around, take some parts back to an inspection area, and check them. By the time the inspector determines that a problem exists, similar parts have probably already made their way downstream in the production process or have been mixed with good parts waiting for transfer to the next operation. In the second case, a "hold for inspection" tag is placed on the parts, which are then moved to an inspection area for 100 percent inspection to separate the good parts from the bad. In both cases, no information is fed back to the production workers to improve the process, and the firm incurs unnecessary expenses. Unfortunately, this scenario is still all too common in many companies.

When Deming revised the 14 Points in 1990, he changed this point to "understand the purpose of inspection." The true purpose of inspection is to provide information to control and improve the process effectively. Thus, inspection activities must be integrated throughout the production process to provide useful information for daily control as well as for long-term improvement.

Inspection and/or testing generally is performed at three major points in the production process: at the receipt of incoming materials, during the manufacturing process, and upon completion of production.

Receiving Inspection If incoming materials are of poor quality, then the final product will certainly be no better. The purpose of receiving inspection is to ensure conformance to requirements before value-adding operations begin. Historically, the quality of incoming materials has been evaluated by the receiving function through reliance on acceptance inspection. The purpose of acceptance inspection is to make decisions on whether to accept or reject a group of items (formally called a *lot*) based on specified quality characteristics. Several different types of acceptance inspection methods are used in industry. The most common are spot checks, 100 percent inspection, and acceptance sampling.

Spot-check procedures select a fixed percentage of a lot for inspection. This amount might typically be 10 percent of the lot, or periodic removal of every tenth (or other specified interval) box of items delivered. The problem with spot checking is its lack of scientific basis. Because spot checking is not based on statistical principles, it does not give an assessment of the risks of making an incorrect decision. In fact, a fixed percentage method gives different levels of risk for different lot sizes. Spot checking is more useful as a quantity-verification tool to reconcile billing invoices than as a decision tool for quality verification.

One hundred percent inspection is essentially a sorting method and theoretically will eliminate all nonconforming items from a lot. Psychologically, 100 percent inspection generates a sense of security and is easy to sell to customers and employees. However, it is usually costly, time consuming, and impractical for large lot sizes or when destructive tests are used. One hundred percent inspection may even give false results, because the monotony and repetition associated with the task can create boredom and fatigue in inspectors. Situations exist where 100 percent inspection is necessary, however. They include inspection of products with critical safety requirements or those with high costs associated with failure.

The third method, which has been used quite extensively since the 1940s, is **acceptance sampling**. With this method, inspectors take a statistically determined random sample and use a decision rule to determine acceptance or rejection of the lot

Figure 11.1 Acceptance Sampling Procedure

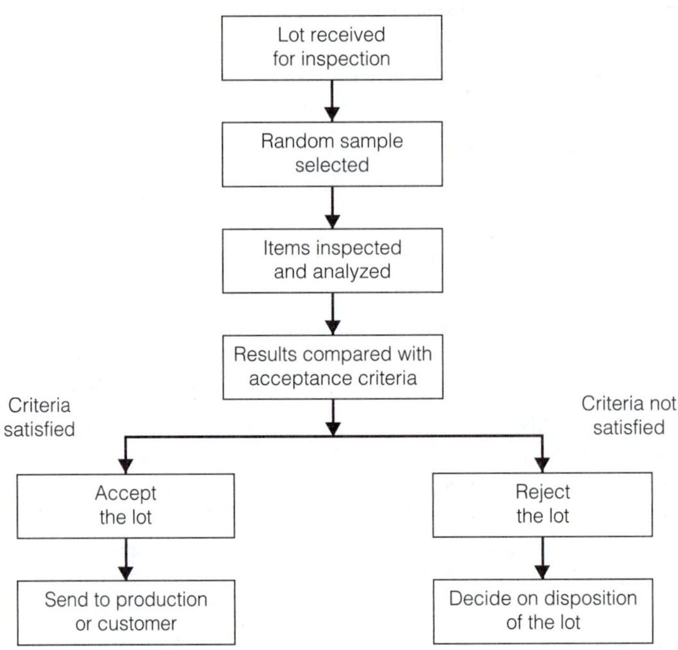

based on the observed number of nonconforming items. The general acceptance sampling procedure is shown in Figure 11.1. A lot is received from a supplier, items from the lot are inspected, and the results are compared with acceptance criteria. If these criteria are satisfied, the lot is accepted and sent to production or shipped to the customers; otherwise, the lot is rejected. Determination of whether to accept or reject a lot is often called **lot sentencing**, which is the true purpose of acceptance sampling. Acceptance sampling is not appropriate for estimating the quality of lots. That is, acceptance sampling techniques should not be used to attempt to determine the percentage of good items or the average value of a quality characteristic. Other statistical sampling schemes are appropriate for those tasks.

Acceptance sampling is based on statistical principles and, therefore, provides an assessment of risk in the decision. In addition, advocates cite other advantages. Acceptance sampling is relatively inexpensive and particularly well suited to destructive testing situations. It takes less time than 100 percent inspection, thus reducing the workload of inspectors. It also requires less handling, decreasing the chance of damage. Finally, acceptance sampling generally does not lead to inspector fatigue as 100 percent inspection does. Acceptance sampling also affords flexibility; the amount of inspection can be varied depending on the quality history. When entire lots are rejected, suppliers feel economic and psychological pressure to improve quality rather than simply to replace the nonconforming items.

Acceptance sampling, which was used extensively during World War II and contributed immensely to improving the quality of manufactured goods to support the war effort, became the foundation of quality control in the decades following the war. Then along came Deming, who condemned acceptance sampling as guaranteeing that "some customers will get defective product." Deming's argument depends on whether or not the supplier's process is a stable system (discussion of this concept can be found in Chapter 9). In a process that is stable, the only changes in the process are caused by random variation—common causes. Because the only difference between "good" lots and "bad" lots is random variation, the likelihood of another bad lot occurring after one bad lot is no greater than of a bad lot occurring after a good one. Thus, nothing can be gained by accepting or rejecting lots that are, in reality, statistically indistinguishable.

If a supplier's process is not stable, however, variation in lots is due to a special cause outside the system of common causes. In this case, sampling inspection can provide an indication of the quality of the lot. Also, the likelihood that a bad lot will occur after one bad lot is much greater than after a good one. Thus, a customer is reasonably motivated to inspect subsequent lots more carefully. Sampling inspection only makes sense when something can be learned from it.

Another argument against acceptance sampling is that it can only detect poor quality, not prevent it. The labor cost and tied-up inventory add no value to the product. It engenders no implicit trust in the supplier's ability to do what it was paid to do—supply conforming items. If a purchased lot is unacceptable, the customer must either (1) keep the lot (often at a reduced price to compensate for lower quality) and remove nonconforming items during production, or (2) return the rejected lot to the supplier. The first alternative is not good and will inevitably result in higher production costs and delays. However, if no other sources of product are available, it may be preferable to a production stoppage. With the second alternative, the supplier must pay the shipping cost, and the rejected lot will be screened, defective units will be reworked or replaced, and the lot will be resubmitted by the supplier. Some argue that the extra burden placed on the supplier often provides good motivation to improve quality. However, the extra costs will eventually be passed on to the customers and ultimately to the consumer—a classic lose-lose situation.

As a temporary measure for quality control, however, acceptance sampling can serve a critical role.[8] In addition, it is useful when testing is destructive or expensive, when 100 percent inspection is not feasible, when a supplier has an excellent quality history but its process capability ratio is sufficiently low to make it risky not to inspect, and when potentially serious product liability risks are involved.[9]

The choice of an acceptance inspection method should be based on the quality history of the supplier. If the quality history is excellent—as evidenced by good statistical control of the supplier's processes and a low process average—no inspection is needed. If, on the other hand, quality history is poor, some form of acceptance sampling should be used. In a TQ environment, however, customers should not have to rely on heavy inspection of purchased items. The burden of supplying high-quality product should rest with the suppliers themselves. Occasional inspection might be used to audit compliance. But suppliers should be expected to provide documentation and statistical evidence that they are meeting required specifications. If supplier documentation is done properly, incoming inspection can be completely eliminated. Japan has been using it for years, and many companies in the West now follow this practice.

In-Process Inspection Because unwanted variation can arise during production, for example, from machines going out of adjustment, worker inattention, or environmental conditions, in-process inspection is needed throughout the production process. When the production operator assumes the role of inspector, the occurrence of special causes of variation can quickly be recognized and immediate adjustments to stabilize the process can be made. Done properly, it can eliminate the need for independent inspection activity.

In designing in-process inspection systems, consideration of three key questions is necessary: *what to inspect, where to inspect*, and *how much to inspect*. Thomas Pyzdek, an experienced consultant in quality, summed up the importance of control: "The objective of SPC [statistical process control] is to control all process factors which cause variation in product features."[10] The critical task is to control the processes that create the products, not the products that result from the processes. The use of flowcharts, cause-and-effect diagrams, and other tools as described in Chapter 9 is the best way to improve understanding of a process and the factors that may cause variation in the output.

Many organizations fall into the trap of trying to inspect every possible quality characteristic. Time and resources preclude this goal. Pyzdek suggests some guidelines for selection:

- The indicator should be closely related to cost or quality.
- The indicator should be easy to measure economically.
- The indicator should show measurable variation.
- The indicator should provide information to help the organization improve quality.

These guidelines and good engineering and managerial judgment will help to define a small, but critical, set of control indicators.

Quality control measurements and indicators fall into one of two categories. An **attribute** is a performance characteristic that is either present or absent in the product or service under consideration. For example, a dimension is either within tolerance or out of tolerance, an order is complete or incomplete, or an invoice can have one, two, three, or any number of errors. Thus, attributes data are discrete and tell whether the characteristic conforms to specifications. Attributes can be measured by visual inspection, such as assessing whether the correct zip code was used in shipping an order; or by comparing a dimension to specifications, such as whether the diameter of a shaft falls within specification limits of 1.60 ± 0.01 inch. Attribute measurements are typically expressed as proportions or rates, for example, the fraction of nonconformances in a group of items, number of defects per unit, or rate of errors per opportunity. The second type of performance characteristic is called a **variable**. Variables data are continuous, such as length or weight. Variables measurements are concerned with the *degree* of conformance to specifications. Thus, rather than determining whether the diameter of a shaft simply meets a specification of 1.60 ± 0.01 inch, a measure of the actual value of the diameter is recorded. Variable measurements are generally expressed with such statistics as averages and standard deviations. Table 11.1 provides additional examples of both attributes and variables measurements.

It is important to understand that collecting attribute data is usually easier than collecting variable data because the assessment can usually be done more quickly by a simple inspection or count, whereas variable data require the use of some type of measuring instrument. In a statistical sense, however, attributes inspection is less efficient than variables inspection. Thus, attributes inspection requires a larger sample than variables inspection to obtain the same amount of statistical information about the quality of the product. This difference can become significant when inspection of each item is time-consuming or expensive. Most quality characteristics in services are attributes, which is perhaps one reason why service organizations have been slow to adopt measurement-based quality management approaches.

The decision of where to perform in-process inspection is fundamentally an economic one. An organization must consider trade-offs between the explicit costs of de-

Table 11.1 Examples of Attributes and Variables Measurements

Attributes

Percentage of accurate invoices
Number of lost parcels
Number of complaints
Mistakes per week
Percentage of shipments on time
Errors per thousand lines of code
Percentage of absenteeism

Variables

Time waiting for service
Hours per week correcting the documents
Time to process travel expense accounts
Days from order receipt to shipment
Cost of engineering changes per month
Time between system crashes
Cost of rush shipments

tection, repair, or replacement and the implicit costs of allowing a nonconformity to continue through the production process. These costs are sometimes difficult or even impossible to quantify. As a result, several rules of thumb influence this decision. The more popular rules include the following:

1. Inspect before all processing operations, such as before every machine or assembly operation.
2. Inspect before relatively high-cost operations or where significant value is added to the product.
3. Inspect before processing operations that may make detection of defectives difficult or costly, such as operations that may mask or obscure faulty attributes, as, for example, painting.
4. Inspect after operations that are likely to generate a high proportion of defectives.
5. Inspect after the finished product is completed.

No one rule is best in all situations. Experience and common sense usually lead to good decisions; however, simulation, economic analysis, and other quantitative tools often are used to evaluate a particular design for inspection activities.

The final question is how much to inspect; that is, whether to inspect all outputs or just a sample. One must first ask: What would be the result of allowing a nonconforming item to continue through production or on to the consumer? If the result might be a safety hazard, costly repairs or correction, or some other intolerable condition, the conclusion would probably be to use 100 percent inspection. If the sampling plan is properly chosen and implemented, lots that are of good quality will be accepted more often than rejected, and lots of poor quality will be rejected more often than accepted. Remember, however, that inherent in sampling is a risk that a small percentage of nonconforming items will be passed.

Unless a product requires destructive testing (in which case, sampling is necessary) or faces critical safety concerns (in which case, 100 percent inspection is warranted), the choice among the three options (no inspection, 100 percent inspection, and sampling) can be addressed on economic grounds. In fact, on a strict economic basis, the choice is to have either no inspection or 100 percent inspection. Deming strongly advocated this viewpoint.

Let C_1 = cost of inspection and removal of a nonconforming item, C_2 = cost of repair if a nonconforming item is allowed to continue to the next point in the production process, and p = the true fraction of nonconforming items in the lot. The expected cost per item for 100 percent inspection is clearly C_1; the expected cost per item for no inspection is pC_2. Setting these equal to each other yields the breakeven value for p.

$$pC_2 = C_1$$

$$p = C_1/C_2$$

Thus, if $p > C_1/C_2$, the best decision is to use 100 percent inspection; if $p < C_1/C_2$, doing nothing at all is more economical.

Example 1: Choosing an Inspection Policy. A radio manufacturer using 100 percent inspection was finding an average of two nonconforming items out of lots of 10,000 purchased electronic components. The estimated cost of inspecting the component is \$0.25, while the cost of replacing a nonconforming component after it has been assembled is about \$25. What is the best economic inspection decision? How much is the manufacturer saving or losing per radio under the current inspection practice if each radio contains 60 of these components?

The error rate is currently 2/10,000 = .0002 nonconformities per unit. Using the definitions of cost given above, C_1 = \$0.25 and C_2 = \$25. Thus, the breakeven point is

$$p = C_1/C_2 = 0.25/25 = .01 \text{ nonconformities per unit.}$$

Because the actual defect rate is much smaller than this breakeven rate, it is not economical to inspect each unit. The expected number of defective components per radio is (.0002)(60) = 0.012. The cost to inspect all components in a radio is \$0.25(60) = \$15. The expected cost of replacing the defective ones would be (0.012)(\$25) = \$0.30 per radio. Therefore, the current inspection policy is incurring a loss of \$15 – 0.30 = \$14.70 per radio.

In practice, however, both the costs C_1 and C_2 and the true fraction nonconforming, p, are difficult to determine accurately. The value of C_1 includes the capital cost of equipment used in the inspection process, depreciation, and residual value, as well as operating costs that include labor, rent, utilities, maintenance, and replacement parts. Included in C_2 are the costs of disassembly and repair, sorting products to find the nonconformances, warranty repair costs if the products are shipped, and cost of lost sales. Many of these costs change over time. In addition, finding p requires sampling inspection in the first place. A useful rule of thumb is that if p is known to be much greater than C_1/C_2, use 100 percent inspection; if p is much less than this ratio, do not inspect. If p is close to C_1/C_2 or is highly variable, use sampling for protection and auditing purposes. In any case, sampling can actually increase costs if performed indiscriminately.

Final Inspection Although final inspection should not be the primary means of quality control, it is still an important part of the overall quality assurance system. Final inspection represents the last point in the manufacturing process at which the producer can verify that the product meets customer requirements, and avoid external failure costs. For many consumer products, final inspection consists of functional testing. For instance, a manufacturer of televisions might do a simple test on every unit to make sure it operates properly. However, the company might not test every aspect of the television, such as picture sharpness or other characteristics. These aspects might already have been evaluated through in-process controls. Computerized test equipment is quite widespread, allowing for 100 percent inspection to be conducted rapidly and cost-effectively.

Visual inspections for aesthetic characteristics such as cosmetic defects often accompany final inspection. Visual inspection is challenging because specifications are subject to interpretation by individual inspectors who may view them in different ways. Considerable training is often required. Inspection error rates of from 10 to 50 percent are not uncommon. As an experiment, ask three people to proofread a lengthy manuscript for typographical errors. Rarely will everyone discover all the errors, much less the same ones. The same is true of complicated industrial inspection tasks, especially those involving detailed microelectronics.

Visual inspection tasks are affected by several factors:

- *Complexity:* The number of defects caught by an inspector decreases with more parts and less orderly arrangement.
- *Defect rate:* When the product defect rate is low, inspectors tend to miss more defects than when the defect rate is higher. (This factor applies to the proofreading task.)
- *Repeated inspections:* Different inspectors will not miss the same defects. Therefore, if the same item is inspected by a number of different inspectors, a higher percentage of total defects will be caught.
- *Inspection rate:* The inspector's performance degrades rapidly as the inspection rate increases.[11]

Understanding these factors leads to several ways to improve inspection:

1. Minimize the number of quality characteristics considered in an inspection task. Five to six different types are approximately the maximum that the human mind can handle well at one time.
2. Minimize disturbing influences and time pressures.
3. Provide clear, detailed instructions for the inspection task.
4. Design the workspace to facilitate the inspection task, and provide good lighting.

The use of poka-yoke devices described in the previous chapter can eliminate the need for human inspection and reduce errors.

Corrective Action and Continual Improvement

Errors in production and service will occur, for example, because of confusing instructions or drawings, unclear verbal directions, inadequate training, poor designs, confusing customer specifications, or incapable equipment. As soon as nonconforming items or errors are identified, they should be brought to the attention of someone who is authorized to take action and prevent further expense. The quality system should clearly state what actions should be taken, and what should be done with any nonconforming items, for example, repair, rework, or scrap. Using techniques for quality improvement described in Chapter 10 to identify the root cause and develop a solution, corrective action should be taken to eliminate or minimize the recurrence of the problem. Permanent changes resulting from corrective actions should be recorded in work instructions, product specifications, or other quality system documentation.

Controlling Inspection, Measuring, and Test Equipment

Measuring quality characteristics generally requires the use of the human senses—seeing, hearing, feeling, tasting, and smelling—and the use of some type of instrument or gauge to measure the magnitude of the characteristic. Before discussing issues of control, we describe common types of measuring instruments used in manufacturing today. These fall into two categories: "low-technology" and "high-technology." Low-technology instruments are primarily manual devices that have been available for many years; high-technology describes those that depend on modern electronics, microprocessors, lasers, or advanced optics.

Gauges can generally be divided into two basic categories: variable gauges and fixed gauges. *Variable gauges*, used for variables inspection, are adjusted to measure each individual part or dimension being inspected. *Fixed gauges*, used for attribute inspection, are preset to a certain dimension; parts being measured are classified according to whether they meet this dimension. The terms *go* and *no-go* are often used to signify this classification. The photographs in Figure 11.2 illustrate many of the types of gauges discussed in this section.

Several types of gauges are used to inspect manufactured dimensions. *Line-graduated gauges* have graduated spacings representing known distances. They include rulers and tapes, various types of inside and outside calipers, and micrometers. Each instrument varies by function and precision of measurement. Rulers and tapes are used to measure length. They are generally accurate to within 1/64 inch. Vernier calipers are used to measure inside and outside diameters and are accurate to within 0.001 inch. Because of their construction, they require a considerable amount of skill to obtain accurate readings. Micrometers are also used to measure outside and inside diameters. Their usual accuracy is 0.001 inch, although some are made to measure in 0.0001-inch graduations. Micrometers have higher reliability in measuring than do vernier calipers.

Dial, digital, and *optical gauges* show variations using a mechanical, electronic, or optical system to obtain dimensional readings. Dial gauges use a mechanical system in which a movable contact touches the part to be measured and translates the dimensional characteristic through a gear train to the dial. The dimension is read from the face of the dial. Digital gauges use electronic systems that translate the movement of the contact touching the part to be measured directly into a number or reading on a dial. This level of sensitivity generally results in greater accuracy than a mechanical dial gauge can provide. Optical gauges use a lens system to magnify the profile of an object and project it onto a screen so that it can be viewed and measured.

Fixed gauges are much simpler than variable gauges. Once they are set for a particular dimension, no adjustment is required as long as wear or deposits on the measuring surfaces are negligible. Types of fixed gauges include plug gauges, ring gauges, snap gauges, and gauge blocks.

Plug gauges measure the inside diameters of bores. They have a machined diameter on one or both ends corresponding to go/no-go dimensions that have been specified for the bore being inspected. If the bore is larger than the no-go dimension of the plug gauge, the part is rejected. If the bore is smaller than the go dimension, it must be rebored to meet the minimum size specification. *Ring gauges* measure outside di-

Figure 11.2 Various Types of Gauges

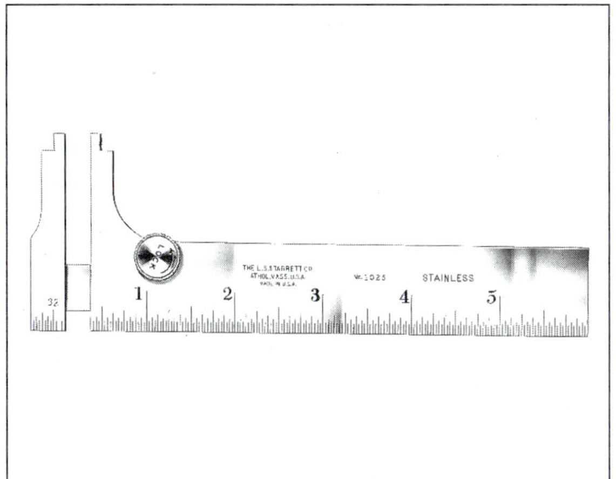

11.2(a) Line-graduated gauge

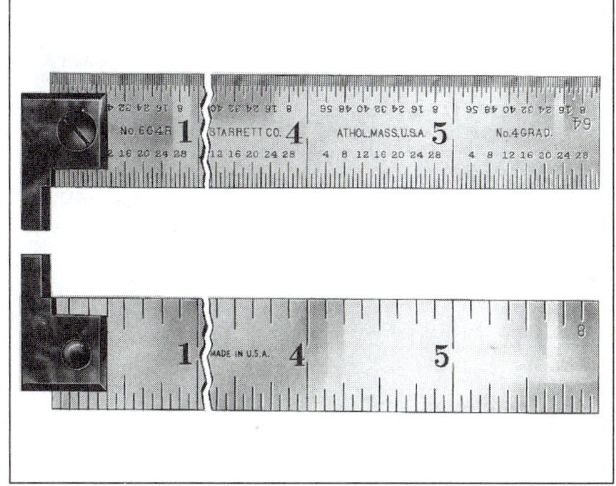

11.2(b) Steel hook rules

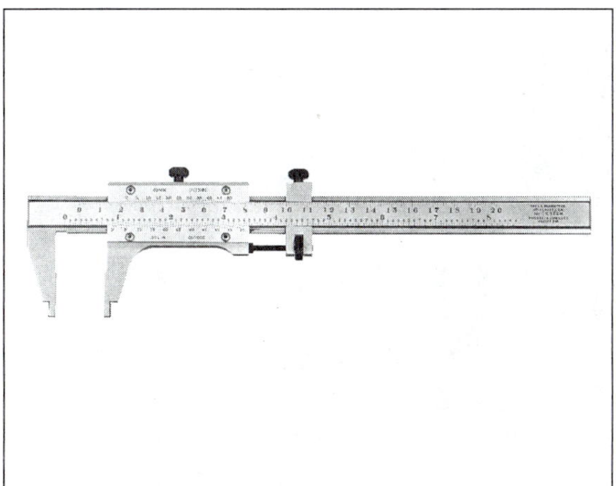

11.2(f) Vernier caliper

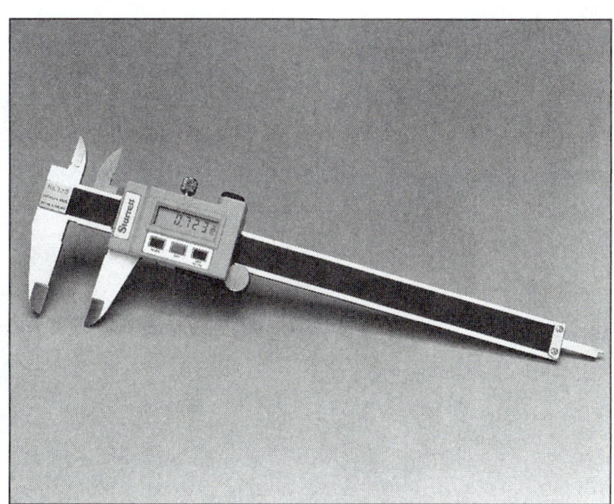

11.2(i) Digital caliper

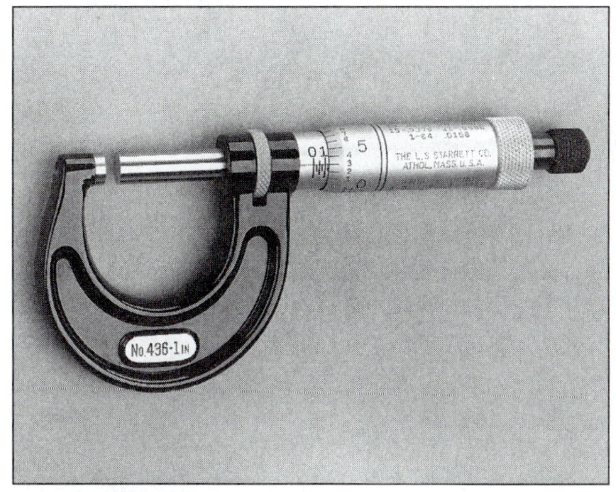

11.2(c) Micrometer

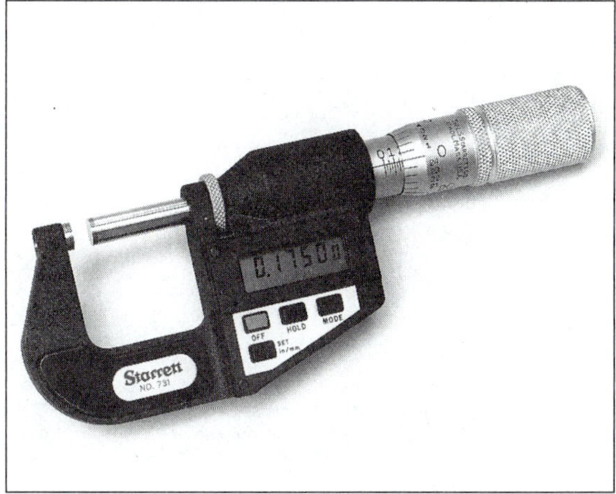

11.2(e) One-inch digital electronic micrometer

(continued)

Figure 11.2 Various Types of Gauges *(continued)*

11.2(g) Dial gauge

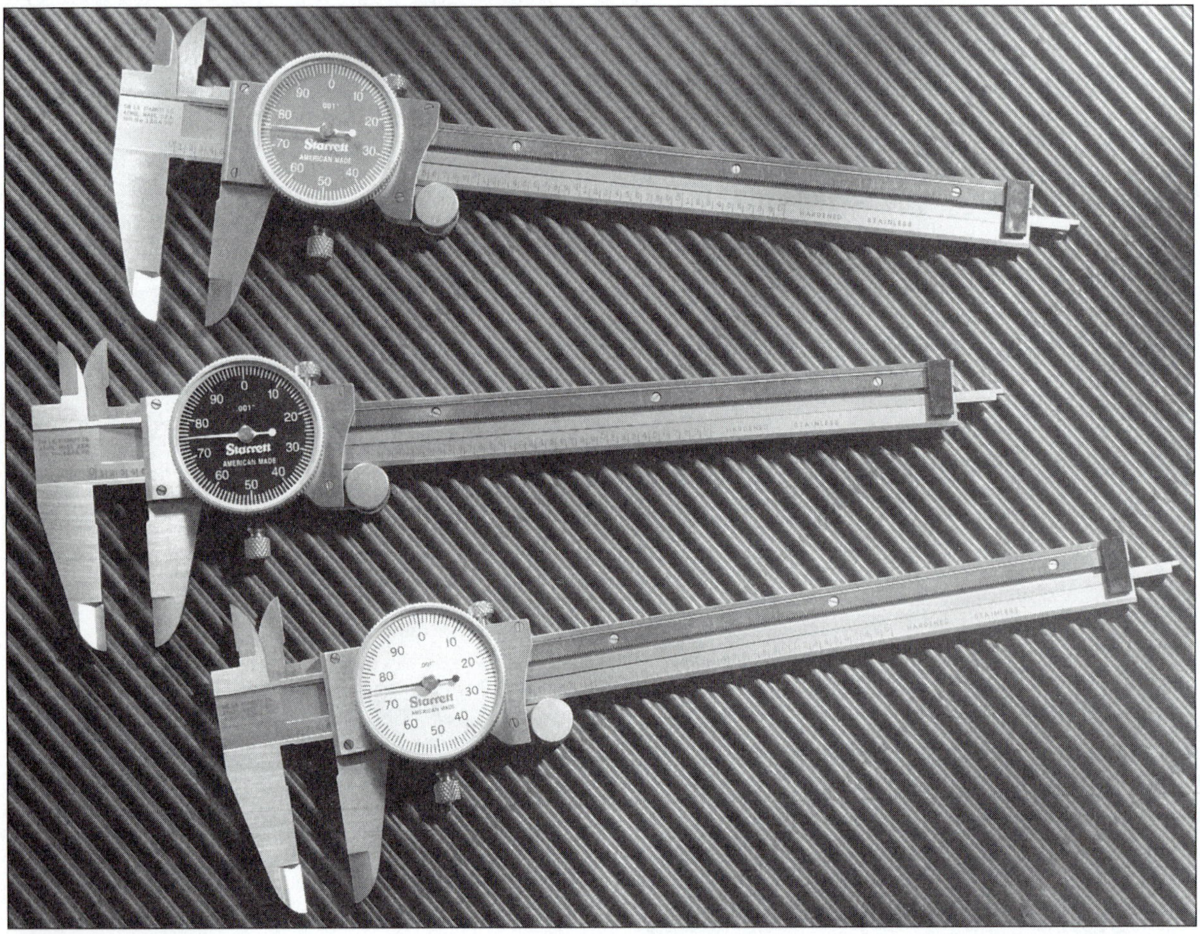

11.2(d) Dial calipers

Source: Courtesy of the L. S. Starrett Company. More information may be found at *http://www.lsstarrett*.com.

ameters of parts using a go/no-go principle. Typically, they are made in pairs, with a no-go ring being used for the minimum dimension and a go ring being used for the maximum size limit. *Snap gauges* are similar to ring gauges in purpose but operate in a different fashion. They measure outside diameters of parts but have an open-ended construction that allows them to snap onto the diameter of the part.

Gauge blocks are special types of fixed gauges designed as a precision measurement standard for calibration of other measuring and inspection instruments. Gauge blocks are constructed of special steel in various lengths and have carefully machined, perfectly parallel, and highly polished measuring end surfaces. When stacked together, various combinations of lengths can be used to produce accurately any desired dimension to the nearest 0.0001 inch.

Computer technology has revolutionized the tasks of inspection and measurement. The potential uses of computers for quality control are being developed at an astonishing rate today. Processes as diverse as manufacturing and microwave cooking can be monitored for correct temperature and timing. Handheld micrometers can run "instant" statistical studies from readings taken on the shop floor. If desired, the readings can be loaded into a desktop personal computer for more thorough analysis. One of the most highly accurate and sophisticated instruments with digital readouts is the *coordinate measuring machine*. This versatile machine, often costing $50,000 to $100,000 or more, combines optics and computer technology in measuring dimensional characteristics that would be impossible to assess using conventional measuring instruments. They can measure three-dimensional forms and use that information in conjunction with computer-aided design systems to provide better knowledge of manufacturing operations. *Photogrammetry* is an indirect, noncontact measurement process by which three-dimensional relationships in real space are determined through mathematical analysis of data extracted from photographic images. This process has applications in the periodic inspection and real-time realignment of assembly tools.

Electro-optical measurements are based on optical digitizing. This technique transforms the optical field of view into an n-dimensional matrix. The system requires an average of one second per measurement with an accuracy of +0.001 inch or less over a 24 × 24-inch measuring range. Fluorescent penetrant inspection involves treating parts with an electrostatic penetrant spray and then inspecting them by blacklight.

Vision systems consist of a camera and video analyzer, a computer, and a display screen. Vision systems can read symbols, identify objects, measure dimensions, and inspect parts for flaws. In quality control applications, vision systems measure, verify, or inspect parts for dimensional tolerances, completeness of assembly, or mechanical defects, and are used in many food processing, pharmaceutical, wood and paper, and plastics manufacturing firms. Costs of vision systems have fallen dramatically in recent years to the $5,000 to $20,000 range, accompanied by vast improvements in performance.

In the automotive industry, vision systems are used in conjunction with robots to weld body seams of varying widths, tighten imprecisely located bolts, and mark identification numbers on engines and transmissions, using lasers. At Mercedes-Benz M Class automotive plant in Alabama, an $800,000 vision system with 38 laser cameras check 84 key measurements preventing out-of-tolerance car bodies from being built, allowing 100 percent inspection to be economically feasible. Other applications include removing blemished vegetables from frozen-food processing lines, examining wood for knots in lumber production, and ensuring that the right drug capsules go into correctly labeled packages.[12]

A Massachusetts company, Cognex, developed a Windows-based image analysis and processing system called Checkpoint that uses point-and-click menus to facilitate its use.[13] A computer can inspect parts on an assembly line in as little as 10 milliseconds and measure each one precisely. The system can be used anywhere along the line to spot missing parts, such as keys from a keyboard, and can also read numbers and characters and store information, which makes it able to "remember" an individual part's movement through the assembly process. This precise information allows the company to track the serial number and manufacturing history in case a critical part fails in use.

Metrology

Gauges and instruments used to measure quality characteristics must provide correct information, which is assured through **metrology**—the science of measurement. Originally, metrology only measured the physical attributes of an object. Today, metrology is defined broadly as the collection of people, equipment, facilities, methods, and procedures used to assure the correctness or adequacy of measurements, and is a vital part of global competitiveness. In testifying before the U.S. Congress, the director of the Office of Standards Services at the National Institute of Standards and Technology noted that efficient national and international trade requires weights and measures organizations that assure uniform and accurate measures used in trade, national or regional measurement standards laboratories, standards development organizations, and accredited and internationally recognized calibration and testing laboratories.[14]

Metrology is vital to quality control because of the emphasis on quality by government agencies, the implications of measurement error on safety and product liability, and the reliance on improved quality control methods such as statistical process control. Cincinnati Milacron's former Machine Tool Group, for example, had an extensive and sophisticated Metrology Services Department that handled more than 30,000 different pieces of measuring and test equipment in an environmentally controlled laboratory.

The need for metrology stems from the fact that every measurement is subject to error. Whenever variation is observed in measurements, some portion is due to measurement system error. Some errors are systematic (called bias); others are random. The size of the errors relative to the measurement value can significantly affect the quality of the data and resulting decisions. The evaluation of data obtained from inspection and measurement is not meaningful unless the measurement instruments are accurate, precise, and reproducible.

Accuracy is defined as the closeness of agreement between an observed value and an accepted reference value or standard. The lack of accuracy reflects a systematic bias in the measurement such as a gauge out of calibration, worn, or used improperly by the operator. Accuracy is measured as the amount of error in a measurement in proportion to the total size of the measurement. One measurement is more accurate than another if it has a smaller relative error.

Precision is defined as the closeness of agreement between randomly selected individual measurements or results. Precision, therefore, relates to the variance of repeated measurements. A measuring instrument with a low variance is more precise than another having a higher variance. Low precision is due to random variation that is built into the instrument, such as friction among its parts. This random variation may be the result of a poor design or lack of maintenance.

A measurement system may be precise but not necessarily accurate at the same time. The relationships between accuracy and precision are summarized in Figure

Example 2: Accuracy and Precision. Suppose that two instruments measure a dimension whose true value is 0.250 inch. Instrument A may read 0.248 inch, while instrument B may read 0.259 inch. The relative error of instrument A is (0.250 – 0.248)/0.250 = 0.8%; the relative error of instrument B is (0.259 – 0.250)/0.250 = 3.6%. Thus, instrument A is said to be more accurate than instrument B.

Now suppose that each instrument measures the dimension three times. Instrument A records values of 0.248, 0.246, and 0.251; instrument B records values of 0.259, 0.258, and 0.259. Instrument B is more precise than instrument A because its values are clustered closer together.

11.3. The figure illustrates four possible frequency distributions of ten repeated measurements of some quality characteristic. In Figure 11.3(a), the average measurement is not close to the true value. Moreover, a wide range of values fall around the average. In this case, the measurement is neither accurate nor precise. In Figure 11.3(b), even though the average measurement is not close to the true value, the range of variation is small. Thus, the measurement is precise but not accurate. In Figures 11.3(c) and (d), the average value is close to the true value—that is, the measurement is

Figure 11.3 Accuracy versus Precision

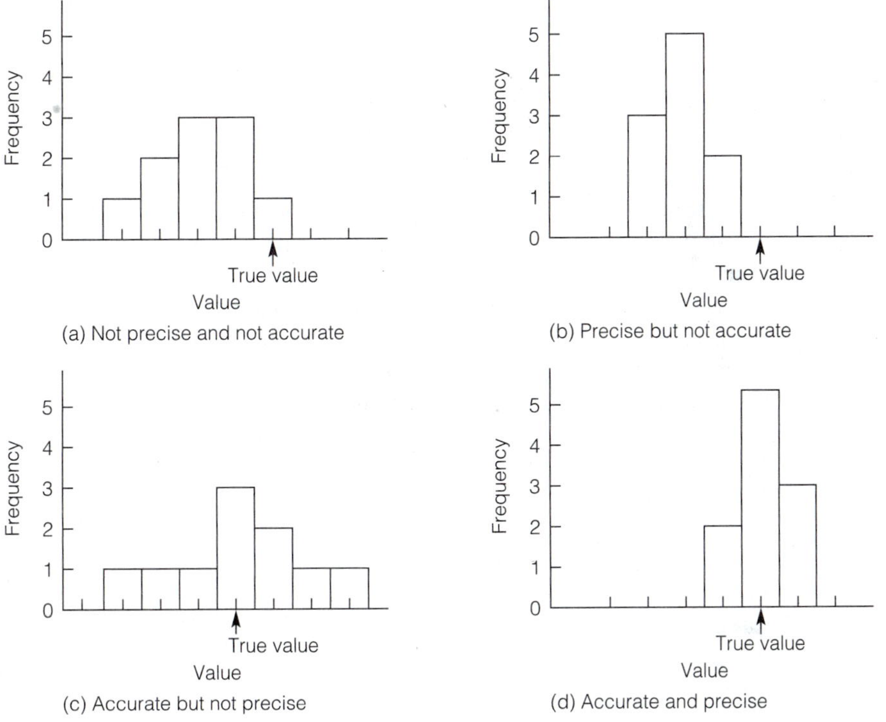

accurate—but in 11.3(c) the distribution is widely dispersed and therefore not precise, while the measurement in 11.3(d) is both accurate and precise. Thus, Figure 11.3 demonstrates the vital nature of properly calibrating and maintaining all instruments used for quality measurements.

When an individual inspector or technician measures the same unit multiple times, the results will usually show some variability. **Repeatability**, or **equipment variation**, is the variation in multiple measurements by an individual using the same instrument. It is a measure of how precise and accurate the equipment is. **Reproducibility**, or **operator variation**, is the variation in the same measuring instrument when it is used by different individuals to measure the same parts, and indicates how robust the measuring process is to the operator and environmental conditions. Causes of poor reproducibility might be poor training of the operators in the use of the instrument or unclear calibrations on the gauge dial. Statistical approaches can be used to quantify and evaluate equipment and operator variation.

The importance of measurement analysis is summed up by the following equation:

$$\sigma^2_{\text{total}} = \sigma^2_{\text{process}} + \sigma^2_{\text{measurement}}$$

It states that the total observed variation in production output (measured by the variance) is the sum of the true process variation, which is what we actually want to measure, plus variation due to measurement. If the measurement variation is high, the observed results will be biased, and process capability measurements, for example, may look worse that they actually are. Thus, an objective of quality control is to reduce measurement error as much as possible.

Measurement System Analysis

The accuracy, repeatability, and reproducibility of any measurement system must be quantified and evaluated. Accuracy can be measured by comparing the observed average of a set of measurements to the true value of a reference standard. Repeatability and reproducibility require a study of variation and can be addressed through statistical analysis. A repeatability and reproducibility study is conducted in the following manner.[15]

1. Select m operators and n parts. Typically at least two operators and 10 parts are chosen. Number the parts so that the numbers are not visible to the operators.
2. Calibrate the measuring instrument (see the next section).
3. Let each operator measure each part in a random order and record the results. Repeat this process for a total of r trials. At least two trials must be used. Let M_{ijk} represent the kth measurement of operator i on part j.
4. Compute the average measurement for each operator:

   $$\bar{x}_i = \left(\sum_j \sum_k M_{ijk}\right) / nr$$

   The difference between the largest and smallest average is

   $$\bar{x}_D = \max_i\{\bar{x}_i\} - \min_i\{\bar{x}_i\}$$

5. Compute the range for each part and each operator:

$$R_{ij} = \max_k\{M_{ijk}\} - \min_k\{M_{ijk}\}$$

These values show the variability of repeated measurements of the same part by the same operator. Next, compute the average range for each operator:

$$\bar{R}_i = \left(\sum_j R_{ij}\right)/n$$

The overall average range is then computed as

$$\bar{\bar{R}} = \left(\sum_i \bar{R}_i\right)/m$$

6. Calculate a "control limit" on the individual ranges R_{ij}:

$$\text{control limit} = D_4\bar{\bar{R}}$$

where D_4 is a constant that depends on the sample size (number of trials, r) and can be found in Appendix B at the end of this book. Any range value beyond this limit might result from some assignable cause, not random error. Possible causes should be investigated and, if found, corrected. The operator should repeat these measurements using the same part. If no assignable cause is found, these values should be discarded and all statistics in step 5 as well as the control limit should be recalculated.

Once these basic calculations are made, an analysis of repeatability and reproducibility can be performed. The repeatability, or equipment variation (EV) is computed as

$$\text{EV} = K_1\bar{\bar{R}}$$

Reproducibility, or operator (or appraisal) variation (AV) is computed as

$$\text{AV} = \sqrt{(K_2\bar{x}_D)^2 - (\text{EV}^2/nr)}$$

The constants K_1 and K_2 depend on the number of trials and number of operators, respectively. Some values of these constants are given in Table 11.2. These constants provide a 99 percent confidence interval on these statistics.

An overall measure of repeatability and reproducibility (R&R) is given by

$$\text{R\&R} = \sqrt{(\text{EV})^2 + (\text{AV})^2}$$

Repeatability and reproducibility are often expressed as a percentage of the tolerance of the quality characteristic being measured. The American Society for Quality suggests the following guidelines for evaluating these measures of repeatability and reproducibility:

Table 11.2 Values of K_1 and K_2

Number of Trials	**2**	**3**	**4**	**5**
K_1	4.56	3.05	2.50	2.21
Number of Operators	**2**	**3**	**4**	**5**
K_2	3.65	2.70	2.30	2.08

Example 3: A Gauge Repeatability and Reproducibility Study. The gauge used to measure the thickness of a gasket having a specification of 0.50 to 1.0 mm is to be evaluated. Ten parts have been selected for measurement by three operators. Each part is measured twice with the results as shown in the spreadsheet in Figure 11.4. (Slight rounding differences from manual calculations may be evident.)

The average measurement for each operator, $\bar{x}_i$, is

$$\bar{x}_1 = 0.830 \qquad \bar{x}_2 = 0.774 \qquad \bar{x}_3 = 0.829$$

Thus, $\bar{x}_D = 0.830 - 0.774 = 0.056$

The average range for each operator is

$$\bar{R}_1 = 0.037 \qquad \bar{R}_2 = 0.034 \qquad \bar{R}_3 = 0.017$$

The overall average range is $\bar{\bar{R}} = (0.037 + 0.034 + 0.017)/3 = 0.0293$. From Appendix B at the end of the book, $D_4 = 3.267$ since the two trials were conducted. Hence the control limit is (3.267) (0.0293) = 0.096. Because all range values fall below this limit, no assignable causes of variation are suspected. Compute the repeatability and reproducibility measures:

$$\text{EV} = (4.56)(0.0293) = 0.134$$

$$\text{AV} = \sqrt{[(0.056)(2.70)]^2 - (0.134)^2/(10)(2)} = 0.147$$

$$\text{R\&R} = \sqrt{(0.134)^2 + (0.147)^2} = 0.199$$

Since the tolerance of the gasket is 1.00 – 0.50 = 0.50, these measures expressed as a percent of tolerance are:

Equipment variation = 100(0.134)/0.50 = 26.8%

Operator variation = 100(0.147)/0.50 = 29.4%

Total *R&R* variation = 100(0.199)/0.50 = 39.8%

While individually, the equipment and operator variation may be acceptable, their combined effect is not. Efforts should be made to reduce the variation to an acceptable level.

Figure 11.4 Spreadsheet for Repeatability and Reproducibility Analysis (R&R.XLS)

	A	B	C	D	E	F	G	H	I	J	K	L	M	N
1	**Gauge Repeatability and Reproducibility**													
2	This spreadsheet is designed for up to three operators, three trials, and ten samples. Enter data ONLY in yellow shaded cells.													
3														
4	**Number of operators**			3		**Upper specification limit**				1				
5	**Number of trials**			2		**Lower specification limit**				0.5				
6	**Number of samples**			10										
7														
8	**Data**	**Operator 1**				**Operator 2**				**Operator 3**				
9		**Trial**				**Trial**				**Trial**				
10	**Sample #**	**1**	**2**	**3**	**Range**	**1**	**2**	**3**	**Range**	**1**	**2**	**3**	**Range**	
11	**1**	0.630	0.590		0.040	0.560	0.560		0.000	0.510	0.540		0.030	
12	**2**	1.000	1.000		0.000	1.040	0.960		0.080	1.050	1.010		0.040	
13	**3**	0.830	0.770		0.060	0.800	0.760		0.040	0.810	0.810		0.000	
14	**4**	0.860	0.940		0.080	0.820	0.780		0.040	0.810	0.810		0.000	
15	**5**	0.590	0.510		0.080	0.430	0.430		0.000	0.460	0.490		0.030	
16	**6**	0.980	0.980		0.000	1.000	1.040		0.040	1.040	1.000		0.040	
17	**7**	0.960	0.960		0.000	0.940	0.900		0.040	0.950	0.950		0.000	
18	**8**	0.860	0.830		0.030	0.720	0.740		0.020	0.810	0.810		0.000	
19	**9**	0.970	0.970		0.000	0.980	0.940		0.040	1.030	1.030		0.000	
20	**10**	0.640	0.720		0.080	0.560	0.520		0.040	0.840	0.810		0.030	
21	**Range average**				0.037				0.034				0.017	
22	**Sample average**				0.830				0.774				0.829	
23														
24												**Tolerance analysis**		
25	**Average range**	0.029		**Repeatability (EV)**						0.134		26.75%		
26	**X-bar range**	0.056		**Reproducibility (AV)**						0.147		29.37%		
27				**Repeatability and Reproducibility (R&R)**						0.199		39.73%		
28				**Control limit for individual ranges**						0.096				
29				Note: any ranges beyond this limit may be the result										
30				of assignable causes. Identify and correct. Discard										
31				values and recompute statistics.										

- Under 10% error: This rate is acceptable.
- 10 to 30% error: This rate may be acceptable based on the importance of the application, cost of the instrument, cost of repair, and so on.
- Over 30% error: Generally, this rate is not acceptable. Every effort should be made to identify the problem and correct it.

Calibration

One of the most important functions of metrology is **calibration**, the comparison of a measurement device or system having a known relationship to national standards against another device or system whose relationship to national standards is unknown. Measurements made using uncalibrated or inadequately calibrated equipment can lead to erroneous and costly decisions. For example, suppose that an inspector has a micrometer that is reading 0.002 inch too low. When measurements are made close to the upper limit, parts that are as much as 0.002 inch over the maximum tolerance limit will be accepted as good, while those at the lower tolerance limit or that are as much as 0.002 inch above the limit will be rejected as nonconforming. A typical calibration system involves the following activities:

- Evaluation of equipment to determine its capability
- Identification of calibration requirements

- Selection of standards to perform the calibration
- Selection of methods and procedures to perform the calibration
- Establishment of calibration frequency and rules for adjusting this frequency
- Establishment of a system to ensure that instruments are calibrated according to schedule
- Implementation of a documentation and reporting system
- Evaluation of the calibration system through an established auditing process

The National Institute of Standards and Technology (NIST) maintains national measurement standards, and provides technical advice on making measurements consistent with national standards. NIST works with various metrology laboratories in industry and government to ensure that measurements made by different people in different places yield the same results. Thus, the measurement of "voltage" or "resistance" in an electrical component has a precise and universal meaning. This process is accomplished in a hierarchical fashion. NIST calibrates the reference-level standards of those organizations requiring the highest level of accuracy. These organizations calibrate their own working-level standards and those of other metrology laboratories. These working-level standards are used to calibrate the measuring instruments used in the field. The usual recommendation is that equipment be calibrated against working-level standards that are 10 times as accurate as the equipment. When possible, at least a four-to-one accuracy ratio between the reference and working-level standards is desired; that is, the reference standards should be at least four times as accurate as the working-level standards.

Many government regulations and commercial contracts require regulated organizations or contractors to verify that the measurements they make are **traceable** to a reference standard. For example, world standards exist for length, mass, and time. For other types of measurement, such as chemical measurements, industry standards exist. Organizations must be able to support the claim of traceability by keeping records that their own measuring equipment has been calibrated by laboratories or testing facilities whose measurements can be related to appropriate standards, generally national or international standards, through an unbroken chain of comparison.[16] The purpose of requiring traceability is to ensure that measurements are accurate representations of the specific quantity subject to measurement, within the uncertainty of the measurement. Not only is an unbroken chain of comparisons necessary, each measurement should be accompanied by a statement of uncertainty associated with the farthest link in the chain from NIST, that is, the last facility providing the measurement value. Traceability can be ensured by purchasing an instrument that is certified against a higher level (traceable) standard, or contracting with a calibration agency who have such instruments to certify the instrument.

Records, Documentation, and Audits

All the elements required for a quality system, such as control processes, measuring and test equipment, and other resources needed to achieve the required quality of conformance, should be documented in a **quality manual**, which serves as a permanent reference for implementing and maintaining the system. A quality manual need not be complex; a small company might need only a dozen pages while a large organization might need manuals for all key functions. Sufficient records should be maintained to demonstrate conformance to requirements and verify that the quality system is operating effectively. Typical records that might be maintained are inspection reports, test data, audit reports, and calibration data. They should be readily retrievable for analysis to identify trends and monitor the effectiveness of corrective actions. Other documents, such as drawings, specifications, inspection procedures and instructions, work instructions, and operation sheets are vital to achieving quality and should likewise be controlled.

Because many documents and data are generated during a product's life cycle, the quality system should include a means of controlling them: keeping documents and data up-to-date and removing obsolete documents, unless they are needed for legal purposes. In many situations it is appropriate to have procedures for identifying and tracing products during all stages of production, delivery, and installation, even down to individual parts or batches. These extensive procedures are critical, for instance, in the food or drug industries in the event of any product recalls.

Keeping the quality control system up to date is not always easy. It is most often facilitated through *internal audits*, which focus on identifying whether documented procedures are being followed and are effective, and reporting issues to management for corrective action. Internal audits generally include a review of process records, training records, complaints, corrective actions, and previous audit reports. Managers must use audit findings as a tool for continuous improvement, not as means of placing blame on individuals.

A typical internal audit begins by asking those who perform a process regularly to explain how it works.[17] Their statements are compared to written procedures, and compliance and deviations are noted. Next, the trail of paperwork or other data are examined to determine whether the process is consistent with the intent of the written procedure and the worker's explanation. Internal auditors also need to analyze whether the process is meeting its intent and objectives, thus focusing on continuous improvement.

Audits should also go beyond the routine procedures of quality control. Juran suggests six key strategic questions that audits should address:[18]

1. Are our quality policies and quality goals appropriate to our company's mission?
2. Does our quality provide product satisfaction to our clients?
3. Is our quality competitive with the moving target of the marketplace?
4. Are we making progress in reducing the cost of poor quality?
5. Is the collaboration among our functional departments adequate to assure optimal company performance?
6. Are we meeting responsibilities to society?

An Example of Quality Control: The FDA's HACCP Approach[19]

The 1993 outbreak of food-borne illness caused by the *E. coli* O157:H7 pathogen focused the attention of the public, the Congress, and USDA on the fact that the common system of meat and poultry inspection based on visible detection did not address the major cause of food-borne illness, which is invisible pathogens. Traditionally, industry regulators have depended on spot-checks of manufacturing conditions and random sampling of final products to ensure safe food. This approach, however, tends to be reactive, rather than preventive. New challenges to the U.S. food supply have prompted the FDA to consider adopting a new approach, called **HACCP** (pronounced has-sip). HACCP stands for Hazard Analysis and Critical Control Points. It is a system of process control developed by the National Aeronautic and Space Administration in preparation for space flight and has been adopted in many industries. HACCP is a management system in which food safety is addressed through the analysis and control of biological, chemical, and physical hazards from raw material production, procurement and handling, to manufacturing, distribution, and consumption of the finished product.

HACCP involves seven principles:

1. *Analyze hazards.* Potential hazards associated with a food and measures to control those hazards are identified. The hazard could be biological, such as a microbe; chemical, such as a toxin; or physical, such as ground glass or metal fragments.
2. *Identify critical control points.* These are points in a food's production—from its raw state through processing and shipping to consumption by the consumer—at which the potential hazard can be controlled or eliminated. Examples are cooking, cooling, packaging, and metal detection.
3. *Establish preventive measures with critical limits for each control point.* For a cooked food, for example, it might include setting the minimum cooking temperature and time required to ensure the elimination of any harmful microbes.
4. *Establish procedures to monitor the critical control points.* Such procedures might include determining how and by whom cooking time and temperature should be monitored.
5. *Establish corrective actions to be taken when monitoring shows that a critical limit has not been met.* Examples include reprocessing or disposing of food if the minimum cooking temperature is not met.
6. *Establish procedures to verify that the system is working properly.* An example includes testing time-and-temperature recording devices to verify that a cooking unit is working properly.
7. *Establish effective record keeping to document the HACCP system.* This principle would include records of hazards and their control methods, the monitoring of safety requirements, and action taken to correct potential problems. Each of these principles must be backed by sound scientific knowledge: for example, published microbiological studies on time and temperature factors for controlling foodborne pathogens.

HACCP is designed for use in all segments of the food industry from growing, harvesting, processing, manufacturing, distributing, and merchandising to preparing food for consumption. Food safety systems based on the HACCP principles have been successfully applied in food processing plants, retail food stores, and food service operations. The HACCP principles have been universally accepted by government agencies, trade associations, and the food industry around the world. HACCP offers a number of advantages over the traditional system. Most importantly, HACCP does the following:

- Focuses on identifying and preventing hazards from contaminating food
- Is based on sound science
- Permits more efficient and effective government oversight, primarily because the record keeping allows investigators to see how well a firm is complying with food safety laws over a period rather than how well it is doing on any given day
- Places responsibility for ensuring food safety appropriately on the food manufacturer or distributor
- Helps food companies compete more effectively in the world market
- Reduces barriers to international trade.

QUALITY CONTROL IN SERVICES

Many people think that "quality control" applies only to manufacturing. This assumption could not be further from the truth. The approach used by The Ritz-Carlton Hotel Company (see the *Quality in Practice* in Chapter 2) to control quality is proactive because of its intensive personalized service environment.[20] Systems for collecting and using quality-related measures are widely deployed and used extensively throughout the organization. For example, Figure 2.5 showed the service quality indicators that each hotel tracks on a daily basis. The Ritz-Carlton recognizes that many customer requirements are sensory, and thus, difficult to measure. However, by selecting, training, and certifying employees in their knowledge of The Ritz-Carlton Gold Standards of service, they are able to assess their work through appropriate sensory measurements—taste, sight, smell, sound, and touch—and take appropriate actions.

The company uses three types of control processes to deliver quality:

1. Self-control of the individual employee based on their spontaneous and learned behavior.
2. Basic control mechanism carried out by every member of the workforce. The first person who detects a problem is empowered to break away from routine duties, investigate and correct the problem immediately, document the incident, and then return to their routine.
3. Critical success factor control for critical processes. Process teams use customer and organizational requirement measurements to determine quality, speed, and cost performance. These measurements are compared against benchmarks and customer satisfaction data to determine corrective action and resource allocation.

In addition, The Ritz-Carlton conducts both self-audits and outside audits. Self-audits are carried out internally at all levels, from one individual or function to an entire hotel. Process walk-throughs occur daily in hotels while senior leaders assess field operations during formal reviews at various intervals. Outside audits are performed by independent travel and hospitality rating organizations. All audits must be documented, and any findings must be submitted to the senior leader of the unit being audited. They are responsible for action and for assessing the implementation and effectiveness of recommended corrective actions.

The most common quality characteristics in services, time (waiting time, service time, delivery time) and number of nonconformances, can be measured rather easily. Insurance companies, for example, measure the time to complete different transactions such as new issues, claim payments, and cash surrenders. Hospitals measure the percentage of infections and the percentage of unplanned readmissions to the emergency room, intensive care, or operating room within, say, 48 hours. Other quality characteristics are observable; they include the types of errors (wrong kind, wrong quantity, wrong delivery date, etc.) and behavior (courtesy, promptness, competency, and so on). Hospitals might monitor the completeness of medical charts and the quality of radiology readings, measured by a double-reading process. An example of a structured quality control process in the service industry is the "10-Step Monitoring and Evaluation Process" set forth by the Joint Commission on Accrediting Health Care Organizations, which was shown in Table 7.3.

Internal measurements of service quality are commonly performed with some type of data sheet or checklist. Time is easily measured by taking two observations: starting time and finishing time. Many observed data assume only "yes" or "no" values. For example, a survey of pharmaceutical operations in a hospital might include the following questions:

- Are drug storage and preparation areas within the pharmacy under the supervision of a pharmacist?
- Are drugs requiring special storage conditions properly stored?
- Are drug emergency boxes inspected on a monthly basis?
- Is the drug emergency box record book filled out completely?

Simple check sheets can be designed to record the types of errors that occur.

Even though human behavior is easily observable, the task of describing and classifying the observations is far more difficult. The major obstacle is developing operational definitions of behavioral characteristics. For example, how does one define courteous versus discourteous, or understanding versus indifferent? Defining such distinctions is best done by comparing behavior against understandable standards. For instance, a standard for "courtesy" might be to address the customer as "Mr." or "Ms." Failure to do so is an instance of an error. "Promptness" might be defined as greeting a customer within five seconds of entering the store, or answering letters within two days of receipt. These behaviors can easily be recorded and counted. Figure 11.5 shows some behavioral questions used in a patient survey by a group of Southern California hospitals.

Even concepts like calibration can be applied to services. A new quality program in the Office of Compensation and Working Conditions (OCWC) at the U.S. Bureau of Labor Statistics (BLS) applies calibration concepts to the office, where the aim of production is largely a cognitive activity and not a tangible product.[21] BLS collects, processes, analyzes, and disseminates essential statistical data to the public, the Congress, and other organizations. The calibration program was designed to increase the consistency of survey data collection. The focus is on the individuals who collect the data and their understanding of the National Compensation Survey concepts. Staffers who ordinarily are out in the field get together to review and discuss the meaning of individual data elements, how the data are collected, and the specifications used to collect the data with the goal of improving the validity of data. During each calibration session, discussion centers on answers to a set of exercises to help identify sources of differences with the ultimate goal of reaching consensus of decisions. Calibration sessions are repeated at preset intervals throughout the survey collection cycle.

For example, differentiating supervisory jobs from managerial jobs can be difficult. One exercise provides descriptions of jobs and asks the staffers to classify the job in one of two occupations: K433 (supervisors, food preparation and service occupations), or B017 (managers, food service and lodging establishments). The manual describes job K433 as "Supervise and coordinate activities of workers in occupations involved in preparing food and beverages and serving them to patrons of such establishments as hotels, clubs, restaurants, and cocktail lounges." Job B017 is described as "Manage and coordinate food service activities of restaurant or other similar eating establishments. Includes caterers, cafeteria directors, banquet managers, and so forth." Now consider the following job description and decide what occupational code you would assign:

> *These employees are the shift captains at a café. They make sure all employees are productively engaged and that the company policy is followed during their shift. They have the power to fire someone on the spot if they break one of the rules. They are generally given permission to hire people. They often have to take over the register or drive-through window when someone misses a shift.*

These employees clearly fit the definition of a supervisor, not a manager. They are enforcing policy, not making it. Their job is to see that assigned work gets done, so the job code would be K433.

Figure 11.5 Sample Hospital Staff Behavior Questions

Admissions

11. Altogether, how long did you have to wait to be admitted?
    More than 1 hour: ______ (1) 1 hour: ______ (2) 30 min.: ______ (3) 15 min.: ______ (4)
12. If you had to wait 30 minutes or longer before someone met with you, were you told why?
    YES: ______ (1) NO: ______ (2) Did not wait 30 minutes: ______ (3)

Nursing Staff

21. Did a nurse talk to you about the procedures for the day?
    Never: ______ (1) Sometimes: ______ (2) Often: ______ (3) Always: ______ (4)
22. Were you on IV fluids?
    YES: ______ (1) NO: ______ (2)
    A. If YES, did the IV fluids ever run out?
    YES: ______ (1) NO: ______ (2)

Medical Staff

28. Did the doctor do what he/she told you he was going to do?
    Never: ______ (1) Sometimes: ______ (2) Often: ______ (3) Always: ______ (4)

Housekeeping

36. Did the housekeeper come into your room at least once a day?
    YES: ______ (1) NO: ______ (2)
39. Was the bathroom adequately supplied?
    Always: ______ (1) Often: ______ (2) Sometimes: ______ (3) Never: ______ (4)

X-Ray

When you received services from the X-ray technician, were the procedures explained to you?
Always: ______ (1) Often: ______ (2) Sometimes: ______ (3) Never: ______ (4)

Food

34. Generally, were your meals served at the same time each day?
    Always: ______ (1) Often: ______ (2) Sometimes: ______ (3) Never: ______ (4)

Source: Adapted from K. M. Casarreal, J. I. Mill, and M. A. Plant, "Improving Service Through Patient Surveys in a Multihospital Organization," Hospital & Health Services Administration, Health Administration Press, Ann Arbor, MI, March/April 1986. 41–52. © 1986, Foundation of the American College of Health Care Executives.

Quality in Practice

Quality Control for an International Wine Producer

J. Boutaris & Sons, S.A. is a major wine producer in Greece with annual sales of about $40 million. The company operates two major wineries and three smaller local wineries, producing 20 different wines and the traditional Greek ouzo. Thirty percent are exported around the world. As international competition increased in the early 1990s, Boutaris decided to become more systematic about quality by shaping a more specific quality policy and designing quality control procedures for incoming materials, for its products, and for its bottling and packaging processes.

A pilot study began with an analysis of the entire production process of two representative wines, from gathering grapes to storing the final products. Activities were grouped into four categories: operations, inspections, transportation, and storage. This analysis resulted in two detailed process flowcharts. Next, the study team identified quality characteristics of the final products and the key quality factors at intermediate steps of the production process, which were classified in a four-level hierarchy. At the first level, they defined three categories: content (wine), bottling (materials and processes), and packaging. At the second level, they classified quality characteristics of the final product according to the three categories of the first level. At the third level, materials supplied by external suppliers and production processes were considered. Finally, at the fourth level, all quality factors for every material and production process of the previous level, as well as the inspection points on the flowchart at which every quality factor may be controlled were recorded. Their efforts resulted in the two tree diagrams shown in Figure 11.6. Figure 11.6(a) shows the first and second levels for one product; Figure 11.6(b) shows the third and fourth levels for a single quality characteristic (hermeticity—the tightness of the seal). The second diagram shows the controllable quality factors in materials and processes that affect the product quality characteristic. For each of the two pilot products, more than 200 factors were identified.

After these quality characteristics were identified, the team established quantitative or qualitative specifications based on current company practice, quality goals, international standards, legislation of the European Economic Community, supplier and internal process capabilities, and accuracy of inspection and measurement methods.

The large number of quality factors made it too difficult to develop detailed quality control schemes for all of them. As an alternative, the team classified quality factors into two categories: procedural and statistical. The first category included all those factors for which deviations from specifications arose from failure to follow established procedures, rather than from random causes—about 20 to 30 factors for the two products. Most of these factors related to the wine-making process, such as the duration of aging and the correspondence between label and actual content. Procedures were written and incorporated into the company's quality manual.

The second category contained the remaining factors that were attributable to common and special causes. The team evaluated the relative importance of these factors along two dimensions: frequency and economic consequence of nonconformance. They used Pareto analysis to identify the most important factors along these dimensions. As a result, they identified approximately 45 critical factors for control using statistical quality control methods.

The team performed repeated measurements to establish the accuracy of measuring methods, especially for quality factors during the wine-making process, such as total acidity. Random samples from lots of incoming materials were drawn, and all critical quality factors were measured and recorded. Finally, they monitored critical processes, such as filling, closely under controlled conditions for several weeks to measure the process capabilities. The analysis of the data indicated that in some cases, specifications were too tight for the process capabilities. After reexamination, some were found to be unnecessarily strict and were relaxed. In some critical cases, specifications were revised to give suppliers the time to improve their quality, with the understanding that they would be gradually tightened to promote continuous improvement.

Figure 11.6 Hierarchy of Quality Characteristics

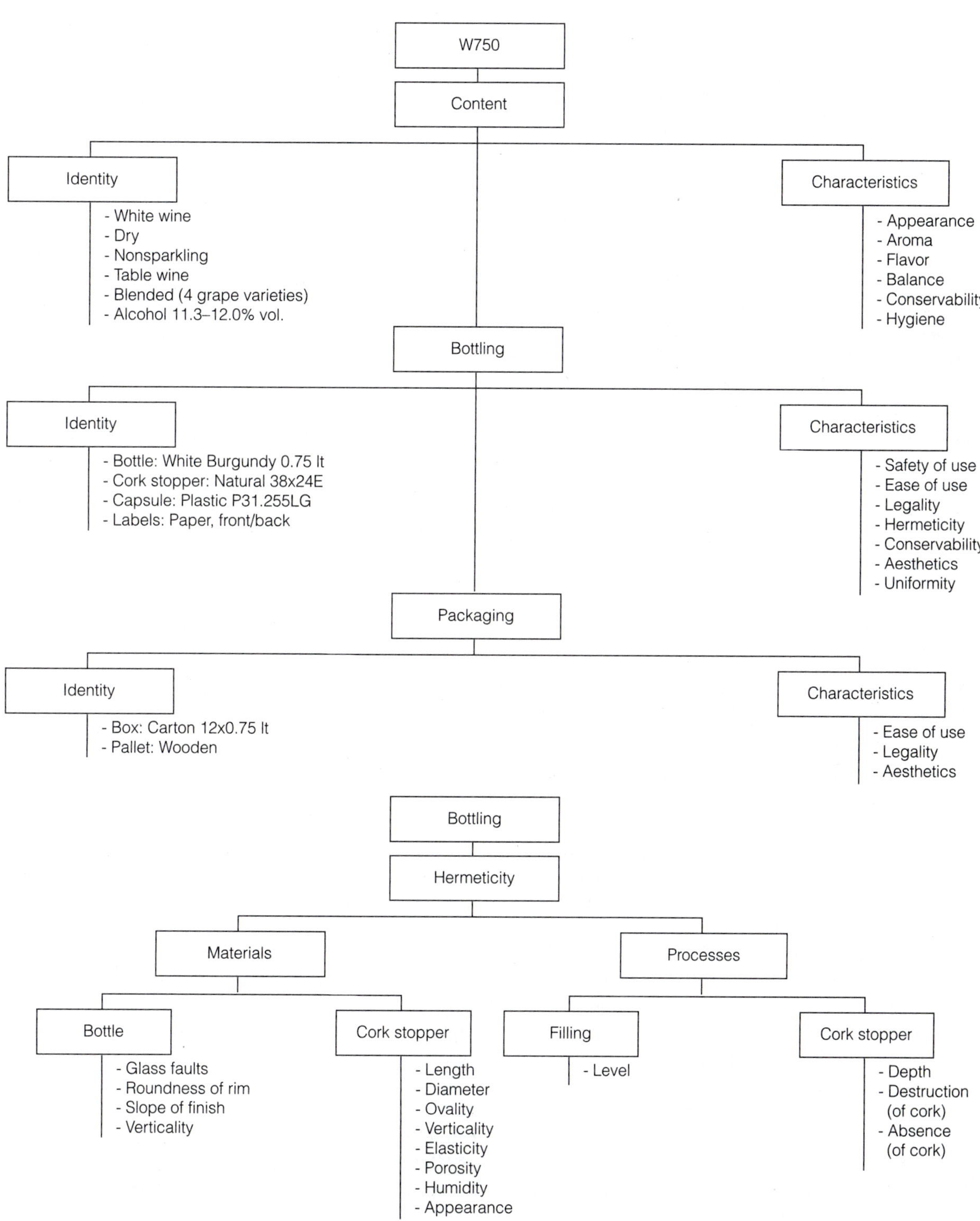

For critical supplier quality factors, acceptance sampling plans were designed, and control charts were developed for process control characteristics. These procedures were implemented in actual production and receiving processes for a trial period to uncover any problems that might result. Training at all levels of managers and operators was an important part of the implementation process. The company revised nearly all job descriptions to reflect the new roles of employees in quality control and improvement. Employees reacted positively to these efforts, mainly because of the personal approach to their quality training and involvement in the project from the early stages.

Before it implemented this quality assurance system, Boutaris's lack of proper analysis of inspection results often led it to make poor decisions. The formal statistical methods allowed the company to make a reliable quantitative evaluation of each lot of incoming materials and each internal process, helping suppliers and process managers understand their weaknesses and improve quality. One example of the success of the program was improved hermeticity. Hermeticity is expressed as the pressure required for air to penetrate the bottle and is the most important factor in the longevity of wine. Bottle characteristics such as roundness of rim and cork length, diameter, and porosity influence this characteristic. In 18 months, the percent nonconforming level fell from 15 percent to less than 5 percent. The positioning of labels, which affects the aesthetics of the final product, was improved through statistical process control from a 10 percent nonconforming level to less than 2 percent. The introduction of these new procedures helped Boutaris achieve ISO 9002 certification a few years later.

Key Issues for Discussion

1. Explain the different approaches the company uses to control its quality.
2. Explain the importance of understanding process capability in setting standards and specifications. How can lessons learned from this case be generalized?

Quality in Practice

Quality Control at Dunlavy Audio Labs, Inc.[22]

Founded in Colorado Springs, Colorado, in 1992 by legendary audio designer, John Dunlavy, Dunlavy Audio Labs (DAL) set forth with one simple goal: to design and manufacture the best high-end loudspeakers and cables in the world. To meet this goal, the company followed strict guidelines of designing products by using proven scientific formulas, sound physics, and solid engineering applications with the goal of outlasting and out-performing every other loudspeaker and audio cable on the market. In order to ensure that customers do indeed receive only the best, Dunlavy Audio Labs has incorporated one of the most rigorous and stringent quality control programs into its loudspeaker manufacturing process.

This quality control begins the moment that a product order is placed by an authorized Dunlavy Audio Labs dealer or distributor and a work order is issued to their cabinet shop. Each cabinet or cabinet pair begins the production process accompanied by a five-page quality control checklist, a portion of which is shown in Figure 11.7, with approximately 100 individual quality control inspections. These individual QC examinations require that the individual DAL employee performing the review sign off and date each step, thus ensuring a high degree of accountability associated with the various individual production steps.

During the initial cabinet-building phase, the cabinets and their corresponding bases, which are hand-built exclusively, are checked for proper dimensions, routering, veneer matching, individual interior driver chamber seals, and cleanliness. The grills, which are machined from 16 gauge cold rolled 1018 steel, and perforated with a laser punch for acoustical transparency, are checked at all weld points for rigidity. After the cabinets are built, veneered, and finished, they enter the primary build area. Immediately an initial QC inspection is conducted identical to the cabinet

Figure 11.7 Samples of Dunlavy Audio Labs Quality Assurance Checklists

DUNLAVY AUDIO LABS
QUALITY ASSURANCE PROGRAM
SC-V & SC-VI PAGE 1
INCOMING Q.C. CHECK LIST

MODEL ________ **SERIAL NO.** ________ **FINISH** ________ **DATE** ________

PAIR ________ **CENTER CHANNEL ONLY ("A")** ________

	"A"		**"B"**	
	INSP.	DATE	INSP.	DATE
Cabinets:				
Finish and color	____	____	____	____
Pair-match	____	____	____	____
Dimensions (outside)	____	____	____	____
Driver depth	____	____	____	____
Mechanical integrity	____	____	____	____
Sealing between chambers	____	____	____	____
Interior foam	____	____	____	____
Cleanliness	____	____	____	____
Hardwood edges (finish, etc.)	____	____	____	____
Excess glue, etc.	____	____	____	____
Wiring Harness:				
Wire lengths	____	____	____	____
Proper labeling	____	____	____	____
Proper connections	____	____	____	____
Air-tight seals	____	____	____	____
Grills:				
Cloth	____	____	____	____
Size/fit	____	____	____	____
Vibration (rattle)	____	____	____	____
Bases:				
Finish (and pair match)	____	____	____	____
Color	____	____	____	____
Pair match	____	____	____	____
Dimensions (outside)	____	____	____	____
Mounting holes	____	____	____	____
Interior nuts	____	____	____	____
Bolt type, size, length	____	____	____	____
Fit to speaker cabinet	____	____	____	____

Figure 11.7 Samples of Dunlavy Audio Labs Quality Assurance Checklists *(continued)*

DUNLAVY AUDIO LABS
QUALITY ASSURANCE PROGRAM
SC-V & SC-VI PAGE 3
INCOMING Q.C. CHECK LIST

MODEL ________ **SERIAL NO.** ________ **FINISH** ________ **DATE** ________

PAIR ________ **CENTER CHANNEL ONLY ("A")** ________

	"A"		"B"	
	INSP.	DATE	INSP.	DATE
Crossover Component Tolerance				
Testing:				
Capacitors	________	________	________	________
Inductors	________	________	________	________
Resistors	________	________	________	________
Crossover:				
Solder joints	________	________	________	________
Component rigidity	________	________	________	________
Cable attachment	________	________	________	________
Match to reference	________	________	________	________
Crossover Installation:				
Proper solder connections (wires to crossover)	________	________	________	________
Correct gasket and seating	________	________	________	________
Correct screws and torque	________	________	________	________
Polarity check (from input)	________	________	________	________

Source: Courtesy of Andrew W. Rigby and Dunlavy Audio Labs, *http://www.dunlavyaudio.com.*

examination performed in the wood shop. At this stage in the production process, the cabinets are prepped for the installation of the dampening material, the internal wiring harnesses, felt, and drivers. This step also has its own QC check sheet. The drivers, prior to installation in the cabinets, have undergone a separate quality control inspection. This inspection includes an initial buzz test as well as anechoic testing of each individual driver, using instrumentation microphones and testing software, for precise pair and set matching determined by frequency response, impulse response, and free air resonance.

After the drivers are installed, the speakers are sent to one of two primary anechoic chambers, where the crossover is tested in conjunction with the loudspeakers. (An anechoic chamber is a nonreflective, enclosed room that enables a loudspeaker designer to accurately establish the performance of a specific speaker in an objective, neutral environment.) The crossovers, prior to this stage of production, have also been subjected to an extensive quality control inspection. All individual parts used in all loudspeaker crossovers are individually measured prior to placement on the fiberglass circuit boards. The completed crossover is checked for component rigidity, circuit continuity, and matched to the set reference standard for that particular model. The anechoic testing of the individual loudspeakers ensures that the highest degree of consistency is maintained in the quality control process. Each loudspeaker is thoroughly tested with even the correct temperature within the anechoic chamber specified for proper testing operations.

As a final QC assurance, DAL CEO and chief designer John Dunlavy must approve each loudspeaker's anechoic test data prior to packaging. If he doesn't like what he sees, the speakers don't ship, much to the chagrin of their test engineers, who spend up to eight hours testing a single pair of speakers.

Prior to shipment, the speakers are buzz tested for the entire audible frequency range (20 Hz to 20 kHz), and are inspected visually. Each screw on the driver units and crossover back plate is individually checked. The products are then packaged using a double box system consisting of impact resistant, industrial grade strength corrugated cardboard, which is then banded to a heavy duty wooden pallet. The quality control sheets are then included in the paperwork and shipped with the speakers.

Key Issues for Discussion

1. Describe the types of quality controls used at DAL. Why does the company use so many checkpoints?
2. Based on the limited information described in this case, in what additional methods or procedures might the company engage to assure the quality of its products?

Summary of Key Points

- An effective quality assurance system includes well-designed and documented procedures for product and process control, inspection and testing, control of measuring and test equipment, and corrective and preventive action.
- A quality policy identifies key objectives of products and services such as fitness for use, performance, safety, and dependability.
- Traditional inspection practices involve heavy inspection of incoming materials and final product, with a focus on separating the good from the bad. These practices are inefficient and ineffective. Inspection should be used as an auditing tool to control processes and identify opportunities for improvement. Three types of inspection are spot-check procedures, 100 percent inspection, and acceptance sampling.
- In-process inspection must consider what to inspect, where to inspect, and how much to inspect. Inspection of critical characteristics should be related to cost or quality and provide useful information for improvement. Where to perform inspection is an economic decision. Generally, it is economical to inspect either all or nothing using a simple breakeven rule. Human factors can dramatically affect inspection performance.
- Various types of gauges, measuring instruments, and automated technology are used in manufacturing to measure quality characteristics. In services, measurement typically is conducted by surveys and other forms of observation. Control of measuring instruments is accomplished through metrology, calibration, and traceability.
- A repeatability and reproducibility study is designed to measure the variation due to measuring equipment and the operators who use the equipment. This variation is commonly expressed as a percentage of tolerance for evaluating the acceptability of measurement error.

- Many service quality characteristics are measurable; others are observable. In either case, they may be controlled in a manner similar to the control of manufacturing characteristics.

Review Questions

1. Describe the components of a basic quality assurance system and the key procedures and approaches used in each.
2. What is a quality policy and why is it important to have one?
3. List the reasons why inspection will always be around to some extent, despite the total quality philosophy.
4. Explain the three major types of procedures commonly used for receiving inspection.
5. What is an acceptance sampling plan? What are the arguments against acceptance sampling?
6. List Pyzdek's guidelines for selecting quality characteristics to inspect.
7. List the rules typically used to select locations for inspection activities.
8. What factors affect visual inspection and how does understanding them lead to improved inspection practices?
9. Briefly describe the different types and applications of fixed and variable gauges.
10. Describe some of the uses of automated technology in inspection and measurement.
11. Describe the science of metrology.
12. What is the difference between accuracy, precision, and reproducibility?
13. What is calibration and why is it important to a good quality assurance system?
14. Contrast the traditional economic model for quality assurance with the modern model. What are the implications of these two models to management?
15. Explain how the HACCP approach reflects the characteristics of a good quality control system.
16. Discuss service quality measurements that would be applicable to the following:
    a. Local and intercity buses
    b. Travel agency
    c. College bookstore
    d. Electric power company
    e. Post office
17. Review the discussion of the use of calibration at the Bureau of Labor Statistics. Classify each of the following jobs as in the example, explaining your reasons. Note any additional information that you might need to make a better decision.
    a. These employees are site managers at small outlets found only in malls and selling only flavored drinks. Two employees are on shift at a time. The site managers have final say on the affairs of the day at their particular location. However, the menu, store appearance, and official procedures are standardized at all locations. Each site employs 10 people, with all but the manager being part-timers. The manager hires, fires, makes sure the site has enough supplies, does quality checks, deals with the mall manage-

ment company on routine issues, and is responsible for any problems that could arise at the location.

b. These employees are restaurant managers. Each of the three employees in this job manages one of the restaurants in the chain, and each restaurant has about 30 employees. The company owner makes all the final decisions but tends to give the managers some flexibility on issues such as specials and displays tailored to local events, and so on. Each restaurant employs shift leaders to make sure operations run smoothly. They provide the owner with suggestions for the menu and are expected to help make decisions about marketing the restaurant at the local level. The manager sometimes will assist with supervision and even cooking during busy periods. Officially, all the employees report to the restaurant manager, although the shift leaders do most of the supervision. The shift leaders may recommend that people get hired or fired, and the restaurant manager will tend to follow their recommendations.

PROBLEMS

1. A manufacturer estimates that the proportion of nonconforming items in one process is 3.5 percent. The estimated cost of inspecting each item is $0.50, while the cost of replacing a nonconforming item after it leaves the production area is $25. What is the best economic inspection decision?
2. The cost to inspect a credit card statement in a bank is $0.75, while correction of a mistake later amounts to $500. What is the breakeven point in errors per thousand transactions for which 100 percent inspection is no more economical than no inspection?
3. Microcard Computer Company is currently experiencing about 50 errors per million lines of code in its software modules. They have been performing 100 percent inspection on each line of code for which the cost of inspecting is $0.04. The average cost of finding and fixing an error in a line of code is $575. The typical software package sold by the firm contains about 10 modules of code (1 million lines per module).
   a. What is the best inspection decision?
   b. At what error rate would it become economical to fix the code?
   c. What is the gain or loss being incurred at the current rate of inspection?
4. Twenty-five (25) parts were measured by quality technicians using two different micrometers. The true dimension for each part is 0.065. Which instrument is more accurate? Which is more precise? Which is the better instrument?

Micrometer A

0.075	0.045	0.045	0.085	0.075
0.065	0.055	0.045	0.050	0.055
0.045	0.050	0.035	0.075	0.055
0.045	0.055	0.055	0.045	0.065
0.075	0.070	0.050	0.025	0.085

Micrometer B

0.064	0.079	0.052	0.075	0.053
0.053	0.058	0.057	0.019	0.071
0.089	0.075	0.073	0.049	0.085
0.082	0.067	0.065	0.025	0.057
0.059	0.070	0.075	0.044	0.069

5. Two scales were used to weigh the same 25 samples of hamburger patties for a fast-food restaurant in Australia. Results are shown as follow. The samples were weighed in grams, and the supplier has assured customers that each patty weighs 114 grams. Which scale is more accurate? Which is more precise? Which is the better scale?

Scale A

113	112	115	115	113
114	115	114	116	114
115	116	112	114	115
114	112	113	113	114
113	114	115	114	114

Scale B

118	116	116	115	116
114	115	115	116	116
115	116	117	116	115
117	117	116	117	118
114	114	116	116	117

6. A gauge repeatability and reproducibility study at Frankford Brake Systems collected the following data. Analyze these data. The part specification is 1.0 ± 0.06 mm.

	Operator 1			Operator 2		
Part/Trial	1	2	3	1	2	3
1	0.97	0.99	0.99	0.96	0.99	1.00
2	0.94	0.96	0.97	0.95	1.00	1.00
3	1.00	1.00	0.99	1.02	1.03	1.00
4	0.97	1.00	0.99	0.96	0.98	0.98
5	0.99	1.00	1.00	1.01	1.01	1.03
6	1.02	1.04	1.03	0.99	1.02	1.02
7	0.96	1.01	0.98	0.97	0.97	0.99
8	1.00	1.02	0.97	1.07	1.02	1.00
9	1.03	1.01	1.00	1.04	1.02	0.98
10	0.96	0.98	0.95	0.99	0.95	0.95

7. A gauge repeatability and reproducibility study at Specialty Motors, Inc., collected the following data. Analyze these data. The part specification for a shim that is being measured is 1.2 ± 0.2 mm.

	Operator 1			Operator 2		
Part/Trial	1	2	3	1	2	3
1	1.05	1.00	0.98	1.05	0.90	0.95
2	1.44	1.42	1.45	1.35	1.45	1.45
3	1.25	1.26	1.22	1.15	1.20	1.20
4	1.25	1.28	1.24	1.15	1.20	1.20
5	0.89	0.85	0.84	0.80	0.85	0.90
6	1.45	1.40	1.45	1.40	1.40	1.40
7	1.35	1.35	1.32	1.35	1.35	1.35
8	1.25	1.20	1.23	1.10	1.20	1.20
9	1.40	1.40	1.40	1.35	1.45	1.45
10	1.08	1.10	1.06	0.90	1.25	1.20

8. A gauge repeatability and reproducibility study was made at Precision Parts, Inc., using three operators, taking three trials each on identical parts. The fol-

lowing data were collected. Do you see any problems after analyzing these data? What should be done? The part specification for a collar that was measured was 1.6 ± 0.2 inches.

	Operator 1			Operator 2			Operator 3		
Part/Trial	1	2	3	1	2	3	1	2	3
1	1.59	1.64	1.72	1.55	1.58	1.80	1.60	1.65	1.62
2	1.66	1.66	1.68	1.68	1.75	1.69	1.68	1.71	1.76
3	1.68	1.68	1.62	1.60	1.42	1.36	1.37	1.30	1.35
4	1.35	1.42	1.48	1.42	1.52	1.59	1.50	1.48	1.51
5	1.68	1.54	1.63	1.75	1.69	1.58	1.59	1.64	1.66
6	1.75	1.74	1.62	1.54	1.52	1.40	1.64	1.71	1.68
7	1.46	1.84	1.52	1.58	1.38	1.57	1.49	1.51	1.44
8	1.66	1.54	1.58	1.59	1.56	1.68	1.47	1.49	1.53
9	1.60	1.58	1.74	1.48	1.58	1.50	1.64	1.67	1.69
10	1.58	1.64	1.60	1.42	1.42	1.54	1.55	1.59	1.53

9. The cost of counting and retrieving a sponge from inside a patient during one type of major surgery is $6.50. The cost of retrieving a sponge to correct a mistake later is $25,000. What is the breakeven point in errors per 10,000 operations for which 100 percent inspection is no more economical than no inspection? Should this approach even be considered in this situation?
10. A genetic researcher is trying to test two laboratory thermometers (that can be read to 1/100,000th of a degree C.) for accuracy and precision. She measured 25 samples with each and obtained the following results. The true temperature being measured is 0 degrees C. Which instrument is more accurate? Which is more precise? Which is the better instrument?

Thermometer A

0.00071	−0.00040	0.00246	0.00130	0.00018
0.00025	0.00245	0.00141	0.00142	0.00015
0.00098	−0.00251	0.00178	0.00221	−0.00129
−0.00065	−0.00027	−0.00136	−0.00039	−0.00063
0.00124	0.00036	−0.00186	0.00118	−0.00089

Thermometer B

0.00126	−0.00221	−0.00011	−0.00071	−0.00032
0.00180	−0.00135	0.00210	0.00027	−0.00076
0.00020	−0.00024	0.00071	−0.00120	−0.00001
0.00079	−0.00165	0.00232	−0.00012	−0.00041
0.00080	−0.00040	−0.00155	0.00114	−0.00149

CASES

I. STUART INJECTION MOLDING COMPANY[23]

Stuart Injection Molding Company (SIMC) is a small business that specializes in custom plastic molding for many different industries, including appliances and various consumer products such as toys. Adele Stuart, daughter of the company's founder and current CEO wishes to expand into the automotive sector. However, she realizes that to do so will require more formalized systems and eventually ISO 9000 registration. Although many basic procedures for assuring quality are in place, most have been conducted informally, and the company has never had a formal quality manual that documents the system and outlines specific responsibilities for managers and workers. Recognizing this major deficiency, they have called you in as a consultant to help. After spending some time in the plant talking with many employees, you have jotted down several notes and observations:

- The plant manager (PM) is responsible for ensuring the success of the quality management system by providing the necessary resources and reviewing system performance. However, SIMC has a quality assurance (QA) department that is responsible for the majority of implementation issues, such as maintaining measuring and test equipment, verifying process capability, performing inspection, selecting methods for monitoring process performance, and auditing the system.
- All functional departments recognize their responsibility for quality planning and producing high-quality products. For example, the marketing and sales department conducts market research to understand customer needs and handles customer complaints; project engineering performs design reviews; manufacturing conducts in-process inspection for the purpose of maintaining control and coordinates continuous improvement processes. These functions are supported by maintenance, supplier relations, receiving, and human resources departments.
- Most products are custom-designed with the customer. When a new job is contracted, a cross-functional team is selected that includes members from project engineering, quality assurance, manufacturing, and sales. This team develops all the specifications to ensure that design meets customer requirements and can be made according to these requirements, selects materials and process tolerances, determines production routings and inspection plans, develops a production control plan and measurement system, and monitors a trial production run. All design changes must be approved by the customer.
- The company uses a variety of contemporary tools to simplify and optimize the product while also focusing on reducing production cost and waste. These include quality function deployment, geometric dimensioning and tolerancing, design for manufacturing and assembly, value engineering, design of experiments, failure mode and effects analysis, and cost/performance/risk analysis.
- Inspection is routine during the production process. QA lab personnel perform all phases of inspection and testing. Production operators use a "first-piece" inspection process application to validate the start-up for a new product. Receiving inspection is performed on material, purchased parts, and subassemblies used in processing, manufacturing, and assembly. Operators also perform in-process inspections during production and final inspection on finished products. When contractually required, statistical process control techniques are used to ensure control of key process characteristics. Gauging instruction sheets are maintained by QA for at least one year.
- Nonconforming products are labeled with a "Do Not Use" tag and kept from being shipped. This tag describes the nonconformance, documents the disposition decision, and records the reinspection results. If they are repaired or reworked, they are reinspected. Products that do not fully comply with specific requirements are not shipped without customer authorization. When nonconformities are detected, they are investigated by a cross-functional team, and corrective actions are initiated to prevent their recurrence.
- SIMC has a continuous improvement philosophy that pervades the entire organization. Processes are improved beyond minimum requirements when further improvements benefit customers. Quality performance and productivity are continuously monitored to identify opportunities for improvement. Everyone in the organization is encouraged to come forward with ideas for improving products, processes, systems, and productivity within the working environment. Some examples of opportunities for quality and productivity improvement are the reduction of cycle times, less scrap, rework and repair rates, less unscheduled machine downtime, and process performance variation.

Based on this information, what would you recommend to the company? Specifically discuss what should be included in the quality manual, and note any additional information that you might need.

II. World-Wide Appliances

World-Wide Appliances (WWA) designs, manufactures, and markets large kitchen appliances such as refrigerators, washers, dryers, and dishwashers for U.S. and international markets. WWA has plants in Durham, North Carolina; Birmingham, Alabama; and St. Louis, Missouri. All design activities are centralized in Durham. The Birmingham plant has approximately 2,500 employees and operates two complete shifts, producing about 750,000 refrigerators each year under several brand names. The international market is growing rapidly and is an important part of WWA strategy; however, domestic sales still account for the majority of revenues.

The Birmingham plant is currently working to obtain ISO 9000 registration. One of the motivations in becoming ISO 9000 certified is to streamline its European operations. In the past, refrigerators were shipped to retrofit companies in Europe that would modify them to meet local electrical requirements. The retrofit company obtained any certification that was necessary to sell the products in Europe. WWA wanted to ship properly configured units directly to distributors in Europe. ISO registration could be a means of gaining this marketing advantage.

The registration effort is not directly opposed by any employees in the Birmingham plant. However, many people do not understand why they need to do certain things required by the standards. The quality manager assigned responsibility for the registration effort, Harold Glenn, does not feel that he has enough higher-level support. The group-level managers who made the decision to seek registration have backed off and left it up to each individual location. Because of their lack of involvement, the upper-level plant management does not perceive it to be high priority. A lack of management support led to a general lack of support for the internal auditing team.

Although the work performed in the plant is highly labor-intensive, few procedures in manufacturing are actually formally written. Glenn feels that the most work will be needed in the areas of gauge calibration, record retention, and corrective action systems. Glenn is not sure whether to use outside consultants to help the plant prepare for registration. If he does not, he feels that he will have to start a major training effort for internal employees. An internal auditing structure is currently being formed. The plan calls for an internal audit in all areas twice a year. The plant plans to use a "bundling" technique to audit each area of the plant. Rather than audit the entire organization at one time, the plant will be divided into small areas, such as the foam injection operation. All requirements will be audited in each area by a small group of auditors. The results will be bundled together to get an overall assessment of the plant. The smaller audits will take place continuously according to an audit schedule. Harold hopes to have at least 50 employees trained to be internal auditors so that he can rotate the responsibilities among many people.

Discussion Questions

1. What criteria should Harold use to decide whether to use outside consultants? If he does not use outside consultants, what types of training should he consider for the plant employees?
2. Evaluate the proposed "bundling" auditing technique. What advantages or disadvantages might it have?

III. Bloomfield Tool Co.

Bloomfield Tool Co. (BTC) is a small manufacturing company that produces precision tools to order. One of BTC's production processes involves producing a metal spacer plate that has a tolerance of 0.05 to 0.100 cm in thickness. Recently, the QA manager was receiving complaints from customers about high levels of nonconforming parts. He suspected problems in the gauges used to check outgoing parts, because they had not been sent out for calibration in some time. However, it was expensive to do, so he wanted to be sure recalibration was needed. He decided to do a gauge R&R test and selected two experienced inspectors to perform the test using 15 identical parts, whose dimensions had

Table 11.4 Data Set for R&R Study

Sample	Operator 1		Operator 2	
1	0.0650	0.0600	0.0650	0.0550
2	0.1000	0.1050	0.1050	0.0950
3	0.0850	0.0800	0.0820	0.0750
4	0.0850	0.0950	0.0820	0.0940
5	0.0550	0.0580	0.0485	0.0525
6	0.0875	0.0915	0.0945	0.0925
7	0.0920	0.0880	0.0990	0.0900
8	0.0850	0.0800	0.0750	0.0700
9	0.0890	0.0980	0.0920	0.0990
10	0.0600	0.0700	0.0550	0.0640
11	0.0680	0.0750	0.0670	0.0720
12	0.0545	0.0500	0.0525	0.0495
13	0.0800	0.0910	0.0870	0.0820
14	0.0700	0.0805	0.0865	0.0830
15	0.0750	0.0650	0.0650	0.0680

Table 11.5 Numbers of Parts versus K_3 Factors

Parts	5	6	7	8	9	10	11	12	13	14	15
K_3 Factors	2.08	1.93	1.82	1.74	1.67	1.62	1.57	1.54	1.51	1.48	1.45

been verified. Table 11.4 shows data provided by the supervisor. Thus, data were from two operators, two gauges, and 15 parts that were measured twice, independently, by the two operators.

A reliability engineer pointed out that variations in the data could be traced to three causes: (1) repeatability problems (equipment variation or EV), (2) reproducibility variations (appraisal variation, or AV), and (3) process variation (part variation, or PV). Thus, total variation (TV) consists of repeatability and reproducibility (R&R) variation and PV. Team members had heard about EV, AV, and R&R in a training class on measurement, but realized that the last item was an obvious, but important point they had not previously considered. They were given the following formulas for computation of the PV and TV:

$$\text{PV} = R_p \times K_3$$

and

$$\text{TV} = \sqrt{(\text{R\&R})^2 + (\text{PV})^2}$$

The R_p value is obtained by calculating the range of the sample averages in a gauge study. The K_3 value depends on the number of parts measured in the study. Some of these values are found in Table 11.5.

Assignment

Calculate the R&R, process, and total variation for the data.*[25] Using the TV as the divisor, calculate the percentage of total variation that the EV, AV, R&R, and PV encompass. (These variations are not directly related to one another, so the percentages will not total to 100 percent.) What conclusions can you draw about the variations that were observed? Based on your analysis, what recommendations could you make on how the measurement system could be improved? What would you tell the production manager?

*Note: Readers who have need for professional software for performing extensive R&R studies or keeping track of gage records and calibration may wish to look at R&Rpack and GAGEpack software developed and distributed by PQ Systems, Inc., P.O. Box 10, Dayton, OH 45474-0010.

NOTES

1. "Coca-Cola: A Taste for Quality," The Coca-Cola Company, Atlanta, Georgia.

2. *http://www.thecoca-colacompany.com/news/NewsDetail.asp?NewsDate=6/15/99.*

3. Walter A. Shewhart, *Economic Control of Quality of Manufactured Product* (New York: Van Nostrand, 1931).

4. "Testing for Conformity: An Inside Job," *Golf Journal*, May 1998, 20–25.

5. "DaimlerChrysler's Quality Practices Pay Off for PT Cruiser," News and Analysis, *Metrologyworld.com*, March 23, 2000.

6. Press Release PR96-14; Milacron Web site: *http://www.milacron.com.*

7. Cincinnati Milacron U.S. Machine Tool Group Quality Manual, September 1997.

8. Dan K. Fitzsimmons, "Gaining Acceptance for Acceptance Sampling," *Quality Progress*, April 1989, 46–48.

9. Douglas C. Montgomery, Introduction to Statistical Quality Control (New York: John Wiley & Sons, 1991).

10. Thomas Pyzdek, *Pyzdek's Guide to SPC, Volume Two—Applications and Special Topics* (Milwaukee, WI: ASQC Quality Press, 1992).

11. Douglas H. Harris and Frederick B. Chaney, *Human Factors in Quality Assurance* (New York: John Wiley, 1969).

12. Stuart F. Brown, "Giving More Jobs to Electronic Eyes," *Fortune*, February 16, 1998, 104[B].

13. *Fortune*, June 27, 1994, 131.

14. Statement made by Belinda Collins before the House Subcommittee on Technology, Committee on Science, June 29, 1995.

15. *ASQC Automotive Division Statistical Process Control Manual* (Milwaukee, WI: American Society for Quality Control, 1986).

16. This section is adopted from NIST Calibration Services Web page at *http://www.nist.gov.*

17. Tom Taormina, "Conducting Successful Internal Audits," *Quality Digest*, June 1998, 44–47.

18. J. M. Juran, *Juran on Leadership for Quality* (New York: Free Press), 1989.

19. U. S. Food and Drug Administration, U.S. Department of Agriculture, National Advisory Committee on Microbiological Criteria for Foods, *Hazard Analysis and Critical Control Point Principles and Application Guidelines*, adopted August 14, 1997; and Food Safety and Inspection Service United States Department of Agriculture, Washington, D.C. 20250, HACCP Questions and Answers/Hazard Analysis and Critical Control Point (HACCP) Systems, January 1998.

20. Adapted from The Ritz-Carlton Hotel Company 1992 and 1999 Application Summaries for the Malcolm Baldrige National Quality Award.

21. Leda Kydoniefs and Carl Lindblom, "Using Calibration in an Office Environment," *Quality Progress*, April 2000, 67–73.

22. Publisher: Dunlavy Audio Labs, P.O. Box 49399, Colorado Springs, CO 80949-9399. Adapted from material provided on the company Web site, *http://www.dunlavyaudio.com*; author: Andrew W. Rigby.

23. We thank our former students Nick Dattilo, Brian Kessler, and Temeka Flowers, on whose research this case is based.

BIBLIOGRAPHY

Case, Kenneth E., and Lynn L. Jones. *Profit Through Quality: Quality Assurance Programs for Manufacturers*. Norcross, GA: American Institute of Industrial Engineers, 1978.

Ferdeber, Charles J. "Measuring Quality and Productivity in a Service Environment." *Industrial Engineering*, July 1981, 193–201.

Griffith, Gary. *Quality Technician's Handbook.* New York: John Wiley, 1986.

Holm, Richard A. "Fulfilling the New Role of Inspection." *Manufacturing Engineering* (May 1988), 43–46.

Lloyd's Register Quality Assurance, Ltd., "Getting the most from ISO 9000," 1999.

MIL-HDBK-53-1A, Military Handbook, Guide for Attribute Lot Sampling Inspection and MIL-STD-105. Washington, DC: Department of Defense, June 30, 1965.

Puma, Maurice. "Quality Technology in Manufacturing," *Quality Progress* 13, no. 8 (August 1980), 16–19.

Rice, George O. "Metrology." In *Quality Management Handbook*, eds., Loren Walsh, Ralph Wurster, and Raymond J. Kimber. New York:

Marcel Dekker, 1986, 517–530.

Sherman, William H. "Inspection: Do We Need It?" *Manufacturing Engineering*, May 1988, 39–42.

Troxell, Joseph R. "Service Time Quality Standards." *Quality Progress* 14, no. 9 (September 1981), 35–37.

———. "Standards for Quality Control in Service Industries." *Quality Progress* 12, no. 1 (January 1979), 32–34.

Tedaldi, Michael, Fred Seaglione, and Vincent Russotti. *A Beginner's Guide to Quality in Manufacturing*. Milwaukee, WI: ASQC Quality Press, 1992.

CHAPTER 12

STATISTICAL PROCESS CONTROL

OUTLINE

Deming's funnel experiment, described in Chapter 9, demonstrates that failure to distinguish between common causes and special causes of variation can actually increase the variation in a process. This problem often results from the mistaken belief that whenever process output is off target, some adjustment must be made. Knowing when to leave a process alone is an important step in maintaining control over a process. Equally important is knowing when to take action to prevent the production of nonconforming product.

Statistical process control (SPC) is a methodology for monitoring a process to identify special causes of variation and signal the need to take corrective action when it is appropriate. When special causes are present, the process is deemed to be *out of control*. If the variation in the process is due to common causes alone, the process is said to be *in statistical control*. A practical definition of statistical control is that both the process averages and variances are constant over time.[1]

SPC relies on *control charts*, one of the basic quality improvement tools that we briefly introduced in Chapter 10. SPC is a proven technique for improving quality and productivity. Many customers require their suppliers to provide evidence of statistical process control. Thus, SPC provides a means by which a firm may demonstrate its quality capability, an activity necessary for survival in today's highly competitive markets. Because SPC requires processes to show measurable variation, it is ineffective for quality levels approaching six-sigma. However, SPC is quite effective for companies in the early stages of quality efforts.

Although control charts were first developed and used in a manufacturing context, they are easily applied to service organizations. Table 12.1 lists just a few of the

Table 12.1 Control Chart Applications in Service Organizations

Organization	Quality Measure
Hospital	Lab test accuracy Insurance claim accuracy On-time delivery of meals and medication
Bank	Check-processing accuracy
Insurance company	Claims-processing response time Billing accuracy
Post Office	Sorting accuracy Time of delivery Percentage of express mail delivered on time
Ambulance	Response time
Police Department	Incidence of crime in a precinct Number of traffic citations
Hotel	Proportion of rooms satisfactorily cleaned Checkout time Number of complaints received
Transportation	Proportion of freight cars correctly routed Dollar amount of damage per claim
Auto service	Percentage of time work completed as promised Number of parts out of stock

many potential applications of control charts for services. The key is in defining the appropriate quality measures to monitor. Most service processes can be improved through the appropriate application of control charts.

In this chapter we describe how to develop and use statistical process control to monitor manufacturing and service processes. The appendix to this chapter provides the statistical details for understanding the theory underlying control charts.

CAPABILITY AND CONTROL

Process capability calculations make little sense if the process is not in statistical control because the data are confounded by special causes that do not represent the inherent capability of the process. Consider Table 12.2, which shows 30 samples measurements of a quality characteristic from a manufacturing process with specifications 0.75 ± 0.25. Each row corresponds to a sample size 5 taken every 15 minutes. The mean of each sample is also given in the last column. A frequency distribution and histogram of these data is shown in Figure 12.1. The data form a relatively symmetric distribution with a mean of 0.762 and standard deviation 0.0738. Using these values, we find that $C_{pk} = 1.075$, indicating that the process capability is at least marginally acceptable.

Table 12.2 Thirty Samples of Quality Measurements

	A	B	C	D	E	F	G	H
1	**Sample**			**Observations**				**Mean**
2	**1**	0.682	0.689	0.776	0.798	0.714		0.732
3	**2**	0.787	0.860	0.601	0.746	0.779		0.755
4	**3**	0.780	0.667	0.838	0.785	0.723		0.759
5	**4**	0.591	0.727	0.812	0.775	0.730		0.727
6	**5**	0.693	0.708	0.790	0.758	0.671		0.724
7	**6**	0.749	0.714	0.738	0.719	0.606		0.705
8	**7**	0.791	0.713	0.689	0.877	0.603		0.735
9	**8**	0.744	0.779	0.660	0.737	0.822		0.748
10	**9**	0.769	0.773	0.641	0.644	0.725		0.710
11	**10**	0.718	0.671	0.708	0.850	0.712		0.732
12	**11**	0.787	0.821	0.764	0.658	0.708		0.748
13	**12**	0.622	0.802	0.818	0.872	0.727		0.768
14	**13**	0.657	0.822	0.893	0.544	0.750		0.733
15	**14**	0.806	0.749	0.859	0.801	0.701		0.783
16	**15**	0.660	0.681	0.644	0.747	0.728		0.692
17	**16**	0.816	0.817	0.768	0.716	0.649		0.753
18	**17**	0.826	0.777	0.721	0.770	0.809		0.781
19	**18**	0.828	0.829	0.865	0.778	0.872		0.834
20	**19**	0.805	0.719	0.612	0.938	0.807		0.776
21	**20**	0.802	0.756	0.786	0.815	0.801		0.792
22	**21**	0.876	0.803	0.701	0.789	0.672		0.768
23	**22**	0.855	0.783	0.722	0.856	0.751		0.793
24	**23**	0.762	0.705	0.804	0.805	0.809		0.777
25	**24**	0.703	0.837	0.759	0.975	0.732		0.801
26	**25**	0.737	0.723	0.776	0.748	0.732		0.743
27	**26**	0.748	0.686	0.856	0.811	0.838		0.788
28	**27**	0.826	0.803	0.764	0.823	0.886		0.820
29	**28**	0.728	0.721	0.820	0.772	0.639		0.736
30	**29**	0.803	0.892	0.740	0.816	0.770		0.804
31	**30**	0.774	0.837	0.872	0.849	0.818		0.830

Figure 12.1 Frequency Distribution and Histogram

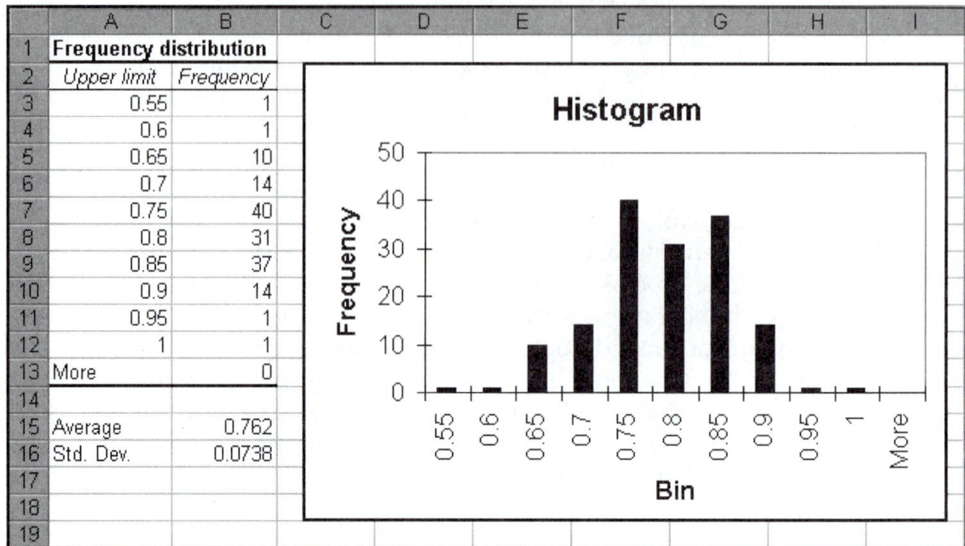

Frequency distribution	
Upper limit	*Frequency*
0.55	1
0.6	1
0.65	10
0.7	14
0.75	40
0.8	31
0.85	37
0.9	14
0.95	1
1	1
More	0
Average	0.762
Std. Dev.	0.0738

Because the data were taken over an extended period of time we cannot determine whether the process remained stable. In a histogram, the dimension of time is not considered. Thus, histograms do not allow you to distinguish between common and special causes of variation. It is unclear whether any special causes of variation are influencing the capability index. If we plot the mean of each sample against the time at which the sample was taken (since the time increments between samples are equal, the sample number is an appropriate surrogate for time), we obtain the run chart shown in Figure 12.2. It indicates that the mean has shifted up at about sample 17. In fact, the process average for the first 16 samples is only 0.738 while the average for the remaining samples is 0.789. Therefore, although the overall average is close to the target specification, at no time was the actual process average centered near the target. We should conclude that this process is not in statistical control, and should not pay much attention to the process capability calculations.

Control and capability are two different concepts. As shown in Figure 12.3, a process may be capable or not capable, or in control or out of control, independently of each other. Clearly, we would like every process to be both capable and in control. If a process is neither capable nor in control, we must first get it in a state of control by removing special causes of variation, and then attack the common causes to improve its capability. If a process is capable but not in control (as the previous example illustrated), we should work to get it back in control.

SPC METHODOLOGY

Control charts, like the other basic tools for quality improvement, are relatively simple to use. Control charts have three basic applications: (1) to establish a state of statistical control, (2) to monitor a process and signal when the process goes out of control, and (3) to determine process capability. The following is a summary of the steps

Figure 12.2 Run Chart of Sample Means

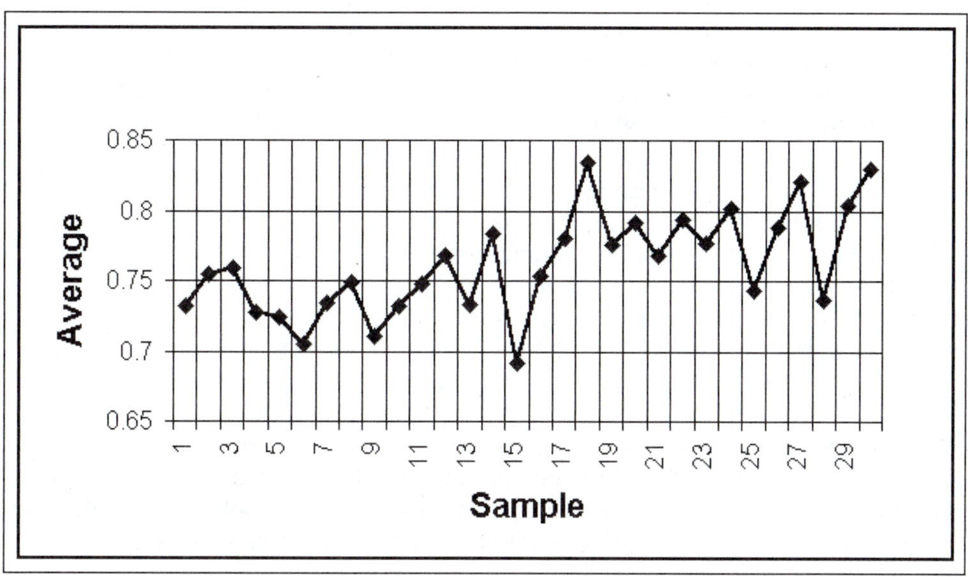

required to develop and use control charts. Steps 1 through 4 focus on establishing a state of statistical control; in step 5, the charts are used for ongoing monitoring; and finally, in step 6, the data are used for process capability analysis.

1. Preparation
    a. Choose the variable or attribute to be measured.
    b. Determine the basis, size, and frequency of sampling.
    c. Set up the control chart.

Figure 12.3 Capability versus Control (Arrows indicate the direction of appropriate management action)

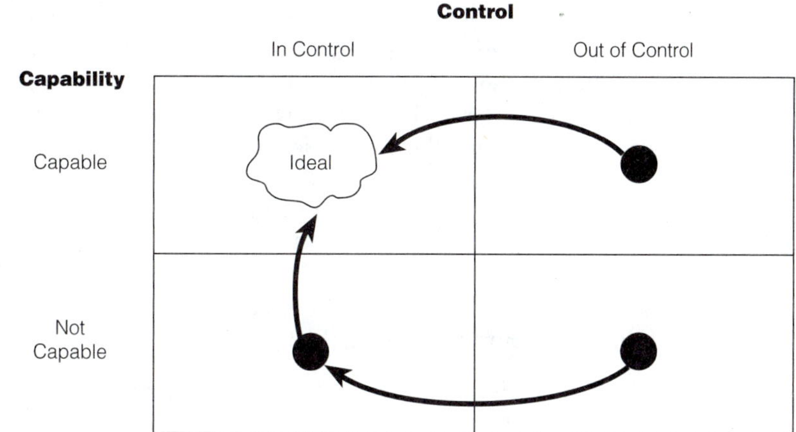

2. Data collection
   a. Record the data.
   b. Calculate relevant statistics: averages, ranges, proportions, and so on.
   c. Plot the statistics on the chart.
3. Determination of trial control limits
   a. Draw the center line (process average) on the chart.
   b. Compute the upper and lower control limits.
4. Analysis and interpretation
   a. Investigate the chart for lack of control.
   b. Eliminate out-of-control points.
   c. Recompute control limits if necessary.
5. Use as a problem-solving tool
   a. Continue data collection and plotting.
   b. Identify out-of-control situations and take corrective action.
6. Use the control chart data to determine process capability, if desired.

In the remainder of this chapter we will discuss the construction, interpretation, and use of control charts following this methodology. Although many different charts are described, they differ only in the type of measurement for which the chart is used; the methodology previously described applies to each of them.

CONTROL CHARTS FOR VARIABLES DATA

Variables data are those that are measured along a continuous scale. Examples of variables data are length, weight, and distance. The charts most commonly used for variables data are the $\bar{x}$-chart ("*x*-bar" chart) and the *R*-chart (range chart). The $\bar{x}$-chart is used to monitor the centering of the process, and the *R*-chart is used to monitor the variation in the process. The range is used as a measure of variation simply for convenience, particularly when workers on the factory floor perform control chart calculations by hand. For large samples and when data are analyzed by computer programs, the standard deviation is a better measure of variability (discussed later in this chapter).

Constructing $\bar{x}$- and *R*-Charts and Establishing Statistical Control

The first step in developing $\bar{x}$- and *R*-charts is to gather data. Usually, about 25 to 30 samples are collected. Samples between size 3 and 10 are generally used, with 5 being the most common. The number of samples is indicated by *k*, and *n* denotes the sample size. For each sample *i*, the mean (denoted $\bar{x}_i$) and the range (R_i) are computed. These values are then plotted on their respective control charts. Next, the *overall mean* and *average range* calculations are made. These values specify the center lines for the $\bar{x}$- and *R*-charts, respectively. The overall mean is the average of the sample means $\bar{x}_i$:

$$\bar{\bar{x}} = \frac{\sum_{i=1}^{k} \bar{x}_i}{k}$$

The average range is similarly computed, using the formula

$$\bar{R} = \frac{\sum_{i=1}^{k} R_i}{k}$$

The average range and average mean are used to compute control limits for the R- and $\bar{x}$-charts. Control limits are easily calculated using the following formulas:

$$UCL_R = D_4\bar{R} \qquad UCL_{\bar{x}} = \bar{\bar{x}} + A_2\bar{R}$$

$$LCL_R = D_3\bar{R} \qquad LCL_{\bar{x}} = \bar{\bar{x}} - A_2\bar{R}$$

where the constants D_3, D_4, and A_2 depend on the sample size and can be found in Appendix B.

The control limits represent the range between which all points are expected to fall if the process is in statistical control. If any points fall outside the control limits or if any unusual patterns are observed, then some special cause has probably affected the process. The process should be studied to determine the cause. If special causes are present, then they are *not* representative of the true state of statistical control, and the calculations of the center line and control limits will be biased. The corresponding data points should be eliminated, and new values for $\bar{\bar{x}}$, $\bar{R}$, and the control limits should be computed.

In determining whether a process is in statistical control, the R-chart is always analyzed first. Because the control limits in the $\bar{x}$-chart depend on the average range, special causes in the R-chart may produce unusual patterns in the $\bar{x}$-chart, even when the centering of the process is in control. (An example of such distorted patterns is given later in this chapter.) Once statistical control is established for the R-chart, attention may turn to the $\bar{x}$-chart.

Figure 12.4 shows a typical data sheet used for recording data and drawing control charts, which is available from the American Society for Quality (ASQ). This form provides space for descriptive information about the process, recording of sample observations and computed statistics, and drawing the control charts. On the back of this form is a work sheet (see Figure 12.5) for computing control limits and process capability information. The construction and analysis of control charts is best seen by example. The ASQ chart is used in the following example.

Example 1: Control Charts for Silicon Wafer Production. The thickness of silicon wafers used in the production of semiconductors must be carefully controlled. The tolerance of one such product is specified as ±0.0050 inches. In one production facility, three wafers were selected each hour and the thickness measured carefully to within one ten-thousandth of an inch. Figure 12.6 on page 694 shows the results obtained for 25 samples. For example, the mean of the first sample is

$$\bar{x}_1 = \frac{41 + 70 + 22}{3} = \frac{113}{3} = 44$$

The range of sample 1 is 70 – 22 = 48. (Note: calculations are rounded to the nearest integer for simplicity.)

The calculations of the average range, overall mean, and control limits are shown in Figure 12.7 on page 695. The average range is the sum of the sample ranges (676) divided by the number of samples (25); the overall mean is the sum of the sample

Figure 12.4 ASQ Control Chart Data Sheet

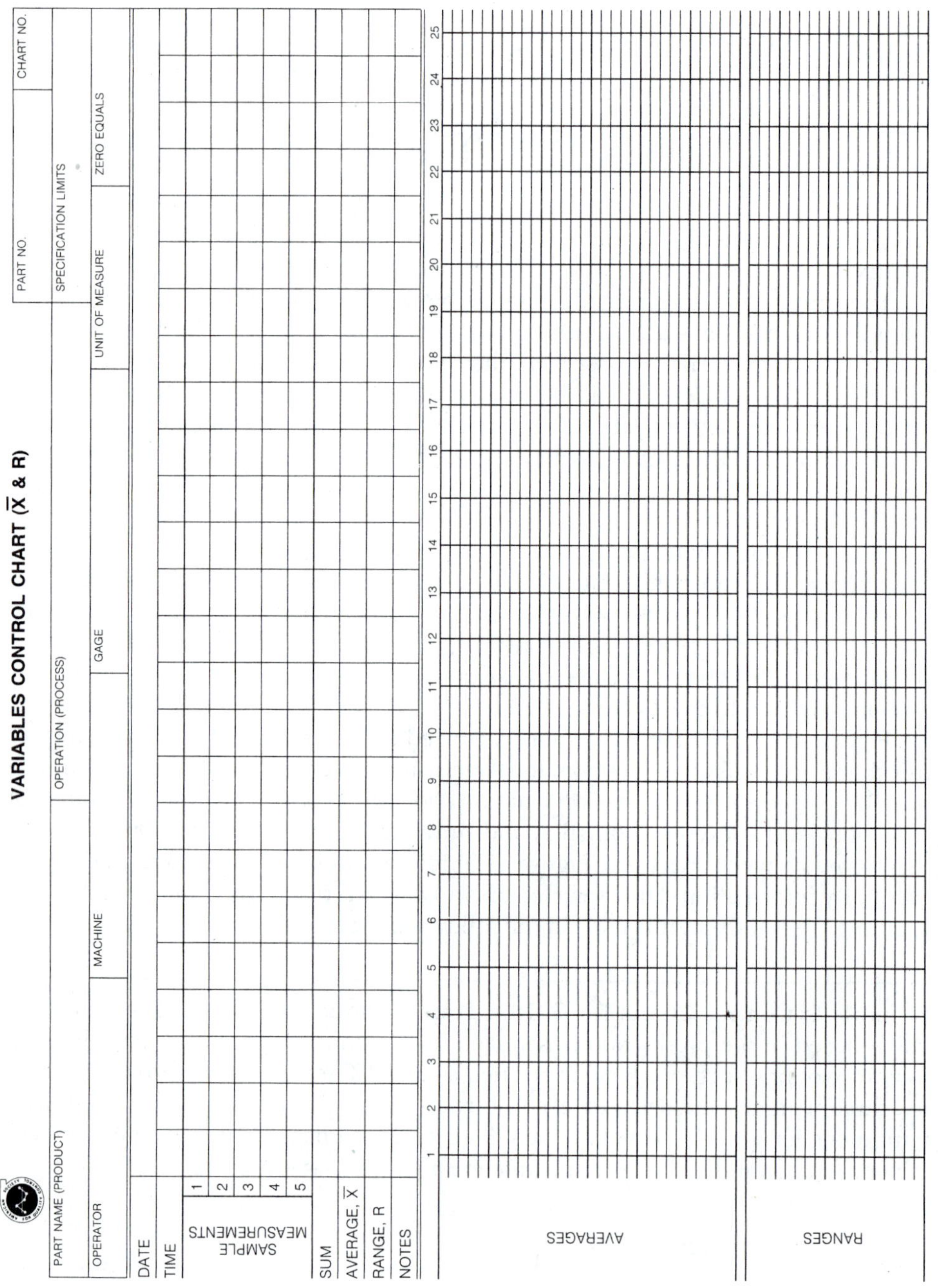

Source: Reprinted with permission of ASQ.

Figure 12.5 ASQ Control Chart Calculation Work Sheet

CALCULATION WORKSHEET

CONTROL LIMITS

SUBGROUPS INCLUDED ______ ______

$\bar{R} = \frac{\Sigma R}{k}$ = ______ = ______ =

$\bar{\bar{X}} = \frac{\Sigma \bar{X}}{k}$ = ______ = ______ =

OR

$\bar{X}'$ (MIDSPEC. OR STD.) = =

$A_2\bar{R}$ = × = ______ × = ______

$UCL_{\bar{X}} = \bar{\bar{X}} + A_2\bar{R}$ = =

$LCL_{\bar{X}} = \bar{\bar{X}} - A_2\bar{R}$ = =

$UCL_R = D_4\bar{R}$ = × = × =

LIMITS FOR INDIVIDUALS

COMPARE WITH SPECIFICATION OR TOLERANCE LIMITS

$\bar{\bar{X}}$ =

$\frac{3}{d_2}\bar{R}$ = × = ______

$UL_x = \bar{\bar{X}} + \frac{3}{d_2}\bar{R}$ =

$LL_x = \bar{\bar{X}} - \frac{3}{d_2}\bar{R}$ =

US =

LS = ______

US − LS =

$6\sigma = \frac{6}{d_2}\bar{R}$ =

MODIFIED CONTROL LIMITS FOR AVERAGES

BASED ON SPECIFICATION LIMITS AND PROCESS CAPABILITY.
APPLICABLE ONLY IF: US − LS > 6σ.

US = LS =

$A_M\bar{R}$ = × = ______ $A_M\bar{R}$ = ______

$URL_{\bar{X}} = US - A_M\bar{R}$ = $LRL_{\bar{X}} = LS + A_M\bar{R}$ =

FACTORS FOR CONTROL LIMITS

n	A_2	D_4	d_2	$\frac{3}{d_2}$	A_M
2	1.880	3.268	1.128	2.659	0.779
3	1.023	2.574	1.693	1.772	0.749
4	0.729	2.282	2.059	1.457	0.728
5	0.577	2.114	2.326	1.290	0.713
6	0.483	2.004	2.534	1.184	0.701

Source: Reprinted with permission of ASQ.

averages (1,221) divided by the number of samples (25). Since the sample size is 3, the factors used in computing the control limits are $A_2 = 1.023$ and $D_4 = 2.574$. (For sample sizes of 6 or less, factor $D_3 = 0$; therefore, the lower control limit on the range chart is zero.) The center lines and control limits are drawn on the chart in Figure 12.8 on page 696.

Examining the range chart first, it appears that the process is in control. All points lie within the control limits and no unusual patterns exist. In the $\bar{x}$-chart, however, sample 17 lies above the upper control limit. On investigation, some defective material had been used. These data should be eliminated from the control chart calculations. Figure 12.9 on page 697 shows the calculations after sample 17 was removed. The revised center lines and control limits are shown in Figure 12.10 on page 698. Customarily, out-of-control points are noted on the chart. The resulting chart appears to be in control.

Interpreting Patterns in Control Charts

When a process is in statistical control, the points on a control chart fluctuate randomly between the control limits with no recognizable pattern. The following checklist provides a set of general rules for examining a process to determine whether it is in control:

1. No points are outside control limits.
2. The number of points above and below the center line is about the same.
3. The points seem to fall randomly above and below the center line.
4. Most points, but not all, are near the center line, and only a few are close to the control limits.

Figure 12.6 Silicon Wafer Thickness Data

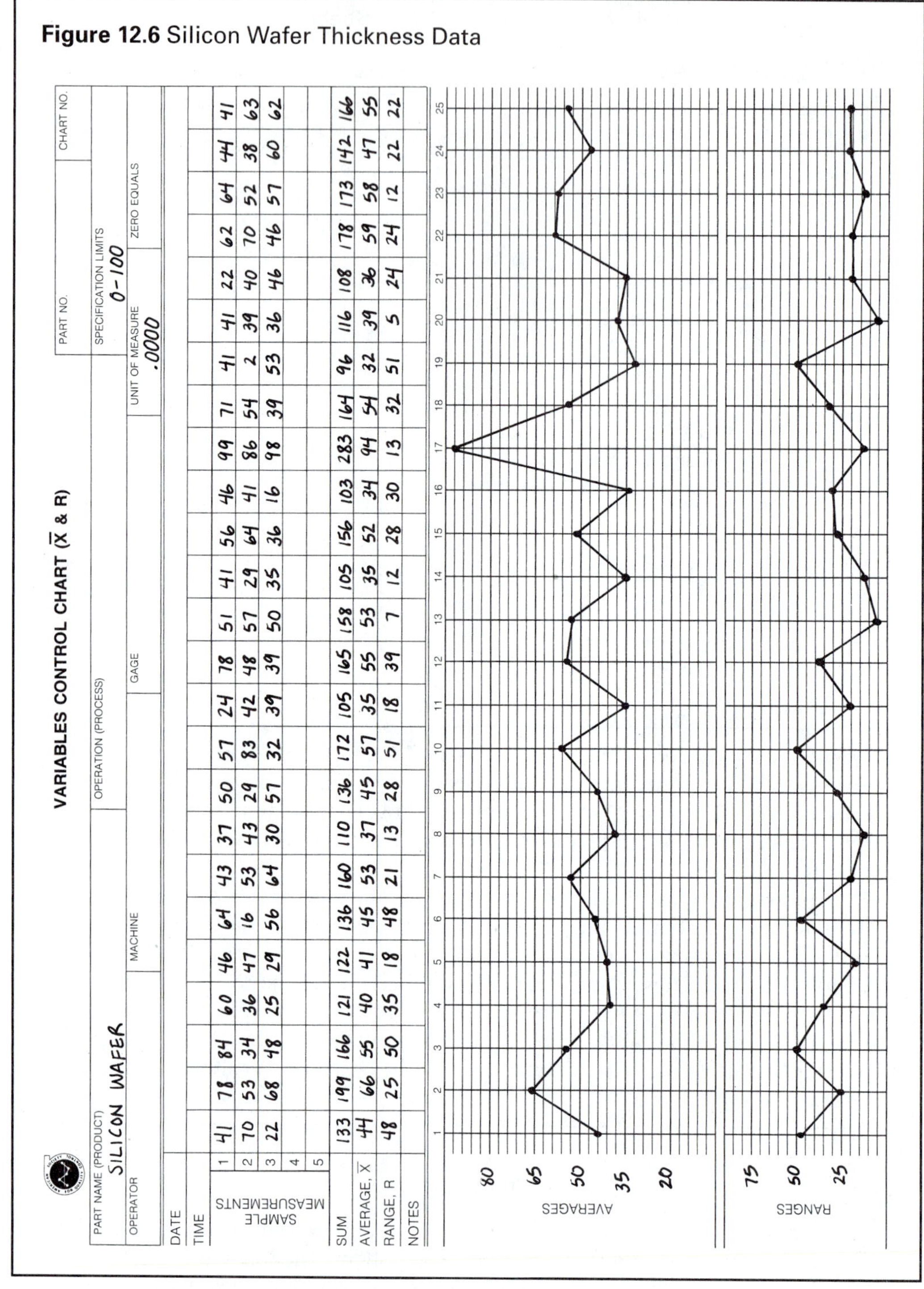

VARIABLES CONTROL CHART ($\bar{X}$ & R)

PART NAME (PRODUCT)	OPERATION (PROCESS)	SPECIFICATION LIMITS	PART NO.	CHART NO.
SILICON WAFER		0-100		
OPERATOR	MACHINE	GAGE	UNIT OF MEASURE	ZERO EQUALS
			.0000	

	1	2	3	4	5	6	7	8	9	10	11	12	13
DATE													
TIME													
SAMPLE MEASUREMENTS 1	41	78	84	60	46	64	43	37	50	57	24	78	51
2	70	53	34	36	47	16	53	43	29	83	42	48	57
3	22	68	48	25	29	56	64	30	57	32	39	39	50
4													
5													
SUM	133	199	166	121	122	136	160	110	136	172	105	165	158
AVERAGE, $\bar{X}$	44	66	55	40	41	45	53	37	45	57	35	55	53
RANGE, R	48	25	50	35	18	48	21	13	28	51	18	39	7
NOTES													

	14	15	16	17	18	19	20	21	22	23	24	25
DATE												
TIME												
SAMPLE MEASUREMENTS 1	41	56	46	99	71	41	41	22	62	64	44	41
2	29	64	41	86	54	2	39	40	70	52	38	63
3	35	36	16	98	39	53	36	46	46	57	60	62
4												
5												
SUM	105	156	103	283	164	96	116	108	178	173	142	166
AVERAGE, $\bar{X}$	35	52	34	94	54	32	39	36	59	58	47	55
RANGE, R	12	28	30	13	32	51	5	24	24	12	22	22
NOTES												

Figure 12.7 Control Limit Calculations

CALCULATION WORKSHEET

CONTROL LIMITS

SUBGROUPS INCLUDED ALL

$\bar{R} = \frac{\Sigma R}{k} = \frac{676}{25} = 27$

$\bar{\bar{X}} = \frac{\Sigma \bar{X}}{k} = \frac{1221}{25} = 48.8$

OR

$\bar{X}'$ (MIDSPEC. OR STD.) $= 50$

$A_2\bar{R} = 1.023 \times 27 = 27.6$

$UCL_{\bar{X}} = \bar{\bar{X}} + A_2\bar{R} = 76.4$

$LCL_{\bar{X}} = \bar{\bar{X}} - A_2\bar{R} = 21.2$

$UCL_R = D_4\bar{R} = 2.574 \times 27 = 69.5$

LIMITS FOR INDIVIDUALS

COMPARE WITH SPECIFICATION OR TOLERANCE LIMITS

$\bar{\bar{X}}$ =

$\frac{3}{d_2}\bar{R} = \quad \times \quad =$

$UL_x = \bar{\bar{X}} + \frac{3}{d_2}\bar{R} =$

$LL_x = \bar{\bar{X}} - \frac{3}{d_2}\bar{R} =$

US =

LS =

US − LS =

$6\sigma = \frac{6}{d_2}\bar{R} =$

MODIFIED CONTROL LIMITS FOR AVERAGES

BASED ON SPECIFICATION LIMITS AND PROCESS CAPABILITY. APPLICABLE ONLY IF: US − LS > 6σ.

US = LS =

$A_M\bar{R} = \quad \times \quad =$ $A_M\bar{R}$ =

$URL_{\bar{X}} = US - A_M\bar{R}$ = $LRL_{\bar{X}} = LS + A_M\bar{R}$ =

FACTORS FOR CONTROL LIMITS

n	A_2	D_4	d_2	$\frac{3}{d_2}$	A_M
2	1.880	3.268	1.128	2.659	0.779
3	1.023	2.574	1.693	1.772	0.749
4	0.729	2.282	2.059	1.457	0.728
5	0.577	2.114	2.326	1.290	0.713
6	0.483	2.004	2.534	1.184	0.701

The underlying assumption behind these rules is that the distribution of sample means is normal. This assumption follows from the central limit theorem of statistics, which states that the distribution of sample means approaches a normal distribution as the sample size increases regardless of the original distribution. Of course, for small sample sizes, the distribution of the original data must be reasonably normal for this assumption to hold. The upper and lower control limits are computed to be three standard deviations from the overall mean. Thus, the probability that any sample mean falls outside the control limits is small. This probability is the origin of rule 1.

Because the normal distribution is symmetric, about the same number of points fall above as below the center line. Also, since the mean of the normal distribution is the median, about half the points fall on either side of the center line. Finally, about 68 percent of a normal distribution falls within one standard deviation of the mean; thus, most—but not all—points should be close to the center line. These characteristics will hold provided that the mean and variance of the original data have not changed during the time the data were collected; that is, the process is stable.

Several types of unusual patterns arise in control charts, which are reviewed here along with an indication of the typical causes of such patterns.[2]

One Point Outside Control Limits A single point outside the control limits (see Figure 12.11 on page 699) is usually produced by a special cause. Often, the *R*-chart provides a similar indication. Once in a while, however, such points are a normal part of the process and occur simply by chance.

A common reason for a point falling outside a control limit is an error in the calculation of $\bar{x}$ or R for the sample. You should always check your calculations whenever this occurs. Other possible causes are a sudden power surge, a broken tool, measurement error, or an incomplete or omitted operation in the process.

Figure 12.8 Initial Control Chart

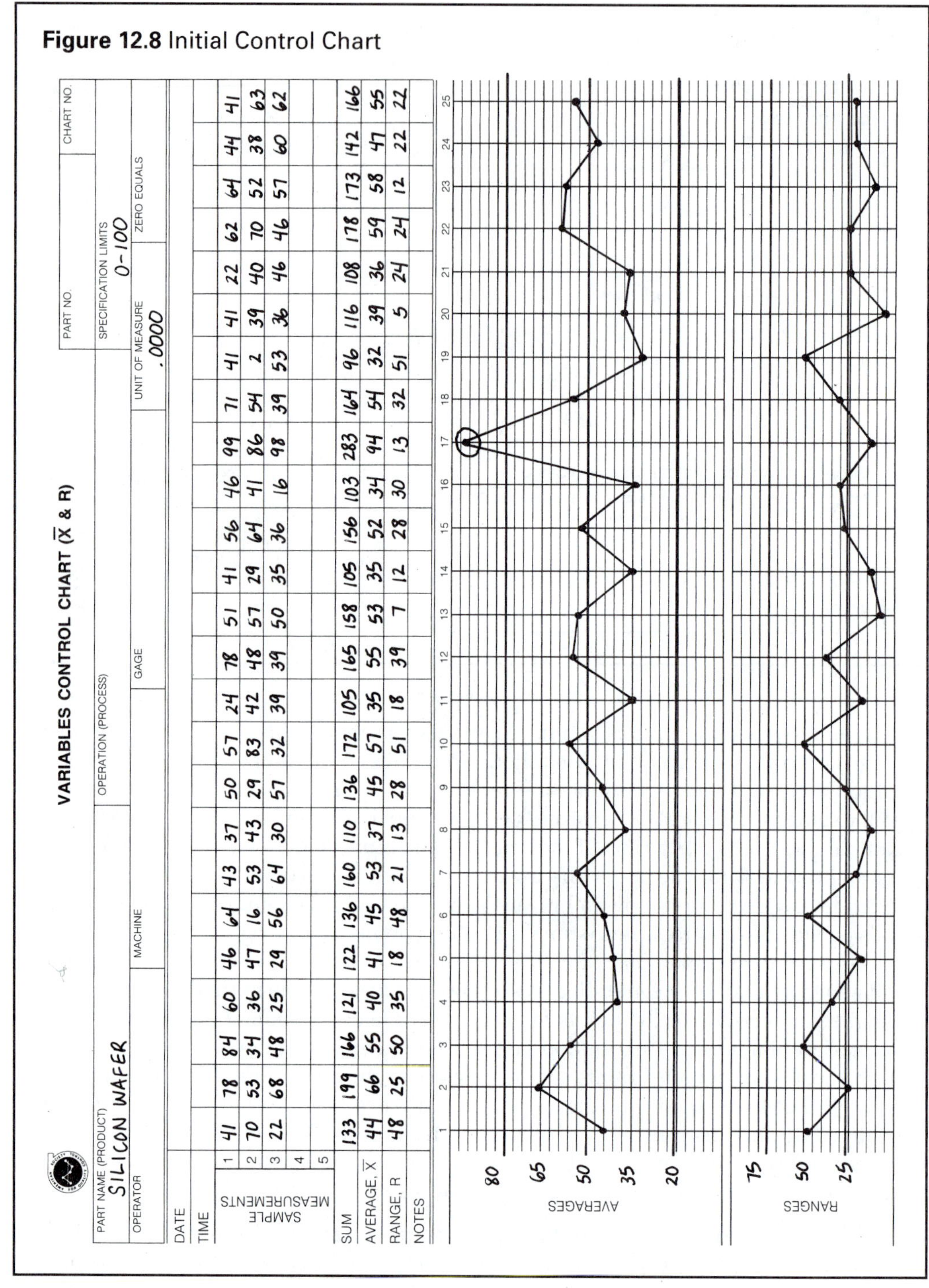

VARIABLES CONTROL CHART ($\bar{X}$ & R)

PART NAME (PRODUCT): SILICON WAFER | OPERATION (PROCESS): | PART NO.: | CHART NO.:
SPECIFICATION LIMITS: 0-100
OPERATOR: | MACHINE: | GAGE: | UNIT OF MEASURE: .0000 | ZERO EQUALS:

	1	2	3	4	5	6	7	8	9	10	11	12	13
DATE													
TIME													
SAMPLE MEASUREMENTS 1	41	78	84	60	46	64	43	37	50	57	24	78	51
2	70	53	34	36	47	16	53	43	29	83	42	48	57
3	22	68	48	25	29	56	64	30	57	32	39	39	50
4													
5													
SUM	133	199	166	121	122	136	160	110	136	172	105	165	158
AVERAGE, $\bar{X}$	44	66	55	40	41	45	53	37	45	57	35	55	53
RANGE, R	48	25	50	35	18	48	21	13	28	51	18	39	7
NOTES													

	14	15	16	17	18	19	20	21	22	23	24	25
DATE												
TIME												
SAMPLE MEASUREMENTS 1	41	56	46	99	71	41	41	22	62	64	44	41
2	29	64	41	86	54	2	39	40	70	52	38	63
3	35	36	16	98	39	53	36	46	46	57	60	62
4												
5												
SUM	105	156	103	283	164	96	116	108	178	173	142	166
AVERAGE, $\bar{X}$	35	52	34	94	54	32	39	36	59	58	47	55
RANGE, R	12	28	30	13	32	51	5	24	24	12	22	22
NOTES												

Figure 12.9 Revised Control Chart Calculations

CALCULATION WORKSHEET

CONTROL LIMITS

SUBGROUPS INCLUDED ALL | #17 REMOVED

$\bar{R} = \frac{\Sigma R}{k} = \frac{676}{25} = 27$ | $\frac{663}{24} = 27.6$

$\bar{\bar{X}} = \frac{\Sigma \bar{X}}{k} = \frac{1221}{25} = 48.8$ | $\frac{1127}{24} = 47.0$

OR

$\bar{X}'$ (MIDSPEC. OR STD.) $= 50$ | $= 50$

$A_2\bar{R} = 1.023 \times 27 = 27.6$ | $1.023 \times 27.6 = 28.2$

$UCL_{\bar{X}} = \bar{\bar{X}} + A_2\bar{R} = 76.4$ | $= 75.2$

$LCL_{\bar{X}} = \bar{\bar{X}} - A_2\bar{R} = 21.2$ | $= 18.8$

$UCL_R = D_4\bar{R} = 2.574 \times 27 = 69.5$ | $2.574 \times 27.6 = 71.0$

LIMITS FOR INDIVIDUALS

COMPARE WITH SPECIFICATION OR TOLERANCE LIMITS

$\bar{\bar{X}}$ =

$\frac{3}{d_2}\bar{R}$ = x =

$UL_x = \bar{\bar{X}} + \frac{3}{d_2}\bar{R}$ =

$LL_x = \bar{\bar{X}} - \frac{3}{d_2}\bar{R}$ =

US =

LS =

US − LS =

$6\sigma = \frac{6}{d_2}\bar{R}$ =

MODIFIED CONTROL LIMITS FOR AVERAGES

BASED ON SPECIFICATION LIMITS AND PROCESS CAPABILITY.
APPLICABLE ONLY IF: US − LS > 6σ.

US = | LS =

$A_M\bar{R}$ = x = | $A_M\bar{R}$ =

$URL_{\bar{X}} = US - A_M\bar{R}$ = | $LRL_{\bar{X}} = LS + A_M\bar{R}$ =

FACTORS FOR CONTROL LIMITS

n	A_2	D_4	d_2	$\frac{3}{d_2}$	A_M
2	1.880	3.268	1.128	2.659	0.779
3	1.023	2.574	1.693	1.772	0.749
4	0.729	2.282	2.059	1.457	0.728
5	0.577	2.114	2.326	1.290	0.713
6	0.483	2.004	2.534	1.184	0.701

Sudden Shift in the Process Average An unusual number of consecutive points falling on one side of the center line (see Figure 12.12 on page 699) is usually an indication that the process average has suddenly shifted. Typically, this occurrence is the result of an external influence that has affected the process, which would be considered a special cause. In both the $\bar{x}$- and R-charts, possible causes might be a new operator, a new inspector, a new machine setting, or a change in the setup or method.

If the shift is up in the R-chart, the process has become less uniform. Typical causes are carelessness of operators, poor or inadequate maintenance, or possibly a fixture in need of repair. If the shift is down in the R-chart, the uniformity of the process has improved. This shift might be the result of improved workmanship or better machines or materials. As mentioned, every effort should be made to determine the reason for the improvement and to maintain it.

Three rules of thumb are used for early detection of process shifts. A simple rule is that if eight consecutive points fall on one side of the center line, one could conclude that the mean has shifted. Second, divide the region between the center line and each control limit into three equal parts. Then if (1) two of three consecutive points fall in the outer one-third region between the center line and one of the control limits or (2) four of five consecutive points fall within the outer two-thirds region, one would also conclude that the process has gone out of control. Examples are illustrated in Figure 12.13 on page 700.

Cycles Cycles are short, repeated patterns in the chart, alternating high peaks and low valleys (see Figure 12.14 on page 701). These patterns are the result of causes that come and go on a regular basis. In the $\bar{x}$-chart, cycles may be the result of operator rotation or fatigue at the end of a shift, different gauges used by different inspectors, seasonal effects such as temperature or humidity, or differences between day and

Figure 12.10 Revised Control Chart

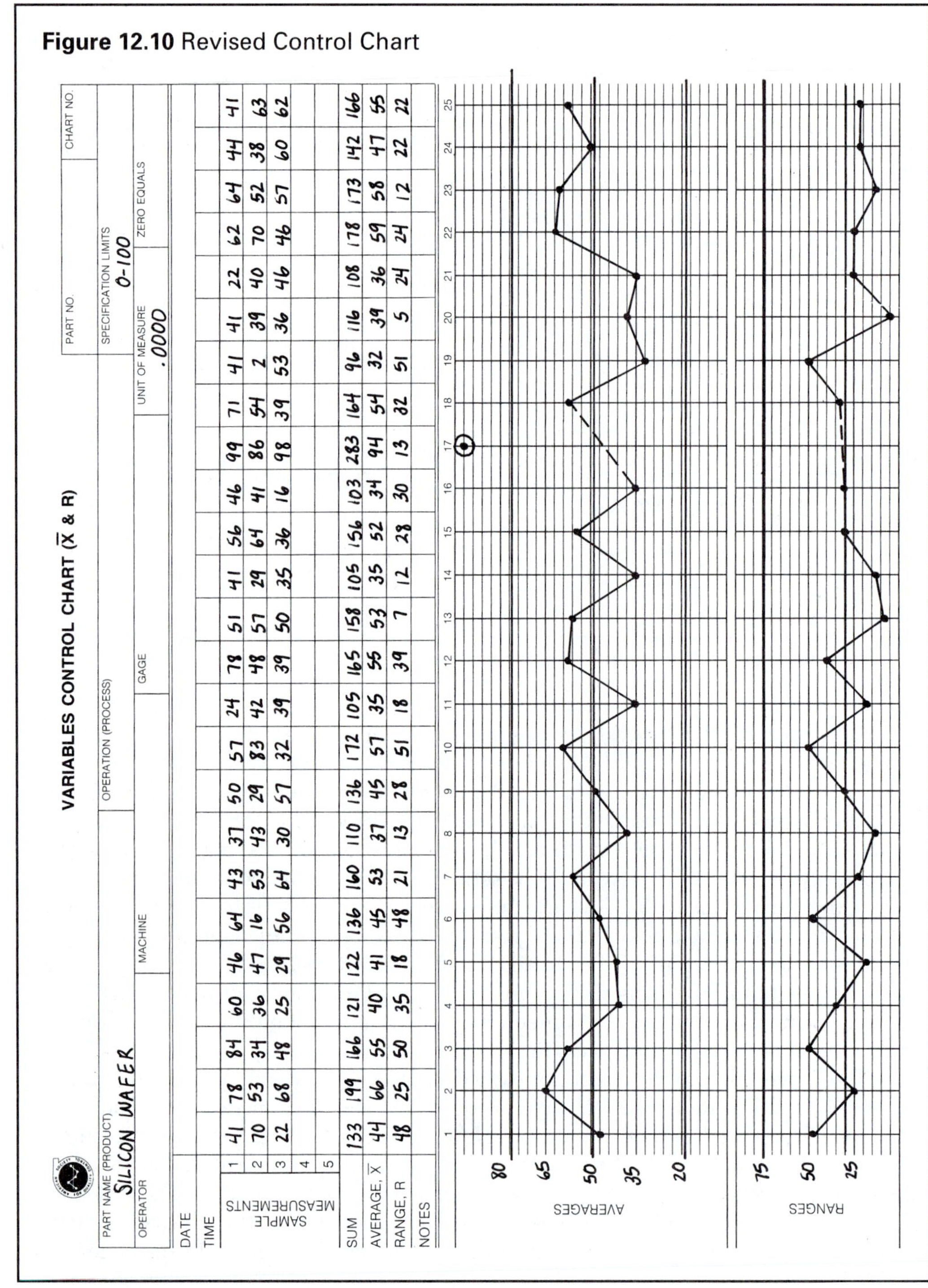

VARIABLES CONTROL CHART ($\overline{X}$ & R)

PART NAME (PRODUCT): SILICON WAFER | OPERATION (PROCESS) | SPECIFICATION LIMITS: 0-100 | PART NO. | CHART NO.

OPERATOR | MACHINE | GAGE | UNIT OF MEASURE: .0000 | ZERO EQUALS

Sample	1	2	3	4	5	6	7	8	9	10	11	12	13	14	15	16	17	18	19	20	21	22	23	24	25
DATE																									
TIME																									
SAMPLE MEASUREMENTS 1	41	78	84	60	46	64	43	37	50	57	24	78	51	41	56	46	99	71	41	41	22	62	64	44	41
2	70	53	34	36	47	16	53	43	29	83	42	48	57	29	64	41	86	54	2	39	40	70	52	38	63
3	22	68	48	25	29	56	64	30	57	32	39	39	50	35	36	16	98	39	53	36	46	46	57	60	62
4																									
5																									
SUM	133	199	166	121	122	136	160	110	136	172	105	165	158	105	156	103	283	164	96	116	108	178	173	142	166
AVERAGE, $\overline{X}$	44	66	55	40	41	45	53	37	45	57	35	55	53	35	52	34	94	54	32	39	36	59	58	47	55
RANGE, R	48	25	50	35	18	48	21	13	28	51	18	39	7	12	28	30	13	32	51	5	24	24	12	22	22
NOTES																									

Figure 12.11 Single Point Outside Control Limits

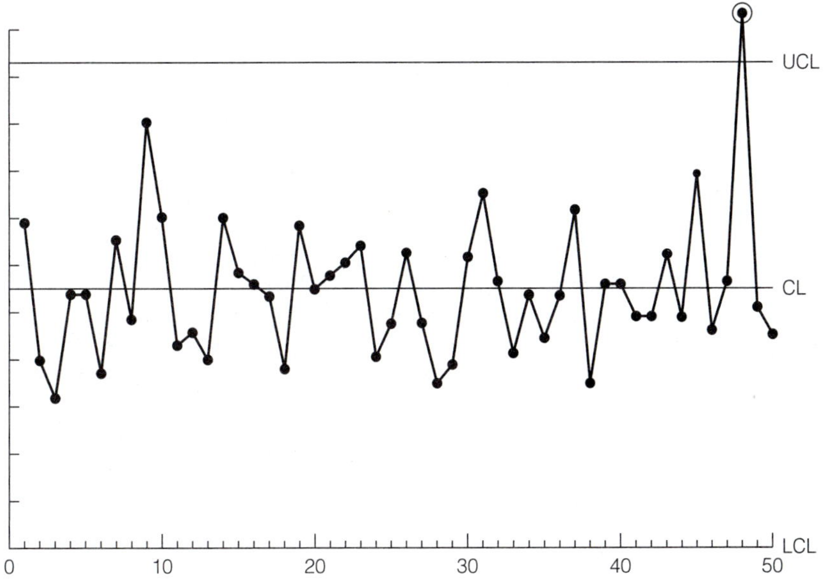

night shifts. In the *R*-chart, cycles can occur from maintenance schedules, rotation of fixtures or gauges, differences between shifts, or operator fatigue.

Trends A trend is the result of some cause that gradually affects the quality characteristics of the product and causes the points on a control chart to gradually move up or down from the center line (see Figure 12.15). As a new group of operators gains experi-

Figure 12.12 Shift in Process Average

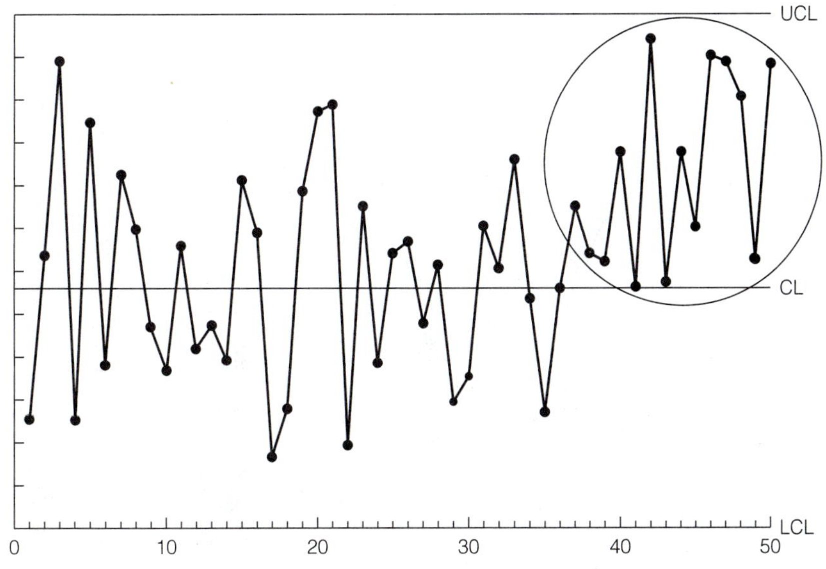

ence on the job, for example, or as maintenance of equipment improves over time, a trend may occur. In the $\bar{x}$-chart, trends may be the result of improving operator skills, dirt or chip buildup in fixtures, tool wear, changes in temperature or humidity, or aging of equipment. In the *R*-chart, an increasing trend may be due to a gradual decline in material quality, operator fatigue, gradual loosening of a fixture or a tool, or dulling of a tool. A decreasing trend often is the result of improved operator skill or work methods, better materials, or improved or more frequent maintenance.

Hugging the Center Line Hugging the center line occurs when nearly all the points fall close to the center line (see Figure 12.16). In the control chart, it appears that the control limits are too wide. A common cause of hugging the center line is that the sample includes one item systematically taken from each of several machines, spindles, operators, and so on. A simple example will serve to illustrate this pattern. Suppose that one machine produces parts whose diameters average 7.508 with variation of only a few thousandths; a second machine produces parts whose diameters aver-

Figure 12.13 Examples of Out-of-Control Processes

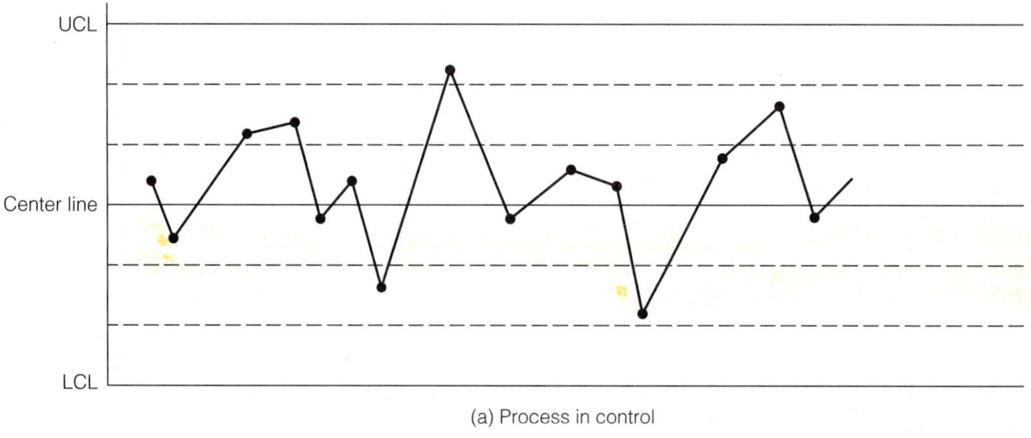

(a) Process in control

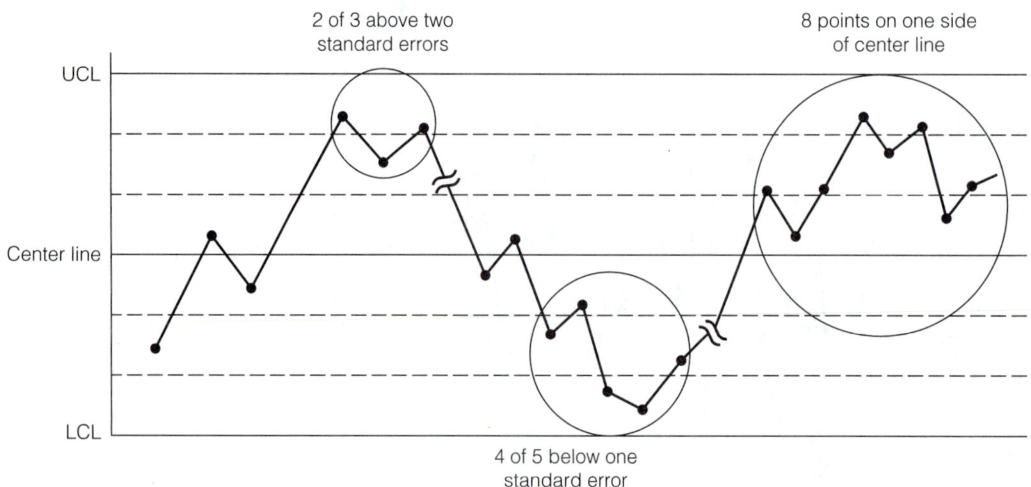

(b) Examples of out-of-control indicators

Figure 12.14 Cycles

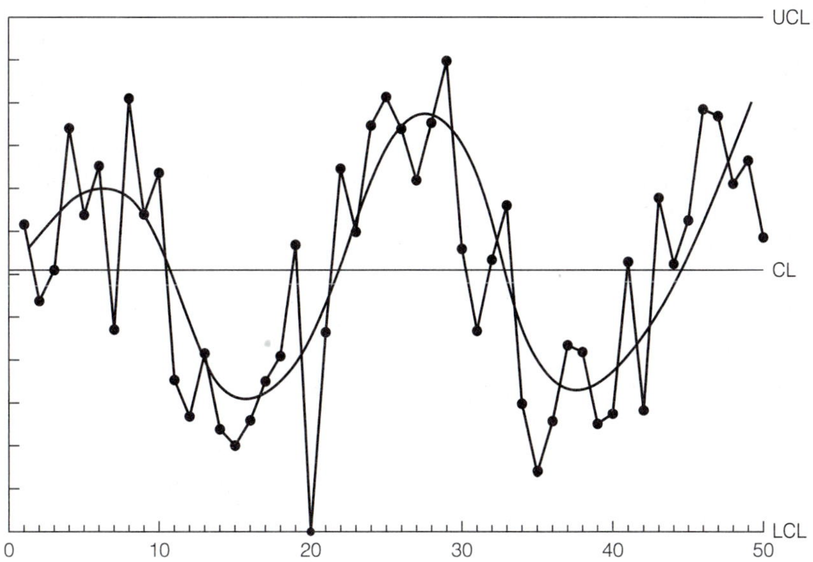

age 7.502, again with only a small variation. Taken together, parts from both machines would yield a range of variation that would probably be between 7.500 and 7.510, and average about 7.505. Now suppose that one part from *each* machine is sampled, and a sample average computed to plot on an $\bar{x}$-chart. The sample averages will consistently be around 7.505, because one will always be high and the second will always be low. Even though a large variation will occur in the parts taken as a whole,

Figure 12.15 Gradual Trend

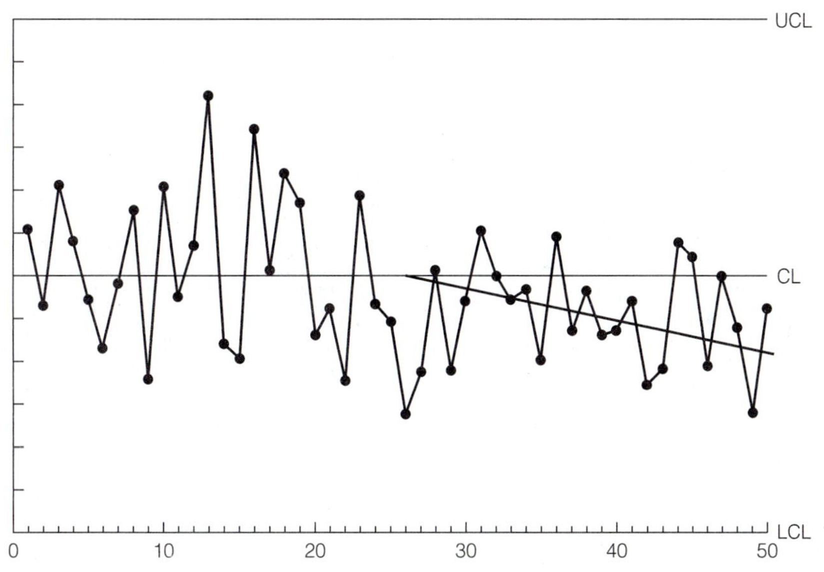

the sample averages will not reflect this variation. In such a case, a control chart should be constructed for *each* machine, spindle, operator, and so on.

An often overlooked cause for this pattern is miscalculation of the control limits, perhaps by using the wrong factor from the table, or misplacing the decimal point in the computations.

Hugging the Control Limits This pattern shows up when many points are near the control limits with few in between (see Figure 12.17). It is often called a mixture and is actually a combination of two different patterns on the same chart. A mixture can be split into two separate patterns, as Figure 12.18 illustrates.

A mixture pattern can result when different lots of material are used in one process, or when parts are produced by different machines but fed into a common inspection group.

Instability Instability is characterized by unnatural and erratic fluctuations on both sides of the chart over a period of time (see Figure 12.19). Points will often lie outside both the upper and lower control limits without a consistent pattern. Assignable causes may be more difficult to identify in this case than when specific patterns are present. A frequent cause of instability is overadjustment of a machine, or the same reasons that cause hugging the control limits.

As suggested earlier, the *R*-chart should be analyzed before the $\bar{x}$-chart, because some out-of-control conditions in the *R*-chart may *cause* out-of-control conditions in the $\bar{x}$-chart. Figure 12.20 on page 703 gives an example of this situation. The range (a) shows a drastic trend downward. If you examine the $\bar{x}$-chart (b), you will notice that the last several points seem to be hugging the center line. As the variability in the process decreases, all the sample observations will be closer to the true population mean, and therefore their average, $\bar{x}$, will not vary much from sample to sample. If this reduction in the variation can be identified and controlled, then new control limits should be computed for both charts.

Figure 12.16 Hugging the Center Line

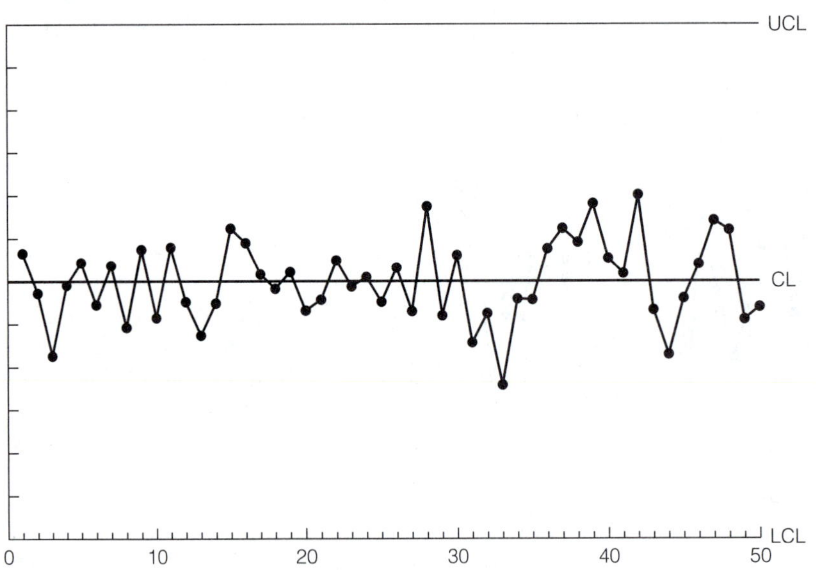

Figure 12.17 Hugging the Control Limits

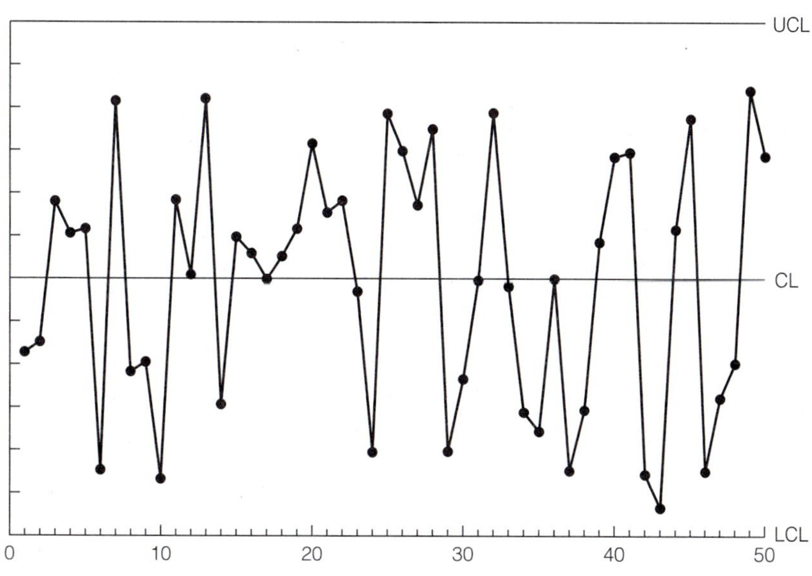

Process Monitoring and Control

After a process is determined to be in control, the charts should be used on a daily basis to monitor production, identify any special causes that might arise, and make corrections as necessary. More important, the chart tells when to leave the process alone! Unnecessary adjustments to a process result in nonproductive labor, reduced production, and increased variability of output.

Figure 12.18 Illustration of Mixture

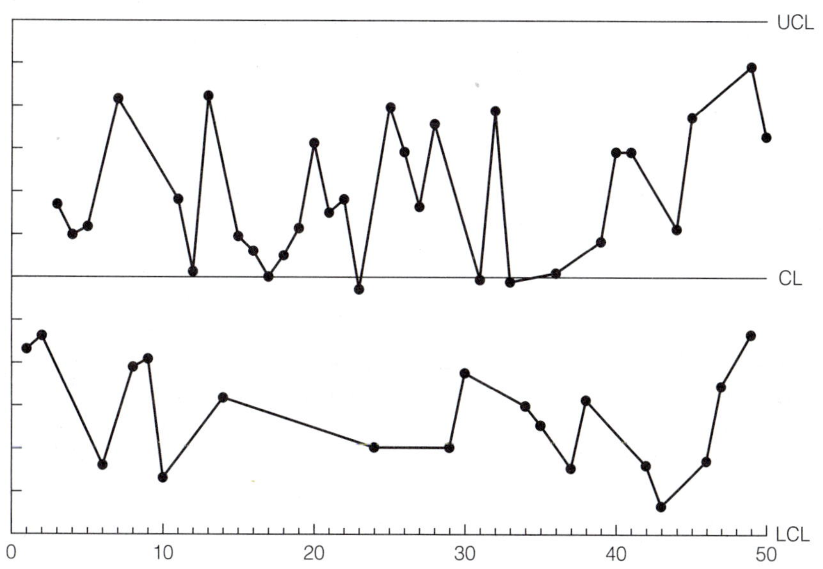

Figure 12.19 Instability

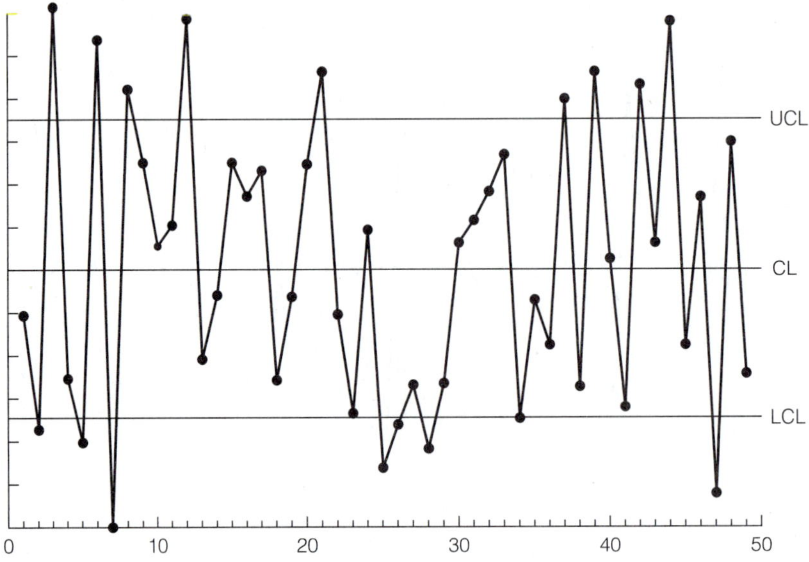

It is more productive if the operators themselves take the samples and chart the data. In this way, they can react quickly to changes in the process and immediately make adjustments. For greatest effectiveness, training of the operators is essential. Many companies conduct in-house training programs to teach operators and supervisors the elementary methods of statistical quality control. Not only does this training provide the mathematical and technical skills that are required, but it also gives the shop-floor personnel increased quality consciousness.

Improvements in conformance typically follow the introduction of control charts on the shop floor, particularly when the process is labor intensive. Apparently, management involvement in operators' work often produces positive behavioral modifications (as first demonstrated in the famous Hawthorne studies). Under such circumstances, and as good practice, management and operators should revise the control limits periodically and determine a new process capability as improvements take place.

Control charts are designed to be used by production operators rather than by inspectors or quality control personnel. Under the philosophy of statistical process control, the burden of quality rests with the operators themselves. The use of control charts allows operators to react quickly to special causes of variation. The range is used in place of the standard deviation for the very reason that it allows shop-floor personnel to easily make the necessary computations to plot points on a control chart. Only simple calculations are required.

Estimating Process Capability

After a process has been brought to a state of statistical control by eliminating special causes of variation, the data may be used to estimate process capability. This approach is not as accurate as that described in Chapter 9 because it uses the average range rather than the estimated standard deviation of the original data. Nevertheless, it is a quick and useful method, provided that the distribution of the original data is reasonably normal.

Under the normality assumption, the standard deviation of the original data can be estimated as follows:

Figure 12.20(a) Trend Down in Range . . .

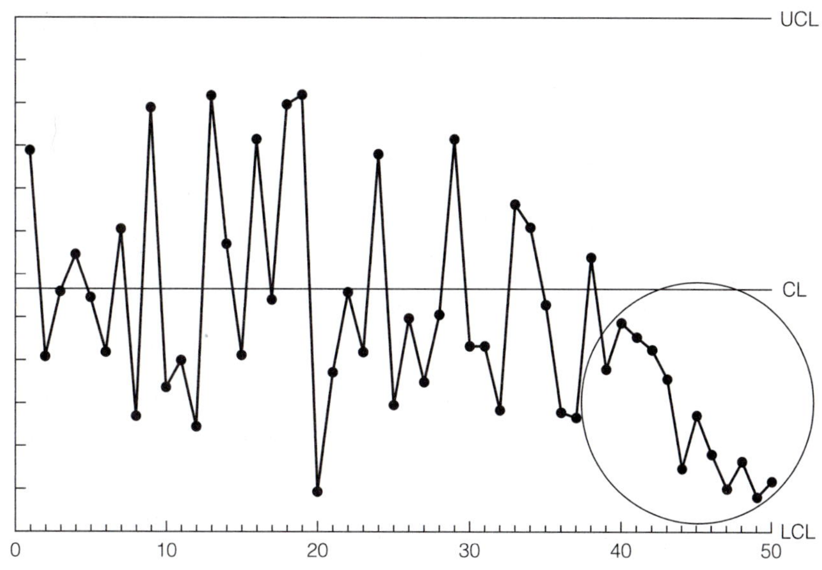

Figure 12.20(b) . . . Causes Smaller Variation in $\bar{x}$

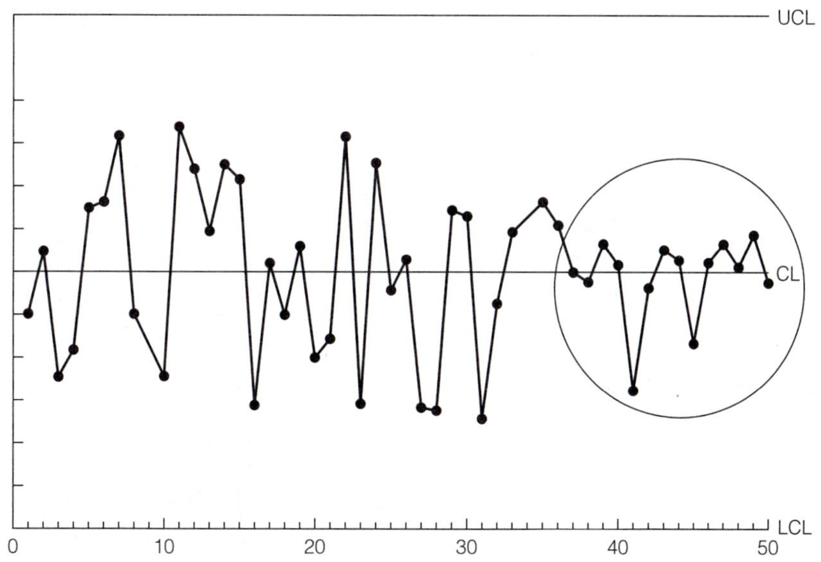

$$\hat{\sigma} = \bar{R}/d_2$$

where d_2 is a constant that depends on the sample size and is also given in Appendix B. Process capability is therefore given by $6\hat{\sigma}$. The natural variation of individual measurements is given by $\bar{\bar{x}} \pm 3\hat{\sigma}$. The back of the ASQ control chart form provides a work sheet for determining this. The following example illustrates these calculations.

Example 2: Estimating Process Capability for the Silicon Wafer Thickness. In Figure 12.21, the calculations for the silicon wafer example discussed earlier are shown in the "Limits for Individuals" section of the form. For a sample of size 3, $d_2 = 1.693$. In Figure 12.21, UL_x and LL_x represent the upper and lower limit on individual observations, based on 3σ limits. Thus, the scaled thickness is expected to vary between –1.9 and 95.9. The zero point of the data is the lower specification, meaning that the thickness is expected to vary from 0.0019 below the lower specification to 0.0959 above the lower specification. The process capability index (see Chapter 9) is

$$C_p = 100/97.8 = 1.02$$

However, the lower and upper capability indexes are

$$C_{pl} = (47 - 0)/48.9 = 0.96$$

$$C_{pu} = (100 - 47)/48.9 = 1.08$$

This analysis suggests that both the centering and the variation must be improved.

Figure 12.21 Process Capability Calculations

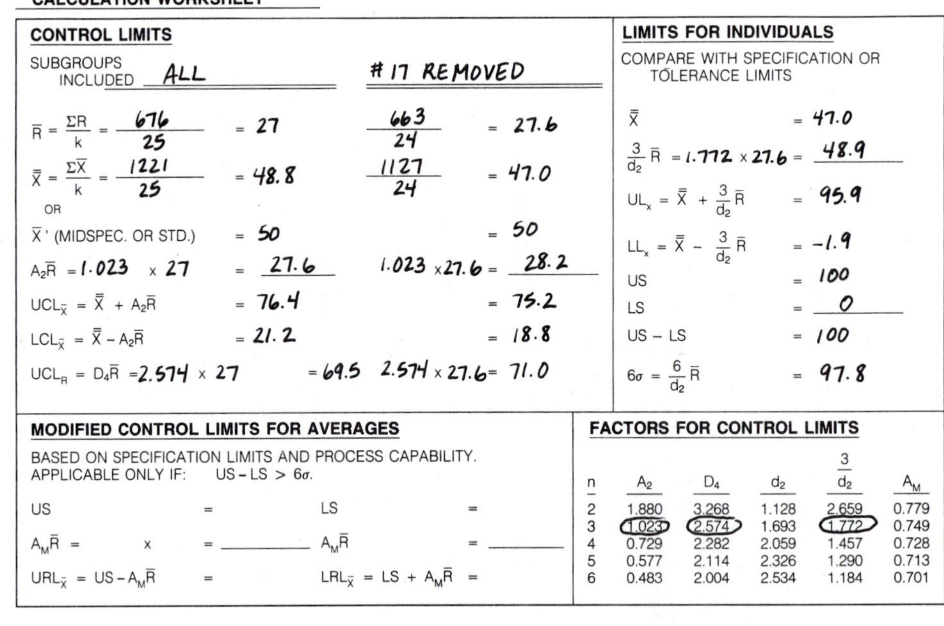

CALCULATION WORKSHEET

CONTROL LIMITS

SUBGROUPS INCLUDED: ALL | #17 REMOVED

	ALL		#17 REMOVED	
$\bar{R} = \frac{\Sigma R}{k}$	676/25	= 27	663/24	= 27.6
$\bar{\bar{X}} = \frac{\Sigma \bar{X}}{k}$	1221/25	= 48.8	1127/24	= 47.0
OR $\bar{X}'$ (MIDSPEC. OR STD.)		= 50		= 50
$A_2\bar{R}$	= 1.023 x 27	= 27.6	1.023 x 27.6	= 28.2
$UCL_{\bar{X}} = \bar{\bar{X}} + A_2\bar{R}$		= 76.4		= 75.2
$LCL_{\bar{X}} = \bar{\bar{X}} - A_2\bar{R}$		= 21.2		= 18.8
$UCL_R = D_4\bar{R}$	= 2.574 x 27	= 69.5	2.574 x 27.6	= 71.0

LIMITS FOR INDIVIDUALS

COMPARE WITH SPECIFICATION OR TOLERANCE LIMITS

$\bar{\bar{X}}$	= 47.0
$\frac{3}{d_2}\bar{R}$ = 1.772 x 27.6	= 48.9
$UL_x = \bar{\bar{X}} + \frac{3}{d_2}\bar{R}$	= 95.9
$LL_x = \bar{\bar{X}} - \frac{3}{d_2}\bar{R}$	= –1.9
US	= 100
LS	= 0
US – LS	= 100
$6\sigma = \frac{6}{d_2}\bar{R}$	= 97.8

MODIFIED CONTROL LIMITS FOR AVERAGES

BASED ON SPECIFICATION LIMITS AND PROCESS CAPABILITY. APPLICABLE ONLY IF: US – LS > 6σ.

US	=	LS	=
$A_M\bar{R}$ = x	=	$A_M\bar{R}$	=
$URL_{\bar{X}} = US - A_M\bar{R}$	=	$LRL_{\bar{X}} = LS + A_M\bar{R}$	=

FACTORS FOR CONTROL LIMITS

n	A_2	D_4	d_2	$\frac{3}{d_2}$	A_M
2	1.880	3.268	1.128	2.659	0.779
3	1.023	2.574	1.693	1.772	0.749
4	0.729	2.282	2.059	1.457	0.728
5	0.577	2.114	2.326	1.290	0.713
6	0.483	2.004	2.534	1.184	0.701

If the individual observations are normally distributed, then the probability of being out of specification can be computed. In the preceding example, assume that the data are normal. The mean is 47 and the standard deviation is 97.8/6 = 16.3. Figure 12.22 shows the calculations for specification limits of 0 and 100. In Appendix A, the area between 0 and the mean (47) is 0.4980. Thus 0.2 percent of the output would

Figure 12.22 Process Capability Probability Computations

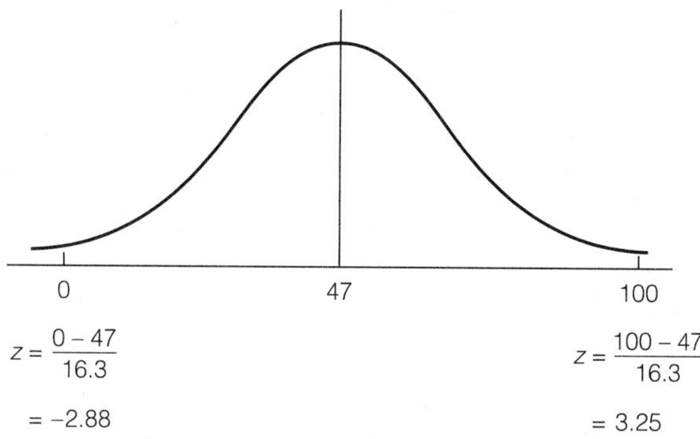

be expected to fall below the lower specification. The area to the right of 100 is approximately zero. Therefore all the output can be expected to meet the upper specification.

A word of caution deserves emphasis here. Control limits are often confused with specification limits. Specification dimensions are usually stated in relation to individual parts for "hard" goods, such as automotive hardware. However, in other applications, such as in chemical processes, specifications are stated in terms of average characteristics. Thus, control charts might mislead one into thinking that if all sample averages fall within the control limits, all output will be conforming. This assumption is not true. Control limits relate to *averages of samples*, while specification limits relate to individual measurements. A sample average may fall within the upper and lower control limits even though some of the individual observations are out of specification. Because $\sigma_{\bar{x}} = \sigma\sqrt{n}$, control limits are narrower than the natural variation in the process and do not represent process capability.

Modified Control Limits

The calculation worksheet on the back of the ASQ control chart form has one additional section entitled "Modified Control Limits for Averages." Modified control limits often are used when process capability is good. For example, suppose that the process capability is 60 percent of tolerance ($C_p = 1.67$) and that the mean can be controlled by a simple adjustment. A company may quickly discover the impracticality of investigating every isolated point that falls outside the usual control limits because the output is probably well within specifications. In such cases, the usual control limits may be replaced with the following:

$$\text{URL}_x = \text{US} - A_m\bar{R}$$

$$\text{LRL}_x = \text{LS} + A_m\bar{R}$$

where URL_x is the upper reject level, LRL_x is the lower reject level, and US and LS are the upper and lower specifications, respectively. Factors for A_m are found on the worksheet. These modified control limits allow for more variation than the ordinary control limits and still provide high confidence that the product produced is within specifications. While the ASQ chart states that these modified limits apply only if the tolerance is greater than 6σ, experts suggest that process capability should be at least 60 to 75 percent of tolerance. If the mean must be controlled closely, a conventional $\bar{x}$-chart should be used even if the process capability is good. Also, if the standard deviation of the process is likely to shift, modified control limits are not appropriate.

Example 3: Computing Modified Control Limits for the Silicon Wafer Case. Figure 12.23 shows the completed worksheet for the silicon wafer thickness example illustrated in this chapter. Because the sample size is 3, $A_m = 0.749$. Therefore, the modified limits are

$$URL_x = US - A_m\bar{R} = 100 - 0.749(27.6) = 79.3$$

$$LRL_x = LS + A_m\bar{R} = 0 + 0.749(27.6) = 20.7$$

Observe that if the process is centered on the nominal, these control limits are looser than the ordinary control limits. In this example, the centering would first have to be corrected from its current estimated value of 47.0.

Figure 12.23 Modified Control Limit Calculations

CALCULATION WORKSHEET

CONTROL LIMITS

SUBGROUPS INCLUDED	ALL		#17 REMOVED	
$\bar{R} = \frac{\Sigma R}{k} =$	676/25	= 27	663/24	= 27.6
$\bar{\bar{X}} = \frac{\Sigma \bar{X}}{k} =$	1221/25	= 48.8	1127/24	= 47.0
OR $\bar{X}'$ (MIDSPEC. OR STD.)		= 50		= 50
$A_2\bar{R}$ =	1.023 x 27	= 27.6	1.023 x 27.6 =	28.2
$UCL_{\bar{X}} = \bar{\bar{X}} + A_2\bar{R}$		= 76.4		= 75.2
$LCL_{\bar{X}} = \bar{\bar{X}} - A_2\bar{R}$		= 21.2		= 18.8
$UCL_R = D_4\bar{R}$ =	2.574 x 27	= 69.5	2.574 x 27.6 =	71.0

LIMITS FOR INDIVIDUALS

COMPARE WITH SPECIFICATION OR TOLERANCE LIMITS

$\bar{\bar{X}}$	= 47.0
$\frac{3}{d_2}\bar{R}$ = 1.772 x 27.6 =	48.9
$UL_x = \bar{\bar{X}} + \frac{3}{d_2}\bar{R}$	= 95.9
$LL_x = \bar{\bar{X}} - \frac{3}{d_2}\bar{R}$	= −1.9
US	= 100
LS	= 0
US − LS	= 100
$6\sigma = \frac{6}{d_2}\bar{R}$	= 97.8

MODIFIED CONTROL LIMITS FOR AVERAGES

BASED ON SPECIFICATION LIMITS AND PROCESS CAPABILITY.
APPLICABLE ONLY IF: US − LS > 6σ.

US	= 100	LS	= 0
$A_M\bar{R}$ = .749 x 27.6 =	20.7	$A_M\bar{R}$	= 20.7
$URL_{\bar{X}} = US - A_M\bar{R}$	= 79.3	$LRL_{\bar{X}} = LS + A_M\bar{R}$	= 20.7

FACTORS FOR CONTROL LIMITS

n	A_2	D_4	d_2	$\frac{3}{d_2}$	A_M
2	1.880	3.268	1.128	2.659	0.779
3	1.023	2.574	1.693	1.772	0.749
4	0.729	2.282	2.059	1.457	0.728
5	0.577	2.114	2.326	1.290	0.713
6	0.483	2.004	2.534	1.184	0.701

Excel Spreadsheet Templates

Figure 12.24 shows an Excel template and solution for the silicon wafer example problem. The template includes an automatic plot of the $\bar{x}$ and R-charts and calculation of process capability indexes. Some scaling of the chart display ranges may be necessary for certain problems. The spreadsheet (XBAR&R.XLS) is available on the CD-rom accompanying this book, as are all other Excel applications in this chapter.

Please note the following:

- The recalculation option for the spreadsheets is set to manual. Therefore, to recalculate any spreadsheet after making changes, press the F9 key or set the recalculation option to automatic in the *Calculation* tab from the *Tools/Options* menu.
- To rescale the vertical axis in a chart to widen the range of the plotted data for instance, double-click on the y-axis, and select the *Scale* tab in the dialog box that appears. Change the "min" and "max" parameters as appropriate.
- When deleting special cause data and recomputing control limits, be sure to update the number of samples used in the calculations to compute the statistics.
- When a sample is deleted from a data set in the templates, do not enter zero for the data; instead, leave the cells blank. The charts are set up to interpolate between nonmissing data points in the *Tools/Options/Chart* tab.

SPECIAL CONTROL CHARTS FOR VARIABLES DATA

Several alternatives to the popular $\bar{x}$- and R-charts for process control of variables measurements are available. This section discusses some of these alternatives.

$\bar{x}$- and s-Charts

An alternative to using the R-chart along with the $\bar{x}$-chart is to compute and plot the standard deviation s of each sample. Although the range has traditionally been used, s involves less computational effort and is easier for shop-floor personnel to understand, making it advantageous. The sample standard deviation is a more sensitive and better indicator of process variability, especially for larger sample sizes. Thus, when tight control of variability is required, s should be used. With the availability of modern calculators and personal computers, the computational burden of computing s is reduced or eliminated, and s has thus become a viable alternative to R.

The sample standard deviation is computed as

$$s = \sqrt{\frac{\sum_{i=1}^{n} (x_i - \bar{x})^2}{n-1}}$$

To construct an s-chart, compute the standard deviation for each sample. Next, compute the average standard deviation $\bar{s}$ by averaging the sample standard deviations over all samples. (Notice that this computation is analogous to computing $\bar{R}$). Control limits for the s-chart are given by

$$UCL_s = B_4\bar{s}$$

$$LCL_s = B_3\bar{s}$$

where B_3 and B_4 are constants found in Appendix B.

Figure 12.24a Excel Spreadsheet and $\bar{x}$- and R-Charts for Examples 1 and 2 (XBAR&R.XLS)

X-bar and R-Chart

This spreadsheet is designed for up to 30 samples, each of a constant sample size from 2 to 10. Enter data ONLY in yellow-shaded cells.

Enter the number of samples in cell D6 and the sample size in cell D7. Then enter your data in the grid below.

Click on sheet tabs for a display of the control charts. Specification limits may be entered in cells N7 and N8 for process capability.

Number of samples (<= 50)	24
Sample size (2 - 10)	3

		A2	D3	D4	d2
Grand Average	47.083333				
Average Range	27.625	1.02	0	2.57	1.69

Process Capability Calculations		Six sigma	97.9
Upper specification	100	Cp	1.02
Lower specification	0	Cpu	1.08
		Cpl	0.96
		Cpk	0.96

DATA	1	2	3	4	5	6	7	8	9	10	11	12	13	14	15	16	17	18	19	20	21	22	23	24	25
1	41	78	84	60	46	64	43	37	50	57	24	78	51	41	56	46		71	41	41	22	62	64	44	41
2	70	53	34	36	47	16	53	43	29	83	42	48	57	29	64	41		54	2	39	40	70	52	38	63
3	22	68	48	25	29	56	64	30	57	32	39	39	50	35	36	16		39	53	36	46	46	57	60	62
4																									
5																									
6																									
7																									
8																									
9																									
10																									
Average	44.33	66.33	55.33	40.33	40.67	45.33	53.33	36.67	45.33	57.33	35	55	52.67	35	52	34.33	#N/A	54.67	32	38.67	36	59.33	57.67	47.33	55.33
LCLx-bar	18.82	18.82	18.82	18.82	18.82	18.82	18.82	18.82	18.82	18.82	18.82	18.82	18.82	18.82	18.82	18.82	18.82	18.82	18.82	18.82	18.82	18.82	18.82	18.82	18.82
Center	47.08	47.08	47.08	47.08	47.08	47.08	47.08	47.08	47.08	47.08	47.08	47.08	47.08	47.08	47.08	47.08	47.08	47.08	47.08	47.08	47.08	47.08	47.08	47.08	47.08
UCLx-bar	75.34	75.34	75.34	75.34	75.34	75.34	75.34	75.34	75.34	75.34	75.34	75.34	75.34	75.34	75.34	75.34	75.34	75.34	75.34	75.34	75.34	75.34	75.34	75.34	75.34
Range	48	25	50	35	18	48	21	13	28	51	18	39	7	12	28	30	#N/A	32	51	5	24	24	12	22	22
LCLrange	0	0	0	0	0	0	0	0	0	0	0	0	0	0	0	0	0	0	0	0	0	0	0	0	0
Center	27.63	27.63	27.63	27.63	27.63	27.63	27.63	27.63	27.63	27.63	27.63	27.63	27.63	27.63	27.63	27.63	27.63	27.63	27.63	27.63	27.63	27.63	27.63	27.63	27.63
UCLrange	71.11	71.11	71.11	71.11	71.11	71.11	71.11	71.11	71.11	71.11	71.11	71.11	71.11	71.11	71.11	71.11	71.11	71.11	71.11	71.11	71.11	71.11	71.11	71.11	71.11

Figure 12.24b $\bar{x}$-Chart for Examples 1 and 2

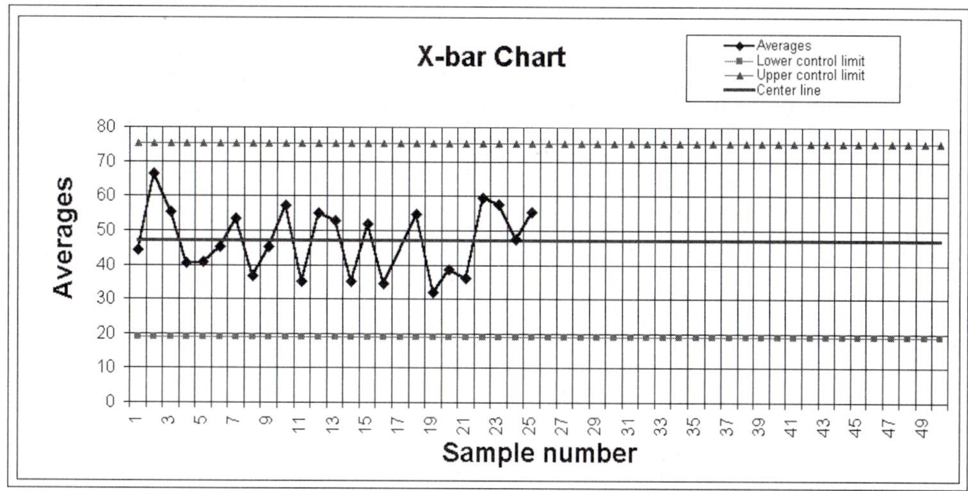

For the associated $\bar{x}$-chart, the control limits derived from the overall standard deviation are

$$UCL_{\bar{x}} = \bar{\bar{x}} + A_3\bar{s}$$

$$LCL_{\bar{x}} = \bar{\bar{x}} - A_3\bar{s}$$

where A_3 is a constant found in Appendix B.

Observe that the formulas for the control limits are equivalent to those for $\bar{x}$- and R-charts except that the constants differ.

Figure 12.24c *R*-Chart for Examples 1 and 2

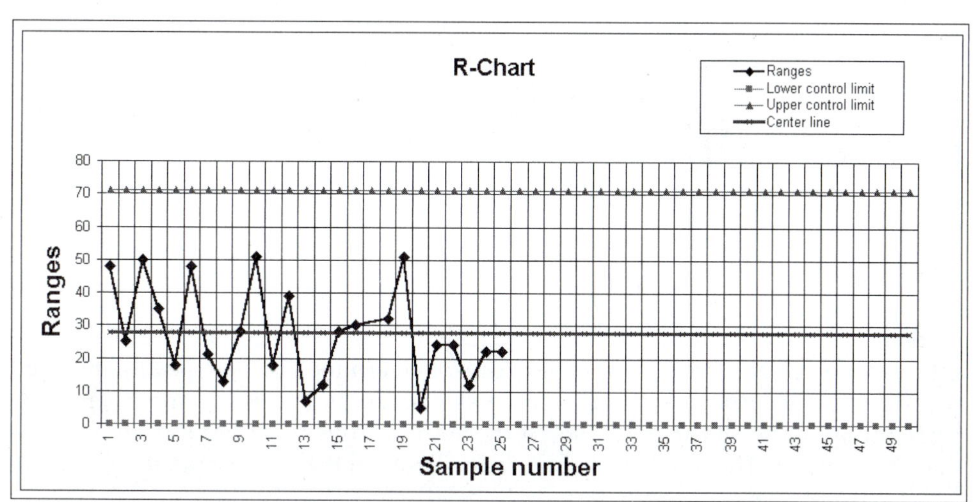

Example 4: Constructing $\bar{x}$- and s-Charts. To illustrate the use of the $\bar{x}$- and s-charts, consider the data given in Figure 12.25. These data represent measurements of deviations from a nominal specification for some machined part. Samples of size 10 are used; for each sample, the mean and standard deviation have been computed.

The average (overall) mean is computed to be $\bar{\bar{x}} = 0.108$, and the average standard deviation is $\bar{s} = 1.791$. For samples of size 10, $B_3 = 0.284$, $B_4 = 1.716$, and $A_3 = 0.975$. Control limits for the s-chart are

$$LCL_s = 0.284(1.791) = 0.509$$

$$UCL_s = 1.716(1.791) = 3.073$$

For the $\bar{x}$-chart, the control limits are

$$LCL_{\bar{x}} = 0.108 - 0.975(1.791) = -1.638$$

$$UCL_{\bar{x}} = 0.108 + 0.975(1.791) = 1.854$$

The $\bar{x}$- and s-charts are shown in Figure 12.26. This evidence indicates the process is not in control, and an investigation as to the reasons for the variation, particularly in the $\bar{x}$-chart, is warranted.

Charts for Individuals

With the development of automated inspection for many processes, manufacturers can now easily inspect and measure quality characteristics on every item produced. Hence, the sample size for process control is $n = 1$, and a control chart for *individual measurements*—also called an *x-chart*—can be used. Other examples in which x-charts are useful include accounting data such as shipments, orders, absences, and accidents; production records of temperature, humidity, voltage, or pressure; and the results of physical or chemical analyses.

With individual measurements, the process standard deviation can be estimated and three-sigma control limits used. As shown earlier, $\bar{R}/d_2$ provides an estimate of the process standard deviation. Thus, an x-chart for individual measurements would have three-sigma control limits defined by

$$UCL_x = \bar{x} + 3\bar{R}/d_2$$

$$LCL_x = \bar{x} - 3\bar{R}/d_2$$

Samples of size 1, however, do not furnish enough information for process variability measurement. Process variability can be determined by using a moving average of ranges, or a *moving range*, of n successive observations. For example, a moving range for $n = 2$ is computed by finding the absolute difference between two successive observations. The number of observations used in the moving range determines the constant d_2; hence, for $n = 2$, from Appendix B, $d_2 = 1.128$. In a similar fashion,

Figure 12.25 Data and Calculations for Example 4 (XBAR&S.XLS)

	A	B	C	D	E	F	G	H	I	J	K	L	M	N	O	P	Q	R	S	T	U	V	W	X	Y	Z
1	**X-bar and s-Chart**																									
2	This spreadsheet is designed for up to 50 samples, each of a constant sample size from 2 to 10. Enter data ONLY in yellow-shaded cells.																									
3	Enter the number of samples in cell D6 and the sample size in cell D7. Then enter your data in the grid below.																									
4	Click on sheet tabs for a display of the control charts (some rescaling may be needed). Specification limits may be entered in cells N7 and N8 for process capability.																									
5																										
6	**Number of samples (<= 50)**				25					Process Capability Calculations						**Six sigma**		2.71								
7	**Sample size (2 - 10)**				10					**Upper specification**						**Cp**										
8										**Lower specification**						**Cpu**										
9	**Grand Average**		**0.108**		**A3**	**B3**	**B4**	**d2**								**Cpl**										
10	**Avg. std. dev.**		**1.7905259**		**0.98**	**0.28**	**1.72**	**3.08**								**Cpk**										
11																										
12	DATA	**1**	**2**	**3**	**4**	**5**	**6**	**7**	**8**	**9**	**10**	**11**	**12**	**13**	**14**	**15**	**16**	**17**	**18**	**19**	**20**	**21**	**22**	**23**	**24**	**25**
13	**1**	1	9	0	1	-3	-6	-3	0	2	0	-3	-12	-6	-3	-1	-1	-2	0	0	1	1	-1	0	1	2
14	**2**	8	4	8	1	-1	2	-1	-2	0	0	-2	2	-3	-5	-1	-2	2	4	3	2	2	0	0	0	2
15	**3**	6	0	0	0	0	0	0	-3	-1	-2	2	0	0	5	-1	-2	-1	0	-3	1	2	2	-1	0	1
16	**4**	9	3	0	2	-4	0	-2	-1	-1	-1	-1	-4	0	0	-2	0	0	0	3	1	1	-1	0	1	2
17	**5**	7	0	3	1	0	2	-1	-2	-3	-1	1	-1	-8	-5	-1	-4	-1	0	3	-3	2	2	1	1	-1
18	**6**	9	0	1	1	1	-1	-1	1	0	0	-2	4	-4	1	0	0	-1	3	1	2	2	2	0	2	2
19	**7**	2	3	2	2	0	2	-3	-3	1	-1	-2	2	-6	5	-2	-2	2	0	0	1	1	-1	0	0	2
20	**8**	7	4	0	0	-2	0	0	0	-3	-2	-1	-3	-1	-4	-1	-4	-1	0	1	-2	1	0	0	0	1
21	**9**	9	8	2	0	0	-3	-2	-3	-1	-2	1	-4	-1	-1	0	-1	1	1	2	3	1	0	-1	-1	-1
22	**10**	7	3	3	1	-2	0	-2	-2	0	0	1	0	-2	-5	-1	0	-2	0	-2	0	2	-1	0	0	2
23	**Average**	6.5	3.4	1.9	0.9	-1.1	-0.4	-1.5	-1.5	-0.6	-0.9	-0.6	-1.6	-3.1	-1.2	-1	-1.6	-0.3	0.8	0.8	0.6	1.5	0.2	-0.1	0.4	1.2
24	**LCLx-bar**	-1.64	-1.64	-1.64	-1.64	-1.64	-1.64	-1.64	-1.64	-1.64	-1.64	-1.64	-1.64	-1.64	-1.64	-1.64	-1.64	-1.64	-1.64	-1.64	-1.64	-1.64	-1.64	-1.64	-1.64	-1.64
25	**Center**	0.108	0.108	0.108	0.108	0.108	0.108	0.108	0.108	0.108	0.108	0.108	0.108	0.108	0.108	0.108	0.108	0.108	0.108	0.108	0.108	0.108	0.108	0.108	0.108	0.108
26	**UCLx-bar**	1.854	1.854	1.854	1.854	1.854	1.854	1.854	1.854	1.854	1.854	1.854	1.854	1.854	1.854	1.854	1.854	1.854	1.854	1.854	1.854	1.854	1.854	1.854	1.854	1.854
27																										
28	**Std. Dev.**	2.838	3.134	2.47	0.738	1.595	2.503	1.08	1.434	1.578	0.876	1.713	4.526	2.807	3.91	0.667	1.506	1.494	1.476	2.098	1.838	0.527	1.317	0.568	0.843	1.229
29	**LCLs**	-1.64	-1.64	-1.64	-1.64	-1.64	-1.64	-1.64	-1.64	-1.64	-1.64	-1.64	-1.64	-1.64	-1.64	-1.64	-1.64	-1.64	-1.64	-1.64	-1.64	-1.64	-1.64	-1.64	-1.64	-1.64
30	**Center**	1.791	1.791	1.791	1.791	1.791	1.791	1.791	1.791	1.791	1.791	1.791	1.791	1.791	1.791	1.791	1.791	1.791	1.791	1.791	1.791	1.791	1.791	1.791	1.791	1.791
31	**UCLs**	3.073	3.073	3.073	3.073	3.073	3.073	3.073	3.073	3.073	3.073	3.073	3.073	3.073	3.073	3.073	3.073	3.073	3.073	3.073	3.073	3.073	3.073	3.073	3.073	3.073

Figure 12.26a $\bar{x}$-Chart for Example 4

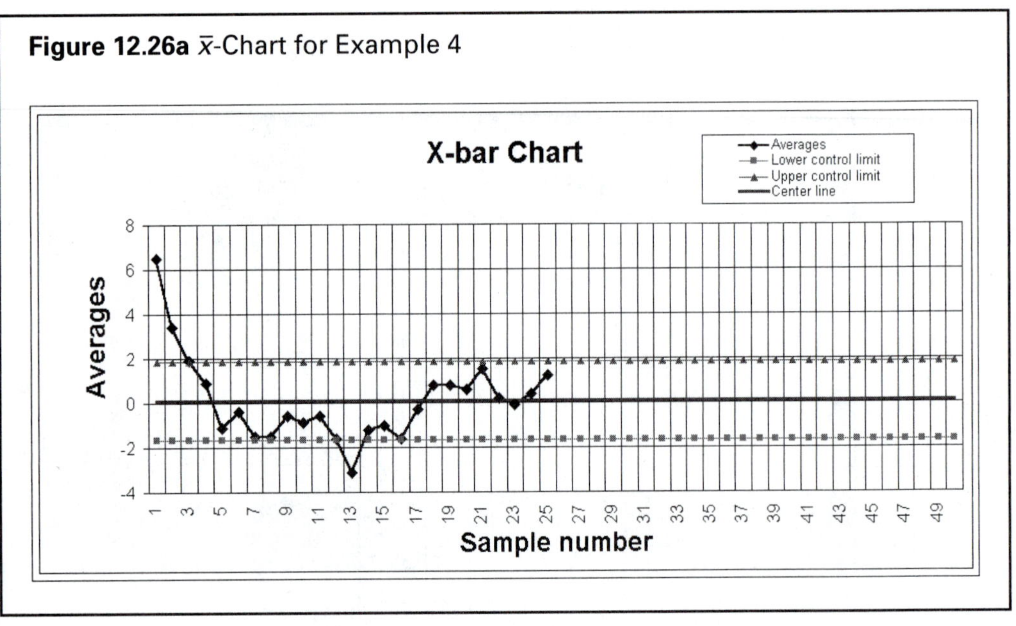

larger values of n can be used to compute moving ranges. The moving range chart has control limits defined by

$$UCL_R = D_4\bar{R}$$

$$LCL_R = D_3\bar{R}$$

which is comparable to the ordinary range chart.

Figure 12.26b s-Chart for Example 4

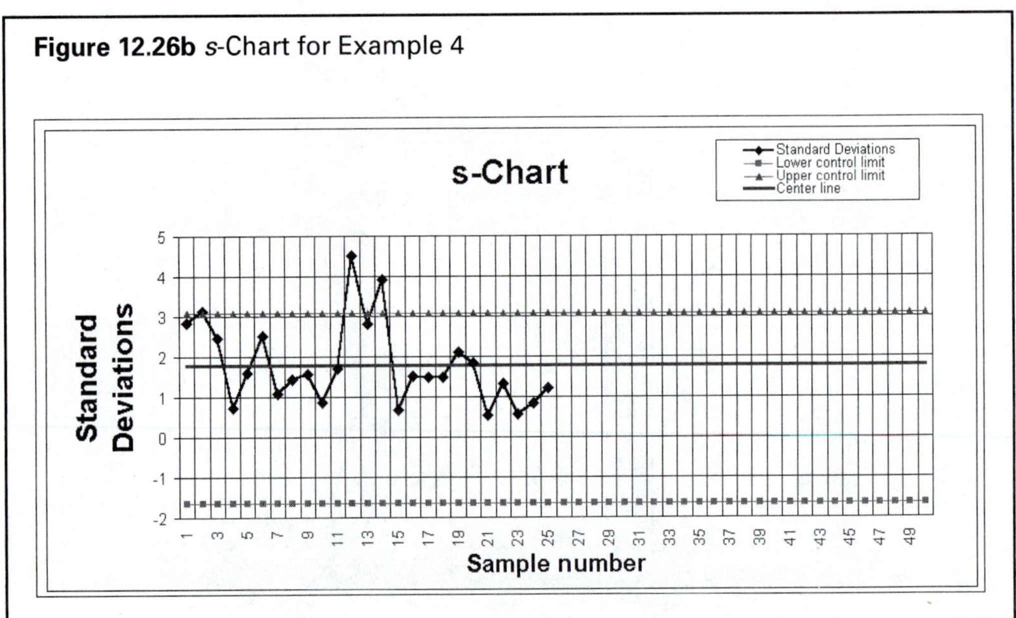

Example 5: Constructing an x-Chart with Moving Ranges. Consider a set of observations measuring the percentage of cobalt in a chemical process as given in Figure 12.27. The moving range is computed as shown by taking absolute values of successive ranges and using the constants in Appendix B. For example, the first moving range is the difference between the first two observations:

$$|3.75 - 3.80| = 0.05$$

The second moving range is computed as

$$|3.80 - 3.70| = 0.10$$

From these data we find that

$$LCL_R = 0$$

$$UCL_R = (3.267)(0.352) = 1.15$$

The moving range chart, shown in Figure 12.28a, indicates that the process is in control.

Next, the x-chart is constructed for the individual measurements:

$$LCL_x = 3.498 - 3(0.352)/1.128 = 2.56$$

$$UCL_x = 3.498 + 3(0.352)/1.128 = 4.43$$

The process, shown in Figure 12.28b, appears to be in control.

Some caution is necessary when interpreting patterns on the moving range chart. Points beyond control limits indicate assignable causes. Successive ranges, however, are correlated, and they may cause patterns or trends in the chart that are not indicative of out-of-control situations. On the x-chart, individual observations are assumed to be uncorrelated; hence, patterns and trends should be investigated.

Control charts for individuals offer the advantage of being able to draw specifications on the chart for direct comparison with the control limits. Some disadvantages also exist. Individuals' charts are less sensitive to many of the conditions that can be detected by $\bar{x}$- and R-charts; for example, the process must vary a lot before a shift in the mean is detected. Also, short cycles and trends may appear on an individual's chart and not on an $\bar{x}$- or R-chart. Finally, the assumption of normality of observations is more critical than for $\bar{x}$- and R-charts; when the normality assumption does not hold, greater chance for error is present.

CONTROL CHARTS FOR ATTRIBUTES

Attributes data assume only two values—good or bad, pass or fail, and so on. Attributes usually cannot be measured, but they can be observed and counted and are useful in many practical situations. For instance, in printing packages for consumer products, color quality can be rated as acceptable or not acceptable, or a sheet of cardboard either is damaged or is not. Usually, attributes data are easy to collect, often by visual inspection. Many accounting records, such as percent scrapped, are readily available. However, one drawback in using attributes data is that large samples are necessary to obtain valid statistical results.

Figure 12.27 Data and Calculations for Example 5 (X&MR.XLS)

X and Moving Range Chart

This spreadsheet is designed for up to 50 observations and a moving range from 2 to 5. Enter data ONLY in yellow-shaded cells.

Enter the number of samples in cell D6 and the sample size in cell D7. Then enter your data in the grid below.

Click on sheet tabs to display the control charts (some rescaling may be needed).

Number of samples (<= 50)	25
Sample size for moving range(2 - 5)	2

		D3	D4	d2
Grand Average	**3.498**			
Average Range	**0.352083333**	**0**	**3.267**	**1.13**

Observation	Value	LCLx	CLx	UCLx	Moving Range	LCLr	CLr	UCLr
1	3.75	2.562	3.498	4.4344				
2	3.8	2.562	3.498	4.4344	0.05	0	0.35	1.15
3	3.7	2.562	3.498	4.4344	0.1	0	0.35	1.15
4	3.2	2.562	3.498	4.4344	0.5	0	0.35	1.15
5	3.5	2.562	3.498	4.4344	0.3	0	0.35	1.15
6	3.05	2.562	3.498	4.4344	0.45	0	0.35	1.15
7	3.5	2.562	3.498	4.4344	0.45	0	0.35	1.15
8	3.25	2.562	3.498	4.4344	0.25	0	0.35	1.15
9	3.6	2.562	3.498	4.4344	0.35	0	0.35	1.15
10	3.1	2.562	3.498	4.4344	0.5	0	0.35	1.15
11	4	2.562	3.498	4.4344	0.9	0	0.35	1.15
12	4	2.562	3.498	4.4344	0	0	0.35	1.15
13	3.5	2.562	3.498	4.4344	0.5	0	0.35	1.15
14	3	2.562	3.498	4.4344	0.5	0	0.35	1.15
15	3.8	2.562	3.498	4.4344	0.8	0	0.35	1.15
16	3.4	2.562	3.498	4.4344	0.4	0	0.35	1.15
17	3.6	2.562	3.498	4.4344	0.2	0	0.35	1.15
18	3.1	2.562	3.498	4.4344	0.5	0	0.35	1.15
19	3.55	2.562	3.498	4.4344	0.45	0	0.35	1.15
20	3.65	2.562	3.498	4.4344	0.1	0	0.35	1.15
21	3.45	2.562	3.498	4.4344	0.2	0	0.35	1.15
22	3.3	2.562	3.498	4.4344	0.15	0	0.35	1.15
23	3.75	2.562	3.498	4.4344	0.45	0	0.35	1.15
24	3.5	2.562	3.498	4.4344	0.25	0	0.35	1.15
25	3.4	2.562	3.498	4.4344	0.1	0	0.35	1.15

Several different types of control charts are used for attributes data. One of the most common is the *p*-chart. Other types of attributes charts are also used. One distinction that we must make is between the terms *defects* and *defectives*. A **defect** is a single nonconforming quality characteristic of an item. An item may have several defects. The term **defective** refers to items having one or more defects. Because certain attributes charts are used for defectives while others are used for defects, one must understand the difference. The term *nonconforming* is often used instead of *defective.*

Figure 12.28a Moving Range Chart for Example 5

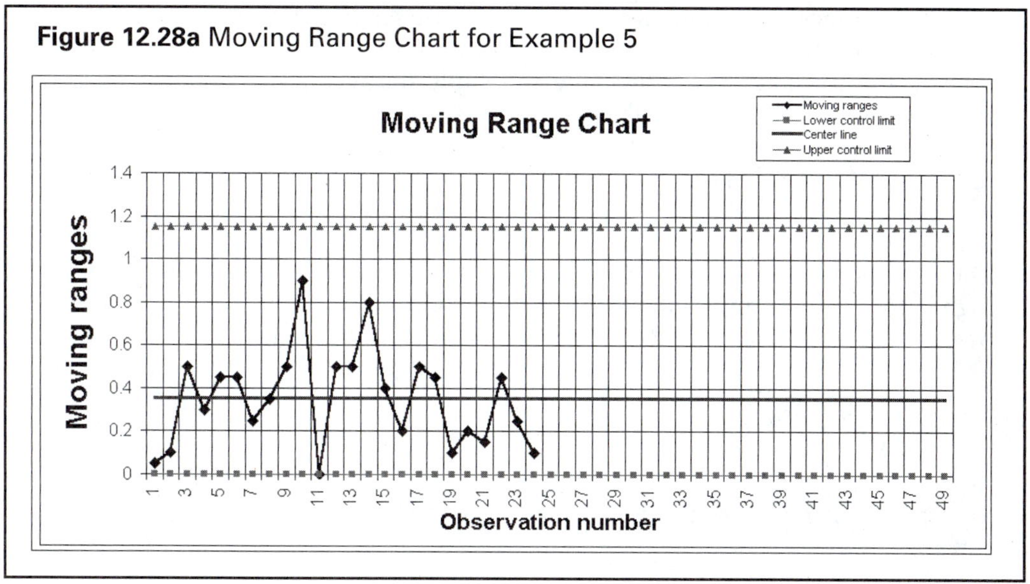

Fraction Nonconforming (*p*) Chart

A ***p*-chart** monitors the proportion of nonconforming items produced in a lot. Often it is also called a **fraction nonconforming** or **fraction defective chart**. As with variables data, a *p*-chart is constructed by first gathering 25 to 30 samples of the attribute being measured. The size of each sample should be large enough to have several nonconforming items. If the probability of finding a nonconforming item is small, a large sample size is usually necessary. Samples are chosen over time periods so that any special causes that are identified can be investigated.

Figure 12.28b *x*–Chart for Example 5

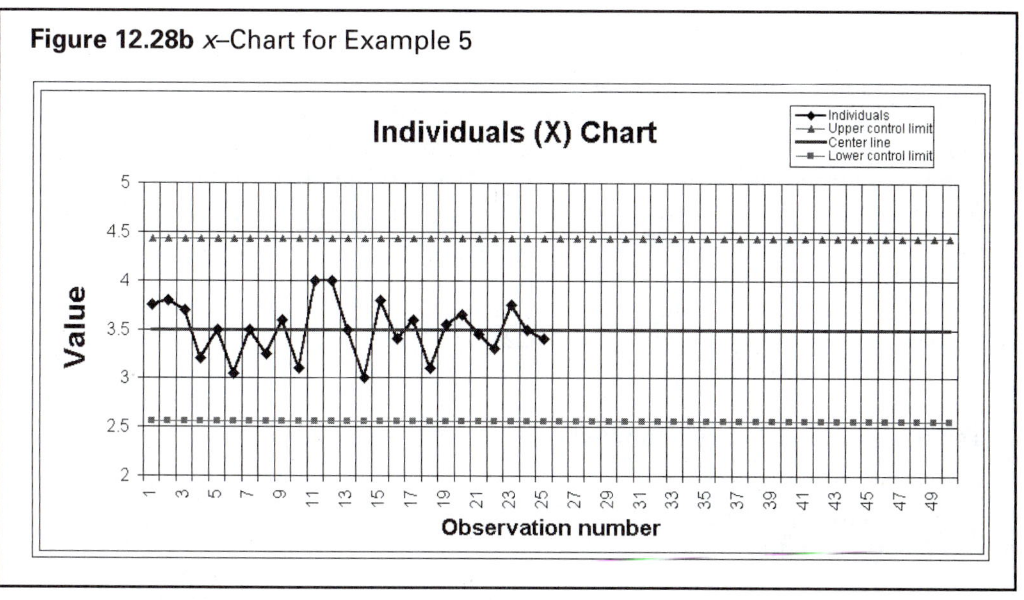

Let us suppose that k samples, each of size n, are selected. If y represents the number nonconforming in a particular sample, the proportion nonconforming is y/n. Let p_i be the fraction nonconforming in the ith sample; the average fraction nonconforming for the group of K samples then is

$$\bar{p} = \frac{p_1 + p_2 + \ldots + p_k}{k}$$

This statistic reflects the average performance of the process. One would expect a high percentage of samples to have a fraction nonconforming within three standard deviations of $\bar{p}$. An estimate of the standard deviation is given by

$$s_{\bar{p}} = \sqrt{\frac{\bar{p}(1-\bar{p})}{n}}$$

Therefore, upper and lower control limits are given by

$$UCL_p = \bar{p} + 3s_{\bar{p}}$$

$$LCL_p = \bar{p} - 3s_{\bar{p}}$$

If LCL_p is less than zero, a value of zero is used.

Analysis of a p-chart is similar to that of an $\bar{x}$- or R-chart. Points outside the control limits signify an out-of-control situation. Patterns and trends should also be sought to identify special causes. However, a point on a p-chart below the lower control limit or the development of a trend below the center line indicates that the process might have improved, since the ideal is zero defectives. Caution is advised before such conclusions are drawn, because errors may have been made in computation. An example of a p-chart is presented next.

Example 6: Constructing a *p*- Chart. The operators of automated sorting machines in a post office must read the ZIP code on a letter and divert the letter to the proper carrier route. Over one month's time, 25 samples of 100 letters were chosen, and the number of errors was recorded. This information is summarized in Figure 12.29. The fraction nonconforming is found by dividing the number of errors by 100. The average fraction nonconforming, $\bar{p}$, is determined to be

$$\bar{p} = \frac{0.03 + 0.01 + \ldots + 0.01}{25} = 0.022$$

The standard deviation is computed as

$$s_{\bar{p}} = \sqrt{\frac{0.022(1-0.022)}{100}} = 0.01467$$

Thus, the upper control limit, UCL_p, is 0.022 + 3(0.01467) = 0.066, and the lower control limit, LCL_p, is 0.022 – 3(0.01467) = –0.022. Because this later figure is negative, zero is used. The control chart for this example is shown in Figure 12.30. The sorting process appears to be in control. Any values found above the upper control limit or evidence of an upward trend might indicate the need for more experience or training of the operators.

Variable Sample Size

Often 100 percent inspection is performed on process output during fixed sampling periods; however, the number of units produced in each sampling period may vary. In this case, the p-chart would have a variable sample size. One way of handling this variation is to compute a standard deviation for each individual sample. Thus, if the number of observations in the ith sample is n_i, control limits are given by

$$\bar{p} \pm 3\sqrt{\frac{\bar{p}(1-\bar{p})}{n_i}}$$

$$\text{where } \bar{p} = \frac{\Sigma \text{number nonconforming}}{\Sigma n_i}$$

Example 7: Variable Sample Size. The data given in Figure 12.31 represent 20 samples with varying sample sizes. The value of $\bar{p}$ is computed as

$$\bar{p} = \frac{18 + 20 + 14 + \ldots + 18}{137 + 158 + 92 + \ldots + 160} = \frac{271}{2{,}980} = .0909$$

The control limits for sample 1 are

$$LCL_p = .0909 - 3\sqrt{\frac{.0909\,(1 - .0909)}{137}} = .017$$

$$UCL_p = .0909 + 3\sqrt{\frac{.0909\,(1 - .0909)}{137}} = .165$$

Because the sample sizes vary, the control limits are different for each sample. The p-chart is shown in Figure 12.32. Note that points 13 and 15 are outside the control limits.

An alternative approach is to use the average sample size, $\bar{n}$, to compute approximate control limits. Using the average sample size, the control limits are computed as

$$UCL_p = \bar{p} + 3\sqrt{\frac{\bar{p}(1-\bar{p})}{\bar{n}}}$$

Figure 12.29 Data and Calculations for Example 6 (P-CHART.XLS)

	A	B	C	D	E	F	G	H	I
1	**Fraction Nonconforming (p) Chart**								
2	This spreadsheet is designed for up to 50 samples. Enter data ONLY in yellow-shaded cells.								
3	Click on the sheet tab to display the control chart (some rescaling may be needed).								
4									
5	**Average (p-bar)**			**0.022**					
6									
7									
8			**Sample**	**Fraction**	**Standard**				
9	**Sample**	**Value**	**Size**	**Nonconforming**	**Deviation**	**LCLp**	**CL**	**UCLp**	
10	1	3	100	0.0300	0.01467	0	0.022	0.066	
11	2	1	100	0.0100	0.01467	0	0.022	0.066	
12	3	0	100	0.0000	0.01467	0	0.022	0.066	
13	4	0	100	0.0000	0.01467	0	0.022	0.066	
14	5	2	100	0.0200	0.01467	0	0.022	0.066	
15	6	5	100	0.0500	0.01467	0	0.022	0.066	
16	7	3	100	0.0300	0.01467	0	0.022	0.066	
17	8	6	100	0.0600	0.01467	0	0.022	0.066	
18	9	1	100	0.0100	0.01467	0	0.022	0.066	
19	10	4	100	0.0400	0.01467	0	0.022	0.066	
20	11	0	100	0.0000	0.01467	0	0.022	0.066	
21	12	2	100	0.0200	0.01467	0	0.022	0.066	
22	13	1	100	0.0100	0.01467	0	0.022	0.066	
23	14	3	100	0.0300	0.01467	0	0.022	0.066	
24	15	4	100	0.0400	0.01467	0	0.022	0.066	
25	16	1	100	0.0100	0.01467	0	0.022	0.066	
26	17	1	100	0.0100	0.01467	0	0.022	0.066	
27	18	2	100	0.0200	0.01467	0	0.022	0.066	
28	19	5	100	0.0500	0.01467	0	0.022	0.066	
29	20	2	100	0.0200	0.01467	0	0.022	0.066	
30	21	3	100	0.0300	0.01467	0	0.022	0.066	
31	22	4	100	0.0400	0.01467	0	0.022	0.066	
32	23	1	100	0.0100	0.01467	0	0.022	0.066	
33	24	0	100	0.0000	0.01467	0	0.022	0.066	
34	25	1	100	0.0100	0.01467	0	0.022	0.066	

and

$$\text{LCL}_p = \bar{p} - 3\sqrt{\frac{\bar{p}(1-\bar{p})}{\bar{n}}}$$

These result in an approximation to the true control limits. For the data in Figure 12.31, the average sample size is $\bar{n} = 2{,}980/20 = 149$. Using this value, the upper control limit is calculated to be 0.1616, and the lower control limit is .0202. However, this approach has several disadvantages. Because the control limits are only approximate, points that are actually out of control may not appear to be so on this chart. Second, runs or nonrandom patterns are difficult to interpret because the standard deviation differs between samples as a result of the variable sample sizes. Hence, this approach should be used with caution.

Figure 12.30 *p*-Chart for Example 6

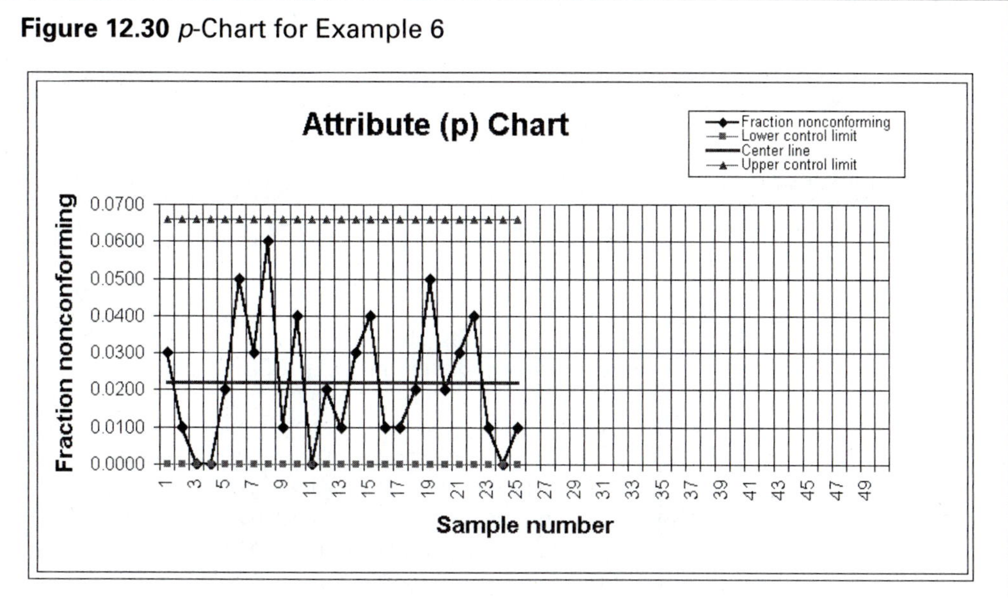

As a general guideline, use the average sample size method when the sample sizes fall within 25 percent of the average. For this example, 25 percent of 149 is 37.25. Thus, the average could be used for sample sizes between 112 and 186. This guideline would exclude samples 3, 6, 9, 11, 13, and 18, whose control limits should be computed exactly. If the calculations are performed on a computer, sample size is not an issue.

np-Charts for Number Nonconforming

In the *p*-chart, the fraction nonconforming of the *i*th sample is given by

$$p_i = y_i/n$$

where y_i is the number found nonconforming and n is the sample size. Multiplying both sides of the equation $p_i = y_i/n$ by n, yields

$$y_i = np_i$$

That is, the number nonconforming is equal to the sample size times the proportion nonconforming. Instead of using a chart for the fraction nonconforming, an equivalent alternative—a chart for the *number* of nonconforming items—is useful. Such a control chart is called an ***np*-chart**.

The *np*-chart is a control chart for the number of nonconforming items in a sample. To use the *np*-chart, the size of each sample *must be constant*. Suppose that two samples of sizes 10 and 15 each have four nonconforming items. Clearly, the fraction nonconforming in each sample is different, which would be reflected in a *p*-chart. An *np*-chart, however, would indicate no difference between samples. Thus, equal sample sizes are necessary to have a common base for measurement. Equal sample

Figure 12.31 Data and Calculations for Example 7 (P-CHART.XLS)

	A	B	C	D	E	F	G	H	I
1	**Fraction Nonconforming (p) Chart**								
2	This spreadsheet is designed for up to 50 samples. Enter data ONLY in yellow-shaded cells.								
3	Click on the sheet tab to display the control chart (some rescaling may be needed).								
4									
5	**Average (p-bar)**		**0.090939597**						
6									
7									
8			**Sample**	**Fraction**	**Standard**				
9	**Sample**	**Value**	**Size**	**Nonconforming**	**Deviation**	**LCLp**	**CL**	**UCLp**	
10	1	18	137	0.1314	0.024565	0.0172	0.091	0.1646	
11	2	20	158	0.1266	0.022874	0.0223	0.091	0.1596	
12	3	14	92	0.1522	0.029976	0.001	0.091	0.1809	
13	4	6	122	0.0492	0.026031	0.0128	0.091	0.169	
14	5	11	86	0.1279	0.031004	0	0.091	0.184	
15	6	22	187	0.1176	0.021026	0.0279	0.091	0.154	
16	7	6	156	0.0385	0.02302	0.0219	0.091	0.16	
17	8	9	117	0.0769	0.026582	0.0112	0.091	0.1707	
18	9	14	110	0.1273	0.027414	0.0087	0.091	0.1732	
19	10	12	142	0.0845	0.024128	0.0186	0.091	0.1633	
20	11	8	140	0.0571	0.0243	0.018	0.091	0.1638	
21	12	13	179	0.0726	0.02149	0.0265	0.091	0.1554	
22	13	5	196	0.0255	0.020537	0.0293	0.091	0.1526	
23	14	15	163	0.0920	0.022521	0.0234	0.091	0.1585	
24	15	25	140	0.1786	0.0243	0.018	0.091	0.1638	
25	16	12	135	0.0889	0.024746	0.0167	0.091	0.1652	
26	17	16	186	0.0860	0.021082	0.0277	0.091	0.1542	
27	18	12	193	0.0622	0.020696	0.0289	0.091	0.153	
28	19	15	181	0.0829	0.021371	0.0268	0.091	0.1551	
29	20	18	160	0.1125	0.022731	0.0227	0.091	0.1591	

sizes are not required for p-charts, because the fraction nonconforming is invariant to the sample size.

The np-chart is a useful alternative to the p-chart because it is often easier to understand for production personnel—the *number* of nonconforming items is more meaningful than a fraction. Also, it requires only a count, making the computations simpler.

The control limits for the np-chart, like those for the p-chart, are based on the binomial probability distribution. The center line is the average number of nonconforming items per sample as denoted by $n\bar{p}$, which is calculated by taking k samples of size n, summing the number of nonconforming items y_i in each sample, and dividing by k. That is,

Figure 12.32 *p*-Chart for Example 7

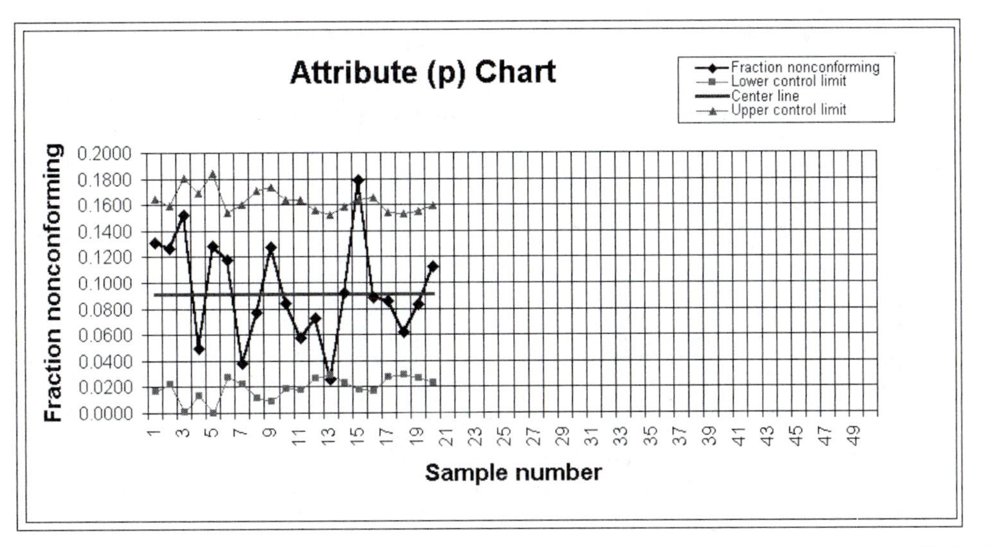

$$n\bar{p} = \frac{y_1 + y_2 + \ldots + y_k}{k}$$

An estimate of the standard deviation is

$$s_{n\bar{p}} = \sqrt{n\bar{p}(1 - \bar{p})}$$

where $\bar{p} = (n\bar{p})/n$. Using three-sigma limits as before, the control limits are specified by

$$\text{UCL}_{n\bar{p}} = n\bar{p} + 3\sqrt{n\bar{p}(1-\bar{p})}$$

$$\text{LCL}_{n\bar{p}} = n\bar{p} - 3\sqrt{n\bar{p}(1-\bar{p})}$$

Example 8: An *np*-Chart for a Post Office. The data for the post office example discussed earlier is given in Figure 12.33. The average number of errors found is:

$$n\bar{p} = \frac{3 + 1 + \ldots + 0 + 1}{25} = 2.2$$

To find the standard deviation, we first compute

$$\bar{p} = \frac{2.2}{100} = 0.022$$

Then,

Figure 12.33 Data and Calculations for Example 8 (NP-CHART.XLS)

	A	B	C	D	E	F	G	H	I
1	**Number Nonconforming (np) Chart**								
2	This spreadsheet is designed for up to 50 samples. Enter data ONLY in yellow-shaded cells.								
3	Each sample must have a constant sample size; enter this in cell C6.								
4	Click on the sheet tab to display the control chart (some rescaling may be needed).								
5									
6	**Sample size**		100						
7									
8	**Average (np-bar)**		**2.2**						
9	**Standard deviation**		**1.466833324**						
10									
11		**Number**							
12	**Sample**	**Nonconforming**	**LCLnp**	**CL**	**UCLnp**				
13	1	3	0	2.2	6.6005				
14	2	1	0	2.2	6.6005				
15	3	0	0	2.2	6.6005				
16	4	0	0	2.2	6.6005				
17	5	2	0	2.2	6.6005				
18	6	5	0	2.2	6.6005				
19	7	3	0	2.2	6.6005				
20	8	6	0	2.2	6.6005				
21	9	1	0	2.2	6.6005				
22	10	4	0	2.2	6.6005				
23	11	0	0	2.2	6.6005				
24	12	2	0	2.2	6.6005				
25	13	1	0	2.2	6.6005				
26	14	3	0	2.2	6.6005				
27	15	4	0	2.2	6.6005				
28	16	1	0	2.2	6.6005				
29	17	1	0	2.2	6.6005				
30	18	2	0	2.2	6.6005				
31	19	5	0	2.2	6.6005				
32	20	2	0	2.2	6.6005				
33	21	3	0	2.2	6.6005				
34	22	4	0	2.2	6.6005				
35	23	1	0	2.2	6.6005				
36	24	0	0	2.2	6.6005				
37	25	1	0	2.2	6.6005				

$$
\begin{aligned}
s_{n\bar{p}} &= \sqrt{2.2(1-.022)} \\
&= \sqrt{2.2(0.978)} \\
&= \sqrt{2.1516} = 1.4668
\end{aligned}
$$

The control limits are then computed as

$$\text{UCL}_{n\bar{p}} = 2.2 + 3(1.4668) = 6.6$$

$$\text{LCL}_{n\bar{p}} = 2.2 - 3(1.4668) = -2.20$$

Because the lower control limit is less than zero, a value of 0 is used. The control chart for this example is given in Figure 12.34.

Figure 12.34 *np*-Chart for Example 8

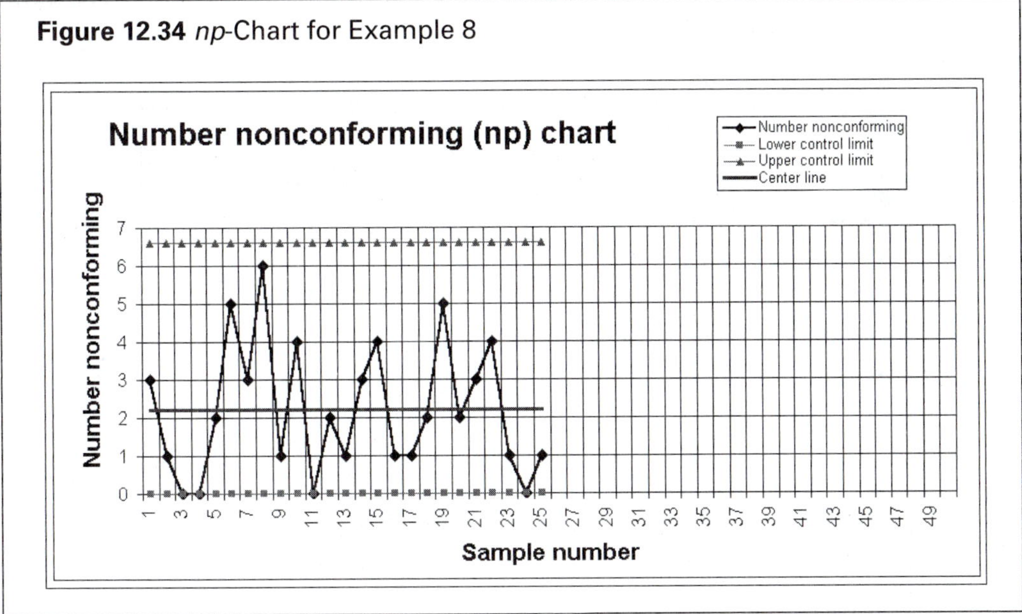

Charts for Defects

Recall that a *defect* is a single nonconforming characteristic of an item, while a *defective* refers to an item that has one or more defects. In some situations, quality assurance personnel may be interested not only in whether an item is defective but also in how many defects it has. For example, in complex assemblies such as electronics, the number of defects is just as important as whether the product is defective. Two charts can be applied in such situations. The **c-chart** is used to control the total number of defects per unit when subgroup size is constant. If subgroup sizes are variable, a ***u*-chart** is used to control the average number of defects per unit.

The *c*-chart is based on the Poisson probability distribution. To construct a *c*-chart, first estimate the average number of defects per unit, $\bar{c}$, by taking at least 25 samples of equal size, counting the number of defects per sample, and finding the average. The standard deviation of the Poisson distribution is the square root of the mean and yields

$$s_c = \sqrt{\bar{c}}$$

Thus, three-sigma control limits are given by

$$\text{UCL}_c = \bar{c} + 3\sqrt{\bar{c}}$$

$$\text{LCL}_c = \bar{c} - 3\sqrt{\bar{c}}$$

Example 9: Constructing a *c*-Chart. Figure 12.35 shows the number of machine failures over a 25-day period. The total number of failures is 45; therefore, the average number of failures per day is

$$\bar{c} = 45/25 = 1.8$$

Figure 12.35 Data and Calculations for Example 9 (C-CHART.XLS)

	A	B	C	D	E	F	G	H
1	**Average Number of Defects (c) Chart**							
2	This spreadsheet is designed for up to 50 samples. Enter data ONLY in yellow-shaded cells.							
3	Click on the sheet tab to display the control chart (some rescaling may be needed).							
4								
5	**Average (c-bar)**		**1.8**					
6	**Standard deviation**		**1.341640786**					
7								
8		**Number**						
9	**Sample**	**of Defects**	**LCLc**	**CL**	**UCLc**			
10	1	2	0	1.8	5.824922			
11	2	3	0	1.8	5.824922			
12	3	0	0	1.8	5.824922			
13	4	1	0	1.8	5.824922			
14	5	3	0	1.8	5.824922			
15	6	5	0	1.8	5.824922			
16	7	3	0	1.8	5.824922			
17	8	1	0	1.8	5.824922			
18	9	2	0	1.8	5.824922			
19	10	2	0	1.8	5.824922			
20	11	0	0	1.8	5.824922			
21	12	1	0	1.8	5.824922			
22	13	0	0	1.8	5.824922			
23	14	2	0	1.8	5.824922			
24	15	4	0	1.8	5.824922			
25	16	1	0	1.8	5.824922			
26	17	2	0	1.8	5.824922			
27	18	0	0	1.8	5.824922			
28	19	3	0	1.8	5.824922			
29	20	2	0	1.8	5.824922			
30	21	1	0	1.8	5.824922			
31	22	4	0	1.8	5.824922			
32	23	0	0	1.8	5.824922			
33	24	0	0	1.8	5.824922			
34	25	3	0	1.8	5.824922			

Control limits for a *c*-chart are therefore given by

$$UCL_c = 1.8 + 3\sqrt{1.8} = 5.82$$

$$LCL_c = 1.8 - 3\sqrt{1.8} = -2.22, \text{ or zero}$$

The chart is shown in Figure 12.36 and appears to be in control. Such a chart can be used for continued control or for monitoring the effectiveness of a quality improvement program.

Figure 12.36 *c*-Chart for Example 9

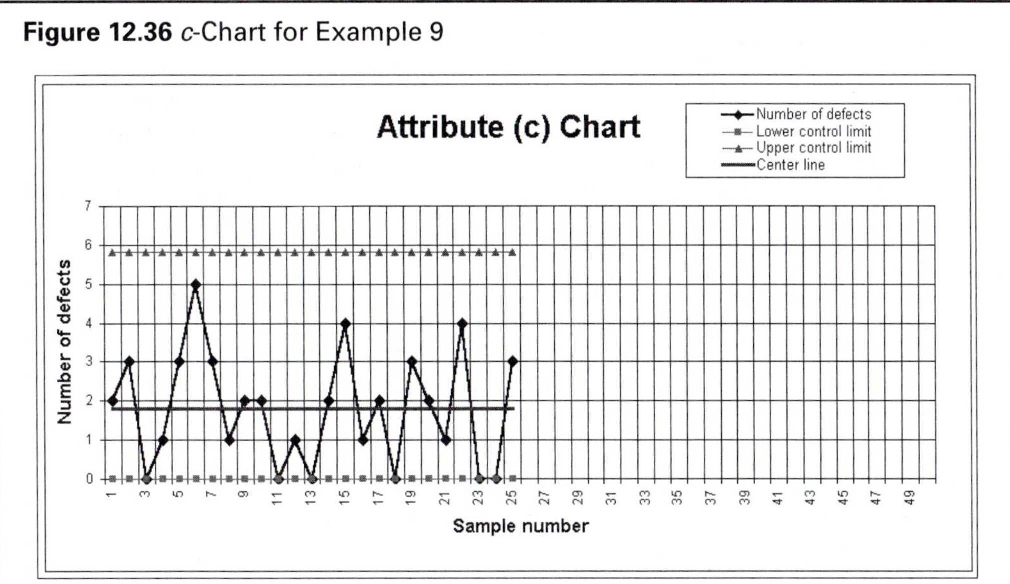

As long as the subgroup size is constant, a *c*-chart is appropriate. In many cases, however, the subgroup size is not constant or the nature of the production process does not yield discrete, measurable units. For example, suppose that in an auto assembly plant, several different models are produced that vary in surface area. The number of defects will not then be a valid comparison among different models. Other applications, such as the production of textiles, photographic film, or paper, have no convenient set of items to measure. In such cases, a standard unit of measurement is used, such as defects per square foot or defects per square inch. The control chart for these situations is the *u*-chart.

The variable u represents the average number of defects per unit of measurement, that is $u = c/n$, where n is the size of the subgroup (such as square feet). The center line $\bar{u}$ for k samples each of size n_i is computed as follows:

$$\bar{u} = \frac{c_1 + c_2 + \ldots + c_k}{n_1 + n_2 + \ldots + n_k}$$

The standard deviation of the ith sample is estimated by

$$s_u = \sqrt{\bar{u}/n_i}$$

The control limits, based on three standard deviations for the ith sample, are then

$$\text{UCL}_u = \bar{u} + 3\sqrt{\bar{u}/n_i}$$

$$\text{LCL}_u = \bar{u} - 3\sqrt{\bar{u}/n_i}$$

Note that if the size of the subgroups varies, so will the control limits. This result is similar to the *p*-chart with variable sample sizes. In general, whenever the sample size n varies, the control limits will also vary.

Example 10: Constructing a *u*-Chart. A catalog distributor ships a variety of orders each day. The packing slips often contain errors such as wrong purchase order numbers, wrong quantities, or incorrect sizes. Figure 12.37 shows the error data collected during August. Because the sample size varies each day, a *u*-chart is appropriate.

To construct the chart, first compute the number of errors per slip as shown in column 3. The average number of errors per slip, $\bar{u}$, is found by dividing the total number of errors (217) by the total number of packing slips (2,843):

$$\bar{u} = 217/2{,}843 = .076$$

The standard deviation for a particular sample size n_i is therefore

$$s_u = \sqrt{.076/n_i}$$

The control limits are shown in the spreadsheet. As with a *p*-chart, individual control limits will vary with the sample size. The control chart is shown in Figure 12.38. One point (#2) appears to be out of control.

One application of *c*-charts and *u*-charts is in a quality rating system. When some defects are considered to be more serious than others, they can be rated, or categorized, into different classes. For instance,

A – very serious
B – serious
C – moderately serious
D – not serious

Each category can be weighted using a point scale, such as 100 for A, 50 for B, 10 for C, and 1 for D.[3] These points, or demerits, can be used as the basis for a *c*- or *u*-chart that would measure total demerits or demerits per unit, respectively. Such charts are often used for internal quality control and as a means of rating suppliers.

Choosing Between *c*- and *u*-Charts

Confusion often exists over which chart is appropriate for a specific application, because the *c*- and *u*-charts apply to situations in which the quality characteristics inspected do not necessarily come from discrete units. The key issue to consider is *whether the sampling unit is constant.* For example, suppose that an electronics manufacturer produces circuit boards. The boards may contain various defects, such as faulty components and missing connections. Because the sampling unit—the circuit board—is constant (assuming that all boards are the same), a *c*-chart is appropriate. If the process produces boards of varying sizes with different numbers of components and connections, then a *u*-chart would apply.

As another example, consider a telemarketing firm that wants to track the number of calls needed to make one sale. In this case, the firm has no physical sampling unit. However, an analogy can be made with the circuit boards. The sale corresponds to the circuit board, and the number of calls to the number of defects. In both examples, the number of occurrences in relationship to a constant entity is being measured. Thus, a *c*-chart is appropriate.

Figure 12.37 Data and Calculations for Example 10 (U-CHART.XLS)

	A	B	C	D	E	F	G	H	I
1	**Average Number of Defects Per Unit (u) Chart**								
2	This spreadsheet is designed for up to 50 samples. Enter data ONLY in yellow-shaded cells.								
3	Click on the sheet tab to display the control chart (some rescaling may be needed).								
4									
5	**Average (u-bar)**		**0.076327823**						
6									
7									
8		**Number**	**Sample**	**Defects**	**Standard**				
9	**Sample**	**of Defects**	**Size**	**per unit**	**Deviation**	**LCLu**	**CL**	**UCLu**	
10	1	8	92	0.0870	0.028804	0	0.076	0.163	
11	2	15	69	0.2174	0.03326	0	0.076	0.176	
12	3	6	86	0.0698	0.029791	0	0.076	0.166	
13	4	13	85	0.1529	0.029966	0	0.076	0.166	
14	5	5	123	0.0407	0.024911	0.002	0.076	0.151	
15	6	5	87	0.0575	0.02962	0	0.076	0.165	
16	7	3	74	0.0405	0.032116	0	0.076	0.173	
17	8	8	83	0.0964	0.030325	0	0.076	0.167	
18	9	4	103	0.0388	0.027222	0	0.076	0.158	
19	10	6	60	0.1000	0.035667	0	0.076	0.183	
20	11	7	136	0.0515	0.02369	0.005	0.076	0.147	
21	12	4	80	0.0500	0.030888	0	0.076	0.169	
22	13	2	70	0.0286	0.033021	0	0.076	0.175	
23	14	11	73	0.1507	0.032336	0	0.076	0.173	
24	15	13	89	0.1461	0.029285	0	0.076	0.164	
25	16	6	129	0.0465	0.024325	0.003	0.076	0.149	
26	17	6	78	0.0769	0.031282	0	0.076	0.17	
27	18	3	88	0.0341	0.029451	0	0.076	0.165	
28	19	8	76	0.1053	0.031691	0	0.076	0.171	
29	20	9	101	0.0891	0.02749	0	0.076	0.159	
30	21	8	92	0.0870	0.028804	0	0.076	0.163	
31	22	2	70	0.0286	0.033021	0	0.076	0.175	
32	23	9	54	0.1667	0.037596	0	0.076	0.189	
33	24	5	83	0.0602	0.030325	0	0.076	0.167	
34	25	13	165	0.0788	0.021508	0.012	0.076	0.141	
35	26	5	137	0.0365	0.023604	0.006	0.076	0.147	
36	27	8	79	0.1013	0.031083	0	0.076	0.17	
37	28	6	76	0.0789	0.031691	0	0.076	0.171	
38	29	7	147	0.0476	0.022787	0.008	0.076	0.145	
39	30	4	80	0.0500	0.030888	0	0.076	0.169	
40	31	8	78	0.1026	0.031282	0	0.076	0.17	

SUMMARY OF CONTROL CHART CONSTRUCTION

Table 12.3 summarizes the formulas used for constructing the different types of control charts discussed thus far. Figure 12.39 provides a summary of guidelines for chart selection.

A wide variety of commercial software is available to implement SPC. For example, one of the more recent packages is *CHARTrunner 2000,* product of PQ Systems (*http://www.pqsystems.com*). *CHARTrunner* generates SPC charts and performs statistical analyses using data that are collected, stored, and managed by other applications such as Microsoft Access or Excel, SQL Server, Oracle, text files, and many others. It generates control charts, as well as histograms, process capability results, Pareto charts, scatter diagrams, and others; performs curve fitting and linear regression; and allows users to customize out-of-control tests, select colors for sigma zones, display multiple sets of control limits, and save charts as image files. Annual software surveys can be found in such professional publications as *Quality Progress* (*http://www.asq.org*) and *Quality Digest* (*http://www.qualitydigest.com*).

Figure 12.38 *u*-Chart for Example 10

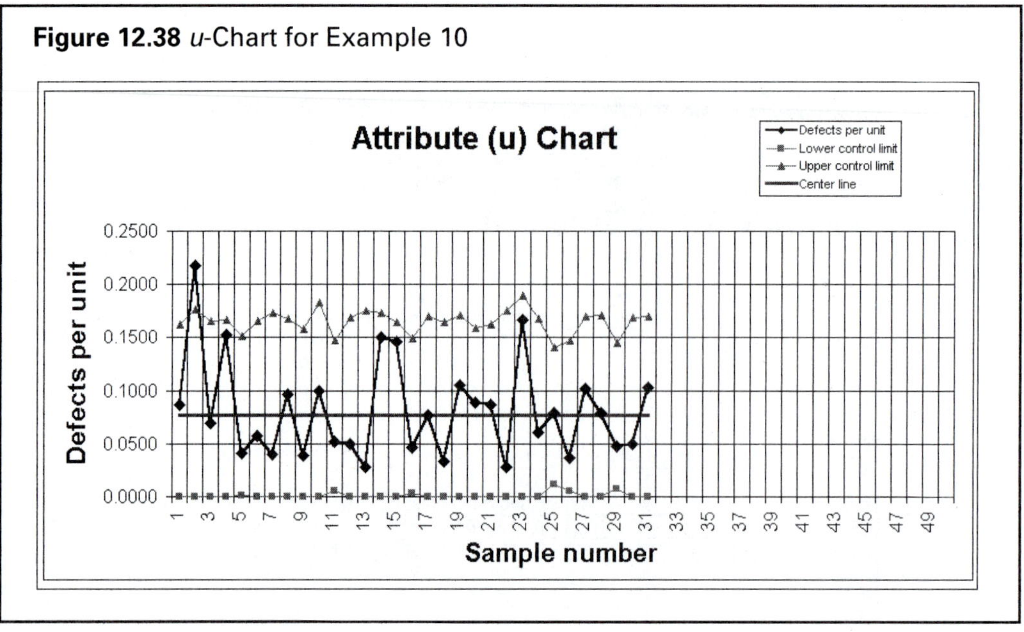

Table 12.3 Summary of Control Chart Formulas

Type of Chart	LCL	CL	UCL
$\bar{x}$ (with R)	$\bar{\bar{x}} - A_2\bar{R}$	$\bar{\bar{x}}$	$\bar{\bar{x}} + A_2\bar{R}$
R	$D_3\bar{R}$	$\bar{R}$	$D_4\bar{R}$
p	$\bar{p} - 3\sqrt{\bar{p}(1-\bar{p})/n}$	$\bar{p}$	$\bar{p} + 3\sqrt{\bar{p}(1-\bar{p})/n}$
$\bar{x}$ (with s)	$\bar{\bar{x}} - A_3\bar{s}$	$\bar{\bar{x}}$	$\bar{\bar{x}} + A_3\bar{s}$
s	$B_3\bar{s}$	$\bar{s}$	$B_4\bar{s}$
x	$\bar{\bar{x}} - 3\bar{R}/d_2$	$\bar{\bar{x}}$	$\bar{\bar{x}} + 3\bar{R}/d_2$
np	$n\bar{p} - 3\sqrt{n\bar{p}(1-\bar{p})}$	$n\bar{p}$	$n\bar{p} + 3\sqrt{n\bar{p}(1-\bar{p})}$
c	$\bar{c} - 3\sqrt{\bar{c}}$	$\bar{c}$	$\bar{c} + 3\sqrt{\bar{c}}$
u	$\bar{u} - 3\sqrt{\bar{u}/n}$	$\bar{u}$	$\bar{u} + 3\sqrt{\bar{u}/n}$

DESIGNING CONTROL CHARTS

Designers of control charts must consider four issues: (1) the basis for sampling, (2) the sample size, (3) the frequency of sampling, and (4) the location of the control limits.

Figure 12.39 Control Chart Selection

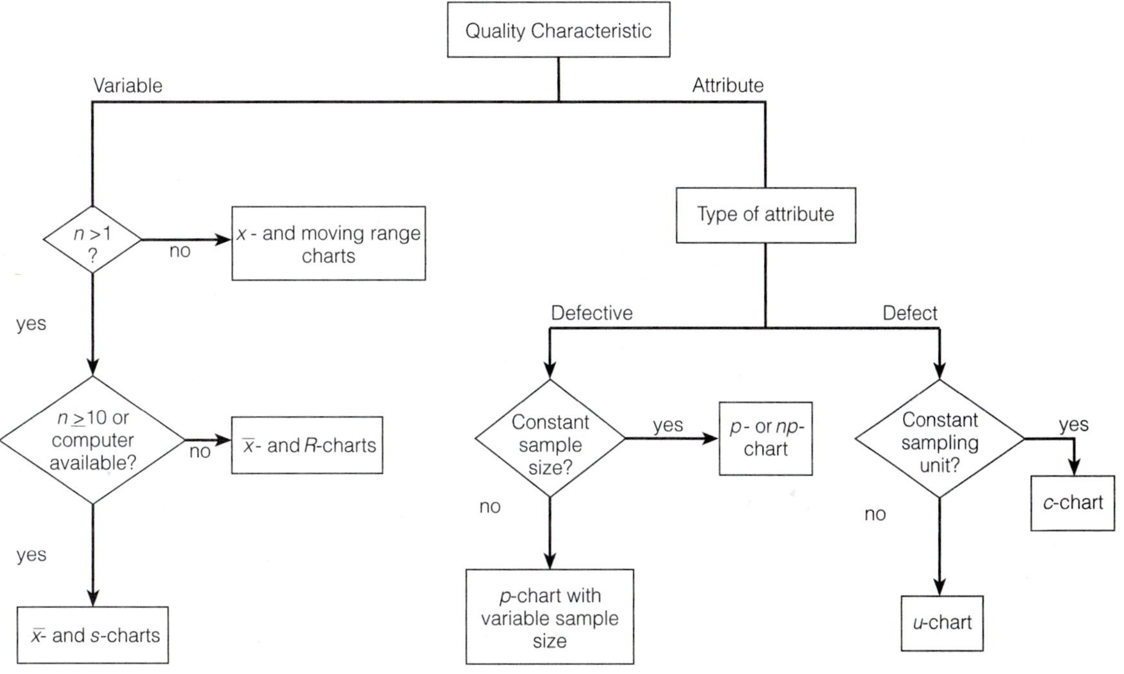

Basis for Sampling

The purpose of a control chart is to identify the variation in a system that may change over time. In one case, a hospital was monitoring the waiting time in its emergency room. In constructing a control chart, five patients were chosen randomly over the course of each shift. In this example, it is unlikely that process conditions would remain stable over an entire working shift. Thus, little useful information was provided in the chart. First, any change in the process average during a shift would not be reflected in the data, and second, a shift in the process level would cause points on the *R*-chart to be out of control, even if no change in the variability of the process actually occurred.

In determining the method of sampling, samples should be chosen to be as homogeneous as possible so that each sample reflects the system of common causes or assignable causes that may be present at that point in time. That is, if assignable causes are present, the chance of observing differences between samples should be high, while the chance of observing differences within a sample should be low. Samples that satisfy these criteria are called **rational subgroups**.

One approach to constructing rational subgroups is to use consecutive measurements over a short period of time. Consecutive measurements minimize the chance of variability within the sample while allowing variation between samples to be detected. This approach is useful when control charts are used to detect shifts in process level. One must also be careful not to overlap production shifts, different batches of material, and so on, when selecting the basis for sampling. Thus, the method of selecting samples should be chosen carefully so as not to bias the results.

Sample Size

Sample size is a second critical design issue. A small sample size is desirable to minimize the opportunity for within-sample variation due to special causes. This issue is important because each sample should be representative of the state of control at one point in time. In addition, the cost of sampling should be kept low. The time an operator spends taking the sample measurements and plotting a control chart represents nonproductive time (in a strict accounting sense only!). On the other hand, control limits are based on the assumption of a normal distribution of the sample means. If the process is not normal, this assumption is valid only for large samples. Large samples also allow smaller changes in process characteristics to be detected with higher probability. In practice, samples of about five have been found to work well in detecting process shifts of two standard deviations or larger. To detect smaller shifts in the process mean, larger sample sizes of 15 to 25 must be used.

Figure 12.40 shows the probability of detecting a shift in the mean in the next sample (that is, the probability of seeing the next point outside the three-sigma control limit when the process has shifted some number of standard deviations) as a function of the sample size for an $\bar{x}$-chart. Thus, if a process has shifted 1.5 standard deviations, a sample size of 5 provides only a 64 percent chance of detection. For a 90 percent chance of detecting this particular process shift, a sample of at least 8 is needed.

Figure 12.40 Probability of Detecting a Shift in Mean

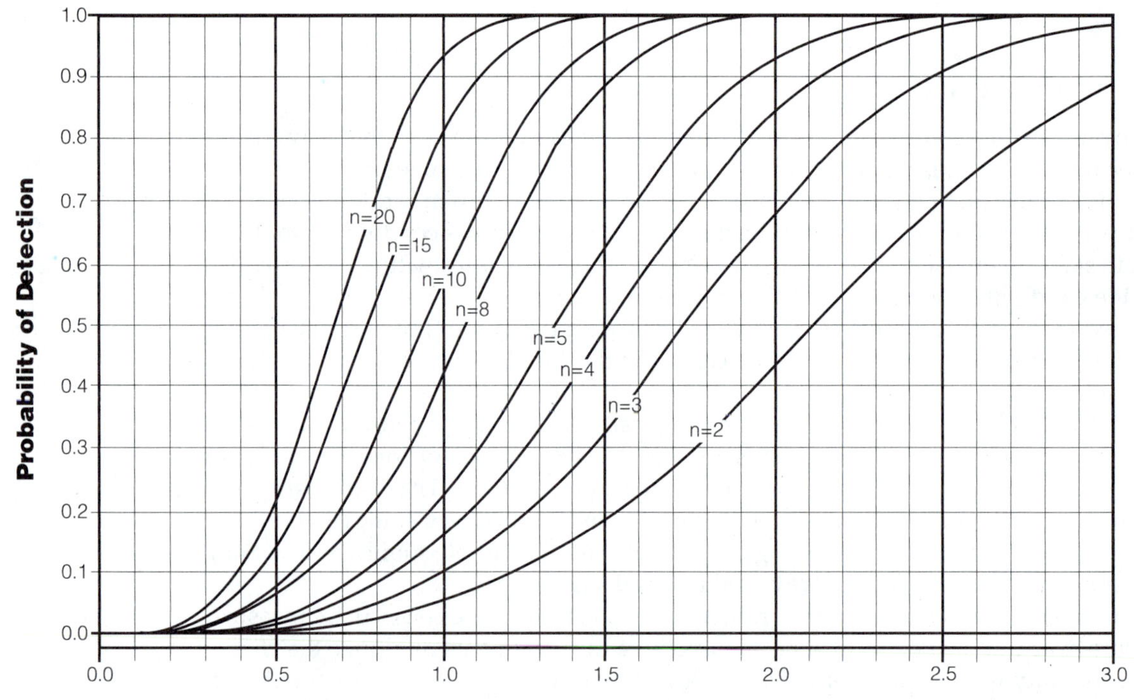

Source: Adapted from Lyle Dockendorf, "Choosing Appropriate Sample Subgroup Sizes for Control Charts," *Quality Progress* 25, no. 10 (October 1992), 160.

For attributes data, too small a sample size can make a p-chart meaningless. Even though many guidelines such as "use at least 100 observations" have been suggested, the proper sample size should be determined statistically, particularly when the true portion of nonconformances is small. If p is small, n should be large enough to have a high probability of detecting at least one nonconformance. For example, if $p = .01$, then to have at least a 95 percent chance of finding at least one nonconformance, the sample size must be at least 300. Other approaches for determining attribute data sample sizes include choosing n large enough to provide a 50 percent chance of detecting a process shift of some specified amount, or choosing n so that the control chart will have a positive lower control limit. The reader is referred to the book by Montgomery in the bibliography for details on these calculations.

Sampling Frequency

The third design issue is the sampling frequency. Taking large samples on a frequent basis is desirable but clearly not economical. No hard-and-fast rules exist for the frequency of sampling. Samples should be close enough to provide an opportunity to detect changes in process characteristics as soon as possible and reduce the chances of producing a large amount of nonconforming output. However, they should not be so close that the cost of sampling outweighs the benefits that can be realized. This decision depends on the individual application and production volume.

Location of Control Limits

The location of control limits is closely related to the risk involved in making an incorrect assessment about the state of control. A Type I error occurs when an incorrect conclusion is reached that a *special cause is present when in fact one does not exist*. This error results in the cost of trying to find a nonexistent problem. A Type II error occurs when *special causes are present but are not signaled in the control chart* because points fall within the control limits by chance. Because nonconforming products have a greater chance to be produced, a cost will eventually be incurred as a result. The size of a Type I error depends only on the control limits that are used; the wider the limits, the less chance of a point falling outside the limits, and consequently the smaller is the chance of making a Type I error. A Type II error, however, depends on the width of the control limits, the degree to which the process is out of control, and the sample size. For a fixed sample size, wider control limits increase the risk of making a Type II error.

The traditional approach of using three-sigma limits implicitly assumes that the cost of a Type I error is large relative to that of a Type II error; that is, a Type I error is essentially minimized. This situation will not always be the case, however. Much research has been performed on economic design of control charts.[4] Cost models attempt to find the best combination of design parameters (center line, control limits, sample size, and sampling interval) that minimize expected cost or maximize expected profit.

Certain costs are associated with making both Type I and Type II errors. A Type I error results in unnecessary investigation for an assignable cause, including costs of lost production time and special testing. A Type II error can be more significant. If an out-of-control process is not recognized, defectives that are produced may result in higher costs of scrap and rework in later stages of production or after the finished good reaches the customer. Unfortunately, the cost of a Type II error is nearly impossible to estimate because it depends on the amount of nonconforming products—a quantity that is unknown.

The costs associated with Type I and Type II errors conflict as control limits change. The tighter the control limits, the greater is the probability that a sample will

Table 12.4 Economic Decisions for Control Chart Construction

Source of Cost	Sample Size	Sampling Frequency	Control Limits
Type I error	large	high	wide
Type II error	large	high	narrow
Sampling and testing	small	low	—

indicate that the process is out of control. Hence, the cost of a Type I error increases as control limits are reduced. On the other hand, tighter control limits will reduce the cost of a Type II error, since out-of-control states will be more easily identified and the amount of defective output will be reduced.

The costs associated with sampling and testing may include lost productive time when the operator takes sample measurements, performs calculations, and plots the points on the control chart. If the testing is destructive, the value of lost products would also be included. Thus, larger sample sizes and more frequent sampling result in higher costs.

The sample size and frequency also affect the costs of Type I and Type II errors. As the sample size or frequency is increased, both Type I and Type II errors are reduced, because better information is provided for decision making. Table 12.4 summarizes this discussion of the three-way interaction of costs. In the economic design of control charts we must consider these simultaneously. Most models for such decisions can become quite complex and are beyond the scope of this text.

As a practical matter, one often uses judgment about the nature of operations and the costs involved in making these decisions. Raymond Mayer suggests the following guidelines:

1. If the cost of investigating an operation to identify the cause of an apparent out-of-control condition is high, a Type I error becomes important, and wider control limits should be adopted. Conversely, if that cost is low, narrower limits should be selected.
2. If the cost of the defective output generated by an operation is substantial, a Type II error is serious, and narrower control limits should be used. Otherwise, wider limits should be selected.
3. If the cost of a Type I error and the cost of a Type II error for a given activity are both significant, wide control limits should be chosen, and consideration should be given to reducing the risk of a Type II error by increasing the sample size. Also, more frequent samples should be taken to reduce the duration of any out-of-control condition that might occur.
4. If past experience with an operation indicates that an out-of-control condition arises quite frequently, narrower control limits should be favored because of the large number of opportunities for making a Type II error. In the event that the probability of an out-of-control condition is small, wider limits are preferred.[5]

ADVANCED CONTROL CHARTS

In addition to the control charts already introduced, several other types of control charts are used in industry. This section briefly reviews three of them: stabilized control charts, exponentially weighted moving average (EWMA) charts, and cumulative sum control charts. The reader is encouraged to study more advanced books on statistical quality control for further details on these and other types of control charts.

Short Production Runs and Stabilized Control Charts

Control charts were developed for high-volume manufacturing situations in which production runs lasted for weeks or months. In some industries, particularly as the pressures for increased manufacturing flexibility increase, short production runs, perhaps for only a few hours, are common. In such situations it may be impossible to collect enough samples to compute control limits. Even if it is possible, by the time the data are collected and the chart is constructed, the production run might be over, thus defeating the purpose of the chart.

Fortunately, classical SPC methods can often be modified to apply to short production runs. Three approaches can be used for variables data. First, tables of special control chart constants for control limits compensate for the fact that a limited number of samples are available. As more data become available, this approach updates control limits until no further updates are needed and standard control chart factors can be used. A second approach is to "code" the data by subtracting the nominal value from the actual measurements. For example, consider a drill press in which each run requires varying depths of cut. Instead of measuring values of the actual depth of cut for a particular part, one can measure the deviation of depth from the target. In this way, differences between products and production runs are removed. In effect, this approach monitors *process* characteristics rather than *product* characteristics.

Finally, the data can be transformed so that they are independent of the unit of measure; such charts are called **stabilized control charts**. The idea is similar to the familiar statistical concept of transforming normally distributed random variables to a normal random variable with mean 0 and variance 1 by subtracting the mean and dividing by the standard deviation. Common transformations are $(\bar{x} - \bar{\bar{x}})/\bar{R}$ and $R/\bar{R}$. For the $\bar{x}$-chart, control limits on the transformation $(\bar{x} - \bar{\bar{x}})/\bar{R}$ are UCL = A_2 and LCL = $-A_2$. Control limits for the R-chart based on the transformation $R/\bar{R}$ are UCL = D_4 and LCL = D_3.

Stabilized charts can be developed for any type of attribute chart by using the transformation

$$z = (\text{sample statistic} - \text{process average})/\text{standard deviation}$$

For example, to develop a stabilized p-chart, use

$$z = (p - \bar{p})/s_p$$

Because z is measured in standard deviations, the upper and lower control limits are +3 and −3, respectively. Readers are encouraged to consult Pyzdek's book cited in the bibliography for further information.

EWMA Charts

The **exponentially weighted moving average (EWMA) chart** was introduced for applications in chemical and process industries in which only one observation per time period may be available. These measurement applications are the same situations in which charts for individuals are used, except that the EWMA chart incorporates information on all the past data, not simply the last observation. The term *exponentially weighted* refers to the fact that the data are weighted, with more weight being given to the most recent data. (You may have studied exponential smoothing as a forecasting technique; the same principle applies.)

The statistic that is plotted on the chart is

$$z_t = \alpha\bar{x}_t + (1 - \alpha)z_{t-1}$$

Here, z_t is the exponentially weighted moving average after observation t is taken; $\bar{x}_t$ is the value of observation t; z_{t-1} is the previous exponentially weighted moving average; and α is a weighting factor between 0 and 1. This formula can be written in an alternate fashion:

$$z_t = z_{t-1} + \alpha(\bar{x}_t - z_{t-1})$$

which states that the current value of the statistic is equal to the previous value plus some fraction of the difference between the current observation and its last estimate. Note that when $\alpha = 1$, the formula reduces to the ordinary $\bar{x}$-chart.

The standard error of the exponentially weighted moving average is

$$\sigma_{z_t} = \sigma_{\bar{x}} \sqrt{\frac{\alpha}{2 - \alpha}} = \frac{\sigma_x}{\sqrt{n}} \sqrt{\frac{\alpha}{2 - \alpha}}$$

Therefore the control limits are given by

$$\text{UCL}_z = \bar{\bar{x}} + 3 \frac{\sigma_x}{\sqrt{n}} \sqrt{\frac{\alpha}{2 - \alpha}}$$

$$\text{LCL}_z = \bar{\bar{x}} - 3 \frac{\sigma_x}{\sqrt{n}} \sqrt{\frac{\alpha}{2 - \alpha}}$$

The EWMA chart is more sensitive to small process level shifts than $\bar{x}$- or individual charts. The smaller the value of α, the more easily are smaller shifts detectable. This chart is useful when the acceptable process limits are narrow. However, this sensitivity can lead to an excessive number of unnecessary adjustments to the process and, consequently, unnecessary costs.

Cumulative Sum Control Charts

The **cumulative sum control chart (CuSum chart)** was designed to identify small but sustained shifts in a process level much more quickly than ordinary $\bar{x}$-charts. Because it gives an early indication of process changes, it is consistent with the management philosophy of doing it right the first time and not allowing the production of nonconforming products.

The CuSum chart incorporates all past data by plotting cumulative sums of the deviations of sample values from a target value; that is,

$$S_t = \sum_{i=1}^{t} (\bar{x}_i - \bar{x}_0)$$

where $\bar{x}_i$ is the average of the ith subgroup, $\bar{x}_0$ is the standard or reference value, and S_t is the cumulative sum when the ith observation is taken. Note that when $n = 1$, $\bar{x}_i$ is the value of the ith observation.

The CuSum chart looks different from ordinary $\bar{x}$- and R-charts. In place of a center line and horizontal control limits, a "mask" is constructed that consists of a location pointer and two angled control limits as illustrated in Figure 12.41. The mask is located on the chart so that the point p lies on the last point plotted. The distance d and the angle θ are the design parameters of the mask. (This text does not discuss how these are computed. Readers are referred to Chapter 10 of Grant and Leavenworth or Chapter 7 of Montgomery [both cited in the bibliography at the end of the chapter] for details.)

If no previous points lie outside the control limits, the process is assumed to be in control. If, for example, a shift in the process mean raises it above the reference value, each new value added to the cumulative sum will cause S_t to increase and result in an upward trend in the chart. Eventually a point will fall outside the upper control limit, indicating that the process has fallen out of control (illustrated in Figure 12.42). The opposite will occur if the mean shifts downward.

PRE-CONTROL[6]

Pre-control is a technique useful in operations such as machining, where quality characteristics are easily monitored and can be adjusted. It is valuable for monitoring process capability over time. A major advantage of pre-control is its direct relationship to specifications, which requires no recording, calculating, or plotting of data.

The idea behind pre-control is to divide the tolerance range into zones by setting two *pre-control lines* halfway between the center of the specification and the tolerance limits (see Figure 12.43). The center zone, called the *green zone*, comprises one-half of the total tolerance. Between the pre-control lines and the tolerance limits are the *yellow zones*. Outside the tolerance limits are the *red zones*.

Pre-control is applied as follows. As a manufacturing run is initiated, five consecutive parts must fall within the green zone. If not, the production setup must be reevaluated before the full production run can be started. Once regular operations commence, two parts are sampled; if the first falls within the green zone, production

Figure 12.41 CuSum Chart for Sample Averages

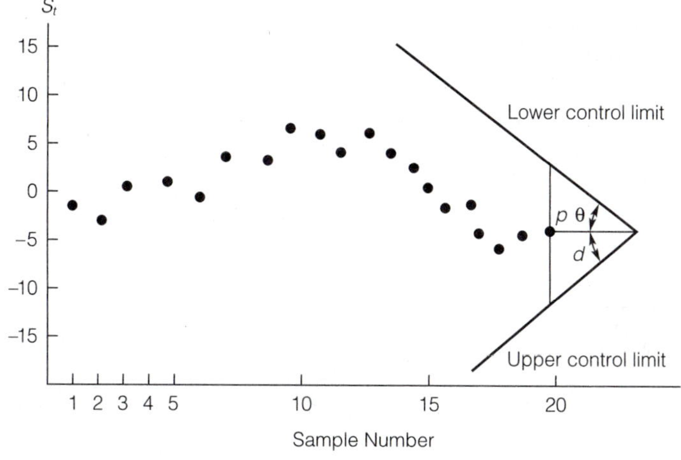

Figure 12.42 CuSum Chart Illustration of Lack of Control

continues, which eliminates the need to measure the second part. If the first part falls in a yellow zone, the second part is inspected. If the second part falls in the green zone, production can continue; if not, production should stop and a special cause should be investigated. If any part falls in a red zone, then action should be taken.

The rationale behind pre-control can be explained using basic statistical arguments. Suppose that the process capability is equal to the tolerance spread (see Figure 12.44). The area of each yellow zone is approximately 0.07, while that of the red zone is less than 0.01. The probability of two consecutive parts falling in a yellow zone is (0.07)(0.07) = 0.0049 if the process mean has not shifted. If $C_p > 1$, this probability is even less. Such an outcome would more than likely indicate a special cause. If both

Figure 12.43 Pre-Control Ranges

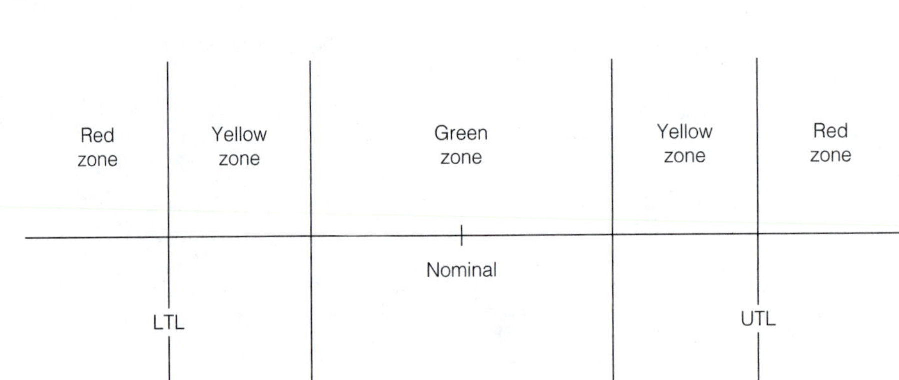

Figure 12.44 Basis for Pre-Control Rules

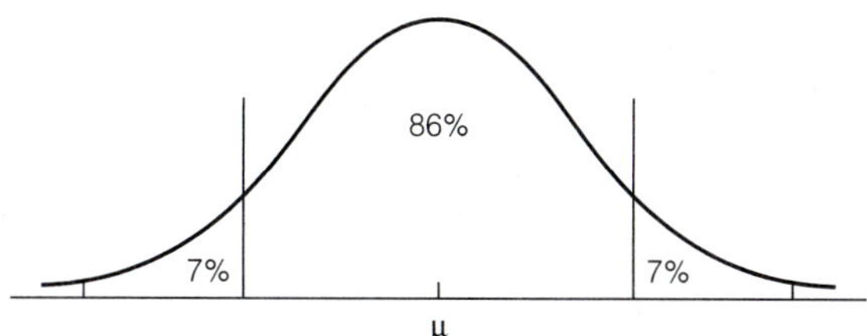

parts fall in the same yellow zone, you would conclude that the mean has shifted; if in different yellow zones, you would conclude that the variation has increased.

The frequency of sampling is often determined by dividing the time period between two successive out-of-control signals by six. Thus, if the process deteriorates, sampling frequency is increased; if it improves, the frequency is decreased.

Example 11: An Example of Pre-Control. The force necessary to break a wire used in electrical circuitry has a specification of 3 gm–7 gm. Thus, the pre-control zones are

Range	Zone
<3	Red
3–4	Yellow
4–6	Green
6–7	Yellow
>7	Red

The following samples were collected:

Sample	First Measurement	Second Measurement
1	4.7	
2	4.5	
3	4.4	
4	4.2	
5	4.2	
6	4.0	
7	4.0	
8	3.7	3.6
9	6.5	3.5

For samples 1 through 7, the first measurement falls in the green zone; thus no further action need be taken. For sample 8, however, the first measurement falls in a yellow zone. The second measurement also falls in a yellow zone. The process should be stopped for investigation of a shift in the mean. At the next time of inspection, both pieces also fall in a yellow zone. In this case, the probable cause is a shift in variation. Again, the process should be stopped for investigation.

Pre-control is not an adequate substitute for control charts and should only be used when process capability is no greater than 88 percent of the tolerance, or equivalently, when C_p is at least 1.14. If the process mean tends to drift, then C_p should be higher. Also, if managers or operators are interested in detecting process shifts even though the product output falls within specifications, pre-control should not be used because it will not detect such shifts.

Quality in Practice

Applying SPC to Pharmaceutical Product Manufacturing[7]

A Midwest pharmaceutical company manufactures (in two stages) individual syringes with a self-contained, single dose of an injectable drug. In the first stage, sterile liquid drug is filled into glass syringes and sealed with a rubber stopper. The remaining stage involves insertion of the cartridge into plastic syringes and the electrical "tacking" of the containment cap at a precisely determined length of the syringe. A cap that is "tacked" at a shorter than desired length (less than 4.920 inches) leads to pressure on the cartridge stopper and, hence, partial or complete activation of the syringe. Such syringes must then be scrapped. If the cap is "tacked" at a longer than desired length (4.980 inches or longer), the tacking is incomplete or inadequate, which can lead to cap loss and potentially a cartridge loss in shipment and handling. Such syringes can be reworked manually to attach the cap at a lower position. However, this process requires a 100 percent inspection of the tacked syringes and results in increased cost for the items. This final production step seemed to be producing more and more scrap and reworked syringes over successive weeks. At this point, statistical consultants became involved in an attempt to solve this problem and recommended SPC for the purpose of improving the tacking operation. The length was targeted as a critical variable to be monitored by $\bar{x}$- and R-charts, which eventually led to the root cause of the problem. The actual case history contains instances in which desired procedures were not always followed. As such, this case illustrates well the properties, problems, pitfalls, and peculiarities in applying such charts, as well as the necessity of having well-trained quality specialists involved.

Operators of the final stage of this syringe assembly process were trained in the basics of process capability studies and control charting techniques. In an attempt to judge the capability of the process, the responsible technician was called in to adjust the tacking machine and to position and secure it at what seemed its best possible position. Then, 35 consecutive samples were taken (see Table 12.5), and a capability study was undertaken.

The process had a sample mean of $\bar{x} = 4.954$ inches, which was close to the nominal aim (or target) of 4.950 inches with a sample standard deviation of $s = 0.0083$ inches. Upper and lower specifications of 4.980 and 4.920 inches, respectively, gave an estimated $C_{pk} = 1.03$. Thus, it was determined that the process was minimally capable and could indeed produce the length desired.

To establish the control charts, the operators collected 15 samples each of size 5 taken every 15 minutes. The $\bar{x}$- and R-charts are shown in Figure 12.45. These charts show that the process is already out of statistical control in both charts.

Table 12.5 Initial 35 Consecutive Samples Taken for the Capability Study

4.95888	4.95533	4.94294	4.95422	4.96679	4.94487	4.95775	4.95710
4.96543	4.95603	4.95210	4.95311	4.95385	4.96014	4.95252	4.96633
4.96255	4.95287	4.93541	4.94840	4.96114	4.93901	4.95966	4.93667
4.95941	4.94539	4.96238	4.94337	4.95550	4.95482	4.96230	4.96175
4.96016	4.94626	4.95904					

Figure 12.45 Initial $\bar{x}$- and R-Charts of the First 15 Samples

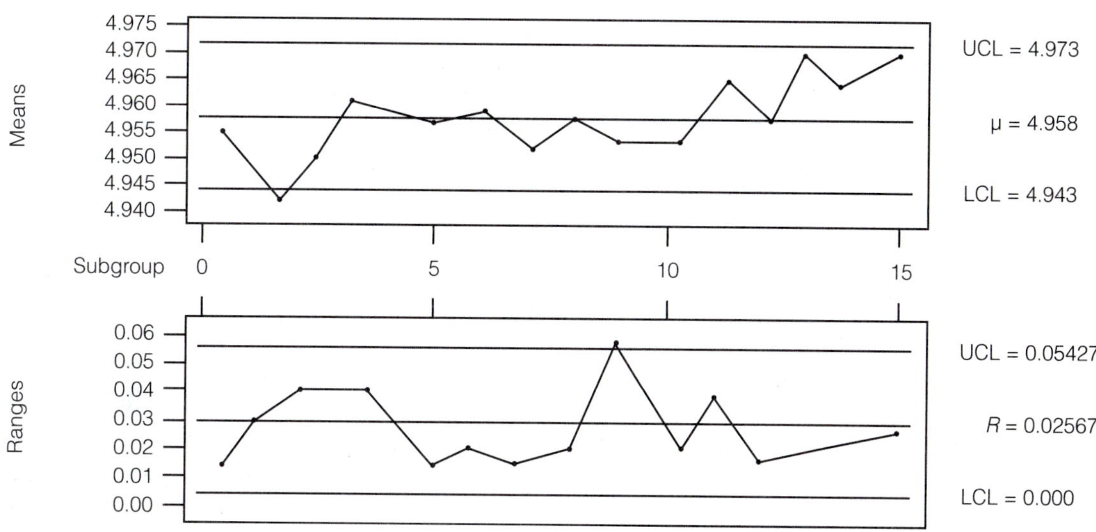

Proper application of SPC procedures would have indicated that special causes be identified and new control limits constructed. Unfortunately, the operators from this shift did not plot these points but only used the control limits they obtained to evaluate future measurements. The operators from this first shift continued to collect samples of size 5 every 15 minutes, but due to their unfamiliarity with charting, they never plotted these 15 new points either. At 4:00 P.M. of the same day, a new shift arrived and did plot this second set of 15 points using the control limits obtained from the first set of 15 points as shown in Figure 12.46. These charts show clearly the centering to be out of statistical control, with the average length far greater than desired. This conclusion was substantiated by

Figure 12.46 $\bar{x}$- and R-Charts, the Next 17 Samples

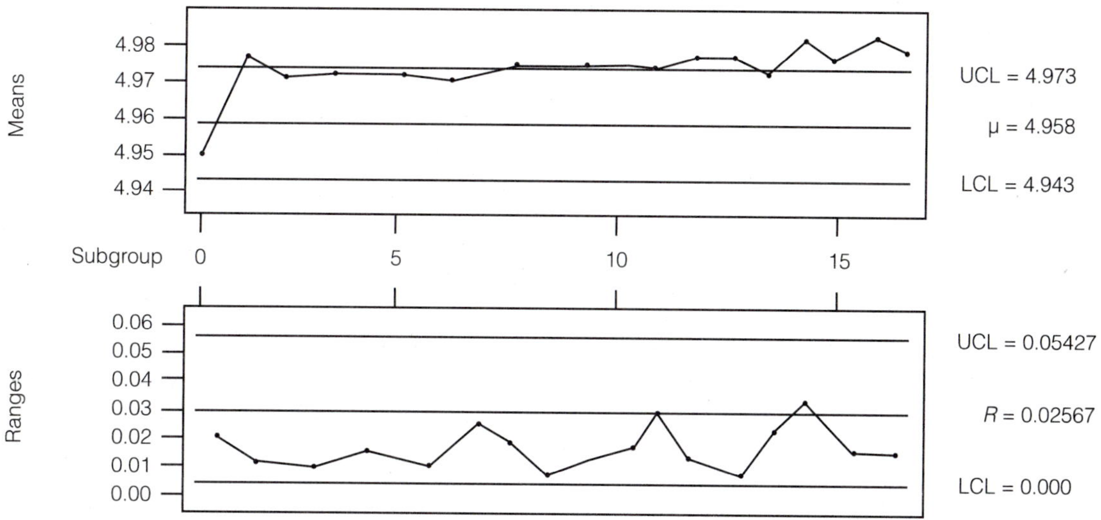

the shift noticing that the caps were not being tacked properly. The maintenance technician was immediately called in to adjust the machine properly.

After this first adjustment by the technician, the plot of the next sample taken 15 minutes later was already beyond the upper control limit for the $\bar{x}$-chart. Thus, the syringes were still too long, although the technician affirmed that he had set the height lower just 15 minutes earlier. The technician was recalled to readjust the machine. The second try was no better, and so the technician was called a third time to adjust the machine. This third try was successful in the sense that the length seemed to be reduced enough to have both the $\bar{x}$ and R values inside their control limits.

This second shift continued sampling and collected 15 additional samples of size 5, at 15-minute intervals. The shift plotted these results (see Figure 12.47), but because no values were beyond the control limits, they took no action. It was at this point that the statistical consultants reviewed what had transpired. They not only determined that the *original* 15 points used to define the $\bar{x}$- and R-charts were themselves showing a process not under statistical control, but that the last 15 points also showed a process not under statistical control. The second shift had failed to notice the string of 15 points of the $\bar{x}$-chart all above the center line and failed to conclude that the center was "not where you wanted it." If they had, they would have once again called the technician to lower the length of the syringes on assembly.

Fortunately, however, the consultants examined the R-chart as well as the $\bar{x}$-chart. Here again, the last 14 points of R were all on one side of the center line, indicating a lack of statistical control. Careful examination of both charts revealed that the points of R were below the center and were indicating that the overall variation has been reduced by what the maintenance technician has done. Yet, in reading the $\bar{x}$-chart (after examining the R-chart), the length of the syringes seemed to have increased. The consultants contacted both the operators and technician in order to try to find out what had happened to cause this confusing "good and bad" thing to occur. The maintenance technician's story was most revealing.

The maintenance technician said that for his first two (unsuccessful) attempts when he was told to adjust the process center (length of syringe) down, he moved the height adjustment stop down on its threaded shaft. However, he found it was difficult to tighten the locknut for this adjustment stop. The third time (the successful one), being frustrated that the thread of the shaft was too bat-

Figure 12.47 $\bar{x}$- and R-Charts for the Last 15 Samples

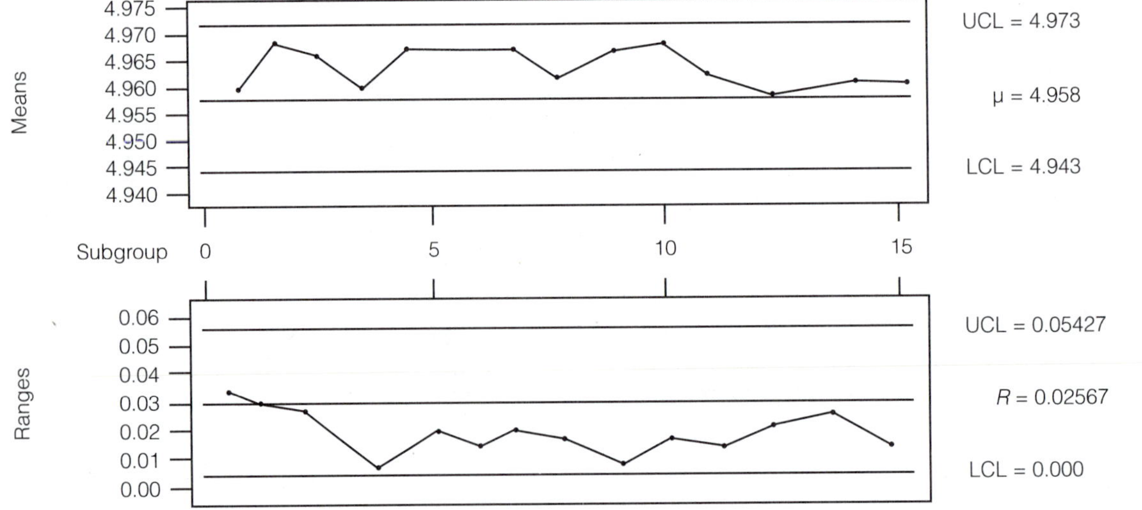

tered at the lower end of the stud, he actually moved the adjustment stop *up* even though he was asked to make the syringe lengths shorter. He thought this would result in still longer syringes being produced, but at least the locknut would hold. When he was told by the shift that the process was now producing the proper length syringes and that the operators were satisfied, he was mystified. He left wondering how a machine adjusted upward (toward longer lengths) could wind up producing shorter-length syringes!

The consultants realized the dramatic improvement (shortening) of the process variation told the important story. When the maintenance technician set the length of the adjustment cap where he was supposed to (lower), the threads were so worn as to make it impossible to hold the locknut in place. Thus, the vibration from the running machine (within about 15 minutes) loosened the locknut and adjustment cap quickly, resulting in drifts off center, producing syringes of erratic lengths. However, when the maintenance technician set the adjustment cap higher (which would make syringes longer), the threads there were good enough for the locknut to hold the cap in place. The lengths, indeed, were a little longer than what was targeted, but the variation had been so dramatically reduced that the overall effect was one of making acceptable syringes; that is, the syringes were a tiny bit longer than desired but very consistent in their length so no plotted points were beyond the upper control limit for the $\bar{x}$-chart.

The operators were satisfied with this situation because now the plotted points of the syringe lengths came under the upper control limit of the $\bar{x}$-chart, which convinced them that they were making syringes to the proper length. The consultants recommended to the managers that the threaded stud on which the adjustment stop moved be replaced. The repair work needed a special part that was fairly expensive and necessitated some downtime for the manufacturing process; nevertheless, on the strength of the control chart data and the explanation of the maintenance technician's and consultant's stories, the recommendation was implemented. Upon replacement of the threaded stud, waste and rework from the final step dropped to virtually zero over the period of many weeks.

Key Issues for Discussion

1. Using the data for the initial process capability study sample given in Table 12.5, compute the process capability indexes and construct a histogram for these data.
2. Explain why it was incorrect that the operators did not plot the initial data, find special causes, and compute new control limits. What might have happened had they done it this way?
3. What lessons can be learned from this case?

Quality in Practice

Using a *u*-Chart in a Receiving Process[8]

Cincinnati Belting and Transmission is a distributor of electrical and power transmission products. The company began to implement a total quality management process in early 1990. One manager was eager to collect data about the organization's receiving process because of a decrease in the organization's on-time deliveries. The manager suspected that the data entry person in the purchasing department was not entering data in the computer in a timely fashion; consequently, packages could not be properly processed for subsequent shipping to the customer. A preliminary analysis indicated that the manager's notion was inaccurate. In fact, the manager was able to see that the data entry person was doing an excellent job. The analysis showed that handling packages that were destined for a branch operation in the same fashion as other packages created significant delays. A simple process change of placing a branch designation letter in front of the purchase order number told the receiving clerk to place those packages on a separate skid for delivery to the branch.

However, this analysis revealed a variety of other problems. Generally, anywhere from 65 to

110 packing slips were processed each day. These were found to contain many errors in addition to the wrong destination designation that contributed to the delays. Errors included

- Wrong purchase order
- Wrong quantity
- Purchase order not on the system
- Original order not on the system
- Parts do not match
- Purchase order was entered incorrectly
- Double shipment
- Wrong parts
- No purchase order

Many packing slips contained multiple errors. Table 12.6 shows the number of packing slips and total errors during early 1992. A *u*-chart was constructed for each day to track the number of packing slip errors—defects—found. A *u*-chart was used because the sample size varied each day. Thus, the statistic monitored was the number of errors per packing slip. Figure 12.48 shows the *u*-chart that was constructed for this period. (This change in the branch designation took place on January 24, resulting in significant improvement, as shown on the chart.)

Although the chart shows that the process is in control (since the branch designation change), the

Table 12.6 Cincinnati Belting and Transmission Packing Slip Error Counts

Date	Packing Slips	Errors	Date	Packing Slips	Errors
21 Jan	87	15	4 Mar	92	8
22 Jan	79	13	5 Mar	69	13
23 Jan	92	23	6 Mar	86	6
24 Jan	84	3	9 Mar	85	13
27 Jan	73	7	10 Mar	101	5
28 Jan	67	11	11 Mar	87	5
29 Jan	73	8	12 Mar	71	3
30 Jan	91	8	13 Mar	83	8
31 Jan	94	11	16 Mar	103	4
3 Feb	83	12	17 Mar	82	6
4 Feb	89	12	18 Mar	90	7
5 Feb	88	6	19 Mar	80	4
6 Feb	69	11	20 Mar	70	4
7 Feb	74	8	23 Mar	73	11
10 Feb	67	4	24 Mar	89	13
11 Feb	83	10	25 Mar	91	6
12 Feb	79	8	26 Mar	78	6
13 Feb	75	8	27 Mar	88	6
14 Feb	69	3	30 Mar	76	8
17 Feb	87	8	31 Mar	101	9
18 Feb	99	13	1 Apr	92	8
19 Feb	101	13	2 Apr	70	2
20 Feb	76	7	3 Apr	72	11
21 Feb	90	4	6 Apr	83	5
24 Feb	92	7	7 Apr	69	6
25 Feb	80	4	8 Apr	79	3
26 Feb	81	5	9 Apr	79	8
27 Feb	105	8	10 Apr	76	6
28 Feb	80	8	13 Apr	92	7
2 Mar	82	5	14 Apr	80	4
3 Mar	75	3	15 Apr	78	8

Figure 12.48 *u*-Chart for Cincinnati Belting and Transmission Packing Slip Errors

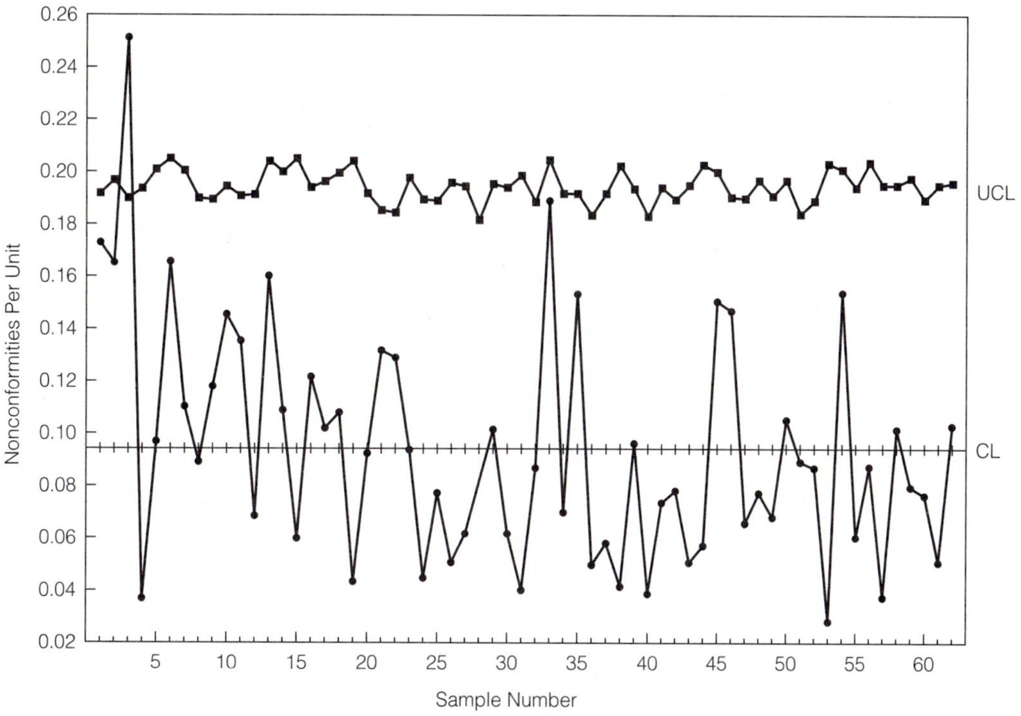

average error rate of more than 9 percent still was not considered acceptable. After consolidating the types of errors into five categories, a Pareto analysis was performed. This analysis showed the following:

Category	Percentage
Purchase order error	35
Quantity error	22
No purchase order on system	17
Original order not on system	16
Parts error	10

The analysis is illustrated in Figure 12.49.

The first two categories accounted for over half of the errors. The remedy for these problems was to develop a training module on proper purchasing methods to ensure that vendors knew the correct information needed on the purchase orders. The third category—no purchase order on the computer system—caused receiving personnel to stage the orders until an investigation could find the necessary information. Because of this problem the company realized it needed to revamp the original order-writing process. Specifically, both the order-writing and purchase order activities needed to be improved.

An analysis of the control chart in Figure 12.48 shows that the average error rate has gradually improved. To a large extent, this improvement was due to the recognition of the problems and enhanced communication among the constituents. While the full training program had not been implemented at the time this case was written, the company believed that a significant reduction in the error rate would result once the training was completed.

Key Issues for Discussion

1. Verify the computation of the center line and control limits in Figure 12.48.
2. What information might a separate chart for each error category provide? Would you recommend spending the time and effort to make these additional computations?

Figure 12.49 Pareto Analysis of Packing Slip Errors

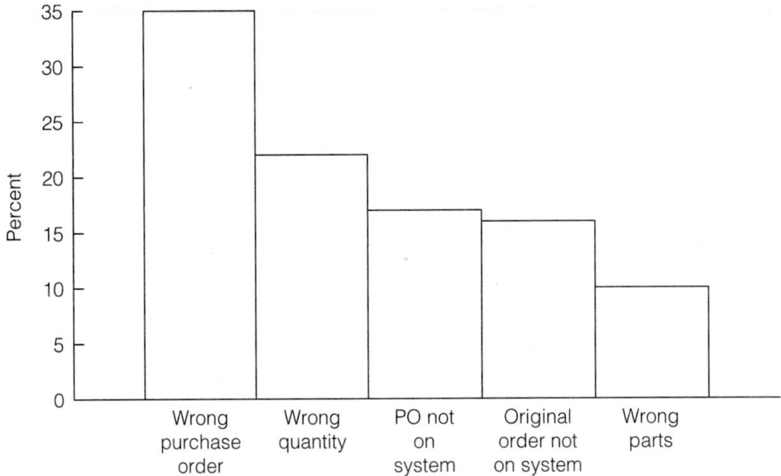

Summary of Key Points

- Statistical process control (SPC) is a methodology for monitoring a process to identify special causes of variation and signal the need to take corrective action when appropriate.
- Capability and control are independent concepts. Ideally, we would like a process to have both high capability and be in control. If a process is not in control, it should first be brought into control before attempting to evaluate process capability.
- Control charts have three basic applications: (1) establishing a state of statistical control, (2) monitoring a process to identify special causes, and (3) determining process capability.
- Control charts for variables data include: $\bar{x}$- and R-charts; $\bar{x}$- and s-charts; and individual and moving range charts. $\bar{x}$- and s-charts are alternatives to $\bar{x}$- and R-charts for larger sample sizes. The sample standard deviation provides a better indication of process variability than the range. Individuals charts are useful when every item can be inspected and when a long lead time exists for producing an item. Moving ranges are used to measure the variability in individuals charts.
- A process is in control if no points are outside control limits; the number of points above and below the center line is about the same; the points seem to fall randomly above and below the center line; and most points (but not all) are near the center line, with only a few close to the control limits.
- Typical out-of-control conditions are represented by sudden shifts in the mean value, cycles, trends, hugging of the center line, hugging of the control limits, and instability.
- Modified control limits can be used when the process capability is known to be good. These wider limits reduce the amount of investigation of isolated points that would fall outside the usual control limits.
- Charts for attributes include p-, np-, c- and u-charts. The np-chart is an alternative to the p-chart, and controls the number nonconforming for attributes data. Charts for defects include the c-chart and u-chart. The c-chart is used for constant sample size and the u-chart is used for variable sample size.

- In designing control charts, one must be concerned with how the sample data are taken, the sample size, the sampling frequency, and the location of the control limits. These factors influence the amount of useful information obtained from the charts, the ability to detect process changes, the potential for error, and the cost of application.
- Various special types of control charts are used for short production runs, for process industries, for improving the sensitivity to detect shifts in the process level, and for easier interpretation. These include stabilized control charts, exponentially weighted moving average charts (EWMA), and CuSum charts.
- Pre-control is a technique for monitoring process capability over time. It is particularly suited to machining applications, but should only be used when process capability is rather good.

Review Questions

1. Define statistical process control and discuss its advantages.
2. What does the term *in statistical control* mean? Explain the difference between capability and control.
3. What are the disadvantages of simply using histograms to study process capability?
4. Discuss the three primary applications of control charts.
5. Describe the difference between variables and attributes data. What types of control charts are used for each?
6. Briefly describe the methodology of constructing and using control charts.
7. What does one look for in interpreting control charts? Explain the possible causes of different out-of-control indicators.
8. How should control charts be used by shop-floor personnel?
9. What are modified control limits? Under what conditions should they be used?
10. How are variables control charts used to determine process capability?
11. Describe the difference between *control limits* and *specification limits*.
12. Why is the s-chart sometimes used in place of the R-chart?
13. Describe some situations in which a chart for individual measurements would be used.
14. Explain the concept of a moving range. Why is a moving range chart difficult to interpret?
15. Explain the difference between defects and defectives.
16. Briefly describe the process of constructing a p-chart. What are the key differences compared with an $\bar{x}$-chart?
17. Does an np-chart provide any different information than a p-chart? Why would an np-chart be used?
18. Explain the difference between a c-chart and a u-chart.
19. Discuss how to use charts for defects in a quality rating system.
20. Describe the rules for determining the appropriate control chart to use in any given situation.
21. What types of charts would be appropriate for the applications listed in Table 12.1?
22. Discuss the concept of rational subgroups.
23. What trade-offs are involved in selecting the sample size for a control chart?
24. Explain the economic trade-offs to consider when determining the sampling frequency to use in a control chart.
25. Discuss the implications of control limit location in terms of Type I and Type II errors.

26. Describe approaches for applying SPC to short production runs.
27. Explain the situations for which EWMA and CuSum charts might be preferred to more traditional control charts.

PROBLEMS

Note: Data sets for many problems in this chapter are available in the Excel workbook *C12Data.xls* on the CD-rom accompanying this text. Click on the appropriate worksheet tab as noted in the problem (e.g., *Prob. 12-1*) to access the data. The Excel templates for control charts used in this chapter are also available on the CD-rom.

1. Thirty samples of size 3 were taken from a machining process over a 15-hour period. These data can be found in the worksheet *Prob. 12-1*.
   a. Compute the mean and standard deviation of the data.
   b. Compute the mean and range of each sample and plot them on control charts. Does the process appear to be in statistical control? Why or why not?
2. The data in worksheet *Prob. 12-2* lists electrical resistance measure values for 50 samples of size 5 that were taken from a computer chip-making process over a 25-hour period.
   a. Compute the mean and standard deviation of the data.
   b. Calculate the control limits and construct the $\bar{x}$- and R-charts, using the first 30 samples. Is the process under control at that point?
   c. After calculating the control limits, the last 20 samples were collected. When plotted using the control limits calculated earlier, does the process appear to be in statistical control? Why or why not? What should be done if it is not under control?
3. Thirty samples of size 6 yielded $\bar{\bar{x}} = 500$ and $\bar{R} = 25$. Compute control limits for $\bar{x}$- and R-charts and estimate the standard deviation of the process.
4. Twenty-five samples of size 5 resulted in $\bar{\bar{x}} = 6.0$ and $\bar{R} = 2.5$. Compute control limits for $\bar{x}$- and R-charts and estimate the standard deviation of the process.
5. Using the data listed in the worksheet *Prob. 12-5*, construct $\bar{x}$- and R-charts. The sample size used is $n = 4$.
6. In testing the voltage of a component used in a mirocomputer, the data listed in the worksheet *Prob. 12-6* were obtained. Construct $\bar{x}$- and R-charts for these data. Determine whether the process is in control. If not, eliminate any assignable causes and compute revised limits.
7. Use the sample data in the worksheet *Prob. 12-7* for a sample size of $n = 4$ for the following exercises:
   a. Construct $\bar{x}$- and R-charts.
   b. After the process was determined to be under control, process monitoring began, using the control limits already established. The results of 20 more samples are shown in the worksheet. Does there appear to be a problem with the process? If so, when should the process have been stopped, and steps taken to correct it?
8. Construct $\bar{x}$- and R-charts for the data in the worksheet *Prob. 12-8*. What conclusions do you reach?
9. General Hydraulics, Inc., is a manufacturer of hydraulic machine tools. It has a history of leakage trouble resulting from a certain critical fitting. Twenty-five samples of machined parts were selected, one per shift, and the diameter of the fitting was measured.
   a. Construct $\bar{x}$- and R-charts for the data listed in the worksheet *Prob. 12-9*.

b. If the regular machine operator was absent when samples 4, 8, 14, and 22 were taken, how will the results in part (a) be affected?

c. A second table in the worksheet represents measurements taken during the next 10 shifts. What information does this table provide to the quality control manager?

10. Fujiyama Electronics, Inc., has been having difficulties with circuit boards, purchased from an outside supplier, because of an unacceptable variability between two drilled holes that are supposed to be 5 cm apart on the circuit boards. Twenty-five samples of four boards each were taken from shipments sent by the supplier as shown in the data listed in the worksheet *Prob. 12-10.*

a. Construct $\bar{x}$- and R-charts for these data.

b. If the supplier's quality manager admitted that they were experiencing quality problems for shipments 18, 19, and 21, how would that affect your control chart? Show the effects on revised $\bar{x}$- and R-charts for these data.

c. Ten more observations were taken, as shown in the second table in the worksheet. Using the revised $\bar{x}$- and R-charts from part (b), comment on what the chart shows after extending it with the new data.

11. Discuss the interpretation of each of the following control charts:

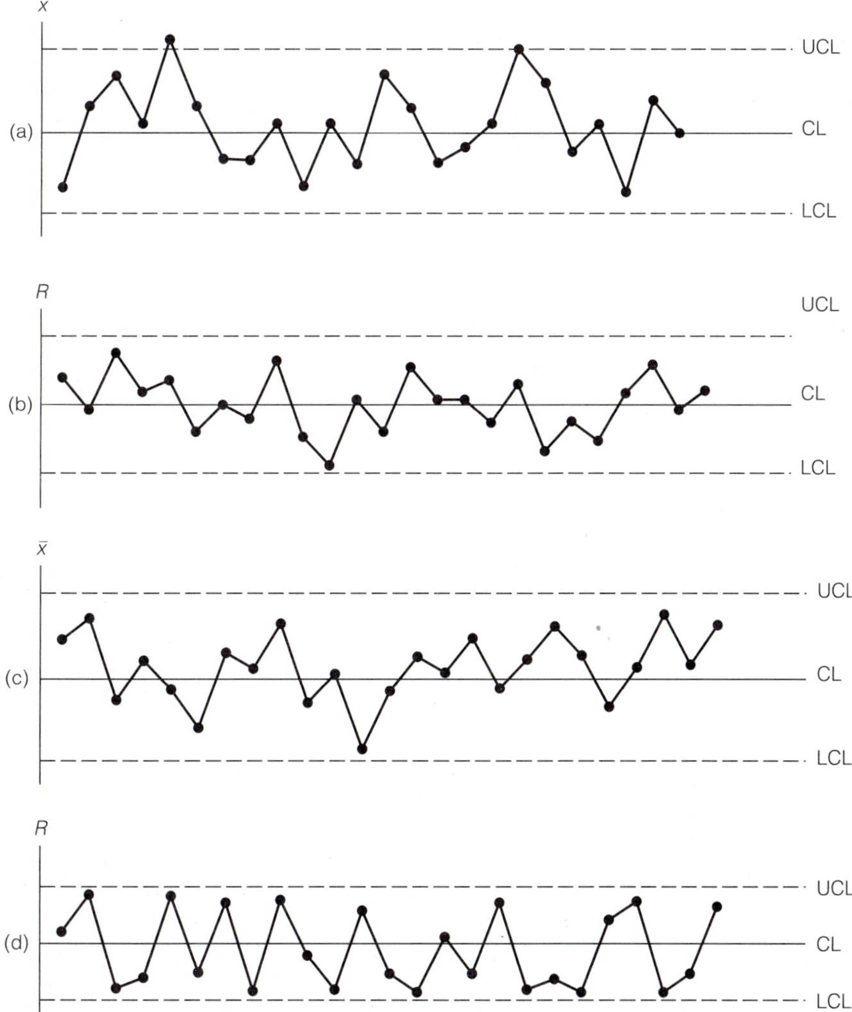

12. For each of the following control charts, assume that the process has been operating in statistical control for some time. What conclusions should the operators reach at this point?

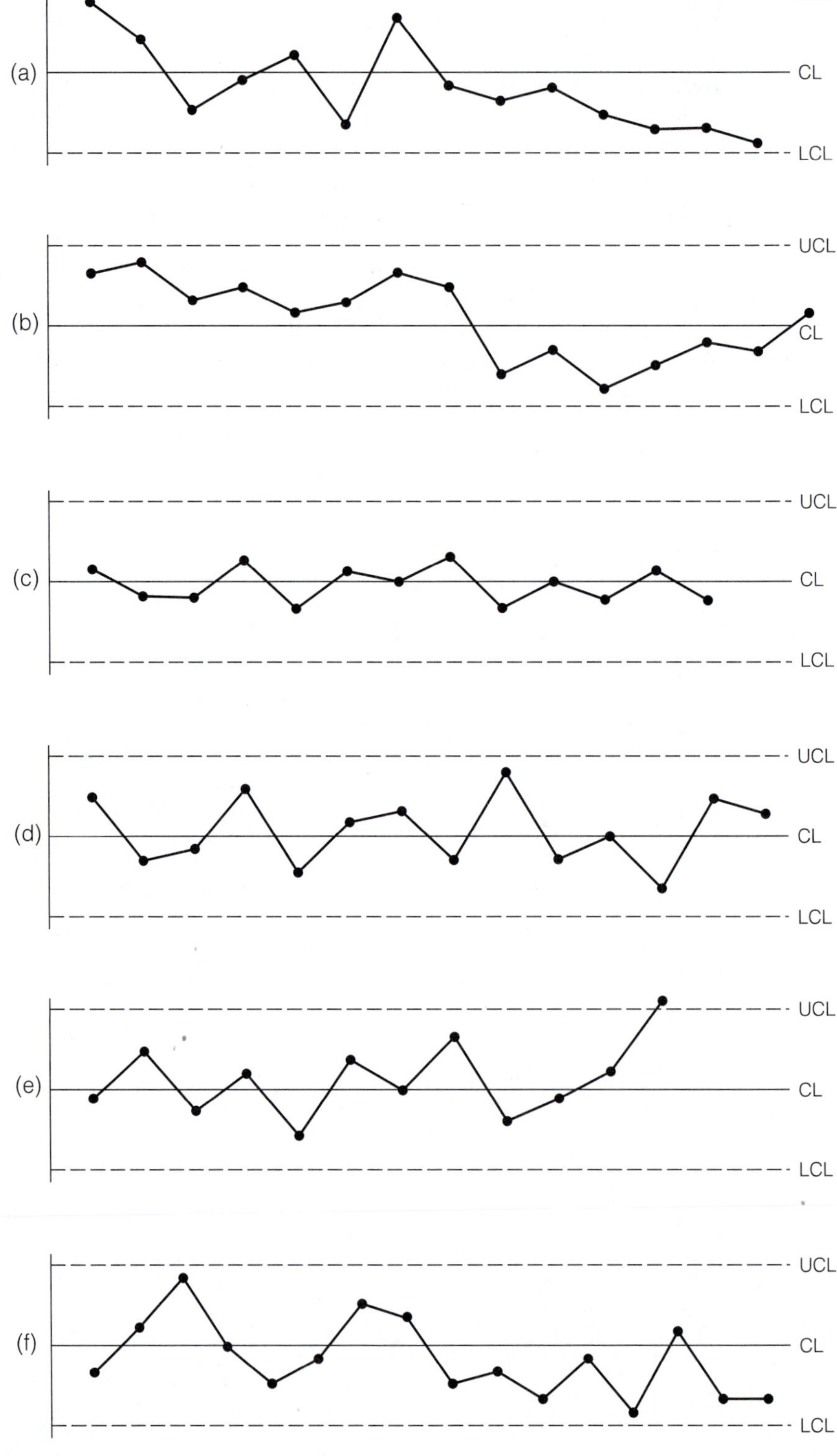

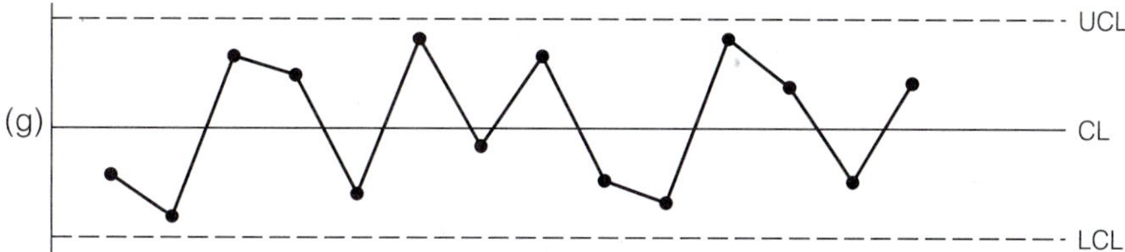

13. Consider the data for 15 samples of size 5 shown in the worksheet *Prob. 12-13*. Specifications are 0.076 ± 0.009.
    a. Compute control limits for an x-chart (chart for individuals) using the statistic $\bar{R}/d_2$ as an estimate of the standard deviation and using the actual standard deviation for the data. Why are they different?
    b. Construct the $\bar{x}$- and R-charts and an x-chart for "individuals" using the data. Interpret the results.
    c. Estimate the process capability by using the actual sample standard deviation.
14. Consider the data for 15 samples of size 4 shown in the worksheet *Prob 12-14*. Specifications are 0.110 ± 0.015.
    a. Computer control limits for an x-chart using the statistic $\bar{R}/d_2$ as an estimate of the standard deviation and using the actual standard deviation for the data. Why are they different?
    b. Construct the $\bar{x}$- and R-charts and a chart for "individuals" using the data. Interpret the results.
    c. Estimate the process capability by using the actual sample standard deviation.
15. Squalk Boxes, Inc., a speaker manufacturer, has a process that is normally distributed and has the following sample means and ranges for eight samples of size 5. Determine process capability limits. If specifications are determined to be 46 ± 5, what percentage will be out of specification?

Sample	**1**	**2**	**3**	**4**	**5**	**6**	**7**	**8**
$\bar{x}$	51.6	40.1	42.3	48.9	36.5	53.1	47.3	49.6
R	5.2	7.1	5.4	5.0	6.3	3.9	4.8	5.9

16. PCDrives has a manufacturing process that is normally distributed and has the following sample means and ranges for eight samples of size 5. Determine process capability limits. If specifications are determined to be 69 ± 7, what percentage will be out of specification?

Sample	**1**	**2**	**3**	**4**	**5**	**6**	**7**	**8**
$\bar{x}$	77.4	60.2	63.5	72.7	54.4	80.4	70.8	74.6
R	6.3	8.1	7.6	7.5	5.3	7.9	6.8	6.6

17. Suppose that in the revised chart in problem 6, the upper specification limit is USL = 475, and the lower specification limit is LSL = 325. Compute the process capability and the modified control limits.
18. Suppose that in the revised chart in problem 10, the upper specification limit is USL = 6.75, and the lower specification limit is LS = 3.25. Compute the process capability and the modified control limits.

19. The Bell Vader Company, which produces heavy-duty electrical motors, machines a part called an end cap. To meet competitive pressures, the company began to apply statistical quality control to its processes. Because each motor produced by the company uses two end caps that could cost as much as $200 each, the company sees the importance of bringing the process under control. The table in the worksheet *Prob. 12-19* shows data collected to construct a control chart.
    a. Compute control limits and construct and analyze the $\bar{x}$- and *R*-charts for this process. What conclusions can you reach about the state of statistical control?
    b. Using the control chart, estimate the process capability. The specification limits for the end cap are 3.9375 to 3.9380. Note that the data are coded, so 75 = 3.9375, 77 = 3.3977, etc. Determine what percentage of end caps would be expected to fall outside specifications. What conclusions and recommendations can you make?
20. An injection molding machine for plastic bottles has four molding heads. The outside diameter of the bottle is an important measure of process performance. The table in the worksheet *Prob. 12-20* shows the results of 20 samples in which the data are coded by subtracting the actual value from the nominal dimension. Construct an $\bar{x}$- and *R*-chart and discuss the results.
21. Suppose that the 20 sample means and standard deviations are observed for samples of size 5, as shown in the worksheet *Prob. 12-21*. Construct $\bar{x}$- and *s*-charts for these data.
22. The sample means and standard deviations are observed for samples of size 10, as shown in the worksheet *Prob. 12-22*. Construct $\bar{x}$- and *s*-charts for these data.
23. Construct $\bar{x}$- and *s*-charts for the data given in Table 12.2 in the chapter.
24. Construct $\bar{x}$- and *s*-charts for the data given in problem 1.
25. Construct $\bar{x}$- and *s*-charts for the data in problem 2.
26. Construct $\bar{x}$- and *s*-charts for the data in problem 6.
27. Construct charts for individuals using both two-period and three-period moving ranges for the following observations (in sequential order):

7.2	8.5	7.4	9.5	16.3	17.1	8.1	7.4	14.7	17.3	15.5
4.3	8.5	16.9	17.2	6.2	15.1	11.5	7.5	12.8	13.5	16.9

28. Assume that the data in problem 13 represent individual measurements instead of samples. Construct charts for individuals and ranges using a five-sample moving range.
29. Twenty-five samples of 50 items each were inspected, and 45 items were found to be defective. Compute control limits for a *p*-chart.
30. Thirty samples of 75 items each were inspected and 50 were found to be defective. Compute control limits for a *p*-chart for this process.
31. The fraction defective for an automotive piston is given in the worksheet *Prob. 12-31* for 20 samples. Two hundred units are inspected each day. Construct a *p*-chart and interpret the results.
32. The fraction defective for a folding process in a printing plant is given in the worksheet *Prob. 12-32* for 25 samples. Fifty units are inspected each shift.
    a. Construct a *p*-chart and interpret the results.
    b. After the process was determined to be under control, process monitoring began, using the control limits already established. The results of 25 more

samples are shown in the second part of the worksheet. Does there appear to be a problem with the process? If so, when should the process have been stopped, and steps taken to correct it?

33. Samples of size 100 have been randomly selected during each shift of 25 shifts in a production process. The data are given in the worksheet *Prob. 12-33*. Construct a p-chart and determine if the process is in control. If not, eliminate any data points that appear to be due to assignable causes and construct a new chart.
34. One hundred insurance claim forms are inspected daily over 25 working days, and the number of forms with errors have been recorded in the worksheet *Prob. 12-34*. Construct a p-chart. If any points occur outside the control limits, assume that assignable causes have been determined. Then construct a revised chart.
35. A hospital surveys all outgoing patients by means of a patient satisfaction questionnaire. The number of patients surveyed each month varies. Control charts that monitor the proportion of unsatisifed patients for key questions are constructed and studied. Construct a p-chart for the data in the worksheet *Prob. 12-35*, which represent responses to a question on satisfaction with hospital meals.
36. A local Internet service provider (ISP) is concerned that customers' level of access is decreasing, due to heavier use. The proportion of peak period time when a customer is likely to receive busy signals is considered a good measure of service level. The percentage of times a customer receives a busy signal during peak periods varies. Based on a sampling process, the ISP has set up control charts to monitor the service level, based on proportion of busy signals received. Construct the p-chart based on the sample data in the table in the worksheet *Prob. 12-36*. What does the chart show? Is this good or bad service, in your opinion?
37. Construct an np-chart for the data in problem 33. What does the chart show?
38. Construct an np-chart for the data in problem 34. What does the chart show?
39. Construct both a c-chart and a u-chart for a situation involving 30 samples of size 7 and having a total of 340 defects and interpret the results.
40. Construct both a c-chart and a u-chart for a situation involving 40 samples of size 10 and having a total of 1,200 defects and interpret the results.
41. A software developer has measured the number of defects per 1,000 lines of code in software modules being developed by the company. Construct a c-chart for data in the table in the worksheet *Prob. 12-41* and interpret the results.
42. Consider the sample data in the worksheet *Prob. 12-42*. Construct a c-chart for these data. What does the chart show?
43. Tom Pyzdek, a noted quality consultant, presented data on falls at a hospital where his father was a patient,[9] shown in the table in the worksheet *Prob. 12-43*. Note that the "sample size" is in hundreds of patient care days (PCDs). Develop a run chart, a frequency histogram, and a u-chart for these data. What insights do you get from each chart? What would you advise the administration of the hospital to do about falls?
44. Find three-sigma control limits for a c-chart with an average number of defects equal to 16.
45. Find three-sigma control limits for a u-chart with $u = 14$ and $n = 4$. What do the limits show?

46. Determine, using Figure 12.40, the appropriate sample size for detecting:
    a. A one-sigma shift in the mean with a 0.80 probability.
    b. A two-sigma shift with 0.95 probability.
    c. A 2.5-sigma shift with 0.90 probability.
47. Develop a stabilized control chart for the silicon wafer example (Figure 12.6). What does the chart show?
48. Develop a stabilized control chart for the post office example (Figure 12.29). What does the chart show?
49. Using a value of $\alpha = 0.4$, construct an EWMA chart for the data shown in the worksheet *Prob. 12-49* as applied to the means of the samples. What does the chart show?
50. Repeat problem 49 for a value of $\alpha = 0.8$. What does the chart show now?

The following questions relate to the chapter Appendix.

51. If control limits are based on 2.75 standard deviations, what percentage of observations will be expected to fall beyond the limits?
52. What are the probability limits corresponding to a Type I error of $\alpha = 0.10$?
53. What is the probability of observing 11 consecutive points on one side of the center line if the process is in control? 10 of 11 points? 9 of 11 points? How many points out of 11 on one side of the center would indicate lack of control?
54. Using Excel, sample three observations from a normal distribution with mean 0 and variance 1. Use this simulation to estimate the value of d_2 in Appendix B and compare your result.

CASES

I. La Ventana Window Company

The La Ventana Window Company (LVWC) manufactures original equipment and replacement windows for residential building and remodeling applications. LVWC landed a major contract as a supplier to Southwestern Vista Homes (SVH), a builder of residential communities in several major cities throughout the southwestern United States. Because of the large volume of demand, LVWC expanded its manufacturing operations to two shifts. Soon, they were working six days per week and hired additional workers and added on to their facility.

Not long after La Ventana began shipping windows to Southwestern, it received some complaints about narrow, misfitting gaps between the upper and lower window sashes. This information alarmed Jim Dean, CEO of La Ventana. He had sold his door business in a cold midwestern city when he decided that he wanted to retire to the desert Southwest. He had played all the golf that he could during the first six months, but then realized that he needed more of a challenge than the game could provide. That was when he started La Ventana, using his experience in manufacturing products for the residential construction market, which was expanding with the amount of construction going on in the Southwest.

LVWC, under Jim's leadership, soon built a reputation as a high-quality manufacturer, which was the principal reason that it was selected as a supplier to SVH. The company based its manufacturing capability on its well-trained and dedicated employees, so it never felt the need to consider formal process control approaches. In view of the recent complaints, Jim suspected that the rapid expansion to a full two-shift operation, the pressures to produce higher volumes, and the push to meet just-in-time delivery requests was causing a breakdown in their quality.

On the recommendation of the plant manager, Jim hired a quality consultant to train the shift supervisors and selected line workers in statistical process control methods. As a trial project, the plant manager wants to evaluate the capability of a critical cutting operation that he suspects might be the source of the gap problem. The nominal specification for this cutting operation is 25.500 inches with a tolerance of 0.030 inch. Thus, the upper and lower specifications are LSL = 25.470 inch and USL = 25.530 inch. The consultant suggested inspecting five consecutive window panels, per operator, in the middle of each shift over a 15-day period and recording the dimension of the cut. The table in the worksheet LVWC Case in the workbook *C12Data.xls* (on your text's CD-rom), shows 15 days' data collected for each shift, by operator.

Assignment

1. Interpret the data in the *LVWC Case* worksheet in the Excel workbook *C12Data.xls*, establish a state of statistical control, and evaluate the capability of the process to meet specifications. Consider the following questions: What do the initial control charts tell you? Do any out-of-control conditions exist? If the process is not in control, what might be the likely causes, based on the information that is available? What is the process capability? What do the process capability indexes tell the company? Is LVWC facing a serious problem that it needs to address? How might the company eliminate the problems found by SVH?
2. The plant manager implemented the recommendations that resulted from the initial study. Because of the success in using control charts, LVWC made a decision to continue using them on the cutting operation. After establishing control, additional samples were taken over the next 20 shifts, shown in second part of the table in the *LVWC Case* worksheet. Evaluate whether the process remains in control, and suggest any actions that should be taken. Consider the following issues: Does any evidence suggest that the process has changed relative to the established control limits? If any out-of-control patterns are suspected, what might be the cause? What should the company investigate?

II. Murphy Trucking, Inc.

Murphy Trucking, Inc. (MTI), supplies contract transportation services to many different manufacturing firms. One of its principal customers, Crawford Consumer Products (CCP), is actively improving quality by using the Malcolm Baldrige National Quality Award criteria. In an effort to improve supplier quality, Crawford Consumer Products mandated, last year, that all suppliers provide factual evidence of quality improvement efforts that lead to highly capable processes.

As part of its supplier development program, CCP held a seminar for all its suppliers to outline this initiative and provide initial assistance. The executive officers of MTI participated in this seminar and recognized that MTI was seriously lacking in its quality improvement efforts. More importantly, Jeff Blaine, who was the purchasing manager at CCP, told them privately that many errors had been found in MTI's shipping documents. CCP would not continue to tolerate this high number of errors; and if no improvements were made, it would seek transportation services elsewhere. Rick Murphy, president and CEO of MTI, was very concerned.

During an off-site meeting, Murphy and other MTI executives developed a comprehensive blueprint to help MTI develop a total quality focus. One of the key objectives was to establish an SPC effort to gain control of key customer-focused processes and establish priorities for improvement.

The Billing Study—After Process Improvement
In a good-faith attempt to respond to CCP's feedback, MTI turned its attention to its billing input errors and worked on them over the following six months. To gain some understanding of the situation, MTI conducted an initial (base case) study by

sampling 20 bills of lading, each day, over a 20-day period. Initial results were dismal, with defective bills averaging a horrible 60 percent!

After process improvement and an intensive effort to train shipping clerks not to make errors, the company was ready to make another study to determine what progress had been made. The first set of tables in the *MTI-Base* worksheet in the Excel workbook *C12Data.xls* shows the results of the initial study. The worksheet *MTI-Rev* shows the results of the second study, after improvements were made. Both studies revealed that field employees were correcting the errors as they found them. In both cases, rework was costing the company almost $2 per error, but the number of errors had been substantially reduced between the two studies. However, field employees still were not always catching the errors, which led to field service and other problems.

Assignment 1

a. At this point, MTI is unsure of how to interpret these results. You have been hired as a consultant by the executive committee to analyze these data and provide additional recommendations for integrating SPC concepts into MTI's quality system. Using the results from the base case data, determine the performance, that is, the process capability, in a qualitative and quantitative sense, of the billing input. What is the average rate of defective bills? Is the process in control? What error rates might the company expect in the future? What general conclusions do you reach?
b. Perform the same statistical analysis with the second set of data. How do the results differ? What is the average rate of defective bills? Is the process in control? What error rates might the company expect in the future? What general conclusions do you reach?

The Billing Study—Part II The revelations from the initial study had been startling. The results from the second study were encouraging, but not yet where the company wanted to be. Rick Murphy personally led a group problem-solving session to address the root causes of the current error rate. During this session, the group members constructed a cause-and-effect diagram to help determine the causes of incorrect bills of lading.

Eight categories of causes were identified:

1. Incomplete shipper name or address
2. Incomplete consignee name or address
3. Missing container type
4. Incomplete description of freight
5. Weight not shown on bill of lading
6. Improper destination code
7. Incomplete driver's signature information
8. Inaccurate piece count

Using Deming's plan-do-study-act process, the group at Murphy designed a plan to examine all bills of lading over a 25-day period and count the number of errors in each of these categories. They repeated the study six months later to determine what progress, if any, had been made in error reduction. The second table in the *MTI Base* worksheet and the second table in the worksheet *MTI-Rev* shows the data for these studies. Rick Murphy thought that the *p*-chart developed in the first study and reapplied to the second study provided significant information about the process; however, he was curious to find out whether another method could tell them more about the nature of the defects they were encountering.

Assignment 2

a. After developing *p*-charts for the first and second studies, you decide to analyze the data to determine whether the system is in control by constructing another appropriate control chart (other than a *p*-chart) that could better tell you about the nature of the defects. You also decide that it would be wise to construct a Pareto diagram to gain additional insight into the problem, and suggest recommendations to reduce billing errors.
b. Complete your analysis by using the three charts from each of the two studies to advise Rick and his managers at Murphy on next steps. How do the results differ from the first to the second study? Is the process in control? What error categories have improved? Which ones might the company need to work on immediately in order to bring about further improvements? What general conclusions do you reach?

CHAPTER 12 APPENDIX

STATISTICAL FOUNDATIONS OF CONTROL CHARTS

Control charts are defined by the center line, upper control limit, and lower control limit. These values are related to the expected value and variance of the statistics plotted on the charts. In Chapter 12, the upper and lower control limits were specified through the use of certain constants given in Appendix B. This section shows how these factors are developed and discusses the statistical basis for the rules used to interpret control charts.

Variables Control Charts

When a process is in control, the distribution of *individual measurements* for variables data is assumed to have a mean μ and a variance σ_x^2. If a sample of size n is chosen, the sampling distribution of $\bar{x}$ will also have a mean μ but will have a variance $\sigma_{\bar{x}}^2 = \sigma_x^2/n$. If the original distribution of individuals is normal, the sampling distribution of averages will also be normal. If not, the central limit theorem states that the sampling distribution of averages will be approximately normal for large sample sizes. Because control chart samples are usually small ($n = 4$ or 5), the central limit theorem does not always apply. However, normality is usually assumed in developing variables control charts.

Under this assumption, $100(1 - \alpha)$ percent of the sample means fall between $\mu - z_{\alpha/2}\sigma_{\bar{x}}$ and $\mu + z_{\alpha/2}\sigma_{\bar{x}}$; these values become the lower and upper control limits. A value of $z_{\alpha/2} = 3$ gives a six-standard deviation range with $\alpha/2 = 0.0014$. Thus, only about 0.3 percent of the sample observations will be expected to fall outside these limits. If the process is in control, the likelihood that a sample will fall outside the control limits is extremely small. On the other hand, if the true mean has shifted, this probability will be much larger. This reasoning is the theoretical basis for assigning three-sigma control limits.

The value of $z_{\alpha/2}$ can, of course, be chosen arbitrarily. In the United States, the value of 3 is commonly accepted. In England, however, $z_{\alpha/2}$ is selected by first setting the probability of a Type I error—usually chosen as $\alpha/2 = 0.001$. Thus, $z_{0.001} = 3.09$ is commonly used to establish control limits. Such limits are called **probability limits**.

***R*-Chart** The range is used as a substitute for the standard deviation primarily because of its simplicity. As noted in Chapter 12, the factor d_2 in Appendix B is used to relate the range to the actual process standard deviation. The factor d_2 is determined as follows. Consider an experiment in which samples of size n are drawn from a normal distribution having a known standard deviation σ_x. If the range R of each sample is computed, the distribution of the statistic R/σ_x can be determined. The expected value of this statistic is the factor d_2, that is

$$E\,(R/\sigma_x) = d_2$$

or, because R is a random variable and σ_x is known,

$$E\,(R)/\sigma_x = d_2$$

This experiment can be performed for each n, and corresponding values of d_2 can be computed.

The expected value of R is estimated by the sample range $\bar{R}$. Thus $\bar{R}/d_2$ is an estimate of the process standard deviation σ_x. To establish control limits for an R-chart, an estimate of the standard deviation of the random variable R, namely σ_R, is needed. From the distribution of the statistic R/σ_x, the ratio σ_R/σ_x can be computed for each n, resulting in another constant d_3.

$$\sigma_R = d_3\sigma_x$$

When $\bar{R}/d_2$ is substituted into the equation as an estimate for σ_x, $d_3\bar{R}/d_2$ then becomes the estimate for σ_R. The control limits for the R-chart are based on three standard deviations about the estimate of the mean. Thus,

$$UCL_R = \bar{R} + 3d_3\bar{R}/d_2 = (1 + 3d_3/d_2)\bar{R} = D_4\bar{R}$$

$$LCL_R = \bar{R} - 3d_3\bar{R}/d_2 = (1 - 3d_3/d_2)\bar{R} = D_3\bar{R}$$

For convenience, the constants $1 + 3d_3/d_2$ and $1 - 3d_3/d_2$ are computed as D_4 and D_3, respectively. The control limits for the R-chart are therefore based on the distribution of the process standard deviation, adjusted to correspond to the range.

$\bar{\bar{x}}$-Chart The statistic $\bar{\bar{x}}$ is an estimate of the population mean μ. Because $\bar{R}/d_2$ is an estimate of σ_x, an estimate of the sample standard deviation is

$$\sigma_{\bar{x}} = \frac{\bar{R}}{d_2\sqrt{n}}$$

Three-sigma limits on $\bar{x}$ are then given by

$$\bar{\bar{x}} \pm \frac{3\bar{R}}{d_2\sqrt{n}}$$

Letting $A_2 = 3/d_2\sqrt{n}$ provides the control limits presented in Chapter 12:

$$UCL_{\bar{x}} = \bar{\bar{x}} + A_2\bar{R}$$

$$LCL_{\bar{x}} = \bar{\bar{x}} - A_2\bar{R}$$

Fraction Nonconforming Control Charts

The theory underlying the p-chart is based on the binomial distribution, because attributes data assume only one of two values: conforming or nonconforming. If p represents the probability of producing a nonconforming item and a sample of n items is selected, the binomial distribution

$$f(x) = \binom{n}{x} p^x (1 - p)^{n-x} \quad x = 0, 1, 2, \ldots, n$$

gives the probability of finding x nonconforming items in the sample.

The sample statistic $\bar{p}$ is an estimate of the population parameter p. An estimate of the standard deviation σ_p is given by

$$\sigma_p = \sqrt{\bar{p}(1 - \bar{p})/n}$$

Figure 12A.1 Area Under the Normal Curve Within One Standard Deviation of the Mean

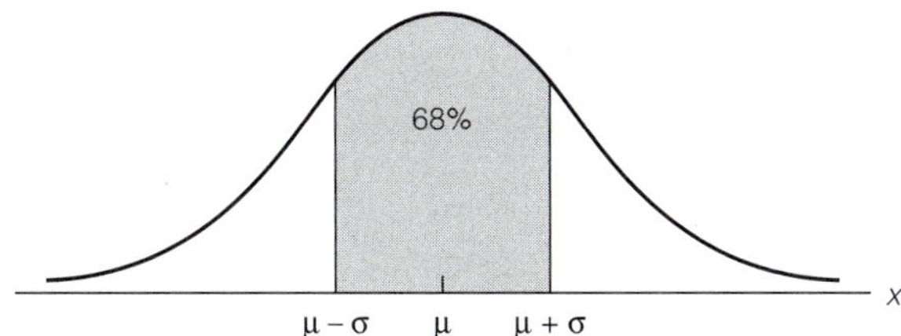

Three-sigma limits on the parameter p are therefore given by

$$UCL_p = \bar{p} + 3\sqrt{\bar{p}(1-\bar{p})/n}$$

$$LCL_p = \bar{p} - 3\sqrt{\bar{p}(1-\bar{p})/n}$$

The critical assumptions in using a p-chart are the constant probability of a defective and the independence of the trials. If these assumptions cannot be assured, the p-chart is not appropriate.

Basis for Control Chart Interpretation Rules

Chapter 12 presented several rules for analyzing and interpreting control charts. For example, a point outside the control limits indicates the possibility that the process is out of control. Under the normality assumption, a 0.9973 probability exists that any sample value will fall within three-sigma limits. Thus a sample value has only a 1 − 0.9973 = 0.0027 probability of exceeding these limits. Unless the process mean, range, or fraction nonconforming has shifted, a point is highly unlikely to fall outside the control limits. The chance remains, however remote, that the process is still under control even though a sample point falls outside the control limits. A person would typically conclude that the process is out of control. This situation represents the probability of a Type I error.

A second rule for interpreting control charts discussed in Chapter 12 was that about two-thirds of the points should fall within the middle one-third of the region between the control limits. This rule follows from the normality assumption that about 68 percent of a normal distribution falls within one standard deviation on either side of the mean (see Figure 12A.1). Therefore, if the process is in control and all samples are chosen from a common population, this assumption should be true. If, however, the value of the population parameter has shifted, the distribution of sample statistics will also change. In such a case, an assignable cause needs to be found.

Another significant indication of an out-of-control situation is the presence of patterns in the control chart over time. If the process is in control, the distribution of sample values should be randomly distributed above and below the center line. A disproportionate number of points either above or below the center line should be suspect. For example, the probability that a point will fall either above or below the center line is 0.5. The probability of obtaining k successive points on one side of the center line is $(0.5)^k$. Thus, the probability that eight consecutive points will fall on one side of the center line is only $(0.5)^8 = 0.0039$. The probability that 10 of 11 consecutive points will fall on one side of the center line can be computed using the binomial formula:

Table 12A.1 Rule Probabilities for $\bar{x}$ Charts When the Process Is in Control

		Probability (sensitivity)						
		x is normal	*x* is slightly skewed			*x* is seriously skewed		
			Sample size			Sample size		
Rule	Description	Sample size is irrelevant	5	10	25	5	10	25
1	$\bar{x}$ is more than $3\sigma_{\bar{x}}$ above $\mu_{\bar{x}}$	0.135%	0.254%	0.209%	0.191%	0.488%	0.380%	0.281%
	$\bar{x}$ is more than $3\sigma_{\bar{x}}$ below $\mu_{\bar{x}}$	0.135%	0.021%	0.046%	0.080%	0.000%	0.008%	0.035%
2	Of three consecutive values of $\bar{x}$, two are above $\mu_{\bar{x}} + 2\sigma_{\bar{x}}$	0.153%	0.237%	0.212%	0.190%	0.342%	0.281%	0.235%
	Of three consecutive values of $\bar{x}$, two are below $\mu_{\bar{x}} - 2\sigma_{\bar{x}}$	0.153%	0.076%	0.098%	0.119%	0.020%	0.048%	0.082%
2a	Two consecutive values of $\bar{x}$ are above $\mu_{\bar{x}} + 2\sigma_{\bar{x}}$	0.052%	0.080%	0.072%	0.064%	0.117%	0.096%	0.080%
	Two consecutive values of $\bar{x}$ are below $\mu_{\bar{x}} - 2\sigma_{\bar{x}}$	0.052%	0.026%	0.033%	0.040%	0.007%	0.016%	0.028%
3	Of five consecutive values of $\bar{x}$, four are above $\mu_{\bar{x}} + 1\sigma_{\bar{x}}$	0.277%	0.284%	0.281%	0.280%	0.273%	0.274%	0.277%
	Of five consecutive values of $\bar{x}$, four are below $\mu_{\bar{x}} - 1\sigma_{\bar{x}}$	0.277%	0.284%	0.284%	0.278%	0.268%	0.273%	0.276%
3a	Four consecutive values of $\bar{x}$ are above $\mu_{\bar{x}} + 1\sigma_{\bar{x}}$	0.063%	0.065%	0.064%	0.064%	0.063%	0.063%	0.063%
	Four consecutive values of $\bar{x}$ are below $\mu_{\bar{x}} - 1\sigma_{\bar{x}}$	0.063%	0.065%	0.065%	0.064%	0.061%	0.063%	0.063%
4	Seven consecutive values of $\bar{x}$ are above $\mu_{\bar{x}}$	0.781%	0.631%	0.680%	0.705%	0.494%	0.568%	0.636%
	Seven consecutive values of $\bar{x}$ are below $\mu_{\bar{x}}$	0.781%	0.961%	0.896%	0.865%	1.202%	1.060%	0.953%
4a	Eight consecutive values of $\bar{x}$ are above $\mu_{\bar{x}}$	0.391%	0.306%	0.333%	0.347%	0.231%	0.271%	0.309%
	Eight consecutive values of $\bar{x}$ are below $\mu_{\bar{x}}$	0.391%	0.495%	0.457%	0.439%	0.639%	0.554%	0.491%
5	Six consecutive values of $\bar{x}$ are in a monotone increasing pattern	0.139%	0.139%	0.139%	0.139%	0.139%	0.139%	0.139%
	Six consecutive values of $\bar{x}$ are in a monotone decreasing pattern	0.139%	0.139%	0.139%	0.139%	0.139%	0.139%	0.139%
6	Of 10 consecutive values of $\bar{x}$, a subset of eight (reading from left to right) are in a monotone increasing pattern	0.069%	0.069%	0.069%	0.069%	0.069%	0.069%	0.069%
	Of 10 consecutive values of $\bar{x}$, a subset of eight (reading from left to right) are in a monotone decreasing pattern	0.069%	0.069%	0.069%	0.069%	0.069%	0.069%	0.069%
7	Of two consecutive values of $\bar{x}$, one is more than $4\sigma_{\bar{x}}$ larger than the other	0.234%	0.229%	0.230%	0.232%	0.282%	0.261%	0.243%

Source: Robert Hoyer and Wayne C. Ellis. "A Graphical Exploration of SPC, Part 2," *Quality Progress* 29, no. 6 (June 1996), 57–64.

$$f(10) = \binom{11}{10}(0.5)^{10}(0.5)^{1} = 0.00537$$

If the process is in control, either of these events is highly unlikely.

Table 12A.1 shows the probabilities associated with seven common rules used for interpreting control charts for normal, slightly skewed, and seriously skewed process outputs. Note that, even for the skewed distributions, almost all of the conditions have probabilities less than 0.01 when the process is in control. Close analysis of this table suggests the following:

- Unless the process is susceptible to small shifts in its center or has low capability, Rule 4a should be used instead of Rule 4.
- The probabilities of the extreme zone rules (1, 2, and 2a) are unusually small for patterns below the center line when the process output is skewed to the right. Observing a pattern below the center line is nearly impossible unless the process is out of control.
- When a pattern is consistent with either Rule 5 or Rule 6, it is almost guaranteed that a trend exists.
- When the distribution of process output is seriously skewed to the right, it is not unusual to observe a point above the upper control limit when the process is in control.

Understanding such issues can help to minimize errors in interpretation.

NOTES

1. Robert W. Hoyer and Wayne C. Ellis, "A Graphical Exploration of SPC, Part 1," *Quality Progress* 29, no. 5 (May 1996), 65–73.
2. This discussion is adapted from James R. Evans, *Statistical Process Control for Quality Improvement: A Training Guide to Learning SPC* (Englewood Cliffs, NJ: Prentice Hall, © 1991). Reprinted with permission of Prentice Hall, Upper Saddle River, NJ.
3. H. F. Dodge and M. N. Torrey, "A Check Inspection and Demerit Weighting Plan," *Industrial Quality Control* 13, no. 1 (July 1956), 5–12.
4. D. C. Montgomery, "The Economic Design of Control Charts: A Review and Literature Survey," *Journal of Quality Technology* 12, no. 2 (1980), 75–87.
5. Raymond R. Mayer, "Selecting Control Limits," *Quality Progress* 16, no 9, (1983), 24–26.
6. Robert W. Traver, "Pre-Control: A Good Alternative to x- R-Charts," *Quality Progress* 18, no. 9 (September 1985).
7. Adapted from LeRoy A. Franklin and Samar N. Mukherjee, "An SPC Case Study on Stabilizing Syringe Lengths," *Quality Engineering* 12, no. 1 (1999–2000), 65–71. Reprinted from *Quality Engineering*, courtesy of Marcel Dekker, Inc.
8. We are grateful to Mr. Rick Casey for supplying this application.
9. Thomas Pyzdek, "Preventing Hospital Falls," *Quality Digest*, May 1999, 26–27.

BIBLIOGRAPHY

American National Standard, Definitions, Symbols, Formulas, and Tables for Control Charts. ANSI/ASQC A1-1987. American Society for Quality Control, 310 W. Wisconsin Ave., Milwaukee, WI 53203.

Brown, Bradford S. "Control Charts: The Promise and the Performance." Presentation at the ASQC/ASA 35th Annual Fall Technical Conference, Lexington, Kentucky, 1991.

Grant, Eugene, L., and Richard S. Leavenworth. *Statistical Quality Control*, 6th ed. New York: McGraw-Hill, 1988.

Ledolter, J., and A. Swersey. "An Evaluation of Pre-Control." *Journal of Quality Technology* 29, no. 2 (April 1997), 163–171.

Montgomery, D. C. *Introduction to Statistical Quality Control*, 4th ed. New York: John Wiley & Sons, 2000.

Nelson, Lloyd S. "Control Charts for Individual Measurements." *Journal of Quality Technology* 14, no. 3 (July 1982), 172–173.

Pyzdek, Thomas. *Pyzdek's Guide to SPC, Volume Two—Applications and Special Topics.* Milwaukee, WI: ASQ Quality Press, 1992.

Rosander, A. C. *Applications of Quality Control in the Service Industries.* New York: Marcel Dekker and ASQ Quality Press, 1985.

Squires, Frank H. "What Do Quality Control Charts Control?" *Quality* (November 1982), 63.

Vance, Lonnie C. "A Bibliography of Statistical Quality Control Chart Techniques, 1970–1980," *Journal of Quality Technology* 15, no. 12 (April 1983).

Wadsworth, Harrison M., Kenneth S. Stephens, and A. Blanton Godfrey. *Modern Methods for Quality Control and Improvement*. New York: John Wiley, 1986.

Chapter 13

Reliability

Outline

Reliability—the ability of a product to perform as expected over time—is one of the principal dimensions of quality. Reliability is an essential aspect of both product and process design. Sophisticated equipment used today in such areas as transportation, communications, and medicine requires high reliability. For example, high reliability is absolutely necessary for safety in space and air travel and for medical products such as pacemakers and artificial organs. High reliability can also provide a competitive advantage for many consumer goods. Japanese automobiles gained large market shares in the 1970s primarily because of their high reliability. As the overall quality of products continues to improve, consumers expect higher reliability with each purchase; they simply are not satisfied with products that fail unexpectedly. However, the increased complexity of modern products makes high reliability more difficult to achieve. Likewise in manufacturing, the increased use of automation, complexity of machines, low profit margins, and time-based competitiveness make reliability in production processes a critical issue for survival of the business.

The subject of reliability became a serious concern during World War II. Sixty percent of the aircraft destined for the Far East proved unserviceable; 50 percent of electronic devices failed while still in storage; the service life of electronic devices used in bombers was only 20 hours; and 70 percent of naval electronics devices failed.[1] The Department of Defense established an ad hoc group in 1950 to study reliability of electronic equipment and components for the armed forces. The official report, released in 1952, led to the development of the Advisory Group on Reliability of Electronic Equipment (AGREE) to further study issues involving reliability, testing, military contracts, packaging, and storage. Military specifications—coded MIL-R for military-reliability—became a mandatory part of military contracts to ensure procurement of equipment and components that met reliability requirements. Because of this military research, which spread rapidly throughout various industries, reliability engineering became a distinct area of expertise.

The American Society for Quality (ASQ) provides a certification program for reliability engineering. ASQ defines a certified reliability engineer as

> *a professional who can understand and apply the principles of performance evaluation and prediction to improve product/systems safety, reliability and maintainability. This body of knowledge and applied technologies include but are not limited to design review and control; prediction, estimation and apportionment methodology; failure mode; the planning, operation and analysis of reliability testing and field failures, including mathematical modeling; understanding of human factors in reliability; the knowledge and ability to develop and administer reliability information systems for failure analysis, design and performance improvement, and reliability program management over the entire product life cycle.*

When products or systems fail, an important customer expectation is the ability to restore them back to a state of operation, such as the reset button on a computer. Thus, a concept closely related to reliability is **maintainability**—the probability that a system or product can be retained in, or one that has failed can be restored to, operating condition in a specified amount of time. Of course, taking preventative maintenance measures to reduce the chance of failure is also critical. This chapter formally defines reliability, presents various techniques for measuring and computing reliability, and discusses methods of reliability engineering, management, and maintainability.

BASIC CONCEPTS AND DEFINITIONS

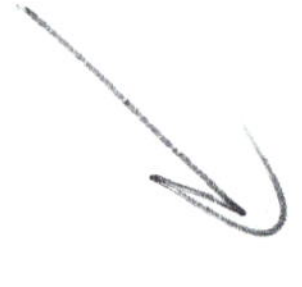

Like quality, reliability is often defined in a similar "transcendent" manner as a sense of trust in a product's ability to perform satisfactorily or resist failure. However, reliability is an issue that requires a more objective, quantitative treatment. Formally, **reliability** is defined *as the probability that a product, piece of equipment, or system performs its intended function for a stated period of time under specified operating conditions.* This definition has four important elements: probability, time, performance, and operating conditions.

First, reliability is defined as a *probability*, that is, a value between 0 and 1. Thus, it is a numerical measure with a precise meaning. Expressing reliability in this way provides a valid basis for comparison of different designs for products and systems. For example, a reliability of 0.97 indicates that, on average, 97 of 100 items will perform their function for a given period of time and under certain operating conditions. Often reliability is expressed as a percentage simply for descriptive purposes.

The second element of the definition is *time*. Clearly a device having a reliability of 0.97 for 1,000 hours of operation is inferior to one having the same reliability for 5,000 hours of operation, assuming that the mission of the device is long life.

Performance is the third element and refers to the objective for which the product or system was made. The term *failure* is used when expectations of performance of the intended function are not met. Two types of failures can occur: **functional failure** at the start of product life due to manufacturing or material defects such as a missing connection or a faulty component, and **reliability failure** after some period of use. Examples of reliability failures include the following: a device does not work at all (car will not start); the operation of a device is unstable (car idles rough); or the performance of a device deteriorates (shifting becomes difficult). Because the nature of failure in each of these cases is different, the failure must be clearly defined.

The final component of the reliability definition is *operating conditions*, which involves the type and amount of usage and the environment in which the product is used. For example, Texas Instruments once manufactured electronic digital and analog watches (the company has since eliminated these products as part of its strategic business plan). The typical operating conditions and environments for a watch are summarized in Table 13.1. Notice that reliability must include extreme environments and conditions as well as the typical on-the-arm use.

By defining a product's intended environment, performance characteristics, and lifetime, a manufacturer can design and conduct tests to measure the probability of product survival (or failure). The analysis of such tests enable better prediction of reliability and improved product and process designs.

Reliability engineers distinguish between **inherent reliability**, which is the predicted reliability determined by the design of the product or process, and the **achieved reliability**, which is the actual reliability observed during use. Actual reliability can be less than the inherent reliability due to the effects of the manufacturing process and the conditions of use.

The field of reliability has evolved through three distinct phases, much like the evolution of quality assurance. Initial efforts were directed at the measurement and prediction of reliability through statistical studies. The major focus was on the

Table 13.1 Some Typical Watch Environments

Environment	Condition	Quantifiable Characteristics	Exposure Time
Typical use	On-the-arm	31°C (88°F)	16 hours/day
Transportation	In packing box	Vibration and shock (–20°C to +80°C)	Specifications for truck/rail/air shipping
Handling accident	Drop to hard floor	1,200 g, 2 milliseconds	1 drop/year
Extreme temperature	Hot, closed automobile	85°C (185°F)	4–6 hours, 5 times/year
Humidity and chemicals	Perspiration, salt, soaps	35°C (95°F) with 90% pH, rain	500 hours/year
Altitude	Pike's Peak	15,000 feet, –40°C	1 time

Source: Adapted from William R. Taylor, "Quality Assessed in New Products Via Comprehensive Systems Approach," *Industrial Engineering* 13, no. 3 (March 1981), 28–32.

determination of failure rates of individual components such as transistors and resistors. Knowledge of component failure rates helps to predict the reliability of complex systems of these components. As knowledge about reliability grew, new methods of analysis were developed to increase the reliability built into products and processes. A new discipline called **reliability engineering** was established. Like total quality management, reliability must become an integral part of all organizational functions: marketing, design, purchasing, manufacturing, and field service. The total process of establishing, achieving, and maintaining reliability objectives is called **reliability management**.

RELIABILITY MEASUREMENT

In practice, reliability is determined by the number of failures per unit time during the duration under consideration (called the **failure rate**). The reciprocal of the failure rate is used as an alternative measure. Some products must be scrapped and replaced upon failure; others can be repaired. For items that must be replaced when a failure occurs, the reciprocal of the failure rate (having dimensions of time units per failure) is called the **mean time to failure (MTTF)**. For repairable items, the **mean time between failures (MTBF)** is used.

Failure Rate and Product Life Characteristics Curve

In considering the failure rate of a product, suppose that a large group of items is tested or used until all fail, and that the time of failure is recorded for each item. Plotting the cumulative percentage of failures against time results in a curve such as the one shown in Figure 13.1. The slope of the curve at any point (that is, the slope of the straight line tangent to the curve) gives the instantaneous failure rate (failures per unit time) at any point in time. Figure 13.2 shows the failure rate curve, generally called a **product life characteristics curve**, corresponding to the cumulative failure curve in Figure 13.1. This curve was obtained by plotting the slope of the curve at every point. Notice that the slope of the curve and thus the failure rate may change over time. Thus, in Figure 13.2, the failure rate at 500 hours is 0.02 failures per hour

Figure 13.1 Cumulative Failure Curve over Time

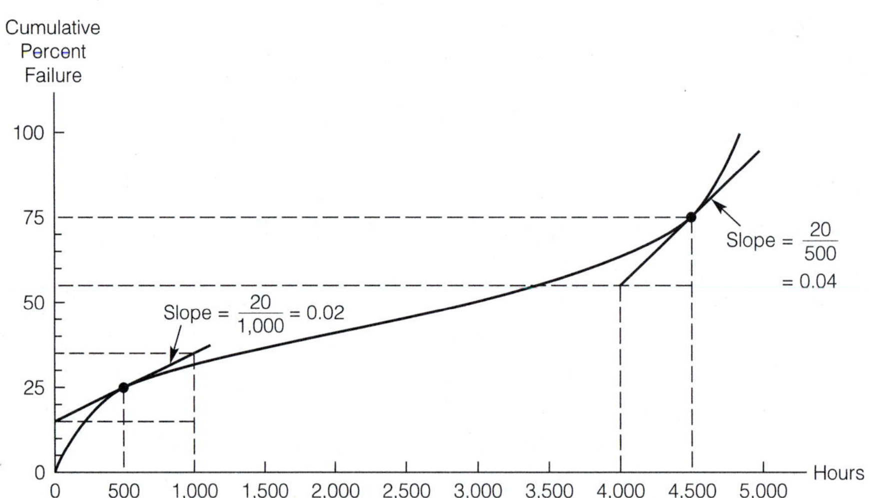

Figure 13.2 Failure Rate Curve

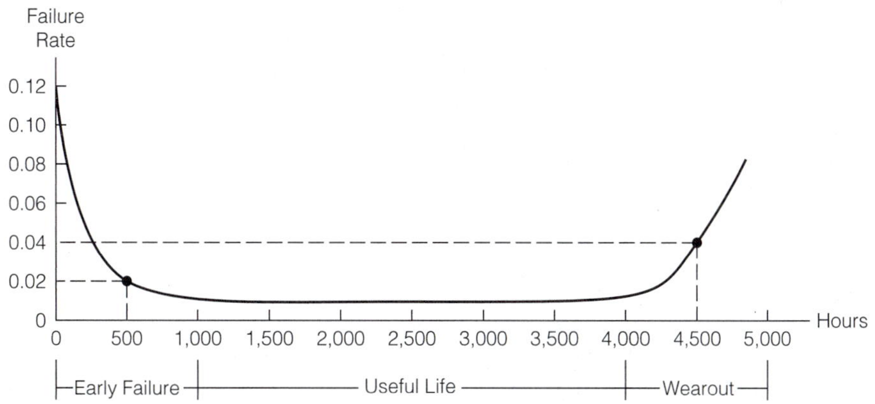

while the failure rate at 4,500 hours is 0.04 failures per hour. The **average failure rate** over any interval of time is the slope of the line between the two endpoints of the interval on the curve. As shown in Figure 13.3, the average failure rate over the entire 5,000-hour time period is 0.02 failures per hour. Many research institutes and large manufacturers conduct extensive statistical studies to identify distinct patterns of failure over time.

Gathering enough data about failures to generate as smooth a curve as is shown in Figure 13.3 is not always possible. If limited data are available, the failure rate is computed using the following formula:

$$\text{Failure rate} = \lambda = \frac{\text{Number of failures}}{\text{Total unit operating hours}}$$

or alternatively,

$$\lambda = \frac{\text{Number of failures}}{(\text{Units tested}) \times (\text{Number of hours tested})}$$

Figure 13.3 Average Failure Rate over a Time Interval

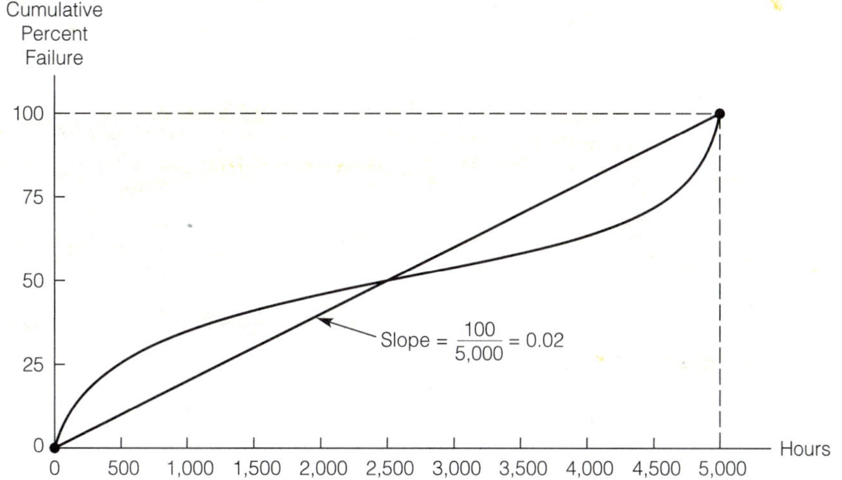

A fundamental assumption in this definition allows for different interpretations. Because the total unit operating hours equal the number of units tested times the number of hours tested, no difference occurs in total unit operating hours between testing 10 units for 100 hours or one unit for 1,000 hours. However, the difference in Figure 13.2 is clear because the failure rate varies over time. For example, if useful life began at 10 hours and the wearout period began at 200 hours, a failure would almost certainly occur before 1,000 hours, whereas a failure would not be likely to occur in 100-hour tests. During a product's useful life, however, the failure rate is assumed to be constant, and different test lengths during this period of time should show little difference. This assumption is the reason that time is an important element of the definition of reliability.

To illustrate the computation of λ, suppose that 10 units are tested over a 100-hour period. Four units failed with one unit each failing after 6, 35, 65, and 70 hours; the remaining six units performed satisfactorily until the end of the test. The total unit operating hours are

$$\begin{aligned} 1 \times 6 &= 6 \\ 1 \times 35 &= 35 \\ 1 \times 65 &= 65 \\ 1 \times 70 &= 70 \\ 6 \times 100 &= \underline{600} \\ & \quad 776 \end{aligned}$$

Therefore, λ = (4 failures)/(776 unit operating hours) = 0.00515 failures per hour. In other words, in a one-hour period, about 0.5 percent of the units would be expected to fail. On the other hand, over a 100-hour period, about (0.00515)(100) = 0.515 or 51.5 percent of the units would be expected to fail. In the actual test, only 40 percent failed.

An electronic component such as a semiconductor commonly exhibits a high, but decreasing, failure rate early in its life (as evidenced by the steep slope of the curve), followed by a period of a relatively constant failure rate, and ending with an increasing failure rate. The failure rate curve in Figure 13.2 is an example of a typical product life characteristics curve for such components.

In Figure 13.2, three distinct time periods are evident: early failure (from 0 to about 1,000 hours), useful life (from 1,000 to 4,000 hours), and wearout period (after 4,000 hours). The first is the early failure period, sometimes called the **infant mortality period**. Weak components resulting from poor manufacturing or quality control procedures will often lead to a high rate of failure early in a product's life. This high rate usually cannot be detected through normal test procedures, particularly in electronic semiconductors. Such components or products should not be permitted to enter the marketplace. The second phase of the life characteristics curve describes the normal pattern of random failures during a product's useful life. This period usually has a low, relatively constant failure rate caused by uncontrollable factors, such as sudden and unexpected stresses due to complex interactions in materials or the environment. These factors are usually impossible to predict on an individual basis. However, the collective behavior of such failures can be modeled statistically, as shown later in the chapter. Finally, as age takes over, the wearout period begins, and the failure rate increases.

New car owners generally experience this phenomenon. During the first few months of ownership, owners may have to return their car to the dealer or remove the initial bugs caused by poor workmanship or manufacturing processes, such as wheel alignment or rattles. Such defects are monitored by J. D. Power's Initial Quality metrics of which you are probably aware. During its prime lifetime, the car may have few failures; however, as parts begin to wear out, the number and rate of failures begin to increase until replacement becomes desirable.

Knowing the product life characteristics curve for a particular product helps engineers predict behavior and make decisions accordingly. For instance, if a manufacturer knows that the early failure period for a microprocessor is 600 hours, it can test the chip for 600 hours (or more) under actual or simulated operating conditions before releasing the chip to the market.

Knowledge of a product's reliability is also useful in developing warranties. As an illustration, consider a tire manufacturer who must determine a mileage warranty policy for a new line of tires. From engineering test data, the reliability curve shown in Figure 13.4 was constructed. This graph shows the probability of tread separation within a certain number of miles. Half the tires will fail by 36,500 miles, 87 percent will wear out by 42,000 miles, and only 14 percent will wear out by 31,000 miles. Thus, if a 31,000-mile warranty is established, management can compute the expected cost of replacing 14 percent of the tires. On the other hand, these data may indicate a poor design in relation to similar products of competitors. Design changes might be necessary to improve reliability. Note that in this example time is not measured chronologically, but in terms of product usage.

Reliability Function

Reliability was defined earlier as the probability that an item will *not* fail over a given period of time. However, the probability distribution of failures is usually a more convenient figure to use in reliability computations. Recall that during the useful life of a product the failure rate is assumed to be constant. Thus, the fraction of good items that fails during any time period is constant. One can assume then that the probability of failure over time can be modeled mathematically by an exponential

Figure 13.4 Cumulative Probability Distribution for Tire Mileage

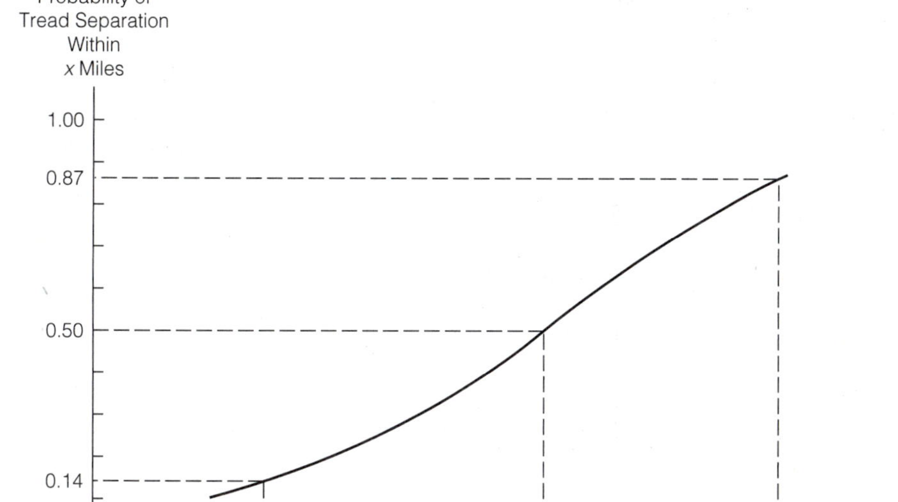

probability distribution. Not only is this model mathematically justified, but it has been empirically validated for many observable phenomena, such as failures of light bulbs, electronic components, and repairable systems such as automobiles, computers, and industrial machinery.

If λ is the failure rate, the probability density function representing failures is given by the exponential density

$$f(t) = \lambda e^{-\lambda t} \quad t \geq 0$$

The probability of failing during a time interval (t_1, t_2) can be shown to be

$$e^{-\lambda(t_2 - t_1)}$$

Specifically, the probability of failure in the interval $(0, T)$ is given by the cumulative distribution function

$$F(T) = 1 - e^{-\lambda T}$$

Because reliability is the probability of *survival*, the **reliability function** is calculated as

$$R(T) = 1 - F(T) = e^{-\lambda T}$$

This function represents the probability that the item will not fail within T units of time.

Consider, for example, an item having a reliability of 0.97 for 100 hours of normal use. Determine the failure rate λ by solving the equation $R = e^{-\lambda T}$ for λ. Substituting $R = 0.97$ and $T = 100$ into this equation yields

$$\begin{aligned} 0.97 &= e^{-\lambda(100)} \\ \ln 0.97 &= -100\lambda \\ \lambda &= -(\ln 0.97)/100 \\ &= 0.0304/100 \\ &\approx 0.0003 \text{ failure per hour} \end{aligned}$$

Thus, the reliability function is $R(T) = e^{-.0003T}$. The cumulative fraction of items that are expected to fail and survive after each 10-hour period may then be tabulated as given in Table 13.2. Note that the fraction failing in any 10-hour period is constant.

The reciprocal of the failure rate is often used in reliability computations. For nonrepairable items, $\theta = 1/\lambda$ is defined as the *mean time to failure* (MTTF). Thus, in the preceding example for $\lambda = 0.0003$ failure per hour, $\theta = 1/.0003 = 3{,}333$ hours. That is, one failure can be expected every 3,333 hours on the average. The probability distribution function of failures and the reliability function can be equivalently expressed using the MTTF as

$$F(T) = 1 - e^{-T/\theta}$$

and

$$R(T) = e^{-T/\theta}$$

Table 13.2 Cumulative Fraction Failing and Surviving

Time, T	Failures, $F(T)$	Survivors, $R(T)$
10	0.003	0.997
20	0.006	0.994
30	0.009	0.991
40	0.012	0.988
50	0.015	0.985
60	0.018	0.982
70	0.021	0.979
80	0.024	0.976
90	0.027	0.973
100	0.030	0.970

Suppose, for example, that an electronic component has a failure rate of $\lambda = 0.0001$ failure per hour. The MTTF is $\theta = 1/0.0001 = 10{,}000$ hours. The probability that the component will not fail in 15,000 hours is

$$\begin{aligned} R(15{,}000) &= e^{-15{,}000/10{,}000} \\ &= e^{-1.5} \\ &= 0.223 \end{aligned}$$

For repairable items, θ is usually called the *mean time between failures* (MTBF). For example, suppose that a machine is operated for 10,000 hours and experiences four failures that are immediately repaired. The mean time between failures is

$$\text{MTBF} = 10{,}000/4 = 2{,}500 \text{ hours}$$

and the failure rate is

$$\lambda = 1/2{,}500 = 0.0004 \text{ failure per hour}$$

MTBF is a useful statistic in many management decisions. Consider a company such as Xerox, which leases copying equipment and maintains a service staff throughout the United States. The MTBF can be used to predict the volume of service calls expected, determine labor requirements for service and geographical assignments, and plan the purchase or manufacture of spare parts. In fact, Xerox actually has used an analytical model to determine service staff size. One of the parameters in the model is the average rate at which machines need service.[2] The failure distribution can also be used to establish preventive maintenance policies for repairable systems.

Other probability distributions are often used for modeling reliability. One of the most common is the Weibull distribution, whose probability density function is

$$f(t) = \alpha\beta t^{\beta-1}e^{-\alpha t^{\beta}} \qquad t > 0$$

The constants α and β are called the **scale** and **shape** parameters, respectively. By varying these constants, the Weibull distribution assumes a variety of shapes as illustrated in Figure 13.5. Thus, it is a flexible modeling tool for fitting empirical failure data to a theoretical distribution. The Weibull distribution is often used in modeling

Figure 13.5 Weibull Distribution for $\alpha = 1$ and $\beta = 0.5, 1, 2,$ and 4

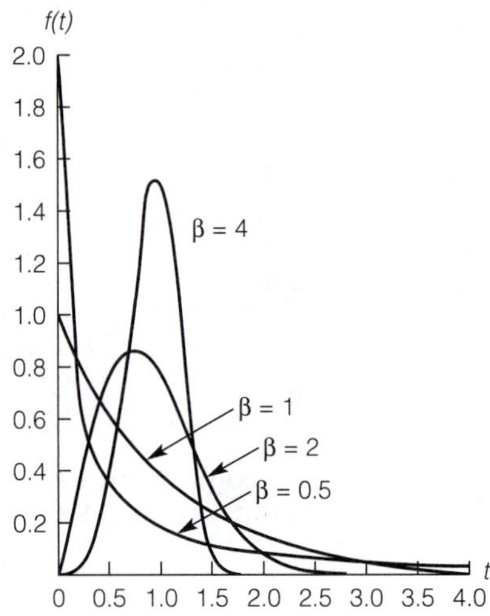

failure data for memory components and structural elements in automobiles and airplanes. The reliability function based on the Weibull distribution is

$$R(T) = e^{-\alpha T^{\beta}}$$

To illustrate the use of the Weibull distribution, suppose that a particular electric component has a Weibull failure distribution with $\alpha = 0.02$ and $\beta = 0.5$. (Determining α and β is an exercise in curve fitting.) Then

$$R(T) = e^{-0.02\sqrt{T}}$$

The fraction of components expected to survive 400 hours is thus

$$R(400) = e^{-0.02\sqrt{400}} = e^{-0.4} = 0.67$$

The following table presents some values of $R(T)$ for selected values of T:

T	*R(T)*
100	0.82
200	0.75
300	0.71
400	0.67
500	0.64
1,000	0.53
5,000	0.24
10,000	0.14

For example, only 24 percent of the components will be expected to survive 5,000 hours or more.

RELIABILITY PREDICTION

Random failures during useful life are uncontrollable, but they can be described by probability distributions. Many systems are composed of individual components with known reliabilities. The reliability data of individual components can be used to predict the reliability of the system. Systems of components may be configured in *series*, in *parallel*, or in some mixed combination. Block diagrams are useful ways to represent system configurations where blocks represent functional components or subsystems. This section presents formulas and techniques for determining system reliability for each of these situations.

Series Systems

A **series system** is illustrated in Figure 13.6. In such a system, all components must function or the system will fail. If the reliability of component i is R_i the reliability of the system is the product of the individual reliabilities, that is

$$R_S = R_1 R_2 \ldots R_n$$

This equation is based on the multiplicative law of probability. For example, suppose that a personal computer system is composed of the processing unit, modem, and printer with reliabilities of 0.997, 0.980, and 0.975, respectively. The reliability of the system is therefore given by

$$R_S = (0.997)(0.980)(0.975) = 0.953$$

Note that when reliabilities are less than one, system reliability decreases as additional components are added in series. Thus, the more complex a series system is, the greater the chance of failure.

If the reliability function is exponential, i.e., $R_i = e^{-\lambda_i T}$, then

$$\begin{aligned} R_S &= e^{-\lambda_1 T} e^{-\lambda_2 T} \cdots e^{-\lambda_n T} \\ &= e^{-\lambda_1 T - \lambda_2 T \ldots - \lambda_n T} \\ &= e^{-\left(\sum_{i=1}^{n} \lambda_i\right) T} \end{aligned}$$

Suppose that a two-component series system has failure rates of 0.004 and 0.001 per hour. Then

$$\begin{aligned} R_S(T) &= e^{-(0.004 + 0.001)T} \\ &= e^{-0.005T} \end{aligned}$$

Figure 13.6 Series System

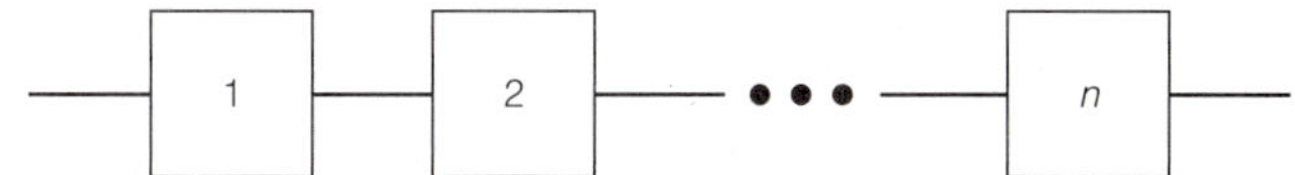

The probability of survival for 100 hours would be

$$\begin{aligned} R_S(100) &= e^{-0.005(100)} \\ &= e^{-0.5} \\ &= 0.6065 \end{aligned}$$

Parallel Systems

A **parallel system** is illustrated in Figure 13.7. In such a system, failure of an individual component is less critical than in series systems; the system will successfully operate as long as one component functions. Hence, the additional components are *redundant*. Redundancy is often built into systems to improve their reliability. However, as mentioned earlier, trade-offs in cost, size, weight, and so on must be taken into account.

The reliability of the parallel system in Figure 13.7 is derived as follows. If R_1, $R_2, \ldots, R_n$ are the reliabilities of the individual components, the probabilities of failure are $1 - R_1, 1 - R_2, \ldots, 1 - R_n$, respectively. Because the system fails only if each component fails, the probability of system failure is

$$(1 - R_1)(1 - R_2) \ldots (1 - R_n)$$

Hence, the system reliability is computed as

$$R_S = 1 - (1 - R_1)(1 - R_2) \ldots (1 - R_n)$$

If all components have identical reliabilities R, then

$$R_S = 1 - (1 - R)^n$$

The computers on the space shuttle were designed with built-in redundancy in case of failure. Five computers were designed in parallel. Thus, for example, if the reliability of each is 0.99, the system reliability is

Figure 13.7 Parallel System

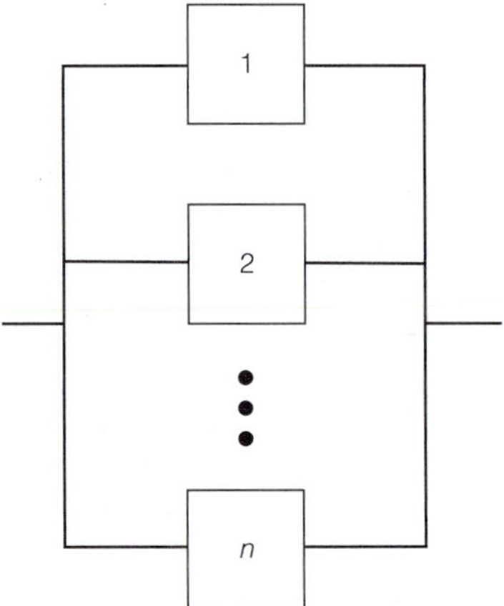

$$R_S = 1 - (1 - 0.99)^5 = 0.9999999999$$

Series-Parallel Systems

Most systems are composed of combinations of series and parallel systems. Consider the system shown in Figure 13.8(a). To determine the reliability of such a system, first compute the reliability of the parallel subsystem B:

$$R_B = 1 - (1 - 0.9)^3 = 0.999$$

This level of reliability is equivalent to replacing the three parallel components B with a single component B having a reliability of 0.999 in series with A, C, and D, as shown in Figure 13.8(b). Next, compute the reliability of the equivalent series system:

$$R_S = (0.99)(0.999)(0.96)(0.98) = 0.93$$

A second type of series-parallel arrangement is shown in Figure 13.9(a). System reliability is determined by first computing the reliability of the series systems ABC and DE:

$$R_{ABC} = (0.95)(0.98)(0.99) = 0.92169$$

$$R_{DE} = (0.99)(0.97) = 0.9603$$

Figure 13.8 Series-Parallel System and Equivalent Series System

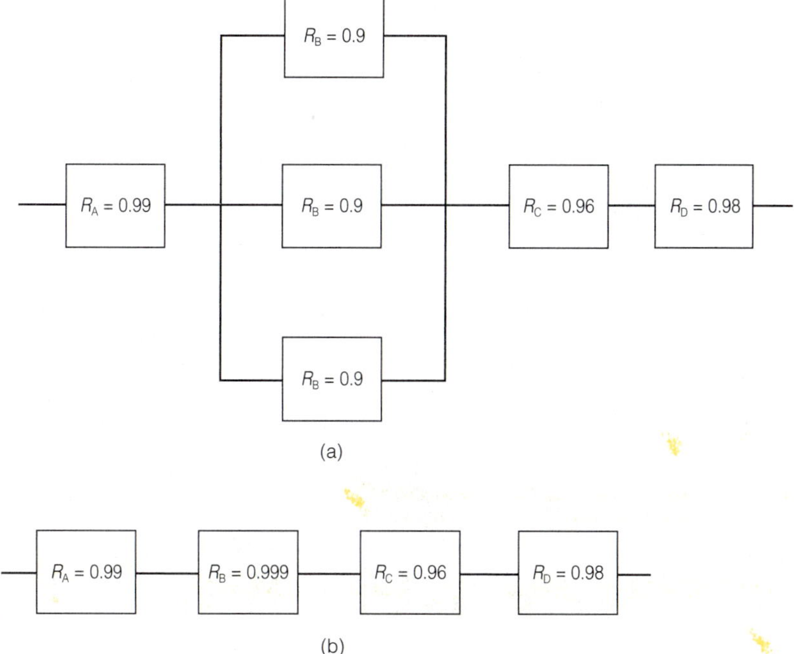

Figure 13.9 Series-Parallel System and Equivalent Series System

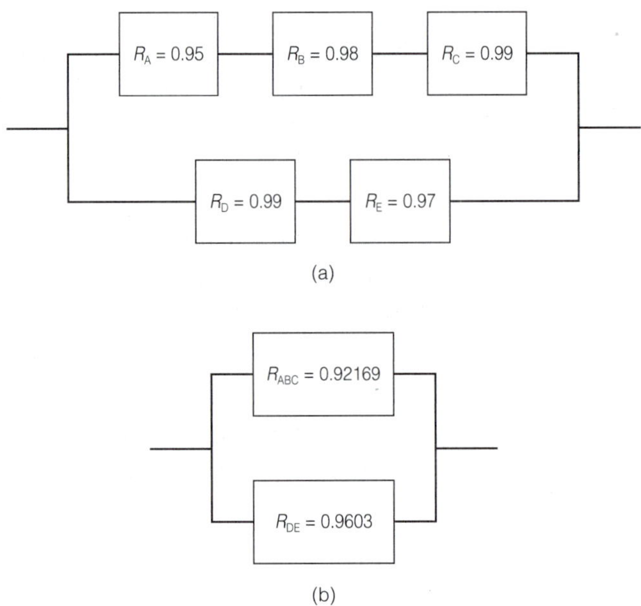

The result is an equivalent parallel system shown in Figure 13.9(b). The system reliability is then computed as

$$R_S = 1 - (1 - 0.92169)(1 - 0.9603) = 0.9969$$

By appropriately decomposing complex systems into series and/or parallel components as shown in these examples, the system reliability can be easily computed. Reliability requirements are determined during the product design phase. The designer may use these techniques to determine the effects of adding redundancy, substituting different components, or reconfiguring the design.

RELIABILITY ENGINEERING

Reliability engineering is a relatively new discipline concerned with the design, manufacture, and assurance of products having high reliability. Many techniques of reliability engineering have been developed. This section provides a review of some of the common methods of reliability engineering.

Standardization

One method of ensuring high reliability is to use components with proven track records of reliability over years of actual use. If failure rates of components can be established, then standard components can be selected and used in the design process. The use of standardized components not only achieves higher reliability, but also reduces costs because standardized components are used in many different products.

Redundancy

Redundancy provides backup components that can be used when the failure of any one component in a system can cause a failure of the entire system. The previous section provided examples of how redundant components can increase reliability dramatically. Redundant components are designed either in a standby configuration or a parallel configuration. In a *standby system*, the standby unit is switched in when the operating unit fails; in the *parallel configuration*, both units operate normally but only one is required for proper functioning. Redundancy is crucial to systems in which failures can be extremely costly, such as aircraft or satellite communications systems. Redundancy, however, increases the cost, size, and weight of the system. Therefore, designers must trade off these attributes against increased reliability.

Physics of Failure

Many failures are due to deterioration because of chemical reactions over time, which may be aggravated by temperature or humidity effects. Understanding the physical properties of materials and their response to environmental effects helps to eliminate potential failures or to make the product robust with respect to environmental conditions that affect reliability. Reliability engineers must work closely with chemists, materials science engineers, and others who can contribute to a better understanding of failure mechanisms.

Reliability Testing

The reliability of a product is determined principally by the design and the reliability of the components of the product. However, reliability is such a complex issue that it cannot always be determined from theoretical analysis of the design alone. Hence, formal testing is necessary, which involves simulating environmental conditions to determine a product's performance, operating time, and mode of failure.

Testing is useful for a variety of other reasons. Test data are often necessary for liability protection, as means for evaluating designs or vendor reliability, and in process planning and selection. Often, reliability test data are required in military contracts. Testing is necessary to evaluate warranties and to avoid high costs related to early field failure. Good testing leads to good reliability and hence good quality.

Product testing is performed by various methods. The purpose of *life testing*, that is, running devices until they fail, is to measure the distribution of failures to better understand and eliminate their causes. However, such testing can be expensive and time-consuming. For devices that have long natural lives, life testing is not practical. *Accelerated life testing* involves overstressing components to reduce the time to failure and find weaknesses. This form of testing might involve running a motor faster than typically found in normal operating conditions. However, failure rates must correlate well to actual operating conditions if accelerated life testing is to be useful.

Other testing studies the robustness of products. For example, one company performed a variety of tests on its computers.[3] Products were disassembled and destructive testing was performed on the electromechanical, mechanical, and physical properties of components. *Environmental testing* consisted of varying the temperature from –40°F (the temperature inside trucks in the northern United States and Canada) to 165°F (the temperature inside trucks in the southwestern United States) to shock the product to see whether it could withstand extremes. Because old wiring exhibits a wide range of variation, AC power was varied from 105 to 135 volts. *Vibration and shock testing* were used to simulate trucks driving from the East to the West Coast to determine the product's ability to withstand rough handling and accidents.

Burn-In

Semiconductors are the basic building blocks of numerous modern products such as videocassette recorders, automotive ignition systems, computers, and military weapons systems. Semiconductors have a small proportion of defects, called *latent defects*, that can cause them to fail during the first 1,000 hours of normal operation. After that, the failure rate stabilizes, perhaps for as long as 25 years, before beginning to rise again as components wear out. These infant mortalities can be as high as 10 percent in a new technology or as low as 0.01 percent in proven technologies. The sooner a faulty component is detected, the cheaper is its replacement or repair. A correction on an integrated circuit fabrication line costs about 50 cents; at the board level it might cost $5; at the system level about $50; and in the field, $500. If a printed circuit board contains 100 semiconductors, a failure rate of 0.01 percent would cause a board failure rate of 1 percent.

Burn-in, or *component stress testing*, involves exposing integrated circuits to elevated temperatures in order to force latent defects to occur. For example, a device that might normally fail after 300 hours at 25°C might fail in less than 20 hours at 150°C. Survivors are likely to have long, trouble-free operating lives.

Studies and experience have demonstrated the economic advantages of burn-in. For example, a large-scale study of the effect of burn-in on enhancing reliability of dynamic MOS memories was conducted in Europe. The failure rate without burn-in conditioning and testing to eliminate infant mortality was 0.24 percent per thousand hours, while burn-in and testing reduced the rate to 0.02 percent per thousand hours. When considering the cost of field service and warranty work, for instance, reduction of semiconductor failure rates in a large system by an order of magnitude translates roughly into an average of one repair call per year versus one repair call per month.

Because burn-in requires considerable time—48 to 96 hours is common—designers attempt to produce equipment that can perform some functional tests during the burn-in cycle rather than after. Modern systems exist to test and burn-in integrated circuits. One system has the capacity of 18,000 DRAMs (dynamic random access memory) per load and is flexible in its burn-in and test procedures to accommodate future types without modification of the hardware. The system can accumulate and display information on the devices under test, both for real-time evaluation and for lot documentation.

Failure Mode and Effects Analysis

The purpose of failure mode and effects analysis (FMEA) is to identify all the ways in which a failure can occur, to estimate the effect and seriousness of the failure, and to recommend corrective design actions. An FMEA usually consists of specifying the following information for each critical component:

- Failure mode (i.e., how the component can fail)
- Cause of failure
- Effect on the product or system within which it operates (safety, downtime, repair requirements, tools required)
- Corrective action (design changes, better user instructions)
- Comments

Figure 13.10 gives an (incomplete) example of a typical FMEA for an ordinary household light socket.

Figure 13.10 FMEA on Common Household Lamp

Failure Mode and Effects Analysis

Analyst *J.A. White*

Product *2C Lamp* Date *10 Jan. 1995*

Component Name	**Failure Mode**	**Cause of Failure**	**Effect of Failure on System**	**Correction of Problem**	**Comments**
Plug part no. P-3	Loose wiring	Use vibration, handling	Will not conduct current; may generate heat	Molded plug and wire	Uncorrected, could cause fire
	Not a failure of plug per se	User contacts prongs when plugging or unplugging	May cause severe shock or death	Enlarged safety tip on molded plug	Children
Metal base and stem	Bent or nicked	Dropping, bumping, shipping	Degrades looks	Distress finish, improved packaging	Cosmetic
Lamp socket	Cracked	Excessive heat, bumping, forcing	May cause shock if contacts metal base and stem; may cause shock upon bulb replacement	Improve material used for socket	Dangerous
Wiring	Broken, frayed, from lamp to plug	Fatigue, heat, carelessness, childbite	Will not conduct current; may generate heat, blow breakers, or cause shock	Use of wire suitable for long life in extreme environment anticipated	Dangerous; warning on instructions
	Internal short circuit	Heat, brittle insulation	May cause electrical shock or render lamp useless	Use of wire suitable for long life in extreme environment anticipated	
	Internal wire broken	Socket slipping and twisting wires	May cause electrical shock or render lamp useless	Use of indent or notch to prevent socket from turning	

Source: K. E. Case and L. L. Jones, *Profit Through Quality: Quality Assurance Programs for Manufacturers*, QC & RE Monograph Series No. 2 (New York: Institute of Industrial Engineers, 1978).

Fault Tree Analysis

Fault tree analysis (FTA) is a logical procedure that begins with a list of potential hazards or undesired states and works backward to develop a list of causes and origins of failure. Its purpose is to show logical relationships between failures and causes, similar to a fishbone diagram (Chapter 10). In this fashion, ways to avoid potential dangers can be uncovered.

An example of an FTA is given in Figure 13.11 for an industrial brake that is assumed to operate like a regular drum type of automobile brake. The fault tree is composed of branches connected to two different types of nodes: AND nodes, denoted by the symbol

and OR nodes, depicted by

If a set of events is connected below an AND node, then *all* events must occur for the event above the node to occur. Below an OR node, *at least one* of the events must occur. Thus, in Figure 13.11 the event "brake doesn't release" can occur if any of the following conditions hold:

broken springs
OR fluid pressure not free to release
OR oversized shoes for drum (width)
OR weak springs
AND
no grease on shoe lands at facing contact.

Figure 13.11 Fault Tree Analysis

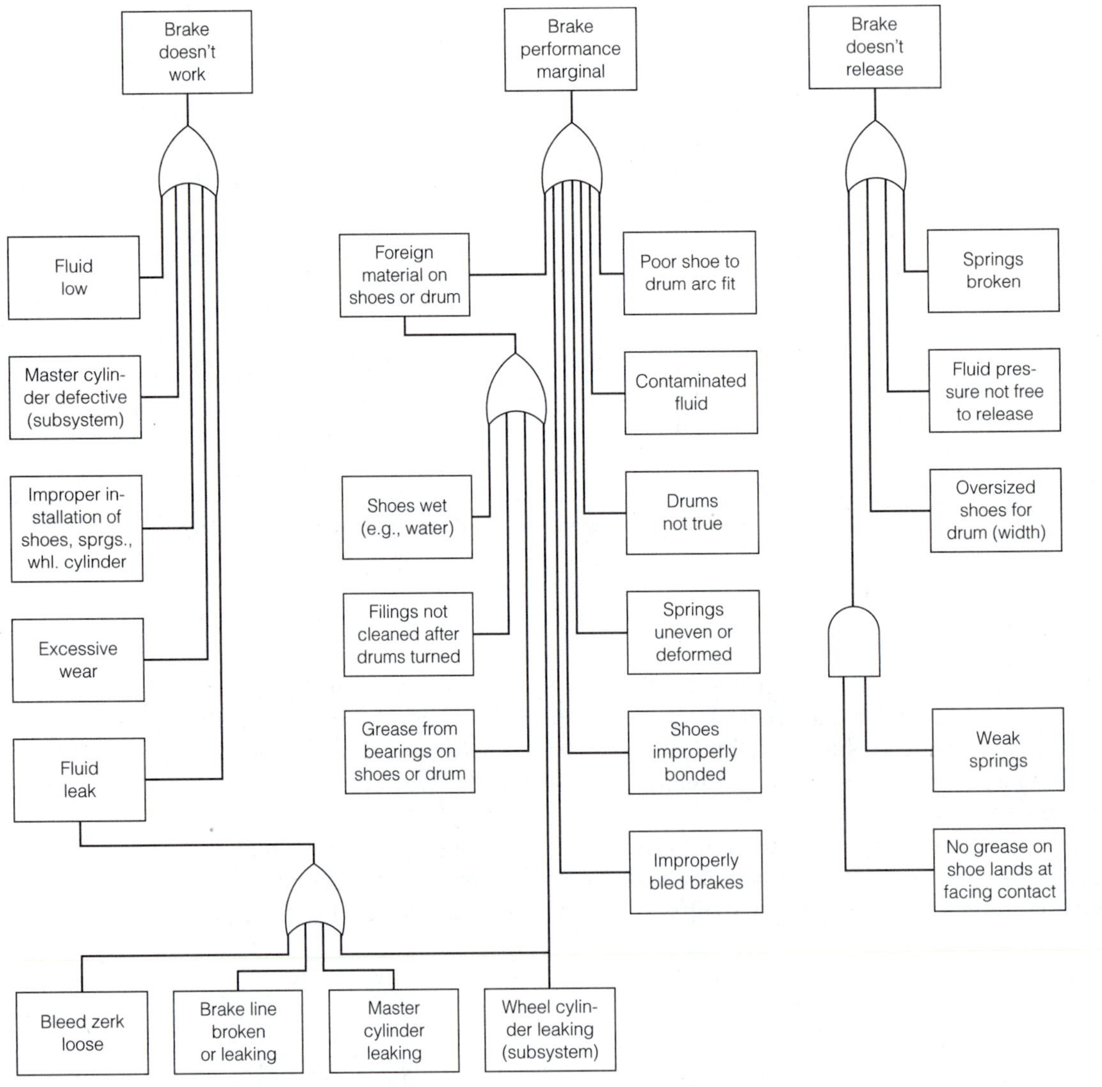

Source: K. E. Case and L. L. Jones, *Profit Through Quality: Quality Assurance Programs for Manufacturers,* QC & RE Monograph Series No. 2 (New York: Institute of Industrial Engineers, 1978).

RELIABILITY MANAGEMENT

Effective reliability management should include the following steps:

- Define customer performance requirements.
- Determine important economic factors and assess their relationship with reliability requirements.
- Define the environment and conditions in which the product will be used.
- Select components, designs, and vendors that meet reliability as well as cost criteria.
- Determine reliability requirements for machines and equipment as well as their impacts on product reliability during manufacturing.
- Analyze field reliability data as a method for quality improvement.

High reliability results in lower costs to society in the context of Taguchi's loss function. Consumers would like products to be 100 percent reliable, which is certainly a worthy goal for manufacturers. However, the production of a product that has perfect reliability under all conditions is impractical. To achieve high reliability, better materials and more precise manufacturing processes must be used. These improvements will increase manufacturing costs to the point that consumers are unwilling to pay the price. Thus, management must balance the economic factors and seek to minimize total cost, keeping in mind that too low a reliability may damage the firm's reputation and result in lost sales or product liability suits. Such decisions must be addressed strategically by upper management.

Reliability is a concern in many areas of the production system and should be an important consideration in design, manufacturing, storage, and transportation, as well as supporting functions such as purchasing, field service, and maintenance.

As a fundamental dimension of quality, reliability must be *designed* into a product. The performance characteristics, operating conditions, and performance duration specified for the product or system drive the technical design. Variations in product performance arise because of the way it is used or because of environmental conditions. Changes take place over time because of chemical changes in components, vibration and stress, or expansion and contraction of materials due to fluctuations in temperature or humidity, for example. Sooner or later, products fail. Creating products that will not fail is nearly impossible. The question is not whether a product will fail, but when. Designers must decide to what extent failure is acceptable and establish specifications for reliability.

Many consumers will not always use a product correctly or follow suggested maintenance procedures. Designers must account for operating errors that will result in failure, and they must maintain safety when failure does occur. Fail-safe designs provide safety in the event of failure. An example is a railway signal that turns red when a failure occurs. Foolproof designs prevent operation in the event of an operating error, thus avoiding failure. An example is a temperature control that prevents overheating by not allowing a heating switch to be closed without prior closure of a fan switch.

Whatever is done in the manufacturing process can and does have an effect on the reliability of the final product sold to customers. To manufacture reliable products from good designs, companies must use good materials, well-maintained machines, and trained workers. The greater the capability of a process to conform to design specifications and targets, the more likely it is that the product will have high reliability. Preventive maintenance in manufacturing is crucial to equipment reliability. Manufacturing, marketing, and financial managers must work together to ensure adequate time, schedules, and budgets for preventive maintenance activities. Operations control strategies such as just-in-time, the use of inspection, and statistical process control all contribute to the achievement of reliability objectives.

Packaging and transportation cannot be neglected. Poor protection and handling can adversely affect the reliability of the product when it reaches the customer. Denton relates a situation in which one company inadvertently packed a half-full load of computers in a 40-foot truck.[4] The boxes dropped from 12 feet high and tumbled around inside the truck from South Carolina to Boston. The cartons were demolished and all the computers were believed to be destroyed. However, not one computer was damaged because of the careful attention to and testing of packaging.

As noted elsewhere in this book, purchasing plays an active role in the final quality of a product. Purchasing must understand the reliability requirements of purchased parts and components and clearly communicate these to suppliers. Field service personnel must understand the nature of failures for preventive maintenance and maintain an adequate supply of spare and replacement parts. Feedback on failures completes the never-ending cycle of product improvement, leading to improved market knowledge and better designs.

Reliability in Computer Software

Many consumer goods are becoming more and more dependent on computers (strictly speaking, microprocessors), which in turn depend on the accompanying software. Reliability failures in computer software are unacceptable departures from requirements. Everyone has undoubtedly experienced a systems crash at an inopportune time. The average software product in the United States contains an estimated 8 to 10 errors per thousand lines of code.

Software reliability problems can cause considerable inconvenience or harm. On January 15, 1990, a software flaw in one programming statement controlling some AT&T switching systems caused a nine-hour nationwide saturation in their telephone network because the switches abnormally shut down.[5]

A more serious problem involved a radiation therapy machine error that resulted in the deaths of several patients.[6] The accidents were caused by software controlling the machine. If the operator entered an unusual but nonetheless possible sequence of commands, the computer control would place the machine into an erroneous and hazardous state, subjecting the patient to a massive overdose. Unfortunately, at that time, the Food and Drug Administration had no requirements regarding software development practices or software quality in medical devices. Only after these incidents occurred did the FDA announce that it would begin reviewing the software in medical devices.

Software with high quality and reliability is essential for global competitiveness. Estimating and predicting software reliability is not easy. Software failures result from inherent design flaws that only reveal themselves under appropriate operational circumstances. These software "bugs" arise from flaws in design specifications, routine coding errors, testing errors, or a variety of incompatibilities with hardware or other support software.

Undoubtedly the biggest software reliability problem in history was the Year 2000 Problem (Y2K Problem), which was conservatively estimated to cost more than $100 billion. As an article in *Business Week* quoted one information systems administrator:

> *"We feel you'll be a lot luckier if the system stops functioning," says Larry Olson, chief information officer for the state of Pennsylvania. "It might be two months before you realize you're getting bad information."*

> *The Year 2000 bug also shows up in microprocessors built into machinery, from automated assembly lines to cellular telephones. "Our biggest concern is that we miss an integrated circuit buried down somewhere that would have a cascade effect," says Bruce Colgate, process control manager at Phillips Petroleum Co. This is one bug whose effects may only be known when it bites.*[7]

Fortunately, Y2K passed without any serious consequences, primarily due to the preventative efforts made ahead of time.

Computer software bears more similarity to services than to manufactured goods. With software, simply inspecting the end product is not practical. Once the program is completed and stored on magnetic media, any bugs have already been included in the product. Hence, particular care must be taken in the design phase. Unfortunately, many software producers are under great pressure to ship products before they are fully tested, which often results in expensive after-market support, not to mention damage to the company's reputation.

The environment in which software is produced has certain characteristics that negatively affect software quality.[8]

- Programmers of widely varying levels of skill
- Small project staffs (often one person)
- Software-naïve customers who are usually interested only in software output
- Poorly defined but often highly complex customer objectives
- High turnover rate for programmers
- Externally or internally generated constraints such as cost and time
- Hardware complexities that occasionally force the applications programmer to operate as a systems programmer, rather than working directly toward the actual goals outlined by the customer
- Poor quality of existing programs that were produced without the benefit of modern support tools

Building quality and reliability into software begins with good planning. A software quality assurance system must be integrated into existing practices and procedures. When software quality assurance is isolated from the software design system, such procedures can be easily ignored or forgotten. All functional groups involved must participate under the guidance of quality assurance personnel. Because quality assurance programs are usually new to software design groups, behavioral and motivational techniques for gaining acceptance are often necessary.

Several techniques have been developed to guide the software development process and to ensure quality and reliability. These techniques include configuration management, reviews and audits, and a variety of testing methods. Each of these activities is based on objective measurement and feedback to the project manager or development team members.

Configuration management has been used extensively for hardware projects in the aerospace and defense industries and has been adapted to software projects. It is an essential requirement in government contracts. Configuration management is a process for designing and maintaining software by tightly controlling the set of software components that make up a complex system. It provides an effective means of incorporating changes during development and use. The process consists of three activities:

1. Establishing approved baseline configurations (designs) for computer programs (configuration definition). These baselines support systematic evaluation, coordination, and disposition of all proposed changes.

2. Maintaining control over all changes in the baseline programs (change control). Many software problems arise due to frequent changes. A rigorous system for monitoring change is an important quality control function.
3. Providing traceability of baselines and changes (configuration accounting). Maintaining a paper trail of configurations and modifications is essential for ensuring that specifications are being met and for determining sources of errors and means of correction.

Through independent reviews, problems or potential problems can be discovered and reported. Software quality assurance groups are responsible for maintaining control over specifications, documentation, and code to assure that performance and design requirements are being met. They also review software designs prior to coding, audit development activities, review and approve testing plans, and monitor actual requirements testing.

A variety of methods for software verification are used. These methods include inspection for requirements that cannot be verified through operational testing such as examination of flow diagrams and program listings; comparing the execution of a program with a standard program with known results; analysis of program outputs to validate complex equations whose results are not directly related to inputs; and conducting tests with known inputs that should generate known outputs.

Achieving reliable software is expensive. One of the most ambitious U.S. projects has been the software for the space shuttle. NASA paid $1,000 for each line of code; a total of $500 million. However, the space shuttle software has been found to contain only 0.1 errors per thousand lines.[9] Correcting software defects is often so expensive that completely rewriting the code is usually cheaper than attempting to modify it. Errors not removed until the maintenance phase of a product's life cycle can cost up to 10 times more to correct than if discovered earlier. Today, more than 50 percent of a data processing department's budget goes to maintenance of software.

In some cases, reliable software is seemingly not even possible. President Reagan's Strategic Defense Initiative was criticized by many computer scientists because the software required for space-based weapons was supposedly too complex to be developed reliably using current technology. Clearly, further research into better methods for achieving quality and reliability in software is necessary as the twenty-first century begins.

MAINTAINABILITY AND AVAILABILITY

Failures will eventually occur, resulting in equipment shutdown and downtime. The amount of downtime is affected by the diagnosis effort required to determine the cause of failure, the ease of access to components, repair procedures, and the availability of spare parts. *Maintainability* is a product's ability to be retained in, or restored to, a specified state of operation within a given period of time. Maintainability depends on two types of maintenance activities: preventive or corrective. *Preventive maintenance* such as oiling equipment, can reduce the risks of failure—even though it requires a certain amount of downtime—and is usually economically justified. *Corrective maintenance* is the response to failures and is a function of reliability. Good maintenance adds to reliability by increasing the probability that the equipment will operate satisfactorily over a period of time. However, a trade-off between reliability and maintainability is inevitable. Higher reliability will usually result in less frequent maintenance but higher design and production costs. Designing for frequent repair or replacement may be a more economical option.

Example 1: Determining a Preventive Maintenance Policy. A part of a bathroom tissue production system is a saw/wrapper machine, which cuts long rolls into smaller pieces and wraps them into packages before they are placed in cartons. Historical data on the time between failures are presented in Table 13.3. From this information, calculate MTBF by adding together the expected values—that is, the midpoint of each time interval—multiplied by their associated probability:

$$\begin{aligned} \text{MTBF} &= 27.5(0.2) + 32.5(0.4) + 37.5(0.3) + 42.5(0.1) \\ &= 34 \text{ hours} \end{aligned}$$

Table 13.3 Historical Data on Time Between Failures

Hours Between Failures	Probability
25–30	0.2
30–35	0.4
35–40	0.3
40–45	0.1
	Total 1.0

At present, the machine is repaired only when it fails, at an average cost of $50. The company is considering a preventive maintenance program that will cost $30 for each inspection and adjustment.

To determine whether this program is economically justified, compute and compare average annual costs. Consider, for instance, the current policy. Assuming 260 working days per year and one shift per day, the machine has 2,080 hours of available time. If the mean time between failures is 34 hours, 2,080/34 = 61.2 breakdowns per year can be expected. Hence, the annual cost will be 61.2 × $50 = $3,060. Now suppose that the machine is inspected every 25 hours and adjusted. If the time until the next failure after adjustment follows the distribution in Table 13.3, the probability of a failure under this policy is zero. However, inspection every 25 hours will occur 2,080/25 = 83.2 times per year, resulting in a cost of 83.2 × $30 = $2,496. Next, suppose the machine receives inspection every 30 hours. From Table 13.3, the probability of a failure occurring before the next inspection is 0.20. Thus, the total expected annual cost will be the cost of inspection, $30 × 2,080/30 = $2,080, plus the expected cost of emergency repair, $50 × (2,080/30) × 0.20 = $693. The total cost is therefore $2,773. Table 13.4 summarizes similar calculations for other maintenance intervals and reveals that a maintenance interval of 25 hours results in a minimal cost policy.

Table 13.4 Cost Computation for Preventive Maintenance

Time Between Inspections	Number of Inspections per Year	Probability of Failure Before Next Inspection	Inspection Cost	Failure Cost	Total Cost
25	83.2	0.0	$2,496	$ 0	$2,496
30	69.3	0.2	2,080	693	2,773
35	59.4	0.6	1,782	1,782	3,564
40	52	0.9	1,560	2,340	3,900

Several design issues are related to maintainability.

- *Access of parts for repair:* One of the biggest consumer complaints about today's automobiles compared to those made before the early 1970s is the difficulty of accessing many parts without special tools. Even though automotive reliability has increased, the complexity of today's engines makes maintenance difficult for a nonprofessional. For good maintainability, components must be easily accessible to maintenance personnel.
- *Modular construction and standardization:* Electronic equipment, such as televisions, is now designed with easily replaceable modular components. This group-type standardization makes diagnosis much easier, allowing problems to be isolated at the board level rather than for individual components. Of course, it also increases the cost of replacement parts. Greater design effort also is necessary. Hence, these trade-offs must be considered on an economic basis. Standardization results in interchangeability of components between products, a reduction in inventory requirements for spare parts, and the increased possibility that parts may not be available when needed.
- *Diagnostic repair procedures:* During the design process, provisions must be made for diagnosis and repair. Clear instructions need to be written. For complex equipment, diagnosis can be time-consuming. Modern information technology and artificial intelligence techniques, known as *expert systems*, are being developed to assist personnel in the diagnosis of equipment.

Availability is the probability that equipment is not down due to failure. The two principal definitions of availability include *operational availability*, which is defined as

$$A_o = \frac{\text{MTBM}}{\text{MTBM} + \text{MDT}}$$

where MTBM = mean time between maintenance, including both corrective and preventive maintenance, and MDT = mean downtime. MDT is the amount of time needed for corrective and preventive maintenance and waiting time. This definition of availability is useful to operations managers in planning equipment utilization but is difficult to employ in design. Instead, designers use *inherent availability*, defined as

$$A_t = \frac{\text{MTBF}}{\text{MTBF} + \text{MTTR}}$$

where MTBF and MTTR represent mean time between failures and mean time to repair, respectively, as previously defined. This equation assumes no preventive maintenance downtime, waiting time, and so on, because these variables cannot be determined in a design environment. Inherent availability assumes ideal conditions and can be used to establish trade-offs between reliability (as measured by MTBF) and maintainability (as measured by MTTR). To illustrate, suppose that availability is specified as 0.99:

$$0.99 = \frac{\text{MTBF}}{\text{MTBF} + \text{MTTR}}$$

or

$$\text{MTBF} = 99\ \text{MTTR}$$

Thus, if MTTR = 2 hours, MTBF must be equal to 198 hours. The designer can use such information to evaluate a proposed design and make appropriate modifications. On the other hand, this information can also be used to reduce MTTR through maintainability improvements, given a specified reliability.

QUALITY IN PRACTICE

TESTING AUDIO COMPONENTS AT SHURE, INC.[10]

Shure Incorporated is a global, privately held company headquartered in Evanston, Illinois, with manufacturing facilities in Illinois, Texas, and Mexico, and sales offices in Germany and Hong Kong. Shure's mission is to

- deliver high-performing, quality, rugged and reliable audio products
- provide superior customer service and support.

Shure's philosophy is to be market-driven and customer-focused in their chosen markets. Each market segment has its own quality and reliability needs.

- *Performance Audio:* musical performers and those who record and monitor their work on stage or in the studio. Anyone who has attended a rock concert can attest to the rough treatment microphones receive from the entertainers, some actually throwing them across the stage.
- *Presentation and Installation Audio:* anywhere a sound system is installed, such as houses of worship, hotels, conference rooms, clubs, theaters, and auditoriums. Many users are unfamiliar with the acoustical characteristics of the equipment they are using and sound technicians are often not on site, so the equipment really needs to run by itself.
- *Radio and TV:* broadcast industry both in studio and on location in the field. Technicians need to have total confidence in the equipment they are using on a live, remote broadcast, because they cannot go back and redo that on-the-spot interview.
- *Consumer Market:* phonograph cartridges and low-cost microphones, including audiophiles, hip-hop DJs, and home recording. Scratch DJs literally take a record and pull it back and forth to the beat of a song, causing tremendous pressure on the phonograph stylus.
- *Mobile Communications:* audio subsystems, like hands-free cellular, within the automotive environment. Microphones need to perform in a variety of temperatures.

S. N. Shure began the company by launching a one-man operation in 1925 that sold radio parts kits. It was the microphone that marked the company's entry into manufacturing in 1932, and the microphone remains Shure's flagship product to this day. Because of its emphasis on engineering research, Shure products became known early on for their outstanding quality and durability. During World War II, Shure was awarded a U.S. government contract to provide microphones to the military, and needed to meet strict specifications for performance and ruggedness. Shure took the extra step to develop a rigorous in-house testing program that remains in place today.

In addition to microphones (both wired and wireless) and phonograph cartridges, Shure manufactures a number of other audio electronics products, including mixers, digital signal processors, personal monitoring systems, and digital feedback reducers. Shure's quality philosophy is reliability oriented. Products are tested for reliability well beyond the warranty period, with the goal of providing the customer long-term service and satisfaction. Testing is designed to simulate actual operating conditions. Shure has more than 80 test procedures in place. The following are a few examples:

- *Microphone Drop Test:* To determine whether a microphone is capable of dynamic shock stress. Initial performance data are taken on the mic. Then the mic is dropped numerous times onto a hardwood floor from a height of 6 feet at random angles. The mic is "talked out" after every two drops. After the drop tests, level and response are tested and compared to the initial data. Any unit not meeting original print specifications is considered a failure.

- *Perspiration Test:* To evaluate the corrosion resistance of painted/plated parts exposed to an acid solution simulating sweat. Parts are placed in a perspiration chamber that consist of a stand supporting the parts over a large glass jar containing acid solution. Parts are inspected daily for amounts of corrosion for a period of seven days. Parts are then compared to good control parts to determine amount of corrosion present.
- *Cable and Cable Assembly Flex:* To insure that any cable that would normally be subjected to random twisting motion under tension will meet field requirements. Cable flex test equipment provides for two independent motions: rocking motion and rotation, and twisting motion and rotation. Cables not meeting flex life specification are considered a failure.
- *Sequential Shipping:* To evaluate the packaging effectiveness and mechanical integrity of the product under simulated shipping conditions. This test is used for all Shure products. Products packaged for shipping are given the following tests, in order: drop test, vibration test, rough handling test. When the product is removed from its packaging, it must appear and operate as new. If appropriate, an electrical test is performed and compared to initial electrical test data.
- *Cartridge Drop and Scrape Test:* To determine ability of stylus to withstand accidental drops and side impacts. A cartridge mounted in a tonearm is dropped onto a moving record at least 100 times. The cartridge is scraped across a moving record 100 times. This test simulates and exceeds any abuse given to the cartridge and stylus in normal use.
- *Temperature Storage:* To determine ability to withstand extreme temperatures for extended periods of time. Initial performance data are taken. For high temperature, the product is placed in a preheated high temperature chamber for seven days. The product is allowed to stabilize at room temperature for 24 hours and then the same performance data are taken. For low temperature, the product is placed in a low temperature chamber for seven days, allowed to stabilize to room temperature for 24 hours, and tested.

By performing these and other rigorous tests, Shure consistently meets its goal of exceeding customers' product performance and reliability expectations.

Key Issues for Discussion

1. Describe how the definition of reliability presented in this chapter applies to the performance tests described here. Do these tests measure inherent reliability or achieved reliability?
2. For the examples of product testing provided in this case, discuss what quality/reliability measurements might be taken and how the data might be analyzed. For example, are the measurements attributes or variables? Would they be analyzed using descriptive statistics, Pareto charts, and so on?

Quality in Practice

Software Quality Assurance at Los Alamos National Laboratory[11]

A quality assurance program was created at Los Alamos National Laboratory to develop software that contained fewer defects and was more maintainable and flexible while also speeding program development. During management planning sessions, objectives were defined that would help produce a quality product, including developing methods for optimizing software maintainability, flexibility, and reliability; facilitating the creation of an environment in which these goals can be accomplished; and monitoring improvement over time. The software features selected for optimization were the ones causing the most problems and therefore representing the greatest opportunity for payoff.

To assure true quality, the quality assurance program was fully integrated into the development process. The program included a structure for project planning, peer reviews of software products, availability of current sets of standards and guidelines, cost-effective testing procedures, accurate measurements of actual effort, and reliable project estimating tools.

Effective product reviews were the most significant element of the quality assurance process. Peer reviews, commonly called *walkthroughs*, consisted of the developer's presentation of the product to a small group of peers to discover errors or potential defects. The results and actions taken during a walkthrough were formally recorded and sent to the developers after the review. Further walkthroughs were scheduled until no defects could be found.

Management decided that the standards to be used had to be current and easily accessible. Before development of the quality assurance program, standards manuals sat unopened and gathering dust, mostly because the methods in the manuals rarely conformed with the way business was normally conducted. The effort involved in writing, editing, and printing such a manual almost guaranteed that a significant portion of the contents would be obsolete before publication. The solution was to enter and update all guidelines and standards using computerized word-processing equipment, with read-only access to all software development personnel.

Traditional software quality assurance programs typically emphasize testing the operation of software in an actual computing environment, which is commonly called *machine testing*. Machine testing uncovers symptoms of problems, not the causes. Unlike the walkthrough process, no amount of machine testing can provide a cure for poorly designed and written computer programs. Dynamic testing is not 100 percent effective for uncovering all possible symptoms of problems, since all possible paths through a program are never exercised in testing. Thus, many problems occur when the program is actually used.

The plan developed at Los Alamos called for taking machine testing out of the hands of developers by creating a separate testing group and rewarding the members on the basis of the number of programs they could break. Testing teams were made responsible for creating test beds as well as for testing programs using live data. Performance evaluations were geared to finding the best new methodologies for testing.

During preliminary management discussions of the plan, management recognized that when projects are estimated accurately from the beginning, quality assurance can be built into the development schedule, allowing a more maintainable, flexible, and reliable product to be delivered. This ability also addressed the problem of budget and schedule slips, which contributed to quality assurance deterioration. An automated estimating system would generate accurate estimates from historical data.

True quality assurance at Los Alamos is achieved by developing reliable methods to detect and remove defects early in the development process and by measuring the actual quality of finished products. By integrating the program into the development process, the entire staff is responsible for producing a quality product, and the program can be accepted by the software organization as a whole.

Key Issues for Discussion

1. Describe the approach used by Los Alamos National Laboratory to assure the quality and reliability of its software.
2. Does the use of the separate testing group conflict with TQ principles? Why or why not?

Summary of Key Points

- Reliability is the probability that a product, piece of equipment, or system performs its intended function for a stated period of time under specified operating conditions.
- Failures in products include functional failure at the start of product life and reliability failure after some period of use.
- Inherent reliability is the predicted reliability determined by the design of the

product or process, and achieved reliability is the actual reliability observed during use.

- Reliability is measured by the number of failures per unit time, called the failure rate. The reciprocal of the failure rate is the mean time to failure (MTTF), or for repairable items, the mean time between failures (MTBF).
- The product life characteristics curve shows the instantaneous failure rate at any point in time. These curves are used to determine design and testing policies as well as for developing warranties.
- The probability of survival as a function of time is called the reliability function, and typically is modeled using an exponential distribution. Reliability functions of individual components can be used to predict reliability for complex systems of series, parallel, or series-parallel configurations.
- Reliability engineering involves techniques such as standardization, redundancy, failure physics, various testing methods, failure mode and effects analysis, and fault tree analysis.
- Reliability management includes the consideration of customer performance requirements, economic factors, environmental conditions, cost, and analysis of field data.
- Reliability in computer software is a difficult, but important issue. Many techniques have been developed to help ensure reliability in software.

Review Questions

1. What is the importance of reliability and why has it become such a prominent area within the quality disciplines?
2. Define reliability. Explain the definition thoroughly.
3. What is the difference between a functional failure and a reliability failure?
4. What is the definition of failure rate? How is it measured?
5. Explain the differences and relationships between the cumulative failure rate curve and the failure rate curve. How is the average failure rate over a time interval computed?
6. Explain the product life characteristics curve and how it can be used.
7. What is a reliability function? Discuss different ways of expressing this function.
8. Explain how to compute the reliability of series, parallel, and series-parallel systems.
9. What is reliability engineering? Briefly discuss some of the major techniques of reliability engineering.
10. Describe different forms of product testing.
11. What does the term *latent defect* mean?
12. Explain the purpose of failure mode and effects analysis and fault tree analysis.
13. What should be included in an effective reliability management program?
14. Discuss the importance of reliability in computer software. Why is it difficult to achieve?
15. What is configuration management? How is it used in quality assurance for software?
16. What is maintainability? Discuss the principal design issues related to it.
17. Discuss the two definitions of availability. What are the differences between them?

PROBLEMS

1. Given the cumulative failure curve in Figure 13.12, sketch the failure rate curve.
2. Compute the average failure rate during the intervals 0 to 30, 30 to 70, and 70 to 100, based on the information in Figure 13.12.
3. The life of a watch battery is normally distributed with a mean of 1,500 days and standard deviation of 60 days.
   a. What fraction of batteries is expected to survive beyond 1,600 days?
   b. What fraction will survive fewer than 1,350 days?
   c. Sketch the reliability function.
   d. What length of warranty is needed so that no more than 10 percent of the batteries will be expected to fail during the warranty period?
4. Treadlife, Inc., makes automobile tires that have a mean life of 50,000 miles with a standard deviation of 4,000 miles.
   a. What fraction of tires is expected to survive beyond 53,500 miles?
   b. What fraction will survive fewer than 42,000 miles?
   c. Sketch the reliability function.
   d. What length of warranty is needed so that no more than 10 percent of the tires will be expected to fail during the warranty period?
5. Compute the failure rate for six transformers that were tested for 400 hours each, three of which failed after 80, 100, and 320 hours.
6. A test of 10 items is conducted for 1,000 hours. Three items fail at 40, 225, and 752 hours. What is the failure rate?
7. Assuming an exponential distribution, a particular light bulb has a failure rate of 0.002 unit per hour. What is the probability of failure within 400 hours? What is the reliability function?
8. An electrical component has a reliability of 0.95 over 1,500 hours of normal use. What is the failure rate? What fraction will survive after 300, 500, and 1,000 hours?
9. Find the mean time to failure (MTTF) for the data in problems 5 and 6.
10. A piece of equipment operated for 3,000 hours and experienced three failures. What is the MTTF?

Figure 13.12 Cumulative Failure Curve

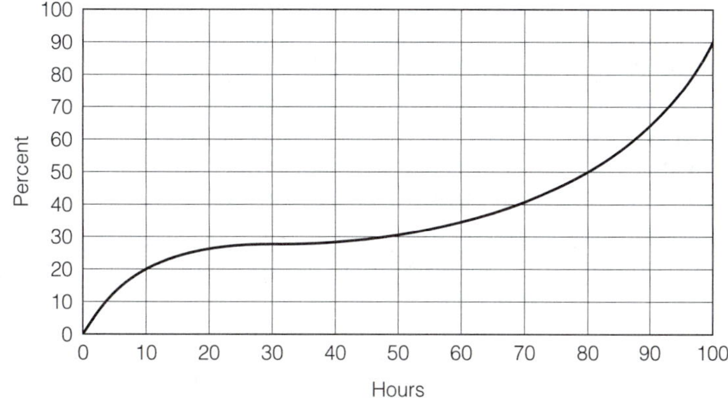

11. The MTBF of a circuit is 1,000 hours. Calculate the failure rate.
12. The MTBF for an Internet service provider's Web server unit is normally distributed with a mean of 180 days and a standard deviation of 10 days. Each failure costs the company $750,000 in lost computing time and repair costs. A shutdown for preventive maintenance can be scheduled during nonpeak times and will cost $500,000. As the manager in charge of computer operations, you are to determine whether a preventive maintenance program is worthwhile. What is your recommendation based on a 1% probability of failure? A 0.5% probability of failure? Assume 365 operating days per year.
13. Refer to the failure data for the equipment maintenance example in Table 13.3. What preventive maintenance period would you recommend if the preventive maintenance cost were $60 and the average costs for an equipment failure were $40? How many breakdowns a year should you expect under your preventive maintenance program?
14. For a particular piece of equipment, the probability of failure during a given week is as follows:

Week of Operation	Probability of Failure
1	0.25
2	0.08
3	0.07
4	0.10
5	0.20
6	0.30

Management is considering a preventive maintenance program that would be implemented at the end of a given week of production. The production loss and downtime costs associated with an equipment failure are estimated to be $2,500 per failure. If it costs $500 to perform the preventive maintenance, when should the firm implement the preventive maintenance program? What is the total maintenance and failure cost associated with your recommendation, and how many failures can be expected each year? Assume 52 weeks of operation per year.
15. An electronic missile guidance system consists of the following components:

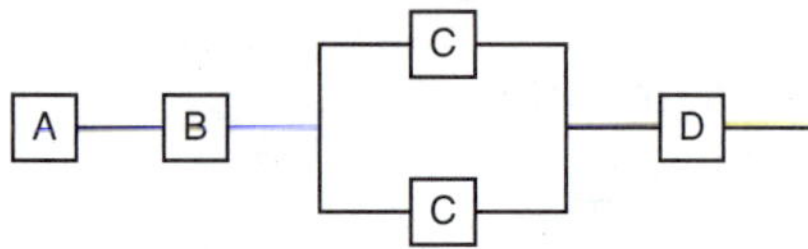

Components A, B, C, and D have reliabilities of 0.97, 0.98, 0.95, and 0.99, respectively. What is the reliability of the entire system?
16. In the previous problem, if A and B only have a reliability of 0.93 each, while C and D have reliabilities of .99, how does this change your answer?
17. A manufacturer of portable radios purchases major electronic components as modules. The reliabilities of components differ by supplier. Suppose that the configuration of the major components is given by

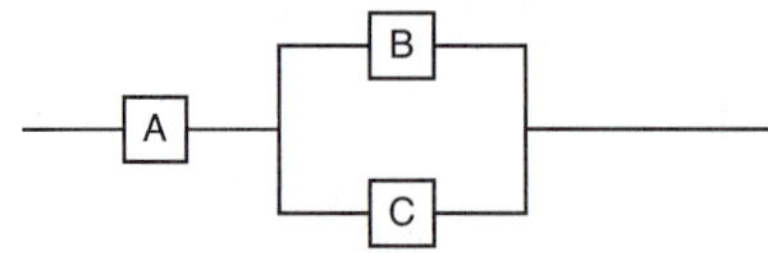

The components can be purchased from three different suppliers. The reliabilities of the components are as follows:

Component	Supplier 1	Supplier 2	Supplier 3
A	.95	.92	.94
B	.80	.86	.90
C	.90	.93	.85

Transportation and purchasing considerations require that only one supplier be chosen. Which one should be selected if the radio is to have the highest possible reliability?

18. In a complex manufacturing process, three operations are performed in series. Because of the nature of the process, machines frequently fall out of adjustment and must be repaired. To keep the system going, two identical machines are used at each stage; thus, if one fails, the other can be used while the first is repaired (see accompanying figure). The reliabilities of the machines are as follows:

Machine	Reliability
A	.75
B	.85
C	.95

a. Analyze the system reliability, assuming only one machine at each stage.
b. How much is the reliability improved by having two machines at each stage?

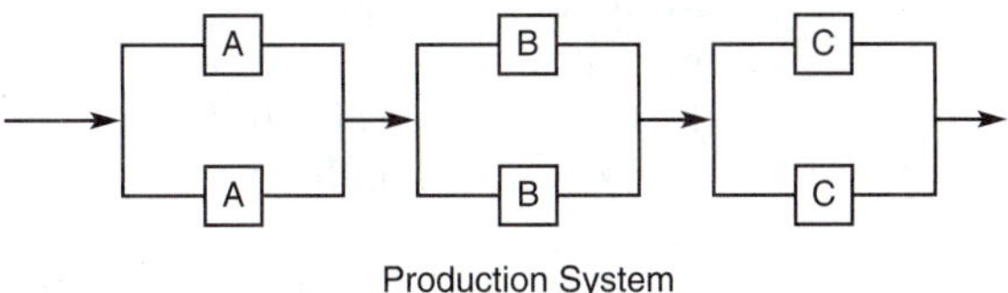

Production System

19. An automated production system consists of three operations: turning, milling, and grinding. Individual parts are transferred from one operation to the next by a robot. Hence, if one machine or the robot fails, the process stops.
    a. If the reliabilities of the robot, turning center, milling machine, and grinder are 0.98, 0.95, 0.98, and 0.93, respectively, what is the reliability of the system?
    b. Suppose that two grinders are available and the system does not stop if one fails. What is the reliability of the system?
20. Military radar and missile detection systems are designed to warn a country of enemy attacks. A system reliability question deals with the ability of the detection system to identify the attack and perform the warning correctly. Assume that a particular detection system has a 0.98 probability of detecting a missile attack.
    a. What is the reliability of the system?
    b. Assume that two detection systems are installed in the same area and that the system operates satisfactorily if at least one of the two detection systems performs correctly. Assume that the probability of detecting an attack is 0.98 for each system. What is the reliability of the two systems?

CASE

AUTOMOTIVE AIR BAG RELIABILITY[12]

Automotive air bags are designed to protect passengers from frontal or near-frontal crashes of about 12 to 14 mph. Sensors are placed on a structural member in the front of the vehicle or in the passenger compartment. The sensor sends a signal to inflate the air bag, which takes about 1/30 second. The bag then quickly deflates. Air bags have significantly improved automotive safety. The Insurance Institute for Highway Safety noted that during 1985–1992, air bags helped reduce deaths by 24 percent. By 1994 air bags were deployed approximately 200,000 times.

One important design question is the reliability of air bags. Two manufacturers set a reliability goal of at least 0.9999. An air bag system has three essential elements: a sensor, an actuating mechanism, and an inflating air bag. Three types of sensors—mechanical, electromechanical, and electronic—are in use. The all-mechanical sensor (AMS) is the simplest. The basic mechanism is shown in Figure 13.13. A steel ball in a tube or cylinder detects the deceleration of a crash. As the ball moves forward in the tube, it is resisted by a bar on a pivot. The other end of the bar is loaded by a bias spring. As the bar moves, it rotates two shafts that move off the edge of spring-loaded firing pins. The pins (called sear pins) stab dual primers, igniting a charge of boron potassium nitrate, which in turn ignites a compound of sodium azide, which then releases nitrogen gas. The gas is filtered and cooled, inflating the bag. The cover (e.g., on the steering wheel) splits open to allow the bag to inflate without damage. Figure 13.14 shows a block diagram of the system with reliability values of the individual components over a 10-year operating life.

Electromechanical sensor systems (EMS) also use a ball-in-tube or ball/cylinder mechanism. The ball is held in place by a magnet instead of a spring. When deceleration occurs, the ball overcomes the magnetic retention forces and travels forward until it touches two electrical contacts, closing a switch that sends current from the battery (or a large capacitor if the battery fails) to heat a bridgewire in a pyrotechnic squib, which then ignites a mixture contained in the squib cavity. The heat ignites a charge of sodium azide, producing nitrogen gas to inflate the bag. This system also

Figure 13.13 AMS Air Bag Sensor

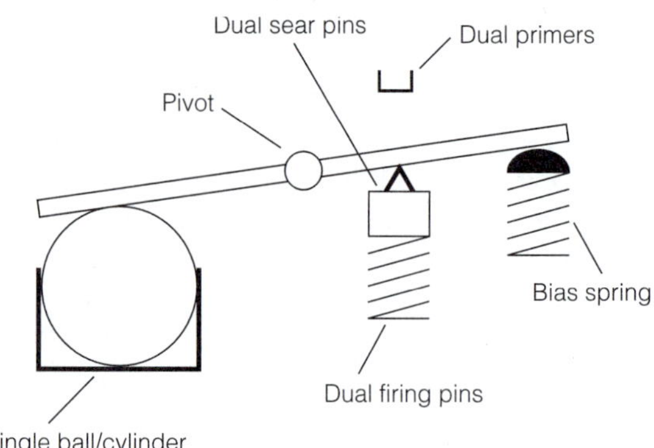

has an arming sensor that prevents unwanted deployment. The electrical portion of the system is monitored by a diagnostic module to pinpoint an electrical failure if it occurs. Figure 13.15 shows this system and some engineering estimates of the reliability of various system components.

The third type of design is an electronic sensor system (ES). Without delving into the details of its operation, which are somewhat more complex than the others, Figure 13.16 shows the system diagram and reliability values.

Discussion Questions

1. What is the role of the dual actuators in the mechanical air bag system? Describe the effect of having only one.
2. Compute the reliabilities of each system. What conclusions do the data suggest?
3. The following table lists some engineering calculations of system reliabilities for each type of system over time when repairability is taken into account. Plot these data on a graph. What do the data suggest?

System	Year 5	10	15	17
AMS	0.999844	0.999716	0.999588	0.999537
EMS	0.999870	0.999759	0.999648	0.999604
ES	0.999190	0.998494	0.997799	0.997521

Figure 13.14 AMS Sensor Block Diagram

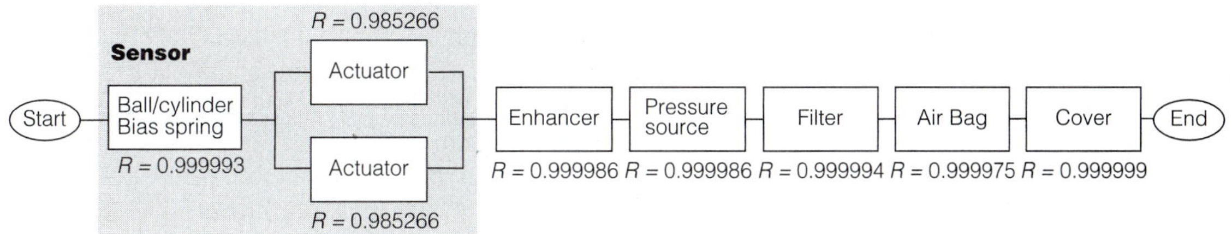

Figure 13.15 EMS Sensor Reliability Diagram

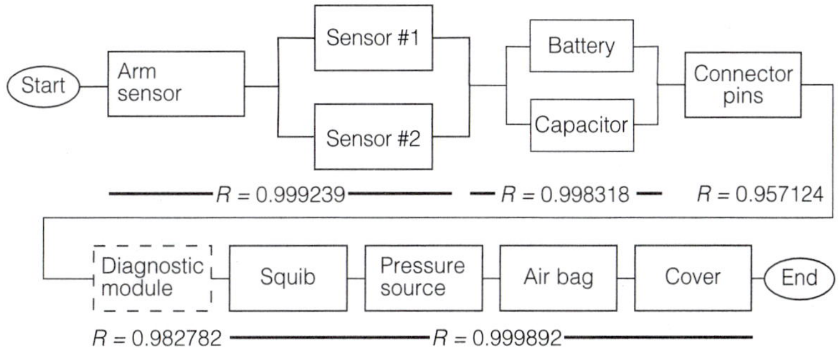

Figure 13.16 ES Sensor Reliability Diagram

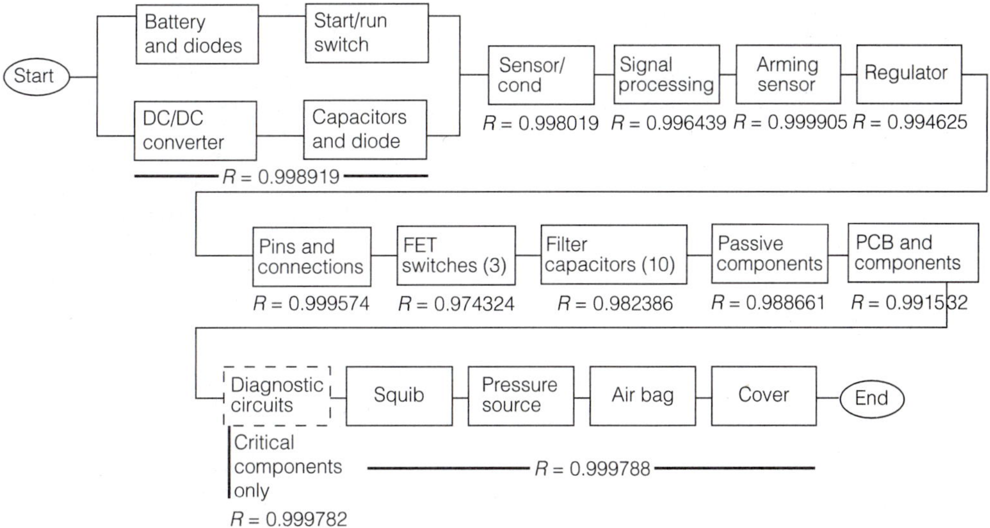

NOTES

1. *Reliability Guidebook*, The Japanese Standards Association (Tokyo: Asian Productivity Organization, 1972), 4.

2. W. H. Blevel, "Management Science's Impact on Service Strategy," *Interfaces* 6, no. 1, pt. 2 (November 1974), 4–12.

3. Keith Denton, "Reducing DOAs (and other Q.C. Problems)," *P&IM Review with APICS News* (December 1989), 35–36.

4. Denton, see note 3.

5. Peter G. Neumann, "Some Reflections on a Telephone Switching Problem," *Communications of the ACM* 33, no. 7 (1990), 154.

6. Jonathan Jacky, "Risks in Medical Electronics," *Communications of the ACM* 33, no. 12 (1990), 138.

7. "How Did We Get in This Mess, Anyway?" sidebar in Peter Mandel, Peter Coy, and Paul C. Judge, "Zap! How the Year 2000 Bug Will Hurt the Economy," *Business Week*, March 2, 1998, 96.

8. G. G. Gustafson and R. J. Kerr, "Some Practical Experience with a Software Quality Assurance Program," *Communications of the ACM* 25, no. 1 (January 1982), 4–12. © 1982, Association for Computing Machinery, Inc.

9. Edward J. Joyce, "Is Error-Free Software Achievable?" *Datamation*, February 15, 1989, 53, 56.

10. Appreciation is expressed to Christine Schyvinck, vice president of Operations, Shure, Inc., for providing this case (October 2000).

11. Adapted from John Connell and Linda Brice, "Practical Quality Assurance," *Datamation*, 1 March, 1985, 106–114. © 1985 by Cahners Publ. Co.

12. Adapted from Howard Frank, "Automotive Air Bag Reliability," Source: *Reliability Review* ISSN 0277-9633, 14, no. 3 (September 1994), 11–22. Published for Reliability Division, ASQ by Williams Enterprises.

BIBLIOGRAPHY

Bernstein, Amy. "Putting Software to the Test." *Business Computer Systems*, December 1984, 48–51.

Buck, Carl N. "Improving Reliability." *Quality*, February 1990, 58–60.

Chowdhury, A. R. "Reliability as It Relates to QA/QC." *Quality Progress* 18, no. 12 (December 1985), 27–30.

Halpern, S. *The Assurance Sciences, an Introduction to Quality Control and Reliability*. Upper Saddle River, NJ: Prentice Hall, 1978.

Juran, J. M., and F. M. Gryna. *Quality Planning and Analysis*, 2d ed. New York: McGraw-Hill, 1980.

Lawrence, Joseph D., Jr. "Semiconductor Quality Considerations," *Quality*, December 1983, 39–41.

Posedel, Rhea J. "Burn-in: The Way to Reliability." *Quality*, August 1982, 22–23.

Singh, B. P. "Reliability, Availability, and Maintainability Program in a Metal Processing Facility." *Proceedings, AIIE 1978 Spring Annual Conference*. Norcross, GA: American Institute of Industrial Engineers, 1978.

Smith, Charles O. *Introduction to Reliability in Design*. New York: McGraw-Hill, 1976.

PART 4

THE QUALITY ORGANIZATION

The concluding section of this book consists of only one chapter—Building and Sustaining Quality Organizations. It is fitting to conclude the book with this chapter, because total quality needs to be viewed as one system that integrates both the managerial system and the technical system. Building a TQ organization necessitates a systems view and the development of a culture that provides the motivation and direction for everyone in the organization to work toward the organization's vision. It requires an understanding of how organizations learn and share best practices.

Fundamentally, it is important to recognize that quality is a journey that must be sustained. As both managers and workers enter and leave the organization, TQ requires constant renewal. This chapter also looks toward the future; as you read it, we hope that you also look toward your future and what these principles will mean to the rest of your lives.

CHAPTER 14

BUILDING AND SUSTAINING TOTAL QUALITY ORGANIZATIONS

OUTLINE

At the Seventh Annual National Conference on Federal Quality in July 1994, 12-year-old Kelly Potter addressed the luncheon crowd of 2,000 participants.[1] Kelly's elementary school in Nazareth, Pennsylvania, participates in Koalaty Kid, a program sponsored by the American Society for Quality, which promotes teaching of quality principles in elementary schools (see Chapter 2). Her message was not earthshaking. She thanked her family and school system members for their support and discussed how quality improvement techniques were used in her school for such things as cafeteria operations and homework assignments. She even applied these techniques to prepare her speech. The audience exploded with a standing ovation. Brad Stratton, past editor of *Quality Progress*, observed, "I don't think they were applauding her verbal message, as much as her nonverbal message which was this: Hey people! This stuff is so simple that kids can do it! Kids!"

The principles of total quality—focus on the customer, involve everyone, and continuously improve—are simple to understand and represent common sense. Yet many companies have experienced great difficulty in implementing total quality and even deciding whether to do it. This difficulty often results from some common misconceptions, such as that TQ means doing lots of "things" like collecting data and organizing teams, or that it only applies to large companies. A total quality strategy does, however, require significant changes in organization design, processes, and culture. Such broad change has been a stumbling block for many companies.

Building and sustaining a TQ organization requires a readiness for change, the adoption of sound practices and implementation strategies, and an effective organization. In this concluding chapter we reflect on many of the concepts discussed throughout this book, and describe what it takes to create a TQ culture and sustain it through learning and sharing best practices.

MAKING THE COMMITMENT TO TQ

A survey of manufacturing firms cited the top three obstacles to TQ implementation among companies that do not have a TQ effort as

1. Lack of a strong motivation
2. Lack of time to devote to quality initiatives
3. Lack of a formalized strategic plan for change[2]

The motivation to adopt a TQ philosophy usually stems from one of two basic sources:

1. A firm reacts to competition that poses a threat to its survival by turning to TQ.
2. TQ represents an opportunity to improve.

Most firms—even Baldrige Award winners—have moved toward total quality because of the first reason. Xerox, for example, watched its market share fall from 80 percent to 13 percent in a little more than a decade (see the *Quality in Practice* case in Chapter 1); Milliken faced increased competition from Asian textile manufacturers; Zytec Corporation found itself in financial difficulties because of reliance on a single customer. Although not facing dire crises, perceived future threats were the impetus for FedEx, Solectron, and Wainwright. When faced with a threat to survival, an organization effects change more easily; under these circumstances, they generally implement TQ quickly and smoothly. However, an organization will generally have more difficulty in gaining support for TQ, or any significant change for that matter, when not facing a crisis. This reluctance is a reflection of the attitude "If it ain't broke, don't fix it." Unfortunately, complacency today often leads to crises tomorrow. Leaders with foresight view TQ as an opportunity to get better, and to maintain or enhance existing market leadership positions. In such cases, one might even attempt to manufacture a crisis mentality to effect change.[3]

When organizations cite a lack of time as the reason for not pursuing TQ, one often finds that the organization has plenty of time to correct errors, rework defective product, and waste time in complex processes that have resulted from years of inefficiency. They do not recognize the Crosby philosophy that "Quality Is Free." In most cases, lack of time is simply an excuse for not wanting to devote the effort necessary to pursue TQ or failure to understand the benefits that can result. The third reason—lack of a change process—also is typically the result of a lack of discipline and a firefighting mentality. We will address organizational change extensively in this chapter.

As we noted in Chapter 5, leadership is the most essential ingredient for success.[4] But gaining commitment from top executives is not easy. As one quality director noted, "It's a hard sell if management is not predisposed. . . ." Dale Crownover, CEO of Texas Nameplate Company, believes the best way to sell quality to top executives is to show them where money is being lost due to absenteeism, downtime, not having procedures in place, lack of job descriptions, and poor training. Other quality managers note the importance of viewing quality as an integrated part of the business, and showing that quality projects are good for business, for example, demonstrating the return on quality that we discussed in Chapter 8. Interviews with Baldrige winners suggest 10 ways to sell the TQ concept:

1. Learn to think like top executives who are paid, after all, to satisfy the concerns of three key groups of stakeholders: customers, investors, and employees.
2. Position quality as a way to address the priority goals of these three groups of stakeholders.
3. Align your objectives with those of senior management. If the organization's goal is to reduce cycle time, show how your program will reduce cycle time. If the goal is to increase market share, show how your plan will do that.
4. Make your arguments as quantitative as possible.
5. When approaching top management, make your first pitch to someone who is likely to be sympathetic to your proposal.
6. Focus on getting an early win, even if it is a small one.
7. Be sure your efforts won't be undercut by corporate accounting policies that may exaggerate the costs of quality or fail to recognize its full financial benefits.
8. Develop allies—both those who are internal and can lend credibility to your position and those who are external and can tell how quality improved the bottom line at their organizations.
9. Develop metrics for return on quality (see Chapter 8), so you can show that your efforts are paying off.
10. Never stop selling quality.

CREATING A TQ CULTURE AND IMPLEMENTING A TQ STRATEGY

Any organizational activity can be viewed in one of three ways, depending on the intensity of commitment to the activity:

1. *Function:* a task or group of tasks to be performed that contribute to the mission or purpose of an organization
2. *Process:* a set of steps, procedures, or policies that define how a function is to be performed and what results are expected
3. *Ideology:* a set of values or beliefs that guide an organization in the establishment of its mission, processes, and functions

Many managers view quality as a set of tasks to be performed by specialists in quality control or individuals in their particular jobs. Other managers have a broader perspective and see quality as a process in which many people at the operating level from a number of functional areas of the organization are involved in cross-functional activities. Still other managers take the broadest viewpoint in which quality is an ideology or philosophy that pervades and defines the culture of the entire organization. For TQ to truly succeed, it must define the culture of the organization.

A corporate culture is a company's value system and its collection of guiding principles. A survey conducted by the Wyatt Company, a Washington, D.C., consulting firm, found that the barriers to change cited most often were employee resistance and "dysfunctional corporate culture"—one whose shared values and behavior are at odds with its long-term health.[5] An example of a dysfunctional culture is a high-tech company that stresses individual rewards while innovation depends on teamwork. To change their management practices, organizations must first address their fundamental values.

Cultural values are often seen in the mission and vision statements of organizations (see Chapter 5). For example, it is not unusual to see statements like "We will continuously strive to improve the level of quality in all our products" or "Teamwork is essential to our mutual success" in corporate mission and vision statements. Culture is a powerful influence on behavior because it is shared widely and because it operates without being talked about, and indeed, often without being thought of.

Culture is reflected by the management policies and actions that a company practices.[6] Therefore, organizations that believe in the principles of total quality are more likely to implement the practices successfully. Conversely, actions set culture in motion. Behavior leads people to think in certain ways. Thus, as total quality practices are used routinely within an organization, its people learn to believe in the principles, and cultural changes can occur.

A concise summary of the principles on which modern, high-performing TQ organizations are built and managed is given in the set of *Core Values and Concepts* that form the basis for the Baldrige criteria.

- Visionary Leadership
- Customer-Driven Excellence
- Organizational and Personal Learning
- Valuing Employees and Partners
- Agility
- Focus on the Future
- Managing for Innovation
- Management by Fact
- Public Responsibility and Citizenship
- Focus on Results and Creating Value
- Systems Perspective

These values must become a living, breathing part of the organization's culture. They often are embodied in the strategies and leadership philosophies of major organizations. For example, the total quality philosophy at Procter & Gamble focuses on delivering superior consumer satisfaction and boils down to four principles:[7]

- Really know our customers and consumers. Know those who resell our products and those who finally use them—and then meet and exceed their expectations.
- Do right things right. This requires hard data and sound statistical analysis to select the "right things" and to direct continual improvement in how well we do those things.
- Concentrate on improving systems. In order to achieve superior customer and consumer satisfaction and leadership financial goals, we must continually analyze and improve the capability of our basic business systems and subsystems.
- Empower people. This means removing barriers and providing a climate in which everyone in the enterprise is encouraged and trained to make his or her maximum contribution to business objectives.

The P&G Statement of Purpose captures the "what," "how," and expected "results" of their quality efforts.

> We will provide products of superior quality and value that best fill the needs of the world's consumers.
>
> We will achieve that purpose through an organization and a working environment which attracts the finest people; fully develops and challenges our

> individual talents; encourages our free and spirited collaboration to drive the business ahead; and maintains the Company's historic principles of integrity, and doing the right thing.
>
> Through the successful pursuit of our commitment, we expect our brands to achieve leadership share and profit positions so that, as a result, our business, our people, our shareholders, and the communities in which we live and work, will prosper.

A similar philosophy is described by the American Express Quality Leadership approach. The fundamental beliefs about quality that provide the philosophical underpinnings and guide decision making at American Express are

- Quality is the foundation of continued success.
- Quality is a journey of continuous improvement and innovation.
- Quality provides a high return, but requires the investment of time and resources.
- Quality requires committed leadership.
- Quality begins by meeting or exceeding the expectations of customers and employees.
- Quality requires teamwork and learning at all levels.
- Quality comes from the energy of a diverse community of motivated and skilled people who are given and take responsibility.

Of course, it is easy to make bold statements like these; making them "real" requires a significant cultural change in many organizations.

Cultural Change

To understand some of the issues associated with changing an organization's culture to a TQ philosophy, it is useful to reflect on the principal differences that distinguish TQ from traditional management practices, many of which we have addressed in earlier chapters. Many traditional practices stem from the fundamental structure of U.S. business, which derives from the Adam Smith principles of division of labor in the eighteenth century and their reinforcement during Frederick Taylor's scientific management era.[8] Even though they were quite appropriate in their time and contributed to past economic success, the principles no longer suffice. Japan, by contrast, built its management system on the teachings of Deming, Juran, Drucker, and other modern business philosophers, whose focus relied on fundamental TQ principles. A clear understanding of these differences can help to avoid many of the problems that firms face when trying to implement TQ, as well as defining the changes necessary to establish a TQ culture. Some of these key differences are described in the following list.[9]

- *Organizational structures:* Traditional management views an enterprise as a collection of separate, highly specialized individual performers and units, linked within a functional hierarchy. Lateral connections are made by intermediaries close to the top of the provinces. TQ views the enterprise as a system of interdependent processes, linked laterally, over time, through a network of collaborating (internal and external) suppliers and customers. Processes are connected to the enterprise's mission and purpose, through a hierarchy of micro and macro processes. Every process contains subprocesses and is itself contained within a higher order process. This structure of processes is repeated throughout the hierarchy.
- *Role of people:* Traditional management views people as a commodity, virtually interchangeable, and to be developed based on the perceived needs of the enterprise. People are passive contributors, with little autonomy, doing what they

are told and nothing more. TQ views people as the enterprise's true competitive edge. Leadership provides people with opportunities for personal growth and development. People take joy and pride through learning and accomplishment, and enhance the capability of the enterprise to succeed. People are active contributors, valued for their creativity and intelligence. Every person is a process manager, presiding over the transformation of inputs to outputs of greater value to the enterprise and to the consumer.

- *Definition of quality:* In traditional management, quality is the adherence to internal specifications and standards. The absence of defects, therefore, defines quality. Inspection of people's work by others is necessary to control defects. Innovation is not required. In TQ, quality is defined in a positive sense as products and services that go beyond the present needs and expectations of customers. Innovation is required.
- *Goals and objectives:* In traditional management, the functional provinces are a zero-sum game in which there must be a loser for every winner. People do not cooperate unless it serves their own or their unit's best interests. Parochialism is a fact of business life. In TQ, self-interest and the greater good are served simultaneously by serving one's customers. Everyone wins or no one wins. Cooperation takes the place of competition.
- *Knowledge:* In traditional management, quality embodies knowledge applicable only to manufacturing and engineering. In TQ, quality embodies knowledge applicable to all the disciplines of the enterprise. All levels of management and the workforce must, as Deming often said, "learn the new philosophy."
- *Management systems:* In traditional management, managers oversee departments or functions or collections of individuals. The pieces do not know they are interdependent. They each act as if they are the whole. Quality problems occur when individual people or departments do not do their best. In TQ, managers oversee interdependent systems and processes and exercise managerial leadership through participative management. Their roles are to act as mentors, facilitators, and innovators. Quality results from the enterprises' systems and individuals working together. People working in the system cannot do better than the system allows (recall the Red Bead experiment in Chapter 9). The majority of problems are prevented and improvement promoted when people understand how they fit in, and have the knowledge to maximize their contribution to the whole system. Only management can create an environment that nurtures a team-oriented culture, which focuses on problem prevention and continuous improvement.
- *Reward systems:* In traditional management, performance appraisal, recognition, and reward systems place people in an internally competitive environment. This environment reinforces individualism to the detriment of teamwork. In TQ, reward systems recognize individual as well as team contributions and reinforce cooperation.
- *Management's role:* Once the organization has found a formula for success it is reluctant to change it. Management's job, therefore, is to maintain the status quo by preventing change. In TQ, the environment in which the enterprise interacts constantly changes. If the enterprise continues to do what it has done in the past, its future performance, relative to the competition, will deteriorate. Management's job, therefore, is to provide the leadership for continual improvement and innovation in processes and systems, products, and services. External change is inevitable, but a favorable future can be shaped.
- *Union-management relations:* In traditional management, the adversarial relationship between union and management is inevitable. The only area for nego-

tiation lies in traditional issues, such as wages, health, and safety. In TQ, the union becomes a partner and a stakeholder in the success of the enterprise. The potential for partnership and collaboration is unlimited, particularly in the areas of education, training, and meaningful involvement of employees in process improvement.

- *Teamwork:* In traditional management, hierarchical "chimney" organization structures promote identification with functions and tend to create competition, conflict, and adversarial relations between functions. In TQ, formal and informal mechanisms encourage and facilitate teamwork and team development across the entire enterprise.
- *Supplier relationships:* In traditional management, suppliers are pitted against each other to submit the lowest price. The more suppliers competing against each other, the better it is for the customer company. In TQ, suppliers are partners with their customers. Partnership aims to encourage innovation, reduce variation of critical characteristics, lower costs, and improve quality. Reducing the number of suppliers and establishing long-term relationships helps to achieve this aim.
- *Control:* In traditional management, control is achieved by preestablished inflexible responsive patterns laid down in the book of rules and procedures. People are customers of the "book," which prescribes appropriate behaviors. In TQ, control results from shared values and beliefs, as well as knowledge of mission, purpose, and customer requirements.
- *Customers:* In traditional management, customers are outside the enterprise and within the domain of marketing and sales. In TQ, everyone inside the enterprise is a customer of an internal or external supplier. Marketing concepts and tools can be used to assess internal customer needs and communicate internal supplier capabilities.
- *Responsibility:* In traditional management, the manager's job is to do the subordinates' planning, and inspect the work to make sure the plans are followed. In TQ, the manager's job is to manage his or her own process and relationships with others and give subordinates the capability to do the same through empowerment. The manager must be a coach and facilitator rather than a director.
- *Motivation:* In traditional management, motivation is achieved by aversive control. People are motivated to do what they do to avoid failure and punishment, rather than contribute something of value to the enterprise. People are afraid to do anything that would displease their supervisor or not be in compliance with company regulations. The system makes people feel like losers. In TQ, managers provide leadership rather than overt intervention in the processes of their subordinates, who are viewed as process managers rather than functional specialists. People are motivated to make meaningful contributions to what they believe is an important and noble cause and of value to the enterprise and society. The system enables people to feel like winners.
- *Competition:* In traditional management, competition is inevitable and inherent in human nature. In TQ, competitive behavior—one person against another or one group against another—is not a natural state. Instead, competitive behavior seeks to improve the methods for pleasing the customer, eliminating waste of nonrenewable resources, or preventing passing on to future generations a damaged planet, incapable of sustaining human life.

One powerful example of cultural change is the case of Wainwright Industries, which has been cited several times in previous chapters.[10] During the 1970s and 1980s, Wainwright lost millions in sales; operations slowed to three days a week; and tensions grew between employees and management. Recognizing that the problem lay with management, the CEO made some radical changes. Workers were called "associates," and everyone was put on salary. Associates are paid even if they miss work and still receive time-and-a-half for overtime. The company has maintained a higher than 99 percent attendance since this change. Managers shed their white shirts and ties, and everyone from the CEO down wears a common uniform, embroidered with the label Team Wainwright. A team of associates developed a profit-sharing plan, whereby everyone receives the same bonus every six months. Everyone has access to the privately held company's financial records. In addition, all reserved parking spaces were removed; walls—including those for the CEO's office—were replaced with glass. Customers, both external and internal, are treated as partners, with extensive communication. The most striking example occurred when one worker admitted having accidentally damaged some equipment, even though most workers were afraid to report such incidents. The CEO called a plantwide meeting and explained what had happened. Then he called the man up, shook his hand, and thanked him for reporting the accident. Reporting of accidents increased from zero to 90 percent, along with suggestions on how to prevent them. As we noted in Chapter 6, Wainwright's culture can be summed up as a *sincere belief and trust in people.*

Impatient managers often seek immediate cultural change by adopting off-the-shelf quality programs and practices, or by imitating other successful organizations. In most cases, this canned approach is setting up for failure. Joshua Hammond of the American Quality Foundation urges business leaders in the United States to develop approaches that maximize their own cultural strengths. A successful quality strategy needs to fit within the existing organization culture, which is the reason the Baldrige Award criteria are nonprescriptive. No magic formula works for everyone. At Zytec, for instance, Deming's 14 Points were chosen as the cornerstone of the company's quality culture. Zytec established a Deming Steering Committee to guide the Deming process, championed individual Deming Points, and acted as advisor to three Deming Implementation Teams. Motorola, on the other hand, invited numerous consultants. In the end, the company decided to develop its own quality approach that fit its needs.

One study of Baldrige Award winners concluded that each has a unique "quality engine" that drives the quality activities of the organization.[11] These individual strengths are summarized in Table 14.1. This table does not suggest that all other aspects of TQ are ignored; they are not. The quality engine customizes the quality effort to the organizational culture and provides focus.

Implementation Barriers

Numerous barriers exist to successfully transforming organizations to a sustained culture of total quality. One reason for TQ failure is a lack of what Deming called "constancy of purpose" in his first version of the 14 Points. The people who implement quality initiatives often have conflicting goals and priorities. For example, the general manager of a large defense electronics contractor unveiled a big quality program, then plunged into dealing with the unit's plummeting revenues and layoffs. Quality went nowhere. Changes in leadership can be devastating. At Florida Power and Light (see the *Quality in Practice* in Chapter 3), John J. Hudiburg drove hard to win the Deming Prize, but his successor reduced the scope of the quality effort.[12] Other organizations continually try to implement the latest fads, only to disband them after a short time in favor of something else. This inconsistency causes an incredible amount of cynicism on the part of the workforce. An organization must have a clear understanding of why it is embarking on a TQ effort and must stay focused for the long haul.

Table 14.1 Quality Engines of Baldrige Award Recipients

Company	Quality Engine	Focus
IBM Rochester	Market-driven quality	Customer needs early in the planning and design process
Motorola	Process control	Defect prevention; Six-Sigma quality
Cadillac	Product development	Integrating manufacturing and design, and partnering with customers and suppliers
Xerox	Benchmarking	Competitive and best-in-class benchmarks
FedEx	Technology	Using technology to speed processes and improve customer service
Milliken	Employee empowerment and involvement	Self-managed teams and active participation of employees in all aspects of the business
Zytec	Strategic planning	Involvement of cross-functional teams, customers, and suppliers in the planning process
Westinghouse	Management by data and facts	Use of measurements to track and improve quality

Another reason for failure is the lack of a holistic view of quality. (The term *Total* in TQ is there for a reason!) Many approaches to "implementing quality" are one-dimensional and consequently prone to failure. For example, some firms emphasize the use of quality tools such as statistical process control, but may only deploy them in a narrow part of the organization such as manufacturing. These firms will see some improvement, but because the entire organization is not involved, success will be limited. Others take a problem-solving approach in which defects in both production and customer service are identified and corrected through quality circles or other team approaches. However, they may ignore customer relationship management processes or strategic planning issues. Again, improvements will be achieved, but they will be sporadic and limited. By essentially delegating quality to front-line employees, management demonstrates a lack of leadership, which will not create the sustained culture required for longevity. A third approach might emphasize design, but ignore many potential means for continuous process improvement. Total quality requires a comprehensive effort that encompasses all of the elements discussed in this book thus far. What is really required is a total change in thinking, not a new collection of tools. A focus on tools and techniques is easy; what is hard is understanding and achieving the changes in human attitudes and behavior that are necessary. We have seen this holistic theme throughout the book as we discussed the "three levels of quality"—individual, process, and organization—all of which are necessary to define a true TQ organization. The level to which an organization has evolved reflects its maturity in developing a TQ culture. Although it is easy to train individuals to perform quality tasks, it is certainly more difficult to establish cross-functional cooperation and to build the entire organization around a TQ framework.

Another danger lies in the lack of understanding cultural issues and the tendency to imitate others—the easy way out. Many of the experts and consultants have rewritten total quality management around their own discipline, such as accounting, engineering, human resources, or statistics. The "one best model" of TQ may not mesh with an organization's culture; most successful companies have developed their own unique approaches to fit their own requirements. Research has shown that imitation of TQ efforts made by one successful organization may not lead to good results in another. To go back to Deming, no knowledge is possible without theory, or to use one of his more descriptive phrases, "There is no instant pudding."

Perhaps the most significant failure encountered in most organizations is a lack of alignment between components of the organizational system. The importance of systems as one of Deming's components of Profound Knowledge cannot be overemphasized. In the Baldrige criteria, **alignment** is defined as consistency of plans, processes, actions, information, decisions, results, analysis, and learning to support key organizationwide goals. Effective alignment requires common understand of purposes and goals and use of complementary measures and information for planning, tracking, analysis, and improvement at each of the three levels of quality. A well-aligned organization has its processes focused on achieving a shared vision and strategy. Aligning the organization is a challenging task that is accomplished through a sound strategy and effective deployment. The most damaging alignment problem to which many TQ failures have been attributed is the lack of alignment between expectations that arise from TQ change processes and reward systems. In one survey, an overwhelming percentage (65.8 percent) of managers surveyed ranked the number one barrier to TQ as "Management's compensation is not linked to achieving quality goals."[13] Although we addressed this issue in Chapter 6, ignoring the "What's in it for me?" question can destroy, and has in numerous cases destroyed, any TQ effort.

Certain mistakes are made repeatedly.[14] Some of the more common mistakes include the following:

1. TQ is regarded as a "program," despite the rhetoric that may state the contrary.
2. Short-term results are not obtained, causing management to lose interest—often either no attempt is made to get short-term results, or management believes that measurable benefits lie only in the distant future.
3. The process is not driven by a focus on the customer, a connection to strategic business issues, and support from senior management.
4. Structural elements in the organization block change—such as compensation systems, promotion systems, accounting systems, rigid policies and procedures, specialization and functionalization, and status symbols such as offices and perks.
5. Goals are set too low. Management does not shoot for stretch goals or use outside benchmarks as targets.
6. The organizational culture remains one of "command and control" and is driven by fear or game playing, budgets, schedules, or bureaucracy.
7. Training is not properly addressed. Too little training is offered to the workforce or it may be of the wrong kind, such as classroom training only or a focus on tools and not problems. Training must be matched to strategy and business needs so as not to be viewed as frivolous.
8. The focus is mainly on products, not processes.
9. Little real empowerment is given and is not supported in actions.
10. The organization is too successful and complacent. It is not receptive to change and learning, and clings to the "not invented here" syndrome.
11. The organization fails to address three fundamental questions: Is this another program? What's in it for me? How can I do this on top of everything else?

12. Senior management is not personally and visibly committed and actively participating.
13. An overemphasis on teams for cross-functional problems leads to the neglect of individual efforts for local improvements.
14. Employees operate under the belief that more data are always desirable, regardless of relevance—"paralysis by analysis."
15. Management fails to recognize that quality improvement is a personal responsibility at all levels of the organization.
16. The organization does not see itself as a collection of interrelated processes making up an overall system. Both the individual processes and the overall system need to be identified and understood.

Even though this list is extensive, it is by no means exhaustive. It reflects the immaturity that many companies exhibit when trying to implement TQ. TQ requires a new set of skills and learning, including interpersonal awareness and competence, teambuilding, encouraging openness and trust, listening, giving and getting feedback, group participation, problem solving, clarifying goals, resolving conflicts, delegating and coaching, empowerment, and continuous improvement as a way of life.[15]

The process must begin by creating a set of feelings and attitudes that lead to lasting values and organizational commitment. It must develop by planning a long-term TQ strategy. Finally, it must be realized through training, continuous feedback and open communications, and empowerment.

Building on Best Practices

The organizational infrastructure, as evidenced by an organization's management systems and practices, is vital to successful TQ implementation. Designing an effective infrastructure requires (1) an understanding of best practices, and (2) a process for continuous evolution toward high-performance management practices.

Research performed in 1992 by H. James Harrington with Ernst & Young and the American Quality Foundation, called the International Quality Study (IQS), suggested that trying to implement all the best practices of world-class organizations may not be a good strategy.[16] In fact, implementing the wrong practices can actually hurt the organization. The study indicated that only five best practices are "universal," and even then, a company faces a 5 percent chance that these practices may not improve its performance. They are:

1. Cycle-time analysis
2. Process value analysis
3. Process simplification
4. Strategic planning
5. Formal supplier certification programs

Beyond these, best practices depend on a company's current level of performance. Three measures of performance are ROA (return on assets: after-tax income divided by total assets), which is a measure of profitability; VAE (value added per employee: sales less the costs of materials, supplies, and work done by outside contractors), a measure of productivity; and quality, as measured by an external customer satisfaction index.

Low performers—those with less than 2 percent ROA and $53,000 VAE (in 1996 dollars), and low quality—can reap the highest benefits by concentrating on fundamentals. These fundamentals include departmental and cross functional teamwork, training in customer relationships, problem solving and suggestion systems, using internal customer complaint systems for new product and service ideas, emphasizing cost reduction when acquiring new technology, using customer satisfaction measures in strategic planning, increased training for all levels of employees, and focusing quality strategy on "building it in" and "inspecting it in." Among those things that low performers should *not* do is use quality as a basis for senior management assessment, use world-class benchmarking or benchmarking marketing and sales processes, rely on surveys to obtain feedback from customers, emphasize empowerment, and remove quality control inspection.

Medium performers—those with ROA from 2 to 6.9 percent, VAE between $53,000 and $84,000, and medium quality levels—achieve the most benefits from promoting department-level improvement teams, training employees in problem solving and other specialized topics, listening to supplier suggestions about new products, emphasizing the role of enforcement for quality assurance, making regular and consistent measurements of progress and sharing quality performance information with middle management, and emphasizing quality as a key to the company's reputation. Medium performers should not emphasize quality and team performance in assessing senior management, increase training in general knowledge subjects, use cross-functional teams or teams with customers on them to create design specifications, shift primary responsibilities for compliance with quality standards away from the quality assurance function, or select suppliers based on their general reputation.

High performers—with ROA exceeding 6.9 percent, VAE over $84,000, and high quality levels respectively—gain the most from providing customer-relationship training for new employees, emphasizing quality and teamwork for senior management assessment, encouraging widespread participation in quality meetings among nonmanagement employees, using world-class benchmarking, communicating strategic plans to customers and suppliers, conducting after-sales service to build customer loyalty, and emphasizing competitor comparison measures and customer satisfaction measures when developing plans. Practices that could get these firms into trouble include increasing participation in department-level improvement teams, focusing technology on production processes, relying on customer surveys as a primary input for improvement, and using cross-functional teams with customers on them to create design specifications.

Strangely, the IQS Best Practices Report has been interpreted by some news media as a criticism of TQ.[17] They translate the report as simply saying that many quality practices are a waste of time and ineffective. On the contrary, the results are the first significant effort to develop a prescriptive theory (back to Deming again) of TQ implementation, rather than relying on intuition and anecdotal evidence. This viewpoint is similar to the contingency approaches in motivation and leadership theory and contradicts the notion of one magic quick fix for quality. Rather, companies advance in stages along a learning curve in their application of TQ and must carefully design their programs to optimize its effect.

This discussion suggests that an organization should begin with a critical self-assessment of where it stands. Such assessment identifies strengths and areas for improvement and determines what practices will yield the most benefit. At a minimum, a self-assessment should address the following:

- *Management involvement and leadership:* To what extent are all levels of management involved?
- *Product and process design:* Do products meet customer needs? Are products designed for easy manufacturability?

- *Product control:* Is a strong product control system in place that concentrates on defect prevention before the fact rather than defect removal after the product is made?
- *Customer and supplier communications:* Does everyone understand who the customer is? To what extent do customers and suppliers communicate with each other?
- *Quality improvement:* Is a quality improvement plan in place? What results have been achieved?
- *Employee participation:* Are all employees actively involved in quality improvement?
- *Education and training:* What is done to ensure that everyone understands his or her job and has the necessary skills? Are employees trained in quality improvement techniques?
- *Quality information:* How is feedback on quality results collected and used?

Many self-assessment instruments that provide a picture of the state of quality in the organization are available.[18] Most self-administered surveys, however, can only provide a rudimentary assessment of an organization's strengths and weaknesses. The most complete way to assess the level of TQ maturity in an organization is to evaluate its practices and results against the Malcolm Baldrige National Quality Award criteria by using trained internal or external examiners, or by actually applying for the Baldrige or a similar state award and receiving comprehensive examiner feedback. Understanding one's strengths and opportunities for improvement creates a basis for evolving toward higher levels of performance. Of course, many companies, especially smaller firms, that are just starting on a quality journey should begin with the basics, for example, a well-documented and consistent quality assurance system such as ISO 9000, which was discussed in Chapter 3.

The Role of Employees

Three key players for successful TQ implementation are senior management, middle management, and the workforce. Each plays a critical role. Senior managers must ensure that their plans and strategies are successfully executed within the organization. Middle managers provide the leadership by which the vision of senior management is translated into the operations of the organization. In the end, the workforce delivers quality and, for TQ to succeed, must feel not only empowerment, but ownership.

Senior Management Many organizations today find themselves in a leadership vacuum because the environment has changed more rapidly than they ever imagined. Their leadership styles have not kept pace, and they find themselves falling back on approaches that were "good enough" for their predecessors, but frequently inadequate today.

In an extensive research project, Henry Mintzberg studied managers who had formal authority and defined 10 managerial roles that leaders must play.[19] These roles were (1) figurehead, (2) leader, (3) liaison, (4) monitor, (5) disseminator, (6) spokesperson, (7) entrepreneur, (8) disturbance handler, (9) resource allocator, and (10) negotiator. Mintzberg pointed out that the importance of each role is contingent on the environmental and organizational factors that face managers who must lead. These contingencies include the industry or environmental surroundings of the organization, its age and size, the organizational level at which the leader operates, and the part of the organization (e.g., operating core, technostructure, or support structure) in which the leader resides. For example, in a pharmaceutical firm, where government regulation and the need for constant protection of the "ethical" quality image abounds, the top management leader must spend a tremendous amount of time as figurehead, liaison, and spokesperson. In a small, family-owned foundry with a history of labor unrest, the CEO would tend to spend much more time as entrepreneur, disturbance handler, and negotiator in order to develop a quality product and image.

Senior managers' responsibilities include the following tasks:

1. Ensure that the organization focuses on the needs of the customer.
2. Cascade the mission, vision, and values of the organization throughout the organization.
3. Identify the critical processes that need attention and improvement.
4. Identify the resources and trade-offs that must be made to fund the TQ activity.
5. Review progress and remove any identified barriers.
6. Improve the macroprocesses in which they are involved, both to improve the performance of the process and to demonstrate their ability to use quality tools for problem solving.[20]

These responsibilities require a commitment of time that is often perceived to take away from other duties. However, if senior managers recognize that quality management is simply good business management, then they are less likely to encounter conflict.

Middle Management Leonard Sayles, a veteran leadership consultant and researcher, observed that middle managers have traditionally not been expected to be leaders, but to be guardians of generally approved management principles (GAMP).[21] GAMP rests on time-honored assumptions and practices:

- Clear and fixed work goals and technology
- Relying on centralized specialist groups
- Focusing on numbers, such as meeting budgeted targets
- Being as autonomous as possible and ignoring the work system
- Delegating as much as possible and managing solely by results
- Compartmentalizing people issues and technology issues

Sayles suggests that GAMP no longer works. The principles were probably effective in simple, stable organizations and the business environment of 30 or 40 years ago; however, critical leadership roles in today's rapidly changing business environment involve coordination, technology development, system and process integration, and continuous improvement. Coordination involves ensuring that strategies and plans are actually carried out at the operating levels of the firm. In the past, employees required direction in the form of precise instructions on what to do and how to do it. Today, managers find themselves monitoring progress, disseminating information and suggestions between local and distant line staff and outside experts, and acting as a spokesperson inside and outside the firm. Technology development requires that managers constantly scan the environment to be aware of technological developments that may threaten or enhance the operations of the company. System and process integration means optimizing the system to meet strategic goals such as customer service, and using tools of quality measurement and continuous improvement.

Middle management has been tagged by many as a direct obstacle to creating a supportive environment for TQ.[22] Because of their position in the company, middle managers have been accused of feeding territorial competition and stifling information flow. They have also been blamed for not developing or preparing employees for change. Middle managers appear to be threatened by continuous improvement efforts, making them unwilling to take initiatives that contribute to continuous improvement. However, middle management's role in creating and sustaining a TQ culture is critical. Middle managers improve the operational processes that are the foundation of customer satisfaction. They can make or break cooperation and teamwork; and they are the principal means by which the remaining workforce prepares for change.

Transforming middle managers into change agents requires a systematic process that dissolves traditional management boundaries and replaces them with an empowered and team-oriented state of accountability for organizational performance. This process involves the following elements:

1. *Empowerment:* Middle managers must be accountable for the performance of the organization in meeting objectives.
2. *Creating a common vision of excellence:* This vision is then transformed into critical success factors that describe key areas of performance that relate to internal and external customer satisfaction.
3. *New rules for playing the organizational game:* Territorial walls must be broken, yielding a spirit of teamwork. Today's managers must assume the role of coach. One new approach is "interlocking accountability" in which managers are accountable to one another for their performance. The second is "team representation" in which each manager is responsible for accurately representing the ideas and decisions of the team to others outside the team.
4. *Implementing a continuous improvement process:* These projects should improve their operational systems and processes.
5. *Developing and retaining peak performers:* Middle managers must identify and develop future leaders of the organization.

Middle managers must also exhibit behaviors that are supportive of total quality, such as listening to employees as customers, creating a positive work environment, implementing quality improvements enthusiastically, challenging people to develop new ideas and reach their potential, setting challenging goals and providing positive feedback, and following through on promises. These changes are often difficult for middle managers to accept. The perceived threats from an empowered workforce, which often lead to flatter organizations, are indeed serious issues that organizations must tackle.

The Workforce If total quality does not occur at the workforce level, it will not occur at all. The workforce implements quality policies. This task requires ownership. Ownership goes beyond empowerment; it gives the employee the right to have a voice in deciding what needs to be done and how to do it.[23] It is based on a belief that what is good for the organization is also good for the individual, and vice versa. At Westinghouse, workers define ownership as "taking personal responsibility for our jobs . . . for assuring that we meet or exceed our customers' standards and our own. We believe that ownership is a state of mind and heart that is characterized by a personal and emotional commitment to approach every decision and task with the confidence and leadership of an owner." Self-managed teams, discussed in Chapter 6, represent one form of ownership.

Increased ownership requires increased sharing of information with the workforce and a commitment to the workforce in good times and in bad. As we discussed earlier in this chapter, Wainwright Industries develops trust and belief in each associate. Its continuous improvement process involves everyone and is associate-driven. Although Wainwright cannot guarantee a job for life, its commitment to job security is based on the philosophy that the training and development Wainwright gives to its employees makes them highly employable and marketable, even if the company should suffer financial hardship. With such commitments, the company can more easily develop the loyalty and commitment needed within the workforce as they jointly strive to apply the principles of total quality.

Union-Management Relations A major stumbling block in the United States in implementing TQ has been the traditional adversarial relationship between unions and management.[24] For example, in 1986 General Motors introduced a team concept for quality improvement in Van Nuys, California, which just barely passed a union membership vote with only 53 percent in support. Since then, the opposition has worked to oppose the concept. In many cases, management must share the responsibility in working with unions as equal partners. Both union and management have important roles in TQ.

Labor's role is, first, to recognize the need for changing its relationship with management and then to educate its members as to how cooperation will affect the organization. This information includes what its members can expect, and how working conditions and job security might change. Labor must carefully select members for such a program and maintain a positive attitude. TQ initiatives must be separated from collective bargaining.

Management must realize that the skills and knowledge of all employees are needed to improve quality and meet competitive challenges. Management must be willing to develop a closer working relationship with labor and be ready to address union concerns and cultivate trust. Both sides should receive training in communication and problem-solving skills. Union and management should have equal representation in committees. External consultants can provide an important role as facilitators and mediators in such efforts.

SUSTAINING THE QUALITY ORGANIZATION

Getting started often seems easy compared to sustaining a quality focus. Numerous organizational barriers and challenges get in the way. New efforts usually begin with much enthusiasm, in part because of the sheer novelty of the effort. After a while, reality sets in and doubts surface. Real problems develop as early supporters begin to question the process. At this point, the organization can resign itself to inevitable failure or persist and seek to overcome the obstacles. Sustaining total quality requires viewing quality efforts as a journey, not an end, as well as the ability to develop into a "learning organization."

Quality as a Journey

Successful TQ organizations realize that quality is a never-ending journey. As an old Chinese proverb says, a journey begins with a single step. Perhaps the best way to understand this concept is through an example.[25] In the 1980s, Techneglas, a Columbus, Ohio, producer of glass for television picture tubes, realized that the quality of its products had to be improved to meet the ever-increasing demands of its customers. Although the company trained its employees in SPC during the mid-1980s, the program was short-lived. In 1992, management realized the need for an organized approach for developing SPC, hired an outside consulting firm, and formed a management steering committee. After their first meeting, they realized that the program they were creating had to be much more than SPC, and had to incorporate a broader notion of TQM. Their initial efforts focused around Deming's principles, for example, using SPC to eliminate mass inspection; improving supervision to provide workers with the proper tools, equipment, and processes, and to drive out fear; establishing new education and training programs; and working with suppliers to ensure statistical evidence of product quality. They also established problem-solving teams, and improved communication between top management and the workforce. By 1993, most operating departments were actively involved, a quality mission statement had been issued, pilot SPC projects were in progress, and teams had been created. A quality council consisting of engineers and assistant supervisors from each department was created to move the implementation process a step down from the management steering committee. Each person on the council was responsible for TQM implementation for his or her respective area. The council focused on SPC applications, teams, and standard operating procedures. In 1996, a TQM facilitator was added to the organization, which eventually expanded to a facilitator for each department. Figure 14.1 shows the key steps in their implementation process. By May of 1997, the quality policy had been drafted and more than 300 employees had received SPC training. Fourteen pilot programs were completed or were in progress. By the end of December, more than 100 standard operating procedures had been written. The entire workforce believes that TQM implementation is the key to continued improvement for the future.

Figure 14.1 Techneglas TQM Implementation Model

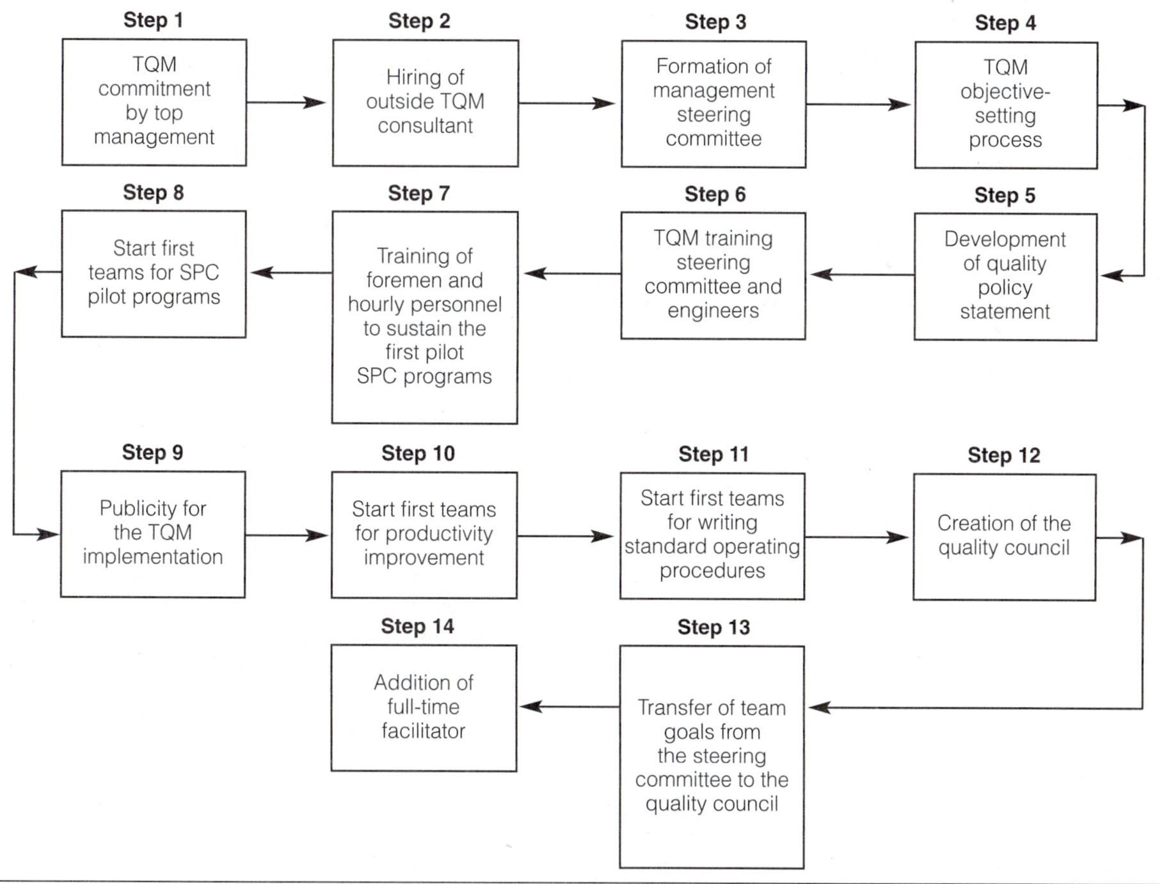

Source: William A. Hines, "The Stops and Starts of Total Quality Management," *Quality Progress,* February 1998, 61–64. ©1998. American Society for Quality. Reprinted with permission.

Even though it is clear that Techneglas has not reached the level of maturity in their management systems as reflected in the Baldrige criteria, they made a serious commitment to the TQ concept and carefully orchestrated a process to make it happen. Surprisingly, or perhaps not, many companies still have not yet made this type of commitment. As the Techneglas example shows, TQ requires discipline, time, and planning just to establish the basics, in which many companies are unwilling to invest.

Many Baldrige-winning companies started from similar humble beginnings. As their systems matured, they discovered the benefits of the Baldrige framework and assessment process as a means for continual improvement. For example, at Armstrong Building Products Operations, the evolution of quality has occurred in several phases since 1983:[26]

Phase I (1983–1985)
Commitment to try
Philip Crosby system
Quality improvement teams

Phase II (1985–1990)
Process improvement
Quality plans added to business plans
Supplier quality management

Phase III (1989–1992)
Vision clearly defined
Empowered employees; flatter organization
Use of Baldrige criteria for self-assessment

Phase IV (1991–1994)
Product and service leadership
Baldrige Award applications (1995 winner)
Business results

Phase V (1994–present)
High-performance change process
"Nonnegotiable" business strategies
Achieving value for employees, customers, shareholders

Similarly, ADAC Laboratories began its TQ approach in 1991 by benchmarking other leading organizations, forming a monthly quality committee, developing a commitment to customer satisfaction, investing in field service, and designing a new strategic planning process.[27] In 1992 ADAC developed its vision, began weekly quality meetings, adopted the Baldrige criteria and conducted a self-assessment, and strengthened quality incentives and rewards. During 1993 the Baldrige criteria were widely deployed, benchmarking was performed in all areas, systematic and comprehensive training programs were started, and quality performance was monitored on a twice-weekly basis. During the next two years, policy deployment (see Chapter 5) was introduced, the ADAC business approach was refined based on TQ and mutual learning principles, the company focused on people-value-added, breakthrough improvement became a priority, and ADAC pursued ISO 9000 registration.

Although the Baldrige Award is not the principal motivator, engaging in the award process can make a difference. Custom Research Incorporated, for example, stated

> *The pursuit [of the Baldrige Award] forced us to improve faster than we would have on our own. As soon as we received the previous year's feed-*

back, we needed to start the current year's application. We were forced to show improvement every year in all aspects of our company. The site visits also motivated our staff. The extensive preparation required for the site visits created tremendous work and tension. But it also created enthusiasm and energy like nothing our company had ever done. . . .We learned from this journey that stubborn persistence does pay off. It paid off for us in both winning the award and in showing us how to improve in order to achieve results. . . . This tremendous opportunity to be reviewed and to receive feedback is one reason we encourage other companies to apply for the Baldrige. Even when we didn't win, it was well worth it. In fact, it was the smartest thing our company ever did. The process of "living under the microscope" proved valuable to our self-awareness. . . . We don't just talk about the Baldrige concept, we implement the principles every day throughout the company. . . . We've actually built an entire company culture around the Baldrige version of performance excellence.[28]

The Learning Organization

Psychologists suggest that individuals go through four stages of learning:

1. *Unconscious incompetence:* You don't know that you don't know.
2. *Conscious incompetence:* You realize that you don't know.
3. *Conscious competence:* You learn to do, but with conscious effort.
4. *Unconscious competence:* Performance comes effortlessly.

As discussed in Chapter 1, many companies in the United States languished in stage 1 until receiving a wake-up call in the 1980s with regard to quality. Unfortunately, as many organizations move into stage 2, they tend to shoot the messenger and refuse to accept their state of incompetence. This attitude can be explained by recognizing that organizations have both static and dynamic components. If organizations exist to structure the work of groups of people, then they must be expected to produce some tangible product or provide some service. The static part of the organization is intended to document, regularize, and maintain the rational requirements for work through relatively stable processes, policies, procedures, rules, and communications on which everyone, at least tacitly, agrees and depends. The static part of an organization thus inherently resists change.

However, organizations are also dynamic entities. Managers must consider the dynamic component in order to deal with instability in the environment, imperfect plans, the need for innovation, and the common human desire for variety and change. The degree of dynamism in organizations is moderated by factors such as culture, leadership, learning, and linkages between people and structures.

Therefore, both the culture and the organizational structure should be designed to support the established direction in which the organization is moving, and modified whenever that direction changes significantly. Managers, especially those who do not understand the nature of leadership, are often hesitant to make needed organizational changes as the organization grows, even when the need for change becomes obvious. This need to change, to move through the four stages of learning repeatedly, is embodied in a concept called **the learning organization**, which we introduced in Chapter 1. In explaining the learning organization, Peter Senge suggests that organizations cannot count on being successful in the long run if they merely have committed leaders who use TQ principles for strategic planning and policy deployment, practice TQ in daily operations, and use it for continuous improvement of the current process. These activities might be called "first generation"

TQ. The key to developing learning organizations, according to Senge, is a new approach to leadership.[29]

Instead of the adaptive approach to learning (first generation TQ), leaders must use a generative approach in which they constantly anticipate the needs of customers to the point of determining what products or services they would truly value but have never experienced and would never think of asking for. Leaders must develop the capability to integrate creative thinking and problem solving throughout the organization. In the words of Walter Wriston, former CEO of Citibank, "The person who figures out how to harness the collective genius of the people in his or her organization is going to blow the competition away." Finally, leaders in learning organizations must help people to restructure their views of reality. Instead of the traditional focus on reacting to events and responding to historical trends, leaders must encourage and model decision making based on understanding the causes of events and the behavior behind the trends in order to make positive changes to the system. Thus, real improvements (second generation TQ) can only be made by understanding the root causes, instead of treating the symptoms.

Garvin criticized Senge and others for not providing an operational framework for implementing a learning organization[30] (something that Senge attempts to correct in another book[31]). Garvin defines the learning organization as

> *. . . an organization that is skilled at creating, acquiring, and transferring knowledge, and at modifying its behavior to reflect new knowledge and insights.*[32]

Interestingly, Garvin observes that simply trying to change and make improvements is not enough. Thus, companies, such as GM, that are trying but failing to make significant changes, have not yet become skilled learning organizations. Also, colleges and universities who know and teach about TQ but don't put the concepts into practice to improve their own teaching, research, and administrative processes, are not exhibiting the characteristics of learning organizations. Companies that are successfully exhibiting the characteristics of learning organizations include L.L. Bean, the Army's Center for Army Lessons Learned and After Action Reviews, Timken, Allegheny Ludlum, and General Electric. Through active management of the learning process, they have become skilled in creating, acquiring, and transferring knowledge and in modifying the behavior of their employees and other contributors to their enterprises.

Garvin points out that learning organizations have to become good at performing five main activities, including "systematic problem solving, experimentation with new approaches, learning from their own experiences and history, learning from the experiences and best practices of others, and transferring knowledge quickly and efficiently throughout the organization."[33] Virtually all of these skills have been defined as TQ terms with the same basic meanings as Garvin suggests:

- Kaizen—continuous quality improvement
- Experimental design
- Santayana review[34]
- Benchmarking
- Dissemination and "holding the gains"

Garvin later raised the important issue of what happens to knowledge when key people leave (retire, die, or move on to other organizations). If knowledge is not widely shared via reports, company intranets, policies and procedures, and face-to-face discussions, it can be easily lost. He states that it must become a part of the organization's norms and values to do such sharing, because it probably is not part of the old style thinking in most organizations, where it is believed that "knowledge is power."

Sitkin and others proposed that a sharp distinction lies between the concepts of what they called "Total Quality Control" (TQC) and "Total Quality Learning" (TQL) approaches (see Table 14.2).[35] They argued that TQC practices applied to the quality precepts of customer satisfaction, continuous improvement, and treating the organization as a system result in a traditional closed cybernetic control system. A closed-loop control system has a standard, a way of measuring actual performance versus the standard, feedback on variances between actual versus standard, and a way to modify the system. The TQL approach, in contrast, applies practices to the precepts in an open-system way that is experimentally oriented, rather than control oriented. The authors argued that the control aspects of TQC are appropriate to stable, routine environments where repetitive operations (such as high-volume manufacturing or service delivery) take place. The environment that contains innovative, highly uncertain operations (such as production of newly designed semiconductors or research and engineering departments) would require a TQL focus that was experimentally oriented and tolerant of mistakes in order to successfully invent new products and approaches. Their theory suggests that TQ implementation practices need to be modified in order to fit various environmental and contextual factors such as stage of the life cycle of the product, industry in which the company operates, and level of education and training of the workforce. Indeed, the Ernst & Young Best Practices report discussed earlier in this chapter confirmed the importance of exploring contingent factors in the implementation of TQ practices.

Organizational learning is considered a fundamental practice in the Baldrige criteria, which defines it as "continuous improvement of existing approaches and processes and adaptation to change, leading to new goals and/or approaches."[36] The criteria view learning as having four distinct stages:

Table 14.2 Linking the Distinctive Principles Associated with TQC and TQL to Common Underlying TQM Precepts

	Principles Derived from Common Precepts	
Shared TQM Precepts	**Control-Oriented Principles (TQC)**	**Learning-Oriented Principles (TQL)**
Customer Satisfaction	Monitor and assess known customer needs Benchmark to better understand existing customer needs Respond to customer needs	Scan for new customers, needs, or issues Test customer need definitions Stimulate new customer need definitions and levels
Continuous Improvement	Exploit existing skills and resources Increase control and reliability	Explore new skills and resources Increase learning and resilience
Treating the Organization as a Total System	First-order learning (cybernetic feedback) Participation enhancement focus	Second-order learning Diversity enhancement focus

Source: Sitkin et al., see note 35.

1. Planning, including the design of processes, selection of measures, and deployment of requirements
2. Execution of plans
3. Assessment of progress, taking into account internal and external results
4. Revision of plans based on assessment findings, learning, new inputs, and new requirements

In the Leadership category, the requirement of Organizational Performance Review compels organizations to provide a picture of their "state of health" and examine how well they are currently performing and also how well they are moving toward the future. This review capitalizes on the information generated from the measurement and analysis of business results and is intended to provide a reliable means to guide both improvement and change at the strategic planning level. It provides a natural linkage among categories 2, 4, and 7 in the criteria as illustrated in Figure 14.2.

As we noted in Chapter 3, many firms use self-assessment against the criteria as a means of identifying and understanding key strengths and opportunities for improvement. Thus, it is not surprising that perhaps the best examples of learning organizations are Baldrige winners. In pursuing their TQ efforts that eventually led to the award, they have continually and systematically translated the examiner feedback into improvements in their management practices. A vice president at Texas Instruments Defense Systems & Electronics (DS&E) Group noted that "participating in the Baldrige Award process energized improvement efforts."[37] By 1997, just before its purchase by Raytheon, DS&E had reduced the number of in-process defects to one-tenth of what they were at the time it won the Baldrige. Production processes that took four weeks several years before were reduced to one week, with costs 20 to 30 percent less.

Figure 14.2 Organizational Learning in the Baldrige Criteria

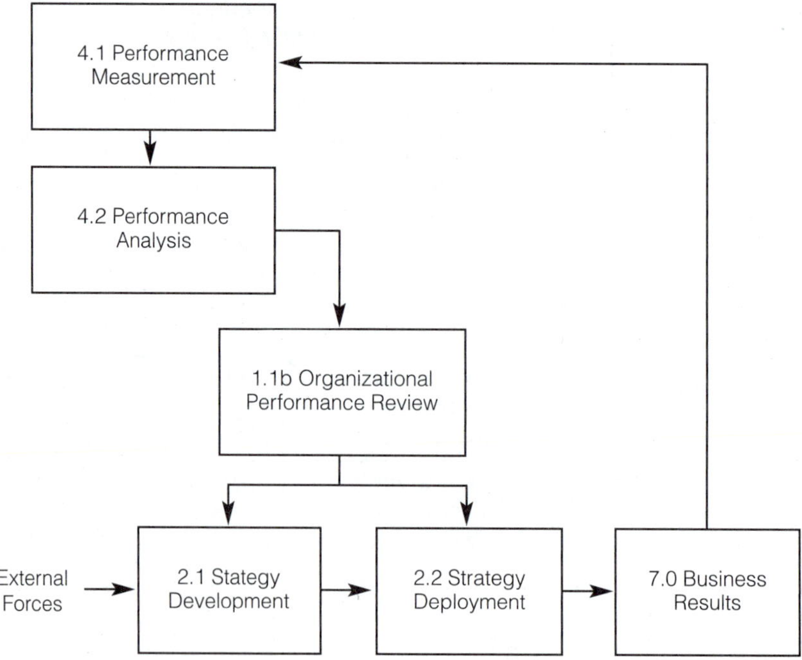

In 1994 the Texas Instruments Corporation launched the TI Business Excellence Standard (TI-BEST), an assessment and improvement process that grew out of DS&E's Baldrige Award experience.[38] The process is applied to TI businesses around the world. The four steps of TI-BEST are:

1. Define business excellence for your business.
2. Assess your progress.
3. Identify improvement opportunities.
4. Establish and deploy an action plan.

This process provides a systematic approach to learning and improvement and benefits the organization by

- Providing a framework that ties efforts together
- Providing a vehicle for identifying best practices
- Providing a structure for sharing knowledge and learning methods and techniques others have used to make improvements
- Allowing employees to speak the same language of quality, thereby increasing communication and organizational alignment toward common goals
- Fostering teamwork across the company
- Improving the ability to measure improvements by documenting processes and results
- Providing a process to accelerate improvement across the organization
- Involving every employee in continuous improvement toward world-class benchmarks.

The complete TI approach to business excellence, displayed on meeting-room walls throughout the organization, is summed up in Figure 14.3. In this model, business excellence is achieved through the three core principles of total quality discussed in Chapter 3. It is supported by a focus on operational excellence through achieving customer satisfaction with processes and teamwork and empowerment (think back to the role of Process Management and Human Resource Focus in the Baldrige framework in Figure 3.6). The approach is implemented by an annual improvement process (Strategic Planning) and measured by a balanced scorecard involving customer, process, HR, and financial measurements and indicators. TI is one of only two semiconductor companies in the world to have gained market share in each of the four consecutive years prior to 1997 and, during that time, has jumped from last place to first in return on net assets, compared to Intel, Motorola, and National Semiconductor.

Solectron's first Baldrige feedback report in 1989 suggested a lack of customer focus and long-range planning. As a result, the company initiated a "customer executive survey" to identify long-term technology and production needs and established a *hoshin kanri* strategic planning process. Since 1991 Solectron Corporation has grown from one site in California employing 2,000 people to 18 sites worldwide employing nearly 20,000 people. In 1997 Solectron became the first repeat winner of the Baldrige Award. Its purpose for reapplying was to "perpetuate that focus on Baldrige compliance worldwide. . . . The big value is moving the discipline up a notch—getting everybody 100-percent involved and having employees see managers implement the quality processes in an even more disciplined fashion."[39] Through its focus on repeated cycles of evaluation and improvement, the Baldrige criteria help organizations develop into true learning organizations. Thus, they provide the means for truly sustaining a quality organization.

Many other companies learn from Baldrige winners. Scott McNealy, CEO of Sun Microsystems, for example, invited three CEOs of Baldrige winners (FedEx,

Figure 14.3 Texas Instruments' Approach to Quality

Office of Best Practices

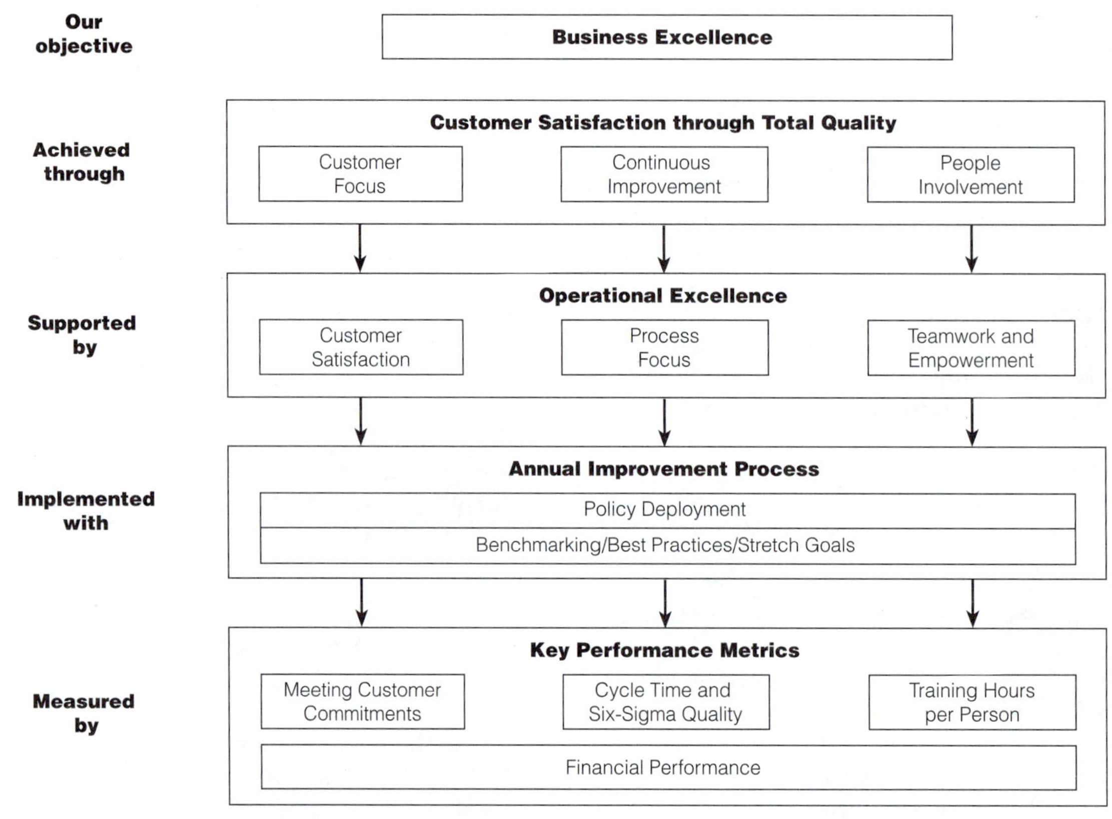

Source: © 1997 American Society for Quality (ASQ). Reprinted with permission.

Motorola, and Xerox) to visit his company to discuss their quality processes. From those meetings came the core principles and strategies that Sun uses today. The key lessons that Sun learned were:

- Quality must be elevated to the level of a "core management process."
- Quality must be the first agenda item of every executive management and board meeting.
- Quality can be managed only if it is measured.
- Quality starts with the employee.
- Achievement in quality must be a factor in compensation.

In explaining this approach, McNealy noted that "Sun was launched as a company in 1982, just about the time that Xerox was starting its Leadership Through Quality process. We wanted to learn as much as we could about what worked and what didn't work before we started solving problems that had already been solved."[40]

Knowledge Management: Sharing Internal Best Practices

Many organizations perform similar activities at different locations or by different people. For example, consider a sales organization with district managers spread out over the country, or a clinical research organization that performs research studies for drug companies in a project environment, or a school district with teachers teaching the same subjects at different locations throughout the district. What happens when one individual develops an innovative practice? How is this knowledge shared among others performing similar jobs? In most organizations, the answer is probably never. A benchmarking study conducted by Arthur Anderson and Co. and the American Productivity and Quality Center reported that 79 percent of managers from the 70 responding companies felt that managing organizational knowledge is central to the organization's strategy, but 59 percent stated that their firm was performing this management function poorly or not at all.[41] Also, 88 percent believed that a climate of openness and trust is important for knowledge sharing, but 32 percent of the respondents believed that their organization did not have such a climate. In many companies, the gap was attributed to a lack of commitment to knowledge management on the part of top managers.

One of the indicators of a true learning organization is the ability to identify and transfer best practices within the organization, sometimes called **internal benchmarking**. It is an area where even the most mature organizations falter, even those that are adept at external benchmarking (see Chapter 10). The American Productivity and Quality Center (APQC) noted that executives have long been frustrated by their inability to identify or transfer outstanding practices from one location or function to another. They know that some facilities have superior practices and processes, yet operation units continue to reinvent or ignore solutions and repeat mistakes.[42] Research has shown that barriers fell into three categories:

1. Lack of motivation to adopt the practice
2. Inadequate information about how to adapt the practice and make it work
3. Lack of "absorptive capacity," the resources and skill to make and manage the change

APQC suggests that although most people have a natural desire to learn and share their knowledge, organizations have a variety of logistical, structural, and cultural hurdles to overcome. These challenges include the following:

- Organizational structures that promote "silo" thinking in which locations, divisions, and functions focus on maximizing their own accomplishments and rewards, or, as Deming called it, suboptimization.
- A culture that values personal technical expertise and knowledge creation over knowledge sharing.
- The lack of contact, relationships, and common perspectives among people who don't work side-by-side.
- An overreliance on transmitting "explicit" rather than "tacit" information—the information that people need to implement a practice that cannot be codified or written down.
- Not allowing or rewarding people for taking the time to learn and share and help each other outside of their own small corporate village.

Internal benchmarking requires a process: first, identifying and collecting internal knowledge and best practices; second, sharing and understanding those practices;

and third, adapting and applying them to new situations and bringing them up to best practice performance levels. Technology, culture, leadership, and measurement are enablers that can help or hinder the process. Many organizations have created internal databases by which employees can share their practices and knowledge. For example, Texas Instruments has a Best Practices Knowledge Base delivered via Lotus Notes, Intranet, and TI's mainframe systems. Information is often organized around business core and support processes. Cultural issues include how to motivate and reward people for sharing best practices and how to establish a supportive culture. As with any TQ effort, senior leadership has to take an active role. This leadership comes through tying initiatives to the company's vision and strategy, communicating success stories at executive meetings, removing implementation barriers, reinforcing and rewarding positive behaviors, leading by example, and communicating the importance of best-practice sharing with all employees. Finally, measuring the frequency of use and satisfaction with best-practices databases, linking practices to financial and customer satisfaction, focusing on cycle time to implement best practices, and measuring the growth of virtual teams that share information are ways in which the organization can monitor the effectiveness of their approaches.

One example of an internal best practice learning process is Royal Mail, the largest business unit within the Post Office Group in the United Kingdom (UK), which handles an average of 64 million letters per day using approximately 160,000 people at 1,900 operational sites throughout the UK.[43] Each potential good practice (a term used to recognize that a practice may not be the best, but is good enough to provide significant performance gains) requires formalized documentation that includes a description of the practice; names and telephone numbers of the contacts; date; process diagram; description of the major steps, who performs them, and what is needed to do the work; implementation resources; and risks and barriers. These practices are scrutinized by a panel for evaluation of their potential for transferability to other parts of the business. The panel characterizes the good practice as either mandatory, where all units and staff are required to adopt it, or recommended, where application is optional, depending on local conditions. Royal Mail uses six measurements for evaluating its approach:

1. The number of potential national good practices reaching national process groups
2. The proportion of national good practices becoming confirmed good practices
3. The extent of implementation
4. The cycle time from first submission to entry in the national database
5. The benefit gained compared to the anticipated benefit
6. Satisfaction from members of the national and business unit process groups

CONCLUSION: A VIEW TOWARD THE FUTURE

In reflecting on quality in the past century, A.V. Feigenbaum and Donald S. Feigenbaum observed:

> *[Quality] has become one of the 20th century's most important management ideas. It has exorcised the traditional business and graduate management school notion that a company's success means making products and offering services quicker and cheaper, selling them hard and providing a product service net to try to catch those that don't work well. It has replaced this notion with the business principle that making products better is the best way to make them quicker and cheaper and that what is done to make quality better anywhere in an organization makes it better everywhere in the organization.*[44]

What the future will hold is never predictable. We face a serious challenge in sustaining the principles of quality amidst the continuing emergence of short-lived management fads, changing leadership driven by pressures of the stock market, e-commerce, and a myriad of other factors. In the January 2000 issue of *Quality Progress*, the American Society for Quality invited 21 individuals to provide comments on quality in the new century.[45] We conclude this book with a sample, and invite you to reflect on what they mean for you as you continue your education and embark on your future careers.

- "Those who understand that quality is derived from effectively managing systems will provide leadership in the new millennium. How many CEOs do you know who arise from the ranks of quality? Few, if any. Yet, I believe tomorrow's business leaders will have deep roots in quality and advanced understanding of how it nourishes their organizations' broader management systems."—Alexander Chong
- "The new millennium presents us with some fundamental challenges:
  - Altered labor markets with higher skill levels, a greater gender balance and increasing diversity.
  - Competitive demands for continuous improvement, customer responsiveness and levels of business excellence which are not price prohibitive.

  These can only be met through an emphasis on quality with equality."—Eileen Drew
- "The 21st century will see leading edge companies apply to information the quality principles successfully applied to manufacturing. This will usher in the next economic revolution—the 'realized' Information Age, created by applying information quality management to information and knowledge processes." —Larry P. English
- "Quality is necessary for public education to thrive in the future. We have a moral imperative to use quality to make a difference in the lives of our children." —Diane Rivers
- "The quality perspective will shape the redefinition of the role of government. This new role will mean serving as a facilitator of relationships and innovative partnerships across all sectors, with less focus on direct delivery of service. Those who understand this context will thrive."—Tina Sung

Finally, Miles Maguire, Editor of *Quality Progress* noted:

> *"In the first 10 seconds of the new century . . . the world will witness the birth of 44 infants . . . by the time a year has passed almost 140 million children will have been born. . . . Consider all the new technologies and products and concepts and ideologies that have taken hold in the last decade: flip phones, fax machines, hip-hop, SUVs, global markets, cyberschooling, eco-tourism, eco-terrorism, extreme sports, e-commerce, gene therapy, streaming media and digital encryption—to name just a few. And now consider how the next decade, the first 1% of the new millennium, will bring at least as great a proliferation of ideas, innovations, and improvements. These developments will set a higher standard of expectations, creating a marketplace with a dizzying diversity of demands that can scarcely be imagined. What will the voice of the 21st century customer be telling us? We'll have to listen carefully to find out."*[46]

Quality in Practice

Xerox 2000: Sustaining Leadership Through Quality[47]

Xerox Corporation's remarkable recovery of global competitiveness was profiled in a *Quality in Practice* in Chapter 1. However, both David Kearns, the CEO who helped to engineer Xerox's successful turnaround, and his successor, Paul Allaire, realized that establishing Leadership Through Quality as part of the corporate culture was only the first critical step in the total quality "race without a finish line."

As Xerox transformed its company vision to "The Document Company" in the early 1990s, it made some radical changes in its organization and leadership system. In addition to changing the organizational structure, Xerox updated the Leadership Through Quality approach that formed the basis for its successful turnaround.[48] In 1994 Allaire outlined the strategy for Xerox 2000. Xerox has used the term *reaffirmation strategy* to emphasize that the company stands firmly behind the basic Leadership Through Quality plan, but that adjustments were needed to broaden the concept from basically a strategic approach to one that better integrates TQ into all aspects of daily business operations. Xerox identified two critical objectives: profitable revenue growth and world-class productivity.

Linking quality to productivity improvement was not part of the initial Leadership Through Quality strategy. Leaders reasoned that team-based quality improvements would inevitably lead to better business results, which proved to be true. However, to remain competitive in the coming years, gradual improvement is not enough; Allaire stated that quantum improvements must be made, and the company is determined to use quality processes to achieve them.

Xerox uses more than 60 specific process improvement initiatives, employee involvement programs, and quality tools to manage its business. It also uses a range of business policies and approaches, quality intensification efforts, and benchmarking. These elements have been integrated into Xerox 2000. To communicate these objectives in a simple manner, Xerox created the Xerox Management Model (see Figure 14.4). The model is a toolbox for all Xerox employees, and

Figure 14.4 Xerox Management Model

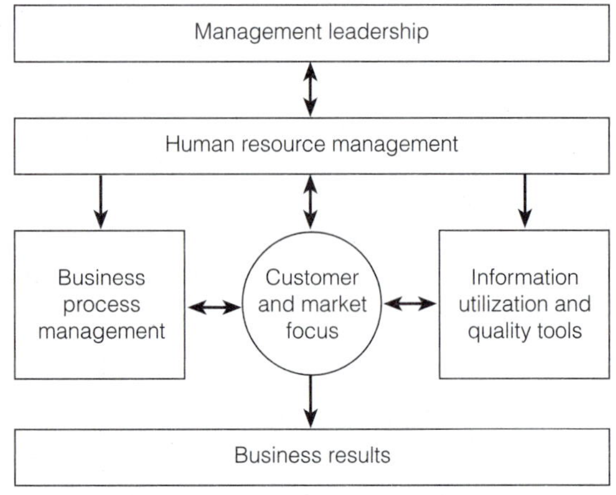

Source: Used with the permission of Richard J. Lee, Xerox Quality Services.

holds everything needed to run the company. It has also been described as a holistic management model because it addresses every aspect of work: planning, creating, leading, managing, changing, organizing, communicating, learning, and rewarding. A description of the six categories follows.

1. *Management leadership.* Xerox management displays a customer focus, exhibits role model behavior, establishes clear long-term goals and annual objectives, establishes strategic boundaries, and provides an empowered environment to achieve world-class productivity and business results.
2. *Human resource management.* Xerox management leads, motivates, develops, and empowers people to realize their full potential. All employees are personally responsible for continuously learning and acquiring competencies required to achieve business objectives and to continuously improve productivity for customers and Xerox.
3. *Business process management.* Business processes are designed to be customer-driven, cross-functional, and value-based.

They create knowledge, eliminate waste, and abandon unproductive work, yielding world-class productivity and higher perceived-service levels for customers.

4. *Information utilization and quality tools.* Fact-based management is led by line management. It is achieved through accurate and timely information and by the disciplined application and widespread use of quality tools.
5. *Customer and market focus.* Current, past, and potential customers define the business. Xerox recognizes and creates markets by identifying patterns of customer requirements. By anticipating and fully satisfying those requirements through the creation of customer value, Xerox achieves its business results.
6. *Business* results. Business results are determined by how well Xerox performs in the first five categories.

The structure of the model mirrors the company's structure. Management leadership is at the top, showing that management commitment and leadership guide all other activities. The arrow leading to and from management leadership emphasizes the importance of open and honest communication with, and feedback from, employees. The remaining components are arranged around customer and market focus. As Allaire explained, "Everything we do begins and ends with the customer." Arrows between the sections represent Xerox's internal and external customers and the markets served.

Allaire expects Xerox employees to use the model to define processes, individual roles, and responsibilities at regular operations reviews; for coaching and training employees; in management meetings; when introducing new business initiatives; for identifying internal benchmarks and best practices; and as the foundation for business assessments and certification. By using the new strategy as its guide, Xerox is preparing its people to grow the company's business results, productivity, and quality performance.

Key Issues for Discussion

1. In what ways is the Xerox Management Model similar to the Baldrige framework? In what ways does it differ?
2. Discuss some of the issues that Xerox would have to face in implementing the new model throughout its vast organization. For example, what types of training might be required? How might computer technology be used in combination with the model?
3. In recent years, Xerox, along with many other "blue chip" companies, has fallen on hard times. Can one place blame on its quality management approaches? How would you respond to such criticism?

Quality in Practice

The Eastman Way[49]

Eastman Chemical Company recognizes that people create quality; this is embodied in a philosophy known as the Eastman Way (see Figure 14.5). The Eastman Way describes a culture based on key beliefs and principles of respect, cooperation, fairness, trust, and teamwork. Developing such a culture depends not only on learning how to recognize and reward behavior, but also understanding the processes and procedures that work against achieving corporate goals.

The wake-up call came in the late 1970s when a key customer told the company that its product was not as good as its competitors' and indicated that if things did not change, Eastman would lose business. Eastman's first realization was that customer feedback was essential to survival. In 1983 the company developed a quality policy; soon after, it began training in statistical process control, flowcharting, and other basic tools. Production employees were encouraged to post their quality results, both good and bad. As one employee stated, "You are asking all of us to post all of our mistakes. How will these things be used?" This clash between the traditional hierarchical, disciplinary organizational culture and the open, honest environment demanded by TQ led to the Eastman Way.

Another key effort started in 1985 was a quality management process that focused on internal

Figure 14.5 The Eastman Way

Eastman people are the key to success. We have recognized throughout our history the importance of treating each other fairly and with respect. We will enhance these beliefs by building upon the following values and principles:

Honesty and integrity. We are honest with ourselves and others. Our integrity is exhibited through relationships with co-workers, customers, suppliers, and neighbors. Our goal is truth in all relationships.

Fairness. We treat each other as we expect to be treated.

Trust. We respect and rely on each other. Fair treatment, honesty in our relationships, and confidence in each other create trust.

Teamwork. We are empowered to manage our areas of responsibility. We work together to achieve common goals for business success. Full participation, cooperation, and open communication lead to superior results.

Diversity. We value different points of view. Men and women from different races, cultures, and backgrounds enrich the generation and usefulness of these different points of view. We create an environment that enables all employees to reach their full potential in pursuit of company objectives.

Employee well-being. We have a safe, healthy, and desirable workplace. Stability of employment is given high priority. Growth in employee skills is essential. Recognition for contributions and full utilization of employees' capabilities promote job satisfaction.

Citizenship. We are valued by our community for our contributions as individuals and as a company. We protect public health and safety and the environment by being good stewards of our products and our processes.

Winning attitude. Our can-do attitude and desire for excellence drive continual improvement, making us winners in everything we do.

Source: "To Be the Best," Eastman Chemical Company publication ECC-67, January 1994. © 1996 American Society for Quality. Reprinted with permission.

and external customers and suppliers and the application of the Deming (PDSA) Cycle. In 1986 senior managers implemented their own quality management process, focusing on understanding customer needs and satisfaction measurements. Later that year the quality focus expanded from individuals to the concept of interlocking teams. (By 1995, 99 percent of employees actively participated in teams.) In 1987 Eastman focused on employee empowerment, and discovered that a company cannot successfully empower employees who don't care, don't have authority, and don't have appropriate skills. Efforts to overcome these obstacles were addressed.

In 1988 Eastman applied for the Baldrige Award, learning a great deal from the site visit and examiners' feedback, and from a Deming seminar attended by 400 managers. In the next year, quality systems were registered to ISO 9000, and Eastman implemented a process, evaluation, control, and improvement system. In 1990 Eastman assessed all of its divisions using the Baldrige criteria. One key improvement made, based on this assessment, was a change in the employee appraisal system, moving from ranking to development. In 1991 Eastman developed its vision: to be the world's preferred chemical supplier. Accomplishing this required measuring performance in many different areas, including customer satisfaction, employee morale, supplier cooperation, and local community support. The company was reorganized from a typical hierarchical structure to a set of strategic business units linked in a hub-and-spoke fashion to the CEO. In 1992 Eastman implemented a supplier recognition program and began helping suppliers in their own quality efforts. In 1993 the company received the Baldrige Award.

During its quality journey, Eastman identified and removed several roadblocks that impede motivation:

- *Fear of losing one's job.* The company promised never to lay anyone off because of quality improvement.
- *The performance appraisal system.* Although those rated near the top complained, it was a clear disincentive to the majority of the workforce.
- *The employee suggestion system.* The original system rewarded individuals with money, which interfered with suggestions for improvements by teams.

To sustain its efforts, Eastman uses seven steps for accelerated continuous improvement.

1. *Focus and pinpoint*. "Focus" is about getting everyone on the same page with regard to goals; "pinpoint" is about specifying in measurable terms what is expected.
2. *Communicate*. Communication is done companywide by publicizing key result areas, the vision, and the mission statement so that employees can answer the questions: What is being improved? Why is it important to the customer, to the company, and to me? What has the management team committed to do to help? And what, specifically, is the company asking me to do?
3. *Translate and link*. Teams translate the companywide objectives into their own language and environment.
4. *Create a management action plan*. Management creates a plan with specific actions to reach a goal, including metrics to measure success. Each team member is asked to know what tasks need to be done, why they are important, and what the team's role is in getting them done.
5. *Improve processes*. Teams use a six-step process similar to those described in Chapter 10.
6. *Measure progress and provide feedback*. Eastman is adamant about the importance of unambiguous, visual feedback to employees and appropriate measures of performance. Eastman's rules include:
   - Feedback should be visual, frequent, simple, and specific.
   - The baseline performance should be shown for comparison.
   - The past, current period, and future goals should be posted.
   - The best-ever score should be posted.
   - A chart should be immediately understandable.
   - A good scorecard allows comments and annotations.
7. *Reinforce behaviors and celebrate results*. Eastman reinforces the learning that leads to positive results by encouraging teams at celebrations to answer the questions: What did you do? Why did it work? Why is it important for the customer, the company, and the team? How did the team accomplish its achievement?

Eastman points out that its formula cannot be blindly followed by others, but must be adapted to the specific corporate culture. Nevertheless, the human principles are universal.

Key Issues for Discussion

1. Trace the development of total quality at Eastman. What lessons can you derive that would be useful to other organizations?
2. How does Eastman exhibit principles of a learning organization?

Summary of Key Points

- Companies adopt TQ to react to competitive threats or take advantage of perceived opportunities. In most cases, threats have provided the incentive to act and change the company's culture. Successful adoption of TQ requires a readiness for change, sound practices and implementation strategies, and an effective organization.
- Gaining commitment for TQ from senior leadership is critical to success, but not easy. Successful strategies for selling the concept include aligning objectives with those of senior management and stakeholder goals, using quantitative arguments such as Return on Quality, developing sympathetic allies, and getting early "wins."
- A corporate culture is a company's value system and collection of guiding principles, and is often reflected in mission and vision statements as well as the management policies and actions that a company practices. The Core Values and Concepts from the Baldrige Criteria are a useful summary of the culture defining a TQ organization.

- Changing the corporate culture is necessary if TQ is to take root in an organization. Change is easier when management has a clear vision, a focus on customers and continuous improvement, strong measurement, cross-functional orientation, and high employee morale. A clear understanding of the differences between TQ and traditional organizations helps define the cultural changes required.
- Organizations encounter numerous barriers to successful implementation. They need to recognize these barriers and avoid the common mistakes that stifle quality efforts, particularly the lack of alignment between components of the organizational system, and ignoring the financial impacts of TQ efforts.
- Designing an effective organizational infrastructure requires an understanding of best practices, a process-oriented quality assurance system, and a process for continuous evolution toward high-performance management practices. Most successful organizations have developed their own unique approaches to implementing TQ.
- Self-assessment provides a starting point to initiate a quality effort. Best practices depend on the level of performance. Low performers must stick to basics such as process simplification, training, and teamwork, while high performers can benefit from benchmarking world-class organizations and using more advanced approaches.
- All employees play a role in TQ implementation. Senior managers must lead the effort and provide resources; middle managers must act as change agents to ensure that strategic goals are met; and the workforce must take personal responsibility for making it happen. Unions must play a part in ensuring the welfare of the organization and work cooperatively with management.
- Quality must be viewed as a never-ending journey. Implementation takes time as well as effort, and organizations must not regard TQ approaches as quick fixes. Organizations must continue to learn and adapt to changing environments. Organizational learning is a key aspect of the Baldrige criteria; thus, it is not surprising that Baldrige winners have demonstrated continual improvement and the ability to change successfully.
- Knowledge management, particularly the sharing of internal best practices (called internal benchmarking), is critical to learning and improvement, yet rarely practiced effectively. Such sharing is inhibited by a variety of logistical, structural, and cultural hurdles.

Review Questions

1. Why do companies decide to adopt TQ? What approach to TQ is more prevalent? Why?
2. Summarize ways by which senior leaders can be sold on the TQ concept.
3. Explain the difference between function, process, and ideology in viewing such organizational activities as TQ.
4. What is corporate culture? How are cultural values reflected in organizations?
5. Explain the term dysfunctional corporate culture. What implications does it have regarding quality?
6. How can an organization develop a TQ-supportive corporate culture?
7. Summarize the differences between a traditional organization and a TQ-focused organization.
8. What lessons can be learned from Wainwright Industries about changing a company's culture?

9. Discuss the barriers to successful TQ implementation. What are some of the common mistakes that organizations make when attempting to implement TQ?
10. Define the term alignment. Of what importance is alignment in successfully implementing TQ?
11. What are the major conclusions and implications of the Best Practices report of Ernst & Young and the American Quality Foundation? How do best practices relate to Deming's philosophy?
12. Explain the importance of self-assessment in building a TQ organization. What issues should self-assessment address?
13. Describe the role of senior management, middle management, the workforce, and unions in TQ implementation. Describe the responsibilities of each group and how they can support one another.
14. Explain the importance of viewing quality as a journey.
15. What is a learning organization? Why is this concept important to total quality?
16. Describe the four stages of learning. How is this model of organizational learning reflected in the Baldrige criteria?
17. Why is it difficult for organizations to successfully manage knowledge and share internal best practices?

Discussion Questions

1. Discuss how each of the Baldrige Core Values and Concepts are explicitly or implicitly reflected in each of the first six categories of the Baldrige criteria.
2. Consider each of the management practices we discussed in this chapter in the context of TQ versus traditional management. Propose some approaches for how an organization might move from the traditional practice to a TQ orientation. What specific organizational changes would be necessary?
3. Create a matrix diagram in which each row is a category of the Baldrige criteria and four columns correspond to
   - Traditional management practices
   - Growing awareness of the importance of quality
   - Development of solid quality management system
   - Outstanding, world-class management practice.

   In each cell of the matrix, list two to five characteristics that you would expect to see for a company in each of the preceding four situations for that category. How might this matrix be used as a self-assessment tool to provide directions for improvement?
4. Develop a hierarchy of the Baldrige Award criteria's Areas to Address that would guide an organization just starting to pursue TQ toward world-class performance. In other words, what Areas to Address would be more appropriate for new organizations to concentrate on, and in what sequence should they progress toward fully meeting the Baldrige criteria?
5. What steps might an organization take to overcome the implementation barriers and common mistakes cited in this chapter?
6. Discuss typical reasons for each of the following barriers to TQ implementation:
   a. Poor planning
   b. Lack of top management commitment
   c. Workforce resistance
   d. Lack of proper training

   e. Teamwork complacency
   f. Failure to change the organization properly
   g. Ineffective measurement of quality improvement
7. Describe some personal experiences in which you traveled through the four stages of learning described in this chapter.
8. What might the "learning organization" concept mean to a college or university?
9. In one company, the overriding focus of implementing TQ was ability to reduce costs. How does this narrow view of TQ inhibit the effectiveness of the organization?
10. You have undoubtedly seen a flock of geese flying overhead. How do the following behaviors of this species provide some insight for organizations wishing to implement TQ?
    a. As each bird flaps its wings, it creates an uplift for the bird behind. By using a "V" formation, the whole flock adds 71 percent more flying range than if each bird flew alone.
    b. Whenever one falls out of formation, it suddenly feels the grad and resistance of trying to fly alone, and quickly gets back into formation to take advantage of the lifting power of the birds immediately in front.
    c. When the lead bird gets tired, it rotates back into formation and another flies at the point position.
    d. The birds in formation honk from behind to encourage those up front to maintain their speed.
    e. When one gets sick or wounded or shot down, two birds drop out of formation and follow their fellow member down to help or provide protection. They stay with this member of the flock until it can fly again or dies. Then they launch out on their own, with another formation or to catch up with their own flock.
11. How might internal benchmarking be applied within your college? What types of activities would be appropriate?
12. What is your opinion on the future of quality? Do you agree with the comments made in the concluding section of this chapter? Why or why not?

Projects, Etc.

1. Examine some corporate Web sites and comment on the cultural values that are reflected by the information you find. How important do these organizations view quality to their success?
2. Talk to individuals that you know from some local organizations (companies, schools, government agencies) about the organization's commitment to quality principles. What factors do they attribute to either the success or failure of their organization's approaches?
3. Interview a manager at a local organization to classify the organization on the scale from "traditional to TQ" based on the list of factors described in this chapter.
4. List some key factors that differentiate quality implementation between small and large companies. What things would smaller companies be better at than large companies? If possible, study some companies to verify your hypotheses.
5. Interview your fellow students to identify a set of "best learning practices." Develop a plan for sharing these practices throughout your school.
6. Research such business publications as *Fortune* and *Business Week* to uncover the reasons for Xerox's sudden stock price fall in 2000. Try to relate your findings to the Baldrige criteria.

Cases

I. The Parable of the Green Lawn[50]

A new housing development has lots of packed earth and weeds, but no grass. Two neighbors make a wager on who will be the first to have a lush lawn. Mr. Fast N. Furious knows that a lawn will not grow without grass seed, so he immediately buys the most expensive seed he can find because everyone knows that quality improves with price. Besides, he'll recover the cost of the seed through his wager. Next, he stands knee-deep in his weeds and tosses the seed around his yard. Confident that he has a head start on his neighbor, who is not making much visible progress, he begins his next project.

Ms. Slo N. Steady, having grown up in the country, proceeds to clear the lot, till the soil, and even alter the slope of the terrain to provide better drainage. She checks the soil's pH, applies weed killer and fertilizer, and then distributes the grass seed evenly with a spreader. She applies a mulch cover and waters the lawn appropriately. She finishes several days after her neighbor, who asks if she would like to concede defeat. After all, he does have some blades of grass poking up already.

Mr. Furious is encouraged by the few clumps of grass that sprout. While these small, green islands are better developed than Ms. Steady's fledgling lawn, they are surrounded by bare spots and weeds. If he maintains these footholds, he reasons, they should spread to the rest of the yard. He notices that his neighbor's lawn is more uniform and is really starting to grow. He attributes this to the Steady children, who water the lawn each evening. Not wanting to appear to be imitating his neighbor, Mr. Furious instructs his children to water his lawn at noon.

The noon watering proves to be detrimental, so he decides to fertilize the remaining patches of grass. Since he wants to make up for the losses the noon watering caused, he applies the fertilizer at twice the recommended application rate. Most of the patches of grass that escape being burned by the fertilizer, however, are eventually choked out by the weeds.

After winning the wager with Mr. Furious, Ms. Steady lounges on the deck enjoying her new grill, which she paid for with the money from the wager. Her lawn requires minimal maintenance, so she is free to attend to the landscaping. The combination of the lawn and landscaping also results in an award from a neighborhood committee that determines that her lawn is a true showplace. Mr. Furious still labors on his lawn. He blames the poor performance on his children's inability to properly water the lawn, nonconforming grass seed, insufficient sunlight, and poor soil. He claims that his neighbor has an unfair advantage and her success is based on conditions unique to her plot of land. He views the loss as grossly unfair; after all, he spends more time and money on his lawn than Ms. Steady does.

He continues to complain about how expensive the seed is and how much time he spends moving the sprinkler around to the few remaining clumps of grass that continue to grow. But Mr. Furious thinks that things will be better for him next year, because he plans to install an automatic sprinkler system and make a double-or-nothing wager with Ms. Steady.

Discussion Questions

1. Within the context of the continual struggles to create a "world-class" lawn and "world-class" business, draw analogies between the events when total quality is implemented.
2. Specifically, translate the problems described here into business language. What are the implementation barriers to achieving total quality?

II. The Yellow Brick Road to Quality[51]

In the film *The Wizard of Oz*, Dorothy learned many lessons. Surprisingly, managers can learn a lot also. For each of the following summaries of scenes in the film, discuss the lessons that organizations can learn in pursuing change and a TQ culture.

1. Dorothy was not happy with the world as she knew it. A tornado came along and transported her to the Land of Oz. Dorothy's house was dropped by the tornado on the Wicked Witch of the East, killing the witch. "Ding, dong, the witch is dead!" rang

throughout Munchkinland, but Dorothy had enraged the dead witch's sister. Dorothy only temporarily lost her home support provided by family back in Kansas. All is not good, however, in the Land of Oz. Dorothy's problem is to find her way home to Kansas. Her call to action was precipitated by a crisis—the tornado that transported her to an alien land.

2. In the throes of a Kansas tornado, Dorothy is transported to an unfamiliar land. Immediately, she realizes her world is different and the processes and people she encounters are different, yet bear some similarity to her Kansas existence. She is lost and confused and uncertain about the next steps to take. She realizes she is in a changed state—the Land of Oz—and must devise a plan to get home.
3. Dorothy is a hero for killing the Wicked Witch of the East. Glinda the Good Witch sends Dorothy on her way to meet the Wizard of Oz who will help her get back to Kansas. The Wicked Witch of the West tries to get Dorothy's newly acquired ruby slippers, but to no avail. Dorothy and Toto leave for Oz via the Yellow Brick Road. Along the way, they are joined by Scarecrow, Tin Man, and Lion. Through their teamwork, they provide mutual support to endure the vexing journey. They overcome many risks and barriers, including the sleeping poppy field, flying monkeys, and a haunted forest on the way to Oz.
4. Dorothy and her entourage finally reach Oz and meet the Wizard. Rather than instantly granting their wishes, the Wizard gives them an assignment—to obtain the Wicked Witch's broom. They depart for the West.
5. Charged with the task of obtaining the broom, Dorothy and company experience several encounters with near disaster, including Dorothy's incarceration in the witch's castle while an hourglass counts the time to her death. In a struggle to extinguish the Scarecrow's fire (incited by the Wicked Witch), Dorothy tosses a bucket of water, some of which hits the Witch and melts her. Dorothy is rewarded with the broomstick and returns to Oz.
6. Returning to Oz, the group talks with the Wizard, expecting him to help Dorothy return to Kansas. After defrocking the Wizard, they find out he does not know how. The Wizard tries to use a hot air balloon to return and accidentally leaves Dorothy and Toto behind upon takeoff. Glinda arrives and helps Dorothy realize she can return to Kansas on her own with the help of the ruby slippers.
7. Dorothy awakens from her dream and experiences a new understanding and appreciation for her home and family in Kansas. "Oh, Auntie Em, there's no place like home."

III. Equipto, Inc.

Equipto, Inc., a division of a *Fortune* 500 corporation, is located in the Midwest. The Industrial Motor Division (IMD) makes motor units that are part of the installation package for large-scale industrial systems. The company has two major competitors in the United States and several smaller competitors abroad. Although its market share has shown a slight decrease, Equipto remains second in U.S. market share and first worldwide.

Three years earlier, management had foreseen the need for adoption of a TQ philosophy. With much fanfare at the corporate level, the new TQ program, called "Quality or Else," was rolled out. It soon became known by its initials QOE. Initial skepticism surfaced within various divisions about whether such a program would help to arrest the progress of Equipto's competitors, especially a rapidly growing Japanese firm that had recently announced plans to build a plant in the United States. However, an enthusiastic middle-level production manager, Bob Green, who had a great deal of creativity as well as credibility, was soon appointed as division director of TQ. He had a vision of TQ that was people-driven, but he had little knowledge of the details of statistical process control (SPC), as his degree was in liberal arts. Also at his level was a division director of quality assurance, Harry Rule, who was steeped in traditional SPC techniques and had many years of quality control experience in the company. Managers and staff alike viewed Rule as a statistical genius. Although he talked a good game about embracing TQ, empowerment, teamwork, listening to the voice of the customer, and other such rhetoric, he acted somewhat condescendingly toward anyone who wasn't his equal in SPC.

After initial planning by Green, Rule, and an outside consultant, the QOE program was rolled out with three days of top management training—led by the outside consulting firm—in TQ philosophy and techniques at the corporate level. All corporate and divisional top managers (the CEO, corporate VPs, divisional presidents and VPs, and a few selected staff people) were included in the executive training session. This TQ training was cascaded down through the divisions, so that every employee received two to five days of training. Much of the training was conducted in-house by facilitators at each plant in every division. Divisions could choose the depth of training in SPC techniques and were encouraged to hire local consultants to help them in this phase of the development. After the "up-front" training, Equipto, Inc. groups were started so that employees could begin to practice their newly learned skills. These activities pretty much consumed the first year of the process.

During the second year, the company began to see some results. Employee skepticism, which had been a major problem in the rank-and-file unionized workforce, began to subside due to three factors:

1. Recognition of teams and team members who had accomplished some significant results. One project that was completed after a nine-month study showed paper savings of $100,000.
2. The enthusiasm of Bob Green, division director of TQ. He went around to all the plants in the division to beat the drum for quality about every three or four months.
3. Emphasis on the human relations aspects of quality, with little being said about SPC, standards, or quantitative analysis of the production processes.

However, middle managers in the divisions had been given little training in how to handle an "empowered" workforce, so they felt somewhat resentful of the process and were left out of team activities.

Equipto and its IMD were in trouble at the beginning of the new fiscal year. Although the Equipto teams had been going strong for more than a year, and they had about 20 percent of the hourly workforce involved, nothing tangible seemed to happen. Apparently, a cyclical downturn was under way, and the company was scrambling for any business that it could get. Middle managers and line supervisors felt pressure to deliver immediate results. The pressure extended up and down the line. Green and Rule at corporate headquarters began to question each other's commitment to TQ, which led to speculation about the outbreak of a major turf war. Green was certain that more training of middle managers could help to turn the corner on quality. Rule was equally certain that more emphasis on SPC was needed at every level in the division.

The IMD had been the most successful division in implementing TQ of any in Equipto. Half the IMD's people in the plants were on a team, and a white-collar accounting department team was just being formed. Estimated savings during the first full year of team operation were $200,000 (including the project that had saved $100,000). Because only about $40,000 in direct out-of-pocket costs had been spent on TQ program development, everyone felt that TQ gave a pretty good return.

At the middle of the year, top management announced that the company had sustained its largest quarterly loss in history. Division managers were told to pare expenses by 15 percent. Bob Green resigned to accept a job with another firm, and Harry Rule was named corporate VP for quality with all phases of TQ and quality assurance under his direction. The divisions were given no specific directives on TQ programs or projects, but many thought that the changes might spell the death of the employee-focused quality program. Others decided to just wait and see. Still others began polishing up their resumes.

Discussion Questions

1. Discuss the way in which the TQ program was launched. Could it have been done differently, and perhaps better?
2. What are the pros and cons of up-front training (training before any projects are begun) versus just-in-time training (training that is done concurrently with development of projects)? Do you think that some momentum might have been lost because employees were trained before they were sent out to work on projects?

3. When and in what form should SPC be introduced to employees at the operating levels in the firm? Was it time for Equipto to do so, or past time?
4. Is it possible for TQ to be a success, and the company to be unprofitable, or worse? What has happened in the recent history of Baldrige Award winners along that line?
5. What should the company do about its TQ process now? Scrap the program, keep the same emphasis, or change to a SPC focus? Why?

NOTES

1. Brad Stratton, "Cynicism vs. Kelly Potter," Editorial Comment, *Quality Progress* 27, no. 9 (September 1994), 5.

2. Gary Salengna and Farzaneh Fazel, "Obstacles to Implementing Quality," *Quality Progress,* July 2000, 53–57.

3. Brian Dumaine, "Times Are Good? Create a Crisis," *Fortune,* June 28, 1993, 123–130.

4. Susan E. Daniels and Mark R. Hagen, "Making the Pitch in the Executive Suite," *Quality Progress,* April 1999, 25–33.

5. Thomas A. Stewart, "Rate Your Readiness to Change," *Fortune,* February 7, 1994, 106–110.

6. James R. Evans and Matthew W. Ford, "Value-Driven Quality," *Quality Management Journal* 4, no. 4 (1997), 19–31.

7. "Total Quality at Procter & Gamble," The *Total Quality Forum,* Cincinnati, OH, August 6–8, 1991.

8. Paul R. Keck, "Why Quality Fails," *Quality Digest,* November 1995, 53–55.

9. Ed Baker, "The Chief Executive Officer's Role in Total Quality: Preparing the Enterprise for Leadership in the New Economic Age," Proceedings of the William G. Hunter Conference on Quality, Madison, WI, 1989.

10. Gregory P. Smith, "A Change in Culture Brings Dramatic Quality Improvements," *The Quality Observer,* January 1997, 14–15, 37.

11. James H. Davis, "Who Owns Your Quality Program? Lessons from Baldrige Award Winners," (New York: Coopers & Lybrand, undated).

12. "Where Did They Go Wrong?" *Business Week/Quality* 1991, October 25, 1991, 34–38.

13. Nabil Tamimi and Rose Sebastianelli, "The Barriers to Total Quality Management," *Quality Progress,* June 1998, 57–60.

14. Core body of knowledge working council findings, "Issues in Implementation of TQ," *A Report of the Total Quality Leadership Steering Committee and Working Councils,* Total Quality Forum, Cincinnati, OH, November 1992, 255–257.

15. Thomas H. Patten, Jr., "Beyond Systems—The Politics of Managing in a TQM Environment," *National Productivity Review,* 1991/1992.

16. "Special Report: Quality," *Business Week,* November 30, 1992, 66–75; and H. James Harrington, "The Fallacy of Universal Best Practices," Report TR 97-003, Ernst & Young, 1997.

17. Cyndee Miller, "TQM's Value Criticized in New Report," *Marketing News,* 1992; Gilbert Fuchsberg, "'Total Quality' Is Termed Only Partial Success," *Wall Street Journal,* October 1, 1992, B1, B7.

18. See, for example, Mark Graham Brown, "Measuring Up Against the 1997 Baldrige Criteria," *Journal for Quality and Participation* 20, no. 4 (September 1997), 22–28.

19. Henry Mintzberg, *Mintzberg on Management* (New York: The Free Press, 1989), 15–21.

20. Arthur R. Tenner and Irving J. DeToro, *Total Quality Management: Three Steps to Continuous Improvement* (Reading, MA: Addison-Wesley, 1992).

21. Leonard Sayles, *The Working Manager* (New York: The Free Press, 1993), 25–32.

22. Mark Samuel, "Catalysts for Change," The *TQM Magazine* 2, no. 4 (1992), 198–202.

23. Davis, see note 11.

24. John Persico, Jr., Betty L. Bednarczyk, and David P. Negus, "Three Routes to the Same Destination: TQM, Part 1," *Quality Progress,* 23, no. 1 (January 1990), 29–33.

25. William A. Hines, "The Stops and Starts of Total Quality Management," *Quality Progress,* February 1998, 61–64.

26. Henry A. Bradshaw, "From Leadership to Customer Satisfaction: The Total Quality Management System," presentation material from the 1996 Regional Malcolm Baldrige Award Conference, Boston, June 6, 1996.

27. Doug Keare, "Lessons Learned and Quality Journey," presentation notes from the 1997 Quest for Excellence Conference, Washington, DC.

28. Custom Research Incorporated, "Six

Lessons Learned From Our Baldrige Journey," *http://www.cresearch.com/mb/mb02/mb02_con.htm.*

29. Peter M. Senge, *The Fifth Discipline: The Art and Practice of the Learning Organization* (New York: Doubleday Currency, 1990), 14.

30. David A. Garvin. "Building a Learning Organization," *Harvard Business Review* (July/August, 1993), 80.

31. Peter M. Senge, Charlotte Roberts, Richard B. Ross, Brian J. Smith, and Art Kleiner, *The Fifth Discipline Field Book: Strategies and Tools for Building a Learning Organization* (New York: Currency-Doubleday, 1994).

32. David A. Garvin, *Learning in Action: A Guide to Putting the Learning Organization to Work* (Boston: Harvard Business School Press), 2000, 11.

33. Garvin, see note 32.

34. This intriguing label deserves a special explanation. It was coined by Joseph Juran in *Juran on Quality by Design* (New York: The Free Press, 1992), 409–413. It refers to the remark once made by philosopher George Santayana, who said, "Those who cannot remember the past are condemned to repeat it."

35. Sim B. Sitkin, Kathleen M. Sutcliffe, and Roger G. Schroeder, "Distinguishing Control from Learning in Total Quality Management: A Contingency Perspective," *Academy of Management Review* 19, no. 3 (1994), 537–564.

36. See Matthew W. Ford and James R. Evans, "Baldrige Assessment and Organizational Learning: The Need for Change Management," *Quality Management Journal* (in press at time of publication).

37. Ann B. Rich, "Continuous Improvement: The Key to Success," *Quality Progress* 30, no. 6 (June 1997).

38. Brad Stratton, "TI Has Eye on Alignment," *Quality Progress* 30, no. 10 (October 1997), 28–34.

39. Marion Harmon, "Solectron Continues to Win With the Baldrige," *Quality Progress* 29, no. 11 (November 1996), 46–48.

40. Larry Hambly, "Sun Microsystems Embeds Quality into Its DNA," *The Quality Observer*, July 1997, 16–20, 45.

41. Robert J. Heibeler. "Benchmarking Knowledge Management," *Strategy and Leadership*, 24, no. 2 (March/April 1996), as cited in Verna Allee, *The Knowledge Evolution: Expanding Organizational Intelligence* (Boston: Butterworth-Heinemann, 1997), 8.

42. Carla O'Dell and C. Jackson Grayson, "Identifying and Transferring Internal Best Practices," APQC White Paper, 2000. *http://www.apqc.org/free/whitepapers/cmifwp/index.htm.*

43. Mohamed Zairi and John Whymark, "The transfer of best practices: how to build a culture of benchmarking and continuous learning—Part 1," *Benchmarking: An International Journal*, 7, no. 1 (2000), 62–78.

44. A.V. Feigenbaum and Donald S. Feigenbaum, "New Quality for the 21st Century," *Quality Progress*, December 1999, 27–31.

45. "21 Voices for the 21st Century," *Quality Progress*, January 2000, 31–39.

46. Miles Maguire, "The Voice of the 21st Century Customer," *Quality Progress*, January 2000, 41.

47. Primary sources for the information in this section include: Robert Howard, "The CEO as Organizational Architect: An Interview with Paul Allaire," *Harvard Business Review*, September/October 1992, 107–119; and David T. Kearns and David A. Nadler, *Prophets in the Dark* (New York: HarperCollins, 1992).

48. Richard J. Leo, "Xerox 2000: From Survival to Opportunity," *Quality Progress* 30, no. 3 (March 1996), 65–71.

49. Adapted from Weston F. Milliken, "The Eastman Way," *Quality Progress* 29, no. 10 (October 1996), 57–62.

50. Adapted from James A. Alloway, Jr., "Laying Groundwork for Total Quality," *Quality Progress* 27, no. 1 (January 1994), 65–67. © 1994 American Society for Quality (ASQ). Reprinted with permission.

51. David M. Lyth and Larry A. Mallak, "'We're Not in Kansas Anymore, Toto' or Quality Lessons from the Land of Oz," *Quality Engineering* 10, no. 30 (1998), 579–588. Copyright © 1998 by David M. Lyth and Larry A. Mallak. All rights reserved.

BIBLIOGRAPHY

AT&T Quality Steering Committee. *Batting 1000: Using Baldrige Feedback to Improve Your Business.* AT&T Bell Laboratories (1992).

AT&T Quality Steering Committee. *Quality Manager's Handbook.* AT&T Bell Laboratories (1990).

Burns, T., and G. M. Stalker. *The Management of Innovation*. London: Tavistock, 1961.

Coud, Dana M. "The Function of Organizational Principles and Process," in *Quality Control and Reliability Management*. ASQC Education and Training Institute. Milwaukee: ASQC, 1969, 6-1 to 6-3.

Emery, F. E., E. L. Trist, and J. Woodward. *Management and Technology*. London: Her Majesty's Stationery Office, 1958.

Kukla, R. E. "Organizing a Manufacturing Improvement Program." *Quality Progress*, November 1983, 28.

Lawrence, P. R., and J. W. Lorsch. *Organization and Environment*. Boston: Harvard University, Division of Research, Graduate School of Business Administration, 1967.

Niven, Daniel. "When Times Get Tough, What Happens to TQM?" *Harvard Business Review*, May/June 1993, 20–33.

Rue, L. W., and L. Byars. Management Skills and Application, 9th ed. New York: McGraw-Hill, 2000.

Schmidt, Warren H., and Jerome P. Finnigan. *A Race Without a Finish Line*. San Francisco: Jossey-Bass Publishers, 1992.

Sinha, Madhav N., and Walter W. O. Willborn. *The Management of Quality Assurance*. New York: John Wiley & Sons, 1985.

Whalen M. J., and M. A. Rahim. "Common Barriers to Implementation and Development of a TQM Program." *Industrial Management* 36, no. 2 (March/April 1994), 19–22.

APPENDIXES

Appendix A

Areas for the Standard Normal Distribution

Entries in the table give the area under the curve between the mean and z standard deviations above the mean. For example, for $z = 1.25$ the area under the curve between the mean and z is 0.3944.

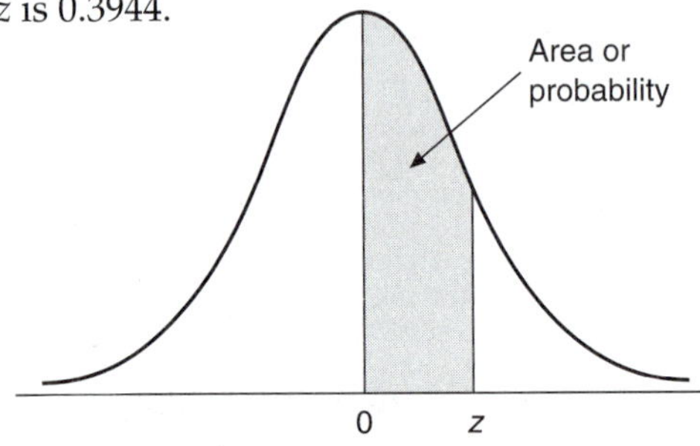

z	0.00	0.01	0.02	0.03	0.04	0.05	0.06	0.07	0.08	0.09
0.0	0.0000	0.0040	0.0080	0.0120	0.0160	0.0199	0.0239	0.0279	0.0319	0.0359
0.1	0.0398	0.0438	0.0478	0.0517	0.0557	0.0596	0.0636	0.0675	0.0714	0.0753
0.2	0.0793	0.0832	0.0871	0.0910	0.0948	0.0987	0.1026	0.1064	0.1103	0.1141
0.3	0.1179	0.1217	0.1255	0.1293	0.1331	0.1368	0.1406	0.1443	0.1480	0.1517
0.4	0.1554	0.1591	0.1628	0.1664	0.1700	0.1736	0.1772	0.1808	0.1844	0.1879
0.5	0.1915	0.1950	0.1985	0.2019	0.2054	0.2088	0.2123	0.2157	0.2190	0.2224
0.6	0.2257	0.2291	0.2324	0.2357	0.2389	0.2422	0.2454	0.2486	0.2518	0.2549
0.7	0.2580	0.2612	0.2642	0.2673	0.2704	0.2734	0.2764	0.2794	0.2823	0.2852
0.8	0.2881	0.2910	0.2939	0.2967	0.2995	0.3023	0.3051	0.3078	0.3106	0.3133
0.9	0.3159	0.3186	0.3212	0.3238	0.3264	0.3289	0.3315	0.3340	0.3365	0.3389
1.0	0.3413	0.3438	0.3461	0.3485	0.3508	0.3531	0.3554	0.3577	0.3599	0.3621
1.1	0.3643	0.3665	0.3686	0.3708	0.3729	0.3749	0.3770	0.3790	0.3810	0.3830
1.2	0.3849	0.3869	0.3888	0.3907	0.3925	0.3944	0.3962	0.3980	0.3997	0.4015
1.3	0.4032	0.4049	0.4066	0.4082	0.4099	0.4115	0.4131	0.4147	0.4162	0.4177
1.4	0.4192	0.4207	0.4222	0.4236	0.4251	0.4265	0.4279	0.4292	0.4306	0.4319
1.5	0.4332	0.4345	0.4357	0.4370	0.4382	0.4394	0.4406	0.4418	0.4429	0.4441
1.6	0.4452	0.4463	0.4474	0.4484	0.4495	0.4505	0.4515	0.4525	0.4535	0.4545
1.7	0.4554	0.4564	0.4573	0.4582	0.4591	0.4599	0.4608	0.4616	0.4625	0.4633
1.8	0.4641	0.4649	0.4656	0.4664	0.4671	0.4678	0.4686	0.4693	0.4699	0.4706
1.9	0.4713	0.4719	0.4726	0.4732	0.4738	0.4744	0.4750	0.4756	0.4761	0.4767
2.0	0.4772	0.4778	0.4783	0.4788	0.4793	0.4798	0.4803	0.4808	0.4812	0.4817
2.1	0.4821	0.4826	0.4830	0.4834	0.4838	0.4842	0.4846	0.4850	0.4854	0.4857
2.2	0.4861	0.4864	0.4868	0.4871	0.4875	0.4878	0.4881	0.4884	0.4887	0.4890
2.3	0.4893	0.4896	0.4898	0.4901	0.4904	0.4906	0.4909	0.4911	0.4913	0.4916
2.4	0.4918	0.4920	0.4922	0.4925	0.4927	0.4929	0.4931	0.4932	0.4934	0.4936
2.5	0.4938	0.4940	0.4941	0.4943	0.4945	0.4946	0.4948	0.4949	0.4951	0.4952
2.6	0.4953	0.4955	0.4956	0.4957	0.4959	0.4960	0.4961	0.4962	0.4963	0.4964
2.7	0.4965	0.4966	0.4967	0.4968	0.4969	0.4970	0.4971	0.4972	0.4973	0.4974
2.8	0.4974	0.4975	0.4976	0.4977	0.4977	0.4978	0.4979	0.4979	0.4980	0.4981
2.9	0.4981	0.4982	0.4982	0.4983	0.4984	0.4984	0.4985	0.4985	0.4986	0.4986
3.0	0.4986	0.4987	0.4987	0.4988	0.4988	0.4989	0.4989	0.4989	0.4990	0.4990

Appendix B

Factors for Control Charts

	x-charts				*s*-Charts				*R*-charts					
n	A	A_2	A_3	c_4	B_3	B_4	B_5	B_6	d_2	d_3	D_1	D_2	D_3	D_4
2	2.121	1.880	2.659	0.7979	0	3.267	0	2.606	1.128	0.853	0	3.686	0	3.267
3	1.732	1.023	1.954	0.8862	0	2.568	0	2.276	1.693	0.888	0	4.358	0	2.574
4	1.500	0.729	1.628	0.9213	0	2.266	0	2.088	2.059	0.880	0	4.698	0	2.282
5	1.342	0.577	1.427	0.9400	0	2.089	0	1.964	2.326	0.864	0	4.918	0	2.114
6	1.225	0.483	1.287	0.9515	0.030	1.970	0.029	1.874	2.534	0.848	0	5.078	0	2.004
7	1.134	0.419	1.182	0.9594	0.118	1.882	0.113	1.806	2.704	0.833	0.204	5.204	0.076	1.924
8	1.061	0.373	1.099	0.9650	0.185	1.815	0.179	1.751	2.847	0.820	0.388	5.306	0.136	1.864
9	1.000	0.337	1.032	0.969	0.239	1.761	0.232	1.707	2.970	0.808	0.547	5.393	0.184	1.816
10	0.949	0.308	0.975	0.9727	0.284	1.716	0.276	1.669	3.078	0.797	0.687	5.469	0.223	1.777
11	0.905	0.285	0.927	0.9754	0.321	1.679	0.313	1.637	3.173	0.787	0.811	5.535	0.256	1.744
12	0.866	0.266	0.886	0.9776	0.354	1.646	0.346	1.610	3.258	0.778	0.922	5.594	0.283	1.717
13	0.832	0.249	0.850	0.9794	0.382	1.618	0.374	1.585	3.336	0.770	1.025	5.647	0.307	1.693
14	0.802	0.235	0.817	0.9810	0.406	1.594	0.399	1.563	3.407	0.763	1.118	5.696	0.328	1.672
15	0.775	0.223	0.789	0.9823	0.428	1.572	0.421	1.544	3.472	0.756	1.203	5.741	0.347	1.653
16	0.750	0.212	0.763	0.9835	0.448	1.552	0.440	1.526	3.532	0.750	1.282	5.782	0.363	1.637
17	0.728	0.203	0.739	0.9845	0.466	1.534	0.458	1.511	3.588	0.744	1.356	5.820	0.378	1.622
18	0.707	0.194	0.718	0.9854	0.482	1.518	0.475	1.496	3.640	0.739	1.424	5.856	0.391	1.608
19	0.688	0.187	0.698	0.9862	0.497	1.503	0.490	1.483	3.689	0.734	1.487	5.891	0.403	1.597
20	0.671	0.180	0.680	0.9869	0.510	1.490	0.504	1.470	3.735	0.729	1.549	5.921	0.415	1.585
21	0.655	0.173	0.663	0.9876	0.523	1.477	0.516	1.459	3.778	0.724	1.605	5.951	0.425	1.575
22	0.640	0.167	0.647	0.9882	0.534	1.466	0.528	1.448	3.819	0.720	1.659	5.979	0.434	1.566
23	0.626	0.162	0.633	0.9887	0.545	1.455	0.539	1.438	3.858	0.716	1.710	6.006	0.443	1.557
24	0.612	0.157	0.619	0.9892	0.555	1.445	0.549	1.429	3.895	0.712	1.759	6.031	0.451	1.548
25	0.600	0.153	0.606	0.9896	0.565	1.435	0.559	1.420	3.931	0.708	1.806	6.056	0.459	1.541

Source: Adapted from Table 27 of ASTM STP 15D ASTM *Manual on Presentation of Data and Control Chart Analysis*. © 1976 American Society for Testing and Materials, Philadelphia, PA.

Appendix C

Random Digits

63271	59986	71744	51102	15141	80714	58683	93108	13554	79945
88547	09896	95436	79115	08303	01041	20030	63754	08459	28364
55957	57243	83865	09911	19761	66535	40102	26646	60147	15702
46276	87453	44790	67122	45573	84358	21625	16999	13385	22782
55363	07449	34835	15290	76616	67191	12777	21861	68689	03263
69393	92785	49902	58447	42048	30378	87618	26933	40640	16281
13186	29431	88190	04588	38733	81290	89541	70290	40113	08243
17726	28652	56836	78351	47327	18518	92222	55201	27340	10493
36520	64465	05550	30157	82242	29520	69753	72602	23756	54935
81628	36100	39254	56835	37636	02421	98063	89641	64953	99337
84649	48968	75215	75498	49539	74240	03466	49292	36401	45525
63291	11618	12613	75055	43915	26488	41116	64531	56827	30825
70502	53225	03655	05915	37140	57051	48393	91322	25653	06543
06426	24771	59935	49801	11082	66762	94477	02494	88215	27191
20711	55609	29430	70165	45406	78484	31639	52009	18873	96927
41990	70538	77191	25860	55204	73417	83920	69468	74972	38712
72452	36618	76298	26678	89334	33938	95567	29380	75906	91807
37042	40318	57099	10528	09925	89773	41335	96244	29002	46453
53766	52875	15987	46962	67342	77592	57651	95508	80033	69828
90585	58955	53122	16025	84299	53310	67380	84249	25348	04332
32001	96293	37203	64516	51530	37069	40261	61374	05815	06714
62606	64324	46354	72157	67248	20135	49804	09226	64419	29457
10078	28073	85389	50324	14500	15562	64165	06125	71353	77669
91561	46145	24177	15294	10061	98124	75732	00815	83452	97355
13091	98112	53959	79607	52244	63303	10413	63839	74762	50289
73864	83014	72457	22682	03033	61714	88173	90835	00634	85169
66668	25467	48894	51043	02365	91726	09365	63167	95264	45643
84745	41042	29493	01836	09044	51926	43630	63470	76508	14194
48068	26805	94595	47907	13357	38412	33318	26098	82782	42851
54310	96175	97594	88616	42035	38093	36745	56702	40644	83514
14877	33095	10924	58013	61439	21882	42059	24177	58739	60170
78295	23179	02771	43464	59061	71411	05697	67194	30495	21157
67524	02865	39593	54278	04237	92441	26602	63835	38032	94770
58268	57219	68124	73455	83236	08710	04284	55005	84171	42596
97158	28672	50685	01181	24262	19427	52106	34308	73685	74246
04230	16831	69085	30802	65559	09205	71829	06489	85650	38707
94879	56606	30401	02602	57658	70091	54986	41394	60437	03195
71446	15232	66715	26385	91518	70566	02888	79941	39684	54315
32886	05644	79316	09819	00813	88407	17461	73925	53037	91904
62048	33711	25290	21526	02223	75947	66466	06232	10913	75336

Source: Reprinted from page 44 of *A Million Digits With 100,000 Normal Deviates,* by the Rand Corporation. New York: The Free Press, 1955. © 1955 by The Rand Corporation. Used by permission.

Appendix D

Binomial Probabilities

Entries in the table give the probability of x successes in n trials of a binomial experiment, where p is the probability of a success on one trial. For example, with six trials and $p = 0.40$, the probability of two successes is 0.3110.

		p									
n	***x***	**0.05**	**0.10**	**0.15**	**0.20**	**0.25**	**0.30**	**0.35**	**0.40**	**0.45**	**0.50**
1	0	0.9500	0.9000	0.8500	0.8000	0.7500	0.7000	0.6500	0.6000	0.5500	0.5000
	1	0.0500	0.1000	0.1500	0.2000	0.2500	0.3000	0.3500	0.4000	0.4500	0.5000
2	0	0.9025	0.8100	0.7225	0.6400	0.5625	0.4900	0.4225	0.3600	0.3025	0.2500
	1	0.0950	0.1800	0.2550	0.3200	0.3750	0.4200	0.4550	0.4800	0.4950	0.5000
	2	0.0025	0.0100	0.0225	0.0400	0.0625	0.0900	0.1225	0.1600	0.2025	0.2500
3	0	0.8574	0.7290	0.6141	0.5120	0.4219	0.3430	0.2746	0.2160	0.1664	0.1250
	1	0.1354	0.2430	0.3251	0.3840	0.4219	0.4410	0.4436	0.4320	0.4084	0.3750
	2	0.0071	0.0270	0.0574	0.0960	0.1406	0.1890	0.2389	0.2880	0.3341	0.3750
	3	0.0001	0.0010	0.0034	0.0080	0.0156	0.0270	0.0429	0.0640	0.0911	0.1250
4	0	0.8145	0.6561	0.5220	0.4096	0.3164	0.2401	0.1785	0.1296	0.0915	0.0625
	1	0.1715	0.2916	0.3685	0.4096	0.4219	0.4116	0.3845	0.3456	0.2995	0.2500
	2	0.0135	0.0486	0.0975	0.1536	0.2109	0.2646	0.3105	0.3456	0.3675	0.3750
	3	0.0005	0.0036	0.0115	0.0256	0.0469	0.0756	0.1115	0.1536	0.2005	0.2500
	4	0.0000	0.0001	0.0005	0.0016	0.0039	0.0081	0.0150	0.0256	0.0410	0.0625
5	0	0.7738	0.5905	0.4437	0.3277	0.2373	0.1681	0.1160	0.0778	0.0503	0.0312
	1	0.2036	0.3280	0.3915	0.4096	0.3955	0.3602	0.3124	0.2592	0.2059	0.1562
	2	0.0214	0.0729	0.1382	0.2048	0.2637	0.3087	0.3364	0.3456	0.3369	0.3125
	3	0.0011	0.0081	0.0244	0.0512	0.0879	0.1323	0.1811	0.2304	0.2757	0.3125
	4	0.0000	0.0004	0.0022	0.0064	0.0146	0.0284	0.0488	0.0768	0.1128	0.1562
	5	0.0000	0.0000	0.0001	0.0003	0.0010	0.0024	0.0053	0.0102	0.0185	0.0312
6	0	0.7351	0.5314	0.3771	0.2621	0.1780	0.1176	0.0754	0.0467	0.0277	0.0156
	1	0.2321	0.3543	0.3993	0.3932	0.3560	0.3025	0.2437	0.1866	0.1359	0.0938
	2	0.0305	0.0984	0.1762	0.2458	0.2966	0.3241	0.3280	0.3110	0.2780	0.2344
	3	0.0021	0.0146	0.0415	0.0819	0.1318	0.1852	0.2355	0.2765	0.3032	0.3125
	4	0.0001	0.0012	0.0055	0.0154	0.0330	0.0595	0.0951	0.1382	0.1861	0.2344
	5	0.0000	0.0001	0.0004	0.0015	0.0044	0.0102	0.0205	0.0369	0.0609	0.0938
	6	0.0000	0.0000	0.0000	0.0001	0.0002	0.0007	0.0018	0.0041	0.0083	0.0156
7	0	0.6983	0.4783	0.3206	0.2097	0.1335	0.0824	0.0490	0.0280	0.0152	0.0078
	1	0.2573	0.3720	0.3960	0.3670	0.3115	0.2471	0.1848	0.1306	0.0872	0.0547
	2	0.0406	0.1240	0.2097	0.2753	0.3115	0.3177	0.2985	0.2613	0.2140	0.1641
	3	0.0036	0.0230	0.0617	0.1147	0.1730	0.2269	0.2679	0.2903	0.2918	0.2734
	4	0.0002	0.0026	0.0109	0.0287	0.0577	0.0972	0.1442	0.1935	0.2388	0.2734
	5	0.0000	0.0002	0.0012	0.0043	0.0115	0.0250	0.0466	0.0774	0.1172	0.1641
	6	0.0000	0.0000	0.0001	0.0004	0.0013	0.0036	0.0084	0.0172	0.0320	0.0547
	7	0.0000	0.0000	0.0000	0.0000	0.0001	0.0002	0.0006	0.0016	0.0037	0.0078
8	0	0.6634	0.4305	0.2725	0.1678	0.1001	0.0576	0.0319	0.0168	0.0084	0.0039
	1	0.2793	0.3826	0.3847	0.3355	0.2670	0.1977	0.1373	0.0896	0.0548	0.0312
	2	0.0515	0.1488	0.2376	0.2936	0.3115	0.2965	0.2587	0.2090	0.1569	0.1094
	3	0.0054	0.0331	0.0839	0.1468	0.2076	0.2541	0.2786	0.2787	0.2568	0.2188
	4	0.0004	0.0046	0.0185	0.0459	0.0865	0.1361	0.1875	0.2322	0.2627	0.2734
	5	0.0000	0.0004	0.0026	0.0092	0.0231	0.0467	0.0808	0.1239	0.1719	0.2188
	6	0.0000	0.0000	0.0002	0.0011	0.0038	0.0100	0.0217	0.0413	0.0703	0.1094
	7	0.0000	0.0000	0.0000	0.0001	0.0004	0.0012	0.0033	0.0079	0.0164	0.0312
	8	0.0000	0.0000	0.0000	0.0000	0.0000	0.0001	0.0002	0.0007	0.0017	0.0039

		p									
n	**x**	**0.05**	**0.10**	**0.15**	**0.20**	**0.25**	**0.30**	**0.35**	**0.40**	**0.45**	**0.50**
9	0	0.6302	0.3874	0.2316	0.1342	0.0751	0.0404	0.0207	0.0101	0.0046	0.0020
	1	0.2985	0.3874	0.3679	0.3020	0.2253	0.1556	0.1004	0.0605	0.0339	0.0176
	2	0.0629	0.1722	0.2597	0.3020	0.3003	0.2668	0.2162	0.1612	0.1110	0.0703
	3	0.0077	0.0446	0.1069	0.1762	0.2336	0.2668	0.2716	0.2508	0.2119	0.1641
	4	0.0006	0.0074	0.0283	0.0661	0.1168	0.1715	0.2194	0.2508	0.2600	0.2461
	5	0.0000	0.0008	0.0050	0.0165	0.0389	0.0735	0.1181	0.1672	0.2128	0.2461
	6	0.0000	0.0001	0.0006	0.0028	0.0087	0.0210	0.0424	0.0743	0.1160	0.1641
	7	0.0000	0.0000	0.0000	0.0003	0.0012	0.0039	0.0098	0.0212	0.0407	0.0703
	8	0.0000	0.0000	0.0000	0.0000	0.0001	0.0004	0.0013	0.0035	0.0083	0.0176
	9	0.0000	0.0000	0.0000	0.0000	0.0000	0.0000	0.0001	0.0003	0.0008	0.0020
10	0	0.5987	0.3487	0.1969	0.1074	0.0563	0.0282	0.0135	0.0060	0.0025	0.0010
	1	0.3151	0.3874	0.3474	0.2684	0.1877	0.1211	0.0725	0.0403	0.0207	0.0098
	2	0.0746	0.1937	0.2759	0.3020	0.2816	0.2335	0.1757	0.1209	0.0763	0.0439
	3	0.0105	0.0574	0.1298	0.2013	0.2503	0.2668	0.2522	0.2150	0.1665	0.1172
	4	0.0010	0.0112	0.0401	0.0881	0.1460	0.2001	0.2377	0.2508	0.2384	0.2051
	5	0.0001	0.0015	0.0085	0.0264	0.0584	0.1029	0.1536	0.2007	0.2340	0.2461
	6	0.0000	0.0001	0.0012	0.0055	0.0162	0.0368	0.0689	0.1115	0.1596	0.2051
	7	0.0000	0.0000	0.0001	0.0008	0.0031	0.0090	0.0212	0.0425	0.0746	0.1172
	8	0.0000	0.0000	0.0000	0.0001	0.0004	0.0014	0.0043	0.0106	0.0229	0.0439
	9	0.0000	0.0000	0.0000	0.0000	0.0000	0.0001	0.0005	0.0016	0.0042	0.0098
	10	0.0000	0.0000	0.0000	0.0000	0.0000	0.0000	0.0000	0.0001	0.0003	0.0010
11	0	0.5688	0.3138	0.1673	0.0859	0.0422	0.0198	0.0088	0.0036	0.0014	0.0005
	1	0.3293	0.3835	0.3248	0.2362	0.1549	0.0932	0.0518	0.0266	0.0125	0.0054
	2	0.0867	0.2131	0.2866	0.2953	0.2581	0.1998	0.1395	0.0887	0.0513	0.0269
	3	0.0137	0.0710	0.1517	0.2215	0.2581	0.2568	0.2254	0.1774	0.1259	0.0806
	4	0.0014	0.0158	0.0536	0.1107	0.1721	0.2201	0.2428	0.2365	0.2060	0.1611
	5	0.0001	0.0025	0.0132	0.0388	0.0803	0.1321	0.1830	0.2207	0.2360	0.2256
	6	0.0000	0.0003	0.0023	0.0097	0.0268	0.0566	0.0985	0.1471	0.1931	0.2256
	7	0.0000	0.0000	0.0003	0.0017	0.0064	0.0173	0.0379	0.0701	0.1128	0.1611
	8	0.0000	0.0000	0.0000	0.0002	0.0011	0.0037	0.0102	0.0234	0.0462	0.0806
	9	0.0000	0.0000	0.0000	0.0000	0.0001	0.0005	0.0018	0.0052	0.0126	0.0269
	10	0.0000	0.0000	0.0000	0.0000	0.0000	0.0000	0.0002	0.0007	0.0021	0.0054
	11	0.0000	0.0000	0.0000	0.0000	0.0000	0.0000	0.0000	0.0000	0.0002	0.0005
12	0	0.5404	0.2824	0.1422	0.0687	0.0317	0.0138	0.0057	0.0022	0.0008	0.0002
	1	0.3413	0.3766	0.3012	0.2062	0.1267	0.0712	0.0368	0.0174	0.0075	0.0029
	2	0.0988	0.2301	0.2924	0.2835	0.2323	0.1678	0.1088	0.0639	0.0339	0.0161
	3	0.0173	0.0853	0.1720	0.2362	0.2581	0.2397	0.1954	0.1419	0.0923	0.0537
	4	0.0021	0.0213	0.0683	0.1329	0.1936	0.2311	0.2367	0.2128	0.1700	0.1208
	5	0.0002	0.0038	0.0193	0.0532	0.1032	0.1585	0.2039	0.2270	0.2225	0.1934
	6	0.0000	0.0005	0.0040	0.0155	0.0401	0.0792	0.1281	0.1766	0.2124	0.2256
	7	0.0000	0.0000	0.0006	0.0033	0.0115	0.0291	0.0591	0.1009	0.1489	0.1934
	8	0.0000	0.0000	0.0001	0.0005	0.0024	0.0078	0.0199	0.0420	0.0762	0.1208
	9	0.0000	0.0000	0.0000	0.0001	0.0004	0.0015	0.0048	0.0125	0.0277	0.0537
	10	0.0000	0.0000	0.0000	0.0000	0.0000	0.0002	0.0008	0.0025	0.0068	0.0161
	11	0.0000	0.0000	0.0000	0.0000	0.0000	0.0000	0.0001	0.0003	0.0010	0.0029
	12	0.0000	0.0000	0.0000	0.0000	0.0000	0.0000	0.0000	0.0000	0.0001	0.0002
13	0	0.5133	0.2542	0.1209	0.0550	0.0238	0.0097	0.0037	0.0013	0.0004	0.0001
	1	0.3512	0.3672	0.2774	0.1787	0.1029	0.0540	0.0259	0.0113	0.0045	0.0016
	2	0.1109	0.2448	0.2937	0.2680	0.2059	0.1388	0.0836	0.0453	0.0220	0.0095
	3	0.0214	0.0997	0.1900	0.2457	0.2517	0.2181	0.1651	0.1107	0.0660	0.0349
	4	0.0028	0.0277	0.0838	0.1535	0.2097	0.2337	0.2222	0.1845	0.1350	0.0873
	5	0.0003	0.0055	0.0266	0.0691	0.1258	0.1803	0.2154	0.2214	0.1989	0.1571
	6	0.0000	0.0008	0.0063	0.0230	0.0559	0.1030	0.1546	0.1968	0.2169	0.2095
	7	0.0000	0.0001	0.0011	0.0058	0.0186	0.0442	0.0833	0.1312	0.1775	0.2095

n	x	0.05	0.10	0.15	0.20	0.25	0.30	0.35	0.40	0.45	0.50
						p					
	8	0.0000	0.0000	0.0001	0.0011	0.0047	0.0142	0.0336	0.0656	0.1089	0.1571
	9	0.0000	0.0000	0.0000	0.0001	0.0009	0.0034	0.0101	0.0243	0.0495	0.0873
	10	0.0000	0.0000	0.0000	0.0000	0.0001	0.0006	0.0022	0.0065	0.0162	0.0349
	11	0.0000	0.0000	0.0000	0.0000	0.0000	0.0001	0.0003	0.0012	0.0036	0.0095
	12	0.0000	0.0000	0.0000	0.0000	0.0000	0.0000	0.0000	0.0001	0.0005	0.0016
	13	0.0000	0.0000	0.0000	0.0000	0.0000	0.0000	0.0000	0.0000	0.0000	0.0001
14	0	0.4877	0.2288	0.1028	0.0440	0.0178	0.0068	0.0024	0.0008	0.0002	0.0001
	1	0.3593	0.3559	0.2539	0.1539	0.0832	0.0407	0.0181	0.0073	0.0027	0.0009
	2	0.1229	0.2570	0.2912	0.2501	0.1802	0.1134	0.0634	0.0317	0.0141	0.0056
	3	0.0259	0.1142	0.2056	0.2501	0.2402	0.1943	0.1366	0.0845	0.0462	0.0222
	4	0.0037	0.0349	0.0998	0.1720	0.2202	0.2290	0.2022	0.1549	0.1040	0.0611
	5	0.0004	0.0078	0.0352	0.0860	0.1468	0.1963	0.2178	0.2066	0.1701	0.1222
	6	0.0000	0.0013	0.0093	0.0322	0.0734	0.1262	0.1759	0.2066	0.2088	0.1833
	7	0.0000	0.0002	0.0019	0.0092	0.0280	0.0618	0.1082	0.1574	0.1952	0.2095
	8	0.0000	0.0000	0.0003	0.0020	0.0082	0.0232	0.0510	0.0918	0.1398	0.1833
	9	0.0000	0.0000	0.0000	0.0003	0.0018	0.0066	0.0183	0.0408	0.0762	0.1222
	10	0.0000	0.0000	0.0000	0.0000	0.0003	0.0014	0.0049	0.0136	0.0312	0.0611
	11	0.0000	0.0000	0.0000	0.0000	0.0000	0.0002	0.0010	0.0033	0.0093	0.0222
	12	0.0000	0.0000	0.0000	0.0000	0.0000	0.0000	0.0001	0.0005	0.0019	0.0056
	13	0.0000	0.0000	0.0000	0.0000	0.0000	0.0000	0.0000	0.0001	0.0002	0.0009
	14	0.0000	0.0000	0.0000	0.0000	0.0000	0.0000	0.0000	0.0000	0.0000	0.0001
15	0	0.4633	0.2059	0.0874	0.0352	0.0134	0.0047	0.0016	0.0005	0.0001	0.0000
	1	0.3658	0.3432	0.2312	0.1319	0.0668	0.0305	0.0126	0.0047	0.0016	0.0005
	2	0.1348	0.2669	0.2856	0.2309	0.1559	0.0916	0.0476	0.0219	0.0090	0.0032
	3	0.0307	0.1285	0.2184	0.2501	0.2252	0.1700	0.1110	0.0634	0.0318	0.0139
	4	0.0049	0.0428	0.1156	0.1876	0.2252	0.2186	0.1792	0.1268	0.0780	0.0417
	5	0.0006	0.0105	0.0449	0.1032	0.1651	0.2061	0.2123	0.1859	0.1404	0.0916
	6	0.0000	0.0019	0.0132	0.0430	0.0917	0.1472	0.1906	0.2066	0.1914	0.1527
	7	0.0000	0.0003	0.0030	0.0138	0.0393	0.0811	0.1319	0.1711	0.2013	0.1964
	8	0.0000	0.0000	0.0005	0.0035	0.0131	0.0348	0.0710	0.1181	0.1647	0.1964
	9	0.0000	0.0000	0.0001	0.0007	0.0034	0.0116	0.0298	0.0612	0.1048	0.1527
	10	0.0000	0.0000	0.0000	0.0001	0.0007	0.0030	0.0096	0.0245	0.0515	0.0916
	11	0.0000	0.0000	0.0000	0.0000	0.0001	0.0006	0.0024	0.0074	0.0191	0.0417
	12	0.0000	0.0000	0.0000	0.0000	0.0000	0.0001	0.0004	0.0016	0.0052	0.0139
	13	0.0000	0.0000	0.0000	0.0000	0.0000	0.0000	0.0001	0.0003	0.0010	0.0032
	14	0.0000	0.0000	0.0000	0.0000	0.0000	0.0000	0.0000	0.0000	0.0001	0.0005
	15	0.0000	0.0000	0.0000	0.0000	0.0000	0.0000	0.0000	0.0000	0.0000	0.0000
16	0	0.4401	0.1853	0.0743	0.0281	0.0100	0.0033	0.0010	0.0003	0.0001	0.0000
	1	0.3706	0.3294	0.2097	0.1126	0.0535	0.0228	0.0087	0.0030	0.0009	0.0002
	2	0.1463	0.2745	0.2775	0.2111	0.1336	0.0732	0.0353	0.0150	0.0056	0.0018
	3	0.0359	0.1423	0.2285	0.2463	0.2079	0.1465	0.0888	0.0468	0.0215	0.0085
	4	0.0061	0.0514	0.1311	0.2001	0.2252	0.2040	0.1553	0.1014	0.0572	0.0278
	5	0.0008	0.0137	0.0555	0.1201	0.1802	0.2099	0.2008	0.1623	0.1123	0.0667
	6	0.0001	0.0028	0.0180	0.0550	0.1101	0.1649	0.1982	0.1983	0.1684	0.1222
	7	0.0000	0.0004	0.0045	0.0197	0.0524	0.1010	0.1524	0.1889	0.1969	0.1746
	8	0.0000	0.0001	0.0009	0.0055	0.0197	0.0487	0.0923	0.1417	0.1812	0.1964
	9	0.0000	0.0000	0.0001	0.0012	0.0058	0.0185	0.0442	0.0840	0.1318	0.1746
	10	0.0000	0.0000	0.0000	0.0002	0.0014	0.0056	0.0167	0.0392	0.0755	0.1222
	11	0.0000	0.0000	0.0000	0.0000	0.0002	0.0013	0.0049	0.0142	0.0337	0.0667
	12	0.0000	0.0000	0.0000	0.0000	0.0000	0.0002	0.0011	0.0040	0.0115	0.0278
	13	0.0000	0.0000	0.0000	0.0000	0.0000	0.0000	0.0002	0.0008	0.0029	0.0085
	14	0.0000	0.0000	0.0000	0.0000	0.0000	0.0000	0.0000	0.0001	0.0005	0.0018
	15	0.0000	0.0000	0.0000	0.0000	0.0000	0.0000	0.0000	0.0000	0.0001	0.0002
	16	0.0000	0.0000	0.0000	0.0000	0.0000	0.0000	0.0000	0.0000	0.0000	0.0000

n	x	p = 0.05	0.10	0.15	0.20	0.25	0.30	0.35	0.40	0.45	0.50
17	0	0.4181	0.1668	0.0631	0.0225	0.0075	0.0023	0.0007	0.0002	0.0000	0.0000
	1	0.3741	0.3150	0.1893	0.0957	0.0426	0.0169	0.0060	0.0019	0.0005	0.0001
	2	0.1575	0.2800	0.2673	0.1914	0.1136	0.0581	0.0260	0.0102	0.0035	0.0010
	3	0.0415	0.1556	0.2359	0.2393	0.1893	0.1245	0.0701	0.0341	0.0144	0.0052
	4	0.0076	0.0605	0.1457	0.2093	0.2209	0.1868	0.1320	0.0796	0.0411	0.0182
	5	0.0010	0.0175	0.0668	0.1361	0.1914	0.2081	0.1849	0.1379	0.0875	0.0472
	6	0.0001	0.0039	0.0236	0.0680	0.1276	0.1784	0.1991	0.1839	0.1432	0.0944
	7	0.0000	0.0007	0.0065	0.0267	0.0668	0.1201	0.1685	0.1927	0.1841	0.1484
	8	0.0000	0.0001	0.0014	0.0084	0.0279	0.0644	0.1134	0.1606	0.1883	0.1855
	9	0.0000	0.0000	0.0003	0.0021	0.0093	0.0276	0.0611	0.1070	0.1540	0.1855
	10	0.0000	0.0000	0.0000	0.0004	0.0025	0.0095	0.0263	0.0571	0.1008	0.1484
	11	0.0000	0.0000	0.0000	0.0001	0.0005	0.0026	0.0090	0.0242	0.0525	0.0944
	12	0.0000	0.0000	0.0000	0.0000	0.0001	0.0006	0.0024	0.0081	0.0215	0.0472
	13	0.0000	0.0000	0.0000	0.0000	0.0000	0.0001	0.0005	0.0021	0.0068	0.0182
	14	0.0000	0.0000	0.0000	0.0000	0.0000	0.0000	0.0001	0.0004	0.0016	0.0052
	15	0.0000	0.0000	0.0000	0.0000	0.0000	0.0000	0.0000	0.0001	0.0003	0.0010
	16	0.0000	0.0000	0.0000	0.0000	0.0000	0.0000	0.0000	0.0000	0.0000	0.0001
	17	0.0000	0.0000	0.0000	0.0000	0.0000	0.0000	0.0000	0.0000	0.0000	0.0000
18	0	0.3972	0.1501	0.0536	0.0180	0.0056	0.0016	0.0004	0.0001	0.0000	0.0000
	1	0.3763	0.3002	0.1704	0.0811	0.0338	0.0126	0.0042	0.0012	0.0003	0.0001
	2	0.1683	0.2835	0.2556	0.1723	0.0958	0.0458	0.0190	0.0069	0.0022	0.0006
	3	0.0473	0.1680	0.2406	0.2297	0.1704	0.1046	0.0547	0.0246	0.0095	0.0031
	4	0.0093	0.0700	0.1592	0.2153	0.2130	0.1681	0.1104	0.0614	0.0291	0.0117
	5	0.0014	0.0218	0.0787	0.1507	0.1988	0.2017	0.1664	0.1146	0.0666	0.0327
	6	0.0002	0.0052	0.0301	0.0816	0.1436	0.1873	0.1941	0.1655	0.1181	0.0708
	7	0.0000	0.0010	0.0091	0.0350	0.0820	0.1376	0.1792	0.1892	0.1657	0.1214
	8	0.0000	0.0002	0.0022	0.0120	0.0376	0.0811	0.1327	0.1734	0.1864	0.1669
	9	0.0000	0.0000	0.0004	0.0033	0.0139	0.0386	0.0794	0.1284	0.1694	0.1855
	10	0.0000	0.0000	0.0001	0.0008	0.0042	0.0149	0.0385	0.0771	0.1248	0.1669
	11	0.0000	0.0000	0.0000	0.0001	0.0010	0.0046	0.0151	0.0374	0.0742	0.1214
	12	0.0000	0.0000	0.0000	0.0000	0.0002	0.0012	0.0047	0.0145	0.0354	0.0708
	13	0.0000	0.0000	0.0000	0.0000	0.0000	0.0002	0.0012	0.0045	0.0134	0.0327
	14	0.0000	0.0000	0.0000	0.0000	0.0000	0.0000	0.0002	0.0011	0.0039	0.0117
	15	0.0000	0.0000	0.0000	0.0000	0.0000	0.0000	0.0000	0.0002	0.0009	0.0031
	16	0.0000	0.0000	0.0000	0.0000	0.0000	0.0000	0.0000	0.0000	0.0001	0.0006
	17	0.0000	0.0000	0.0000	0.0000	0.0000	0.0000	0.0000	0.0000	0.0000	0.0001
	18	0.0000	0.0000	0.0000	0.0000	0.0000	0.0000	0.0000	0.0000	0.0000	0.0000
19	0	0.3774	0.1351	0.0456	0.0144	0.0042	0.0011	0.0003	0.0001	0.0002	0.0000
	1	0.3774	0.2852	0.1529	0.0685	0.0268	0.0093	0.0029	0.0008	0.0002	0.0000
	2	0.1787	0.2852	0.2428	0.1540	0.0803	0.0358	0.0138	0.0046	0.0013	0.0003
	3	0.0533	0.1796	0.2428	0.2182	0.1517	0.0869	0.0422	0.0175	0.0062	0.0018
	4	0.0112	0.0798	0.1714	0.2182	0.2023	0.1491	0.0909	0.0467	0.0203	0.0074
	5	0.0018	0.0266	0.0907	0.1636	0.2023	0.1916	0.1468	0.0933	0.0497	0.0222
	6	0.0002	0.0069	0.0374	0.0955	0.1574	0.1916	0.1844	0.1451	0.0949	0.0518
	7	0.0000	0.0014	0.0122	0.0443	0.0974	0.1525	0.1844	0.1797	0.1443	0.0961
	8	0.0000	0.0002	0.0032	0.0166	0.0487	0.0981	0.1489	0.1797	0.1771	0.1442
	9	0.0000	0.0000	0.0007	0.0051	0.0198	0.0514	0.0980	0.1464	0.1771	0.1762
	10	0.0000	0.0000	0.0001	0.0013	0.0066	0.0220	0.0528	0.0976	0.1449	0.1762
	11	0.0000	0.0000	0.0000	0.0003	0.0018	0.0077	0.0233	0.0532	0.0970	0.1442
	12	0.0000	0.0000	0.0000	0.0000	0.0004	0.0022	0.0083	0.0237	0.0529	0.0961
	13	0.0000	0.0000	0.0000	0.0000	0.0001	0.0005	0.0024	0.0085	0.0233	0.0518
	14	0.0000	0.0000	0.0000	0.0000	0.0000	0.0001	0.0006	0.0024	0.0082	0.0222
	15	0.0000	0.0000	0.0000	0.0000	0.0000	0.0000	0.0001	0.0005	0.0022	0.0074
	16	0.0000	0.0000	0.0000	0.0000	0.0000	0.0000	0.0000	0.0001	0.0005	0.0018

n	x	0.05	0.10	0.15	0.20	0.25	0.30	0.35	0.40	0.45	0.50
						p					
	17	0.0000	0.0000	0.0000	0.0000	0.0000	0.0000	0.0000	0.0000	0.0001	0.0003
	18	0.0000	0.0000	0.0000	0.0000	0.0000	0.0000	0.0000	0.0000	0.0000	0.0000
	19	0.0000	0.0000	0.0000	0.0000	0.0000	0.0000	0.0000	0.0000	0.0000	0.0000
20	0	0.3585	0.1216	0.0388	0.0115	0.0032	0.0008	0.0002	0.0000	0.0000	0.0000
	1	0.3774	0.2702	0.1368	0.0576	0.0211	0.0068	0.0020	0.0005	0.0001	0.0000
	2	0.1887	0.2852	0.2293	0.1369	0.0669	0.0278	0.0100	0.0031	0.0008	0.0002
	3	0.0596	0.1901	0.2428	0.2054	0.1339	0.0716	0.0323	0.0123	0.0040	0.0011
	4	0.0133	0.0898	0.1821	0.2182	0.1897	0.1304	0.0738	0.0350	0.0139	0.0046
	5	0.0022	0.0319	0.1028	0.1746	0.2023	0.1789	0.1272	0.0746	0.0365	0.0148
	6	0.0003	0.0089	0.0454	0.1091	0.1686	0.1916	0.1712	0.1244	0.0746	0.0370
	7	0.0000	0.0020	0.0160	0.0545	0.1124	0.1643	0.1844	0.1659	0.1221	0.0739
	8	0.0000	0.0004	0.0046	0.0222	0.0609	0.1144	0.1614	0.1797	0.1623	0.1201
	9	0.0000	0.0001	0.0011	0.0074	0.0271	0.0654	0.1158	0.1597	0.1771	0.1602
	10	0.0000	0.0000	0.0002	0.0020	0.0099	0.0308	0.0686	0.1171	0.1593	0.1762
	11	0.0000	0.0000	0.0000	0.0005	0.0030	0.0120	0.0336	0.0710	0.1185	0.1602
	12	0.0000	0.0000	0.0000	0.0001	0.0008	0.0039	0.0136	0.0355	0.0727	0.1201
	13	0.0000	0.0000	0.0000	0.0000	0.0002	0.0010	0.0045	0.0146	0.0366	0.0739
	14	0.0000	0.0000	0.0000	0.0000	0.0000	0.0002	0.0012	0.0049	0.0150	0.0370
	15	0.0000	0.0000	0.0000	0.0000	0.0000	0.0000	0.0003	0.0013	0.0049	0.0148
	16	0.0000	0.0000	0.0000	0.0000	0.0000	0.0000	0.0000	0.0003	0.0013	0.0046
	17	0.0000	0.0000	0.0000	0.0000	0.0000	0.0000	0.0000	0.0000	0.0002	0.0011
	18	0.0000	0.0000	0.0000	0.0000	0.0000	0.0000	0.0000	0.0000	0.0000	0.0002
	19	0.0000	0.0000	0.0000	0.0000	0.0000	0.0000	0.0000	0.0000	0.0000	0.0000
	20	0.0000	0.0000	0.0000	0.0000	0.0000	0.0000	0.0000	0.0000	0.0000	0.0000

Source: Reprinted from *Handbook of Probability and Statistics with Tables,* 2nd ed., by R. S. Burington and D. C. May. New York: McGraw-Hill Book Company, Inc., 1970, by permission of the authors' trustee.

Appendix E

Poisson Probabilities

Entries in the table give the probability of x occurrences for a Poisson process with a mean μ. For example, when $\mu = 2.5$, the probability of four occurrences is 0.1336.

					μ					
x	0.1	0.2	0.3	0.4	0.5	0.6	0.7	0.8	0.9	1.0
0	0.9048	0.8187	0.7408	0.6703	0.6065	0.5488	0.4966	0.4493	0.4066	0.3679
1	0.0905	0.1637	0.2222	0.2681	0.3033	0.3293	0.3476	0.3595	0.3659	0.3679
2	0.0045	0.0164	0.0333	0.0536	0.0758	0.0988	0.1217	0.1438	0.1647	0.1839
3	0.0002	0.0011	0.0033	0.0072	0.0126	0.0198	0.0284	0.0383	0.0494	0.0613
4	0.0000	0.0001	0.0002	0.0007	0.0016	0.0030	0.0050	0.0077	0.0111	0.0153
5	0.0000	0.0000	0.0000	0.0001	0.0002	0.0004	0.0007	0.0012	0.0020	0.0031
6	0.0000	0.0000	0.0000	0.0000	0.0000	0.0000	0.0001	0.0002	0.0003	0.0005
7	0.0000	0.0000	0.0000	0.0000	0.0000	0.0000	0.0000	0.0000	0.0000	0.0001

					μ					
x	1.1	1.2	1.3	1.4	1.5	1.6	1.7	1.8	1.9	2.0
0	0.3329	0.3012	0.2725	0.2466	0.2231	0.2019	0.1827	0.1653	0.1496	0.1353
1	0.3662	0.3614	0.3543	0.3452	0.3347	0.3230	0.3106	0.2975	0.2842	0.2707
2	0.2014	0.2169	0.2303	0.2417	0.2510	0.2584	0.2640	0.2678	0.2700	0.2707
3	0.0738	0.0867	0.0998	0.1128	0.1255	0.1378	0.1496	0.1607	0.1710	0.1804
4	0.0203	0.0260	0.0324	0.0395	0.0471	0.0551	0.0636	0.0723	0.0812	0.0902
5	0.0045	0.0062	0.0084	0.0111	0.0141	0.0176	0.0216	0.0260	0.0309	0.0361
6	0.0008	0.0012	0.0018	0.0026	0.0035	0.0047	0.0061	0.0078	0.0098	0.0120
7	0.0001	0.0002	0.0003	0.0005	0.0008	0.0011	0.0015	0.0020	0.0027	0.0034
8	0.0000	0.0000	0.0001	0.0001	0.0001	0.0002	0.0003	0.0005	0.0006	0.0009
9	0.0000	0.0000	0.0000	0.0000	0.0000	0.0000	0.0001	0.0001	0.0001	0.0002

					μ					
x	2.1	2.2	2.3	2.4	2.5	2.6	2.7	2.8	2.9	3.0
0	0.1225	0.1108	0.1003	0.0907	0.0821	0.0743	0.0672	0.0608	0.0550	0.0498
1	0.2572	0.2438	0.2306	0.2177	0.2052	0.1931	0.1815	0.1703	0.1596	0.1494
2	0.2700	0.2681	0.2652	0.2613	0.2565	0.2510	0.2450	0.2384	0.2314	0.2240
3	0.1890	0.1966	0.2033	0.2090	0.2138	0.2176	0.2205	0.2225	0.2237	0.2240
4	0.0992	0.1082	0.1169	0.1254	0.1336	0.1414	0.1488	0.1557	0.1622	0.1680
5	0.0417	0.0476	0.0538	0.0602	0.0668	0.0735	0.0804	0.0872	0.0940	0.1008
6	0.0146	0.0174	0.0206	0.0241	0.0278	0.0319	0.0362	0.0407	0.0455	0.0540
7	0.0044	0.0055	0.0068	0.0083	0.0099	0.0118	0.0139	0.0163	0.0188	0.0216
8	0.0011	0.0015	0.0019	0.0025	0.0031	0.0038	0.0047	0.0057	0.0068	0.0081
9	0.0003	0.0004	0.0005	0.0007	0.0009	0.0011	0.0014	0.0018	0.0022	0.0027
10	0.0001	0.0001	0.0001	0.0002	0.0002	0.0003	0.0004	0.0005	0.0006	0.0008
11	0.0000	0.0000	0.0000	0.0000	0.0000	0.0001	0.0001	0.0001	0.0002	0.0002
12	0.0000	0.0000	0.0000	0.0000	0.0000	0.0000	0.0000	0.0000	0.0000	0.0001

					μ					
x	3.1	3.2	3.3	3.4	3.5	3.6	3.7	3.8	3.9	4.0
0	0.0450	0.0408	0.0369	0.0344	0.0302	0.0273	0.0247	0.0224	0.0202	0.0183
1	0.1397	0.1304	0.1217	0.1135	0.1057	0.0984	0.0915	0.0850	0.0789	0.0733
2	0.2165	0.2087	0.2008	0.1929	0.1850	0.1771	0.1692	0.1615	0.1539	0.1465
3	0.2237	0.2226	0.2209	0.2186	0.2158	0.2125	0.2087	0.2046	0.2001	0.1954
4	0.1734	0.1781	0.1823	0.1858	0.1888	0.1912	0.1931	0.1944	0.1951	0.1954

x	μ 3.1	3.2	3.3	3.4	3.5	3.6	3.7	3.8	3.9	4.0
5	0.1075	0.1140	0.1203	0.1264	0.1322	0.1377	0.1429	0.1477	0.1522	0.1563
6	0.0555	0.0608	0.0662	0.0716	0.0771	0.0826	0.0881	0.0936	0.0989	0.1042
7	0.0246	0.0278	0.0312	0.0348	0.0385	0.0425	0.0466	0.0508	0.0551	0.0595
8	0.0095	0.0111	0.0129	0.0148	0.0169	0.0191	0.0215	0.0241	0.0269	0.0298
9	0.0093	0.0040	0.0047	0.0056	0.0066	0.0076	0.0089	0.0102	0.0116	0.0132
10	0.0010	0.0013	0.0016	0.0019	0.0023	0.0028	0.0033	0.0039	0.0045	0.0053
11	0.0003	0.0004	0.0005	0.0006	0.0007	0.0009	0.0011	0.0013	0.0016	0.0019
12	0.0001	0.0001	0.0001	0.0002	0.0002	0.0003	0.0003	0.0004	0.0005	0.0006
13	0.0000	0.0000	0.0000	0.0000	0.0001	0.0001	0.0001	0.0001	0.0002	0.0002
14	0.0000	0.0000	0.0000	0.0000	0.0000	0.0000	0.0000	0.0000	0.0000	0.0001

x	μ 4.1	4.2	4.3	4.4	4.5	4.6	4.7	4.8	4.9	5.0
0	0.0166	0.0150	0.0136	0.0123	0.0111	0.0101	0.0091	0.0082	0.0074	0.0067
1	0.0679	0.0630	0.0583	0.0540	0.0500	0.0462	0.0427	0.0395	0.0365	0.0337
2	0.1393	0.1323	0.1254	0.1188	0.1125	0.1063	0.1005	0.0948	0.0894	0.0842
3	0.1904	0.1852	0.1798	0.1743	0.1687	0.1631	0.1574	0.1517	0.1460	0.1404
4	0.1951	0.1944	0.1933	0.1917	0.1898	0.1875	0.1849	0.1820	0.1789	0.1755
5	0.1600	0.1633	0.1662	0.1687	0.1708	0.1725	0.1738	0.1747	0.1753	0.1755
6	0.1093	0.1143	0.1191	0.1237	0.1281	0.1323	0.1362	0.1398	0.1432	0.1462
7	0.0640	0.0686	0.0732	0.0778	0.0824	0.0869	0.0914	0.0959	0.1002	0.1044
8	0.0328	0.0360	0.0393	0.0428	0.0463	0.0500	0.0537	0.0575	0.0614	0.0653
9	0.0150	0.0163	0.0188	0.0209	0.0232	0.0255	0.0280	0.0307	0.0334	0.0363
10	0.0061	0.0071	0.0081	0.0092	0.0104	0.0118	0.0132	0.0147	0.0164	0.0181
11	0.0023	0.0027	0.0032	0.0037	0.0043	0.0049	0.0056	0.0064	0.0073	0.0082
12	0.0008	0.0009	0.0011	0.0014	0.0016	0.0019	0.0022	0.0026	0.0030	0.0034
13	0.0002	0.0003	0.0004	0.0005	0.0006	0.0007	0.0008	0.0009	0.0011	0.0013
14	0.0001	0.0001	0.0001	0.0001	0.0002	0.0002	0.0003	0.0003	0.0004	0.0005
15	0.0000	0.0000	0.0000	0.0000	0.0001	0.0001	0.0001	0.0001	0.0001	0.0002

x	μ 5.1	5.2	5.3	5.4	5.5	5.6	5.7	5.8	5.9	6.0
0	0.0061	0.0055	0.0050	0.0045	0.0041	0.0037	0.0033	0.0030	0.0027	0.0025
1	0.0311	0.0287	0.0265	0.0244	0.0225	0.0207	0.0191	0.0176	0.0162	0.0149
2	0.0793	0.0746	0.0701	0.0659	0.0618	0.0580	0.0544	0.0509	0.0477	0.0446
3	0.1348	0.1293	0.1239	0.1185	0.1133	0.1082	0.1033	0.0985	0.0938	0.0892
4	0.1719	0.1681	0.1641	0.1600	0.1558	0.1515	0.1472	0.1428	0.1383	0.1339
5	0.1753	0.1748	0.1740	0.1728	0.1714	0.1697	0.1678	0.1656	0.1632	0.1606
6	0.1490	0.1515	0.1537	0.1555	0.1571	0.1584	0.1594	0.1601	0.1605	0.1606
7	0.1086	0.1125	0.1163	0.1200	0.1234	0.1267	0.1298	0.1326	0.1353	0.1377
8	0.0692	0.0731	0.0771	0.0810	0.0849	0.0887	0.0925	0.0962	0.0998	0.1033
9	0.0392	0.0423	0.0454	0.0486	0.0519	0.0552	0.0586	0.0620	0.0654	0.0688
10	0.0200	0.0220	0.0241	0.0262	0.0285	0.0309	0.0334	0.0359	0.0386	0.0413
11	0.0093	0.0104	0.0116	0.0129	0.0143	0.0157	0.0173	0.0190	0.0207	0.0225
12	0.0039	0.0045	0.0051	0.0058	0.0065	0.0073	0.0082	0.0092	0.0102	0.0113
13	0.0015	0.0018	0.0021	0.0024	0.0028	0.0032	0.0036	0.0041	0.0046	0.0052
14	0.0006	0.0007	0.0008	0.0009	0.0011	0.0013	0.0015	0.0017	0.0019	0.0022
15	0.0002	0.0002	0.0003	0.0003	0.0004	0.0005	0.0006	0.0007	0.0008	0.0009
16	0.0001	0.0001	0.0001	0.0001	0.0001	0.0002	0.0002	0.0002	0.0003	0.0003
17	0.0000	0.0000	0.0000	0.0000	0.0000	0.0001	0.0001	0.0001	0.0001	0.0001

					μ					
x	6.1	6.2	6.3	6.4	6.5	6.6	6.7	6.8	6.9	7.0
0	0.0022	0.0020	0.0018	0.0017	0.0015	0.0014	0.0012	0.0011	0.0010	0.0009
1	0.0137	0.0126	0.0116	0.0106	0.0098	0.0090	0.0082	0.0076	0.0070	0.0064
2	0.0417	0.0390	0.0364	0.0340	0.0318	0.0296	0.0276	0.0258	0.0240	0.0223
3	0.0848	0.0806	0.0765	0.0726	0.0688	0.0652	0.0617	0.0584	0.0552	0.0521
4	0.1294	0.1249	0.1205	0.1162	0.1118	0.1076	0.1034	0.0992	0.0952	0.0912
5	0.1579	0.1549	0.1519	0.1487	0.1454	0.1420	0.1385	0.1349	0.1314	0.1277
6	0.1605	0.1601	0.1595	0.1586	0.1575	0.1562	0.1546	0.1529	0.1511	0.1490
7	0.1399	0.1418	0.1435	0.1450	0.1462	0.1472	0.1480	0.1486	0.1489	0.1490
8	0.1066	0.1099	0.1130	0.1160	0.1188	0.1215	0.1240	0.1263	0.1284	0.1304
9	0.0723	0.0757	0.0791	0.0825	0.0858	0.0891	0.0923	0.0954	0.0985	0.1014
10	0.0441	0.0469	0.0498	0.0528	0.0558	0.0588	0.0618	0.0649	0.0679	0.0710
11	0.0245	0.0265	0.0285	0.0307	0.0330	0.0353	0.0377	0.0401	0.0426	0.0452
12	0.0124	0.0137	0.0150	0.0164	0.0179	0.0194	0.0210	0.0227	0.0245	0.0264
13	0.0058	0.0065	0.0073	0.0081	0.0089	0.0098	0.0108	0.0119	0.0130	0.0142
14	0.0025	0.0029	0.0033	0.0037	0.0041	0.0046	0.0052	0.0058	0.0064	0.0071
15	0.0010	0.0012	0.0014	0.0016	0.0018	0.0020	0.0023	0.0026	0.0029	0.0033
16	0.0004	0.0005	0.0005	0.0006	0.0007	0.0008	0.0010	0.0011	0.0013	0.0014
17	0.0001	0.0002	0.0002	0.0002	0.0003	0.0003	0.0004	0.0004	0.0005	0.0006
18	0.0000	0.0001	0.0001	0.0001	0.0001	0.0001	0.0001	0.0002	0.0002	0.0002
19	0.0000	0.0000	0.0000	0.0000	0.0000	0.0000	0.0000	0.0001	0.0001	0.0001

					μ					
x	7.1	7.2	7.3	7.4	7.5	7.6	7.7	7.8	7.9	8.0
0	0.0008	0.0007	0.0007	0.0006	0.0006	0.0005	0.0005	0.0004	0.0004	0.0003
1	0.0059	0.0054	0.0049	0.0045	0.0041	0.0038	0.0035	0.0032	0.0029	0.0027
2	0.0208	0.0194	0.0180	0.0167	0.0156	0.0145	0.0134	0.0125	0.0116	0.0107
3	0.0492	0.0464	0.0438	0.0413	0.0389	0.0366	0.0345	0.0324	0.0305	0.0286
4	0.0874	0.0836	0.0799	0.0764	0.0729	0.0696	0.0663	0.0632	0.0602	0.0573
5	0.1241	0.1204	0.1167	0.1130	0.1094	0.1057	0.1021	0.0986	0.0951	0.0916
6	0.1468	0.1445	0.1420	0.1394	0.1367	0.1339	0.1311	0.1282	0.1252	0.1221
7	0.1489	0.1486	0.1481	0.1474	0.1465	0.1454	0.1442	0.1428	0.1413	0.1396
8	0.1321	0.1337	0.1351	0.1363	0.1373	0.1382	0.1388	0.1392	0.1395	0.1396
9	0.1042	0.1070	0.1096	0.1121	0.1144	0.1167	0.1187	0.1207	0.1224	0.1241
10	0.0740	0.0770	0.0800	0.0829	0.0858	0.0887	0.0914	0.0941	0.0967	0.0993
11	0.0478	0.0504	0.0531	0.0558	0.0585	0.0613	0.0640	0.0667	0.0695	0.0722
12	0.0283	0.0303	0.0323	0.0344	0.0366	0.0388	0.0411	0.0434	0.0457	0.0481
13	0.0154	0.0168	0.0181	0.0196	0.0211	0.0227	0.0243	0.0260	0.0278	0.0296
14	0.0078	0.0086	0.0095	0.0104	0.0113	0.0123	0.0134	0.0145	0.0157	0.0169
15	0.0037	0.0041	0.0046	0.0051	0.0057	0.0062	0.0069	0.0075	0.0083	0.0090
16	0.0016	0.0019	0.0021	0.0024	0.0026	0.0030	0.0033	0.0037	0.0041	0.0045
17	0.0007	0.0008	0.0009	0.0010	0.0012	0.0013	0.0015	0.0017	0.0019	0.0021
18	0.0003	0.0003	0.0004	0.0004	0.0005	0.0006	0.0006	0.0007	0.0008	0.0009
19	0.0001	0.0001	0.0001	0.0002	0.0002	0.0002	0.0003	0.0003	0.0003	0.0004
20	0.0000	0.0000	0.0001	0.0001	0.0001	0.0001	0.0001	0.0001	0.0001	0.0002
21	0.0000	0.0000	0.0000	0.0000	0.0000	0.0000	0.0000	0.0000	0.0001	0.0001

					μ					
x	8.1	8.2	8.3	8.4	8.5	8.6	8.7	8.8	8.9	9.0
0	0.0003	0.0003	0.0002	0.0002	0.0002	0.0002	0.0002	0.0002	0.0001	0.0001
1	0.0025	0.0023	0.0021	0.0019	0.0017	0.0016	0.0014	0.0013	0.0012	0.0011
2	0.0100	0.0092	0.0086	0.0079	0.0074	0.0068	0.0063	0.0058	0.0054	0.0050
3	0.0269	0.0252	0.0237	0.0222	0.0208	0.0195	0.0183	0.0171	0.1060	0.0150
4	0.0544	0.0517	0.0491	0.0466	0.0443	0.0420	0.0398	0.0377	0.0357	0.0337

x	μ 8.1	8.2	8.3	8.4	8.5	8.6	8.7	8.8	8.9	9.0
5	0.0882	0.0849	0.0816	0.0784	0.0752	0.0722	0.0692	0.0663	0.0635	0.0607
6	0.1191	0.1160	0.1128	0.1097	0.1066	0.1034	0.1003	0.0972	0.0941	0.0911
7	0.1378	0.1358	0.1338	0.1317	0.1294	0.1271	0.1247	0.1222	0.1197	0.1171
8	0.1395	0.1392	0.1388	0.1382	0.1375	0.1366	0.1356	0.1344	0.1332	0.1318
9	0.1256	0.1269	0.1280	0.1290	0.1299	0.1306	0.1311	0.1315	0.1317	0.1318
10	0.1017	0.1040	0.1063	0.1084	0.1104	0.1123	0.1140	0.1157	0.1172	0.1186
11	0.0749	0.0776	0.0802	0.0828	0.0853	0.0878	0.0902	0.0925	0.0948	0.0970
12	0.0505	0.0530	0.0555	0.0579	0.0604	0.0629	0.0654	0.0679	0.0703	0.0728
13	0.0315	0.0334	0.0354	0.0374	0.0395	0.0416	0.0438	0.0459	0.0481	0.0504
14	0.0182	0.0196	0.0210	0.0225	0.0240	0.0256	0.0272	0.0289	0.0306	0.0324
15	0.0098	0.0107	0.0116	0.0126	0.0136	0.0147	0.0158	0.0169	0.0182	0.0194
16	0.0050	0.0055	0.0060	0.0066	0.0072	0.0079	0.0086	0.0093	0.0101	0.0109
17	0.0024	0.0026	0.0029	0.0033	0.0036	0.0040	0.0044	0.0048	0.0053	0.0058
18	0.0011	0.0012	0.0014	0.0015	0.0017	0.0019	0.0021	0.0024	0.0026	0.0029
19	0.0005	0.0005	0.0006	0.0007	0.0008	0.0009	0.0010	0.0011	0.0012	0.0014
20	0.0002	0.0002	0.0002	0.0003	0.0003	0.0004	0.0004	0.0005	0.0005	0.0006
21	0.0001	0.0001	0.0001	0.0001	0.0001	0.0002	0.0002	0.0002	0.0002	0.0003
22	0.0000	0.0000	0.0000	0.0000	0.0001	0.0001	0.0001	0.0001	0.0001	0.000

x	μ 9.1	9.2	9.3	9.4	9.5	9.6	9.7	9.8	9.9	10
0	0.0001	0.0001	0.0001	0.0001	0.0001	0.0001	0.0001	0.0001	0.0001	0.0000
1	0.0010	0.0009	0.0009	0.0008	0.0007	0.0007	0.0006	0.0005	0.0005	0.0005
2	0.0046	0.0043	0.0040	0.0037	0.0034	0.0031	0.0029	0.0027	0.0025	0.0023
3	0.0140	0.0131	0.0123	0.0115	0.0107	0.0100	0.0093	0.0087	0.0081	0.0076
4	0.0319	0.0302	0.0285	0.0269	0.0254	0.0240	0.0226	0.0213	0.0201	0.0189
5	0.0581	0.0555	0.0530	0.0506	0.0483	0.0460	0.0439	0.0418	0.0398	0.0378
6	0.0881	0.0851	0.0822	0.0793	0.0764	0.0736	0.0709	0.0682	0.0656	0.0631
7	0.1145	0.1118	0.1091	0.1064	0.1037	0.1010	0.0982	0.0955	0.0928	0.0901
8	0.1302	0.1286	0.1269	0.1251	0.1232	0.1212	0.1191	0.1170	0.1148	0.1126
9	0.1317	0.1315	0.1311	0.1306	0.1300	0.1293	0.1284	0.1274	0.1263	0.1251
10	0.1198	0.1210	0.1219	0.1228	0.1235	0.1241	0.1245	0.1249	0.1250	0.1251
11	0.0991	0.1012	0.1031	0.1049	0.1067	0.1083	0.1098	0.1112	0.1125	0.1137
12	0.0752	0.0776	0.0799	0.0822	0.0844	0.0866	0.0888	0.0908	0.0928	0.0948
13	0.0526	0.0549	0.0572	0.0594	0.0617	0.0640	0.0662	0.0685	0.0707	0.0729
14	0.0342	0.0361	0.0380	0.0399	0.0419	0.0439	0.0459	0.0479	0.0500	0.0521
15	0.0208	0.0221	0.0235	0.0250	0.0265	0.0281	0.0297	0.0313	0.0330	0.0347
16	0.0118	0.0127	0.0137	0.0147	0.0157	0.0168	0.0180	0.0192	0.0204	0.0217
17	0.0063	0.0069	0.0075	0.0081	0.0088	0.0095	0.0103	0.0111	0.0119	0.0128
18	0.0032	0.0035	0.0039	0.0042	0.0046	0.0051	0.0055	0.0060	0.0065	0.0071
19	0.0015	0.0017	0.0019	0.0021	0.0023	0.0026	0.0028	0.0031	0.0034	0.0037
20	0.0007	0.0008	0.0009	0.0010	0.0011	0.0012	0.0014	0.0015	0.0017	0.0019
21	0.0003	0.0003	0.0004	0.0004	0.0005	0.0006	0.0006	0.0007	0.0008	0.0009
22	0.0001	0.0001	0.0002	0.0002	0.0002	0.0002	0.0003	0.0003	0.0004	0.0004
23	0.0000	0.0001	0.0001	0.0001	0.0001	0.0001	0.0001	0.0001	0.0002	0.0002
24	0.0000	0.0000	0.0000	0.0000	0.0000	0.0000	0.0000	0.0001	0.0001	0.0001

x	μ = 11	12	13	14	15	16	17	18	19	20
0	0.0000	0.0000	0.0000	0.0000	0.0000	0.0000	0.0000	0.0000	0.0000	0.0000
1	0.0002	0.0001	0.0000	0.0000	0.0000	0.0000	0.0000	0.0000	0.0000	0.0000
2	0.0010	0.0004	0.0002	0.0001	0.0000	0.0000	0.0000	0.0000	0.0000	0.0000
3	0.0037	0.0018	0.0008	0.0004	0.0002	0.0001	0.0000	0.0000	0.0000	0.0000
4	0.0102	0.0053	0.0027	0.0013	0.0006	0.0003	0.0001	0.0001	0.0000	0.0000
5	0.0224	0.0127	0.0070	0.0037	0.0019	0.0010	0.0005	0.0002	0.0001	0.0001
6	0.0411	0.0255	0.0152	0.0087	0.0048	0.0026	0.0014	0.0007	0.0004	0.0002
7	0.0646	0.0437	0.0281	0.0174	0.0104	0.0060	0.0034	0.0018	0.0010	0.0005
8	0.0888	0.0655	0.0457	0.0304	0.0194	0.0120	0.0072	0.0042	0.0024	0.0013
9	0.1085	0.0874	0.0661	0.0473	0.0324	0.0213	0.0135	0.0083	0.0050	0.0029
10	0.1194	0.1048	0.0859	0.0663	0.0486	0.0341	0.0230	0.0150	0.0095	0.0058
11	0.1194	0.1144	0.1015	0.0844	0.0663	0.0496	0.0355	0.0245	0.0164	0.0106
12	0.1094	0.1144	0.1099	0.0984	0.0829	0.0661	0.0504	0.0368	0.0259	0.0176
13	0.0926	0.1056	0.1099	0.1060	0.0956	0.0814	0.0658	0.0509	0.0378	0.0271
14	0.0728	0.0905	0.1021	0.1060	0.1024	0.0930	0.0800	0.0655	0.0514	0.0387
15	0.0534	0.0724	0.0885	0.0989	0.1024	0.0992	0.0906	0.0786	0.0650	0.0516
16	0.0367	0.0543	0.0719	0.0866	0.0960	0.0992	0.0963	0.0884	0.0772	0.0646
17	0.0237	0.0383	0.0550	0.0713	0.0847	0.0934	0.0963	0.0936	0.0863	0.0760
18	0.0145	0.0256	0.0397	0.0554	0.0706	0.0830	0.0909	0.0936	0.0911	0.0844
19	0.0084	0.0161	0.0272	0.0409	0.0557	0.0699	0.0814	0.0887	0.0911	0.0888
20	0.0046	0.0097	0.0177	0.0286	0.0418	0.0559	0.0692	0.0798	0.0866	0.0888
21	0.0024	0.0055	0.0109	0.0191	0.0299	0.0426	0.0560	0.0684	0.0783	0.0846
22	0.0012	0.0030	0.0065	0.0121	0.0204	0.0310	0.0433	0.0560	0.0676	0.0769
23	0.0006	0.0016	0.0037	0.0074	0.0133	0.0216	0.0320	0.0438	0.0559	0.0669
24	0.0003	0.0008	0.0020	0.0043	0.0083	0.0144	0.0226	0.0328	0.0442	0.0557
25	0.0001	0.0004	0.0010	0.0024	0.0050	0.0092	0.0154	0.0237	0.0336	0.0446
26	0.0000	0.0002	0.0005	0.0013	0.0029	0.0057	0.0101	0.0164	0.0246	0.0343
27	0.0000	0.0001	0.0002	0.0007	0.0016	0.0034	0.0063	0.0109	0.0173	0.0254
28	0.0000	0.0000	0.0001	0.0003	0.0009	0.0019	0.0038	0.0070	0.0117	0.0181
29	0.0000	0.0000	0.0001	0.0002	0.0004	0.0011	0.0023	0.0044	0.0077	0.0125
30	0.0000	0.0000	0.0000	0.0001	0.0002	0.0006	0.0013	0.0026	0.0049	0.0083
31	0.0000	0.0000	0.0000	0.0000	0.0001	0.0003	0.0007	0.0015	0.0030	0.0054
32	0.0000	0.0000	0.0000	0.0000	0.0001	0.0001	0.0004	0.0009	0.0018	0.0034
33	0.0000	0.0000	0.0000	0.0000	0.0000	0.0001	0.0002	0.0005	0.0010	0.0020
34	0.0000	0.0000	0.0000	0.0000	0.0000	0.0000	0.0001	0.0002	0.0006	0.0012
35	0.0000	0.0000	0.0000	0.0000	0.0000	0.0000	0.0000	0.0001	0.0003	0.0007
36	0.0000	0.0000	0.0000	0.0000	0.0000	0.0000	0.0000	0.0001	0.0002	0.0004
37	0.0000	0.0000	0.0000	0.0000	0.0000	0.0000	0.0000	0.0000	0.0001	0.0002
38	0.0000	0.0000	0.0000	0.0000	0.0000	0.0000	0.0000	0.0000	0.0000	0.0001
39	0.0000	0.0000	0.0000	0.0000	0.0000	0.0000	0.0000	0.0000	0.0000	0.0001

Source: Reprinted from *Handbook of Probability and Statistics with Tables*, 2nd ed., by R. S. Burington and D. C. May. New York: McGraw-Hill Book Company, Inc., 1970, by permission of the authors' trustees.

APPENDIX F

VALUES OF e^{-iN}

To find $e^{-1.5}$, choose $N = 15$ and $i = .10$.

	i											
N	**.01**	**.02**	**.03**	**.04**	**.05**	**.06**	**.07**	**.08**	**.09**	**.10**	**.11**	**.12**
1	0.990	0.980	0.970	0.961	0.951	0.942	0.932	0.923	0.914	0.905	0.896	0.887
2	0.980	0.961	0.942	0.923	0.905	0.887	0.869	0.852	0.835	0.819	0.803	0.787
3	0.970	0.942	0.914	0.887	0.861	0.835	0.811	0.787	0.763	0.741	0.719	0.698
4	0.961	0.923	0.887	0.852	0.819	0.787	0.756	0.726	0.698	0.670	0.644	0.619
5	0.951	0.905	0.861	0.819	0.779	0.741	0.705	0.670	0.638	0.607	0.577	0.549
6	0.942	0.887	0.835	0.787	0.741	0.698	0.657	0.619	0.583	0.549	0.517	0.487
7	0.932	0.869	0.811	0.756	0.705	0.657	0.613	0.571	0.533	0.497	0.463	0.432
8	0.923	0.852	0.787	0.726	0.670	0.619	0.571	0.527	0.487	0.449	0.415	0.383
9	0.914	0.835	0.763	0.698	0.638	0.583	0.533	0.487	0.445	0.407	0.372	0.340
10	0.905	0.819	0.741	0.670	0.607	0.549	0.497	0.449	0.407	0.368	0.333	0.301
11	0.896	0.803	0.719	0.644	0.577	0.517	0.463	0.415	0.372	0.333	0.298	0.267
12	0.887	0.787	0.698	0.619	0.549	0.487	0.432	0.383	0.340	0.301	0.267	0.237
13	0.878	0.771	0.677	0.595	0.522	0.458	0.403	0.353	0.310	0.273	0.239	0.210
14	0.869	0.756	0.657	0.571	0.497	0.432	0.375	0.326	0.284	0.247	0.214	0.186
15	0.861	0.741	0.638	0.549	0.472	0.407	0.350	0.301	0.259	0.223	0.192	0.165
16	0.852	0.726	0.619	0.527	0.449	0.383	0.326	0.278	0.237	0.202	0.172	0.147
17	0.844	0.712	0.600	0.507	0.427	0.361	0.304	0.257	0.217	0.183	0.154	0.130
18	0.835	0.698	0.583	0.487	0.407	0.340	0.284	0.237	0.198	0.165	0.138	0.115
19	0.827	0.684	0.566	0.468	0.387	0.320	0.264	0.219	0.181	0.150	0.124	0.102
20	0.819	0.670	0.549	0.449	0.368	0.301	0.247	0.202	0.165	0.135	0.111	0.091
21	0.811	0.657	0.533	0.432	0.350	0.284	0.230	0.186	0.151	0.122	0.099	0.080
22	0.803	0.644	0.517	0.415	0.333	0.267	0.214	0.172	0.138	0.111	0.089	0.071
23	0.795	0.631	0.502	0.399	0.317	0.252	0.200	0.159	0.126	0.100	0.080	0.063
24	0.787	0.619	0.487	0.383	0.301	0.237	0.186	0.147	0.115	0.091	0.071	0.056
25	0.779	0.607	0.472	0.368	0.287	0.223	0.174	0.135	0.105	0.082	0.064	0.050
26	0.771	0.595	0.458	0.353	0.273	0.210	0.162	0.125	0.096	0.074	0.057	0.044
27	0.763	0.583	0.445	0.340	0.259	0.198	0.151	0.115	0.088	0.067	0.051	0.039
28	0.756	0.571	0.432	0.326	0.247	0.186	0.141	0.106	0.080	0.061	0.046	0.035
29	0.748	0.560	0.419	0.313	0.235	0.176	0.131	0.098	0.074	0.055	0.041	0.031
30	0.741	0.549	0.407	0.301	0.223	0.165	0.122	0.091	0.067	0.050	0.037	0.027

N	13	.14	.15	.16	.17	.18	.19	.20	.21	.22	.23	.24
1	0.878	0.869	0.861	0.852	0.844	0.835	0.827	0.819	0.811	0.803	0.795	0.787
2	0.771	0.756	0.741	0.726	0.712	0.698	0.684	0.670	0.657	0.644	0.631	0.619
3	0.677	0.657	0.638	0.619	0.600	0.583	0.566	0.549	0.533	0.517	0.502	0.487
4	0.595	0.571	0.549	0.527	0.507	0.487	0.468	0.499	0.432	0.415	0.399	0.383
5	0.522	0.497	0.472	0.449	0.427	0.407	0.387	0.368	0.350	0.333	0.317	0.301
6	0.458	0.432	0.407	0.383	0.361	0.340	0.320	0.301	0.284	0.267	0.252	0.237
7	0.403	0.375	0.350	0.326	0.304	0.284	0.264	0.247	0.230	0.214	0.200	0.186
8	0.353	0.326	0.301	0.278	0.257	0.237	0.219	0.202	0.186	0.172	0.159	0.147
9	0.310	0.284	0.259	0.237	0.217	0.198	0.181	0.165	0.151	0.138	0.126	0.115
10	0.273	0.247	0.223	0.202	0.183	0.165	0.150	0.135	0.122	0.111	0.100	0.091
11	0.239	0.214	0.192	0.172	0.154	0.138	0.124	0.111	0.099	0.089	0.080	0.071
12	0.210	0.186	0.165	0.147	0.130	0.115	0.102	0.091	0.080	0.071	0.063	0.056
13	0.185	0.162	0.142	0.125	0.110	0.096	0.085	0.074	0.065	0.057	0.050	0.044
14	0.162	0.141	0.122	0.106	0.093	0.080	0.070	0.061	0.053	0.046	0.040	0.035
15	0.142	0.122	0.105	0.091	0.078	0.067	0.058	0.050	0.043	0.037	0.032	0.027
16	0.125	0.106	0.091	0.077	0.066	0.056	0.048	0.041	0.035	0.030	0.025	0.021
17	0.110	0.093	0.078	0.066	0.056	0.047	0.040	0.033	0.028	0.024	0.020	0.017
18	0.096	0.080	0.067	0.056	0.047	0.039	0.033	0.027	0.023	0.019	0.016	0.013
19	0.085	0.070	0.058	0.048	0.040	0.033	0.027	0.022	0.018	0.015	0.013	0.010
20	0.074	0.061	0.050	0.041	0.033	0.027	0.022	0.018	0.015	0.012	0.010	0.008
21	0.065	0.053	0.043	0.035	0.028	0.023	0.018	0.015	0.012	0.010	0.008	0.006
22	0.057	0.046	0.037	0.030	0.024	0.019	0.015	0.012	0.010	0.008	0.006	0.005
23	0.050	0.040	0.032	0.025	0.020	0.016	0.013	0.010	0.008	0.006	0.005	0.004
24	0.044	0.035	0.027	0.021	0.017	0.013	0.010	0.008	0.006	0.005	0.004	0.003
25	0.039	0.030	0.024	0.018	0.014	0.011	0.009	0.007	0.005	0.004	0.003	0.002
26	0.034	0.026	0.020	0.016	0.012	0.009	0.007	0.006	0.004	0.003	0.003	0.002
27	0.030	0.023	0.017	0.013	0.010	0.008	0.006	0.005	0.003	0.003	0.002	0.002
28	0.026	0.020	0.015	0.011	0.009	0.006	0.005	0.004	0.003	0.002	0.002	0.001
29	0.023	0.017	0.013	0.010	0.007	0.005	0.004	0.003	0.002	0.002	0.001	0.001
30	0.020	0.015	0.011	0.008	0.006	0.005	0.003	0.002	0.002	0.001	0.001	0.001

Solutions to Even-Numbered Problems

Chapter 5

2. The Affinity Diagram for the Creative Design Group may be constructed similar to Figure 5.8 in the chapter. The diagram should show categories such as customer service, team environment, facilities/technology, design goals, worker amenities, project/financial controls, competitive personnel issues, and business/financial issues.

   From this analysis, Trendy could see that human resources and technology had some issues that needed to be addressed in her long-range plans. In addition, she suspected that the competitive business/financial issues had impacts on, but were also impacted by, the competitive personnel and technology issues.

4. a) and b)
   Using data from the interrelationship digraph (see problem 1), an arrow diagram can be established. The Arrow Diagram shows precedent relationships for each activity.

   The technique may be extended a little further by the use of the PERT/CPM technique in order to calculate the critical path and the estimated project completion time, which are shown on the diagram. The diagram indicates that Joe and his team have a minimum of 21 days to complete the project, if their single time estimates for each activity are accurate.

   If a PERT-type analysis were to be used, then the probability of completion within a specified time frame could also be established. However, this method requires that three time estimates be made for each activity, which is a little more difficult and time consuming.

Chapter 7

2. The Taguchi Loss Function is $L(x) = k(x - T)^2$
   $\$3 = k(0.022)^2$
   $k = 6198.35$
   $\therefore L(x) = k(x - T)^2 = 6198.35(x - T)^2$

4. The Taguchi Loss Function is $L(x) = k(x - T)^2$
   a) $\$2 = k(0.022)^2$
      $k = 4132.23$
      $\therefore L(x) = k(x - T)^2 = 4123.23(x - T)^2$
   b) $L(x) = 4132.23(x - T)^2$
      $\therefore L(0.018) = 4132.23\ (0.018)^2 = \$1.34$

6. For a specification of 150 ± 5 ohms:
   a) $L(x) = k(x - T)^2$
      $\$100 = k(5)^2$
      $k = 4$
   b) $EL(x) = k(\sigma^2 + D^2) = 4(2^2 + 0^2) = \$16$

8. For a specification of 2.000 ± .002 mm and a $4 scrap cost:
$\overline{x} = 2.00008$; $D = 2.00008 - 2.00 = 0.00008$
$\sigma = 0.00104$
a) $L(x) = k(x - T)^2$
$\$4 = k(0.002)^2$; $\therefore k = 1{,}000{,}000$
b) $EL(x) = k(\sigma^2 + D^2) = 1{,}000{,}000\ (0.00104^2 + 0.00008^2) = \$1.088$

10. a) The Taguchi Loss function is: $L(x) = k(x - T)^2$
$400 = k(25)^2$
$k = 0.64$
So, $L(x) = 0.64(x - T)^2$
b) $\$1.50 = 0.64\ (x - 120)^2$
$2.34 = (x - 120)^2$
$(x - T)_{\text{Tolerance}} = \sqrt{2.34} = 1.53$ volts
$\therefore x = 121.53$

12. $L(x) = 100{,}000(x - T)^2$

For a typical calculation:
$\therefore L(0.21) = 100{,}000(0.21 - 0.24)^2 = \$90.00$

Weighted loss = $0.14 \times \$90.00 = \$12.60$

Value	Loss ($)	Process P Probability	Weighted Loss ($)	Process Q Probability	Weighted Loss ($)
0.20	160.00	0.00	0	0.02	3.20
0.21	90.00	0.14	12.60	0.03	2.70
0.22	40.00	0.14	5.60	0.15	6.00
0.23	10.00	0.14	1.40	0.15	1.50
0.24	0	0.16	0	0.30	0
0.25	10.00	0.14	1.40	0.15	1.50
0.26	40.00	0.14	5.60	0.15	6.00
0.27	90.00	0.14	12.60	0.03	2.70
0.28	160.00	0.00	0	0.02	3.20
Expected losses			39.20		26.80

Therefore, Process Q incurs a smaller loss than Process P, even though some output of Q falls outside specifications.

14. Analysis of customer responses from Bob's Big Burgers indicates a likelihood of several strong relationships between customer requirements and associated technical requirements of the burger design, such as value vs. price; nutrition vs. calories (and other nutritional content values, such as sodium and percent fat).

Note three customer response categories are unrelated to the design of the burgers—order accuracy, speedy service, and menu board. These factors would require a separate analysis as part of a facility and process design.

16. Analysis of customer responses for Fingerspring's proposed Personal Digital Assistant (PDA) indicates a likelihood of several strong relationships between customer requirements and associated technical requirements of the design, such as value vs. price; features vs. compactness, ease of use vs. features. Operating costs may possibly be distantly related to initial cost and features.

Technical characteristics required to translate the "voice of the customer" into operational or engineering terms might be measures of purchase cost, operating programs (e.g., Windows CE, or other similar systems), number and type of features, weight, dimensions, battery life, cost of replacement batteries, and peripherals.

CHAPTER 8

2. Because no values for percentages of sales attributable to quality costs were indicated, it is not possible to calculate an index base for the various cost categories. However, it is possible to draw some general conclusions from the data. The data show that both internal and external failure costs are too high for Product A, appraisal costs are too high for Product B, and both internal failure and appraisal costs are too high for Product C. Managers of all product lines should put more emphasis on prevention and attempt to reduce costs in other categories.

4. The composite index for quality costs for Midwest Sales shows that total quality cost has been stable at \$0.07/total sales dollars. Internal failure rates have been reduced substantially, from \$468.20 in the first quarter to \$166.40 in the fourth quarter. External failure rates have also shown substantial improvement since the first quarter, dropping from \$280.80 to \$128.60 in the fourth. Increases in prevention and appraisal expenditures have apparently led to improvements in failure costs. The overall index has fallen slightly. Management should maintain or increase the level of prevention and appraisal in an effort to reduce quality costs, especially failure costs. See the following table.

Total Sales and Quarterly Quality Costs (in \$ millions)

	1	2	3	4
Total Sales	4,120.0	4,206.0	4,454.0	4,106.0
External failure	280.8	208.2	142.8	128.6
Internal failure	468.2	372.4	284.4	166.4
Appraisal	194.2	227.7	274.4	266.2
Prevention	28.4	29.2	50.2	80.2
Total Quality Cost	971.6	837.5	751.8	641.4

Index of Quality Costs as a % of Sales

	1 Qtr.	2 Qtr.	3 Qtr.	4 Qtr.
External failure	6.82	4.95	3.21	3.13
Internal failure	11.36	8.85	6.39	4.05
Appraisal	4.71	5.41	6.16	6.48
Prevention	0.69	0.69	1.13	1.95
Total Quality Cost	23.58	19.91	16.88	15.62
Total Sales/Base Sales	100	102.09	108.11	99.66

6. The following table shows that total quality costs as a percent of sales ranges from very high to moderate between products. Internal and external failure costs are large for Product A, because little appraisal or prevention is done. For Product B, defects are being screened out, causing much higher appraisal costs, in total and as a percent of quality costs. However, this method does reduce

overall quality costs as a percent of sales (25%), somewhat. Product C has attained a pretty good balance among quality cost categories, although a larger percentage of prevention costs might prove to be advantageous.

Sales and Quality Costs (in $ thousands)

Total Sales	$2.500	$1.800	$2.600			
% Quality Costs	35%	25%	18%			
	Product A	Product B	Product C	Product A	Product B	Product C
External failure	$0.368	$0.090	$0.070	42%	20%	15%
Internal failure	0.394	0.113	0.187	45%	25%	30%
Appraisal	0.105	0.234	0.164	12%	52%	40%
Prevention	0.009	0.014	0.047	1%	3%	15%
Total Quality Cost	$0.875	$0.450	$0.468			

8. The spreadsheet data show that the printing company is spending too much on appraisl and internal failure cost and too little on prevention. Improvement efforts should concentrate on the categories of proofreading, press downtime, and correction of typos.

	Quality Costs (in $ thousands)
External failure	$ 28
Internal failure	615
Appraisal	542
Prevention	21
Total Quality Cost	1,206

	Quality Costs (%)
External failure	2.32
Internal failure	51.00
Appraisal	44.94
Prevention	1.74
Total Quality Cost	100.00

10. For the Hamilton Bank, a detailed report might be prepared by an internal or external quality consultant to the bank as follows:

Cost Elements	Quality Cost Categories Costs	Subtotal	Proportion
APPRAISAL			
1. Run credit checks	26.13		
Loan Payment & Loan Payoffs			
Receive & process (2 items)	1,058.92		
Inspection			
Review documents	3,021.63		
Prepare tickler file, etc.	156.75		
Review all output	2,244.14	$6,507.57	0.496

PREVENTION			
Conduct training	1,366.94	$1,366.94	0.104
INTERNAL FAILURE COSTS			
Scrap and Rework			
Make document corrections	1,013.65		
Correct rejects	425.84		
Reconcile incomplete collateral reports	78.34		
Compensate for system downtime	519.38		
Loan Payment or Payoff			
Respond to inquiries, no coupon	783.64		
Research payoff problems	14.34	$2,820.85	0.215
EXTERNAL FAILURE COSTS			
Respond to dealer calls, etc.	2,418.88	$2,418.88	0.185
Total Costs	$13,114.24		

Abbreviated analysis:
As one would hope, the external failure costs for the bank are not *extremely* high at $2,418.88. However, they do represent 18.5% of the total quality costs.

The highest cost category is in appraisal costs at $6,507.57 and 49.6% of total quality costs.

The largest internal failure costs are being incurred in the document correction and "Respond to inquiries, no coupon" areas and in the "Compensate for system downtime" categories.

In the prevention area, it appears that not much attention is being given to the need for this activity.

12. Data in the following table when developed into a Pareto chart, will show that Oakton Paper Co. is experiencing problems in two major categories: rejected paper and customer complaints. These categories, which could be related to each other, account for 74.7% of their quality costs.

Oakton Paper Co.
Quality Costs and Percentages

	Percent	Cumulative %	Cost
Rejected paper	61.0%	61.0%	$427,000
Customer complaints	14.0	75.0	98,000
Odd lot	9.0	84.0	63,000
High material costs	7.0	91.0	49,000
Downtime	4.0	95.0	28,000
Excess inspection	3.0	98.0	21,000
Testing costs	2.0	100.0	14,000
Total Costs			$700,000

14. **National Computer Repairs**
Quality Costs and Percentages

	Percent	Cumulative %	Cost
Customer returns	45.33%	45.33%	$160,000
Workstation downtime	22.67	68.00	80,000
Rework costs	11.33	79.33	40,000
Inspection costs, outgoing	8.77	88.10	31,000
Training/system improvement	7.65	95.75	27,000
Inspection costs, incoming	4.25	100.00	15,000
Total Costs			353,000

The data for National Computer Repairs show that two categories of customer returns, and workstation downtime total 68 percent of the defects. These two are possibly related and may indicate "short staffing" and lack of training of setup personnel. Steps should be taken to analyze root causes for these problem areas in order to correct them as quickly as possible.

16. Because nothing is mentioned to suggest that a discounted present value is required, simplified calculating methods, not considering the time value of the money invested, are used in the following solutions:

a) Lost profits = ($20/sale × 940,020)/5 = $3,760,080 per year

b) Recovered profits = .05 × $3,760,080 = $188,004

So, return on quality for each year is $188,004/$85,000 = 2.212 or 221.2% return, which means that each year the investment will pay for itself in less than six months of savings.

CHAPTER 9

2. One of the advantages of using Excel® spreadsheets is that a great deal of analysis can be done easily. The summary statistics follow. A histogram may also be constructed by using Excel's Data Analysis tools (found under the "Tools" heading on the spreadsheet). For best results in constructing the histogram, it is suggested that you set up your "bins" so as to provide 7 to 10 approximately equal-sized class intervals for the data. Note that if the program finds that the classes shown in the bins do not extend over the upper or lower range of the data, it will automatically compensate by adding a "Less" or "More" category for the outliers.

Column1	
Mean	3.581
Standard Error	0.073356677
Median	3.6
Mode	3.6
Standard Deviation	0.733566767
Sample Variance	0.538120202
Kurtosis	−0.30271777
Skewness	0.107636406
Range	3.4
Minimum	1.9
Maximum	5.3

Sum	358.1
Count	100
Confidence Level(95.0%)	0.145555587

The conclusion that can be reached from looking at the summary statistics and the histogram is that these data are fairly uniformly distributed, with some slight skewing to the right.

4. The mean, $\mu = 2000$ ml; the standard deviation, $\sigma = 20$ ml

$$P(x > 2000) = 0.5000 - P\left(\frac{x-\mu}{\sigma}\right) = 0.5000 - .4950 = 0.005$$

Using the Normal Table, Appendix A, $Z_1 = 2.575$, and by symmetry $Z_2 = -2.575$

$$Z_1 = \frac{x-\mu}{\sigma} = \frac{(x_1 - 2{,}000)}{20} = -2.575$$

$x_1 = 2{,}051.5$ ml

$$Z_2 = \frac{x-\mu}{\sigma} = \frac{(x_2 - 2{,}000)}{20} = -2.575$$

$x_2 = 1{,}948.5$ ml

∴ The maximum cutoff for filling should be 2,051.5 ml and the minimum should be 1,948.5 ml

6. (Using the Standard Normal Distribution Table, Appendix A)

$$z = -2.05 = \frac{16-\mu}{0.6}\ ;\ \therefore\ \mu = 17.23 \text{ oz.}$$

8. The mean, $\mu = 12.05$; the standard deviation, $\sigma = 0.02$

$$P(x < 12.0) = 0.5000 - P\left(\frac{x-\mu}{\sigma}\right)$$

$$Z = \frac{x-\mu}{\sigma} = \frac{(12.0 - 12.05)}{0.02} = -2.5$$

$$Z = \frac{x-\mu}{\sigma} = \frac{(12.10 - 12.05)}{0.02} = -2.5$$

(Using Normal Table, Appendix A)

$$P(Z < 12.0) = 0.5000 - P(-2.5 < Z < 0) = 0.5000 - 0.4938 = 0.0062$$

$$P(x > 12.10) = 0.5000 - P\left(\frac{x-\mu}{\sigma}\right)$$

$$Z = \frac{x-\mu}{\sigma} = \frac{(12.0 - 12.05)}{0.02} = 2.5$$

(Using Normal Table, Appendix A)

$$P(Z > 12.10) = 0.5000 - P(0 < Z < 2.5) = 0.5000 - 0.4938 = 0.0062$$

10. Note: You may need to brush up on calculations of mean and standard deviations using grouped data from a statistics textbook. See the following, using class midpoints estimated from the given cells.

	Class mp x	f	fx	fx^2
1	39.75	1	39.75	1,580.063
2	39.45	4	157.80	6,225.210
3	39.15	13	508.95	19,925.393
4	38.85	15	582.75	22,639.838
5	38.55	29	1,117.95	43,096.973
6	38.25	26	994.50	38,039.625
7	37.95	8	303.60	11,521.620
8	37.65	3	112.95	4,252.568
9	37.35	1	37.35	1,395.023
		100	3,855.60	148,676.313

$$\bar{x} = \frac{\Sigma fx}{n} = \frac{3,855.6}{100} = 38.556$$

$$s = \sqrt{\frac{\Sigma fx^2}{n-1} - \frac{\Sigma (fx)^2/n}{n-1}} = \sqrt{\frac{148,815.992}{99} - \frac{(3,857.4)^2/100}{99}} = 0.4472$$

A normal probability plot shows that the data are approximately normally distributed, with some a R-square value of 0.939.

12. Note: use s, calculated in problem 10, as an estimate of $\sigma = 0.447$

$$C_p = \frac{\text{UTL} - \text{LTL}}{6\sigma} = \frac{41.1 - 36.3}{6(0.447)} = 1.790\text{; not satisfactory}$$

$$C_p = \frac{41.1 - 36.3}{6\sigma} = 2.5\text{; Therefore, } \sigma = 0.32 \text{ would be required, instead of the current } \sigma = 0.447$$

14. For sample statistics of $\bar{x} = 0.5750$; $\sigma = 0.0065$

$$C_p = \frac{\text{UTL} - \text{LTL}}{6\sigma} = \frac{0.582 - 0.568}{6(0.0065)} = 0.359\text{; not satisfactory}$$

16. Summary statistics and a histogram that can be constructed from spreadsheet data show:

Column1	
Mean	24.0014
Standard Error	0.00097
Median	24.001
Mode	24
Standard Deviation	0.00967
Sample Variance	9.4E-05
Kurtosis	0.531132
Skewness	0.05271
Range	0.058
Minimum	23.971
Maximum	24.029
Confidence Level(95.0%)	0.00192

	Bin	Frequency
	23.971	1
	23.977	0
	23.983	0
	23.988	7
	23.994	14
	24.000	26
	24.006	20
	24.012	19
	24.017	7
	24.023	5
More		1

For sample statistics of: $\bar{x} = 24.0014$; $s = 0.0097$
Specification limits for the process are: $23.97 \le \mu \le 24.03$

$$Z = \frac{24.0300 - 24.0014}{0.0097} = 2.95;\ P(Z > 2.94) = (0.5 - 0.4984) = 0.0016 \text{ that items will exceed upper limit}$$

$$Z = \frac{23.9700 - 24.0014}{0.0097} = -3.24;\ P(Z < -3.24) = 0.00 \text{ that items will exceed lower limit}$$

Therefore, the percent outside is 0.0016, or 0.16%

$$C_p = \frac{\text{UTL} - \text{LTL}}{6s} = \frac{24.030 - 23.970}{6(0.0097)} = 1.031$$

$$C_{pu} = \frac{\text{UTL} - \bar{x}}{3s} = \frac{24.030 - 24.0014}{3(0.0097)} = 0.983$$

$$C_{pl} = \frac{\bar{x} - \text{LTL}}{3s} = \frac{24.0014 - 23.970}{3(0.0097)} = 1.079$$

The process capability indexes are slightly out of tolerance for the upper index, and within minimum limits for the lower and overall index. These results indicate that the process may be minimally adequate if it can be centered on the nominal dimension of 24. However, the ideal situation would be to launch process improvement studies so that the capability indexes could be at least doubled.

18. Omega Parts Ltd. Solution

Process capability results from the Excel spreadsheet software are shown here.

Average	0.0764	
Standard deviation	0.0104	

C_p	0.8019
C_{pl}	0.8468
C_{pu}	0.7569
C_{pk}	0.7569

These data show that the process has a rather low overall capability, with C_p = 0.8019 and a total of 1.71% of the values falling outside of the specification limits of 0.05 – 0.10.

Process statistics: $\bar{x} = 0.0764$; $\sigma = 0.0104$

$Z = \dfrac{0.10 - 0.0764}{0.0104} = 2.27$; $P(Z > 2.27) = (0.5 - 0.4884) = 0.0116$ that the part will exceed upper limit

$Z = \dfrac{0.05 - 0.0764}{0.0104} = -2.54$; $P(Z < -2.54) = (0.5 - 0.4945) = 0.0055$ that the part will exceed lower limit

Therefore, the percent outside is: 0.0171, or 1.71%

$$C_p = \frac{UTL - LTL}{6\sigma} = 2.0 = \frac{5.60 - 5.20}{6\sigma} = \frac{0.4}{6\sigma}; \text{ Therefore, } \sigma = 0.033$$

$$C_{pu} = \frac{UTL - \bar{x}}{3\sigma} = \frac{5.60 - \bar{x}}{3\sigma} = 2.0; \text{ Therefore, we get } \bar{x} = 5.4$$

$$C_{pl} = \frac{\bar{x} - LTL}{3\sigma} = \frac{\bar{x} - 5.20}{3\sigma} = 2.0; \text{ Therefore, we get } \bar{x} = 5.4$$

22. The proper sample size for the proportion of sorting errors at a post office, using a 95% confidence level is:

    $n = (z_{\alpha/2})^2\, p(1 - p)/E^2 = (1.96)^2\,(0.022)(0.978)/(0.01)^2 = 826.56$, use 827

24. First, we must find an estimated p:

    $p = \dfrac{27}{150} = 0.18$

    Then, using the formula for sample size:

    $n = (z_{\alpha/2})^2\, p(1 - p)/E^2$, we can solve for n as follows:

    $n = (1.645)^2\,(0.18)(0.82)/(0.05)^2$

    $n = [(2.706)\,(0.1476)]/(0.0025) = 159.76$

    Thus, the telephone company can be 90% confident of their results based on this sample size (of 160). It means that they need to take 10 more surveys in order to meet the required sample size.

26. Using Table 9.1, for a population of 2,000 the sample size required for a critical 1% rate, with a 99% confidence level is approximately 400 (use 98.9% confidence, critical rate of 1%).

Chapter 10

2. To calculate the dpmo, we use 21/42 to get the number of defects per unit (DPUs). However, 67 opportunities per aircraft checked must be taken into consideration, as shown, in order to calculate dpmo.

   dpmo = (21/42) × 1,000,000/67 = 7,462.6, which is slightly less than 4 sigma with off-centering of 1.5 sigma.

4. No indication of how many opportunities for defects per component is given, so we will simply have to assume that the defect rate is 1 per 1,000 units produced. Therefore, only 750 defective items (0.001 × 750,000) were produced. To calculate dpmo, we see:

dpmo = (1/1,000) × 1,000,000 = 1,000, which is slightly better than 4.5 sigma with off-centering of 1.5 sigma.

6. The frequency distribution for the following data shows that, although the data are fairly uniformly distributed, 14 points are above the upper specification limit of 2.55 cm and 3 points are below the lower specification limit of 2.45 cm. It is likely that the process needs to be improved, with the first step being the removal of any special causes. A control chart would have to be constructed and/or a process capability study performed in order to get a fuller picture of the process. (Note the cell represented by 2.56 cm also contains 5 values at 2.55 not considered to be "above" the 2.55 cm limit.)

Dimension (cm)	Frequency
2.42	0
2.44	3
2.46	10
2.48	13
2.50	23
2.52	39
2.54	18
2.56	13
2.58	5
2.60	1

8. The scatter diagram shows an interesting and counterintuitive result. As the production rate increases, the defect rate decreases. This effect could be because of the "learning curve." Thus, as operators become more skilled and familiar with the process and production runs are longer, the defect rate can be improved.

10. The following data and a Pareto diagram will show that approximately 55% of the problems are with long delays and another 25.2% are due to shipping errors, for a total in the top two categories of 80.2%. These categories should be improved first.

Dot.Com Apparel House
Quality Errors and Percentages

	Percent	Cumulative %	Frequency
Long delays	54.98%	54.98%	5,372
Shipping errors	25.18	80.16	2,460
Delivery errors	7.70	87.85	752
Electronic charge errors	6.65	94.50	650
Billing errors	5.50	100.00	537

12. The data on the syringes, when plotted on a scatter diagram, show a suspicious pattern that indicates the process may be unstable. Nine values from samples 20 to 29 alternate above and below the average, indicating that some instability may be found in the system if it is carefully investigated.

CHAPTER 11

2. For $C_1 = \$0.75$ and $C_2 = \$500.00$
   $p = C_1/C_2 = 0.75/500 = 0.0015$ *or* 1.5 errors/1,000 transactions

4. Accuracy of: Instrument A

$$100 \times \frac{\text{Abs}\ [0.057 - 0.065]}{0.065} = 12.3\%$$

Accuracy of: Instrument B

$$100 \times \frac{\text{Abs}\ [0.0626 - 0.065]}{0.065} = 3.69\%$$

Instrument B is more accurate.

The frequency data, taken from the Excel printout, shows that Instrument A is more precise than Instrument B. Instrument A is a better instrument, because it is likely that it can be adjusted to center on the nominal value of 0.065.

INSTRUMENT A

	Upper Cell Boundaries	Frequencies	Standard Statistical Measures	
Cell 6	0.085	2	Mean	0.057
Cell 5	0.075	8	Median	0.055
Cell 4	0.055	8	Mode	0.045
Cell 3	0.045	7	Standard deviation	0.0151
Cell 2	0.035	0	Variance	0.00023
Cell 1	0.025	1	Max	0.085
			Min	0.025
			Range	0.06

INSTRUMENT B

	Upper Cell Boundaries	Frequencies	Standard Statistical Measures	
Cell 7	0.089	4	Mean	0.0626
Cell 6	0.077	8	Median	0.065
Cell 5	0.066	6	Mode	0.075
Cell 4	0.054	5	Standard deviation	0.01689
Cell 3	0.042	0	Variance	0.00029
Cell 2	0.031	1	Max	0.089
Cell 1	0.019	1	Min	0.019
			Range	0.07

6. Detailed calculations for the first operator are as follows:

   $\bar{x}_1 = (\Sigma\Sigma M_{ijk})/nr = 29.721/30 = 0.9907$

   $\bar{R}_1 = (\Sigma M_{ij})/n = 0.280/10 = 0.028$

   Use this method to calculate values for the second operator:

   $\bar{x}_2 = 29.901/30 = 0.9967$; $\bar{R}_2 = 0.380/10 = 0.038$

   $\bar{x}_D = \max\{\bar{x}_i\} - \min\{\bar{x}_i\} = 0.9967 - 0.9907 = 0.0060$

   $\bar{\bar{R}} = (\Sigma\bar{R}_1)/m = (0.028 + 0.038)/2 = 0.033$

   $D_4 = 2.574$; $UCL_R = D_4\bar{\bar{R}} = (2.574)\ (0.033) = 0.0849$, all ranges below

$K_1 = 3.05; K_2 = 3.65$ (from Table 11.2)

$EV = K_1\overline{\overline{R}} = (3.05)(0.033) = 0.10065$

$OV = \sqrt{(K_2\,\overline{x}_D)^2 - (EV^2/nr)} = 0.0119$

$RR = \sqrt{(EV)^2 + (OV)^2} = 0.1014$

Equipment variation = 100(0.10065/0.12) = 83.88%
Operator variation = 100(0.0119/0.12) = 9.92%
R&R variation = 100(0.1014/0.12) = 84.50%

Spreadsheet results confirm prior calculations, as follows:

				Tolerance analysis
Average range	0.033	Repeatability (EV)	0.10065	83.88%
X-bar range	0.006	Reproducibility (OV)	0.01191	9.93%
		Repeatability and Reproducibility (R&R)	0.10135	84.46%
		Control limit for individual ranges	0.08514	
		Note: any ranges beyond this limit may be the result of assignable causes. Identify and correct. Discard values and recompute statistics.		

∴ Concentrate on reducing equipment variation.

8. This analysis follows the same form as problem 6. Note that the control limit of 0.302 was exceeded by the range in sample 7 for the first operator. This sample could have been due to a misreading of the gauge. If so, this sample should be thrown out, another one taken, and the values recomputed. Spreadsheet results are as follows:

				Tolerance analysis
Average range	0.117	Repeatability (EV)	0.3579	89.47%
X-bar range	0.058	Reproducibility (OV)	0.1423187	35.58%
		Repeatability and Reproducibility (R&R)	0.3851275	96.28%
		Control limit for individual ranges	0.30272	
		Note: any ranges beyond this limit may be the result of assignable causes. Identify and correct. Discard values and recompute statistics.		

10. Accuracy of: Thermometer A

$$100 \times \frac{\text{Abs }[0.00031 - 0]}{1\text{ deg.}} = 0.031\%$$

Accuracy of: Thermometer B

$$100 \times \frac{\text{Abs }[-0.00005 - 0]}{1\text{ deg.}} = 0.005\%$$

Thermometer B is more accurate.

The Excel-calculated statistics show that Thermometer B is also more precise than Thermometer A, as indicated by a smaller standard deviation. Thermometer B is a better instrument, because it is likely that it can be adjusted to center on the nominal value of 0.

a) **Thermometer A**

	Upper Cell Boundaries	Frequencies	Standard Statistical Measures	
Cell 7	0.00246	4	Mean	0.00031
Cell 6	0.00163	6	Median	0.00025
Cell 5	0.00080	5	Mode	#N/A
Cell 4	−0.00003	5	Standard deviation	0.00134
Cell 3	−0.00086	3	Variance	0.000002
Cell 2	−0.00169	1	Max	0.002456
Cell 1	−0.00251	1	Min	−0.002514
			Range	0.00497

b) **Thermometer B**

	Upper Cell Boundaries	Frequencies	Standard Statistical Measures	
Cell 5	0.00232	3	Mean	−0.00005
Cell 4	0.00156	7	Median	−0.00012
Cell 3	0.00005	7	Mode	#N/A
Cell 2	−0.00070	7	Standard deviation	0.001204
Cell 1	−0.00221	1	Variance	0.
			Max	0.00232
			Min	−0.00221
			Range	0.00453

CHAPTER 12

2. a) Descriptive statistics, based on all 50 samples, are shown below. The histogram shows the "classic" bell curve shape.

Descriptive Statistics—Problem 12-2	
Mean	9.046
Standard Error	0.070
Median	9.011
Mode	9.215
Standard Deviation	1.103
Sample Variance	1.218
Kurtosis	−0.323
Skewness	0.071
Range	5.716
Minimum	6.341
Maximum	12.057
Sum	2261.440
Count	250.000
Confidence Level(95.0%)	0.137

Bin	Frequency
6.0	0
6.6	3
7.2	9
7.8	23
8.4	36
9.0	52
9.6	48
10.2	44
10.8	19
11.4	12
12.0	3
12.6	1

b) Results from first 30 samples of 5 show that both the $\bar{x}$ and $\bar{R}$ charts are apparently in control.

For the Center Lines, $CL_{\bar{x}}: \bar{\bar{x}} = 9.155;\ CL_R: \bar{R} = 2.271$

Control limits for the $\bar{x}$-chart are $\bar{\bar{x}} \pm A_2\bar{R}$
$UCL_{\bar{x}} = \bar{\bar{x}} + A_2\bar{R} = 9.155 + (0.577)2.271 = 10.465$
$LCL_{\bar{x}} = \bar{\bar{x}} - A_2\bar{R} = 9.155 - (0.577)2.271 = 7.845$

For the R-chart: $UCL_R = D_4\bar{R} = (2.114)2.271 = 4.800$
$LCL_R = D_3\bar{R} = 0$

c) When using control limits to monitor the last 20 samples, two unusual occurrences can be noted. Sample #32 goes slightly above the upper control limit on the R-chart, and sample #36 on the $\bar{x}$-bar chart almost touches the upper control limit. The out-of-control point on the R-chart should have resulted in the process being stopped and an assignable cause should have been searched for and corrected.

The sample #36 variation in the $\bar{x}$-chart could have been due to chance, but the situation should be carefully observed.

4. For the Center Lines, $CL_{\bar{x}}: \bar{\bar{x}} = 6.0;\ CL_R: \bar{R} = 2.5$

Control limits for the $\bar{x}$-chart are
$\bar{\bar{x}} \pm A_2\bar{R} = 6.0 \pm (0.577)2.5 = 4.56$ to 7.44

For the R-chart: $UCL_R = D_4\bar{R} = 2.114(2.5) = 5.29$
$LCL_R = D_3\bar{R} = 0$

Estimated $\sigma = \bar{R}/d_2 = 2.5/2.326 = 1.08$

6. From the initial control charts, it appears that there are two out-of-control points, one on the $\bar{x}$-chart and one on the R-chart. We must throw out outliers #16 and #23, and revise the charts.

The **initial** chart has Center Lines, $CL_{\bar{x}}: \bar{\bar{x}} = 402.92;\ CL_R: \bar{R} = 33.20$

Control limits for the $\bar{x}$-chart are
$\bar{\bar{x}} \pm A_2\bar{R} = 402.92 \pm 1.023(33.20) = 368.96$ to 436.88

For the R-chart: $UCL_R = D_4\bar{R} = 2.574(33.20) = 85.46$
$LCL_R = D_3\bar{R} = 0$

For the **revised** $\bar{x}$-chart
$\bar{\bar{x}} \pm A_2\bar{R} = 400.29 \pm 1.023(30.96) = 368.62 \text{ to } 431.96$

For the **revised** R-chart: $UCL_R = D_4\bar{R} = 2.574(30.96) = 79.69$
$LCL_R = D_3\bar{R} = 0$

8. For 30 samples of 5 given in the problem, we obtain the following control limits. We can conclude from the $\bar{x}$-chart that the process is probably out of control, because almost all of the points in the first half of the chart are "hugging the center line" (e.g., within the inner 1/3 region closest to the center line). Also, the second point on the R chart appears to be out of control. Steps must be taken to bring it under control before charts can be used for continuing control.

   For the Center Lines, $CL_{\bar{x}} : \bar{\bar{x}} = 0.053$; $CL_R : \bar{R} = 0.986$

   Control limits for the $\bar{x}$-chart are
   $\bar{\bar{x}} \pm A_2\bar{R} = -0.053 \pm 0.577(0.986) = -0.622 \text{ to } 0.516$

   For the R-chart: $UCL_R = D_4\bar{R} = 2.11(0.986) = 2.081$
   $LCL_R = D_3\bar{R} = 0$

10. The data can be used to calculate the center line and control limits as shown. Control charts can also be plotted from the data.
    a) Center Lines, $CL_{\bar{x}} : \bar{\bar{x}} = 5.103$; $CL_R : \bar{R} = 1.105$

       Control limits for the $\bar{x}$-chart are
       $\bar{\bar{x}} \pm A_2\bar{R} = 5.103 \pm 0.729(1.105) = 4.298 \text{ to } 5.908$

       For the R-chart: $UCL_R = D_4\bar{R} = 2.282(1.105) = 2.521$
       $LCL_R = D_3\bar{R} = 0$

    b) An $\bar{x}$-chart will show that Samples 19 and 21 are out of control and the R-chart that sample 18 is out of control on its range. We obtain the following control limits after dropping these 3 points:

       New Center Lines: Center Lines, $CL_{\bar{x}} : \bar{\bar{x}} = 5.026$; $CL_R : \bar{R} = 1.076$

       Control limits for the $\bar{x}$-chart are
       $\bar{\bar{x}} \pm A_2\bar{R} = 5.026 \pm 0.729(1.076) = 4.242 \text{ to } 5.810$

       For the R-chart: $UCL_R = D_4\bar{R} = 2.282(1.076) = 2.455$
       $LCL_R = D_3\bar{R} = 0$

    c) The additional data show that the process is operating within control limits. A control chart using the same limits will show that the last 10 samples are also within limits.

12. a) The first control chart shows an out-of-control process with a definite downward trend. The last 4 out of 5 points are below one standard error away from the mean. The process needs adjustment upward.

    b) The second control chart shows an out-of-control condition, with the first eight points above the centerline. Then there appears to be a sudden shift in the process average, putting the next six points below the centerline. It is possible that the process is being **overadjusted.** It needs to be centered and then watched for out-of-control indications with no unnecessary operator intervention.

c) The third control chart shows the data hugging the centerline, indicating that the process is possibly out of control. If the process has multiple machines or operators, a control chart should be constructed for each machine to avoid "masking" the variation brought on by mixing data from several sources.

d) The fourth control chart shows a process that is stable and in control.

e) The fifth control chart shows an out-of-control condition, with a point above the upper-control limit.

f) The sixth control chart shows that seven out of eight of the most recent points are below the centerline, indicating that the process is out of control.

g) The last control chart shows too many points close to the upper and lower control limits, indicating an out-of-control condition.

14. a) From the data, the following centerline and control limits are calculated:

$CL_{\bar{x}}: \bar{\bar{x}} = 0.1115;\ CL_R: \bar{R} = 0.0101$

Estimated $\sigma = \bar{R}/d_2 = 0.0101/2.059 = 0.0049$; actual $\sigma = 0.0055$, close to the estimate.
$\bar{\bar{x}} \pm 3\sigma_{est} = 0.1115 \pm 3(0.0049) = 0.0968$ to 0.1262;
for $\bar{\bar{x}} \pm 3\sigma = 0.1115 \pm 3(0.0055) = 0.0950$ to 0.1280

The limits above apply to individual items only. Individual items can only be plotted on x-charts. See the chart for individuals, when constructed, and the previous problem, for a more thorough discussion.

b) Detailed comparisons of process capability using actual σ can be constructed with spreadsheets provided on the student CD-rom.

Although individual values must be plotted on x-charts as shown, you need to understand their relationship to $\bar{x}$-chart and $\bar{R}$-chart results for comparison with the charts for individuals.

For the $\bar{x}$-chart:

$\bar{\bar{x}} \pm A_2\bar{R} = 0.1115 \pm 0.729(0.0101) = 0.1041$ to 0.1189

For the R-chart: $UCL_R = D_4\bar{R} = 2.282(0.0101) = 0.0230$
$LCL_R = D_3\bar{R} = 0$

The limits apply to sample groups of 5 items each.

c) The comparisons of process capability using the actual σ value are shown by the following data:

Nominal specification	**0.110**
Upper tolerance limit	**0.125**
Lower tolerance limit	**0.095**

Average	0.1115	
Standard deviation	0.0055	

C_p	0.912
C_{pl}	1.003
C_{pu}	0.821
C_{pk}	0.821

16. For the Center Lines, $CL_{\bar{x}} : \bar{\bar{x}} = 69.25$; $CL_R : \bar{R} = 7.012$
Control limits for the $\bar{x}$-chart are

$$\bar{\bar{x}} \pm A_2\bar{R} = 69.25 \pm 0.577(7.012) = 65.204 \text{ to } 73.296$$

For the R-chart: $UCL_R = D_4\bar{R} = 2.114(7.012) = 14.824$
$LCL_R = D_3\bar{R} = 0$

The limits apply to sample groups of 5 items each.

Estimated $\sigma = \bar{R}/d_2 = 7.012/2.326 = 3.015$

The problem asks that you perform a process capability analysis, which is only justified if the process is in control. The fact that the process is thought to be normally distributed does not establish that it is in control. The $\bar{x}$-chart shows that the process is, in fact, out of control. The percent outside calculation can be performed as follows. Note the warning given, however.

Percent Outside Specification Limits (62 to 76)

% Below LSL: $Z = \dfrac{LSL - \bar{\bar{x}}}{\sigma}$

$Z = \dfrac{-62 - 69.5}{3.015} = -2.49$; $P(Z < -2.49) = (0.5 - 0.4936) = 0.0064$ that items will exceed lower limit

% Above USL: $Z = \dfrac{USL - \bar{\bar{x}}}{\sigma}$

$Z = \dfrac{76 - 69.25}{3.015} = 2.24$; $P(Z > 2.24) = (0.5 - 0.4875) = 0.0125$ that items will exceed upper limit

Therefore, the percent outside is calculated as: 1.89%

Although the percent outside calculations seem to show that the process has a relatively small percent outside specifications, it should be noted that the x-chart shows that the process is not even **close** to being in control. Hence, the percent outside calculation is going to generate questionable results.

18. With data from problem 10 and USL = 6.75 and LSL = 3.25, from spreadsheet data we see:

Upper specification	6.75	C_p	1.1165
Lower specification	3.25	C_{pl}	1.1331
Nominal specification	5.00	C_{pu}	1.0999
		C_{pk}	1.0999

Note that the spreadsheet uses an estimated standard deviation of:
Estimated $\sigma = \bar{R}/d_2 = 1.076/2.059 = 0.5226$

From this, we obtain:

Percent Outside Specification Limits (3.25 to 6.75)

% Below LSL: $Z = \dfrac{LSL - \bar{\bar{x}}}{\sigma}$

$Z = \dfrac{3.25 - 5.026}{0.5226} = -3.40$; $P(Z < -3.40) = (0.5 - 0.499663^*) = 0.000337$ that items will exceed lower limit

*Note: This figure was taken from an outside table because Appendix A extends only to $z = 3.09$.

% Above USL: $Z = \dfrac{USL - \bar{\bar{x}}}{\sigma}$

$Z = \dfrac{6.75 - 5.026}{0.5226} = 2.87$; $P(Z > 2.82) = (0.5 - 0.4979) = 0.0021$ that items will exceed upper limit

Therefore, the percent outside is calculated as: 0.24%

These calculations show that the process has a relatively small percent outside specification. In problem 10, points that showed assignable causes were eliminated, so the process should be in control. The process still needs some "fine tuning" in order to become capable as shown by the percent outside calculation and the capability indexes.

The modified control limits are

$URL_x = US - A_m\bar{R} = 6.75 - (0.728)(1.076) = 5.967$
$LRL_x = LS + A_m\bar{R} = 3.25 + (0.728)(1.076) = 4.033$

20. From the data, the following can be calculated

a) For the Center Line, $CL_{\bar{x}} : \bar{\bar{x}} = 0.0481$; $CL_R : \bar{R} = 0.1035$

Control limits for the $\bar{x}$-chart are
$\bar{\bar{x}} \pm A_2\bar{R} = 0.0481 \pm 0.729(0.1035) = -0.0273$ to 0.1236

For the R-chart: $UCL_R = D_4\bar{R} = 2.282(0.1035) = 0.2362$
$LCL_R = D_3\bar{R} = 0$

b) $\bar{x}$-chart and the R-chart show that the process is "hugging the center line" creating an out-of-control condition on the means and their ranges. The cause for this condition may be judged from the structure of the data. It appears that each of the heads on the molding machine has a separate distribution of data. Thus, control charts should be prepared for each head, rather than treating the data as if they came from the same population.

22. The data can be used to calculate the center line and control limits shown below.

a) For the Center Line, $CL_{\bar{x}} : \bar{\bar{x}} = 1.321$; $CL_s : \bar{s} = 0.018$

Control limits for the $\bar{x}$- and s-charts are
$\bar{\bar{x}} \pm A_3\bar{s} = 1.321 \pm 0.975(0.018) = 1.304$ to 1.339

For the s-chart: $UCL_s = B_4\bar{s} = 1.716(0.018) = 0.031$
$LCL_s = B_3\bar{s} = 0.284(0.018) = 0.005$

Revised $\bar{x}$- and s-charts

The $\bar{x}$-chart shows that the process is out of control. After removing points 7 and 18 (the latter point was just on the control limit on this chart), the results showed no significant difference, because the points virtually offset each other in a positive and negative direction.

For the Center Line, $CL_{\bar{x}}: \bar{\bar{x}} = 1.321$; $CL_s: \bar{s} = 0.018$

Control limits for the $\bar{x}$- and s-charts are 1.304 to 1.339

For the s-chart: $UCL_s = 0.031$
$LCL_s = 0.005$

The process is now under control.

24. The data can be used to calculate the center line and control limits shown here.

a) For the Center Line, $CL_{\bar{x}}: \bar{\bar{x}} = 0.762$; $CL_s: \bar{s} = 0.066$

Control limits for the $\bar{x}$- and s-charts are
$\bar{\bar{x}} \pm A_3\bar{s} = 0.762 \pm 1.427(0.066) = 0.667$ to 0.856

For the s-chart: $UCL_s = B_4\bar{s} = 2.089(0.066) = 0.138$
$LCL_s = B_3\bar{s} = 0$

The $\bar{x}$-chart shows an out-of-control condition, with points 11 through 18 below the center line. Causes must be investigated and the process must be brought under control before $\bar{x}$- and s-charts can be used for process monitoring.

26. The data can be used to calculate the center line and control limits shown here.

For the Center Line, $CL_{\bar{x}}: \bar{\bar{x}} = 400.290$; $CL_s: \bar{s} = 16.404$

Control limits for the $\bar{x}$- and s-charts are
$\bar{\bar{x}} \pm A_3\bar{s} = 400.290 \pm 1.954(16.404) = 368.263$ to 432.344

For the s-chart: $UCL_s = B_4\bar{s} = 2.089(16.404) = 42.127$
$LCL_s = B_3\bar{s} = 0$

Based on the revised data from problem 6(b) with 23 samples, the process is under control, with no apparent problems.

28. Using data from problem 13 as individual measures, with 5 sample moving ranges, the calculations for the $\bar{x}$-chart for individuals and R-chart show:

From the data summary: $\bar{x} = 0.076$; $\bar{R} = 0.006$

Control Limits on x:

$UCL_x = \bar{x} + 3(\bar{R}/d_2) = 0.076 + 3(0.006)/2.326 = 0.084$
$LCL_x = \bar{x} - 3(\bar{R}/d_2) = 0.076 - 3(0.006)/2.326 = 0.068$

Control limits on R: $UCL_R = D_4\bar{R} = 2.114(0.006) = 0.013$
$LCL_R = D_3\bar{R} = 0(0.0048) = 0$

The process is probably out of control, with points 25–36 "hugging" the center line on the $\bar{x}$-chart and points 33–60 on the Moving Range Chart above the center line. Reasons for the out-of-control condition need to be sought out and corrected.

30. $CL_p = 50/2{,}250 = 0.0222$

$s_p = \sqrt{\bar{p}(1 - \bar{p})/n}$

$s_p = \sqrt{(0.0222)(0.9778)/75} = 0.0170$

Control limits:

$UCL_p = \bar{p} + 3s_p$

$UCL_p = 0.0222 + 3(0.0170) = 0.0732$

$LCL_p = \bar{p} - 3s_p$

$LCL_p = 0.0222 - 3(0.0170) = -0.0288$, use 0

32. From the data, control limits and a control chart may be constructed. Control limits are

$CL_p = 0.06$

$s_p = \sqrt{\bar{p}(1 - \bar{p})/n} = \sqrt{(0.06)(0.94)/50} = 0.0336$

Control limits:

$UCL_p = \bar{p} + 3s_p = 0.06 + 3(0.0336) = 0.1608$

$LCL_p = \bar{p} - 3s_p = 0.06 - 3(0.0336) = -0.0408$, use 0

The process appears to be under control.

b) The process starts to go out of control, with samples 29, 30, 31 being the first indicator. Two out of three of these are more than 2σ away from the mean, $\bar{p}$. Later, four out of five samples between 37–41 are more than 1σ away from the mean, $\bar{p}$. Finally, sample 48 exceeds the upper control limit.

34. From the data, control limits and a control chart may be constructed. Control limits are

a) Initially, $CL_p = 0.53/25 = 0.0212$

$s_p = \sqrt{\bar{p}(1 - \bar{p})/n} = \sqrt{(0.0212)(0.9788)/100} = 0.0144$

$UCL_p = \bar{p} + 3s_p = 0.0212 + 3(0.0144) = 0.0644$

$LCL_p = \bar{p} - 3s_p = 0.0212 - 3(0.0144) = -0.0022$, use 0

Throw out samples 9 and 23, which are out-of-control values, and revise the chart.

b) Revised:

$CL_p = 0.3795/23 = 0.0165$

$s_p = \sqrt{\bar{p}(1-\bar{p})/n} = \sqrt{(0.0165)(0.9835)/100} = 0.0127$

Control limits:

$UCL_p = \bar{p} + 3s_p = 0.0165 + 3(0.0127) = 0.0546$

$LCL_p = \bar{p} - 3s_p = 0.0165 - 3(0.0127) = -0.0217$, use 0

36. From the data, control limits and a control chart may be constructed. Control limits are

The average sample size = 521.04

$CL_p = 173/13{,}026 = 0.0133$

$s_p = \sqrt{(\bar{p}(1-\bar{p})/n} = \sqrt{(0.0133)(0.9867)/521.04} = 0.0050$

$UCL_p = \bar{p} + 3s_p = 0.0133 + 3(0.0050) = 0.0283$

$LCL_p = \bar{p} - 3s_p = 0.0133 - 3(0.0050) = -0.0017$, use 0

All points fall within the control limits.

38. From the data control limits and a control chart may be constructed. Using data from problem 34, we get these control limits:

$CL_{np} = n\bar{p} = \dfrac{y_1 + y_2 + y_3 + \dots y_M}{M} = 53/25 = 2.12;\ \bar{p} = 2.12/100 = 0.0212$

$s_{np} = \sqrt{n\bar{p}(1-\bar{p})} = \sqrt{100(0.0212)(0.9788)} = 1.44$

$UCL_{n\bar{p}} = \bar{p} + 3s_{n\bar{p}} = 2.12 + 3(1.44) = 6.44$

$LCL_{n\bar{p}} = \bar{p} - 3s_{n\bar{p}} = 2.12 - 3(1.44) = -2.20$, use 0

As was shown in the previous control chart for problem 34, values for samples 9 and 23 are outside the control limits. Eliminating these points, we get revised control limits shown for the final control chart.

Revised:

$CL_{np} = n\bar{p} = 38/23 = 1.65;\ \bar{p} = 1.65/100 = 0.0165$

$s_{np} = \sqrt{n\bar{p}(1-\bar{p})} = \sqrt{100(0.0165)(0.9835)} = 1.274$

Control limits:

$UCL_{np} = n\bar{p} + 3s_{n\bar{p}} = 1.65 + 3(1.274) = 5.47$

$LCL_{np} = n\bar{p} + 3s_{n\bar{p}} = 1.65 - 3(1.274) = -2.172$, use 0

The *np* chart shows that all points are now in control.

40. For the u-chart conditions: 40 samples; $n = 10$, number of defects $= 1{,}200$

Center Line for the u-chart: $\bar{u} = 1{,}200/400 = 3.0$

$\bar{u} \pm 3\sqrt{\bar{u}/n} = 3.0 \pm 3\sqrt{(3.0/10)} = 3.0 \pm 1.64 = -0.29$ to 4.64

Center Line for the c-chart: $\bar{c} = 1{,}200/40 = 30$

$\bar{c} \pm 3\sqrt{\bar{c}} = 30 \pm 3\sqrt{30} = 30 \pm 16.43 = 13.57$ to 46.43

42. For the c-chart: number defective $= 176$; number of samples $= 10$

Center Line for the c-chart: $\bar{c} = 176/10 = 17.6$

$\bar{c} \pm 3\sqrt{\bar{c}} = 17.6 \pm 3\sqrt{17.6} = 17.6 \pm 12.59 = 5.01$ to 30.19

By inspection of the data, it can be seen that the first point is below the lower control limit and should be discarded. The result is $\bar{c} = 19.111$ and $\sigma_{\bar{c}} = 4.372$.

44. For the c-chart: Center Line: $\bar{c}$ (average number of defects) $= 16$

$\bar{c} \pm 3\sqrt{\bar{c}} = 16 \pm 3(4) = 16 \pm 12 = 4$ to 28

46. This is simply an exercise in reading values from the curves to fit required conditions.
   a) For a 1σ shift and a 0.80 probability, use $n = 15$ (if rounded to next higher value).
   b) For a 2σ shift and a 0.95 probability, use $n = 8$ (rounded to next higher value).
   c) For a 2.5σ shift and a 0.90 probability, use $n = 3$ (rounded to next higher value).

48. The stabilized p-chart, based on the post office example, plots the "transformed Z statistic" instead of p, and it shows the process is in control. To verify calculations, for example, the first data point is

$\bar{p} = 0.022;\ \sigma_{\text{process}} = \sqrt{\bar{p}(1 - \bar{p})} = \sqrt{0.022(1 - 0.022)} = 0.1467$

Note that $\bar{p}(1 - \bar{p})$ is not divided by n, because it is the estimated *process* standard deviation, not the sample standard devision. Thus variations in sample and lot sizes can be tolerated here, where they might cause problems with the standard p-chart.

$$z = \frac{p - \bar{p}}{\sigma_p} = \frac{0.03 - 0.022}{0.1467} = 0.0545$$

50. The control chart for the EMWA versus observed valus, with an $\alpha = 0.8$ shows that the process is under control, and the EMWA estimate closely anticipates the next observed value. The conclusion is that a better "forecast" of future values was obtained (versus those in problem 49) for volatile values such as these by using a larger α value, which gave greater weight to more recent values.

52. $\frac{\alpha}{2} = \frac{0.10}{2} = 0.05$; from the normal probability table, $P(Z) = 0.4500$

Therefore, $Z_{0.02} = 1.64$ or 1.65, because it is equidistant (0.4495 and 0.4505, respectively) between the closest table values to 0.4500.

54. Results will vary, depending on the random numbers generated. For example, one simulation of 100 sets of 3 values yielded an average of 1.754 versus d_2 = 1.693 for $n = 3$.

CHAPTER 13

2. From 0–30, slope = 29/30 = 0.967
From 30–70, slope = (40 – 29)/(70 – 30) = 0.275
From 70 – 100, slope = (90 – 40)/(100 – 70) = 1.667
From 0–100, slope = 90/100 = 0.9

4. a) $P(x > 53{,}500) = 0.5 - P(50{,}000 < x < 53{,}500)$

$P(50{,}000 < x < 53{,}500) = P\left(Z < \frac{53{,}500 - 50{,}000}{4{,}000}\right) = P(0 < Z < 0.875) =$ 0.3108 (using Z = 0.88)

Therefore, $P(x > 53{,}500) = 0.5 - 0.3108 = 0.1892$ should survive beyond 53,500 miles.

b) $P(x < 42{,}000) = P\left(Z < \frac{42{,}000 - 50{,}000}{4{,}000}\right) = P(Z < -2.00) = 0.5 - P(42{,}000 < x < 50{,}000) = 0.5 - 0.4772 = 0.0228$

c) The distribution looks approximately like this:

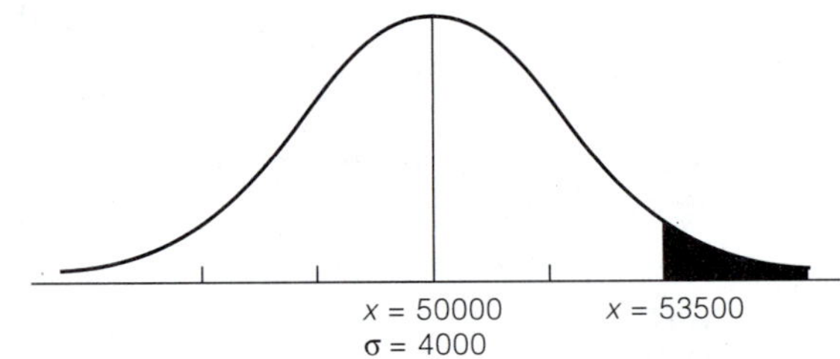

d) Let x_w be the limit of the warranty period.

$P(x < x_w) = 0.10;\ Z = -2.33,$ for $Z = \frac{x - 50{,}000}{4000} = -2.33,$

$x_w = 40{,}680$ miles for the warranty limit

6. $\lambda = \frac{3}{[(7 \times 1{,}000) + 40 + 225 + 752]} = \frac{3}{8{,}017} = 0.000374$ failures/hour

8. $R = e^{-\lambda T} = 0.95 = e^{(-1)1{,}500}$
$\ln 0.95 = -1{,}500\lambda$
$-0.0513 = -1{,}500\lambda$

$$\lambda = \frac{\ln 0.95}{-1{,}500} = \frac{0.0513}{1{,}500} = 0.0000342 \text{ failures/hour}$$

Time, t	Failures, $F(T)$	Survivors, $R(T)$
300	0.0103	0.9897
500	0.0171	0.9828
1000	0.0342	0.9658

10. For $\theta = \dfrac{3{,}000}{3} = 1{,}000$ hours

12. Mean days between breakdown $\bar{x} = 180$, $s = 10$, using 365 days per year
For no preventive maintenance: $365/180 = 2.023$ breakdowns per year
2.023 breakdowns/year × \$750,000/breakdown = \$1,517,250
For a 1% chance of breakdown, let x be time between maintenance

$$\frac{x - 180}{10} = -2.33, \ x = 156.7 \text{ days}$$

365/156.7 = 2.329 maintenance checks per year

2.329 × \$500,000/check	=	\$1,164,500.00
+ 0.01 × 2.329 × \$750,000	=	17,467.50
Total		\$1,181,967.50

For a 0.5% chance of breakdown, let x be time between maintenance be:

$$\frac{x - 180}{10} = -2.58, \ x = 154.2 \text{ days}$$

365/154.2 = 2.367 maintenance checks

2.367 × \$500,000/check	=	\$1,183,500.00
+ 0.005 × 2.367 × \$750,000	=	8,876.25
Total		\$1,192,376.25

Therefore, we may conclude that preventive maintenance is worthwhile.

14. MTBF = (0.5)(0.25) + 1.5(0.08) + 2.5(0.07) + 3.5(0.10) + 4.5(0.20) + 5.5(0.30)
= 3.32 wks
52/3.32 = 15.66 failures/year

Time Between Maintenance	Failure Expense	Maintenance Expense	Total
1 wk	0.25 × 52 × \$2,500 = \$32,500	52 × \$500 = \$26,000	\$58,500
2 wk	0.33 × 52/2 × \$2,500 = \$21,450	26 × \$500 = \$13,000	\$34,450
3 wk	0.40 × 52/3 × \$2,500 = \$17,333	17.3 × \$500 = \$ 8,650	\$25,983
4 wk	0.50 × 52/4 × \$2,500 = \$16,250	13 × \$500 = \$ 6,500	\$22,750
5 wk	0.70 × 52/5 × \$2,500 = \$18,200	10.4 × \$500 = \$ 5,200	\$23,400
6 wk	1.00 × 52/6 × \$2,500 = \$21,667	8.7 × \$500 = \$ 4,350	\$26,017

15.66 × \$2,500 = \$39,000/year, with no maintenance. Therefore, perform maintenance every 4 weeks for minimum cost.

16. $R_{cc} = 1 - (1 - 0.99)^2 = 0.9999$

$R_a R_b R_{cc} R_d = (0.93)(0.93)(0.9999)(0.99) = 0.856$

18. a) $R_a R_b R_c = (0.75)(0.85)(0.95) = 0.605$

b) $R_{aa} R_{bb} R_{cc} = [1 - (1 - 0.75)^2][1 - (1 - 0.85)^2][1 - (1 - 0.95)^2] =$ $(0.9375)(0.9775)(0.9975) = 0.914$

20. a) $R_T = 0.98$

b) Because these systems are parallel, $R = 1 - (1 - 0.98)^2 = 0.9996$

Index

R

S